They enhance the **learning of critical thinking, problem solving, and performance skills** of individuals with ELN, and increase their self-awareness, self-management, self-control, self-reliance, and self-esteem. Moreover, special educators emphasize the **development, maintenance, and generalization** of knowledge and skills across environments, settings, and the lifespan.

Special Education Content Standard 5:
LEARNING ENVIRONMENTS AND SOCIAL INTERACTIONS

Special educators actively **create learning environments** for individuals with ELN that foster cultural understanding, safety and emotional well-being, positive social interactions, and **active engagement** of individuals with ELN. In addition, special educators **foster environments in which diversity is valued** and individuals are taught to live harmoniously and productively in a culturally diverse world. Special educators shape **environments to encourage the independence,** self-motivation, self-direction, personal empowerment, and self-advocacy of individuals with ELN. Special educators **help their general education colleagues integrate individuals** with ELN in regular environments and engage them in meaningful learning activities and interactions. Special educators use **direct motivational and instructional interventions** with individuals with ELN to teach them to respond effectively to current expectations. When necessary, special educators can safely **intervene with individuals with ELN in crisis.** Special educators coordinate all these efforts and provide **guidance and direction to paraeducators and others,** such as classroom volunteers and tutors.

Special Education Content Standard 6:
COMMUNICATION

Special educators understand **typical and atypical language development** and the ways in which exceptional conditions can interact with an individual's experience with and use of language. Special educators use individualized strategies to **enhance language development** and **teach communication skills** to individuals with ELN. Special educators are familiar with **augmentative, alternative, and assis-**tive technologies to support and enhance communication of individuals with exceptional needs. Special educators match their communication methods to an individual's language proficiency and cultural and linguistic differences. Special educators provide **effective language models** and they use communication strategies and resources to **facilitate understanding of subject matter for individuals with ELN whose primary language is not English.**

Special Education Content Standard 7:
INSTRUCTIONAL PLANNING

Individualized decision-making and instruction is at the center of special education practice. Special educators develop **long-range individualized instructional plans** anchored in both general and special curricula. In addition, special educators systematically translate these individualized plans into carefully selected **shorter-range goals and objectives,** taking into consideration an individual's abilities and needs, the learning environment, and a myriad of cultural and linguistic factors. Individualized instructional plans emphasize **explicit modeling** and **efficient guided practice** to assure acquisition and fluency through maintenance and generalization. Understanding of these factors, as well as the implications of an individual's exceptional condition, guides the special educator's selection, adaptation, and creation of materials, and the use of powerful instructional variables. Instructional plans are **modified based on ongoing analysis of the individual's learning progress.** Moreover, special educators facilitate this instructional planning in a **collaborative context** including the individuals with exceptionalities, families, professional colleagues, and personnel from other agencies as appropriate. Special educators also develop a variety of **individualized transition plans,** such as transitions from preschool to elementary school and from secondary settings to a variety of postsecondary work and learning contexts. Special educators are comfortable using **appropriate technologies** to support instructional planning and individualized instruction.

Special Education Content Standard 8:
ASSESSMENT

Assessment is integral to the decision-making and teaching of special educators, and special educators use **multiple types of assessment information** for a variety of educational decisions. Special educators use the results of assessments to help identify exceptional learning needs and to develop and implement individualized instructional programs, as well as to adjust instruction in response to ongoing learning progress. Special educators understand the **legal policies and ethical principles of measurement and assessment** related to referral, eligibility, program planning, instruction, and placement for individuals with ELN, including those from culturally and linguistically diverse backgrounds. Special educators understand **measurement theory and practices** for addressing issues of validity, reliability, norms, bias, and interpretation of assessment results. In addition, special educators understand the appropriate **use and limitations** of various types of assessments. Special educators collaborate with families and other colleagues to assure **non-biased, meaningful assessments and decision-making.** Special educators conduct **formal and informal assessments** of behavior, learning, achievement, and environments to design learning experiences that support the growth and development of individuals with ELN. Special educators use assessment information to **identify supports and adaptations** required for individuals with ELN to access the general curriculum and to participate in school-, system-, and statewide assessment programs. Special educators **regularly monitor the progress** of individuals with ELN in general and special curricula. Special educators use **appropriate technologies** to support their assessments.

Special Education Content Standard 9:
PROFESSIONAL AND ETHICAL PRACTICE

Special educators are guided by the profession's ethical and professional practice standards. Special educators practice in multiple roles and complex situations across wide age and developmental ranges. Their practice requires ongoing attention to **legal matters** along with serious professional and **ethical considerations.** Special educators engage in **professional activities** and participate in learning communities that benefit individuals with ELN, their families, colleagues, and their own professional growth. Special educators view themselves as **life-long learners** and regularly reflect on and adjust their practice. Special educators are aware of how their own and others' attitudes, behaviors, and ways of communicating can influence their practice. Special educators understand that culture and language can interact with exceptionalities, and [they] are **sensitive to the many aspects of diversity** of individuals with ELN and their families. Special educators actively plan and engage in activities that foster their professional growth and keep them **current with evidence-based best practices.** Special educators know their own limits of practice and practice within them.

Special Education Content Standard 10:
COLLABORATION

Special educators routinely and effectively **collaborate with families, other educators, related service providers, and personnel from community agencies in culturally responsive ways.** This collaboration assures that the needs of individuals with ELN are addressed throughout schooling. Moreover, special educators embrace their special role as advocates for individuals with ELN. Special educators promote and advocate the learning and well-being of individuals with ELN across a wide range of settings and a range of different learning experiences. Special educators are viewed as specialists by a myriad of people who actively seek their collaboration to effectively include and teach individuals with ELN. Special educators are a **resource to their colleagues** in understanding the laws and policies relevant to individuals with ELN. Special educators use collaboration to **facilitate the successful transitions** of individuals with ELN across settings and services.

HUMAN EXCEPTIONALITY

School, Community, and Family

NINTH EDITION

HUMAN EXCEPTIONALITY

School, Community, and Family

MICHAEL L. HARDMAN
University of Utah

CLIFFORD J. DREW
University of Utah

M. WINSTON EGAN
Brigham Young University

Houghton Mifflin Company
Boston   New York

This book is dedicated to people with differences everywhere, who have risen to the challenge of living in a society that is sometimes nurturing, but all too often ambivalent.

To our families, a loving and appreciative thank you for being so patient and caring during the more than 25 years of writing, rewriting, and revising this text.

MLH
CJD
MWE

Editor in Chief/Publisher: Pat Coryell
Sponsoring Editor: Shani Fisher
Marketing Manager: Amy Whitaker
Development Editor: Julia Giannotti
Project Editor: Nan Lewis-Schulz
Senior Art and Design Coordinator: Jill Haber Atkins
Cover Design Director: Tony Saizon
Senior Photo Editor: Jennifer Meyer Dare
Senior Composition Buyer: Chuck Dutton
New Title Project Manager: James Loneragan
Editorial Assistant: Dayna Pell
Marketing Assistant: Samantha Abrams
Editorial Assistant: Katherine Roz
Cover Image: Black-eyed Susans © Rebecca Grantham

Photo credits appear on page 626, which constitutes a continuation of the copyright page.

Printed in the U.S.A.

Library of Congress Control Number: 2007920938

Instructor's examination copy
   ISBN-10: 0-618-91730-6
   ISBN-13: 978-0-618-91730-3
For orders, use student text ISBNs
   ISBN-10: 0-618-92042-0
   ISBN-13: 978-0-618-92042-6

123456789-VH-11 10 09 08 07

Brief Contents

Contents

1 UNDERSTANDING EXCEPTIONALITY   2

2 EDUCATION FOR ALL   22

3 INCLUSION AND MULTIDISCIPLINARY COLLABORATION IN THE EARLY CHILDHOOD AND ELEMENTARY SCHOOL YEARS   54

6 EXCEPTIONALITY AND THE FAMILY   134

7 LEARNING DISABILITIES   160

8 | ATTENTION-DEFICIT/ HYPERACTIVITY DISORDER   202

9 EMOTIONAL/BEHAVIORAL DISORDERS 226

10 INTELLECTUAL DISABILITIES   262

13 AUTISM SPECTRUM DISORDER 346

Selected Features

INCLUSION THROUGH THE LIFESPAN

REFLECT ON THIS

About the Authors

MICHAEL L. HARDMAN is Dean of the College of Education and Professor in the Department of Special Education at the University of Utah. He has also served as Chair of the Department of Special Education and the Department of Teaching and Learning at the University. He also serves as the University Coordinator for the Eunice Kennedy Shriver National Center for Community of Caring. In 2004–2005, Dr. Hardman was appointed the Matthew J. Guglielmo Endowed Chair at California State University, Los Angeles, and the Governor's Representative to the California Advisory Commission on Special Education. Additionally, Dr. Hardman is Senior Education Advisor to the Joseph P. Kennedy, Jr. Foundation in Washington, D.C., and a member of the Board of Directors for the Council for Exceptional Children.

Dr. Hardman has numerous publications in national journals throughout the field of education and has authored several college textbooks of which *Human Exceptionality* is now in its ninth edition. As a researcher, he has directed international and national demonstration projects in the areas of educational policy and reform, developmental disabilities, professional development, inclusive education, transition from school to adult life, and preparing tomorrow's leaders in special education.

CLIFFORD J. DREW is Associate Dean for Research and Outreach in the College of Education at the University of Utah. He is also a professor in the Special Education and Educational Psychology Departments. Dr. Drew came to the University of Utah in 1971 after serving on the faculties of the University of Texas at Austin and Kent State University. He received his master's degree from the University of Illinois and his Ph.D. from the University of Oregon. He has published numerous articles in education and related areas including intellectual disabilities, research design, statistics, diagnostic assessment, cognition, evaluation related to the law and information technology. His most recent book, *Intellectual Disabilities Across the Lifespan* (Pearson, 2007) is Dr. Drew's 28th text. His professional interests include research methods in education and psychology, human development and disabilities, applications of information technology, and outreach in higher education.

M. WINSTON EGAN, chair of the Teacher Education Department in the David O. McKay School of Education at Brigham Young University, has taught children of all ages, preschool through high school. He began his special education career at Utah Boys Ranch. His writings appear in *Behavior Disorders, Journal of Teacher Education, Teacher Education and Special Education, Journal of Technology and Teacher Education, American Journal of Distance Education, Journal of Special Education, Rural Special Education Quarterly,* and *Teaching and Teacher Education.* He has been honored with several university teaching awards including Professor of the Year, Blue Key National Honor Society at Brigham Young University, and Excellence in Teaching Award, Graduate School of Education, University of Utah. He has also been an associate of the National Network of Education Renewal (NNER). His interests include youth development, video-anchored instruction, teacher socialization and development, and emotional/behavior disorders.

Preface

> When some people are excluded from the social fabric of our communities, that fabric contains a "hole." When there is a hole, the entire fabric is weakened. It lacks richness, texture and the strength of diversity.
>
> —Anonymous

Welcome to *Human Exceptionality: School, Community, and Family!* In this our ninth edition, we are very pleased to be joining the Houghton Mifflin family of college textbooks and look forward to a lasting and productive collaboration for years to come. For most of you, this book is the beginning of your journey into the lives of people with disabilities and those with extraordinary gifts and talents. As authors, we would like to provide our perspectives on the continuing features of this book as well as on what is new and exciting in this ninth edition. This text is about people—people with diverse needs, desires, characteristics, and lifestyles—people who for one reason or another are described as exceptional. What does the word *exceptional* mean to you? For that matter, what do the words *disordered, deviant, disabled, challenged, different,* or *handicapped* mean to you? Who or what influenced your knowledge and attitudes toward the people and words we use to describe them? Up to this point in your life, you were probably most influenced by life experiences and not by any formal training. You may have a family member, friend, or casual acquaintance who is exceptional in some way. It may be that you are a person who is exceptional in some way. Then again, you may be approaching a study of human exceptionality with little or no background. You will find that the study of human exceptionality is the study of being human. Perhaps you will come to understand yourself better in the process. As suggested by the novelist Louis Bromfield,

> There is a rhythm in life, a certain beauty which operates by a variation of lights and shadows, happiness alternating with sorrow, content with discontent, distilling in this process of contrast a sense of satisfaction, of richness that can be captured and pinned down only by those who possess the gift of awareness.

New in This Edition

➤ We have significantly increased our topical coverage of multidisciplinary and collaborative approaches to education, health care, and social services for people who are exceptional.

➤ A popular feature of the book, *Inclusion through the Lifespan,* has added the term *collaboration* to the title in order to reflect our multidisciplinary approach to including people who are exceptional in schools, communities, and families.

➤ The ninth edition also has an expanded emphasis on "education for all." Several chapters discuss the most current information available on the *No Child Left Behind Act* and the *Individuals with Disabilities Education Improvement Act of 2004 (IDEA 2004).* Enhanced education topics include discussions on school reform, highly qualified teachers, assessment and accountability for all students, school-wide collaboration among general and special educators, and evidence-based practices in education.

➤ We are also very proud of the fact that the ninth edition contains over 1,200 citations from sources that have been published since the year 2000—the majority of these citations have been published within the past three years. As such, we are very comfortable in saying to our readers that the ninth edition of *Human Exceptionality* is one of the most current sources available on the lives of people with disabilities and those with gifts and talents.

Organizational Features

In addition to providing you with current and informative content, we are committed to making your experience with people with disabilities and those with gifts and talents informative, interesting, enjoyable, and productive. To this end, we have incorporated features within this ninth edition that will significantly enhance your desire to learn more and become acquainted with human exceptionality.

➤ FOCUS PREVIEW, QUESTIONS, AND REVIEW

At the beginning of the chapter and throughout the book, we've provided tools to help you learn more effectively about the key topics within each section. New to the ninth edition is **Focus Preview** which serves as an advanced organizer for your reading. It lists each of the **Focus Questions** that occur throughout the chapter, setting the stage for upcoming chapter content. The margins of each chapter contain a series of **Focus Questions** on information within the chapter that is important for you to learn and know. Each chapter concludes with a **Focus Review** that repeats the Focus Questions and provides brief highlights based on chapter material.

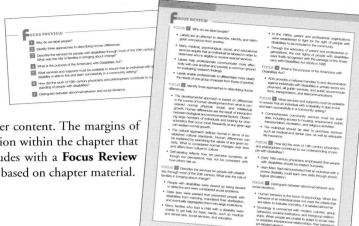

◄ TO BEGIN WITH . . .

To Begin With . . . excerpts, found at the beginning of each chapter, are designed to introduce and stimulate interest. They offer a variety of fascinating and current anecdotes, facts, and figures related to the chapter content.

➤ SNAPSHOT

Snapshot features are personal insights into the lives of real people. These insights may come from the teachers, family members, friends, peers, and professionals, as well as from the person who is exceptional. Each chapter in the book opens with a *Snapshot* of an individual who is exceptional. We believe you will find the Snapshots to be one of the most enriching aspects of your introduction to human exceptionality.

◄ INCLUSION AND COLLABORATION THROUGH THE LIFESPAN

Another feature in this new edition is *Inclusion and Collaboration Through the Lifespan,* which has been expanded to provide more information on ways to interact with, include, communicate with, or teach people who are exceptional across a variety of settings (home, school, and community) and age spans (early childhood through the adult years). Hopefully these ideas provide a stimulus for further thinking on ways to include these individuals as family members, school peers, friends, or neighbors, as well as collaborate with other professionals concerned with improving the lives of people who are exceptional.

◄ REFLECT ON THIS

Every chapter includes one or more boxes entitled *Reflect on This*. Each box highlights additional interesting and relevant information beyond the chapter narrative that will add to your learning and enjoyment of the topic.

➤ ASSISTIVE TECHNOLOGY

The ninth edition offers new information on the expanding use of technology for people who are exceptional. *Assistive Technology* features highlight important innovations in computers, biomedical engineering, and instructional systems.

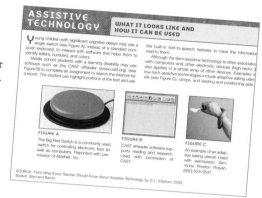

◄ DEBATE FORUM

Every chapter includes a *Debate Forum* to broaden your view of issues that affect the lives of people with differences. The *Debate Forums* are an inside look into differing philosophies and opinions on various issues, such as whether the Americans with Disabilities Act actually levels the playing field or creates advantage, the pros and cons of inclusive education for students with disabilities, the meaning of a high school diploma or the appropriateness of an intervention strategy. For each topic, a position is taken (*point*) and an alternative to that position (*counterpoint*) is given. The purpose of the *Debate Forum* is not to establish right or wrong answers, but to better understand the diversity of issues concerning individuals who are exceptional.

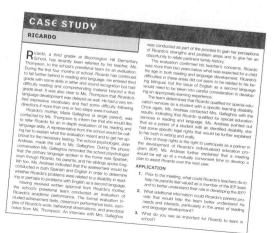

➤ CASE STUDY

Each chapter includes a *Case Study* feature, which is an in-depth look at a personal story of exceptionality. Each *Case Study* also includes Application Questions to extend your knowledge and apply what you learned from each vignette.

CHAPTER-CLOSING RESOURCES

The closing section of each chapter contains several resources to expand your knowledge of the topics addressed. *Further Readings* lists selected books and journals that provide information about each chapter topic. *Web Resources* discusses informative websites that you can visit to build your knowledge of exceptionalities. *Building Your Portfolio* is a resource for teacher candidates in general and special education. It explains the Council for Exceptional Children (CEC) standards that are covered in each chapter and gives you tips for collecting the materials you prepare for this class in order to build a professional portfolio based on the standards.

Instructor Supplements: A Complete Instructional Package

A variety of teaching tools are available to assist instructors in organizing lectures, planning evaluations, and ensuring student comprehension.

INSTRUCTOR'S RESOURCE MANUAL AND TEST BANK. Prepared by Sarah Overall, University of Utah, the Instructor's Resource Manual includes a wealth of interesting ideas and activities designed to help instructors teach the course. Each chapter of the Manual includes: at-a-glance grids, chapter outline, introducing the chapter, lecture outline, related discussion/activities, case study feedback, related media, and handout masters. Prepared by the textbook authors, the Test Bank has been significantly improved to include more challenging essay, multiple-choice, true/false, short answer and case study questions for every chapter. Page number references, suggested answers, and skill level have been added to each question to better help instructor's create and evaluate student tests.

COMPUTERIZED OR PRINT TEST BANK. The Test Bank is available electronically or through a computerized testing program. Instructors can use the Test Bank to create exams in just minutes by selecting from the existing database of questions, editing questions, or writing original questions.

POWERPOINT™ PRESENTATION. Prepared by Matt Jameson, chapter PowerPoint™ slides are ideal for lecture presentations or student handouts. The PowerPoint™ presentation created for this text provides dozens of ready-to-use graphic and text images including illustrations from the text.

STUDENT STUDY GUIDE

Prepared by Christine K. Ormsbee, the student Study Guide that accompanies the text features numerous ways of helping students apply and practice what they have learned in the text including:

- ➤ Guided Review—guides students through the key concepts in each chapter using a KWL process model
- ➤ Best Practices—websites, videos, books, and models to help students understand how best to serve children, youth, and adults with disabilities
- ➤ Community Activities—activities that let students understand how IDEA is implemented in their local system
- ➤ Case Study—case studies with multiple-choice and critical thinking questions that ask students to apply what they have learned in each chapter
- ➤ Getting Involved—a list of contacts to help students identify ways of becoming involved
- ➤ Practice Test—up to 20 questions per chapter.

COMPANION WEBSITE

The Online Study Center extends the textbook content and provides resources for further exploration into special education. The site offers links to relevant websites, practice tests, and activities to help prepare for the Praxis and other Certification exams. The Online Study Center also includes access to Houghton Mifflin's Video Cases. Organized by topic, each case is a 4- to 6-minute module consisting of video files presenting actual classroom scenarios that depict the complex problems and opportunities teachers face every day. The video clips are accompanied by "artifacts" to provide background information and allow preservice teachers to experience true classroom dilemmas in their multiple dimensions.

The Online Teaching Center includes an online version of the Instructor Resource Material, a guide to using the student website, and PowerPoint™ slides to accompany each chapter.

Acknowledgments

We begin with a very big thank you to our colleagues from around the country who provided such in-depth and constructive feedback on the ninth edition of *Human Exceptionality*

Sherry Best, California State University, Los Angeles

Amanda Boutot, University of Las Vegas, Nevada

Peggy Hypes, Carson-Newman College

Jodi Katsafanas, Duquesne University

Patricia Mason, Bridgewater State College

Michelle Moriarty, Johnson County Community College

Gary Troia, Michigan State University

Special thanks to the people with disabilities and their families who participated in the Snapshot case studies and Assistive Technology features for this new edition. These are the people who make up the heart of what this book is all about. Throughout the writing and production of this book, they made us keenly aware that this book is first and foremost about people.

For a job exceptionally well done, we extend our gratitude to Sarah Overall and Matt Jameson at the University of Utah for their first-rate effort in taking the lead in revising the instructor's manual and PowerPoint™ slides for the book. Sarah spent untold hours developing and editing lecture notes, creating related activities, and locating the most current and informative media available in the area of exceptionality. Matt, as he has consistently done in past editions, produced an easy-to-use and high-quality PowerPoint™ presentation for every chapter in the book. Sarah and Matt were always on time with a high-quality product. We also extend our thanks to the faculty and students at the University of Utah and Brigham Young University who continue to teach us a great deal about writing textbooks. Many of the changes incorporated into this ninth edition are a direct result of critiques from university colleagues and students in our classes.

As authors, we are certainly grateful for the commitment and expertise of the Houghton Mifflin editorial and production team in bringing to fruition the highest quality text possible. This team has sought to consistently improve the readability, utility, and appearance of this book. We want to especially thank our Executive Editor, Mary Finch. This is our first opportunity to work with Mary and we appreciate her welcoming us to Houghton Mifflin and consistently supporting our product. Our Sponsoring Editor, Shani Fisher, has been a wonderful addition to the editorial team who kept us on track and informed during production. A special thanks to Julia Giannotti who worked closely with us to ensure quality supplements, including the instructor's manual and test bank, student study guide companion website, and PowerPoint™ slides.

We genuinely appreciate the opportunity to work with Tom Conville and Nesbitt Graphics who handled the editorial production of the book. Tom has been great to work with, attending not only to the quality of the content but also ensuring that the book maintains its strong user-friendly approach to instruction. Connie Day's careful and in-depth editing of the manuscript has been crucial in presenting a product of which we are all very proud. The photo researcher for this book was Kate Cebik who did an outstanding job of locating photos that brought to life the text's printed word. Under Kate's direction, we have included the most recent photographs from photo shoots in general education classes including school systems that work with the inclusion model around the country. This photo resource also contains families with children and adults with disabilities.

Last, but certainly not least, we express our appreciation to Lacy Egbert for her painstaking work on locating permissions for this edition. She did excellent work on a thankless but critical task.

To those professors who have chosen this book for adoption, and to those students who will be using this book as their first information source on people with differences, we hope our ninth edition of *Human Exceptionality* meets your expectations.

A loving thank you to our families who have always been there during the past two decades of writing and re-writing this text. We have strived oh so hard to produce a product of which you can be proud.

Michael L. Hardman

Clifford J. Drew

M. Winston Egan

HUMAN EXCEPTIONALITY

School, Community, and Family

1

Understanding Exceptionality

TO BEGIN WITH . . .

THE SUPER-CRIP STEREOTYPE

"Physicist Stephen Hawking is confined to a wheelchair, a virtual prisoner in his own body," began a *Time* magazine piece on the world's leading theoretical scientist. If Hawking were black, any mawkish reference to race in a lead would bring outraged charges from civil rights groups. But reporters know better than to call attention to race—or gender. Yet despite gains in rights for people [with disabilities], the press continues to sensationalize when doing stories in which a disability is involved to the exclusion of real news. Features on "courageous" individuals surmounting handicaps—we call them "in-spite-of stories"—greatly outnumber disability issues reporting. . . . Reporters flaunt demeaning and inaccurate clichés; "afflicted" and "victim" are routine. . . . So what's wrong with an occasional tug at the heartstrings? There's been too much of it. The "super-crip" approach has become the staple, comparable to the "credit-to-the-race" angle once epidemic in stories involving black people. [Major league] pitcher Jim Abbott has felt the frustration ever since the press focused on Abbott's lack of a right hand. Abbott has put it this way: "It seems weird to me sometimes that I'm a first-round pick and yet . . . since I turned professional the only thing anyone wants to talk about is playing with one hand." (Johnson, 2006)

IT'S THE "PERSON FIRST"

If you saw a person in a wheelchair unable to get up the stairs into a building, would you say "There is a handicapped person unable to find a ramp"? Or would you say "There is a person with a disability who is handicapped by an inaccessible building"? What is the proper way to speak to or about someone who has a disability? Consider how you would introduce someone—Jane Doe—who doesn't have a disability. You would give her name, where she lives, what she does or what she is interested in—she likes swimming, or eating Mexican food, or watching Robert Redford movies. Why say it differently for a person with disabilities? Every person is made up of many characteristics—mental as well as physical—[and] few want to be identified only by their ability to play tennis or by their love for fried onions or by the mole that's on their face. Those are just parts of us. In speaking or writing, remember that children or adults with disabilities are like everyone else—except they happen to have a disability. (Autism Society, 2006)

AN ERA OF RIGHTS AND RESPECT

Attitudes toward persons with disabilities have undergone profound changes during the past three decades. Society's view that these individuals represented a burden to be segregated and medically treated has largely given way, replaced by notions that people with disabilities are entitled to rights and respect. A philosophical orientation of normalization has gradually edged out segregationist conceptions of the role of people with disabilities in contemporary American society. . . . Public institutions, the mainstay of state service systems since the 19th century, have increasingly been supplanted by a network of community-based residential programs and supports. The magnitude of this transformation is such that since 1967, when the public institutional population peaked at nearly 200,000 persons, the census has declined by more than 140,000 persons. . . . Furthermore, the complete closure of institutional facilities has accelerated. (Parish, 2002, p. 353)

FOCUS PREVIEW

1 Why do we label people?

2 Identify three approaches to describing human differences.

3 Describe the services for people with disabilities through most of the 20th century. What was the role of families in bringing about change?

4 What is the purpose of the Americans with Disabilities Act?

5 What services and supports must be available to ensure that an individual with a disability is able to live and learn successfully in a community setting?

6 How did the work of 19th-century physicians and philosophers contribute to our understanding of people with disabilities?

7 Distinguish between abnormal behavior and social deviance.

▼ SNAPSHOT

FRANKLIN DELANO ROOSEVELT

This snapshot was adapted from the remarks of Senator Robert Dole to his colleagues in the United States Senate on April 14, 1995. Senator Dole, disabled himself following a serious injury in World War II, remembers President Franklin Roosevelt as a master politician; an energetic and inspiring leader during the dark days of the Depression; a tough, single-minded commander-in-chief during World War II; a statesman; the first elected leader in history with a disability; and a disability hero.

FDR'S Splendid Deception

In 1921, at age 39, Franklin Roosevelt was a young man in a hurry. He was following the same political path that took his cousin Theodore Roosevelt to the White House. He was elected to the New York State Senate in 1910 and later was appointed assistant secretary of the Navy. In 1920, he was the Democratic candidate for vice president. Then, on the evening of August 10, while on vacation, he felt ill and went to bed early. Within three days he was paralyzed from the chest down. Although the muscles of his upper body soon recovered, he remained paralyzed below the waist. His political career screeched to a halt. He spent the next seven years in rehabilitation, determined to walk again. He never did. He mostly used a wheelchair. Sometimes he was carried by his sons or aides. Other times he crawled on the floor. But he did perfect the illusion of walking—believing that otherwise his political ambitions were dead. He could stand upright only with his lower body painfully wrapped in steel braces. He moved forward by swinging his hips, leaning on the arm of a family member or aide. It worked for only a few feet at a time. It was dangerous. But it was enough

to convince people that FDR was not a "cripple." FDR biographer Hugh Gallagher has called this effort, and other tricks used to hide his disability, "FDR's splendid deception." This deception was aided and abetted by many others. The press were co-conspirators. No reporter wrote that FDR could not walk, and no photographer took a picture of him in his wheelchair. For that matter, thousands saw him struggle when he "walked." Maybe they didn't believe or understand what they saw. In 1928, FDR ended his political exile and was elected governor of New York. Four years later, he was president. On March 4, 1933, standing at the East Front of this Capitol, he said, "The only thing we have to fear is fear itself." He was 35 feet from his wheelchair. Few people knew from what deep personal experiences he spoke. Perhaps the only occasion where FDR fully acknowledged the extent of his disability in public was a visit to a military hospital in Hawaii. He toured the amputee wards in his wheelchair. He went by each bed, letting the men see him exactly as he was. He didn't need to give any pep talks—his example said it all.

FDR: A Disability Hero

Earlier I called FDR a "disability hero." But it was not for the reasons some might think. It would be easy to cite his courage and grit. But FDR would not want that. "No sob stuff," he told the press in 1928 when he started his comeback. Even within his own family, he did not discuss his disability. It was simply a fact of life. In my view, FDR is a hero for his efforts on behalf of others with a disability. In 1926, he purchased a run-down resort in Warm Springs, Georgia and, over the next 20 years, turned it into a unique, first-class rehabilitation center. It was based on a new philosophy of treatment—one where psychological recovery was as important as medical treatment. FDR believed in an independent life for people with disabilities—at a time when society thought they belonged at home or in institutions. Warm Springs was run by people with polio, for people with polio. In that spirit, FDR is the father of the modern independent living movement, which puts people with disabilities in control of their own lives. He also founded the National Foundation for Infantile Paralysis—known as the "March of Dimes"—and raised millions of dollars to help others with polio and find a cure. In public policy, FDR understood that government help in rehabilitating people with disabilities is "good business"—often returning more in taxes and savings than it costs. It is unfortunately a philosophy that we often pay more lip service than practice.

Disability Today and Tomorrow

Our nation has come a long way in its understanding of disability since the days of President Roosevelt. For example, we recognize that disability is a natural part of life. We have begun to build a world that is accessible. No longer do we accept that buildings—through either design or indifference—be inaccessible, which is a "Keep Out" sign for the disabled. We have come a long way in another respect—in attitudes. Fifty years ago, we had a president who could not walk and believed it was necessary to disguise that fact from the American people. Today, I trust that Americans would have no problem in electing as president a man or woman with a disability. (Dole, 1995)

Franklin Delano Roosevelt (FDR) has been hailed as one of the greatest U.S. presidents in history. *Time* magazine (Goodwin, 2006) named FDR as one of the runners-up (behind Albert Einstein) for the most important person of the 20th century, describing him as a statesman who helped define the political and social fabric of our time. What *Time* didn't talk about was FDR's life as a person with a disability and why he was forced to hide the fact that he had polio and couldn't walk. In our opening snapshot, we learn of Roosevelt's deception and why he is considered by many to be a disability hero even though he publicly denied his physical differences. Throughout his life, FDR did everything possible to avoid being "labeled" as a person with a disability. In Roosevelt's time, disability meant weakness, and he believed that revealing a paralysis would jeopardize his standing as a national leader (Sidey/Washington, 2006). Fortunately, we have a much better understanding of human diversity in today's society; that is, we know everyone is unique in some way. In fact, a national survey (N.O.D./Harris & Associates, 1995) found that more than 80% of Americans knew FDR was paralyzed. Of those who knew of his disability, 75% favored the depiction of him in a wheelchair at the new FDR national monument in Washington, D.C. This became a reality when a life-size bronze statue of FDR was unveiled at the monument in January 2001.

Describing People with Differences

To address differences, society creates descriptors to identify people who vary significantly from the norm. This process is called *labeling*. Sociologists use labels to describe people who do not follow society's expectations; educators and psychologists use labels to identify and provide services for students with learning, physical, and behavioral differences; and physicians use labels to distinguish the sick from the healthy.

Common Terminology

Common descriptors used to describe people with differences include *disorder, disability*, and *handicap*. These terms are not synonymous. **Disorder**, the broadest of the three terms, refers to a general disturbance in mental, physical, or psychological functioning. A **disability** is more specific than a disorder and results from a loss of physical functioning (such as a loss of sight, hearing, or mobility) or from difficulty in learning and social adjustment that significantly interferes with typical growth and development. A **handicap** is a limitation imposed on the individual by the demands in the environment and is related to the individual's ability

Focus 1
Why do we label people?

➤ **Disorder**
A disturbance in normal functioning (mental, physical, or psychological).

➤ **Disability**
A condition resulting from a loss of physical functioning; or, difficulties in learning and social adjustment that significantly interfere with normal growth and development. A person with a disability has a physical or mental impairment that substantially limits the person in some major life activity.

➤ **Handicap**
A limitation imposed on an individual by the environment and by the person's capacity to cope with that limitation.

to adapt or adjust to those demands. For example, Franklin Roosevelt used a wheelchair because of a physical disability—the inability to walk. He was dependent on the wheelchair to move from place to place. When the environment didn't accommodate his wheelchair (for example, when he encountered a building without ramps, accessible only by stairs), his disability became a handicap.

When applied as an educational label, *handicapped* has a narrow focus and a negative meaning. The word *handicapped* literally means "cap in hand"; it originates from a time when people with disabilities were forced to beg in the streets merely to survive.

Exceptional is a more comprehensive term. It may be used to describe an individual whose physical, intellectual, or behavioral performance differs substantially from the norm, either higher or lower. People described as exceptional include those with extraordinary abilities (such as **gifts and talents**) and/or disabilities (such as **learning disabilities** or **intellectual disabilities**). People who are exceptional, whether gifted or disabled, often benefit from individualized assistance, supports, or accommodations in school and society.

Labels are only rough approximations of characteristics. Some labels, such as **deaf**, might describe a permanent characteristic—loss of hearing; others, such as *overweight*, might describe a temporary characteristic. Some labels are positive, others negative. Labels communicate whether a person meets the expectations of the culture. A society establishes criteria that are easily exceeded by some but are unreachable for others. For example, a society may value creativity, innovation, and imagination and will reward those who have such attributes with positive labels, such as *bright, intelligent,* and *gifted.* A society, however, may brand anyone whose ideas drastically exceed the limits of conformity with negative labels, such as *radical, extremist,* and *rebel.*

Moreover, the same label may have different meanings for different groups, depending on each group's viewpoint. For example, Ellen is labeled by her high school teachers as a *conformist* because she always follows the rules. From the teacher's point of view, this is a positive characteristic, but to the student's peer group, it may have more negative connotations. Ellen may be described by her high school classmates as a "brown noser" or "teacher's pet."

What are the ramifications of using labels to describe people? Labels are often based on ideas, not facts. Thus, even though labels have been the basis for developing and providing services to people, they can also promote stereotyping, discrimination, and exclusion. Some professionals believe that the practice of labeling people has perpetuated and reinforced both the label and the behaviors it implies (Cook, 2001; Hardman & Nagle, 2004; National Council on Disability, 2000).

If the use of labels may have negative consequences, why is labeling used so extensively? One reason is that many social services and educational programs for people who are exceptional require the use of labels to distinguish those who are eligible for services from those who are not. Woolfolk (2004), discussing the need to label students with "special education needs," suggested that labeling protects the child. "If classmates know a student has [intellectual disabilities], they will be more willing to accept his or her behaviors. Of course, labels still open doors to special programs, useful information, special technology and equipment, or financial assistance" (p. 106). To illustrate, Maria, a child with a hearing loss, must be assessed and labeled as having a hearing loss in her local school district before specialized educational or social services can be made available to her. Another reason for the continued use of labels is the "useful information" they provide professionals for communicating effectively with one another and the common ground they offer for evaluating research findings. Labeling also helps to identify the specific needs of a particular group of people. Labeling can help to determine degrees of needs or to set priorities for services when societal resources are limited.

> **Exceptional**
A term describing any individual whose physical, mental, or behavioral performance deviates so substantially (higher or lower) from the average that additional support is required to meet the individual's needs.

> **Gifts and talents**
Extraordinary abilities in one or more areas.

> **Learning disabilities**
A condition in which one or more of an individual's basic psychological processes in understanding or using language are deficient.

> **Intellectual disabilities**
Substantial limitations in functioning, characterized by significantly subaverage intellectual functioning concurrent with related limitations in two or more adaptive skills. Intellectual disability manifests itself prior to age 18.

> **Deaf**
A term used to describe individuals who have hearing losses greater than 75 to 80 dB, have vision as their primary input, and cannot understand speech through the ear.

Council for Exceptional Children

Standard 1: Foundations

Labels have been the basis for developing and providing services to people with disabilities. Can they also promote stereotyping, discrimination, and exclusion?

When Someone Doesn't Conform to the Norm

Significant physical, behavioral, and learning differences are found infrequently in every society. Most people in any given culture conform to its established standards. Conformity—doing what we are supposed to do—is the rule for most of us, most of the time (Baron Byrne, & Branscombe, 2006). Usually, we look the way we are expected to look, behave the way we are expected to behave, and learn the way we are expected to learn. When someone differs substantially from the norm, three approaches may be used to describe the nature and extent of these differences (see Figure 1.1).

A DEVELOPMENTAL APPROACH. To understand human differences, which result from an interaction of biological and environmental factors, we must first establish what is typical (normal) development. According to the developmental view, typical development can be described statistically, by observing in large numbers of individuals those characteristics that occur most frequently at a specific age. For example, when we state that the average 3-month-old infant is able to follow a moving object visually, *average* is a statistical term based on observations of the behavior of 3-month-old infants. When an individual child's growth pattern is compared to that group average, differences in development (either advanced or delayed) are labeled accordingly.

A CULTURAL VIEW. From a cultural perspective, *normal* is defined by societal values. Whereas a developmental view considers only the frequency of behaviors to define differences, a cultural approach suggests that differences can be explained partly by examining the *values* inherent within a culture. What constitutes a significant difference varies over time, from culture to culture, and among the social classes within a culture. People are considered *deviant* when they do something that is disapproved of by other members within the dominant culture. For example, in some cultures, intelligence is described in terms of how well someone

FIGURE 1.1

Three Approaches to Describing Human Differences

Developmental Approach

Cultural View

Self-Labeling

Match the names to the descriptions:

1. He was diagnosed with amyotrophic lateral sclerosis (ALS–Lou Gehrig's disease) at the age of 21. He must use a wheelchair and have round-the-clock nursing care. His speech has been severely affected, and he communicates through a computer by selecting words from a screen that are expressed through a speech synthesizer. Acknowledged as one of the greatest physicists in history, he developed a theory on black holes that provided new insights into the origin of the universe. Currently, he is professor of mathematics at Cambridge University, a post once held by Sir Isaac Newton.

a. Abert Einstein

b. Sarah Berhardt

c. Nelson Rockefeller

d. Stephen Hawking

e. Whoopi Goldberg

f. George S. Patton Jr.

g. Walt Disney

h. Tom Cruise

i. James Earl Jones

term governor of New York and was appointed vice president of the United States during the Nixon administration.

6. He is the voice of Darth Vader and the most in-demand narrator in Hollywood. Virtually mute as a child, he stuttered throughout most of his youth. With the help of his high school English teacher, he overcame stuttering by reading Shakespeare aloud to himself and then to audiences. He went on to debating and finally to stage and screen acting.

7. He was regarded as a slow learner during his school years and never had much success in public education. Later, he became the best-known cartoonist in history, producing the first full-length animated motion picture.

2. He did not learn to read at all until he was 12 years old and continued having difficulty reading all his life. He was able to get through school by memorizing his teachers' entire lectures. Acknowledged as one of the greatest strategists in military history, he gained fame as a four-star general in World War II.

3. She was disabled by an accident in 1914 and eventually had to have part of her leg amputated. Regarded as one of the greatest French actresses in history, she continued her career on stage until her death in 1923.

4. A well-known, tireless humanitarian advocate for children, the homeless, and human rights, also involved in the battles against substance abuse and AIDS, this Oscar-winning actress and Grammy winner is a high school dropout with an acknowledged reading disability.

5. He was diagnosed with severe dyslexia, which made reading very difficult for him throughout life. He became a four-

8. He did not speak until the age of 3. Even as an adult he found that searching for words was laborious. Schoolwork, especially math, was difficult for him, and he was unable to express himself in written language. He was thought to be "simple-minded" (retarded) until he discovered that he could achieve through visualizing rather than the use of oral language. His theory of relativity, which revolutionized modern physics, was developed in his spare time. *Time* magazine named him the most important person of the 20th century.

9. He has never learned to read due to severe dyslexia and was unable to finish high school. Today he is regarded as one of most accomplished actors of his time. Although unable to read, he can memorize his lines from an auditory source (cassette tape or someone reading to him).

SOURCE: The source of this quiz is unknown. It was adapted from the Family Village website (http://www.familyvillage.wisc.edu/index.htmlx) and from *Take a Walk in My Shoes—A Guide Book for Youth on Diversity Awareness Activities* by Yuri Morita, June 1996, Office of Affirmative Action, Division of Agriculture & National Resources, University of California, 300 Lakeside Drive, 6th Floor, Oakland, CA 94612-3560. Phone 510/987-0096.

Answers: 1(d), 2(f), 3(b), 4(e), 5(c), 6(i), 7(g), 8(a), 9(h)

scores on a test measuring a broad range of abilities, and in other cultures, intelligence is much more closely related to how skillful someone is at hunting or fishing. The idea that people are the products of their cultures has received its greatest support from anthropology, which emphasizes the diversity and arbitrary nature of cultural rules regarding dress, eating habits, sexual habits, politics, and religion.

SELF-LABELING. Everyone engages in a self-labeling process that others may not recognize. Thus, self-imposed labels reflect how we perceive ourselves, not how others see us. Conversely, a person may be labeled by society but not accept that label. Such was the case with Thomas Edison. Although the schools labeled Edison an intellectually incapable child, he eventually recognized that he was an individualist. He proved himself by ignoring the label imposed on him and pursuing his own interests as an inventor. (See the nearby Reflect on This feature on page 7 and take a quiz on other famous people with disabilities.)

The Effects of Being Labeled

Reactions to a label differ greatly from one person to another but can often be negative (Dajini, 2001; Persaud, 2000; Woolfolk, 2004). In two studies of college students' reactions to various labels used to describe people with intellectual disabilities (mental retardation) and learning disabilities, researchers found that older terms, such as *mental subnormality* and *mental handicap,* generate a more negative reaction than newer terms, such as *learning difficulty* and *learning disability* (Hastings & Remington, 1993; Hastings, Songua-Barke, & Remington, 1993). However, only one term, *exceptional,* received a positive rating from the college students studied. The authors attributed this positive reaction to the students defining *exceptional* as meaning "much above average."

SEPARATING THE PERSON AND THE LABEL. Once a label has been affixed to an individual, the two may become inseparable. For example, Becky has been identified as having mental retardation. The tendency is to refer to Becky and her condition as one in the same—Becky is retarded. Becky is described by her label (retardation), which loses sight of the fact that she is first and foremost a human being, and that her exceptional characteristics (intellectual and social differences) are only a small part of who she is. To treat Becky as a label rather than as a person with special needs is an injustice, not only to Becky but to everyone else as well.

ENVIRONMENTAL BIAS. The environment in which we view someone can clearly influence our perceptions of that person. For example, it can be said that if you are in a mental hospital, you must be insane. In a classic study, Rosenhan (1973) investigated this premise by having himself and seven other "sane" individuals admitted to a number of state mental hospitals across the United States. Once in the mental hospitals, these subjects behaved normally. The question was whether the staff would perceive them as people who were healthy instead of as patients who were mentally ill. Rosenhan reported that the seven pseudopatients were never detected by the hospital staff (although several of the real patients recognized them as imposters). Throughout their hospital stays, the pseudopatients were incorrectly labeled and treated as schizophrenics. Rosenhan's investigation demonstrated that the environment in which the observations are made can bias the perception of what is normal.

Including People with Disabilities in Family and Community Settings

FOCUS 3
Describe the services for people with disabilities through most of the 20th century. What was the role of families in bringing about change?

A Brief History

Throughout recorded history, people perceived as disabled have been vulnerable to practices such as infanticide, slavery, physical abuse, and abandonment. These practices reflected a common societal fear that the so-called mentally and morally defective would defile the human race. It was widely believed that most deviance was caused by hereditary factors that, if left unchecked, would result in widespread social problems (Braddock & Parrish, 2002).

Humanitarian reform in the last half of the 18th century brought an era of optimism concerning the treatment and eventual cure of people described as deviant. However, when deviance wasn't cured and continued to be a major social problem well into the 19th century, many professionals became convinced that it was necessary to sterilize and segregate large numbers of "mental and social degenerates," as they were called at the time. Legal measures were taken to prohibit these people from marrying. Eventually, legislation was expanded to include their compulsory **sterilization**, and laws were passed in an effort to reduce the number of so-called *deviates.* Laws in some countries contained provisions for sterilizing people with mental retardation, individuals with epilepsy, the sexually promiscuous, and criminals. In addition to marriage and sterilization laws, measures were passed to move large numbers of individuals from their local communities to isolated special-care facilities. These facilities became widely known as **institutions** and have been variously called schools, hospitals, colonies, prisons, and asylums.

The institutions of the early 20th century became concerned with social control as they grew in size and as financial resources diminished. To manage large numbers of individuals on a limited financial base, these facilities had to establish rigid rules and regulations, stripping away individual identities and forcing people into group regimentation. For example, individuals could not have personal possessions, were forced to wear institutional clothing, and were issued identification tags and numbers. Locked living units, barred windows, and high walls enclosing the grounds characterized institutions. Organized treatment programs declined, and the number of "terminal," uncured patients grew, resulting in institutional expansion and the erection of new buildings. Given the public skepticism and professional pessimism concerning the value of treatment programs, this growth meant diminishing funds for mental health care. This alarming situation remained unchanged for nearly five decades and declined even further during the Great Depression of the 1930s. By the early 1950s, thousands of people had been committed to mental hospitals throughout the United States, and comparable numbers of persons with mental retardation lived in segregated institutions referred to as colonies, hospitals, or training schools. Several attempts to reform institutions were initiated. The American Psychiatric Association led efforts to inspect and rate the nation's mental hospitals and called attention to their lack of therapeutic intervention and their deplorable living conditions. (For more in-depth information on the history of institutions in the United States, see Blatt & Kaplan, 1974; Wolfensberger, 1975.)

> **Sterilization**
> The process of making an individual unable to reproduce, usually accomplished surgically.

> **Institution**
> An establishment or facility governed by a collection of fundamental rules.

Parents and Professionals Organize to Bring About Change

In spite of the growth of segregated institutions in the 20th century, the vast majority of people with disabilities remained at home within their families. For families, the choice to keep the child at home meant they were on their own, receiving little or no outside support. Government resources were very limited, and available funding was directed to support services outside of the family, often even beyond the community where they lived (Braddock & Parrish, 2002). For the better part of this century, many families who had a child with a disability were unable to get help for basic needs, such as medical and dental care, social services, and education.

In response to the lack of government support, and in an effort coinciding with the civil rights movement in the United States, parents of children with disabilities began to organize in about 1950. United Cerebral Palsy (UCP) was founded in 1949, and the National Association for Retarded Children[1] (NARC) began in 1950. The UCP and NARC joined other professional organizations already in existence, such as the National Association for the Deaf, the American Association on Mental Deficiency,[2] the Council for Exceptional Children, and the American Federation for the Blind, to advocate for the rights of persons with disabilities. The purpose of these national organizations was to get accurate information to families with disabilities, professionals, policy makers, and the general public. Each organization focused on the rights of people with disabilities to be included in family and community life and have access to medical treatment, social services, and education. Other parent groups followed, including the National Society for Autistic Children (1961) and the Association for Children with Learning Disabilities[3] (1964). Over the next three decades, litigation ensued on the

[1]Now the ARC—A National Organization on Intellectual Disabilities (The ARC).
[2]Now the American Association on Intellectual and Developmental Disabilities (AAIDD).
[3]Now the Learning Disabilities Association (LDA).

rights of people with disabilities to access services within their own communities. Through the advocacy of parent and professionals organizations, the civil rights of people with disabilities were finally recognized with the passage of the Americans with Disabilities Act (ADA) in 1990. We will now examine the ways in which the rights of people with disabilities to participate as equal members of society were reaffirmed through ADA.

The Americans with Disabilities Act (ADA)

In 1973, the U.S. Congress passed an amendment to the Vocational Rehabilitation Act that included a provision prohibiting discrimination against persons with disabilities in federally assisted programs and activities. **Section 504** of the Act stated,

> No otherwise qualified person with a disability . . . shall, solely on the basis of disability, be denied access to, or the benefits of, or be subjected to discrimination under any program or activity provided by, any entity/institution that receives federal financial assistance.

Section 504 has been hailed as the first civil rights law for people with disabilities, and it set the stage for passage of the most sweeping civil rights legislation in the United States since the **Civil Rights Act of 1964**: the **Americans with Disabilities Act (ADA)** signed into law in 1990. The purpose of ADA is to prevent discrimination on the basis of disability in employment, programs and services provided by state and local governments, goods and services provided by private companies, and commercial facilities. (See the nearby Reflect on This, "One City's Response to ADA," on page 11.)

In the past, people with disabilities have had to contend with the harsh reality that learning to live independently did not guarantee access to all that society had to offer in terms of services and jobs. Although several states have long had laws that promise otherwise, access to places such as public restrooms and restaurants and success in mainstream corporate America have often eluded those with disabilities, primarily because of architectural and attitudinal barriers. ADA is intended to change these circumstances, affirming the rights of more than 50 million Americans with disabilities to participate in the life of their community. Much as the Civil Rights Act of 1964 gave clout to the African American struggle for equality, ADA has promised to do the same for those with disabilities. Whether it will succeed in eliminating the fears and prejudices of the general community remains to be seen, but the reasons for such legislation were obvious. First, it was clear that people with disabilities faced discrimination in employment, access to public and private accommodations (hotels, theaters, restaurants, grocery stores), and services offered through state and local governments (N.O.D./Harris & Associates, 2000, 2004). Second, because the historic Civil Rights Act of 1964 did not even mention people with disabilities, they had no federal protection against discrimination except through the somewhat limited provisions in Section 504. As the United States Department of Justice (2006) put it,

> Barriers to employment, transportation, public accommodations, public services, and telecommunications have imposed staggering economic and social costs on American society and have undermined our well-intentioned efforts to educate, rehabilitate, and employ individuals with disabilities. The Americans with Disabilities Act gives civil rights protections to individuals with disabilities similar to those provided to individuals on the basis of race, color, sex, national origin, age, and religion. It guarantees equal opportunity for individuals with disabilities in public accommodations, employment, transportation, State and local government services, and telecommunications.

In 2002, The National Organization on Disability (N.O.D.) and Harris and Associates released the results of a survey on how Americans perceived ADA 12 years after its passage. The survey revealed strong and sustained public endorsement of this landmark civil rights legislation. Seventy-seven percent were aware of ADA. Of those who had heard of the act, 93% approved of what it is trying to accomplish.

Sidebar

➤ **Section 504**

Provision with the Vocational Rehabilitation Act of 1973 that prohibits discrimination against persons with disabilities in federally assisted programs and activities.

➤ **Civil Rights Act of 1964**

Legislation passed in the United States that prohibits discrimination against individuals on the basis of race, sex, religion, or national origin.

➤ **Americans with Disabilities Act (ADA)**

Civil rights legislation in the United States that provides a mandate to end discrimination against people with disabilities in private-sector employment, all public services, public accommodations, transportation, and telecommunications.

Focus 4

What is the purpose of the Americans with Disabilities Act?

Council for Exceptional Children

Standard 1: Foundations

Building a Barrier-Free Community for 10-Year-Old Brittany and Her Friends

Fernandina Beach, Florida, a resort community of 8,800 residents on Amelia Island between the Atlantic Ocean and the Amelia River, is Florida's second-oldest city and the state's first resort area. With its 50-block downtown historic district, golf courses, parks and nature areas, beaches, and a resident shrimping fleet, the community welcomes visitors and vacationers from all corners of the country. And recently, Fernandina Beach became an even more welcoming place for people with disabilities.

The city of Fernandina Beach made a decision—and a commitment—to go above and beyond the minimum ADA requirements and to make the city as usable and accessible as possible for everyone. To do this, city officials and residents worked together to find new approaches to accessibility, an experience they found both gratifying and exciting.

The city is working to make all its playgrounds accessible. Each city playground will have new accessible equipment, accessible playground surfaces, and accessible paths to the playground equipment. Cheri Fisher is thrilled with the changes. She no longer has to lift her daughter onto the play

equipment and can happily watch as Brittany and her buddy go down the slide together. "What's really good is that Brittany now can play longer because she's not as tired from trudging to the playground. She also can play on pretty much all the equipment and play together with her friends; she's not being excluded now." Ten-year-old Brittany, who uses crutches and sometimes a wheelchair to get around, agrees. "I like the rope things that go round and round and I like the slide with the bumps and I liked the three of us sliding together!" In addition to creating accessible playgrounds, the city installed an accessible route to the picnic pavilions in each of its city parks and accessible picnic tables in every pavilion.

The city constructed a beach walkover at the Main Beach and constructed an accessible viewing area connected to the accessible beach path, allowing as many as eight people using wheelchairs to sit together on the beach and enjoy an unobstructed view of the surf. The city plans to construct two additional walkovers at opposite ends of the city at the North Park and Seaside Park Beaches to give wheelchair users access to the beach nearest them. The city also purchased two beach wheelchairs for those who wish to join family and friends near the water on the sandy beach. It has plans to buy more.

SOURCE: United States Department of Justice (2006). A resort community improves access to city programs and services for residents and vacationers. Available: http://www.usdoj.gov/crt/ada/fernstor.htm (retrieved February 18, 2006).

The ADA Definition of Disability

Under ADA, a person with a disability is defined as (1) having a physical or mental impairment that substantially limits him or her in some major life activity, and (2) having experienced discrimination resulting from this physical or mental impairment. Federal regulations define a physical or mental impairment as

(1) any physiological disorder, or condition, cosmetic disfigurement, or anatomical loss affecting one or more of the following body systems: neurological, musculoskeletal, special sense organs, respiratory (including speech organs), cardiovascular, reproductive, digestive, genito-urinary, hemic and lymphatic, skin, and endocrine; or

(2) any mental or psychological disorder, such as mental retardation, organic brain syndrome, emotional or mental illness, and specific learning disabilities. (29 C.F.R. § 1630.2[h])

Federal regulations do not establish an exclusive list of specific impairments covered by ADA. Instead, they describe the type of condition that constitutes a physical or mental impairment. ADA does, however, specify certain conditions that are *not* considered "impairments." These include homosexuality and bisexuality; environmental, cultural, and economic disadvantages such as a prison record or a lack of education; and age (42 U.S.C. § 12211[a]; 29 C.F.R. pt. 1630 app. § 1630.2[h]). A person does not have an impairment simply because he or she is advanced in years.

Major Provisions of ADA

➤ **Reasonable accommodations**

Requirements within ADA to ensure that a person with a disability has an equal chance of participation. The intent is to create a "fair and level playing field" for the person with a disability. A reasonable accommodation takes into account each person's needs resulting from her or his disability. Accommodations may be arranged in the areas of employment, transportation, or telecommunications.

ADA mandates protections for people with disabilities in public- and private-sector employment, all public services, and public accommodations, transportation, and telecommunications. The U.S. Department of Justice is charged with the responsibility of ensuring that these provisions are enforced on behalf of all people with disabilities. The intent of ADA is to create a "fair and level playing field" for eligible persons with disabilities. To do so, the law specifies that **reasonable accommodations** need to be made that take into account each person's needs resulting from his or her disabilities. As defined in law, the principal test for a reasonable accommodation is its effectiveness: Does the accommodation provide an opportunity for a person with a disability to achieve the same level of performance and to enjoy benefits equal to those of an average, similarly situated person without a disability? See the Debate Forum, "Leveling the Playing Field or Creating Advantage? Casey's Story," below.

DEBATE FORUM

LEVELING THE PLAYING FIELD OR CREATING ADVANTAGE? CASEY'S STORY

Casey Martin was born on June 2, 1972, with a very rare congenital disorder (Klippel-Trenauny-Weber syndrome), a condition with no known cure. The disorder is degenerative and causes serious blood circulation problems in Casey's right leg and foot. His right leg is about half the size of his left, and when forced to walk on it, Casey experiences excruciating pain and swelling. Casey can only expect these problems to worsen as he grows older, and there is a possibility that leg amputation will be necessary in the future.

Obviously, this condition would be difficult and very painful under any circumstances, but Casey's occupation is professional golf—a career that was fostered early in life and one that he is very good at. During his college years, Casey went to Stanford and played with Tiger Woods on the team that won the 1994 NCAA championship. In 1995, Casey joined the Nike pro tour and was just one step away from the pinnacle of golf, the Professional Golf Association (PGA) tour. However, his condition continued to deteriorate, and the pain in his right leg and foot grew steadily worse. He finally reached the point where he could no longer walk a golf course but had to use a cart to get around. Although the PGA had modified the rules of golf for players with disabilities in recreational settings, the organization did not permit the use of a golf cart during *competitions*. Given the progressive state of his disability, Casey requested an exemption that would allow him to ride rather than walk. The PGA refused his request, and Casey took the matter to court, claiming discrimination

on the basis of the Americans with Disabilities Act. In February of 1998, a U.S. magistrate found in Casey's favor. Casey played the events on the Nike tour throughout 1998 and 1999, qualifying for his first PGA tour event in January 2000. Meanwhile, the PGA appealed the decision to allow Casey to ride a cart, and in a 7-to-2 decision on May 29, 2001, the U.S. Supreme Court ruled that Casey Martin must be allowed to ride a cart during competition. The Court ruled that allowing Casey access to the cart would not "fundamentally alter" the game of golf or give him any advantage over other golfers on the course.

Although the U.S. Supreme Court ruled in Casey's favor, the debate continues over whether he has been given an advantage over his fellow pro golfers by being able to ride a golf cart when others must walk. Is riding a cart an advantage for Casey, or does the golf cart simply allow the "playing field" to be leveled, as intended in the Americans with Disabilities Act? What is your view?

The PGA's attempt to disallow Casey Martin's use of a golf cart was an act of discrimination against a person with a disability. The PGA is a public entity, and golf courses are places of public accommodation under the Americans with Disabilities Act. Therefore, the association must provide *reasonable accommodations* for someone with a permanent disability. As the Supreme Court ruling notes, Casey met all the ADA requirements. He has a permanent disability, and without a reasonable accommodation (riding in a golf cart) he could not participate in his chosen profession. The PGA argues that riding in a cart creates an advantage for Casey. Couldn't it be argued that riding is actually a disadvantage? From a sitting position, Casey can't get the same perspective on and feel for the course that his competitors have. The PGA also argued that it should have the right to determine its own rules for competitions. Fine! Change the rules to allow Casey and any other golfer with disabilities to use a cart. In the end, if letting Casey Martin ride means that the PGA must allow every golfer to use a cart, so be it. Isn't the PGA's motto "anything is possible"?

One cannot help but express admiration for the grit and determination of Casey Martin. There is no doubt that he is a person with a tragic medical disability. However, with all due respect to the decision of the U.S. Supreme Court, Congress never intended for ADA to require an organization such as the PGA to change its basic rules of operation and thus create an advantage for one golfer over another. Physical requirements, including walking up to five miles on any given day in unfavorable weather, is an *essential element* of golf at its highest level. Any golfer who is allowed to ride in a cart, disabled or not, will have an unfair advantage over other competitors. If the PGA allows this for one player, it will create hardship for others, which is exactly what ADA did not want. The real issue here is that a fundamental rule of golf has stood from its beginning hundreds of years ago: Players in the highest levels of competition must walk the course as part of the test of their skills. One set of rules must apply to all players.

The major provisions of the ADA include the following:

➤ *Employment.* ADA mandates that employers not discriminate in any employment practices, including job application procedures, hiring, firing, advancement, compensation, training, and other terms, conditions, and privileges of employment. It applies to recruitment, advertising, tenure, layoff, leave, fringe benefits, and all other employment-related activities. The law applies to any business with 15 or more employees. (See the nearby Reflect on This, "Top Ten Reasons to Hire People with Disabilities" below.)

REFLECT ON THIS

TOP 10 REASONS TO HIRE PEOPLE WITH DISABILITIES

1. Employees with disabilities can ease concerns about labor supply.

2. People with disabilities have equal or higher job performance ratings, higher retention rates, and lower absenteeism.

3. Employees with disabilities can relate better to customers with disabilities, who represent $1 trillion in annual aggregate consumer spending.

4. Diverse work groups can create better solutions to business challenges.

5. People with disabilities are better educated than ever, and are proven to have met and/or exceeded challenges.

6. A person with a disability motivates work groups and increases productivity.

7. Companies that hire and accommodate people with disabilities in their workplaces can receive tax benefits.

8. Employing people with disabilities is good for the individual, the business, and society. This is a "win-win-win" strategy.

9. People with disabilities are motivated by the desire to give something back, and have opportunities for personal growth, job flexibility, and social inclusion.

10. It's ability, not disability, that counts.

SOURCE: National Organization on Disability (2006) Top ten reasons to hire people with disabilities. Retrieved May 8, 2006, from http://www.nod.org/index.cfm?fuseaction=page.viewPage&pageID=1430&nodeID=1&FeatureID=253&redirected=1&CFID=7245299&CFTOKEN=6043927

➤ *Transportation.* ADA requires that all new public-transit buses, bus and train stations, and rail systems be accessible to people with disabilities. Transit authorities must provide transportation services to individuals with disabilities who cannot use fixed-route bus services. All Amtrak stations must be accessible to people with disabilities by the year 2010. Discrimination by air carriers in areas other than employment is not covered by ADA but rather by the Air Carrier Access Act (49 U.S.C. 1374 [c]).

➤ *Public accommodations.* Restaurants, hotels, and retail stores may not discriminate against individuals with disabilities. Physical barriers in existing facilities must be removed, if removal is readily achievable. If not, alternative methods of providing the services must be offered. All new construction and alterations of facilities must be accessible.

➤ *Government.* State and local agencies may not discriminate against qualified individuals with disabilities. All government facilities, services, and communications must be accessible to people with disabilities.

➤ *Telecommunications.* ADA requires that all companies offering telephone service to the general public must offer telephone relay services to individuals with hearing loss who use telecommunication devices or similar equipment.

Making the ADA Dream a Reality

Focus 5
What services and supports must be available to ensure that a person with a disability is able to live and learn successfully in a community setting?

Legislating against discrimination is one thing; enforcing laws against it is another. The purpose of ADA was to ensure that comprehensive services (such as employment, housing, educational programs, public transportation, restaurant access, and religious activities) were available to all individuals within, or as close as possible to, their family and community settings. In 1999, the U.S. Supreme Court ruled in *L. C. & E. W. v. Olmstead* (now known as the *Olmstead* decision) that it is a violation of ADA to discriminate against people with disabilities by providing services only in institutions when they could be served in a community-based setting. This historic decision encouraged states to reevaluate how they deliver publicly funded long-term care services to people with disabilities. A state can be in compliance with ADA if it has (1) a comprehensive, effective working plan for placing qualified people in less restrictive settings, and (2) a waiting list for community-based services that ensures people can receive services and be moved off the list at a reasonable pace (Fox-Grage, Folkemer, Straw, & Hansen, 2002).

Individuals with disabilities must have access to generic community services, including dental care, medical treatment, life insurance, and so forth. Access to these services allows people the opportunity to be included in community life. Successful inclusion is based on two factors: (1) the individual's ability, with appropriate education and training, to adapt to societal expectations, and (2) the willingness of society to adapt to and accommodate individuals with differences.

Access to adequate housing and to a barrier-free environment is essential for people with physical disabilities. A **barrier-free facility** may be created by renovating existing facilities and requiring that new buildings and public transportation incorporate barrier-free designs. People in wheelchairs or on crutches need entrance ramps to and within public buildings; accessibility to public telephones, vending machines, and restrooms; and lifts for public transportation vehicles. Available community living environments could include private homes, specialized boarding homes, supervised apartments, group homes, and foster homes.

Recreation and leisure opportunities within the community vary substantially according to the individual's age and the severity of his or her disability, and the availability of such opportunities also varies from community to community. Thus many persons with disabilities may not have access to dance and music lessons, gymnastics training, swimming lessons, and scouting activities that are generally available to others within the community. Similar problems exist for children, adolescents, and adults with disabilities, many of whom may do little with their leisure time beyond watching television.

Recreational programs must be developed to assist individuals in developing worthwhile leisure activities and more satisfying lifestyles. Therapeutic recreation is a profession con-

➤ **Barrier-free facility**

A building or other structure that is designed and constructed so that people with mobility disabilities (such as those in wheelchairs) can move freely through all areas without encountering architectural obstructions.

Council for Exceptional Children

Standard 5: Learning Environments and Social Interactions

cerned specifically with this goal: using recreation to help people adapt their physical, emotional, or social characteristics to take advantage of leisure activities more independently in a community setting.

Work is essential to the creation of successful lifestyles for all adults, including those with disabilities. Yet many individuals with disabilities are unable to gain employment during their adult years. A poll conducted by the National Organization on Disability and Harris Associates (2004) found significant gaps between the employment rates of people with disabilities and the employment rates of their peers who were not disabled. Only 35%

The inclusion of children and adults with disabilities in recreation and sports activities recognizes and accepts the range of human diversity. What are some other reasons for people with disabilities to participate in community recreation and sports activities?

CASE STUDY

SARINA

Over the past several years, many changes have occurred in Sarina's life. After spending most of her life in a large institution, Sarina, now in her late 30s, moved into an apartment with two other women, both of whom have a disability. She receives assistance from a local supported-living program in developing skills that will allow her to make her own decisions and become more independent in the community.

Over the years, Sarina has had many labels describing her disability, including mental retardation, epilepsy, autism, physical disability, chronic health problems, and serious emotional disturbance. She is very much challenged both mentally and physically. Medical problems associated with epilepsy necessitate the use of medications that affect Sarina's behavior (motivation, attitude, etc.) and her physical well-being. During her early 20s, while walking up a long flight of stairs, Sarina had a seizure that resulted in a fall and a broken neck. The long-term impact from the fall was a paralyzed right hand and limited use of her left leg.

Sarina's life goal has been to work in a real job, make money, and have choices about how she spends it. For most of her life, the goal has been out of reach. Her only jobs have been in sheltered workshops, where she worked for next to nothing, doing piecemeal work such as sorting envelopes, putting together cardboard boxes, or folding laundry. Whereas most of the focus in the past has been on what Sarina "can't do" (can't read, can't get along with supervisors, can't handle the physical requirements of a job), her family and the professionals on her support team are looking more at her very strong desire to succeed in a community job.

A job has opened up for a stock clerk at a local video store about 3 miles from Sarina's apartment. The store manager is willing to pay minimum wage for someone to work 4 to 6 hours a day stocking the shelves with videos and handling some basic tasks (such as cleaning floors, washing windows, and dusting furniture). Sarina loves movies and is really interested in this job. With the support of family and her professional team, she has applied for the job.

APPLICATION

1. As Sarina's potential employer, what are some of the issues you would raise about her capability to perform the essential functions of the job?

2. What would you see as the "reasonable accommodations" necessary to help Sarina succeed at this job if she were to be hired?

of people with disabilities (ages 18 to 64) work full- or part-time, compared to 78% of people who are not disabled. A comparison of working and nonworking individuals with disabilities revealed that working individuals were more satisfied with life, had more money, and were less likely to blame their disability for preventing them from reaching their potential. For more insight into the employment of a person with disabilities, see the nearby Case Study, "Sarina," on page 15.

Multidisciplinary Collaboration

This chapter concludes with a brief examination of three disciplines concerned with supporting people with disabilities and their families in community settings: medicine, psychology, and sociology. Each discipline is unique in its understanding of, and approach to, people with disabilities. Figure 1.2 explains some of the terms associated with each field.

The Role of Health Care Professionals

The **medical model** has two dimensions: normalcy and pathology. *Normalcy* is defined as the absence of a biological problem. **Pathology** is defined as alterations in an organism caused by disease, resulting in a state of ill health that interferes with or destroys the integrity of the organism. The medical model, often referred to as the *disease model*, focuses primarily on biological problems and on defining the nature of the disease and its pathological effects on the individual. The model is universal and does not have values that are culturally relative. It is based on the premise that being healthy is better than being sick, regardless of the culture in which one lives.

When diagnosing a problem, a physician carefully follows a definite pattern of procedures that includes questioning the patient to obtain a history of the problem, conducting a physical examination and laboratory studies, and (in some cases) performing surgical exploration. The person who has a biological problem is labeled the *patient*, and the deficits are then described as the patient's *disease*.

We must go back more than 200 years to find the first documented attempts to personalize health care to serve the needs of people with differences. In 1799, as a young physician and

FOCUS **6**

How did the work of 19th-century physicians and philosophers contribute to our understanding of people with disabilities?

➤ **Medical model**

Model by which human development is viewed according to two dimensions: normal and pathological. *Normal* refers to the absence of biological problems, *pathological* to alterations in the organism caused by disease.

➤ **Pathology**

Alterations in an organism that are caused by disease.

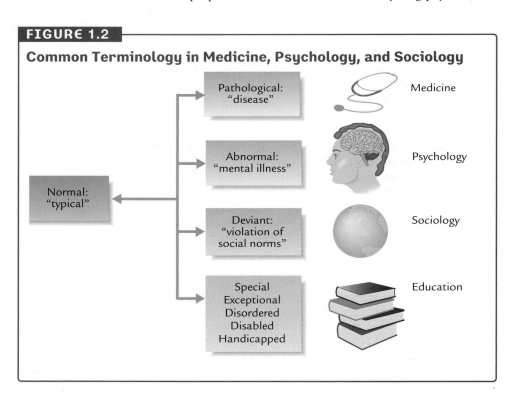

FIGURE 1.2

Common Terminology in Medicine, Psychology, and Sociology

Normal: "typical"

Pathological: "disease" — Medicine

Abnormal: "mental illness" — Psychology

Deviant: "violation of social norms" — Sociology

Special Exceptional Disordered Disabled Handicapped — Education

authority on diseases of the ear and on the education of those with hearing loss, Jean Marc Itard (1775–1838) believed that the environment, in conjunction with physiological stimulation, could contribute to the learning potential of any human being. Itard was influenced by the earlier work of Philippe Pinel (1742–1826), a French physician concerned with mental illness, and of John Locke (1632–1704), an English philosopher. Pinel maintained that people characterized as insane or idiots needed to be treated humanely, but his teachings emphasized that they were essentially incurable and that any treatment to remedy their disabilities would be fruitless. Locke, in contrast, described the mind as a "blank slate" that could be opened to all kinds of new stimuli. The positions of Pinel and Locke represent the classic controversy of **nature versus nurture:** What are the roles of heredity and environment in determining a person's capabilities?

Itard tested the theories of Pinel and Locke in his work with Victor, the so-called wild boy of Aveyron. Victor was 12 years old when found in the woods by hunters. He had not developed any language, and his behavior was virtually uncontrollable, described as savage or animal-like. Ignoring Pinel's diagnosis that the child was an incurable idiot, Itard took responsibility for Victor and put him through a program of sensory stimulation that was intended to cure his condition. After five years, Victor developed some verbal language and became more socialized as he grew accustomed to his new environment. Itard's work with Victor documented for the first time that learning is possible even for individuals described by most professionals as totally helpless.

Health care services for people with disabilities have evolved considerably since Itard's groundbreaking work. The focus today is directly on the individual in family and community settings. In many cases, the physician is the first professional with whom parents have contact concerning their child's disability, particularly when the child's problem is identifiable immediately after birth or during early childhood. The physician is the family adviser and communicates with parents regarding the medical prognosis and recommendations for treatment. However, too often physicians assume that they are the family's only counseling resource (Drew & Hardman, 2007). Physicians should be aware of additional resources within the community, including other parents, social workers, mental health professionals, and educators.

Health care services are often taken for granted simply because they are readily available to most people. This is not true, however, for many people with disabilities. It is not uncommon for a pediatrician to suggest that parents seek treatment elsewhere for their child with a disability, even when the problem is a common illness such as a cold or a sore throat.

It would be unfair to stereotype health care professionals as unresponsive to the needs of people with disabilities. On the contrary, medical technology has prevented many disabilities from occurring and has enhanced the quality of life for many people. However, to ensure that people with disabilities receive comprehensive health care services in a community setting, several factors must be considered. Physicians in community practice (such as general practitioners and pediatricians) must receive more training in the medical, psychological, and educational aspects of disability conditions. This training could include instruction regarding developmental milestones; attitudes toward children with disabilities; disabling conditions; prevention; screening, diagnosis, and assessment; interdisciplinary collaboration; effective communication with parents; long-term health care and social treatment programs; and community resources.

Health care professionals must also be willing to treat people with disabilities for

➤ **Nature versus nurture**
Controversy concerning how much of a person's ability is related to sociocultural influences (nurture) and how much to genetic factors (nature).

Physicians in community practice must be willing to provide medical care to people with disabilities. What additional training do you think is needed in order for physicians to care for people with disabilities?

➤ **Geneticist**

A professional who specializes in the study of heredity.

➤ **Genetic counselor**

A specially trained professional who counsels people about their chances of producing a seriously ill infant, in reference to their genetic history.

➤ **Physical therapist**

A professional who provides services that help restore function, improve mobility, relieve pain, and prevent or limit permanent physical disabilities. Physical therapists help restore, maintain, and promote overall fitness and health for people of all ages.

➤ **Occupational therapist**

A professional who specializes in developing self-care, work, and play activities to increase independent function and quality of life, enhance development, and prevent disability.

➤ **Conditioning**

The process by which new objects or situations elicit responses that were previously elicited by other stimuli.

➤ **Ecological approach**

An approach in psychology that ascribes abnormal behavior more to the interaction of an individual with the environment than to disease.

FOCUS **7**

Distinguish between abnormal behavior and social deviance.

➤ **Neurotic disorders**

Patterns of behavior characterized by combinations of anxieties, compulsions, obsessions, and phobias.

➤ **Psychotic disorders**

Serious behavior disorders resulting in a loss of contact with reality and characterized by delusions, hallucinations, or illusions.

common illnesses when the treatment is irrelevant to the patient's disability. Physicians need not become disability specialists, but they must have enough knowledge to refer patients to appropriate specialists when necessary. For instance, physicians must be aware of, and willing to refer patients to, other community resources, such as social workers, educators, and psychologists. The health care profession must continue to support physician specialists and other allied health personnel who are well equipped to work with people with disabilities. These specialized health professionals include **geneticists** and **genetic counselors, physical therapists** and **occupational therapists,** public health nurses, and nutritional and dietary consultants.

The Role of Psychologists

Modern psychology is the science of human and animal behavior, the study of the overt acts and mental events of an organism that can be observed and evaluated. Broadly viewed, psychology is concerned with every detectable action of an individual. Behavior is the focus of psychology, and when the behavior of an individual does not meet the criteria of normalcy, it is labeled *abnormal.*

Psychology, as we know it today, is more than 125 years old. In 1879, Wilhelm Wundt (1832–1920) defined psychology as the science of conscious experience. His definition was based on the *principle of introspection*—looking into oneself to analyze experiences. William James (1842–1910) expanded Wundt's conception of conscious experience in his treatise *The Principles of Psychology* (1890) to include learning, motivation, and emotions. In 1913, John B. Watson (1878–1958) shifted the focus of psychology from conscious experience to observable behavior and mental events.

In 1920, Watson conducted an experiment with an 11-month-old child named Albert. Albert showed no fear of a white rat when he was initially exposed to the animal, seeing it as a toy and playing with it freely. Watson then introduced a loud, terrifying noise directly behind Albert each time the rat was presented. After a period of time, the boy became frightened by the sight of any furry white object, even though the loud noise was no longer present. Albert had learned to fear rats through **conditioning,** the process in which new objects or situations elicit responses that were previously elicited by other stimuli. Watson thus demonstrated that abnormal behavior could be learned through the interaction of the individual with environmental stimuli (Watson & Rayner, 1920).

In spite of Watson's work, most theorists during the first half of the 20th century considered the medical model to be the most logical and scientific approach to understanding abnormal behavior. The public was more accepting of the view that people with psychological disturbances were sick and not fully responsible for their problems.

The **ecological approach**, which emerged in the latter half of the 20th century, supported Watson's theories. This approach views abnormal behavior more as a result of an individual's interaction with the environment than as a disease. It reflects the belief that social and environmental stress, in combination with the individual's inability to cope, lead to psychological disturbances.

We cannot live in today's society without encountering the dynamics of abnormal behavior. The media are replete with stories of murder, suicide, sexual aberration, burglary, robbery, embezzlement, child abuse, and other incidents that display abnormal behavior. Each case represents a point on the continuum of personal maladjustment that exists in society. Levels of maladjustment range from behaviors that are slightly deviant or eccentric (but still within the confines of normal human experience) through **neurotic disorders** (partial disorganization characterized by combinations of anxieties, compulsions, obsessions, and phobias) to **psychotic disorders** (severe disorganization resulting in loss of contact with reality and characterized by delusions, hallucinations, and illusions).

In Western culture, the study of abnormal behavior historically has been based in philosophy and religion. Until the Middle Ages, the disturbed or mad person was thought to have "made a pact with the devil," and the psychological affliction was believed to be a result of divine punishment or the work of devils, witches, or demons residing within the person. The earliest known treatment for mental disorders, called *trephining,* involved drilling holes in a person's skull to permit evil spirits to leave (Carlson et al., 2007).

Today's psychologists use myriad approaches in the treatment of mental disorders, including behavior therapy, rational-emotive therapy, group psychotherapy, family therapy, and client-centered therapy. According to Carlson et al. (2007), the majority of psychologists describe their therapeutic philosophy as eclectic. They choose from many different approaches in determining the best way to work with an individual in need of psychological help.

The Role of Social Services Professionals

Whereas psychology focuses primarily on the behavior of the individual, social services professionals are concerned with modern cultures, group behaviors, societal institutions, and intergroup relationships. These professionals examine individuals in relation to their physical and social environment. When individuals meet the social norms of the group, they are considered normal. When individuals are unable to adapt to social roles or to establish appropriate interpersonal relationships, their behaviors are labeled **deviant**. Unlike medical pathology, social differences cannot be defined in universal terms. Instead, they are defined within the context of the culture, in any way the culture chooses to define them.

Even within the same society, different social groups often define human differences in various ways. Groups of people who share the same norms and values develop their own rules about what is and what is not acceptable social behavior. Four principles serve as guidelines in determining who will be labeled socially different:

1. Normal behavior must meet societal, cultural, or group expectations. Difference is defined as a violation of social norms.

2. Social differences are not necessarily illnesses as defined by the medical model. Failure to conform to societal norms does not imply that the individual has pathological or biological deficits.

3. Each culture determines the range of behaviors that are defined as normal or deviant and then enforces these norms. Those people with the greatest power within the culture can impose their criteria for normalcy on those who are less powerful.

4. Social differences may be caused by the interaction of several factors, including genetic makeup and individual experiences within the social environment.

Today, many different kinds of social services professionals specialize across more than 50 subfields and specialties. Within each specialty, these professionals undertake a systematic study of the workings of social groups, organizations, cultures, and societies and their influence on individual and group behavior. The social services professional accumulates and disseminates information about social behavior (including disability) in the context of the society as a whole. The following are just a few examples of specialties that may include an emphasis on disability: sociology, social work, gerontology (the study of aging), criminology and criminal justice, and family and marriage. This chapter has examined many different perspectives on people with disabilities, including terms commonly used to describe these individuals, bringing about social change and inclusion through the Americans with Disabilities Act, and understanding people with disabilities from the perspectives of medicine, psychology, and sociology. In the next chapter, we focus on the education of students with disabilities in America's schools. Chapter 2, "Education for All," is an examination of the origins of special education, the characteristics of effective instruction, the Individuals with Disabilities Education Act, and current trends in educational services and supports.

➤ **Deviant**
A term used to describe the behavior of individuals who are unable to adapt to social roles or to establish appropriate interpersonal relationships.

FOCUS REVIEW

FOCUS 1 Why do we label people?

- Labels are an attempt to describe, identify, and distinguish one person from another.

- Many medical, psychological, social, and educational services require that an individual be labeled in order to determine who is eligible to receive special services.

- Labels help professionals communicate more effectively with one another and provide a common ground for evaluating research findings.

- Labels enable professionals to differentiate more clearly the needs of one group of people from those of another.

FOCUS 2 Identify three approaches to describing human differences.

- The developmental approach is based on differences in the course of human development from what is considered normal physical, social, and intellectual growth. Human differences are the result of interaction between biological and environmental factors. Observing large numbers of individuals and looking for characteristics that occur most frequently at any given age can explain normal growth.

- The cultural approach defines *normal* in terms of established cultural standards. Human differences can be explained by examining the values of any given society. What is considered normal changes over time and differs from culture to culture.

- Self-labeling reflects how we perceive ourselves, although our perceptions may not be consistent with how others see us.

FOCUS 3 Describe the services for people with disabilities through most of the 20th century. What was the role of families in bringing about change?

- People with disabilities were viewed as being deviant or defective and were considered social problems.

- State laws were passed that prevented people with disabilities from marrying, mandated their sterilization, and eventually segregated them into large institutions.

- Many families who had a child with a disability were unable to get help for basic needs, such as medical and dental care, social services, and education.

- In the 1960s, parent and professional organizations were established to fight for the right of people with disabilities to be included in the community.

- Through the advocacy of parent and professional organizations, the civil rights of people with disabilities were finally recognized with the passage of the Americans with Disabilities Act (ADA) in 1990.

FOCUS 4 What is the purpose of the Americans with Disabilities Act?

- ADA provides a national mandate to end discrimination against individuals with disabilities in private-sector employment, all public services, and public accommodations, transportation, and telecommunications.

FOCUS 5 What services and supports must be available to ensure that an individual with a disability is able to live and learn successfully in a community setting?

- Comprehensive community services must be available, including access to housing, employment, public transportation, recreation, and religious activities.

- The individual should be able to purchase services such as medical and dental care, as well as adequate life insurance.

FOCUS 6 How did the work of 19th-century physicians and philosophers contribute to our understanding of people with disabilities?

- Early 19th-century physicians emphasized that people with disabilities should be treated humanely.

- Jean-Marc Itard demonstrated that an individual with a severe disability could learn new skills through physiological stimulation.

FOCUS 7 Distinguish between abnormal behavior and social deviance.

- Human behavior is the focus of psychology. When the behavior of an individual does not meet the criteria that are taken to indicate normalcy, it is labeled *abnormal.*

- Sociology is concerned with modern cultures, group behaviors, societal institutions, and intergroup relationships. When people are unable to adapt to social roles or establish interpersonal relationships, their behaviors are labeled *deviant.*

Council for
Exceptional
Children

BUILDING YOUR PORTFOLIO

If you are thinking about a career in special education, you should know that many states use national standards developed by the Council for Exceptional Children (CEC) to assess a teacher candidate's knowledge and skills for working with students with disabilities. See a complete listing of the ten CEC Content Standards on the inside front cover of this text.

CEC Content Standards Addressed in This Chapter

1 Foundations

2 Development and Characteristics of Learners

5 Learning Environments and Social Interactions

9 Professional and Ethical Practice

Assess Your Knowledge of the CEC Standards Addressed in This Chapter

Some states require that teacher candidates develop a portfolio of products that demonstrate their mastery of the CEC content standards. To assist in the development of products for this portfolio, you may wish to complete the following activities.

- Complete a written test of the chapter's content.

  If your instructor requires a written test of your content knowledge for this chapter, keep a copy for your portfolio. A practice test on the

information covered in this chapter is available through the Human Exceptionality Companion Website and the Student Study Guide.

- Respond to the Application Questions for the Case Study "Sarina."

  Review the Case Study and respond in writing to the application questions. Keep a copy of the Case Study and of your written response for your portfolio.

- Participate in a Community Service Learning Activity.

  Community service learning is a valuable way to enhance your learning experience. Visit our companion website (college.hmco.com/ pic/hardman9e) for suggested community service learning activities that correspond to the information presented in this chapter. Develop a reflective journal of the service learning experience for your portfolio.

WEB RESOURCES

The Americans with Disabilities Act

http://www.usdoj.gov/crt/ada/adahom1.htm

This website contains up-to-date information on ADA, along with often-asked questions about the law, stories of people with disabilities, and analysis of the law's major provisions.

The Council for Exceptional Children

http://www.cec.sped.org

The Council for Exceptional Children (CEC) is the largest international professional organization dedicated to improving educational outcomes for individuals with exceptionalities, students with disabilities, and the gifted. This site contains information on professional development opportunities, reviews of publications and products, and updates on the Individuals with Disabilities Education Act.

National Council on Disability

http://www.ncd.gov/

The National Council on Disability (N.C.D.) is a federal agency that advocates for policies, programs, and services that guarantee equal opportunity for people with disabilities. Its purpose is to empower people with disabilities to achieve economic self-sufficiency, independent living, and inclusion and integration into all aspects of society.

National Organization on Disability

http://www.nod.org/

The mission of the National Organization on Disability (N.O.D.) is to expand the participation and contribution of America's 54 million men, women, and children with disabilities in all aspects of life. This site contains information on opportunities for community involvement and economic participation for people with disabilities.

FURTHER READINGS

Jones, N. L. (2004). The Americans with Disabilities Act: Overview, regulations, and interpretations. New York: Novinka Books.

This book summarizes the major provisions of the Americans with Disabilities Act (ADA) and discusses recent issues, including rules, Supreme Court decisions, regulations, and information sources. ADA provides broad protection for individuals with disabilities from discrimination in employment, public accommodations and services operated by public entities, transportation, and telecommunications.

Braddock, D. (Ed.) (2002). *Disability at the Dawn of the 21st Century and the State of the States.* Washington, DC: The American Association on Mental Retardation.

This book provides an excellent historical perspective on the history of programs and services for people with developmental disabilities from the

age of institutions to inclusion in the 21st century. The authors also provide interesting facts and figures on state financing of services for people with disabilities.

Fleisher, D. J., & Zames, F. (2001). *The Disability Rights Movement.* Philadelphia: Temple University Press.

Based on interviews with almost a hundred activists, this book provides a detailed history of the struggle for disability rights in the United States. It is a complex story of shifts in consciousness, shifts in policy, and changing focuses on particular disabilities such, as blindness, deafness, polio, quadriplegia, psychiatric and developmental disabilities, chronic conditions (for example, cancer and heart disease), and AIDS.

COMPANION WEBSITE

Visit the companion website at college.hmco.com/pic/hardman9e for additional resources that support this text:

- HM Video Cases that present actual classroom scenarios that you may face every day as a teacher

- Practice ACE Exams that will help you prepare for quizzes, tests, and certification exams

- Flashcards of key terms

- Weblinks

Education for All

EDUCATION FOR SOME, BUT NOT ALL

In 1970, before the enactment of the federal protections in IDEA, schools in America educated only one in five students with disabilities. More than one million students were excluded from public schools and another 3.5 million did not receive appropriate services. Many states had laws excluding certain students, [such as] those who were blind, deaf, or labeled "emotionally disturbed" or "mentally retarded." Almost 200,000 school-age children with mental retardation and emotional disabilities were institutionalized. The likelihood of exclusion was greater for children with disabilities living in low-income, ethnic and racial minority, or rural communities. (National Council on Disability, 2000, p. 6)

MUCH HAS BEEN ACCOMPLISHED AND MUCH REMAINS TO BE DONE

Four decades ago, [the U.S.] Congress began to lend the resources of the federal government to the task of educating children with disabilities. Since then, special education has become one of the most important symbols of American compassion, inclusion, and educational opportunity. Over the years, what has become known as the Individuals with Disabilities Education Act has moved children with disabilities from institutions into classrooms, from the outskirts of society to the center of class instruction. Children who were once ignored are now protected by the law and given unprecedented access to a "free and appropriate public education." But America's special education system presents new and continuing challenges. . . . Hundreds of thousands of parents have seen the benefit of America's inclusive education system. But many more see room for improvement. . . . Although it is true that special education has created a base of civil rights and legal protections, children with disabilities remain those most at risk of being left behind. (President's Commission on Excellence in Special Education, 2002)

FROM ACCESS TO RESULTS IN THE EDUCATION OF CHILDREN WITH DISABILITIES

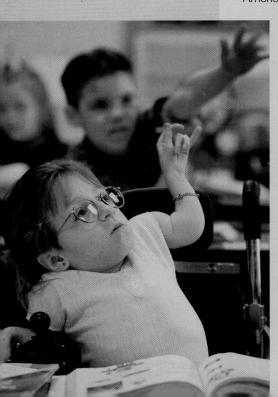

Disability is a natural part of the human experience and in no way diminishes the right of individuals to participate in or contribute to society. Improving educational results for children with disabilities is an essential element of our national policy of ensuring equality of opportunity, full participation, independent living, and economic self-sufficiency for individuals with disabilities. Almost 30 years of research and experience has demonstrated that the education of children with disabilities can be made more effective by [1] having high expectations for such children and ensuring their access to the general education curriculum in the regular classroom, to the maximum extent possible . . . [2] providing appropriate special education and related services, and aids and supports in the regular classroom, to such children, whenever appropriate . . . and [3] providing incentives for whole-school approaches, scientifically based early reading programs, positive behavioral interventions and supports, and early intervening services to reduce the need to label children as disabled. (Individuals with Disabilities Education Act [IDEA] 2004, PL 108-446, Sec. 601[c][1])

1. What educational services were available for students with disabilities during most of the 20th century?

2. Identify the principal issues in the right-to-education cases that led to eventual passage of the national mandate to educate students with disabilities.

3. Indentify five major provisions of the Individuals with Disabilities Education Act.

4. Discuss the special education referral, assessment, planning, and placement process.

5. Identify four principles for school accountability as required in the No Child Left Behind Act (NCLB). Under IDEA 2004, what must a student's IEP include to ensure access to the general curriculum?

6. What does it mean to be a "highly qualified" teacher as required in NCLB and IDEA 2004?

7. Identify three characteristics of evidence-based special education that enhance learning opportunities for students with disabilities.

8. Distinguish between students with disabilities who are eligible for services under Section 504/ADA and those who are eligible under IDEA.

9. Distinguish between the principles of zero tolerance and zero exclusion in America's schools.

▼SNAPSHOT

EDUCATING REED

I was just a mom who wanted a program for my son. That really is the whole story. Eleven years ago we adopted a little boy with Down syndrome. We were excited and nervous and overwhelmed. He was our sixth child, the fourth one we adopted, and the only one with disabilities. . . . [Our local neighborhood] school wasn't ready to have Reed in a regular classroom, but they got ready. . . . Reed has been in the neighborhood school for five years now. We've had our ups and downs but we've worked things out. The [special education] resource teacher was wonderful at working with the regular education teachers. For instance, Reed's second-grade teacher did creative writing for part of the day. But Reed wasn't at the point where he could sit down and compose something on his own. So his resource teacher had Reed dictate something to her in the morning. (She found out all our family secrets!) Then in the afternoon, when his regular class did creative writing, he would take what she had written down and copy it. They adapted the curriculum like that throughout the year.

One day that year, I overheard Reed talking to one of his friends. His friend said, "I did really good on my test today." Reed said, "I didn't. I don't do good on tests." So I went back to talk to his teacher. Apparently, every Thursday they had a multiple-choice and fill-in-the-blank history test that was about six pages long. I told the teacher that Reed didn't do very well with that format. The process of reading and understanding the questions and filling in the bubbles and blanks just took him longer. I also told his teacher that I was really concerned about Reed's self-esteem because he feels he doesn't do well on tests. "I know what we can do," the teacher said. "We can send the test home on Wednesday night and he can do it at home." I thought, "Oh, great! One more thing to do with everything else." But I wanted it to work, so I said, "Let's try it." Reed started bringing home his history tests. Often when we were in the car going somewhere, he would read the test aloud and fill in the blanks and the bubbles. It blew me away how much of the stuff he knew! I knew that he wasn't just guessing because he got so many of the questions right. He had successes in science that year too. His teachers told me, "I'm delighted with what he knows. He raises his hand to answer just about every question, and even if he doesn't know the right answer, he knows the context. He knows how to make the experiments work. He figures things out faster than some of the other kids."

His homeroom teacher called me after a few weeks and said, "I figured out what you want."

"What's that?" I said.

"You want me to have him in the regular class as much as I can, and just have him be part of the class with the rest of the kids. You don't want me to overwhelm him, or frustrate him, but you don't want me to underestimate him either."

I said, "That's it. You've just spelled out inclusion. That's exactly what my dream is." (Hahne, K., 2000, p. 105, 109–111)

$\Large A$ccess to education is a basic American value, reflecting the conviction that all children should have an opportunity to learn and develop to the best of their ability. Schools are responsible for every student, from the most academically capable to those in need of specialized services and supports, such as Reed from our opening Snapshot. All Karen wanted for her son was an opportunity to learn the skills that would facilitate his success in school, family, and community. Karen's dream for Reed was no different from what all parents want from their child's education: literacy, personal autonomy, economic self-sufficiency, personal fulfillment, and citizenship. She believed that the dream could be best accomplished in an educational setting where general and special education teachers work together to understand and meet Reed's educational needs.

Origins of Special Education

FOCUS 1
What educational services were available for students with disabilities during most of the 20th century?

The goal of education is full participation for everyone, regardless of race, cultural background, socioeconomic status, physical disability, or mental limitation. Unfortunately, it wasn't until 1975 that this value was translated into actual practice for all students with disabilities in the United States. This section discusses early special education programs, the concept of education as a privilege rather than a right for students with disabilities, and the expanding role of the federal government in the 1960s.

Early Special Education Programs

Throughout most of the last three centuries, many families who had a child with a disability were unable to get help addressing that child's most basic needs, such as medical and dental care, social services, and education. In the 18th and 19th centuries, educational services for children with disabilities were primarily confined to residential schools for students with physical disabilities and those who were deaf and blind. In the early 1900s, educational programs for children with disabilities gained some momentum through the efforts of many dedicated professionals. Those efforts consisted largely of programs that were separate from the public schools, established mainly for children who were described as "slow learners" or had hearing or sight loss. These students were usually placed in segregated classrooms in a public school building or in separate schools. Special education meant segregated education. Moreover, students with substantial differences were excluded from public education entirely.

Education as a Privilege But Not a Right

From 1920 to 1960, the availability of public school programs for children with disabilities continued to be sporadic and selective. Most states merely allowed for special education; they did not mandate it. Services to children with mild emotional disorders (such as discipline problems or inappropriate behavior) were initiated in the early 1930s, but mental hospitals continued to be the only alternative for most children with severe emotional problems. Special classes for children with physical disabilities expanded in the 1930s, primarily for those described as having "crippling" conditions, heart defects, and other health-related problems that interfered with participation in a general education classroom. Separate schools for these children, very popular during the late 1950s, were often specially equipped with elevators, ramps, and modified doors, toilets, and desks.

During the 1940s, the question of placement in a special school versus placement in a general education class emerged as an important policy issue in the education of students with disabilities. Educators became more aware of the need for these students to be educated in an environment that would promote more "typical" social interaction with peers without disabilities.

By the 1950s, many countries around the world began to expand educational opportunities for students with disabilities in special schools and classes. In some countries, parents of children with disabilities organized to lobby policy makers for more appropriate social and ed-

Council for
Exceptional
Children

Standard 1: Foundations

ucational services for their children. Additionally, many health care and social services professionals began to advocate on behalf of individuals with disabilities, thus enriching knowledge through research and incorporating that knowledge into effective practice.

The number of public school classes for students with mild mental retardation and those with behavior disorders increased in the late 1950s. For the most part, these children continued to be educated in a school setting that isolated them from peers without disabilities. However, the validity of segregated programs continued to be questioned. Several studies in the 1950s and 1960s (e.g., Cassidy & Stanton, 1959; Johnson, 1961; Jordan & deCharms, 1959; Thurstone, 1959) examined the efficacy of special classes for children with mild mental retardation. Summarizing this research, Johnson (1962) suggested that the academic achievement of learners with mental retardation was consistent, regardless of whether they were placed in special or general education classes, and that the child's social adjustment was not harmed by the special program. Although numerous criticisms regarding the design of efficacy studies have been made over the years, they did result in a movement toward expanding services beyond special classes in public schools. An example of this outcome was the development of a model whereby a child could remain in the general class program for the majority (if not the entirety) of the school day, receiving special education when and where it was needed.

Expanding the Role of the Federal Government

The 1960s brought significant changes in the education of students with disabilities. President John F. Kennedy expanded the role of the federal government, providing financial support to university programs for the preparation of special education teachers. The Bureau of Education for the Handicapped (BEH) in the Office of Education (presently the Office of Special Education and Rehabilitative Services in the U.S. Department of Education) was created as a clearinghouse for information at the federal level. Demonstration projects were funded nationwide to establish a research base for the education of students with disabilities in the public schools.

The Right to Education

The right to education for children with disabilities came to the public forum as a part of a larger social issue in the United States: the civil rights of people from differing ethnic and racial backgrounds. The civil rights movement of the 1950s and 1960s awakened the public to the issues of discrimination in employment, housing, access to public facilities (such as restaurants and transportation), and public education.

Education was reaffirmed as a right and not a privilege by the U.S. Supreme Court in the landmark case of *Brown v. Topeka, Kansas, Board of Education* (1954). In its decision, the court ruled that education must be made available to everyone on an equal basis. A unanimous Supreme Court stated, "In these days, it is doubtful that any child may reasonably be expected to succeed in life if he is denied the opportunity of an education. Such an opportunity, where the state has undertaken to provide it, is a right which must be made available to all on equal terms" (*Brown v. Topeka, Kansas, Board of Education*, 1954).

Although usually heralded for striking down racial segregation, this decision also set a precedent for the education of students with disabilities. However, nearly 20 years passed before federal courts were confronted with the issue of a free and appropriate education for these students.

The 1970s have often been described as a decade of revolution in the education of students with disabilities. Many of the landmark cases were brought before the courts to address the right to education for students with disabilities. Additionally, major pieces of state and federal legislation were enacted to reaffirm the right of students with disabilities to a free public education.

In 1971, the Pennsylvania Association for Retarded Citizens filed a class-action suit on behalf of children with mental retardation who were excluded from public education on the basis of intellectual deficiency (*Pennsylvania Association for Retarded Citizens v. Commonwealth of Pennsylvania*, 1971). The law suit charged that these children were being denied their right to

FOCUS **2**
Identify the principal issues in the right-to-education cases that led to eventual passage of the national mandate to educate students with disabilities.

Council for
Exceptional
Children

Standard 1: Foundations

TABLE 2.1

**Major Court Cases and Federal Legislation Focusing on the
Right to Education for Individuals with Disabilities (1954–2005)**

COURT CASES AND FEDERAL LEGISLATION	PRECEDENTS ESTABLISHED
Brown v. Topeka, Kansas, Board of Education (1954)	Segregation of students by race is held unconstitutional. Education is a right that must be available to all on equal terms.
Hobsen v. Hansen (1969)	The doctrine of equal educational opportunity is a part of the law of due process, and denying an equal educational opportunity is a violation of the Constitution. Placement of children in educational tracks based on performance on standardized tests is unconstitutional and discriminates against poor and minority children.
Diana v. California State Board of Education (1970)	Children tested for potential placement in a special education program must be assessed in their native or primary language. Children cannot be placed in special classes on the basis of culturally biased tests.
Pennsylvania Association for Retarded Citizens v. Commonwealth of Pennsylvania (1971)	Pennsylvania schools must provide a free public education to all school-age children with mental retardation.
Mills v. Board of Education of the District of Columbia (1972)	Exclusion of individuals with disabilities from free, appropriate public education is a violation of the due-process and equal protection clauses of the Fourteenth Amendment to the Constitution. Public schools in the District of Columbia must provide a free education to all children with disabilities regardless of their functional level or ability to adapt to the present educational system.
Public Law 93-112, Vocational Rehabilitation Act of 1973, Section 504 (1973)	Individuals with disabilities cannot be excluded from participation in, denied benefits of, or subjected to discrimination under any program or activity receiving federal financial assistance.
Public Law 94-142, Part B of the Education of the Handicapped Act (1975)	A free and appropriate public education must be provided for all children with disabilities in the United States. (Those up through 5 years old may be excluded in some states.)
Hendrick Hudson District Board of Education v. Rowley (1982)	The U.S. Supreme Court held that in order for special education and related services to be appropriate, they must be reasonably calculated to enable the student to receive educational benefits.
Public Law 99-457, Education Handicapped Act amendments (1986)	A new authority extends free and appropriate education to all children with disabilities of the ages 3 through 5 and provides a new early intervention program for infants and toddlers.
Honig v. Doe (1988)	The U.S. Supreme Court holds that the Education for All Handicapped Children Act (now IDEA) does not allow for students with disabilities who exhibit dangerous or disruptive behavior that is related to their disability to be suspended from school for more than 10 days or to be expelled without their parent's consent, a hearing decision, or a court order.
Public Law 99-372, Handicapped Children's Protection Act (1986)	Reimbursement of attorneys' fees and expenses is given to parents who prevail in administrative proceedings or court actions.
Public Law 101-336, Americans with Disabilities Act (1990)	Civil rights protections are provided for people with disabilities in private-sector employment, all public services, and public accommodations, transportation, and telecommunications.
Public Law 101-476, Individuals with Disabilities Education Act (1990)	The Education of the Handicapped Act amendments are renamed the Individuals with Disabilities Education Act (IDEA). Two new categories of disability are added: autism and traumatic brain injury. IDEA requires that an individualized transition plan be developed no later than age 16 as a component of the IEP process. Rehabilitation and social work services are included as related services.
Public Law 105-17, Amendments to the Individuals with Disabilities Education Act (1997) (Commonly referred to as IDEA 97)	IDEA 97 expands the emphasis for students with disabilities from public school access to improving individual outcomes (results). The 1997 amendments modify eligibility requirements, IEP requirements, public and private placements, disciplining of students, and procedural safeguards.
Public Law 108-446, Individuals with Disabilities Education Improvement Act of 2004	IDEA 2004 eliminates IEP short-term objectives for most students, new state pilot programs for multi-year IEPs and paperwork reduction; establishes qualifications to become a highly qualified special education teacher.

a free public education. The plaintiffs claimed that children with mental retardation can learn if the educational program is adjusted to meet their individual needs. The primary issue was whether public school programs should be required to accommodate the needs of children with intellectual differences. The court ordered Pennsylvania schools to provide, to all children with mental retardation of ages 6 to 21, a free public education commensurate with their individual learning needs. In addition, preschool education was to be provided for children with mental retardation if the local school district provided it for children who were not disabled.

The case of *Mills v. District of Columbia Board of Education* (1972) expanded the Pennsylvania decision to include all children with disabilities. District of Columbia schools were ordered to provide a free and appropriate education to every school-age child with a disability. The court further ordered that when general public school assignment was not appropriate, alternative educational services had to be made available. Thus, the right of students with disabilities to an education was reaffirmed. The *Pennsylvania* and *Mills* cases served as catalysts for several court cases and pieces of legislation in the years that followed. Table 2.1 on page 26 summarizes precedents regarding the right of students with disabilities to education.

The Individuals with Disabilities Education Act (IDEA)

In 1975, the U.S. Congress assembled various pieces of state and federal legislation into one comprehensive national law. **The Education for All Handicapped Children Act** (Public Law 94–142) made a free and appropriate public education available to nearly four million school-age students with disabilities in the United States between the ages of 6 and 21. The law included provisions for an individualized education program, procedural safeguards to protect the rights of students and their parents, nondiscriminatory and multidisciplinary assessment, and education with peers without disabilities to the greatest extent appropriate (a concept also known as the least restrictive environment). Each of these provisions is discussed in more depth later in this chapter.

In 1986, Congress amended the Education for All Handicapped Children Act to make a free and appropriate public education available to preschool-age students. **Public Law 99-457** extended all the rights and protections of school-age children (ages 6 through 21) to preschoolers ages 3 through 5. PL 99-457 also established a state grant program for infants and toddlers up through 2 years old. Infants and toddlers with developmental delays, as defined by each state, became eligible for services that included a multidisciplinary assessment and an **Individualized Family Service Plan (IFSP).** Although this provision did not mandate that states provide services to all infants and toddlers with developmental delays, it did establish financial incentives for state participation. (The IFSP and other provisions of PL 99-457 are discussed at length in Chapter 3.)

In 1990, the same year that ADA was signed into law, Congress renamed the Education for All Handicapped Children Act (Public Law 94-142) the **Individuals with Disabilities Education Act** (IDEA). The purpose in this name change was to reflect "people first" language ("putting the person before the disability") and to promote the use of the term *disabilities* rather than *handicapped.*

What Are Special Education and Related Services?

IDEA establishes what is called the **zero-exclusion principle**; that is, it requires that public schools provide special education and related services to meet the individual needs of all eligible students, regardless of the extent or type of their disability. **Special education** means specially designed instruction provided, at no cost to parents, in all settings (such as the classroom, physical education facilities, the home, and hospitals or institutions). IDEA also mandates that students with disabilities receive any related services necessary to ensure that they benefit from their educational experience. **Related services** include

> transportation, and such developmental, corrective, and other supportive services (including speech-language pathology and audiology services, interpreting services, psychological services, physical and occupational therapy, recreation, including therapeutic recreation, social work services, school nurse services designed to enable a child with a disability to receive a

> ➤ **The Education for All Handicapped Children Act (Public Law 94-142)**
> Passed in 1975, this federal law mandated a free and appropriate public education to all eligible students, regardless of the extent or type of handicap (disability). Eligible students must receive special education and related services necessary to meet their individual needs.

> ➤ **Public Law 99-457**
> Legislation that extended the rights and protections of Public Law 94-142 to preschool-age children (ages 3 through 5). The law also established an optional state program for infants and toddlers with disabilities.

> ➤ **Individualized Family Service Plan (IFSP)**
> A plan of services for infants and toddlers and their families. It includes statements regarding the child's present developmental level, the family's strengths and needs, the major outcomes of the plan, specific interventions and delivery systems to accomplish outcomes, dates of initiation and duration of services, and a plan for transition into public schools.

> ➤ **Individuals with Disabilities Education Act (IDEA-Public Law 101-476)**
> The new name for the Education for All Handicapped Children Act (Public Law 94-142) per the 1990 amendments to the law.

> ➤ **Zero-exclusion principle**
> No person with a disability can be rejected for a service, regardless of the nature, type, or extent of their disabling condition.

> ➤ **Special education**
> Specially designed instruction provided at no cost to parents in all settings (such as the classroom, physical education facilities, the home, and hospitals or institutions).

> ➤ **Related services**
> Those services necessary to ensure that students with disabilities benefit from their educational experience. Related services may include special transportation, speech pathology, psychological services, physical and occupational therapy, recreation, rehabilitation counseling, social work, and medical services.

Standard 1: Foundations

Standard 2: Development and Characteristics of Learners

free appropriate public education as described in the individualized education program of the child, counseling services, including rehabilitation counseling, orientation and mobility services, and medical services, except that such medical services shall be for diagnostic and evaluation purposes only) as may be required to assist a child with a disability to benefit from special education, and include the early identification and assessment of disabling conditions in children. (Exception: The term does not include a medical device that is surgically implanted, or the replacement of such device. (IDEA 2004, PL 108-446, Sec. 602[26])

Who Is Eligible for Special Education and Related Services?

In order for a student to receive the specialized services available under IDEA, two criteria must be met. First, the student must be identified as having one of the disability conditions cited in federal law or a corresponding condition defined in a state's special education rules and regulations. These conditions include mental retardation (intellectual disabilities), hearing impairments (including deafness), speech or language impairments, visual impairments (including blindness), serious emotional disturbance, **orthopedic impairments**, **autism**, **traumatic brain injury**, multiple disabilities, other health impairments, or specific learning disabilities (IDEA 2004, PL 108-446, Sec. 602[3][A][i]). Each disability will be defined and described in depth in subsequent chapters of this text.

In the 1997 amendments to IDEA, states and school districts/agencies were given the option of eliminating categories of disability (such as mental retardation or specific learning disabilities) for children ages 3 through 9. For this age group, a state or school district may define a child with a disability as

> experiencing developmental delays, as defined by the State and as measured by appropriate diagnostic instruments and procedures, in one or more of the following areas: physical development; cognitive development; communication development; social or emotional development; or adaptive development. (IDEA 2004, PL 108-446, Sec. 602[3][b][i][ii])

The second criterion for eligibility is the student's demonstrated need for specialized instruction and related services in order to receive an appropriate education. This need is determined by a team of professionals and parents. Both criteria for eligibility must be met. If this is not the case, it is possible for a student to be identified as disabled but not be eligible to receive special education and related services. These students may still be entitled to accommodations or modifications in their educational program. (See Providing Reasonable Accommodations under Section 504/ADA later in this chapter.)

► **Orthopedic impairments**
Bodily impairments that interfere with an individual's mobility, coordination, communication, learning, and/or personal adjustment.

► **Autism**
A childhood disorder with onset prior to 36 months of age. It is characterized by extreme withdrawal, self-stimulation, intellectual deficits, and language disorders.

► **Traumatic brain injury**
Direct injuries to the brain, such as tearing of nerve fibers, bruising of the brain tissue against the skull, brain stem trauma, and swelling.

Major Provisions of IDEA

The five major provisions of IDEA are as follows:

1. All students with disabilities are entitled to a free and appropriate public education designed to meet their unique needs and prepare them for employment and independent living.

FOCUS **3**
Identify five major provisions of the Individuals with Disabilities Education Act.

IDEA mandates a free and appropriate public education for students with disabilities ages 3 to 21. What are the major provisions of IDEA?

2. Schools must use nondiscriminatory and multidisciplinary assessments in determining a student's educational needs.

3. Parents have the right to be involved in decisions regarding their son's or daughter's special education program.

4. Every student must have an individualized education program (IEP).

5. Every student has the right to receive her or his education with peers who are not disabled to the maximum extent appropriate.

A FREE AND APPROPRIATE PUBLIC EDUCATION (FAPE). IDEA is based on the principle that every student can learn. Consequently, all students with disabilities are entitled to a **free and appropriate public education (FAPE)** designed to meet their unique needs. Schools must provide special education and related services at no cost to parents. The IDEA provisions related to FAPE are based on the Fourteenth Amendment to the U.S. Constitution, which guarantees equal protection of the law. No student with a disability can be excluded, on the basis of that disability, from a public education (the zero-exclusion principle). A major interpretation of FAPE was handed down by the U.S. Supreme Court in *Hendrick Hudson District Board of Education v. Rowley* (1982). The Supreme Court declared that an appropriate education consists of "specially designed instruction and related services" that are "individually designed" to provide "educational benefit." Often referred to as the "some educational benefit" standard, this ruling stipulates that a state need not provide an ideal education but must provide a beneficial one for students with disabilities.

NONDISCRIMINATORY AND MULTIDISCIPLINARY ASSESSMENT. IDEA incorporated several provisions related to the use of nondiscriminatory testing procedures in labeling and placement of students for special education services. Among those provisions are the following:

➤ The testing of students in their native or primary language, whenever possible

➤ The use of evaluation procedures selected and administered to prevent cultural or racial discrimination

➤ Validation of assessment tools for the purpose for which they are being used

➤ Assessment by a team of school professionals, utilizing several pieces of information to formulate a placement decision.

Historically, students with disabilities were too often placed in special education programs on the basis of inadequate or invalid assessment information. This resulted in a disproportionate number of children from differing ethnic backgrounds, as well as a disproportionate number from disadvantaged backgrounds (living in poverty), being inappropriately placed in special education.

PARENTAL SAFEGUARDS AND INVOLVEMENT. IDEA granted parents the following rights in the education of their children:

➤ To give consent in writing before the child is initially assessed to determine eligibility for special education and related services

➤ To consent in writing to the educational setting in which the child will receive special education and related services

➤ To request an independent educational assessment if the parents believe the school's assessment is inappropriate

➤ To request an educational assessment at public expense if the parent disagrees with the school's assessment and recommendations

➤ To participate on the committee that considers the assessment of, placement of, and programming for the child

➤ To inspect and review educational records and challenge information believed to be inaccurate, misleading, or in violation of the privacy or other rights of the child

➤ To request a copy of information from the child's educational record

➤ To request a due-process hearing concerning the school's proposal (or refusal) to initiate or change the identification, educational assessment, or placement of the child or the provision of a free and appropriate public education.

➤ **Free and Appropriate Public Education (FAPE)**

Provision within IDEA that every eligible student with a disability be included in public education. The U.S. Supreme Court declared that an appropriate education consists of "specially designed instruction and related services" that are "individually designed" to provide "educational benefit."

Standard 8: Assessment

Standard 3: Individual Learning Differences

Standard 7: Instructional Planning

Standard 9: Professional and Ethical Practice

The development of the IEP is a collaborative process involving parents, educators, and students. Why is it important for parents to participate in the development of the IEP?

The intent of these safeguards is twofold: first, to create an opportunity for parents to be more involved in decisions regarding their child's education program; and second, to protect the student and family from decisions that could adversely affect the child's education. Families thus can be secure in the knowledge that every reasonable attempt is being made to educate their child appropriately.

Some professionals and parents have argued that IDEA's promise for a parent and professional partnership has never been fully realized. In a survey conducted by Johnson, Duffett, Farkas, & Wilson (2002), the vast majority of parents were convinced that their child needed special education, but they had to fight an uphill battle to secure services. At the same time, parents reported they could not "envision what their children's lives would be like without the special services their school offers" (p. 10).

Several barriers may exist between the school and the home, including poor communication, a lack of trust, and inadequate coordination of services (Friend & Bursuck, 2006; Schaller, Yang, & Chang, 2004). Byrnes (2002) suggested that schools go beyond the procedural due-process requirements in IDEA and "make parents an integral part of the school community" (p. 201). Every attempt should be made to prevent adversarial relationships, such as those that often arise in due-process hearings. Such hearings may lead to mistrust and long-term problems. IDEA responds to the need for a mediation process to resolve any conflict between parents and school personnel and to prevent long-term adversarial relationships. The law requires states to establish a mediation system in which parents and schools voluntarily participate. In such a system, an impartial individual would listen to parents and school personnel and attempt to work out a mutually agreeable arrangement in the best interest of the student with a disability. Although mediation is intended to facilitate the parent and professional partnership, it must not be used to deny or delay a due-process hearing.

THE INDIVIDUALIZED EDUCATION PROGRAM (IEP). The **individualized education program (IEP)** is a written statement that is the framework for delivering a free and appropriate public education to every eligible student with a disability. The IEP provides an opportunity for parents and professionals to join together in developing and delivering specially designed instruction to meet student needs.

The team responsible for developing the IEP consists of the student's parents; at least one special education teacher; at least one general education teacher if the child is, or may be, participating in the general education environment; and a school district representative. The school district representative must be qualified to provide, or supervise the provision of, specially designed instruction to meet the unique needs of children with disabilities. This educator must also be knowledgeable about the **general curriculum** and the availability of resources within the school district (LEA).

The IEP team must also include a professional(s) who can interpret the eligibility and instructional implications of the various assessment results. Other professionals who have knowledge or special expertise regarding the child (including related-services personnel), as well as the student with a disability, when appropriate, may be included at the discretion of the parents or school district.

The purpose of the IEP process is to ensure continuity in the delivery of special education services and supports for each student on a daily and annual basis. The IEP is also intended to promote more effective communication between school personnel and the child's family. IDEA 2004 requires that each child's IEP include

Council for Exceptional Children

Standard 3: Individual Learning Differences

Standard 7: Instructional Planning

➤ **Individualized education program (IEP)**

Provision in IDEA that students with disabilities must receive an educational program based on multidisciplinary assessment and designed to meet individual needs. The program must include consideration of the student's present level of performance, annual goals, short-term instructional objectives, related services, percent of time in general education, timeline for special education services, and an annual evaluation.

➤ **General curriculum**

Instructional content that all students are expected to learn as they progress through school and earn a high school diploma. The specific content and performance standards for student achievement are set by each individual state or local school district.

➤ A statement of the child's present levels of academic achievement and functional performance, including how the child's disability affects the child's involvement and progress in the general education curriculum. For preschool children, as appropriate, how the disability affects the child's participation in appropriate activities.

➤ A statement of measurable annual goals, including academic and functional goals, designed to meet the child's needs that result from the child's disability, to enable the child to be involved in and make progress in the general education curriculum; and meet each of the child's other educational needs that result from the child's disability. For children with disabilities who take *alternate assessments* aligned to alternate achievement standards, a description of benchmarks or short-term objectives.

➤ A description of how the child's progress toward meeting the annual goals described will be measured and when periodic reports on the progress the child is making toward meeting the annual goals will be provided.

➤ A statement of the special education and related services and supplementary aids and services, based on peer-reviewed research to the extent practicable, to be provided to the child, or on behalf of the child, and a statement of the program modifications or supports for school personnel that will be provided for the child to (a) advance appropriately toward attaining the annual goals and (b) be involved in and make progress in the general education curriculum and to participate in extracurricular and other nonacademic activities, and (c) be educated and participate with other children with disabilities and children without disabilities.

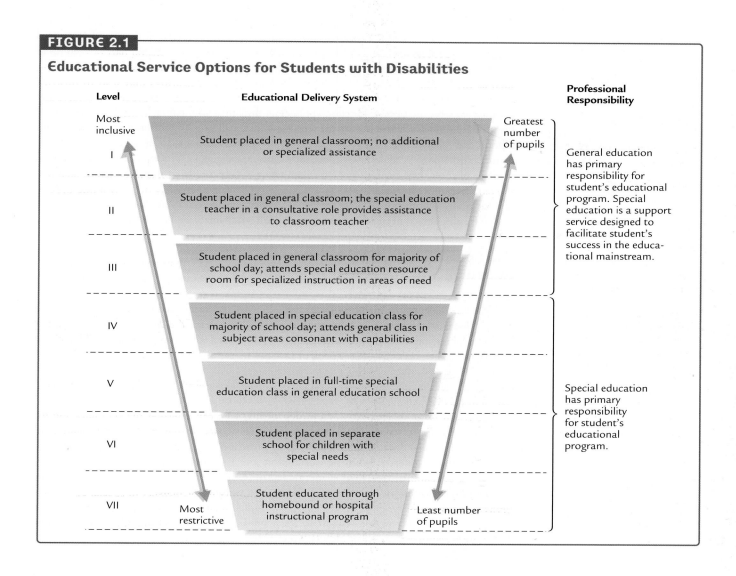

FIGURE 2.1

Educational Service Options for Students with Disabilities

> An explanation of the extent, if any, to which the child will not participate with children without disabilities in the regular [general education] class.

> A statement of any individual appropriate accommodations that are necessary to measure the academic achievement and functional performance of the child on State and districtwide assessments, or if the IEP Team determines that the child shall take an alternate assessment of student achievement, a statement of why the child cannot participate in the regular assessment; and the particular alternate assessment selected is appropriate for the child. (IDEA, 2004, P.L. 108-446, Sec. 614[d])

EDUCATION IN THE LEAST RESTRICTIVE ENVIRONMENT. All students with disabilities have the right to learn in an environment consistent with their academic, social, and physical needs—the **least restrictive environment (LRE).** IDEA mandated that

> To the maximum extent appropriate, children with disabilities, including children in public or private institutions or other care facilities, are educated with children who are not disabled, and that special classes, separate schooling, or other removal of children with disabilities from the regular [general] education environment occurs only when the nature or severity of the disability is such that education in regular classes with the use of supplementary aids and services cannot be achieved satisfactorily. (IDEA, 2004, P.L. 108-446, Sec 614[d])

To be certain that schools meet this mandate, federal regulations required districts to develop a continuum of educational placements based on the individual needs of students. The continuum may range from placement in a general classroom with support services to homebound and hospital programs. Placement in a setting along this continuum is based on the premise that this is the most appropriate environment to implement a student's individualized program as developed by the IEP team. An educational services model depicting seven levels on the continuum of placements is presented in Figure 2.1 on page 31.

Some parents and professionals have criticized the concept of "a continuum of placements" in recent years. The concern is that, despite IDEA's strong preference for students with disabilities to be educated with their peers who are not disabled, the continuum has legitimized and supported the need for more restrictive, segregated settings. Additionally, the continuum has created the perception that students with disabilities must "go to" services, rather than those services coming to them. In other words, as students move farther from the general education class, the resources available to meet their needs increase concomitantly. Of the nearly six million students with disabilities age 6 to 21 in America's schools, 4% receive their education in separate schools, residential facilities, and homebound programs (U.S. Department of Education, 2006). For a closer look at who is being served in special education programs, and where, see Figure 2.2 on page 33.

The Special Education Referral, Assessment, Planning, and Placement Process

The purpose of special education, as mandated in IDEA, is to ensure that all eligible students with disabilities have the opportunity to receive a free and appropriate public education. The process involves four sequential phases: (1) initiating the referral, (2) assessing student eligibility and educational need, (3) developing the individualized education program (IEP), and (4) determining the student's educational placement in the least restrictive environment. (See Table 2.2 on page 34.)

PHASE 1: INITIATING THE REFERRAL. Referral for special education can occur at different times for different students, depending on the type and severity of the need. Students with more severe disabilities are likely to be referred prior to elementary school and to have received early intervention and preschool services. For children with more mild disabilities, referral could be initiated at any time during elementary school when they appear to have difficulty in academic learning, in exhibiting appropriate behavior, or in overall development. For these children, the general education teacher is the most likely referral source.

The referral begins with a request to the school's *special services committee or child-study team* for an assessment to determine whether the student qualifies for special education services.

Focus 4

Discuss the special education referral, assessment, planning, and placement process.

FIGURE 2.2

A Profile of Special Education in the United States

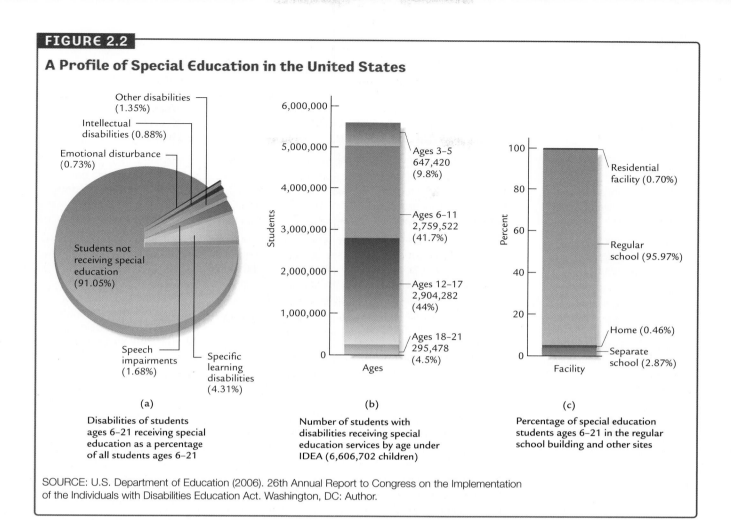

(a) Disabilities of students ages 6–21 receiving special education as a percentage of all students ages 6–21

- Other disabilities (1.35%)
- Intellectual disabilities (0.88%)
- Emotional disturbance (0.73%)
- Students not receiving special education (91.05%)
- Speech impairments (1.68%)
- Specific learning disabilities (4.31%)

(b) Number of students with disabilities receiving special education services by age under IDEA (6,606,702 children)

- Ages 3–5 647,420 (9.8%)
- Ages 6–11 2,759,522 (41.7%)
- Ages 12–17 2,904,282 (44%)
- Ages 18–21 295,478 (4.5%)

(c) Percentage of special education students ages 6–21 in the regular school building and other sites

- Residential facility (0.70%)
- Regular school (95.97%)
- Home (0.46%)
- Separate school (2.87%)

SOURCE: U.S. Department of Education (2006). 26th Annual Report to Congress on the Implementation of the Individuals with Disabilities Education Act. Washington, DC: Author.

Once the team receives the referral, it may either: (1) attempt to modify or adapt current instruction in the general education class through **coordinated early intervening services**, or (2) conduct a formal evaluation to determine the student's eligibility for special education services.

The first step, coordinated early intervening services, involves instructional adaptations, modifications, or accommodations designed to provide children who are at risk for educational failure with additional support before referring them for special education services, if needed. Parents are notified that the child is having difficulty and are asked to meet with the school team. The team and the parents discuss the student's needs and recommend possible changes. Adaptations vary according to student need, but most often involve modifying curriculum, changing a seating arrangement, changing the length and difficulty of homework or classroom assignments, using peer tutors or volunteer parents to assist with instructional programs, or implementing a behavior management program. It is the responsibility of the general education teacher to implement the modified instruction and to assess the student's progress over a predetermined period of time. If the modifications are successful, there will be no further need to make a referral for special education. To assist school districts in developing and implementing coordinated early-intervening services, IDEA 2004 allows up to 15% of a school's allocation of federal funds, in combination with other funds, to be spent on such services. This funding is intended for students who are not yet identified as needing special education but who require additional academic and behavioral support to achieve in the general education classroom. Instructional activities may include professional development to assist teachers in delivering scientifically based interventions, as well as to provide behavioral evaluations, services, and supports (IDEA, 2004, P.L. 108-446, Sec 613[i]).

Should the team determine that the student's educational progress is not satisfactory, even with the use of early intervening services, a formal referral for special education may be initiated. The formal referral begins with the team's review and analysis of the information provided by education professionals and parents in order to further understand the child's educational

> ➤ **Coordinated early intervening services**
>
> The provision of services and supports for student who have not yet been identified as needing special education and related services but who need extra academic and behavior support to succeed in the general education classroom.

Standard 3: Individual Learning Differences

TABLE 2.2

The Special Education Referral, Assessment, Planning, and Placement Process

PHASE 1 INITIATING THE REFERRAL	PHASE 2 ASSESSING STUDENT ELIGIBILITY AND EDUCATIONAL NEED	PHASE 3 DEVELOPING THE INDIVIDUALIZED EDUCATION PROGRAM (IEP)	PHASE 4 DETERMINING THE LEAST RESTRICTIVE ENVIRONMENT (LRE)

• School personnel or parents indicate concern about student's learning, behavior, or overall development.
 	
• If referral is made by school personnel, parents are notified of concerns.
 	
• Child-study team decides to provide additional support services and adapt student's instructional program prior to initiating formal assessment for eligibility. (This step may be bypassed, and team may choose to immediately seek parental permission to evaluate the student's eligibility for special education.)
 	
• School seeks and receives parents' permission to evaluate student's eligibility for special education services. (This will occur if the additional support services and adaptive instruction are unsuccessful OR if the team has chosen to move directly to a formal evaluation to determine student eligibility.)
	• Multidisciplinary and nondiscriminatory assessment tools and strategies are used to evaluate student's eligibility for special education services.
	
	• Child-study team reviews assessment information to determine (1) whether student meets eligibility requirements for special education services under 1 of 12 disability classifications or meets the definition of developmentally delayed (for students between ages 3 and 9), and (2) whether student requires special education services.
	
	• If team agrees that the student is eligible for and needs special education services, then the process moves to phase 3: developing the IEP.
		• Appropriate professionals to serve on an IEP team are identified. A team coordinator is appointed.
		
		• Parents (and student when appropriate) participate as equal members of the team and are provided with written copies of all assessment information.
		
		• Team meets and agrees upon the essential elements of the student's individualized education program plan:
		  • Measurable annual goals
		  • Skill areas needing special education and related services
		  • Persons responsible for providing services and supports to meet student's identified needs
		  • Criteria/evaluation procedures to assess progress
		  • Student's access to the general education curriculum
		  • Student's participation in state-wide or school district assessments
		  • Beginning and end dates for special education services
		  • A process for reporting to parents on student's progress toward annual goals
		  • Positive behavioral intervention plan if needed
			• Identify potential educational placements based on student's annual goals and special education services to be provided.
			
			• Adhering to the principle that students with disabilities are to be educated with their peers without disabilities to the maximum extent appropriate, justify any removal of the child from the general education classroom.
			
			• With parents involved in the decision-making process, determine student's appropriate educational placement.
			
			• Document, on the student's IEP, justification for any removal from the general education classroom.
			
			• Team members agree in writing to the essential elements of the IEP and to the educational placement where special education and related services are to be provided.
			
			• As members of the IEP team, parents must consent in writing to the agreed-upon educational placement for their child.

needs. Documentation may include results from achievement tests, classroom performance tests, samples of student work, behavioral observations, or anecdotal notes (such as teacher journal entries). The team must also decide whether additional assessment information is needed in order to determine the child's eligibility for special education. At this time a written notice must be provided to parents that includes all of the following:

➤ A full explanation of the procedural safeguards available to the parents

➤ A description of the action proposed (or refused) by the school, why the school proposes or refuses to take the action, and a description of any options the school considered and the reasons why those options were rejected

Early intervening services involves adapting instruction to the need of the student before initiating a referral for special education services. What are some early intervening strategies that teachers can use in their classroom?

➤ A description of each evaluation procedure, test, record, or report the school used as a basis for the proposal or refusal

➤ A description of any other factors relevant to the school's proposal or refusal to take action

Following such written notice, the school must seek consent in writing from the parents in order to move ahead with the evaluation process. Informed consent means that parents

➤ have been fully informed of all information relevant to the activity for which consent is sought, in their native language or other mode of communication.

➤ understand and agree in writing to the carrying out of the activity for which their consent is sought (the consent describes that activity and indicates any record) that will be released and to whom.

➤ understand that the granting of consent is voluntary on the part of the parent and may be revoked at any time.

PHASE 2: ASSESSING STUDENT ELIGIBILITY AND EDUCATIONAL NEED.
Once written consent to evaluate has been obtained from parents, the school child-study team moves ahead to assess the student's eligibility for special education services under IDEA. The assessment should include the student's performance in both school and home environments. When the assessment process is complete, a decision is made regarding the student's eligibility for special education and his or her disability classification. Presently, the most common way to classify students for special education is to categorize them into one of the disability areas discussed earlier in this chapter (such as specific learning disabilities, autism, and so on).

Council for Exceptional Children

Standard 3: Individual Learning Differences

Standard 8: Assessment

PHASE 3: DEVELOPING THE INDIVIDUALIZED EDUCATION PROGRAM (IEP).
The IEP is the cornerstone of a free and appropriate public education (Huefner, 2006; National Information Center for Children and Youth with Disabilities, 2003). Once it has been determined that the student is eligible for special education services under IDEA, the next step is to establish an IEP team. At a minimum this team consists of the student's parents, the student (when appropriate), a special education teacher, a general education teacher (if the student is participating in the general education environment), and a representative of the local education agency (LEA). As stated in IDEA, the LEA representative must be qualified to provide, or supervise the provision of, specially designed instruction to meet the unique needs of children with disabilities; is knowledgeable about the general education curriculum; and is knowledgeable about the availability of resources of the local educational agency (IDEA 2004, P.L. 108-446, Sec 614[b][D][iv]). Additionally, IDEA requires that someone (either a current team member or someone from outside of the team, such as a school psychologist) be available to interpret each student's assessment results. At the discretion of the parents or school district, other individuals with knowledge or special expertise, including related-services specialists, may also be invited to participate on the IEP team.

Each IEP team should have a coordinator (such as the special education teacher, school psychologist, or school principal) who serves as liaison between the school and the family. The coordinator has the responsibility to (1) inform parents and respond to any concerns they may have regarding the IEP process, (2) help parents develop specific goals they would like to see their child achieve, (3) schedule IEP meetings that are mutually convenient for both team members and parents, and (4) lead the IEP meetings. Prior to the initial IEP meeting, parents should be provided with written copies of all assessment information on their child. Individual conferences with members of the IEP team or a full team meeting may be necessary before development of the IEP. This will further assist parents in understanding and interpreting assessment information. Analysis of the assessment information should include a summary of the child's strengths, as well as areas in which the child may require special education or related services.

Once there is mutual agreement between educators and parents on the interpretation of the assessment results, the team coordinator organizes and leads the IEP meeting(s). Such meeting(s) are meant to achieve the following purposes:

➤ Document each student's present levels of performance.

➤ Agree on measurable annual goals (and objectives/benchmarks for children with disabilities who take alternate assessments aligned to alternate achievement standards).

➤ Identify skill areas where special education (including physical education) and related services are needed, the persons responsible for delivering these services, and the criteria/evaluation procedures that will be applied to assess progress.

➤ Document student access to the general curriculum.

➤ Document student participation in state- and district-wide assessment programs with individual modifications or adaptations made, as necessary, in how the tests are administered. For children who cannot participate in regular assessments, the team must document the use of state-developed **alternate assessments.**

➤ Establish beginning and end dates for special education services.

➤ Determine a process for reporting to parents on student progress toward annual goals.

See Figure 2.3, a sample individualized education program for Diane, an elementary school-age student with disabilities.

PHASE 4: DETERMINING THE LEAST RESTRICTIVE ENVIRONMENT. A student's educational placement is determined only after educators and parents have agreed on annual goals (and on short-term objectives/benchmarks for children with disabilities who take alternate assessments aligned to alternate achievement standards). The decision regarding placement rests upon the answers to two questions: First, what is the appropriate placement for the student, given his or her annual goals? Second, which of the placement alternatives under consideration is consistent with the least restrictive environment? As stated in IDEA, to the maximum extent appropriate, the student is to be educated with peers who are not disabled. To ensure that this principle is applied in making placement decisions, IDEA begins with the premise that the general education classroom is where all children belong. Thus any movement away from the general education class must be justified and documented on the student's IEP.

Finally, decisions regarding the appropriate placement for a student are most successful when parents are viewed as valued and equal participants in the process. Parents must be fully involved in, and must eventually consent to, the educational placement for their child. Parents should be encouraged not only to share their expectations for the child, but also to express approval for or concerns about the goals, objectives, resources, or timelines that are being proposed by educators. The IEP must be the result of a collaborative process that reflects the views of both the school and the family. For more insight into the important issues that professionals, parents, and students must consider in developing IEP goals and objectives and determining the most appropriate educational placement, see the Case Study, "Jerald," on page 40.

➤ **Alternate assessments**

Assessments mandated in IDEA for students who are unable to participate in required state- or district-wide assessments. They ensure that all students, regardless of the severity of their disabilities, are included in the state's accountability system.

Council for Exceptional Children

Standard 3: Individual Learning Differences

FIGURE 2.3

A Sample Individualized Education Program (IEP) for Diane: An Elementary-Age Student with Disabilities

STUDENT'S PRIMARY CLASSIFICATION: SERIOUS EMOTIONAL DISTURBANCE SECONDARY CLASSIFICATION: NONE

Student Name _Diane_

Date of Birth _5-3-93_

Primary Language:

HOME _English_ Student _English_

Date of IEP Meeting _April 27, 2006_

Entry Date to Program _April 27, 2006_

Projected Duration of Services _One school year_

Services Required _Specify amount of time in educational and/or related services per day or week_

General Education Class _4–5 hours p/day_

Resource Room _1–2 hours p/day_

Special Ed Consultation in General Ed Classroom _Co-teaching and consultation with general education teacher in the areas of academic and adaptive skills as indicated in annual goals._

Self-Contained _None_

Related Services _Group counseling sessions twice weekly with guidance counselor. Counseling to focus on adaptive skill development as described in annual goals and short-term objectives_

P.E. Program _45 min. daily in general ed PE class with support from adapted PE teacher as necessary_

Assessment

Intellectual _WISC_R_

Educational _Key Math Woodcock Reading_

Behavioral/Adaptive _Burks_

Speech/Language

Other

Vision _Within normal limits_

Hearing _Within normal limits_

Classroom Observation Done

Dates _1/15-2/25/2006_

Personnel Conducting Observation _School Psychologist, Special Education Teacher, General Education Teacher_

Present Level of Performance Strengths

1) _Polite to teachers and peers_

2) _Helpful and cooperative in the classroom_

3) _Good grooming skills_

4) _Good in sports activities_

Access to General Education Curriculum

Diane will participate in all content areas within the general education curriculum. Special education supports and services will be provided in the areas of math, reading, and social skills development.

Effect of Disability on Access to General Education Curriculum

Emotional disabilities make it difficult for Diane to achieve at expected grade level performance in general education curriculum in the areas of reading and math. It is expected that this will further impact her access to the general education curriculum in other content areas (such as history, biology, English) as she enters junior high school.

Participation in Statewide or District Assessments

Diane will participate in all state and districtwide assessments of achievement. No adaptations or modifications required for participation.

Justification for Removal from General Education Classroom

Diane's objectives require that she be placed in a general education classroom with support from a special education teacher for the majority of the school day. Based on adaptive behavior assessment and observations, Diane will recive instruction in a resource room for approximately one to two hours per day in the areas of social skills development.

Reports to Parents on Progress toward Annual Goals

Parents will be informed of Diane's progress through weekly reports of progress on short-term goals, monthly phone calls from general ed teachers, special education teachers, and school psychologist, as well as regularly scheduled report cards at the end of each term.

FIGURE 2.3

A Sample Individualized Education Program (IEP) for Diane, An Elementary School-Age Student with Disabilities *(continued)*

STUDENT'S PRIMARY CLASSIFICATION: SERIOUS EMOTIONAL DISTURBANCE
SECONDARY CLASSIFICATION: NONE

Areas Needing Specialized Instruction and Support

Team Signatures   IEP Review Date _____

LEA Rep. _____

1. Adaptive Skills

Parent _____

• *Limited interaction skills with peers and adults*

Sp Ed Teacher _____

• *Excessive facial tics and grimaces*

Gen Ed Teacher _____

• *Difficulty staying on task in content subjects, especially reading and math*

School Psych _____

• *Difficulty expressing feelings, needs, and interests*

Student (as appropriate) _____

2. Academic Skills

Related Services Personnel (as appropriate) _____

• *Significantly below grade level in math—3.9*

Objective Criteria and Evaluation Procedures _____

• *Significantly below grade level in reading—4.3*

Annual Review: _____ Date: _____

Comments/Recommendations

_____

_____

_____

_____

_____

FIGURE 2.3

A Sample Individualized Education Program (IEP) for Diane, An Elementary School-Age Student with Disabilities *(continued)*

IEP—ANNUAL GOALS	PERSONS RESPONSIBLE	OBJECTIVE CRITERIA AND EVALUATION PROCEDURES
#1 Annual Goal: Diane will improve her interaction skills with peers and adults.	General education teacher and special ed teacher (resource room) School psychologist consultation	Classroom observations and documented data on target behavior
#2 Annual Goal: Diane will increase her ability to control hand and facial movements.	General education teacher and special ed teacher (resource room) School psychologist consultation	Classroom observations and documented data on target behavior
#3 Annual Goal: Diane will improve her ability to remain on task during academic work.	General education teacher and special ed teacher (resource room) School psychologist consultation	Classroom observations and documented data on target behavior
#4 Annual Goal: Diane will improve her ability to express her feelings.	General education teacher and special ed teacher (resource room) School psychologist consultation	Classroom observations and documented data on target behavior
#5 Annual Goal: Diane will improve math skills by one grade level.	Collaboration of general education teacher and special education teacher through co-teaching and consultation	Precision teaching Addison Wesley Math Program Scope and Sequence Districtwide Assessment of Academic Achievement
#6 Annual Goal: Diane will improve reading skills by one grade level.	Collaboration of general education teacher and special education teacher through co-teaching and consultation	Precision teaching Barnell & Loft Scope and Sequence Districtwide Assessment of Academic Achievement

CASE STUDY

JERALD

Jerald is finishing up his last two months in a second-grade classroom at Robert F. Kennedy Elementary School. Kennedy is a large urban school with a number of students from low economic and culturally diverse backgrounds. Many of its students are described as "disadvantaged" and at significant risk of school failure.

Next year, Jerald will move to third grade, and his parents and teachers have expressed some concerns. "Jerry is an outgoing kid who loves to talk about anything to anyone at any time," says his mother. His current second grade teacher, Miss Robins, complains that he is "hyperactive, inattentive, and a behavior problem." His mom, his dad, and his teacher agree that Jerald has a great deal of difficulty with controlling his emotions.

MOTHER: I just wish he wasn't so easily frustrated at home when things aren't going his way.

MISS ROBINS: He's always in a state of fight or flight. When he is in a fighting mode, he hits, teases, and screams at me or the other students. When in a state of "flight," he withdraws and refuses to comply with any requests. He may even put his head on his desk and openly cry to vent his frustrations.

During second grade, his "fight" behavior has increased considerably. Miss Robins reported that "he has made very little progress and is uncontrollable—a very disruptive influence on the other children in the class." With permission from Jerald's parents, she initiated a referral to the school's child-study team to assess his eligibility for special education services. His overall assessment indicated that he was falling further behind in reading (word decoding skills at grade level 1.5; reading comprehension at grade level 1.0) and math (grade level 1.9). Behaviorally, he has difficulty expressing his feelings in an appropriate manner. He is impulsive, easily distracted, and not well liked by his peers. After determining his eligibility for special education services, the school IEP team developed Jerald's third-grade annual goals and objectives. The focus will be on

1. improving Jerald's reading and math achievement by ensuring access to general curriculum with specialized academic instruction and support—Jerald is to be included in the district and state testing program.

2. teaching Jerald the skills to (a) manage his own behavior when faced with difficult or frustrating situations and (b) improve daily interactions with teachers and peers—the

activities for these goals will be included on the IEP as components of Jerald's *behavioral intervention plan*.

Once the team had agreed on annual goals, for Jerald, they discussed various classroom and school settings that would be appropriate to his needs as described in the IEP. Miss Robins and the school principal are concerned that his disruptive behavior will be too difficult to control in a general education classroom. They would like to see him placed in a special self-contained class for students who are emotionally disturbed. They are concerned not only for Jerald's education but also about the negative effect he has on his classroom peers. Miss Robins reported that she had to spend a disproportionate amount of her time dealing with Jerald's inappropriate behavior.

Taking into account the views of Jerald's teachers and the school principal, the team is considering placement in a special education class for students with serious behavior problems. Such a class is not available at his home school, so Jerald would have to be transported to a special education program in another location. Ms. Beckman, the special education consulting teacher, has an alternative point of view. She proposes that Jerald stay at Kennedy Elementary and that his behavioral intervention plan and specialized academic instruction be implemented in next year's third-grade classroom. Working in collaboration with Jerald's general education teacher and other members of the school's assistance team, Ms. Beckman suggests using cooperative learning techniques, co-teaching among the general and special education teachers, and ongoing support from the school psychologist.

Jerald's parents, although they recognize that his disruptive behavior is increasing and that he is falling further behind academically, are reluctant to have him transferred to another school. They feel it would remove him from his family and neighborhood supports. His brother, who will be in the fifth grade, also goes to Kennedy Elementary.

APPLICATION

1. What do you see as the important issues for the team to consider in deciding what educational setting would be most appropriate to meet Jerald's needs?

2. In addition to the recommendations made by Ms. Beckman, the special education resource room teacher, what suggestions would you have to adapt Jerald's academic and behavioral program if he were to remain in his third-grade class at Kennedy Elementary?

3. Should he remain in his third-grade class at Kennedy Elementary?

Current Trends in the Education of Students with Disabilities

The education of students with disabilities has gone through many changes during the past three decades. In this section, we take a closer look at four major factors that directly affect each student's opportunity for a free and appropriate public education in 21st-century American schools. The major influences are (1) the No Child Left Behind Act (NCLB) and IDEA 2004; (2) evidenced-based special education practice; (3) ensuring reasonable accommodations for students under Section 504/ADA; and (4) establishing safe schools.

NCLB and IDEA 2004: From Access to Accountability

STANDARDS AND SCHOOL ACCOUNTABILITY. The rallying cry in today's schools is "higher expectations for all students." This call for more accountability for student progress culminated in the passage of the *No Child Left Behind Act of 2001* (NCLB). NCLB espouses a **standards-based approach** to reforming schools: Set high standards for what should be taught and how student performance should be measured. Four principles characterize school accountability under NCLB:

1. A focus on student achievement as the primary measure of school success

2. An emphasis on challenging academic standards that specify the knowledge and skills students should acquire and the levels at which they should demonstrate mastery of that knowledge

3. A desire to extend the standards to all students, including those for whom expectations have traditionally been low

4. Heavy reliance on achievement testing to spur the reforms and to monitor their impact (U.S. Department of Education, 2003)

NCLB's push for a standards-driven educational system was a strong influence on reform in the education of students with disabilities. Prior to the congressional reauthorizations of IDEA in 1997 and 2004, federal policy concentrated on ensuring *access* to a free and appropriate public education (FAPE). In clarifying the definition of FAPE, the courts required schools to make available individualized, specially designed instruction and related services resulting in "some educational benefit." Eventually, the "some educational benefit standard" was further expanded to ensure meaningful progress that could be measured for each student.

Advocates for standards-based reform have strongly emphasized the importance of acknowledging the inclusion of students with disabilities in a state and school district accountability system. They contend that in spite of the call to include all students in school reform initiatives, students with disabilities and other disadvantaged students were being left out. Research suggested that the participation of students with disabilities in

OCUS 5

Identify four principles for school accountability as required in the No Child Left Behind Act (NCLB). Under IDEA 2004, what must a student's IEP include to ensure access to the general curriculum?

➤ **Standards-based approach**
Instruction that emphasizes challenging academic standards of knowledge and skills and the levels at which students should demonstrate mastery of them.

Council for Exceptional Children

Standard 3: Foundations

Students with disabilities must have access to the general curriculum and must be included in statewide testing programs when appropriate. Do you think participation in the general curriculum results in higher academic achievement for students with disabilities?

the general curriculum and in statewide assessments of student performance varied considerably from state to state and district to district (Thurlow, 2000). Hehir (2002) suggests that "one of the reasons students with disabilities are not performing better is that they have not had sufficient access to the general curriculum" (p. 6). States and school districts were keeping students with disabilities out of their accountability systems because of fear that these students would pull down scores.

In response to these concerns, IDEA 2004 stipulates that a student's IEP must describe how the disability affects the child's involvement and progress *in the general curriculum*. The law requires an explanation of any individual modifications in the administration of state- or district-wide assessment of student achievement that are needed in order for the child to participate.

The promise of NCLB and IDEA 2004 is straightforward: All students can and will learn more than they are currently learning, and all students will succeed if schools set the highest academic standards. If students don't succeed, then public schools must be held accountable for their failure. The definition of success is determined by student proficiency on content specified by the state and as measured by state performance standards. The promise of "all means all" includes students with disabilities. Therefore, students with disabilities must be (1) assured access to a "highly qualified" teacher who is knowledgeable in the subject matter area(s) being taught; (2) a curriculum on which the standards are based; (3) assessments that measure performance on the standards; and (4) inclusion in the reported results that determine how well a school is meeting the established performance criteria. The promise that every student will learn and succeed has been translated into public policy in both NCLB and IDEA 2004. Although public policy provides the impetus for every student to learn and succeed, the critical issue is whether the promise becomes reality. Many questions are yet to be answered. Among them:

➤ Are the characteristics of evidence-based special education practice compatible with a standards-based approach to education?

➤ Will participation of students with disabilities in a standards-based curriculum result in higher academic achievement, or is failure an inevitable outcome?

➤ Are general and special education teachers being adequately prepared to work in a standards-based system?

For a more in-depth look at contrasting perspectives on the inclusion of students with disabilities in a standards-driven system as mandated by NCLB and IDEA 2004, see the Debate Forum "NCLB and Students with Disabilities: High Academic Achievement or Inevitable Failure?" on page 43.

NCLB AND IDEA 2004: WHAT IT MEANS TO BE A "HIGHLY QUALIFIED" TEACHER. Throughout history, definitions of teacher quality have been left primarily to individual states and local school districts. This changed under NCLB and IDEA 2004. For the first time in history, federal policy was very explicit about what constitutes a "highly qualified" teacher. An individual is considered highly qualified if he or she has obtained full state certification (licensure) or successfully passed a state's teacher licensing examination. A highly qualified teacher must not merely have had state requirements waived on an emergency, temporary, or provisional basis. New elementary school teachers must hold a bachelor's degree and demonstrate *subject knowledge and teaching skills* in the basic elementary school curriculum, including (but not limited to) reading, writing, and mathematics. Subject matter competency and teaching skills must be measured by "a rigorous state test." New middle school and secondary school teachers must also hold a bachelor's degree and demonstrate a *high level of competency in the academic subjects they teach*. Subject matter competency must be measured by "a rigorous state subject matter test" or must be evidenced by having completed an undergraduate major in the subject area, a graduate degree, or coursework equivalent to an undergraduate academic major.

Effective 2002–2003, the law required that all new teachers working with disadvantaged children in **Title I schools** must have met the above requirements. Additionally, a state had to ensure that *all* teachers providing instruction in core subjects (such as English, math, science, social studies, foreign languages, and art) meet the "highly qualified" criterion by the end of the 2005–2006 school year. Qualifications for veteran teachers were also specified in the law. Veteran teachers must hold at least a bachelor's degree and must meet the same standard as new elementary, middle,

FOCUS 6

What does it mean to be a "highly qualified" teacher as required in NCLB and IDEA 2004?

➤ **Title I schools**

Public schools that enroll a significant percentage of children who are living at or below the poverty level as established by the U.S. federal government. Title I schools serve millions of disadvantaged children to ensure their fair, equal, and significant opportunity to obtain a high-quality education and demonstrate proficiency on challenging state academic assessments.

DEBATE FORUM

NCLB AND STUDENTS WITH DISABILITIES: HIGH ACADEMIC ACHIEVEMENT OR INEVITABLE FAILURE?[2]

Standards-based reform in the No Child Left Behind Act (NCLB) is based on the premise that improving student performance is highly correlated with a standards system and high-stakes accountability. However, the issue has generated considerable debate within the field of education. In this Debate Forum, we examine contrasting perspectives on including students with disabilities in a standards-driven system with high-stakes accountability.

POINT

Proponents of including students with disabilities in a standards-driven system argue that doing so will enable these students to experience a wider variety of subjects at a deeper level. This would give students with disabilities exposure to higher-order thinking skills such as problem solving, enable them to develop collaborative skills, and engender a sense of responsibility and self-esteem (McLaughlin & Tilstone, 2000). A standards-driven system also promotes more collaboration among special and general educators, requiring them to develop more challenging learner goals and raise expectations for students with disabilities.

Proponents also argue that if students know their promotion to a higher grade level or high school graduation is dependent on their attainment of a particular standard, they will be motivated to achieve at a higher performance level. Traditionally, special education students have not been held accountable for the achievement of IEP goals. This has sometimes resulted in a lowering of individual expectations and a failure to learn essential skills. As a corollary, special educators were not held accountable for the poor performance of their students and largely regarded the IEP as paper compliance rather than an accountability tool (Sebba, Thurlow, & Goertz, 2000). Including students in a standards-driven system forces teachers to use the IEP as an accountability blueprint, altering goals and objectives as necessary to ensure student progress in the general curriculum.

Some educators, although they accept the premise that standards-based reform should apply to all students, are uneasy about the inclusion of test scores from students with disabilities in the accountability system and about the impact on teachers. Teachers and principals may become anxious about the consequences of published low scores. General education teachers may be concerned that students with disabilities will negatively affect publicly available scores and that schools will blame them.

COUNTERPOINT

Opponents to the standards-based approach as espoused in NCLB raise several concerns. First, they maintain, failure is inevitable because there is insufficient instructional time and resources to meet the instructional needs of students with disabilities. Second, there is no evidence that a standards-driven system will actually lead to sustained higher levels of achievement among students with disabilities and no indication "whether the skills gained through this curriculum are the ones that will prove necessary for successful transition from school" (McLaughlin & Tilstone, p. 62).

It can be argued that establishing content standards for students with disabilities at the state level is inconsistent with the concept of individualization and not in the best interests of either students with disabilities or their peers without disabilities. There is a fear that if all students are expected to reach the same standard, then the bar will be lowered to accommodate those with less ability. If the bar isn't lowered, then students with disabilities will routinely fail to meet the standard. Teachers may feel powerless because they believe it is not possible for all students to reach the required standards.

Another issue is that including students with disabilities within a standards-driven system will affect their rate of high school graduation. The failure to graduate has serious repercussions in today's society. Students who continually fail to reach required standards won't receive a high school diploma in a high-stakes system. One reason for ensuring student access to the general curriculum was the need to improve results. Ironically, it is possible that the requirement of high standards in the general curriculum may instead further compromise the graduation rate for students with disabilities.

Some educators believe that inclusion in a standards-driven system will damage the self-esteem of students with disabilities if they do not perform well. Valuable instruction time would be spent teaching content in academic areas, rather than concentrating on the acquisition of critical functional skills. In order to facilitate a student's mastery of academic skills, teachers could be forced to remove students from the general education class, thus compromising the inclusion of students with their same-aged peers. Kauffman (1999) argues that it is unrealistic and potentially damaging to expect all students to cope with a common standard. There is no denying the need to improve results in both general and special education, but students with disabilities will never catch up with their peers who are not disabled. In fact, they may fall even further behind.

[2]Major portions of this Debate Forum are drawn from Hardman, M. & Mulder, M. (2004). Critical issues in public education: Federal reform and the impact on students with disabilities. In L. M. Bullock, & R. A. Gable (Eds.), *Quality personnel preparation in emotional/behavior disorders* (pp. 12–36), Dallas, TX: Institute for Behavioral and Learning Differences.

and secondary teachers. They may, however, demonstrate their competency in the teaching of academic subjects based on "a high objective uniform state standard of evaluation" (HOUSSE).

In November 2004, Congress passed into law IDEA 2004. A major purpose of this law was to align its accountability provisions with NCLB, including what it means to be a highly qualified special education teacher. IDEA 2004 states that the term *highly qualified* has the same meaning as applied to elementary, middle, and secondary teachers in NCLB. This means that new and veteran special education teachers at the elementary level must have subject knowledge and teaching skills in reading, writing, mathematics, and other areas of the basic elementary curriculum in which they have the primary responsibility for instruction (teacher of record). New and veteran special education teachers at the middle and secondary level must have subject knowledge and teaching skills in academic subjects in which they have the primary teacher of record has responsibility for instruction.

Specifically, IDEA 2004 requires that special education teachers hold a bachelor's degree and obtain full state certification as a special education teacher (including certification obtained through alternative routes to certification) *or* pass the state's special education teacher licensing examination. As is true of elementary and secondary teachers, highly qualified special education teachers must not have had their certification or licensure requirements waived on an emergency, temporary, or provisional basis.

In addition to the above requirements, special education teachers who are teaching core academic subjects "exclusively to children who are assessed against alternate achievement standards" must meet the same requirements as highly qualified elementary teachers, unless the instruction is "above the elementary level." In that case, the special education teacher must have subject matter knowledge appropriate to instruction at the middle school or secondary school level.

New and veteran special education teachers who teach two or more subjects at the middle or secondary level must also meet the applicable requirements in NCLB. New special education teachers who teach multiple subjects must be highly qualified in one subject area (mathematics, arts, or science) and will have two years from the date of employment to demonstrate competence in the additional core academic subjects they teach by passing a state's HOUSSE or meeting NCLB content requirements. Veteran special education teachers at the middle or secondary level who teach multiple subjects must also demonstrate competence in all core academic subjects they teach by passing a state's HOUSSE or meeting NCLB content requirements. However, these teachers are not given a two-year grace period to demonstrate competence in the core academic subjects they teach.

Finally, there was no statutory language in IDEA 2004 regarding special education teachers who provide only **consultative services** to a highly qualified elementary or secondary teacher. However, federal regulations for IDEA 2004 clarify that special education teachers in consultative roles are considered highly qualified if such individuals meet all other applicable requirements under the law.

Although NCLB and IDEA 2004 are explicit in their definition of a highly qualified teacher, there is considerable disagreement among educators about whether *highly qualified* is equivalent to *high quality*. What are the qualifications necessary to become an effective teacher? NCLB stresses that highly qualified teachers have "subject matter competency" in areas in which they are the primary instructor (teacher of record). As suggested by Brownell, Sindelar, Bishop, Langley, and Seo (2002), the emphasis is on a thorough knowledge of the content being taught and on the verbal ability to deliver that content. It is not on pedagogy. However, Darling-Hammond and Young (2002) report that there is a body of research suggesting that both pedagogy and content knowledge have had a significant impact on student performance and increase the likelihood of teachers remaining in the field. This view is echoed by the National Commission on Teaching and America's Future (NCTAF) (1996). In their report, *What Matters Most: Teaching for America's Future*, the commission stresses the importance of what teachers know *and* what they do. It recommends that university teacher preparation programs emphasize cognitive, social, and cultural foundations; mentoring and instruction; content pedagogy; and technology and teaming.

Characteristics of Evidence-Based Special Education Practice

Ensuring an appropriate educational experience for students with disabilities means providing evidence-based (scientifically based) special education services and supports. The characteris-

➤ **Consultative services**
With respect to special education teachers, services provided to a highly qualified general education teacher that adjust the learning environment, modify instructional methods, adapt curricula, use positive behavior supports and interventions, and select and implement appropriate accommodations to meet the individual needs of children. The special education teacher may provide such services in a co-teaching or other consultative role.

FOCUS 7
Identify three characteristics of evidence-based special education that enhance learning opportunities for students with disabilities.

For some time, the general classroom teacher has had to work with students who have disabilities without the assistance of any effective support. This is no longer the case in many of today's schools. The emergence of inclusive education programs in elementary schools throughout the United States has strengthened collaborative efforts between the general education classroom teacher and the network of supports available in the schools. When student need and ability make it appropriate, instruction in functional life skills can be implemented. Students are taught only those skills that will help them succeed in accessing and participating in a natural setting, whether it is the classroom, family, or neighborhood. Functional life skills may include daily living (such as self-help, personal finances, and community travel), personal-social development (such as learning **self-determination** and socially responsible behaviors), communication skills, recreational and leisure activities, and employment skills.

The functional life skills approach is based on the premise that if these practical skills are not taught through formal instruction, they will not be learned. Most students do not need to be taught functional skills because they have already learned them through everyday experience. This does not mean that students being taught through a functional approach are not also learning core academic skills. Instruction may occur in academic content areas, but not in the same sequence. For example, a functional life skills approach to reading would initially teach frequently used words that are necessary for survival within the environment (examples include danger, exit, and rest room signs) and then pair them directly with an environmental cue.

Providing Reasonable Accommodations Under Section 504/ADA

America's schools must provide supports and services to two groups of students with disabilities. One group qualifies for special education services under IDEA because their disability limits their access to an appropriate education. Another group, though not viewed as educationally limited by their disability and therefore ineligible for special education, are protected against discrimination under Section 504 of the Vocational Rehabilitation Act and the Americans with Disabilities Act (ADA).[1] Although these two laws are comparable in focus, ADA includes conditions such as HIV infections, heart disease, drug addiction, and alcoholism under the definition of disability. However, Section 504 has more specific information on "what it would mean not to discriminate on the basis of disability in various educational settings" (Jarrow, 1999, p. 3). Together, Section 504 and ADA comprehensively address issues of nondiscrimination and equal opportunity for students with disabilities.

Students eligible under Section 504/ADA are entitled to have a *written plan* that assures them access to an education comparable to that of students who are not disabled. A **504/ADA plan** is different from an IEP in its scope and intent. Whereas an IEP is concerned with ensuring access to a free and appropriate education designed to provide educational benefit, a 504 plan provides for reasonable accommodations or modifications as a means to "create a fair and level playing field" for the student. For example, a student who uses as wheelchair but does not require special education services may still need a written 504/ADA plan covering access to adapted transportation or physical therapy (Huefner, 2006). A comparison of IDEA and 504/ADA provisions is found in Table 2.3 on page 48.

Numerous accommodations or modifications can be made for students, depending on identified need. Examples include untimed tests, extra time to complete assignments, changes in seating arrangements to accommodate vision or hearing loss or distractibility, opportunity to respond orally on assignments and tests, taped textbooks, access to peer tutoring, access to a study carrel for independent work, and use of supplementary materials such as visual or auditory aids.

Safe Schools: Zero Tolerance versus Zero Exclusion

In the past several years, maintaining a safe school environment for America's children has become a critical priority for parents, school personnel, policy makers, and government officials. The National Center for Education Statistics (2000) reports that 7% of students in grades 9 through 12 report carrying a weapon such as a gun or knife to school. One out of every 620

> ➤ **Self-determination**
> The ability of a person to consider options and make appropriate choices regarding residential life, work, and leisure time.

FOCUS 8
Distinguish between students with disabilities who are eligible for services under Section 504/ADA and those who are eligible under IDEA.

> ➤ **504/ADA plan**
> A written plan that provides for reasonable accommodations or modifications in assessment and instruction as a means to "create a fair and level playing field" for students who qualify as disabled under Section 504 of the Vocational Rehabilitation Act and the Americans with Disabilities Act.

Council for Exceptional Children

Standard 1: Foundations

FOCUS 9
Distinguish between the principles of zero tolerance and zero exclusion in America's schools.

---

[1] See Chapter 1 for a more detailed description of Section 504 and ADA.

TABLE 2.3

A Comparison of the Purposes and Provisions of IDEA and Section 504/ADA

	IDEA	SECTION 504/ADA
General Purpose	This federal funding statute provides financial aid to states in their efforts to ensure adequate and appropriate services for children and youth with disabilities.	This broad civil rights law prevents discrimination on the basis of disability in employment, programs and services provided by state and local governments, goods and services provided by private companies, and commercial facilities.
Definition of Disability	IDEA identifies 12 categories of disability conditions. However, the law also allows states and school districts the option of eliminating categories for children ages 3 through 9 and defining them as developmentally delayed.	504/ADA identifies students as disabled if they meet the definition of a qualified handicapped [disabled] person (i.e., student has or has had a physical or mental impairment that substantially limits a major life activity, or student is regarded as disabled by others).
Responsibility to Provide a Free and Appropriate Public Education (FAPE)	Both require the provision of a free and appropriate education, including individually designed instruction, to students covered under specific eligibility criteria.	
	IDEA requires a written IEP document.	504/ADA does not require a written IEP document but does require a written plan.
	"Appropriate education" means a program designed to provide "educational benefit."	"Appropriate" means an education comparable to the education provided to students who are not disabled.
Special Education or General Education	A student is eligible to receive IDEA services only if the child-study team determines that the student is disabled under 1 of the 12 qualifying conditions and requires special education. Eligible students receive special education and related services.	An eligible student meets the definition of qualified person with a disability: one who currently has or has had a physical or mental impairment that substantially limits a major life activity or who is regarded as disabled by others. The student is not required to need special education in order to be protected.
Funding	IDEA provides additional funding if a student is eligible.	504/ADA does not provide additional funds.
Accessibility	IDEA requires that modifications be made, if necessary, to provide access to a free and appropriate education.	504/ADA includes regulations regarding building and program accessibility.
Notice Safeguards	Both require notice to the parent or guardian with respect to identification, evaluation, and/or placement.	
	IDEA requires written notice.	504/ADA does not require written notice, but a district would be wise to provide it.
	It delineates required components of written notice.	Particular components are not delineated.
	It requires written notices prior to *any* change in placement.	It requires notice only before a "significant change" in placement.
Evaluations	IDEA requires consent before an initial evaluation is conducted.	504/ADA does not require consent but does require notice.
	It requires reevaluations at least every 3 years.	It requires periodic reevaluations.
	It requires an update and/or review before *any* change in placement.	Reevaluation is required before a significant change in placement.
	It provides for independent educational evaluations.	Independent educational evaluations are not mentioned.
Due Process	Both statutes require districts to provide impartial hearings for parents or guardians who disagree with the identification, evaluation, or placement of a student with disabilities.	
	Specific requirements are detailed in IDEA.	504/ADA requires that the parent have an opportunity to participate and be represented by counsel. Other details are left to the discretion of the local school district. These should be covered in school district policy.
Enforcement	IDEA is enforced by the Office of Special Education Programs in the Department of Education.	504/ADA is enforced by the Office for Civil Rights in the Department of Justice.

school-age children in America is killed by gunfire before the age of 20—that's about 13 children every day (Children's Defense Fund, 2005). About 8% of America's children are victims of crimes at school each year (National Center for Education Statistics, 2002). In 1994, the U.S. Congress passed the Gun-Free Schools Act. This federal legislation mandated that every state receiving federal education funds enact a law requiring all local educational agencies (school districts) to expel for at least one year any student who brings a firearm to school.

The federal law and the corresponding state legislation employ the principle of **zero tolerance**. This principle states that the consequences for a student's misbehavior (such as a one-year expulsion) are predetermined and that no individual reasons or circumstances are considered.

The zero-tolerance principle has both supporters and detractors, but it has posed a particularly serious issue for students with disabilities receiving services under the provisions of IDEA. IDEA employs a zero-rejection principle, requiring that an eligible student with a disability cannot be denied access to a free and appropriate public education (FAPE). How, then, can a student with a disability be expelled from school under any circumstances?

Many professionals and parents of students with disabilities are concerned that if schools allow a cessation of services, it will undermine IDEA's zero-exclusion principle. Others argue that students with disabilities should be treated no differently than students without disabilities when the individual is likely to cause injury to self and others.

In dealing with this controversial issue, IDEA 2004 reiterated that a free and appropriate public education must be available to all students with disabilities and that there should be no cessation of services. Schools must seek to employ instructional alternatives to expulsion—that is, helping children to learn decision-making and problem-solving skills that promote acceptable behavior. Hartwig and Ruesch (2000) suggested that it is important to have a balanced approach to discipline that includes "both proactive strategies to prevent problem behavior and well-specified, procedurally sound responses to problem behavior" (p. 246).

This chapter has briefly traced the history of special education services within the United States, the movement to reaffirm the rights of students with disabilities to a free and appropriate public education, the basic tenets of the Individuals with Disabilities Education Act, and current policy and practice in the field of special education. In Chapter 3, we continue our discussion with an in-depth examination of effective practices for inclusion and collaboration in the early childhood and elementary school years.

One out of every ten children is a victim of crime in America's schools. Thirteen children are killed every day by gunfire in America. This school is conducting a drill to prepare children for a potential terrorist attack. What else can society do to make America's schools safe?

> **Zero tolerance**

Approach whereby the consequences for a student's misbehavior are predetermined, and no individual reasons or circumstances are not to be considered.

Council for Exceptional Children

Standard 1: Foundations

Standard 9: Professional and Ethical Practice

FOCUS REVIEW

FOCUS 1 What educational services were available for students with disabilities during most of the 20th century?

- Educational programs at the beginning of the 20th century were provided primarily in separate, special schools.

- For the first 75 years of the 20th century, the availability of educational programs for students with disabilities was sporadic and selective. Special education was allowed in many states but required in only a few.

- Research on the efficacy of special classes for students with mild disabilities suggested that there was little or no benefit in removing students from general education classrooms.

FOCUS 2 Identify the principal issues in the right-to-education cases that led to eventual passage of the national mandate to educate students with disabilities.

- The U.S. Supreme Court reaffirmed education as a right and not a privilege.

- In Pennsylvania, the court ordered the schools to provide a free public education to all children aged 6 to 21 with mental retardation.

- The *Mills* case extended the right to a free public education to all school-age children with disabilities.

FOCUS 3 Identify five major provisions of the Individuals with Disabilities Education Act.

- The labeling and placement of students with disabilities in educational programs requires the use of nondiscriminatory and multidisciplinary assessment.

- Parental consent is required for students' testing and placement, and their participation as team members in the development of an IEP is crucial.

- Procedural safeguards (such as due process) protect the child and family from decisions that could adversely affect their lives.

- Every student with a disability is entitled to a free and appropriate public education.

- The delivery of an appropriate education occurs through an individualized education program (IEP).

- All children have the right to learn in an environment consistent with their academic, social, and physical needs. The law mandated that children with disabilities receive their education with peers without disabilities to the maximum extent appropriate.

FOCUS 4 Discuss the special education referral, assessment, planning, and placement process.

- Initiating the referral: A student is referred for an assessment to determine whether he or she qualified for special education services. Once the school's child-study team receives the referral, it may try to modify or adapt instruction in the general education classroom or conduct a formal assessment to determine whether the student is eligible for special education.

- Assessing student eligibility and educational need: A multidisciplinary team of professionals conducts a nondiscriminatory assessment of the student's needs, including assessment of performance in both school and home environments, to determine eligibility for special education.

- Developing the individualized education program (IEP): An IEP team is established that includes professionals, parents, and the student when appropriate. This team is responsible for documenting the student's present level of performance, agreeing on measurable annual goals, identifying skill areas where special education and related services are needed; documenting access to the general curriculum and participation in state- and district-wide assessments; establishing beginning and ending dates for special education services; and determining a process for reporting to parents on student progress in meeting annual goals.

- Determining the least restrictive environment: Once the IEP team has agreed on annual goals, it decides what educational placement is most appropriate to the student's individual needs.

FOCUS 5 Identify four principles for school accountability as required in the No Child Left Behind Act. Under IDEA 2004, what must a student's IEP include to ensure access to the general curriculum?

- The four principles are

  1. A focus on student achievement as the primary measure of school success

  2. An emphasis on challenging academic standards that specify the knowledge and skills students should acquire and the levels at which they should demonstrate mastery of that knowledge

  3. A desire to extend the standards to all students, including those for whom expectations have traditionally been low

  4. Heavy reliance on achievement testing to spur the reforms and to monitor their impact

- IDEA 2004 requires that a student's IEP describe how the disability affects the child's involvement and progress in the general curriculum. IEP goals must enable the child to access the general curriculum when appropriate.

FOCUS 6 What does it mean to be a "highly qualified" teacher as required in NCLB and IDEA 2004?

- An individual is considered highly qualified if he or she has obtained full state certification/licensure or has successfully passed a state's teacher licensing examination. (It is not enough for a teacher merely to have had state requirements waived on an emergency, temporary, or provisional basis.)

- New elementary teachers must hold a bachelor's degree and demonstrate *subject knowledge and teaching skills* in the basic elementary school curriculum.

- New middle school and secondary school teachers must also hold a bachelor's degree and demonstrate a *high level of competency in the academic subjects they teach*.

- A state must ensure that *all* teachers providing instruction in "core subjects" (such as English, math, science, social studies, foreign languages, and art) meet the "highly qualified" definition.

- Veteran teachers must hold at least a bachelor's degree and be held to the same standard as new elementary, middle, and secondary teachers. They may, however, demonstrate their competency in the teaching of academic subjects based on "a high objective uniform state standard of evaluation" (HOUSSE).

- The term *highly qualified* has the same meaning as applied to elementary, middle, and secondary teachers in NCLB.

- Special education teachers must hold a bachelor's degree and obtain full state certification as a special education teacher *or* pass the state's special education teacher licensing examination.

- Highly qualified special education teachers must not merely have had their certification or licensure requirements waived on an emergency, temporary, or provisional basis.

- Special education teachers who are teaching core academic subjects "exclusively to children who are assessed against alternate achievement standards" must meet the same requirements as highly qualified elementary teachers unless the instruction is "above the elementary level." In that case, the special education teacher must have subject matter knowledge appropriate to middle school or secondary school instruction.

- New and veteran special education teachers who teach two or more subjects at the middle or secondary level must also meet the applicable requirements in NCLB. New special education teachers who teach multiple subjects must be highly qualified in one subject area (mathematics, arts, or science) and will have two years from the date of employment to demonstrate competence in the additional core academic subjects they teach by passing a state's HOUSSE or meeting NCLB content requirements.

- Veteran special education teachers at the middle or secondary level who teach multiple subjects must also demonstrate competence in all core academic subjects in which they have primary teaching responsibility by passing a state's HOUSSE or meeting NCLB content requirements.

- There is no statutory language in IDEA 2004 regarding special education teachers who provide only *consultative services* to a highly qualified elementary or secondary teacher. However, federal regulation state that special education teachers in consultative roles are considered highly qualified if such individuals meet all other applicable requirements under the law.

FOCUS 7 Identify three characteristics of evidence-based special education practice that enhance learning opportunities for students with disabilities.

- Individualization: A student-centered approach to instructional decision making

- Intensive instruction: Frequent instructional experiences of significant duration

- The explicit teaching of academic, adaptive, and/or functional life skills

FOCUS 8 Distinguish between students with disabilities who are eligible for services under Section 504/ADA and those who are eligible under IDEA.

- Students eligible under ADA are entitled to accommodations and/or modifications to their educational program that will ensure that they receive an appropriate education comparable to that of their peers without disabilities.

- Students eligible under IDEA are entitled to special education and related services to ensure that they receive a free and appropriate education.

FOCUS 9 Distinguish between the principles of zero tolerance and zero exclusion in America's schools.

- The principle of zero tolerance states that the consequences for a student's misbehavior are predetermined and that no individual reasons or circumstances are considered.

- The principle of zero exclusion states that no student with a disability can be denied a free and appropriate public education, regardless of the nature, type, or extent of his or her disabling condition.

BUILDING YOUR PORTFOLIO

Council for Exceptional Children

If you are thinking about a career in special education, you should know that many states use national standards developed by the Council for Exceptional Children (CEC) to assess a teacher candidate's knowledge and skills for working with students with disabilities. See a complete listing of the ten CEC Content Standards on the inside front cover of this text.

CEC Content Standards Addressed in This Chapter

1 Foundations

2 Development and Characteristics of Learners

3 Individual Learning Differences

7 Instructional Planning

8 Assessment

9 Professional and Ethical Practice

Assess Your Knowledge of the CEC Standards Addressed in This Chapter

Some states require that teacher candidates develop a portfolio of products that demonstrate their mastery of the CEC content standards. To assist in the development of products for this portfolio, you may wish to complete the following activities.

- Complete a written test of the chapter's content.

  If your instructor requires a written test of your content knowledge for this chapter, keep a copy for your portfolio. A practice test on the information covered in this chapter is available through the Human Exceptionality Companion Website and the Student Study Guide.

- Respond to the application questions for the Case Study "Jerald."

  Review the Case Study and respond in writing to the application questions. Keep a copy of the Case Study and of your written response for your portfolio.

- Participate in a community service learning activity.

  Community service is a valuable way to enhance your learning experience. Visit our companion website for suggested community service learning activities that correspond to the information presented in this chapter. Develop a reflective journal of the service learning experience for your portfolio.

WEB RESOURCES

The Office of Special Education Program, U.S. Department of Education

http://www.ed.gov/offices/OSERS/OSEP/Resources/link.html

The Office of Special Education Programs (OSEP) is dedicated to improving results for infants, toddlers, children, and youth with disabilities ages birth through 21 by providing leadership and financial support to assist states and local districts. This website provides information on IDEA grants to states and discretionary grants to universities/colleges and other not-for-profit organizations to support research, demonstrations, technical assistance, dissemination of information, technology and personnel development, and parent-training and information centers.

IDEA Partnerships: Results for Kids Resources

http://ideapartnership.org/ebp.cfm

This library responds to several challenges and opportunities inherent in the Individuals with Disabilities Education Act (IDEA 2004) and

the No Child Left Behind Act, such as early intervening to prevent learning difficulties from leading to academic failure; the need for instruction that works for culturally and/or linguistically diverse students; the imperative to reduce referrals of children who do not need special education; the impetus to increase success for all students in the general curriculum; and the contribution of nonacademic services to improving academic performance.

National Information Center for Children and Youth with Disabilities

http://www.nichcy.org/

NICHCY is a national information center that provides information on disabilities and disability-related issues. NICHCY's website has information on specific disabilities, special education and related services for children in school, individualized education programs; parent materials, disability organizations, professional associations, education rights and what the law requires, early-intervening services for infants and toddlers, and transition to adult life.

FURTHER READINGS

Edelman, M. W. (2005). *The State of America's Children.* Washington, DC: The Children's Defense Fund.

The book provides comprehensive and state-by-state data on family income, child health, children and families in crisis, child care and early childhood development, child nutrition, education, adolescent pregnancy, and violence. It features information on national trends in child poverty, births to teens, mothers in the work force, and youth unemployment.

Huefner, D. (2006). *Getting Comfortable with Special Education Law: A Framework for Working with Children with Disabilities.* Norwood, MA: Christopher-Gordon Publishers.

This book is a guide to understanding the needs of children with disabilities; the complex legal relationship between federal and state governments; the contributions being made by legislation, regulations, and court decisions; and the ultimate responsibility of parents and teachers to make appropriate education a reality for all children with disabilities.

Pitaski, V. M. (2002). *What Do I Do When . . . The Answer Book on Placement Under the IDEA and Section 504.* Alexandria, VA: L R P Publications.

In a question-and-answer format, this book provides solutions to educational placement under IDEA and Section 504/ADA. Legal obligations for schools and agencies are described, including cross references to judicial decisions and administrative rulings.

Sorrells, A. M., Rieth, H. J., & Sindelar, P. T. (Eds.) (2004). *Critical Issues in Special Education: Access, Diversity, and Accountability.* Boston: Allyn and Bacon.

This book includes contributions from researchers, policy makers, teachers, and parents on effective practices and critical thinking to ensure that students with disabilities receive a free and appropriate education in the least restrictive environment. Each chapter raises issues and concerns that revolve around a given topic and challenges students to reframe their thinking about how to teach students with disabilities effectively.

COMPANION WEBSITE

Visit the companion website at college.hmco.com/pic/hardman9e for additional resources that support this text:

- HM Video Cases that present actual classroom scenarios that you may face every day as a teacher

- Practice ACE Exams that will help you prepare for quizzes, tests, and certification exams
- Flashcards of key terms
- Weblinks

3

Inclusion and Multidisciplinary Collaboration in the Early Childhood and Elementary School Years

TO BEGIN WITH . . .

LEARNING TO TEACH SO THAT ALL STUDENTS CAN LEARN

As schools educate more students who were earlier excluded from school altogether or segregated in "special" classes, teachers increasingly need knowledge about learning differences that is typically reserved to a very few. . . . As more and more of these students are included in [general] education classrooms, expected to meet the same standards as other students, teachers need a more diagnostic approach to assessing learners' needs and a much wider repertoire of teaching strategies to address them. In addition to students with identified [disabilities], there is a full continuum of perceptual and expressive abilities that create distinctive learning profiles for all students, most of whom can be better taught by teachers who are sensitive to how they learn. . . . These students are present in virtually all classrooms, but few teachers have had the preparation to teach them effectively. (Darling-Hammond, 2006, p. 257)

WHAT TEACHERS NEED TO KNOW IN AN INCLUSIVE CLASSROOM

Special education teachers often report their lack of knowledge about the general education curriculum, whereas general education teachers often report their lack of knowledge about individualizing instruction. However, after a year of collaboration, both report greater knowledge and comfort in these areas. They use many of the same instructional strategies in the inclusive classroom that are effective for students in general classrooms. These include cooperative learning, hands-on learning, peer and cross-age tutoring and support models. . . . Special education should be understood as a service, not a place. Thus, a student (labeled either special or general education) may receive services in a variety of settings or groups. Although not a legal term, inclusion is best expressed in the student who is on the regular register, attends homeroom with her or his peers, participates equally in school activities, receives instruction suited to her or his needs, is held to the school's common standards and receives the same report card as other students. (Lipsky & Gartner, 2002, p. 202)

DOES INCLUSION DELIVER A GOOD EDUCATION?

In some schools, "fully included" children sit isolated in the back of general education classrooms, their education addressed by a team of specialists with whom they work individually or in small groups. Interaction with the rest of the class is limited. This arrangement offers the worst of both options—the student with disabilities receives a separate education in a way that prominently advertises his [or her] difference. He [or she] is a class of one. Increasing numbers of schools—particularly at the elementary level—are discovering creative ways of addressing the academic needs of a wider range of students in general education classrooms. Supportive adults become functional classroom members rather than appendages. Extensive summer workshops foster faculty communication about universally designed educational practices. And differentiated instruction—so much the rage in general education—embraces all children, especially in these days of high content standards. (Byrnes, 2002, p. 219)

▼SNAPSHOT

SUPPORTING BILL, THE NEW KID AT SCHOOL

Bill lived in an institution until he was 12. When his new foster parents brought him home, they enrolled him in the local elementary school. Bill's first IEP meeting included his foster parents, teachers, specialists, some schoolmates, and Bill. First they discussed Bill's strengths. Though they had just met, and Bill didn't talk, his classmates thought he was very friendly and nice to be around. "Great smile" went up on his list of strengths. His foster parents added, "Loves music." His teacher, Mr. Lewis, noted that Bill seemed to be enjoying the meeting and added, "Likes to be involved." The listing continued.

Bill's goals were discussed. He needed to work on "tracking"—visually following and focusing on key people and things in his environment. Bill was assigned to work with a sixth grade math teacher who was famous for his animated teaching and for pacing around the classroom. Bill would have lots of opportunity to "track" this teacher while he also worked on responding vocally and helping to pass out materials to classmates. In PE, classmates decided "being cool" was a goal they thought Bill would want, so they cued his foster parents in on clothes that Bill would need and on the latest in backpack styles. They also arranged to meet Bill at his bus, taking him with them to hang out with friends before school each day. Other goals were discussed. Learning to operate a switch so that he might eventually operate an electric wheelchair was one. Another goal was improving the coordination of his movements and broadening the range of motion of his stiffened joints by helping to reshelve books in the library.

After a while, his teachers and classmates worked on their own creative-thinking goals by beginning each lesson by brainstorming about how Bill could be included in the lesson. The day frogs were dissected in a biology lesson, Bill's group decided to dissect theirs on his wheelchair tray. Bill squealed like everyone else when the frog parts were held up for inspection. His goal of "vocalizing" was easily met that day! Another student had Bill help him color the frog anatomy hand-out with marker pens: practice in coordinated movement.

When Bill's homeroom teacher told the class they could listen to music for ten minutes each day, it took them exactly two days to teach him to operate the switch that turned on the music for everyone. In Home Skills class, he was the only one allowed to operate the switch on the mixer that made the cookies that the class eventually named "Bill's Cool Cookies" and sold as a fundraiser for their field trip. In PE, Bill's classmates put the bat in his hands, helped him hit the ball, and raced the wheelchair around the bases with Bill laughing all the way. The next year Bill died unexpectedly in his sleep. Hundreds of kids from his school went to the funeral.

(Adapted from National Institute for Urban School Improvement, 2003, p. 11.)

This chapter explores inclusive education, collaboration, and programs and services in the early childhood and elementary school years. For infants, toddlers, and preschool-age children, the world is defined primarily through family and a small group of same-age peers. As the child progresses in age and development, the world expands to include the neighborhood, the school, and (eventually) the community. For Bill in our opening snapshot, the first 12 years of his life were confined within the walls of an institution, where he had few personal possessions, wore clothing designed more for utility than for fashion, and lived under a regimented set of rules that controlled when he ate, when he played, and when he slept. Bill's life was dramatically changed when he left the institution and his new foster parents enrolled him in the neighborhood elementary school. Bill became the new kid on the block. Inclusion for Bill meant hanging out with friends, learning new skills side-by-side with peers, and racing around the bases in his wheelchair during PE class.

Inclusive Education

The history of education has seen continuous evolution in the terms used to describe the concept of educating students with disabilities in a general education setting, side-by-side with their peers without disabilities. The most common terms are *mainstreaming*, *least restrictive environment*, and *inclusive education*. We discussed the least restrictive environment in the context of IDEA 2004 in Chapter 2. The expression *mainstreaming* dates back to the very beginnings of the field of special education. It didn't come into widespread use until the 1960s, however, with the growth of classes for children with disabilities in the public schools, most of which separated students with disabilities from their peers without disabilities.

At that time, some professionals called into question the validity of separate programs. Dunn (1968) charged that classes for children with mild retardation could not be justified: "Let us stop being pressured into continuing and expanding a special education program that we know now to be undesirable for many of the children we are dedicated to serve" (p. 5). Dunn, among others, called for a placement model whereby students with disabilities could remain in the general education class program for at least some portion of the school day and receive special education when and where needed. This model became widely known as **mainstreaming.**

Although mainstreaming implied that students with disabilities would receive individual planning and support from both general and special educators, this did not always happen in actual practice. In fact, the term *mainstreaming* fell from favor when it became associated with placing students with disabilities in general education classes without providing additional support, as a means to save money and limit the number of students who could receive additional specialized services. (Such practices gave rise to the term *maindumping* as an alternative to mainstreaming.) However, the term *mainstreaming* remains in some use today as one way to describe educating students with disabilities in general education settings.

What Is Inclusive Education?

The terms *mainstreaming* and *inclusive education*, although often used interchangeably, are not synonymous. Whereas mainstreaming implies the physical placement of students with disabilities in the same school or classroom as students without disabilities, inclusive education suggests that placement alone is not enough. **Inclusive education** *means students with disabilities receive the services and supports appropriate to their individual needs within the general education setting.* Peterson and Hittie (2005) described this paradigm as "push-in services" (p. 21). Whereas the traditional model for special education has been "pulling the student out" of the general education class to receive support, inclusive education focuses on "pushing services and supports into" the general education setting for both students and teachers.

Council for Exceptional Children

Standard 3: Individual Learning Differences

Standard 5: Learning Environments and Social Interactions

➤ **Mainstreaming**
A term used to describe the placement of students with disabilities into general education classrooms for some or all of the school day.

FOCUS **1**
Define inclusive education.

➤ **Inclusive education**
Students with disabilities receive the services and supports appropriate to their individual needs within the general education setting.

Inclusive education may also be defined by the extent of the student's access to, and participation in, the general education classroom. **Full inclusion** is an approach whereby students with disabilities receive all instruction in a general education classroom; support services come to the student. **Partial inclusion** involves students with disabilities receiving some of their instruction in a general education classroom, with "pull out" to another instructional setting when appropriate to their individual needs. The success of full and partial inclusion programs depends on several factors, including a belief in the value of inclusion on the part of professionals and parents, the availability of a support network of general and special education professionals, and access to a curriculum that meets the needs of each student.

A number of educators have argued that in spite of certain accomplishments, pull-out programs have caused negative effects or obstacles to the appropriate education of students with disabilities (Lipsky & Gartner, 2002; Sailor, Gee, & Karasoff, 2000; Shapiro et al., 2002). On the other hand, proponents of pull-out programs have argued that the available research doesn't support the premise that full-time placement in a general education classroom is superior to special education classes for all students with disabilities (Chesley & Calaluce, 2002; Dorn & Fuchs, 2004; Hallahan, 2002). For a more in-depth look at the differing perspectives on full inclusion, see the Debate Forum on page 58.

Characteristics of Evidence-Based Inclusive Schools

The passage of the *No Child Left Behind Act* and *IDEA 2004* launched a great deal of discussion about which characteristics, taken together, constitute an evidence-based (that is, supported by scientific research) school for all students. There seems to be considerable agreement that schools are most effective in promoting student achievement and valued postschool outcomes when they

➤ promote the values of diversity, acceptance, and belonging.

➤ ensure the availability of formal and natural supports within the general education setting.

➤ provide services and supports in age-appropriate classrooms in neighborhood schools.

➤ ensure access to the general curriculum while meeting the individualized needs of each student.

➤ provide a multidisciplinary schoolwide support system to meet the needs of all students.

DIVERSITY, ACCEPTANCE, AND BELONGING. An evidence-based inclusive school promotes acceptance and belonging within a diverse culture (Gollnick & Chinn, 2006; Hollins & Gutzman, 2005). Wade and Zone (2000) described this value as "building community and affirming diversity. . . . Struggling learners can be actively involved, socially accepted, and motivated to achieve the best of their individual and multiple abilities" (p. 22). Landers and Weaver (1997) indicated that "inclusion is an attitude of unqualified acceptance and the fostering of student growth, at any level, on the part of all adults involved in a student's education" (p. 7). These authors further suggested that the responsibility for ensuring a successful inclusive program lies with adults. "Adults must be able to design appropriate educational opportunities that foster the individual student's growth within the context of the student's talents and interests among age-appropriate peers" (p. 7). (See the nearby Reflect on This, "Including Ross," on page 60.)

FORMAL AND NATURAL SUPPORTS. Within an effective inclusive school, students with disabilities must have access to both formal and natural support networks (Friend & Bursuck, 2006; McDonnell, Hardman, & McDonnell, 2003). **Formal supports** are those provided by, and funded

➤ **Full inclusion**

Students with disabilities receive all instruction in a general education classroom; support services come to the student.

➤ **Partial inclusion**

Students with disabilities receive some of their instruction in a general education classroom, with "pull out" to another instructional setting when appropriate to their individual needs.

OCUS 2
Describe the characteristics of evidence-based inclusive schools.

Council for Exceptional Children

Standard 3: Individual Learning Differences

Standard 9: Professional and Ethical Practice

➤ **Formal supports**

Educational supports provided by, and funded through, the public school system. They include qualified teachers, paraprofessionals, and access to instructional materials designed for, or adapted to, individual needs.

Inclusive classrooms promote diversity, acceptance, and belonging for all children. What are the responsibilities of professionals to ensure a successful inclusive program?

DEBATE FORUM

PERSPECTIVES ON FULL INCLUSION

*F*ull inclusion: Students are placed in a general education classroom for the entire school day. The supports and services necessary to ensure an appropriate education come to the student in the general education class; the student is not "pulled out" into a special education classroom for instruction.

POINT

We must rethink our current approach to the educational placement of students with disabilities. Pulling these students out of general education classrooms and into separate settings does not make sense in today's schools from the standpoint of both values and "what works." As a moral imperative, inclusion is the right thing to do.

Inclusion goes beyond returning students who have been in separate placements to the general education classroom. It incorporates an end to labeling students and shunting them out of the regular [general eduation] classroom to obtain needed services. It responds to . . . the call for "neverstreaming" by establishing a refashioned mainstream, a restructured and unified school system that serves all students together. (Lipsky & Gartner, 2004, p. 203)

COUNTERPOINT

No one is questioning the value of children belonging, of their being a part of society. However, it is not necessarily true that removing a child with a disability from the general education classroom is a denial of human rights. Is it a denial of human rights to remove a student with a disability from a setting where that child receives inadequate academic support to meet his or her instructional needs? Isn't it a denial of human rights to leave a child in a classroom where she or he is socially isolated? How do you translate the moral imperative into action when the social and academic needs of these students are beyond the expertise of a general education teacher? We must separate the vision from the reality. General education does not have the inclination or the expertise to meet the diverse needs of all students with disabilities. General education is already overburdened with the increasing number of at-risk students, large class sizes, and an inadequate support system.

POINT

Let's do separate vision from reality. The reality is that traditional special education has failed; it does not work (Lipsky & Gartner, 2002; Meyer, 2001; Peterson & Hittie, 2005). Setting aside the values inherent in the inclusion of all students, let's look at the reality:

- Only 35% of people with disabilities reported being employed full- or part-time, compared to 78% of those who do not have disabilities.

- Three times as many people with disabilities live in poverty with annual household incomes below $15,000 (26% versus 9%).

- People with disabilities remain twice as likely to drop out of high school (21% versus 10%).

- They are twice as likely to have inadequate transportation (31% versus 13%), and a much higher percentage go without needed health care (18% versus 7%).

- People with disabilities are less likely to socialize, eat out, or attend religious services than their counterparts without disabilities.

- Not surprisingly given the persistence of these gaps, life satisfaction for people with disabilities also trails. Only 34% say they are very satisfied, compared to 61% of those without disabilities. (National Organization on Disability[N.O.D.]/Harris Survey, 2004)

Positive and sucessful experiences in school, including interactions with nondisabled peers, put students with disabilities

COUNTERPOINT

There is always a flip side to the research coin. What about the following research findings?

- Research doesn't support the premise that full-time placement in a general education classroom is superior to special education pull-out programs for all students with disabilities (Chesley & Caladuce, 2002; Hallahan, 2002).

- General education teachers have little expertise in assisting students with learning and behavioral difficulties and are already overburdened with large class sizes and inadequate support services (Kavale & Forness, 2000; Mastropieri & Scruggs, 2007).

- Special educators have been specifically trained to individualize instruction, develop instructional strategies, and use proven techniques that facilitate learning for students with disabilities (Hallahan, 2002).

- In general, both parents and professionals are quite satisfied with the special education continuum of placements (Johnson & Duffett, 2002).

Additionally, on what basis do you attach blame to special education for low graduation and high dropout rates or for the lack of access to postsecondary education? Given that 96% of all students with disabilities are spending at least a portion of their day in general classes, shouldn't we be looking at the system as a whole, not just special education, in trying to deal with student failure? Concerning the high unemployment rate for people with disabilities, shouldn't we look at the failure of adult services to expand opportunities for individuals to receive

on a better trajectory toward successful transition into adult life. Falvey, Rosenberg, Monson, and Eschillian (2006) have noted that there is no evidence that pulling them out of general education classrooms benefits students with disabilities.

the training and support they need to find and succeed in community employment settings?

The conclusions from researchers that special education has failed can be countered by other investigators who offer a very different interpretation (Dorn & Fuch, 2004; Lane, Hoffmeister, & Bahan, 2002). These researchers, while calling for improvements in special education, don't support its abolition.

POINT

We could argue forever about what the research supports or doesn't support, and still not reach any agreement. Let's come back to the issue of values and reality. The goal behind full inclusion is to educate students with disabilities with their peers without disabilities in a general education class, as a means to increase their access to, and participation in, all natural settings. The general education classroom is a microcosm of the larger society. For the preschool-age child, the world is defined primarily through family and a small same-age peer group. As the child gets older, the world expands to the neighborhood, to the school, and eventually to the larger heterogeneous community. As educators, we must ask how we can educate the child with a disability to foster full participation as the life space of the individual is expanded. What are the barriers to full participation, and how do we work to break them down? A partnership between general and special education is a good beginning to breaking down barriers. Each professional brings his or her knowledge and resources into a single setting in the development of an instructional program that is directly oriented to student needs. This unified approach to instruction will provide teachers with the opportunity to work across disciplines and gain a broader understanding of the diversity in all children. Pull-out programs result in a fragmented approach to instruction, with little cooperation between general and special education.

Finally, students in pull-out programs are much more likely to be stigmatized. Separate education on the basis of a child's learning or behavioral characteristics is inherently unequal.

COUNTERPOINT

The value of full inclusion is a laudable goal, but nevertheless one that is not achievable or even desirable for many students with disabilities. The reality is that specialized academic and social instruction can best be provided, at least for some students, in a pull-out setting. These more restricted settings *are* the least restrictive environment for some students. Pull-out programs will more effectively prepare the student to return to less restricted settings, such as the general education class. A move to full inclusion will result in the loss of special education personnel who have been trained to work with students who have diverse needs. In spite of the rhetoric about collaboration between general and special education, the responsibilities for the student's education in a full-inclusion classroom will move to the general education class teacher with little or no support. The result will be dumping these students into an environment that will not meet their needs.

---

through, the public school system. They include qualified teachers, paraprofessionals, and access to instructional materials designed for, or adapted to, individual needs. **Natural supports** consist of the student's family and classmates. These individuals constitute a support network of mutual caring that promotes greater inclusion within the classroom and school, access to effective instruction, and the development of social relationships (friendships). The importance of formal and natural support networks cannot be overstated. Through these networks, students with disabilities achieve success in an inclusive school. High-quality formal supports, including teachers and paraprofessionals, are the key to students learning valued instructional content. Through the natural support network, students are able to bond with others who will listen, understand, and support them as they attempt to cope with the challenges of being in an inclusive setting.

AGE-APPROPRIATE CLASSROOMS IN A NEIGHBORHOOD SCHOOL. Evidence-based inclusive schools provide services and support to students with disabilities in age-appropriate classrooms within a neighborhood school. The National Association of School Psychologists (2003) defines inclusive education as the opportunity for students with disabilities to attend the same school they would attend if they were not disabled.

> **Natural supports**

The student's family and classmates. These individuals make up a support network of mutual caring that promotes greater inclusion within the classroom and school, access to effective instruction, and the development of social relationships (friendships).

Ross, age 11, has achdroplasia, a skeletal disorder that causes short limbs and other orthopedic problems. The bones of his head and face do not develop normally, and this has left him with a small amount of permanent hearing loss necessitating the use of hearing aids. Ross, who also has a learning disability, attends Public School 234 in Lower Manhattan. His mother, Tracey, reflects on how easy it is for his classmates to include him.

Standing outside the school yard at recess on a warm winter day, I watch Ross at the center of a swirl of children playing blackboard, which looks like tag on steroids. He is smaller than the others, with legs that are again starting to look short and bowed because they do not grow at the same rate as his torso. Still, I am amazed to see him playing like this. Best of all, the other children instinctively adapt their games so he can participate, including him as a matter of course, changing the rules slightly. If only the adults at school were this flexible, I tell myself. That has been another story entirely.

SOURCE: From "The Disabilities You Can See May Be Easier to Deal with Than the Ones You Can't," by T. Harden, 2003, *New York Times,* April 13, Section 4a, p. 2. Copyright © 2003 by The New York Times Co. Reprinted by permissions.

> Inclusive programs are those in which students, regardless of the severity of their disability, receive appropriate specialized instruction and related services within an age-appropriate general education classroom in the school that they would attend if they did not have a disability.

ACCESS TO THE GENERAL CURRICULUM. Access to the general curriculum for students with disabilities is a critical provision of IDEA 2004. As suggested within the law, "almost 30 years of research and experience has demonstrated that the education of children with disabilities can be made more effective by having high expectations for such children and ensuring their access in the general curriculum to the maximum extent possible" (IDEA 2004, PL 108-446, Sec. 682[C][5]). A student's IEP must describe how the disability affects the child's involvement and progress in the general curriculum. An evidence-based inclusive school promotes meaningful participation for each student within the subject matter content areas identified in the general curriculum (e.g., reading, mathematics, science, etc.) Meaningful participation in the general curriculum will necessitate the development and use of effective strategies, such as universally designed curriculum, instructional adaptations, multilevel instruction, assistive technology, and cooperative learning. Each of these strategies is discussed in detail later in this chapter.

MULTIDISCIPLINARY SCHOOLWIDE INSTRUCTIONAL SUPPORT. Evidence-based inclusive schools are characterized by a schoolwide support system that uses both general and special education resources in combination to benefit all students in the school (Lewis & Norwich, 2005; Mastropieri & Scruggs, 2007; Peterson & Hittie, 2005). The leadership of the school principal is vital. The principal should openly support the inclusion of all students in the activities of the school, advocate for the necessary resources to meet student needs, and strongly encourage cooperative learning and peer support programs (Friend & Cook, 2003). Inclusive classrooms are characterized by a philosophy that celebrates diversity, rewards collaboration among professionals, and teaches students how to help and support one another. In the next section, we discuss the essential elements of schoolwide collaboration, why it is an important concept within an inclusive school, and who must be involved for it to be effective.

Multidisciplinary Collaboration

➤ **Collaboration**

Professionals, parents, and students *working together* to achieve the mutual goal of delivering an effective educational program designed to meet individual needs.

Multidisciplinary collaboration is defined as professionals from across different disciplines, parents, and students *working together* to achieve the mutual goal of delivering an evidence-based educational program designed to meet individual needs. It should always be viewed as a cooperative, not a competitive, endeavor. As suggested by Friend and Bursuck (2006), collaboration is not *what* those involved do, it is *how* they do it. This process can be described as a *collaborative ethic*, in which everyone works together as a multidisciplinary team to meet the needs of all students, including those with disabilities. The team focuses on mastering the process of collaboration as well as cultivating the professional values and skills necessary to work effectively as part of a team.

> No one teacher can be skillful at teaching so many different students. She [He] needs a little help from her colleagues. When teachers with different areas of expertise and skill work together, they can individually tailor learning better for all their students. (National Institute for Urban School Improvement, 2003, p. 9)

In an inclusive school, effective multidisciplinary collaboration has several key characteristics:

➤ Parents are viewed as active partners in the education of their children.

➤ Team members from various disciplines (such as education, health care, and pychological and social services) share responsibility; individual roles are clearly understood and valued.

➤ Team members promote peer support and cooperative learning.

Parents as Valued Partners

Inclusive schools are most effective when they value families and establish positive and frequent relationships with parents. A strong relationship between home and school is characterized by a clear understanding of the philosphical and practical approaches to meeting the needs of the student with a disability within the general education setting. Collaboration among parents and professionals is most effective when everyone

➤ acknowledges and respects each other's differences in values and culture.

➤ listens openly and attentively to the other's concerns.

➤ values opinions and ideas.

➤ discusses issues openly and in an atmosphere of trust.

➤ shares in the responsibility and consequences for making a decision. (Drew & Hardman, 2007).

When parents feel valued as equal members of the team, they are more likely to develop a positive attitude toward school professionals. Consequently, educators are able to work more closely with parents to understand each student's needs and functioning level. Home-school collaboration will work only if communication is a two-way process where everyone feels respected.

Sharing the Responsibility

An inclusive school is effective when professionals from across the disciplines work together to achieve a common goal: a free and appropriate education for students with disabiliteis. Unfortunately, professional isolation was the norm for teachers of students with disabilities for more than a century. Special education meant separate education. However, in the late 1980s, some parents and professionals questioned whether it was in the best interest of students with disabilities to be taught solely by special education teachers in separate classrooms or schools. A merger of general and special education was proposed to ensure that these students would have access to qualified professionals from both disciplines. The proposed

FOCUS 3
Define multidisciplinary collaboration and identify its key characteristics.

Council for Exceptional Children

Standard 10: Collaboration

When parents feel valued as members of the IEP team, they are likely to have positive attitudes toward teachers and school administrators. What are some strategies that professionals could use to develop an effective home-school partnership?

REFLECT ON THIS

WHAT'S MY ROLE ON THE MULTIDISCIPLINARY SCHOOLWIDE ASSISTANCE TEAM?

A team is a group of professionals, parents, and/or students who join together to plan and implement an appropriate educational program for a student at risk or with a disability. Team members may be trained in different areas of study, including education, health services, speech and language, school administration, and so on. In the team approach, these individuals sit down together and coordinate their efforts to help the student, regardless of where or how they were trained. For this approach to work, each team member must clearly understand his or her role and responsibilities as a member of the team. Let's visit with some team members and their role in working with a student.

SPECIAL EDUCATION TEACHER

It's my responsibility to coordinate the student's individualized education program. I work with each member of the team to assist in selecting, administering, and interpreting appropriate assessment information. I maintain ongoing communication with each team member to ensure that we are all working together to help the student. It's my responsibility to compile, organize, and maintain good, accurate records on each student. I propose instructional alternatives for the student and work with others in the implementation of the recommended instruction. To carry this out, I locate or develop the necessary materials to meet each student's specific needs. I work directly with the student's parents to ensure that they are familiar with what is being taught at school and can reinforce school learning experiences at home.

PARENTS

We work with each team member to ensure that our child is involved in an appropriate educational program. We give the team information about our child's life outside school and suggest experiences that might be relevant to the home and the community. We also work with our child at home to reinforce what is learned in school. As members of the team, we give our written consent for any evaluations of our child and any changes in our child's educational placement.

SCHOOL PSYCHOLOGIST

I select, administer, and interpret appropriate psychological, educational, and behavioral assessment instruments. I consult directly with team members regarding the student's overall educational development. It is also my responsibility to directly observe the student's performance in the classroom and assist in the design of appropriate behavioral management programs in the school and at home.

SCHOOL ADMINISTRATOR

As the school district's representative, I work with the team to ensure that the resources of my school and district are used appropriately in providing services to the student. I am ultimately responsible for ensuring that the team's decisions are implemented properly.

GENERAL EDUCATION CLASSROOM TEACHER

I work with the team to develop and implement appropriate educational experiences for the student during the time that he or she spends in my classroom. I ensure that the student's experiences outside my classroom are consistent with the instruction he or she receives from me. In carrying out my responsibilities, I keep an accurate and continuous record of the student's progress. I am also responsible for referring any other students in my classroom who are at risk and may need specialized services to the school district for an evaluation of their needs.

ADAPTED PHYSICAL EDUCATION TEACHER

I am an adapted physical education specialist who works with the team to determine whether the student needs adapted physical education services as a component of his or her individualized education program.

RELATED-SERVICES SPECIALIST

I may be a speech and language specialist, social worker, school counselor, school nurse, occupational or physical therapist, juvenile court authority, physician, or school technology coordinator. I provide any additional services necessary to ensure that the student receives an appropriate educational experience.

▶ **Regular education initiative**

A merger of general and special education proposed in the late 1980s so that all educators would share responsibility in ensuring an appropriate educational experience for students with disabiities.

merger became known as the **regular education initiative** (REI). The goal of REI was for general and special education teachers to share responsibility in ensuring an appropriate educational experience for students with disabilities. Ultimately, the separate special education system would be eliminated. Although REI was viewed by some as an attempt on the part of the federal government to reduce the number of students with mild disabilities receiving special education, and thus ultimately to reduce the cost of special education, it did result in a re-examination of the roles of general and special educators within the inclusive school. "Shared responsibility" became the means by which students with disabilities could receive both the formal and the natural supports necessary for them to participate in the general curriculum and in the inclusive classroom.

MULTIDISCIPLINARY SCHOOLWIDE ASSISTANCE TEAMS. To meet the needs of a diverse group of students, including those with disabilities, schools have developed support networks that facilitate collaboration among professionals. **Multidisciplinary schoolwide assistance teams** (SWATs), sometimes referred to as *teacher assistance teams* (TATs), involve groups of professionals from several different disciplines, students, and/or parents working together to solve problems, develop instructional strategies, and support classroom teachers. SWATs use a variety of strategies to assist teachers in making appropriate referrals for students who may need specialized services, to adapt instruction or develop accommodations consistent with individual student needs, to involve parents in planning and instruction, and to coordinate services across the various team members. (See the nearby Reflect on This, "What's My Role on the Multidisciplinary Schoolwide Assistance Team?" on page 62.)

WORKING TOGETHER AS A PROFESSIONAL AND PARENT TEAM. Students with disabilities have very diverse needs, ranging from academic and behavioral support to functional life skills, communication, and motor development. These needs require that students have access to many different education and related-services specialists who work together in delivering instruction and providing appropriate resources. Examples of these specialists include general and special education teachers, speech and language specialists, physical therapists, and behavior specialists.

Multidisciplinary collaborative teaming involves bringing key specialists together to develop an instructional program that views the student from a holistic perspective. All members of the team work together to integrate instructional strategies and therapy concurrently within the classroom—and to evaluate the effectiveness of their individual roles in meeting the needs of each student.

Collaborative teaming is advantageous in an inclusive setting, but it may be difficult to implement because of differing philosophical orientations on the part of team members. If a professional believes that only he or she is qualified to provide instruction or support in particular area of need (e.g., communication or motor development), then efforts to share successful strategies are inhibited (McDonnell et al., 2003; Vaughn, Bos, & Schumm, 2005). To overcome this barrier, several strategies could be used to facilitate successful multidisciplinary collaborative teaming:

➤ Always focus on the needs of the student first, rather than on the individual philosophy or expertise of each professional.

➤ View team members as collaborators rather than experts. Understand what each professional has to offer in planning, implementing, integrating, and evaluating instructional strategies in an inclusive setting.

➤ Openly communicate the value of each professional's role in meeting student needs. Maintain an open and positive attitude toward other professionals' philosophy and practices.

➤ Meet regularly and consult one another on how the student is progressing. Identify what is working, what barriers to progress exist, and what steps will be taken next in furthering the student's learning and development. (Pettig, 2000; Spencer, 2005.)

Peer Support and Cooperative Learning

Peers may serve as powerful natural supports for students with disabilities in both academic and social areas (Maheady, Harper, & Mallette, 2001). They often have more influence on their classmates' behavior than the teacher does. Peer support programs may range from simply creating opportunities for students with disabilities to interact socially with peers without disabilities to highly structured programs of peer-mediated instruction. **Peer-mediated instruction** involves a structured interaction between two or more students under the direct supervision of a classroom teacher. The instruction may use peer and cross-age tutoring and/or cooperative learning. **Peer and cross-age tutoring** emphasize individual student learning, whereas **cooperative learning** emphasizes the simultaneous learning of students as they seek to achieve group goals. Although they are often an underrated and underused resource in general education, peers are very reliable

> ➤ **Multidisciplinary Schoolwide Assistance Teams (SWATS)**
> Groups of professionals, students, and/or parents working together to solve problems, develop instructional strategies, and support classroom teachers.

> ➤ **Peer-mediated instruction**
> A structured interaction between two or more students under the direct supervision of a classroom teacher. Peers assist in teaching skills to other students.

> ➤ **Peer tutoring**
> An instructional method to facilitate learning of students with disabilities in a general education class. One student provides instruction and/or support to another student or group of students.

> ➤ **Cross-age tutoring**
> An instructional method that pairs older students with younger students to facilitate learning.

> ➤ **Cooperative learning**
> Emphasizes the simultaneous learning of students as they work together to achieve group goals.

In addition to being effective teaching strategies, peer support and cooperative learning build self-esteem and increase the acceptance of students with disabilities in inclusive classrooms. Why do you think these strategies are often underutilized in general education classrooms?

Council for Exceptional Children

Standard 4: Instructional Strategies

FOCUS **4**

Why is it so important to provide early intervention services as soon as possible to young children at risk?

and effective in implementing both academic and social programs with students who have disabilities (Gillies & Ashman, 2000). In addition, cooperative learning is beneficial to all students, from the highest achievers to those at risk of school failure. It builds self-esteem, strengthens peer relationships, and increases the acceptance of students with disabilities in inclusive classrooms. The effectiveness of peers, however, is dependent on carefully managing the program so that students both with and without disabilities benefit. It is important for teachers to carefully select, train, and monitor the performance of students working as peer tutors. Cooperative learning appears to be most effective when it includes goals for the group as a whole, as well as for individual members (Eggen & Kauchak, 2004; McDonnell, et al., 2003; Vaughn, et al., 2005).

The Early Childhood Years

The past two decades have seen a growing recognition of the educational, social, and health needs of young children with disabilities. This is certainly true for Yvonne from the nearby Snapshot. Yvonne was born with cerebral palsy, requiring immediate services and supports from many different professionals. Yvonne's early learning experiences provided a foundation for her future learning, growth, and development. Early intervention was also crucial to the family's understanding of Yvonne's needs and of the importance of a strong parent-professional partnership.

The first years of life are critical to the overall development of children, including those at risk for disabilities. Moreover, classic studies in the behavioral sciences from the 1960s and 1970s in-

▼ SNAPSHOT

YVONNE

THE EARLY CHILDHOOD YEARS

Anita was elated. She had just learned during an ultrascan that she was going to have twin girls. As the delivery date neared, she thought about how much fun it would be to take them on long summer walks in the new double stroller. Two weeks after her estimated delivery date, she was in the hospital, giving birth to her twins. The first little girl arrived without a problem. Unfortunately, this was not the case for the second.

There was something different about her; it became obvious almost immediately after the birth. Yvonne just didn't seem to have the same body tone as her sister. Within a couple of days, Yvonne was diagnosed as having cerebral palsy. Her head and the left side of her body seemed to be affected

most seriously. The pediatrician calmly told the family that Yvonne would undoubtedly have learning and physical problems throughout her life. She referred the parents to a division of the state health agency responsible for assisting families with children who have disabilities. Further testing was done, and Yvonne was placed in an early intervention program for infants with developmental disabilities. When she reached the age of 3, Yvonne's parents enrolled her in a preschool program where she would have the opportunity to learn communication and social skills, while interacting with children of her own age with and without disabilities. Because neither of the parents had any direct experience with a child with disabilities, they were uncertain how to help Yvonne. Would this program really help her that much, or should they work with her at home only? It was hard for them to see this little girl go to school so very early in her life.

dicated that early stimulation is critical to the later development of language, intelligence, personality, and a sense of self-worth (Bloom, 1964; Hunt, 1961; Piaget, 1970; White, 1975).

Advocates of **early intervention** for children at risk for disabilities believe that intervention should begin as early as possible in an environment free of traditional disability labels (such as "mentally retarded" and "emotionally disturbed"). Carefully selected services and supports can reduce the long-term impact of the disability and counteract any negative effects of waiting to intervene. The postponement of services may, in fact, undermine a child's overall development, as well as his or her acquisition of specific skills (Batshaw, 2003; Berk, 2005).

Bringing About Change for Young Children with Disabilities

For most of the 20th century, comprehensive educational and social services for young children with disabilities were nonexistent or were provided sporadically at best. For families of children with more severe disabilities, often the only option outside of the family home was institutionalization. As recently as the 1950s, many parents were advised to institutionalize a child immediately after birth if he or she had a recognizable physical condition associated with a disability (such as Down syndrome). By doing so, the family would not become attached to the child in the hospital or after returning home.

The efforts of parents and professionals to gain national support to develop and implement community services for young children at risk began in 1968 with the passage of Public Law (PL) 90-538, the Handicapped Children's Early Education Program (HCEEP). A primary purpose of HCEEP was to fund model demonstration programs focused on experimental practices for young children with disabilities. Many of the best approaches that emerged from these experimental projects were transferred to other early intervention programs through outreach efforts funded through HCEEP. The documented success of HCEEP eventually culminated in the passage of PL 99-457, in the form of amendments to the Education of the Handicapped Act, passed in 1986. The most important piece of legislation ever enacted on behalf of infants and preschool-age children with disabilities, this law opened up a new era of services for young children with disabilities. It required that all states ensure a free and appropriate public education to every eligible child with a disability between 3 and 5 years of age. For infants and toddlers (birth to 2 years of age), a new program, Part H (changed to Part C in the 1997 Amendments to IDEA), was established to help states develop and implement programs for early intervention services. Part C has several purposes:

1. Enhance the development of infants and toddlers with disabilities, to minimize their potential for developmental delay, and to recognize the significant brain development that occurs during a child's first 3 years of life;

2. Reduce the educational costs to our society, including our nation's schools, by minimizing the need for special education and related services after infants and toddlers with disabilities reach school age;

3. Maximize the potential for individuals with disabilities to live independently in society;

4. Enhance the capacity of families to meet the special needs of their infants and toddlers with disabilities; and

5. Enhance the capacity of state and local agencies and service providers to identify, evaluate, and meet the needs of all children, particularly minority, low-income, inner city, and rural children, and infants and toddlers in foster care. (IDEA 2004, PL 108-446, Part C Sec. 631[a])

Although states are not *required* to participate, every state provides at least some services under Part C of IDEA.

Early Intervention Under Part C of IDEA

Early intervention focuses on the identification and provision of education, health care, and social services as a means to enhance learning and development, reduce the effects of a disability, and prevent the occurrence of future difficulties for young children. IDEA 2004 defines eligible infants and toddlers as those under 3 years of age who need early intervention services

➤ **Early intervention**
Comprehensive services for infants and toddlers who are disabled or at risk of acquiring a disability. Services may include education, health care, and/or social or psychological assistance.

Council for Exceptional Children

Standard 1: Foundations

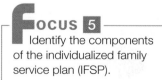
FOCUS **5**
Identify the components of the individualized family service plan (IFSP).

for one of two reasons: (1) there is a developmental delay in one or more of the areas of cognitive development, physical development, communication development, social or emotional development, and adaptive development; or (2) there is a diagnosis of a physical or mental condition that has a high probability of resulting in a developmental delay.

Timing is critical in the delivery of early intervention services. The maxim "the earlier, the better" says it all. Moreover, early intervention may be less costly and more effective than providing services later in the individual's life (Niccols, Atkinson, & Pepler, 2003; Siegler, 2003). Effective early intervention services are directed not only to the young child with a disability but to family members as well (McDonnell et al., 2003). All early intervention services must be designed and delivered within the framework of informing and empowering family members. Comprehensive early intervention is broad in scope, as illustrated in the listing of IDEA, Part C services found in Figure 3.1.

The services under Part C of IDEA that are needed for the child and the family are identified through the development of an **individualized family service plan** (IFSP). The IFSP is structured much like the individualized education program (IEP), but it broadens the focus to include all members of the family. Figure 3.2 lists the required components of the IFSP. The nearby Reflect on This, "It Takes a Whole Village to Develop an IFSP," on page 67, describes how each component is incorporated into the development and implementation of the IFSP.

Evidence-Based Early Intervention

This section examines evidence-based models for delivering services and supports to infants and toddlers, including developmentally supportive care in hospitals, and center-based and family-centered programs. In order for these models to be effective, services and supports should focus on individualization, intense interventions, and a comprehensive approach to meeting the needs of each child and that child's family.

SERVICE DELIVERY. Advancements in health care have increased the number of infants at-risk who survive birth. **Intensive care specialists**, working with sophisticated medical technologies in newborn intensive care units and providing developmentally supportive care, are able to save the lives of infants who years ago would have died in the first days or weeks of life. **Developmentally supportive care** views the infant as "an active collaborator" in determining what services are necessary to enhance survival. With this approach, infant behavior is carefully observed to determine what strategies (such as responding to light, noise, or touch) the infant is using to try to survive. Specially trained developmental specialists then focus on understanding the infant's "developmental agenda" in order to provide appropriate supports and services to enhance the infant's further growth and development.

Standard 3: Individual Learning Differences

➤ **Individualized Family Service Plan (IFSP)**

Service plan intended to to ensure that infants and toddlers receive appropriate services under Part C of IDEA. The IFSP is structured much like the individualized education program (IEP), but it broadens the focus to include all members of the family.

➤ **Intensive care specialists**

Health care professionals (such as physicians and nurses) trained specifically to provide medical care to newborns who are seriously ill, disabled, or at risk of serious medical problems; also referred to as *neonatal specialists.*

➤ **Developmentally supportive care**

Approach to care that views the infant as "an active collaborator" in determining what services are necessary to enhance survival.

IT TAKES A WHOLE VILLAGE TO DEVELOP AN IFSP

The African saying "It takes a whole village to raise a child," best illustrates the individualized family service plan (IFSP). No one person can accurately decide what is the best treatment or care for a child with special needs. That's why Part C of IDEA stipulates that infants and toddlers with disabilities must have an IFSP. The IFSP is an ongoing written service plan for children from birth to age 3 until they transition into preschool. Anything of concern to a family is outlined and highlighted in the IFSP:

The IFSP is a team effort involving families and professionals.

- *Medical history/developmental information:* Includes diagnosis, medications, strengths, concerns such as a breakdown of the child's fine and gross motor skills, communication, social-emotional issues, and self-help as well as play and cognitive skills.

- *Family interest and concerns:* Everything from housing, transportation, health, and financial issues to employment, social service programs, legal services, early intervention programs, and therapy.

- *Timeline:* A breakdown in months detailing when the family would like to see events occur in a child's development; includes a plan of action, a service provider, cost, and outcome.

- *Preschool transition plan:* Includes what school district the child resides in, the district contact person, and a plan of action for how and when the transition to preschool services will take place.

An assigned person, known as a service coordinator, generally initiates an IFSP and works with the family to complete it as the child approaches preschool age. The service coordinator works with a variety of people and agencies to ensure that the child's and family's needs are met. A family's priorities can easily change, and for that reason, the IFSP is a working, flexible document. Its focus is to help provide families with support and encourage them to seek community resources.

SOURCE: *The Individualized Family Service Plan*, by Resources for Young Children and Families, 2000, Colorado Springs, CO. Author. Retrieved from: http://www.rycf.org/ifsp.html

In addition to the intensive services provided in hospital newborn intensive care units, early intervention may be delivered through center-based and family-based programs or a combination of the two (Bruder, 2001). The center-based model requires families to take their child from the home to a setting where comprehensive services are provided. These sites may

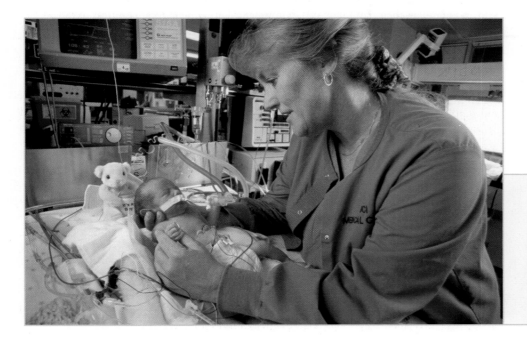

Infant care specialists save the lives of many seriously ill newborns who only a few years ago would have died in the first days or weeks of life. Why is developmentally supportive care an important concept in early intervention services?

Required Components of the IFSP

1. Infant's or toddler's present levels of physical development, cognitive development, communication development, social or emotional development and adaptive development, based on objective criteria;

2. Family's resources, priorities, and concerns related to enhancing the development of the family's infant or toddler with a disability;

3. Measurable results or outcomes expected to be achieved for the infant or toddler and the family, including pre-literacy and language skills, as developmentally appropriate for the child, and the criteria, procedures, and timelines used to determine the degree to which progress toward achieving the results or outcomes is being made and whether modifications or revisions of the results or outcomes or services are necessary;

4. Specific early intervention services based on peer-reviewed research, to the extent practicable, necessary to meet the unique needs of the infant or toddler and the family, including the frequency, intensity, and method of delivering services;

5. Natural environments in which early intervention services will appropriately be provided, including a justification of the extent, if any, to which the services will not be provided in a natural environment;

6. Projected dates for initiation of services and the anticipated length, duration, and frequency of the services;

7. Identification of the service coordinator from the profession most immediately relevant to the infant's or toddler's or family's needs who will be responsible for the implementation of the plan and coordination with other agencies and persons, including transition services; and

8. Steps to be taken to support the transition of the toddler with a disability to preschool or other appropriate services. (IDEA 2004, PL 108-446, Sec. 636[d])

be hospitals, churches, schools, or other community facilities. The centers use various instructional approaches, including both developmental and therapeutic models, to meet the needs of infants and toddlers. Center-based programs tend to look like hospitals or health care facilities in which the primary orientation is therapy.

In contrast to the center-based model, a family-centered program provides services to the child and family in their natural living environment. Using the natural resources of the home, professionals address the needs of the child in terms of individual family values and lifestyles. As suggested by Bruder (2001), the focus on natural environments

> has created multiple opportunities for children with disabilities to participate in a variety of home and community activities as environments for learning. Home activities are events that occur on either a regular or periodic basis in a child' primary living setting (e.g., getting dressed, taking a bath), and community activities include a wide range of informal (e.g., visits to the park, taking a walk) and formal (e.g., storytime at the library) experiences. . . . (p. 210)

Finally, early intervention may be provided through a combination of services at both a center and the home. Infants or toddlers may spend some time in a center-based program, receiving instruction and therapy in individual or group settings, and also receive in-home family-centered services to promote learning and generalization in their natural environment.

INDIVIDUALIZED, INTENSIVE, AND COMPREHENSIVE SERVICES. Early intervention programs for infants and toddlers should be based on individual need, and they should be intensive over time and comprehensive. Intensity reflects the frequency and amount of time an infant or child is engaged in intervention activities. An intensive approach requires that the child participate in intervention activities that involve two to three hours of contact

Council for Exceptional Children

Standard 5: Learning Environments and Social Interactions

Council for Exceptional Children

Standard 4: Instructional Strategies

each day, at least four or five times a week. Until the 1980s, this child-centered model of service delivery placed parents in the role of trainers who provided direct instruction to the child and helped him or her transfer the learning activities from the therapeutic setting to the home environment. The model of parents as trainers eventually was questioned by many professionals and family members. Families were dropping out of programs, and many parents either did not use the intervention techniques effectively with their children or simply preferred to be parents, not trainers (McDonnell et al., 2003). With the passage of PL 99-457 in 1986 (now IDEA), early intervention evolved into a more family-centered approach in which individual family needs and strengths became the basis for determining program goals, supports needed, and services to be provided.

Providing the breadth of services necessary to meet the individual needs of an infant or toddler within the family constellation requires a *multidisciplinary intervention team*. It should include professionals with varied experiential backgrounds—such as speech and language therapy, physical therapy, health care, and education—and the parents or guardian. The multidisciplinary team should review the IFSP at least annually and issue progress updates to the parents every six months. Coordination of early intervention services across disciplines and with the family is crucial if the goals of the program are to be realized.

The traditional academic-year programming (lasting approximately nine months) that is common to many public school programs is not in the best interests of infants and toddlers who are at risk or have disabilities. Continuity is essential. Services and supports must be provided throughout the early years without lengthy interruptions.

Preschool Services: Referral, Assessment, and IEP Development

Four-year old Matt from the nearby Snapshot began receiving preschool services as soon as he came out of the coma that resulted from his being hit by a car. Although he suffered a severe head trauma and still has to wear a helmet and use a walker, Matt is doing well in his kindergarten class. Preschool services for Matt began with a referral to his local school in order to assess the type and extent of his perceived delays relative to same-age peers without disabilities. Once Matt's needs were identified and the multidisciplinary team determined his eligibility for preschool special education services, appropriate developmental and age-appropriate instructional strategies were implemented in a school-based classroom.

FOCUS **6**

Identify evidence-based instructional approaches for preschool-age children with disabilities.

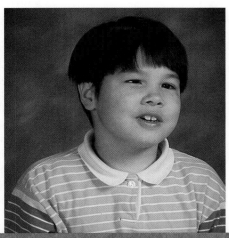

▼SNAPSHOT

MATT

One day, 4-year-old Matt was playing across the street from his house. As he crossed the street to return home, he was hit by a car. Matt suffered a severe trauma as a result of the accident and was in a coma for more than two months. Now he's in school and is doing well.

Matt wears a helmet to protect his head, and he uses a walker in his general education kindergarten class in the morning and special education class in the afternoon. The general education kindergarten children sing songs together and work on handwriting, before they work at centers in the classroom. Matt's favorite center is the block area. He spends most of his time there. Recently, however, he has become interested in the computer and math centers.

He is working on his fine motor skills and speech skills so he can learn to write and use a pencil again. The focus of his academic learning is mastering the alphabet, learning how to count, and recognizing numbers. He also receives regular speech therapy. He speaks in sentences, but it is very difficult for others to understand what he is saying.

Matt is well liked by his classmates. His teacher enjoys seeing his progress. "Well, it's our hope that he'll be integrated with the other kids eventually, and through the activities we do in the classroom here (in special education) and in the kindergarten, we hope the kids will get to know him and interact with him and that this will help pull up his skills to the level where he can go back to the general education classroom for all his schoolwork."

REFERRAL. Programs for preschool-age children with disabilities have several important components. First, a **child-find system** is set up in each state to locate preschool-age (ages 3 to 5) children at risk and to make referrals to the local education agency. Referrals may come from parents, the family physician, health care or social service agencies, or the child's day care or preschool teacher. Referrals for preschool services may be based on a child's *perceived* delays in physical development (such as not walking by age 2), speech and language delays (such as nonverbal by age 3), excessive inappropriate behavior (such as frequent temper tantrums, violent behavior, extreme shyness, or excessive crying), or sensory difficulties (unresponsive to sounds or unable to visually track objects in the environment).

MULTIDISCIPLINARY ASSESSMENT. Following a referral, a child-study team initiates assessments to determine whether the child is eligible for preschool special education services under IDEA 2004. A preschool-age child with disabilities is eligible if he or she meets both of the following requirements. First, developmental delays are evident as measured by appropriate diagnostic instruments and procedures, in one or more of the following areas: physical development, cognitive development, communication development, social or emotional development, or adaptive development. Second, as a result of these delays, the child needs special education and related services (IDEA 2004, PL 108-446, Sec. 602[3]).

DEVELOPING AN IEP FOR THE PRESCHOOL-AGE CHILD. If the child is eligible, an individualized education program (IEP) is developed. Specialists from several disciplines—including physical therapy, occupational therapy, speech and language therapy, pediatrics, social work, and special education—participate in the development and implementation of IEPs for preschool-age children. The purpose of preschool programs for young children with disabilities is to assist them in living in and adapting to a variety of environmental settings, including home, neighborhood, and school. Depending on individual needs, preschool programs may focus on developing skills in communication, social and emotional learning, physical well-being, self-care, and coping (Klein, Cook, & Richardson-Gibbs, 2001; Odom & Bailey, 2001). The decision regarding which skill areas are to be taught should be based on a functional assessment of the child and of the setting where he or she spends time. **Functional assessments** determine the child's skills, the characteristics of the setting, and the family's needs, resources, expectations, and aspirations (Horner, Albin, Sprague, & Todd, 2006). Through a functional assessment, professionals and parents come together to plan a program that supports the preschool-age child in meeting the demands of the home, school, or community setting.

Evidence-Based Practices in Preschool Education

This section reviews the concept of developmentally appropriate practice (DAP) for preschool-age children and explains how it serves as a foundation to meet the individual needs of young children with disabilities in age-appropriate placements. We also examine the importance of teaching functional skills in inclusive preschool settings.

DEVELOPMENTALLY APPROPRIATE PRACTICE. Early child educators share the conviction that programs for young children should be based on **developmentally appropriate practice** (DAP). DAP is grounded in the belief that there has been too much emphasis on preparing preschool-age children for academic learning and not enough on activities that are initiated by the child, such as play, exploration, social interaction, and inquiry. As suggested by the National Association for the Education of Young Children (NAEYC, 2006), "high quality early childhood programs do much more than help children learn numbers, shapes, and colors. Good programs help children learn how to learn: to question why and discover alternative answers; to get along with others; and to use their developing language, thinking, and motor skills."

DAP is viewed as culturally sensitive because it emphasizes interaction between children and adults. Adults become "guides" for student learning rather than controlling what, where, and how students acquire knowledge. DAP is strongly advocated by the NAEYC, the nation's largest national organization for professionals in early childhood education. NAEYC has developed several guiding principles for the use of DAP; these are illustrated in Figure 3.3.

➤ Child-find system

A system within a state or local area that attempts to identify all children who are disabled or at risk in order to refer them for appropriate support services.

Standard 7: Instructional Planning

Standard 4: Instructional Strategies

➤ Functional assessments

Assessments to determine the child's skills, the characteristics of the setting, and the family's needs, resources, expectations, and aspirations.

➤ Developmentally appropriate practices (DAPs)

Instructional approaches that use curriculum and learning environments consistent with the child's developmental level. These approaches provide young children with opportunities to explore, discover, choose, and acquire skills that are sensitive and responsive for their ages and abilities.

FIGURE 3.3

Guiding Principles for the Use of Developmentally Appropriate Practices (DAPs)

- *Create a caring community of learners*. Developmentally appropriate practices occur within a context that supports the development of relationships between adults and children, among children, among teachers, and between teachers and families.

- *Teach to enhance development and learning*. Adults are responsible for ensuring children's healthy development and learning. From birth, relationships with adults are critical determinants of children's healthy social and emotional development, and they also serve as mediators of language and intellectual development.

- *Construct an appropriate curriculum*. The content of the early childhood curriculum is determined by many factors, including the subject matter of the disciplines, social or cultural values, and parental input. In developmentally appropriate programs, decisions about curriculum content also take into consideration the age and experience of the learners.

- *Assess children's learning and development*. Assessment of individual children's development and learning is essential for planning and implementing an appropriate curriculum. In developmentally appropriate programs, assessment and curriculum are integrated, with teachers continually engaging in observational assessment for the purpose of improving teaching and learning.

- *Establish reciprocal relationships with families*. Developmentally appropriate practices derive from deep knowledge of individual children and of the context within which they develop and learn. The younger the child, the more important it is for professionals to acquire this knowledge through relationships with the child's family.

SOURCE: Adapted from National Association for the Education of Young Children (2006). *NAEYC position statement*. Retrieved July 16, 2006, from http://www.naeyc.org/about/positions/pdf/PSDAP98.PDF

AGE-APPROPRIATE PLACEMENT. As we have noted, DAP is widely accepted throughout the early childhood community, but many special education teachers and related services personnel (such as speech and language pathologists and physical therapists) see DAP as a base or foundation to build on in order to meet the individual needs of young children with disabilities. These professionals indicate that early childhood programs for students with disabilities must also take into account age-appropriate placements and functional skill learning.

Age-appropriate placements emphasize the child's chronological age over developmental level. Thus a 2-year-old with developmental delays is first and foremost a 2-year-old, regardless of whether he or she has disabilities. A young child with disabilities should be exposed to the same instructional opportunities and settings as a nondisabled peer of the same chronological age. Age-appropriate learning prepares the child to live and learn in inclusive environments with same-age peers. Arguing that DAP and age-appropriate practice are compatible, McDonnell et al. (2003) suggested that there are many ways to create learning experiences for young children that are both developmentally appropriate and age-appropriate. The following is one example:

> Mark is a 5-year-old with limited gross and fine motor movement and control. His cognitive development is similar to a typically developing 11-month-old. Mark is learning to use adaptive switches to activate toys and a radio or [CD] player. Mark enjoys listening to music and toys that make noise and move simultaneously. Mark would also enjoy the lullabies and battery-operated lamb and giraffe toys that might usually be purchased for an 11-month-old. However, he also enjoys Raffi songs and songs from Disney movies, as well as automated race tracks and battery-operated dinosaurs and robots. The latter selection of music and toys would also interest other children of his age . . . and could provide some familiar and pleasurable experiences for Mark to enjoy in classroom and play settings with typical peers. (p. 239)

➤ **Age-appropriate placement**
A child's educational placement is based on the need for instructional programs consistent with chronological age rather than developmental level.

TEACHING FUNCTIONAL SKILLS. Consistent with the individualized needs of the child and the expectations of the family, teaching functional skills facilitates the young child's learning in the natural setting (such as home and family). Functional skill development helps the child adapt to the demands of a given environment—that is, it creates an adaptive fit between the child and the setting in which he or she must learn to function. Functional skills focus on teaching and assisting the child to become more independent and to interact appropriately with family, friends, and professsionals In fact, it may be more important for some children to be able to dress themselves, brush their teeth, comb their hair, and take care of other personal hygiene needs than to be able to name six breeds of dogs.

Council for
Exceptional
Children

Standard 5: Learning Environments and Social Interactions

INCLUSIVE PRESCHOOL CLASSROOMS. In the evidence-based inclusive classroom, young children with disabilities receive their educational program side-by-side with peers without disabilities in a regular preschool or day care program. Effective programs are staffed by child care providers, special education preschool teachers in a co-teaching or consultant role, paraprofessionals, and other related-services personnel as needed by the children. Figure 3.4 describes the values that are at the foundation of an evidence-based inclusion preschool program, and the multidsicplinary resources that are essential in implementing it.

In a study of child care providers, Devore & Hanley-Maxwell (2000) identified five critical factors that contributed to successfully serving young children with disabilities in inclusive, community-based child care settings: (1) a willingness on the part of the child care provider to make inclusion work; (2) a realistic balance between the resources available in the program and the needs of the student; (3) continual problem solving with parents; (4) access to emotional support and technical assistance from special educators and early intervention therapists; and (5) access to other supports, such as other child care providers, respite care providers, and houses of worship.

There are many reasons for the increasing number of inclusive classrooms for preschool students with disabilities. Inclusive classrooms create opportunities for social interaction and for the development of friendships among children with disabilities and same-age peers without disabilities. The social development skills learned in inclusive settings are applied at home and community as well as in future educational and social settings. Preschool-age children without disabilities learn to value and accept diversity (Drew & Hardman, 2007).

➤ **Head Start**

A federally funded preschool program for children from a background of economic disadvantage. Designed to give each child a "head start" prior to elementary school.

Head Start, the nation's largest federally funded early childhood program, was enacted into law in 1965 and has served over 16 million children. The program was developed around a strong research base suggesting that early enrichment experiences for children with economic disadvantages would better prepare them for elementary school (Phillips & Cabrera, 2006). Although the original legislation did not include children with disabilities, the law was eventually expanded in 1992 to require that at least 10% of Head Start enrollment be reserved for these children. The U.S. Department of Health and Human Services (2006) reported that of the 906,903 children in Head Start programs, children with disabilities accounted for 12.5% of this population. Head Start has been hailed through the years as a major breakthrough in federal support for early childhood education.

Federal regulations under Head Start have been expanded to ensure that a disabilities service plan be developed to meet the needs of all children with disabilities and their families, that the programs designate a coordinator of services for children with disabilities, and that the necessary special education and related services be provided for children who are designated as disabled under IDEA.

Indicators of Quality in an Inclusive Preschool Program

- Inclusion, as a value, supports the right of all children, regardless of abilities, to participate actively in natural settings within their communities. Natural settings are those in which the child would spend time if he or she did not have a disability. These settings include (but are not limited to) home, preschool, nursery schools, Head Start programs, kindergartens, neighborhood school classrooms, child care, places of worship, recreational venues (such as community playgrounds and community events) and other settings that all children and families enjoy.

- Young children and their families have full and successful access to health, social, educational, and other support services that promote full participation in family and community life. The cultural, economic, and educational diversity of families is valued and supported as a process for identifying a program of services.

- As young children participate in group settings (such as preschool, play groups, child care, and kindergarten), their active participation should be guided by developmentally and individually appropriate curricula. Access to and participation in the age-appropriate general curriculum becomes central to the identification and provision of specialized support services.

- To implement inclusive practices, there must be
  - the continued development, implementation, evaluation, and dissemination of full inclusion supports, services, and systems that are of high quality for all children;
  - the development of preservice and inservice training programs that prepare families, services providers, and administrators to develop and work within inclusive settings;
  - collaboration among key stakeholders to implement flexible fiscal and administrative procedures in support of inclusion;
  - research that contributes to our knowledge of recommended practice; and
  - the restructuring and unification of social, educational, health, and intervention supports and services to make them more responsive to the needs of all children and families.

SOURCE: Adapted from Division for Early Childhood, Council for Exceptional Children (2006). *Position statement on inclusion*. Retrieved July 17, 2006, from http://www.decsped.org/pdf/positionpapers/Position%20Inclusion.pdf

Transition from Preschool to Elementary School

Transitions, although a natural and ongoing part of everyone's life, are often difficult under the best of circumstances. For preschool-age children with disabilities and their families, the transition from early childhood programs to kindergarten can be very stressful. Early childhood programs for preschool-age children with disabilities commonly employ many adults (both professional and paraprofessional). In contrast, kindergarten programs are often not able to offer the same level of staff support, particularly in more inclusive educational settings. Therefore, it is important for preschool professionals responsible for transition planning to attend not only to the needs and skills of the individual student, but also to how he or she can match the performance demands of the elementary school and classroom setting. Sainato and Morrison (2001) indicated that successful transition from preschool to elementary programs is a critical factor in inclusion. These authors make several suggestions for professionals engaged in the transition process:

- ➤ The child's skill level is viewed as the predictor of the potential for success.
- ➤ Kindergarten teachers identify functional, social, and behavioral skills as more important for successful transition than academic skills.
- ➤ Readiness skills, language competence, self-care skills, appropriate social behavior, and independent performance during group activities are identified as prerequisites to inclusive placements in elementary school programs.

Council for Exceptional Children

Standard 7: Instructional Planning

➤ Focusing on the prerequisite skills that are likely to increase the child's success in inclusive elementary settings is important, but it must not be used to prevent young children from participating in inclusive placements.

In order to identify the skills needed in the elementary school environment, a preschool transition plan should begin at least one to two years before the child's actual move. This move is facilitated when the early intervention specialist, the child's future kindergarten teacher, and the parents engage in a careful planning process that recognizes the significant changes that the child and the family will go through as they enter a new and unknown situation (Rosenkoetter, Whaley, Hains, & Pierce, 2001).

In summary, early childhood programs for children with disabilities focus on teaching skills that will improve a child's opportunities for living a rich life and on preparing the child to function successfully in family, school, and neighborhood environments. Young children with disabilities are prepared as early as possible to share meaningful experiences with same-age peers. Additionally, early childhood programs lessen the impact of conditions that may deteriorate or become more severe without timely and adequate intervention and that may prevent children from developing other, secondary disabling conditions. The intended outcomes of these programs will not, however, be accomplished without consistent family participation and professional collaboration.

The Elementary School Years

In the elementary school years, the focus is on supporting children as they attempt to meet the expectations of the general education curriculum. The degree to which a child is able to cope with these expectations depends on how effectively the school accommodates individual needs. For Ricardo in the Case Study on page 75, the school's expectations were difficult to meet, and he fell significantly behind his classmates in reading and language. His third-grade teacher initiated a referral to evaluate Ricardo's eligibility for special education services. Once it was determined that Ricardo qualified as a student with a learning disability, a multidiscplinary team of special educators, general educators, related-services personnel, and his parents worked together to develop his individualized education program (IEP) and meet his reading and language needs.

Meeting Student Needs Through a General Education/Special Education Partnership

Today's teachers face the challenges of preparing the next generation for a changing world and responding to an increasingly diverse group of students. The growing student diversity includes increasing numbers from ethnically diverse backgrounds, those with disabilities, and children at risk of educational failure. Each of these factors contributes to the critical need for general education and special education teachers to work together in preparing all students for the many challenges of the next century, while at the same time not losing sight of individual learning needs, styles, and preferences.

The current wave of reform in America's schools, as mandated in federal law through No Child Left Behind and IDEA 2004, is focused on finding new and more effective ways to increase student learning by establishing high standards for *what* should be taught and *how* performance will be measured. Accountability for meeting high standards rests at several levels, but the ultimate test of success is what happens between teacher and student in the day-to-day classroom.

Increasing student diversity in the schools will require general educators to teach students whose needs exceed those of the traditionally defined "typical child." Correspondingly, special education teachers must have the specialized skills to meet the needs of students with disabilities, but they will also be called upon to apply this expertise to a much broader group of high- risk and disadvantaged students in a collaborative educational environment. The combination of these factors makes a very strong case for a partnership between general education and special education.

THE MANY ROLES OF THE SPECIAL EDUCATION TEACHER. In an inclusive school, special educators are called upon to fill multiple roles, including the "three Cs": collaborator, consultant, and coordinator. In the role of *collaborator*, special educators

RICARDO

Ricardo, a third grader at Bloomington Hill Elementary School, has recently been referred by his teacher, Ms. Thompson, to the school's prereferral team for an evaluation. During the first four months of school, Ricardo has continued to fall further behind in reading and language. He entered third grade with some skills in letter and sound recognition but had difficulty reading and comprehending material beyond a first grade level. It was also clear to Ms. Thompson that Ricardo's language development was delayed as well. He had a very limited expressive vocabulary and had some difficulty following directions if more than one or two steps were involved.

Ricardo's mother, Maria Galleghos (a single parent), was contacted by Ms. Thompson to inform her that she would like to refer Ricardo for an in-depth evaluation of his reading and language skills. A representative from the school would be calling her to explain what the evaluation meant and to get her approval for the necessary testing. The school psychologist, Jean Andreas, made the call to Ms. Galleghos. During the phone conversation Ms. Galleghos reminded the school psychologist that the primary language spoken in the home was Spanish, even though Ricardo, his parents, and his siblings spoke English too. Ms. Andreas indicated that the assessment would be conducted in both Spanish and English in order to determine whether Ricardo's problems were related to a disability in reading or perhaps to problems with English as a second language.

Having received written approval from Ricardo's mother, the school's prereferral team conducted an evaluation of Ricardo's academic performance. The formal evaluation included achievement tests, classroom performance tests, samples of Ricardo's work, behavioral observations, and anecdotal notes from Ms. Thompson. An interview with Mrs. Galleghos was conducted as part of the process to gain her perceptions of Ricardo's strengths and problem areas and to give her an opportunity to relate pertinent family history.

The evaluation confirmed his teacher's concerns. Ricardo was more than two years below what was expected for a child his age in both reading and language development. Ricardo's difficulties in these areas did not seem to be related to his being bilingual, but the issue of English as a second language would need to be taken into careful consideration in developing an appropriate learning experience.

The team determined that Ricardo qualified for special education services as a student with a specific learning disability. Once again, Ms. Andreas contacted Mrs. Galleghos with the results, indicating that Ricardo qualified for special education services in reading and language. Ms. Andreas pointed out that as a parent of a student with an identified disability, she had some specific legal rights that would be further explained to her both in writing and orally.

One of those rights is the right to participate as a partner in the development of Ricardo's individualized education program (IEP). Ms. Andreas further explained that a meeting would be set up at a mutually convenient time to develop a plan to assist Ricardo over the next year.

APPLICATION

1. Prior to the meeting, what could Ricardo's teachers do to help his parents feel valued as a member of the IEP team and to better understand their role in developing the IEP?

2. What additional information could Ricardo's parents provide that would help the team better understand his needs and interests, particularly in the areas of reading and language development?

3. What do you see as important for Ricardo to learn in school?

> ➤ work with school personnel (such as general educators, the school principal, related-services personnel) and parents to identify the educational needs of students with disabilities;

> ➤ link student assessment information to the development of the IEP and access to the general curriculum;

> ➤ determine appropriate student accommodations and instructional adaptations; and

> ➤ deliver intensive instruction using specialized teaching methods.

Special educators provide instruction and support in academic, behavioral and/or adaptive/functional areas, as well as fostering student self-determination and self-management skills. As collaborators, special education teachers use effective problem-solving strategies to facilitate student learning, co-teach with general educators, and apply effective accountability measures to evaluate individual students' progress and long-term results.

In the role of *consultant*, the special education teacher must be able to serve as a resource to general educators and parents on effective instructional practices for students with disabilities. Expertise may be provided in content areas (such as effective approaches to teaching reading to students with special needs) and/or problem-solving skills (such as strategies to motivate students to participate in class activities).

Council for Exceptional Children

Standard 10: Collaboration

General education teachers face the challenges of working with students from different ethnic backgrounds and students with disabilities. What training and support do general education teachers need to implement an inclusive education program successfully?

In the role of *coordinator*, the special education teacher takes the lead responsibility for organizing the activities of the school team in developing, implementing, and evaluating student IEPs. He or she also may be responsible for organizing school resources to best meet the needs of students with disabilities; may initiate professional development activities for school team members; may supervise paraprofessionals, peer support, and volunteers; and facilitates positive communication with parents.

THE GENERAL EDUCATION TEACHER: MEETING THE CHALLENGE OF "LEAVING NO CHILD BEHIND." The Study of Personnel Needs in Special Education (SPeNSE, 2006) reported that 95% of all general education teachers are currently working directly with students with disabilities in their classrooms, with an average caseload of 3.5 students. General education teachers must meet the challenges of achieving increased academic excellence as mandated in NCLB, as well as responding to students with many different needs coming together in a common environment. The inclusion of students with disabilities in general education classes need not be met with teacher frustration, anger, or refusal. These reactions are merely symptomatic of the confusion surrounding inclusive education. Huefner (2006) suggested that the IDEA 2004 requirement for general educators to be members of the IEP team gives them leverage to obtain the supports they need to be more effective with special education students and to work more collaboratively with special education teachers. As members of the IEP team, general educators are in a better position to share their knowledge and insight on individual students and to provide important information on how the student will fare in the general education curriculum and the classroom setting.

Specific roles for general educators in working collaboratively with special education and related-services personnel include

➤ identifying and referring students who may be in need of additional support in order to succeed in an inclusive setting;

➤ understanding each student's individual strengths and limitations, and the affects on learning;

➤ implementing an appropriate individualized instructional program that is focused on supporting student success in the general education curriculum; and

➤ initiating and maintaining ongoing communication with parents.

Unfortunately, inclusive education is sometimes synonymous with dumping a student with disabilities into a general education class without the necessary supports to the teacher or to the student, and at the expense of others in the class. In their responses to a survey (Hobbs, 1997), general education teachers identified four major problems that they encountered in their attempts to meet the needs of students with disabilities:

➤ disruptive students who lacked the necessary social and behavioral skills to succeed in a general education setting;

➤ lack of specialized assistance from a special education teacher or other school personnel;

➤ lack of information regarding the appropriate instructional adaptations necessary to meet the needs of any given student with a disability; and

➤ concerns regarding the social acceptance of students with disabilities (peers sometimes isolate, tease, or bully these students).

However, in a review of the literature on the attitudes and beliefs of general educators regarding students with disabilities, Pugach (2005) suggested that the discussion has shifted away from focusing on the barriers to inclusion to what it is that teachers need to know, and what they can do, to meet the needs of these students. To address these needs, Pugach further asserts,

> it will be crucial to take advantage of the natural progression [in universities] toward collaborative [teacher education] programs . . . conducted in a joint fashion, teams comprised of teacher educators from special and general teacher education, across content areas and multicultural education. . . . By joining forces in this manner we can begin to provide answers to a new generation of questions about how best to achieve the goal of delivering instruction of the highest quality to students with disabilities." (p. 578)

(See the Reflect on This, "Competencies for General Education and Special Education Teachers in an Inclusive Classroom," below.)

The role of the general education teacher extends not only to working with students with mild disabilities, but also to involvement with those with more severe disabilities. Success in a general education class for students with severe disabilities depends critically on the cooperative relationship among the general education teacher, the special education teacher, and the school support team. The general educator works with the team to create opportunities to include students with more severe disabilities. Inclusion may be achieved by having the general education class serve as a homeroom for the student; by developing opportunities for students with severe disabilities to be with their peers without disabilities as often as possible both within the general education class and in school activities such as recess, lunch, and assemblies; by developing a peer support program; and by using effective practices, such as multilevel instruction, universal design, direct instruction, assistive technology, and curriclum-based measurement.

Evidenced-Based Practices in Inclusive Elementary School Programs

In today's schools, we are seeing a greater emphasis on access to the general curriculum and on accountabilty for student learning in the United States. What does access to the general curriculum mean for students with disabilities? How can schools make the curriculum accessible to all students in an inclusive setting? What approaches are needed to measure student progress effectively? In this section, we take a closer look at evidence-based instructional approaches that

Focus 8

Why are multilevel instruction, universal design for learning, direct instruction, assistive technology, and curriculum-based assessment/measurement considered evidence-based practice in an inclusive classroom?

REFLECT ON THIS

COMPETENCIES FOR GENERAL EDUCATION AND SPECIAL EDUCATION TEACHERS IN AN INCLUSIVE CLASSROOM

- Ability to solve problems and to informally assess the skills a student needs (rather than relying solely on a standardized curriculum).

- Ability to take advantage of children's individual interests and use their internal motivation for developing skills.

- Ability to set high but alternative expectations that are suitable for the students; this means developing alternative assessments.

- Ability to make appropriate expectations for *each* student, regardless of the student's capabilities. If teachers can do this, it allows all students to be included in a class and school.

- Ability to determine how to modify assignments for students and to design classroom activities with so many

levels that all students have a part. This teaching skill can apply not just at the elementary or secondary level, but at the college level as well. It will mean more activity-based teaching rather than seat-based teaching.

- Ability to learn how to value all kinds of skills that students bring to a class, not just the academic skills. In doing this, teachers will make it explicit that in their classrooms they value all skills, even if that is not a clear value of a whole school.

- Ability to provide daily success for all students. Teachers have to work to counteract the message that all students get when certain students are continually taken out of class for special work.

SOURCE: University of Northern Iowa (2006). *Children that learn together, learn to live together*. Cedar Falls, Iowa, University of Northern Iowa, Department of Special Education. Retrieved July 24, 2006, from http://www.uni.edu/coe/inclusion/standards/index.html

have proved effective in creating access to the general education curriculum and facilitating student learning in an inclusive setting.

MULTILEVEL (DIFFERENTIATED) INSTRUCTION. Today's classrooms include children with many different needs and abilities. Haager and Klinger (2005) describe what it is like for teachers to face the challenges of a mixed-ability class:

> Mrs. Ryan [an elementary special education teacher] co-teaches in Mrs. Crawford's fourth-grade class during language arts time. Today Mrs. Crawford is explaining an assignment after reading aloud a chapter of a literature book. The students have their own copies of the literature book to use as a reference. The assignment is to write each vocabulary word written on the board, draw an illustration of the word, and write a sentence demonstrating its meaning. The students are using the class dictionaries and will complete any work they do not finish in class for homework. The will also write an entry in their reading journals for homework. Mrs. Ryan observes Marcel and Tomika, two students on her special education roster, during the reading time and makes some notes in her consultation log regarding Marcel's approved attention. He has refrained from talking aloud during reading, one of his goals. When the students begin their seat work, she [Mrs. Ryan] implements *adaptations* for both students. The will both do only half of the words, and she and the teacher [Mrs. Crawford] have re-arranged which words are most critical. They will do journal entries later with Mrs. Ryan's assistance. She quietly explains the modifications to Marcel and Tomika and directs them to begin with the assignment, reminding them that they should spell the vocabulary words correctly since they are copying them, but they need not worry about spelling all the words right in their sentences; the important thing is getting their ideas down. (pp. 54–55)

In a mixed-ability class, students of the same age are clearly not alike in *how* they learn or in their *rate* of acquiring new knowledge. Therefore, teachers must use **multilevel instruction** (also referred to as differentiated instruction), in which a variety of teaching approaches within the same curriculum are *adapted* to individual need and functioning level. At its most basic level, multilevel instruction provides students with many different ways to access and learn content within the general education curriculum. Peterson and Hittie (2005) describe multilevel instruction as "designing for diversity" and suggest several strategies for its implementation:

- ➤ Design lessons at multiple levels.
- ➤ Challenge students at their own level.
- ➤ Provide support to push children ahead to their next level of learning.
- ➤ Engage children in learning via activities related to the real world—to their lives at home and in the community.
- ➤ Engage the **multiple intelligences** and learning styles of children so that many pathways for learning and demonstrating achievement are available.
- ➤ Involve students in collaborative pair or group work in which children draw on each other's strengths. (p. 46)

To be effective, multilevel instruction requires that general and special education teachers work together to ensure access to the curriculum for all children in the class, while at the same time accepting individual goals for each child (Gartin, Murdick, Imbeau, & Perner, 2002; Haager & Klinger, 2005). Together with related-services personnel (such as speech and language pathologists, school psychologists, and physical therapists), these teachers use many different instructional strategies that are consistent with a student's level and rate of learning. Finally, students are able to demonstrate progress in many different ways (such as orally instead of in writing).

UNIVERSAL DESIGN FOR LEARNING. **Universal design for learning** (UDL) goes one step beyond multilevel instruction, creating instructional programs and environments that work for all students, to the greatest extent possible, *without the need for adaptation or special-*

Standard 4: Instructional Strategies

─────────────

➤ **Multilevel instruction (differentiated instruction)**

Differing levels of instruction that provide students with many different ways to access and learn content within the general education curriculum.

➤ **Multiple intelligences**

A theory that people have intelligence across several domains, including linguistic, logical-mathematical, spatial, musical, bodily-kinesthetic, interpersonal (responds to the needs of others), intrapersonal (self-knowledge), and naturalistic (knowledge of the natural world).

➤ **Universal design for learning**

Instructional programs and environments that work for all students, to the greatest extent possible, without the need for adaptation or specialized design. Such a curriculum must be accessible and applicable to students, teachers, and parents with different backgrounds, learning styles, abilities, and disabilities in widely varied learning contexts.

ized design. (The concept was adapted from architecture, where buildings are created with diverse users in mind from the beginning in order to avoid costly retrofitting of features such as curb cuts, ramps, and automatic doors that accommodate the needs of people with disabilities.)

As is true for multilevel instruction, the basic premise of universal design for learning is to make the curriculum accessible and applicable to all students, regardless of their abilities or learning styles. A range of options is available to each student that supports access to and engagement with the learning materials (Rose & Meyer, 2002). Figure 3.5 describes the basic principles of the universal design curriculum and provides an example of its application in the teaching of mathematics.

Universal design for learning helps make the curriculum accessible and applicable to all students, regardless of their abilities or learning styles. Here students are using a digital talking textbook. What are some other ways in which universal design for learning can help students with disabilities in an inclusive classroom?

FIGURE 3.5

Principles of the Universal Design Curriculum and Their Application to Teaching Mathematics

In a UDL curriculum . . .

- *Goals* provide an appropriate challenge for all students.
- *Materials* have a flexible format, supporting transformation between media and multiple representations of content to support all students' learning.
- *Methods* are flexible and diverse enough to provide appropriate learning experiences, challenges, and supports for all students.
- *Assessment* is sufficiently flexible to provide accurate, ongoing information that helps teachers adjust instruction and maximize learning.

Teaching Math Using UDL

Suppose a math teacher uses the UDL approach to convey the critical features of a right triangle. With software that supports graphics and hyperlinks, a document is prepared that shows:

- Multiple examples of right triangles in different orientations and sizes, with the right angle and the three points highlighted.
- An animation of the right triangle morphing into an isosceles triangle or into a rectangle, with voice and on-screen text to highlight the differences.
- Links to reviews on the characteristics of triangles and of right angles.
- Links to examples of right triangles in various real-world contexts.
- Links to pages that students can go to on their own for review or enrichment on the subject.
- The teacher could then project the documentation onto a large screen in front of the class. Thus the teacher would present the concept not simply by explaining it verbally or by assigning a textbook chapter or workbook page, but by using many modalities and with options for extra support or extra enrichment.

SOURCE: From "Providing New Access to the General Curriculum: Universal Design for Learning, *Teaching Exceptional Children,*" by C. Hitchcock, A. Meyer, D. Rose, & R. Jackson, 2002, November/December, pp. 8, 13.

ASSISTIVE TECHNOLOGY

WHAT IT LOOKS LIKE AND HOW IT CAN BE USED

Young children with significant cognitive delays may use a single switch (see Figure A), instead of a standard computer keyboard, to interact with software that helps them to identify letters, numbers, and colors.

Middle school students with a learning disability may use software such as the CAST eReader (www.cast.org) (see Figure B) to complete an assignment to search the Internet for a report. The student can highlight portions of the text and use the built-in text-to-speech features to have the information read to them.

Although the term *assistive technology* is often associated with computers and other electronic devices (high-tech), it also applies to a whole array of other devices. Examples of low-tech assistive technologies include adaptive eating utensils (see Figure C), ramps, and seating and positioning aids.

FIGURE A

The Big Red Switch is a commonly used switch for controlling electronic toys as well as computers. Reprinted with permission of AbleNet, Inc.

FIGURE B

CAST eReader software supports reading and research. Used with permission of CAST.

FIGURE C

An example of an adaptive eating utensil. Used with permission. Simmons Preston Rolyan, (800) 523-5547.

SOURCE: From *What Every Teacher Should Know About Assistive Technology,* by D. L. Edyburn, 2003, Boston: Allyn and Bacon. Copyright © 2003 by Allyn & Bacon. Reprinted with permission.

DIRECT INSTRUCTION. A primary characteristic of special education is the *explicit teaching* of academic, adaptive, and functional skills. (See Chapter 2 for more information on the characteristics of effective special education). Research suggests that students with disabilities learn more efficiently through the structured, teacher-directed approach often referred to as **direct instruction** (Adams & Carnine, 2003; Carnine, 2000). Direct instruction has several key elements (Friend & Bursuck, 2006):

➤ **Direct instruction**

Instruction that focuses on the explicit teaching of academic, adaptive, and functional skills. A structured, teacher-directed approach is used to teach children new skills.

➤ The teacher presents new content or skills in small steps, incorporating illustrations and concrete examples.

➤ Under direct guidance and questioning from the teacher, the student practices on new content or skills.

➤ Students receive immediate feedback on all correct or incorrect responses, correction, and re-teaching as necessary.

➤ Students practice independently on skills that have been presented until they reach a high rate of correct responses.

➤ Learned material is reviewed systematically through homework or exams.

➤ Re-teaching takes place when material is missed in homework assignments or exams.

ASSISTIVE TECHNOLOGY. Have you ever watched a program with closed-captioning or a foreign movie with subtitles? Do you turn on your television and open your garage door with a remote control device? Do you speed dial or use a digital address book on your cell phone? If so, you use assistive technology. **Assistive technology** is "any item, piece of equipment, or product system, whether acquired commercially off the shelf, modified, or customized, that is used to increase, maintain, or improve the functional capabilities of a child with disabilities" (Technology Related Assistance for Individuals with Disabilities Act, 20 U.S.C. 1401[1]).

Assistive technology can take many forms (high-tech or low-tech) and can be helpful to students with disabilities in several different ways. For students with reading problems, a high-tech digital textbook could assist with decoding and comprehending text. Students who have difficulty in verbally communicating with others might use a low-tech language board on which they point to pictures cut from magazines to indicate what they would like for lunch. Students with motor difficulties could learn to operate a joystick so they can move their power wheelchair in any direction. For more information, see the Assistive Technology feature, "What It Looks Like and How It Can Be Used," on page 80.

> **Assistive technology**
> Any item, piece of equipment, or product system, whether acquired commercially off the shelf, modified, or customized, that is used to increase, maintain, or improve the functional capabilities of a child with disabilities.

CURRICULUM-BASED ASSESSMENT/MEASUREMENT. In this era of accountability, developing *assessments* that reliably *measure* student learning is an essential component of instruction (Hosp & Hosp, 2003). As Howell and Nolet (2000) put it, "Assessment is the process of collecting information by reviewing the products of student work, interviewing, observing, or testing" (p. 3). Educators assess students for the purpose of deciding whether they are making adequate progress and, if not, what additional or different services and supports are needed.

The hallmarks of any good assessment are its accuracy, fairness, and utility (For a more in-depth discussion of nondiscriminatory and multidisciplinary assessment, see Chapter 5). Traditional standardized tests (such as intelligence [IQ] or achievement tests) compare one student to another in order to determine how each individual compares to the overall average. For example, an average score on the Stanford-Binet IQ test is 100. Any score (higher or lower) would be described as deviating from the average. Significantly higher scores may lead to the use of such descriptors as *gifted* or *talented*. Significantly lower scores may result in the label *intellectual disabilities*.

Traditional assessments may be useful in determining a student's eligibility for special education (comparing the student to the average performance of peers), but many educators question their use in planning for instruction and measuring day-to-day student learning. An

REFLECT ON THIS

DISTINGUISHING AMONG CBAs, CBMs, AND OTHER TYPES OF READING ASSESSMENT TOOLS

CURRICULUM-BASED ASSESSMENT (CBA)

Assessment is based on the reading curriculum materials used in the class.

CURRICULUM-BASED MEASUREMENT (CBM)

Students take brief tests of reading speed, accuracy, and comprehension. These scores are monitored over time to determine whether progress is adequate.

STANDARDIZED, NORM-REFERENCED ASSESSMENT

A published reading acheivement test is admnistered under standardized condiions. Students may answer test questions on computerized answer sheets or give answers to an examiner in an individual administration. Student's score is compared with scores of a normative sample of students.

CRITERION-REFERENCED ASSESSMENT

Students' test scores are compared with a certain predetermined criterion level that they must meet to be considered competent in reading at their grade level.

PERFORMANCE ASSESSMENT

Students can be asked to "perform" on a variety of reading-related tasks, such as summarizing a passage, looking up a reference, or identifying a certain printed label in a store.

PORTFOLIO ASSESSMENT

A variety of the student's products relevant to reading are collected—for example, a list of books read, book reports written, or tape recordings of reading selections.

SOURCE: Adpated from Mastropieri, M. A., & Scruggs, T. E. (2007). *The inclusive classroom: Strategies for effective instruction.* Upper Saddle River, NJ: Merrill, p. 271.

> **Curriculum-based assessment (CBA)**

Any procedure that evaluates student performance in relation to the school curriculum. CBA uses probes as indicators, or benchmarks, of student progress.

> **Curriculum-based measurements (CBMs)**

Frequent, direct measurements of critical school behaviors, which could include timed (1–5 minute) tests of performance.

alternative approach to traditional assessment is the use of **curriculum-based assessments** (CBAs) and **curriculum-based measurements** (CBMs). CBAs include "any procedure that evaluates student performance in relation to the school curriculum, such as weekly spelling tests," whereas CBMs are the "frequent, direct measurements of critical school behaviors, which could include timed (1–5 minute) tests of performance on reading, math, and writing skills" (Mastropieri & Scruggs, 2007, p. 271). See the Reflect on This feature, "Distinguising Among CBAs, CBMs, and Other Types of Reading Assessment Tools," on page 81.

As we conclude this section on the elementary years, it is important to review some of the factors associated with an effective inclusive education program. First, teachers must work together with related services professionals to develop and use evidence-based instructional practices that promote access to the general curriculum and increase student learning and achievement. Evidence-based practices include the use of multilevel instruction, universal design for learning, direct instruction, assistive technology, and curriclum-based assessment/measurement.

FOCUS REVIEW

FOCUS 1 Define inclusive education.

- Inclusive education may be defined as placing students with disabilities in a general education setting within their home or neighborhood school while making available both formal and natural supports to ensure an appropriate educational experience.

- Full inclusion occurs when the student with a disability receives all instruction and support within the general education classroom. Partial inclusion occurs when the student with a disability receives most instruction within the general education classroom but is "pulled out" for specialized services part of the school day.

FOCUS 2 Describe the characteristics of evidence-based inclusive schools.

Evidence-based inclusive schools

- promote the values of diversity, acceptance, and belonging.

- ensure the availability of formal and natural supports within the general education setting.

- provide services and supports in age-appropriate classrooms in neighborhood schools.

- ensure access to the general curriculum while meeting the individualized needs of each student.

- provide a schoolwide support system to meet the needs of all students.

FOCUS 3 Define multidisciplinary collaboration and identify its key characteristics.

- Collaboration is defined as professonals, parents, and students *working together* to achieve the mutual goal of delivering an effective educational program

designed to meet individual needs. Collaboration is not what those involved do; it is how they do it.

- In an inclusive school, effective collaboration has several key characteristics:
  - Parents are viewed as active partners in the education of their children.
  - Team members share responsibility; individual roles are clearly understood and valued.
  - Team members promote peer support and cooperative learning.

FOCUS 4 Why is it so important to provide early intervention services as soon as possible to young children at risk?

- The first years of life are critical to the overall development of all children—normal, at risk, and disabled.

- Early stimulation is crucial to the later development of language, intelligence, personality, and self-worth.

- Early intervention may prevent or reduce the overall impact of disabilities, as well as counteracting the negative effects of delayed intervention.

- Early intervention may in the long run be less costly and more effective than providing services later in the individual's life.

FOCUS 5 Identify the components of the individualized family service plan (IFSP).

- The infant's or toddler's present levels of physical development, cognitive development, communication development, social or emotional development, and adaptive development.

- The family's resources, priorities, and concerns related to enhancing the development of the young child with a disability.

- The major outcomes to be achieved for the infant or toddler and the family, and the criteria, procedures, and timelines used to determine progress toward achieving those outcomes.

- Specific early intervention services necessary to meet the unique needs of the infant or toddler and the family. The natural environments in which early intervention services are to be provided, including a justification of the extent, if any, to which the services will not be provided in a natural environment.

- The projected dates for initiation of services and the anticipated duration of the services.

- Identification of the service coordinator.

- The steps to be taken to support the transition of the toddler with a disability to preschool or other appropriate services.

FOCUS 6 Identify evidence-based instructional approaches for preschool-age children with disabilities.

- A child-find system in each state to locate young children at risk and make referrals to appropriate agencies for preschool services.

- An individualized education program (IEP) that involves specialists across several disciplines.

- Instruction that reflects developmentally appropriate practice, age-appropriate practice, and the teaching of functional skills.

- Inclusive preschool classrooms where young children with disabilities are educated side-by-side with peers without disabilities.

FOCUS 7 Describe the roles of special education and general education teachers in an inclusive classroom setting.

- Special education teachers have multiple roles that may be referred to as the "three Cs": collaborator, consultant, and coordinator.

- In the role of *collaborator*, special educators work with school to assess student needs, develop the IEP, determine appropriate accommodations and instructional adaptations, and deliver intensive instruction in academic, behavioral, and/or adaptive functional areas. Special education teachers use effective problem-solving strategies to facilitate student learning, co-teach with general educators, and apply effective accountability measures to evaluate individual student progress and long-term results.

- In the role of *consultant*, the special education teacher serves as a resource to general educators and parents on effective instructional practices for students with disabilities.

- In the role of *coordinator*, the special education teacher takes the lead responsibility for organizing the activities of the school team in developing, implementing, and evaluating student IEPs. Special education teachers may also be responsible for organizing school resources; spearheading professional development activities; supervising paraprofessionals, peer support, and volunteers; and facilitating positive communication with parents.

- General educators must be able to identify and refer students who may be in need of additional support; to understand each student's individual strengths and limitations, and the affects on learning; to implement an appropriate individualized instructional program that is focused on supporting student success in the general education curriculum; and to initiate and maintain ongoing communication with parents.

FOCUS 8 Why are multilevel instruction, universal design for learning, direct instruction, assistive technology, and curriculum-based assessment/measurement considered evidence-based practice in an inclusive classroom?

- Students of the same age are clearly not alike in how they learn or in their rate of learning. For this reason, teachers must use multilevel instruction (also referred to as *differentiated instruction*) in which multiple teaching approaches within the same curriculum are *adapted* to individual need and functioning level.

- Universal design goes one step beyond multilevel instruction, creating instructional programs and environments that work for all students, to the greatest extent possible, without the need for adaptation or specialized design.

- A primary characteristic of special education is the *explicit teaching* of academic, adaptive, and functional skills. Research suggests that students with disabilities learn more efficiently through the structured, teacher-directed approach often referred to as *direct instruction*.

- Assistive technology can take many forms and can be helpful to students with disabilities in several different ways (examples include a high-tech digital textbook, a low-tech language board, and a joystick to guide a power wheelchair).

- Although traditional assessments may be useful in determining a student's eligibility for special education, many educators question their use in planning for instruction and measuring day-to-day student learning. An alternative to traditional tests is the use of curriculum-based assessments (CBAs) and curriculum-based measurements (CBMs). CBAs include any procedure that evaluates student performance in relation to the school curriculum. CBMs are frequent, direct measurements of critical school behaviors, which could include timed (1–5 minute) tests of performance.

BUILDING YOUR PORTFOLIO

If you are thinking about a career in special education, you should know that many states use national standards developed by the Council for Exceptional Children (CEC) to assess a teacher candidate's knowledge and skills for working with students with disabilities. See a complete listing of the ten CEC Content Standards on the inside front cover of this text.

CEC Content Standards Addressed in This Chapter

1 Foundations

2 Development and Characteristics of Learners

3 Individual Learning Differences

4 Instructional Strategies

5 Learning Environments and Social Interactions

6 Communication

7 Instructional Planning

9 Professional and Ethical Practice

10 Collaboration

Assess Your Knowledge of the CEC Standards Addressed in This Chapter

Some states require that teacher candidates develop a portfolio of products that demonstrate mastery of the CEC content standards. To assist in the development of products for this portfolio, you may wish to complete the following activities.

- Complete a written test of the chapter's content.

  If your instructor requires a written test of your content knowledge for this chapter, keep a copy for your portfolio. A practice test on the information covered in this chapter is available through the Human Exceptionality Companion Website and the Student Study Guide.

- Respond to the Application Questions for the Case Study "Ricardo."

  Review the Case Study and respond in writing to the application questions. Keep a copy of the Case Study and of your written response for your portfolio.

- Participate in a Community Service Learning Activity.

  Community service is a valuable way to enhance your learning experience. Visit our companion website for suggested community service learning activities that correspond to the information presented in this chapter. Develop a reflective journal of the service learning experience for your portfolio.

WEB RESOURCES

Center for Applied Special Technology (CAST)

http://www.cast.org/

CAST is a not-for-profit organization that uses technology to expand opportunities for all people, especially those with disabilities. This website contains information on how technology can help students with disabilities by improving their access to, and progress and participation in, the general education curriculum and through advances in universal design for learning.

Inclusive Education Website: The "Whats" and "How Tos" of Inclusive Education

http://www.uni.edu/coe/inclusion/

Whether you're familiar with inclusive education or have little idea what the term means, this website is designed to help you learn more. It answers some of the most frequently asked questions on inclusion and offers basic guidelines for teaching in an inclusive classroom. Resources for learning more about inclusive education are also included.

Special Education Resources on the Internet

http://seriweb.com/

Special Education Resources on the Internet (SERI) is a collection of Internet-accessible information resources of interest to those involved in the education of students with disabilities. This collection exists in order to make on-line special education resources more easily and readily available in one location.

The Division for Early Childhood (DEC) of the Council for Exceptional Children

http://www.dec-sped.org/

The Division for Early Childhood (DEC) of the Council for Exceptional Children advocates for individuals who work with or on behalf of children with special needs, birth through age 8, and their families. This website contains information on early childhood conferences, publications, government information, and jobs.

FURTHER READINGS

Peterson, J. M., & Hittie, M. M. (2005). *Inclusive Teaching: Creating Effective Schools for All Learners* (Mylabschool Edition). Boston: Allyn and Bacon.

A comprehensive book designed to help educators meet the needs of all students in inclusive settings. Topics include celebrating difference, a *vision for inclusive schools, parent and community partnerships, planning for instruction with diverse learners, collaboration, and strategies for inclusive teaching.*

Lerner, J. W., Lowenthal, B., & Egan, R. W. (2002). *Preschool Children with Special Needs: Children At Risk, Children with Disabilities* (2nd ed.). Boston: Allyn and Bacon.

This book examines issues in early childhood general and special education, emphasizing the needs of preschoolers aged 3 to 6. It provides information to teachers and others who work with young children in all settings. Current models of curricula, which incorporate research and practical experiences with children who have special needs, are described and discussed.

Friend, M., & Cook, L. (2003*). Interactions: Collaboration Skills for School Professionals* (4th ed.). Boston: Allyn and Bacon.

This book looks at how teams of school professionals—classroom teachers, special education teachers, and counselors—can effectively work together to provide a range of essential services to students with special needs. Future teachers learn how to collaborate with school professionals and families to help special education students who are more and more often being placed in general education classroom settings.

COMPANION WEBSITE

Visit the companion website at college.hmco.com/pic/hardman9e for additional resources that support this text:

- HM Video Cases that present actual classroom scenarios that you may face every day as a teacher

- Practice ACE Exams that will help you prepare for quizzes, tests, and certification exams
- Flashcards of key terms
- Weblinks

4

Transition and Adult Life

STUDENTS WITH DISABILITIES AND ACADEMIC STANDARDS

Secondary-age students with disabilities are expected to meet the same high academic standards as their peers without disabilities in general education classrooms, yet many do not experience success during their middle and high school years. This lack of success for students with disabilities at the secondary level often is impacted by miscommunication between educators . . . an increasing difficulty with assignments, and an inability to address diverse learning needs given the strong focus on content mastery. (Murawski & Dieker, 2004, p. 52)

TOO MANY YOUNG ADULTS WITH DISABILITIES SITTING AT HOME

Young people leaving the school system frequently find there is no coordinated adult system of services and supports to help them find work, housing, [or] recreational and leisure activities. Many have difficulty finding jobs because they have not learned the academic, technical, and social skills necessary to find and/or maintain employment. Too many young adults end up sitting at home with very little involvement in their communities. The transition requirements of the IDEA are designed to help students successfully leave school to live and work within the community. Transition planning and activities cover the student's school years from age [16] until school completion, which may be through age 21 if there are continuing educational needs. (The ARC, 2006)

COLLEGE-BOUND STUDENTS WITH DISABILITIES

Today, there are more students with documented disabilities in higher education than ever before—over 9.5% of all freshmen as compared with only 2.6% in 1978. Although the process has been slow, colleges and universities have made their programs more and more accessible, sometimes in good faith, sometimes due to coercion . . . by federal agencies and courts. Only modest progress was made between 1973 and 1990; however, once the ADA [Americans with Disabilities Act] was passed . . . [universities and colleges] that had made little or no progress in making their building and programs accessible increased their efforts. . . . Of particular significance in recent years has been the growth in the number of students with learning disabilities. Over 35% of the freshmen in 1996 who reported having a disability were purported to have a learning disability. . . . The growth in the number of students with learning disabilities has created a new challenge to professors and colleges. . . . Many professors prefer that all students meet the same set of requirements, within the same time period . . . and in the same way, and are ill-prepared to adapt their instruction to address the individual needs of students or to identify appropriate, fair, and reasonable accommodations. (Thomas, 2000, p. 248)

1. What do we know about access to community living and employment for people with disabilities after they leave school?

2. What are the requirements for transition planning in IDEA?

3. Identify the purpose of person-centered transition planning and the basic steps in its formulation.

4. Why is it important for students with disabilities to receive instruction in self-determination, academics, adaptive and functional life skills, and employment preparation during the secondary school years?

5. Describe government-funded and natural supports for people with disabilities.

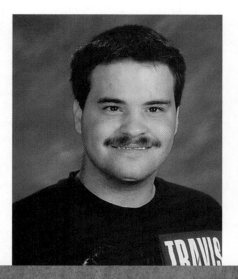

▼ SNAPSHOT

LEE

Lee is a high school student with a part-time job stocking shelves at a local store. Lee walks from his high school to catch the bus to work. On his way to the bus, everyone says hello to Lee. He's a great friend to everybody. Everyone makes it a point to stop and ask how he's doing.

At work, his employer gives him a checklist indicating how many cases of each item Lee needs to bring from the backroom to stock on the shelves. Lee can't read, but he can associate the item with the cases in the backroom. Most of Lee's education occurs in the community with the assistance of peer tutors who help him learn to purchase foods, bank, use the bus, and perform various work functions.

In his high school classes, Lee also has access to peer tutors who work with him. They may provide one-on-one tutoring or participate with him in a weight-lifting class. They are invaluable to him and his teachers.

Lee has become much more independent because of the skills he has learned in school and practiced in the community. Eventually, he plans to live independently.

What are society's expectations of an individual leaving school and moving into adult life? Early adulthood marks a time of transition from relative dependence on the family to an increasing responsibility for one's own life. Young adults are concerned with furthering their education, earning a living, establishing their independence, and creating social networks. As an adolescent leaves high school, decisions need to be made. A person may reflect on several questions: What kind of career or job do I desire? Should I further my education to increase my career choices? Where shall I live and with whom shall I live? How shall I spend my money? With whom do I choose to spend time? Who will be my friends?

Although most adolescents face these choices as a natural part of growing into adult life, the issues confronting individuals with disabilities and their families may be very different. For many, the choice may be to disappear into the fabric of society and try to make it on their own without the supports and services that were so much a part of their public school experience. Others may choose to go to college, seeking the needed accommodations (such as more time to take tests, large-print books, or interpreters) that will give them a fighting chance to succeed in an academic world. Still others will need ongoing supports to find and keep a job and to live successfully in the community.

Given these expectations of adult life, the school's responsibility is to teach the critical skills that will facilitate access to valued postschool outcomes for students with disabilities. For Lee, in the opening Snapshot, instruction focused on increasing his independence by teaching him how to ride the bus, work in the community, take care of his personal needs (such as shopping and having a checking account), and enjoy his free time lifting weights. Much has been done to improve the quality of life for adults with disabilities, but many individuals are still unable to access the services or supports necessary for success following graduation.

Research on the Lives of Adults with Disabilities

One measure of an educational program's effectiveness is the success of its graduates. The year 2010 marks the 35th anniversary of the passage of Public Law 94-142), now the Individuals with Disabilities Education Act (IDEA 2004), and the educational opportunities afforded by this landmark legislation have not yet led to full participation of special education graduates in the social and economic mainstream of their local communities (National Organization on Disability [N.O.D.]/Harris, 2004). However, there has been considerable improvement. Whereas follow-up studies of special education graduates in the 1990s suggested that these individuals had higher unemployment rates, lower rates of participation in postsecondary education, and less extensive support networks than their peers without disabilities (Hasazi, Furney, & Destefano, 1999; Wagner & Blackorby, 1996), a more recent study, the National Longitudinal Study-2 (Wagner, Newman, Cameo, & Levine, 2005), reports that progress has been made in several areas (high school completion, living arrangements, social involvement, further education, and employment rates). The Reflect on This on page 89 highlights some of the positive changes, as reported by Wagner et al., three decades since the passage of IDEA and nearly two decades after the passage of ADA.

High School Completion and Access to Valued Postschool Outcomes

The increasing emphasis that policymakers, professionals, and parents place on the transition from school to adult life has altered many earlier perceptions about people with disabilities. Without question, the potential of adults with disabilities has been significantly underestimated. In recent years, professionals and parents have begun to address some of the crucial issues facing students with disabilities as they prepare to leave school and face life as adults in their local communities. Nearly 400,000 students with disabilities exit school each year. Since the pas-

CHANGES OVER TIME IN THE POSTSCHOOL OUTCOMES OF YOUNG ADULTS WITH DISABILITIES

Two studies commissioned by the U.S. Department of Education documented changes experienced by young adults with disabilities two years after they exited high school. The National Longitudinal Study (NLTS) followed up on students with disabilities who had been receiving special education services in 1985, and the National Longitudinal Study-2 (NLTS2) assessed the status of young adults with disabilities who exited in 2001. The following presents highlights of comparisons between these two studies.

SCHOOL COMPLETION

- The school completion rate of young adults with disabilities increased, and the dropout rate decreased by 17 percent between 1987 and 2003. With these changes, 70% of the young adults with disabilities from the 2003 study completed high school.

COMMUNITY LIVING AND SOCIAL ACTIVITIES

- The living arrangements of young adults with disabilities have been stable over time. Two years after exiting high school, approximately 75% of young adults with disabilities from both studies lived with their parents, one in eight lived independently, and 3% lived in a residential facility or institution.

- Ninety percent of young adults with disabilities from the 1987 and 2003 studies were single. However, membership in organized community groups (such as hobby clubs, community sports, and performing groups) more than doubled, such that 28% of young adults with disabilities from the 2003 study belonged to a group.

- Between 1987 and 2003, there was a large increase in adults with disabilities who had ever been subject to disciplinary action at school, fired from a job, or arrested.

More than 50% of the young adults with disabilities from the 2003 study had negative consequences for their behavior, compared to 33% from the 1987 study.

ENGAGEMENT IN SCHOOL AND WORK, OR PREPARATION FOR WORK

- Overall engagement in school, work, and job training increased only slightly (from 70% to 75%) between 1987 and 2003. Although their overall rate of engagement in these activities did not increase markedly over time, the modes of engagement did change.

  - Engagement in the combination of postsecondary education and paid employment nearly quadrupled, to 22% for students in the 2003 study.

  - There was a significant increase in employment (11%) from 1987 to 2003, and 44% of the young adults in the 2003 study had been employed since high school.

EMPLOYMENT

- In 2003, 70% of young adults with disabilities who had been out of school up to two years had worked for pay at some time since leaving high school; only 55% had done so in 1987. However, 18% of young adults in the 2003 study were less likely than those in the 1987 study to be working full-time in their current job. Approximately 39% of the young adults in the 2003 study were employed full-time.

- Over time, considerably more young adults with disabilities earned above the federal minimum wage (70% in 1987 vs. 85% in 2003). Yet the average hourly wage did not increase when adjusted for inflation; earnings averaged $7.30 per hour in 2003.

SOURCE: Wagner, M., Newman, L., Cameto, R., & Levine, P. (2005). *Changes over time in the early postschool outcomes of youth with disabilities. A report from the National Longitudinal Study* (NLTS) *and the National Longitudinal Transition Study-2* (NLTS2). Menlo Park, CA: SRI International, p. ES-1-ES-3.

sage of IDEA, schools have made significant strides in preparing youth with disabilities for adult life, but much remains to be done. Of the students with disabilities exiting school (ages 14–21), only 51% leave with a high school diploma, compared to 90% of their peers without disabilities (U.S. Department of Education, 2006). Although there has been improvement, as evidenced by the results of the NLTS-2 (Wagner et al., 2005), too many of the current graduates from special education programs are not adequately prepared for employment and have difficulty accessing further education. They are also unable to locate the critical programs and services necessary for success as adults in their local communities (N.O.D./Harris, 2004; Wehman, 2006a). For people with more severe disabilities, long waiting lists for employment and housing services prove frustrating (McDonnell, Hardman, & McDonnell, 2003). Prouty, Smith, and Lakin (2001) reported that nearly 72,000 adults with severe disabilities were on waiting lists for residential, day treatment, or family support services. Furthermore, individuals with disabilities who enroll in

Council for Exceptional Children

Standard 5: Learning Environments and Social Interactions

postsecondary education often find that the supports and services they need in order to achieve success in college are also not available (Babbitt & White, 2002; Thomas, 2000).

Employment

The U.S. Department of Education's National Longitudinal Transition Study-2 (NLTS-2) (Wagner et al., 2005) reported that the *probability* of young adults with disabilities working for pay at some time during the first few years out of high school had increased significantly (from 55% to 70%) between 1987 and 2003. However, the current rate of employment for young adults with disabilities lagged significantly behind that of same-age peers without disabilities (41% vs. 63%) in 2003. Worse yet, the unemployment rate reported by Wagner et al. in 2005 is significantly higher than the findings of the 2004 N.O.D./Harris poll, in which only 35% of the people with disabilities indicated that they were working full- or part-time.

Closing the Gap: Transition Planning and Services

Standard 7: Instructional Planning

The transition from school to adult life is a complex and dynamic process. Transition planning should culminate with the transfer of support from the school to an adult service agency, access to postsecondary education, or life as an independent adult. The planning process involves a series of choices about which experiences in their remaining school years will best prepare students with disabilities for what lies ahead in the adult world. A successful transition from school to the adult years requires both formal (government-funded) and natural supports (Steere, Rose, & Cavaiuolo, 2007; Tymchuk, Lakin, & Luckasson, 2001; Wehman, 2006a). Historically, providing *formal supports*, such as health care, employment preparation, and supported living, has been emphasized. Only recently has society begun to understand the importance of the family and other *natural support* networks in preparing the adolescent with disabilities for adult life. Research suggests that the family unit may be the single most powerful force in preparing the adolescent with disabilities for the adult years (Drew & Hardman, 2007).

The principal components of an effective transition system include

> ➤ Effective middle (junior high) and high school programs that link instruction to further education (such as college or trade schools) and to valued postschool outcomes (such as employment, independent living, and recreation/leisure activities).

> ➤ A cooperative system of transition planning that involves public education, adult services, and an array of natural supports (family and friends) in order to ensure access to valued postschool outcomes.

> ➤ The availability of formal government-funded programs following school that meet the unique educational, employment, residential, and leisure needs of people with disabilities in a community setting.

IDEA Transition Planning Requirements

IDEA requires that every student with a disability receive transition services. **Transition services** for a student with a disability consist of a coordinated set of activities with the following attributes:

> ➤ Designed to be within a results-oriented process—that is, focused on improving the academic and functional achievement of the child with a disability to facilitate the child's movement from school to postschool activities, including postsecondary education, vocational education, integrated employment (including supported employment), continuing and adult education, adult services, independent living, and community participation.

> ➤ Based on the individual child's needs, taking into account the child's strengths, preferences, and interests.

FOCUS **2**
What are the requirements for transition planning in IDEA?

> ➤ **Transition services**
A coordinated set of activities for students with disabilities that are designed to facilitate the move from school to employment, further education, vocational training, independent living, and community participation.

> Designed to include instruction, related services, community experiences, the development of employment and other postschool adult living objectives, and, when appropriate, acquisition of daily living skills and functional vocational evaluation. (IDEA 2004, PL 108-446, Sec. 602[34])

IDEA requires that, beginning at age 16 and updated annually, a student's individualized program should include measurable postsecondary goals based on age-appropriate transition assessments related to training, education, employment, and, where appropriate, independent living skills. The IEP must include a statement of transition services related to various courses of study (such as participation in advanced placement courses or a vocational education program) that will assist the student in reaching her or his goals (IDEA 2004, PL 108-446, Sec. 614[d]).

Other Federal Laws Linked to IDEA and Transition Planning

Five other pieces of federal legislation are linked directly to the IDEA transition requirements to facilitate an effective transition planning process. They are the Vocational Rehabilitation Act, the Carl Perkins Vocational and Applied Technology Education Act, the Americans with Disabilities Act (ADA), the School-to-Work Opportunities Act, and the Ticket to Work and Work Incentives Improvement Act. The Vocational Rehabilitation Act provides services through rehabilitation counselors in several areas (such as guidance and counseling, vocational evaluation, vocational training and job placement, transportation, family services, interpreter services, and telecommunication aids and devices). Recent amendments to the act encourage stronger collaboration and outreach between the schools and the rehabilitation counselors in transition planning.

Greater connections between education and vocational rehabilitation are expected to help students with disabilities in moving on to postsecondary education or in obtaining employment. The Carl Perkins Vocational and Technical Education Act provides students with disabilities greater access to vocational education services (for more information, see http://www.ed.gov/offices/OVAE/CTE/legis.html). ADA addresses equal access to public accommodations, employment, transportation, and telecommunication services following the school transition years. (See Chapter 1.) Such services are often directly targeted as a part of the student's transition plan.

The School-to-Work Opportunities Act provides all students in the public schools with education and training to prepare them for first jobs in high-skill, high-wage careers and for further education following high school (for more information, see http://www.ncrel.org/sdrs/areas/issues/envrnmnt/stw/sw0stw94.htm). Students with disabilities are specifically identified as a target population of the act. The Ticket to Work and Work Incentives Improvement Act provides greater opportunities for the employment of people with disabilities by allowing them to work and still keep critical health care coverage. Prior to the passage of this act, many people with disabilities were not able to work because federal Social Security laws put them at risk of losing Medicaid and Medicare coverage if they accrued any significant earnings. Thus there was little incentive for people with disabilities to work because they could not access health insurance. The Work Incentives Improvement Act made health insurance available and affordable when a person with a disability goes to work or develops a significant disability while working (for more information, see http://www.ssa.gov/work/Ticket/ticket_info.html).

Person-Centered Transition Planning

Transition involves much more than the mere transfer of administrative responsibility from the school to an adult service agency. **Person-centered transition planning** is based on an understanding of and commitment to each student's needs and preferences, and it must be developed and implemented within each student's IEP. Planning should include access to the general education curriculum and a focus on the adaptive and functional skills that will facilitate life in the community following school (deFur, 2000; Steere et al., 2007; Wehman, 2006b).

See Figure 4.1 for an illustration of person-centered transition planning in the area of employment preparation. The purpose of the transition statement is to (1) identify the type and

Standard 1: Foundations

Standard 7: Instructional Planning

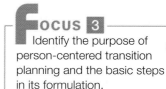

Focus 3
Identify the purpose of person-centered transition planning and the basic steps in its formulation.

> **Person-centered transition planning**
Planning process that is based on an understanding of and commitment to each student's needs and preferences, and that must be developed and implemented within each student's IEP. The process includes access to the general education curriculum and a focus on the adaptive and functional skills that will facilitate life in the community following school.

range of transitional services and supports, and (2) establish timelines and personnel responsible for completing the plan. Wehman (2006a) identifies six basic steps in the person-centered transition planning process. These are listed in Figure 4.2.

Facilitating Student and Parent Involvement

In the transition from school to adult life, many students and parents receive quite a shock. Once they leave school, students may not receive any further assistance from government programs or, at the least, they may be placed on long waiting lists for employment training, housing, or education assistance. Thus the person with a disability may experience a significant loss

Standard 9: Professional and Ethical Practice

FIGURE 4.2

Basic Steps in the Formulation of Person-Centered Transition Planning

1. Convene IEP teams, individualized to reflect the wants and needs of each transition-age student.
   - Identify all transition-age students.
   - Identify appropriate school service personnel.
   - Identify appropriate adult service agencies.
   - Identify appropriate members of the student's networks.

2. Review assessment data and conduct additional assessment activities.
   - Meet with transition-age student and a small circle of friends, family members, co-workers, neighbors, church members, and/or staff to establish the individual's needs and preferences for adult life.

3. Teams develop IEPs/Transition IEPs.
   - Schedule the IEP meeting.
   - Conduct the IEP meeting.
   - Open the IEP/transition IEP meeting.

4. Implement the IEP or transition IEP.
   - Operate according to guidelines defined in interagency agreements.
   - Use the **Circle of friends/Circle of support** to implement the IEP or Transition IEP.

5. Update the IEP/transition IEP annually and implement follow-up procedures.
   - Phase out involvement of school personnel, while increasing involvement of adult service agencies.
   - Contact persons responsible for completion of IEP/transition IEP goals to monitor progress.

6. Hold an exit meeting.
   - Ensure most appropriate employment outcome or access to further education.
   - Ensure most appropriate community living and recreation outcome.
   - Ensure referrals to all appropriate adult agencies and support services.

SOURCE: Wehman, P. (2006a). Individualized transition planning. In P. Wehman (Ed.), *Life beyond the classroom: Transition strategies for young people with disabilities* (4th ed.) Baltimore: Paul H. Brookes, pp. 78–95.

➤ **Circle of friends/Circle of support**

A group of individuals who meet regularly to work on behalf of and support a person with disabilities. These circles work to "open doors" to new opportunities for the person with disabilities, including establishing new friendships.

in services at a crucial time. Many students and their parents know little, if anything, about what life may bring during the adult years.

To fully prepare for the transition from school, students and parents must be educated about critical components of adult service systems, including the characteristics of service agencies and what constitutes a good program, as well as current and potential opportunities for employment, independent living, or further education (deFur, 2000). There are several strategies that schools can use to facilitate family involvement in the transition process. These include the adoption of a person-centered approach to transition planning, where the student is at the core of the planning process, and school work with parents to identify the student's preferences and expectations.

Working with Adult Services

In addition to the student, parents, and school personnel, professionals from adult service agencies (such as vocational rehabilitation counselors, representatives from university or college centers for students with disabilities, and the state developmental disability agency) may also be involved in transition planning. **Adult service agencies** assist individuals with disabilities in accessing postsecondary education, employment, supported living, and/or leisure activ-

➤ **Adult service agencies**

Agencies with a major focus on providing services and supports to help people with disabilities become more independent as adults. Adult service agencies include rehabilitation services, social services, mental health services, and the like.

Schools have many roles in the transition planning process. What do you think are a school's most important responsibilities in facilitating a successful transition from school to adult life?

ities. Agencies may provide support in vocational rehabilitation, social services, and mental health. Examples of supports include career, education, or mental health counseling, job training and support (such as a job coach), further education (college or trade school), attendant services, and interpreter services. Adult service agencies should become involved early in transition planning to begin targeting the services that will be necessary once the student leaves school. Adult service professionals should collaborate with the school in establishing transition goals and identifying appropriate activities for the student during the final school years. Additionally, adult service professionals must be involved in developing information systems that can effectively track students as they leave school and should monitor the availability and appropriateness of services to be provided during adulthood (Wehman, 2006b).

Preparing Students for Adult Life: The Role of Secondary Schools

Successful transition begins with a solid foundation—the school. Secondary schools have many roles in the transition process: assessing individual needs; helping each student develop an IEP/transition plan; coordinating transition planning with adult service agencies; participating with parents and students in the planning process; and providing experiences to facilitate access to community services and employment. For Lee, in the opening Snapshot, these experiences included learning to shop in a neighborhood grocery store and training for a job in the community. For another student with a disability who has different needs and abilities, the activities may be more academically oriented and college preparation the immediate goal.

Several outcomes are expected for students with disabilities as they enter adulthood. First, they should be able to function as independently as possible in their daily lives; their reliance on others to meet their needs should be minimized. As students with disabilities leave school, they should be able to make choices about where they will live, how they will spend their free time, and whether they will be employed in the community or go on to college. For students with disabilities considering college, Babbitt and White (2002) have devised a process to help them to identify their readiness for further education. Figure 4.3 lists questions intended to facilitate the transition of students with disabilities from school to college.

Secondary schools are in the unique position of being able to coordinate activities that enhance student participation in the community and link students, such as Lee, with needed programs and services. Several instructional practices are at the core of evidence-based secondary programs for students with disabilities. These include teaching self-determination, aca-

FOCUS **4**

Why is it important for students with disabilities to receive instruction in self-determination, academics, adaptive and functional life skills, and employment preparation during the secondary school years?

FIGURE 4.3

Helping Students with Disabilities Assess Their Readiness for College

- *Carlos, a student with a learning disability, failed two classes his first semester at college before seeking help from the Disability Resource Center.*
- *DeVon, who uses a wheelchair, often arrives late for class because she didn't schedule enough time between classes to get from building to building.*
- *Erik, an emotionally challenged student, does well in class but finds paying bills and getting along with his new roommates overwhelming.*

What do these three adolescents have in common? They are all students with various disabilities, and they are all having difficulty making the transition from high school to college. To help adolescents with disabilities assess their readiness for college, Babbitt and White (2002) developed a questionnaire focused directly on the attitudes and needs of these students. For example, students are asked to what extent the following statements are true of them.

1. I want to continue my education after high school.
2. I have taken the classes needed in high school to prepare me for college.
3. I know what type of employment I want after college.
4. I know how to use the phone book.
5. I know how to budget money.
6. I have access to regular transportation.
7. My family is helping me make plans for college.
8. I know how to use a course catalog.
9. I know how to use an ATM.
10. I will seek assistance at the Disability Resource Center at the institution I attend if needed.
11. I will be living at home while attending college.
12. I plan to have a job while attaining my postsecondary education.
13. I have health/dental/vision insurance.
14. I know how to apply for financial aid to continue my education.
15. I will need help filling out all necessary paperwork that is required to go to college.
16. I know how to schedule an appointment.
17. I am aware of how my disability will affect me during college.
18. I can identify the areas that I need to improve on to be successful in college.
19. I have the skills to make new friends
20. I know how to advocate for myself.
21. My individualized education program (IEP) is written to help me prepare for postsecondary education.
22. I am comfortable in groups.
23. I have the skills to use a computer or word processor.
24. My academic assignments are modified.
25. I will need help in the following areas to be successful in college.

_____

_____

SOURCE: Adapted from Babbitt, B. C., & White, C. M. (2002). RU ready? Helping students assess their readiness for postsecondary education. *Teaching Exceptional Children*, 35(2), 64–65.

demic skills, adaptive and functional life skills, and employment preparation (McDonnell, Hardman, & McGuire, 2007).

Teaching Self-Determination

Standard 4: Instructional Strategies

Standard 3: Individual Learning Differences

Self-determination plays a critical role in the successful transition from school to adult life (Bremer, Kachgal, & Schoeller, 2003; Morgan, Ellerd, Gerity, & Blair, 2000; Wehmeyer, Gragoudas, & Shogren, 2006). Definitions of self-determination focus on a person's ability to consider options and make appropriate decisions and to exercise free will, independence, and individual responsibility (University of Illinois at Chicago National Research and Training Center, 2003). The need for secondary schools to teach self-determination skills is evident from research on positive transition outcomes (Algozzine, Browder, Karvonen, Test, & Wood, 2001). Wehmeyer et al. indicate that "teaching effective decision-making and problem-solving skills has been shown to enhance positive transition outcomes for youth and young adults" (p. 45). These include the reduction of problem behaviors, improved outcomes in community-based instruction, and the promotion of choice-making opportunities in vocational tasks. Teaching self-determination skills to students with disabilities helps them become more efficient in acquiring knowledge and solving problems (Bambara, Browder, & Koger, 2006). Students grow better able to achieve goals that will facilitate their transition out of school and become aware of the specific challenges they will face in the adult years. Ultimately, the student leaves school with a more highly developed sense of personal worth and social responsibility and with better problem-solving skills.

Creating opportunities for individual choice and decision-making is an important element in the transition from school to adult life. Each individual must be able to consider options and make appropriate choices. This means less problem solving and decision making on the part of service providers and family members and a greater focus on teaching and promoting choice. The planning process associated with the development of a student's IEP is an excellent opportunity to promote self-determination. Unfortunately, very few adolescents with disabilities attend their IEP meetings, and even fewer actively participate (Wehman, 2006a). Figure 4.4 reviews some of the things families and professionals can do to promote self-determination in youth with disabilities.

Teaching Academic Skills and Access to the General Curriculum

Research suggests that students with disabilities are not faring as well as they could be in the academic content of high school programs or in postsecondary education (U.S. Department of Education, 2006). These students have higher school dropout rates and lower academic achievement than their peers without disabilities. However, the research also suggests that students with mild disabilities, particularly those with learning disabilities, can achieve in academic content beyond their current performance (Friend & Bursuck, 2006). Getzel and Gugerty (2001) propose that high school programs for students with mild disabilities must

Standard 2: Development and Characteristics of Learners

Standard 4: Instructional Strategies

➤ develop teaching strategies based on the unique learning characteristics of each student;

➤ take into account the cultural background of each student and its effect on learning;

➤ determine each student's strongest learning modes (visual, auditory, and/or tactile) and adapt instruction accordingly;

➤ use assistive technology (e.g., laptop computers, personal data managers, pocket-size spellcheckers, etc.) to help students capitalize on their strengths; and

➤ create positive learning environments to enable students to feel motivated and build their self-esteem.

For students with moderate to severe disabilities, the purpose of academic learning may be more functional and compensatory—to teach skills that have immediate and frequent use in the student's environment (Browder, Ahlgrim-Delzell, Courtade-Little, & Snell, 2006). Instruction concentrates on skills needed in the student's daily living routine. For example, safety skills may include reading street signs, railroad crossings, entrance/exit signs, or product labels. Information skills may include reading job application forms, classified ads, maps, telephone directories, or catalogs.

FIGURE 4.4

Promoting Self-Determination in Youth with Disabilities: Tips for Families and Professionals

Promote Choice Making

- Identify strengths, interests, and learning styles.
- Provide choices about clothing, social activities, family events, and methods of learning new information.
- Hold high expectations for youth.
- Teach youth about their disability.
- Involve children and youth in self-determination/self-advocacy; opportunities in school, home and community.
- Prepare children and youth for school meetings.
- Speak directly to children and youth.
- Involve children and youth in educational, medical, and family decisions.
- Allow for mistakes and natural consequences.
- Listen often to children and youth.

Encourage Exploration of Possibilities

- Promote exploration of the world every day.
- Use personal, tactile, visual, and auditory methods for exploration.
- Identify young adult mentors with similar disabilities.
- Talk about future jobs, hobbies, and family lifestyles.
- Develop personal collages/scrap books based on interests and goals.
- Involve children and youth in service learning (4H, Ameri-Corps, local volunteering).

Promote Reasonable Risk Taking

- Make choice maps listing risks, benefits, and consequences of choice.
- Build safety nets through family members, friends, schools, and others.
- Develop skills in problem solving.
- Develop skills in evaluating consequences.

Encourage Problem Solving

- Teach problem solving skills.
- Allow ownership of challenges and problems.
- Accept problems as part of healthy development.
- Hold family meetings to identify problems at home and in the community.
- Hold class meetings to identify problems in school.
- Allow children and youth to develop a list of self-identified consequences.

Promote Self-Advocacy

- Encourage communication and self-representation.
- Praise all efforts of assertiveness and problem solving.
- Develop opportunities at home and in school for self-advocacy.

- Provide opportunities for leadership roles at home and in school.
- Encourage self-advocates to speak in class.
- Teach about appropriate accommodation needs.
- Practice ways to disclose disability and accommodation needs.
- Create opportunities to speak about the disability in school, home, church, business and community.

Facilitate Development of Self-Esteem

- Create a sense of belonging within schools and communities.
- Provide experiences for children and youth to use their talents.
- Provide opportunities to youth for contributing to their families, schools, and communities.
- Provide opportunities for individuality and independence.
- Identify caring adult mentors at home, school, church, or in the community.
- Model a sense of self-esteem and self-confidence.

Develop Goal Setting and Planning

- Teach children and youth family values, priorities, and goals.
- Make posters that reflect values and are age-appropriate.
- Define what a goal is and demonstrate the steps to reach a goal.
- Make a road map to mark the short-term identifiers as they work toward a goal.
- Support children and youth in developing values and goals.
- Discuss family history and culture—make a family tree.
- Be flexible in supporting youth to reach their goals; some days they may need much motivation and help; other days they may want to try alone.

Help Youth Understand Their Disabilities

- Develop a process that is directed by youth for self-identity: Who are you? What do you want? What are your challenges and barriers? What supports do you need?
- Direct children and youth to write an autobiography.
- Talk about the youth's disability.
- Talk about the youth's abilities.
- Involve children and youth in their IEP.
- Use good learning style inventories and transition assessments.
- Identify and utilize support systems for all people.

SOURCE: Self-determination: Supporting successful transition by C. D. Bremer, M. Kachgal, & K. Schoeller, 2003, April, *Research to Practice Brief of the National Center on Secondary Education and Transition*, 2 (1), p. 3.

In many school districts, students with disabilities must meet the same requirements as their peers without disabilities in order to receive a high school diploma. Do you think students with disabilities should be held to the same standard as those who are not disabled?

With an increasing emphasis on academics and increasing access to the general curriculum, there is a growing concern about students with disabilities and the opportunity to earn a high school diploma. Since employers views the high school diploma as a minimum requirement signaling competence, what does this mean for students with disabilities who are unable to meet academic criteria? Many students with disabilities do not receive the same high school diploma as their peers without disabilities. Some states and local school districts have adopted graduation requirements that specify successful completion of a number of credits in order to receive a diploma. Students with disabilities must meet the same requirements as their peers in order to receive a "regular" high school diploma. If a student with a disability fails to meet graduation requirements, he or she may be awarded an "IEP diploma," marking progress toward annual goals, or a certificate of high school completion (or attendance). IEP diplomas and certificates of completion communicate that a student was unable to meet the requirements to obtain a standard diploma.

Other states award students with disabilities the standard high school diploma based on modified criteria that are individually referenced, reflecting the successful completion of IEP goals and objectives as determined by a multidisciplinary team of professionals and the student's parents. For more insight into the controversy surrounding this issue, see the Debate Forum, "Students with Disabilities and the Meaning of a High School Diploma" on page 99.

Teaching Adaptive and Functional Life Skills

Students with disabilities in the secondary school years need access to social activities. Adaptive and functional life skills training may include accessing socialization activities in and outside school and learning to manage one's personal affairs. It may be important to provide basic instruction on how to develop positive interpersonal relationships and the behaviors that are conducive to successfully participating in community settings (McDonnell et al., 2003; Wehman, 2006b). Instruction may include co-teaching among general and special education teachers, as well as the use of peer tutors to both model and teach appropriate social skills in community settings such as restaurants, theaters, or shopping malls. See the Reflect on This, "Tips and Strategies for Co-Teaching at the Secondary Level" on page 100.

Employment Preparation

People with disabilities are often characterized as consumers of society's resources rather than as contributors, but employment goes a long way toward dispelling this idea. Paid employment means earning wages, through which individuals can buy material goods and enhance their quality of life; it also contributes to personal identity and status (Drew & Hardman, 2007).

In the past, high schools have been somewhat passive in their approach to employment training, focusing primarily on teaching vocational readiness through simulations in a classroom setting. More recently, high schools have begun to emphasize employment preparation for students with disabilities through work experience, career education, and community-referenced instruction. In a work experience program, the student spends a portion of the school day in classroom settings (which may emphasize academic and/or vocational skills) and the rest of the day at an off-campus site receiving on-the-job training. The responsibility for

DEBATE FORUM

STUDENTS WITH DISABILITIES AND THE MEANING OF A HIGH SCHOOL DIPLOMA

Should students with disabilities be required to demonstrate the same academic competence as their peers without disabilities in order to receive a high school diploma? Or, if they are unable to meet graduation requirements, should they receive an IEP diploma or certificate of completion?

POINT

The purpose of a high school diploma is to communicate to employers, colleges, and society in general that an individual has acquired a specified set of knowledge and skills that prepares him or her to leave school and enter postsecondary education or the world of work. All students must be held to the same standards, or the diploma will have no meaning as a "signal" of competence and will make no impression on employers or colleges. For those students with disabilities who cannot meet graduation requirements, there is certainly a need to signal what the individual has achieved during high school, even though it is not to the same performance level as those who are awarded the diploma. This can be accomplished through a certificate of completion with modified criteria for graduation. What is most important is not to devalue the high school diploma by lowering the requirements for earning it. Otherwise, employers and colleges will continue to lose faith in public education as a credible system for preparing students for the future.

COUNTERPOINT

Although the move to hold all students to specific requirements (or standards) is to be applauded, it is discriminatory to expect all students to meet the same standards in order to receive a high school diploma. The purpose of a high school diploma is to communicate that the individual has demonstrated a "personal best" while in school, thus acquiring knowledge and a set of skills consistent with his or her ability. I would also support the viewpoint that students with disabilities can achieve at much higher levels than they do now, and expectations should be raised. However, some will never be able to satisfy the graduation requirements now in place in many states and school districts. Students with disabilities who cannot perform at the level mandated in graduation requirements should still be awarded a standard diploma based on their having met requirements consistent with their individual needs and abilities. This is the basis of a free and appropriate public education for students with disabilities. If a standard diploma is not awarded, students with disabilities will be immediately singled out as incompetent and will be at a major disadvantage with employers, regardless of the skills they possess.

---

the training may be shared among the high school special education teacher, vocational rehabilitation counselor, and vocational education teacher.

Career education includes training in social skills development as well as general occupational skills. Career education programs usually concentrate on developing an awareness of various career choices, exploring occupational opportunities, and developing appropriate attitudes, social skills, and work habits.

Whereas career education is oriented to developing an awareness of various occupations, community-referenced instruction involves direct training and ongoing support, as necessary, in a community employment site. The demands of the work setting and the functioning level, interests, and wishes of each individual determine the goals and objectives of the training. The most notable difference between community-referenced instruction and work experience programs is that the former focuses on the activities to be accomplished at the work site rather than on the development of isolated skills in the classroom. An employment training program based on a community-referenced approach includes the following elements:

➤ Primary focus on student and family needs and preferences

➤ A balance between time spent in inclusive general education classrooms and in placement and employment preparation at least until age 18

Council for Exceptional Children

Standard 4: Instructional Strategies

- A curriculum that reflects the job opportunities available in the local community
- An employment training program that takes place at actual job sites
- Training designed to sample the student's performance across a variety of economically viable alternatives
- Ongoing opportunities for students to interact with peers without disabilities in a work setting
- Training that culminates in employment placement
- Job placement linked to comprehensive transition planning, which focuses on establishing interagency agreements that support the student's full participation in the community (Drew & Hardman, 2007; Inge & Moon, 2006)

For more insight into employment preparation during the high school years, see the Case Study, "Maria" on page 101.

REFLECT ON THIS

TIPS AND STRATEGIES FOR CO-TEACHING AT THE SECONDARY LEVEL

PREPARING TO CO-TEACH

ACTIONS	QUESTIONS TO ASK YOURSELF OR OTHERS
Assess the current environment.	What type of collaboration currently exists between general and special education? Has there been any discussion of inclusion, collaboration, or co-teaching? How do teachers react when they hear about students with special needs in general education classes? Are there any who react favorably?
Move in slowly.	What is our joint understanding of co-teaching as a service delivery model? May I teach or co-teach a lesson with you? Are there any areas that you feel less strongly about, in which I might be able to assist?
Involve an administrator.	How is the district addressing the least restrictive environment (LRE) mandate and the inclusive movement? Would our school site be willing to be proactive by including co-teaching? What discipline areas will we target first? How will we ensure that support is provided across all content areas, including electives? Would we be able to count on administrative support, especially with co-planning time and scheduling assistance?
Get to know your partner.	Could we complete a co-teaching checklist to help guide us in discussing our personal and professional preferences? Are there any pet peeves or issues that I should know about prior to our working together? Do we both have the same level of acquaintance with the curriculum and expertise in instructing students with disabilities? How shall we ensure that we both are actively involved and that neither feels over- or underutilized? What feedback structure can we create to assist in our regular communication?
Create a workable schedule.	How often will co-teaching occur (daily, a few times a week, for a specific unit)? What schedule would best meet the needs of the class and of both instructors? How can we ensure that this schedule will be maintained consistently so that both co-teachers can trust it? How will we maintain communication between co-taught sessions?

IF ONE OF YOU IS DOING THIS . . .	THE OTHER CAN BE DOING THIS . . .
Lecturing	Modeling note taking on the board/overhead; ensuring "brain breaks" to help students process lecture information
Taking roll	Collecting and reviewing last night's homework; introducing a social or study skill
Passing out papers	Reviewing directions; modeling the first problem on the assignment
Giving instructions orally	Writing down instructions on board; repeating or clarifying any difficult concept
Checking for understanding with large heterogeneous group of students	Checking for understanding with small heterogeneous group of students
Circulating, providing one-on-one support as needed	Providing direct instruction to the whole class
Prepping half of the class for one side of a debate	Prepping the other half of the class for the opposing side of the debate
Facilitating a silent activity	Circulating, checking for comprehension
Providing large-group instruction	Circulating, using proximity control for behavior management
Running last-minute copies or doing errands	Reviewing homework; providing a study or test-taking strategy
Re-teaching or preteaching with a small group	Monitoring a large group as members work on practice materials
Facilitating sustained silent reading	Reading aloud quietly with a small group; previewing upcoming information
Reading a test aloud to a group of students	Proctoring a test silently with a group of students
Creating basic lesson plans for standards, objectives, and content curriculum	Providing suggestions for modifications, accommodations, and activities for diverse learners
Facilitating stations or groups	Also facilitating stations or groups
Explaining new concept	Conducting role playing or modeling a concept; asking clarifying questions
Considering modification needs	Considering enrichment opportunities

SOURCE: Murawski, W. W., & Dieker, L. A. (2004). Tips and strategies for co-teaching at the secondary level. *Teaching Exceptional Children* 36(5), 54, 56.

CASE STUDY

MARIA

Maria is 19 years old and leaving high school to begin her adult life. For most of her high school years, she was in special education classes for reading and math, because she was about three grade levels behind her peers without disabilities. During the last term of high school, she attended a class on exploring possible careers and finding and keeping a job. The class was required for graduation, but it didn't make much sense to Maria because she had never had any experience with this area before. It just didn't seem to be related to her other schoolwork.

Although Maria wants to get a job in a retail store (such as stocking clothing or shoes), she isn't having much success. She doesn't have a driver's license, and her parents don't have time to run her around to apply for various jobs. The businesses she approached are close by her home and know her

well, but they keep telling her she isn't *qualified* for the jobs available. She has never had any on-the-job training in the community. Maria's parents are not very enthusiastic about her finding employment because they are afraid she might lose some of her government-funded medical benefits.

APPLICATION

1. In retrospect, what transition planning services would you have recommended for Maria during her last years of high school?

2. How would you help Maria now? Do you see the Americans with Disabilities Act playing a role in Maria's story?

3. Whose responsibility is it to work with potential employers to explore "the reasonable accommodations" that would facilitate the opportunity for Maria to succeed in a community job?

The Adult Years

Much of the attention paid to people with disabilities in the past focused on children and youth. More recently, professionals and parents have been addressing the challenges encountered by adults, altering our overall perspective of disability and broadening the views across the disciplines. Would Adolphe's life in the nearby Snapshot have been better if intervention had occurred when he was younger? What can be done *now* to ensure that Adolphe has the supports he needs to actively participate in the life of his community?

When we reach adulthood, we leave home, go to college or get a job, and become more self-reliant. For adults with disabilities, living situations and lifestyles vary greatly. Many people with disabilities lead a somewhat typical existence, living and working in their community, perhaps marrying, and for the most part supporting themselves financially. These adults may still need support, however, as do some people who are not disabled. That support is most often "time-limited" (such as vocational rehabilitation services) or informal (attention from family members and friends). Those with more severe disabilities reach adulthood still in need of a formal support system that facilitates their opportunities for paid employment, housing in the community, and access to recreation and leisure experiences.

The next section examines some of the decisions facing individuals with disabilities and their families during the adult years. This chapter concludes with a discussion of what it takes to build a support network for adults with disabilities.

Self-Determination

Council for Exceptional Children

Standard 1: Foundations

Adult life for people with disabilities and their families is often paradoxical. On the one hand, many parents struggle with their son's or daughter's "right to grow up." On the other hand, some families must deal with his or her continuing need for support, further complicated by the issues surrounding what legally, or even in practical terms, constitutes adult status. Just as there is a great deal of variability in the needs and functioning level of people with disabilities, there is also considerable variability in lifestyle during the adult years. Some adults with mild disabilities go on to college and become self-supporting, eventually working and living inde-

▼SNAPSHOT

ADOLPHE

Adolphe was 31 when he came to what may have been the most startling realization of his life: he was learning disabled! Adolphe was uncertain what this label meant, but at least he now had a term for what had mostly been a difficult life. The label came from a clinical psychologist who had administered a number of tests after Adolphe had been referred by his counselor, whom he had been seeing since his divorce a year ago. The past year had been particularly rough, although most of Adolphe's life had been troublesome.

As a young child, Adolphe was often left out of group activities. He was not very adept at sports, was uncoordinated, and could not catch or hit a baseball no matter how hard he tried. School was worse. Adolphe had a difficult time completing assignments and often forgot instructions. Paying attention in class was difficult, and it often seemed as though there were more interesting activities than the assignments. Adolphe finally gave up on school when he was a junior and took a job in a local service station. That employment did not last long, for he was terminated because of frequent billing errors. The owners said they could not afford to lose so much money because of "stupid mistakes on credit card invoices."

The loss of that job did not bother Adolphe much. An enterprising young man, he had already found employment in the post office, which paid much more and seemed to have greater respectability. Sorting letters presented a problem, however, and loss of that job did trouble Adolphe. He began to doubt his mental ability further and sought comfort in his girlfriend, whom he had met recently at a YMCA dance. They married quickly when she became pregnant, but things did not become easier. After 12 years of marriage, two children, a divorce, and five jobs, Adolphe is finally gaining some understanding of why he has been so challenged throughout his life.

pendently. Just as is true for people without disabilities, however, some of these adults may still need assistance, whether it be government-funded or from family, friends, and neighbors. For adults with more severe disabilities, ongoing formal and natural supports are critical in order to ensure access to and participation in employment, supported residential living, and recreation in their local community. Parents and family members of people with severe disabilities often face the stark reality that their caregiving role may not diminish during the adult years and could well extend through a lifetime. About 526,000 Americans with disabilities are 60 years of age or older, and 60% of these individuals are living at home with their aging parents and/or siblings (Hodapp, Glidden, & Kaiser, 2005).

Whereas most people confront many choices as a natural part of the transition into adult life, the questions facing a person with disabilities and his or her family may be quite different. Issues concerning the competence of the person with a disability to make decisions in his or her best interest, as well as the role of formal and informal support networks to assist in such decision making, may also arise.

Building a Support Network

Adults with disabilities and their families not only must come to terms with making choices relative to planning for the future but also must deal with the maze of options of government-funded programs. Over the past 30 years, adult services have gone through major reform. The system has evolved from a sole focus on protecting, managing, and caring for persons with disabilities in segregated settings to a broader focus on providing what is necessary in order for the person to participate in family and community life. As we move through the 21st century, adult services will continue to adapt to the changing needs and preferences of the person with a disability and his or her network of family and friends. However, as suggested by a recent survey of Americans with disabilities (N.O.D./Harris, 2004), there is still a long way to go.

GOVERNMENT-FUNDED PROGRAMS. Federal and state governments provide funding for several different programs for people with disabilities. These include income support, health care, Medicare, supported residential living, and employment.

Income Support Government **income support** programs, enacted through Social Security legislation (Supplemental Security Income [SSI] and Social Security Disability Insurance [SSDI]), make direct cash payments to people with disabilities, thus providing basic economic assistance. Income support programs have been both praised and criticized. They have been praised because money is made available to people in need who otherwise would have no means to support themselves. They have been criticized because such support programs can make it economically advantageous for people with disabilities to remain unemployed and dependent on society. For many years, individuals who went to work at even 50% of minimum wage could lose income support and medical benefits that far exceeded the amount they would earn on a job. This disincentive to work was significantly reduced with passage of the Work Incentives Improvement Act. Many people with disabilities can now go to work and not worry about losing critical health care coverage.

Health Care Government-sponsored health care for people with disabilities comes under two programs: Medicaid and Medicare. **Medicaid**, established in 1965, pays for health care services for individuals receiving SSI cash payments, as well as for families receiving welfare payments. Medicaid is an example of a federal–state partnership program that requires participating states to provide matching funds to available federal dollars. The state match can be as low as 22% and as high as 50%, depending on state per capita income.

The Medicaid program can pay for inpatient and outpatient hospital services, for laboratory services, and for early screening, diagnosis, treatment, and immunization for children. Working within federal regulations, states design their own plans for the delivery of Medicaid services. Thus, a service provided in one state may not be provided in another.

Medicare is a national insurance program for individuals over the age of 65 and for eligible people with disabilities. Medicare has two parts: hospital insurance and supplementary medical insurance. The Hospital Insurance Program pays for short-term hospitalization, related care in skilled nursing facilities, and some home care. The Supplementary Medical Insurance

FOCUS **5**
Describe government-funded and natural supports for people with disabilities.

➤ **Income support**
A government-sponsored program whereby the individual receives cash payments to support living needs.

Council for Exceptional Children

Standard 1: Foundations

➤ **Medicaid**
A government-sponsored health care program for people with disabilities and others that can pay for inpatient and outpatient hospital services, laboratory services, and early screening, diagnosis, treatment, and immunization for children.

➤ **Medicare**
A government-sponsored national insurance program for people over 65 years of age and eligible people with disabilities. Medicare may pay for hospital and physician-related costs.

Standard 5: Learning Environments and Social Interactions

▶ **Group home**

A supported living arrangement for people with disabilities, in which professionals provide ongoing training and support in a community home setting.

▶ **Semi-independent apartment or home**

Housing for persons with disabilities who require less supervision and support.

▶ **Foster family care**

A supported living arrangement for persons with disabilities, whereby an individual lives in a family setting, learns adaptive skills, and works in a community job.

▶ **Vocational rehabilitation**

A government-sponsored program to help people with disabilities find employment consistent with their needs and abilities.

▶ **Supported employment**

Employment in an integrated setting provided for people with disabilities who need some type of continuing support and for whom competitive employment has traditionally not been possible.

Program covers physician services, outpatient services, ambulance services, some medical supplies, and medical equipment.

Supported Residential Living For most of the 20th century, federal government support for residential living was directed to large congregate care settings (institutions and nursing homes). In the 21st century, however, people with disabilities, their families, and professionals are advocating for smaller community-based residences within local neighborhoods and communities. In the past 20 years, spending for smaller community residences increased sevenfold (Braddock, Hemp, Rizzolo, Parish, & Pomeranz, 2002). People with disabilities and their families are also advocating for choice, individualization, and a focus on the abilities of people, rather than on their disabilities, in making decisions about community living.

Three of the most widely used models for residential living are group homes, semi-independent homes and apartments, and foster family care. **Group homes** may be large (as many as fifteen or more people) or small (four or fewer people). In the group home model, professionals provide ongoing training and support to people with disabilities, aiming to make their daily living experiences as similar as possible to those of people who are not disabled. The **semi-independent apartment or home** provides housing for people with disabilities who require less supervision and support. This model for residential living may include apartment clusters (several apartments located close together), a single co-residence home or apartment in which a staff member shares the dwelling, or a single home or apartment occupied by a person with a disability who may or may not receive assistance from a professional.

Foster family care provides a surrogate family for persons with a disability. The goal of foster care is to integrate individuals with disabilities into a family setting where they will learn adaptive skills and work in the community. Foster family care settings may accommodate up to six adults with disabilities.

Employment Sustained competitive employment for people with disabilities is important for many reasons (such as monetary rewards, adult identity, social contacts, and inclusion in a community setting). Yet the reality is that adults with disabilities are significantly underemployed and unemployed, compared to their peers without (N.O.D./Harris, 2004).

In spite of the disappointing data on the unemployment rates of people with disabilities, there is good reason to be optimistic about their future employment opportunities. A greater emphasis is being placed on employment opportunities for these people than ever before (Braddock et al., 2002; Ryan, 2000; Wagner et al., 2005). Competitive employment can now be described in terms of three alternatives: employment with no support services, employment with time-limited support services, and employment with ongoing support services.

An adult with a disability may be able to locate and maintain employment without support from government-funded programs. Many find jobs through contacts with family and friends, the local job service, want ads, and the like. For people with mild disabilities, the potential for locating and maintaining a job is enhanced greatly if the individual has received employment training and experience during the school years.

An adult with a disability may also have access, on a time-limited, short-term basis, to several employment services, including vocational rehabilitation, vocational education, and on-the-job training. Time-limited employment services provide intensive, short-term support to people with disabilities who have the potential to make it on their own after receiving government assistance. For example, **vocational rehabilitation** provides services to enable people with disabilities, including those with the most severe disabilities, to pursue meaningful careers by securing gainful employment commensurate with their preferences and abilities. Through the vocational rehabilitation program, federal funds pass to the states to provide services in counseling, training, and job placement. Vocational rehabilitation services may also include short-term job training for those who are in a supported employment program.

Supported employment is work in an integrated setting provided for people with disabilities who need some type of continuing support and for whom competitive employment has traditionally not been possible. The criteria for supported employment require that the job provide at least 20 hours of work per week in a real job setting.

Over the past two decades, supported employment has become a viable program for people with disabilities in need of long-term support. In the United States, federal and state funding for supported employment programs increased by 33% from 1996 to 2000. The number of people with disabilities participating in supported employment increased by 22%. The efficacy of supported employment has been documented through a variety of research studies (Braddock et al., 2002; Kregel, 2001; Morgan, Ellerd, Jensen, & Taylor, 2000).

Vocational rehabilitation services include intensive short-term training and support for people with disabilities who are seeking gainful employment. What are some other community employment and support living services available to people with disabilities?

Supported employment consists of four main features: wages, social inclusion with peers who are not disabled, ongoing support provided as necessary by a job coach or through natural supports (co-workers), and application of a zero-exclusion principle. A zero-exclusion principle differs from the more traditional approach of "getting individuals with disabilities ready for work"; instead, it focuses on placing the individual on a job and providing the necessary supports to ensure success. The essential element of a successful supported employment program is establishing a match between the needs and abilities of the individual and the demands of a particular job.

NATURAL SUPPORTS. The importance of natural supports for adults with disabilities (including family, friends, neighbors, and co-workers) cannot be overstated. As is true for all of us, adults with disabilities need a support network that extends beyond government-funded programs. Some adults with disabilities may never move away from their primary family. Parents, and in some cases siblings, assume the major responsibilities of ongoing support for a lifetime (Hodapp et al., 2005). It is estimated that eight out of ten adults with more severe disabilities live with their parents for most of their lives (Braddock et al., 2002). This "perpetual parenthood" results from a son or daughter's continuing dependence through the adult years, either because of a lack of formal resources for the family or because the family simply chooses to care for the individual at home.

Siblings appear to have attitudes similar to those of their parents. Over time, siblings seem to have frequent contact with their brother or sister and are knowledgeable about their lives. In addition, they play a major role in their parents' support network. Interestingly, however, only about 10% of these siblings move in with their brother or sister with a disability at some point during adult life (Drew & Hardman, 2007).

Extended family members (grandparents, aunts, uncles, and so on) often remain important sources of support as well. Extended family members may help with transportation, meals, housecleaning, or just "being there" for the individual. Similar support may also come from friends, neighbors, and co-workers. The nature and type of support provided by individuals outside of the family will be unique to the individuals involved and will depend on a mutual level of comfort in both seeking and providing assistance. Clear communication regarding what friends or neighbors are willing to do, and how that matches the needs and preferences of each individual, is essential.

From the high school transition years through adult life, the issues surrounding quality services and supports for people with disabilities are ever-changing, varied, and complex. With the information in Chapters 1 through 4 as a foundation, we in Chapter 5, move on, to a discussion of multicultural and diversity issues in the education of students with disabilities.

FOCUS 1 What do we know about access to community living and employment for people with disabilities after they leave school?

- The educational opportunities afforded under IDEA have not yet led to full participation of special education graduates in the social and economic mainstream of their local communities.

- However, there has been considerable improvement. The National Longitudinal Study-2 reports that progress has been made in several areas (high school completion, living arrangements, social involvement, further education, and employment rates).

- Adult service systems do not have the resources to meet the needs of students with disabilities following the school years.

- The capabilities of adults with disabilities are often underestimated.

FOCUS 2 What are the requirements for transition planning in IDEA?

- IDEA requires that every student with a disability receive transition services.

- Transition planning is designed to be a results-oriented process focused on improving the academic and functional achievement of the child with a disability to facilitate the child's movement from school to postschool activities.

- Transition services must be based on the individual student's needs, taking into account the student's preferences and interests

- Transition services must include a focus on postsecondary education, vocational education, integrated employment (including supported employment), continuing and adult education, adult services, independent living, and/or community participation.

- IDEA requires that, beginning at age 16 and updated annually, a student's individualized program should include measurable postsecondary goals based on age-appropriate transition assessments related to training, education, employment, and, where appropriate, independent living skills.

- The IEP must include a statement of transition services related to various courses of study (such as participation in advanced placement courses or a vocational education program) that will assist the student in reaching her or his goals.

FOCUS 3 Identify the purpose of person-centered transition planning and the basic steps in its formulation.

- Person-centered transition planning is based on an understanding of and commitment to each student's needs and preferences, and it must be developed and implemented within each student's IEP.

- It is a process that ensures each student's access to the general education curriculum and/or a focus on the adaptive and functional skills that will facilitate life in the community following school. The basic steps in person-centered transition planning include

  - Convening the IEP team organized in terms of the preferences and needs of each student

  - Reviewing assessment data and conducting additional assessment activities.

  - Developing IEPs/transition IEPs

  - Implementing the IEP or transition/IEP

  - Updating the IEP/transition IEP annually and implementing follow-up procedures

  - Holding an exit meeting

FOCUS 4 Why is it important for students with disabilities to receive instruction in self-determination, academics, adaptive and functional life skills, and employment preparation during the secondary school years?

- Self-determination skills help students to solve problems, consider options, and make appropriate choices as they make the transition into adult life.

- Academic skills are essential in meeting high school graduation requirements and preparing students with disabilities for college. A functional academic program helps students learn applied skills in daily living, leisure activities, and employment preparation.

- Adaptive and functional life skills help students learn how to socialize with others, maintain personal appearance, and make choices about how to spend free time.

- Employment preparation during high school increases the probability of success on the job during the adult years and places the person with a disability in the role of a contributor to society.

FOCUS 5 Describe government-funded and natural supports for people with disabilities.

- Income support programs are direct cash payments to people with disabilities, providing basic economic assistance.

- Medicaid and Medicare are government-supported health care programs. The Medicaid program can pay for inpatient and outpatient hospital services, laboratory services, and early screening, diagnosis, treatment, and immunization for children. Medicare is a national insurance program with two parts: hospital insurance and supplementary medical insurance.

- Residential services indicate a trend toward smaller, community-based residences located within local neighborhoods and communities. These residences may include group homes, semi-independent homes and apartments, or foster family care. The purpose of residential services is to provide persons with disabilities a variety of options for living in the community.

- There are essentially three approaches to competitive employment for people with disabilities: employment with no support services, employment with time-limited support services, and employment with ongoing support services. The purpose of all three approaches is to help people with disabilities get a job and maintain it over time.

- Natural supports include family, friends, neighbors, and co-workers.

BUILDING YOUR PORTFOLIO

If you are thinking about a career in special education, you should know that many states use national standards developed by the Council for Exceptional Children (CEC) to assess a teacher candidate's knowledge and skills for working with students with disabilities. See a complete listing of the ten CEC Content Standards on the inside front cover of this text.

CEC Content Standards Addressed in This Chapter

1 Foundations

2 Development and Characteristics of Learners

3 Individual Learning Differences

4 Instructional Strategies

5 Learning Environments and Social Interactions

7 Instructional Planning

9 Professional and Ethical Practice

Assess Your Knowledge of the CEC Standards Addressed in This Chapter

Some states require that teacher candidates develop a portfolio of products that demonstrate mastery of the CEC content standards. To assist in the development of products for this portfolio, you may wish to complete the following activities.

- Complete a written test of the chapter's content.

  If your instructor requires a written test of your content knowledge for this chapter, keep a copy for your portfolio. A practice test on the information covered in this chapter is available through the Human Exceptionality Companion Website and the Student Study Guide.

- Respond to the Application Questions for the Case Study "Maria."

  Review the Case Study and respond in writing to the application questions. Keep a copy of the Case Study and of your written response for your portfolio.

- Participate in a Community Service Learning Activity.

  Community service is a valuable way to enhance your learning experience. Visit our companion website for suggested community service learning activities that correspond to the information presented in this chapter. Develop a reflective journal of the service learning experience for your portfolio.

WEB RESOURCES

National Center on Secondary Education and Transition

http://www.ncset.org

The National Center on Secondary Education and Transition (NCSET) at the University of Minnesota coordinates national resources, offers technical assistance, and disseminates information related to secondary education and transition for youth with disabilities, in order to create opportunities for them to achieve successful futures. This website contains information on transition issues, publications, other links, and state resources.

Transition Research Institute at the University of Illinois at Urbana-Champaign

http://www.ed.uiuc.edu/SPED/tri/institute.html

The Transition Research Institute at the University of Illinois at Urbana-Champaign (TRI) identifies effective practices, conducts intervention and evaluation research, and provides technical assistance activities that promote the successful transition of youth with disabilities from school to adult life. This website contains resources (such as recent publications, videos, and curricula) for teachers, service providers, and researchers on transition.

APSE, The Network on Employment

http://www.apse.org

APSE, formally the Association for Persons in Supported Employment, provides information on improving and expanding integrated employment opportunities, services, and outcomes for persons with disabilities. This website provides information on supported employment resources and education for professionals, consumers, family members, and employers.

FURTHER READINGS

Wehman, P. (Ed.) (2006). *Life beyond the classroom: Transition Strategies for Young People with Disabilities* (4th ed.). Baltimore: Paul H. Brookes.

This book provides comprehensive coverage of transition issues, including defining and planning transition, facilitation and support of transition, and ways of customizing transition service delivery to people with specific types of disabilities. Information is also provided on person-centered planning and consumer choice, control, and satisfaction, as well as on independent living, mobility, and assistive technology.

Steere, D. E., Rose, E., & Cavaiuolo, D. (2007). *Growing Up: Transition to Adult Life for Students with Disabilities.* Boston: Allyn and Bacon.

This book provides a comprehensive overview of the development of transition services for students with disabilities who are exiting the education system. Chapter discussions include specific aspects of the transition process and the central role that students with disabilities and their families play in ensuring an effective planning system. Case studies are used to illustrate effective practices.

Brinckerhoff, L. C., McGuire, J. M., & Shaw, S. F. (2001). *Transition to Postsecondary Education: Strategies for Students with Learning Disabilities* (2nd ed.). Austin, TX: ProEd.

This book provides in-depth information on planning the transition from high school to college; determining eligibility for services and testing accommodations; policy development; accommodation provisions; service delivery options for college students with learning disabilities and attention-deficit/hyperactivity disorder (ADHD); advances in assistive technology; and approaches to professional development and program evaluation.

COMPANION WEBSITE

Visit the companion website at college.hmco.com/pic/hardman9e for additional resources that support this text:

- HM Video Cases that present actual classroom scenarios that you may face every day as a teacher

- Practice ACE Exams that will help you prepare for quizzes, tests, and certfication exams

- Flashcards of key terms

- Weblinks

5

Multicultural and Diversity Issues

TO BEGIN WITH . . .

MINORITY CHILDREN OVERREPRESENTED IN DISABILITIES

Children from minority backgrounds are found more frequently in disability categories than would be expected on the basis of population makeup. This high rate of identification often involves assessment using psychological and educational testing, which suggests that the assessment and uses of test information may include serious cultural and racial bias. (Erevelles, Kanga, & Middleton, 2006; Ferri & Connor, 2005; Spinelli, 2006)

POVERTY RELATED TO MULTIPLE PROBLEMS IN SOME MINORITY GROUPS

Poverty is often associated with poor health care and a lifetime of increased risk, can be detrimental to a child's development, and is seen by some researchers as a threat to academic performance. Poverty occurs more often in cultural and ethnic minorities than in those from the cultural majority. Nearly three times as many African Americans and Hispanics as non-Hispanic whites live in poverty. (Bratter & Eschbach, 2005; Durant, 2004; U.S. Bureau of the Census, 2000)

EARLY LEARNING MAY ACCOUNT FOR SOME CULTURAL DIFFERENCES

Learning during the early years plays a vitally important role in later behavior. The content of what is learned during this period may produce sociocultural differences that set minority youngsters apart from their peers in the cultural majority. (Fiese, Eckert, & Spagnola, 2006; Rueda & Yaden, 2006)

MULTICULTURAL EDUCATION AIMED AT ALL STUDENTS

Multicultural education is intended to teach all students about different cultures. It teaches all students about cultural diversity, shows them how to function in a multicultural society, and has the goal of enhancing equity for marginalized groups of children. (Banks & Banks, 2006; Gollnick & Chinn, 2006)

1 Identify three ways in which the purposes of and approaches to general education in the United States sometimes differ from the purposes of and approaches to special education and multicultural education.

2 Describe population trends among culturally diverse groups in the United States. How do these changes affect the educational system?

3 Identify two ways in which assessment may contribute to the overrepresentation of culturally diverse students in special education programs.

4 Identify three ways in which language diversity may contribute to assessment difficulties with students who are from a variety of cultures.

5 Cite three ways in which differing sociocultural customs may affect the manner in which parents become involved in the educational process.

6 Indicate two areas that require particular attention in the development of an individualized education plan (IEP) for a student from a culturally diverse background.

7 Identify two considerations that represent particular difficulties in serving children from culturally diverse backgrounds in the least restrictive environment.

8 Identify two ways in which poverty may contribute to the academic difficulties of children from culturally diverse backgrounds, often resulting in their referral to special education.

9 Identify two ways in which migrancy among culturally diverse populations may contribute to academic difficulties.

10 Cite three conceptual factors that have contributed to heightened attention and concern regarding the placement of children from ethnic and cultural groups in special education.

▼ SNAPSHOT

MARY

Mary had come to the United States as a baby. She remembered little about the process. Her mother came across the border with her brother, wading through a river and crossing the desert while carrying Mary. When they reached Phoenix there was little to welcome them except the heat, even though it was the middle of the night.

When Mary began to talk, she spoke mostly Spanish with smatterings of English that she heard from other children. As she started school, her language was still mostly Spanish. She heard her mother speak Spanish, she watched Spanish television programs, and there were few printed materials in her house at all. She still could not identify letters or numbers and could not read words, and she identified signs on the street largely by their shape.

Mary started going to school because the other children around her did and also because her mother had to work during part of the day. Mary's first teacher found her unable to read in either Spanish or English, although she communicated with her friends in a combination of both languages. Mary was sent to be tested, and her low scores resulted in her being placed in another classroom where the teacher spent a lot of time teaching her new words in English.

Mary's progress was slow at first, but as her ability to identify words increased, she began to read the English in the books at school. Mary had a slow start, but her ability to speak English improved. Her communication with classmates continued to be a blend of Spanish and English, and her interactions with her mother at home were conducted mostly in Spanish. At school she was moved back to a general classroom curriculum, and she became increasingly adept at compartmentalizing life at school from life at home. Conversations with her mother were limited to things they both knew, which tended to involve fixing meals and other home-related topics. She didn't talk about school, and her mom didn't ask.

RAPHAEL

Ten-year-old Raphael lives with his adoptive parents. He is proud of his deafness—he accepts it and is comfortable with it. His mother is very conscientious about using sign language whenever Raphael is in the room, even if she is speaking to someone else. "If Raphael is watching, then I will sign. He deserves it."

Raphael does very well integrating with his hearing peers at recess. There are a group of guys—little boys—10 or 11 years old who are always coming around, "Can Raphael come out? Can Raphael do this? . . . Just ask him if he'll play with me." A lot of them are picking up the basic signs. So there's a lot of interaction going on.

"He's one of the most popular kids in the neighborhood, and he can play with anybody. He knows how to get his point of view across to the others, and the others—they make up their own little signs that are not really sign language or anything, but they know what they're talking about. When we first moved to this neighborhood, the responses we got from our neighbors, that we have a deaf kid is, 'Wow. That's neat,' and then they'd kind of go, 'All right, now let's hold back.' But when he goes out there, they see that he can play basketball with any kid in his neighborhood, that he can play street hockey, he can rollerblade, he can ride bikes, and he's not a problem to anybody. In fact, he's the most popular kid in the neighborhood.

"I see Raphael's future as . . . I'm really not sure yet. He's really getting involved in his computers at school. And I'd like to see him continue that way. His working with computers has made a whole new person out of him."

DANIEL

Daniel is an 8-year-old second-grader. He and his family arrived in the United States from Mexico two years ago. Daniel has a 14-year-old brother, Julian, who is in middle school. Julian fills a role that is common for children in recently immigrated families, serving as the family's link to the English-speaking world through his ability to translate. Three additional siblings born between Daniel and his brother are still in Mexico. The family's support system includes the father's brothers and their wives, all recent immigrants from Mexico. Daniel's father is a construction worker, and his mother is a housewife.

"Daniel's academic performance has been average. He has consistently submitted required assignments, he has perfect attendance, and his interactions with teachers and peers have been good. Recently, Daniel's academic performance has declined, and he has become withdrawn. His teacher, Mrs. Strickland, noted that Daniel has failed several tests, that he has not had his parents sign the required school folder (which includes the tests he failed), and that he has not had his parents sign permission slips needed for planned field trips. As a result, Daniel has lost recess privileges, has had to eat by himself at lunch time, and has not been allowed to participate in two field trips. (Although he had earned the right to participate in the field trips, the fact that he did not have written parental permission prevented him from doing so.)

"Mrs. Strickland wrote the parents a note on Daniel's folder, explaining that they needed to sign his folder and that Daniel needed to study for his tests. She also telephoned Daniel's home and talked to 'someone' there about the situation who said, 'OK.' Mrs. Strickland had become extremely frustrated because there had been no change. Every morning, she reprimanded Daniel for not bringing the required signed folder and demanded an explanation. Daniel did not respond."[1]

[1]SOURCE: Excerpted from "Counseling Hispanic Children and Youth," by J. T. Zapata. In *Counseling for Diversity*, edited by C. C. Lee, 1995, pp. 103–104. Boston: Allyn & Bacon. Copyright © 1995. Reprinted by permission.

Mary's situation presents a significant challenge for the education system and raises a number of questions. Should someone in the school system have been fighting to keep Mary from being labeled? Or was her testing satisfactory even though it was probably suspected that she had disabilities? She received specialized help, and it appears that she learned English to a level that made academic progress possible despite her slow start. Should she have been considered as having disabilities because of her academic difficulties? Mary managed to separate her home life from school, but will that successfully continue or will her slow start put her continually behind her peers? In this chapter, we will examine many complicated issues related to cultural and ethnic diversity and their impact on public education.

A goal of many educators is to promote an understanding of the world's diverse cultures.

Our complex culture reflects an enormous array of needs because a wide variety of individuals take part in our society. Meeting those needs tests seriously the capacities of service organizations such as the education system and of many other private and governmental agencies. Because so many groups require special attention, advocacy groups have emerged to champion certain causes. In some of these cases, a particular group's educational needs have not been adequately met by school systems that are structured to serve the majority.

Multicultural education arose from a belief that the needs of certain children—children whose cultural backgrounds differ from those of the majority—were not being appropriately met. Broad societal unrest related to racial discrimination fueled and augmented this belief. Similarly, **special education** evolved from the failure of general education to meet the needs of youngsters who were not learning as rapidly or in the same way as their peers. Reformers believed that two particular groups of students were being mistreated—in one case, because of their cultural or racial background, and in the other, because of their disabilities.

To explore multiculturalism and diversity, we will first discuss the basic purpose of general education and the conventional approaches used to achieve this purpose. We will also compare the underlying purposes and approaches of special education and multicultural education and discuss the connections between the two. After building this foundation, we will examine multicultural and diversity issues in the context of this book's focus: human exceptionality in society, school, and family. This process will highlight an interesting twist on one of the major themes of the book: collaboration among general and special educators. In the context of multicultural and diversity issues, this notion of collaboration becomes more complex, as we shall see. Professionals and advocates in multicultural education face a troubling reality: Not all children from multicultural backgrounds need special education, but specialized instruction and services may fill important needs for many of them.

➤ **Multicultural education**
Education that promotes learning about multiple cultures and their values.

➤ **Special education**
As defined in IDEA, specially designed instruction provided to students with disabilities in all settings, including the workplace and training centers.

Purposes of and Approaches to Education

The fundamental purpose of education in the United States is to produce literate citizens. According to this perspective, education is presumably intended for everyone; all children should have access to public education through the level of high school. In general terms, this goal is implemented by grouping and teaching students according to chronological age and evaluating their performance on the basis of what society expects children of each age to achieve. Society uses what youngsters of each age typically can learn as its yardstick for assessing their progress. Thus American education is aimed at the masses, and performance is judged in terms of an average. Through this system, schools attempt to bring most students to a similar, or at least a minimal, level of knowledge.

FOCUS **1**

Identify three ways in which the purposes of and approaches to general education in the United States sometimes differ from the purposes of and approaches to special education and multicultural education.

Cultural Pluralism and the Role of Education

Understanding diverse cultures and the impact of collective culture on individuals is an ongoing challenge for research in social science (Deaux, Reid, & Martin, 2006; Oyserman, Coon, & Kemmelmeier, 2002; Quezada & Osajima, 2005). Multicultural education values and promotes **cultural pluralism**. It teaches all students about cultural diversity and how to function in a multicultural society and thus is not aimed only at students of cultural or racial minorities (Mirel, 2002; Ornstein & Moses, 2005). Gollnick and Chinn (2006), asserting that multicultural education is a concept that addresses cultural diversity, cited six beliefs and assumptions on which it is based:

1. Cultural differences have strength and value.
2. Schools should be models for the expression of human rights and respect for cultural differences.
3. Social justice and equality for all people should be of paramount importance in the design and delivery of curricula.
4. Attitudes and values necessary for the continuation of a democratic society can be promoted in schools.
5. Schooling can provide the knowledge, skills, and dispositions—[and the] values, attitudes, and commitments—to help students from diverse groups learn.
6. Educators working with families and communities can create an environment that is supportive of multiculturalism. (p. 7)

Rather than seeking to homogenize the population, current multicultural education promotes the notion that schools should encourage students to gain information about multiple cultures and to attain competence in understanding both those present in our society and those existing throughout the world. This perspective opposes the once-prevalent view that schools should minimize cultural differences (Baldwin, Faulkner, & Hecht, 2006).

Multicultural education is intended to teach all students about different cultures. Yet despite some progress, we still largely lack an awareness of how members of different cultural groups have contributed to major developments in our country's history. To illustrate, the 1990s PBS series on the Civil War, produced by Kenneth Burns, highlighted significant roles played by African Americans—a contribution that many of us did not learn about in school. Also, during World War II, Native Americans known as "Code Talkers" served in critical communications roles by transmitting messages in their native language, which could not be decoded by Axis forces. And despite the degrading abuse inflicted on them from many sources, Japanese Americans volunteered for critical assignments and served the United States with distinction during World War II. Such stories need to be told.

Young people develop many of their enduring attitudes and a significant knowledge base at school. Their thoughts and feelings about diverse cultures are at least partially shaped by what they learn in the classroom. Incomplete information and stereotypical presentations about different cultures detract from students' understanding of the variety of people that characterizes our world (e.g., Arredondo & Perez, 2006; Cohen & Steele, 2002; Vasquez, Lott, & Garcia-Vazquez, 2006). Careless treatment of this important topic perpetuates two problems: a lack of factual information about numerous cultures and a lack of skill in relating to those of different backgrounds. A complete education must include recognition of the roles of many peoples in shaping our country and our world and must foster respect and appreciation.

There are some very important differences between the fundamental purposes of general education, special education, and multicultural education. Indeed, the primary purpose of general education runs counter to those of the other two. Aimed at serving the masses, general education attempts to achieve a leveling effect by bringing everyone to more or less the same level of understanding, teaching similar topics in groups, and evaluating achievement on the basis of a norm, or average. Special education, in contrast, tends to focus on the individual. Special education professionals would agree that the basic purpose of special education is to provide an opportunity for each child with a disability to learn and develop to his or her individual potential. Current special education efforts focus on individual needs, strengths, and preferences. This individualized approach is important because many students in special education seem unable to learn well through instruction that is broadly directed at large groups.

> ➤ **Cultural pluralism**
> Multiple cultural subgroups living together in a manner that preserves group differences, thereby maintaining each group's cultural or ethnic traditions.

Thus special education tends to emphasize individuals and specific skill levels. Evaluation is based, at least in part, on individual attainment of a specified mastery level, not entirely on comparison with **norm-based averages** (that is, the average performance scores of peers).

At a certain level, the overarching goal of multicultural education is also somewhat at odds with general education's goal of achieving consistency (bringing the population to a comparable level of performance in similar areas of knowledge). Further, general education largely reflects a societal self-portrait of the United States as a "melting pot" for peoples of all backgrounds, emphasizing similarities and downplaying differences. Contemporary multicultural education, on the other hand, sees the school as a powerful tool for appreciating and promoting diversity.

The differences among the goals and approaches of general, special, and multicultural education can create considerable difficulty within school systems and can generate disagreements among educators. As one faction (multicultural education) attempts to make inroads into the broader domain of another (general education), an adversarial or competitive situation may result. Yet such misunderstandings can be diminished through thoughtful discussion and examination of the issues.

➤ **Norm-based averages**
Comparison of a person's performance with the average performance scores of age-mates.

Multiculturalism/Diversity and Special Education

Connections between multicultural education and special education have not always been comfortable. They have often involved issues of racial discrimination and inappropriate educational programming. For example, one uneasy interface between multicultural and special education involves special education's role of serving children who are failing in the general education system. Unfortunately, a disproportionately large number of students placed in special education are from minority backgrounds (Ferri & Connor, 2005; Green, McIntosh, & Cook-Morales, 2005). This issue continues to surface (Erevelles et al., 2006; Skiba, Poloni-Staudinger, & Simmons, 2005; Spinelli, 2006), fueling suspicion that special education has been used as a tool of discrimination or as a means of separating racial and ethnic minorities from the majority. Still, certain instructional approaches common to both special and multicultural education can meet a student's academic needs.

Our discussion of special and multicultural education will focus on the prevalence of culturally diverse students in special education, along with four major elements of the Individuals with Disabilities Education Act (IDEA, presented in Chapter 1): nondiscriminatory and multidisciplinary assessment, parental involvement in developing each child's educational program, a free and appropriate public education delivered through an individualized education plan (IEP), and education in the least restrictive environment.

FOCUS **2**

Describe population trends among culturally diverse groups in the United States. How do these changes affect the educational system?

Prevalence and Overrepresentation of Culturally Diverse Students in Special Education

The term *prevalence* generally refers to the number of people in a given population who exhibit a condition, problem, or particular status (those who have a hearing loss, for example, or who have red hair). In general terms, a phenomenon's prevalence is determined by counting how often it occurs. In this section, we will examine prevalence in a somewhat different sense, discussing certain factors relevant to the relationship between human exceptionality and multicultural issues, and we will examine the proportion of students from culturally diverse backgrounds in special education.

There are several factors associated with students at risk for academic failure. They include diverse cultural background, limited background in speaking English, and poverty. It is important to emphasize that these factors indicate only risk for difficulties in school; they do not necessarily destine a student for a special education placement. Yet a disproportionate number of special education students are from nonmainstream cultural backgrounds (Green, et al., 2005; Skiba et al., 2005). The overrepresentation of students of color in groups labeled as having disabilities is cause

Some culturally diverse students may be inappropriately placed into special education classes, resulting in overrepresentation.

for concern. African American children, for instance, appear more frequently than expected (on the basis of their numbers) in classes for students with serious emotional disturbance and intellectual disabilities, and Latinos also represent a large and rapidly growing group in special education (Drew & Hardman, 2007). At the other end of the spectrum, disproportionately few ethnic minority students are found in academically rigorous and gifted programs (Gollnick & Chinn, 2006). The Case Study "Overrepresentation, Finances, and School Reform" illustrates a tangled web of issues, pertaining to school funding, assessment, and misdiagnosis/discrimination, that contribute to the overrepresentation of nonmainstream students in special education.

These are issues concerning school placement and assessments that are heavily influenced by the academic context (Erevelles et al., 2006; Spinelli, 2006). Some contend that in these circumstances, social factors play a significant role in shaping definitions, diagnoses, and resulting intervention or treatment (Green et al., 2005; Rueda & Yaden, 2006). Practically speaking, this means that the mainstream culture largely determines the definitions, diagnoses, and treatments that result in more nonmainstream children than expected being identified as needing specialized education. Even so, however, the evidence is mixed. Some results indicate that people of color and some other ethnicities are equally represented or are underrepresented compared to their Caucasian counterparts, in disability categories such as mood and anxiety disorders (Cuffe, McKeown, Addy, & Garrison, 2005; Ferrell, Beidel, & Turner, 2004).

Furthermore, cultural minority students do not complete school in the same proportions as their peers from the cultural majority. School dropout figures are about 13% for African American youngsters and between 28.6% and 38.2% for Latinos, (Anderson, 2004; Banks & Banks, 2006; Taylor, 2005). This compares with just over 7% for whites in the same age range. Dropout rates also correlate closely with family school history and vary across income groups (Banks & Banks, 2006; Martinez, DeGarmo, & Eddy, 2004; Jozefowicz, 2003). In an outcome related to these circumstances, Caucasian children from more privileged neighborhoods tend to have higher educational and occupational expectations than their minority counterparts (Buckner, Bassuk, & Weinreb, 2002; Charles, Dinwiddie, & Massey, 2004). Accordingly, some researchers see poverty as a threat to academic performance (Durant, 2004; McGee, 2004). However, poverty does not exert a simple, singular influence; rather, it is accompanied by a complex set of other influences, including detrimental physical elements of the environment (such as limited or substandard health care and increased risks related to health and development), the children's assessment of their own abilities, teachers' judgments of the children's performance, and other environmental influences (Farmer et al., 2004). Impoverished environmental effects surface as topics of serious concern in most discussions of educational problems, related reforms, and early intervention efforts. Research evidence does indicate that thoughtfully developed early intervention programs have beneficial effects on poor children's academic performance, cognitive development, and general health (Halfon & McLearn, 2002; Li, 2003; McGee, 2004). Family assistance generally has very positive outcomes; examples include home visitation programs, nutrition assistance and guidance, and the availability of family health care and guidance in accessing it (Zigler, Finn-Stevenson, & Hall, 2002).

Several culturally or ethnically diverse populations are growing rapidly because of increasing birthrates and immigration levels. For example, African Americans represented approximately 13% of the total population in the United States in 2002, a modest increase from 2000 but one that follows many years of growth (McKinnon, 2001; McKinnon, 2003). Figure 5.1 graphically portrays the U.S. population by ethnic background, with growth projections through 2050. The increase of culturally and ethnically diverse groups will have a profound impact on education, presenting diverse needs that demand a broad spectrum of additional educational services.

Council for Exceptional Children

Standard 2: Development and Characteristics of Learners

CASE STUDY

OVERREPRESENTATION, FINANCES, AND SCHOOL REFORM

An associate dean of education, who happens to be African American, was labeled as having intellectual disabilities and placed in special education for a significant portion of his school life. This is just one example of egregious misdiagnosis and possible discrimination in special education placement. Although IDEA is aimed at integrating youngsters with disabilities into the educational mainstream and guarding against ethnic discrimination, overrepresentation still occurs at the beginning of the 21st century. In fact, a 1993 report prepared by *U.S. News & World Report* suggests that placement of minority students in special education programs continues to be far higher than what would be expected on the basis of population demographics (Separate and Unequal, 1993). This report indicates that African American students are overrepresented in special education in nearly 80% of the states. This information is based on Department of Education survey data provided by the states themselves.

Disproportionately high representation of students of color in special education has been a continuing concern, as indicated throughout this chapter. Concerns regarding misdiagnosis (which occurred in the case of the associate dean) and discriminatory practices have always surfaced in examinations of this problem; sociocultural issues are raised, as well as the personal implications for individual children and their families. Other matters that also seem notable are related to serious and broad-based school reform.

Cost factors, for example, cannot be overlooked. The national price tag for special education services has risen 30-fold, to over $30 billion, since 1977. And there is considerable inducement for school districts to expand special education (even in separate rather than integrated programs). First, districts often receive more funding for special education students than for those not so identified. Texas, for example, pays local districts 10 times the normal per-student rate for teaching a youngster in a special education class (the national average is 3 times the normal per-student rate). Second, many states exclude special education scores in the statistical analysis of statewide competency exams. Consequently, their average scores are higher, and these districts receive more favorable publicity and have more supportive boards of education. Such circumstances may translate into a better budget once again, to say nothing of enhancing the reputation of the administrator.

This, then, is a multihorned dilemma. An administrator can increase his or her budget and enhance the prestige of a district by channeling low-achieving students into special education. Such pragmatism, however, runs counter to the fundamental concepts of IDEA and contributes to overrepresentation of minorities in special education. In addition to these serious moral issues, litigation has become an increasing significant alternative for remedying educational problems. Lawsuits can be very disruptive to the operation of a school district, as well as to an administrator's personal life. Of five district administrators at a meeting in August 1994 (a meeting unrelated to any administrative problems), the one with the fewest crises had "only one half-million-dollar lawsuit pending."

APPLICATION

1. How can we balance the various facets of cultural diversity, integrated special services to students with disabilities, and a large public educational system within the context of our general society?

2. How should school finances and other incentives be coordinated with public policy and federal and state legislation?

    Some vocal critics claim that the educational system should be discarded and a new approach developed "from scratch." However, there is no clear evidence that financial savings would result or that reforming our existing system would not be an equally effective alternative.

3. What would you do as an administrator? Does there need to be a new or restructured and expanded infrastructure within the public school system to improve service delivery? How would this be organized and what elements should be included from the ground up? What would the cost structure look like and where would the money come from? Would it require new revenue sources or reconfigured deployment of existing revenue sources?

4. If you redesigned the delivery system in Question 3, how would you measure outcomes?

5. What would you suggest as the parent of a minority child?

Language differences also often contribute to academic difficulties for students from diverse backgrounds who are educated in a system designed by the cultural majority (Chiappe, Siegel, & Gottardo, 2002; Drew & Hardman, 2007; Vaughn et al., 2006). Census data indicate that over 21 million people 5 years of age or older speak English less than "very well" (U.S. Bureau of the Census, 2000). This represents nearly 18 percent of the total population in this age range and has an enormous impact on schools in general. Particular challenges arise when youngsters have a disability and also have limited English skills.

Council for Exceptional Children

Standard 3: Individual Learning Differences

FIGURE 5.1

Percentage of Population by Race and Hispanic Origin: 1990 to 2050

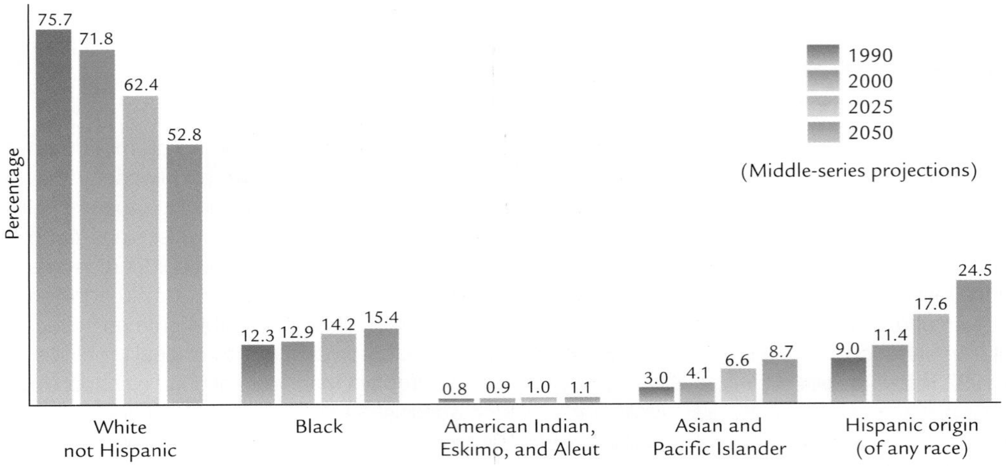

Legend:
- 1990
- 2000
- 2025
- 2050

(Middle-series projections)

White not Hispanic: 75.7, 71.8, 62.4, 52.8
Black: 12.3, 12.9, 14.2, 15.4
American Indian, Eskimo, and Aleut: 0.8, 0.9, 1.0, 1.1
Asian and Pacific Islander: 3.0, 4.1, 6.6, 8.7
Hispanic origin (of any race): 9.0, 11.4, 17.6, 24.5

SOURCE: From *"National Population Projections,"* by G. Spencer and F. W. Hollman. In *Population Profile of the United States: 1997,* 1998, pp. 8–9, U. S. Bureau of the Census, Current Population Reports, Series P23-194. Washington, DC U.S. Government Printing Office.

People with different language backgrounds constitute a rapidly growing sector of the U.S. population. This has had a major impact on school systems; the number of youngsters speaking languages other than English has significantly increased recently (Barnum-Martin et al., 2006; Choi & Harachi, 2002; Wiese, 2006). Growth in the diverse languages spoken places a heavy demand on U.S. school systems to provide linguistically appropriate instruction and to exercise vigilance and caution in assessment (Hambleton, Merenda, & Spielberger, 2006; Harrington & Brisk, 2006). And this trend continues. The number of students with limited English proficiency (LEP) is expected to grow more rapidly than the numbers of other groups of students (e.g., Barrera, 2006; de Valenzuela & Baca, 2004; Solarsh & Alant, 2006).

Such figures only broadly reflect students who are either bilingual or linguistically diverse. Certainly, many come from backgrounds that enable them to achieve academically in a school system based primarily on the English language. Not all students accounted for here will need special supports or programs. However, some require a substantial amount of supplementary assistance, even if they are not best placed in what we have traditionally conceived of as special education. Students with different language backgrounds will have varying levels of skill with the language being used for instruction, ranging from literally no understanding to the student who not only can communicate but also can succeed academically in the language being used for teaching. This alters the overall school landscape enormously, because extraordinary instructional effort is necessary for students with limited English proficiency, as well as for those who need more intense focus because of disabilities. The broad range of educational curricula requires reevaluation if we are to provide optimal learning opportunities (Baca & Baca, 2004; Edelsky, 2006; Vaughn et al., 2006).

Broadly analyzing and re-conceptualizing educational curriculum as suggested above requires significant effort (Wiese, 2006). Estimates and actual census data are always subject to error. However, analyses thus far suggest that such error is relatively small and that, if anything, these data are likely to underestimate the problem somewhat. The importance of linguistically appropriate instruction is magnified considerably when we consider other multicultural factors, such as the need for a careful examination of educational goals and the methods of achieving them (Barrera, 2006; Heredia & Altarriba, 2002; Rueda & Yaden, 2006). However, these issues become politicized and complex as legislators enact laws that dictate matters of language (see the Debate Forum, "English-Only or Bilingual Education?").

Declaring English the official or national language of the United States has had some support by lawmakers at several levels during the past few years, as recently as 2006. Initiatives to promote such legislation at the state level are fluid and politically volatile. The same is true nationally, with legislators passing such legislation and at the same time arguing about whether it has racist overtones (Montgomery, 2006). Yet English is not the primary language for many Americans. Students from culturally diverse backgrounds represent a very large proportion of the school enrollment across the country. Even when they are not maneuvering for political position, critics claim that bilingual education places an unacceptable burden on the educational system, compromising its ability to provide specialized educational services to meet students' needs. There is a significant cost to the daily or weekly instructional schedule that may already be available from kindergarten through the twelfth grade in many districts. Added to this are the various components of different integration models that are needed to meet individual student needs (Collier, 2004).

POINT

Children from different cultures must have certain skills to survive in the world of the cultural majority. For their own good, they should be taught in English and taught the knowledge base of the cultural majority. This knowledge will prepare them for success and will more efficiently utilize the limited funds available, because specialized culturally sensitive services will not be required.

COUNTERPOINT

Children from cultures different from that of the majority must have an equal opportunity to learn in the most effective manner possible. This may mean teaching them in their native language, at least some of the time. To do otherwise is a waste of talent and doesn't prepare them to become maximally productive tax-paying citizens (thereby helping to pay the costs incurred for their education). To force students who are culturally diverse to use English is also an example of discrimination by the cultural majority.

Multidisciplinary Collaboration in Meeting the Needs of Culturally and Linguistically Diverse (CLD) Students

Multidisciplinary collaboration is essential to nearly every area of educational service delivery for those with disabilities. Such collaboration is crucial to addressing the needs of culturally and linguistically diverse (CLD) students because such a range of expertise is required among stakeholders (Dettmer, Thurston, & Dyck, 2005; Friend & Cook, 2007). Cultural, ethnic, and linguistic diversity presents special challenges necessitating multidisciplinary collaboration in areas of assessment, language diversity, and professional preparation.

Collaborating on Nondiscriminatory Assessment

The history of assessment for children of diverse cultures raises serious issues of accuracy, fairness, and our ability to provide appropriate services to children. Perhaps nowhere is the interface between special and multicultural education more prominent than in issues of **nondiscriminatory assessment**. As noted earlier, disproportionate numbers of minority students are found in special education classes (Ferri & Connor, 2005; Green, McIntosh, & Cook-Morales, 2005). Decisions regarding referral and placement in these classes are based on

> ➤ **Nondiscriminatory assessment**
> One of the provisions of IDEA, which requires that testing be done in a child's native or primary language. Procedures to prevent cultural or racial discrimination are also stipulated, as is the use of validated assessment tools. Assessment must be conducted by a multidisciplinary team using several kinds or sources of information to make a placement decision.

▶ **Measurement bias**

An unfairness or inaccuracy of test results that is related to cultural background, sex, or race.

▶ **Test bias**

An unfairness of a testing procedure or test instrument, which gives one group a particular advantage or another a disadvantage as a consequence of factors unrelated to ability, such as culture, sex, or race.

Educators must avoid test bias in assessing children for potential special education placement.

psychological assessment, which typically is based on standardized evaluations of intellectual and social functioning. Such assessments often discriminate, or are biased, against children from ethnically and culturally diverse backgrounds (Barrett, 2005; Linn & Miller, 2005; Venn, 2004). All assessment requires collaboration to ensure appropriate and effective data-based instructional practice. Assessment of children from diverse cultures heightens the need for professional collaboration and its importance for appropriate provision of services.

In several early cases, courts determined that reliance on academic and psychological assessments discriminated against Latino students (Diana v. State Board of Education, 1970, 1973) and African American students (Larry P. v. Riles, 1972, 1979). Assessment and instruction for Asian American children were addressed in the case of *Lau v. Nichols* (1974). These California cases had a national impact and greatly influenced the drafting of IDEA. Two prominent precedents in IDEA, for example, were established in the case of *Diana v. State Board of Education*: (1) children tested for potential placement in special education must be assessed in their native or primary language, and (2) children cannot be placed in special classes on the basis of culturally biased tests. Finally, IDEA also mandates that evaluation involve a multidisciplinary team using several sources of information to make a placement decision. To put these safeguards in context, it is necessary to examine the assessment process and how cultural bias can occur.

Because assessment for special education must avoid cultural bias, it is a source of major controversy. **Measurement bias** produces error during testing, leading to unfair or inaccurate test results that do not reflect the student's actual mental abilities or skills (de Valenzuela & Baca, 2004; Manly & Jacobs, 2002). In many cases, cultural bias taints both the construction and development of assessment instruments and their use (Barrett, 2005; Gregory, 2007; Reynolds, Livingston, & Willson, 2006). Standardized, norm-referenced instruments have been particularly criticized because the performances of children from different cultures are often compared with norms developed on the basis of other populations. Under these testing conditions, children from nonmainstream backgrounds often appear disadvantaged by cultural differences (Erevelles, et al., 2006; McMillan, 2007; Spinelli, 2006).

Bias in psychological assessment has been recognized as a problem for many years and continues to concern professionals (Cohen, 2002; Gregory, 2007; Linn & Miller, 2005). Some assessment procedures simply fail to document the same level of performance by individuals from mainstream and diverse cultural backgrounds, even if they have similar abilities. This phenomenon is referred to as **test bias**.

Considerable effort has been expended to develop tests that are culture-free or culture-fair (one example is using only test items that do not ask for information available primarily in the majority culture). This effort was rooted in the belief that the test itself was the major element contributing to bias or unfairness. But this simplistic perspective was flawed, because it focused solely on the test instrument itself and did not adequately address bias in the use of an instrument or the interpretation of data. (In other words, administration and interpretation should include adjustment for cultural differences). Over the years, however, this effort did lead to some improvements in areas where cultural bias was involved in instrument construction and to some procedural adaptations. Revision minimized the most glaring problems by reducing both the amount of culture-specific content (e.g., naming items more familiar to middle-class Caucasians than to others) and the culture-specific language proficiency required to perform test tasks (e.g., using language more commonly heard in middle-class, English-speaking homes than in others).

However, refinements to test instruments have limited effectiveness when the use of the test and the interpretation of results are not appropriate and conceptually sound. Although concern about administration and interpretation is not new, recent attention has led to a more balanced focus on procedures as well as on the test instrument itself (Downing & Haladyna, 2006; Linn, 2002; Willingham, 2002). One of the best ways to ensure fair testing is to prepare those who give tests and interpret the results so that they understand cultural issues in assessment. Adjustments may entail interpersonal interaction during test sessions that may be unfamiliar or offensive to a child from a different culture. Professionals need explicit and focused training to help them see how easily bias can creep in (Merrell, 2003; Reynolds et al., 2006). Personal preferences, such as racial biases, may substantially influence evaluation and, in turn, result in the incorrect assessment of a student.

Collaborating on the Needs of Students from Diverse Cultural Backgrounds

Multidisciplinary collaboration is essential to meet the significant challenges presented by the language differences of students with diverse cultural backgrounds. Assessment of non-English-speaking children has often been biased, providing an inaccurate reflection of those children's abilities (Gregory, 2007; Solarsh & Alant, 2006). If language diversity is not considered during assessment and educational planning, a child may receive an inappropriate educational placement (Cohen & Spenciner, 2007; Harrington & Brisk, 2006; Pena, Iglesias, & Lidz, 2001).

A particularly difficult situation exists for students with limited English proficiency and a language disorder, such as delayed language development (Battle, 2002; Puckett & Black, 2005; Trawick-Smith, 2006). Determining the degree to which each factor contributes to academic deficiency is difficult. In fact, it may not be important to assign a certain proportion of performance deficit to language differences and another proportion to intellectual or academic ability. What may be vitally important, however, is identifying students with language differences and finding appropriate educational services, other than special education, to help them. Such services may include intensive language assistance or other tutorial help, but not placement in special education classes or the special education system. It may be hard to decide whether such a child should be placed in special education. Special education placement will surely raise questions about whether such placement is occurring because the child is linguistically diverse as a consequence of his or her cultural background or is linguistically deficient for developmental reasons. Although these questions are not easily answered, the field is enormously strengthened because they are at last being asked and addressed (e.g., Cohen & Spenciner, 2007; Scheffner-Hammer, Pennock-Roman, Rzasa, & Tomblin, 2002).

As indicated earlier, census data show a substantially increasing number of children in the American educational system who speak languages other than English (Choi & Harachi, 2002; Wiese, 2006). Therefore, all teachers, related education personnel, social workers, psychologists, and administrators must become aware of the challenges to making appropriate educational assessments of students with language diversity (Cohen & Spenciner, 2007). In many cases this means that specific, focused training must be included in professional preparation programs.

One of the seemingly positive safeguards in IDEA, requiring assessment of a child in his or her native language, also raises new questions. Although this law represents a positive step toward fair treatment of students with linguistically diverse backgrounds, some difficulties have emerged in its implementation. Specifically, the legislation defines *native language* as the language used in the home, yet a regulation implementing IDEA defined it as the language the youngster normally uses in school. This latter definition may present problems for a bilingual student who has achieved a conversational fluency in English, yet whose proficiency may not be adequate to sustain academic work. For this child, testing in English is likely to be biased, even though it is considered a proper procedure according to regulations.

FOCUS 3
Identify two ways in which assessment may contribute to the overrepresentation of culturally diverse students in special education programs.

Council for Exceptional Children

Standard 2: Development and Characteristics of Learners

Standard 3: Individual Learning Differences

FOCUS **4**

Identify three ways in which language diversity may contribute to assessment difficulties with students who are from a variety of cultures.

Council for
Exceptional
Children

Standard 1: Foundations

Standard 8: Assessment

Standard 9: Professional and Ethical Practice

Collaboration and Professional Preparation

Proper training of professionals working with children from diverse backgrounds is particularly important to achieve effective collaboration for all students with disabilities (Dettmer et al., 2005; Friend & Cook, 2007). Such preparation is essential in order for professionals to obtain accurate data and minimize interpretations that may lead to bias (Gregory, 2007; Merrell, 2003). Professionals must be constantly alert to potential bias due to language differences as well as other factors that may mask students' true abilities. In many cases, information about the child's home life and other environmental matters can provide valuable insight to aid evaluators in both administering assessment and interpreting results. That information includes what languages are spoken in the household and by whom, who the child's caregivers are (parents and others), how much time the child spends with caregivers, and the child's out-of-school activities. Uninformed assumptions about family and related circumstances can lead to inaccurate assessment, so the evaluator must obtain as much information as possible about the child and her or his life.

It is vitally important to understand the child in the context of that child's family (De Von Figueroa-Moseley, Ramey, & Keltner, 2006; Quinones-Mayo & Dempsey, 2005). Such understanding includes the child and his or her family, as well as interaction patterns between family members and professionals such as teachers and social workers. This understanding is not readily available and often is not included in professional preparation programs. Professional training challenges are often addressed unsuccessfully in programs in psychology, teacher education, and a number of related areas (see, for example, Causey, Thomas, & Armento, 2000; Guadarrama, 2000).

Multidisciplinary collaboration is a very important tool in education, particularly in special and multicultural education. Effective collaboration requires that all of the professionals have a student-centered focus and be progressing toward the same general objective. To that end, the purposes of education itself must be considered from the outset: Are we attempting to bring the bulk of the citizenry to a similar point in education or knowledge? Are we creating a leveling effect, trying to make all people alike to some degree? Or are we promoting individual growth and development and encouraging cultural diversity and individual differences?

Parents from Different Cultures and Involvement in Special Education

FOCUS **5**

Cite three ways in which differing sociocultural customs may affect the manner in which parents become involved in the educational process.

Council for
Exceptional
Children

Standard 5: Learning Environments and Social Interactions

Parental involvement in the education of students with disabilities is required by IDEA. Parent rights, however, are based on certain assumptions. One fundamental assumption is that parents are consistently proactive and will challenge the school if their child is not being treated properly. Although this assumption is true of some parents of children in special education, it is not true for all. Some parents are reluctant or afraid to interact with the educational system. The manner in which parents are involved, their goals for such involvement, and evaluation of the outcomes of family participation are important to achieving maximum benefit (De Von Figueroa-Moseley et al., 2006; Quinones-Mayo & Dempsey, 2005; Wolfendale, 2005).

The acceptance of a child's disability is not easy for any parent, and a family's attitude toward exceptionality can influence how a child's intervention proceeds. People of diverse cultural backgrounds have perspectives and beliefs regarding illness, disability, and specialized services that may differ from those of the majority culture (Baca & Cervantes, 2004; Drew & Hardman, 2007). For example, some cultures have great difficulty accepting disabilities because of religious beliefs and values. Views about the family also can affect treatment of children with disabilities. The extended family structures common in African American and Latin cultures can cause hesitation about accepting care from outside the family and result in anxieties about special education. Parents of children with disabilities who are from lower socioeconomic levels, have a minority background, and speak a primary language other than English face enormous disadvantages in interacting with the special education system.

Sensitivity in interpersonal communication is very important when professionals deliver services to children of families who are culturally diverse (De Von Figueroa-Moseley et al., 2006; Quinones-Mayo & Dempsey, 2005). The meaning and interpretation of certain facial expressions, the expression of emotions, manners, and behaviors denoting respect and interpersonal matters vary greatly among cultures. Such connotations affect the interactions between minority family members, between these individuals and those of the cultural majority, and certainly with educational professionals. Some families from nonmainstream cultures may be reluctant to receive assistance from outside the family for a variety of reasons. For example, some parents may feel shame that their child has been identified as having disabilities, and this response is likely to influence their acceptance of the situation (Drew & Hardman, 2007). Moreover, professionals should keep in mind that the immigration status of some families may affect the way they react to attempts to provide services for their children. Although this constitutes a pragmatic consideration rather than a cultural difference, a family that is residing in the United States illegally or feels uncertain about its residency status may avoid interacting with an educational system.

U.S. public education predominantly reflects the philosophy of the cultural majority. This is not surprising, since social institutions—in this case, formal schooling—are typically founded on such mainstream views. Yet the social customs of the minority subcultures may continue to flourish in private and often emerge in individual interactions and behaviors (Collier, 2004; Dika & Singh, 2002; Gollnick & Chinn, 2006). Such differences surface in discussions of disabilities. For example, although intellectual disability is recognized by all cultures, its conceptualization, social interpretation, and treatment are culture-specific (Drew & Hardman, 2007; Webb, 2004). The condition may be regarded as negative (being viewed as a punishment visited on the family, for example) or may be viewed favorably (as offering the blessing of knowing an unusual person, for instance), depending on the cultural context. Similarly, certain behaviors that a professional of the majority culture might view as a learning problem may in fact be a product of the acculturation process or be considered normal within a child's cultural background. For example, a Native American child may not respond to some questions in a testing situation because his or her cultural custom is not to speak of such matters. The white test administrator, however, interprets this lack of response as meaning that the child does not know the answer and therefore classifies it as an error on the test. Some level of cultural bias and insensitivity is present in many aspects of professional work, including the research reports we read. This is important to remember as we attempt to understand cultural differences and to provide services in a

Council for Exceptional Children

Standard 5: Learning Environments and Social Interactions

society characterized by cultural pluralism (Banks & Banks, 2006; Deaux, Reid, & Martin, 2006; Quezada & Osajima, 2005).

Educating Students with Disabilities from Culturally Diverse Backgrounds

Individualized Education

FOCUS 6

Indicate two areas that require particular attention in the development of an individualized education plan (IEP) for a student from a culturally diverse background.

Developing an individualized education plan (IEP) for each student with a disability is required by IDEA. Most school districts have considerable experience in this process, but they must also meet further requirements when addressing the needs of a child with cultural and/or linguistic differences (Hendrick & Weissman, 2007; Morrison, 2007). Depending on her or his background and capabilities, such a student may need remediation for a specific disability, catch-up work in academic subjects, and instruction in English as a second language. The IEP must consider cultural factors, such as language differences, as well as learning and behavior disabilities, and it may have to provide for specialized instruction from different professionals for each facet of education. Rarely will a single professional have the training and background in the student's culture and language and in the specialized skills needed to remediate disabilities. Rather, effective educational programming for culturally diverse students requires a team effort (Baca & Cervantes, 2004; Gollnick & Chinn, 2006).

When developing an IEP for a student from a culturally diverse background, education professionals should avoid making stereotypical assumptions about his or her ethnic and cultural background. These may involve well-intentioned but misguided efforts to integrate into instruction culturally relevant foods, activities, or holidays. The utmost care should be taken to make sure that such content is specifically correct (not just an uninformed generalization about a religious celebration or folk dance) and is actually related to the student's experience—some foods typically associated with a student's ethnic group may not be eaten in that particular child's family or neighborhood. Insensitive use of such material may do more to perpetuate an unfortunate stereotype than to enrich a child's understanding of his or her heritage. Selection of culturally appropriate instructional materials requires a knowledge base that is beyond that of many educational professionals and demands a thorough analysis (Hoover & Collier, 2004; Kroeger & Bauer, 2004). IEPs written for children from culturally diverse backgrounds must truly be developed in an individualized fashion, perhaps even more so than for children with disabilities who come from the cultural majority.

The Least Restrictive Environment

FOCUS 7

Identify two considerations that represent particular difficulties in serving children from culturally diverse backgrounds in the least restrictive environment.

Education in the least restrictive environment (LRE) involves a wide variety of placement options (see Chapter 2). The guiding principle is that instruction for students with disabilities should take place in an environment as similar to that of the educational mainstream as possible and alongside peers without disabilities to the greatest extent appropriate. The

Children from culturally diverse backgrounds receiving special education services must be taught in settings with nondisabled peers to the maximum extent appropriate.

same is true for a child from a culturally diverse background who is receiving appropriate special education services, although some unique circumstances require additional attention (such as attention to a developmental language delay as well as to limited English skill). In all cases, these inclusive settings must also be sensitive to family and cultural differences (such as a family that speaks primarily a language other than English in the home). If possible, these cultural differences may be used as instructional tools or enhancements. For example, the teacher might ask the youngster to help teach part of a lesson on Spanish culture. What may seem like a subtle nuance can become an important positive lesson in cultural difference and respect.

Children with exceptionalities who have language differences may also receive assistance from bilingual education staff. In some cases, the language instruction may be incorporated into other teaching (Dong, 2002; Harrington & Brisk, 2006). In situations where the disability is more severe or the language difference is extreme (perhaps the child has little or no English proficiency), the student may be placed in a separate setting for a portion of instructional time.

Cultural and language instruction will vary with the child's needs, according to the model used in a given school district. Figure 5.2 illustrates varying levels of student fluency

Standard 1: Foundations

> **Pull-out programs**
Programs that move the student with a disability from the general education classroom to a separate class for at least part of the school day.

FIGURE 5.2

Degree of Inclusion Grid

	Preproduction	Early production	Speech emergence	Intermediate fluency	Intermediate advanced fluency	Advanced fluency
Needs total assistance to interact	Inclusion with targeted pull-out					
Needs a great deal of assistance						
Needs a lot of assistance						
Has a moderate level of needs	Inclusion with pull-out/push-in combination of services					
Has moderate but specific needs			Inclusion with push-in			
Has specific need to be addressed					Total inclusion	
Needs minimal assistance						

	Total inclusion
	Push-in for targeted assistance
	Pull-out/push-in combination for targeted assistance
	Pull-out for targeted assistance

	AQS	CLIC	IPT	LAS-O	Muñoz	SOLOM
Does not speak the language	0	0	0	0	0	0
Preproduction, has receptive comprehension	1	1–4	A	1	1	1–5
Early production, limited social fluency	2	5–10	B	2	2	6–10
Speech emergence, limited academic fluency	3	11–17	C	3	3	11–15
Intermediate social and academic fluency	4	18–32	D	4	4	16–20
Advanced intermediate social and academic fluency	5	33–44	E	5	5	21–25
Advanced social and academic fluency	6	45–55	F			

SOURCE: Collier, C. (2004). Including bilingual exceptional children in the general education classroom. In L. M. Baca & H. T. Cervantes (Eds.), *The bilingual special education interface* (4th ed., pp. 301). Columbus, OH: Merrill/Macmillan.

on a grid outlining the degree of assistance needed. Each intersection leads to different levels of integration recommended. For example, if the student needs total assistance to interact and is in a *very* early stage of language development (designated "preproduction" in Figure 5.2), this child may be provided inclusive instruction with targeted pull-out to provide very focused assistance. Programming options vary along the continuum of needs and levels of fluency to a point where the student is involved in totally inclusive instruction to meet specific needs and thereby achieve intermediate advanced or advanced fluency. This model allows consideration of language development and bilingual student's needs and represents an important framework for factoring in potential disability needs as well as language diversity status. Although this concept is logical, Collier noted that "there is still considerable debate concerning how and where the bilingual exceptional child should be served" (2004, p. 305). We saw earlier, in the preceding Case Study and Debate Forum, that Collier's statement is multifaceted. It involves overrepresentation and political components, and weaving throughout this complex set of influences is a need to serve students with maximum effectiveness.

Other Multicultural and Diversity Issues

Many influences come into play as we consider multicultural and diversity issues in education. In some cases, societal problems contribute to a child's development of learning difficulties; an example is parental neglect for extensive periods of time, resulting in little language and cognitive development occurring in a very young child. In other cases, the complications involved in educating people from a variety of cultures who also have differing abilities produce a host of challenges in assessment and instruction. It is important to note that the study of culture and associated variables, such as poverty and migrancy, is seldom well served by attempts to identify simplistic causal relationships. For example, findings of differences in self-esteem between people of differing ethnic backgrounds may be due to racial differences, differences in economic status, or a combination of influences. Research on race and culture involves complex and interacting variables that defy simple conclusions (Ram, 2005; Li, 2003; Twenge & Crocker, 2002).

Children Living in Poverty

One important example of how social and cultural factors are interrelated is found in the conditions associated with poverty. A child from an impoverished environment may be destined for special education even before birth. Increased health risks during pregnancy arise from more limited prenatal health care, poorer maternal nutrition, and potential exposure to other risk factors that are associated with birth complications (Gelfand & Drew, 2003; McDonough, Sacker, & Wiggins, 2005). Children who begin their lives facing such challenges are more likely to have difficulty later than those who do not. Children who live in poverty may be more frail, be sick more often, experience greater stress, and exhibit more neurological problems that later contribute to academic difficulties (Drew & Hardman, 2007; Gallo & Matthews, 2003; Skiba et al., 2005). These conditions are more prevalent in the lives of cultural and ethnic minorities (e.g., Bratter & Eschbach, 2005; Buckner et al., 2002). Census data published in 2000 indicated that 22.1% of all African Americans and 21.2% of Latinos lived below the poverty level, compared to 7.5% of the non-Hispanic white population. Other census data present an even more disturbing picture for children: 20.8% of all children were considered to be living below the poverty level (U.S. Bureau of the Census, 2000).

The effects of impoverished environments continue to cast the shadow of health risk beyond childhood and often over a lifetime. These influences frequently include shortened

Focus 8
Identify two ways in which poverty may contribute to the academic difficulties of children from culturally diverse backgrounds, often resulting in their referral to special education.

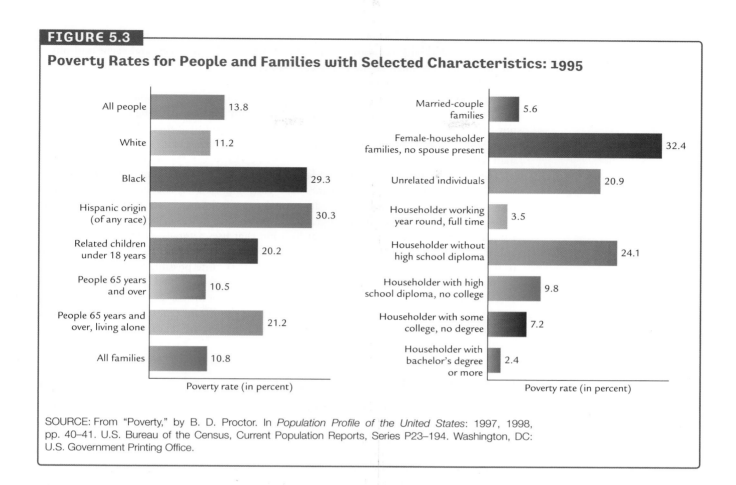

FIGURE 5.3

Poverty Rates for People and Families with Selected Characteristics: 1995

Characteristic	Poverty rate (in percent)
All people	13.8
White	11.2
Black	29.3
Hispanic origin (of any race)	30.3
Related children under 18 years	20.2
People 65 years and over	10.5
People 65 years and over, living alone	21.2
All families	10.8

Characteristic	Poverty rate (in percent)
Married-couple families	5.6
Female-householder families, no spouse present	32.4
Unrelated individuals	20.9
Householder working year round, full time	3.5
Householder without high school diploma	24.1
Householder with high school diploma, no college	9.8
Householder with some college, no degree	7.2
Householder with bachelor's degree or more	2.4

SOURCE: From "Poverty," by B. D. Proctor. In *Population Profile of the United States*: 1997, 1998, pp. 40–41. U.S. Bureau of the Census, Current Population Reports, Series P23–194. Washington, DC: U.S. Government Printing Office.

life expectancy, relatively poorer physical health, and more chronic health problems (Abernathy, Webster, & Vermeulen, 2002; McDonough et al., 2005; Ram, 2005). Poverty is found more often in populations having multicultural education needs than in populations without such needs, and it is also associated with homelessness and academic risk, contributing to the link between special and multicultural education. Figure 5.3 summarizes poverty rates across several characteristics (Feldman, 2005; Gelfand & Drew, 2003; Skiba et al., 2005).

Children from Migrant Families

Although migrancy is often associated with minority status and poverty, this is not always the case. Frequent mobility sometimes characterizes affluent families, such as those who move from a summer home to a winter home or take extended trips when it suits parents, rather than school schedules. Similarly, children of military personnel may change schools frequently on a schedule that does not coincide with the academic year.

Forces that interrupt the continuity of schooling have an impact on learning, teacher and peer relationships, and general academic progress (Nakagawa, Stafford, Fisher, & Matthews, 2002; Neven, 2005). Often this is a detrimental influence. The mobility of wealthy people and others subject to frequent reassignment also has an impact, but it is frequently offset by other circumstances that contribute to a child's general education (such as the opportunity for travel and the assistance of tutors). These children are not subject to the same risks as children from families who migrate as a way of life without the financial resources to offset negative impacts. Unlike military personnel, for example, migrant workers are not assured of employment, housing, or a welcoming sponsor.

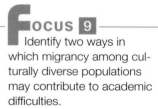

FOCUS 9

Identify two ways in which migrancy among culturally diverse populations may contribute to academic difficulties.

In many cases, the circumstances of migrancy are associated with ethnic or cultural diversity, as well as with economic disadvantage, language differences, and social and physical isolation from much of the larger community. Often the proportion of migrant workers from minority backgrounds is extremely high, and it varies geographically. For example, evidence indicates that over 80% of the farm laborers employed in California and other western states are recent immigrants from Mexico. Although reliable data are not available for other regions, migrancy is rather widespread and involves seasonal or migrant workers throughout the nation (Barranti, 2005; Buckner et al., 2002; Drew & Hardman, 2007).

The issues created by poverty and language diversity are even more difficult to address when a child moves three or four times each year. Children experience limited continuity and considerable inconsistency in educational programming. These children may begin the school year in one reading program and finish only a lesson or two before they are moved to another school in a different location that uses a totally different program and approach to the topic. They often have little access to services because of short-term enrollment or a school's limited service capabilities. It is quite possible for these children to be in each school for such a short time that they are never identified or referred as needing specialized instructional assistance. It is difficult to pinpoint the exact effects of mobility on children's academic progress, but the problem is significant. Even a consistent tracking system that could "move with the child" would be helpful to the receiving school or district.

Factors Contributing to Student Placement in Special Education

Focus 10
Cite three conceptual factors that have contributed to heightened attention and concern regarding the placement of children from ethnic and cultural groups in special education.

A number of other factors link special and multicultural education. Some of them raise serious concerns about the placement of minority children in special education, and others pertain to how such placements might best occur.

Special education focuses on differences. If a young girl has academic difficulty, perhaps failing in reading and math, she is singled out as different. She is different in that her math and reading performances are far below those of her peers, and so she may receive special help in these subjects. Several questions emerge as we consider this example: How do we determine that the student is doing poorly in reading and math? Is the student a candidate for special education? What is the primary reason why the student might be a candidate for special education?

What if the student comes from a culturally different background, as does Mary in the opening Snapshot? Should Mary be considered disabled because of her academic performance or because of her culturally different background? This question may not have a clear answer, for contributing factors may be so intertwined that they cannot be separated and weighed in a meaningful manner. Mary might have been inappropriately considered for specialized education as long as her performance was primarily a language and cultural matter (attributable merely to her being from a background different from that of the majority). It might be argued that the reason for Mary's receiving special help is irrelevant as long as she received that extra help. This perspective may have intuitive appeal, but it is not a satisfactory position for professionals involved in multicultural education. If Mary received special education because of her cultural and language background, not primarily because she was disabled, she was being labeled and placed inappropriately.

Furthermore, special education often carries a stigma. Many people infer that children in special education are somehow inferior to those who do not require such instruction. Will this early assistance place Mary at a disadvantage later? Unfortunately, the negative view of specialized education persists despite efforts by professionals to change it. Peers may ridicule children who are in special education. Some parents are more comfortable with having their child placed in the general education classes—even if the child might do better in special education. And parents of children who are gifted and talented are often quick to point out that their children are in an accelerated class so that no one assumes that they are attending a special education class.

This negative perspective on special education is especially harmful to children like Mary if their placement stems from mislabeling or flawed assessment. Multicultural advocates may correctly claim that placing students in special education because of cultural differences is an example of discrimination (and perhaps oppression) by the cultural majority. This view explains why the advocates of multicultural education become concerned—even angry—when children with culturally diverse backgrounds appear to be overrepresented in special education.

An additional problem may occur if a child's special education placement is not multiculturally sensitive and appropriate. The wrong special education intervention can do more harm than good. For instance, even the best instruction will be ineffective if it is provided in English and the student does not comprehend English or speak it fluently. As noted earlier, designing appropriate instructional programs for children from culturally different backgrounds is complex and is likely to involve a number of different specialists operating as a team. Such instruction may also require some changes or adaptations in the organization of the educational system so that these children may progress satisfactorily through the academic material (Gollnick & Chinn, 2006; Morrison, 2007).

Mary's placement in special education could have impeded her academic progress to the extent that her failure became a self-fulfilling prophecy. In short, Mary could have become what she had been labeled. Her poor academic and social performance may be due to cultural differences, not to disability. Mary could have been turned into a poor student by the system itself. The concept of the self-fulfilling prophecy has been discussed for many years and continues to receive attention in a variety of contexts from marketing to education (Snyder, Shorey, & Rand, 2006; Spangenberg & Sprott, 2006; Trouilloud, Sarrazin, & Bressoux, 2006). This factor warrants particular attention as we study multicultural issues and specialized instruction.

Meeting the Needs of Students with Disabilities from Culturally Diverse Backgrounds

Specialized instruction for students with disabilities who come from culturally diverse backgrounds must be based on individual need. The IEP must include specific cultural considerations that are relevant for a particular child, addressing language dominance and language proficiency in terms of both conversational and academic skills. The IEP may need to address the type of language intervention needed, which might include enrichment (either in a native language or in English) or language development intervention, which also may be either in a native language or in English. Instruction may target language enhancement through a strategy integrated with existing curriculum material, such as children's literature.

These are only examples of the considerations that may need attention, and they are issues related primarily to language diversity. Environmental conditions, such as extreme poverty and developmental deprivation, may dictate that services and supports focus on environmental stimulation that was lacking in the child's early learning (Hendrick & Weissman, 2007; Li, 2003). The possible individual strategies are as varied as the factors that make up a child's background.

It is also important to note that most children from culturally diverse backgrounds do not require special education. Although the factors discussed here may place such students at risk for special education referral, general instruction may meet their needs without special education services. When this is possible, it is a mistake to label such students as disabled. Table 5.1 on page 130 outlines points that educators should consider as they address various elements of the referral process for children from diverse backgrounds.

TABLE 5.1

Process Checklist for Serving Children from Diverse Backgrounds

This checklist provides professionals with points to consider in the process of educating children from culturally diverse backgrounds. These matters should be considered during each of the following: referral and testing or diagnostic assessment; classification, labeling, or class assignment change; teacher conferences or home communication.

PROCESS	ISSUES	QUESTION TO BE ASKED
Referral, Testing, or Diagnostic Assessment	Language issues	Is the native language different from the language in which the child is being taught, and should this be considered in the assessment process? What is the home language? What is the normal conversational language? In what language can the student be successfully taught or assessed (academic language)?
	Cultural issues	What are the views toward schooling of the culture from which the child comes? Do differences exist in expectations between the school and family for the child's schooling goals? What are the cultural views toward illness or disability?
	Home issues	What is the family constellation, and who are the family members? What is the family's economic status?
Classification, Labeling, or Class Assignment Change	Language issues	Does the proposed placement change account for any language differences that are relevant, particularly academic language?
	Cultural issues	Does the proposed placement change consider any unique cultural views regarding schooling?
	Home issues	Does the proposed change consider pertinent family matters?
Teacher Conferences or Home Communication	Language issues	Is the communication to parents or other family members in a language they understand?
	Cultural issues	Do cultural views influence communication between family members and the schools as a formal governmental organization? Is there a cultural reluctance of family members to come to the school? Are home visits a desirable alternative? Is communication from teachers viewed positively?
	Home issues	Is the family constellation such that communication with the schools is possible and positive? Are family members positioned economically and otherwise to respond to communication from the schools in a productive manner? If the family is of low SES, is transportation a problem for conferences?

FOCUS REVIEW

FOCUS 1 Identify three ways in which the purposes of and approaches to general education in the United States sometimes differ from the purposes of and approaches to special education and multicultural education.

- A major purpose of general education is to provide education for everyone and to bring all students to a similar level of performance.

- Special education focuses on individual differences and often evaluates performance in terms of an individually set or prescribed performance level.

- Multicultural education promotes cultural pluralism and, therefore, promotes differences.

FOCUS 2 Describe population trends among culturally diverse groups in the United States. How do these changes affect the educational system?

- Ethnically and culturally diverse groups (such as Latinos, African Americans, and others) represent substantial portions of the U.S. population.

- Population growth in ethnically and culturally diverse groups is increasing at a phenomenal rate—in some cases, at twice the rate of growth in the Caucasian population. Both immigration and birthrates contribute to this growth.

- Increased demands for services will be placed on the educational system as growth continues among culturally diverse populations.

FOCUS 3 Identify two ways in which assessment may contribute to the overrepresentation of culturally diverse students in special education programs.

- Using assessment instruments that are designed and constructed with specific language and content that "favors" the cultural majority.
- Using assessment procedures that are biased, either implicitly or explicitly, against people from culturally different backgrounds.

FOCUS 4 Identify three ways in which language diversity may contribute to assessment difficulties with students who are from a variety of cultures.

- Students with limited or no English proficiency may be thought to have speech or language disorders and hence may be referred and tested for special education placement.
- A child's native language may appear to be English because of conversational fluency at school, but he or she may not be proficient enough to engage in academic work or assessment in English.
- Because of his or her language differences, a child's academic or psychological assessment may inaccurately represent his or her ability.

FOCUS 5 Cite three ways in which differing sociocultural customs may affect the manner in which parents become involved in the educational process.

- Parents from some cultural backgrounds may view special assistance differently than educational institutions do.
- Parents from some cultural backgrounds may be reluctant to take an active role in interacting with the educational system.
- Certain behaviors that may suggest a disabling condition that calls for special education assistance are viewed as normal in some cultures, and parents from those cultures may not see them as problematic.

FOCUS 6 Indicate two areas that require particular attention in the development of an individualized education plan (IEP) for a student from a culturally diverse background.

- Coordination of different services and professional personnel becomes crucial.
- Cultural stereotypes should not be perpetuated by as-

sumptions that are inappropriate for an IEP or otherwise improper for education.

FOCUS 7 Identify two considerations that represent particular difficulties in serving children from culturally diverse backgrounds in the least restrictive environment.

- Cultural or language instruction may be needed in addition to other teaching that focuses on remediation of a learning problem, making integration into the educational mainstream more difficult.
- Training limitations of school staff, rather than the child's needs, may influence placement decisions.

FOCUS 8 Identify two ways in which poverty may contribute to the academic difficulties of children from culturally diverse backgrounds, often resulting in their referral to special education.

- Circumstances resulting in disadvantaged prenatal development and birth complications occur much more frequently among those of low socioeconomic status and among nonmainstream populations.
- Environmental circumstances that place children at risk, such as malnutrition and toxic agents, are found most frequently in impoverished households, and poverty often afflicts ethnic minority populations.

FOCUS 9 Identify two ways in which migrancy among culturally diverse populations may contribute to academic difficulties.

- In many cases, migrant families are characterized by economic disadvantages and language differences.
- Children in migrant households may move and change educational placements several times a year, which limits continuity and contributes to inconsistent educational programming.

FOCUS 10 Cite three conceptual factors that have contributed to heightened attention and concern regarding the placement of children from ethnic and cultural groups in special education.

- Stigma is attached to special education.
- Special education placement for children from culturally and ethnically diverse groups may not be educationally effective in meeting their academic needs.
- A self-fulfilling prophecy may occur, resulting in youngsters becoming what they are labeled.

If you are thinking about a career in special education, you should know that many states use national standards developed by the Council for Exceptional Children (CEC) to assess a teacher candidate's knowledge about and skills for working with students with disabilities. See a complete listing of the ten CEC Content Standards on the inside front cover of this text.

CEC Content Standards Addressed in This Chapter

1 Foundations

2 Development and Characteristics of Learners

3 Individual Learning Differences

5 Learning Environments and Social Interactions

8 Assessment

9 Professional and Ethical Practice

Assess Your Knowledge of the CEC Standards Addressed in Chapter 5

Some states require that teacher candidates develop a portfolio of products that demonstrate mastery of the CEC content standards. To assist in the development of products for this portfolio, you may wish to complete the following activities.

- Complete a written test of the chapter's content.

If your instructor requires a written test of your content knowledge for this chapter, keep a copy for your portfolio. A practice test on the information covered in this chapter is available through the *Human Exceptionality* companion website (college.hmco.com/pic/hardman9e) and the *Student Study Guide.*

- Respond to the Application Questions for the Case Study, "Overrepresentation, Finances, and School Reform."

Review the Case Study and respond in writing to the application questions. Keep a copy of the Case Study and of your written response for your portfolio.

- Participate in a Community Service Learning Activity.

Community service is a valuable way to enhance your learning experience. Visit our companion website for suggested community service learning activities that correspond to the information presented in this chapter. Develop a reflective journal of the service learning experience for your portfolio.

WEB RESOURCES

National Association for Multicultural Education

http://www.nameorg.org

The National Association for Multicultural Education was founded to bring together individuals and groups with an interest in multicultural education from all levels of education, different disciplines, and diverse professions and organizations. This website provides information about the organization, its activities, and a variety of other resources pertaining to multicultural education.

Electronic Magazine of Multicultural Education

http://www.eastern.edu/publications/emme

This is an on-line magazine for scholars, practitioners, and students of multicultural education. EMME includes material for both the general public and professionals working in multicultural education. Content is compiled as theme-based issues that contain articles, teaching ideas, and reviews of juvenile and professional books.

Center for Multilingual, Multicultural Research (CMMR)

http://www.usc.edu/dept/education/cmmr

This website provides a rich source of bilingual, ESL, and multicultural education resources. The visitor will find articles and links to websites that include full text presentations and a broad array of other resources. The full spectrum of age ranges may be seen in the material available.

Center for Multicultural Education at the University of Washington

http://depts.washington.edu/centerme/home.htm

This website reports on research and activities aimed at improving practice related to equity issues, intergroup relations, and achievement by students of color. This site includes information about the center's research and teaching missions, successful K–12 programs, and events that are scheduled at the center.

FURTHER READINGS

Anderson, J., Anderson, A., Lynch, J., & Shapiro, J. (2003). "Storybook reading in a multicultural society: Critical perspectives." In *On Reading Books to Children: Parents and Teachers,* ed. A. Van Kleeck, S. Stahl, and E. Bauer. Mahwah, NJ: Erlbaum.

This chapter discusses storybook reading from a multicultural perspective and within the context of literacy.

Jewel, P. (2002). "Multicultural counseling research: An evaluation with proposals for future research." In *Multicultural Counseling: A Reader,* ed. S. Palmer. Thousand Oaks, CA: Sage.

This chapter attempts to answer the frequent criticism that traditional counseling lacks relevance for multicultural circumstances.

Nieto, S. (2002). *Language, Culture, and Teaching: Critical Perspectives for a New Century.* Mahwah, NJ: Erlbaum.

This book presents realistic examples of dilemmas about diversity faced by teachers in their classrooms.

Utley, C., Obiakor, F., & Ford, B. (2002). "Professional Development: An Essential Component for Educating Teachers as Lifelong Learners."

In *Educating All Learners: Refocusing the Comprehensive Support Model,* ed. F. Obiakor and P. Grant. Springfield, IL: Charles C Thomas.

This chapter examines the crucial aspects of professional development for teachers and describes key elements of a multicultural professional development training program.

COMPANION WEBSITE

Visit the companion website at college.hmco.com/pic/hardman9e for additional resources that support this text:

- HM Video Cases that present actual classroom scenarios that you may face every day as a teacher

- Practice ACE Exams that will help you prepare for quizzes, tests, and certfication exams
- Flashcards of key terms
- Weblinks

6 Exceptionality and the Family

TO BEGIN WITH . . .

PARENTS BAND TOGETHER TO FIGHT FOR THEIR SONS

Mothers have a certain sixth sense when it comes to their children. Often, they predict illness before symptoms are obvious—they just know. When Nicole took her five-year-old son Tyler to the doctor after he complained of leg pain, she thought they would be sent home with the usual answer, "He's fine, there's nothing to worry about." But this time, the answer was different. She was about to find out that both Tyler and her other son, Spencer (age 2), have a genetic disorder known as Duchenne Muscular Dystrophy (DMD). A progressive muscle disorder caused by mutations in a gene located on the X-chromosome, DMD causes loss of muscle function and loss of independence. To date, there is no cure.

After getting through the initial shock and grief, Nicole and her husband, Richard, decided to take action. They would not let this devastating disorder get the better of them and their sons and determined to do everything in their power to fight DMD. While surfing the Internet, they found an organization called Parent Project Muscular Dystrophy (PPMD). PPMD gave them what they were so desperately looking for—a community of other families going through the same thing, accurate and clear information about DMD, and a foundation through which fundraising efforts could be channeled in the effort to find a cure (Furlong, 2005, pp. 61–62).

NOTHING IN MY BACKGROUND OR UPBRINGING PREPARED ME TO HANDLE THIS NEW, UNEXPECTED CHALLENGE

I was living in Manhattan with my six-year-old son Allesandro and my newborn daughter Allegra. We had a very happy life with no sign of trouble on the horizon. Allesandro was in kindergarten and was doing fine and Allegra was a happy, healthy baby. This continued for four years, but then our lives took a turn that forever altered the course of our future. My daughter began to exhibit what I thought at first was a small behavior problem. This problem soon escalated into something I had never seen or imagined before. When I tried to find help, I was confronted by a medical establishment that offered me conflicting opinions and seemed to know as little about her condition as I did. This uncertainty was the beginning of a terrifying and bewildering ordeal, filled with dire predictions from all sides telling me that my child's education and future prospects and even her happiness were in question.

. . . I had no idea what to do or who to turn to. Worst of all was the crushing sense of isolation, the feeling that I was the only one going through it and that no one—no one—could possibly understand. I even had difficulty talking to my own family about this. My father was extremely busy as the head of the Ford Motor Company and was always traveling. My mother, although she was nearby, had instilled the concepts of discretion and stoicism in us at an early age—problems were something to be handled quietly, preferable without imposing them on anyone else. Nothing in my background or upbringing prepared me to handle this new, unexpected challenge. (Ford, 2003, p. xii)

1. Identify five factors that influence the ways in which families respond to infants with birth defects or disabilities.

2. What three statements can be made about the adjustments that parents experience in responding to infants or young children with disabilities?

3. Cite three ways in which a newborn child with disabilities influences the family social/ecological system.

4. Identify three aspects of raising a child with a disability that contribute to spousal stress.

5. Identify four general phases that parents may experience in rearing a child with a disability.

6. Cite four factors that influence the relationship that develops between infants with disabilities and their mothers.

7. Identify three ways in which fathers may respond to their children with disabilities.

8. Identify four ways in which siblings respond to a brother or sister with a disability.

9. Indicate three ways in which grandparents and other extended family members may render support to families with children who have disabilities.

10. Describe five behaviors that skilled and competent professionals exhibit when interacting with and relating to families that include children with disabilities.

11. What are five goals of family support systems?

12. Identify the critical aspects of collaborative training for parents, families, and professionals

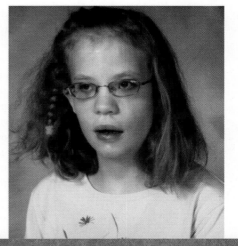

▼SNAPSHOT

TEELA

Teela is an 11-year-old girl with some challenging disabilities. Doctors have not been able to give her a specific diagnosis. We do know that her brain did not form properly and has several physical deformities within it. Because of this, Teela has substantial global delay, has epilepsy, and is nonverbal.

In spite of her challenges, Teela has been able to develop some good abilities. She loves to do puzzles—she even likes to turn the pieces over and do her puzzles on the wrong side. Teela is also learning how to read and knows quite a lot of sign language. She uses her "talking machine" to help her communicate. Teela's dad wrote a program for a pocket PC that she wears around her neck. The program includes pictures that represent Teela's vocabulary words. As Teela touches the pictures, she is able to "talk." Between her talking machine and her sign language, Teela is actually quite a talkative girl.

Teela's family is very important to her. Whenever someone is gone from home, she often asks where that person is. She has to be told several times a day that "Dad is at work and he'll be home tonight." Teela has a 9-year-old sister, Marissa, and a 3-year-old brother, Travis. Although Teela has significant difficulties with social interactions, she shows a lot of affection for her siblings. Marissa likes to make Teela laugh—not an easy task. Travis likes to feed her snacks. Both have learned sign language from Teela.

As a mother of a handicapped child and two normally developing children, I try to provide the most "normal" or typical family life that I can. We do a lot of activities together with adjustments made for Teela. Anywhere we go we bring a bag of Teela's puzzles, alphabet books, and other items to keep her happy. Teela's favorite stuffed animal, Big Soft Betty the dog, goes absolutely everywhere with us. Teela always attracts a certain amount of stares and other reactions but her siblings are not bothered by it. It's what they've always known. When other children are scared of Teela, Marissa will often reassure them by saying, "That's just my sister." Teela especially likes to go camping with her family. She is a good hiker in spite of some problems with balance and gross motor skills. She falls down a lot but still loves to be with her family in the mountains. Marissa and Travis are genuinely proud of Teela for small accomplishments such as completing a hike, writing her name, or winning medals at Special Olympics.

Sometimes people tell me I must be a "special" person to have a handicapped child. The truth is I'm just a regular person trying to cope with a difficult and unexpected situation the best that I can. (Ellen Burkett, personal communication, June 11, 2006)

Focus 1

Identify five factors that influence the ways in which families respond to infants with birth defects or disabilities.

Nowhere is the impact of an individual who is exceptional felt so strongly as in the family (Hauser-Cram, 2006; McHugh 2003, Strohm, 2005). The birth of an infant with disabilities may alter the family as a social unit in a variety of ways. Parents and siblings may react with shock, disappointment, anger, depression, guilt, and confusion (Harris & Glasberg, 2003; Hastings, Daley, Burns, & Beck, 2006; McHugh, 2003; Strohm, 2005). Over time, many parents and siblings develop coping skills that enhance their sense of well-being and their capacity to deal with the stressful demands of caring for a child, youth, or adult with a disability (Baskin & Fawcett, 2006; Gray, 2002; Hauser-Cram 2006; Pipp-Siegel, Sedey, & Yoshinaga-Itano, 2002). Many family members become resilient (Blacher, 2002), and many adapt well to having a child with a disability (Hastings & Taunt, 2002; Poston et al., 2003; Raver, 2005; Snow, 2001). For many families, humor plays an important role in releasing negative emotions, remedying stress, connecting in unique ways with family members, and moving away from "terminal seriousness," a malady no one wants or needs (Rieger, 2004). Consider the humor found in this short musing of a mother of a child with a disability.

My son is very direct and obsessive in his questions. He asks what he wants to ask: "Who are you? What is your name?" Over and over again. So I often use him in these social situations where I'm not quite sure of people's names, and I need to talk to them. I just make sure I'm near my son, because he will ask, "What is your name again?" [laughs]. (Rieger, 2004, p. 205)

A child with physical, intellectual, or behavioral disabilities presents unique and diverse challenges to the family unit (Orgassa, 2005). In one instance, the child may hurl the family into crisis, precipitating major conflicts among its members. Family relationships may be weakened by the added and unexpected physical, emotional, and financial stress. In another instance, a child with a disability may be a source of unity that bonds family members together and strengthens their relationships (Ferguson, 2002; Snow, 2001). Many factors influence the reactions of the family, including the emotional stability of each individual, religious values and beliefs, socioeconomic status, time constraints, and the severity and type of the child's disability (Poston & Turnbull, 2004; Turnbull & Turnbull, 2002). Twenty-eight percent of the children with disabilities in the United States live in poverty. They and their families experience hunger, greatly diminished access to health care, often overcrowded and unclean housing, unsafe neighborhoods and schools, and a host of other, equally challenging circumstances (Park, Turnbull, & Turnbull, 2002).

In this chapter we discuss how raising children with disabilities affects parents, siblings, grandparents, and other extended family members. We also explore the family as a **social/ecological system** defined by a set of purposes, cultural beliefs, parent and child roles, expectations, and family socioeconomic conditions (Fine & Simpson, 2000; Jackson & Turnbull, 2004; Ortiz, 2006; Turnbull & Turnbull, 2002; Zhang & Bennett, 2001). A social/ecological approach looks at how each family member plays roles consistent with expectations established by discussions, traditions, beliefs, or cultures. In the process, each member functions in an interdependent manner with other members to pursue family and individual goals and to fulfill various expectations (Poston et al., 2003). This approach also examines the **ecocultural** and socioeconomic factors that impinge on the children with disabilities and their families (Turnbull & Turnbull, 2002). For example, a family who has experienced substantial income loss because of layoffs or a family whose par-

➤ **Social/ecological system**
An organization that provides structure for human interactions, for defining individual and group roles, for establishing expectations about behavior, and for specifying individual and group responsibilities in a social environment. Also called a social system. The system is ecological; changes in one individual or element in the environment often spell changes for other individuals within the system.

➤ **Ecocultural**
A term referring to cultural and environmental factors that influence family functioning, such as unemployment, the primary language spoken in the home, traditions in the country of origin, parental illness, number of children in the family, and educational background.

ents are drug abusers may not be as effective, resilient, or resourceful in responding to an infant, child, or youth with a disability. A social/ecological framework makes it easy for us to see how changes in one family member can affect every other member and, consequently, the entire family system (Ferguson, 2002; Fox, Vaughan, Wyatte, & Dunlap, 2002; Hauser-Cram et al., 2001). This chapter also addresses the ways in which children with disabilities affect the quality of life experienced by families and their individual members. In general, families that include children with disabilities experience more frequent and intense concerns about quality-of-life issues than families with children without disabilities. These concerns center on such factors as financial well-being, emotional wellness, social well-being, family interaction, and parenting (Poston et al., 2003).

Understanding Families

Reacting to Crisis

The birth of an infant with significant disabilities has a profound impact on the family (Fox et al., 2002; Thies & Travers, 2006). The expected or fantasized child whom the parents and other family members have anticipated does not arrive, and the parents are thrown into a state of emotional shock.

Some conditions, such as **spina bifida** and **Down syndrome,** are readily apparent at birth, whereas others, such as hearing impairments and learning disabilities, are not detectable until later. Even if attending physicians and other professionals suspect the presence of a disabling condition, they may be unable to give a confirmed diagnosis without the passage of some time and further testing. When parents also suspect that something is wrong, waiting for a diagnosis can be agonizing (Frost, 2002; Fox et al., 2002).

The most immediate and predictable reaction to the birth of a child with a disability is shock, characterized by feelings of disappointment, sadness, loneliness, fear, anger, frustration, devastation, numbness, uncertainty, and a sense of being trapped. Courtney, the mother of a preschooler with a disability put it this way: "I really think I am on the verge of getting lost. Well, I probably am lost. Things that used to be important issues in my daily life—like weight, clothes, and all that material stuff—seem so senseless now" (Baskin & Fawcett, 2006, p. 97). Another reaction is depression, often exhibited in the form of grief or mourning. Some parents describe such emotions as very much like those suffered after the death of a loved one. Recurrent sorrow and frequent feelings of inadequacy are persistent emotions that many parents experience as they gradually adjust to having an infant with a disability (Lee, Strauss, Wittman, Jackson, & Carstens, 2001). These ongoing feelings of grief may be triggered by health or behavior challenges presented by the child, by unusual child care demands, by lack of achievement of developmental milestones in the child, and/or by insensitivity of extended family and community members (Gray, 2002; Lee et al., 2001). Consider this statement made by a woman who had been both the sister and the mother of a child with a disability:

> ➤ **Spina bifida**
> A developmental defect of the spinal column.
>
> ➤ **Down syndrome**
> A condition caused by a chromosomal abnormality that results in unique physical characteristics and varying degrees of mental retardation. This condition was once described as "mongolism," a term that is no longer acceptable.

I felt my mother's deep sorrow inside me, and there was nothing I could do for her. Later in my life, I would feel that same helpless grief when one of my own children became blind and I couldn't stop it from happening. There is nothing more terrible than not being able to keep harm away from your child. And for a sibling, there is nothing more painful than watching your mother's heart break because one of her children is wounded. (McHugh, 2003, p. 6)

Although parents of children with disabilities share many of the same feelings and reactions, their responses and their

Receiving the news that your child might have a disability produces powerful emotions.

FOCUS 2
What three statements can be made about the adjustments that parents experience in responding to infants or young children with disabilities?

eventual adjustments vary from one person to another (Poston et al., 2003; Turnbull & Turnbull, 2002). There is no linear movement through specific stages of adjustment (Hauser-Cram, 2006). The stage approach simply helps us think about the ways in which parents might respond, over time, to a child or sibling with a disability. The "stages" associated with various kinds of emotions may overlap one another and resurface during another period. Some parents go through distinct periods of adjustment, whereas others adjust without passing through any identifiable sequence of stages. The process of adjustment for parents is continuous and distinctively individual (Baxter, Cummins, & Yiolitis, 2000; Fine & Nissenbaum, 2000; Ulrich, 2003).

Some parents, siblings, and even relatives of children with disabilities employ a kind of cognitive or accommodative coping that enables them to think about the child, sibling, or grandchild with disabilities in ways that enhance their sense of well-being and capacity for responding positively (Baskin & Fawcett, 2006). For example, read the following account of one mother's response to the birth of a child with a disability.

> Something like this could tear a marriage apart . . . but instead it has brought us closer.
>
> Right after she was born, I remember this revelation. She was teaching us something . . . how to keep things in perspective . . . to realize what's important. I've learned that everything is tentative and that you never know what life will bring.
>
> I've learned that I'm a much stronger person than I had thought. I look back, see how far I've come, and feel very pleased.
>
> The good that's come from this is that I marvel at what a miracle she is . . . it is a miracle that she's alive and that we are going to take her home. (Affleck & Tennen, 1993, p. 136)

This mother was able to interpret the birth and subsequent events in a positive manner. Her thinking or cognitive coping helped her reduce or successfully manage feelings of shock, distress, and depression. Additionally, her positive interpretation of this event contributed to her capacity to respond effectively to her child's needs.

SHOCK. The initial response to the birth of an infant with a disability is generally shock, distinguished variously by feelings of anxiety, guilt, numbness, confusion, helplessness, anger, disbelief, denial, and despair (Friend & Cook, 2003; Gray, 2002). Parents sometimes have feelings of grief, detachment, bewilderment, or bereavement. At this time, when many parents are most in need of assistance, the least amount of help may be available. The ways in which parents react during this period depend on their psychological makeup, the types of assistance rendered, and the nature and severity of the disability (Turnbull & Turnbull, 2002). Over time, many parents move from being victims to being survivors of the trauma (Gray, 2002).

> I'll guarantee that every parent, at some point between the thrill of conception and the anxiety of the delivery room, has experienced the same fear, "What if something is wrong with my baby?"
>
> Most of us like to think we would do anything, make any sacrifice, for our children. But when the vague fear you have tried to stifle becomes a reality, when your child is born with a severe physical or mental disability that threatens your own freedom and lifestyle, that commitment is put to the test.
>
> After you have experienced the shock, the denial, the grief, it slowly begins to dawn on you. Your life has changed forever, in ways you never expected, never wanted, never dared to imagine.
>
> I know. It happened to me. (Anton, 2002, p. 28)

During the initial period of shock, parents may be unable to process or comprehend information provided by medical and other health-related personnel. For this reason, essential information may need to be communicated to parents several times until they have fully grasped it. Parents may experience the greatest assaults on their self-worth and value systems during this time. They may blame themselves for their child's disabilities and may seriously question their positive self-perceptions. Likewise, they may be forced to reassess the meaning of life and the reasons for their present challenges.

REALIZATION. The stage of realization is characterized by several types of parental behavior. Parents may be anxious or fearful about their ability to cope with the demands of caring for a child with unique needs. They may be easily irritated or upset and spend considerable time in self-accusation, self-pity, or self-hate. They may continue to reject or deny information provided by health care professionals. During this stage, however, parents do come to understand the actual demands and constraints that will come with raising a child with a disability (Lee et al., 2001). For example, one parent wrote,

> "It's probably Cerebral Palsy," said the Early Intervention therapist. Rachel was only four months old during this initial evaluation. She couldn't hold her head up, roll over, sit up, or crawl. She couldn't even lift her arms or legs. She had no eye contact, cried constantly, and never slept. I knew something was wrong and feared she would never bond with me.
>
> I remember starting to cry. The grandmothers looked on, tried to hold back their tears, but they couldn't. My perfect child was officially not perfect. After collecting my thoughts and trying to shed the feeling of devastation, I tried to think of the positives. As long as it's CP, I thought, this diagnosis meant that she would be physically disabled, but her mental faculties would be intact. We called to make an appointment with a neurologist within 10 minutes of the initial CP diagnosis. Unfortunately, two months passed before we could get an appointment. (Epstein & Bessell, 2002, p. 56)

DEFENSIVE RETREAT. During the stage of defensive retreat, parents attempt to avoid dealing with the anxiety-producing realities of their child's condition. Some try to solve their dilemma by seeking placement for the child in a clinic, institution, or residential setting. Other parents disappear for a while or retreat to a safer and less demanding environment. One mother, on returning home from the hospital with her infant with Down syndrome, quickly packed her suitcase and left with her infant in the family car, not knowing what her destination would be. She simply did not want to face her immediate family or relatives. After driving around for several hours, she decided to return home. Within several months, she adapted very well to her daughter's needs and began to provide the stimulation necessary for gradual, persistent growth. Her daughter is now married and works full-time in a day care center for young children.

ACKNOWLEDGMENT. Acknowledgment is the stage in which parents mobilize their strengths to confront the conditions created by having a child with a disability. At this time, parents begin to involve themselves in the intervention and treatment process. They are also better able to comprehend information or directions provided by specialists and other care providers concerning their child's condition and treatment. Some parents become interested in joining an advocacy organization that is suited to their child's condition and to the needs of the family (Fuller & Olsen, 1998). Parents begin to accept the child with the disability (Friend & Cook, 2003). It is during this stage that parents can direct their energies to challenges external to themselves.

Family Characteristics and Interactions

The birth of a child with disabilities and the continued presence of that child strongly influence how family members respond to one another, particularly if the child is severely disabled or has multiple disabilities. In many families, the mother experiences the greatest amount of trauma and strain. In caring for such a child, she may no longer be able to handle many of the tasks she once performed, and her attention to other family members may be greatly reduced.

When the mother is drawn away from the tasks she used to perform, other family members often must assume more responsibility. Adjusting to new roles and routines may be difficult, and family members may need to alter their personal routines in order to assist the mother. Responses of family and extended family members may vary according to their cultural backgrounds and related beliefs about children with disabilities (Banks, 2003; Bui & Turnbull, 2003; Frankland, Turnbull, & Wehmeyer, & Blackmountain, 2004; Park, Turnbull & Turnbull, 2002). In this regard, we are just beginning to understand the influence of various cultures on the ways

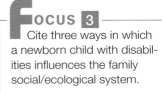

FOCUS **3**
Cite three ways in which a newborn child with disabilities influences the family social/ecological system.

in which children with disabilities are viewed and treated within these cultures (Banks, 2003; Boscardin, Brown-Chidsey, & Gonzales-Matinez, 2001; McHatton & Correa, 2005). Teachers and other treatment providers need to be sensitive to child-rearing practices and the roles of family members, as well as to parents' religious beliefs and views about the role of education (Rivers, 2000; McHatton & Correa, 2005; Poston & Turnbull, 2004; Zhang & Bennett, 2001). Professionals also need to be aware of the different meanings that parents assign to their children with disabilities (Banks, 2003). Furthermore, greater efforts must be directed at finding appropriate interpreters for IFSP and IEP meetings, becoming adept in cross-cultural communication, learning how to do home visits, and connecting with diverse families and communities.

As the child with disabilities grows older, the mother frequently faces a unique dilemma: how to strike a balance between the nurturing activities she associates with her role as caregiver and the activities associated with fostering the child's independence. Seeing her child struggle with new tasks and suffer the setbacks that naturally occur in trying new behaviors can be difficult. For many mothers, conquering overprotectiveness is extremely difficult, but it can be accomplished with help from those who have already experienced and surmounted this problem. If the mother or other care providers continue to be overprotective, the results can be counterproductive, especially when the child reaches late adolescence and is unprepared for entry into adulthood or semi-independent living.

➤ **Dyadic relationship**
A relationship involving two individuals who develop and maintain a significant affiliation over time.

Mothers often develop strong **dyadic relationships** with their children with disabilities (Hauser-Cram, 2006). Dyadic relationships are evidenced by very close ties between these children and their mothers. Rather than communicating with all members of the family, a child may use his or her mother as the exclusive channel for communicating needs and making requests. Dyadic relationships may also develop between other members of the family. Certain siblings may turn to each other for support and nurturing. Older siblings may take on the role of parent substitutes as a result of their new caregiving responsibilities, and their younger siblings, who come to depend on older siblings for care, then tend to develop strong relationships with them.

Every family has a unique power structure. In some families the father holds most of the power or control, and in others the governance of the family lies with the mother or the family at large. *Power*, in the context of this discussion, is defined as the amount of control or influence one or more family members exert in managing family decisions, assigning family tasks, and implementing family activities. Just as families vary greatly in their membership and their organization, the power structure within each family varies with the characteristics of its members. That power structure may be altered substantially by the arrival of an infant with disabilities. Siblings, for example, may need to assume greater power as they take on more responsibilities for themselves and others.

Many children with disabilities are being raised by foster parents, single parents, parents of blended families, and lesbian and gay parents. Furthermore, about half a million children are cared for through various state social services organizations and agencies (Fish, 2000). It is clear that all child care professionals need to work effectively and respectfully with all families, learning about their unique needs and responding with family-sensitive programs and interventions (Ulrich, 2003). A number of organizations and publications provide support to these families, including the Single Parent Resource Center, *Gay Parent* magazine, Single Parents, the Family Pride Coalition, SafeTPlace, the Single Parents Association Online, Parents Without Partners, and the Single Parent Network.

The nature of families may vary, but one common factor is the presence of a child with a disability. This child deserves the attention and support of school personnel and other professionals, no matter what type of family unit the child is part of. The people who serve as primary caregivers or legal guardians of the child should be invited to participate fully in all programs and support services (Fish, 2000).

Spousal Relationships

The following statement illustrates the interactions and outcomes that a couple may experience in living with a child with a disability.

> When I think about having another child, I panic. In fact, I have consumed hours of psychological time thinking about my little boy and our response to him. Actually, my husband and I really haven't dealt successfully with our feelings. Two years ago, I gave birth to a little boy who is severely disabled. I was about 26 years old and my husband was 27.

FOCUS **4**
Identify three aspects of raising a child with a disability that contribute to spousal stress.

We didn't know much about children, let alone children with disabilities, nor did we ever think that we would have a child who would be seriously disabled. When the pediatrician suggested institutionalization for the child, we just nodded our heads. Believe it or not, I had merely looked at him through the observation windows once or twice.

Recently, my husband gave me an ultimatum: "Either you decide to have some children, or I'm going to find someone who will." (There are, of course, other things that are bothering him.) Since the birth of this child, I have been absolutely terrified of becoming pregnant again. As a result, my responses to my husband's needs for physical affection have been practically absent—or should I say, nonexistent. I guess you could say we really need some help.

Parents of children with disabilities need time to be together. This is often made possible through respite care.

An infant with a chronic health condition or disability may require more immediate and prolonged attention from the mother for feeding, treatment, and general care, and her attention may become riveted on the life of the child. The balance that once existed between being a mother and being a partner no longer exists. The mother may become so involved with caring for the child that other relationships lose their quality and intensity. The following statements express the feelings that may surface as a result:

Angela spends so much time with Juan that she has little energy left for me. It is as if she has become consumed with his care.

You ask me to pay attention to Juan, but you rarely spend any time with me. When am I going to be a part of your life again?

I am developing a resentment toward you and Juan. Who wants to come home when all your time is spent waiting on him?

Although these feelings are typical of some fathers, other fathers have the opposite reaction. Some may become excessively involved with their disabled children's lives, causing their partners to feel neglected. Mothers deeply involved in caregiving may feel overworked, overwhelmed, and in need of a break or reprieve. They may wonder why their spouses are not more helpful and understanding. However, fathers who assist with the burdens of caring serve as a buffer, contributing to their partner's well-being and resilience. Day-to-day physical and psychological support provided by fathers is invaluable to mothers of children with disabilities (Simmerman, Blacher, & Baker, 2001). This support is also predictive of couple satisfaction and contentment (Simmerman et al., 2001). Moreover, fathers who effectively employ problem-focused coping, actively confronting stressful problems associated with rearing a children with disabilities, contribute to higher marital adjustment in their spouses (Stoneman & Gavidia-Payne, 2006).

Fear, anger, guilt, and resentment often interfere with a couple's capacity to communicate and seek realistic solutions. Fatigue itself profoundly affects how couples function and communicate. As a result, some parents of children with disabilities join together to create **respite care** programs, which give them a chance to get away from the demands of childrearing and to relax and renew their relationship (Baskin & Fawcett, 2006). Other factors also contribute to spousal stress: unusually heavy financial burdens for medical treatment or therapy; frequent visits to treatment facilities; forgone time in couple-related activities; lost sleep and fatigue, particularly in the early years of the child's life; and social isolation from relatives and friends.

Research related to spousal stress and instability is often contradictory (Seltzer et al., 2001). Some families experience extreme spousal turmoil, often culminating in separation and eventually divorce, yet others experience the usual joys and challenges of being married. Recent

➤ **Respite care**

Assistance provided by individuals outside the immediate family to give parents and other children within the family time away from the child with a disability for a recreational event, a vacation, and so on. Some states provide funding to families to secure this kind of care.

research suggests that there is "a detectable overall negative impact on marital adjustment, but this impact is small and much lower than would be expected given earlier assumptions about the supposed inevitability of damaging impacts of children with disabilities on family well-being" (Risdal & Singer, 2004, p. 101).

Parent-Child Relationships

The relationships between parents and children with disabilities are a function of many factors. Some of the most crucial are the child's age and gender; the family's socioeconomic status, coping strength, and composition (one-parent family, two-parent family, or blended family); and the nature and seriousness of the disability. Families go through a developmental sequence in responding to the needs and nuances of caring for children with disabilities:

1. The time at which parents learn about or suspect a disability in their child.
2. The period in which the parents make plans regarding the child's education.
3. The point at which the individual with a disability has completed his or her education.
4. The period when the parents are older and may be unable to care for their adult off-spring (Turner, 2000).

The nature and severity of the disability and the willingness of the parents to adapt and to educate themselves regarding their role in helping the child have an appreciable influence on the parent-child relationship that eventually emerges.

Many mothers of children with severe disabilities or serious illnesses face the dilemma of finding suitable baby-sitters. The challenge is far greater than one might imagine:

> Marcia's a very mature girl for her age, but she becomes almost terrified when she thinks that she might have to hold our new son, Jeremy. He has multiple disabilities.
>
> I don't dare leave him with our other two children, Amy and Mary Ann. They're much too young to handle Jeremy. But I need to get away from the demands that seem to be ever present in caring for Jeremy. If I could just find one person who could help us, even just once a month, things would be a lot better for me and my family.

Locating a youth or adult who is willing and able to provide quality care for an evening or weekend is extremely difficult. In some areas of the country, however, enterprising teenagers have developed baby-sitting businesses that specialize in tending children with disabilities. Frequently, local disability associations and parent-to-parent programs help families find qualified baby-sitters or other respite care providers.

Time away from the child with a disability or serious illness gives parents and siblings a chance to meet some of their own needs (Chan & Sigafoos, 2000). Parents can recharge themselves for their demanding regimens, and siblings can use the exclusive attention of their parents to reaffirm their importance in the family and their value as family members. Consider the challenges one mother faces in caring for her children (see Case Study: Rita). Imagine for a moment what is must be like to demonstrate this kind of care and commitment as a parent.

MOTHER-CHILD RELATIONSHIPS. If a child's impairment is congenital and readily apparent at birth, the mother often becomes primarily responsible for relating to the child and attending to his or her needs. If the infant is born prematurely or needs extensive, early medical assistance, that relationship and bonding may be slow to emerge, for many reasons. The mother may be prevented from engaging in the anticipated feeding and caregiving activities, because the child may need to spend many weeks in an isolette supported by sophisticated medical

RITA

Please review this brief description of Rita's activities as a single parent of two children with disabilities. As you read through the case, think about what you might do if you were approached to identify ways in which the community, neighbors, service providers, and others might be helpful to her in caring for her children and herself.

My weekdays start about 4:45 in the morning. I get up, take my shower, get everything ready for the day. Pull their snack packs, put their ice packs in there, put them by the door—just get it organized. Around 6:30–6:45 in the morning I wake them up. I usually dress them—at least once because they will take something off and throw it around and around the house. Both of the children—I do this individually to each of the children. I come downstairs and we normally eat breakfast. We are out of the house somewhere around 7:30, if I'm lucky, and they remember to leave everything at the door . . . .

[We] get home around 6:45–7:00 in the evening. Right away . . . normally on the weekend I cook enough so I just pull out a portion; defrost it in the microwave and heat it up. That's their first meal of the night.

I put them down initially for bedtime around 8:30 but they have difficulty going to sleep at night so between 8:30 and 11:00 they are constantly up, walking down(stairs); I put them back to bed—they'll come down, put them back to bed; they'll come down. I'll put them back to bed. There's usually another snack in there. Up, down, back to bed. Around 11:00 at night that's when I get a chance to finish my ironing—finishing their snack packs for the next day and their lunches. That's all set up in the fridge. I just line it all up in there and it's ready to go. Put all the clothes out for the next day before I get to bed. I normally don't get more than about five hours of sleep a night. If I'm lucky, five. (Segal, 2004, p. 337)

APPLICATION

1. What could you do as a neighbor to be helpful to Rita?
2. What family-centered services might be useful to Rita?
3. What might you do, as Rita's employer, to help her meet the challenges of raising her children?
4. How might grandparents and other family members be involved in a meaningful fashion?
5. What ought to be the primary goals of the assistance provided by friends, associates, and family members?

equipment. As a consequence of the remoteness they experience in interacting with their infants in a personally satisfying manner, some mothers even come to question whether they really had a baby. For all these reasons, the development of mother-child attachment may be impeded.

In other cases, a mother may be forced into a close physical and emotional relationship with her child with a disability or injury (Baskin & Fawcett, 2006). The bond that develops between mother and child is one that cannot be severed. She assumes primary responsibility for fostering the child's emotional adjustment and encouraging the child's initial skills. She may function as the child's personal representative or interpreter. In this role, the mother becomes responsible for communicating the child's needs and desires to other family members.

Because of the sheer weight of these responsibilities, other relationships may wane or even disappear. The mother who assumes this role and develops a very close relationship with her offspring with a disability often walks a variety of tightropes (Larson, 2000). In her desire to protect her child, she may become overprotective and thus deny the child opportunities to practice the skills and participate in the activities that ultimately lead to independence. The mother may also underestimate her child's capacities and may be reluctant to allow her child to engage in challenging or risky ventures. In contrast, other mothers may neglect their children with disabilities and not provide the stimulation so critical to their optimal development. The mother's long-term vision for her child with a disability dramatically influences her behavior in preparing her son or daughter for adulthood and appropriate independence.

FATHER-CHILD RELATIONSHIPS. Information about fathers of children with disabilities is primarily anecdotal in nature or appears in case studies, websites, magazine articles, and books (Dollahite, 2001; Meyer, 1995). Some research suggests that the child care involvement of fathers with children with disabilities is not significantly different from that of fathers of other children (Turbiville, 1997; Young & Roopnarine, 1994). Moreover, fathers are generally more reserved and guarded in expressing their feelings than other family members (Lamb &

FOCUS **7**
Identify three ways in which fathers may respond to their children with disabilities.

In our society, individuals with appearances that are seen as atypical or unattractive are often rejected. . . . Today, many individuals with Down syndrome are able to read, write, and function at near normal levels due to educational and medical advances such as early intervention and cardiac surgery. . . . A persistent obstacle to full acceptance of individuals with Down syndrome in both school and society may be their characteristic appearance. . . . Facial plastic surgery is an intervention that has been proposed to improve the physical functioning, appearance, and social acceptance of individuals with Down syndrome.

Facial reconstructive surgery for children with Down syndrome has involved multiple procedures to correct one or all of the distinct facial features of Down syndrome. These procedures may include tongue reduction, implants in the bridge of the nose, chin, cheeks, and jawbone, and Z-plasty on the eyelids to erase characteristic epicanthal folds. . . . Other procedures may be done on soft tissue areas of the face, such as removal of part of the lower lip to prevent drooping, removal of fatty tissue under the chin, and correction of the position and size of the ears. . . .

Results of investigations into the benefits of surgery on appearance, physical functioning, and social acceptance are similar. As noted by Goeke et al. (in press), studies using impressionistic data based on the responses of parents and doctors who were directly involved showed evidence for the surgery's positive outcomes. (Goeke, 2003, p. 323)

Meyer, 1991). Fathers are more likely to internalize their feelings and may respond with coping mechanisms such as withdrawal, sublimation, and intellectualization. Fathers of children with mental retardation are typically more concerned than mothers about their children's social development and eventual educational status, particularly if the children are boys (Turbiville, 1997). Likewise, they are more affected than mothers by the visibility and severity of their children's condition (Lamb & Meyer, 1991; Turbiville, 1997; Wang et al., 2004). Often, fathers of children with severe disabilities spend less time interacting with them, playing with them, and engaging in school-related tasks. Also, fathers are more likely to be involved with their children with disabilities if the children are able to speak or interact with words and phrases.

The relationships that emerge between fathers and children with disabilities are affected by the same factors as mother-child relationships. One important factor may be the gender of the child (Turbiville, 1997). If the child is male and if the father had idealized the role he would eventually assume in interacting with a son, the adjustment for the father can be very hard. The father may have had hopes of playing football with the child, of his eventually becoming a business partner, or of participating with his son in a variety of recreational activities. Many of these hopes will not be realized with a son who has a severe disability.

Some parents consider medical interventions for altering the appearance of children with Down syndrome, hoping to contribute to or to enhance their social acceptance by peers and others (see Reflect on This, "Would You Consider This?").

When fathers withdraw or remain uninvolved with the child, other family members, particularly mothers, shoulder the caregiving responsibilities (Lamb & Meyer, 1991; Turbiville, 1997). This withdrawal often creates significant stress for mothers and other family members.

Fathers of children with disabilities prefer events and learning activities that are directed at the whole family, not just themselves (Turbiville & Marquis, 2001). They want to learn with other family members and other families how

Supportive fathers contribute to the happiness of their children and their spouses by being available for child care and other home-centered support.

to encourage learning, language development, and so on (Johnson, 2000). Service providers often neglect fathers, not realizing what important contributions they are capable of making. Fathers prefer programs that clearly address their preferences and priorities—programs that focus on their needs (Turbiville & Marquis, 2001). Children whose fathers are involved in their education perform better in school, evidence better social skills, are more highly motivated to succeed in school, and are less likely to exhibit violent or delinquent behavior later in their lives (Johnson, 2000; Turbiville, 1997).

Sibling Relationships

The responses of siblings to a sister or brother with a disability vary (Brown, 2004; Harris & Glasberg, 2003; McHugh, 2003; Meyer, 2005; Strohm, 2005). Upon learning that a brother or sister has a disability, siblings are frequently encumbered with different kinds of concerns. A number of questions are commonly asked: "Why did this happen?" "Is my brother contagious? Can I catch what he has?" "What am I going to say to my friends?" "I can't baby-sit him!" "Am I going to have to take care of him all of my life?" "Will I have children who are disabled too?" "How will I later meet my responsibilities to my brother with a disability and also meet the needs of my future wife and children?"

FOCUS **8**
Identify four ways in which siblings respond to a brother or sister with a disability.

Like their parents, siblings want to know and understand as much as they can about the disability of their sibling. They want to know how they should respond and how their lives might be different as a result of having a brother or sister with a disability. If these concerns can be adequately addressed, the prognosis for positive sibling involvement with the brother or sister with a disability is much better (Brown, 2004; Darley, Porter, Werner, & Eberly, 2002). (See the nearby Reflect on This for some young people's thoughts on the "up side" of having a sibling with a disability.)

Parents' attitudes and behaviors significantly affect those of their children toward siblings with disabilities (Grissom & Borkowski, 2002). If parents are optimistic and realistic in their views toward the child with a disability, then siblings are likely to mirror these attitudes and related behaviors. Generally, siblings have positive feelings about having a sister or brother with a disability and believe that their experiences with these siblings with disabilities have made them better individuals (Connors & Stalker, 2003; McHugh, 2003). Siblings who are kindly disposed toward assisting the child with a disability can be a real source of support (Brown, 2004; Harland & Cuskelly, 2000). One mother of an 11-year-old son put it this way: "In the past he has said, 'I wish I had a regular brother, I wish I had someone to play with.' And there are really some hard, sad things like that. But over the years, he has been such a support, and he will help in any way that we ask. I'm pleased with the qualities that I see in him" (Darley et al., 2002, pp. 34–35). Many siblings play a crucial role in fostering the intellectual, social, and affective development of a brother or sister with a disability.

However, negative feelings do exist among siblings of children with disabilities (Brown, 2004; Fine & Nissenbaum, 2000; Gray 2002; Masson et al., 2000). Loneliness, anxiety, guilt, and envy are common. Feelings of loneliness may surface in children who wanted a brother or sister with whom they could play. Anxiety may be present in a youth who wonders who will care for the sibling with a disability when the parents are no longer able to do so or are no longer alive. Guilt may arise for many reasons. Siblings, feeling they are obligated to care for the sibling with a disability, believe that failing to provide such care would make them bad or flawed. Similarly, they may feel guilty about the thoughts and feelings they have about their sibling, such as anger, frustration, resentment, and even hate. Realizing that

Siblings may play many roles in nurturing and supporting a brother or sister with a disaiblity.

WHAT ARE SOME ADVANTAGES—GOOD PARTS—OF HAVING A SIBLING WITH A DISABILITY?

You get more clothes because she doesn't care about them.
—Lydia Q., 13, Massachusetts

If my sister wasn't a part of my life, I would be so ignorant about people who have disabilities.
—Margaret C., 14, Illinois

It gives you a different outlook on life. You don't take anything in life for granted. Jeremy helps me to slow down and just take a moment to relax and love life.
—Lindsay D., 17, North Carolina

One thing is that we have a handicap sticker for parking. She also brings happiness to our family.
—Matt M., 15, Illinois

He changed who I was and opened my eyes about life.
—Alicia F., 17, Illinois

You don't have the little brother that picks up and listens to your phone calls, then tattles on you.
—Katelyn C., 16, Virginia

You become sensitive to other people's needs and more understanding and accepting of people's differences. You also get to be part of special groups like Sibshops.
—Christiana R., 13, Wisconsin

I've learned tolerance and respect, traits others may never learn and qualities that I value beyond everything else.
—Erin G., 14, Alberta

I think David's made me a better person. Definitely a less judgmental one.
—Katie J., 19, Illinois

SOURCE: Don Meyer, 2005, *The Sibling Slam Book* (pp. 72–73). Bethesda, Maryland: Woodbine House.

many parents would not respond positively to the expression of such feelings, some siblings carry them inside for a long time. One sibling put it this way:

> I love hanging out with my sib. Like any sibling, sometimes you love your brother one day and hate him the next. That is how it is with me. One day we will watch a movie, go on the Internet, and wrestle. The next day he may embarrass me. I have come to the realization that not all sibs, not just sibs with disabilities, like their sib every day. This was very important for me to learn. I hang out with my brother when I feel comfortable and I am in the mood, not because I feel obligated. — Emma F., 15, Michigan (Meyer, 2005, p. 33)

With increased inclusion of students with disabilities in neighborhood schools and other general education settings, siblings are often "called into action." They may be asked to explain their brother or sister's behavior, to give ongoing support or modeling, and respond to questions that teachers and others ask. Furthermore, they may be subject to teasing and related behaviors. Because of these and other factors, some siblings experience a greater risk for behavior problems.

Many siblings resent the time and attention that parents devote to their sister or brother with a disability. This resentment may also take the form of jealousy. Some siblings feel emotionally neglected, convinced that their parents are oblivious to their needs for attention and emotional support (McHugh, 2003). For some siblings, the predominant feeling is bitter resentment or even rage. For others, the predominant attitude toward the family experience of growing up with a brother or sister with a disability is a feeling of deprivation—the sense that their social, educational, and recreational pursuits have been seriously limited.

The following statements are examples of such feelings: "We never went on a family vacation because of my brother, Steven." "How could I invite a friend over? I never knew how my autistic brother would behave." "How do you explain to a date that you have a sister who is retarded?" "Many of my friends stopped coming to my house because they didn't know how to handle my brother, Mike, who is deaf. They simply could not understand him." "I was always shackled with the responsibilities of tending my little sister. I didn't have time to have fun with my friends." "I want a real brother, not a retarded one."

Siblings of children with disabilities may also believe they must compensate for their parents' disappointment about having a child with a disability (McHugh, 2003). They may feel an undue amount of pressure to excel or to be successful in a particular academic or artistic pursuit. Such perceived pressure can have a profound effect on siblings' physical and mental health, as can the expressed expectations of parents: "Why do I always feel as if I have to be the perfect child or the one who always does things right? I'm getting tired of constantly having to win my parents' admiration. Why can't I just be average for once?"

Support groups play an integral role in helping families understand and plan for their children with disabilities.

Support groups for siblings of children with disabilities are emerging and can be particularly helpful to adolescents. These groups introduce children and youth to the important aspects of having such a sibling in the family. They establish appropriate expectations and discuss questions that children or youth may be hesitant to ask in a family context. These groups also provide a therapeutic means by which these individuals analyze family needs and identify practical solutions (McHugh, 2003).

The best way to help siblings of children with disabilities is to support their parents and families. Participating in programs that encourage them to share information, to express feelings, and to learn how to be meaningfully involved with their sister or brother with a disability contributes much to their well-being.

FOCUS **9**

Indicate three ways in which grandparents and other extended family members may render support to families with children who have disabilities.

Extended Family Relationships

The term *extended family* is frequently used to describe a household in which an immediate (nuclear) family lives with relatives. For the purposes of this section, we use this term to refer to close relatives with whom the immediate family has regular and frequent contact, even though they do not necessarily live in the same household. These individuals may include grandparents, uncles, aunts, cousins, close neighbors, or friends.

When a grandchild with a disability is born, the joy of the occasion may dissipate. Like parents, grandparents are hurled into a crisis that necessitates reevaluation and reorientation (Scherman, Gardner, & Brown, 1995; Seligman & Darling, 1989). They must decide not only how they will respond to their child, who is now a parent, but also how they will relate to the new grandchild. Many grandparents, having grown up in a time when deviation from the norm was barely tolerated, much less understood, enter the process of weathering this crisis without much understanding.

Research indicates that grandparents, particularly during the diagnostic phase, play an influential role in how their children—the new parents—respond to the child with a disability. If the grandparents are understanding and emotionally supportive and provide good role models of effective coping, they may have a positive impact on their own children, the mother and father. If the grandparents are critical or not accepting, they may add to the parents' burden and complicate it even further (Seligman & Darling, 1989).

Grandparents and other family members may contribute a great deal to the primary family unit (Darley et al., 2002; Fox et al., 2002; Luckner & Velaski, 2004). The correlation

Grandparents or other close relatives may be very helpful in providing respite care.

between grandparent support and positive paternal adjustment is significant (Sandler, Warren, & Raver, 1995). One mother of a child with a disability described a grandmother's actions in this way: "She would play with my son and make a big game out of things that the therapist wanted him to practice. I believe [it is] because of her . . . [that my son] is able to walk today" (Baranowski & Schilmoeller, 1991, p. 441). If grandparents live near the family, they may become an integral part of the resource network and, as such, may be able to provide support before the energies of their children are so severely depleted that they require additional, costly help. To be of assistance, grandparents must be prepared and informed, which can be achieved in a variety of ways. They must have an opportunity to voice their questions, feelings, and concerns about the disability and its complications, and they must have means by which they can become informed. Parents can aid in this process by sharing, with their own parents and siblings, the pamphlets, materials, and books suggested by health, advocacy, and educational personnel.

Grandparents may be helpful in several other ways, providing much-needed respite care and sometimes financial assistance in the form of a "special needs" trust for long-term support of the grandchild (Carpenter, 2000). Furthermore, they may be able to give parents a weekend reprieve from the pressures of maintaining the household and to assist with transportation or baby-sitting. Grandparents often serve as third-party evaluators, providing solutions to seemingly unresolvable problems. The child with a disability profits from the unique attention that only grandparents can provide. This attention can be a natural part of special occasions such as birthdays, vacations, fishing trips, and other traditional family activities.

Multidisciplinary Collaboration and Family-Centered Support

Council for Exceptional Children

Standard 5: Learning Environments and Social Interactions

Family-centered services and programs encourage families to take the lead in establishing and pursuing their priorities (Brown, 2004) (see Figure 6.1). Professionals from many disciplines, including teachers, health care providers, and social services professionals, who embrace a family-centered philosophy focus on the strengths and capabilities of families, not on their deficits (Muscott, 2002, Raver, 2005; Ulrich, 2003). Furthermore, family-centered services are directed at the entire family, not just at the mother and the child or youth with a disability (Brown, 2004). "The pivotal element of family-centered care is the recognition that the family is constant and the intervention setting is temporary. . . . Family members are the hour-to-hour, day-to-day therapists and teachers" (Cantu, 2002, p. 48). Unfortunately, multidisciplinary family-centered support is primarily an early childhood phenomenon. The term *family-centered* and its variants are rarely found in the research literature on elementary schools (Dunst, 2002, p. 142). The picture is even more bleak in secondary schools, whose structural and organizational features do not promote effective collaboration with parents and families (Dunst, 2002).

Patterns of family-centered support vary as a function of the life cycle of the family, in parallel with the changing needs of parents, children with disabilities, and their siblings (Dunst, 2002; Turnbull & Turnbull, 2002; Vacca & Feinberg, 2000). Family support during the early childhood years focuses on delivering appropriate services in natural environments and on helping family members develop an understanding of the child's disability, deal with child-related behavior problems, become knowledgeable about their legal rights, learn how to deal with the stress in their lives, and learn how to communicate and work effectively with caregivers (Bruder, 2000; Gallagher, Rhodes, & Darling, 2004; Hauser-Cram et al., 2001; Raver, 2005; Shelden & Rush, 2001).

Family-centered, home-based services delivered by educational and social services professionals are directed at fostering appropriate motor development, promoting speech and language development, assisting with toilet training, and stimulating cognitive development. Other assistance may be targeted at helping parents address specific physical or health conditions that may require special diets, medications, or therapy regimens. The thrust of these services is compentency enhancement (Raver, 2005).

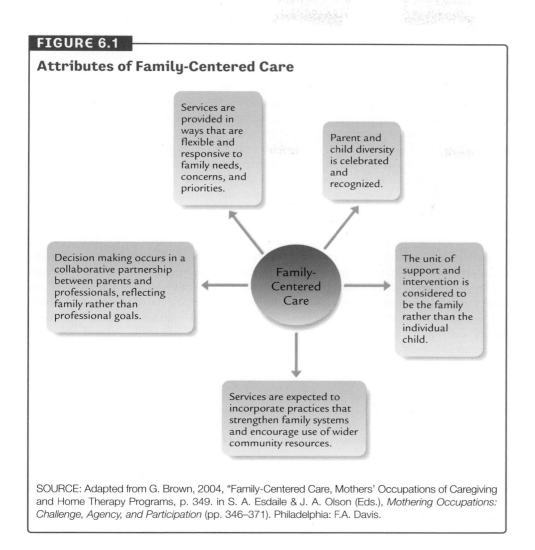

FIGURE 6.1

Attributes of Family-Centered Care

Services are provided in ways that are flexible and responsive to family needs, concerns, and priorities.

Parent and child diversity is celebrated and recognized.

Decision making occurs in a collaborative partnership between parents and professionals, reflecting family rather than professional goals.

Family-Centered Care

The unit of support and intervention is considered to be the family rather than the individual child.

Services are expected to incorporate practices that strengthen family systems and encourage use of wider community resources.

SOURCE: Adapted from G. Brown, 2004, "Family-Centered Care, Mothers' Occupations of Caregiving and Home Therapy Programs, p. 349. in S. A. Esdaile & J. A. Olson (Eds.), *Mothering Occupations: Challenge, Agency, and Participation* (pp. 346–371). Philadelphia: F.A. Davis.

During the elementary school years, parents become increasingly concerned about their children's academic achievement and social relationships. With the movement in many school systems to more inclusionary programs, parents may be particularly anxious about their children's social acceptance by peers without disabilities and about the intensity and appropriateness of instructional programs delivered in general education settings. Overall, parents seem to be pleased with the possibilities associated with inclusion, particularly its social aspects. Intervention efforts during this period are based on the individualized education program (IEP). Consistent collaboration between parents and various multidisciplinary team members is crucial to the actual achievement of IEP goals and objectives. Interestingly, little is known from a research perspective about the actual achievement outcomes of the IEP process (Turnbull & Turnbull, 2002).

Many children with disabilities attend their own neighborhood schools and are fully included in most every activity.

The secondary school years frequently pose significant challenges for adolescents with disabilities, their parents, and their families. Judith, the mother of a teenager with several disabilities, put it this way: "I am very worried about her future. We have joined the local ARC trust, but otherwise haven't made many plans for the future with her. I am hoping that she will be able to live in a supported setting as an adult, and that we might regain a little freedom, although that might be overly optimistic" (Baskin & Fawcett, 2006, p. 205). Like their peers, adolescents with disabilities confront significant physical and psychological issues, including learning how to deal with their emergent sexuality, developing satisfactory relationships with individuals outside of the home environment, and becoming appropriately independent. Parents of adolescents with disabilities agree that academic achievement is vitally important; nevertheless, they want their sons and daughters to develop solid social skills and other behaviors associated with empathy, perseverance, and character (Geisthardt, Brotherson, & Cook, 2002; Kolb & Hanley-Maxwell, 2003). Other issues must also be addressed during these years, such as preparing for employment, achieving appropriate self-regulation, learning how to access adult services, and developing community living skills.

During their children's adolescence, parents often experience less compliance with their requests and greater resistance to their authority. Parents who are attuned to the unique challenges and opportunities of this developmental phase work closely with education professionals and other personnel to develop IEPs that address these issues and prepare the adolescent with disabilities for entry into adulthood. As appropriate, youth with disabilities are now actively prepared for IEP meetings and participate in them with parents and professionals (Martin et al., 2006).

During their child's adolescence, parents are taught how to "let go," how to access adult services, and how to further their son or daughter's independence. Parents need information about the steps necessary to develop trusts and other legal documents for the welfare of all of their children.

The movement from high school to community and adult life can be achieved successfully by adolescents with disabilities if parents and professionals from a number of disciplines plan for this transition (Levinson, McKee, & DeMatteo, 2000). Transition planning is mandated by IDEA and is achieved primarily through the IEP planning process. IEP goals during this period are directed at providing instruction that is specifically related to succeeding in the community and functioning as an adult. These adult skills include behaviors related to self-regulation, self-realization, pychological empowerment, and autonomy. The challenge for parents and care providers is to help adolescents with disabilities achieve as much independence as possible, given their unique strengths and challenges.

Collaborating with Professionals

The interaction between professionals and parents is too often marked by confusion, dissatisfaction, disappointment, and anger (Blue-Banning, Summers, Frankland, Nelson, & Beegle, 2004; Carpenter, 2000). Consider the concern this father expresses:

> When the physician walked in to deliver the message he looked squarely into my wife's eyes. Even though we were sitting side by side on a chair turned hospital bed, his eyes never made contact with mine. I can surely empathize with the physician, who no doubt recognized the pain in my beautiful wife's eyes. The fact remained however that I, the father, was also in a state of complete emotional collapse. The failure of this particular physician to even make eye contact with me seemed to send the message that either I was not hurting, or I was to simply "take it like a man." I have to believe that this extremely capable physician did not do this with any degree of premeditation. Rather, he avoided eye contact with me, much less a dialogue, out of conditioning. While the mother-child bond is undeniably powerful, . . . our health care providers [must recognize] the equally powerful father-child bond. . . . Countless nights spent with grieving fathers over late night coffee has made me realize that many of my brothers are hurting and have minimal outlets for emotional expression. (Fischer, 2003, p. 1)

Available research and other new developments have led many observers to believe that relationships between parents and professionals can be significantly improved (Carpenter, 2000; Fine & Nissenbaum, 2000; Johnson, 2000; Lake & Billingsley, 2000; McKay, 2000; Ulrich, 2003). One parent described the emotional support she received in this way: "[T]here was no time that I didn't think I could call Dr. Tiehl and just cry, or, you know, bring all the boys in and Dr. Tiehl would just scoop up Matthew for me and walk away for a while so that I could talk to Matthew's teacher" (Fox et al., 2002, p. 444).

Council for Exceptional Children

Standard 10: Collaboration

Another parent, in speaking about a physician, said the following: "[E]very time I talk to him he'll give me words of encouragement. He'll say something like, 'You know you are Devante's primary caretaker and the best thing you can do for him is to love him.' I mean, this is regardless of if I bring him in for a scraped knee or ear infection, it's always something about just loving him and being there for him and understanding" (Fox et al., 2002, p. 444).

Indeed, progress has been made in helping professionals communicate and relate more effectively to parents and others responsible for children and youth with disabilities (Lake & Billingsley, 2000; Simpson & Zurkowski, 2000). This is particularly true in the preparation of special educators and others who serve as direct and indirect service providers in family, school, and community-based programs (Correa, Hudson, & Hayes, 2004; Rupiper & Marvin, 2004). The Debate Forum "Univeral Health Care" addresses this much-discussed issue in the context of services for children with disabilities.

One such collaborative approach that involves families and professionals from many different disciplines is positive behavior support (PBS) (Fox & Dunlap, 2002; Frankland, Edmonson, & Turnbull, 2001). This approach focuses on changing disruptive behaviors and supporting behaviors that are needed and valued by parents, neighbors, teachers, and other community members. In effect, all important players in the child's or youth's life become interveners, working together to achieve well-defined outcomes. These may include skills related to making and keeping friends, replacing loud vocalizations with more appropriately toned speech and language, and developing new ways of responding to events that normally spur aggression or property destruction (Fox et al., 2002). The primary focus of PBS is to develop behaviors that are useful and highly valued at home, at school, and in the community.

Effective collaborators establish rapport with the families, create supportive environments, demonstrate sensitivity to family issues, affirm the positive features of the child with a disability, share valuable information, contribute to the parent's confidence, clarify expectations, and listen well (Blue-Banning et al., 2004; Luckner & Velaski, 2004). Care providers seek to understand the family, its ecology, and its culture, taking the time to listen and to build relationships (Fox et al., 2002; Franklin et al., 2004; Rivers, 2000; Zhang & Bennett, 2001). Superb family support programs help keep families together, enhancing their capacity to meet the needs of the individual with a disability, reducing the need for out-of-home placement, and giving families access to typical social and recreational activities. The following statement expresses a parent's wonderment at the effectiveness of family-centered support: "They never give up. I am just astounded by the many creative ways they keep coming up with to help him. Oftentimes they do not understand him, but they never give up. At one point I had to ask myself: Are these people for real? . . . I cannot believe how genuine and real they really are" (Worthington, Hernandez, Friedman, & Uzzell, 2001, p. 77).

Strengthening Family Supports

The primacy of the family in contributing to the well-being of all children is obvious. Research indicates that family members provide one another with the most lasting, and often the most meaningful, support (Cantu, 2002; Raver, 2005; Turnbull & Turnbull, 2002). Much of what has been done to assist children with disabilities, however, has supplanted rather than supported families in their efforts to care and provide for their children. Monies and resources have been directed historically at services and supports outside the family environment or even beyond the neighborhood or community in which the family lives.

Increasingly, policy makers and program providers are recognizing the importance of the family and its crucial role in the development and ongoing care of a child with a disability. Services are now being directed at the family as a whole, rather than just at the child with the disability (Raver, 2005). This support is particularly evident in the individualized family service plan (IFSP), as discussed earlier in this chapter and in Chapter 3. Such an orientation honors the distinctive and essential role of parents, siblings, and other extended family members as primary caregivers, nurturers, and teachers. Additionally, these services provide parents and siblings with opportunities to engage in other activities that are important to their physical, emotional, and social well-being.

Family supports are directed at several goals. These include enhancing the caregiving capacity of the family; giving parents and other family members respite from the often tedious and sometimes unrelenting demands of caring for a child with a serious disability; assisting

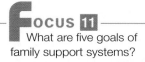

Focus 10
Describe five behaviors that skilled and competent professionals exhibit when interacting with and relating to families that include children with disabilities.

Focus 11
What are five goals of family support systems?

Council for Exceptional Children

Standard 5: Learning Environments and Social Interactions

the family with persistent financial demands related to the disability; providing valuable training to families, extended family members, concerned neighbors, and caring friends; and improving the quality of life for all family members.

Research suggests that family support services, particularly parent-to-parent programs, have reduced family stress, increased the capacity of family members to maintain arduous care routines, improved the actual care delivered by family members, provided substantial emotional support, and increased their capacity to cognitively cope with the demands of parenting (Singer et al., 1999). Parent-to-parent programs carefully match a parent in a one-to-one relationship with a trained and experienced supporting parent. The supporting parent is a volunteer who has attended a training program and is open to listening, sharing, and being available when a parent needs support (Herbert, Klemm, & Schimanski, 1999).

Because of these family support services and parent-to-parent programs, many children and youth enjoy the relationships and activities that are a natural part of living in their own homes, neighborhoods, and communities. These services enable children and youth with disabilities to be truly a part of their families, neighborhoods, and communities.

Collaborative Training for Parents, Families, and Professionals

FOCUS 12

Identify the critical aspects of collaborative training for parents, families, and professionals.

PARENT AND FAMILY TRAINING. Parent training is an essential part of most early intervention programs for children with disabilities. As part of IDEA, the thrust of parent training is directed at helping parents acquire the essential skills that will assist them in implementing their child's IEP or IFSP (Tynan & Wornian, 2002). No longer is the child viewed as the

DEBATE FORUM

UNIVERSAL HEALTH CARE: SHOULD IT BE A REALITY FOR ALL—EVEN CHILDREN WITH DISABILITIES?

WHAT IS IT?

Universal health care is a health care system in which all residents of a geographic or political entity have their health care paid for by the government, regardless of what medical condition is involved.

WHAT WOULD BE COVERED?

Universal health care systems vary in which services are covered completely, which are covered partially, and which are not covered at all. Some of these services may include medically necessary services from physicians, physical therapy, occupational therapy, mammography screenings, immunization services, treatment of sexually transmitted diseases, HIV testing, optometry and vision services, alcohol and drug abuse treatment and rehabilitation services, mental health services, gambling addiction services, dentistry services, prescription drugs, medical supplies and appliances, podiatry services, chiropractic services, emergency medical transportation, nursing home care, and home care services.

HOW WOULD IT BE FUNDED?

The majority of universal health care systems are funded primarily by tax revenue. Some nations, such as Germany and France, employ a multipayer system in which health care is funded by private and public contributions.

WHAT IS A "SINGLE-PAYER" SYSTEM?

The term, *single-payer*, refers to a health care system in which only one entity is billed for all medical costs, typically a government-run universal health care agency or department. Instead of billing the patient directly, government agencies (such as Medicare and DSHS), and any number of private insurance companies, a doctor or pharmacist need only bill the universal health care agency. This service is also offered in the private sector by entities known as "cash flow companies" in the medical billing industry. Such entities provide some of the benefits of single-payer plans, including reduced paperwork and guaranteed payment. However, these benefits are often neutralized by the fees associated with employing a cash flow company's services. Such fees typically would not exist in a government-run universal health care system, because a government agency does not need to concern itself with turning a profit.

WHAT COUNTRIES PROVIDE UNIVERSAL HEALTH CARE?

Australia, Austria, Belgium, Canada, Cuba, Denmark, Finland, France, Germany, Japan, The Netherlands, New Zealand, Norway, Portugal, Seychelles, South Africa, Spain, Sweden, Taiwan, and The United Kingdom are among the many countries that have various types of universal health care systems.

POINT

- Health care is a right.
- Universal health care provides coverage to all citizens, regardless of ability to pay.
- Health care becomes increasingly unaffordable for businesses and individuals.
- Universal health care provides for uninsured adults who may forgo treatment needed for chronic health conditions.
- Universal health care reduces wastefulness and inefficiencies in the delivery of health care.
- A centralized national database makes diagnosis and treatment easier for doctors.
- Health care professionals would be able to concentrate on treating patients rather than focusing on administrative duties.
- Universal health care would encourage patients to seek preventive care, enabling problems to be detected and treated earlier.
- The profit motive in the current health care systems adversely affects the cost and quality of health care.

COUNTERPOINT

- Health care is not a right.
- Universal health care would increase waiting times for medical treatments.
- Universal health care would lessen the overall quality of health care.
- Unequal access and health disparities still exist in some universal health care systems.
- Government agencies are less efficient because of bureaucratic procedures.
- Citizens may not exercise restraint in their drug costs and doctor visits; thus costs increase.
- Universal health care must be funded with higher taxes and/or spending cuts in other areas.
- Profit motives, competition, and individual ingenuity lead to greater cost control and effectiveness in providing health care.
- Uninsured citizens can sometimes receive health and emergency care from alternative sources such as non-profits and government-run hospitals.
- Government-mandated procedures reduce doctor flexibility and lead to poor patient care.
- Healthy people who take care of themselves have to pay for the burden of those who smoke, are obese, and the like.
- Some systems have banned physicians from selling services outside the system, forcing universal compliance with one system, which some say violates human liberties.
- Loss of the option of going into private practice and possible reduced pay may dissuade many would-be doctors from pursuing the profession.
- Implementation of universal health care would cause losses in insurance industry jobs and set the stage for other business closures in the private sector.

SOURCE: Adapted from *Universal Health Care*, Wikipedia. Retrieved June 2, 2006; from http://en.wikipedia.org/wiki/Universal_health_care

---

primary recipient of services; instead, services and training are directed at the complex and varied needs of each family and its members (Adams, 2001). Much of the training is conducted by experienced and skilled parents of children with disabilities, who volunteer their time as part of their affiliation with an advocacy or support group. These support groups play an invaluable role in helping parents, other family members, neighbors, and friends respond effectively to the child or youth with a disability. In describing her experiences with parent training, one mother made the following comments:

Standard 10: Collaboration

> Oh yes, she [the parent trainer] was excellent. Our third child was a 29 weeker. We didn't know any of that stuff. . . . I enjoyed finding out what was going on and knowing the signals, because if he's going to throw up a red flag to me, I want to know how to react. . . . I couldn't believe all the stuff that she told me that I didn't know. . . . she related to all members of the family. . . . I appreciated what she did. (Ward, Cronin, Renfro, Loman, & Cooper, 2000)

Training may be focused on feeding techniques, language development activities, toilet training programs, reducing and replacing challenging behaviors, motor development activities, or other issues important to parents (Buschbacker, Fox, & Clarke, 2004; Kazdin, 2005;

Training provides parents with skills for promoting cognitive development, for dealing with challenging behaviors, and for setting appropriate expectations.

Tynan & Wornian, 2002). For parents of youth or adults with disabilities, the training may be directed at accessing adult services, using functional assessment and positive behavior support, accessing recreational programs, finding postsecondary vocational programs, locating appropriate housing, or legal planning for guardianship (Chambers, Hughes, & Carter, 2004; Russell & Grant, 2005). In some instances, the training centers on giving parents meaningful information about their legal rights, preparing them to participate effectively in IEP meetings, helping them understand the nature of their child's disability, making them aware of recreational programs in their communities, or alerting them to specific funding opportunities. Through these training programs, parents learn how to engage effectively in problem solving and conflict resolution and thus are empowered and prepared to advocate for their children and themselves. Parent involvement with the education of their children with disabilities significantly benefits the children's learning and overall school performance.

The training of families is directed at siblings, grandparents, and other relatives. It may even involve close neighbors or caring friends who wish to contribute to the well-being of the family. Often these are individuals who are tied to the family through religious affiliations or long-standing friendships (Poston & Turnbull, 2004). Some families use a process referred to as GAP (group action planning). In this process, family members meet with service providers (case workers, speech clinicians, and other professionals) on a regular basis to learn together, to plan, and to make adjustments in the interventions currently in place (Devlin & Harber, 2004).

Siblings of children with disabilities need information about the nature and possible course of disabilities affecting their brother or sister (Chambers, Hughes, & Carter, 2004). Furthermore, they need social and emotional support and acknowledgment of their own needs for nurturing, attention, and affirmation. Some research suggests that many siblings know very little about their brother's or sister's disability, its manifestations, and its consequences. Siblings need to understand that they are not responsible for a particular condition or disability. Other questions also need addressing. These questions deal with the heritability of the disability, the siblings' future role in providing care, the ways in which siblings might explain the disability to their friends, and how the presence of the brother or sister with a disability will affect their family and themselves.

In most instances, the training of siblings occurs through support groups that are specifically designed for a particular age group. In these groups, siblings can express feelings, vent frustrations, and learn from others. They may also pick up pointers on how to deal with predictable situations—that is, what to say or how to respond. They may learn sign language, how to complete simple medical procedures, how to manage misbehavior, or how to use certain incentive systems. In some cases, they may become prepared for the eventual death of a brother or sister who has a life-threatening condition.

Training of grandparents, other relatives, neighbors, and friends is also crucial. They, like the siblings of children with disabilities, must be informed, must have opportunities to express feelings, must be able to ask pertinent questions, and must receive training that is tailored to their needs. If informed and well trained, they often provide the only consistent respite care that is available to families. Also, they may contribute invaluable transportation, recreational activities, baby-sitting, critical emotional support, and/or short-term and long-term financial assistance (Gorman, 2004).

COLLABORATIVE TRAINING FOR PROFESSIONALS. Collaborative training involves professionals, such as educators, social workers, psychologists, and health care professionals. This training focuses primarily on relationship building, communication, collaboration skills, and cross-cultural understanding (Correa & Jones, 2000; Raver, 2005; Santarelli, Koegel, Casas, & Koegel, 2001; Taylor & Baglin, 2000; Zhang & Bennett, 2001). Collaborative training

Council for Exceptional Children

Standard 9: Professional and Ethical Practice

is also aimed at helping professionals understand the complex nature of family cultures, structures, functions, and interactions, as well as at encouraging them to take a close look at their own attitudes, feelings, values, and perceptions about families that include children, youth, and adults with disabilities (Correa & Jones, 2000; Gorman, 2004; Stone, 2005; Turnbull & Turnbull, 2002). Unfortunately, some professionals see parents as part of the child's problem rather than as partners on a team. Moreover, they may be insensitive to the daily demands inherent in living with a child, youth, or adult who presents persistent challenges. As a consequence, they may use vocabulary that is unfamiliar to parents, may speak a language that is foreign to parents, may not give parents enough time to express their feelings and perceptions, and may be insensitive to cultural variations in ways of relating and communicating. Hence the communication and collaboration skills that are stressed in training for professionals include effective communication, problem-solving strategies, negotiation, and conflict resolution (Ortiz, 2006). See the Reflect on This "What I'd Tell That Doctor" for one youngster's advice to his obstetrician.

REFLECT ON THIS

WHAT I'D TELL THAT DOCTOR

When I was born, the obstetrician said that I cannot learn, never see my mom and dad and never learn anything and send me to an institution. Which I think it was wrong.

Today we were talking about if I could see my obstetrician and talk to him, here are things I would say . . .

I would say, "People with disabilities *can learn!*"

Then I would tell the obstetrician how smart I am. Like learning new languages, going to other foreign nations, going to teen groups and teen parties, going to cast parties, becoming independent, being . . . a lighting board operator, an actor, the backstage crew. I would talk about history, math, English, algebra, business math, global studies. One thing I forgot to tell the obstetrician is I plan to get a academic diploma when I pass my RCTs.* . . .

I will tell him that I play the violin, that I make relationships with other people, I make oil painting, I play the piano. I can sing, I am competing in sports, in the drama group, that I have many friends, and I have a full life.

So I want the obstetrician will never say that to any parent to have a baby with a disability any more. If you send a baby with a disability to an institution, the baby will miss all the opportunities to grow and to learn . . . and also to receive a diploma. The baby will miss relationships and love and independent living skills. Give a baby with a disability a chance to grow a full life. To experience a half-full glass instead of the half-empty glass. And think of your abilities not your disabilities.

I am glad that we didn't listen to the obstetrician . . .

Jason Kingsley, who was born with Down syndrome, as he appeared at age 3 on Sesame Street demonstrating his letter identification skills.

Living independently, Jason proudly opens the door of his new apartment.

*New York State Regents Competency Tests

SOURCE: Adapted from Jason Kingsley, 2004, "What I'd Tell That Doctor." In S. D. Klein & J. D. Kemp (Eds.), *Reflections from a Different Journey: What Adults with Disabilities Wish All Parents Knew* (pp. 14–15). New York: McGraw-Hill.

FOCUS 1 Identify five factors that influence the ways in which families respond to infants with birth defects or disabilities.

- The emotional stability of each family member
- Religious values and beliefs
- Socioeconomic status
- The severity of the disability
- The type of disability

FOCUS 2 What three statements can be made about the adjustments that parents experience in responding to infants or young children with disabilities?

- There is no linear movement through various stages of adjustment.
- Emotions of one period may overlap each other and resurface during another period.
- The adjustment process, for most parents, is continuous and distinctively individual.

FOCUS 3 Cite three ways in which a newborn child with disabilities influences the family social/ecological system.

- The communication patterns within the family may change.
- The power structure within the family may be altered.
- The roles and responsibilities assumed by various family members may be modified.

FOCUS 4 Identify three aspects of raising a child with a disability that contribute to spousal stress.

- A decrease in the amount of time available for the couple's activities
- Heavy financial burdens
- Fatigue

FOCUS 5 Identify four general phases that parents may experience in rearing a child with a disability.

- The diagnostic period: Does the child truly have a disability?
- The school period (elementary and secondary, with its inherent challenges: dealing with teasing and other peer-related behaviors, as well as learning academic, social, and vocational skills): Included in this period are the challenges of adolescence.
- The postschool period: The child makes the transition from school to other educational or vocational activities.
- The period when the parents are no longer able to provide direct care and guidance for their son or daughter.

FOCUS 6 Cite four factors that influence the relationship that develops between infants with disabilities and their mothers.

- The mother may be unable to engage in typical feeding and caregiving activities because of the intensive medical care being provided.
- Some mothers may have difficulty bonding to children with whom they have little physical and social interaction.
- Some mothers are given little direction in becoming involved with their children. Without minimal involvement, some mothers become estranged from their children and find it difficult to begin the caring and bonding process.
- The expectations that mothers have about their children and their own functions in nurturing them play a significant role in the relationship that develops.

FOCUS 7 Identify three ways in which fathers may respond to their children with disabilities.

- Fathers are more likely than mothers to internalize their feelings.
- Fathers often respond to sons with disabilities differently from the way they respond to daughters.
- Fathers may resent the time their wives spend in caring for their children with disabilities.

FOCUS 8 Identify four ways in which siblings respond to a brother or sister with a disability.

- Siblings tend to mirror the attitudes and behaviors of their parents toward a child with disabilities.
- Siblings may play a crucial role in fostering the intellectual, social, and affective development of the child with a disability.
- Some siblings may attempt to compensate for their parents' disappointment by excelling in an academic or artistic pursuit.
- Some siblings respond with feelings of resentment or deprivation.

FOCUS 9 Indicate three ways in which grandparents and other extended family members may render support to families with children who have disabilities.

- They may provide their own children with weekend respite from the pressures of the home environment.
- They may assist occasionally with baby-sitting or transportation.
- They may support their children in times of crisis by listening and helping them deal with seemingly unresolvable problems and by providing short-term or long-term financial assistance.

FOCUS 10 Describe five behaviors that skilled and competent professionals exhibit when interacting with and relating to families that include children with disabilities.

- They establish rapport.
- They create supportive environments.
- They demonstrate sensitivity to the needs of these families and seek to understand the culture and ecology of each family.
- They share valuable information.
- They listen well.

FOCUS 11 What are the five goals of family support systems?

- Enhancing the caregiving capacity of the family
- Giving parents and other family members respite from the demands of caring for a child with a disability
- Assisting the family with persistent financial demands related to the child's disability
- Providing valuable training to families, extended family members, concerned neighbors, and caring friends
- Improving the quality of life for all family members

FOCUS 12 Identify the critical aspects of collaborative training for parents, families, and professionals.

- To help parents with specific activities, such as feeding their children, teaching them language skills, helping them become toilet trained; accessing adult services; finding appropriate housing; and locating appropriate postsecondary vocational training.
- To help parents understand their legal rights and contribute to their understanding of the nature of their child's disability.
- To make them aware of services in the community and of available financial assistance.
- The training of families is directed at siblings, grandparents, and other relatives. It may even involve close neighbors or caring friends who wish to contribute to the well-being of the family.
- Some families use group action planning, a process in which family members meet with service providers on a regular basis to learn together, to plan, and to make adjustments in the interventions currently in place.
- Siblings need social and emotional support and acknowledgment of their own needs for nurturing, attention, and affirmation.
- Collaborative training for professionals focuses primarily on relationship building, communication, collaboration skills, and cross-cultural understanding.

BUILDING YOUR PORTFOLIO

Council for Exceptional Children

If you are thinking about a career in special education, you should know that many states use national standards developed by the Council for Exceptional Children (CEC) to assess a teacher candidate's knowledge and skills for working with students with disabilities. See a complete listing of the ten CEC Content Standards on the inside front cover of this text.

CEC Content Standards Addressed in This Chapter

1 Foundations
3 Individual Learning Differences
5 Learning Environments and Social Interactions
9 Professional and Ethical Practice
10 Collaboration

Assess Your Knowledge of the CEC Standards Addressed in This Chapter

Some states require that teacher candidates develop a portfolio of products that demonstrate mastery of the CEC content standards. To

assist in the development of products for this portfolio, you may wish to complete the following activities.

- Complete a written test of the chapter's content.

  If your instructor requires a written test of your content knowledge for this chapter, keep a copy for your portfolio. A practice test on the information covered in this chapter is available through the Human Exceptionality Companion Website and the Student Study Guide.

- Respond to the Application Questions for Case Study "Rita."

  Review the Case Study and respond in writing to the application questions. Keep a copy of the Case Study and of your written response for your portfolio.

- Participate in a Community Service Learning Activity.

  Community service is a valuable way to enhance your learning experience. Visit our companion website for suggested community service learning activities that correspond to the information presented in this chapter. Develop a reflective journal of the service learning experience for your portfolio.

The Fathers Network

http://www.fathersnetwork.org

The Fathers Network offers resources and information for fathers, family members, and care providers. The network provides news, press releases, and recent articles about children and youth with disabilities and their families.

Beach Center on Disability

http://www.beachcenter.org

This website is designed for parents and other family members who are interested in children, youth, and adults with disabilities. The Beach Center provides meaningful materials, training, and other services to families that include children with disabilities.

National Respite Care Network

http://www.archrespite.org/index.htm

This website provides valuable information for parents, families, and other care providers who are seeking temporary relief in caring for children, youth, and adults with disabilities, chronic or terminal illnesses, or related conditions.

Gabriel's Angel Network: Celebrating the Lives of Children with Disabilities

http://www.gabrielsangelnetwork.org/html/gabe_s_story.html

This website contains some very tender and compelling videos and other valuable information provided by parents about their children with disabilities. It is also a site where fathers, mothers, and other care providers can connect in real time with other parents of children with disabilities.

National Dissemination Center for Children with Disabilities (NICHCY)

http://www.nichcy.org

This center, funded by the federal government, provides up-to-date information about disabilities and special education issues. If you are thinking about a career in special education, you should know that many states use national standards developed by the Council for Exceptional Children (CEC) to assess a teacher candidate's knowledge about and skills for working with students with disabilities. See a complete listing of the ten CEC Content Standards on the inside front cover of this text.

PACER Center

http://www.pacer.org/

The primary mission of the PACER Center is to enhance the quality of life for children and youth with disabilities, as well their families. It provides high-quality workshops and excellent materials for parents, professionals, and other care providers.

Technical Assistance Alliance for Parent Centers

http://www.taalliance.org/Centers/index.htm

A great resource for parents seeking help on a variety of fronts: obtaining appropriate services for their children with disabilities; working to improve achievement for all children; training and informing families, parents, and professionals on a variety of topics; assisting with the resolution of problems between families and schools or other agencies; and connecting children and youth with disabilities to community resources.

DisabilitiesResources.org

http://www.disabilityresources.org/

This website is a wonderful source of well-organized materials for parents, siblings, families, and professionals. It not only provides multiple links to other sites but also describes in some depth each link and its connection to the disability of interest.

FURTHER READINGS

Exceptional Parent (EP) Magazine.

For years, the editors and writers of Exceptional Parent (EP) Magazine *have provided parents, families, and professionals with insightful information related to children, youth, and adults with disabilities. Many of the articles are written by parents or siblings of children with disabilities. This magazine is published in River Edge, New Jersey. Its website is http://www.exceptionalparent.com.*

Klein, S. D., & Kemp, J. D. (2004). *What adults with disabilities wish all parents knew.* New York: McGraw-Hill.

This very insightful book contains first-rate, first-person recommendations and accounts of adults with disabilities. Parents, teachers, health care, and social services professionals will profit much from these very personal portrayals written by talented and capable individuals with disabilities.

Baskin, A., & Fawcett, H. (2006). *More than a mom: Living a full and balanced life when your child has special needs.* Bethesda, MD: Woodbine House.

As its title indicates, this book provides invaluable suggestions about living a full and balanced life as a mother of a child with disabilities. Each chapter is packed with wonderful ideas about caring for oneself, creating meaningful family times, and other topics highly relevant for mothers.

Meyer, D. (2005). *The sibling slam book: What it's really like to have a brother or sister with special needs.* Bethesda, MD: Woodbine House.

This is a highly readable, even entertaining book for siblings of children and youth with disabilities. It begins with a list of very interesting and relevant questions answered by siblings of children and youth with special needs.

Strohm, K. (2005). *Being the other one: Growing up with a brother or sister who has special needs.* Boston, MA: Shambhala Publications.

This excellent resource for siblings, parents, and professionals is especially effective when discussing sibling-related issues and opportunities. It is an insightful and compelling book written by a sibling of a sister with cerebral palsy.

COMPANION WEBSITE

Visit the companion website at college.hmco.com/pic/hardman9e for additional resources that support this text:

- HM Video Cases that present actual classroom scenarios that you may face everyday as a teacher

- Practice ACE Exams that will help you prepare for quizzes, tests, and certification exams
- Flashcards of key terms
- Weblinks

7

Learning Disabilities

TO BEGIN WITH . . .

HIGH PREVALENCE OF LEARNING DISABILITIES

During the early part of the 21st century, specific learning disabilities continued to be the most prevalent kind of disability in the United States from the elementary years into adolescence and early adulthood. In 2004 over 2.8 million children and youth (aged 6 through 21) with learning disabilities were served under IDEA. (Dietz & Montague, 2006; U.S. Department of Education, 2006a)

BOYS WITH LEARNING DISABILITIES OUTNUMBER GIRLS—MAYBE

Conventional wisdom has suggested that boys identified with learning disabilities substantially outnumber girls. However, some recent research calls into question the levels cited in the past, questioning the referral processes and reading assessment (Lerner & Kline, 2006; Siegel & Smyth, 2005; Young, 2005).

LEARNING DISABILITY ACCOMMODATIONS ON SAT INCREASING

The number of students requesting accommodations on SAT tests—the great majority involving claims for a learning disability—has increased, although questions have been raised regarding the benefits and validity of such accommodations. (Lighthouse, 2006; Ungerleider & Maslow, 2001)

DIRECT INSTRUCTION EFFECTIVE WITH THOSE HAVING LEARNING DISABILITIES

Direct instruction is an efficient and reliable instructional approach for students with LD; in some cases, it is even more effective than for students in general education. (Tournaki, 2003; Walker, Shippen, Alberto, Houchins, & Cihak, 2005)

FOCUS PREVIEW

1. Cite four reasons why definitions of learning disabilities have varied.

2. Identify three classification schemes that have been used with people who have learning disabilities.

3. Give two current estimated ranges for the prevalence of learning disabilities.

4. Identify seven characteristics attributed to those with learning disabilities, and explain why it is difficult to characterize this group.

5. List four causes thought to be involved in learning disabilities.

6. Cite four questions that are addressed by screening assessment of students who seem to have learning disabilities.

7. Identify three types of interventions or treatments employed with people diagnosed as having learning disabilities.

8. How are the services and supports for adolescents and adults with learning disabilities different from those used with children?

▼ SNAPSHOT

JAMAAL

Jamaal's difficulties first became evident in kindergarten, which is somewhat unusual because learning disabilities are more typically identified later in the school years. His parents were frustrated and, like so many parents of children with disabilities, felt that they were not doing something correctly. Jamaal was also aware of some difficulties; he mentioned to the teacher that he sometimes had trouble concentrating.

Jamaal expresses himself well verbally and comes up with great ideas; however, he has particular problems with reading and writing. It appears that he trails his classmates in sight word vocabulary, which influences both academic areas. His fourth-grade teachers are now working very hard to integrate into his instruction the important skills that he will need in order to succeed as he moves on in school. Although he exhibits some disruptive behaviors, they are relatively minor in the overall context of Jamaal's world. He fundamentally has a positive outlook and already has plans for attending college—rather long-range planning for a fourth grader!

MATHEW

Note: The following is an excerpt from a statement prepared by an upper-division psychology undergraduate student who has learning disabilities. Mathew tells his story in his own words, recounting some of his school experiences, his diagnosis, and how his learning disabilities affect his academic efforts.

Imagine having the inability to memorize times tables, not being able to "tell time" until the ninth grade, and taking several days to read a simple chapter from a school textbook.

In elementary and high school, I was terrified of math classes for several reasons. First, it did not matter how many times I practiced my times tables or other numerical combinations relating to division, subtraction, and addition. I could not remember them. Second, I dreaded the class time itself for inevitably the teacher would call on me for an answer to a "simple" problem. Multiplication was the worst! Since I had to count on my fingers to do multiplication, it would take a lot of time and effort. Do you know how long it takes to calculate 9×7 or 9×9 on your fingers? Suffice it to say too long, especially if the teacher and the rest of the class are waiting.

When I was a sophomore at a junior college, I discovered important information about myself. After two days of clinical cognitive testing, I learned that my brain is wired differently than most individuals. That is, I think, perceive, and process information differently. They discovered several "wiring jobs" which are called learning disabilities. First, I have a problem with processing speed. The ability to bring information from long-term memory to consciousness (into short-term memory) takes me a long time. Second, I have a deficit with my short-term memory. This means that I cannot hold information there very long. When new information is learned, it must be put into long-term memory. This is an arduous process requiring the information to be rehearsed several times. Third, I have a significant problem with fluid reasoning. Fluid reasoning is the ability to go from A to G without having to go through B, C, D, E, and F. It also includes drawing inferences, coming up with creative solutions to problems, solving unique problems, and the ability to

transfer information and generalize. Hence, my math and numerical difficulties. . . .

With all of this knowledge, I was able to use specific strategies that will help me in compensating for these neurological wiring patterns. Now I tape all lectures rather than trying to keep up taking notes. I take tests in a room by myself and they are not timed. Anytime I need to do mathematical calculations I use a calculator. . . .

SOURCE: From *Understanding Child Behavior Disorders* (4th ed., p. 238), by D. M. Gelfand and C. J. Drew, 2003, Belmont, CA: Wadsworth. Used with permission.

The field of learning disabilities was virtually unrecognized prior to the 1960s. These disabilities are often considered mild because people with learning disabilities usually have average or near-average intelligence, although learning disabilities can occur at all intelligence levels. People with learning disabilities achieve at unexpectedly low levels, particularly in reading and mathematics. Recently, the term *learning disabilities* has come to be regarded as a generic label representing a very heterogeneous group of conditions, which range from mild to severe in intensity (Keogh, 2005; Mather & Gregg, 2006; Smith, 2004). In many cases, people with learning disabilities have been described as having "poor neurological wiring." Individuals with learning disabilities exhibit a highly variable and complex set of characteristics and needs. Consequently, they present a substantial challenge to family members and professionals. This set of challenges, however, is repeatedly met with significant success, as evidenced by many stories of outstanding achievement by adults who have histories of learning disabilities in childhood.

Definitions and Classifications

Confusion, controversy, and polarization have been associated with **learning disabilities** as long as they have been recognized as a family of disabilities. In the past, many children now identified as having specific learning disabilities would have been labeled remedial readers, remedial learners, emotionally disturbed, or even children with intellectual disabilities—if they received any special attention or additional instructional support at all. Impaired academic performance is a major element in most current definitions of learning disabilities (Cornett-DeVito & Worley, 2005; Mather & Gregg, 2006; Stone & May, 2002). Today, services related to learning disabilities represent the largest single program for exceptional children in the United States. Although this program is relatively new, its growth rate has been unparalleled by any other area in special education: Those with learning disabilities represented about 25% of all students with disabilities in 1975, but that figure had grown to nearly 50% in 2000 (U.S. Department of Education, 2006a). Both definition and classification in the field of learning disabilities are still under discussion in many forums (e.g., Fletcher, Francis, & Morris, 2005; Keogh, 2005; Wallach, 2005).

Definitions

The definitions of learning disabilities vary considerably. This inconsistency may be due to the field's unique evolution, rapid growth, and strong interdisciplinary nature. The involvement of multiple disciplines (such as medicine, psychology, speech and language, and education) has also contributed to confusing terminology. For example, education coined the phrase *specific*

FOCUS 1
Cite four reasons why definitions of learning disabilities have varied.

➤ **Learning disability**
A condition in which one or more of the basic psychological processes involved in understanding or using language are deficient.

Council for Exceptional Children
Standard 1: Foundations

learning disabilities; psychology uses this term as well as others, such as *perceptual disorders* and *hyperkinetic behavior*; the speech and language field employs the terms *aphasia* and *dyslexia*; and medicine uses the labels *brain damage, minimal brain dysfunction, brain injury,* and *impairment*. *Brain injury, minimal brain dysfunction,* and *learning disabilities* are the most commonly used terms, though all appear in various disciplines (Keogh, 2005; Mather & Gregg, 2006).

A child with a brain injury is described as having an organic impairment resulting in perceptual problems, thinking disorders, and emotional instability. A child with minimal brain dysfunction manifests similar problems but often shows evidence of difficulties in language, memory, motor skills, and impulse control. Individuals with minimal brain dysfunction are often characterized as average or above average in intelligence, which clearly distinguishes the disorder from intellectual disabilities.

EARLY HISTORY. Samuel Kirk, an educator, introduced the term *specific learning disabilities* in 1963. His original concept remains largely intact today. The condition is defined by delays, deviations, and performance discrepancies in basic academic subjects (such as arithmetic, reading, spelling, and writing) and by speech and language problems that cannot be attributed to intellectual disabilities, sensory deficits, or emotional disturbance. The common practice in education is to describe individuals with learning disabilities on the basis of what they are *not*. For example, although they may have a number of problems, they do not have intellectual disabilities, emotional disturbance, or hearing loss. *Learning disabilities* is an umbrella label that includes a variety of conditions and behavioral and performance deficits (Gelfand & Drew, 2003).

IDEA AND JOINT COMMITTEE DEFINITIONS. The Individuals with Disabilities Education Act (IDEA) of 2004 stated that

> "Specific learning disability" means a disorder in one or more of the basic psychological processes involved in understanding or in using language, spoken or written, which may manifest itself in an imperfect ability to listen, think, speak, read, write, spell, or to do mathematical calculations. The term includes such conditions as perceptual disabilities, brain injury, minimal brain dysfunction, dyslexia, and developmental aphasia. The term does not include children who have learning problems which are primarily the result of visual, hearing, or motor disabilities, of [intellectual disabilities], of emotional disturbance, or of environmental, cultural, or economic disadvantage. (IDEA 2004, PL 108-446, Sec. 602[30]).

This definition codified into federal law many of the concepts found earlier in Kirk's description. It also furnished a legal focus for the provision of services in the public schools. Providing service guidelines through the IDEA definition matured over the years with criteria from the companion "Rules and Regulations." Figure 7.1 summarizes the criteria for identifying a specific learning disability that were published in the *Federal Register* in 2006. These criteria are consistent with the IDEA definition presented earlier.

The IDEA definition and the guidelines in Figure 7.1 primarily describe conditions that are not learning disabilities and give little substantive explanation of what *does* constitute a learning disability (i.e., a discrepancy between achievement and ability in areas of oral expression, listening, written expression, and so on). This use of exclusionary criteria still surfaces in a variety of circumstances (e.g., Mayes & Calhoun, 2005; Picton & Karki, 2002). The IDEA definition is also somewhat ambiguous because it prescribes no clear way to measure a learning disability. Another definition statement presented by the National Joint Committee for Learning Disabilities (1998) included certain important elements not expressed in IDEA:

> Learning disabilities is a general term that refers to a heterogeneous group of disorders manifested by significant difficulties in the acquisition and use of listening, speaking, reading, writing, reasoning, or mathematical abilities. These disorders are intrinsic to the individual, [are] presumed to be due to central nervous system dysfunction, and may occur across the lifespan. Problems in self-regulatory behaviors, social perception, and social interaction may exist with learning disabilities but do not by themselves constitute a learning disability. Although learning disabilities may occur concomitantly with other handicapping conditions (e.g., sensory impairment, [intellectual disabilties], serious emotional disturbance), or with extrinsic influences (such as cultural differences, insufficient or inappropriate instruction), they are not the result of those conditions or influences. (1998, p. 187)

FIGURE 7.1

Criteria for Identifying a Specific Learning Disability

1. A team may determine that a child has a specific learning disability if the child does not achieve adequately for the child's age or meet state-approved grade-level standards in one or more of the seven areas noted below, when provided with learning experiences and instruction appropriate for the child's age or state-approved grade-level standards. Criteria adopted by a state must permit the use of a process based on the child's response to research-based intervention and cannot prohibit the use of a severe discrepancy between intellectual ability and achievement.

    i. Oral expression

    ii. Listening comprehension

    iii. Written expression

    iv. Basic reading skill

    v. Reading comprehension

    vi. Mathematical calculation

    vii. Mathematical reasoning

2. The team may *not* identify a child as having a specific learning disability if the lack of achievement is primarily the result of:

    i. A visual, hearing, or motor impairment,

    ii. [Intellectual Disabilities],

    iii. Limited English proficiency,

    iv. Emotional disturbance,

    v. Environmental, cultural, or economic disadvantage, or

    vi. Lack of instruction

SOURCE: Adapted from "Rules and Regulations," August 14, 2006, section [300.541, *Federal Register*, p. 12457] (b).

This definition is important to our discussion for several reasons. First, it describes *learning disabilities* as a generic term that refers to a heterogeneous group of disorders. Second, a person with learning disabilities must manifest significant difficulties. The word *significant* is used in an effort to remove the connotation that a learning disability constitutes a mild problem. Finally, this definition makes it clear that learning disabilities are lifelong problems and places them in a context of other disabilities and cultural differences. These are important refinements of earlier definitions.

OTHER ISSUES IN DEFINING LEARNING DISABILITIES. Varying definitions and terminology related to learning disabilities emerged partly because of different theoretical views of the condition. For example, perceptual-motor theories emphasize an interaction between various channels of perception and motor activity. Perceptual-motor theories of learning disabilities focus on contrasts between the normal sequential development of motor patterns and the motor development of children with learning disabilities. Children with learning disabilities are seen as having unreliable and unstable perceptual-motor abilities, which present problems when such children encounter activities that require an understanding of time and space.

Language disability theories, on the other hand, concentrate on a child's reception or production of language (Wallach, 2005). Because language is so important in learning, these theories emphasize the relationship between learning disabilities and language deficiencies. Just looking at these two theories, then, makes it clear that very different viewpoints exist regarding these disabilities. This field encompasses many theoretical perspectives on the nature of learning problems, as well as on their causation and treatment.

Still another view of learning disabilities has emerged in the past several years. Some researchers have suggested that many different, specific disorders have been grouped under one term. They see *learning disabilities* as a general umbrella term that includes both academic and behavioral problems, and they have developed terminology to describe particular conditions falling within the broad category of learning disabilities. Some of these terms refer to particular areas of functional academic difficulty (such as math, spelling, and reading), whereas others reflect difficulties that are behavioral in nature. This perspective was adopted by the American Psychiatric Association in the fourth edition of its *Diagnostic and Statistical Manual of Mental Disorders* (American Psychiatric Association, 2000). This manual uses the term *learning disorders* to refer specifically to disorders in areas such as reading, mathematics, and written expression.

In one sense, this strategy is not surprising. It has long been acknowledged that people with learning disabilities make up a very heterogeneous group, yet professionals have continued to describe them as though they were much alike. Such characterizations typically reflect the theoretical or disciplinary perspective of the professional, rather than an objective behavioral description of the individual being evaluated. This has resulted in a tendency to focus on defining a particular disorder and then categorizing people according to such definitions, rather than objectively evaluating the individual with problems. This approach often leads to error when members of a population that exhibits a wide variety of disorders are evaluated.

Research on learning disabilities also reflects the problems of definition. The wide range of characteristics associated with children who have learning disabilities, along with various methodological challenges (such as heterogeneous populations and measurement error) has caused many difficulties in conducting research on learning disabilities (Gall, Gall, & Borg, 2007; Salkind, 2006; Suter, 2006). Generalizing research results is hazardous, and replication of studies is very difficult. Efforts to standardize and clarify definitions continue, and they are important for both research and intervention purposes.

The notion of severity has largely been ignored in earlier definitions and concepts related to learning disabilities. Although this has changed somewhat, severity still receives only limited attention (see Pierangelo & Giuliani, 2006; Porter, 2005). Learning disabilities have probably been defined in more ways by more disciplines and professional groups than any other type of disability (Keogh, 2005; Mather & Gregg, 2006; Mayes & Calhoun, 2005). We describe the behavioral characteristics of learning disabilities from different theoretical viewpoints, because it is important to know how a person might be classified as having a learning disability according to different perspectives.

Classification

Learning disabilities is a term applied to a complex constellation of behaviors and symptoms. Many of these symptoms or characteristics have been used for classification purposes at one time or another. Three major elements have a substantial history of being employed in classifying learning disabilities: discrepancy, heterogeneity, and exclusion—all points that we noted earlier (Fletcher, Denton, & Francis, 2005; Pierangelo & Giuliani, 2006). Discrepancy approaches to classification are based on the notion that there is an identifiable gap between intelligence and achievement in particular areas, such as reading, math, and language. Heterogeneity classification addresses the differing array of academic domains where these children often demonstrate performance problems (as in the seven areas noted in Figure 7.1). The exclusion approach reflects the idea that the learning disabilities cannot be due to selected other conditions. The evidence supporting the use of discrepancy and exclusion as classification parameters is not strong, whereas heterogeneity seems to be supported. Some of the literature on learning disabilities asserts that discrepancy is a worthwhile definition element. Some theorists also contend that the approach to definition should be inclusive, focused on the specific attributes that need attention rather than on what learning disabilities are not (Francis, Fletcher, & Stuebing, 2005; Keogh, 2005).

Reference to severity appears in the literature on learning disabilities fairly often, even though it is not accounted for in most definitions (Gangadharan, Bretherton, & Johnson, 2001; Porter, 2005). Prior to 2004, IDEA mandated that any criterion for classifying a child as having learning disabilities must be based on a preexisting severe discrepancy between intel-

FOCUS **2**

Identify three classification schemes that have been used with people who have learning disabilities.

lectual capacity and achievement. The determination of referral for special services and type of educational placement was related to the following criteria:

1. Whether a child achieves commensurate with his or her age and ability when provided with appropriate educational experiences

2. Whether the child has a severe discrepancy between achievement and intellectual ability in one or more of seven areas related to communication skills and mathematical abilities

A child's learning disability must be determined on an individual basis, and there must be a severe discrepancy between achievement and intellectual ability in one or more of the following areas: oral expression, listening comprehension, written expression, basic reading skill, reading comprehension, mathematical calculation, or mathematical reasoning.

The meaning of the term *severe discrepancy* is debated among professionals (e.g., Burns & Senesac, 2005; Mayes & Calhoun, 2005; Stanovich, 2005). Although it is often stipulated as a classification parameter, there is no broadly accepted way to measure it. What is an "acceptable" discrepancy between a child's achievement and what is expected at his or her grade level? 25 percent? 35 percent? 50 percent? Research on discrepancy classifications, particularly in reading, reveals that the discrepancy concept has mixed empirical support, particularly in field applications (Dean, Burns, & Grialou, 2006; Fletcher, Denton, & Francis, 2005; Stuebing et al., 2002).

REFLECT ON THIS

REDEFINING LEARNING DISABILITIES USING A RESPONSE-TO-INTERVENTION MODEL

Many professionals and policy makers in the field have raised concerns about the concept of using a discrepancy-based formula for identifying students with learning disabilities, including under- and overidentification of different groups of students as having learning disabilities, inconsistencies in how the formula is applied, and the denial of assistance to students until upper elementary years. Many students show early signs of struggling with academic skills but do not qualify until later grades when the discrepancy between cognitive and academic functioning widens. This essentially denies assistance to stuents until they have experienced years of failure. Researchers are currently investigating a response-to-intervention model for identifying students with learning disabilities.

Key to a response-to-intervention model is using systematic and ongoing measurement of progress of academic skills for all students. This allows teachers to both identify students who need additional help and monitor progress closely. By tracking student's progress closely, teachers will see that some students respond well to supplemental intervention and do not require specialized services such as special education. Students who do not respond well, or more slowly, may need more intensive, specialized instruction and are likely candidates for consideration of a learning disabilities designation. This moves the focus of identification away from nebulous and hard-to-measure psychological constructs and onto instruction. Students who fail to progress despite adequate opportunities to learn may require special consideration.

Current conceptualization of a response-to-intervention approach have three tiers of instruction designed to provide appropriate educational support to all students regardless of labels or designations. These tiers are as follows:

Tier One consists of a well-designed, comprehensive core academic program (most current research is focusing on reading). All students receive adequate instruction and are assessed at regular intervals to determine which students are not making satisfactory progress in this tier.

Tier Two is supplemental instruction for students showing early signs of academic difficulty according to systematic progress monitoring assessment. After approximately 10 weeks of instruction, teachers would identify students for supplemental intervention. These students would receive 20 to 30 minutes of supplemental instruction in addition to continuing in the core program. Students are assessed at regular intervals (e.g., every 10 weeks) to determine if they are ready to exit Tier Two, continue, or move on to Tier Three.

Tier Three represents more specialized and intensive instruction for students who have not responded to intervention in Tier Two. After receiving a significant amount of comprehensive instruction in the first tier and supplemental instruction in the second, some students will continue to have difficulty. At this point, teachers may decide to make a referral to special education or another type of service that would provide more intensive, focused, specialized intervention in the third tier.

SOURCE: Excerpted from Haager, D., & Klinger, J.K. (2005). *Differentiating instruction in inclusive classrooms: The special educator's guide.* Boston: Pearson–Allyn & Bacon, p. 32.

In recognizing the controversy surrounding the use of a "discrepancy formula" as the only criterion for determining eligibility for special education services, current IDEA regulations no longer *require* that school districts determine whether a child has a severe discrepancy between intellectual ability and achievement. Schools now have the option of using a process that determines a child's **response to intervention (RTI)**, which is aimed at evidence-based decisions and is research based (U.S. Department of Education, 2006b). The basic concept of RTI is empirically based decision making—that is, determining intervention success on the basis of data reflecting the student's performance. This approach has considerable appeal for several reasons. In particular, RTI is focused on the child's academic response to specific instruction, and it is also another perspective for assessing children with learning disabilities. This latter rationale is very useful for some children who are struggling with early academic work but may not evidence a severe discrepancy. RTI is attracting increased interest generally— and particularly regarding children with learning disabilities (Bradley, Danielson, & Doolittle, 2005; Dean et al., 2006; Deshler, Mellard, & Tollefson, 2005). The Reflect on This box summarizes key elements of the RTI model.

Lack of agreement about concepts basic to the field has caused difficulties in both research and treatment for those with learning disabilities. Nonetheless, many people who display the challenging characteristics of learning disabilities are successful in life and have become leaders in their fields (an example is Charles "Pete" Conrad, Jr., who became an astronaut).

➤ **Response to Intervention (RTI)**

A student's response to instructional interventions that have been determined to be effective through scientifically based research.

Prevalence

Problems in determining the numbers of people with learning disabilities are amplified by differing definitions, theoretical views, and assessment procedures. Prevalence estimates are highly variable, ranging from 2.7% to 30% of the school-age population (Dietz & Montague, 2006; Lerner & Kline, 2006). The most reasonable estimates range from 5% to 10%, as shown in Figure 7.2.

One of the major recurring themes in this text is that assessment of and accountability for all students are essential, but these are challenging tasks in the area of learning disabilities because of the varying prevalence estimates. Accuracy and reliability are vital cornerstones of

FOCUS **3**
Give two current estimated ranges for the prevalence of learning disabilities.

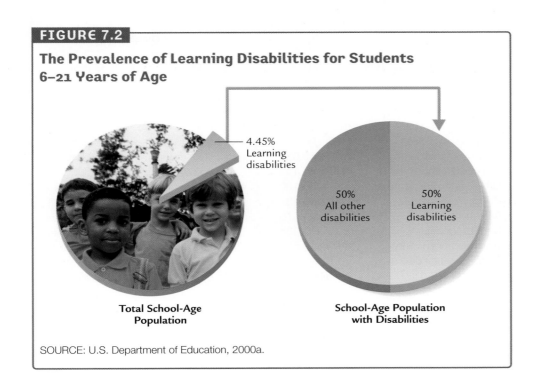

FIGURE 7.2

The Prevalence of Learning Disabilities for Students 6–21 Years of Age

4.45% Learning disabilities

50% All other disabilities

50% Learning disabilities

Total School-Age Population

School-Age Population with Disabilities

SOURCE: U.S. Department of Education, 2000a.

Much has changed from the educational delivery for these children with learning disabilities to that found in today's schools.

assessment and accountability. The variation in prevalence estimates is partially due to changing definition statements, along with the pressing need to provide service to a very large number of children having academic problems. Variation in estimates of the prevalence of learning disabilities raises the issue of what is acceptable public and educational policy and is directly related to assessment accuracy.

Since learning disabilities emerged as a category, their prevalence has been high compared to that of other exceptionalities and so has been controversial for many years. Learning disabilities are among the most common of all reported causes of disability. However, it is difficult to find one prevalence figure that is agreed on by all involved in the field. In 2004, over 6.1 million children with disabilities (ages 6 to 21) were being served under IDEA in the United States. Of that number, over 2.8 million were classified as having learning disabilities, a figure that represents nearly 50% of the population with disabilities being served (U.S. Department of Education, 2006a).

Professionals and parents involved with other disability groups often question the high prevalence of learning disabilities. In some cases, they simply know they must compete for the limited funds distributed among groups of people with different disabilities. Others, however, are concerned that the learning disabilities category is being overused to avoid the stigma associated with other labels or because of misdiagnosis, which may result in inappropriate treatment. And the heavy use of the learning disabilities label in referrals for services continues to grow, as illustrated in Table 7.1.

TABLE 7.1

Changes in Number of Students Ages 6 Through 21 Served Under IDEA by Disability Category, 1995 and 2004

DISABILITY	1995	2004	CHANGE IN NUMBER
Specific learning disabilities	2,601,825	2,839,694	237,869
Speech or language impairments	1,026,878	1,151,260	124,382
[Intellectual Disabilities]	585,571	567,780	−17,791
Emotional disturbance	439,164	484,488	45,324
Multiple disabilities	94,529	133,364	38,835
Hearing impairments	68,035	72,626	4,591
Orthopedic impairments	63,152	65,452	2,300
Other health impairments	134,160	511,869	377,709
Visual impairments	25,487	26,130	643
Autism	29,076	166,424	137,348
Deaf-blindness	1,385	1,725	340
Traumatic brain injury	9,579	23,248	13,669
Developmental delay[1]	—	74,377	—
All disabilities	5,078,841	6,118,437	1,039,596

[1]Beginning in 1997, states had the option of reporting children aged 3 through 9 in the developmental delay category.

SOURCE: U.S. Department of Education (2006). Twenty-sixth Annual Report to Congress on the Implementation of the Individuals with Disabilities Act. (a)

Although discrepancies in prevalence estimates occur in all fields of exceptionality, the area of learning disabilities seems more variable than most. This can be partly attributed to the different procedures used by the agencies, states, and researchers who do the counting and estimating (e.g., Booth, Booth, & McConnell, 2005; Dietz & Montague, 2006; Fuchs, 2005). Another source of discrepancy may be differing or vague definitions of learning disabilities. Prevalence figures gathered through various studies are unlikely to match when different definitions determine what is counted. This situation is common in the field of learning disabilities.

Albert Einstein failed math in elementary school and demonstrated little ability or interest in school work. His intellectual genius and capability in science and mathematics was not evident until his early teens. Einstein represents the discrepancy that can exist in an individual student.

Characteristics

Although specific learning disabilities are often characterized as representing mild disorders, few attempts have been made to validate this premise empirically. Identification of subgroups, subtypes, or severity levels in this heterogeneous population was largely neglected in the past. However, some attempts have been made in recent years to address these issues (Porter, 2005; Wakely, Hooper, & de Kruif, 2006). Subtype and **comorbidity** research are appearing in the current literature at increasing rates (Deitz & Montague, 2006; van Lang, Bouma, & Sytema, 2006). Subtype research investigates the characteristics of youngsters to identify distinctive groups within the broad umbrella of learning disabilities. Comorbidity research investigates the degree to which youngsters exhibit evidence of multiple disabilities or conditions (such as learning disabilities and ADHD, or learning disabilities and personality disorders) (Brook & Boaz, 2005; Daley, 2006; McNamara, Willoughby, & Chalmers, 2005). In some ways these approaches are exploring similar questions from differing perspectives. Certainly, the learning disabilities category has multiple subgroups, because the definitions have been so broad and the group is so heterogeneous. Likewise, many students who have learning disabilities also exhibit characteristics of other disorders, such as emotional difficulties.

Researchers have investigated a broad array of subgroups ranging from people with reading problems to those with hyperactivity (e.g., Dietz & Montague, 2006; van Lang et al., 2006). Attention-deficit/hyperactivity disorder (ADHD) is a condition often associated with learning disabilities (Sparks, Javorsky, & Philips, 2005). Several characteristics of ADHD have long been recognized in many children with learning disabilities, and there is a significant level of comorbidity between the two conditions (some estimates are as high as 25%). However, there is certainly not complete correspondence in characteristics between the two (e.g., Filippatou & Livaniou, 2005; McNamara, Willoughby, & Chalmers, 2005). Because of the co-occurrence, distinctions between learning disabilities and ADHD as categories are not always clear. This is not surprising, given the historical overlap in definitions and the very heterogeneous groups of people being considered (Brook & Boaz, 2005; Fussell, Macias, & Saylor, 2005). Chapter 8 examines ADHD in detail.

In time, subtype and comorbidity research may lead to more effective intervention, geared precisely to the specific needs of distinctive groups within the large, heterogeneous population with learning disabilities (Bender, 2004; Fletcher, 2005; Dietz & Montague, 2006).

Perceptions of teachers and other professionals have also been solicited in an effort to understand more about learning disabilities (Eckert, Dunn, Codding, Begeny, & Kleinmann, 2006; Ring & Travers, 2005). Although they too exhibit some error and variability, such ratings are stable enough to support reliable distinctions, in terms of both subtype and severity,

➤ **Comorbidity**
The occurrence together of multiple medical conditions or disabilities.

Focus **4**
Identify seven characteristics attributed to those with learning disabilities, and explain why it is difficult to characterize this group.

Council for Exceptional Children

Standard 2: Development and Characteristics of Learners

Standard 3: Individual Learning Differences

Many students with learning disabilities have difficulties with word recognition, word knowledge, and the use of context in learning to read.

among students with learning disabilities. Some research suggests that teachers have mixed judgments about the nature of a disability and its severity, depending on the particular child and the academic content involved (Berry, 2006; Eckert et al., 2006). Teacher perceptions and knowledge have long been cited as a badly overlooked source of assessment information; their input is vital in designing instructional adaptation for students with learning problems. Also, teachers working with students with learning disabilities quite often encounter youngsters who they firmly believe should not be considered as having a learning disability. Such reports support the contention that many students currently being served as having learning disabilities may have been inappropriately referred. Thirty years ago, Larsen (1978) commented on this phenomenon:

> It is . . . likely that the large number of students who are referred for mild to moderate underachievement are simply unmotivated, [are] poorly taught, come from home environments where scholastic success is not highly valued, or are dull [to] normal in intelligence. For all intents and purposes, these students should not automatically be considered as learning disabled, since there is little evidence that placement in special education will improve their academic functioning. (p. 7)

Academic Achievement

Problems and inconsistencies in academic achievement largely prompted the recognition of learning disabilities as an area of exceptionality. Individuals with learning disabilities, though generally of or above-average or near-average intelligence, seem to have many academic problems. These problems usually persist from the primary grades through the end of formal schooling, including college (Sams, Collins, & Reynolds, 2006; Sparks et al., 2005). However, researchers are suggesting that educational planning for students with learning disabilities should offer a variety of long-range alternatives, including options and academic preparation for postsecondary education (Luna, 2003; Roer-Strier, 2002; Tarleton & Ward, 2005).

READING. Reading problems are observed among students with learning disabilities more often than problems in any other area of academic performance. Historically, as the learning disabilities category began to take shape, it was applied to youngsters who had earlier been identified as remedial reading students. Estimates have suggested that as many as 90% of students with learning disabilities have reading difficulties, and the *low* estimates are around 60% (Bender, 2004). Clearly, problems with the reading process are very prevalent among students identified as having learning disabilities (Schmidt, Rozendal, & Greenman, 2002; Rix, 2006;

Siegel & Smythe, 2005; Silliman & Scott, 2006). However, the specific problems that they have in reading vary as much as the many components of the reading process.

Both word knowledge and word recognition are vitally important parts of reading skill, and they both cause problems for people with learning disabilities (Gonzalez, 2002; Wilber & Cushman, 2006). When most of us encounter a word that we know, we recall its meaning from our "mental dictionary," but for unfamiliar words we must "sound out" the letters and pronounce the words by drawing on our knowledge of typical spelling patterns and pronunciation rules. This ability is very important in reading, both because we cannot memorize all words and because we constantly encountered new ones.

Students must also be able to generalize letter patterns and draw analogies with considerable flexibility. Good readers usually accomplish this task rather easily, quite quickly, and almost automatically after a little practice (Kamhi & Catts, 2002). Students with reading disabilities, however, experience substantial difficulty with this process, and when they can do it, they seem to manage it only slowly and laboriously. Such students need specific training and practice in strategies that will help them succeed at recognizing words (Manset-Williamson & Nelson, 2005; Wilber & Cushman, 2006).

Another important component of reading involves the use of context to determine meaning. Here again, good readers tend to be rather adept, but poor readers have trouble. Although poor readers encounter substantial problems in using context information to recognize words or infer their meaning, specific instruction improves their performance. Moreover, students with learning disabilities do not use background information effectively. Good and poor readers differ in the degree to which they use background knowledge for reading (Coyne, Kame'enui, & Simmons, 2001; Smith, 2004). Similarly, some students with learning disabilities focus on minor details within a text, without distinguishing the important ideas from those of less significance. A specific focus on learning strategies can help these students. Teaching them skills such as organizing and summarizing, using mnemonics, problem solving, and relational thinking can offset these difficulties and enhance their academic performance (Gerber, 2005; Prater, 2007).

Reading involves many skills (such as the ability to remember and the ability to focus on important, rather than irrelevant, aspects of a task) that also affect performance in other

➤ **Dyslexia**

A very severe type of learning disability that affects the ability to read, sometimes characterized by letter reversals such as reading b for d.

REFLECT ON THIS   DYSLEXIA: SEARCHING FOR CAUSES

Throughout history, people have always speculated about the cause of learning disabilities, particularly the most severe forms, such as **dyslexia** (a very rare condition). The constant search for the single or most prominent cause is jokingly called looking for the "bullet theory" by professionals in the field, most of whom believe that matters are more complicated than singular causation. However, "bullet theory" reports continue to make news in the popular press, perhaps because they are simple enough to present in short accounts (or in sound bites on television) and attribution is simple—"The cause is—" (fill in the blank).

Time magazine followed this trend on August 29, 1994, with "Brain Bane," an article reporting that researchers might have found a cause for dyslexia. Beginning with background information on dyslexia, its prevalence, and its characteristics, this article then moves to the final paragraph (where

barely one-third of the article is devoted to the main topic, causation). Here it is noted that Dr. Albert Galaburda of Harvard and Beth Israel Hospital in Boston has been conducting research on the brains of people with dyslexia who have died. Essentially, the research team sampled brain tissue from people with dyslexia (postmortem) and compared it with brain tissue collected from people who did not have dyslexia. Interestingly enough, these researchers found a difference in the size of nerve cells between the left and right hemispheres in tissue from people with dyslexia, but they found no such difference in the tissue from individuals without dyslexia. The researchers were careful to note that the size differential is only between 10 and 15%, but that was enough to capture the attention of *Time*. The public thirst for bullet theories is alive and well.

SOURCE: Adapted from "Brain Bane: Researchers May Have Found a Cause for Dyslexia" by C. P. Alexander, 1994, *Time*, 144(9), p. 61.

subject areas (Baxter, Woodward, & Olson, 2005; Bayliss, Jarrold, & Baddeley, 2005). Some difficulties experienced by people with learning disabilities emerge in more than one area, making it hard to pinpoint and explain the exact deficit. For example, does a child with reading disabilities have attention difficulties or working memory deficits? The problem could be caused by either disability or by a combination of the two. Specific instruction may improve performance, but if the focus of the training is too limited, the student may not generalize it to other relevant areas. Instruction that combines different methods (such as using both phonological awareness and instruction in specific skills) may serve students with reading disabilities better than applying only a single method (Boets, Wouters, & van Wieringen, 2006; Manset-Williamson & Nelson, 2005; Swanson & Howard, 2005). In cases of more severe disability (such as dyslexia), it may be necessary to teach the person to compensate for the problem by accessing information through other means (see the nearby Reflect on This, "Dyslexia: Searching for Causes"). In some cases the most effective instruction combines compensatory instruction with a direct focus on problem areas.

WRITING AND SPELLING. Children with learning disabilities often exhibit quite different writing performance than their peers without disabilities. This problem affects their academic achievement and frequently persists into adulthood. Difficulties may occur in handwriting (slow writing, spacing problems, poor formation of letters), spelling, and composition or general written expression (Chalk, Hagan-Burk, & Burke, 2005; Richards, et al., 2005; Wakely et al., 2006). Several such problems are illustrated in Figure 7.3.

Some children are poor at handwriting because they have not mastered the basic developmental skills required for the process, such as grasping a pen or pencil and moving it in a fashion that results in legible writing. In some cases, fine motor development seems delayed in children with learning disabilities, and that of course contributes to physical difficulty in using writing materials. Handwriting also involves an understanding of spatial concepts, such as up, down, top, bottom, and letter alignment. These abilities frequently are less well developed in youngsters with learning disabilities than in their peers without disabilities (Graham, Struck, Stantoro, & Berninger, 2006; Wakely et al., 2006). The physical actions involved in using pencil or pen, as well as problems in discerning spatial relationships, can make it difficult to form letters and to use spacing between letters, words, and lines. Some children with rather mild handwriting problems may be exhibiting slowness in development, which will

FIGURE 7.3

Writing Samples of a College Freshman with a Learning Disability

As I seT hare Thinking abouT This simiTe I wundr How someone Like Me Cood posblee make iT thou This cors. BuT some Howl I muse over come my fers and Wrese So I muse Be Calfodn in my sef and be NoT aferad To Trie

3 Reasens I Came To College

Reasen#1   To fofel a Drem that my Parens, Teichers and I hadd — Adrem that I codd some day by come ArchuTeck.

Reasen#2   To pouv rong those who sed I codd NoT make iT.

Reasen#3   Becos I am a bulheded.

The text of these samples reads as follows:

As I sit here thinking about this semester, I wonder how someone like me could possibly make it through this course. But somehow I must overcome my fears and worries. So I must be confident in myself and be not afraid to try.

Three Reasons I Came To College

Reason #1. To fulfill a dream that my parents, teachers, and I had—a dream that I could some day become architect.

Reason #2. To prove wrong those who said I could not make it.

Reason #3. Because I am bullheaded.

improve as they grow older, receive instruction, and practice. However, in more severe cases, age and practice may not bring about mastery of the handwriting skill.

Some researchers view the handwriting, writing, and composition skills of students with learning disabilities as closely related to their reading ability. For example, research does not clearly indicate that children with learning disabilities write more poorly than their normally achieving peers who are reading at a similar level. A number of sub-processes, ranging from basic skills to strategies employed, seem to contribute significantly to writing problems among students with learning disabilities (Berry, 2006; Chalk et al., 2005). Letter reversals and, in severe cases, **mirror writing** have often been used as illustrations of poor handwriting. Again, however, it is questionable whether children with learning disabilities make these types of errors more often than their peers without disabilities at the same reading level.

The logic connecting writing and reading abilities has intuitive appeal. Most children write to some degree on their own, even before receiving instruction in school. In general, children who write spontaneously also seem to read spontaneously and tend to have considerable practice at both before they enter school. Their homes tend to have writing materials readily available for experimentation and practice. Spontaneous writers may often observe their parents writing, and the parents and child may write together. Further research concerning the relationship between reading and writing is definitely in order (Vaid, Singh, Sakhuja, & Gupta, 2002; Wakely et al., 2006). Instruction in writing for children with learning disabilities has historically been somewhat isolated from the act of reading and other content areas, which may have led to another challenge—the lack of skill transfer (Swanson & Howard, 2005; Troia & Graham, 2002).

Poor spelling (also evident in Figure 7.3) is often a problem among students with learning disabilities. These children frequently omit letters or add incorrect ones. Their spelling may also show evidence of letter-order confusion and developmentally immature pronunciation (Richards et al., 2005; Silliman, Bahr, & Peters, 2006; Smith, 2004). Relatively little research has been conducted on these spelling difficulties, and teaching methods have been based primarily on individual opinion rather than on proven approaches (Gerber, 2005; van Aarle, van den Bercken, & Krol, 2005). Recent literature suggests that the spelling skills of students with learning disabilities follow developmental patterns similar to those of their peers without disabilities but that they are delayed (Bender, 2004; Lerner & Kline, 2006; Romani, Olson, & Di Betta, 2005). Characteristics such as problems in memory and visual and auditory processing, deficiencies in auditory discrimination, phonic generalizations, and impulsivity have also been implicated in the spelling difficulties that accompany learning disabilities. Data are mixed on these characteristics, and further research on spelling is needed for a clearer understanding of this area (Donfrancesco, Mugnaini, & Dell'Uomo, 2005; Savage, Frederickson, & Goodwin, 2005).

MATHEMATICS. Arithmetic is another academic area that causes individuals with learning disabilities considerable difficulty. They often have trouble with counting, writing numbers, and mastering other simple math concepts (Brosvic, Dihoff, & Epstein, 2006; Eisenmajer, Ross, & Pratt, 2005; Mazzocco & Thompson, 2005). Counting objects is perhaps the most fundamental mathematics skill and provides a foundation for the development of the more advanced, yet still basic, skills of addition and subtraction. Some youngsters omit numbers when counting sequences aloud (e.g., 1, 2, 3, 5, 7, 9), and others can count correctly but do not understand the relative values of numbers. Students with arithmetic learning disabilities have additional difficulties when asked to count beyond 9, which requires the use of more than one digit. This skill is somewhat more advanced than single-digit counting and involves knowledge about place value.

Place value is a more complex concept than the counting of objects and is fundamental to understanding addition and subtraction, since it is essential to the processes of carrying and borrowing. Many students with learning disabilities in math have problems understanding place value, particularly the idea that the same digit (such as 6) represents different magnitudes when placed in various positions (as in 16, 61, and 632). Such complexities require strategic problem solving, which presents particular difficulties for students with learning disabilities (Butler, Beckingham, & Lauscher, 2005; Rock, 2005). Research on the provision of specific math problem-solving instruction indicates significant success at both elementary and middle-school levels (Jitendra, Sczesniak, & Deatline-Buchman, 2005; Xin, Jitendra, &

> **Mirror writing**
Writing backwards from right to left, making letters that look like ordinary writing seen in a mirror.

Deatline-Buchman, 2005). Evidence also suggests that students with learning disabilities benefit even more than general education students from very focused direct instruction in math (Tournaki, 2003).

Some of these basic mathematics difficulties are often major obstacles in the academic paths of students with learning disabilities; they frequently continue to cause problems throughout high school and into the college years (McGlaughlin, Knoop, & Holliday, 2005). Mastery of fundamental quantitative concepts is vital to learning more abstract and complex mathematics, a requirement for youth with learning disabilities who are seeking to complete high school and attend colleges or universities (Jorgensen, Fichten, & Havel, 2005; Sullivan, 2005). These young adults are increasing in number, and it is essential for them to master algebra and geometry during secondary education. These topics have traditionally received minimal or no attention in curricula designed for students with learning disabilities. Such coursework has tended to emphasize computational skills, although change is occurring as parents and educators recognize the need for more advanced instruction in mathematics (McGlaughlin et al., 2005; Sullivan, 2005). Further research on difficulties with mathematics and on effective instruction for students who encounter such problems grows more important as such young people seek to attain more challenging educational goals.

ACHIEVEMENT DISCREPANCY. Students with learning disabilities perform below expectations based on their measured potential, in addition to scoring below their peers in overall achievement. This discrepancy between academic achievement and the student's assessed ability and age has prompted considerable research and theorizing. Attempts to quantify the discrepancy between academic achievement and academic potential for students with learning disabilities have appeared in the literature for some time, but the field still lacks a broadly accepted explanation of the phenomenon (Dean et al., 2006; Mayes & Calhoun, 2005; Stanovich, 2005). Early in the school years, youngsters with learning disabilities may find themselves two to four or more years behind their peers in level of academic achievement, and many fall even farther behind as they continue in the educational system. This discouraging pattern often results in students dropping out of high school or graduating without proficiency in basic reading, writing, or math skills (U.S. Department of Education, 2006a).

Intelligence

Certain assumptions about intelligence are being reexamined in research on learning disabilities. Typically, populations with behavior disorders and learning disabilities are thought to include

This teacher is providing several cues to help her students grasp the meaning of the word cytoplasm. She has linked a shaded illustration, the whole word cytoplasm, cytoplasm broken syllable-by-syllable, and the actual writing and visualizing of the word and what it represents. A combination of cues is often important for students with learning disabilities.

people generally considered above average or near average in intelligence (Sabornie, Cullinan, & Osborne, 2005; Sams et al., 2006). Differences between students with behavior disorders and those with specific learning disabilities have been defined on the basis of social skill levels and learner characteristics. However, individuals with learning disabilities may also exhibit secondary behavioral disorders, and students with behavior disorders may also have learning difficulties. To complicate the matter further, student classroom performance suggests that behavior problems are not associated with a particular level of intellectual functioning. It is well known that individuals with intellectual deficits and those with learning disabilities may both exhibit a considerable amount of maladaptive social and interpersonal behavior (Bryan, 2005; Fussell et al., 2005). Problems in social adjustment must be viewed as a shared characteristic.

These insights have affected traditional ideas about the distinctions between learning disabilities and intellectual disabilities. Marked discrepancy between measured intelligence and academic performance has long been viewed as a defining characteristic of people with learning disabilities (Mayes & Calhoun, 2005; Sabornie et al., 2005). Also, descriptions of learning disabilities have often emphasized great intraindividual differences between skill areas. For example, a youngster may exhibit very low performance in reading but not in arithmetic. Frequently, this variability in aptitude has been used to distinguish populations with learning disabilities from those with intellectual disabilities. A typical view holds that individuals with intellectual disabilities exhibit a consistent profile of abilities (generally, low performance in all areas), in contrast to the pronounced intraindividual variability associated with learning disabilities. However, intraindividual variability is sometimes evident in students with intellectual disabilities and in those with behavior disorders. Furthermore, the widely touted intraindividual variability in students with learning disabilities does not always appear; here again, the research evidence is mixed (Dean et al., 2006; Sabornie et al., 2005).

Cognition and Information Processing

People with learning disabilities have certain characteristics related to **cognition**, or **information processing**. Long used in psychology as a model for studying the processes of the mind, theories about cognition focus on the way a person acquires, retains, and manipulates information (e.g., Bauminger, Edelsztein, & Morash, 2005; Geary & Hoard, 2005; Gettinger & Seibert, 2002). These processes often emerge as problematic for individuals with learning disabilities. For example, teachers have long complained that such children have poor memory. In many cases, these students seem to learn material one day but cannot recall it the next. Research on the memory skills of these children has been relatively scanty, although it is crucial to understanding how information is acquired, stored, selected, and recalled. Memory function is also centrally involved in language skill and development, a challenging area for many children with learning disabilities (Barrett, Tugade, & Engle, 2004; Mammarella & Cornoldi, 2005; Woltz, 2003). Certain evidence has suggested that children with learning disabilities do not perform as well as normal children on some memory tasks, whereas on other tasks, research results have shown no differences (Bayliss et al., 2005; Pretorius, Naude, & Becker, 2002).

Research also suggests that children with learning disabilities have differing, rather than uniformly deficient, cognitive abilities (Eisenmajer et al., 2005; Geary & Hoard, 2005). This finding has led to the development of specific, highly focused instruction for individuals with learning disabilities to replace generic curricula reflecting the assumption that their cognitive skills are generally poor.

Attention problems have also been associated with learning disabilities. Such problems have often been clinically characterized as short attention span. Parents and teachers often note that their children with learning disabilities cannot sustain attention for more than a very short time and that some of them exhibit considerable daydreaming and high distractibility. Some researchers have observed **short attention spans** in these children, but others have indicated that they have difficulty in certain types of attention problems and, in some cases, attend selectively (Bender, 2004; Semrud-Clikeman, 2005). **Selective attention** problems make it difficult to focus on centrally important tasks or information rather than on peripheral or less relevant stimuli. Such problems might emerge when children with learning disabilities are asked to compute simple math problems that are on the chalkboard (which also means they must copy from the board). They may attend to the copying task rather than to the math

➤ **Cognition**
The act of thinking, knowing, or processing information.

➤ **Information processing**
A model used to study the way people acquire, remember, and manipulate information.

➤ **Short attention span**
An inability to focus one's attention on a task for more than a few seconds or minutes.

➤ **Selective attention**
Attending that often does not focus on centrally important tasks or information.

problems. In this situation, the teacher can easily modify the task (for example, by using worksheets rather than asking students to copy from the board) to facilitate completion of an important lesson. Attention problems remain in the spotlight as the information-processing problems of children with learning disabilities are investigated (e.g., Stone & Carlisle, 2006; Tsal, Shalev, & Mevorach, 2005).

Learning Characteristics

Although the study of perceptual problems played a significant role early in the history of learning disabilities, interest in this topic has declined. Some researchers, however, continue to view perception difficulties as important. Perception difficulties in people with learning disabilities represent a constellation of behavior anomalies, rather than a single characteristic. Descriptions of these problems have referred to the visual, auditory, and **haptic** sensory systems. Difficulty in visual perception has been closely associated with learning disabilities. It is important to remember that the definitions of learning disabilities exclude impaired vision in the traditional sense; visual perception problems in persons with learning disabilities are something distinctly different. This type of abnormality can cause a child to see a visual stimulus as unrelated parts rather than as an integrated pattern; for example, a child may not be able to identify a letter in the alphabet because he or she perceives only unrelated lines, rather than the letter as a meaningful whole. Clearly, such perception would cause severe performance problems in school, particularly during the early years (Smith, 2004).

Visual perception problems may emerge in **figure–ground discrimination**, which is the process of distinguishing an object from its background. Whereas most of us have little difficulty with figure–ground discrimination, certain children labeled as having learning disabilities may have trouble focusing on a word or sentence on the page of a textbook because they cannot distinguish it from the rest of the page. This, of course, results in difficulties with schoolwork. This deficit illustrates one of the problems in research on learning disabilities: It could represent a figure–ground discrimination disorder, but it could also reveal an attention deficit or a memory problem. Thus the same abnormal behavior can be accounted for differently by several theories (e.g., Barrett et al., 2004; Baum & Olenchak, 2002; Sams et al., 2006).

Other discrimination problems have also surfaced in descriptions of people with learning disabilities. Individuals with difficulties in **visual discrimination** may be unable to distinguish one visual stimulus from another (they cannot tell the difference between words such as *sit* and *sat,* for example, or between letters such as V and W); they commonly reverse letters such as b and d. This type of error is common among young children, causing great concern for parents. Yet most youngsters overcome this problem in the course of normal development, and by about 7 or 8 years of age, show few reversal or rotation errors with visual images. Children who make frequent errors beyond that age might be viewed as potential problem learners and may need additional instruction specifically aimed at improving such skills.

Auditory perception problems have historically been associated with learning disabilities. Some children have been characterized as unable to distinguish between the sounds of different words or syllables or even to identify certain environmental sounds (such as a ringing telephone) and differentiate them from others. These problems have been termed **auditory discrimination** deficits. People with learning disabilities have also been described as having difficulties in auditory blending, auditory memory, and auditory association. Those with **auditory blending** problems may not be able to blend word parts into an integrated whole as they pronounce the word. **Auditory memory** difficulties may result in an inability to recall information presented orally. **Auditory association** deficiencies may result in an inability to process such information. Difficulties in these areas can obviously create school performance problems for a child. Although some research related to auditory elements of teaching students with learning disabilities continues, research attention has diminished in recent years (Brosvic et al., 2006; Eisenmajer et al., 2005).

Another area of perceptual difficulty long associated with learning disabilities involves haptic perception (touch, body movement, and position sensation). Such difficulties are thought to be relatively uncommon but may be important in some areas of school performance. For example, handwriting requires haptic perception, because tactile information about the grasp of a pen or pencil must be transmitted to the brain. In addition, **kinesthetic** information regarding

> **Haptic**
>
> Related to the sensation of touch and to information transmitted through body movement or position.

> **Figure–ground discrimination**
>
> The process of distinguishing an object from its background.

> **Visual discrimination**
>
> Distinguishing one visual stimulus from another.

> **Auditory discrimination**
>
> Distinguishing between the sounds of different words, syllables, or environmental noises.

> **Auditory blending**
>
> The skill of blending the parts of a word into an integrated whole when speaking.

> **Auditory memory**
>
> The ability to recall verbally presented material.

> **Auditory association**
>
> The ability to process ideas or information presented verbally.

> **Kinesthetic**
>
> Related to the sensation of body position, presence, or movement, resulting chiefly from stimulation of sensory nerve endings in the muscles, tendons, and joints.

hand and arm movements is transmitted as one writes. Children with learning disabilities have often been described by teachers as having poor handwriting and difficulties in spacing letters and staying on the lines of the paper (Sanson, 2005; Voss, 2005). Such problems could also be due to abnormalities in visual perception, however, so definitively attributing some behaviors to a single factor is difficult. Figure 7.3 on page 172 offers an example of writing by a college freshman with learning disabilities. The two samples in this figure were written on consecutive days, each in a 40-minute period. The note beside the samples translates what was written.

Not all individuals labeled as having learning disabilities exhibit behaviors that suggest perceptual problems. Patterns of deficiencies vary widely. Also, empirical evidence of perceptual problems in those labeled as having learning disabilities is generally lacking. Overall, the notion of perceptual dysfunction is founded on clinical impressions rather than on rigorous research, but even so, this viewpoint is widespread.

Hyperactivity

Hyperactivity has commonly been linked to children labeled as having learning disabilities, although current literature more often associates it with attention-deficit/hyperactivity disorder (ADHD) (Dietz & Montague, 2006; McNamara et al; 2005). Also termed **hyperkinetic behavior, hyperactivity** is typically defined as a general excess of activity. Professionals working in the area of learning disabilities, particularly teachers, often mention this behavior first in describing their students, depicting them as fidgeting a great deal and as unable to sit still for even a short time (e.g., Fussell et al., 2005; Smith, Barkley, & Shapiro, 2006). Most descriptions portray an overly active child with limited ability to self-monitor and attend.

Certain points need to be clarified as we discuss hyperactivity in children with learning disabilities. First, not all children with learning disabilities are hyperactive, and not all hyperactive children have learning disabilities. As many as half the children with learning disabilities may not be hyperactive—certainly it is not a universal characteristic. Mixed research results and confusion currently mark our understanding of how learning disabilities are related to hyperactivity (Dietz & Montague, 2006; McNamara et al., 2005).

Social and Emotional Characteristics

Thus far we have discussed academically related characteristics and behavior of students with learning disabilities. Definitions and labels used for these students tend to focus on the academic perspective. Yet children and adolescents with learning disabilities often have emotional and interpersonal difficulties that are quite serious and highly resistant to treatment (Bryan, 2005; Fussell et al., 2005). Because of their learning problems, they frequently experience low self-esteem and negative emotional consequences (Manning, Bear, & Minke, 2006; Mather & Ofiesh, 2005). They may not be able to interact effectively with others because they misunderstand social cues or cannot discriminate among, or interpret the subtleties of, typical interpersonal associations.

In some cases the social dimensions of life pose greater problems for students with learning disabilities than their specific academic deficits, and yet this trait is essentially ignored in the definitions and labels related to learning disabilities. Some researchers view the broad category of learning disabilities as less functional than specific terminology that more precisely describes particular problems. Many professionals would not support broadening the definition of learning disabilities to incorporate social and emotional dimensions, although it is clear that these are substantial (Brook & Boaz, 2005).

Causation

Researchers have theorized about a number of possible causes for learning disabilities. However, despite substantial work related to this field, determining precise causation has been elusive, and the effort to do so still continues. There are probably many different causes of learning disabilities, and in some cases, a specific type of learning disability may have multiple causes (Loomis, 2006; Mather & Gregg, 2006; Tomblin, 2006). Also, a single cause may underlie multiple disor-

➤ **Hyperkinetic behavior**
An excess of behavior in circumstances where it is not appropriate.

➤ **Hyperactivity**
Perhaps the most frequently mentioned behavior characteristic in the literature on ADHD. In some cases, the term *hyperactivity* refers to too much activity. In others cases, the term refers to activity inappropriate for a given situation or context.

FOCUS **5**
List four causes thought to be involved in learning disabilities.

ders, such as learning disabilities and ADHD, in the same child (Dietz & Montague, 2006; McNamara et al., 2005; Smith & Williams, 2005). But because it is imperative to help affected students even though we do not yet fully understand the cause of learning disabilities, the practical issues of assessment and intervention have frequently taken priority in research so that specialized instruction can be offered to such students (Bender, 2005).

Neurological Factors

For many years, some have viewed the cause of learning disabilities as structural neurological damage, abnormal neurological development, or some type of abnormality in neurological function. A substantial portion of the literature in the field has reflected the interest in this proposition (e.g., Galaburda, 2005; Smith, 2004). Neurological factors have been the focus of some research and have been discussed as identification criteria in some literature (Brumback & Coffey, 2006; Hynd & Reynolds, 2005).

Neurological damage associated with learning disabilities can occur in many ways. Damage may be inflicted on the neurological system at birth by conditions such as anoxia (a lack of oxygen), low birth weight, or abnormal fetal positioning during delivery (Litt, Taylor, & Klein, 2005; Pierangelo & Giuliani, 2006). Infections may also cause neurological damage and learning disabilities, as can certain types of physical injury. In many cases, neurological damage as a cause of learning disability must be largely inferred because direct evidence is not available (Drew & Hardman, 2007; Gelfand & Drew 2003). (Chapter 10 discusses the relationship between the effects of neurological damage and intellectual disabilities). However, advancing technology such as magnetic resonance imaging (MRI) is generating research that supports some unusual neurological functioning in these children (Shaywitz et al., 2002).

Maturational Delay

Some theories have suggested that a delay in maturation of the neurological system results in the difficulties experienced by some individuals with learning disabilities. In many ways, the behavior and performance of children with learning disabilities resemble those of much younger individuals (Lerner & Kline, 2006). They often exhibit delays in skills maturation, such as slower development of language skills, and problems in the visual-motor area and several academic areas, as already noted. Although maturational delay is probably not a causative factor in all types of learning disabilities, there is considerable evidence that it contributes to some (Pierangelo & Giuliani, 2006).

Genetic Factors

Genetic causation has also been implicated in learning disabilities. Genetic abnormalities, which are inherited, are thought to cause or contribute to one or more of the problems categorized as learning disabilities (Holman, 2006; Plomin & Kovas, 2005). This is always a concern for parents, whatever the learning or behavior disorder. Over the years some research, including studies of **identical twins** and **fraternal twins**, has suggested that such disorders may be inherited (Hayiou-Thomas, Oliver, & Plomin, 2005; Wadsworth & DeFries, 2005). These findings must be viewed cautiously because of the well-known problems in separating the influences of heredity and environment, but some evidence supports the idea that some learning disabilities are inherited (Petrill, Deater-Deckard, & Thompson, 2006; Walker & Plomin, 2005).

Environmental Factors

The search for the causes of learning disabilities has also implicated certain environmental influences. Dietary inadequacies, food additives, radiation stress, fluorescent lighting, unshielded television tubes, drinking, drug consumption, and inappropriate school instruction have all been investigated at one time or another (Loomis, 2006; Walker & Plomin, 2005). Some environmental factors, such as irradiation, lead ingestion, maternal smoking, illicit drugs, and family stress, are known to have negative effects on development (Cone-Wesson, 2005; Taylor & Rogers, 2005; U.S. Department of Education, 2006a). In some cases, these influences appear to be primarily prenatal concerns; in others, the problems seem limited to the postnatal environment or are attributable to both. Research on environmental causation related specifically to learning disabilities remains inconclusive, but it is the focus of continuing study.

➤ **Identical twins**

Twins that develop from a single fertilized egg in a single placental sac. Such twins are of the same sex and usually resemble one another closely.

➤ **Fraternal twins**

Twins that develop from two fertilized eggs and develop in two placental sacs. Often such twins do not resemble each other closely.

Assessment

Psychoeducational assessment, or the evaluation of individuals with learning disabilities, has several purposes. The ultimate goal is to provide an appropriate intervention, if warranted, for the child or adult being evaluated. Assessment and intervention involve a series of related step, which include screening, identification, placement, and delivery of specialized assistance. This may mean additional help with academic work, instruction in social skills, or support related to any aspect of life and may involve professionals from a number of human service disciplines. Deciding how to meet an individual student's needs requires information obtained through a variety of assessment procedures (Aiken & Groth-Marnat, 2006; McMillan, 2007; Gregory, 2007). This section will examine the purposes and domains of assessment for learning disabilities and will focus on intelligence, adaptive behavior, and academic achievement.

Formal and Informal Assessment

An individual's status in performance, skills, and ability can be evaluated in a number of ways, either formally or informally. Formal versus informal assessment has come to mean standardized tests versus teacher-made tests or techniques. Standardized instruments, such as intelligence tests and achievement tests, are published and distributed on a commercial basis. Teacher-made techniques or instruments (or those devised by any professional) are ones that are not commercially available. These may be constructed for specific assessment purposes and are often quite formal, in the sense that great care is taken in the evaluation process (Airasian, 2005; Gronlund, 2006). Both formal and informal assessment techniques are effective ways of evaluating students with learning disabilities and other students as well (Linn & Miller, 2005; Mellard, Deshler, & Barth, 2004). Both are used for evaluation purposes in a number of performance or behavior areas.

Other distinguishing characteristics can be used to describe assessment instruments. **Norm-referenced assessment** compares an individual's skills or performance with that of others, such as peers, usually on the basis of national average scores. Thus a student's counting performance might be compared with that of his or her classmates, with that of others in the school district of the same age, or with state or national average scores. In contrast, **criterion-referenced assessment** compares an individual's skills not with a norm but with a desired level (criterion) of performance or a specific goal. For example, the goal may involve counting to 100 with no errors by the end of the school year. One application of criterion-referenced assessment, **curriculum-based assessment**, has received increasing

Council for Exceptional Children

Standard 8: Assessment

➤ **Norm-referenced assessment**
Assessment wherein a person's performance is compared with the average of a larger group.

➤ **Criterion-referenced assessment**
Assessment that compares a person's performance to a specific established level (the criterion). This performance is not compared with that of other people.

➤ **Curriculum-based assessment**
Assessment in which the objectives of a student's curriculum are used as the criteria against which progress is evaluated.

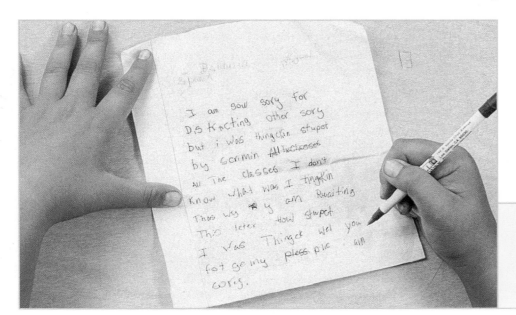

By comparing a student's skill level with a criterion-based assessment, a teacher is able to make a specific instruction plan for the student.

attention recently. It uses the objectives in a student's curriculum as the criteria against which progress is evaluated (Cleary & Zimmerman, 2006; Macy, Bricker, & Squires, 2005). The relationship between evaluation and instructional objectives makes instruction planning and assessment more efficient. Other terms (such as *objectives-referenced measurement*) have been used for similar procedures, but they all involve assessment referenced to instruction (Gronlund, 2004).

Both norm- and criterion-referenced assessment are useful for working with students with learning disabilities. Norm-referenced assessment is often used for administrative purposes, such as compiling census data on how many students are achieving at or above the state or national average. Criterion-referenced assessment is helpful for specific instructional purposes and planning.

These two types of assessment do not require entirely separate types of assessment instruments or procedures. Depending on how a technique, instrument, or procedure is employed, it may be used in a norm-referenced or a criterion-referenced manner. Some areas, such as intelligence, are more typically evaluated using norm-referenced procedures. However, even a standardized intelligence test can be scored and used in a criterion-referenced fashion (the test would then function as a source of test items, and a student's performance could not be evaluated exactly as the test developer intended). Assessment should always be undertaken with careful attention to the purpose and future use of the evaluation (Drew & Hardman, 2007; Gregory, 2007).

Screening

Screening of students who seem to have learning disabilities has always been an important facet of assessment. Such assessment occurs prior to labeling or treatment of the student, although clinicians or others (often parents) in contact with the child often suspect that a problem exists. Some individuals are screened at a rather young age, and their assessment compares them to children of a similar age. But assessment for potential learning disabilities most often takes place during the school years. This is partly because the types of performance that are most problematic for these children are not often required until the child goes to school and partly because one of the important markers for learning disabilities (a discrepancy between ability and achievement) does not seem to show as well very early. However, screening and further assessment steps may be undertaken earlier if a child's difficulties attract attention before school. Such assessment may result in intervention at a very early age, which can be very beneficial for these children.

The role of screening is to "raise a red flag," or suggest that investigation is needed. Four questions are pertinent at this point of the assessment process:

1. Is there a reason to investigate the abilities of the child more fully?

2. Is there a reason to suspect that the child in any way has disabilities?

3. If the child appears to have disabilities, what are their characteristics, and what sort of intervention is appropriate?

4. How should we plan for the future of the individual?

Answers to these questions might point to a variety of needs: further classification of the disability, planning of such intervention services as psychological treatment or individualized instruction, or ongoing evaluation of progress. For students with learning disabilities, assessment is not a simple, isolated event that results in a single diagnosis but, rather, a complex process involving many different steps (Gregory, 2007; Scott, Delgado, & Tu, 2005). After diagnosis, continuing assessment undergirds all decision making while an individual receives services related to learning disabilities. For our purposes, approaches to assessment focus on intelligence, adaptive skills, and academic achievement.

Intelligence

For the most part, individuals with learning disabilities are described as having above average or near-average intelligence, although they experience problems in school that are typical of students with lower intelligence levels. In many cases, measures of intelligence may be inaccu-

---

➤ **Screening**

A preliminary assessment process that may suggest that further evaluation of a child's needs and functioning level is necessary. The role of screening is to "raise a red flag" if a problem is indicated.

FOCUS **6**

Cite four questions that are addressed by screening assessment of students who seem to have learning disabilities.

rate because of specific visual, auditory, or other limitations that may affect the student's performance (Dean et al., 2006; Sabornie et al., 2005). However, intelligence assessment remains an important matter for individuals with learning disabilities and is often carried out with a standardized instrument such as an intelligence test.

Where measured intelligence fits into the definition of learning disabilities is somewhat controversial. Some researchers argue that intelligence is irrelevant to the definition of learning disabilities, whereas others see it as important. Still others believe that the traditional way of measuring intelligence is problematic, but not the concept of intelligence per se (Klassen, Neufeld, & Munro, 2005; Watkins, Kush, & Schaefer, 2002). Such a divergence of opinion is not unusual in the field of learning disabilities.

Adaptive Skills

People with learning disabilities are frequently described as exhibiting poor adaptive skills—that is, they lack a sense of what constitutes appropriate behavior in a particular environment. Such descriptions have appeared primarily in clinical reports, and evaluation of adaptive skills has not historically been a routine part of assessment of learning disabilities to the same degree as in other areas of exceptionality, such as intellectual disabilities. However, some work has been undertaken to address adaptive and social skills and their assessment for individuals with learning disabilities (e.g., Smith, & Williams, 2005; Whitaker, 2004). Such efforts are based on the assumption that a discrepancy between ability and academic achievement alone is insufficient to describe learning disabilities fully. The study of adaptive skills has contributed to greater understanding of subtypes and severity levels in learning disabilities and is beginning to receive greater attention in the field as researchers focus more on the emotional well-being of students with learning disabilities (see Fussell et al., 2005; Bauminger et al., 2005; Singer, 2005).

Academic Achievement

Academic achievement has always been a major problem for students with learning disabilities. Assessment of academic achievement determines whether there is an overall discrepancy between a student's ability and his or her academic achievement. Such assessment also helps evaluate the student's level of functioning in one or more specific academic areas. Instruments have been developed and used to diagnose specific academic problems. For example, a number of reading tests, including the Woodcock Reading Mastery Tests, the Diagnostic Reading Scales, and the Stanford Diagnostic Reading Test, are used to determine the nature of reading problems. Likewise, mathematics assessment employs instruments such as the Key Math Diagnostic Arithmetic Test and the Stanford Diagnostic Mathematics Test (Gronlund, 2006). All of these assessments may be important for Alice, the young student we met earlier and whom we see again in the nearby Snapshot.

▼SNAPSHOT

ALICE

Alice found herself very frustrated with school. She was in the fourth grade, and her grades were very bad. She had worked hard, but many of the things that were required just didn't seem to make sense.

History was a perfect example. Alice had looked forward to learning more about history; it was so interesting when her grandfather told his stories. Alice thought it would have been fun to live back then, when all the kids got to ride horses. But history in school was not fun, and it didn't make any sense at all. Alice had been reading last night, supposedly about a girl who was her age and was moving west with a wagon train. As she looked at the book, Alice read strange things. One passage said, "Mary pelieveb that things would get detter. What they hab left Missouri they hab enough foob dut now there was darely enough for one meal a bay. Surely the wagon-master woulb finb a wet to solve the brodlem." Alice knew that she would fail the test, and she cried quietly in her room as she dressed for school.

Academic assessment for students with learning disabilities is very important. For the most part, assessment techniques resemble those used in other areas of exceptionality, because deficits in academic achievement are a common problem among students with a variety of disabilities. Diagnosis of deficits in specific skills, however, has a more prominent history in learning disabilities and has prompted the development of focused, skills-oriented assessment of academic achievement in other disability areas as well. As with other exceptionalities, issues of inclusion and collaboration are major considerations in choosing the types of assessments employed; they have a significant impact on instructional placement and implementation in the educational program (Hardman, 2005; Rix, 2006; Stecker, 2006). Assessment with maximum relevance to the setting of application, often termed authentic or alternative assessment, also has attracted growing interest. These methods assess progress or skill using settings and procedures in a context like that in which the student must function, in contrast to the sterile, formal style of test administration used in the past.

The Elementary School Years

Services and supports for children with learning disabilities have changed over time as professionals have come to view learning disabilities as a constellation of specific individualized needs, rather than as a single generic category. Specific disabilities, such as cognitive learning problems, attention deficit and hyperactivity, social and emotional difficulties, and problems with spoken language, reading, writing, spelling, and mathematics, are receiving research attention (e.g., Brosvic et al., 2006; Romani, Olson, & Di Betta, 2005; Wakely et al., 2006). This approach has resulted in services and supports focused on individual need, rather than on general treatment of learning disabilities. Greater attention is being paid to social skills instruction for children with learning disabilities and to the effective use of tutors and of peers as tutors (Dettmer et al., 2005; Vadasy, Sanders, & Peyton, 2005). Some services and supports focus on strategic instruction (e.g., teaching the children how to learn), counseling and/or peer and family support (e.g., parent training), and medical treatment, all in the context of a structured educational environment (Grunow, Spaulding, Gomez, & Plante, 2006; Prater, 2007). Early intervention with the most effective instruction possible is viewed as a crucial factor in the child's overall academic success (Compton, Fuchs, & Fuchs, 2006; Gersten & Jordan, 2005).

An overarching concept for this approach to intervention is the RTI model for making decisions about instructional focus. RTI tends to be associated with assessment because of its prominent and ongoing measurement components (Ardoin, 2006; Vellutino, Scanlon, Small, & Fanuele, 2006). Although the assessment element is important, the comprehensive RTI concept also includes other important components related to evidence-based decisions about interventions (Fuchs & Fuchs, 2006; Haager & Klinger, 2005). As indicated in Figure 7.4, the three-tiered service triangle involves a carefully designed comprehensive academic core to which a very large proportion of students with learning disabilities will respond—perhaps as high as 80 to 85%. In tier two, more intensive or supplemental instruction is undertaken to help the next 10 to 15% make progress, and tier three involves the even more specialized and intense instruction needed by about 5% of students with the most serious academic challenges. Of course these proportions are rough estimates and will vary depending on the children involved, the nature of the instruction, and certainly the context (Klinger & Edwards, 2006; Wilber & Cushman, 2006). A balanced RTI concept focuses on both the assessment and intervention elements of the evidence-based decision making that is crucial for both general and special education.

Services and supports for adolescents or adults with learning disabilities may differ from those for children. Some changes in approach are due to shifting goals as individuals grow older (for example, the acquisition of basic counting skills versus math instruction in preparation for college). Educational support requires a broad range of specialized instruction tailored to individual needs that change as the person grows older. See the Inclusion and Collaboration Through the Lifespan, "People with Learning Disabilities," for more information about inter-

FIGURE 7.4

RTI Model for Instruction and Service Delivery

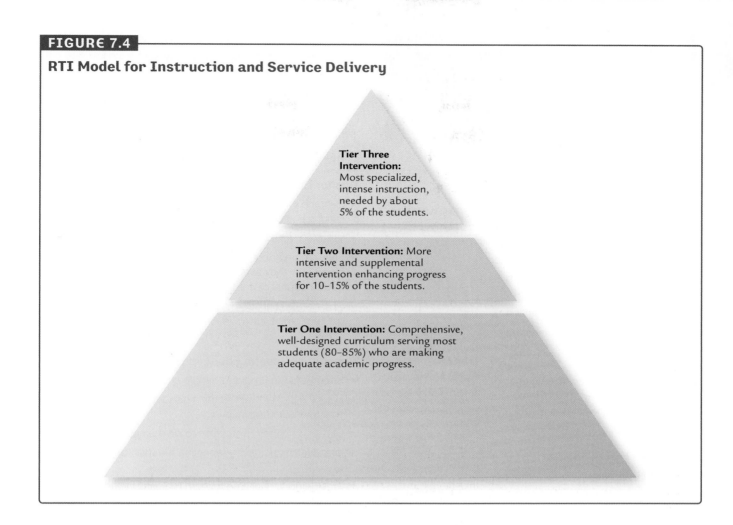

Tier Three Intervention: Most specialized, intense instruction, needed by about 5% of the students.

Tier Two Intervention: More intensive and supplemental intervention enhancing progress for 10–15% of the students.

Tier One Intervention: Comprehensive, well-designed curriculum serving most students (80–85%) who are making adequate academic progress.

acting effectively with people with learning disabilities at all ages. Individuals from varied professions must function as a team and also as unique contributors to create a well-balanced program for the student with learning disabilities (Dettmer et al., 2005; Wilkinson, Ortiz, Robertson, & Kushner, 2006).

Academic Instruction and Support

A wide variety of instructional approaches have been used over the years for children with learning disabilities. These include strategies to develop cognition, attention, spoken language, and skill in reading, writing, and mathematics (Jitendra et al., 2005; Lerner & Kline, 2006; Rock, 2005; Walker et al., 2005). Even within each area, a whole array of instructional procedures have been used to address specific problems. For example, cognitive training has incorporated problem solving, strategies for attacking problems, and instruction in social competence (Bryan, 2005; Okada, Goto, & Ueno, 2005).

Various approaches to cognitive instruction are needed to teach the heterogeneous population of children with learning disabilities. Such strategies or tactics are often customized or reconfigured to individualize the program and target a student's specific needs. For example, if a youngster exhibits adaptive skills deficits that interfere with inclusion in general education, such skills may form an instructional focus. Flexible and multiple services or supports may make inclusion possible, providing a well-defined instructional environment, teaching the child important skills, and addressing interpersonal or social-emotional needs (Hardman, 2005). Coordinating or orchestrating such an instructional package is not a casual or simple task. Successful inclusion requires determining the intensity and duration of instruction appropriate for the child, choosing supports that will meet the child's needs, accomplishing this early in the child's

INCLUSION AND COLLABORATION THROUGH THE LIFESPAN

People with Learning Disabilities

EARLY YEARS*

Tips for the Family

- Play verbal direction games, such as finding certain words or sounds, interspersing those that are difficult with those that are easy for the child with learning disabilities.
- Read to the child daily for 20 minutes or more.
- Give the child practice in identifying different sounds (e.g., the doorbell and phone).
- Reinforce the child for paying attention.
- Promote family learning about learning disabilities, their child's specific strengths and limitations, and their respect for their child as a person.
- Work and collaborate across different professions to coordinate the child's services, including educators, psychologists, health care professionals, and others involved in assessment and intervention.

Tips for the Preschool Teacher

- Collaborate with parents, other educators, and service providers to plan and implement the child's comprehensive program.
- Limit verbal instructions to simple sentences, presented briefly, one at a time.
- Determine appropriate content carefully, paying attention to the developmental level of the material.
- Provide multiple examples to clarify points and reinforce meaning.
- Provide more practice than usual, particularly on new material or skills.

Tips for Preschool Personnel

- Collaborate with all school personnel and others who are providing services for all children. Participate in developing a child-centered model that coordinates services from all professions so that there is a planning and implementation protocol for each child.
- Promote a school environment and attitude that encourage respect for children of all abilities.
- Promote the development of instructional programs focusing on preacademic skills, which may not be necessary for all children but may be very important for young students with learning disabilities.

---

*Very young children who may have learning disabilities typically have not been formally diagnosed with the disability, although they may exhibit what appears to be maturational slowness.

- Be alert for students who seem to be of average or higher intelligence but, for reasons that may not be evident, are not performing up to ability.
- Community activities should be arranged to include a broad range of maturational levels so that children with learning disabilities are not shut out and do not experience unnecessary failure at this early age.

ELEMENTARY SCHOOL YEARS

Tips for the Family

- Become involved in the school through parent-teacher organizations and conferences.
- Volunteer as a tutor.
- Learn more about learning disabilities as you begin to understand how they affect your child, perhaps through reading relevant material or enrolling in a short course.
- Collaborate and coordinate all information about the child from different professionals, such as psychologists, physicians, social workers, and others who may be providing services.

Tips for the General Education Classroom Teacher

- Keep verbal instructions simple and brief.
- Have the student with learning disabilities repeat directions to you, to ensure understanding.
- Use mnemonics in instruction to aid memory.
- Intensify instruction by repeating the main points several times to aid memory.
- Provide additional time to learn material, including repetition or re-teaching.
- Collaborate, communicate, and coordinate the various services a student with learning disabilities might be receiving, such as counseling and psychological assessment, and be certain that the parents are active team participants.

Tips for Preschool Personnel

- Encourage individual athletic activities (e.g., swimming) rather than competitive team sports.
- Involve the child in appropriate school activities (e.g., chorus or music) where interests are apparent.
- Develop peer tutoring programs, in which older students assist children who are having difficulty, and collaborate across all school personnel who have become stakeholders by virtue of the child's enrollment.

Tips for Neighbors and Friends

- Make contact and collaborate with advocacy or other groups that can help you learn about and interact with the child with learning disabilities.
- Maintain a relationship with the child's parents, talking with them about the child if and when they feel comfortable doing so.
- As a friend, encourage parents to seek special assistance from agencies that might provide services such as "talking books."
- If you are interested, offer assistance to the child's parents in whatever form they may need, or even volunteer to work with the child as a tutor.

SECONDARY SCHOOL AND TRANSITION YEARS

Tips for the Family

- Provide extra support for your youngster in the family setting, encouraging good school performance despite academic problems that may be occurring.

- Encourage your adolescent to talk about and think about future plans as he or she progresses into and through the transition from school to young adult life.

- Try to understand the academic and social difficulties the student may encounter. Encourage impulse control if impulsiveness may be causing some of the problems.

- Do not shy away from the difficult task of encouraging the student to associate with peers who are success-oriented rather than with those who may be involved in inappropriate behavior.

- Collaborate with the participating professionals as well as with parents of other children who are not encountering challenges in order to maintain a balanced perspective for your adolescent.

- Encourage your adolescent to consider and plan for the years after high school, whether the student wants to go to college or find employment.

Tips for the General Education Classroom Teacher

- Specifically teach self-recording strategies, such as asking oneself, "Was I paying attention?"

- Relate new material to knowledge the student with learning disabilities already has, making specific connections with familiar information.

- Teach the use of external memory enhancers (e.g., lists and note taking).

- Encourage the use of other devices to improve class performance (e.g., tape recorders).

Tips for School Personnel

- Promote involvement in social activities and clubs that will enhance interpersonal interaction.

- Where students with learning disabilities have such interests and abilities, encourage participation in athletics or other extracurricular activities.

- Where interests and abilities are present, involve students in support roles to extracurricular activities (e.g., as team equipment manager).

- Promote the development of functional academic programs that are combined with transitional planning and programs. Collaborate with professionals from areas the student may encounter as he or she transitions to young adulthood.

- Provide information on college for students with learning disabilities, and encourage them to seek counseling about educational options, where appropriate.

Tips for Neighbors and Friends

- Encourage students to seek assistance from agencies that may provide services (e.g., special newspapers, talking books, and special radio stations).

- Promote involvement in community activities (e.g., scouting, Rotary Club, Chamber of Commerce, or other service organizations for adults).

- Encourage a positive understanding of learning disabilities among neighbors, friends, and community agencies (e.g., law enforcement officials) who may encounter adolescents or adults with disabilities.

ADULT YEARS

Tips for the Family

- Interact with your adult family member with learning disabilities on a level that is consistent with his or her adult status. Despite all the difficulties he or she may have experienced in school and while maturing, remember that this person is now an adult.

- While recognizing the person's adult status, also remember that your adult family member with learning disabilities will probably continue to experience specific difficulties related to his or her disability.

- Help the person to devise ways of compensating for areas of challenge and collaborate with community professionals who may interact with the individual.

Tips for Therapists or Other Professionals

- In adulthood, it is unlikely that basic academic instruction will be the focus of professional intervention. It may be worthwhile to focus on compensatory skills for particularly difficult problem areas.

- Be alert for signs of emotional stress that may require intervention. This person may have a very deep sense of frustration accrued over a lifelong history of difficulties and failure.

Tips for Neighbors and Friends

- It may be necessary to be more flexible or understanding with adult friends or neighbors with learning disabilities. There may be good explanations for deviations from what is considered normal behavior. However, if certain behaviors are persistent and are particularly aggravating to you, you owe it to your friend to discuss the matter rather than letting it interfere with a friendship. You may have numerous friends, but the adult with learning disabilities may have precious few; thus your understanding and honesty are particularly valuable.

life, and continuing the strategy through upper grades as well (Hardman, 2005; Huefner, 2006). Some educators believe that early intervention with a focus on excellent instruction can avoid academic failure for many children who might otherwise be diagnosed as having learning disabilities and thus can obviate the need, in their case, for either special education or mainstreaming. Such a program for elementary-level children can build and improve their deficient skills, giving them a more promising prognosis for success in later school programs.

MATHEMATICS. Mathematics instruction for students with learning disabilities exemplifies how building a foundation of basic skills can enhance later learning. Earlier, we noted that children with difficulties learning arithmetic may have trouble with basic counting and with understanding place value. For these students, counting may be most effectively taught with manipulative objects. Repetitive experience with counting buttons, marbles, or any such objects provides practice in counting, as well as exposure to the concepts of magnitude associated with numbers. Counting and grouping sets of ten objects can help children begin to grasp rudimentary place-value concepts. These activities must often be quite structured for students with learning disabilities, although it is clear they can effectively be taught problem-solving strategies for math (Jitendra et al., 2005; Xin et al., 2005).

Commercial programs of instruction in basic math concepts are also available. Cuisenaire Rods, sets of 291 color-coded rods used for manipulative learning experiences, are an example. These rods, whose differing lengths and colors are associated with numbers, can be used to teach basic arithmetic processes to individual students or groups.

Computer technology has also found its way into math skills instruction for students with learning disabilities (Bitter & Pierson, 2005; Roblyer, 2006). Personal computers are particularly appealing for teaching math, because content can be presented in whatever sequence is most helpful. Computers can also provide drill and practice exercises for those who need it, an instructional goal that is often difficult for teaching staff to attain in a classroom with several children. Concern exists, however, regarding the use of computer technology primarily for drill and practice. Although reinforcement of learning is clearly a strength of many math programs, some focus excessively on drill and practice. Many researchers strongly contend that a broad range of instructional applications is needed, extending beyond the development of elementary skills, to serve more students (McNergney & McNergney, 2007; O'Bannon & Puckett, 2007). Computer technology has yet to meet the high expectations many have had for its application to instruction. It can provide some effective instruction for some students with learning disabilities, but students for whom the manipulation of objects is helpful in understanding math concepts may find microcomputers less useful. Long-term research is needed to study the effectiveness of computer instruction and to determine its most useful application for these children.

READING. It has long been recognized that students with learning disabilities have great difficulty with reading. Because of this, reading instruction has received considerable attention, and many different strategies have been developed to address the problem (Kamhi & Catts, 2005a; Rix, 2006; Van der Bijl, Alant, & Lloyd, 2006). Each procedure has succeeded with certain children, but none with all. This result lends credence to the current belief that many different disabilities may affect students who experience problems in the same area. Research on particular types of skill instruction, such as pre-reading activities, guided practice with feedback, and the direct teaching of skills in summarizing, has produced significant improvements for students with learning disabilities (see Manset-Williamson & Nelson, 2005; Ullman, 2005; Wilber & Cushman, 2006). Information gained from such research is being incorporated into instructional programs more than ever before and in many different content areas (see the nearby Assistive Technology, "Software for Writing." Combined with the realization that no single approach fits all students, this trend promises improved instruction and positive outcomes for students with learning disabilities.

Reading programs that base and sequence instruction within a developmental framework often help students with learning disabilities (Kamhi & Catts, 2005b; Smith, 2004). Typically, such programs methodically introduce sight vocabulary based on developmental status, with an emphasis on analytic phonics. Developmental approaches to reading involve basal readers such as *Holt Basic Reading*; the Ginn 720 Series; Scott, Foresman Reading; and the

ASSISTIVE TECHNOLOGY

SOFTWARE FOR WRITING

Writing has long been recognized as an academic area that presents considerable difficulty for children with learning disabilities. Advances in educational applications of technology, especially the development of new computer software, have the potential to assist children with writing problems (Englert et al., 2005; Hetzroni & Shrieber, 2004). An example of such software is *Write: OutLoud*, a talking word processor. Write: OutLoud cues the user with a beep or a flash on the screen in response to an incorrectly spelled word. This program can also speak! It will read back a sentence or a word so that the user can check his or her work for accuracy.

Another software package with a speaking component is the *Co: Writer*, a word prediction program. It lets users write almost as quickly as they can think by predicting words through a program using artificial intelligence. For example, typing in the first letter or two of a word that the user is unsure how to spell will produce a list of possible words from which to choose. It helps those with spelling difficulties and low motor ability; it also helps with grammar and spelling problems.

A third package is marketed for students with learning disabilities in particular. This software, *WordQ* writing software, may be used with widely available word processing packages. It suggests words for the student and provides feedback to help him or her find mistakes. WordQ enables the student to write ideas unaided and check spelling, grammar, and punctuation. One option with this software also allows for a speech recognition adaptor named *SpeakQ*, which is helpful for individuals who "cannot fluently dictate at a fast rate, remember verbal commands, and/or get through training" (Bloorview MacMillan Children's Centre, www.wordq.com, 2006).

Macmillan Series E. Such basal readers are most useful for group instruction (they are often designed for three levels), are well sequenced on a developmental basis, and typically provide enough detail to be used effectively by somewhat inexperienced teachers. The orientation toward group instruction, however, is likely to present some limitations for those students with learning disabilities who need a great deal of individual attention. Houghton Mifflin's Soar to Success program presents an appealing small-group intervention package that focuses on students performing at a two- to three-grade reading deficit. Earlier this program focused on grades 3 to 6, but grades 7 and 8 were added during the spring of 2000. SRA reading programs (such as Reading Mastery and Open Court) are considered appropriate in both scope and sequence for children with learning disabilities; they also incorporate recommended teaching techniques.

Many teachers successfully use whole-language strategies to teach reading to students with learning disabilities. This approach tends to deemphasize isolated exercises and drills. Some are concerned, however, that this population needs a balance between a whole-language approach and focused, intensive, direct instruction related to problem areas (e.g., Kozlof, 2005; Lerner & Kline, 2006; Pavri, 2006). To make significant progress, a student with a serious reading disability often needs individualized reading instruction. A wide variety of materials (e.g., trade books) may be selected to match the student's reading level and cover topics of high interest to the student. The teacher responsible for developing and providing individualized instruction needs to have considerable knowledge of reading skills and the procedures that facilitate learning them.

Effective individualized instruction also requires ongoing monitoring of progress, and explicit attention to student needs. Good teachers are constantly evaluating the learning environment and fine-tuning instructional elements to enhance their students' learning. Prater (2003, 2007) outlines five characteristics for teachers to focus on in this strategy for instructional enhancement. She uses the acronym "CRIME" to help teachers identify these characteristics. (See the nearby Reflect on This, "It's a CRIME to Ignore the Classroom.")

Several commercially available reading programs also provide specific skill-oriented reading instruction that functions in a diagnostic/prescriptive manner. Examples include the Fountain Valley Reading Support System, available from Zweig and Associates, and the Ransom Program from Addison-Wesley. Computer-assisted instruction is employed in some diagnostic/prescriptive reading programs, such as the Harcourt Brace CAI Remedial Reading Program and the Stanford University CAI Project. Individualized instruction is a hallmark of diagnostic/prescriptive reading programs. Such materials let students work at their own pace. These mate-

IT'S A CRIME TO IGNORE THE CLASSROOM

Five elements for evaluation and adjustment in an effective classroom:

CURRICULUM

What determines the curriculum in my classroom?

What are the state and/or district standards?

How difficult, comprehensive, and important is the material?

RULES

What are my posted rules?

How well do I make students accountable for keeping the rules?

What behaviors are important to me that are not posted?

INSTRUCTION

How do I usually present new information?

What kind of assignments and tests do I require?

Do I expect individual or group work or both?

How important is homework?

MATERIALS

What supplementary teaching materials are available to me?

Do students have access to support materials such as computers, calculators, and cassette players?

Are students expected to supply their own basic materials?

ENVIRONMENT

How is the furniture in my classroom arranged?

What are the visual and auditory distracters in my classroom?

What time of day am I teaching this content?

SOURCES: Prater, M. A. (2003). She will succeed! Strategies for success in inclusive classrooms. *Teaching Exceptional Children, 35,* 58–64.

Prater, M. A. (2007). *Teaching strategies for students with mild to moderate disabilities.* Boston: Allyn & Bacon, pp. 235–238.

rials teach only those skills that lend themselves to the particular program's format, but notwithstanding this limitation, they have considerable strengths. For example, they do not require that the teacher possess the high degree of knowledge and skill that is essential for totally individualized, teacher-generated reading instruction. Additionally, diagnostic/prescriptive programs generally provide ongoing assessment and feedback, and developmental skills are usually well sequenced. Even so, such remedial reading programs are somewhat controversial in terms of both methodology and conceptual arguments about their function and appropriateness (e.g., Manset-Williamson & Nelson, 2005; Rix, 2006; Wilber & Cushman, 2006).

A variety of other programs and approaches to reading instruction are available, and each has its own strengths and limitations. Other developmentally based approaches include synthetic phonics basals, linguistic phonemic programs, and language experience approaches. Some procedures use multisensory techniques to maximize the student's learning. Selection of method and application of instructional technique should be based on a student's particular disability profile and other relevant needs.

Computer software for assessment and instruction in reading can assist students with learning disabilities, and its use will become increasingly common in the future. Computer-presented reading instruction offers some particular advantages. It provides individual instruction, as well as never-ending drill and practice, as mentioned earlier. Programs can also combine feedback with corrective instruction in areas such as writing (Englert, Wu, & Shao, 2005; Voss, 2005). As computer programs advance, reading instruction software will improve (right now, word-recognition programs seem to be of higher quality than comprehension software) and will become more widely available. However, there is continuing concern about the appropriate use of software and about the need for long-range planning, faculty training, and other staff development related to applications of technology in instruction (see Bitter & Pierson, 2005). There continues to be a gap between developments in technology and their effective broad implementation in education, and many matters require debate and resolution before information technology can realize its full potential in education (McNergney & McNergney, 2007; O'Bannon & Puckett, 2007; Roblyer, 2006).

As children progress into the upper-elementary grades, they may need instruction in compensatory skills or methods to "work around" deficits not yet remedied. This instruction may involve tutoring by an outside agency or an individual specializing in the problem, or it may involve placement in a resource room or even a self-contained class for students with learning disabilities. The approach that is chosen will depend on the severity of the difficulty, the particular area of deficiency, and sometimes (for better or for worse) the resources and attitudes of the decision makers (such as families and school districts).

Behavioral Interventions

Distinctions between behavioral and academic interventions are not always sharp and definitive. Both involve students in learning skills and changing behavior. Behavioral interventions, however, generally use practical applications of learning principles such as reinforcement. Behavioral interventions such as the structured presentation of stimuli (e.g., letters or words), reinforcement for correct responses (e.g., specific praise), and self-monitoring of behavior and performance are used in many instructional approaches (Persampieri, Gortmaker, Daly, Sheridan, & McCurdy, 2006; Rock, 2005; Twyman, McCleery, & Tindal, 2006). In this section, we briefly discuss some behavioral interventions that are used outside of traditional academic areas.

With certain children, instruction may focus on social skills training. Some students with learning disabilities who experience repeated academic failure, despite their great effort, become frustrated and depressed (e.g., Brook et al., 2005). They may not understand why their classmates without disabilities seem to do little more than they do and yet achieve more success. These students may withdraw or express frustration and anxiety by acting out or becoming aggressive. When this type of behavior emerges, it may be difficult to distinguish individuals with learning difficulties from those with behavior disorders as a primary disability, so both diagnosis of the problem and treatment may be quite difficult (e.g., Bryan, 2005; Cartledge, 2005). In fact, these groups of students often exhibit many similar behaviors. The social and behavioral difficulties of students with learning disabilities are receiving increasing attention in the research literature (Bender, 2004; Fussell et al., 2005).

Behavioral contracts are one type of intervention that is often used to change undesirable behavior. Using this approach, a teacher, behavior therapist, or parent establishes a contract with the child that provides him or her with reinforcement for appropriate behavior. Such contracts are either written or spoken, usually focus on a specific behavior (such as remaining in his or her seat for a given period of time), and reward the child with something that she or he really likes and considers worth striving for (such as going to the library or using the class computer). It is important that the pupil understand clearly what is expected and that the event or consequence be appealing to the child, so that it really does reinforce the appropriate behavior. Behavioral contracts have considerable appeal because they give students some responsibility for their own behavior (Gelfand & Drew, 2003; McDougal, Chafouleas, & Waterman, 2006). They can also be used effectively by parents at home. Contracts in various forms can be applied for students at widely differing ages.

Token reinforcement systems represent another behavioral intervention often used with youngsters experiencing learning difficulties. **Token reinforcement systems** allow students to earn tokens for appropriate behavior and eventually to exchange them for a reward of value to them (DuPaul & Weyandt, 2006; Gelfand & Drew, 2003; Prater, 2007). Token systems resemble the work-for-pay lives of most adults and therefore can be generalized to later life experiences. Although token systems require considerable time and effort to plan and implement, they can be truly effective.

Behavioral interventions are based on fundamental principles of learning largely developed from early research in experimental psychology. These principles have been widely applied in many settings for students with learning disabilities as well as other exceptionalities. One of their main strengths is that once the basic theory is understood, behavioral interventions can be modified to suit a wide variety of needs and circumstances.

➤ **Behavioral contract**

An agreement, written or oral, between people, stating that if one party behaves in a certain manner (for example, the student completes homework), the other (for example, the teacher or parent) will provide a specific reward.

➤ **Token reinforcement system**

A system in which students, by exhibiting positive behavior changes, may earn plastic chips, marbles, or other tangible items that they can exchange for activities, food items, special privileges, or other rewards.

The Adolescent Years

Services and supports for adolescents and young adults with learning disabilities differ somewhat from those used for children. Age is an important factor to consider when planning services. Even the services and supports used during childhood vary according to age: assistance appropriate for a child 6 years of age will not typically work for one who is 12. New issues crop up during the teenage years. Adolescents and young adults with learning disabilities may, like their peers without such disabilities, become involved in alcohol or drug use and sexual activity (Brook & Boaz, 2005; Hechtman, 2005; Unruh & Bullis, 2005). Certainly, they are vulnerable to peer pressure and to the temptation of engaging in misconduct. However, adolescents are also influenced by their parents' expectations, which may be an important positive factor in academic achievement. Age-appropriate modifications are essential to effective instruction and services for adolescents with learning disabilities, and most often they must be individually designed.

Academic Instruction and Support

Academic instruction for adolescents with learning disabilities differs from such programs for younger children. Research suggests that the educational system often fails adolescents with learning disabilities. These students have lower school completion rates than their peers without learning disabilities, as well as higher unemployment rates (U.S. Department of Education, 2006a). The goal of secondary education is to prepare individuals for postschool lives and careers. These findings suggest a serious doubt that youth with learning disabilities are being adequately supported in meeting this goal. Often these adolescents find that they still need to develop basic academic survival skills (and, for some, preparation for college), and they may also lack social skills and comfortable interpersonal relationships (Bryan, 2005; Cartledge, 2005; Milsom & Hartley, 2005). Adolescents with learning disabilities are attending college in greater numbers than ever, but they tend to drop out at higher rates than their peers without disabilities (U.S. Department of Education, 2006a). Clearly, a comprehensive model, with a variety of components, needs to be developed to address a broad spectrum of needs for adolescents and young adults with learning disabilities (Kaiser, 2005; Luftig & Muthert, 2005).

Relatively speaking, adolescents with learning disabilities have received considerably less attention than their younger counterparts. Academic deficits that first appeared during the younger years tend to grow more marked as students face progressively more challenging work, and by the time many reach secondary school or adolescence, they may be further behind academically than they were in the early grades (Bender, 2004). Although academic performance figures prominently in the federal definition of learning disabilities, there still has been relatively little research on factors that influence academic development in adolescents with learning disabilities. Problems in motivation, self-reliance, learning strategies, social competence, and skill generalization all emerge repeatedly in the literature on such adolescents and young adults (e.g., Brook & Boaz, 2005; Reiff, 2004).

Time constraints represent one difficulty that confronts teachers of adolescents with learning disabilities. A limited amount of time is available for instruction, student progress can be slow, and determining what to focus on is difficult. In some areas, high school students may not

The goals of adolescents with learning disabilities will vary among individuals. Some students may look forward to employment after high school while others might plan some type of continuing education.

have progressed beyond fifth-grade level academically, and they may have only a rudimentary grasp of some academic topics (Bender, 2004). Yet they are reaching an age at which life grows more complex. A broad array of issues must be addressed, including possible college plans (an increasingly frequent goal for students with learning disabilities), employment goals, and preparation for social and interpersonal life during the adult years. In many areas, instead of building and expanding on a firm foundation of knowledge, many adolescents with learning disabilities are operating on a beginning to intermediate level. They may appear less than fully prepared for the challenges ahead of them, but a well-planned program of supports can do much to smooth the transition to adulthood.

The challenge of time constraints has led researchers to seek alternatives to and supplements for traditional teaching of academic content to students with learning disabilities. Even with the press of time, each individual requires specific instructional planning. For example, evidence suggests that direct instruction may also be effective when focused on key areas such as writing skills (Walker et al., 2005). However, in other cases, learning strategies may be the focus of instruction. Teaching learning strategies to students is one widely used approach that focuses on the learning process. In this approach, students are taught how to learn in addition to the content of a given lesson (e.g., Garrett, Mazzocco, & Baker, 2006; Prater, 2007). Thus the learning strategies approach promotes self-instruction and frequently emphasizes "thinking about" the act being performed. This metacognition process may focus on rather complex academic content, such as math or writing (Garrett et al., 2006; Wakely et al., 2006; Woltz, 2003). Learning strategies instruction often employs mnemonic acronyms that help the student remember steps for the strategy process. Prater (2007) summarizes several acronyms that are useful for writing and composition (see in the nearby Reflect on This, "Writing Strategies").

Secondary school instruction for adolescents with learning disabilities may also involve teaching compensatory skills to make up for those not acquired earlier. Compensatory skills often address specific areas of need, such as writing, listening, and social skills. For example, tape recorders may be used in class to offset difficulties in taking notes during lectures and thus compensate for a listening (auditory input) problem. For some individuals, personal problems related to disabilities require counseling or other mental health assistance. And to complicate matters further, hormonal changes with strong effects on interpersonal behavior come into play during adolescence; research results are just beginning

REFLECT ON THIS

WRITING STRATEGIES

Acronyms are often used to help students remember the broad steps involved in various instructional strategies. Below are three strategies that can be used for writing and composition with students who have learning disabilities. These acronyms are mnemonic cues to facilitate their use by students and teachers.

POWER
- **P**lan
- **O**rganize
- **W**rite
- **E**dit
- **R**ewrite/Revise

STOP & LIST
- **Stop**
- Think of Purpose
- **List** Ideas
- Sequence Them

PLEASE
- **P**ick a topic
- **L**ist ideas
- **E**valuate ideas
- **A**ctivate ideas
- **S**upply supporting details
- **E**nd with closing sentence/Evaluation

SOURCE: From Prater, M. A. (2007). *Teaching strategies for students with mild to moderate disabilities.* Boston: Allyn & Bacon, pp 349–350.

to emerge on such issues for adolescents with learning disabilities (Floyd, 2006; Galaburda, 2005; Gutstein & Sheely, 2002). These students tend to have low social status among nearly all the people around them, including peers, teachers, and even parents. Some may become involved in criminal activities, although the research evidence linking learning disabilities and juvenile delinquency is mixed (Chitsabesan & Bailey, 2006; Grigorenko, 2006; Smith, 2004). Generally, research results do not suggest that individuals with learning disabilities are arrested or sentenced to serve jail terms at substantially higher rates than peers without disabilities.

Transition from School to Adult Life

Some adolescents and adults with learning disabilities have successfully adapted by themselves to a variety of challenges. However, many of the difficulties that adolescents with learning disabilities experience do not disappear as they grow older, and specialized services are often needed throughout adolescence and perhaps into adulthood (Flanagan, Bernier, Keiser, & Ortiz, 2003; Hudson, 2006; Lipka & Siegel, 2006). The National Research Center on Learning Disabilities emphasized this developmental need, noting that "specific learning disabilities persist across the lifespan, though manifestations and intensity may vary as a function of developmental stage and environmental demands" (NRCLD, 2002). The importance of this statement is that it explicitly addresses the lifespan and acknowledges the variations that may occur at different ages. We currently do not understand all the factors that contribute to success or lack of it in young adults with learning disabilities. Some ingredients that would seem to contribute to success as a young adult (such as verbal intelligence and length of school enrollment) have not proved to be accurate predictors. Perhaps these findings reflect difficulties and inaccuracies in measurement as well as challenges in prediction (Flanagan & Harrison, 2005; Gregory, 2007). Accumulating research on the transition years of adolescents with learning disabilities may begin to illuminate some of these methodological problems. We may find that this period of life is characterized by some unique challenges, just as it is for young people with other disabilities (Flanagan et al., 2003; Hudson, 2006).

TRANSITION SERVICES. Transition services remain rather sparse for adolescents with learning disabilities. However, this area is beginning to receive increased research attention. We are beginning to learn more about how emotional, interpersonal, and social competence issues affect adults with learning disabilities, and such research will have an impact on transition planning. Research is emerging on factors such as substance abuse; results suggest a possible association between alcohol abuse and learning disabilities (e.g., Kelly, 2006; Kennemer & Goldstein, 2005). Services and supports that address this problem are beginning to be reported (Brown & Coldwell, 2006; Cummings, Davies, & Campbell, 2002; Edelman & Remond, 2005). Although the picture remains unclear at this point, there is some evidence that adults with learning disabilities are at risk of engaging in violence and violent crime (Moore, 2001; Wenar & Kerig, 2006). Research on interpersonal relationships is also under way, and preliminary findings point to a need for transition services for young adults with learning disabilities in areas of emotional well-being, interpersonal intimacy, and sexuality (e.g., Floyd, 2006; Lipka & Siegel, 2006). Results suggest that the competence of young adults with learning disabilities in these areas is not notably positive.

Those who are planning transition programs for adolescents with learning disabilities must consider that these adolescents' life goals may approximate those of adolescents without disabilities. Some students look forward to employment that will not require education beyond high school. Some plan to continue their schooling in vocational and trade schools (Lerner & Kline, 2006). As with other areas of exceptionality, schooling should play a significant role in preparing young adults with learning disabilities for the transition from school to work (Hudson, 2006). Employment preparation activities such as occupational awareness programs, work experience, career and vocational assessment, development of job-related academic and interpersonal skills, and information about specific employment should be part of transition plans and should benefit these students. In addition, professionals may need to negotiate with employers to secure some accommodations at work for young adults with learning disabilities. Limited data are available on the employment success of young adults with

ALICE REVISITED

Remember Alice, whom we met in the last Snapshot? When we last saw her, Alice was in the fourth grade and was extremely frustrated with school. Unfortunately, she failed the history test for which she was preparing. She could not obtain enough information from the narrative and consequently could not answer the questions on the test. The exam was a paper-and-pencil test, which, to Alice, looked like the book that she was supposed to read about the family who was moving west with the wagon train. When she received her graded test, Alice broke into tears. This was not the first time she had wept about her schoolwork, but it was the first time her teacher had observed it.

Alice's teacher, Mr. Dunlap, was worried about her. She was not a troublesome child in class, and she seemed attentive. But she could not do the work. On this occasion, Mr. Dunlap consoled Alice and asked her to stay after school briefly to chat with him about the test. Since it was early in the year, he had no clue what was wrong, except that he knew this charming girl could not answer his test questions. He was astonished when they sat together and he determined that Alice could not even read the questions. If she could not read the questions, he thought, then she undoubtedly can't read the book. But he was fairly certain that she was not lacking in basic intelligence. Her conversations simply didn't indicate such a problem.

After further consoling Alice about her test, Mr. Dunlap sent her home and then contacted her parents. He knew a little about exceptional children and the referral process. He set that process in motion, meeting with the parents, the school psychologist, and the principal, who also sat in on all the team meetings at this school. After a diagnostic evaluation, the team met again to examine the psychologist's report. Miss Burns, the psychologist, had tested Alice and found that her scores fell in the average range in intelligence (with a full-scale WISC-III score of 114). She had also assessed Alice's abilities with a comprehensive structural analysis of reading skills. This led her to believe that Alice had a rather severe form of dyslexia, which interfered substantially with her ability to read.

Alice's parents expressed a strong desire for her to remain in Mr. Dunlap's class. This was viewed as a desirable choice by each member of the team, and the next step was to determine how an intervention could be undertaken to work with Alice while she remained in her regular class as much as possible. All team members, the parents included, understand that effectively meeting Alice's educational and social needs will be challenging for everyone. However, they are all agreed that they are working toward the same objectives—a very positive first step.

APPLICATION

Placing yourself in the role of Mr. Dunlap, and given the information that you now have about Alice, respond to the following questions.

1. How can you facilitate Alice's social needs, particularly focusing on her relationships with her classmates?

2. Should information about Alice's reading difficulties be shared with classmates, or would this be detrimental to their interactions with her?

3. Who should be a part of this broad educational planning?

4. Should you talk with Alice about it?

---

learning disabilities; most reports combine information on people with a number of disabilities. Most authorities agree, however, that the employment years for these individuals usually are not any easier than their school years, and a definite need exists for programs to facilitate the transition from school to work (Carter, Lane, & Pierson, 2006; O'Brien, 2006).

COLLEGE BOUND. As we have noted, growing numbers of young people with learning disabilities plan to attend a college or university (Cornett-DeVito & Worley, 2005; Estrada, Dupoux, & Wolman, 2006; U.S. Department of Education, 2006a). There is little question that they will encounter difficulties and that careful transition planning is essential to their success. Their dropout rates are higher and their academic performance indicators are lower than those of their counterparts without learning disabilities. It is also clear that with some additional academic assistance, they not only will survive but also can be competitive college students (Hartman-Hall & Haaga, 2002; Rath & Royer, 2002). These students need substantial college preparatory counseling before they leave secondary school. There is a considerable difference between the relatively controlled setting of high school and the more unstructured environment of college. In their preparation for this significant transition, students profit from focused assistance, transition planning, and goal setting, perhaps in conjunction with their high school counselors (e.g., Proctor, Hurst, Prevatt, Petscher, Adams, 2006; Trusdell & Horowitz, 2002).

College-bound students with learning disabilities may find that many of their specific needs are related to basic survival skills in higher education. At the college level, it is assumed that students can already take notes and digest lecture information auditorily and that they have adequate writing skills, reading ability, and study habits. Transition programs must strengthen these abilities as much as possible and show the students how to compensate for deficits, using a range of perspectives and strategies to plan the student's pursuit of postsecondary education (Kaiser, 2005 Proctor et al., 2006). Taped lectures can be replayed many times to help the student understand the information. Students with reading disabilities can obtain the help of readers who tape-record the content of textbooks so that they can listen to the material, rather than making painfully slow progress if reading is difficult and time-consuming. College students with learning disabilities must seek out educational support services and social support networks to offset emotional immaturity and personality traits that may impede college achievement (Estrada et al., 2006). There is also a shift under way that reconceptualizes students with learning disabilities in higher education settings and includes increasing the services available to them (Roer-Strier, 2002).

Perhaps the most helpful survival technique that can be taught to an adolescent with learning disabilities is actually more than a specific skill; it is a way of thinking about survival—an overall attitude of resourcefulness and a confident approach to solving problems. Recall Mathew, the psychology student in one of this chapter's first Snapshots. Mathew has an amazing array of techniques that he uses to acquire knowledge while compensating for the specific areas where he has deficits. Students need both proven techniques to deal with problem areas and the ability to generate new ways to tackle the challenges that inevitably arise in college. This positive attitude also includes knowing how to seek help and how to advocate for oneself. Transition programs that can instill such a mind-set in students preparing for college have truly served an important purpose.

Another key transition element involves establishing a support network. Students with learning disabilities should be taught how to establish an interpersonal network of helpers and advocates. An advocate on the faculty can often be more successful than the student in requesting special testing arrangements or other accommodations (at least to begin with). A word of caution is in order, however. Faculty in higher education are bombarded with student complaints and requests, many of which are not based on extreme needs. Consequently, many faculty are wary of granting special considerations such as extra time. However, a request from a faculty colleague may carry more weight. It should also be noted that many faculty are uninformed about learning disabilities, and overtures from a colleague can enhance the credibility of the student's request.

Concern about the accommodations requested by students who claim to have learning disabilities is genuine and is growing. Because these disabilities are "invisible," they are hard to understand, and there is much room for abuse in requests for accommodations. Such requests have increased dramatically, and many faculty are skeptical about their legitimacy. Research suggests that some cynicism is understandable; some claims indeed lack a sound justification, and the diagnostic documentation provided for many college students who claim to need accommodations because of a learning disability is seriously flawed. Although the Americans with Disabilities Act clearly mandates accommodation, college students with learning disabilities should be aware that many higher-education faculty are skeptical about the merits of this mandate and that the process of getting special arrangements approved is not simple (Flanagan et al., 2003; Lipka & Siegel, 2006). Some incidents related to this issue have been widely publicized and politicized, and they may have a detrimental effect on the general higher-education environment for those with learning disabilities. Providing clear diagnostic evidence of a learning disability will enhance the credibility of a request for accommodation. Even faculty in special education have encountered those who have diagnosed themselves and claim to have a learning disability; this behaviour is counterproductive to improving the experiences of students with learning disabilities in higher education. The accompanying Debate Forum, "Reasonable Accommodataion versus Unreasonable Costs," illustrates some elements of these issues.

Students with learning disabilities can lead productive, even distinguished, adult lives. But some literature suggests that even after they complete a college education, adults with learning disabilities have limited career choices (Bender, 2004). A more comprehensive research base is needed in this area. However, we do know that notable individuals have been identified as having learning disabilities. They include scientist and inventor Thomas Edison, U.S. president Woodrow Wilson, scientist Albert Einstein, and governor of New York and vice president of the United States Nelson Rockefeller. We also know that the young man whose writing we saw in Figure 7.3 became a successful architect. Such achievements are not accomplished without considerable effort, but they show that the outlook for people with learning disabilities is very promising.

Multidisciplinary Collaboration: Education and Other Services

Council for
Exceptional
Children

Standard 5: Learning Environments and Social Interactions

Standard 7: Instructional Planning

Multidisciplinary collaboration is particularly crucial for those with learning disabilities because of the wide range of characteristics that may emerge in these individuals. Providing effective inclusive education and the full range of other services requires a wide variety of professionals (Dettmer, Thurston, & Dyck, 2005.) Clear and ongoing communication among all stakeholders must address all elements of planning for the student and adult with learning disabilities, as well as implementation of these plans. There is an enormous heterogeneity of ability and disability configurations that emerge and evolve at various ages in those with learning disabilities. An individual may exhibit several important developmental, academic, social, or health-related characteristics that warrant attention from professional and family members (Tarleton & Ward, 2005; Wenar & Kerig, 2006). Effective collaboration among all participants, including the person with learning disabilities, can promote maximum levels of life achievements.

Collaboration on Inclusive Education

Definitions and descriptions of various approaches to inclusive education were introduced in earlier chapters. Much of the impetus for the inclusive education movement emerged from efforts of parents and advocacy organizations, and the concept has been known as mainstreaming, as the regular education initiative, and as integration service models. A very large proportion of students with learning disabilities receive educational services in settings that are either fully or partially inclusive (Atkinson, 2006; Prater, 2003). From 1995 to 2004, less than 12% of students with learning disabilities from 6 to 21 years of age were served mostly outside the regular classroom. The U.S. Department of Education defines this service pattern as being more than 60% of the time outside the regular class (U.S. Department of Education, 2006a).

Inclusive education is an important part of the academic landscape for students with learning disabilities, and a variety of specific instructional strategies are employed to enhance success. Inclusive approaches have received increasing attention in the learning disability literature, which has prompted thought-provoking debate about appropriate formats and the advantages and limitations of placing students with learning disabilities in fully inclusive educational environments (Bender, 2005; Klinger & Vaughn, 2002). To be successful, inclusive education requires commitment to collaboration among general and special educators and other team members.

Instructing students with learning disabilities in inclusive settings requires significant advance planning. Increasingly, the education of these students is guided by complex, comprehensive plans incorporating instructional services and supports and multiple approaches. IEPs at this stage have evolved with the student's chronological age and as his or her skills develop. Each student's instructional plan targets specific areas where the individual needs more intense or specialized attention. The academic focus may be on a reading problem or on difficulties in some content area. Social and behavioral issues may emerge in the inclusive environment, and related interventions may form part of the spectrum of services and supports (Peterson & Hittie, 2005; Rix, 2006). To be effective, instructional supports must be directly related to the student's needs in the context of a general education classroom.

Several factors affect the success of inclusive education for students with learning disabilities. For example, teacher attitudes are very influential. Some evidence suggests that general education teachers feel unprepared to teach students with disabilities, to collaborate with special educators, and to make academic adaptations. Adequate teacher preparation is a crucial factor in effective inclusive education. Such preparation requires a significant collaborative partnership between general education and special education teacher education programs—a partnership that has largely been lacking to date. This defect continues to be criticized in teacher education literature and reflects many dilemmas in higher education (Chang, Early, & Winton, 2005; DeSimone & Parmar, 2006). In addition to teachers' curriculum and instructional skills, their personal attitudes toward inclusive education are vitally important. General education teachers often have less positive attitudes toward and perceptions of inclusive education than special education teachers do, although such attitudes can be changed (Bishop & Jones, 2002; Butin, 2005; Romi & Leyser, 2006).

Successful inclusion requires much more than just placing students with learning disabilities in the same classroom with their peers without disabilities. Some researchers have noted that because these students need supports and adaptations, successful inclusion might better be described as supported inclusion than simply as inclusion. Inclusive education must be undertaken only after careful planning of the instructional approach, services, and supports (Hardman, 2005; Huefner, 2006). Such a program can effectively promote academic support, motivation, and development of social-emotional skills for students with learning disabilities.

Collaboration on Health and Other Services

A variety of other services may be marshaled for students and adults with learning disabilities, and here again, collaboration and communication are essential. In some cases these relationships are established during the school years, and the collaboration linkage is connected to both education and family components of the child's life. Collaboration between educators, speech and language specialists, physical therapists, and occupational therapists is essential for a smoothly functioning personal plan (Graner, Faggetta-Luby, & Fritschmann, 2005; Rodger, & Brown, 2005; Troia, 2005). Services can continue for some time and will surely evolve over time. One area that often receives attention for those with learning disabilities involves health care professionals. Medical personnel are sometimes involved in the diagnosis of learning disabilities and in prescribing medications used in treating conditions that may coexist with learning disabilities. The involvement of physicians varies somewhat according to the age of the person with disabilities.

CHILDHOOD. Physicians often diagnose a child's abnormal or delayed development in the areas of language, behavior, and motor functions. It is not uncommon for pediatricians to participate in diagnosing physical disabilities that may significantly affect learning and behavior and then to interpret medical findings to the family and other professionals. Physicians may have early involvement with a child with learning disabilities because of the nature of the problem, such as serious developmental delay or hyperactivity. More often a medical professional sees the young child first because he or she has not entered school yet, and the family physician is a primary adviser for parents (Drew & Hardman, 2007; Martin, 2005). When other professional expertise is needed, the physician may refer the family to other specialists and then function as a team member in meeting a child's needs.

One example of medical service appropriate for some children with disabilities involves controlling hyperactivity and other challenging behaviors. Many children with learning disabilities receive medication such as Ritalin (generic name, methylphenidate) to control hyperactivity. Although their action is not completely understood, such psychostimulants appear to result in general improvement for a large proportion of children with ADHD (Pelham et al., 2002; Seidman et al., 2006; Sutcliffe, 2006). Some researchers have expressed caution about such treatment, however, focusing on matters of effectiveness, overprescription, and side effects (e.g., Chapman, Gledhill, Jones, Burton, & Soni, 2006; Rapport & Moffitt, 2002; Shireman, Reichard, & Rigler, 2005). Concerns have also been expressed about the soundness of research methods used to investigate the effects of medication (e.g., De Haan, 2006; Gelfand, & Drew, 2003).

Too little is known about the effects of medication on hyperactivity, even as evidence continues to accumulate. For example, there are a number of situations where it is not known which drug will be effective until after treatment has begun. Uncertainty regarding dosage level and the fact that high doses may have toxic effects are adding to the confusion. Although there are clear benefits to the use of medication, it may be overprescribed (Pelham et al., 2002; Shireman et al., 2005; Zuvekas, Vitiello, & Norquist, 2006). Continued research is crucial to clarifying many aspects of this treatment.

ADOLESCENCE. As in other treatment areas, medical services for adolescents and young adults with learning disabilities differ somewhat from those for children. The literature directly addressing medical services during adolescence is unfortunately scarce, although some studies have explored specific needs that may require medical attention. For example, stress and serious emotional difficulty, including depression, during the adolescent years are receiving attention (e.g., Brook & Boaz, 2005; Maag & Reid, 2006; Young & Chesson, 2006). In some cases, psychiatry may be involved in treatment, through either interactive therapy or the prescribing of antidepressant medication. Some efforts are under way to improve the assessment of medical, developmental, functional, and growth variables for individuals with learning difficulties, in a variety of settings (e.g., Collishaw, Maughan, & Pickles, 2005; Mayes & Calhoun, 2006). These efforts too are expanding and may soon systematically address individuals with learning disabilities at various age levels.

Some adolescents receiving medication to control hyperactivity may have been taking it for a number of years, since many such physician assessments and prescriptions are made during childhood. On the other hand, some treatments are of rather short duration and many terminate within two years (Allsopp, Minskoff, & Bolt, 2005; Zuvekas et al., 2006). This finding raises serious questions about which type of treatment is most suitable. Other unanswered questions concern problems with side effects and with determining which medications are effective in dealing with particular symptoms (Chapman et al., 2006; Rapport & Moffitt, 2002; Shireman et al., 2005). A number of adolescent youth and adults with learning disabilities have struggled through their earlier years and have not received medication until after childhood. In many cases, the medication to assist with behavior and attention problems is again an amphetamine and appears to have the same beneficial results noted earlier (Pelham et al., 2002, Shireman et al., 2005; Sutcliffe, 2006).

The field of learning disabilities and the individuals served within it represent an interesting array of challenges, perhaps the most perplexing among the high-incidence disabilities. In the overall picture of disabilities, these challenges are not trivial, both because they are complex and because they involve such a very large proportion of those who have disabilities. Progress is evident, though it is also clear that intense and systematic research efforts are essential if improvement in service is to continue.

FOCUS 1 Cite four reasons why definitions of learning disabilities have varied.

- *Learning disabilities* is a broad, generic term that encompasses many different specific problems.
- The study of learning disabilities has been undertaken by a variety of different disciplines.
- The field of learning disabilities per se has existed for only a relatively short period of time and is therefore relatively immature with respect to conceptual development and terminology.
- The field of learning disabilities has grown at a very rapid pace.

FOCUS 2 Identify three classification schemes that have been used with people who have learning disabilities.

- Discrepancy—based on notion that there is an identifiable gap between intelligence and achievement in particular areas such as math, reading, and language. Discrepancy evaluation has been controversial, and IDEA 2004 now allows schools to use a "response to intervention" process.
- Heterogeneity—classification based on the differing academic domains where those with learning disabilities experience performance challenges.
- Exclusion—notes what those with learning disabilities are not. Might be more useful if it focused instead on what attributes need attention.

FOCUS 3 Give two current estimated ranges for the prevalence of learning disabilities.

- From 2.7% to 30% of the school-age population, depending on the source.
- From 5% to 10% is a reasonable current estimate.

FOCUS 4 Identify seven characteristics attributed to those with learning disabilities, and explain why it is difficult to characterize this group.

- Typically, of above-average or near-average intelligence
- Uneven skill levels in various areas
- Hyperactivity
- Perceptual problems
- Problems with visual and auditory discrimination
- Cognition deficits, such as in memory
- Attention problems
- The individuals included under the umbrella term *learning disabilities* are so varied that they defy simple characterization in terms of a single concept or label.

FOCUS 5 List four causes thought to be involved in learning disabilities.

- Neurological damage or malfunction
- Maturational delay of the neurological system
- Genetic abnormality
- Environmental factors

FOCUS 6 Cite four questions that are addressed by screening assessment of students who seem to have learning disabilities.

- Is there a reason to investigate the abilities of the child more fully?
- Is there a reason to suspect that the child in any way has disabilities?
- If the child appears to have disabilities, what are their characteristics, and what sort of intervention is appropriate?
- How should we plan for the future of the individual?

FOCUS 7 Identify three types of interventions or treatments employed with people diagnosed as having learning disabilities.

- Medical treatment, in some circumstances involving medication to control hyperactivity
- Academic instruction and support in a wide variety of areas that are specifically aimed at building particular skills
- Behavioral interventions aimed at improving social skills or remediating problems in this area (behavioral procedures may also be a part of academic instruction)

FOCUS 8 How are the services and supports for adolescents and adults with learning disabilities different from those used with children?

- Services and supports for children focus primarily on building the most basic skills.
- Instruction during adolescence may include skill building but also may involve assistance in compensatory skills to circumvent areas where deficits exist.
- Services during adolescence should include instruction and assistance in transition skills that will prepare students for adulthood, employment, and further education, taking into account the students' own goals.
- Information for adults with learning disabilities should include an awareness of how "invisible" their disability is to others and how requests for accommodation might be viewed with skepticism.

Council for Exceptional Children

If you are thinking about a career in special education, you should know that many states use national standards developed by the Council for Exceptional Children (CEC) to assess a teacher candidate's knowledge about and skills for working with students with disabilities. See a complete listing of the ten CEC Content Standards on the inside front cover of this text.

CEC Content Standards Addressed in This Chapter

1 Foundations

2 Development and Characteristics of Learners

3 Individual Learning Differences

5 Learning Environments and Social Interactions

7 Instructional Planning

8 Assessment

Assess Your Knowledge of the CEC Standards Addressed in This Chapter

Some states require that teacher candidates develop a portfolio of products that demonstrate mastery of the CEC content standards. To assist in the development of products for this portfolio, you may wish to complete the following activities.

- Complete a written test of the chapter's content.

  If your instructor requires a written test of your content knowledge for this chapter, keep a copy for your portfolio. A practice test on the information covered in this chapter is available through the Human Exceptionality Companion Website (college.hmco.com/pic/hardman9e) and the Student Study Guide.

- Respond to the Application Questions for the Case Study "Alice Revisited."

  Review the Case Study and respond in writing to the application questions. Keep a copy of the Case Study and of your written response for your portfolio.

- Participate in a Community Service Learning Activity.

  Community service is a valuable way to enhance your learning experience. Visit our companion website for suggested community service learning activities that correspond to the information presented in this chapter. Develop a reflective journal of the service learning experience for your portfolio.

WEB RESOURCES

The Learning Disabilities Council

http://www.ldcouncil.org

This site provides a variety of helpful materials for parents of children with learning disabilities and for adults with learning disabilities. Includes information on parent guides and workbooks, support groups for adults, and various links to other sites that address useful topics.

National Center for Learning Disabilities

http://www.ncld.org

This site includes many resources and fact sheets related to learning disabilities. Topics range from living with learning disabilities to advocacy and lobbying links for those interested in public policy.

Technical Assistance Alliance for Parent Centers

http://www.taalliance.org

This site provides a newsline service with information on federal programs and many listings of upcoming events such as conferences.

Public law and policy debates are reviewed. Resources include consortia, fundraising opportunities, and a wide array of parent-related information pertaining to family issues and learning disabilities.

Learning Disabilities Association of America (LDA)

http://www.ldanatl.org

This association is a not-for-profit organization of individuals with learning disabilities, professionals working with learning disabilities, and family members. The aim of this organization is to advance the education and welfare of children and adults with learning disabilities. The site links to resources, news and alerts about learning disabilities, and announcements of upcoming events. Legislative action bulletins are also included.

FURTHER READINGS

Crawford, V. (Ed.) (2002). *Embracing the Monster: Overcoming the Challenges of Hidden Disabilities*. Baltimore, MD: Paul H. Brookes.

Learning disabilities are often characterized as hidden disabilities. This book provides a first-hand account of Veronica's life with learning disabilities and related challenges. It describes challenges with school, personal relationships, and resulting emotions.

Nadeau, K. G. and Quinn, P. O. (Eds.) (2000). *Understanding Women with AD/HD*. Silver Spring, MD: Advantage Books.

This volume includes discussions on both learning disabilities and attention-deficit/hyperactivity disorders. The focus is on women with these

disabilities who want to return to school in order to enhance their self-esteem and personal fulfillment, as well as to increase their career opportunities and earning capacity.

Sternberg, R. J. (Ed.) (2002). *Why Smart People Can Be So Stupid*. New Haven, CT: Yale University Press.

This book includes information on people with learning disabilities and describes how some of their behaviors appear different to outside observers. Discussion of the reasoning approaches used by individuals with learning disabilities reveals why others may view them as unusual, may treat them differently, and may even discriminate against them.

Whittlesey, V. (2001). *Diversity Activities for Psychology*. Boston: Allyn and Bacon.

This book covers a broad range of activities related to topics that are seldom addressed in the context of learning disabilities and other disabilities. *Diversity is a main topic, and issues related to culture, ethnicity, gender, and sexual orientation are explored. Activities are included for the topics of emotion, motivation, personality, and human sexuality—discussions that are difficult to find in most sources.*

COMPANION WEBSITE

Visit the companion website at college.hmco.com/pic/hardman9e for additional resources that support this text:

- HM Video Cases that present actual classroom scenarios that you may face every day as a teacher

- Practice ACE Exams that will help you prepare for quizzes, tests, and certfication exams
- Flashcards of key terms
- Weblinks

8 Attention-Deficit/ Hyperactivity Disorder

TO BEGIN WITH . . .

ADHD: IT'S NOT JUST FOR KIDS ANYMORE

Once considered primarily a childhood condition, ADHD . . . is now known to be a lifelong condition for as many as half of those troubled with its hallmark symptoms of inattention, distractibility, impulsivity and emotional instability starting before age 7. (ARMC News, 2006 Barkley, 2006)

DIAGNOSIS: ADHD NOT AIRHEADS

While the great majority of those diagnosed are boys, experts now believe ADHD may be just as prevalent in girls. . . . The main reason girls are undiagnosed is that the disorder often exhibits itself differently in them, says Dr. Kathleen Nadeau. . . . Boys with ADHD tend to be more disruptive and act out physically, while girls tend to be less rebellious and are written off as airheads. (CBSNEWS.com, "Health News," December 13, 2002)

MEDICATION OF YOUNG CHILDREN INCREASING

Ritalin, which is commonly used to treat attention-deficit/hyperactivity disorder (ADHD), carries a warning against its use in children under six. . . . [However,] recent studies show a doubling to tripling of the number of children under age 4 taking Ritalin. (Livni, 2000)

OUT OF CONTROL: IMPERFECT SOLUTIONS

Wendy Snider and Paul Kirchmeyer asked counselors for help with their son Alex. Dr. William Pelham, who works with Alex and other children [with ADHD], helped them take Alex off the medication patch and start him on a pill: Adderall, another ADHD medication. They tested him on different doses. . . . Dr. Pelham also intensified Alex's behavior program. (CBSNEWS.com, 2002)

▾SNAPSHOT

JAMES

James has been driving his mother crazy since he was an infant. When he was a baby, he was irritable, colicky, and difficult to predict or manage. His mother recalls that he could run before he could walk, and that he was constantly getting into things. In fact, he was such an active and exploring pre-schooler [that] he poisoned himself and was well known in the emergency room for a series of accidents.

However, trouble really started to occur for James when he entered school. He had difficulty listening to the teacher and staying on task. He had particular problems with acting before thinking. For example, he would raise his hand even before the teacher finished a question and would invariably not know the answer. He would blurt out comments in the classroom, and he seemed incapable of keeping his hands to himself. He always seemed to be on the move, particularly in structured classrooms. In addition to his classroom and academic problems, James also had social problems. His peers did not like him. They commented that he seemed bossy and uncooperative: "He always had to do things his way."

At first, the teacher thought he was immature, and he was retained for a year. This only made things worse. He did not grow out of his problems, and his peers made fun of him for being stupid. James hated school. He became defiant with the teacher and started fights with the other children on the playground.

Things have improved for James since last year. His doctor has him on a stimulant medication, and he spends part of the school day in a resource room classroom. This classroom is particularly good for James because the teacher has a good program that rewards him for being on task and completing work. The teacher also runs a social skills training group, and James is starting to learn how to cooperate with other children. In addition, James' mother and father have taken a parenting class on how to manage children with ADHD and things have started to improve at home.

SOURCE: From *Understanding Child Behavior Disorders*, (3rd ed., p. 117), by D. M. Gelfand, W. R. Jenson, and C. J. Drew, 1997, Fort Worth: Harcourt.

➤ **Attention-deficit/ hyperactivity disorder (ADHD)**

A disorder characterized by difficulties in maintaining attention because of a limited ability to concentrate. Children with ADHD exhibit impulsive actions and hyperactive behavior.

➤ **Hyperactivity**

Perhaps the most frequently mentioned behavioral characteristic in the literature on ADHD. In some cases, the term *hyperactivity* refers to too much activity; in other cases, it refers to activity inappropriate for a given situation or context.

➤ **Executive function**

The ability to monitor and regulate one's own behavior. Executive function reflects an individual's ability to exercise impulse control and to think about and anticipate the consequences of actions.

FOCUS 1

Identify three behavioral symptoms commonly associated with ADHD.

Council for Exceptional Children

Standard 1: Foundations

Standard 2: Development and Characteristics of Learners

Standard 3: Individual Learning Differences

FOCUS 2

Identify two ways in which the behavior of children with ADHD detrimentally affects instructional settings.

Behaviors of children with ADHD often challenge teachers in both instruction and classroom management.

Attention-deficit/hyperactivity disorder (ADHD) took center stage as a separate disability during the 1990s. The puzzling characteristics associated with ADHD, descriptions of affected individuals, and collections of symptoms first appeared in historical writings as early as 100 years ago (Nigg, Hinshaw, & Huang-Pollock, 2006; Rafalovich, 2004). In the past few decades, ADHD was viewed as a set of symptoms accompanying other conditions, such as learning disabilities and emotional or behavior disorders. In more recent years, however, ADHD has come increasingly to be treated as a separate and distinct disability, although it is still not viewed as such in IDEA (U.S. Department of Education, 2006).

People with ADHD may exhibit a variety of characteristics, including unusually impulsive behavior, fidgeting or **hyperactivity**, an inability to focus attention, or some combination of these behaviors. In many cases, we define ADHD by what we see—hyperactivity, disruptiveness, and perhaps aggressive behavior. In fact, ADHD is actually a variety of physical processes (such as neurological or chemical malfunctions) interacting with social, psychological, or environmental factors (e.g., frustration, social isolation, poor teaching). In grappling with such behaviors, researchers in ADHD have begun to look beyond these characteristics and to conceptualize the disability as an intense disorder of self-regulation, impulse control, attention span, and activity level. Increasingly, the literature on ADHD reflects attention to impulse control and thinking about the consequences of one's actions, via studies on concepts such as **executive function**, which is the ability to monitor and regulate one's own behavior (Brown, 2006; Happe, Booth, & Charlton, 2006; Nigg et al., 2006).

For people with ADHD, their symptoms are often intense enough to interfere with performance and life activities in a number of ways. Children with ADHD often have significant difficulties in school and frequently present a substantial challenge to teachers in terms of both instruction and classroom management (e.g., Kapalka, 2005). Such children may be in and out of their seats, pestering others, or even exhibiting aggressive behaviors such as hitting or pulling hair. They may be unable to focus on the teacher's instructions and may impulsively start assignments before they have heard all the directions. In many cases an assignment may not be completed, either because the child did not hear the work objective or because he or she darted to another activity that captured his or her roving attention.

Although much of the attention on ADHD has focused on children and adolescents, this condition may also present major difficulties for adults. Some researchers estimate that ADHD is a lifelong disability for perhaps one-third to one-half of those affected during childhood (Barkley, Fischer, Smallish, & Fletcher, 2006; Halperin & Schulz, 2006; Seidman, 2006). ADHD during adulthood may make it difficult to focus on specific work responsibilities long enough to see them through to completion. The affected worker may flit from task to task, making a little headway on each but completing none. Such individuals may have difficulty focusing during discussions with their supervisors. They may exhibit well-rehearsed social survival skills such as nodding and looking at the boss, but their thoughts may be far away on a jumble of tasks that are not finished.

ADHD and Other Disabilities

ADHD has long been associated with learning disabilities. As research evidence has accumulated on both learning disabilities and ADHD, it has become increasingly clear that there is a certain amount of overlap, or comorbidity (conditions occurring together) (Adler, Barkley, Wilens, & Ginsberg, 2006; Daley, 2006; Sutcliffe, 2006). Some researchers describe the co-occurrence as common, and estimates vary from 25% to 70% overlap between learning disabilities and ADHD (Dietz & Montague, 2006; Mayes & Calhoun, 2006; U.S. Department of Education, 2004). This is clearly evident in the Snapshot of Nancy, who is diagnosed as having ADHD combined type, with a number of elements of learning disabilities.

▼SNAPSHOT

NANCY

Nancy makes an impression, and she always has. As an infant, she was fussy and cried a lot. Despite all attempts to soothe her, it seemed impossible to make her comfortable or happy. Her mother wondered if she would ever sleep through the night. As she grew and as her physical abilities increased, life in the house was devoted to keeping her safe, twenty-four hours a day. She learned how to climb the bars and get out of her crib by her first birthday. Child safety latches and gates proved inadequate to the task of keeping Nancy and harm apart. When she was 3, her parents were awakened one morning at 4:30 to the screams of the family cat. They followed the sound, arriving in the bathroom just in time to save the cat from being flushed down the toilet by Nancy. Her pediatrician felt that Nancy was just an active, inquisitive preschooler and that judgment would come with maturity. Time was the remedy.

At 5, Nancy was enrolled in kindergarten. The teacher quickly realized that Nancy was different. Her attention span was much shorter than that of the other children, and her levels of impulsivity and activity were much higher. She was not benefiting from the kindergarten program, and the decision was made to move her to the prekindergarten class, assuming that with time, she would develop the attention abilities required to be successful in school—that she was developmentally immature. Life was no better in the prekindergarten class. She talked incessantly, grabbed whatever she wanted, and was in constant motion. Nancy wasn't learning, and neither was anyone else.

Finally, when Nancy was in second grade, the school and her parents concluded that a psychological evaluation was in order to find an explanation for Nancy's problems. The results indicated normal ability and, surprisingly, normal development of cognitive concepts and language. What stood out was her constant movement and her dangerous and disruptive impulsivity, as well as her academic problems in the classroom. Her performance levels in reading, writing, and math lagged well behind her peers. A medical examination was suggested, and the diagnosis was attention-deficit/hyperactivity disorder, combined type. On the basis of this information, as well as the discrepancy between her achievement and ability, and the absence of other disabling conditions, the school's multidisciplinary team determined that she qualified for services as a student with a learning disability.

Today, Nancy is a reasonably successful fourth grader. She still stands out, and she probably always will. A combination of behavioral interventions and psychostimulant medication has brought her behavior under control, although she still has a shorter attention span, is somewhat fidgety, and displays more impulsivity and activity than other fourth graders. She has learned to self-monitor her attention as a result of cognitive behavior modification interventions implemented by the consultant teacher. Counseling sessions with the guidance counselor have helped her to accept responsibility for her actions and not to blame her actions on the ADHD or the medication. Nevertheless, her homeroom teacher has a hard time accepting that her behaviors are the result of a disability. Mr. Smith finds it hard to accept that a student who is obviously as capable as Nancy, and who *sometimes* pays attention and can control her behavior reasonably well, has a "real" learning disability. He suspects that the "attention disorder" is an excuse for letting Nancy do what she pleases.

SOURCE: Raymond, E. B. (2004). *Learners with Mild Disabilities: A Characteristics Approach* (2nd ed., pp. 209–210). Boston: Allyn and Bacon.

► **Tourette's syndrome**
A condition characterized by motor
or verbal tics that cause the person
to make repetitive movements, emit
strange involuntary sounds, or say
words or phrases that are
inappropriate for the context.

FOCUS **3**
Identify four other areas
of disability that are often
found to be comorbid with
ADHD.

A number of other conditions appear to have a notable level of comorbidity with ADHD (Drabick, Gadow, & Sprafkin, 2006; Masi et al., 2006; Nadeau & Quinn, 2002). One is **Tourette's syndrome**, a condition characterized by motor or verbal tics that cause the person to make repetitive movements, emit strange involuntary sounds, and/or say inappropriate words or phrases (sometimes intense swearing) (Robertson, 2006; Termine et al., 2006). Tourette's does not appear with great frequency among those with ADHD, although about half of the individuals with Tourette's exhibit some ADHD symptoms. There is some evidence that causal culprits in Tourette's may include some of the chemical malfunctions thought to be related to ADHD, although further research is needed in this area (Brand et al., 2002; Kurlan, 2005).

As indicated in the Case Study below, another area of disability that overlaps with ADHD is that of behavior, conduct, and emotional disorders. This covers a very large area, so some level of comorbidity is not surprising. Some of the behaviors exhibited by individuals with ADHD are quite disruptive. In some cases, the level of aggression can easily be interpreted as a conduct or behavior disorder. The literature suggests that such behavior disorders occur in as many as half of those with ADHD (Burns & Walsh, 2002; Masi et al., 2006; Kurlan, 2005; Mayes & Calhoun, 2006). There are also interesting overlaps between ADHD and certain conditions that might be considered emotional disorders, such as anxiety, depression, obsessive-compulsive disorder, and some levels of neurotic behavior (Bettencourt, Talley, Benjamine, & Valentine, 2006; Drabick et al., 2006; Termine et al., 2006).

As we examine ADHD, it is important to realize it has many faces. ADHD is not a simple condition that can be defined and categorized easily. The distinctions between ADHD and other conditions are often not clear, in part because certain definitions have historically overlapped and in part because groups of people who have been diagnosed with one condition or another represent very heterogeneous populations (Cukrowicz, Taylor,

CASE STUDY

ADHD AND OTHER DISABILITIES: COEXISTING CONDITIONS

Jim was a 10-year-old boy enrolled in a mental health day program that treated severely behaviorally disordered children. In this program he was treated for a major fire-setting problem. Jim's developmental history was characterized by deprivation, inadequate parenting, chaotic home life, and a series of foster home placements. He was diagnosed as having both a conduct disorder and attention-deficit disorder. His list of referral problems included stealing, hyperactivity, tantrums, learning disabilities, aggression, noncompliance, zoophilia, and fire setting. The fire setting had been a problem since Jim was 3, when he burned down the family home. Since his foster placements, Jim had averaged approximately one fire setting every two weeks.

It was assumed that Jim set fires partly because he enjoyed seeing the fires and partly as a reaction to stress. The stress was related to a series of skill deficits in the social and academic areas. In addition, it was assumed that Jim did not fully realize the dangerous consequences of his behavior. His

therapy involved a multiple-treatment approach. . . . After treatment, Jim's fire setting dropped from an average of one every two weeks to virtually zero fires at a one-year follow-up. Jim improved his basic social skills and appeared better prepared to handle stressful situations, although some of his inappropriate behaviors, such as stealing and family problems, have persisted.

APPLICATION

1. List the different professionals who may have contact with Jim and his parents as a result of the different types of problems he presents.

2. How important do you believe communication between the various professionals that you listed is? What difficulties are likely to arise if they do not communicate in a coordinated manner?

3. In order to coordinate communication and treatment, who is the best candidate to be the focal point for organizing Jim's case? Should it be his parents? Or should it be one of the professionals involved in his treatment?

SOURCE: From *Understanding Child Behavior Disorders* (3rd ed.), by D. M. Gelfand, W. R. Jenson, & C. J. Drew, 1997, p. 127. Fort Worth: Harcourt.

Schatschneider, & Iacono, 2006; Martin, Levy, Pieka, & Hay, 2006). Evidence suggests that a large percentage of those with ADHD demonstrate comorbidity with some other identifiable condition (Dietz & Montague, 2006; Gelfand & Drew, 2003; Mayes & Calhoun, 2006).

Definitions

ADHD characteristics have often been described in the context of other prominent disabilities where there is substantial comorbidity, most frequently learning disabilities and emotional or behavior disorders. The definition of ADHD that is used most often is that provided by the American Psychiatric Association (APA) in the fourth edition of its *Diagnostic and Statistical Manual of Mental Disorders* (DSM-IV) (APA, 2000). The APA definition is presented in Table 8.1.

The APA includes three subcategories of ADHD in its description of diagnostic criteria: (1) ADHD, combined type; (2) ADHD, predominantly inattentive type; and (3) ADHD, predominantly hyperactive-impulsive type (APA, 2000). The diagnostic criteria for these categories, as outlined in DSM-IV, are summarized in Figure 8.1. Although many people exhibit symptoms that combine inattention, impulsivity, and hyperactivity, others have a predominant feature that corresponds to one of the other two subtypes.

The American Academy of Pediatrics has issued a set of clinical practice guidelines that build on DSM-IV criteria. These guidelines are intended to provide primary-care clinicians with further suggestions for making diagnostic decisions for these children. They include the points summarized in Figure 8.2.

FOCUS 4
Identify the three major types of ADHD according to DSM-IV.

Council for Exceptional Children

Standard 2: Development and Characteristics of Learners

TABLE 8.1

APA Definitions of ADHD

CRITERION	DESCRIPTION
Criterion A	• The essential feature of attention-deficit/hyperactivity disorder is a persistent pattern of inattention and/or hyperactivity-impulsivity that is more frequent and severe than is typically observed in individuals at a comparable level of development.
Criterion B	• Some hyperactive-impulsive or inattentive symptoms that cause impairment must have been present before age 7 years, although many individuals are diagnosed after the symptoms have been present for a number of years.
Criterion C	• Some impairment from the symptoms must be present in at least two settings (e.g., at home and at schoolwork).
Criterion D	• There must be clear evidence of interference with developmentally appropriate social, academic, or occupational functioning.
Criterion E	• The disturbance does not occur exclusively during the course of a pervasive developmental disorder, schizophrenia, or other psychotic disorder and is not better accounted for by another mental disorder (e.g., mood disorder, anxiety disorder, dissociative disorder, or personality disorder).

SOURCE: From *Diagnostic and Statistical Manual of Mental Disorders* (4th ed. Text Revision, p. 85), by the American Psychiatric Association, 2000, Washington, DC: Author.

FIGURE 8.1

Diagnostic Criteria for Attention-Deficit/Hyperactivity Disorder

A. Either (1) or (2):

1. Six (or more) of the following symptoms of *inattention* have persisted for at least 6 months to a degree that is maladaptive and inconsistent with developmental level:

Inattention

a. Often fails to give close attention to details or makes careless mistakes in schoolwork, work, or other activities.

b. Often has difficulty sustaining attention in tasks or play activities.

c. Often does not seem to listen when spoken to directly.

d. Often does not follow through on instructions and fails to finish schoolwork, chores, or duties in the workplace (not due to oppositional behavior or failure to understand instructions).

e. Often has difficulty organizing tasks and activities.

f. Often avoids, dislikes, or is reluctant to engage in tasks that require sustained mental effort (such as schoolwork or homework).

g. Often loses things necessary for tasks or activities (e.g., toys, school assignments, pencils, books, or tools).

h. Is often easily distracted by extraneous stimuli.

i. Is often forgetful in daily activities.

2. Six (or more) of the following symptoms of *hyperactivity-impulsivity* have persisted for at least 6 months to a degree that is maladaptive and inconsistent with developmental level:

Hyperactivity

a. Often fidgets with hands or feet or squirms in seat.

b. Often leaves seat in classroom or in other situations in which remaining seated is expected.

c. Often runs about or climbs excessively in situations in which it is inappropriate (in adolescents or adults, may be limited to subjective feelings or restlessness).

d. Often has difficulty playing or engaging in leisure activities quietly.

e. Is often "on the go" or often acts as if "driven by a motor."

f. Often talks excessively.

Impulsivity

g. Often blurts out answers before questions have been completed.

h. Often has difficulty awaiting turn.

i. Often interrupts or intrudes on others (e.g., butts into conversations or games).

B. Some hyperactive-impulsive or inattentive symptoms that caused impairment were present before age 7 years.

C. Some impairment from the symptoms is present in two or more settings (e.g., at school [or work] and at home).

D. There must be clear evidence of clinically significant impairment in social, academic, or occupational functioning.

E. The symptoms do not occur exclusively during the course of a pervasive developmental disorder, schizophrenia, or other psychotic disorder and are not better accounted for by another mental disorder (e.g., mood disorder, anxiety disorder, dissociative disorder, or a personality disorder).

Code based on type:

Attention-Deficit/Hyperactivity Disorder, Combined Type: if both Criteria A1 and A2 are met for the past 6 months.

Attention-Deficit/Hyperactivity Disorder, Predominantly Inattentive Type: if Criterion A1 is met but Criterion A2 is not met for the past 6 months.

Attention-Deficit/Hyperactivity Disorder, Predominantly Hyperactive-Impulsive Type: if Criterion A2 is met but Criterion A1 is not met for the past 6 months.

Coding note: For individuals (especially adolescents and adults) who currently have symptoms that no longer meet full criteria, "In Partial Remission" should be specified.

SOURCE: Reprinted with permission from the *Diagnostic and Statistical Manual of Mental Disorders*, (4th ed. Text Revision, p. 92). Copyright 2000 American Psychiatric Association.

American Academy of Pediatrics Clinical Practice Guidelines

1. In a child 6 to 12 years old who presents with inattention, hyperactivity, impulsivity, academic underachievement, or behavior problems, primary-care clinicians should initiate an evaluation for ADHD.

2. The diagnosis of ADHD requires that a child meet criteria in *Diagnostic and Statistical Manual of Mental Disorders*, Fourth Edition.

3. The assessment of ADHD requires evidence directly obtained from parents or caregivers regarding the core symptoms of ADHD in various settings, the age of onset, the duration of symptoms, and the degree of functional impairment.

4. The assessment of ADHD requires evidence directly obtained from the classroom teacher (or other school professional) regarding the core symptoms of ADHD, the duration of symptoms, the degree of functional impairment, and associated conditions.

5. Evaluation of the child with ADHD should include assessment for associated (coexisting) conditions.

6. Other diagnostic tests are not routinely indicated to establish the diagnosis of ADHD but may be used for the assessment of other, coexisting conditions (e.g., learning disabilities and mental retardation).

This clinical practice guideline is not intended as a sole source of guidance in the evaluation of children with ADHD. Rather, it is designed to assist primary-care clinicians by providing a framework for diagnostic decision making. It is not intended to replace clinical judgment or to establish a protocol for all children with this condition and may not provide the only appropriate approach to this problem.

SOURCE: From "Diagnosis and Evaluation of the Child with Attention-Deficit/Hyperactivity Disorder (AC0002)," by the American Academy of Pediatrics, 2000, *Pediatrics*, 105, 1158–1170.

Prevalence

Prevalence estimates for ADHD most often suggest that 3% to 7% of all school-aged children may have the disorder, although some researchers believe this is too low (APA, 2000; Faraone & Biederman, 2005; Smith, Barkley, & Shapiro, 2006). The literature generally indicates that more males than females are identified with ADHD; the average male/female ratio ranges from 2.5:1 to 3.5:1 (Cuffe, Moore, & Mckeown, 2005; Gelfand & Drew, 2003). There is wide variation in the gender data, however, with male/female ratios ranging from 2:1 to 10:1, depending on the population sampled (Faraone & Biederman, 2005; Zahn-Waxler, Crick, Shirtcliff, & Woods, 2006). Young children show higher male/female ratios than older groups. It should be noted that identifying ADHD in children under 4 or 5 years of age is very difficult (APA, 2000). Males and females with ADHD seem to exhibit different symptoms and may have different intervention needs, which could account for differences in identification and incidence. Young males may exhibit more disruptive or aggressive behaviors, which may more readily bring them to the attention of their teachers or parents (Marshal & Molina, 2006; Radford & Ervin, 2002; Thapar, van den Bree, Fowler, Langley, & Whittinger, 2006). Young females may exhibit inattentiveness or daydreaming more often. Some questions have been raised about the possibility of gender bias in identification and diagnosis. This assertion suggests that boys may be overidentified, and girls underidentified, partly because of the differing predominant behaviors (Derks et al., 2006; McGoey, Eckert, & DuPaul, 2002; Zahn-Waxler et al., 2006). The literature remains mixed on this issue, suggesting that although some gender bias may be present, the substantial gender differences may reflect some actual difference in the prevalence of ADHD in males and females (Jackson, 2002). More

FOCUS 5

Identify two prevalence estimates for ADHD that characterize the difference in occurrence by gender.

recent research shows mixed results on gender prevalence, with some evidence of an increase among young females (Cuffe et al., 2005; Robison, Skaer, Sclar, & Galin, 2002).

There is some evidence that different types of ADHD have differing prevalence levels (inattentive, hyperactive-impulsive, and combined types), although these levels vary considerably between studies (Mayes & Calhoun, 2006). There also appears to be some variation between subgroups by age, gender, and comorbidity with other conditions, although considerably more evidence needs to be accumulated on these issues (Kessler et al., 2006; Mayes & Calhoun, 2006; Zahn-Waxler et al., 2006). Prevalence appears somewhat higher in younger children and in males, although these youngsters may stand out because the disruptive or high-activity symptoms evident in such groups attract attention.

There has been substantial growth in services to ADHD students during the last decade, particularly since the U.S. Department of Education stipulated that such students are eligible for services under the IDEA category of Other Health Impairments. Such eligibility is certainly not the only factor affecting the growing number of people in this category, but it is thought to have a substantial impact (U.S. Department of Education, 2006).

Multidisciplinary Collaboration

Standard 4: Instructional Strategies

Standard 7: Instructional Planning

The process of assessing, diagnosing, and providing services to those with ADHD is a joint venture between multiple disciplines that come together as a team. This collaborative team most often includes professionals from medicine, psychology, and education and may also involve others, such as social workers or counselors, depending on the family circumstances (Adler et al., 2006; Dehon & Scheeringa, 2006). We have discussed collaboration between multiple disciplines previously with other disabilities. However, children with ADHD present characteristics that broaden the diversity of this team perhaps more than any other disability.

Because of the behavioral diversity found in ADHD, these children, adolescents, and adults may come in contact with many professionals, such as physicians, law enforcement personnel, psychologists, and (as always) educators. At the most basic level, referrals may emerge from several stakeholders, most notably parents and teachers or other educational personnel (Ambalavanan & Molten, 2005; Pappas, 2006). Such initial assessments are likely to emerge when the child's behavior or academic performance brings him or her to someone's attention. For these children, disruptive behavior may be the triggering characteristic, or this type of behavior may be accompanied by lack of attention to directions, failure to complete their academic work, impulsivity, and perhaps challenges in developing social relationships (e.g., Barkley, 2006). Complete assessment, diagnosis, and resulting interventions for those with ADHD frequently include many professionals, ranging from physicians, who may prescribe medication, to educators and psychologists, who focus on instruction and behavioral management (DuPaul, 2006a; Santosh, Baird, & Pityaratstian, 2006; Wells, Chi, & Hinshaw, 2006). As the child reaches adolescence and transitions into adulthood, the context changes, but the need for multidisciplinary collaboration on assessments and intervention continues (e.g., Dowson, 2006).

Assessment and Diagnosis

FOCUS **6**

Identify the two broad categories of assessment information useful in diagnosing ADHD.

Standard 8: Assessment

The most frequent behaviors and features of ADHD include what appears to be a high level of activity that may include aggressive and disruptive behavior that causes concerns for parents or teachers (Barkley, 2006; Daley, 2006). Parents often seek advice and help from medical, psychological, and/or educational personnel. In many cases, these professionals collaborate to provide information and to help plan interventions. Such collaboration becomes essential for a comprehensive evaluation that leads to implementing an intervention with multiple facets. Making this collaboration effective is essential for the well-being of the child and usually includes the full range of activities from referral through assessment and implementation of the program that results (Efron, 2005; Rappley, 2005; Wolraich, Bickman, Lambert, Simmons, & Doffing, 2005). Assessment and diagnostic information for

ADHD falls into two broad categories: data that are medical in nature, and data that provide information about educational, behavioral, and contextual circumstances.

Medical data are collected through examinations by pediatricians or other health care professionals. In many cases, these health care professionals are family doctors or referred physicians whom are sought out by the parents outside the school system. Clinical interviews and other psychological assessments are undertaken by psychologists who may be on staff in the schools or in private practice. This process is likely to entail compilation of both psychological and environmental data, including information about family and school matters. Additionally, direct information from parents and teachers is sought and quantified through the completion of rating scales and other such instruments (Derks, Hudziak, Dolan, Ferinand, & Boomsma, 2006; Pappas, 2006; Power, Werba, Watkins, Angelucci, & Eirldi, 2006).

An important part of the diagnostic evaluation of ADHD is information collected by health care professionals.

One instrument used to assess ADHD is the Child Behavior Checklist (CBCL). The CBCL is considered a very useful assessment procedure in child psychopathology (Derks et al., 2006; Oldehinkel, Veenstra, Ormel, de Winter, & Vulhulst, 2006; Tripp & Schaughency, 2006). It provides parent data, teacher ratings, and classroom observation protocols to assess academic competence and social problems beginning at age 4 and to evaluate adolescents through age 18. The Snapshot on Doug shows a portion of the CBCL reporting protocol used by parents. The information outlines several challenges facing Doug, as well as the need to use multiple assessment procedures. Other evaluation protocols include the Behavior Assessment System for Children—Teacher Rating Scales (BASC–TRS), the Behavior Rating Inventory of Executive Function (BRIEF), and the School Situations Questionnaire (SSQ) (Jarratt, Riccio, & Siekierski, 2005;

REFLECT ON THIS

INSURANCE AS A FACTOR IN ASSESSMENT

On the surface, insurance coverage would not seem to play a significant role in assessment and diagnosis of ADHD. However, in many cases it may play more of a role than we might expect. The National Institutes of Health reported that "The lack of insurance coverage for psychiatric or psychological evaluations, behavior modification programs, school consultation, parent management training, and other specialized programs presents a major barrier to accurate classification, diagnosis, and management of ADHD. Substantial cost barriers exist in that diagnosis results in out-of-pocket costs to families for services not covered by managed care or other health insurance" (1998, p. 10).

Consider the situation of a parent of a child who has just completed a series of tests that have led to a long conversation with the family pediatrician. She has outlined what she believes are the next steps of information gathering, suggested that ADHD may be involved, and discussed the fact that some treatment recommendations may not be covered by insurance. The costs may be significant: several hundred dollars per month for a while and then unknown after that. This is a predicament that is familiar to many parents of children with ADHD.

SOURCE: *From Diagnosis and Treatment of Attention-Deficit/Hyperactivity Disorder,* (pp.1–37), by National Institutes of Health, 1998, *NIH Consensus Statement Online,* 16(2), November 16–18.

Pelletier, Collett, Gimpel, & Crowley, 2006). The SSQ is different from many rating scales in that it presents situations where the child being evaluated may encounter problems.

The referral process for evaluating a child typically begins with the educational and psychological data-gathering process outlined in the preceding paragraphs, and information may come from educational professionals or parents. The initial referral is very important, because it sets in motion a course of action that it is hoped will significantly affect the child's life for the better, in the form of effective treatment (Pappas, 2006; Power et al., 2006). As with most referrals, a child with ADHD will enter the process because of some aspect of performance or behavior that sets him or her apart and causes concern for the person or professional who initiates the referral process (such as a parent or classroom teacher). Parental concerns may focus on the aggressive and disruptive behavior exhibited by many children with ADHD. Evidence sug-

▼ SNAPSHOT

DOUG

Doug is an 11-year-old, fifth grade male who was referred because of parental and teacher concerns about his school performance. He is suspected of having significant attention problems.

Doug also has significant trouble in peer and other relationships. He often fights and argues with peers, resulting in his often playing by himself.

Doug has a history of significant medical difficulties. He is the product of an at-risk pregnancy. Although he achieved most developmental milestones within normal timeframes, he has a history of motor delays. In second grade he was diagnosed with muscular dystrophy. He also suffers from inflammatory bowel disease, resulting in ongoing treatment for ulcers. He does not tolerate many foods well and consequently his appetite is poor.

In first grade Doug was also diagnosed as learning-disabled, with problems in reading. He is in a resource special education program. He is described by his teacher as "socially inept." He is often disrespectful of teachers and peers. His grades deteriorated significantly toward the end of the last academic year. His teachers consider him to be a capable underachiever with behavior problems such as inattention, excessive talking, fighting, arguing, and poor work completion.

[Doug was evaluated on the CBCL Scales listed below, which indicated a broad range of difficulties for this youngster.] . . .

- Internalizing
- Withdrawn
- Somatic complaints
- Anxious/depressed
- Externalizing

- Social problems
- Thought problems
- Attention problems
- Delinquent behavior
- Aggressive behavior

His mother's report [was] more severe than the majority of the three teacher ratings. His mother's responses to the Parenting Stress Index were also highly significant, revealing stress beyond the 99th percentile on the majority of the PSI scales.

All raters and observations were needed in order to clarify the CBCL results. Aggressive behavior, attention problems, somatic complaints, and depression symptoms were identified by the majority of indices. Enough information was gleaned to make the diagnosis of attention-deficit/hyperactivity disorder and oppositional defiant disorder. Recommendations for intervention also included treatment for significant sadness, although the criteria for a depressive disorder were not met at the time of the evaluation.

Indications of thought problems were not corroborated by other findings. The clinicians thought that the thought problems scale was elevated for some raters due to interpretation of the items by raters as indicators of hyperactivity or inattention. CBCL Social Problems scores were corroborated by low scores on social skills measures. The social skills measures were used to develop behavioral objectives for Doug's intervention.

This CBCL profile highlights the need, more pressing in a case like this, to complement the CBCL with other measures. In this case, teacher ratings, observations, self-reports, measures of parent stress, history taking, and observations were all needed to clarify diagnostic impressions and identify treatment objectives.

SOURCE: From *Clinical Assessment of Child and Adolescent Personality and Behavior* (p. 131), by R. W. Kamphaus & P. J. Frick, 1996, Needham Heights, MA: Allyn and Bacon. Reprinted by permission.

gests that raising children with such disabilities is likely to contribute to significant parental life stress, which often triggers the referral process (Johnson & Reader, 2002; Power et al., 2006).

An initial referral is a precursor to a complete evaluation and diagnostic analysis, including a comprehensive clinical interview conducted by a psychologist. At the clinical interview stage, more information is collected on the nature of the child's behavior and on the environment in which it occurs (both school and family settings). This stage may also involve the use of behavior checklists, functional assessment, or other protocols that quantify observations in a structured fashion (Radford & Ervin, 2002). One such protocol is the Diagnostic Interview Schedule for Children (DISC-IV) (Canivez & Sprouls, 2005; Derks, Hudziak, & Dolan, 2006). The DISC is a structured interview designed for use by trained psychologists or lay interviewers.

The final source of diagnostic evaluation is the medical examination. This assessment takes into account all information that has been gathered; its goal is to determine whether other physical conditions may contribute to the behavior observed. The medical examination may also generate the first step in intervention if medication is prescribed.

Much of the referral and diagnostic assessment outlined here involves some professional judgment that might be considered subjective. This is no different from the evaluation process for other disabilities—trained professional judgment is extremely critical. However, for ADHD, some have questioned whether bias affects the accuracy of the assessment process (Hall, Ashley, Bramlett, Dielmann, & Murphy, 2005; Jarratt, Riccio, & Siekierski, 2005). Such questions also raise concern about how well professionals are prepared to conduct assessments. For example, a teacher may play a very important part in the identification of ADHD. And there is some evidence that a teacher's decision to refer a student for assessment or identification for ADHD may be influenced considerably by his or her general attitude, style, and beliefs about teaching practices (Hepperlen, Clay, Henly, & Barke, 2002). As illustrated earlier, observations and ratings of children through standardized ADHD protocols are an important part of the evaluation process. Despite the standardized nature of these tools, their accuracy and usefulness depend in large part on the knowledge and experience of those who complete them. Some research suggests that considerable error may occur because the raters' own characteristics influence how they rate a child's behavior problems (Barry, Dunlap, Cotton, Lochman, & Wells, 2005; Martell & Evans, 2005).

If there are significant inaccuracies in the way teachers evaluate children with ADHD, then programs that prepare these professionals need to respond (Orford, 2006). Some researchers have raised concerns about the way teachers are prepared to work with children who have ADHD. Some evidence suggests that recent graduates from teacher preparation programs are not better prepared than teachers who graduated earlier. Such findings imply that the teacher education curriculum needs to be enhanced with more information and strategies related to disabilities in general, and to ADHD as a part of that experience (Chang, Early, & Winton, 2005; DeSimone & Parmar, 2006).

Characteristics

The opening Snapshot presented James, a child with characteristics associated with ADHD that appeared at a very early age. James's story also illustrates how one type of behavior problem can lead or contribute to another as a child grows older. Discussion of the characteristics of ADHD can clearly become mired in "chicken or egg" issues: which came first, impulsivity and problems with self-regulation, or inattention, hyperactivity, and aggression? This is an important debate to the extent that it helps to identify effective interventions.

James's behavior before he received medication included hyperactivity with disruptive and aggressive tendencies. James seemed not to think ahead about the outcomes or consequences of his actions. He appeared to be impulsive, and an observer could easily infer that he had difficulty regulating his own behavior.

Self-Regulation, Impulsivity, and Hyperactivity

Difficulty in self-regulation and behavioral inhibition are receiving more attention as theoretical explanations and research models for ADHD (Happe et al., 2006; Nigg et al., 2006;

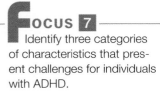

FOCUS **7**

Identify three categories of characteristics that present challenges for individuals with ADHD.

Council for Exceptional Children

Standard 2: Development and Characteristics of Learners

Individuals with ADHD have difficulty paying attention. Here is a young woman lost in a daydream during a teacher's lecture.

Seidman, 2006). Some researchers have suggested that these efforts are crucial to understanding ADHD (e.g., Brown, 2006). Discussions include concepts such as behavioral inhibition and executive function, as well as impulse control, self-regulation, and self-management. Problems encountered by the individual under all of these rubrics are quite similar and seem to involve substantial difficulty in thinking through one's actions to see what the effects of certain behaviors might be (Gureasko-Moore, DuPaul, & White, 2006; Happe et al., 2006; Seidman, 2006). People with ADHD are not able to consider the following question: "If I behave in a certain manner, what is the probable outcome, and how will it affect those around me?" This was true with James when he raised his hand before the question was asked and without having the answer in mind.

Hyperactivity is a primary characteristic of ADHD, as suggested in the diagnostic criteria summarized in Figure 8.1 on page 208. In accordance with these criteria, the hyperactive behavior must persist for at least six months and must be intense enough to create maladaptive problems for the individual. Many parents, teachers, and others describe such youngsters as those who fidget and squirm constantly; are continually running, jumping, and climbing around; and are generally on the move all the time (Pelletier et al., 2006; Rowland, Lesesne, & Abramowitz, 2002; Tripp & Schaughency, 2006). As most parents will confirm, all children can be characterized in these terms from time to time, but the hyperactive child with ADHD far exceeds the norm. The behaviors are seemingly continuous and occur in inappropriate settings and times.

Hyperactivity may be the most frequently mentioned characteristic in the literature addressing various facets of ADHD. Being overly active seems to affect about half of the children diagnosed with ADHD. Although the high-activity characteristic appears to diminish as some children get older, for others this is not true. In some cases, the hyperactive behavior begins to surface in adolescence and may be evident through the adult years (Barkley, 2006; Chronis, Jones, & Raggi, 2006).

Social Relationships

Youngsters with ADHD often encounter difficulties in their social relationships with peers (Chronis et al., 2006; Kazdin, 2005). Some children have trouble getting along because they exhibit aggressive behavior toward their classmates, and of course this does not promote positive social interactions (Donovan, 2006; Pappadopulos et al., 2006; Radford & Ervin, 2002). Other children with ADHD exhibit seriously antisocial or pathological social behavior, such as cruelty to animals, that may suggest other mental health problems (Danforth, Harvey, Ulaszek, & McKee, 2006; Hirshfeld-Becker et al., 2002; Miller et al., 2006). These behaviors can contribute to low social status among peers, which may persist for years. This pattern may evolve in a variety of ways over time; for example, it may lead to increased risk for criminal activity (Diamond et al., 2006; Monastra, 2005; Spencer, 2005). Such behavioral patterns present enormous challenges for schools as these children proceed through the system.

Individuals with ADHD often feel isolated from others. Social relationships can be a difficult challenge.

The level of severity of ADHD is significant in both males' and females' social relationships, and the outcomes are varied and often serious (Heiman, 2005; Hoza et al., 2005). Some youngsters with ADHD grow increasingly frantic as they try to gain friends, which can easily aggravate their already poor self-regulating behavior. They may thereby seem even more of a nuisance to the peers whom they wish to befriend. Accumulated frustration due to low social status and to having few friends may prompt even stranger behaviors aimed at gaining attention from classmates. Some research also suggests that substance abuse may be more likely among those with ADHD (Monastra, 2005; Winstanley, Eagle, & Robbins, 2006). Some investigators have claimed that this may be due to the use of psychostimulants as treatment, but there is not a great deal of research evidence to support such an assertion (McCabe, Teter, & Boyd, 2006). Some researchers have found that other, comorbid disabilities may be more predictive than ADHD of substance abuse; these conditions include social impairment, conduct disorders, and aggressive behavior (e.g., Lambert, 2005; Marshal & Molina, 2006). Thus research results have so far failed to reveal whether substance abuse is more closely related to ADHD or to other, coexisting conditions, but the combination appears to increase risk substantially.

Academic Characteristics

Students with ADHD experience significant challenges in an academic setting. Research suggests that a very large proportion of these children and adolescents experience substantial learning problems in school (e.g., Dodding, Lewandowski, & Eckert, 2005; Rappley, 2005). Such problems increase as the students progress through the educational system and schoolwork demands more and more of the skills with which they have the greatest difficulty: self-management and thinking ahead (Brown, 2006; Gureasko-Moore et al., 2006; Seidman, 2006). Although these children may have some specific memory difficulties, their academic performance is more likely to suffer from their being inattentive, impulsive, and less "planful" in addressing their studies (Gorman, Klorman, Thatcher, & Borgstedt, 2006; Klingberg, Forssberg, & Westerberg, 2002; Nigge et al., 2006). Failure and poor academic performance also affect other areas, such as self-esteem, creating a repeating cycle of circumstances and symptoms that some researchers believe accumulate dynamically, increasing the likelihood of further problems (Barkley, 2006; Brook & Boaz, 2005; Davids & Gastpar, 2005).

Children and adolescents with ADHD are characterized by a lack of academic success compared to their peers without disabilities, and often they do not graduate from high school (Evans, 2005; Galili-Weisstub & Segman, 2003). Poor academic achievement by students with ADHD is usually associated with their disruptive and nonproductive social behaviors, their poor capacity to self-manage, and a reduced social support network that might otherwise help enhance their academic performance (DuPaul, 2006b; Gureasko-Moore et al., 2006). In academic environments that adapt instruction to individual student needs and abilities, students with ADHD can learn, achieve academically, and improve their self-management skills (DuPaul, 2006a; Harris, Friedlander, Saddler, Frizzelle, & Graham, 2006).

Causation and Interventions

FOCUS 8

Identify three possible causes of ADHD.

Causation

There is considerable difference of opinion about the causes of ADHD, and both biological and environmental influences have been identified (e.g., Krain & Castellanos, 2006; Monastra, 2005; Ravenel, 2002). Speculation has included genetic inheritance, neurological injury during birth complications, and negative impacts of a variety of environmental factors (Daley, 2006; Ehringer, Rhee, Young, Corley, & Hewitt, 2006). As we begin to understand ADHD better, we will probably find that multiple causes are associated with this condition.

Neurological causes of ADHD have been suspected for many years, although viewpoints on the nature of such neurological dysfunction have varied considerably. Early investigation on behaviors exhibited by World War I soldiers who had sustained head injuries focused on a trauma-based or physical cause for brain malfunction. Current theories still include injury-induced brain malfunction, although more current thinking also views chemical imbalances in serotonin and dopamine as possible causes (Mill et al., 2006; Moore et al., 2006; Winstanley et al., 2006).

Documentation of neurological causes for ADHD has progressed enormously through new and developing technology, particularly neuroimaging procedures (Fassbender & Schweitzer, 2006; Pliszka et al., 2006). Where previously the medical profession speculated about neurological dysfunction on the basis of observed behavior, we are now able to examine the brain directly. For example, neuroimaging shows that people with ADHD seem to exhibit brain abnormalities in three areas: the **frontal lobes**, selected areas of the **basal ganglia**, and the **cerebellum** (Archibald, Kerns, Mateer, & Ismay, 2005; Fredericksen et al., 2002). Figure 8.3 indicates the general areas in the brain that have been identified as having abnormalities associated with ADHD.

➤ **Frontal lobes**

The front parts of the brain, which are nearest to the forehead.

➤ **Basal ganglia**

Sections of the brain that are near the stem, close to where the spinal cord meets the bottom of the brain matter.

➤ **Cerebellum**

The part of the brain that coordinates muscle movement. It is located right below the large main sections of the brain.

In some cases the actual brain structures appear different for individuals with ADHD, whereas in other cases the chemical functioning in the brain may be different from that in people who do not have the condition (Halperin & Schulz, 2006; Moore et al., 2006; Seidman, 2006). Such differences in structure and chemical function may have a variety of causes, including physical injury to the brain and developmental factors. It is widely known that environmental influences during prenatal or neonatal periods can have serious detrimental effects. For example, lead exposure, pregnant mothers' alcohol abuse, nutrition, and exposure to tobacco smoke place developing embryos and infants at high risk for serious learning and developmental delays. Likewise, low birthweight and delivery complications are high-risk circumstances that may be related to ADHD (Button, Thapar, & McGuffin, 2005; Nash et al., 2006; Schmidt & Georgieff, 2006). Emotional and general health status for both the pregnant mother and the developing fetus appear to be important predictive factors in ADHD causation (Gelfand & Drew, 2003; Lee, Chang, & Lung, 2006). Serious problems during this critical prenatal period of development can have a wide variety of undesirable outcomes for the baby that may result in developmental delays or deficiencies in both intellectual and behavioral functioning (Drew & Hardman, 2007; Mathews et al., 2006).

Heredity has long been associated with ADHD, which suggests that there may be a genetic transmission of traits that result in the condition. Youngsters appear to be at higher risk of being diagnosed with ADHD if parents or siblings have the condition (Daley, 2006; Seidman et al., 2006; Wigg et al., 2002). Research on twins also implies a hereditary link in that identical twins (same egg) have a higher coincidence of the condition than fraternal twins (different eggs) (Ehringer et al., 2006; Martin et al., 2006; Reich, Huang, & Todd, 2006). Evidence supports the concept that multiple genes may be involved and that they may present a tendency or predisposition in an affected individual that may be triggered by various environmental circumstances (Knopik et al., 2005; Martin, Levy, Pieka, & Hay, 2006; Mill et al., 2006). Research on the genetic bases of ADHD is ongoing, and results continue to emerge.

Interventions

ADHD requires multiple interventions that fall into two broad categories: behavioral and medical. As is true in many disability areas, effective treatment involves a multidisciplinary team approach and includes combinations of techniques as determined by individual need

FOCUS 9

Identify two approaches to intervention that appear to show positive results with individuals who have ADHD.

FIGURE 8.3

Brain Malfunctions in Some Areas of the Brain
Frontal lobes, basal ganglia, and cerebellum seem to be associated with ADHD.

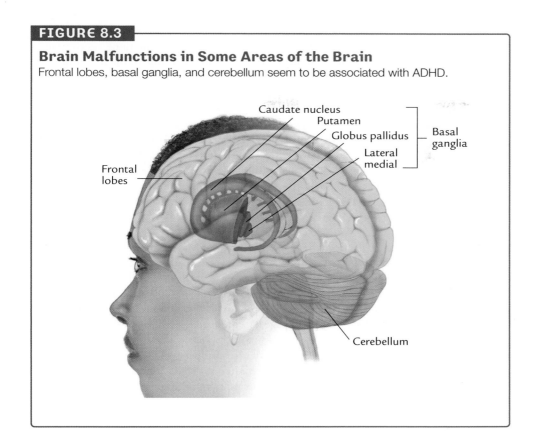

(Coghill, Nigg, Rothenberger, Sonuga-Barke, & Tannock, 2005; Hechtman, Abikoff, & Jensen, 2005; Jensen et al., 2005).

THE ELEMENTARY SCHOOL YEARS. On a practical level, psychostimulants (e.g., methylphenidate, the generic name for Ritalin) appear to result in behavioral improvement for about 80% of children with ADHD (Gorman et al., 2006; Miranda, Jarque, & Tarraga, 2006; Reich et al., 2006). However, administration of such medication has long presented some perplexing ironies to physicians. Whereas a medication may work well for a child with ADHD, the same medication would make most of us hyperactive. Self-regulation theories tend to approach the problem primarily as a functional deficit in self-regulation or impulse control. Administration of methylphenidate arouses the frontal lobes of the brain, which exert a regulatory influence. This regulatory function affects regions of the nervous system that monitor motor activity and distractibility (Gorman et al., 2006; Sutcliffe, 2006).

Controlling hyperactive and impulsive behavior appears to be most effectively accomplished with medication (often methylphenidate) (Connor, 2002; Pelham et al., 2005; Reich et al., 2006). Evidence is emerging that pharmacological control of behavioral challenges is more effective than nonmedical interventions, such as behavioral treatment (Hechtman, Abikoff, & Jensen, 2005; Miranda et al., 2006; Pappadopulos et al., 2006). Research supporting the effectiveness of medication is accumulating, but such medical intervention shows no effect, or very limited influence, on academic performance (DuPaul, 2006a; 2006b; Pelham et al., 2005). Current thinking suggests that even though there are clear benefits to the use of medication, it may be overprescribed, and there are side effects and issues of potential abuse that need further research (Diller, 2006; McGough et al., 2006; White, Becker-Blease, & Grace-Bishop, 2006). Some evidence also suggests that medication has positive effects on ADHD combined subtypes, whereas further research is clearly needed on the efficacy of medical intervention for the impulsivity and inattentive types (Barkley, 2006; Reich et al., 2006).

Some researchers advise caution in the use of psychostimulants for both theoretical and practical reasons. First, there are concerns regarding side effects, as one would expect with any pharmacological treatment in such widespread use. In some cases, it is difficult to distinguish

Council for Exceptional Children

Standard 4: Instructional Strategies

Standard 5: Learning Environments and Social Interactions

Standard 7: Instructional Planning

psychological characteristics that may appear to be side effects (such as increased anxiety) from the symptoms of ADHD itself. Investigators examining these questions are constantly trying to determine whether an increase in anxiety, for example, is due to the use of medication over time or occurs because a child becomes increasingly anxious as a result of negative personality or interpersonal effects of ADHD (e.g., Jensen et al., 2002; Null & Feldman, 2005; Rafalovich, 2005). Additionally, some researchers express uneasiness about appropriate dosage, overprescription, and unhealthy side effects such as increased tobacco and alcohol use. There are also matters of potential for abuse, and issues related to management planning and implementation for children being treated with medication (Dierker, Canino, & Merikangas, 2006; Rush et al., 2005; Wilens & Biederman, 2006). Table 8.2 summarizes a variety of medications, their uses, and some of the side effects observed.

Children who are young when they begin to receive medication may take it over a very long period, and it is unclear what the cumulative effects may be on physical or intellectual development (Kutcher, 2002). For preschoolers, there is some evidence that susceptibility to side effects might be greater (Kratochvil, Egger, Greenhill, & McGough, 2006). Further investigation in both of these areas is certainly warranted. Concerns about medication interventions have been raised in the popular press and continue to arise periodically as the field grapples with the challenges presented by these children (e.g., Diller, 2006; McCabe et al., 2006). Alternatives to medication have sometimes been proposed, as the Reflect on This "Exploring Other Options" and the Debate Forum on page 219 indicate.

The hyperactive and impulsive behaviors of many children with ADHD clearly present a significant challenge to parents, teachers, and other school personnel during the elementary school years. Elementary teachers describe these children as fidgety, impulsive, often off-task, and constantly disruptive (Hoerger & Mace, 2006; Vile Junod, Dupaul, Jitendra, Volpe, & Cleary, 2006). These behaviors are often accompanied by deficits in academic performance (Marshal & Molina, 2006; Radford & Ervin, 2002). From a teacher's viewpoint, it is difficult for the child to focus on learning if he or she is in constant motion. This point emphasizes two major and recurring themes in this text: collaboration among general and special educators, and focusing on a single system of educational services and supports. The hyperactive and impulsive behaviors exhibited by many children with ADHD sorely test their inclusion in

---

TABLE 8.2

Medications, Uses, and Side Effects

	MEDICATIONS	WHEN PRESCRIBED	SIDE EFFECTS
Neuroleptics	Haloperidol (Haldol), Chlorpromazine (Thorazine), Thioridazine (Mellaril)	Overt psychosis, unmanageable destructive behavior, severe aggression, Tourette's syndrome	Sedation, dystonic reactions
Antidepressants	Amitriptyline (Elavil), Nortriptyline (Aventyl), Imipramine (Tonfranil)	Depression, school refusal with panic, attention-deficit disorder with hyperactivity	(Some effects related to dosage level)—dry mouth, blurred vision, constipation, sedation, cardiac toxicity, seizures
Stimulants	d-Amphetimine (Dexedrine), Methylphenidate (Ritalin), Pemoline (Cylert)	Attention-deficit disorder with hyperactivity	Appetite suppression, insomnia, dysphoric reaction, growth delay
Major Tranquilizers and Sedatives	Diazepam (Valium), Chlordiazepoxide (Librium), Hydroxyzine (Atrax, Vistaril)	Distorted reality perception	Sedation, common misuse
Lithium Carbonate	Lithium	Manic depressive or bipolar illness	Tremor, nausea, vomiting, weakness

SOURCE: From *Learning Disabilities: Characteristics, Identification, and Teaching Strategies* (5th ed., p. 63), by W. N. Bender, 2004, Boston: Allyn and Bacon.

general education settings. Because of these behaviors, children with ADHD are often disruptive to the instructional environment and require a great deal of focused time and effort on the part of teachers. It is crucial for these youngsters that the inclusion model not be discarded just because it is difficult to apply for those with ADHD.

Nonmedical, school-based interventions can also be effective in improving the classroom behaviors of elementary-age school children with ADHD, and some are more potent than others. In general, targeted behavior modification strategies appear to be more effective for controlling behavioral problems than those that involve cognitive-behavioral or cognitive interventions. Cognitive-behavioral therapies are based on combining behavioral techniques with efforts to change the way a person thinks about his or her behaviors—that is, attempting

DEBATE FORUM

IS MEDICATION BEING APPROPRIATELY USED AS A TREATMENT FOR ADHD?

Concern continues regarding the use of medication, particularly psychostimulants, to treat students with ADHD. The evidence continues to mount that medication is the most effective intervention. Some professionals, however, have seriously questioned the administration of medication as currently practiced.

POINT

Several points must be raised regarding the administration of medication to children with ADHD. Medication is very widely used for treating ADHD, and it may be overprescribed. Some estimates place the number of children receiving psychostimulant treatment near one million. In the context of such widespread use, how little we actually know about long-term influences and side effects is a serious concern.

COUNTERPOINT

For some children with ADHD, medication is the only approach that will bring their hyperactivity under control and thereby allow effective instruction to occur. Without such treatment, these students will be unable to attend to their academic work and will be so disruptive in classroom situations that other students will not be effectively taught. Side effects such as insomnia, irritability, and decreased appetite, among others, are relatively minor and temporary for the most part. Research suggests that according to teachers, a substantial proportion of those children receiving medication show an improvement in behavior.

to enhance the cognitive control that a person has over his or her actions. Research evidence does not suggest beneficial results from cognitive-behavioral interventions for children with ADHD (Gureasko-Moore et al., 2006; Miranda et al., 2006). Using behavior modification interventions aimed at controlling a child's behavioral activity and giving structure to the classroom environment both seem to be academically productive. Descriptions of effective instructional settings for children with ADHD consistently include a good deal of structure.

Educators should arrange the classroom setting in such a way as to enhance the child's ability to respond, attend, and behave in a manner that is conducive to learning. Teachers may have to monitor constantly the directions they give students with ADHD, often cuing them to the fact that a direction or message is about to be delivered. This might be done with a prompt such as "Listen, John" or some other signal that the teacher is comfortable making and is well understood by the student as meaning a directive is to follow. The signal may be accompanied by other signals or procedures that add structure and direct the student's attention to the learning task at hand. Such cues or signals must be designed in a developmentally appropriate manner (Gelfand & Drew, 2003; Kapalka, 2005).

Academic instructions must directly target the specific content area wherein the child is experiencing problems. Student learning is enhanced by strategies that involve considerable structure (Lohman, 2002; Prater, 2007). Instruction, such as writing lessons, may be more effective if reinforcement is combined with modeling and increased practice (Danforth et al., 2006; Miller et al., 2006; U.S. Department of Education, 2004). With these children, there is a need to demonstrate the learning strategy rather than just describing it. They often require individualized instruction from a teacher or aide, focused on the specific content area that needs attention, such as reading, math, or spelling. Such individual work is clearly a labor-intensive undertaking but may be enhanced by the use of assistive technology in areas such as focusing reading attention (see Assistive Technology below). Further research on the practical implementation and effectiveness of such approaches is needed, but early results seem promising (Higgins, Boone, & Lovitt, 2002).

Multiple treatment approaches (often termed multimodal treatments), such as drug and behavior therapies, are more effective than just one kind of treatment for children with ADHD (Evans et al., 2006; Hechtman et al., 2005; Swanson et al., 2002). But this approach

ASSISTIVE TECHNOLOGY

STUDENT ASSISTANT FOR LEARNING FROM TEXT (SALT): FOCUSING ATTENTION TO IMPROVE READING

Software has been developed that enables teachers to develop hypermedia versions of textbooks that emphasize a variety of characteristics. One approach has been to provide prompting and guidance by highlighting text with color or distinctive fonts in order to focus the attention of students reading the text. Called Student Assistant for Learning from Text (SALT), this software was developed and tested on students with learning disabilities (MacArthur & Haynes, 1995). The powerful features of the software appear to be helpful for various students who have difficulty attending to main ideas in the text, as often happens with students having ADHD.

Because teachers have the ability to modify the text, they can focus the features of the material to best suit a student's needs. Teachers also have the capacity to intensify student engagement by linking supplementary graphics and video, as well as challenging the students with questions about their reading. Student assessment regarding use of the software has been overwhelmingly favorable. Although further research is needed, SALT appears to be an effective software package for a variety of students with disabilities (Higgins, Boone, & Lovitt, 2002).

SOURCES: Higgins, K., Boone, R., & Lovitt, T. C. (2002). "Adapting Challenging Texbooks to Improve Content Area Learning." In M. R. Shinn, H. M. Walker, G. Stoner (Eds.), *Interventions for Academic and Behavior Problems II: Preventive and Remedial Approaches* (pp. 755–790). Washington, DC: National Association of School Psychologists.

MacArthur, C. A., & Haynes, J. B. (1995). Student Assistant for Learning from Text (SALT): A hypermedia reading aid. *Journal of Learning Disabilities, 28,* 150–159.

creates a risk factor that may not emerge with a single treatment. The National Institutes of Health consensus report (1998) noted that communication or coordination among educational (school-based) and health-related (medical) assessments and services is often poor. Diagnosticians and interventionists from both disciplines may have difficulty communicating outside of their field, and this may lead to a worsening of the child's condition or promote additional problems, such as antisocial behaviors. Less than perfect communication and coordination among multiple disciplines has been one of the obstacles that must be overcome in providing services to all people with disabilities (Drew & Hardman, 2007; Montague & Dietz, 2006). And this problem is exacerbated in the case of children with ADHD, because such a high proportion are receiving both medical treatment and school-based instruction. The situation can be improved if all parties pay special attention to facilitating communication among attending physicians and others providing treatment. However, this is unlikely to occur unless it is explicitly included in the intervention plan prepared for a child.

ADOLESCENCE AND ADULTHOOD. Once viewed as a childhood condition, ADHD is now known to have a significant presence beyond those early years and is accompanied by an array of other behaviors and conditions in adolescence and adulthood (e.g., Barkley et al., 2006; Halperin & Schulz, 2006; Seidman, 2006). Current research suggests that ADHD is far more persistent into adulthood than once was thought and that it often requires continuing adult treatment (Barkley, Fischer, Smallish, & Fletcher, 2002). Interventions appropriate for adolescents and adults with ADHD must be reassessed and, where appropriate, modified in an age-appropriate manner (Gureasko-Moore et al., 2006). However, certain characteristics described for children with ADHD—and certain interventions—seem also to apply to adolescents and adults. For example, cognitive challenges such as the impulse control and memory problems found in ADHD children occur in many adults with ADHD as well (Nigg et al., 2006; Seidman, 2006). The structured environment that is beneficial for school-based instruction appears to facilitate other interventions later in life, such as psychological therapy and self-management (Gureasko-Moore et al., 2006; Toner, O'Donoghue, & Houghton, 2006). Also reminiscent of treatment at younger ages, instruction for adolescents with ADHD is more effective when the students can employ learning strategies (such as mnemonics and conceptual organizers) to assist in their acquisition of academic content (Barkley, 2006). Further, medication remains an effective treatment for the impulsivity and difficulty in focusing on tasks that continue into the adolescent and adult years for many people with ADHD. Stimulant medications, such as methylphenidate, remain effective, although some investigators are exploring alternative medications in order to reduce side effects or lessen the potential for abuse (Biederman, 2005; Connor, 2002). As is the case with other treatments, adaptations and modifications are often necessary to ensure that the treatment is age-appropriate and to achieve the most effective intervention during these years. ADHD may present lifelong symptoms that require intervention or compensatory action by those around the individual, as indicated in this chapter's Inclusion and Collaboration Through the Lifespan.

Adolescents and adults with ADHD may not exhibit hyperactivity but may still have considerable difficulty in focusing on tasks and controlling impulses. Again, medication may be an effective treatment for some of these behaviors. However, it is likely that these individuals will also require significantly more structure in their environment than their peers without disabilities. Counseling that emphasizes behavior modification may be enormously helpful. This represents the adult-appropriate remnants of the structured environment that was productive for the individual during childhood. At this point in life, it is probably best to communicate openly with the person about his or her areas of strength and the areas in which ADHD presents the person with the greatest challenges. This type of frank communication will be most effective if used by adult family members, such as spouses, as well as by professional therapists. Such conversations are not always easy, but they become easier over time, especially if they are aimed at a positive enhancement of the lives of all involved.

People with ADHD face significant challenges at every age. Although behaviors of adults with ADHD may look somewhat different from those of children with ADHD, there are some similarities, and adults with ADHD face many difficulties. Many mysteries remain to be solved, but there also has been significant progress in treating this disability.

INCLUSION AND COLLABORATION THROUGH THE LIFESPAN

People with Attention-Deficit/Hyperactivity Disorder

EARLY YEARS

Tips for the Family

- Learn about the simple applications of behavior modification in a home environment, perhaps by enrolling in a parent training class.

- Try to structure the home environment in terms of family activities and tasks for the child, perhaps using a similar structure for all family members. This may mean setting a daily routine that is somewhat fixed, or even a fixed routine for portions of the day. Organize activities into groupings so that each is somewhat isolated from the others.

- Learn about ADHD from a practical standpoint that makes sense to family members. Do your best not to focus explicitly on the affected child in a manner that has negative implications for him or her (for example, avoid direct comments about disability or about how difficult life is because of the child's condition). Instead, try to arrange the environment and activities in a manner that can best meet the child's needs as a routine approach to family life.

- Collaborate and communicate across different professions to coordinate the child's services. Family members, especially parents or guardians, are the central coordination point for all of the child's interactions with professionals, including educators, psychologists, counselors, and health care professionals. This focal point will include evaluations and treatments or interventions (medications, special behavioral interventions, and so on).

- Give directions while looking the child in the eyes, thereby gaining attention and building eye contact as a control mechanism.

Tips for the Preschool Teacher

- Initiate and maintain communication with the child's parents or guardians to enhance the information flow and, if possible, to promote consistent collaboration across environments in rules and reward structures.

- Structure the environment and activities. For instance, divide activities into short sessions, each focusing on a single subactivity.

- Signal or alert the student when a verbal directive is to be given in order to focus attention. For example, say, "Jim, listen. I want you to . . ."

- Use a kitchen timer to facilitate time management, and gradually increase periods for activities where attention is focused.

- Monitor stress in the child; exceeding his or her stress thresholds may trigger disruptive behavior or inattention.

- Collaborate and communicate with other school personnel in order to promote a consistent environment throughout the school regarding appropriate behavior and interactions (e.g., praise, structuring).

Tips for Preschool Personnel

- Collaborate and communicate with other preschool staff who are involved in the child's instruction. This effort may be directed primarily at the teacher, but it is important to communicate and work cooperatively with all school personnel who have direct interactions with the child (e.g., transportation personnel, custodial and building managers).

- Try to communicate and interact with the child in a manner consistent with the teacher's program. The setting may be different (e.g., hallways, playground, or bus), but the contingencies for appropriate behavior should be consistent to the greatest extent possible.

Tips for Neighbors and Friends

- These children may be noisier and more active than others in the neighborhood. Try to ignore minor transgressions.

- Communicate and collaborate with the child's parents to learn what techniques they use for control. Be proactive in initiating conversations with the parents, while remaining respectful of the parents' primary role. In other words, be a helper, not an intrusive busybody.

- Encourage appropriate behavior in a manner that is consistent with the parents' plan. This may seem awkward at first, but the parents are probably working very hard to provide a good family environment for the child. They will appreciate your help.

ELEMENTARY YEARS

Tips for the Family

- Think about modifying the structured family environment to be appropriate for the developmental level of the child.

- While continuing the overall structure begun during the younger years, gradually lengthen the activity periods.

- Consider varying somewhat the distinctive breaks between activities, and modify rewards for older children.

- Be proactive in communicating with the child's teacher, and facilitate communication between medical and educational professionals. Family members, particularly parents or guardians, are the focal point of collaboration and coordination for all information about the child from psychologists, physicians, social workers, and others who may be providing services.

Tips for the General Education Classroom Teacher

- Maintain distinctive signals and age-appropriate alerting messages as cues for attention. Minimize drawing the attention of other students to the child's challenges.

- Divide assignments into smaller or shorter segments as necessary.

- Shorten work sessions as needed. Make clear breaks between activities or subjects.

- Give positive rewards for good academic work and appropriate behavior. Such reinforcement is very important for these children.

- Collaborate, communicate, and coordinate the various services a student with ADHD might be receiving (such as counseling, psychological assessment, and medication), and be proactive in inviting the parents to be active team participants.

Tips for School Personnel

- Collaborate in ongoing communication with other school staff who are involved with the child, including his or her teacher(s), the bus driver, counselors, and any extracurricular staff.
- Try to use communication and rules consistent with those employed by the other school team members, looking to the child's teacher and parents as key leaders in formulating the child's environment.

Tips for Neighbors and Friends

- Recognize that during the elementary years, these children may appear more active or noisy than their playmates in the neighborhood.
- Communicate and collaborate with the child's parents in order to provide a reasonably consistent neighborhood environment. For example, if behavior modification is being used in the home to shape other elements of the youngster's behavior, learn the simple components of reinforcement and contingency setting.

SECONDARY AND TRANSITION YEARS

Tips for the Family

- Make age-appropriate modifications of the family environment.
- Maintain structuring, but add more adult-like modeling, and demonstrate how to focus attention.
- Continue to proactively collaborate and communicate with school personnel, especially the teacher, in order to maintain consistent ways of supporting and challenging the person with ADHD.
- Begin thinking ahead as the adolescent or young adult matures toward adulthood. Collaboration and communication have involved the young person with ADHD for a few years now, and everyone should begin looking forward with confidence to future plans.

Tips for the General Education Classroom Teacher

- Help the youngster to direct or modify annoying behavior and characteristics to achieve more appropriate and acceptable ways of behaving. Handle this delicately, because the youngster is on the brink of adulthood in some ways and yet is very immature in many others.
- Initiate communication and collaboration with other school personnel who are involved in the academic and nonacademic life of the youngster, as well as with the parents. Proactively initiate collaboration on a plan to provide a relatively consistent environmental structure for the individual.
- Help the youngster to learn strategies for organizing both academic and nonacademic activities. By now in the young person's life, this may involve open acknowledgment of limitations such as a short attention span and difficulties with self-management.

Tips for School Personnel

- Collaborate and help open lines of communication with all school personnel who are involved with the youngster.
- Depending on your particular role within the school, don't hesitate to visit with the youngster's parents and

others in the broader community (e.g., employers, police organizations).

- Help to shape a positive growth environment for the youngster within your realm of responsibility (e.g., coach). Facilitate this young adult's skill development, while acknowledging that her or his daily life may differ from the lives of others. Communicate with other school personnel to collaborate on the educational development planning in a comprehensive manner.

Tips for Neighbors and Friends

- Communicate with the youngster's parents about how this period of development is proceeding for the youngster and how you, as a nonfamily adult, can participate with the youngster, if that is a comfortable role.
- Recognize that this young person, who is beginning to look like an adult, still may encounter great difficulty with impulse control and task focus. If you are working with him or her, perhaps as an employer, structure the environment to take advantage of strengths and minimize the effect of limitations.

ADULT YEARS

Tips for the Family

- Communicate directly with this family member about his or her personal strengths and limitations. Opening such lines of communication will facilitate adapting the structure of the family environment for this new stage in the individual's life.
- Work with the affected person and other family members to help structure or organize the family environment. The adult with ADHD may not be hyperactive but still may have some challenges with impulse control and task focus.
- Communicate and collaborate openly with physicians or other health care professionals who are treating the family member with ADHD. This should not be done without the knowledge of the affected individual and will be more productive if all team members work together.

Tips for Therapists or Other Professionals

- Open lines of communication with other adult family members in order to promote a consistent and productive environment for the client.
- Help your client organize his or her life in such a way as to emphasize personal strengths and lessen the demands in areas where challenges are most evident.

Tips for Neighbors, Friends, and Employers

- This adult is likely to test your patience. He or she may appear to be a busybody, flitting from one task to another without finishing any. If you are an employer, you may find yourself presented with partially completed assignments. Try to be patient, persistent, and direct in communicating with the individual.
- Speak directly with the person about his or her strengths, and help the person maintain focus on staying organized.
- Structure the environment in order to take advantage of strengths and minimize the effects of limitations. Limit the areas of responsibility in order to help the individual focus.

FOCUS 1 Identify three behavioral symptoms commonly associated with ADHD.

- Impulsive behavior
- Fidgeting or hyperactivity
- Inability to focus attention

FOCUS 2 Identify two ways in which the behavior of children with ADHD detrimentally affects instructional settings.

- Children with ADHD challenge teachers' skills in classroom management, because they are in and out of their seats a lot, pestering their classmates and perhaps exhibiting aggressive behavior toward other students.
- Children with ADHD challenge teachers' skills in instruction in that they may be unable to focus on instructions, they may impulsively start assignments before hearing all the directions, and they may submit incomplete assignments because they did not listen to all the instructions.

FOCUS 3 Identify four other areas of disability that are often found to be comorbid with ADHD.

- Learning disabilities
- Tourette's syndrome
- Conduct disorders
- Emotional disorders

FOCUS 4 Identify the three major types of ADHD according to DSM-IV.

- Attention-deficit/hyperactivity disorder, combined type
- Attention-deficit/hyperactivity disorder, predominantly inattentive type
- Attention-deficit/hyperactivity disorder, predominantly hyperactive-impulsive type

FOCUS 5 Identify two prevalence estimates for ADHD that characterize the difference in occurrence by gender.

- Estimates for the ratio of males with ADHD to females with the disorder range from 2:1 to 10:1.
- On average, the male/female ratio is about 2.5:1 to 3.5:1.

FOCUS 6 Identify the two broad categories of assessment information useful in diagnosing ADHD.

- Information about medical status
- Information about educational, behavioral, and contextual circumstances

FOCUS 7 Identify three categories of characteristics that present challenges for individuals with ADHD.

- Difficulties in self-regulation, impulsivity, and hyperactivity
- Difficulties in social relationships
- Significant challenges in academic performance

FOCUS 8 Identify three possible causes of ADHD.

- Neurological dysfunction that is trauma-based
- Neurological dysfunction due to differences in brain structure
- Hereditary transmission

FOCUS 9 Identify two approaches to intervention that appear to show positive results with individuals who have ADHD.

- Medication
- Behavior modification

BUILDING YOUR PORTFOLIO

Council for Exceptional Children

If you are thinking about a career in special education, you should know that many states use national standards developed by the Council for Exceptional Children (CEC) to assess a teacher candidate's knowledge and skills for working with students with disabilities. See a complete listing of the ten CEC Content Standards on the inside front cover of this text.

CEC Content Standards Addressed in This Chapter

1 Foundations
2 Development and Characteristics of Learners
3 Individual Learning Differences
4 Instructional Strategies
5 Learning Environments and Social Interactions
7 Instructional Planning
8 Assessment

Assess Your Knowledge of the CEC Standards Addressed in This Chapter

Some states require that teacher candidates develop a portfolio of products that demonstrate mastery of the CEC content standards. To assist in the development of products for this portfolio, you may wish to complete the following activities.

- Complete a written test of the chapter's content.

  If your instructor requires a written test of your content knowledge for this chapter, keep a copy for your portfolio. A practice test on the information covered in this chapter is available through the companion website (*college.hmco.com/pic/hardman9e*) *and the Student Study Guide.*

- Respond to the Application Questions for the Case Study "ADHD and Other Disabilities: Coexisting Conditions."

  Review the Case Study and respond in writing to the application questions. Keep a copy of the Case Study and of your written response for your portfolio.

- Participate in a Community Service Learning Activity.

  Community service is a valuable way to enhance your learning experience. Visit our companion website for suggested community service learning activities that correspond to the information presented in this chapter. Develop a reflective journal of the service learning experience for your portfolio.

WEB RESOURCES

ADHD Owner's Manual

http://www.edutechsbs.com/adhd

This site is a resource that includes information about both learning disabilities and ADHD. It discusses educational and behavioral interventions, medication, and tips for teachers. There is a section entitled "The Feeling of Having ADHD" for those who want to have that perspective as they learn more about this condition.

Troubled Teen Advisor

http://troubled-teen-advisor.com/
index.php?source=ov&kw=adhd

This site is for parents who are facing the challenges of understanding their teenage children. It places ADHD in the context of the social world of these teens, along with school challenges, legal issues, substance abuse, runaway behaviors, and depression.

Diamond Ranch Academy

http://strugglingteens.us/academic.html

This private commercial website is for an academic program aimed particularly at teens with ADHD and other conditions that result in challenging behaviors. It is representative of the private academic and treatment organizations that some families turn to for assistance with their children or teens who are having difficulty in public school settings.

FURTHER READINGS

Cimera, R. E. (2002). *Making ADHD a Gift: Teaching Superman How to Fly.* Lanham, MD: Scarecrow Press.

This book is for parents and beginning teachers who encounter children, teens, or adults with ADHD. The book is aimed at general audiences and is expressed in a nontechnical manner. It is written by an author who has ADHD and offers insights from that perspective.

Rosenthal, D., and Lovgy, R., (2002). *ADHD: A Survival Guide for Parents and Teachers.* Duarte, CA: Hope Press.

This book is written for parents and other caretakers of children with ADHD. Practical and easily understood, it presents strategies for working with these children. Readers will turn repeatedly to this user-friendly resource.

Nylund, D. (2002). *Treating Huckleberry Finn: A New Narrative Approach to Working with Kids Diagnosed ADD/ADHD.* Hoboken, NJ: Wiley.

Could or would Huck Finn be diagnosed with ADHD in today's world? Would he be on Ritalin? This interesting set of questions occurred to the author one night while he was reading to his son. It is a perspective that resonates with issues raised in the popular press about overprescription and the drawbacks of medication.

COMPANION WEBSITE

Visit the companion website at college.hmco.com/pic/hardman9e for additional resources that support this text:

- HM Video Cases that present actual classroom scenarios that you may face every day as a teacher

- Practice ACE Exams that will help you prepare for quizzes, tests, and certfication exams
- Flashcards of key terms
- Weblinks

9

Emotional/Behavioral Disorders

KATIE[1]

No matter what I offer, she's not happy. Whenever she doesn't get what she wants, she throws a temper tantrum. Putting on her seat belt in the car is a major struggle. Taking her to the grocery store is a nightmare. She won't sit down in the cart and cries when I insist. She always demands candy as we are leaving the store. When I take her to the doctor, she runs the other way. It takes both a nurse and the doctor to hold her down for her shots. It's embarrassing to have people look at her and think she is a brat and that I am an incompetent mom. I've tried everything to get her to listen to me and do what I want her to do. Time-out just doesn't work. She doesn't get along well with other children because she is so rough and demanding. I can't leave her with anyone because she cries the whole time I'm gone or they come to get me because she is so upset. I feel like a prisoner.

One day as she and I were crossing the street, Katie threw herself on the ground and refused to go one step farther. With cars whizzing by in both directions, I frantically tried everything—cajoling, bribing, begging. Finally, in despair, I grabbed Katie by the arm and pulled her to the other side of the street. Katie screamed in pain. To my horror, I realized that I had pulled Katie's elbow out of joint. After attending to the elbow, my pediatrician asked how it had happened. Upon hearing the story, he recommended that I seek psychological help for myself and for Katie. (Booth & O'Hara, 2005, pp. 91–92)

"THAT *$@%# JUST DOESN'T LIKE ME!!"

Jamarian sits in the hall beside the classroom door. When asked what happened, he replies, "Nothing!! That *$@%# just doesn't like me!! I hate this school!!" His teacher has a different view: "How do you expect me to teach when students just don't want to learn? Kids like Jamarian should be in special classes so the rest of the class can learn!" (Algozzine & White, 2002, p. 85)

DEPRESSION AND GIRLS

Depression is rare in preschoolers, with estimates ranging from 0.4% to 0.9%, and is uncommon in school-aged children, with estimates from 1.8% to 6.3%. The prevalence of depression increases dramatically after puberty, particularly in girls. The lifetime prevalence of major depression in adolescent females is between 20.8% and 31.6%, and the estimated prevalence of subclinical depression in adolescent girls is as high as 59%. The 1-year first incidence of major depression for girls is 7.14%. . . . [Thirty-five percent] of girls will have had at least one episode of major depression by the age of 19 years.

[1]SOURCE: Adapted from "Mood Disorders and Symptoms in Girls," by C. Zahn-Waxler, E. Race, & S. Duggal, 2005, in *Handbook of Emotional and Behavioral Problems in Girls*, New York: Kluwer Academic/Plenem Publishers, p. 29.

1 Identify six essential parts of the federal definitions for emotional/behavioral disorders.

2 Identify five factors that influence the ways in which we perceive the behaviors of others.

3 Cite three reasons why classification systems are important to professionals who identify, treat, and educate individuals with EBD.

4 What differentiates externalizing disorders from internalizing disorders?

5 Identify five general characteristics (intellectual, adaptive, social, and achievement) of children and youth with EBD.

6 What can accurately be said about the causes of EBD?

7 What four important outcomes are achieved through a functional behavioral assessment?

8 What five guiding principles are associated with systems of care?

9 What are three goals that schools can pursue to significantly reduce the entry of youth into delinquency and related behaviors?

10 What two factors should be considered when placing a child or youth with EBD in general education settings and related classes?

▼ SNAPSHOT

DEBBIE

I was in kindergarten when I was molested and raped by my teenage cousin. I was afraid to tell anyone what he had done to me because he had threatened me with harm and said that he would tell everyone what happened was my idea. Shortly after that, I started to have difficulty when things did-n't go as planned or as I expected at school. I literally would go into a panic and cry hysterically. I had low self-esteem because I felt like I had done something so terribly wrong. I thought I was a bad child. I tried to overcompensate by not making mistakes and by trying to do everything perfect.

As I became older my Post-Traumatic Stress Disorder Symptoms manifested more as severe stomach aches and rashes on my arms and legs. I had reoccurring nightmares related to my trauma that prevented me from getting a good night's sleep, and in the evening I would become anxious about going to bed. I was going to school tired, and it made it very difficult for me to focus on my schoolwork. I also wanted to disappear into my own world to escape such a painful childhood memory.

Different teachers responded differently to my behavior by being critical, or trying to be helpful and supportive. Even though there were adults who offered kindness and support, I never felt safe.

Fortunately I was given a wonderful teacher in the fourth grade, and then I had her again in the sixth grade. Even though she was my teacher in regular education classes, she had experience working with children who had emotional and behavior problems. The gifts this teacher gave to me were self-esteem and self-confidence [about] my intellectual, artistic and creative abilities. She encouraged me to develop my artistic abilities and recommended me for advanced art in junior high school. Even though I continued to have many difficult challenges in junior and senior high school, I credit this elementary teacher for helping me develop skills that enabled me to make it through what may have been impossible achievements. My talent in art and creativity helped me in my day-to-day struggles. I had an avenue to help me deal with my emotional and behavior challenges, and somewhere deep down inside it gave me hope.

SOURCE: Deborah (Debbie) K. Burt, M.Ed., BCET (personal communication, August 10, 2007).

ZACHARY

I would describe Zachary as having movie-star looks, a heart the size of Montana, and a spunky personality that draws people to him. He is a real give-the-shirt-off-his-back kind of guy. As a young child he learned to read by memorization instead of the use of phonics. He was into skateboarding, snowboarding—a real risk taker in sports. The straw that seemed to break the camel's back occurred at age 16 when his low citizenship grades prevented his participating in football. Shortly after that he was cut from the high school basketball team . . . and then drank a beer, smoked a joint, and participated in sexual activity—all in the same night.

In the last ten years he has shown amazing signs of talent. He has made wonderful woodworking pieces, cooks amazing dishes for the family, and is a natural salesman. However, his life seems to be interrupted by what I refer to as episodes. From 1 to 10 on a ten-point scale: 1 is using the "F" word and throwing something, and 10 would be "call the police due to drugs and assault." There is no rhyme or reason to when these episodes occur. Within Zachary, there are red flags that he sees, but he does not always respond to their warning signals. These episodes have caused most of his friends and family to draw back and feel cautious. He often leaves family events to associate with his drug buddies, and so the cycle of addiction and related behaviors continues.

As parents, we feel we have tried it all. My father was a medical doctor who tutored me often. Medications of all kinds, multiple evaluations over the years, and excellent medical care seemed only to frustrate Zachary. We did the *tough love*, the kick-him-out-of-the-home intervention, applied severe consequence for his misbehaviors, and enrolled him in expensive rehab programs. But nothing seems to turn the tide of disaster in his life.

I love my son. His dad has said, "It's me or him in this house." He has also said, "Zachary represents everything I abhor." This gives you little feel for the conflict his personality has inflicted on our marriage. I have said to God, "If you need to take my son into your arms to assist him to feel success at last . . . I give him to you." I have also told Zachary not to take his own life, or take someone else's life, or conceive a grandchild we may never have association with. That is all I have asked of him for many years. He can only take care of Zachary and then only minimally. I hold on to him with my faith, and I love his very soul and he knows it. When he is in our home now at age 26, I keep my arms and feet in the car and hold on for the ride!

> ➤ **Emotional disorders**
> Behavior problems that are frequently internal in nature. Persons with these problems may have difficulty in expressing or dealing with emotions evoked in normal family-, school-, or work-related experiences.

> ➤ **Behavior disorders**
> Conditions in which the emotional or behavioral responses of individuals in various environments significantly differ from those characteristic of their peer, ethnic and/or cultural groups. These responses seriously affect social relationships, personal adjustment, schooling, and employment.

Individuals with **emotional and behavioral disorders (EBD)**—such as Deborah and Zachary in the opening snapshot—experience great difficulty in relating appropriately to peers, siblings, parents, and teachers. Students with EBD also have difficulty responding to academic and social tasks that are essential parts of their schooling. They may be deficient in important academic and social behaviors. In other cases, individuals with EBD may not have learned the skills necessary for successful participation in school settings. Statistically, students with EBD are more likely to be economically disadvantaged, male, and African American (Kea, Cartledge, & Bowman, 2002; Yeh, Forness, Ho, McCabe, & Hough, 2004). In fact, African American students are "2.21 times more likely to be classified as having emotional disturbance than all other [disability] groups combined" (U.S. Department of Education, 2005, p. 31).

Definitions

As you will see, several terms have been developed to describe individuals with EBD. These terms include *socially maladjusted, emotionally disturbed, conduct disordered,* and *behavior disordered.* In reading this section, think about the words or labels you have used over time to describe peers, relatives, classmates, or other acquaintances who frequently exhibited deviant and/or unusual behaviors.

The IDEA Definition

Emotional disturbance is defined in the Individuals with Disabilities Education Act (IDEA) as follows:

(I) A condition exhibiting one or more of the following characteristics over a long period of time and to a marked degree, which adversely affects educational performance:

    (A) An inability to learn that cannot be explained by intellectual, sensory, or health factors;

    (B) An inability to build or maintain satisfactory relationships with peers and teachers;

    (C) Inappropriate types of behavior or feelings under normal circumstances;

    (D) A general pervasive mood of unhappiness or depression; or

    (E) A tendency to develop physical symptoms or fears associated with personal or school problems.

(II) The term does not include children who are socially maladjusted, unless it is determined that they are seriously emotionally disturbed.

Focus 1

Identify six essential parts of the federal definitions for emotional/behavioral disorders.

This description of severe emotional disturbance, or EBD, was adapted from an earlier definition created by Bower (1959). The IDEA definition for EBD has been criticized for its lack of clarity, for its incompleteness, and for its exclusion of individuals described as *socially maladjusted*—sometimes referred to as juvenile delinquents (Cullinan, 2004; Hughes & Bray, 2004; Merrell & Walker, 2004; U.S. Department of Education, 2006). Furthermore, this definition mandates that assessment personnel demonstrate that the disorder is adversely affecting students' school performance. In many cases, students with serious EBD—such as eating disorders, depression, suicidal tendencies, and social withdrawal—do not receive appropriate care and treatment merely because their academic achievement in school appears to be normal or above average. In some cases, these students are gifted (see Chapter 18).

The National Mental Health and Special Education Coalition Definition

The National Mental Health and Special Education Coalition has proposed a definition for EBD that goes beyond the language of IDEA (Forness & Knitzer, 1992):

(i) The term emotional or behavioral disorder means a disability characterized by behavioral or emotional responses in school so different from appropriate age, cultural, or ethnic norms that they adversely affect educational performance. Educational performance includes academic, social, vocational, and personal skills. Such a disability (A) is more than a temporary, expected response to stressful events in the environment; (B) is consistently exhibited in two different settings, at least one of which is school-related; and (C) is unresponsive to direct intervention in general education or the child's condition is such that general education interventions would be insufficient.

(ii) Emotional and behavioral disorders can coexist with other disabilities.

(iii) This category may include children or youth with schizophrenic disorders, affective disorders, anxiety disorders, or other sustained disorders of conduct or adjustment when they adversely affect educational performance in accordance with section (i). (Forness & Knitzer, 1992, p.13)

Council for Exceptional Children

Standard 1: Foundations

This definition shares some of the same problems as those related to the IDEA definition of EBD (Cullinan, 2004). First, it does not clearly specify how the behaviors identified would be measured or quantified. Second, little legitimate and valid information exists about the norms of behavior for various ethnic and/or cultural groups, and it is very difficult to make determinations based on data that simply do not currently exist. Third, this definition implies that prereferral interventions delivered by general education personnel were ineffective or "insufficient." Cullinan (2004) questions this definitional provision: "Its implementation would would mean that whether or not a particular student qualifies as [EBD] is determined in part by the abilities of other people—prereferral team members and other educators—to cope with his or her problems" (Cullinan, 2004, p. 46).

FOCUS 2
Identify five factors that influence the ways in which we perceive the behaviors of others.

Identifying Normal Behavior

Many factors influence the ways in which we perceive the behaviors of others. Our perceptions of others and their behaviors are significantly influenced by our personal beliefs, standards, and values about what constitutes normal behavior. Our range of tolerance varies greatly, depending on the behaviors and the situations. What may be viewed as normal by some may be viewed by others as abnormal. For example, parents may have little foundation for determining what is normal behavior, since their perceptions are often limited by their lack of experience with children in general. They may see their child's behavior as somewhat challenging but not abnormal (Newcomer, 2003).

The context in which behaviors occur also dramatically influences our view of their appropriateness. For example, teachers and parents expect children to behave reasonably well in settings where they have interesting things to do or where children are doing things they seem to enjoy. Often children with emotional/behavioral disorders misbehave in these settings. At times, they seem to be oblivious to the environments in which they find themselves. Some have the social skills to act appropriately but choose not to use them (Meadows & Stevens, 2004). Sometimes the intensity or sheer frequency of some behaviors forces parents and others to ask, "Is this behavior really normal?"

Many factors influence the types of behaviors that individuals with EBD exhibit or suppress: (1) the parents' and teachers' management styles, (2) the school or home environment, (3) the social and cultural values of the family, (4) the social and economic climate of the community, (5) the responses of peers and siblings; and (5) the biological, academic, intellectual, and social-emotional characteristics of the individuals (Coleman & Webber, 2002).

Classification

FOCUS 3
Cite three reasons why classification systems are important to professionals who identify, treat, and educate individuals with EBD.

We use classification systems to describe various subsets of challenging behaviors. These systems serve several purposes for professionals. First, they provide them with a means for describing various types of behavior problems in children and youth. Second, they provide professionals with common terms for communicating with each other (Cullinan, 2004). Third, physicians and other mental health specialists use these characteristics and other information as a basis for diagnosing and treating individuals. Unfortunately, "[c]lassifications as yet have limited validity for the most important purpose of classification: specifying interventions [and treatments] that are best suited to improve any particuler form of EBD" (Cullinan, 2004, p. 41).

The field of EBD includes many different types of problems, so it is not surprising that many approaches have been used to classify these individuals. Some classification systems describe individuals according to statistically derived categories, whereby patterns of strongly related behaviors are identified through sophisticated statistical techniques. Other classification systems are clinically oriented; they are derived from the experiences of physicians and other mental health specialists who work directly with children, youth, and adults with EBD (Cullinan, 2004).

Statistically Derived Classification Systems

FOCUS 4
What differentiates externalizing disorders from internalizing disorders?

Council for Exceptional Children

Standard 2: Development and Characteristics of Learners

Standard 3: Individual Learning Differences

For a number of years, researchers have collected information about children with EBD. Data collected from parent and teacher questionnaires, interviews, and behavior rating scales have been analyzed via advanced statistical techniques. Certain clusters or patterns of related behaviors have emerged from these studies. For example, Peterson (1987) found that the EBD exhibited by elementary school children could be accounted for by two dimensions: withdrawal and aggression. Similarly, several researchers have intensively studied young psychiatric patients to develop a valid classification system (Achenbach, 1966, 1991a, 1991b, & 2000). Statistical analysis of data generated from these studies revealed two broad categories of behavior: externalizing symptoms and internalizing symptoms. The latter category is made up of behaviors that seem to be directed more at the self than at others. Withdrawal, depression, shyness, and phobias are examples of internalized behaviors; some clinicians would describe individuals with these conditions as *emotionally disturbed.*

Children or youth who exhibit externalizing disorders may be described as engaging in behaviors that are directed more at others than at themselves. These behaviors could be characterized as aggressive, noncompliant, defiant, resistive, disruptive, and dangerous. Such behaviors significantly affect parents, siblings, classmates, and teachers. Despite the outward differences between internalizing and externalizing behaviors, the distinction between these two categories is not always clear-cut. For example, adolescents who are severely depressed certainly have an impact on their families and others, although the primary locus of their distress is internal.

Other researchers (Quay, 1975, 1979; Von Isser, Quay, & Love, 1980), using similar methodologies, have reliably identified four distinct categories of EBD in children:

Youth with EBD often engage in destructive behaviors directed at themselves or others.

1. Conduct disorders involve such characteristics as overt aggression, both verbal and physical; disruptiveness; negativism; irresponsibility; and defiance of authority—all of which are at variance with the behavioral expectations of the school and other social institutions.

2. Anxiety–withdrawal contrasts sharply with conduct disorders. It involves overanxiety, social withdrawal, seclusiveness, shyness, sensitivity, and other behaviors that imply a retreat from the environment rather than a hostile response to it.

3. Immaturity characteristically involves preoccupation, short attention span, passivity, daydreaming, sluggishness, and other behaviors not consistent with developmental expectations.

4. Socialized aggression typically involves gang activities, cooperative stealing, truancy, and other manifestations of participation in a delinquent subculture. (Von Isser et al., 1980, pp. 272–273)

The fourth category, socialized aggression, is related to social maladjustment. Presently, children and youth identified as socially maladjusted are not necessarily eligible for services through IDEA. Socialized aggression is also related to another term we have mentioned very briefly, *conduct disorder*. We will review conduct disorders in greater depth later in this section.

Clinically Derived Classification Systems

Several clinically derived classification systems have been developed, but the system predominantly used by medical and psychological personnel is the *Diagnostic and Statistical Manual of Mental Disorders* (DSM-IV-TR) (First & Tasman, 2004). This and previous editions were developed and tested by committees of psychiatric, psychological, and health care clinicians—hence the term *clinically derived classifications*. Professionals in each of these groups included people who worked closely with children, adolescents, and adults with mental disorders, or, in our terminology, emotional/behavioral disorders (EBD). The categories and subcategories of DSM-IV-TR (First & Tasman, 2004) were developed after years of investigation and field testing. Unfortunately, these psychiatric categories are not generally used by school personnel in identifying children or adolescents for special education services. However, some professionals are beginning to push for the adoption of these categories for use in school settings (Forness, 2004).

The current manual, DSM-IV-TR (First & Tasman, 2004), identifies nine major groups of childhood disorders that may be exhibited by infants, children, or adolescents. These

Young people with anorexia nervosa have grossly distorted perceptions about their bodies.

include mental retardation; learning and motor skills disorders; communication disorders; pervasive developmental disorders; attention-deficit and disruptive behavior disorders; feeding and eating disorders of infancy or early childhood; tic disorders; elimination disorders and childhood anxiety disorders; and reactive attachment disorders of infancy or early childhood. Several of these disorders often overlap with other exceptionalities, such as mental retardation and autism.

PERVASIVE DEVELOPMENTAL DISORDERS. Children with pervasive developmental disorders exhibit severe deficits in several areas of development. The current term for these disorders is autism spectrum disorders (ASDs). These disorders include significant problems in relating to parents, siblings, and others; very poor communication skills; and unusual behaviors evidenced in gestures, postures, and facial expressions (DuCharme & McGrady, 2005). Generally these disorders are accompanied by chromosomal abnormalities, structural abnormalities in the nervous system, and congenital infections. Also, these disorders are generally evident at birth or present themselves very early in a child's life. They include autistic disorder, Rett's disorder, childhood disintegration disorder, and Asperger's disorder. Autism Spectrum Disorders will be addressed in Chapter 13.

ATTENTION-DEFICIT AND DISRUPTIVE BEHAVIOR DISORDERS. Children with these disorders manifest a variety of symptoms (see Figures 9.1 and 9.2). For example, children with attention deficits have difficulty responding well to typical academic and social tasks and find it hard to control their level of physical activity. Often their activity appears to be very random or purposeless in nature. See Chapter 8 for information on attention-deficit disorders.

Children with disruptive behavior disorders frequently cause physical harm to other individuals or to animals, often engage in behaviors destructive to others' property, repeatedly participate in theft and deceitful activities, and regularly violate rules and other social conventions. In some instances, children with these disorders are highly oppositional. They exhibit a pattern of recurrent negativism, opposition to authority figures, and loss of temper. Other typical behaviors include disobeying, arguing, blaming others for problems and mistakes, and being spiteful. Most of the students with EBD who are served in special education through IDEA have a conduct disorder or are oppositionally defiant.

FEEDING AND EATING DISORDERS. The disorder known as pica consists of the persistent eating of nonnutritive materials for at least one month. Materials consumed may be cloth, string, hair, plaster, or even paint. Often children with pervasive developmental disorders manifest pica.

Anorexia and bulimia are common eating disorders evidenced by gross disturbances in eating behaviors (Levitt, Sansone, & Cohn, 2004). In the case of anorexia nervosa, the most distinguishing feature is bodyweight that is 15% below the norm (Smolak, 2005). These individuals are intensely afraid of weight gain and exhibit grossly distorted perceptions of their bodies. Bulimia is characterized by repeated episodes of binging, followed by self-induced vomiting or other extreme measures to prevent weight gain. Both of these conditions may result in depressed mood, social withdrawal, irritability, and other, more serious medical conditions. Rumination disorder is characterized by repeated regurgitation and rechewing of food. Five to 10% of the girls and women receiving treatment for anorexia and bulimia will die from complications of these conditions (Smolak, 2005).

TIC DISORDERS. Tic disorders involve stereotyped movements or vocalizations that are involuntary, rapid, and recurrent over time. Tics may take the form of eye blinking, facial gestures, sniffing, snorting, repeating certain words or phrases, or grunting. Stress often exacerbates the nature and frequency of tics. These disorders include Tourette's disorder, chronic motor or vocal tic disorder, and transient tic disorder.

ELIMINATION DISORDERS AND CHILDHOOD ANXIETY DISORDERS. Elimination disorders entail soiling (econpresis) and wetting (enuresis) in older children. Children who continue to have consistent problems with bowel and bladder control past their fourth or fifth birthday may be diagnosed as having an elimination disorder, particularly if the condition is not a function of any physical aberration.

Children and youth with anxiety disorders have difficulty dealing with anxiety-provoking situations and with separating themselves from parents or other attachment figures (e.g., close friends, teachers, coaches). Unrealistic worries about future events, overconcern about achievement, excessive need for reassurance, and somatic complaints are characteristic of young people who exhibit anxiety disorders. Behaviors indicative of this disorder include persistent refusal to go to school, excessive worry about personal harm or injury to self or other family members, reluctance to go to sleep, and repeated complaints about headaches, stomachaches, nausea, and related conditions.

The last condition included within this subset of disorders is selective mutism. Young children with this condition are able to speak but do not speak in specific social situations. Most commonly, this disorder appears in the first days or weeks of attending school or participating in a new social environment. These children are able to talk, and they do speak at home with their parents or other care providers, but they are verbally silent in school and other social settings.

REACTIVE ATTACHMENT DISORDER. Reactive attachment disorder of infancy or early childhood is represented by noticeably abnormal and developmentally inept social relatedness. This disorder appears as a result of grossly inadequate care—such as physical or emotional neglect, frequent changes in major caregivers, and other abuse. Behaviors common to this disorder include extreme inhibitions, inability to form appropriate attachments, complete lack of ability to respond to or instigate social interaction with others, and either hypervigilence or complete absense of attention to surrounding social opportunities.

Prevalence

Standard 1: Foundations

Estimates of the prevalence of EBD vary greatly from one source to the next, ranging from 1% to 33.5% (Wicks-Nelson & Israel, 2006; Rosenberg, Wilson, Maheady, & Sindelar, 2004). During the past ten years in the United States, fewer than 1% of children and youth 3 to 21 years of age have been identified and served as exhibiting EBD (National Center for

Education Statistics, 2006). Researchers suggest that 10 to 20% of children experience severe EBD (Walker, Ramsey, & Gresham, 2004).

Unfortunately, significant numbers of children and youth with EBD remain unidentified and do not receive the mental health care or special education they so critically need. Equally distressing is the disproportionate number of young African American males who are identified as having EBD, vastly exceeding the percentage that would be expected in the general population of school-age students (Kea et al., 2002; Osher et al., 2004; U.S. Department of Education, 2005).

Some researchers have suggested that the number of students who receive special education for EBD is less than one-third of those who actually need this assistance. The low number of students served is due in part to the lack of standardized identification criteria, to varying definitions, and to meager research about the processes related to identifying students as having EBD (Rosenberg et al., 2004). Also contributing to the problems of identification, classification, and provision of service is the fact that many children and youth with EBD manifest other disabling conditions.

Characteristics

If you had to describe children and youth with EBD, what would you say about their intellectual capacity, their behavior, their academic performance, and their long-term prospects for employment and success? This section will give you answers to some of these questions. However, note that the facts and figures introduced here represent averages. Service providers, teachers, and friends must view each child or youth with EBD individually, focusing on his or her strengths and potential for growth and change.

Intelligence

Researchers from a variety of disciplines have studied the intellectual capacity of individuals with EBD. In an early national study of children with EBD enrolled in public school programs, the majority of these students exhibited above-average intelligence (Morse, Cutler, & Fink, 1964). However, recent research paints a different picture. Children and youth with EBD tend to have average to below-average IQs compared to their peers without EBD (Algozzine et al., 2001; Coleman & Webber, 2002; Seifert, 2000). Obviously, either the characteristics of students with EBD have changed or the sampling procedures employed in the earlier study were flawed.

What impact does intelligence have on the educational and social-adaptive performance of children with EBD? Is the intellectual capacity of a child with EBD a good predictor of other types of achievement and social behavior? The answer is yes. The IQs of students with EBD are the best predictors of future academic and social achievement (Kauffman, 2005). The below-average IQs of many of these children contribute significantly to the challenges they experience in mastering academic and social tasks in school and other environments.

Social and Adaptive Behavior

Individuals with EBD exhibit a variety of problems in adapting to their home, school, and community environments (Bradley, Henderson, & Monfore, 2004; Algozzine et al., 2001; McEvoy & Welker, 2000). Furthermore, they have difficulties in relating socially and responsibly to persons such as peers, parents, teachers, and other authority figures. In one study, 89% of the students with EBD met established criteria for psychiatric disorders (Cassidy, James, & Wiggs, 2001). The two most common diagnoses were ADHD and conduct disorder. In short, students with EBD are difficult to teach and to parent. In contrast to their peers who generally follow rules, respond well to their teachers and parents, finish classwork and home chores, and comply promptly with adult requests, children and youth with EBD often defy their parents and teachers, disturb others, do not complete tasks, and behave in ways that invite rejection by those around them. These behaviors lead to referral for special education and related services.

Focus 5
Identify five general characteristics (intellectual, adaptive, social, and achievement) of children and youth with EBD.

Council for Exceptional Children

Standard 3: Individual Learning Differences

Socially, children and youth with EBD may have difficulty sharing, playing typical age-appropriate games, and apologizing for actions that hurt others. They may be unable to deal appropriately with situations that produce strong feelings, such as anger and frustration. Problem solving, self-control, accepting consequences for misbehavior, negotiating, expressing affection, and reacting appropriately to failure are behaviors that do not come naturally. Because these children have deficits in these social-adaptive behaviors, they frequently experience difficulties in meeting the demands of the classrooms and other social environments in which they live and participate (Hansen & Lignugaris-Kraft, 2005; Polsgrove & Smith, 2004).

A recent study sheds some light on the social difficulties experienced by children with EBD. Researchers have found that about three out of four children with EBD show clinically significant language deficits (Cross, 2004; Forness, 2004; Mattison, Hooper, & Carlson, 2006; Nungesser & Watkins, 2005). These include problems related to processing and understanding verbal communication and using language to communicate (Benner, Nelson, & Epstein, 2002). These researchers also found that one out of two children with language deficits is identified as having EBD. These language deficits may contribute significantly to the social problems experienced by children with EBD and their care providers.

When we discussed classification earlier in this chapter, we reviewed the statistically derived categories of behaviors that were common to children and adolescents with EBD. These categories included conduct disorders, anxiety–withdrawal, immaturity, and **socialized aggression**. Children and adolescents with conduct disorders engage in verbal and physical aggression. They may threaten or bully other children, extort money from them, or physically hurt them, often without any provocation. In classrooms, these students often defy authority, refuse to follow teachers' directions, and frequently engage in power struggles with parents, teachers, and administrators (Rosenberg et al., 2004; Seifert, 2000; Wicks-Nelson & Israel, 2006). Students with EBD are "13.3 times more likely than other students with disabilities to be arrested while in school" (U.S. Department of Education, 1999, p. II-4). Also, 42% of the youth with disabilities in correctional facilities are youngsters with identified EBD (Burrell & Warboys, 2000).

Children and adolescents who are anxious and withdrawn frequently exhibit behaviors such as seclusiveness and shyness. They may find it extremely difficult to interact with others in normal social events. They tend to avoid contact with others and may often be found daydreaming. In the extreme, some of these youth begin to avoid school or refuse to attend

Council for Exceptional Children

Standard 6: Communication

➤ **Socialized aggression**
Participation in a delinquent subculture that involves activities such as gang behavior, cooperative stealing, and truancy.

Youth with EBD drop out of school at a higher rate than other students with identified disabilities.

(Graczyk, Connolly, & Corapci, 2005). Their school avoidance or refusal is marked by persistent fear of social situations that might arise in school or related settings. These youth fear being humiliated or embarrassed. Their anxiety may be expressed by tantrums, crying, freezing, and other bodily complaints (stomachaches, sickness, etc.). Such children and youth with EBD, who lack personal and social skills, are more likely than other youth with disabilities to be victimized during their school years.

Other children and youth with EBD may struggle with depression (Ialongo, Poduska, Werthamer, & Kellam, 2001; Roberts & Bishop, 2005). Left untreated, these individuals are at risk for suicide, poor school performance, and relationship problems with peers, siblings, parents, and teachers. Manifestations of depression in children and youth include sleep disturbance (nightmares, night terrors, etc.), fatigue or loss of energy, excessive feelings of guilt or worthlessness, inability to concentrate, and suicidal thoughts.

Youth gang activities, drug abuse, truancy, violence toward others, and other delinquent acts characterize children and adolescents who are identified as "undersocialized aggressive" or "socially maladjusted" or as having a conduct disorder. Serious conduct problems in children and youth often foreshadow poor adult adjustment—substance abuse, spousal and friendship violence, and serious criminal activity (Capali & Eddy, 2005).

Adolescents with conduct problems are often seen as impulsive, hyperactive, irritable, and excessively stubborn. Research studies suggest that as many as 40% to 70% of students with EBD exhibit attention-deficit/hyperactivity disorder (ADHD) (Place, Wilson, Martin, & Hulsmeier, 1999; Forness & Kavale, 2001). Furthermore, many students with EBD engage in behaviors that draw attention to themselves, are cruel to others, and are sometimes involved in drug trafficing and other illegal activities (Capali & Eddy, 2005). It is easy to see how the behaviors associated with these categories are maladaptive and interfere with success in school, family, community, and (eventually) employment.

Academic Achievement

As we have noted; students with EBD experience significant difficulties and deficits in academic subject areas, and they rarely catch up academically (Barton-Arnwood, Wehby, & Falk, 2005; Bradley, Henderson, & Monfore, 2004; Lane, 2004; Nelson, Benner, Lane, & Smith, 2004; Pierce, Reid, & Epstein, 2004; Weaster, 2004). In contrast to other students with high-incidence disabilities such as learning disabilities, students with EBD exhibit the "poorest academic outcomes" (Shriner & Wehby, 2004, p. 216). Some attribute these poor performance outcomes to the preparation of the teachers who work with these students and to the poor quality of the academic instruction these students subsequently receive (Gable, 2004; Lane, 2004; Shriner & Wehby, 2004). Additionally, interventions for students with EBD are generally directed at developing social behaviors rather than academic achievement (Ryan, Reid, & Epstein, 2004). Thus many, if not most, students with EBD are not well prepared to take and perform well on state or federally mandated tests or on other measures of academic achievement (Carter et al., 2005).

The dropout and graduation rates for students with EBD are staggering. About 51% to 70% of these students drop out of school—most before they finish the tenth grade—a greater percentage than found for any other disabilitiy group (Sitlington & Neubert, 2004; U.S. Department of Education, 2005). Students with EBD consistently have the lowest graduation rates of all disability groups (25% to 29%) (U.S. Department of Education, 2005).

Studies dealing with employment rates of students after high school are frankly depressing (Bullis, 2001; Carter & Wehby, 2003; Sitlington & Neubert, 2004). Only 41% of students with EBD who have exited high school are employed two years later, compared with 59% of typical adolescents who have left or completed high school. Three to five years later, the contrasts are even stronger: 69% of students without disabilities are employed, compared with 42% to 70% of students with EBD. Significant challenges persist in preparing young people with EBD for meaningful employment and involvement in our communities (Carter & Wehby, 2003; Bullis, 2001). Unfortunately, transition services to bridge schooling with employment are sorely lacking for youth with behavior disorders (Carter & Wehby, 2003). Later in this chapter, we will talk about collaborative approaches to intervention that are designed to address social, educational, transition, and employment problems.

Causation

Council for Exceptional Children

Standard 1: Foundations

What causes children and youth to develop EBD? As you read this section, think about your own patterns of behavior. How would you explain these patterns? What has given rise to them?

Throughout history, philosophers, physicians, theologians, and others have attempted to explain why people behave as they do. Historically, people who were mentally ill were described as possessed by evil spirits, for which the treatment of choice was religious in nature. Later, Sigmund Freud (1856–1939) and others advanced the notion that behavior could be explained in terms of subconscious phenomena or early traumatic experiences. More recently, some theorists have attributed disordered behaviors to inappropriate learning and complex interactions that take place between individuals and their environments (Rutter, 2006). Others, approaching the issue from a biological perspective, have suggested that aberrant behaviors are caused by certain biochemical substances, brain abnormalities or injuries, and chromosomal irregularities.

With such a wide array of explanations, it is easy to see why practitioners might choose different approaches in identifying, treating, and preventing various behavioral disorders. However, the variety of theoretical frameworks and perspectives provides clinicians with a number of avenues for explaining the presence of certain behaviors (Coleman & Webber, 2002). As you will see, the causes of behavioral disorders are multifaceted and often complex (Heilbrun, 2004; Rutter, 2006).

The Biophysical Approach

The biophysical framework explains EBD as a function of inherited or abnormal biological conditions. Behavior problems are assumed to result from some physiological, biochemical, or genetic abnormality or disease (Coleman & Webber, 2002; Rosenberg et al., 2004; Wicks-Nelson & Israel, 2006). For example, consider diabetes. This condition is not caused by psychological factors. It has a biophysical basis: a malfunctioning pancreas that does not produce insulin. Another example is schizophrenia, which is far more likely to manifest itself in young adults both of whose parents have been diagnosed as having the disorder. Thus there appears to be a strong genetic basis for the emergence of this serious behavioral disorder. Some individuals with schizophrenia benefit from medications that address biological factors or deficits that give rise to their challenging behaviors.

The Psychoanalytic Approach

Subconscious processes, predispositions, and early traumatic experiences explain the presence of EBD from a psychoanalytic perspective. These internal processes are unobservable events that occur in the mind. As individuals gain insight into their psychic conflicts via psychotherapy, they may be able to eliminate or solve their behavior problems. The return to normalcy may also be aided by a caring therapist or teacher. For children, this process theoretically occurs through play therapy, in which inner conflicts are revealed and subsequently resolved through family therapy and therapeutic play experiences with understanding adults (Coleman & Webber, 2002; Rosenberg et al., 2004; Seifert, 2000; Wicks-Nelson & Israel, 2006). Also, some youth with EBD may receive various forms of psychotherapy in hospitals or other intensive care settings. Few if any school-based intervention programs are founded on principles derived strictly from the psychoanalytic approach.

The Behavioral Approach

The behavioral approach focuses on aspects of the environment that prompt, reward, diminish, or punish certain behaviors. Through treatment, adults and children are given opportunities to learn new adaptive behaviors by identifying realistic goals, understanding what environmental features trigger both functional and maladaptive behaviors, and receiving positive reinforcement for attaining these goals. Gradually, aberrant behaviors are eliminated or replaced by more appropriate ones (Rosenberg et al., 2004; Wicks-Nelson & Israel, 2006). This approach has had a profound impact on the practices and interventions of special educators and other clinicians. And this approach, more than most others, has a significant research base affirming its effectiveness in treating a broad array of disorders and challenging behaviors (Coleman & Webber, 2002; Rosenberg et al., 2004).

The Phenomenological Approach

From a phenomenological point of view, abnormal behaviors arise from feelings, thoughts, and past events tied to a person's self-perception or self-concept. Faulty perceptions or feelings are thought to cause individuals to behave in ways that are counterproductive to self-fulfillment. Therapy is centered on helping people develop satisfactory perceptions and behaviors that are in agreement with their self-selected values.

The Sociological–Ecological Approach

The sociological–ecological model is by far the most widely encompassing explanation of EBD (Anderson & More, 2003). Aberrant behaviors are presumed to be caused by a variety of interactions and transactions with other people. For some theorists, the deviant behaviors are taught as part of the person's culture. For others, the behaviors are a function of labeling. According to this perspective, individuals labeled as juvenile delinquents gradually adopt the patterns of behavior that are associated with their assigned labels. In addition, others who are aware of the labels begin to treat these individuals as though they were truly delinquent. Such responses are assumed to promote the delinquent behaviors (Coleman & Webber, 2002; Rosenberg et al., 2004; Wicks-Nelson & Israel, 2006).

This model also specifies another source of aberrant behavior: *differential association*. This concept is closely related to the cultural-transmission explanation of deviance: People exhibit behavior problems in an attempt to conform to the wishes and expectations of a group they want to join or be affiliated with—such as a gang. Finally, the sociological–ecological perspective views the presence of aberrant behavior as a function of a variety of interactions and transactions that are derived from a broad array of environmental settings. For example, a community may sanction or informally support certain aberrant behaviors associated with delinquency, violence, drug abuse, and teen pregnancy.

Each model contributes different explanations for the causes of EBD. Mental health professionals agree that the pathways to EBD are multidimensional—some are environmentally induced, others involve co-interactions with environmental factors and genetic endowments, and others are primarily genetic (Rutter, 2006).

Clearly, many factors contribute to the emergence of EBD. Family and home environments play a critical role (Barber, Stolz, & Olsen, 2005). Poverty, involvement of primary caregivers with drugs and alcohol, child abuse and neglect, malnutrition, dysfunctional family environments, family discord, and incompetent parenting have a profound impact on the behaviors exhibited by children and adolescents (Conroy & Brown, 2004; Henry, Tolan, & Gorman-Smith, 2001; Wicks-Nelson & Israel, 2006). For example, "minimal rules in the home, poor monitoring of children, and inconsistent rewards and punishments create an environment in which behavior problems flourish" (Sampers et al., 2001, p. 94).

Children reared in low-income families bear increased risks for wide-ranging challenges, including lower intellectual development, deficient school achievement, and high rates of emotional/behavioral problems. Antisocial behaviors often emerge in children whose family poverty is accompanied by other stressors, such as homelessness, the death of a parent, placement in foster care, or persistent child abuse or neglect.

Family discord also plays a role in the development of EBD in some children. Extended marital conflict and distress are associated with several serious child outcomes, including aggressive behavior, difficulty with schoolwork, depression, health problems, and inferior social competence (Wicks-Nelson & Israel, 2006).

Procedures used in child management and discipline also play important roles in the development of EBD. However,

Interactions with family members play a significant role in the expression of emotional/behaviour problems.

the way in which child management may trigger EBD is highly complex. Parents who are extremely permissive, who are overly restrictive, or who are aggressive often produce children with conduct disorders. Home environments that are devoid of consistent rules and consequences for child behavior, that lack parental supervision, that reinforce aggressive behavior, and that use aggressive child management practices produce children who are very much at risk for developing conduct disorders (Wicks-Nelson & Israel, 2006).

Child abuse plays a major role in the development of aggression and other problematic behaviors in children and adolescents (Crosson-Tower, 2002; Horton & Cruise, 2001). Effects of child abuse on young children include withdrawal, noncompliance, aggression, enuresis (bed wetting), and physical complaints. Physically abused children exhibit high rates of adjustment problems of all kinds (Wicks-Nelson & Israel, 2006). Neglected children have difficulty in academic subjects and receive below-average grades. Children who have been sexually abused manifest an array of problems, including inappropriate, premature sexual behavior; poor peer relationships; and often serious mental health problems. Similar difficulties are evident in adolescents who have been abused. These include low self-esteem, depression, poor peer relationships and school problems, and self-injurious and suicidal behaviors.

As this section shows, the pathways to EBD are many and varied. However, the more we learn about these pathways, the greater our opportunity to prevent disorders from occurring or to lessen their overall impact. Much can be done for children, at-risk youth, and their families if appropriate preventive measures and interventions are actively pursued and put in place (Hester et al., 2004; Quinn & Poirier, 2004).

Assessment

Screening, Prereferral Interventions, and Referral

Screening is the first step in the assessment process. Screening is based on the belief that early identification leads to early treatment, which may reduce the overall impact of the EBD on the individual and family. As suggested earlier in this chapter, significant numbers of children and youth with EBD are *not* identified and thus do not receive appropriate services.

Screening approaches are multiagent, mutimethod, and multigated; that is, they do not rely on one professional, one method, or one observation for assessing a child or youth when EBD is suspected (Conroy, Hendricksen, & Hester, 2004). Screeners move through successive "gates" in order to identify children or youth for more intensive assessment and prereferral interventions.

One such approach is *Systematic Screening for Behavior Disorders* (SSBD), developed by Walker and Severson (1992). This approach has been very effective in identifying young children who need prereferral interventions and other services. SSBD is a three-stage process, beginning with nominations by a general education teacher. Teachers think about the children in their classes and then group them according to various behavior patterns, some of which mirror the characteristics of children with EBD, including externalizing and internalizing disorders. Once the children have been grouped, each child is ranked within the group according to the severity and frequency of his or her behaviors. The last step is a series of systematic observations conducted in classrooms and in other school environments to see how the children who were ranked as most severely affected behave in these environments. As children are progressively and systematically identified through this multiple-gating process, assessment team members determine which children ought to be considered for prereferral interventions or for other, more intensive assessments.

COLLABORATION. Prereferral interventions are designed to address the students' identified behavioral and academic problems and to reduce the likelihood of further, more restrictive actions or placements. Often these interventions are developed, planned, and implemented under the direction of multidisciplinary collaborative teams. Many states now require prereferral interventions before referrals may be received and processed by school personnel (Rosenberg et al., 2004). Prereferral interventions generally include efforts to remediate the students' difficulties by altering instruction and classroom management procedures, providing additional support for academic and behavioral success, and helping parents, professionals, and other key individuals respond more effectively to these children and youth.

The actual submission of a referral for a student is generally preceded by several parent-teacher conferences. These conferences help the teacher and parents determine what actions should to be taken. For example, the student's difficulties may be symptomatic of family problems such as a parent's extended illness, marital difficulties, or severe financial challenges. If the parents and related teachers continue to be perplexed by a child's or youth's behavior, a referral may be initiated. Referrals are generally processed by principals, who review them, consult with parents, and then forward the referrals to a psychologist or other qualified professionals.

Once a referral has been appropriately processed and a parent's or guardian's permission for testing and evaluation has been obtained, assessment team members carefully observe and assess a child's present levels of performance: intellectually, socially, academically, physically, and emotionally. Their task is to determine whether the child has EBD and whether he or she qualifies for special education services.

Assessment Factors

As we noted earlier in this chapter, emotional/behavioral disorders have many causes. Likewise, the behaviors of children and youth being assessed for EBD serve many functions. In other words, behaviors are purposeful. For example, a young child may tantrum in order to avoid schoolwork that is too difficult. Or a youth may engage in destructive behavior to gain attention that he or she does not otherwise receive from peers or parents. Behavior is also a function of interactions with environmental factors. Some conditions set off negative behaviors, and other conditions reward or reinforce these same behaviors. Interpersonal factors (such as depression, anxiety, or erroneous interpretations of environmental events) may contribute to a child's or youth's problems. If a child or youth is showing behaviors that are highly problematic, teachers and other professionals have an obligation to look at them from a functional point of view—that is, to see what purposes these behaviors serve and what conditions give rise to them (see the Reflect on This on page 242).

Current IDEA regulations require assessment team members to conduct functional behavioral assessments and to document the impact of the EBD on the child's or youth's academic achievement (U.S. Department of Education, 2006; Witt, VanDerHeyden, & Gilbertson, 2004). Simply defined, "Function assessment is a collection of methods for obtaining information about antecedents (things a child experiences before the behavior of concern), behaviors (what the child does), and consequences (what the child experiences

> Multidisciplinary team members play critical roles in assessing the seriousness of emotional/behavioral problems as well as planning appropriate interventions.

Standard 10: Collaboration

FOCUS **7**
What four important outcomes are achieved through a functional behavioral assessment?

Standard 8: Assessment

ONE BEHAVIORAL SPECIALIST'S APPROACH TO FUNCTIONAL BEHAVIORAL ASSESSMENT

WHAT IS FUNCTIONAL BEHAVIORAL ASSESSMENT?

Functional behavioral assessment (FBA) is a process of gathering information about the things or events that influence a person's problem behaviors. These could be either external events in the person's environment (e.g., interactions with others, work demands) or internal things (e.g., illness, fatigue, depression).

WHY IS FBA CARRIED OUT?

FBA gathers information that is used to guide the development of a treatment or intervention plan. This plan should focus both on reducing or eliminating the problem behaviors and on increasing appropriate, desired behaviors.

HOW IS FBA CARRIED OUT?

There are three major strategies for collecting FBA information:

1. **Indirect/informant methods.** This involves collecting information from teachers, parents, or other relevant persons through interviews or the use of checklists, rating scales, or questionnaires.

2. **Systematic observation in typical settings.** This involves conducting structured observations to collect data on the occurrence of the behavior and on things that may be related to it. These observations are usually done during the person's regular activities (e.g., during classroom work periods, on the playground).

3. **Experimental manipulations (functional analysis).** This involves setting up situations in which different events are directly manipulated (i.e., presented and withdrawn) to assess their effects on the person's problem behaviors. Data on the behavior are systematically collected to allow for comparisons of the effects of different manipulations.

WHAT SHOULD BE THE OUTCOMES OF A GOOD FBA?

- A thorough description of all the problem behaviors of concern, including how often they occur, how long they last, and how intense or potentially damaging they are. Also, it is important to identify behaviors that seem typically to occur together (e.g., the student yells, then throws things).

- Identification of the general and more specific things and events that seem to "set off" the problem behaviors, or predict when and where they are going to occur (e.g., when the student is not getting attention, is asked to do particular activities, or is ill, tired, or hungry).

- Identification of any outcomes or consequences of the behavior that may be reinforcing and maintaining it (e.g., getting attention, getting help with work, avoiding or escaping work demands or activities).

- Summarization of this information into statements or hypotheses about the behavior (e.g., "When Janna gets little sleep the night before and is asked to do math problems that are difficult for her, she will put her head down, refuse, and/or throw or destroy her books to escape having to do the task").

- Some level of systematic observational data that support the statements or hypotheses you've developed. These data could be the systematic observations or experimental manipulations mentioned above.

- The whole purpose of FBA is to guide the development of a plan. Such a plan should include a comprehensive array of strategies, such as changing the curriculum and instruction, teaching alternative skills, and rewarding appropriate behaviors.

SOURCE: From "One Behavioral Specialist's Approach to Functional Behavioral Assessment" by R. O'Neill, in *Getting Comfortable with Special Education Law*, 2000, p. 288, by D. Snow Huefner, Norwood, MA: Christopher-Gordon Publishers.

after the behavior of interest). The purpose is to identify potential reasons for the behavior and to use the information to develop strategies that will support positive student performance while reducing the behaviors that interfere with the child's successful functioning" (Witt, Daly, & Noell, 2000, p. 3). The purpose of functional behavioral assessment is to identify the functions of a student's behavior in relation to various school, home, or community settings. Assessment team members collect information through interviews, make careful observations, and examine the effects of probes or experimental manipulations over a period of several days (see the nearby Reflect on This, "Amy and Jay," and Figure 9.3). Through these procedures, team members and parents discover reliable relationships among specific problem behaviors, the settings or events that give rise to these behaviors, and their consequences.

If the functional behavioral assessment is done well, it provides grounding for the development of behavior intervention plans (BIPs) that may be used to assist the child or youth in developing new, more adaptive behaviors (Meadows & Stevens, 2004; Witt, VanDerHeyden,

& Gilbertson, 2004). Additionally, the BIP may include new curricular or instructional approaches tailored to the student's learning needs and preferences. The BIP may also identify changes to be implemented in the school or home environment. These might include peer and paraprofessional support, use of conflict resolution specialists, home-based programs, and other carefully selected interventions.

Assessment Techniques

Several techniques and procedures are used to identify children with EBD, and all closely parallel the theoretical framework or philosophical perspective of their evaluators. As we have seen, the identification and classification of a child or youth with EBD are preceded by a set of screening procedures accompanied by a functional behavioral assessment, teacher and parent interviews, diagnostic academic assessments, behavior checklists, a variety of sociometric devices (such as peer ratings), and the use of teacher rating scales (Conroy, Hendricksen, & Hester, 2004; Rosenberg et al., 2004).

Typically, parents and teachers are asked to respond to a variety of rating-scale items that describe behaviors related to various classifications of EBD. The number of items marked and the rating given to each item contribute to the behavior profiles generated from the ratings (see Figure 9.4). In making their assessments, parents and professionals are asked to consider the child's behavior during the past several months.

A postive development in assessing children and youth for EBD is **strength-based assessment** (Epstein, 1998; Lyons, 1997). In contrast to deficit-oriented instruments, this approach focuses on the individual's strengths. One such instrument is the *Behavioral and Emotional Rating Scale*–Second Edition (BERS2) (Epstein & Sharma, 1997). Using this instrument, parents, teachers, and other caregivers rate the child's or youth's strengths in several important areas, including interpersonal strength, involvement with family, intrapersonal strength, school functioning, and affective or emotional strength. Skilled clinicians use the BERS and other, similar approaches to develop strength-centered, rather than deficit-centered, IEPs for children and youth with EBD (see Figure 9.5).

Once the screening process has been concluded, specialists and/or consultants—including psychologists, special educators, social workers, and psychiatrists—complete in-depth assessments of the child's academic and social-emotional strengths and weaknesses in various settings, such as the classroom, home, and playground. The assessment team may analyze classroom and playground interactions with peers, using functional behavioral assessment techniques; may administer various tests to evaluate personality, achievement, and intellectual factors; and may interview the parents and the child. Additionally, they may observe the child at home, again making use of functional behavioral assessment procedures.

➤ **Strength-based assessment**

An assessment procedure in which parents, teachers, and other caregivers rate a child's or youth's strengths and use this information to develop strength-centered, rather than deficit-centered, individualized education programs for children and youth with EBD.

FIGURE 9.3

Results of a Functional Behavioral Assessment for Amy and Jay

	EVENT	PROBLEM PATHWAY	REPLACEMENT PATHWAY	POSSIBLE INTERVENTIONS
Amy				
	Setting event	Peer altercation ↓	Peer Altercation ↓	Teach problem-solving skills
	Antecedent	Verbal insult ↓	Verbal insult ↓	Use prompts and cues
	Behavior	Physical aggression ↓	Move away or tell teacher ↓	Teach anger management skills
	Consequence	Escape altercation	Escape altercation and access teacher reinforcement	Provide reinforcement for appropriate behavior and response cost for inappropriate behavior
Jay				
	Setting event	Classroom setting ↓	Classroom setting ↓	Use group contingency
	Antecedent	Peer holds class attention ↓	Peer holds class attention ↓	Use prompts and cues
	Behavior	Disruptive sounds and actions ↓	Raise hand and make appropriate comment ↓	Teach student to access peer attention in positive manner
	Consequence	Peer attention	Peer attention	Provide praise along with student attention and have peers ignore inappropriate behavior under group contingency

SOURCE: From "Using Functional Behavioral Analysis to Develop Effective Intervention Plans," by T. M. Scott and C. M. Nelson, 1999, *Journal of Positive Behavior Intervention*, 1(4), p. 249. Copyright © 1999 by Pro-Ed, Inc. Reprinted by permission.

A particularly complex problem for clinicians is the assessment of children and youth who have limited English proficiency and/or are culturally diverse (Goh, 2004; Obiakor et al., 2004). Unfortunately, many of these children and youth are disproportionately represented in special education settings for students with EBD (Osher et al., 2004). Some optimism is warranted, however, especially as practitioners collaborate and employ functional behavioral assessment and related procedures, prereferral interventions, and positive behavioral support (PBS) with all students.

The development of essential social skills is important to many children with emotional/behavior disorders.

Positive behavior support holds great promise for helping students from diverse backgrounds remain and succeed in general education classrooms and in other less restrictive settings (Heineman, Dunlap, & Kincaid, 2005; Reinke, Herman & Tucker, 2006). PBS "is a systems approach for establishing a continuum of proactive, positive discipline procedures for all students and staff members in all types of school settings" (Eber, Sugai, Smith, & Scott, 2002, p. 171). Instead of treating the symptom(s) and ignoring the underlying problems, the thrust of PBS is to address all the features and factors that may be related to a child's or youth's negative behaviors. The primary goals of PBS systems are improved behaviors for all children and youth at home, at school, and in the community; enhanced academic performance; and the prevention of serious violent, aggressive, or destructive behaviors. Schools in which PBS systems are adopted define schoolwide expectations and rules; actively and regularly build social competence through active teaching and social skills programming; reward targeted, prosocial behaviors on a regular basis; and make decisions on the basis of frequently collected, pertinent data (Lewis, Hudson, Richter, & Johnson, 2004; Meadows & Stevens, 2004; Miller, Lane, & Wehby, 2005; Reinke, Herman, & Tucker, 2006). Individually tailored plans are developed and put into action by collaborative teams of

SHOULD KARL STAY AT HOME OR BE HELPED ELSEWHERE?

Karl is a 7-year-old boy who was referred to the study by a staff member at the mental health clinic where he was receiving weekly outpatient therapy. Though his mother, Ms. S., found their current therapist to be helpful, she felt her family needed more comprehensive assistance. As Karl grew older, his aggressive behaviors were increasingly difficult to manage and residential placement had been discussed. Ms. S. was adamant that "even with all of his problems, he belongs at home." On referral to the study, Karl was randomly assigned to FCICM (Family-Centered Intensive Case Management).

Karl likes to bowl, fish, and play soccer. His mother described him as a very loving and generous child who could be helpful when he wanted to be. Karl liked school but had low-average school achievement and received additional help in reading and math. Karl's teacher reported that he had some behavioral problems in school and difficulty with peer relationships.

At home, Karl behaved aggressively toward his younger sister and mother. Ms. S. reported that he had violent temper tantrums. He was found once putting a pillow over his sister's face, and he had harmed her in other ways. Ms. S. did not feel that she could leave the two children alone for even a few minutes. Karl had purposely injured a pet hamster and animals he found, and he had also set several small fires. His mother was concerned about his increasing withdrawal and "not telling me how he was feeling." He had tried to hang himself with a belt, dashed into busy roads, and engaged in other risk-taking behaviors. He experienced sleep problems, was diagnosed with depression, and was assessed as functionally impaired in social relationships and self-direction.

Karl's needs contributed to the tension between his mother and stepfather, and the relationship between Karl and his stepfather was difficult. Karl was confused and distressed by the lack of contact with his birth father and imagined his father to be coming for a visit or being able to live with him when there was virtually no contact between them. Karl and his mother had made allegations of psychological abuse and neglect (Evans et al., pp. 563–564).

APPLICATION

1. With appropriate human and material resources, what would need to be arranged so Karl could remain at home rather than be placed in a residential setting?

2. What family-centered services would help his mother and other family members?

3. What advocacy assistance might the mother profit from in working with Karl's school?

4. On what basis should Karl be removed from his home for other, more intensive treatments or services?

---

professionals for students who present chronic, challenging behaviors. These plans evolve from carefully completed functional behavioral assessments conducted by key individuals in the child's or youth's school, home, and community settings.

Interventions

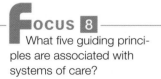

Focus 8
What five guiding principles are associated with systems of care?

Historically, most children and youth with EBD received treatments and interventions in isolation from their families, homes, neighborhoods, and communities. These treatments and interventions were based on the assumption that students' problems were exclusively of their own making. Services, if delivered at all, were rarely coordinated. Fragmentation was the rule (Eber & Keenan, 2004). Significant changes are beginning to take place, thanks to brave and vocal advocates who chronicled the deplorable plight of children and youth with EBD (Duchnowski & Friedman, 1990; Knitzer, 1982; Peacock Hill Working Group, 1990; Stroul & Friedman, 1986).

Multidisciplinary Collaboration: Systems of Care

Standard 5: Learning Environments and Social Interactions

Increasingly, care providers for children and youth with EBD are establishing systems of care (Adelman & Taylor, 2006; Anderson & Mohr, 2003; National Mental Health Information Center, 2006). One very promising practice is the wraparound process (Eber & Keenan, 2004; Kendziora, Bruns, Osher, Pacchiano, & Mejia, 2001). "Wraparound is not a service or set of services; it is a [collaborative] planning process. This process is used to build consensus within a team of professionals, family members, and natural support providers to improve the effectiveness, efficiency, and relevance of supports and services developed for children and their families" (Eber et al., 2002, p. 173). We will have more to say about the wraparound process in subsequent sections of this chapter.

Community-based and family-centered systems for delivering services to children and youth with EBD are also emerging (Eber et al., 2002). In these systems, educational, medical, and community care providers are beginning to pay greater attention to youth with EBD and their families, as well as to the communities in which they live (Hernandez, Gomez, Lipien, Greenbaum, Armstrong, Gonzalez, 2001; Koyanagi & Feres-Merchant, 2000; Worthington, Hernandez, Friedman, & Uzzell, 2001) (see Figure 9.6). This new approach is based on several core values and guiding principles (see Figure 9.7). One of the basic features of the systems-of-care concept is that it does not represent a prescribed structure for assembling a network of services and agencies. Rather, it reflects a philosophy about the way in which services should be delivered to children, youth, and their families. The child and family become the focus of the delivery system, with vital services surrounding them. These services might include home-based services, placement in special classes, therapeutic foster care, financial assistance, primary health care, outpatient treatment, career education, after-school programs, and family support. An integral part of the systems of care is schoolwide primary prevention (Adelman & Taylor, 2006; Eber et al., 2002; Greenburg, Domitrovich, & Bumbarger, 2001). Interventions associated with this kind of prevention include systems for positive development, early or prereferral interventions (as noted earlier); multidisciplinary collaboration, teaching conflict resolution, emotional literacy, **cognitive-behavioral therapy**, and anger management for all students in the school—not just for those identified with EBD (Guerra, Boxer, & Kim, 2005; Mayer, Lochman, & Van Acker, 2005). These kinds of interventions can avert 75% to 85% of student adjustment and behavior problems.

The Early Childhood Years: Multidisciplinary/Multi-Agency Collaboration

The early childhood years are important for all children, particularly those at risk for developing EBD (Hester et al., 2004). Recent research suggests that EBD can be prevented (Kendziora, 2004). Many children would not develop serious EBD if they and their families

➤ **Cognitive-behavior therapy**
A form of therapy that focuses on the important role of thinking and how it influences behavior(s) and related feelings. Cognitive-behavioral interventionists teach youth to review carefully their thoughts about a given event or experiences, learning how to address and successfully interpret distortions in thinking, skills that subsequently improve their behaviors and feelings.

FIGURE 9.6

The System of Care Framework

Mental health services

Social services

Operational services

Recreational services

Child and Family

Educational services

Vocational services

Health services

Substance abuse services

SOURCE: Adapted from *A System of Care for Children and Adolescents with Severe Emotional Disturbances* (p. xxvi), by B. Stroul and R. M. Friedman, 1986 (Rev. ed.), Washington, DC: Georgetown University Child Development Center, National Technical Assistance Center for Children's Mental Health. Copyright 1986 by B. Stroul and R. M. Friedman. Adapted by permission.

FIGURE 9.7

Core Values and Guiding Principles of Systems of Care

Core Values

1. The system of care should be child-centered and family focused, with the needs of the child and family dictating the types and mix of services provided.

2. The system of care should be community-based, with the locus of services as well as management and decision-making responsibility resting at the community level.

3. The system of care should be culturally competent, with agencies, programs, and services that are responsive to the cultural, racial, and ethnic differences of the population they serve.

Guiding Principles

1. Children with emotional disturbances should have access to a comprehensive array of services that address physical, emotional, social, and educational needs.

2. Children with emotional disturbances should receive individualized services in accordance with the unique needs and potentials of each child and guided by an individualized service plan.

3. Children with emotional disturbances should receive services within the least restrictive, most normative environment that is clinically appropriate.

4. The families and surrogate families of children with emotional disturbances should be full participants in all aspects of the planning and delivery of services.

5. Children with emotional disturbances should receive services that are integrated, with linkages between child-serving agencies and programs and mechanisms for planning, developing, and coordinating services.

6. Children with emotional disturbances should be provided with case management or similar mechanisms to ensure that multiple services are delivered in a coordinated and therapeutic manner and that they can move through the system of services in accordance with their changing needs.

7. Early identification and intervention for children with emotional disturbances should be promoted by the system of care in order to enhance the likelihood of positive outcomes.

8. Children with emotional disturbances should be ensured smooth transitions to the adult service system as they reach maturity.

9. The rights of children with emotional disturbances should be protected, and effective advocacy efforts for children and youth with emotional disturbances should be promoted.

10. Children with emotional disturbances should receive services without regard to race, religion, national origin, sex, physical disability, or other characteristics, and services should be sensitive and responsive to cultural differences and special needs.

SOURCE: From *A System of Care for Children and Adolescents with Severe Emotional Disturbances* (p. xxiv), by B. Stroul and R. M. Friedman, 1986 (Rev. ed.), Washington, DC: Georgetown University Child Development Center, National Technical Assistance Center for Children's Mental Health. Copyright 1986 by B. Stroul and R. M. Friedman, Reprinted by permission.

had received early, child-centered, intensive, community-based, and family-focused services and interventions. Moreover, the cost of delivering these prevention services would be far less than that of providing services to these same individuals as teens, young adults, and adults. Society seems unwilling to make investments that would yield remarkable financial, social, and emotional dividends for us, our children, and our communities (Lopez, 2005). Key elements of the prevention process include early identification, family-driven needs assessment, home-based and community-based interventions, and collaboration among an array of educational and community agencies (Hester et al., 2004; Kendziora, 2004).

Interventions for young children with EBD are child-, family-, and home-centered. Often they are directed at reducing the effects of the EBD or even preventing them (Joseph & Strain, 2003; Kendziora, 2004). Thus the goals associated with individualized family service plans (IFSPs) go well beyond the typical educational goals found in individualized education programs (IEPs) for older children. Interventions for young children with EBD include building positive replacement behaviors for challenging behaviors, promoting appropriate social interactions with peers and others, and creating positive behavioral support across a child's natural environments (Essa, 2003; Hester et al., 2004). Family-centered interventions focus on such things as respite care; parent training directed at managing the young child with EBD at home and in other community settings; the delivery of family, marital, or drug therapy; and the provision of specialized day care or day treatment (Eddy, Reid & Fetron, 2000; Simpson et al., 2001). The nature, intensity, and duration of these multi-agency services and interventions are determined by the needs of the families and the speed with which they develop new skills and coping strategies. The interventions are delivered in multiple contexts—the places where children, family members, and others play, work, learn, and grow.

Often the interventions for young children with EBD are directed at beginning communication skills; appropriate social interaction with siblings, parents, and peers; beginning social skills; and responding effectively to developmentally appropriate tasks. Also, in keeping with the movement toward inclusion, family intervention and transition specialists pay greater attention to preparing young children for successful participation in less restrictive environments (Kennedy, Long, Jolivette, Cox, Tang, & Thompson, 2001).

Much progress can be achieved through parent-training programs that help parents develop effective management and motivation skills.

Council for Exceptional Children

Standard 7: Instructional Planning

The Elementary School Years

Elementary school children with EBD often present overlapping behavioral problems. These problems center on accepting appropriate consequences for behavior, interacting successfully with others, using self-control and self-regulation, following directions, and expressing strong feelings. Such behaviors become the focus of intervention efforts. With the assistance of parents, IEP team members strive to construct a complete picture of each child, determining his or her present levels of intellectual, social, emotional, and academic performance and the contexts that give rise to and support these behaviors (Beard & Sugai, 2004). These levels of performance and the outcomes derived from the functional behavioral assessment become the basis for identifying important goals for the child's IEP and for developing behavior intervention plans (Lewis, Lewis-Palmer, Newcomer, & Sticher, 2004).

Typically, programs for children with EBD focus on replacing maladaptive with adaptive behaviors, increasing self-regulation; building appropriate academic skills and dispositions, increasing self-awareness, increasing cooperative behavior, building self-esteem, and acquiring age-appropriate self-control (Barton-Arnwood et al., 2005; Henley, 2003; Lane, Wehby, Barton-Arnwood, 2005; Lien-Thorne & Kamps, 2005; Reid, Trout, & Schartz, 2005). Children need these skills and behaviors to succeed in their classrooms, homes, and communities.

In the past, many programs for children with EBD were restrictive, controlling, and punitive in nature (Knitzer et al., 1990). Rather than teaching new behaviors, these programs focused on controlling the behaviors of children and youth. These programs employed the **curriculum of control** (Knitzer et al., 1990) or the *curriculum of noninstruction* (Shores & Wehby, 1999, p. 196). Rather than developing replacement behaviors or new behaviors, children and

Council for Exceptional Children

Standard 4: Instructional Strategies

➤ **Curriculum of control**

Classroom routines, structures, and instructional strategies focused on controlling children and youth rather than on teaching them new, success-related social and academic behaviors.

INCLUSION AND COLLABORATION THROUGH THE LIFESPAN

People with Emotional/Behavioral Disorders (EBD)

EARLY CHILDHOOD YEARS

Tips for the Family

- Become involved with parent training and other community support services.
- Work collaboratively with multidisciplinary personnel (such as educators, social workers, health care professionals, and parent group volunteers) in developing effective child management strategies.
- Use the same evidence-based intervention strategies at home that are taught in the preschool or specialized intervention setting.
- Establish family routines, schedules, and incentive systems that reward and build positive behaviors.
- Participate in advocacy or parent support groups.
- Understand your rights regarding health care, education, and social services and benefits.

Tips for the Preschool Teacher

- Work collaboratively with the multidisciplinary professionals in your preschool (such as the director, psychologist, social worker, parent trainers, special educators, and health care professionals) to identify evidence-based instructional strategies.
- Establish clear schedules, class routines, rules, and positive consequences for all children in your classroom.
- Create a learning and social environment that is nurturing and supportive for everyone.
- Explicitly teach social behaviors (such as following directions, greeting other children, sharing toys, and using words to express anger) to all children.
- Ask for help from the multidisciplinary teacher support team. Remember, collaboration is the key to success.

Tips for Preschool Personnel

- Engage older, socially competent peers to assist with readiness skills and social skills training.
- Help others (such as teaching assistants, aides, and volunteers) know what to do in managing children with challenging behaviors.
- Make every effort to involve children with EBD in schoolwide activities and special performances.
- Orient and teach preschool children without disabilities about how to appropriately respond and relate to classmates with challenging behaviors. Such responses include ignoring, walking away, getting help from the teacher, and the like.
- Collaborate with parents in using the same management systems and strategies in your preschool classroom that are used in the home.

Tips for Neighbors and Friends

- Become familiar with the things you can do in responding to the challenging behaviors of a child with EBD.
- Be patient with parents who are attempting to cope with their child's temper tantrum or other challenging behaviors in a natural setting (such as a grocery store, in the mall, or in the park).
- Assist parents who would benefit from some time away from their preschooler by offering respite care for short periods of time.
- Involve the neighborhood child with EBD in your family activities.
- Help parents' awareness of advocacy or support groups.
- Encourage parents to involve their child in neighborhood and community events (such as parades, holiday celebrations, and birthday parties).

ELEMENTARY YEARS

Tips for the Family

- Use in your home environment the effective management techniques that are being used in your child's classroom.
- Help your other children develop an understanding of EBD.
- Establish clear rules, set routines, and consequences that are consistent with your child's developmental age and interests.
- Take advantage of parent training and support groups that are available in your community.
- Obtain counseling, when appropriate, for yourself, your other children, and your spouse from a community mental health agency or other public or private sources.
- Help your other children and their friends understand the things they can do to support your child with EBD.

Tips for the General Education Classroom Teacher

- Provide a positive, structured classroom environment (examples include clearly stated rules, helpful positive and negative consequences, well-conceived classroom schedules, and carefully taught classroom routines).
- Teach social skills (such as dealing with bullying and accepting criticism) to all of the children with the help of members of the school's multidisciplinary teacher assistance team.
- Teach self-management skills (such as goal selection, self-monitoring, self-reinforcement) to all children with the aid of the school's multidisciplinary teacher assistance team.
- Use cooperative learning strategies and peer tutoring to promote the learning of all children and to develop positive relationships among students.
- Ask for help from members of your school's multidisciplinary teacher assistance team or the child's parents.

Tips for School Personnel

- Use same-age or cross-age peers to provide tutoring, coaching, and other kinds of assistance in developing the academic and social skills of children with EBD.
- Establish schoolwide management programs and positive behavior supports that reinforce individual and group accomplishments.

- Work closely and collaboratively with members of the multidisciplinary teacher assistance team to create a school environment that is positive and caring.
- Use collaborative problem-solving techniques in dealing with difficult or persistent behavior problems—work with your school multidisciplinary teacher assistance team.
- Help children develop an understanding of how to respond appropriately to students with challenging behaviors.

Tips for Neighbors and Friends

- Involve the child with EBD in appropriate after-school activities (such as computer games, and informal sports).
- Invite the child to spend time with your family in appropriate recreational events (such as swimming, hiking, boating).
- Teach your children how to support appropriate behavior and to ignore inappropriate behavior when it occurs.
- Catch the child being good rather than looking for "bad" behaviors.
- As a youth leader, coach, or recreational specialist, get to know each child with behavior disorders well so that you can respond with confidence when providing support.

SECONDARY AND TRANSITION YEARS

Tips for the Family

- Continue your efforts to focus on the positive behaviors of your child with EBD.
- Assist your child in understanding and selecting appropriate postsecondary training, education, and/or employment.
- Give yourself a regular break from the task of being a parent, and engage in activities that are totally enjoyable for you.
- Ask for help from community mental health services, clergy, or a close friend when you are feeling overwhelmed or stressed.
- Consult regularly with support personnel to monitor progress and develop ideas for maintaining the behavioral and academic gains made by your child.
- Maintain involvement in advocacy and parent support groups.

Tips for the General Education Classroom Teacher

- Create positive relationships within your classroom through cooperative learning teams and group-oriented assignments.
- Engage all students in creating standards for conduct as well as consequences for positive and negative behaviors.
- Focus your efforts on developing positive relationships with students with EBD by greeting them regularly in your class, informally talking with them at appropriate times, attending to improvements in their performance, and becoming aware of their interests and concerns.
- Work closely with the members of the school multidisciplinary teacher assistance team to be aware of teacher behaviors that may affect the student's performance.
- Understand that changes in behavior often occur very gradually, with periods of regression and sometimes tumult.

Tips for School Personnel

- Create a school climate that is positive and supportive.
- Provide students with an understanding of their roles and responsibilities in responding to peers with disabilities.
- Engage peers in providing social skills training, job coaching, and academic tutoring.
- Engage members of the school multidisciplinary teacher assistance team to help you deal with crisis situations and to provide other supportive therapies and interventions.
- Establish schoolwide procedures for dealing quickly and efficiently with particularly difficult behaviors.

Tips for Neighbors, Friends, and Potential Employers

- If you have some expertise in a content area (such as math, English, or history), offer to provide assistance with homework or school assignments for students with behavior EBD.
- Provide opportunities for students with EBD to be employed in your business.
- Give parents an occasional respite by inviting the adolescent with EBD to join your family for a family-oriented activity.
- Encourage other children and adolescents to volunteer as peer partners, job coaches, and social skills trainers.
- Do not allow others to tease, harass, or ridicule an adolescent with emotional/behavioral disorders in your presence.

ADULT YEARS

Tips for the Family

- Build on efforts to develop appropriate independence and interdependence.
- Maintain contact with appropriate multidisciplinary personnel (such as health care or social services personnel), particularly if the adult with EBD is on medication or receiving counseling.
- Work collaboratively with appropriate adult service agencies that are required by law to assist with your adult child's employment, housing, and recreation.
- Prepare your other children or other caregivers as appropriate to assume the responsibilities that you may be unable to assume over time.

Tips for Neighbors, Friends, and Employers

- As an employer, be willing to make sensible and reasonable adjustments in work environments.
- Understand adjustments that may need to take place with new medications or treatment regimens.
- Get to know the individual as a person—the individual's likes and dislikes, whom she or he admires, and any preferred leisure activities.
- Be willing to involve the individual in appropriate holiday events and special occasions, such as birthdays, athletic activities, and other social gatherings.
- Understand what might be uncomfortable to the individual.
- Be available to communicate with others who may be responsible for the individual's well-being—a job coach, an independent-living specialist, and others.

youth in many of these programs languished or regressed (Knitzer, 1982; Knitzer et al., 1990). Even today, many children and youth with behavior disorders are served in settings that remove them from natural interactions with students without disabilities. Most young people with EBD form friendships that are neighborhood-based rather than school-centered—just the opposite of young people without disabilities (Panacek & Dunlap, 2003).

DEBATE FORUM

DESPERATE BARGAIN: CUSTODY FOR CARE, PARENTS GIVE UP KIDS AS LAST RESORT

Christy Mathews struggled for years to pay for treatment for her mentally ill daughter, a 15-year-old who burns and cuts herself and last year threatened to stab her mom with a steak knife.

Desperate and afraid, Mathews tried to get Hamilton County officials to pay for Lauren to live in a psychiatric facility. A social worker finally told her she could get help—if Mathews gave up custody of her daughter to the county.

"I shouldn't be forced to give my daughter up to get her the help she needs, but that's how the system works," she says. "What you have to go through is unreal."

Mathews refused to turn over Lauren, but thousands of parents in Ohio and elsewhere have been forced to give in.

In the past three years, Ohio parents who've run out of insurance or money have given up custody of as many as 1,800 children so the government will pay to treat their mental illness, a Cincinnati Enquirer investigation has found.

Even then, kids don't always get the help they need. An examination of inspection records, court documents, and interviews reveals that Ohio counties place more than 7,000 children a year in centers where some are abused, molested, improperly drugged and left in wretched conditions.

At least 38 of Ohio's 88 counties acknowledge taking children from parents, who give up their rights to say where their kids are sent for treatment, how long they stay, or even what kind of medicine they are given.

County officials say that obtaining custody is the only way they can tap federal money to cover treatment costs that run as high as $1,000 a day. But not even Michael Hogan, director of Ohio's Department of Mental Health, defends the practice. "We must stop trading custody for care. It's terrible," he says. "A civilized society should not do this."

Trading custody for care is a "travesty," adds Gayle Channing Tenenbaum, a lobbyist for the Ohio Public Children Services Association.

"As a state," she says, "we've totally given up on these kids."

POINT

Universal health care should be available to all children. The laws of supply and demand do not provide well for the common good of families who cannot access or pay for needed health care. Children, youth, and families experiencing profound needs for mental health care should not be excluded because they cannot pay, nor should parents or families be encouraged to give the government custody of their children so that the children may receive critical psychiatric or medical care. Access to health care should be considered a basic human right, not a privilege.

COUNTERPOINT

Government programs are rarely well managed or cost-effective. A universal health system for all children would become nothing more than bloated bureaucracy that would eventually collapse of its own weight. Competition is absolutely essential to the well-being of any health care system. Without competition, the quality, availability, and cost of health care would be severely compromised. Also, billions of dollars that would otherwise go to cost-effective private health providers would be wasted in a universal health care system administered by government bureaucrats.

SOURCE: Adapted from Spencer Hunt and Debra Jasper, "Desperate Bargain: Custody for Care," The Enquirer, March 21, 2004, Cincinnati, Ohio.

FIGURE 9.8

Elements of Wraparound

1. Community-based

2. Individualized and strength-based

3. Culturally competent [and sensitive]

4. Families as full and active partners

5. Team-based process involving family, child, natural supports, agencies, and community supports

6. Flexible approach and funding

7. Balance of formal and informal community and family resources

8. Unconditional commitment

9. Development and implementation of an individualized service/support plan based on a community/neighborhood, interagency, collaborative process

10. Outcomes determined and measured through team process (Eber & Keenan, 2004, p. 507)

COLLABORATION: WRAPAROUND SERVICES. New systems of care for children and youth with EBD have emerged (Eber & Keenan, 2004). These systems deliver wraparound services to children and youth with EBD and their families (see Reflect on This, "Seth: Part One"). As is implied by the word *wraparound,* children, youth, and their families receive the multidisciplinary support that they need to address the problems in the family, home, and school that give rise to the EBD. Services may include in-home child management training, employment assistance, and family therapy—whatever is needed to help families become successful. Figure 9.8 lists essential features of these *wraparound* systems and related programs.

Again, at the heart of many new programs is positive behavioral support (PBS). Instead of trying to eliminate or control behaviors, teachers, parents, and clinicians collaborate, working together to understand the purposes and functions of children's or youth's behaviors. The goal of PBS is to apply various strategies to lessen challenging behaviors and to build resilient behaviors that culminate in long-lasting changes (Lewis, Hudson, Richter, & Johnson, 2004). PBS may be implemented on a schoolwide basis for all children, on a classroom level, or with individual students (Liaupsin, Jolivette, & Scott, 2004; Safran & Oswald, 2003). Salient

Council for Exceptional Children

Standard 10: Collaboration

REFLECT ON THIS — SETH: PART ONE

Connie Thomas is a single mother of three children: Sarah, Molly, and Seth, who are now ages 16, 14, and 13. Connie is incredibly open. She is willing to share the most painful details of her life in a way that communicates both genuine acceptance of her family situation and the fatigue of struggle. All of her children have had challenges related to emotional or behavioral problems at one point or another. Connie is quick to note that she herself is a recovering alcoholic and addict. She has been sober for over 20 years now, but until 9 years ago, she was married to a man who abused alcohol and drugs.

When Seth was 7, the Wraparound process began for the Thomas family. Not only was he at imminent risk of removal from his home because of his behavior, but he was also having serious problems in school. Susan, who had been connected to the family as Seth's social worker since he was 4, recalled the school referral that in part began Seth's Wraparound plan of care. "[The principal] called up and said, 'Do something or get this kid out of my school.'" It is at the point when a child has needs across multiple service systems that Stark County's Creative Community Options process kicks in.

SOURCE: Adapted from Kendziora, Bruns, Osher, Pacchiano, & Mejia (2001) *Systems of Care: Promising Practices in Children's Mental Health*, 2001 series, vol. I. Washington, DC: Center for Effective Collaboration and Practice, American Institutes for Research.

SETH: PART TWO

One thing that Connie needed was help at home with Seth. This help was provided in part through an intensive home-based program. Rick was a supervisor and therapist in this program. . . . Rick recalled his early experiences with the Thomas family.

[Seth] was just running crazy around the house—that's the best way to describe it. It was all we could do to try to get him to sit down and participate in some very structured exercises. . . . He was [also] doing some more gross stuff with his sisters, and Sarah and Molly were just not liking it too much—and I don't blame them. So we were going out and trying to do some stabilization in the home.

Since entering middle school, Seth has been placed in a self-contained classroom for children with severe behavioral problems, with five or six students, a teacher, and an aide. Last school year, Seth was not able to stay in this classroom and wound up receiving one-on-one tutoring for half days. . . . After leaving school at about 11:30, Seth would go to his pastor's home, where the pastor's children were home-schooled. Seth would study with them for the remainder of the school day. This combination of formal and informal supports worked well for the Thomas family, and Seth was able to finish out the school year fairly successfully.

SOURCE: Adapted from Kendziora, Bruns, Osher, Pacchiano, & Mejia (2001) *Systems of Care: Promising Practices in Children's Mental Health*, 2001 series, vol. I. Washington, DC: Center for Effective Collaboration and Practice, American Institutes for Research.

characteristics of schoolwide PBS include a shared vision of the primary purposes of the school, positive school leadership, collaborative teams, and decisions driven by ongoing data regarding achievment and behavior (Liaupsin, Jolivette, & Scott, 2004).

As highlighted in the assessment section of this chapter, professionals use functional behavioral assessment to determine the patterns and functions of certain behaviors. Once these patterns and functions are well understood, teachers, parents, and others help children develop positive approaches to achieving their goals and learning how to deal with their thoughts and feelings in positive ways (Beard & Sugai, 2004).

Children who exhibit moderate to severe EBD may be served in special classes (see Reflect on This, "Seth: Part Two"). In some school systems, special classes are found in elementary, middle, and high schools. They may be grouped in small clusters of two to three classes in selected buildings. Other special classes may be found within hospital units, special schools, residential programs, juvenile units, and specialized treatment facilities. Preliminary research regarding the impact of self-contained classes on students' progress in social, academic, and behavior domains is disappointing at best. Most students in self-contained classes make very little progress in these domains, and some fall even farther behind (Lane, Wehby, Little, & Cooley, 2005).

Most special classes for children with moderate to severe disorders share certain characteristics. The first is a high degree of structure and specialized instruction; in other words, rules are clear and consistently enforced; helpful routines are in place; high-quality academic and social instruction are provided; and both adult–child relationships and child–child relationships are fostered and developed (Kauffman, Bantz, & McCullough, 2002). Other features include close teacher monitoring of student performance, frequent feedback, and reinforcement based on students' academic and social behaviors. Students learn how to express themselves, how to address individual and group problems, and how to deal with very strong feelings and emotions. Point systems

Council for Exceptional Children

Standard 5: Learning Environments and Social Interactions

Classrooms for students with EBD provide for academic as well as social growth.

FIGURE 9.9

Point Card for IEP goals

Name: _Mike_   **Date:** _26 November_

1. My IEP goal today is: *Raising my hand to get teacher help, to answer questions, or to participate in class discussions.*

Goal "Positives"	Goal "Negative"		Percent "Positives"
7/// ///	//		*8/10 = 80%*

Points Earned on IEP Goal Today   _8_

2. Returned Daily Home Note: Yes   ✔   No _____   Points Earned on Daily Home Note   _10_

3. Bus Report: Poor   ✔   Good ____ Excellent ____   Points Earned on Bus Report   _3_

Positive Classroom Behaviors	Appropriate Location	On Task, Listened, Worked Consistently, Etc.	Appropriate Langauge	Respectful of Others and Their Things	Appropriate Social Skills
Time					
8:30 to 9:00	2	0	2	2	0
9:00 to 10:00	2	2	2	2	2
11:00 to 12:00	2	0	2	2	0
12:00 to 1:00	2	2	2	2	0
1:00 to 2:00	2	0	2	2	0
2:00 to 3:00	2	2	2	2	0
3:00 to 3:30	2	2	2	2	0
Points Earned	14	8	14	14	2

Total Positive Classroom Points Earned Today	52
Total Points Earned Today	73
Total Points Spent Today	–10
Total Points Banked Today	63

or token economies are often used, although some concerns have been raised about them. These systems provide students with a specific number of points or tokens when they maintain certain behaviors or achieve certain goals. The points can be exchanged for various rewards, such as treats, school supplies, or activities that students enjoy. Furthermore, all members of special classes are well informed about behavioral and academic expectations (see Figure 9.9). One of the greatest challenges in teaching and treating students with EBD is encouraging them to generalize their newly learned knowledge and social skills to settings outside their "treatment" environments— that is, to the home, community, and workplace (Wicks-Nelson & Israel, 2006).

EasyChild is a wonderful piece of software that provides parents with excellent tools for encouraging and supporting positive behaviors in their children and students. After entering basic information about the child, parents may produce weekly behavior charts, token incentive systems, graphic summaries of performance, privileges charts, and management and encouragement-support materials. Charts and graphs are easily produced for refrigerator placement and for monitoring the child's ongoing behavior. The software also provides a means for parents to handle major incidents with advance planning, establishing appropriate rules and consequences (EasyChild Software, 2006).

In addition to behaviorally oriented interventions, students may also receive individual counseling or group and family therapy (Wicks-Nelson & Israel, 2006). Also, many children with EBD profit from carefully prescribed and monitored drug therapies and regimens; about 50% of the youth identified with behavior disorders take medications for their conditions (U.S. Department of Education, 2005; Konopasek & Forness, 2004; Wicks-Nelson & Israel, 2006). These medications help students who struggle with depression, hyperactivity, impaired attention, and mood variations. These medications may be prescribed by a psychiatrist, pediatrician, or primary-care physician.

The Adolescent Years

Individually and collectively, adolescents with EBD pose significant challenges for parents, teachers, and other care providers. These problems include violent exchanges with parents and others, delinquency, school refusal, bullying, fighting, withdrawal, and substance abuse. In the past, interventions and programs for adolescents with EBD, like those created for elementary children, were often punitive, controlling, and negative. As indicated in the previous section, the curriculum of control, or of noninstruction, predominated.

MULTIDISCIPLINARY COLLABORATION. Fortunately, perspectives are changing. Professionals in education, medicine, social work, and mental health are developing systems of care. Again, these systems of care are characterized by family-friendly, multidisciplinary collaboration (Kendziora et al., 2001; Woodruff et al., 1999). Ideally, the care is community-based, family-driven, individualized, based on strengths rather than weaknesses, sensitive to diversity, and team-based. In these systems, the knowledge and views of parents and family members are taken very seriously. These key people help design, shape, and assess intervention and transition programs (Sitlington & Neubert, 2004). If a family needs parent training, family therapy, and employment assistance, the agencies and school work together to provide these services. If the youth needs services beyond those typically delivered in a school, they are provided.

Another approach that is beginning to gather momentum is **individualized care (IC)**. IC is linked to the **wraparound approach (WRAP)** (Kendziora et al., 2001). WRAP focuses on improving the outcomes for children and adolescents with EBD through coordinated, flexible approaches to integrated, family-centered care. Rather than being served in school settings or at a mental health agency, services are delivered to children and adolescents, their parents, and families where they are needed—frequently in their homes. The case study of Seth provides powerful examples of IC and WRAP in action (see Reflect on This, "Seth: Part Three").

Increasingly, professionals, particularly teachers in concert with other support personnel and adult services, are attempting to prepare young people with EBD for employment (Bullis & Yovanoff, 2006). These programs center on developing the necessary social, academic, vocational, and self-management skills and related behaviors for successful entry-level employment. Additionally, they focus on student involvement, workplace supports, community linkages, and family participation (Benitez, Lattimore, & Wehmeyer, 2005; Carter & Lunsford, 2005).

GANGS. In the United States, youth gangs represent the largest segment of criminally active, peer-centered groups (Howell, 2003). Prominent researchers view gang affiliation as a developmental phenomenon emanating from a variety of family, neighborhood, and other

➤ **Individualized care (IC)**

Improving the outcomes for children and adolescents with EBD through coordinated, flexible approaches to integrated, family-centered care. Services are delivered to children and adolescents, their parents, and families where those services are needed, frequently in their homes.

➤ **Wraparound approach (WRAP)**

Care that provides comprehensive services to youth and their families, addressing individual and family needs through flexible approaches coordinated and orchestrated by a team of caring professionals and paraprofessionals.

➤ **Full inclusion**

The delivery of appropriate specialized services to children or adolescents with EBD or other disabilities in general education settings. These services are usually directed at improving students' social skills, developing satisfactory relationships with peers and teachers, building targeted academic skills, and improving the attitudes of peers without disabilities.

In the Thomas family's case, there is little question that the Wraparound process helped them "make it work." The element that made the most difference was that their Wraparound plan of care was truly family-driven. Connie said,

> Up until five years ago, when all of [the family advocacy] started taking place, we were in pretty sad shape, but the grant and that whole mindset of letting parents drive their program, and letting them be in the driver's seat, and you just stick in the services—that helped. Ever since then, things have been much easier, much easier. I don't feel like I'm clawing and fighting anymore. Or trying to prove that I haven't done anything wrong that's caused my kid to be this way.

The Wraparound process has helped the Thomas family meet their major life goals—to stay together at home, to keep the children at school, and to get along better with one another. Connie emphasized the progress that Seth has made.

> He has grown from someone I really thought would be institutionalized into—"he's not half bad, is he?" He's not half bad. I think with more work and I'm not sure how much emotionally he'll grow, but each year, I see a little bit more maturity.

SOURCE: Adapted from Kendziora, Bruns, Osher, Pacchiano, & Mejia (2001) *Systems of Care: Promising Practices in Children's Mental Health,* 2001 series, vol. I. Washington, DC: Center for Effective Collaboration and Practice, American Institutes for Research.

variables, some of which include nonintact families, unsafe neighborhoods, availability of and access to drugs, high community crime rates, and poor schools (Howell & Egley, 2005). As indicated earlier in this chapter, 42% of youth in correctional facilities are young people with identified EBD, who are often referred to as socially maladjusted or delinquent (Burrell & Warboys, 2000). The primary age range for gang members is 12 to 24 years of age. The peak range for gang activity and involvment is 15 to 16 years of age, and numbers are increasing at each end of the age continuum. Adolescents who are chronically delinquent or are found guilty of felony offenses (e.g., physical assault, armed robbery) present considerable challenges for parents and community members. Additionally, the proliferation of gangs in many communities poses serious problems for schools, teachers, law enforcement officers, and gang members themselves (Borg & Dalla, 2005).

Standard 7: Instructional Planning

Many youth involved in gangs mirror the characteristics and behaviors associated with conduct disorders that we discussed in the classification section of this chapter. As early as first grade, antisocial behaviors and learning failure are significant predictors of potential gang involvement. Family factors related to gang involvment include minimal or no parental support or supervision, poverty, abuse and neglect, and single or no-parent families (youth being raised by grandparents or others). Availability of drugs, unsafe neighborhoods, low-quality schools, inconsistent or negative social norms—all of these community factors contribute to gang membership and related behaviors.

Generally speaking, gang prevention, intervention, and suppression programs have not been particularly effective (Borg & Dalla, 2005; Thornberry, et al., 2003;). In part, this lack of success reflects the challenges inherent in addressing larger societal issues such as poverty, racism, and discrimination.

Gangs pose serious problems for schools, neighborhoods, and their families.

FOCUS 9

What are three goals that schools can pursue to significantly reduce the entry of youth into delinquency and related behaviors?

Council for Exceptional Children

Standard 10: Collaboration

EMERGING COLLABORATIVE APPROACHES. Endorsed by the U.S. Department of Justices's Office of Juvenile Justice and Delinquency Prevention (OJJDP), the *Comprehensive Strategy Framework* (CSF) (Howell, 2003) is a collaborative, integrated approach to delinquency prevention, suspression, and treatment. The approach is two-tiered; that is, it focuses first on preventing delinquency and intervening early when youth initially engage in delinquent acts. In this regard, schools play a major role in preventing or reducing delinquency by significantly reducing academic failure, suspensions, and dropping out. Schools that are successful in these pursuits are characterized by "supportive leadership, dedicated and collegial staff, schoolwide behavior management, and effective academic instruction" (Christle, Jolivette, & Nelson, 2005, p. 1).

If first-tier efforts are ineffective, high-quality, second-tier interventions are activated. These include involvement and activation of core social institutions in the community, family-centered care, multi-agency collaboration, use of appropriate adjudication measures and sanctions, and community-based treatment and rehabiliation services. The *comprehensive strategy framework* (CFS) is characterized as follows:

➤ It encompasses the entire juvenile justice enterprise—prevention, intervention, and suppression—in the form of graduated sanctions.

➤ Although it specifically targets serious, violent, and chronic offenders, it provides a framework for dealing with all juvenile offenders as well as at-risk children and adolescents.

➤ It calls for an integrated, multi-agency response to childhood and adolescent problems that promotes a unified effort on the part of the juvenile justice, mental health, child welfare, education, and law enforcement systems and community organizations.

➤ It links all juvenile justice system resources in an interactive manner, reflecting the belief that comprehensive juvenile justice is not a zero-sum game.

➤ It guides jurisdictions in developing response continuums that parallel offender and gang member careers, beginning with early intervention and followed by a combination of prevention and graduated sanctions. Such a continuum allows a community to organize an array of programs that corresponds to how gang member careers develop over time (Borg & Dalla, 2005, p. 358).

Increasingly, communities, agencies, and schools are embracing collaborative approaches or systems of care for preventing and treating delinquency and gang-related problems.

Inclusive Education

The term *full inclusion* is generally defined as the delivery of appropriate, specialized services to children or adolescents with EBD or other disabilities in general education settings. These services are usually directed at improving students' social skills, helping them develop satisfactory relationships with peers and teachers, building targeted academic skills, and improving the attitudes of peers without disabilities.

Another aspect of the full-inclusion movement is that some professionals have recommended elimination of the present delivery systems and variety of placement options (Kauffman et al., 2002; Kavale & Forness, 2000; Stainback & Stainback, 1992). They would be replaced by a model in which all students, regardless of disabling condition, would be educated in their neighborhood schools. These schools would serve all students with disabilities, including those with EBD; thus special schools, special classes, and other placements associated with the typical continuum of placements would no longer be available.

Despite the emphasis on inclusion, many students with EBD are served in settings separated from general education classrooms. In fact, students with EBD are far more likely to be served in special schools and separate facilities than are

Children with emotional/behavior disorders can pose challenges for general education teachers.

students with learning disabilities, mental retardation, and hearing impairments. A little more than 18% of all students identified with EBD are served in separated environments—settings removed from regular education settings (U.S. Department of Education, 2005).

Inclusion of students with EBD in general education settings should be determined ultimately by what the child or adolescent with EBD genuinely needs (Kauffman et al., 2002). These needs are established through the thoughtful deliberations of parents, professionals, and (as appropriate) the child or adolescent, via the IEP process. This process creates the basis for determining the services and supports required to address the child's or adolescent's needs, both present and anticipated. If the identified services and supports can be delivered with appropriate intensity in the general education environment without adversely affecting the learning and safety of other students, placement in this environment should occur. However, if the needs of the student cannot be successfully met in the general education setting, other placement alternatives should be explored and selected. Inclusion of students with EBD is greatly enhanced when school personnel develop schoolwide structures that support inclusion, when collaborative teaching is fostered, and when general education personnel receive targeted training, timely consultation, and appropriate in-class assistance.

Focus 10

What two factors should be considered when placing a child or youth with EBD in general education settings and related classes?

Council for Exceptional Children

Standard 9: Professional and Ethical Practice

Focus Review

FOCUS 1 Identify six essential parts of the definitions of emotional/behavioral disorders.

- The behaviors in question must be exhibited to a marked extent.
- Learning problems that are not attributable to intellectual, sensory, or health deficits are common.
- Satisfactory relationships with parents, teachers, siblings, and others are few.
- Behaviors that are considered inappropriate occur in many settings and under normal circumstances.
- Pervasive unhappiness or depression is frequently displayed by children with EBD.
- Physical symptoms or fears associated with the demands of school are common in some children.

FOCUS 2 Identify five factors that influence the ways in which we perceive the behaviors of others.

- Our personal beliefs, standards, and values
- Our tolerance for certain behaviors and our emotional fitness at the time the behaviors are exhibited
- Our perceptions of normalcy, which are often based on a personal perspective rather than on an objective standard of normalcy as established by consensus or research
- The context in which a behavior takes place
- The frequency with which the behavior occurs or its intensity

FOCUS 3 Cite three reasons why classification systems are important to professionals who identify, treat, and educate individuals with EBD.

- They provide a means of describing and identifying various types of EBD.

- They provide a common language for communicating about various types and subtypes of EBD.
- They sometimes provide a basis for treating a disorder and making predictions about treatment outcomes.

FOCUS 4 What differentiates externalizing disorders from internalizing disorders?

- Externalizing disorders involve behaviors that are directed at others (e.g., fighting, assaulting, stealing, vandalizing).
- Internalizing disorders involve behaviors that are directed inwardly, or at oneself, more than at others (e.g., fears, phobias, depression).

FOCUS 5 Identify five general characteristics (intellectual, adaptive, social, and achievement) of children and youth with EBD.

- Children and youth with EBD tend to have average to below-average IQs compared to their normal peers.
- Children and youth with EBD have difficulties in relating socially and responsibly to peers, parents, teachers, and other authority figures.
- Three out of four children with EBD show clinically significant language deficits.
- More than 40% of the youth with disabilities in correctional facilities are youngsters with identified EBD.
- Compared to other students with disabilities, students with EBD are absent more often, fail more classes, are retained more frequently, and are less successful in passing minimum-competency examinations.

FOCUS 6 What can accurately be said about the causes of EBD?

- Continuously interacting biological, genetic, cognitive, social, emotional, and cultural variables contribute to EBD.

FOCUS 7 What four important outcomes are achieved through a functional behavioral assessment?

- A complete description of all of the problem behaviors, including their intensity, their length, their frequency, and their impact

- A description of the events that seem to set off the problem behaviors

- One or more predictions about when and under what conditions the problem behaviors occur

- Identification of the "purposes" or consequences that the individual achieves by exhibiting the problem behaviors

FOCUS 8 What five guiding principles are associated with systems of care?

- Children with emotional disturbances have access to services that address physical, emotional, social, and educational needs.

- Children receive individualized services that are based on their unique needs and potentials and are guided by an individualized service plan.

- Children receive services within the least restrictive environment that is appropriate.

- Families are full participants in all aspects of the planning and delivery of services.

- Children receive integrated services with connections between child-serving agencies and programs and mechanisms for planning, developing, and coordinating services.

FOCUS 9 What are four goals that schools can pursue to significantly reduce the entry of youth into delinquency and related behaviors?

- Providing effective academic instruction

- Securing dedicated and collegial school personnel

- Implementing schoolwide positive behavior management systems

- Significantly reducing academic failure, suspensions, and dropping out

FOCUS 10 What two factors should be considered when placing a child or youth with EBD in general education settings and related classes?

- Will the services and supports be sufficently intensive to meet IEP goals and objectives?

- Will the safety and learning of other children or youth in the classroom be adversely affected?

BUILDING YOUR PORTFOLIO

If you are thinking about a career in special education, you should know that many states use national standards developed by the Council for Exceptional Children (CEC) to assess a teacher candidate's knowledge and skills for working with students with disabilities. See a complete listing of the ten CEC Content Standards on the inside front cover of this text.

CEC Standards Addressed in This Chapter

1 Foundations
2 Development and Characteristics of Learners
3 Individual Learning Differences
4 Instructional Strategies
5 Learning Environments and Social Interactions
7 Instructional Planning
8 Assessment
9 Professional and Ethical Practice
10 Collaboration

Assess Your Knowledge of CEC Standards Addressed in This Chapter

Some states require that teacher candidates develop a portfolio of products that demonstrate mastery of the CEC content standards. To assist in the development of these products for your portfolio, you may wish to complete the following activities.

- Complete a written test of the chapter's content.

  If your instructor requires a written test of your content knowledge for this chapter, keep a copy for your portfolio. A practice test on the information covered in this chapter is available through the companion website (college.hmco.com/pic/hardman9e) and the Student Study Guide.

- Respond to the Application Questions for the Case Study "Should Karl Stay at Home or Be Helped Elsewhere?"

  Review the Case Study and respond in writing to the application questions. Keep a copy of the case study and of your written response for your portfolio.

- Participate in a Community Service Learning Activity.

  Community service is a valuable way to enhance your learning experience. Visit our companion website for suggested community service learning activities that correspond to the information presented in this chapter. Develop a reflective journal of the service learning experience for your portfolio.

WEB RESOURCES

Council for Children with Behavior Disorders (CCBD)

http://www.ccbd.net

CCBD is a division of the Council for Exceptional Children. CCBD, whose members include educators, parents, mental health providers, and other professionals. It vigorously pursues quality services and programs for children and youth with EBD.

Center for Effective Collaboration and Practice (CECP)

http://cecp.air.org

CECP improves services for children and youth with EBD and helps neighborhoods and communities create schools that promote emotional well-being, effective instruction, and safe learning. The center is an integral part of the American Institutes for Research and is funded by a cooperative agreement with the Office of Special Education Programs in the U.S. Department of Education.

Center for Evidenced-Based Practice: Young Children with Challenging Behavior

http://challengingbehavior.fmhi.usf.edu/about.html

The center is supported by the U.S. Department of Education, Office of Special Education Programs. Its purpose is to increase the use of evidence-based practices in working with children with behavior disorders.

The Technical Assistance Center on Positive Behavioral Interventions and Supports (PBIS)

http://www.pbis.org/english/default.htm

PBIS was established by the Office of Special Education Programs, U.S. Department of Education, to give schools technical assistance in identifying, adapting, and sustaining effective schoolwide disciplinary programs.

National Association of School Psychologists

http://www.naspcenter.org/

This association promotes promising and data-driven practices in education and mental health for children, youth, and their families, capitalizing on family strengths, supporting diversity, and sustaining families.

The National Alliance for the Mentally Ill (NAMI)

http://www.nami.org/

NAMI is an advocacy organization of individuals who are interested in people with severe mental illnesses, such as schizophrenia, major depression, bipolar disorder, obsessive-compulsive disorder, and anxiety disorders.

FURTHER READINGS

Bell, D. J., Foster, S. L., & Mash, E. J. (Eds.) (2005). *Handbook of Behavioral and Emotional Problems in Girls*. New York: Kluwer Academic/Plenum Publishers.

These authors have assembled an interesting and timely collection of chapters about behavior problems in girls. Topics include mood disorders, attention-deficit/hyperactivity disorder, substance abuse, aggresssion and antisocial behaviors, homelessness, and other conditions.

Gullatta, T. P., & Adams, R. A. (Eds.) (2005). *Handbook of Adolescent Behavioral Problems: Evidence-Based Approaches to Prevention and Treatment*. New York: Springer.

This handbook presents the work of talented scholars who address evidence-based approaches to preventing and treating depression, eating disorders, obesity, suicide, substance abuse, and other behavior disorders.

Wicks-Nelson, R., & Israel, A. C. (2006). *Behavior Disorders of Childhood* (5th ed.). Upper Saddle River, NJ: Prentice-Hall.

This book presents a comprehensive, in-depth view of behavior disorders in children and youth. It is replete with research findings, interesting case studies, and illustrative materials that are engaging and informative.

Davis, D. L. (2004). *Your Angry Child: A Guide for Parents*. New York: The Haworth Press.

This is a very readeable book for parents who are interested in helping the child who seems to be very angry and out of control. Practical suggestions are provided for connecting with angry children and teenagers and building more functional behaviors.

Lock, J., & Le Grange, D. (2005). *Help Your Teenager Beat an Eating Disorder*. New York: Guilford Press.

This is a very useful book for parents or teachers who are interested in assisting a youth with an eating disorder. A number of helpful suggestions and strategies are provided for giving support to youth who struggle with these disorders.

COMPANION WEBSITE

Visit the companion website at college.hmco.com/pic/hardman9e for additional resources that support this text:

- HM Video Cases that present actual classroom scenarios that you may face every day as a teacher

- Practice ACE Exams that will help you prepare for quizzes, tests, and certification exams
- Flashcards of key terms
- Weblinks

10 Intellectual Disabilities

TO BEGIN WITH . . .

PROMOTING SELF-DETERMINATION AND SELF-ADVOCACY

Change that fosters self-determination, self-advocacy and social freedom is limited. Most laws and judicial decisions recognize these concepts but do not provide for their enforcement. More than 100,000 people with intellectual and developmental disabilities remain institutionalized in the United States. Many others, while not institutionalized, have little control over where, with whom, and how they live in their communities. Large numbers of these people want opportunities to contribute to their communities through useful part-time employment. Tens of thousands of individuals and their families have no access to basic services that would offer, at the least, a modicum of control over their lives. (Lakin, 2005, p. 11–12)

I HEAR THE MUSIC THAT IS THOMAS

Retard! My ninth-grade students toss this word around as if its meaning is clear . . . someone who is slow and stupid. "You retard!" Sometimes I quietly ask them not to call one another names. But some days I feel like making a point, so I just quietly mention that my youngest son, Thomas, is retarded [has intellectual disabilities]. Their faces reveal embarrassment, and I wonder if they know the musical meaning of the word. I hear the music that is Thomas—slow down to a different pace . . . ritard. (Corum, 2003, D1)

TROY DANIEL'S CLASS GRADUATION SPEECH

Troy Daniels, a young man with Down syndrome who uses a wheelchair, was selected to stand before the graduating class at Northfield High School in Vermont and deliver the senior speech. Here is an excerpt:

> Not long ago people with disabilities could not go to school with other kids, they had to go to special schools. They could not have real friends; they call people like me "retard." That breaks my heart. . . . The law says that I can come to school but no law can make me have friends. But then some kids started to think that I was okay, first just one or two kids were nice to me. . . . Others started to hang out with me and they found out we could be friends. I cared about them and they cared about me. . . . I want all people to know and see that these students I call my friends are the real teachers of life. (Troy Daniels, personal communication, 2003)

THE KEYS ARE MINE!

When I lived at Lake Owasso State Institution in Minnesota, you had to ask for everything. Can you let me out? Can I have a can of pop? Can I stay up a little longer? When I moved into a group home, I had to follow all of the rules. I had to go to bed at a certain time, and when I was in bed, I had to be asleep; that was that. Two years ago I got married. My wife and I moved into our own apartment. Now that I have my own place, I make my own decisions. I have my own keys. I can let myself out, and let myself back in. Now I can come and go when I want. I can make my own food, and I decide whether I want to have breakfast or lunch. My wife and I decide when the staff come over. They help us with some things but we make our own decisions. (Otley, 2006, p. 24)

1. Identify the major components of the AAIDD definition of intellectual disabilities.

2. Identify four approaches to classifying people with intellectual disabilities.

3. What is the prevalence of intellectual disabilities?

4. Identify intellectual, self-regulation, and adaptive skills characteristics of individuals with intellectual disabilities.

5. Identify the academic, motivational, speech and language, and physical characteristics of children with intellectual disabilities.

6. Identify the causes of intellectual disabilities.

7. Why are early intervention services for children with intellectual disabilities so important?

8. Identify five skill areas that should be addressed in programs for elementary-age children with intellectual disabilities.

9. Identify four educational goals for adolescents with intellectual disabilities.

10. Why is the inclusion of students with intellectual disabilities in general education settings important to an appropriate educational experience?

▼SNAPSHOT

LILLY

Lilly is an 8-year-old with mental retardation. When she was adopted at the age of 2, her new parents were told she would never talk and might not walk. Through the untiring efforts of her family during the early childhood years, Lilly is able to say some words and use short sentences that are understood by her family and friends. She can now walk without support. Lilly's greatest challenge, according to her mother, is to stay focused. If directed step by step, Lilly is capable of participating in family activities and helping out around the house. Her brother Josh is always there for Lilly, helping her with homework, reading to her, and helping her get dressed in the morning.

At school, Lilly spends part of her day in a classroom with other students who also have mental retardation and part of the day in a general education class with second grade students without disabilities. While in the special education classroom, Lilly works with peer tutors from the sixth grade general education class to help her with schoolwork. Her two peer tutors, Nita and Amy, work with Lilly on using the computer to better develop her communication skills. A computer is a wonderful tool for Lilly because all she has to do is learn to hit the right buttons on the Touch Talker program to communicate with family, friends, and teachers. Lilly's second grade teacher, Mrs. Roberts, describes Lilly as one of the most popular students in her class. The second grade students love her "neat talking machine." When in the second grade class,

Lilly participates in learning centers where she is paired up with students without disabilities working on a variety of activities.

Lilly's mother and teachers are optimistic about her future. The special education teacher hopes that Lilly will be able to go to her neighborhood school next year and spend even more time with "typical" students of her own age. "And from there, with her great social skills and her persistence, I see her as being independent in the future, working in a job setting."

ROGER

Roger is 19 years old and lives at home with his parents. During the day, he attends high school and works in a local toy company on a small work crew with five other individuals who also have disabilities. Roger and his working colleagues are supervised by a job coach. Roger assembles small toys and is learning how to operate power tools for wood- and metal-cutting tasks. His wages are not enough to allow Roger to be financially independent, so he will probably always need some financial support from his family or society.

Roger is capable of caring for his own physical needs. He has learned to dress and feed himself and understands the importance of personal care. He can communicate many of his needs and desires verbally but is limited in his ability to participate in social conversations, such as discussing the weather or what's new at the movies. Roger has never learned to read, and his leisure hours are spent watching television, listening to the radio, and visiting with friends.

BECKY

Becky is a 6-year-old who has significant delays in intellectual, language, and motor development. These developmental differences have been evident from very early in her life. Her mother experienced a long, unusually difficult labor, and Becky endured severe dips in heart rate; at times, her heart rate was undetectable. During delivery, Becky suffered from birth asphyxiation and epileptic seizures. The attending physician described her as flaccid (soft and limp), with abnormal muscle reflexes. Becky has not yet learned to walk, is not toilet trained, and has no means of communication with others in her environment. She lives at home and attends a local elementary school during the day.

Her education program includes work with therapists to develop her gross motor abilities in order to improve her mobility. Speech and language specialists are examining the possibility of teaching her several alternative forms of communication (e.g., a language board or manual communication system) because Becky has not developed any verbal skills. The special education staff is focusing on decreasing Becky's dependence on others by teaching some basic self-care skills such as eating, toileting, and grooming. The professional staff does not know what the ultimate long-term impact of their intervention will be, but they do know that although Becky is a child with severe mental retardation, *she is learning.*

This chapter discusses people whose intellectual and social capabilities may differ significantly from the average. Their growth and development depend on the educational, social, and medical supports made available throughout life. Lilly from the opening Snapshot is a child with intellectual disabilities who has a wonderful support network of family, friends, and teachers. As she grows older, she may achieve at least partial independence economically and socially within her community. Most likely, Lilly will continue to need some assistance from family, friends, and government programs to help her adjust to adult life.

Roger has completed school and is just beginning life as an adult in his community. Roger is a person with moderate **intellectual disabilities**. Although he will probably require continuing support on his job, he is earning wages that contribute to his success and independence as an adult. Within a few years, Roger will most likely move away from his family and into a supported living arrangement, such as a house or apartment of his own.

Becky has severe intellectual disabilities. Although the long-term prognosis is unknown, she has many opportunities for learning and development that were not available until recently. Through a positive home environment and a school program that supports her learning and applying skills in natural settings, Becky can reach a level of development that was once considered impossible.

Lilly, Roger, and Becky are people with intellectual disabilities (historically referred to as *mental retardation*), but they are not necessarily representative of the wide range of people who are characterized as having intellectual disabilities. A 6-year-old child described as having mild intellectual disabiliteis may be no more than one or two years behind in the development of academic and social skills. Many children with mild intellectual disabilities are not identified until they enter elementary school at age 5 or 6, because they may not exhibit physical or learning delays that are readily identifiable during the early childhood years. As these children enter school, developmental delays become more apparent. During early primary grades, it is not uncommon for the cognitivie and social differences of children with intellectual disabilities to be attributed to immaturity. However, within a few years, educators generally recognize the need for specialized services to support the child's development in the natural settings of school, neighborhood, and home.

People with moderate to severe intellectual disabilities have challenges that transcend the classroom. Some have significant multiple disabling conditions, including sensory, physical, and emotional problems. People with moderate intellectual disabilities are capable of learning adaptive skills that allow a degree of independence, with ongoing support. These skills include the abilities to dress and feed themselves, to meet their own personal care and health needs, and to develop safety skills that enable them to move without fear wherever they go. These individuals have some means of communication. Most can develop spoken language skills, but some may be able to learn only manual communication (signing). Their social interaction skills are limited, however, which makes it a challenge for for them to relate spontaneously to others.

People with profound intellectual disabilities often depend on others to maintain even their most basic life functions, including eating, toileting, and dressing. They may not be capable of self-care and often do not develop functional communication skills. This does not mean that education and treatment beyond routine care and maintenance are not beneficial. The nature of these disabilities is the primary reason why such individuals were excluded from the public schools for so long. Exclusion was often justified on the basis that schools did not have the resources, facilities, or trained personnel to deal with the needs of students who functioned at lower levels.

Definitions and Classification

People with intellectual disabilities have been studied for centuries, by a variety of professional disciplines. They are often stereotyped as a homogeneous group of individuals—"the retarded"—with similar physical characteristics and learning capabilities. Nothing could be further from the truth. In fact, intellectual disabilities encompass a broad range of functioning levels and learning capabilities.

Standard 1: Foundations

Evolving Terminology

Varying perspectives exist on the use of the term *intellectual disabilities*. In the United States, *mental retardation* was in use for most of the 20th century and into the early 21st century, although this term is no longer widely accepted. Many individuals, family members, and professionals questioned the continued use of the term *mental retardation*. As suggested by Warren (2002), "[the term *mental retardation*] has been attacked as promoting stigma and negative stereotyping" (p. 1). In 2006, members of the **American Association on Mental Retardation (AAMR)**, the most widely known professional association in the United States whose mission is progressive policies, sound research, effective practices, and universal human rights, officially changed its name to the **American Association on Intellectual and Developmental Disabilities (AAIDD)**. Herein, for purposes of our discussion, we will refer to this organization as AAIDD, while inserting AAMR in parentheses when appropriate.

➤ **American Association on Mental Retardation (AAMR)**

An organization of professionals from many disciplines involved in the study and treatment of intellectual disabilities. In 2006, the organization changed its name to the American Asssociation on Intellectual and Developmental Disabilities.

➤ **American Association on Intellectual and Developmental Disabiities (AAIDD)**

See *American Association on Mental Retardation*

Definition

The most widely accepted definition of intellectual disabilities is that of the AAIDD:

> Intellectual disability [is] characterized by significant limitations both in intellectual functioning and in adaptive behavior as expressed in conceptual, social and practical adaptive skills. This disability originates before age 18. (AAIDD [AAMR], 2002, p. 1)

The AAIDD definition has evolved through years of effort to more clearly reflect the ever-changing perception of intellectual disabilities. Historically, definitions of mental retardation (now referred to as intellectual disabilities) were based solely on the measurement of intellect, emphasizing routine care and maintenance rather than treatment and education. In recent years, the concept of adaptive behavior has played an increasingly important role in defining and classifying people with intellectual disabilities.

In the next section, we address six major dimensions of the AAIDD definition: (a) intellectual abilities, (b) adaptive behavior, (c) participation, interactions, and social roles, (d) health, (e) environmental context, and (f) age of onset.

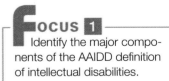

FOCUS **1**
Identify the major components of the AAIDD definition of intellectual disabilities.

INTELLECTUAL ABILITIES. Intellectual abilities include reasoning, planning, solving problems, thinking abstractly, comprehending complex ideas, learning quickly, and learning from experience (AAIDD [AAMR], 2002). They are assessed by a standardized intelligence test where a person's score is compared to the average of other people who have taken the same test (referred to as a *normative sample*). The statistical average for an intelligence test is generally set at 100. We state this by saying that the person has an intelligence quotient (IQ) of 100. Psy-

➤ **Intellectual abilities**

A person's ability to reason, plan, solve problems, think abstractly, comprehend complex ideas, learn quickly, and learn from experience.

➤ Standard deviation

A statistical measure of the amount that an individual score deviates from the average.

➤ Adaptive behavior

A collection of conceptual, social, and practical skills that people have learned in order to function in their everyday lives.

Standard 2: Development and Characteristics of Learners

chologists use a mathematical concept called the **standard deviation** to determine the extent to which any given individual's score deviates from this average of 100. An individual who scores more than two standard deviations below 100 on an intelligence test meets AAIDD's definition of subaverage general intellectual functioning. This means that people with IQs of approximately 70 to 75 and lower would be considered as having intellectual disabilities.

ADAPTIVE BEHAVIOR. AAIDD defines **adaptive behavior** as a collection of conceptual, social, and practical skills that "have been learned by people in order to function in their everyday lives" (p. 41). (Figure 10.1 provides several examples of adaptive behavior.) If a person has limitations in these adaptive skills, he or she may need some additional assistance or supports in order to participate more fully in both family and community life. Consider Becky from the chapter-opening Snapshot. She has significant limitations in her adaptive skills. She is unable to walk or take care of her basic needs (practical skills). And at 6 years old, she has limited means of communicating with others (conceptual skills).

As is true with intelligence, adaptive skills also may be measured by standardized tests. These tests, most often referred to as *adaptive behavior scales*, generally use structured interviews or direct observations to obtain information. Adaptive behavior scales measure the individual's ability to take care of personal needs (such as hygiene) and to relate appropriately to others in social situations. Adaptive skills may also be assessed through informal appraisal, such as observations by family members or professionals who are familiar with the individual, or through anecdotal records.

PARTICIPATION, INTERACTION, AND SOCIAL ROLES. AAMR emphasizes the importance of a positive environment for fostering growth, development, and individual well-being. Thus a person's participation and interaction within the environment are indicators of adaptive functioning. The more an individual engages in valued activities, the more likely that an "adaptive fit" exists between the person and his or her environment. (See Chapter 2 for information about the concept of "adaptive fit.") Valued activities may include an appropriate education, living arrangements, employment settings, and community participation.

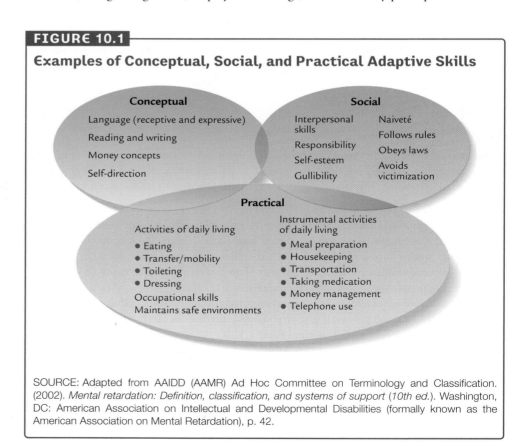

FIGURE 10.1

Examples of Conceptual, Social, and Practical Adaptive Skills

Conceptual
- Language (receptive and expressive)
- Reading and writing
- Money concepts
- Self-direction

Social
- Interpersonal skills
- Responsibility
- Self-esteem
- Gullibility
- Naiveté
- Follows rules
- Obeys laws
- Avoids victimization

Practical

Activities of daily living
- Eating
- Transfer/mobility
- Toileting
- Dressing
Occupational skills
Maintains safe environments

Instrumental activities of daily living
- Meal preparation
- Housekeeping
- Transportation
- Taking medication
- Money management
- Telephone use

SOURCE: Adapted from AAIDD (AAMR) Ad Hoc Committee on Terminology and Classification. (2002). *Mental retardation: Definition, classification, and systems of support* (*10th ed.*). Washington, DC: American Association on Intellectual and Developmental Disabilities (formally known as the American Association on Mental Retardation), p. 42.

The concept of participation in valued activities was introduced by Bengt Nirje from Sweden over three decades ago through the **principle of normalization.** This principle emphasizes the need to make available to the person with intellectual disabilities "the patterns and conditions of everyday life which are as close to the norms and patterns of mainstream society" as possible (Nirje, 1970, p. 181). Normalization goes far beyond the mere physical inclusion of the individual in a community. It also promotes the availability of needed supports, such as training and supervision, without which the individual with intellectual disabilities may not be prepared to cope with the demands of community life.

Learning and applying adaptive skills in a community work setting contributes to the individual's independence and is consistent with the principle of normalization.

PHYSICAL AND MENTAL HEALTH. The physical and mental health of an individual influences his or her overall intellectual and adaptive functioning. AAIDD indicates that the functioning level for people with intellectual disabilities is signficantly affected (facilitated or inhibited) by the effects of physical and mental health. "Some individuals [with intellectual disabilities] enjoy robust good health with no significant activity limitations. . . . On the other hand, some individuals have a variety of significant health limitations, such as epilepsy or cerebral palsy, that greatly impair body functioning and severely restrict personal activities and social participation" (p. 45).

ENVIRONMENTAL CONTEXT. As defined by AAIDD, *context* is the term for the interrelated conditions in which people live their lives. It is based on an environmental perspective with three different levels: (a) the immediate social setting that includes the person and her or his family, (b) the broader neighborhood, community, or organizations that provide services and supports (such as public education), and (c) the overarching patterns of culture and society. The various levels are important to people with mental intellectual disabilities because they provide differing opportunities and can foster well-being.

AGE OF ONSET. The AAIDD defines the age of onset for intellectual disabilities as prior to 18 years. The reason for choosing age 18 as a cutoff point is that intellectual disabilities belong to a family of conditions referred to as **developmental disabilities**. Developmental disabilities are mental and/or physical impairments that are diagnosed at birth or during the childhood and adolescent years. A developmental disability results in substantial functional limitations in at least three areas of major life activity (such areas include self-care, language, learning, mobility, self-direction, capacity for independent living, and economic self-sufficiency).

PUTTING THE DEFINITION INTO PRACTICE. Based on the dimensions described above, AAIDD cites five criteria that professionals should apply as they put the definition into practice.

1. Limitations in a person's present funtioning must be considered within the context of community environments typical of the individual's age, peers, and culture.

2. Valid assessment considers cultural and linguistic diversity as well as differences in communication, sensory, motor, and behavioral factors.

3. Within an individual, limitations often coexist with strengths.

4. An important purpose of describing limitations is to develop a profile of needed supports.

5. With appropriate personalized supports over a sustained period, the life functioning of the person with [intellectual disabilities] generally will improve. (AAIDD [AAMR], 2002)

➤ **Principle of normalization**

Making the patterns and conditions of everyday life and of mainstream society available to persons with disabilities.

➤ **Developmental disabilities**

Mental and/or physical impairments that are diagnosed at birth or during the childhood and adolescent years. Result in substantial functional limitations in at least three areas of major life activity (e.g., self-care, language, learning, mobility, self-direction, capacity for independent living, or economic self-sufficiency).

Focus **2**
Identify four approaches to classifying people with intellectual disabilities.

➤ **Assistive technology**
Technology devices that help an individual with disabilities adapt to the natural settings of home, school, and family. The technology may include computers, hearing aids, wheelchairs, and so on.

Classification

To more clearly understand the diversity of people with intellectual disabilities, several classification systems have been developed. Each classification method reflects an attempt by a particular discipline (such as medicine or education) to better understand and respond to the needs of individuals with intellectual disabilities. Here are four of these methods.

SEVERITY OF THE CONDITION. The extent to which a person's intellectual capabilities and adaptive skills differ from what is considered "normal" can be described by using terms such as *mild, moderate, severe,* or *profound. Mild* describes the highest level of performance; *profound* describes the lowest level. Distinctions between severity levels associated with intellectual disabilities are determined by scores on intelligence tests and by limitations in adaptive skills.

A person's adaptive skills can also be categorized by severity. Adaptive skill limitations can be described in terms of the degree to which an individual's performance differs from what is expected for his or her chronological age. Let's look at Lilly, Roger, and Becky from our opening Snapshot. As an 8-year-old, Lilly has learned some of the self-care skills required for a child of her age, and although her socialization and communication skills are below what is expected, she is able to interact with others successfully through the use of **assistive technology**. Roger, at age 19, has developed many skills that allow him to live successfully in his own community with some supervision and support. It took longer for Roger to learn to dress and feed himself than it did for Lilly, but he has learned these skills. Although his verbal communication skills are somewhat rudimentary, he is capable of communicating basic needs and desires. Becky is a child with severe to profound intellectual disabilities. At age 6, her development is significantly delayed in nearly every area. However, it is clear that with appropriate intervention, she is learning.

EDUCABILITY EXPECTATIONS. To distinguish among the diverse needs of students with intellectual disabilities, the field of education developed its own classification system. As implied by the word *expectatons,* students with intellectual disabilities have been classified according to how well they are expected to achieve in a classroom situation. The specific descriptors used vary greatly from state to state, but they most often indicate an approximate IQ range, and a statement of predicted achievement:

Educable (IQ 55 to about 70). Second- to fifth-grade achievement in school academic areas. Social adjustment skills will result in independence with intermittent or limited support in the community. Partial or total self-support in a paid community job is a strong possibility.

Trainable (IQ 40 to 55). Learning primarily in the area of self-care skills; some achievement in functional academics. A range of more extensive support will be needed to help the student adapt to community environments. Opportunities for paid work include supported employment in a community job.

The classification criterion for educability expectation was originally developed to determine who would be able to benefit from school and who would not. The term *educable* implied that the child could cope with at least some of the academic demands of the classroom, meaning that the child could learn basic reading, writing, and arithmetic skills. The term *trainable* indicated that the student was not educable and was capable only of being trained in settings outside the public school. In fact, until the passage of PL 94–142 in 1975 (now IDEA), many children who were labeled trainable could not get a free public education. In some school systems, the terms *educable* and *trainable* have been replaced by symptom-severity classifications (mild through severe intellectual disabilities).

MEDICAL DESCRIPTORS. Intellectual disabilities may be classified on the basis of the biological origin of the condition. A classification system that uses the cause of the condition to differentiate people with intellectual disabilities is often referred to as a *medical classification* system because it emerged primarily from the field of medicine. Common medical descriptors include fetal alcohol syndrome, chromosomal abnormalities (e.g., Down syndrome), metabolic disorders (e.g., phenylketonuria, thyroid dysfunction), and infections (e.g., syphilis, rubella). These medical conditions will be discussed more thoroughly in the section on causation.

CLASSIFICATION BASED ON NEEDED SUPPORT. AAIDD uses a classification system based on the type and extent of the support that the individual requires to function in the natural settings of home and community. AAIDD recommends four levels of support:

- ➤ *Intermittent.* Supports are provided on an "as-needed basis." These supports may be (1) episodic—that is, the person does not always need assistance; or (2) short-term, occurring during lifespan transitions (e.g., job loss or acute medical crisis). Intermittent supports may be of high or low intensity.

- ➤ *Limited.* Supports are characterized by consistency; the time required may be limited, but the need is not intermittent. Fewer staff may be required, and costs may be lower than those associated with more intensive levels of support (examples include time-limited employment training and supports during transition from school to adulthood).

- ➤ *Extensive.* Supports are characterized by regular involvement (e.g., daily) in at least some environments, such as work or home; supports are not time-limited (e.g., long-term job and home-living support will be necessary).

- ➤ *Pervasive.* Supports must be constant and of high intensity. They have to be provided across multiple environments and may be life-sustaining in nature. Pervasive supports typically involve more staff and are more intrusive than extensive or time-limited supports.

The AAIDD's emphasis on classifying people with intellectual disabilities on the basis of needed support is an important departure from the more restrictive perspectives of the traditional approaches. Supports may be described not only in terms of the level of assistance needed, but also by type—that is, as formal or natural support systems. Formal supports may be funded through government programs, such as income maintenance, health care, education, housing, or employment. Another type of formal support is the advocacy organization (e.g., **ARC, A National Organization of and for People with Intellectual and Related Developmental Disabilities**) that lobbies on behalf of people with intellectual disabilities for improved and expanded services, as well as giving family members a place to interact and support one another. **Natural supports** differ from formal supports in that they are provided not by agencies or organizations, but by the nuclear and extended family members, friends, or neighbors. Natural supports are often more effective than formal supports in helping people with intellectual disabilities access and participate in a community setting. Research suggests that adults with intellectual disabililities who are successfully employed following school find more jobs through their natural support network of friends and family than through formal support systems (McDonnell, Hardman, & McDonnell, 2003).

> School and community programs are moving away from pejorative classification categories (such as "trainable" and "custodial") to descriptions of the individual based on type and extent of support needed to function in natural settings.

> ➤ **ARC, A National Organization of and for People with Intellectual and Related Developmental Disabilities**
>
> A national organization of and for people with intellectual and related developmental disabilities, their parents, their friends, and professionals who assist them. The Arc works to enhance the quality of life for people with intellectual disabilities in family, school, and community settings.

> ➤ **Natural supports**
>
> Supports for people with disabilities that are provided by family, friends, and peers.

Prevalence

The U.S. Department of Education (2006) reported that 591,440 students between the ages of 6 and 21 were labeled as having intellectual disabilities (mental retardation) and receiving service under IDEA. Approximately 10% of all students with disabilities between the ages of 6 and 21 have intellectual disabilities. Overall, students with intellectual disabilities constitute about 0.88% of the total school population (see Figure 10.2).

Based on an intelligence test score of 70 or lower, people with intellectual disabilities would constitute about 3% of the total population, or about 6.6 million people in the United

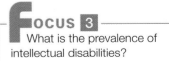

FOCUS 3
What is the prevalence of intellectual disabilities?

FIGURE 10.2

Prevalence of Intellectual Disabilities

1%
with mental
retardation

10% with
moderate,
severe, or
profound
mental
retardation

90% with mild
mental retardation

**Total School-Age
Population**

**School Population
with Mental Retardation**

SOURCE: U.S. Department of Education. (2006). To Assure the Free Appropriate Public Education of All Children with Disabilities. *Twenty-sixth Annual Report to Congress on the Implementation of the Individuals with Disabilities Education Act.* Washington, DC: U.S. Government Printing Office.

States. The President's Committee for People with Intellectual Disabilities (2006) estimates that approximately seven to eight million Americans of all ages have intellectual disabilities. Intellectual disabilities affect about one in ten families in the United States. Note that we are able only to estimate prevalence, because no one has actually counted the number of people with intellectual disabilities.

Characteristics

In this section, we examine the many characteristics of people with intellectual disabilities that can affect their academic learning, as well as their ability to adapt to home, school, and community environments.

Learning and Memory

Intelligence is the ability to acquire, remember, and use knowledge. A primary characteristic of intellectual disabilities is diminished intellectual ability that translates into a difference in the rate and efficiency with which the person acquires, remembers, and uses new knowledge, compared to the general population.

The learning and memory capabilities of people with intellectual disabilities are significantly below average in comparison to peers without disabilities. Children with intellectual disabilities, as a group, are less able to grasp abstract, as opposed to concrete, concepts. Accordingly, they benefit from instruction that is meaningful and useful, and they learn more from contact with real objects than they do from representations or symbols.

Intelligence is also associated with learning how to learn and with the ability to apply what is learned to new experiences. This process is known as establishing learning sets and generalizing them to new situations. Children and adults with intellectual disabilities develop learning sets at a slower pace than peers without disabilities, and they are deficient in relating information to new situations (Beirne-Smith, Patton, & Kim, 2006). **Generalization** happens "when a child appplies previously learned content or skills to a situation in which the information has not been taught (Drew & Hardman, 2007). The greater the severity of intellectual deficit, the

---

Focus 4
Identify intellectual, self regulation, and adaptive skills characteristics of individuals with intellectual disabilities.

Council for Exceptional Children

Standard 2: Development and Characteristics of Learners

➤ **Generalization**

The process of applying previously learned information to new settings or situations.

greater the difficulties with memory. Memory problems in children with intellectual disabilities have been attributed to several factors. People with intellectual disabilities have trouble focusing on relevant stimuli in learning and in real-life situations, sometimes attending to the wrong things (Kittler, Krinsky-McHall, & Devenny, 2004; Westling & Fox, 2004).

Self-Regulation

People with intellectual disabilities do not appear to develop efficient learning strategies, such as the ability to rehearse a task (to practice a new concept, either out loud or to themselves, over and over). The ability to rehearse a task is related to a broad concept known as **self-regulation**, or the ability to mediate or regulate one's own behavior (Shonkoff & Phillips, 2000). Whereas most people will rehearse to try to remember, it does not appear that individuals with intellectual disabilities are able to apply this skill.

Some researchers have begun to focus on **information-processing theories** to better understand learning differences in people with intellectual disabilities. Information-processing theorists study how a person processes information from sensory stimuli to motoric output (Sternberg, 2003). In information-processing theory, the learning differences in people with intellectual disabilities are seen as the underdevelopment of metacognitive processes. Metacognitive processes help the person plan how to solve a problem. First, the person decides which strategy he or she thinks will solve a problem. Then the strategy is implemented. During implementation, the person monitors whether the strategy is working and makes any adaptions necessary. Finally, the results of the strategy are evaluated in terms of whether the problem has been solved and how the strategy could be used in other situations (Sternberg, 2003). Even though children with intellectual disabilities may be unable to use the best strategy when confronted with new learning situations, they can be taught ways to do so.

> **➤ Self-regulation**
> The ability to regulate one's own behavior.

> **➤ Information-processing theories**
> Theories on how a person processes information from sensory stimuli to motor output.

Adaptive Skills

The abilities to adapt to the demands of the environment, relate to others, and take care of personal needs are all important aspects of an independent lifestyle. In the school setting, adaptive behavior is defined as the ability to apply skills learned in a classroom to daily activities in natural settings.

The adaptive skills of people with intellectual disabilities are often not comparable to those of their peers without disabilities. A child with intellectual disabilities may have difficulty in both learning and applying skills for a number of reasons, including a higher level of distractibility, inattentiveness, failure to read social cues, and impulsive behavior. Thus these children will need to be taught appropriate reasoning, judgment, and social skills that lead to more positive social relationships and personal competence. Adaptive skill differences for people with intellectual disabilities may also be associated with a lower self-image and a greater expectancy for failure in both academic and social situations. Lee, Yoo, and Bak (2003) investigated the quality of social relationships among children with mild intellectual disabilities and peers who were not disabled and found that the children without disabilities did perceive their classmates with intellectual disabilities as friends. However, they had concerns that limitations in communication and some behavior problems made it difficult to maintain a friendship with a child who had an intellectual disability.

Academic Achievement

Research on the academic achievement of children with mild to moderate intellectual disabilities has suggested that they will experience significant delays in the areas of literacy and mathematics. Reading comprehension is usually considered the weakest area of learning. In general, students with mild intellectual disabilities are better at decoding words than comprehending their meaning (Drew & Hardman, 2007) and read below their own mental-age level (Katims, 2000).

Children with intellectual disabilities also perform poorly on mathematical computations, although their performance may be closer to what is typical for their mental age. These children may be able to learn basic computations but may be unable to apply concepts appropriately in a problem-solving situation (Beirne-Smith et al., 2006).

A growing body of research has indicated that children with moderate or severe intellectual disabilities can be taught academics as a means to gain information, participate in social set-

FOCUS 5
Identify the academic, motivational, speech and language, and physical characteristics of children with intellectual disabilities.

The academic performance of children with intellectual disabilities varies greatly, depending on the level of intellectual ability and adaptive skills. Many children with mild intellectual disabilities may learn to read, though at a slower rate, whereas those with moderate intellectual disabilities benefit from a functional academic program.

tings, increase their orientation and mobility, and make choices (Browder, Ahlgrim-Delzell, Courtade-Little, & Snell, 2006). Reading helps students develop a useful vocabulary that will facilitate their inclusion in school and community settings (Browder, et al., 2006). These children may be able to recognize their names and those of significant others in their lives, as well as common survival words, including *help, hurt, danger*, and *stop*. Math assists students in learning such skills as how to tell time, add and subtract small sums to manage finances (such as balancing a checkbook), and appropriately exchange money for products in community settings (e.g., grocery stores, movie theaters, and vending machines).

Motivation

People with intellectual disabilities are often described as lacking motivation, or outer-directed behavior. They may seem unwilling or unable to complete tasks, take responsibility, and be self-directed. Although people with intellectual disabilities may appear to be less motivated than their peers without disabilities, such behavior may be attributable to the way they have learned to avoid certain situations because of a fear of failure. A child with intellectual disabilities may have a history of failure, particularly in school, and may be afraid to take risks or participate in new situations. The result of failure is often **learned helplessness**—"No matter what I do or how hard I try, I will not succeed." To overcome a child's feelings of learned helplessness, professionals and family members should focus on providing experiences that have high probabilities for success. The opportunity to strive for success, rather than to avoid failure, is a very important learning experience for these children.

Speech and Language

One of the most serious and obvious characteristics of individuals with intellectual disabilities is delayed speech and language development. The most common speech difficulties involve **articulation problems, voice problems**, and **stuttering**. Language problems are generally associated with delays in language development rather than with a bizarre use of language (Beirne-Smith et al., 2006; Moore-Brown & Montomery, 2006). Kaiser (2000) emphasized that "the overriding goal of language intervention is to increase the functional communication of students" (p. 457).

There is considerable variation in the language skills of people with intellectual disabilities. In general, the severity of the speech and language problems is positively correlated with the cause and severity of the intellectual disabilities: the milder the intellectual disabilities, the less pervasive the language difficulty (Moore-Brown & Montgomery, 2006). Speech and language difficulties may range from minor speech defects, such as articulation problems, to the complete absence of expressive language. Speech and language pathologists are able to correct minor speech differences for most students with intellectual disabilities.

➤ **Learned helplessness**

Refusal or unwillingness to take on new tasks or challenges, resulting from repeated failures or control by others.

➤ **Articulation problems**

Speech problems such as omissions, substitutions, additions, and distortions of words.

➤ **Voice problems**

Abnormal acoustical qualities in a person's speech.

➤ **Stuttering**

A speech problem involving abnormal repetitions, prolongations, and hesitations as one speaks.

TABLE 10.1

Speech and Language Skills for People with Moderate to Profound Intellectual Disabilities

SEVERITY OF MENTAL RETARDATION

Moderate	Severe	Profound
Most individuals have delays or deviations in speech and language skills, but many develop language abilities that make possible some level of communication with others.	Individuals exhibit significant speech and language delays and deviations (such as lack of expressive and receptive language, articulation difficulties, and little, if any, spontaneous interaction).	Individuals do not exhibit spontaneous communication patterns. Echolalic speech, speech out of context, and purposeless speech may be evident.

Intellectual disabilities may cause speech problems, but some speech difficulties (such as **echolalia**) may also directly contribute to the severity of the intellectual disabilities. Table 10.1 describes the range of speech and language skills for people with moderate to profound intellectual disabilities.

➤ Echolalia

A meaningless repetition or imitation of words that have been spoken.

Physical Development

The physical appearance of most children with intellectual disabilities does not differ from that of same-age children who are not disabled. However, a relationship exists between the severity of the intellectual disabilities and the extent of physical differences for the individual (Drew & Hardman, 2007; Horvat, 2000). For the person with severe intellectual disabilities, there is a significant probability of related physical problems; genetic factors are likely to under lie both disabilities. The individual with mild intellectual disabilities, in contrast, may exhibit no physical differences because the intellectual disabilities may be associated with environmental, not genetic, factors. Table 10.2 describes the range of physical characteristics associated with individuals who have moderate to profound intellectual disabilities.

The majority of children with severe and profound intellectual disabilities have multiple disabilities that affect nearly every aspect of intellectual and physical development (Westling &

TABLE 10.2

Physical Characteristics of People with Moderate to Profound Intellectual Disabilities

SEVERITY OF MENTAL RETARDATION

Moderate	Severe	Profound
Gross and fine motor coordination is usually delayed. However, the individual is often ambulatory and capable of independent mobility. Perceptual–motor skills exist (e.g., body awareness, sense of touch, eye–hand coordination) but are often delayed in comparison to the norm.	As many as 80% have significant motor difficulties (i.e., poor or no ambulatory skills). Gross or fine motor skills may be present, but the individual may lack control, resulting in awkward or uncontrolled movement.	Some gross motor development is evident, but fine motor skills are delayed. The individual is usually nonambulatory and not capable of independent mobility within the environment. The individual may lack perceptual–motor skills.

Fox, 2004). Increasing health problems for children with intellectual disabilities may be associated with genetic or environmental factors. For example, people with Down syndrome have a higher incidence of congenital heart defects and respiratory problems directly linked to their genetic condition. On the other hand, some children with intellectual disabilities experience health problems because of their living conditions. A significantly higher percentage of children with intellectual disabilities come from low socioeconomic backgrounds in comparison to peers without disabilities. Children who do not receive proper nutrition and are exposed to inadequate sanitation have a greater susceptibility to infections (Drew & Hardman, 2007). Health services for families in these situations may be minimal or nonexistent, depending on whether they are able to access government medical support, so children with intellectual disabilities may become ill more often than those who do not have disabilities. Consequently, children with intellectual disabilities may miss more school.

Causation

Intellectual disabilities result from multiple causes, some known, many unknown. For about 30% of all people with intellectual disabilities, the cause of the condition is unknown. This percentage is much higher for people with mild intellectual disabilities, wherein the specific cause cannot be determined in 75% of cases (The ARC, 2006). Possible known causes of intellectual disabilities include sociocultural influences, biomedical factors, behavioral factors, and unknown prenatal influences.

Sociocultural Influences

For individuals with mild intellectual disabilities, the cause of the problem is not generally apparent. A significant number of these individuals come from families of low socioeconomic status and diverse cultural backgrounds; their home situations often offer few opportunities for learning, which only further contributes to their challenges at school. Additionally, because these high-risk children live in such adverse economic conditions, they generally do not receive proper nutritional care. In addition to poor nutrition, high-risk groups are in greater jeopardy of receiving poor medical care and living in unstable families (Children's Defense Fund, 2005).

An important question to be addressed concerning people who have grown up in adverse sociocultural situations is this: How much of the person's ability is related to sociocultural influences, and how much to genetic factors? This issue is referred to as the **nature-versus-nurture** controversy. Numerous studies over the years have focused on the degree to which heredity and environment contribute to intelligence. These studies show that although we are reaching a better understanding of the interactive effects of both heredity and environment, the exact contribution of each to intellectual growth remains unknown.

The term used to describe intellectual disabilities that may be attributable to both sociocultural and genetic factors is **cultural-familial intellectual disabilities**. People with this condition are often described as (1) having mild intellectual disabilities, (2) having no known biological cause for the condition, (3) having at least one parent or sibling who has mild intellectual disabilities, and (4) growing up in a low-socioeconomic-status (low-SES) home environment.

Biomedical Factors

For the majority of people with more severe intellectual disabilities, problems are evident at birth. As defined by the AAIDD, **biomedical factors** "relate to biologic processes, such as genetic disorders or nutrition" (AAIDD [formerly AAMR], 2002, p. 126).

Many biomedical factors are associated with intellectual disabilities. In this section, we will discuss three major influences: chromosomal abnormalities, metabolism and nutrition, and postnatal brain disease.

CHROMOSOMAL ABNORMALITIES. Chromosomes are thread-like bodies that carry the genes that play the critical role in determining inherited characteristics. Defects resulting from **chromosomal abnormalities** are typically severe and accompanied by visually evident abnor-

FOCUS **6**
Identify the causes of intellectual disabilities.

Council for Exceptional Children

Standard 2: Development and Characteristics of Learners

Standard 8: Assessment

➤ **Nature versus nurture**
Controversy concerning how much of a person's ability is related to sociocultural influences (nurture) as opposed to genetic factors (nature).

➤ **Cultural-familial intellectual disabilities**
Intellectual disabilities that may be attributable to both sociocultural and genetic factors.

➤ **Biomedical factors**
Biologic processes, such as genetic disorders or inadequate nutrition, that can cause intellectual disabilities or other disabilities.

➤ **Chromosomal abnormalities**
Defects or damage in the chromosomes of an individual. Chromosomes are thread-like material that carries the genes and therefore plays a central role in inherited characteristics.

malities. Fortunately, genetically caused defects are relatively rare. The vast majority of humans have normal cell structures (46 chromosomes arranged in 23 pairs) and develop without accident. Aberrations in chromosomal arrangement, either before fertilization or during early cell division, can result in a variety of abnormal characteristics.

One of the most widely recognized types of intellectual disabilities, Down syndrome, results from chromosomal abnormality. About 3,000 to 5,000 children are born with this order each year in the United States (about one in every 800 to one in every 1,100 live births) (The ARC, 2006). A person with Down syndrome is characterized by slanting eyes with folds of skin at the inner corners (epicanthal folds); excessive ability to extend the joints; short, broad hands with a single crease across the palm on one or both hands; broad feet with short toes; a flat bridge of the nose; short, low-set ears; a short neck; a small head; a small oral cavity; and/or short, high-pitched cries in infancy.

The most common cause of Down syndrome is a chromosomal abnormality known as trisomy 21, in which the 21st chromosomal pair carries one extra chromosome.

Down syndrome has received widespread attention in the literature and has been a favored topic in both medical and special education textbooks for many years. Part of this attention is due to the ability to identify a cause with some degree of certainty. The cause of such genetic errors has become increasingly associated with the age of both the mother and the father. The most common type of Down syndrome is **trisomy 21**. In about 25% of the cases associated with trisomy 21, the age of the father (particularly when he is over 55 years old) is also a factor. For more insight into the myths and truths about Down syndrome, see the nearby Reflect on This feature.

Other chromosomal abnormalities associated with intellectual disabilities include **Williams syndrome** and **fragile X syndrome**. Williams syndrome is a rare genetic disease that occurs in about 1 in every 20,000 births and is characterized by an absence of genetic materials on the seventh pair of chromosomes. Most people with Williams syndrome have some degree of intellectual disabilities and associated medical problems (such as heart and blood vessel abnormalities, low weight gain, dental abnormalities, kidney abnormalities, hypersensitive hearing, musculoskeletal problems, and elevated blood calcium levels). While exhibiting deficits in academic learning and spatial ability typical of people with intellectual disabilities, they are often described as highly personable and verbal, exhibiting unique abilities in spoken language.

Fragile X syndrome is a common hereditary cause of intellectual disabilities associated with genetic anomalies in the 23rd pair of chromosomes. Males are usually more severely affected than females because they have an X and a Y chromosome. Females have more protection because they have two X chromosomes; one X contains the normal functioning version of the gene and the other is nonfunctioning. The normal gene partially compensates for the nonfunctioning gene. The term *fragile X* refers to the fact that this gene is pinched off in some blood cells. For those affected with fragile X, intellectual differences can range from mild learning disabilities and a normal IQ to severe intellectual disabilities and autism. Physical features may include a large head and flat ears; a long, narrow face with a broad nose; a large forehead; a squared-off chin; prominent testicles; and large hands. People with fragile X are also characterized by speech and language delays or deficiencies and by behavioral problems. Some people with fragile X are socially engaging and friendly, but others have autistic-like characteristics (poor eye contact, hand flapping, hand biting, and fascination with spinning objects) and may be aggressive. Males may also exhibit hyperactivity.

METABOLISM AND NUTRITION. **Metabolic disorders** are characterized by the body's inability to process (metabolize) certain substances that can then become poisonous and damage tissue in the central nervous system. With **phenylketonuria** (PKU), one such inherited

➤ **Trisomy 21**

Type of Down syndrome in which the chromosomal pairs do not separate properly during the formation of sperm or egg cells, resulting in an extra chromosome on the 21st pair; also called *nondisjunction*.

➤ **Williams syndrome**

A rare genetic disease that occurs in about one in every 20,000 births and is characterized by an absence of genetic materials on the seventh pair of chromosomes.

➤ **Fragile X Syndrome**

A condition involving damage to the chromosome structure, which appears as a breaking or splitting at the end of the X chromosome.

➤ **Metabolic disorders**

Problems in the body's ability to process (metabolize) substances that can become poisonous and damage the central nervous system.

➤ **Phenylketonuria (PKU)**

A metabolic disorder that may cause intellectual disabilities if left untreated.

MYTH: Down syndrome is a rare genetic disorder.

TRUTH: Down syndrome is the most commonly occurring genetic condition. One in every 733 live births is a child with Down syndrome, representing approximately 5,000 births per year in the United States alone. Today, Down syndrome affects more than 350,000 people in the United States.

MYTH: Most children with Down syndrome are born to older parents.

TRUTH: Eighty percent of children born with Down syndrome are born to women younger than 35-years-old. However, the incidence of births of children with Down syndrome increases with the age of the mother.

MYTH: People with Down syndrome are severely retarded.

TRUTH: Most people with Down syndrome have IQs that fall in the mild to moderate range of retardation. Children with Down syndrome are definitely educable, and educators and researchers are still discovering the full educational potential of people with Down syndrome.

MYTH: Most people with Down syndrome are institutionalized.

TRUTH: Today people with Down syndrome live at home with their families and are active participants in the educational, vocational, social, and recreational activities of the community. They are integrated into the regular education system and take part in sports, camping, music, art programs and all the other activities of their communities. In addition, they are socializing with people with and without disabilities and, as adults, are obtaining employment and living in group homes and other independent housing arrangements.

MYTH: Parents will not find community support in bringing up their child with Down syndrome.

TRUTH: In almost every community of the United States there are parent support groups and other community organizations directly involved in providing services to families of individuals with Down syndrome.

MYTH: Children with Down syndrome must be placed in segregated special education programs.

TRUTH: Children with Down syndrome have been included in regular academic classrooms in schools across the country. In some instances they are integrated into specific courses, while in other situations students are fully included in the regular classroom for all subjects. The degree of mainstreaming is based in the abilities of the individual; but the trend is for full inclusion in the social and educational life of the community.

MYTH: Adults with Down syndrome are unemployable.

TRUTH: Businesses are seeking young adults with Down syndrome for a variety of positions. They are being employed in small and medium-sized offices: by banks, corporations, nursing homes, hotels, and restaurants. They work in the music and entertainment industry, in clerical positions, and in the computer industry. People with Down syndrome bring to their jobs enthusiasm, reliability, and dedication.

MYTH: People with Down syndrome are always happy.

TRUTH: People with Down syndrome have feelings just like everyone else in the population. They respond to positive expressions of friendship, and they are hurt and upset by inconsiderate behavior.

MYTH: Adults with Down syndrome are unable to form close interpersonal relationships leading to marriage.

TRUTH: People with Down syndrome date, socialize, and form ongoing relationships. Some marry. Women with Down syndrome can and do have children, but there is a 50% chance that their child will have Down syndrome. Men with Down syndrome are believed to be sterile, with only one documented instance of a male with Down syndrome who has fathered a child.

MYTH: Down syndrome can never be cured.

TRUTH: Research on Down syndrome is making great strides in identifying the genes on chromosome 21 that cause the characteristics of Down syndrome. Scientists now feel strongly that it will be possible to improve, correct or prevent many of the problems associated with Down syndrome in the future.

SOURCE: Adapted from *Down Syndrome: Myths and Truths,* by the National Down Syndrome Society (2006). Retrieved September 27, 2006, from http://www.ndss.org/content.cfm?fuseaction=NDSS.article&article=443

metabolic disorder, the baby is not able to process phenylalanine, a substance found in many foods, including the milk ingested by infants. The inability to process phenylalanine results in an accumulation of poisonous substances in the body. If it goes untreated or is not treated promptly (mostly through dietary restrictions), PKU causes varying degrees of intellectual disabilities, ranging from moderate to severe deficits. If treatment is promptly instituted, however, damage may be largely prevented or at least reduced. For this reason, most states now require mandatory screening for all infants in order to treat the condition as early as possible and prevent lifelong problems.

Milk also presents a problem for infants affected by another metabolic disorder. With **galactosemia**, the child is unable to properly process lactose, which is the primary sugar in milk and is also found in other foods. If galactosemia remains untreated, serious damage results, such as cataracts, heightened susceptibility to infection, and reduced intellectual functioning. Dietary controls must be undertaken, eliminating milk and other foods containing lactose.

POSTNATAL BRAIN DISEASE. Some disorders are associated with gross postnatal brain disease. **Neurofibromatosis** is an inherited disorder that results in multiple tumors in the skin, peripheral nerve tissue, and other areas such as the brain. Intellectual disability does not occur in all cases, although it may be evident in a small percentage of patients. The severity of intellectual disabilities and other problems resulting from neurofibromatosis seems to be related to the location of the tumors (e.g., in the cerebral tissue) and to their size and pattern of growth. Severe disorders due to postnatal brain disease occur with a variety of other conditions, including **tuberous sclerosis**, which also involves tumors in the central nervous system tissue and degeneration of cerebral white matter.

Behavioral Factors

Intellectual disabilities may result from behavioral factors that are not genetically based. Behavioral causes of intellectual disabilities include infection and intoxication (such as HIV and **fetal alcohol syndrome**), as well as traumas and physical accidents. As defined by AAMR, **behavioral factors** are "potentially causal behaviors, such as dangerous (injurious) activities or maternal substance abuse" (AAMR, 2002, p. 126).

INFECTION AND INTOXICATION. Several types of **maternal infections** may result in difficulties for the unborn child. In some cases, the outcome is spontaneous abortion of the fetus; in others, it may be a severe birth defect. The probability of damage is particularly high if the infection occurs during the first three months of pregnancy. **Congenital rubella** (German measles) causes a variety of conditions, including intellectual disabilities, deafness, blindness, cerebral palsy, cardiac problems, seizures, and a variety of other neurological problems. The widespread administration of a rubella vaccine is one major reason why the incidence of intellectual disabilities as an outcome of rubella has declined significantly in recent years.

Another infection associated with intellectual disabilities is the **human immunodeficiency virus (HIV)**. When transmitted from the mother to the unborn child, HIV can result in significant intellectual deficits. The virus actually crosses the placenta and infects the fetus, damaging the infant's immune system. HIV is a major cause of preventable infectious intellectual disabilities (Kowalski, 2006).

Several prenatal infections can result in other severe disorders. **Toxoplasmosis**, an infection carried by raw meat and fecal material, can result in intellectual disabilities and other problems such as blindness and convulsions. Toxoplasmosis is primarily a threat if the mother is exposed during pregnancy, whereas infection prior to conception seems to cause minimal danger to the unborn child.

Intoxication is cerebral damage that results from an excessive level of some toxic agent in the mother–fetus system. Excessive maternal use of alcohol or drugs or exposure to certain environmental hazards, such as x-rays or insecticides, can damage the child. Damage to the fetus from maternal alcohol consumption is characterized by facial abnormalities, heart problems, low birthweight, small brain size, and intellectual disabilities. The terms *fetal alcohol syndrome (FAS)* and *fetal alcohol effects (FAE)* (a lesser number of the same symptoms associated with FAS) refer to a group of physical and mental birth defects resulting from a woman's drinking alcohol during pregnancy. FAS is recognized as a leading preventable cause of intellectual disabilities. The National Organization on Fetal Alcohol Syndrome (2006) estimated that one in every 100 live births involves FAS and that more than 40,000 babies with alcohol-related problems are born in the United States each year. Similarly, pregnant women who smoke are at greater risk of having a premature baby with complicating developmental problems such as intellectual disabilities (Centers for Disease Control, 2006). The use of drugs during pregnancy has varying effects on the infant, depending on frequency of use, and drug type. Drugs known to produce serious fetal damage include LSD, heroin, morphine, and cocaine. Prescription drugs such as **anticonvulsants** and antibiotics have also been associated with infant malformations.

> **Galactosemia**
>
> A metabolic disorder that causes an infant to have difficulty processing lactose. The disorder may cause intellectual disabilities and other problems.

> **Neurofibromatosis**
>
> An inherited disorder resulting in tumors of the skin and other tissue (such as the brain).

> **Tuberous sclerosis**
>
> A birth defect that does not appear until late childhood, is related to intellectual disabilities in about 66% of cases, and is characterized by tumors on many organs.

> **Fetal alcohol syndrome (FAS)**
>
> Damage caused to the fetus by the mother's consumption of alcohol.

> **Behavioral factors**
>
> Behaviors, such as dangerous activities or maternal substance abuse, that can cause intellectual disabilities or other disabilities.

> **Maternal infection**
>
> Infection in a mother during pregnancy, sometimes having the potential to injure the unborn child.

> **Congenital rubella**
>
> German measles contracted by a mother during pregnancy, which can cause a variety of conditions, including intellectual disabilities, deafness, blindness, and other neurological problems.

> **Human immunodeficiency virus (HIV)**
>
> A virus that impairs immune system function and has been linked to AIDS.

> **Toxoplasmosis**
>
> An infection caused by protozoa carried in raw meat and fecal material.

> **Anticonvulsants**
>
> Medication prescribed to control seizures (convulsions).

➤ **Prematurity**

Status of infants delivered before 37 weeks from the first day of the mother's last menstrual period.

➤ **Low birthweight**

A weight of 5 1/2 pounds (2,500 grams) or less at birth.

➤ **Encephalitis**

An inflammation of brain tissue that may damage the central nervous system.

➤ **Anoxia**

A lack of oxygen that may result in permanent damage to the brain.

➤ **Anencephaly**

A condition in which the person has a partial or complete absence of cerebral tissue.

➤ **Hydrocephalus**

An excess of cerebrospinal fluid, often resulting in enlargement of the head and pressure on the brain, which may cause intellectual disabilities.

Maternal substance abuse is also associated with gestation disorders involving prematurity and low birthweight. **Prematurity** refers to infants delivered before 35 weeks from the first day of the last menstrual period. **Low birthweight** characterizes babies that weigh 2,500 grams (5.5 pounds) or less at birth. Prematurity and low birthweight significantly increase the risk of serious problems at birth, including intellectual disabilities.

Another factor that can seriously affect the unborn baby is blood-type incompatibility between the mother and the fetus. The most widely known form of this problem occurs when the mother's blood is Rh-negative, whereas the fetus has Rh-positive blood. In this situation, the mother's system may become sensitized to the incompatible blood type and produce defensive antibodies that damage the fetus. Medical technology can now prevent this condition through the use of a drug known as Rhogam.

Intellectual disabilities can also occur as a result of postnatal infections and toxic excess. For example, **encephalitis** may damage the central nervous system following certain types of childhood infections (e.g., measles or mumps). Reactions to certain toxic substances—such as lead, carbon monoxide, and drugs—can also damage the central nervous system.

TRAUMAS OR PHYSICAL ACCIDENTS. Traumas or physical accidents can occur prior to birth (e.g., exposure to excessive radiation), during delivery, or after the baby is born. Consider Becky from the chapter opening Snapshot: The cause of her intellectual disabilities was trauma during delivery. She suffered from birth asphyxiation as well as epileptic seizures. The continuing supply of oxygen and nutrients to the baby is a critical factor during delivery. One threat to these processes involves the position of the fetus. Normal fetal position places the baby with the head toward the cervix and the face toward the mother's back. Certain other positions may result in damage to the fetus as delivery proceeds. The baby's oxygen supply may be reduced for a period of time until the head is expelled and the lungs begin to function, and this lack of oxygen may result in damage to the brain. Such a condition is known as **anoxia** (oxygen deprivation).

Unknown Prenatal Influences

Several conditions associated with unknown prenatal influences can result in severe disorders. One such condition involves malformations of cerebral tissue. The most dramatic of these malformations is **anencephaly**, a condition in which the individual has a partial or even complete absence of cerebral tissue. In some cases, portions of the brain appear to develop and then degenerate. In **hydrocephalus**, which also has unknown origins, an excess of cerebrospinal fluid accumulates in the skull and results in potentially damaging pressure on cerebral tissue. Hydrocephalus may involve an enlarged head and cause decreased intellectual functioning. If surgical intervention occurs early, the damage may be slight because the pressure will not have been serious or prolonged.

Although we have presented a number of possible causal factors associated with intellectual disabilities, the cause is unknown and undeterminable in many cases. Additionally, many conditions associated with intellectual disabilities are due to the interaction of hereditary and environmental factors. Although we cannot always identify the causes of intellectual disabilities, measures can be taken to prevent their occurrence.

Educational Services and Supports

We now turn our attention to educating students with intellectual disabilities from early childhood through the transition from school to adult life. The provision of appropriate services and supports for individuals with intellectual disabilities is a lifelong process. For children with mild intellectual disabilities, educational services may not begin until they are in elementary school. However, for those with more severe intellectual disabilities, services and supports will begin at birth and may continue into the adult years.

The Early Childhood Years

The child with mild intellectual disabilities may exhibit subtle developmental delays in comparison to agemates, but parents may not view these discrepancies as significant enough to seek intervention during the preschool years. Even if parents are concerned and seek help for their child prior to elementary school, they are often confronted with professionals who are apathetic toward early childhood education. Some professionals believe that early childhood services may actually create, rather than remedy, problems, because the child may not be mature enough to cope with the pressures of structured learning in an educational environment. Simply stated, the maturation philosophy means that before entering school, a child should reach a level of growth at which he or she is ready to learn certain skills. Unfortunately, this philosophy has kept many children out of the public schools for years.

The antithesis of the maturation philosophy is the prevention of further problems in learning and behavior through intervention. **Head Start**, initially funded as a federal preschool program for students who are disadvantaged, is a prevention program that attempts to identify and instruct at-risk children before they enter public school. Although Head Start did not generate the results that were initially anticipated (the virtual elimination of school adjustment problems for students with disadvantages), it has represented a significant move forward and continues to receive widespread support from parents and professionals alike. The rationale for early education is widely accepted in the field of special education and is an important part of the IDEA mandate.

Intervention based on normal patterns of growth is referred to as the *developmental milestones approach* because it seeks to develop, remedy, or adapt learner skills based on the child's variation from what is considered normal. This progression of skills continues as the child ages chronologically; rate of progress depends on the severity of the condition. Some children with profound intellectual disabilities may never exceed a developmental age of 6 months. Those with moderate intellectual disabilities may develop to a level that will enable them to lead fulfilling lives as adults, with varying levels of support.

The importance of early intervention cannot be overstated. Significant advances have been made in the area of early intervention, including improved assessment, curricula, and instructional technologies; increasing numbers of children receiving services; and appreciation of the need to individualize services for families as well as children (Batshaw, 2003; Berk, 2005; Guralnick, 2001). Early intervention techniques, such as **infant stimulation** programs, focus on the acquisition of sensorimotor skills and intellectual development. Infant stimulation involves learning simple reflex activity and equilibrium reactions. Subsequent intervention then expands into all areas of human growth and development.

The Elementary School Years

Public education is a relatively new concept as it relates to students with intellectual disabilities, particularly those with more severe characteristics. Historically, many of these students were defined as *noneducable* by the public schools because they did not fit the programs offered by general education. Because such programs were built on a foundation of academic learning that emphasized reading, writing, and arithmetic, students with intellectual disabilities could not meet the academic standards set by the schools and thus were excluded. Public schools were not expected to adapt to the needs of students with intellectual disabilities; rather, the students were expected to adapt to the schools.

With the passage of Public Law 94-142 (now IDEA 2004), schools that excluded these children for so long now face the challenge of providing an appropriate education for all children with intellectual disabilities. Education has been redefined on the basis of a new set of values. Instruction and support for children of elementary school age with intellectual disabilities focus on decreasing dependence on others, while concurrently teaching

FOCUS 7
Why are early intervention services for children with intellectual disabilities so important?

➤ **Head Start**
A federally funded preschool program for students with disadvantages to give them "a head start" prior to elementary school.

Council for Exceptional Children

Standard 3: Individual Learning Differences

Standard 7: Instructional Planning

➤ **Infant stimulation**
Early intervention procedures that provide an infant with an array of visual, auditory, and physical stimuli to promote development.

FOCUS 8
Identify five skill areas that should be addressed in programs for elementary-age children with intellectual disabilities.

adaptation to the environment. Therefore, instruction must concentrate on those skills that facilitate the child's interaction with others and emphasize independence in the community. Instruction for children with intellectual disabilities generally includes development of motor skills, self-help skills, social skills, communication skills, and academic skills.

MOTOR SKILLS. The acquisition of motor skills is fundamental to the developmental process and a prerequisite to successful learning in other content areas, including self-help and social skills. Gross motor development involves general mobility, including the interaction of the body with the environment. Gross motor skills are developed in a sequence, ranging from movements that make balance possible to higher-order locomotor patterns. Locomotor patterns are intended to move the person freely through the environment. Gross motor movements include controlling the head and neck, rolling, body righting, sitting, crawling, standing, walking, running, jumping, and skipping.

Fine motor development requires more precision and steadiness than the skills developed in the gross motor area. The development of fine motor skills, including reaching, grasping, and manipulating objects, is initially dependent on the ability of the child to visually fix on an object and visually track a moving target. Coordination of the eye and hand is an integral factor in many skill areas, as well as in fine motor development. Eye-hand coordination is the basis of social and leisure activities and is essential to the development of the object-control skills required in employment.

SELF-HELP SKILLS. The development of self-help skills is critical to a child's progression toward independence from caregivers. Self-help skills include eating, dressing, and maintaining personal hygiene. Eating skills range from finger feeding and drinking from a cup to using proper table behaviors (such as employing utensils and napkins), serving food, and following etiquette. Dressing skills include buttoning, zipping, buckling, lacing, and tying. Personal hygiene skills are developed in an age-appropriate context. Basic hygiene skills include toileting, face and hand washing, bathing, tooth brushing, hair combing, and shampooing. Skills associated with adolescent and adult years include skin care, shaving, hair setting, and the use of deodorants and cosmetics.

Fine motor skill development and eye-hand coordination are important in fostering independence for the young child with intellectual disabilities.

SOCIAL SKILLS. Social skills training emphasizes the importance of learning problem-solving and decision-making skills and of using appropriate communication in a social context. Difficulty with problem solving and decision making have been barriers to the success of people with intellectual disabilities in community and school settings. Students with intellectual disabilities will not learn these skills through observation but must be specifically taught how to solve problems.

Westling and Fox (2004) suggested several learning outcomes for students in the use of appropriate communication in a social context. They must be able to initiate and maintain a conversation (whether it be verbal, signed, or pictorial) while using appropriate social conventions and courtesies (e.g., staying on topic, not interrupting the speaker, appropriate body posture). These authors suggested a list of social skills that are important instructional targets for students with intellectual disabilities. (See Figure 10.3)

COMMUNICATION SKILLS. The ability to communicate with others is an essential component of growth and development. Without communication, there can be no interaction. Communication systems for children with intellectual disabilities take three general forms: verbal language, augmentative communication (including sign language and language boards), and a combination of the verbal and augmentative approaches. The approach used depends on the child's capability. A child who can develop the requisite skills for spoken language will have greatly enhanced everyday interactive skills. For a child unable to develop verbal skills as an effective means of communication, manual communication must be considered. Such children must develop some form of communication that will facilitate inclusion with peers and family members throughout their lives. For some specific tips on ways to effectively include people with intellectual disabilities from early childhood through the adult years, see this chapter's Inclusion and Collaboration Through the Lifespan.

Some students with intellectual disabilities benefit from the use of assistive technology and communication aids. Assistive technology may involve a variety of communication approaches that assist a person with intellectual disabilities who has limited speech ability. These approaches may be low-tech (a language board with pictures) or high-tech (a laptop computer with voice output). Regardless of the approach, a communication aid can be a valuable tool in

Standard 5: Learning Environments and Social Interactions

FIGURE 10.3

Instructional Targets in Social Skills Training

Establish eye contact.

Establish appropriate proximity.

Maintain appropriate body posture during conversation.

Speak with appropriate volume, rate, and expression.

Maintain attention during exchange.

Initiate greetings.

Respond to greetings.

Initiate partings.

Respond to partings.

Discriminate appropriate times to greet or part.

Answer questions.

Ask questions.

Make requests.

Respond to requests.

Ask for information.

Provide information.

Ask for clarification.

Respond to requests for clarification.

Extend social invitation.

Deliver refusals.

Respond to refusals.

Use social courtesies (please, thank you, apology).

Maintain topic.

Initiate a new topic.

SOURCE: From *Teaching Students with Severe Disabiilties*, by D. Westling & L. Fox (2004). Upper Saddle River, NJ: Merrill, p. 279.

INCLUSION AND COLLABORATION THROUGH THE LIFESPAN

People with Intellectual Disabilities

EARLY CHILDHOOD YEARS

Tips for the Family

- Promote family learning about the diversity of all people in the context of understanding the child with intellectual differences.

- Create opportunities for friendships to develop between your child and children without disabilities, in preschool and in family and neighborhood settings.

- Help facilitate your child's opportunities and access to neighborhood preschools by actively participating in the education planning process and collaborating with professionals with multidisciplinary backgrounds (health care, social services, education, etc.) Become familiar with the individualized family service plan (IFSP) and how it can serve as a planning tool to support the inclusion of your child in preschool programs that involve students without disabilities.

Tips for the General Education Preschool Teacher

- Focus on the child's individual abilities first. Whatever labels have been placed on the child (e.g., "mentally retarded") will have little to do with instructional needs.

- When teaching the child, focus on presenting each component of a task clearly, while reducing outside stimuli that may distract the child from learning.

- Begin with simple tasks, and move to more complex ones as the child masters skills.

- Verbally label stimuli, such as objects or people, as often as possible to provide the child with both auditory and visual input.

- Provide a lot of practice in initial learning phases, using short but frequent sessions to ensure that the child has mastered the skill before moving on to more complex tasks.

- Create success experiences by rewarding correct responses to tasks as well as appropriate behavior with peers who are not disabled.

- It is important for the young child with intellectual disabilities to be able to transfer learning from school to the home and neighborhood. Facilitate such transfer by providing information that is meaningful to the child and noting how the initial and transfer tasks are similar.

TIPS FOR PRESCHOOL PERSONNEL

- Support the inclusion of young children with intellectual disabilities in classrooms and programs.

- Collaborate with the team of multidisciplinary professionals, including teachers, staff, related-services professionals (such as speech and language pathologists), and volunteers as they attempt to create success experiences for the child in the preschool setting.

- Integrate families as well as children into the preschool programs. Offer parents as many opportunities as possible to be part of the program (e.g., advisory boards, volunteer experiences).

Tips for Neighbors and Friends

- Look for opportunities for young neighborhood children who are not disabled to interact during play times with the child who has an intellectual disability.

- Provide a supportive community environment for the family of a young child who has an intellectual disability. Encourage the family, including the child, to participate in neighborhood activities (e.g., outings, barbecues, outdoor yard and street cleanups, crime watches).

- Try to understand how the young child with intellectual disabilities is similar to other children in the neighborhood rather than different. Focus on those similarities in your interactions with other neighbors and children in your community.

ELEMENTARY YEARS

Tips for the Family

- Actively participate with the multidisciplinary team in the development of your son or daughter's individualized education program (IEP). Through active participation, advocate for those goals that you would like to see on the IEP that will focus on your child's developing social interaction and communication skills in natural settings (e.g., the general education classroom).

- To help facilitate your son's or daughter's inclusion in the neighborhood elementary school, help the multidisciplinary team of professionals to better understand the importance of inclusion with peers who are not disabled (e.g., riding on the same school bus, going to recess and lunch at the same time, participating in schoolwide assemblies).

- Participate in as many school functions for parents (e.g., PTA, parent advisory groups, volunteering) as is reasonable, to connect your family to the mainstream of the school.

- Create opportunities for your child to make friends with same-age children without disabilities.

Tips for the General Education Classroom Teacher

- View children with intellectual disabilities as children, first and foremost. Focus on their similarities to other children rather than on their differences.

- Recognize children with intellectual disabilities for their own accomplishments within the classroom, rather than comparing them to those of peers without disabilities.

- Employ cooperative learning strategies wherever possible to promote effective learning by all students. Use peers without disabilities as support for students with intellectual disabilities. This may include establishing peer-buddy programs or peer and cross-age tutoring.

- Consider all members of the classroom when you organize the physical environment. Find ways to meet the individual needs of each child (e.g., establishing aisles that will accommodate a wheelchair and organizing desks to facilitate tutoring on assigned tasks).

Tips for School Personnel

- Integrate the multidisciplinary resources within the school to meet the needs of all children.

- Wherever possible, help general classroom teachers access the collaborative and multidisciplinary resources necessary to meet the needs of students with intellectual disabilities. Instructional materials and programs should be made available to whoever needs them, not just to those identified as being in special education.

- Help general and special education teachers to develop peer-partner and support networks for students with intellectual disabilities.

- Promote the heterogeneous grouping of students. Avoid clustering large numbers of students with intellectual disabilities in a single general education classroom. Integrate no more than two in each elementary classroom.

- Maintain the same schedules for students with intellectual disabilities as for all other students in the building. Recess, lunch, school assemblies, and bus arrival and departure schedules should be identical for all students.

- Create opportunities for the multidisciplinary personnel in the school to collaborate in the development and implementation of instructional programs for individual children.

Tips for Neighbors and Friends

- Support families who are seeking to have their child with intellectual disabilities educated with children who are not disabled. This will give children with intellectual disabilities more opportunities for interacting with children who are not disabled, both in school and in the local community.

SECONDARY AND TRANSITION YEARS

Tips for the Family

- Create opportunities for your son or daughter to participate in activities that are of interest to him or her, beyond the school day, with same-age peers who are not disabled, including high school clubs, sports, or just hanging out in the local mall.

- Promote opportunities for students from your son's or daughter's high school to visit your home. Help arrange get-togethers or parties involving students from the neighborhood and/or school.

- Become actively involved in the development of the individualized education and transition program. Explore with the high school its views on what should be done to assist your son or daughter in the transition from school to adult life.

Tips for the General Education Classroom Teacher

- Collaborate with the school's multidisciplinary team (special educators, related-services personnel, administrators, paraeducators) to adapt subject matter in your classroom (e.g., science, math, or physical education) to the individual needs of students with intellectual disabilities.

- Let students without disabilities know that the student with intellectual disabilities belongs in their classroom. The goals and activities of this student may be different from those of other students, but with support, the student with intellectual

disabilities will benefit from working with you and the other students in the class.

- Support the student with intellectual disabilities in becoming involved in extracurricular activities. If you are the faculty sponsor of a club or organization, explore whether this student is interested and how he or she could get involved.

Tips for School Personnel

- Advocate for parents of high-school-age students with intellectual disabilities to participate in the activities of the school (e.g., committees and PTA).

- Help facilitate parental collaboration in the IEP process during the high school years by helping the school's multidisciplinary team value parental input that focuses on a desire to include their child in the mainstream of the school. Parents will be more active when school personnel have general and positive contact with the family.

- Provide human and material support to high school special education or vocational teachers seeking to develop community-based instruction programs that focus on students learning and applying skills in actual community settings (e.g., grocery stores, malls, theaters, parks, and work sites).

Tips for Neighbors, Friends, and Potential Employers

- Work with the family and school personnel to create opportunities for students with intellectual disabilities to participate in community activities (such as going to the movies, "hanging out" with peers without disabilities in the neighborhood mall, and going to high school sports events).

- As a potential employer, work with the high school to locate and establish community-based employment training sites for students with intellectual disabilities.

ADULT YEARS

Tips for the Family

- Become aware of what life will be like for your son or daughter in the local community during the adult years. What formal supports (government-funded advocacy organizations) from various disciplines (such as health care and social services) and informal supports are available in your community? What are the characteristics of adult service programs? Explore adult support systems in the local community in the areas of supported living, employment, and recreation and leisure.

Tips for Neighbors, Friends, and Potential Employers

- Seek ways to become part of the community support network for the individual with intellectual disabilities. Be alert to ways in which this individual can become and remain actively involved in community employment, neighborhood recreational activities, and functions at a local house of worship.

- As potential employers in the community, seek information on employment of people with intellectual disabilities. Find out about programs (e.g., supported employment) that focus on arranging work for people with intellectual disabilities while meeting your needs as an employer.

helping a person with intellectual disabilities communicate with others. For a more in-depth look at assistive technology and communication aids for people with intellectual disabilities, see the Assistive Technology, "Ryan's Story" on page 287.

ACADEMIC SKILLS. Students with intellectual disabilities can benefit from instruction in basic or functional academic programs. In the area of literacy, students with mild intellectual disabilities will require a systematic instructional program that takes into account for differences in the rate of learning, but they will learn to read when given "rich, intensive, and extensive literary experiences" (Katims, 2000). In fact, these students may achieve as high as a fourth- or fifth-grade level in reading. Katims indicated that students with intellectual disabilities make significant progress in literacy programs that emphasize **direct instruction** (the direct teaching of letters, words, and syntactic, phonetic, and semantic analysis) in conjunction with written literature that is meaningful to the student or that draw on the student's own writings.

A significant relationship exists between measured IQ and reading achievement: Students with intellectual disabilities read well below nondisabled students of the same age. This relationship seems to suggest that reading instruction should be limited to higher-functioning students with intellectual disabilities. A growing body of research, however, indicates that students with more severe intellectual disabilities can learn academic skills. According to Browder and colleagues (2006), "The emerging research shows that students with severe disabiities can master academic skills. However, educators continue to have substantial work ahead to demonstrate effective practices for teaching them the wide range of academic skills typical of the general curriculum" (p. 493).

A functional reading program uses materials that are a part of a person's normal routines in work, everyday living, and leisure activities. For example, functional reading involves words that are frequently encountered in the environment, such as those used on labels or signs in public places; words that warn of possible risks; and symbols such as the skull and crossbones to denote poisonous substances.

Students with intellectual disabilities also have challenges in developing math skills, but the majority of those with mild intellectual disabilities can learn basic addition and subtraction. However, these children will have significant difficulty in the areas of mathematical reasoning and problem-solving tasks (Beirne-Smith et al., 2006). Math skills are taught most efficiently through the use of money concepts. For example, functional math involves activities such as learning to use a checkbook, shop in a grocery store, or operate a vending machine. The immediate practical application motivates the student. Regardless of the approach used, arithmetic instruction must be concrete and practical to compensate for the child's deficiencies in reasoning ability.

For more insight into instruction that facilitates interaction with others and emphasizes independence for students of elementary-school age with intellectual disabilities, read the nearby Case Study and respond to the application questions.

Transitioning from School to Adult Life

The goals of an educational program for adolescents with intellectual disabilities are to increase personal independence, enhance opportunities for participation in the local community, prepare for employment, and facilitate a successful transition to the adult years.

PERSONAL INDEPENDENCE AND PARTICIPATION IN THE COMMUNITY. The term *independence* refers to the development and application of skills that lead to greater self-sufficiency in daily personal life, including personal care, self-help, and appropriate leisure activities. Participation in the community includes access to programs, facilities, and services that people without disabilities often take for granted: grocery stores, shopping malls, restaurants, theaters, and parks. Adolescents with intellectual disabilities need opportunities for interaction with peers without disabilities (other than caregivers), access to community events, sustained social relationships, and involvement in choices that affect their lives. An illustration of the range of community services and supports that can facilitate the transition of an adolescent with intellectual disabilities into the adult years is shown in Figure 10.4.

> ➤ **Direct instruction**
> Teaching academic subjects through precisely sequenced lessons involving drill, practice, and immediate feedback. In reading, direct instruction involves the focused teaching of letters and words, as well as syntactic, phonetic, and semantic analysis.

FOCUS 9
Identify four educational goals for adolescents with intellectual disabilities.

Council for Exceptional Children

Standard 1: Foundations

CASE STUDY

INCLUDING SCOTT

Scott's parents, Heather and Bill Bonn, discuss their son's educational experiences:

By the time Scott was 10 years old, he had been in five different schools. Because he has Down syndrome, he began his schooling at 18 months, attending the only public special education school in the county once a week. At that time, all children [with intellectual disabilities] were bussed to this central location. Scott stayed at the special education school until he was 3 1/2 years old. He could have stayed there until he was 21, but we wanted something different for him. . . . The transition to Coleridge Elementary School wasn't easy. . . . Scott spent most of the day working on academics in the special education classroom; he was included in the general education classroom for only short periods for art, music, lunch, and show-and-tell. At first, he didn't like going into the general education classroom, but before long it was the reverse: He didn't want to leave. . . . Scott is now fully included. Lately we've noticed that he is more verbal. . . . He is less dependent on an assistant at school and has started to develop independent work skills. (Bonn, 2000a, p. 174; Bonn, 2000b, pp. 210–211)

APPLICATION

1. What skills are important for Scott to learn and apply now that he is fully included in a general education classroom?

2. Scott will move to a middle school next year. Can you identify some strategies that teachers might use to help Scott make a successful transition from elementary school to middle school?

EMPLOYMENT PREPARATION. Work is a crucial measure of any person's success during adulthood, providing the primary opportunity for social interaction, a basis for personal identity and status, and a chance to contribute to the community. These needs are basic to adults who have intellectual disabilities, just as they are to their peers without disabilities.

FIGURE 10.4

Categories of Supports Needed During the Adult Years

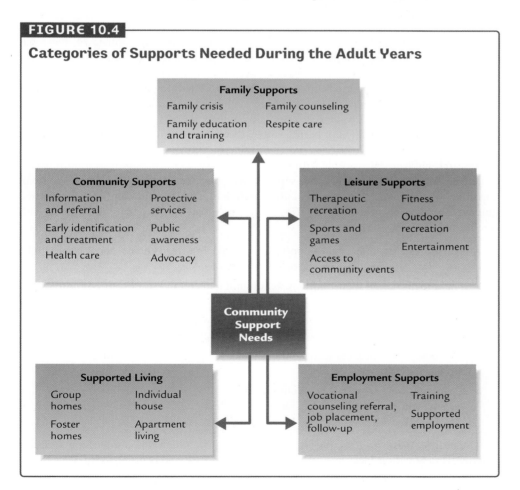

For adolescents with moderate and severe intellectual disabilities, employment preparation during high school is shifting away from segregated sheltered workshops to supported employment in inclusive community settings.

➤ **Sheltered workshop**

A segregated vocational training and employment setting for people with disabilities.

➤ **Supported employment**

Paid work in integrated community settings for individuals with more severe disabilities who are expected to need continuous support services, and for whom competitive employment has traditionally not been possible.

Fortunately, employment training for students with intellectual disabilities is shifting from the isolation and "getting ready" orientation of a **sheltered workshop** to activities accomplished in community employment. Goals and objectives are developed according to the demands of the community work setting and the functioning level of the individual. The focus is on helping each person to learn and apply skills in a job setting while receiving the support necessary to succeed. Providing ongoing assistance to the individual on the job is the basis of an approach known as supported employment. **Supported employment** is defined as work in an inclusive setting for individuals with severe disabilities (including those with intellectual disabilities) who are expected to need continuous support services and for whom competitive employment has traditionally not been possible. (See Chapter 4 for more information about supported employment.)

Research indicates that people with intellectual disabilities can work in community employment if adequate training and support are provided (Braddock, Hemp, Rizzolo, Parish, & Pomeranz, 2002; Kregel, 2001; Wehman, 2006). Below are some suggested guidelines in developing a comprehensive employment training program for students with intellectual disabilities.

➤ The student should have the opportunity to make informed choices about what jobs he or she wants to do and where he or she wants to work.

➤ The student should receive employment training in community settings prior to graduation from high school.

➤ Employment training should focus on work opportunities present in the local area where the individual currently lives.

➤ The focus of the employment training should be on specific job training as the student approaches graduation.

➤ Collaboration between the school and adult service agencies must be part of the employment-training program. (Drew & Hardman, 2007; Morgan, Ellerd, Gerity, & Blair, 2000).

The nearby Assistive Technology feature describes how a high school transition specialist working closely with a local business and using assistive technology developed a successful community-based employment training program.

ASSISTIVE TECHNOLOGY

Ryan is a 20-year-old with intellectual disabilities. Using motion video on CD-ROM, he was able to learn about the complexities of several possible jobs without having to observe any of them in person. Working with a transition specialist at a computer, Ryan was able to learn about and select a list of preferred jobs from a CD-ROM program. The CD-ROM program distinguished six job domains based on various characteristics (e.g., work location, required physical stamina, and level of social activity). Ryan initially identified general work conditions. This screening process then allowed him to identify preferences in employment conditions (e.g., inside vs. outside work, heavy vs. light physical involvement, working mostly alone vs. mostly with people). Below is Ryan's story as told by his transition specialist, Becky Blair.

I first met Ryan when he was referred after a series of unsuccessful community-based job placements. The background information I received from his previous service provider described him as unmotivated and sloppy in both appearance and job performance. The professionals who had worked with Ryan in the past recommended that he return to a sheltered day program for "work skills training."

During the intake process, I asked Ryan to name his three most desired jobs. The jobs he identified as most preferred were the same ones from which he had been fired due to extensive absence or poor performance. Documentation indicated that although Ryan was able to perform the tasks associated with each job, he would lose interest after a short time.

To further assist Ryan in identifying and obtaining employment, staff from a local university project, the *Yes Program,* gave him the opportunity to view a number of jobs on a video. After watching the video, Ryan identified motel housekeeping as a desired job. He seemed really excited about this particular job, so together, he and I began our job search. After a few weeks of job development, we found a rather reluctant employer who was willing to give Ryan a job on a 30-day trial basis. I explained the agreement to Ryan, and again he assured me that this was the job he wanted.

Within 3 weeks, Ryan had become the fastest and most dependable housekeeper on the motel's staff. His employer was so impressed with his work that she asked me if I had other people with disabilities looking for employment. Within 6 weeks of his start date, Ryan was awarded Employee of the Month and was given a cash bonus. Less than 2 months after starting the job, he was promoted to "second floor supervisor" and received a raise. In my last contact with him, Ryan was supervising a crew of employees—adults without disabilities—on an entire motel wing. The once hesitant and skeptical employer now brags about Ryan's performance to anyone who will listen.

SOURCE: Adapted from R. L. Morgan, D. A. Ellerd, B. P. Gerity, & R. J. Blair. (2000). "That's the Job I Want": How Technology Helps Young People in Transition. *Teaching Exceptional Children, 32*(4), 44–49.

Inclusive Education

Historically, special education for students with intellectual disabilities meant segregated education. Today, however, the focus is on including these students in general education schools and classrooms. Some students with intellectual disabilities are included for only a part of the school day and attend only those general education classes that their individualized education program (IEP) teams consider consistent with their needs and functioning levels (such as physical education, industrial arts, home economics). Other students with intellectual disabilities attend general education classes for all or the majority of the school day. For these students, special education consists primarily of services and supports intended to facilitate their opportunities and success in the general education classroom. Placement information from the U.S. Department of Education (2006) indicated that approximately 94% of students with intellectual disabilities between the ages of 6 and 21 were placed in general education schools for the entire day. Of these students, about 11% were served in a general education class for at least 80% of the time, and 53% spent more than half of their time outside the general education class.

Another placement option for students with disabilities is the special school. Special schools are defined as facilities exclusively for students with intellectual disabilities or other disabilities. Approximately 4.1% of students with intellectual disabilities were found to attend public special schools, and less than 1% attended private special schools (U.S. Department of Education, 2006). In this era of inclusion, considerable controversy exists as to whether there is *any* justification for placing students with intellectual disabilities in special schools. For more insight into this controversy, see the nearby Debate Forum.

FOCUS 10
Why is the inclusion of students with intellectual disabilities in general education settings important to an appropriate educational experience?

Council for Exceptional Children
Standard 5: Learning Environments and Social Interactions

DEBATE FORUM

CAN SPECIAL SCHOOLS FOR STUDENTS WITH INTELLECTUAL DISABILITIES BE JUSTIFIED?

POINT

There will always be a need for special schools. Although inclusion may be appropriate for many students with intellectual disabilities, special schools are the least restrictive environment for a small number of children who require intensive instruction and support that cannot be provided in a general education school or classroom. Special schools provide for greater homogeneity in grouping and programming. Teachers can specialize in particular areas such as art, language, physical education, and music. Teaching materials can be centralized and, thus, used more effectively with larger numbers of students. A special school more efficiently uses available resources. In addition, some parents of students with severe intellectual disabilities believe that their children will be happier in a special school that "protects" them.

COUNTERPOINT

Research on the efficacy of special schools does not support the contention that such a placement is ever the least restrictive environment (Sailor, Gee, & Karasoff, 2000). On the contrary, investigations over the past 20 years have strongly indicated that students with intellectual disabilities, regardless of the severity of their condition, benefit from placement in general education environments where opportunities for interaction with students who are not disabled are systematically planned and implemented (Sailor et al., 2000). Inclusion for students with intellectual disabilities embodies a variety of opportunities, both within the general education classroom and throughout the school. Besides interaction in a classroom setting, ongoing inclusion occurs in the halls, on the playground, in the cafeteria, and at school assemblies.

Stainback, Stainback, and Ayres (1996) also reported that general education teachers who have the opportunity for interaction with children with intellectual disabilities are not fearful of or intimidated by their presence in the school building. Special schools generally offer little, if any, opportunity for interaction with normal peers and deprive the child of valuable learning and socialization experiences. Special schools cannot be financially or ideologically justified. Public school administrators must now plan to include children with intellectual disabilities in existing general education schools and classes.

FOCUS REVIEW

FOCUS 1 Identify the major components of the AAIDD definition of intellectual disabilities.

- There are significant limitations in intellectual abilities.

- There are significant limitations in adaptive behavior as expressed in conceptual, social, and practical adaptive skills.

- Disability originates before the age of 18.

- The severity of the condition is tempered by the individual's participation, interactions, and social roles within the community; by her or his overall physical and mental health; and by the environmental context.

FOCUS 2 Identify four approaches to classifying people with intellectual disabilities.

- Severity of the condition may be described in terms of mild, moderate, severe, or profound intellectual disabilities.

- Educability expectations are designated for groups of children who are educable and children who are trainable.

- Medical descriptors classify intellectual disabilities on the basis of the origin of the condition (e.g., infection, intoxication, trauma, chromosomal abnormality).

- Classification based on the type and extent of support needed categorizes people with intellectual disabilities as having intermittent, limited, extensive, or pervasive needs for support in order to function in natural settings.

FOCUS 3 What is the prevalence of intellectual disabilities?

- There are 591,440 students between the ages of 6 and 21 labeled as having intellectual disabilities (mental retardation) and receiving service under IDEA. Approximately 10% of all students with disabilities between the ages of 6 and 21 have intellectual disabilities.

- Overall, students with intellectual disabilities constitute about 0.88% of the total school population.
- Based on an intelligence test score of 70 or lower, people with intellectual disabilities would constitute about 3% of the total population, or about 6.6 million people in the United States.

FOCUS **4** Identify intellectual, self-regulation, and adaptive skills characteristics of individuals with intellectual disabilities.

- Intellectual characteristics may include learning and memory deficiencies, difficulties in establishing learning sets, and inefficient rehearsal strategies.
- Self-regulation characteristics include difficulty in mediating or regulating behavior.
- Adaptive skills characteristics may include difficulties in coping with the demands of the environment, developing interpersonal relationships, developing language skills, and taking care of personal needs.

FOCUS **5** Identify the academic, motivational, speech and language, and physical characteristics of children with intellectual disabilities.

- Students with intellectual disabilities exhibit significant deficits in the areas of reading and mathematics.
- Students with mild intellectual disabilities have poor reading mechanics and comprehension, compared to their same-age peers.
- Students with intellectual disabilities may be able to learn basic computations but be unable to apply concepts appropriately in a problem-solving situation.
- Motivational difficulties may reflect learned helplessness—"No matter what I do or how hard I try, I will not succeed."
- The most common speech difficulties involve articulation problems, voice problems, and stuttering.
- Language differences are generally associated with delays in language development rather than with the bizarre use of language.
- Physical differences generally are not evident for individuals with mild intellectual disabilities because these intellectual disabilities are usually not associated with genetic factors.
- The more severe the intellectual disabilities, the greater the probability of genetic causation and of compounding physiological problems.

FOCUS **6** Identify the causes of intellectual disabilities.

- Intellectual disabilities are the result of multiple causes, some known, many unknown. The cause of intellectual disabilities is generally not known for the individual with mild intellectual disabilities.
- Causes associated with moderate to profound intellectual disabilities include sociocultural influences, biomedical factors, behavioral factors, and unknown prenatal influences.

FOCUS **7** Why are early intervention services for children with intellectual disabilities so important?

- Early intervention services are needed to provide a stimulating environment for the child to enhance growth and development.
- Early intervention programs focus on the development of communication skills, social interaction, and readiness for formal instruction.

FOCUS **8** Identify five skill areas that should be addressed in programs for elementary-age children with intellectual disabilities.

- Motor development skills
- Self-help skills
- Social skills
- Communication skills
- Academic skills

FOCUS **9** Identify four educational goals for adolescents with intellectual disabilities.

- To increase the individual's personal independence
- To enhance opportunities for participation in the local community
- To prepare for employment
- To facilitate a successful transition to the adult years

FOCUS **10** Why is the inclusion of students with intellectual disabilities in general education settings important to an appropriate educational experience?

- Regardless of the severity of their condition, students with intellectual disabilities benefit from placement in general education environments where opportunities for inclusion with nondisabled peers are systematically planned and implemented.

BUILDING YOUR PORTFOLIO

If you are thinking about a career in special education, you should know that many states use national standards developed by the Council for Exceptional Children (CEC) to assess a teacher candidate's knowledge and skills for working with students with disabilities. See a complete listing of the ten CEC Content Standards on the inside front cover of this text.

CEC Content Standards Addressed in This Chapter

1 Foundations

2 Development and Characteristics of Learners

3 Individual Learning Differences

5 Learning Environments and Social Interactions

7 Instructional Planning

8 Assessment

Assess Your Knowledge of the CEC Standards Addressed in This Chapter

Some states require that teacher candidates develop a portfolio of products that demonstrate mastery of the CEC content standards. To assist in the development of products for this portfolio, you may wish to complete the following activities.

- Complete a written test of the chapter's content

  If your instructor requires a written test of your content knowledge for this chapter, keep a copy for your portfolio. A practice test on the information covered in this chapter is available through the companion website (college.hmco.com/pic/hardman9e) and the Student Study Guide.

- Respond to the Application Questions for the Case Study "Including Scott"

  1. *Review the Case Study and respond in writing to the application questions.*

  2. *Keep a copy of the case study and of your written response for your portfolio.*

- Participate in a Community Service Learning Activity

  Community service is a valuable way to enhance your learning experience. Visit our companion website for suggested community service learning activities that correspond to the information presented in this chapter. Develop a reflective journal of the service learning experience for your portfolio.

WEB RESOURCES

American Association on Intellectual and Developmental Disabilities (AAIDD)

http://www.aamr.org

AAIDD (formerly AAMR) is the oldest and largest interdisciplinary organization of professionals (and others) concerned about intellectual disabilities and related disabilities. This website contains AAMR publications, products, and information on the definition of intellectual disabilities.

The ARC, A National Association of and for People with Intellectual and Related Developmental Disabilities

http://www.thearc.org

The Arc is the national organization of and for people with intellectual disabilities and related developmental disabilities and their families.

This website provides information on promoting and improving supports and services for people with intellectual disabilities and their families, as well as research and education resources on the prevention of intellectual disabilities in infants and young children.

National Down Syndrome Society

http://www.ndss.org

The National Down Syndrome Society (NDSS) was established to ensure that people with Down syndrome have the opportunity to achieve their full potential in community life. Other than the U.S. government, it is largest supporter of Down syndrome research. This website is a resource for research, educational opportunities, health issues, and life planning. An advocacy center provides up-to-date information on policy issues and national legislation.

FURTHER READINGS

Beirne-Smith, M., Patton, J. R., & Kim., S. H. (2006). *Mental Retardation: An Introduction to Intellectual Disability* (7th edition). Upper Saddle River, NJ: Merrill.

Provides an overview of the basic concepts; biology, psychology, and sociology of intellectual disabilities; intervention issues; and family considerations.

Drew, C. J., & Hardman, M. L. (2007). *Intellectual Disabilities across the Lifespan* (9th ed.). Columbus, OH: Merrill.

Offers an interdisciplinary introduction to intellectual disabilities with an emphasis on stages of human development and the lifespan. The book

includes chapters on family and social issues, early development, education, and multicultural issues.

Shriver, M. (2001). *What's Wrong with Timmy?* New York: Little, Brown.

Uses storytelling to answer children's questions about intellectual disabilities. Maria Shriver tells the story of 8-year-old Kate, who, while at the park with her mother, notices Timmy, a boy who looks and behaves differently from the other children she knows. Kate wonders if there is something "wrong" with Timmy, but when her mother introduces her to Timmy, the seeds of friendship are planted.

Trainer, M., & Featherstone, H. (2003). *Differences in Common: Straight Talk on Mental Retardation, Down Syndrome, and Your Life.* Bethesda, MD: Woodbine House.

A collection of almost fifty essays that span more than 20 years of a mother's experience with Down syndrome. A wide variety of issues are explored; including family adjustment, public attitudes, inclusion, and independence.

COMPANION WEBSITE

Visit the companion website at college.hmco.com/pic/hardman9e for additional resources that support this text:

- HM Video Cases that present actual classroom scenarios that you may face every day as a teacher

- Practice ACE Exams that will help you prepare for quizzes, tests, and certfication exams
- Flashcards of key terms
- Weblinks

11

Communication Disorders

TO BEGIN WITH . . .

DISABILITIES IN COMMUNICATION NOT UNCOMMON

Nearly 19% of the children (6–21 years old) with disabilities who were served under federal law during 2004 had speech or language difficulties. (U.S. Department of Education, 2006)

TECHNOLOGY HELPS HER EXPRESSION

"It's her self-expression, her ability to express her feelings and goals. Just being understood makes her feel valued. . . . That's the purpose of technology—to not hold people back." (Norma Velez, speaking about her daughter's voice machine, as quoted by Horiuchi, 1999)

FREE SPEECH: HELP FOR STUTTERING

A story about Dr. Joe Kalinowsky on *Good Morning America* captures the embarrassment and feelings that often accompany stuttering. "'And I prayed every night' Kalinowsky said. 'Take off an arm. Take off my arm, God. 'Cause I know kids will tease me for not having an arm. But if I can talk the same as every other kid, that'll be OK.'" (abcNEWS.com, *Good Morning America*, December 27, 2002)

TWELVE MONTHS OR SO

Parents can become overly concerned about the development of their baby's language skills if they interpret the age expectations too rigidly. Dr. Caroline Bowen, a certified speech patholo-gist, reminds parents that "children vary quite considerably with regard to the rate at which they reach the various speech and language 'milestones.' There is no need to put out an SOS for a speech pathologist if your child does not do the things . . . at precisely the ages stated! When you see language ages and stages and read an age like '12 months,' say to yourself, '12 months or so.'" (Bowen, 2002)

1. Identify four ways in which speech, language, and communication are interrelated.

2. Explain how language delay and language disorder differ.

3. Identify three factors that are thought to cause language disorders.

4. Describe how treatment approaches for language disorders generally differ for children and for adults.

5. Cite three factors that are thought to cause stuttering.

6. Identify two ways in which learning theory and home environments are related to delayed speech.

7. Identify two reasons why some professionals are reluctant to treat functional articulation disorders in young schoolchildren.

▼SNAPSHOT

MEGHAN

Meghan is 12 years old. She is a respected member of her sixth-grade class in a school that has become a powerful inclusive community for her. People are drawn to Meghan because of her courage, her humor, and her belief in living for her dreams.

Meghan has a strong circle of friends who pay attention to who she is as a person and know how to be with her and share in many different mutual experiences. Meghan enjoys skiing, playing tennis, swimming, music, and movies. Meghan's friends call her on the phone and talk to her—even if she chooses only to listen. If they could just see her smile over the telephone! She goes to birthday parties and has slumber parties. Her friends have given her the opportunity to be a typical sixth grader.

When Meghan was born, we knew she had cerebral palsy. We saw that she had a projected motor delay and cognitive delay, but how much was uncertain. As parents, we wanted a language-based environment, not a life skills environment, for Meghan. We wanted her to have a childhood where her strengths were recognized and her hopes for learning encouraged. Meghan may never tell us on demand the 26 letters of the alphabet, a readiness requirement in the developmental center program, but she was able to return to an inclusive fourth grade community, where she learned the history of California. She knew the people who built the railroad and could tell us this through an adapted curriculum and picture cues, and she was accurate.

Meghan is apraxic. It is hard for her to come up with words—it is hard for her to retrieve them and it is hard for her to summon the motor skills to utter them. But she is driven to talk and to get her messages out. We use many forms of communication with her: verbal modeling, singing because it builds vocabulary (music uses another part of the brain), sign language for a visual way to focus, and a Dynavox. The Dynavox is touch-activated and creates verbal speech. We can program information on its screen to increase practical language skills as well as link up with the curriculum she is being taught in school.

Meghan just completed an oral presentation on the Alaskan oil spill. We created a page on the Dynavox with picture cues that had verbal messages sequencing the key topics of her report.

One of Meghan's friends helped her program "I'm having a bad hair day" into her Dynavox diary. She uses sassy sixth-grade language now, and we think of it as an increase in language skills! We can be the great Mom, Dad, and teachers in her life, but it is her peers who are the most valuable resources, for they see Meghan as a person first and her disability second. They will make the difference in her tomorrows, for they pay attention to what they have in common, not to what makes them different.

We communicate many times each day. We order food in a restaurant, thank a friend for doing a favor, ask a question in class, call for help in an emergency, follow instructions regarding the assembly of a piece of furniture, or give directions to someone who is lost. Our lives revolve around communication in many crucial ways. Despite its importance and constant presence in our lives, we seldom think much about communication unless we have a problem with it. Communication is also one of the most complicated processes people undertake. Speech and language are two highly interrelated components of communication. Problems in either can significantly affect a person's daily life. Because of their complexity, determining the cause of a problem in these areas is often perplexing.

Communication is the exchange of ideas, opinions, or facts between senders and receivers. It requires that a sender (an individual or group) compose and transmit a message and that a receiver decode and understand the message (Anderson, Shames, & Chabon, 2006; Bernstein, 2002). The sender and receiver are therefore partners in the communication process.

Although they are related, speech and language are not the same thing. Speech is the audible representation of language. It is one means of expressing language but not the only means. Language represents the message contained in speech. It is possible to have language without speech, such as sign language used by people who are deaf, and speech without language, such as the speech of birds that are trained to talk. Communication is the broader concept. Language is a part of communication. Speech is often thought of as a part of language, although language may exist without speech. Figure 11.1 illustrates the interrelationship of speech, language, and communication.

FOCUS **1**

Identify four ways in which speech, language, and communication are interrelated.

FIGURE 11.1

A Conceptual Model of Communication, Language, and Speech

Language can exist without speech (left), and not all speech constitutes language (right), but spoken language (center) is one outcome of typical human development. Communication is the broad umbrella concept that includes speech and language. Although communication *can* be achieved without these components, it is greatly enhanced by them.

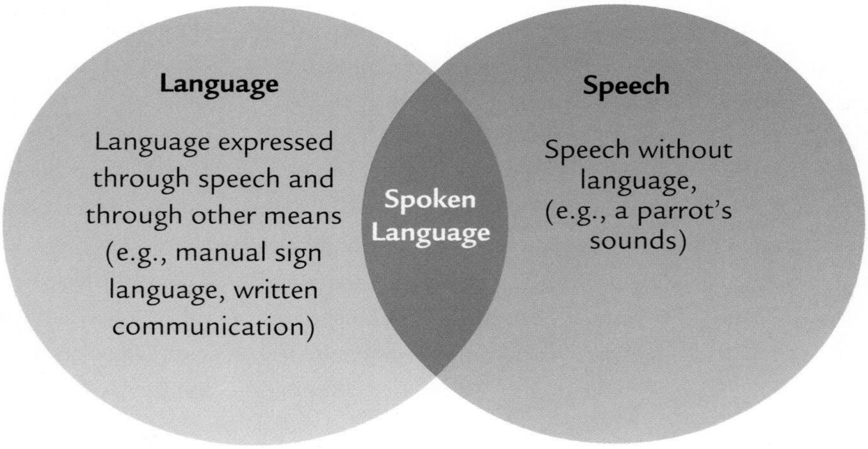

Language

Language expressed through speech and through other means (e.g., manual sign language, written communication)

Spoken Language

Speech

Speech without language, (e.g., a parrot's sounds)

The Structure of Language

Language consists of several major components, including phonology, syntax, morphology, semantics, and pragmatics. Phonology is the system of speech sounds that an individual utters—that is, rules regarding how sounds can be used and combined (Nicolosi, Harryman, & Krescheck, 2003; Owens, Metz, & Haas, 2007). For example, the word *cat* has three phonemes, C-A-T. Syntax involves the rules governing sentence structure, the way sequences of words are combined into phrases and sentences. For example, the sentence *Will you help Janice?* changes in meaning when the order of the words is changed to *You will help Janice.* Morphology is concerned with the form and internal structure of words—that is, the transformations of words in terms of areas such as tense (for example, present to past tense) and number (singular to plural), and so on. When we add an *s* to *cat*, we have produced the plural form, *cats*, with two morphemes, or units of meaning: the concept of cat and the concept of plural. Such transformations involve prefixes, suffixes, and inflections (Feldman, Barac-Cikoja, & Kostic, 2002; Owens, 2006). Grammar is constituted from a combination of syntax and morphology. Semantics represents the understanding of language, the component most directly concerned with meaning. Semantics addresses whether the speaker's intended message is conveyed by the words and their combinations in an age-appropriate manner. It involves the meaning of a word to an individual, which may be unique in each of our personal mental dictionaries (e.g., the meaning of the adjective *nice* in the phrase *nice house*).

Pragmatics is a component of language that is receiving increased attention in recent literature (e.g., Schauer, 2006; Tomasello, 2003; Verhoeven & Vermeer, 2002). It represents the "rules that govern the reason(s) for communicating (called communicative functions or intentions) as well as the rules that govern the choice of codes to be used when communicating" (Bernstein, 2002, p. 9). Pragmatics can be illustrated by the fact that teachers talk differently depending on whether they are providing direct instruction, making a point in a faculty meeting, or chatting at a party. Pragmatics includes processes such as turn taking and the initiating, maintaining, and ending of a conversation. Figure 11.2 illustrates how the various components constitute language.

> ➤ **Pragmatics**
> A component of language that represents the rules that govern the reason(s) for communicating.

FIGURE 11.2

Components in the Structure of Language

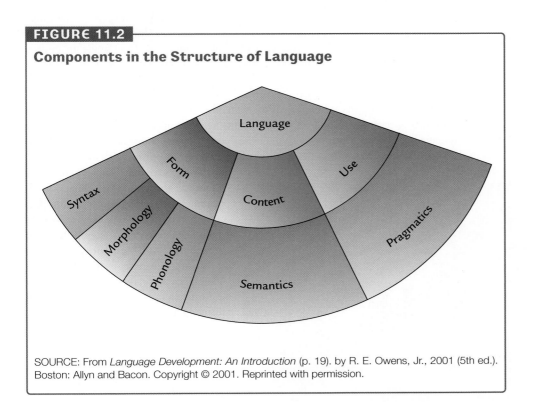

SOURCE: From *Language Development: An Introduction* (p. 19). by R. E. Owens, Jr., 2001 (5th ed.). Boston: Allyn and Bacon. Copyright © 2001. Reprinted with permission.

Language Development

In a vast percentage of cases, children develop language in a normal fashion, without significant delays or disruptions to the process. It is important to understand this typical developmental process as we examine and describe language characteristics that differ from the norm and interfere with the effectiveness of communication.

The development of language is a complex process. It is also one of the most fascinating to observe, as parents of infants know well. Young children normally advance through several stages in acquiring language, from a preverbal stage to the use of words in sentences. An infant's initial verbal output is primarily limited to crying and hence is usually associated with discomfort (from hunger, pain, or being soiled or wet). Before long (around 2 months), babies begin to coo as well as cry, verbally expressing reactions to pleasure as well as discomfort. At about 3 to 6 months of age, they begin to babble, which involves making some consonant and vowel sounds. At this point, babies often make sounds repeatedly when they are alone, seemingly experimenting with their sound making and not necessarily trying to communicate with anyone (Locke, 2006; Owens, 2005). They may also babble when their parents or others are playing with or otherwise handling them.

A baby's first word is a momentous, long-anticipated event. In fact, eager parents often interpret as "words" sounds that stretch the imagination of more objective observers and probably have no meaning to the child. What usually happens is that the baby begins to string together sounds that occasionally resemble words. To the parents' delight, these sounds frequently include utterances such as "Da-Da" and "Ma-Ma," which, of course, are echoed, repeated, and reinforced greatly by the parents. As the baby actually begins to listen to the speech of adults, exchanges, or "conversations," seem to occur, where the youngster responds by saying "Da-Da" when a parent says that sound. Although this type of interchange sounds like a conversation, the child's vocal productions may be understood only by those close to him or her (such as parents or siblings); people other than immediate family members may not be able to interpret their meaning at all. The baby also begins to use different tones and vocal intensity, which makes his or her vocalization vaguely resemble adult speech. The interactions between babies and their parents can do much to enhance babies' developing language at this time. Parents often provide a great deal of reinforcement, such as praise in excited tones, or hugs, for word approximations. They also provide stimulus sounds and words for the baby to mimic, giving the youngster considerable directed practice.

The timing of a baby's actual first word is open to interpretation, although it usually happens between 9 and 14 months. These words often involve echoing (repeating what has been heard) or mimicking responses based on verbalizations by those around the baby. At first the words may have little or no meaning, although they soon become attached to people or objects in the child's immediate environment, such as Daddy, Mommy, or milk. Before long these words begin to have more perceptible intent, as the child uses them for requests and as a means of pleasing parents. Strings of two and three words that resemble sentences typically begin between 18 and 24 months of age. At this stage, meaning is usually unmistakable because the child can clearly indicate that he or she wants something. The child uses fairly accurate syntax, with word order generally consisting of subject-verb-object.

Most children with normally developing language are able to use all the basic syntactical structures by 3 to 4 years of age. By 5 years, they have progressed to using six-word sentences, on the average. A child who is developing language

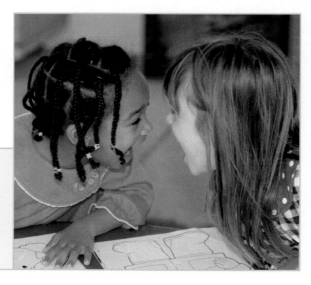

Within a broad range of 4 to 8 years of age, children with normal language development can correctly articulate most speech sounds in context.

TABLE 11.1

Normal Language and Prelanguage Development

AGE	BEHAVIOR
Birth	Crying and making other physiological sounds
1 to 2 months	Cooing as well as crying
3 to 6 months	Babbling as well as cooing
9 to 14 months	Speaking first words as well as babbling
18 to 24 months	Speaking first sentences as well as words
3 to 4 years	Using all basic syntactical structures
4 to 8 years	Articulating correctly all speech sounds in context

SOURCE: Reprinted with permission of Merrill, an imprint of Macmillan Publishing Company, from Drew, C. J., & Hardman, M. L. (2007). *Intellectual Disabilities Across the Lifespan* (9th ed., p. 208). Columbus, OH: Merrill. Copyright © 2004 by Macmillan Publishing Company.

at a normal pace articulates nearly all speech sounds correctly, and in context, somewhere between 4 and 8 years of age. These illustrations are couched in terms of when children produce language—that is, in terms of expressive language development. However, some observations suggest that a child's receptive skills precede his or her ability to express language. Thus children are able to understand a great deal more than they can express. Most children show some understanding of language as early as 6 to 9 months, often responding first to commands such as "no-no" and their names (Hulit & Howard, 2006; Owens, 2005).

Variable age ranges are used for each milestone in outlining normal language development, some with rather broad approximations. Several factors contribute to this variability. For one thing, even children who are developing normally exhibit substantial differences in their rates of development. Some variations are due to a child's general health and vitality, others to inheritance, and still others to environmental influences, such as the amount and type of interaction with parents and siblings (Petrill, Deater-Deckard, & Thompson, 2006; Stromswold, 2006; Weigel, Martin, & Bennett, 2006). Note also that age ranges become wider in more advanced stages of development (e.g., 3 to 6 months for babbling; 18 to 24 months for two- and three-word strings). These advanced developments are also more complex, some involving subtleties that are not as singularly obvious as, say, the first "Da-Da." Therefore, observation of when they first occur is perhaps less accurate. Table 11.1 summarizes general milestones of normal language and prelanguage development.

Considerable variability also occurs with abnormal language and speaking ability. In some cases, the same factors that contribute to variability in normal language are considered disorders if they result in extreme performance deviations. In other cases, the definitions differ and characteristics vary among people—the same variability we have encountered with other disorders.

Standard 3: Individual Learning Differences

Multidisciplinary Collaboration

A wide range of topics will be addressed as we discuss the details of communication disorders. These extend from developmental delays to physical characteristics, all factors that may influence a person's ability to communicate. Some of these may have genetic causes, whereas others are influenced primarily by environmental factors. Thus the communication features are widely varied, and effective intervention components must reflect that variation in order to adequately serve the needs of the individual. As we discuss these various communication challenges and their assessment and treatment, it is important to return to a recurring theme: multidisciplinary collaboration. Such cooperation is crucial for students with communication disorders because of the broad array of challenges that fall into the purview of different disciplines ranging from medical and health-related specialties to those involving teaching and behavior modification.

Standard 4: Instructional Strategies

Standard 5: Learning Environments and Social Interactions

Interventions for all communication disorders must consider multiple elements. These include the nature of the problem, the manner in which an individual is affected, what services are provided, and where they are delivered, as well as when and how (Anderson et al., 2006). It is also important to consider cultural and linguistic background as an intervention is being planned (Payne & Taylor, 2006). The influences of different cultures and linguistic circumstances have been noted as significant in previous chapters, but it is their direct impact on communication that is especially clear. Assessment and intervention are an individualized undertaking, just as with other types of disorders (Bacon & Wilcox, 2006; Markham & Dean, 2006). Some causes are rather easily identified and may or may not be remedied by mechanical or medical intervention.

As we have seen with other disabilities, referrals may come from several stakeholders, notably parents and teachers or other educational personnel (Broomfield & Dod, 2004; Farmer & Oliver, 2005). Parents play a significant role in initial identification of a potential problem, because their child's communication, and sometimes her or his communication disability, develop during the early years. Such initial assessments are likely to emerge when the child's communication performance attracts someone's attention. Parents working with speech and language pathologists become key leaders in coordinating multidisciplinary team collaboration, although they often acquire knowledge about services from professionals in health and educational fields (Alexander & Solomon, 2006; Anderson et al., 2006). Referrals, screening procedures, diagnoses, and interventions will follow trajectories that are mapped specifically on the features of a child's communication disability and other contextual matters, such as family circumstances (Moore-Brown & Montgomery, 2001). We will discuss the nature of such interventions as we examine specific communication disorders. You will see that individualized language plans are required as outlined in IDEA, as well as multidisciplinary teams of professionals (Bacon & Wilcox, 2006; McCauley & Fey, 2006).

Language Disorders

Council for Exceptional Children

Standard 6: Communication

History has witnessed language in many different forms. Some early Native Americans communicated using systems of clucking or clicking sounds made with the tongue and teeth. These sounds were also used in combination with hand signs and spoken language that often differed greatly between tribes. Such differing language systems have been described extensively in a variety of historical documents and continue to be of interest (e.g., Bartens, 2000; Sims, 2005).

Current definitions of language reflect the breadth necessary to encompass diverse communication systems. For the most part, these definitions refer to the systems of rules and symbols that people use to communicate, including matters of phonology, syntax, morphology, and semantics (Owens, 2005; Reed, 2005). In these definitions of language, considerable attention is given to meaning and understanding. For example, Bernstein (2002) defined language as encompassing the "complex rules that govern sounds, words, sentences, meaning, and use. These rules underlie an individual's ability to understand language (language comprehension) and his or her ability to formulate language (language production)" (p. 5).

Speech disorders include problems related to verbal production—that is, vocal expression. Language disorders represent serious difficulties in the ability to understand or express ideas in the communication system being used. The distinction between speech disorders and language disorders is like the difference between the sound of a word and the meaning of a word. As we examine language disorders, we will discuss both difficulties in expressing meaning and difficulties in receiving it. Figure 11.3 lists a number of behaviors that might emerge if a child has a language disorder.

Definition

A serious disruption of the language acquisition process may result in language disorders. Such irregular developments may involve comprehension (understanding) or expression in written or spoken language (Anderson et al., 2006; Nicolosi et al., 2003). Such malfunctions may occur in one or more of the components of language. Because language is one of the most complex sets of behaviors exhibited by humans, language disorders are complex and present perplexing assess-

Focus 2
Explain how language delay and language disorder differ.

FIGURE 11.3

Behaviors Resulting in Teacher Referral of Children with Possible Language Impairments

The following behaviors may indicate that a child in your classroom has a language impairment that is in need of clinical intervention. Please check the appropriate items.

- Child mispronounces sounds and words.
- Child omits word endings, such as plural *–s* and past tense *–ed.*
- Child omits small unemphasized words, such as auxiliary verbs or prepositions.
- Child uses an immature vocabulary, overuses empty words, such as *one* and *thing*, or seems to have difficulty recalling or finding the right word.
- Child has difficulty comprehending new words and concepts.
- Child's sentence structure seems immature or overreliant on forms such as subject-verb-object. It's unoriginal, dull.
- Child's question and/or negative sentence style is immature.
- Child has difficulty with one of the following:

Verb tensing	Articles	Auxiliary verbs
Pronouns	Irregular verbs	Prepositions
Word order	Irregular plurals	Conjunctions

- Child has difficulty relating sequential events.
- Child has difficulty following directions.
- Child's questions are often inaccurate or vague.
- Child's questions are often poorly formed.
- Child has difficulty answering questions.
- Child's comments are often off topic or inappropriate for the conversation.
- There are long pauses between a remark and the child's reply or between successive remarks by the child. It's as if the child is searching for a response or is confused.
- Child appears to be attending to communication but remembers little of what is said.
- Child has difficulty using language socially for the following purposes:

Request needs	Pretend/imagine	Protest
Greet	Request information	Gain attention
Respond/reply	Share ideas, feelings	Clarify
Relate events	Entertain	Reason

- Child has difficulty interpreting the following:

Figurative language	Humor	Gestures
Emotions	Body language	

- Child does not alter production for different audiences and locations.
- Child does not seem to consider the effect of language on the listener.
- Child often has verbal misunderstandings with others.
- Child has difficulty with reading and writing.
- Child's language skills seem to be much lower than skills in other areas, such as mechanical, artistic, or social skills.

SOURCE: From R. E. Owens, Jr. *Language Disorders: A Functional Approach to Assessment and Intervention* (4th ed., p. 355). Copyright © 2004, All rights reserved. Reprinted by permission of Allyn and Bacon.

ment problems. Language involves memory, learning, message reception and processing, and expressive skills. An individual with a language disorder may have deficits in any of these areas, and it may be difficult to identify the nature of the problem (Doehring, 2002; Owens et al., 2007). In addition, language problems may arise in the form of language delays.

Language delay occurs when the normal rate of developmental progress is interrupted but the systematic sequence of development remains essentially intact. For youngsters with a language delay, the development follows a normal pattern or course of growth but is substantially slower than in most children of the same age; in other words, children with delays use the language rules typical of a younger child. In language disorders, by contrast, language acquisition is not systematic and/or sequential; children with language disorders do not acquire rule-governed linguistic behavior in a sequential progression. The term *language disorder* is used in a general sense to refer to several types of behaviors. Where evidence suggests that delay may be a major contributor, we discuss it as such.

Classification

The terminology applied to the processes involved in language, and to disorders in those processes, varies widely. In many cases, language disorders are classified according to their causes, which may be known or only suspected (Anderson & Shames, 2006; Owens et al., 2007). In other cases, specific labels, such as aphasia, tend to be employed. One fruitful approach is to view language disorders in terms of receptive and expressive problems (Mildenberger, Noterdaeme, Sitter, & Amorosa, 2001; Reed, 2005). We shall examine both of these categories, as well as aphasia, a problem that may occur in both children and adults.

➤ **Receptive language disorders**

Difficulties in comprehending what others say.

RECEPTIVE LANGUAGE DISORDERS. People with **receptive language disorders** have difficulty comprehending what others say. In many cases, receptive language problems in children are noticed when they do not follow an adult's instructions. These children may seem inattentive, as though they do not listen to directions, or they may be very slow to respond. Individuals with receptive language disorders have great difficulty understanding other people's messages and may process only part (or none) of what is being said to them (Nicolosi et al., 2003; Owens et al., 2007). They have a problem in language processing, which is basically half of language (the other part being language production). Language processing is essentially listening to and interpreting spoken language.

It is not uncommon for receptive language problems to appear in students with learning disabilities (Lerner & Kline, 2006; Long, 2005). Such language deficits contribute significantly to problems with academic performance and to difficulties in social interactions for these students. Receptive language disorders appear as high-risk indicators of other disabilities and may remain undiagnosed because they are not as evident as problems in language production (Reed, 2005).

➤ **Expressive language disorders**

Difficulties in producing language.

EXPRESSIVE LANGUAGE DISORDERS. Individuals with **expressive language disorders** have difficulty in language production, or formulating and using spoken or written language. Those with expressive language disorders may have limited vocabularies and use the same array of words regardless of the situation. Expressive language disorders may appear as immature speech, often resulting in interaction difficulties (Reed, 2005). People with expressive disorders also use hand signals and facial expressions to communicate.

➤ **Aphasia**

An acquired language disorder caused by brain damage and characterized by complete or partial impairment of language comprehension, formulation, and use.

APHASIA. **Aphasia** involves a loss of the ability to speak or comprehend because of an injury or developmental abnormality in the brain. Aphasia most often affects those in whom a specific brain injury has resulted in impairment of language comprehension, formulation, and use. Thus definitions of aphasia commonly link the disorder to brain injury, through either mechanical accidents or other damage, such as that caused by a stroke. Many types of aphasia and/or conditions associated with aphasia have been identified (Basso, 2003; Holland, 2006; Spreen, 2002). Aphasic language disturbances have also been classified in terms of receptive and expressive problems.

Aphasia may be found both during childhood and in the adult years. The term *developmental aphasia* has been widely used for children, despite the long-standing association of aphasia with neurological damage. Children with aphasia often begin to use words at age 2 or later and to use phrases at age 4. The link between aphasia and neurological abnormalities in children is of interest to researchers, and some evidence suggests a connection. In many cases of aphasia in children, however, objective evidence of neurological dysfunction has been difficult to acquire.

Adult aphasia typically is linked to accidents or injuries likely to occur during this part of the lifespan, such as gunshot wounds, motorcycle and auto accidents, and strokes. For this group, it is clear why terms such as *acquired language disorder* emerge. These disorders are typically acquired through specific injury. Current research suggests that different symptoms result from damage to different parts of the brain (e.g., Holland, 2006; Owens et al., 2007). Those with injury to the front part of the brain often can comprehend better than they can speak; they also have considerable difficulty finding words, have poor articulation with labored and slow speech, omit small words such as *of* and *the*, and generally have reduced verbal production. Individuals with aphasia resulting from injury to the back part of the brain seem to have more fluent speech, but it lacks content. Speech may also involve using an unnecessarily large number of words to express an idea or employing unusual or meaningless terms. The speech of these individuals appears to reflect impaired comprehension (Basso, 2003).

Causation

Pinpointing the causes of different language disorders can be difficult. We do not know precisely how normal language acquisition occurs or how malfunctions influence language disorders. We do know that certain sensory and other physiological systems must be intact and developing normally for language processes to develop normally. For example, if vision or hearing is seriously impaired, a language deficit may result (Owens et al., 2007; Reed, 2005). Likewise, serious brain damage might inhibit normal language functioning. Learning must also progress in a systematic, sequential fashion for language to develop appropriately. For example, children must attend to communication before they can mimic it or attach meaning to it. Language learning is like other learning. It must be stimulated and reinforced to be acquired and mastered (Bernstein & Levey, 2002).

Many physiological problems may cause language difficulties. Neurological damage that may affect language functioning can occur prenatally, during birth, or anytime throughout life (Gleason, 2005; Hulit & Howard, 2006). For example, language problems clearly can result from oxygen deprivation before or during birth (e.g., Drew & Hardman, 2007). Likewise, a serious accident later in life can disrupt a person's language skills. Serious emotional disorders may accompany language disturbances if an individual's perception of the world is substantially distorted (Owens et al., 2007; Reed, 2005).

Language disorders may also occur if learning opportunities are seriously deficient or are otherwise disrupted. As with speech, children may not learn language if the environment is not conducive to such learning (Annoussamy, 2006; Culatta & Wiig, 2006). Modeling in the home may be so infrequent that a child cannot learn language in a normal fashion. This might be the case in a family where no speaking occurs because the parents have hearing impairments, even though the children hear normally. Such circumstances are rare, but when they do occur, a language delay may result. The parents cannot model language for their children, nor can they respond or reinforce speaking.

Learning outcomes are highly variable. In situations that seem normal, we may find a child with serious language difficulty. In circumstances that seem lacking, we may find a child whose language facility is normal. The Snapshot presents an example involving four brothers with normal hearing who were born to and raised by parents who both had severe hearing impairments and no spoken-language facility. They have distinguished themselves in various ways, from earning Ph.D.s and M.D.s (one holds both degrees) to other achievements (one became a millionaire with patented inventions). Although the Snapshot represents a rare set of circumstances, it illustrates how variable and poorly understood language learning is.

Distinctions between speech problems and language problems are blurred because they overlap as much as the two functions of speech and language overlap. Receptive and expressive language disorders are as intertwined as speech and language. When someone does not express language well, does he or she have a receptive problem or an expressive problem? These disorders are not easily separated, nor can their causes be clearly categorized.

FOCUS **3**

Identify three factors that are thought to cause language disorders.

Council for Exceptional Children

Standard 2: Development and Characteristics of Learners

Standard 6: Communication

Standard 4: Instructional
Strategies

Standard 7: Instructional
Planning

FOCUS **4**
Describe how treatment
approaches for language
disorders generally differ
for children and for adults.

Intervention

As outlined in our discussion of multidisciplinary collaboration, treatments of language disorders must account for many elements as a plan is developed (Anderson et al., 2006; Payne & Taylor, 2006). Interventions are individualized, and significant planning is required (Bacon & Wilcox, 2006; Markham & Dean, 2006).

INDIVIDUALIZED LANGUAGE PLANS. A number of integrated steps are involved in effective language training. They include identification, assessment, development of instructional objectives, development of a language intervention program, implementation of the intervention program, reassessment of the child, and re-teaching, if necessary. These steps are similar to the general stages of specialized educational interventions that are outlined in IDEA. Specific programs of intervention may also involve other activities aimed at individualized intervention (see, for example, Gillon, 2002; Moore-Brown & Montgomery, 2001; McCauley & Fey, 2006). Teams of professionals must collaborate, and often others, such as health care deliverers, are involved (Bacon & Wilcox, 2006; Theodore, Bray, Kehle, & DioGuardi, 2006; Weiss, 2002). Speech-language pathologists and parents may collaborate as leaders on this team. Such collaboration among professionals reflects the federal law and is also one of our important recurring themes.

Programs of language training are tailored to an individual's strengths and limitations. In fact, current terminology labels them individualized language plans (ILPs), similar in concept to the individualized education plans (IEPs) mandated by IDEA (Nelson, 2002). These intervention plans include several components:

➤ Long-range goals (annual)

➤ Short-range and specific behavioral objectives

➤ A statement of the resources to be used in achieving the objectives

➤ A description of evaluation methods

➤ Program beginning and ending dates

➤ Evaluation of the individual's generalization of skills.

▼SNAPSHOT

CY

LANGUAGE DIFFERENCES: WE DIDN'T KNOW THEY WERE DIFFERENT

My name is Cy, and I am one of the four brothers mentioned. Both of my parents were deaf from a very early age; they never learned to speak. When you ask me how we learned speech, I can't really answer, knowing what I now know about how important those very early years are in this area. When we were really young, we didn't even know they were deaf or different (except for Dad's active sense of humor). Naturally, we didn't talk; we just signed. We lived way out in the country and didn't have other playmates. Grandma and Grandpa lived close by, and I spent a lot of time with them. That is when I began to know something was different. We probably began learning to talk there.

When we were about ready to start school, we moved into town. My first memory related to school is sitting in a sandbox, I guess on the playground. We had some troubles in school, but they were fairly minor as I recall. I couldn't talk or pronounce words very well. I was tested on an IQ test in the third grade and they said I had an IQ of 67. Both Mom and Dad worked, so we were all sort of out on our own with friends, which probably helped language, but now I wonder why those kids didn't stay away from us because we were a bit different. Probably the saving grace is that all four of us seem to have pretty well developed social intelligence or skills. We did get in some fights with kids, and people sometimes called us the "dummys' kids." I would guess that all four of us pretty much caught up with our peers by the eighth grade. One thing is for certain: I would not trade those parents for any others in the world. Whatever they did, they certainly did right.

Cy, Ph.D.

This student uses a computer that prints in large type that he can easily read. An individual using a computer to communicate probably has a severe physical or cognitive disability that affects communication.

For young children, interventions often focus on beginning language stimulation. Treatment is intended to mirror the conditions under which children normally learn language, but the stimulation may be intensified and more systematic.

Many different approaches have been used to remediate aphasia, although consistent and verifiable results have been slow to emerge. Intervention typically involves the development of an individual's profile of strengths, limitations, age, and developmental level, monolingual or bilingual background, and literacy, as well as considerations regarding temperament that may affect therapy (Alison, Winslow, Merchant, & Brumfitt, 2006; Holland, 2006; Worrall, Mc-Cooey, Davidson, Larkins, & Hickson, 2002). From such a profile, an individualized treatment plan can be designed.

Several questions immediately arise, including what to teach or remediate first and whether teaching should focus on an individual's strong or weak areas. These questions have been raised from time to time with respect to many disorders. Teaching exclusively to a child's weak areas may result in more failure than is either necessary or helpful to his or her progress. That is, the child may experience so little success and receive so little reinforcement that he or she becomes discouraged about the whole process. Good clinical judgment needs to be exercised in deciding how to divide one's attention between the aphasic child's strengths and his or her weaknesses. Intervention programs include the collaborative participation of parents and other family members, as well as any other professionals who may be involved with the overall treatment of the youngster (Nelson, 2002; Tiegerman-Farber, 2002; Turner & Whitworth, 2006).

The perspective for remediation of adults with aphasia begins from a point different from that for children, in that it involves relearning or reacquiring language function. Views regarding treatment have varied over the years. Early approaches included an expectation that adults with aphasia would exhibit spontaneous recovery. This approach has largely been replaced by a view that patients are more likely to progress if direct therapeutic instruction is implemented.

Strengths and limitations must both receive attention when an individualized remediation program is being planned. However, development of an aphasic adult's profile of strengths and deficits may involve some areas different from those that apply to children. For example, social, linguistic, and vocational readjustments are three broad areas that need attention for most adults with aphasia. Furthermore, the notion of readjustment differs substantially from initial skill acquisition. Language learning treatment (relearning) is often employed in a way that focuses on the individual's needs and is practical in terms of service

Computer technology has made inroads in many areas of human disability in the past few years and will become increasingly important in the future. Language disability intervention is one area where technology is being used effectively. Advances in both hardware and software have already affected language training and have great potential for future development.

First Words is a language tutorial program that may have a number of applications for teaching those who are developing or reacquiring language functions. This program uses graphic presentations combined with synthesized speech to teach high-frequency nouns and test a student's acquisition of them. The student is presented with two pictures of an object and asked to decide which one represents the word being taught. Students can select an answer using a computer keyboard or a special selection switch or by touching the object on the screen. First Words is a relatively inexpensive program costing about $200. The voice synthesizer and the touch-screen options must be added to the basic package, but they may be essential to effective intervention, depending on the student's capability.

delivery (Fridriksson, Nettles, Davis, Morrow, & Montgomery, 2006; Hopper, Holland, & Rewega, 2002). Some individuals with aphasia are effectively treated in group settings, whereas individual therapy works well for others (e.g., Hickin, Best, Herbert, Howard, & Osborne, 2002; Ross et al., 2006; Van-Slyke, 2002). Advances in technology are often used in diagnosis and treatment (Beveridge & Crerar, 2002; Fink, Brecher, Sobel, & Schwartz, 2005; Stark, Martin, & Fink, 2005); see the Assistive Technology, "Computers: A Language Tutorial Program."

An individualized treatment plan for adults with aphasia also involves evaluation, profile development, and teaching/therapy in specific areas within each of the broad domains (Melton & Shadden, 2005; Owens et al., 2007; Worrall et al., 2002). Such training should begin as soon as possible, depending on the person's condition. Some spontaneous recovery may occur during the first 6 months after an incident resulting in aphasia, but waiting beyond 2 months to begin treatment may seriously delay whatever degree of recovery is possible.

AUGMENTATIVE COMMUNICATION. Some individuals require intervention via means of communication other than oral language. In some cases, the person may be incapable of speaking because of a severe physical or cognitive disability, so a nonspeech means of communication must be designed and implemented. Known variably as assistive, alternative, and **augmentative communication**, these strategies may involve a variety of approaches, some employing new technological developments. Augmentative communication strategies have received increasing attention in the past few years, partly because of the development of technology applications in unusual settings and partly because of coverage in the popular press (Mechling & Cronin, 2006; Waller, 2006). Applications include a range of circumstances and disability conditions, such as intellectual disabilities, autism, and multiple disabilities that are often in the severe functioning range (Fager, Hux, Beukelman, & Karantounis, 2006; Johnston, Reichle, & Evans, 2004). These strategies must also be individualized to meet the specific needs of those being treated and to take into account their strengths and limitations in operating the technology. Augmentative communication strategies are providing therapists with important new alternatives for intervention with individuals who have language disorders. Research results suggest that carefully chosen techniques and devices can be quite effective (e.g., Noens, van Berckelaer-Onnes, Verpoorten, & van Duijn, 2006; Wolpaw, Birbaumer, McFarland, Pfurtscheller, & Vaughan, 2002). Two examples of specific devices are communication boards with graphics or symbols and electronic appliances that simulate speech sounds. Other approaches include systems of manual communication (such as gestures and signs) that do not depend on mechanical or electronic aids. See the Assistive Technology, "Assistive Devices to Help Level the Playing Field."

➤ **Augmentative communication**

Forms of communication that employ nonspeech alternatives.

Council for
Exceptional
Children

Standard 6: Communication

Using a pink cap rigged with a long gold stick and pencil eraser, 11-year-old Marisa Velez punches a few buttons on a computerized box.

"Hello, my name is Marisa Velez," the box says in a computerized voice, customized to sound like a girl. "This device lets me speak like anyone else."

For Marisa, who was born with quadriplegia cerebral palsy, the Liberator and other devices in her home and school are the key to a productive life.

Such assistive technology usually is associated with devices that help people with a disability, but it also includes commonplace items such as glasses, hearing aids, and canes.

Assistive technology has enabled Marisa to attend regular classes at Westvale Elementary School like any other student.

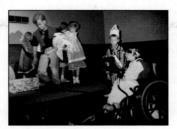

Marisa uses a Liberator voice machine to talk, a computer touch-screen to write, and a motorized wheelchair. All these devices enable her to participate in a school play.

She uses a motorized wheelchair to get around the building and a computer touch-screen to write papers. She also can use the Liberator voice machine, which has a built-in printer, to complete assignments and quizzes.

"It's her self-expression, her ability to express her feelings and goals. Just being understood makes her feel valued," said Marisa's mother, Norma Velez. "That's the purpose of technology—to not hold people back." Even so, Norma Velez had to scream and shout to get her insurance to pay for Marisa's Liberator. "Marisa was the first individual our [insurance] company provided a speech device for," she said. "At first, they said it was not a medical necessity. But the object is to not give up. If she is ill and cannot communicate what is wrong, of course that is a medical necessity."

SOURCE: Adapted from "Assistive Devices Help to Level Playing Field: Machines Can Be Key to Productive Life and Individual Self-Esteem," by V. Horiuchi, 1999, Salt Lake Tribune, April 10, p. D8.

Speech Disorders

Speech disorders involve deviations great enough to interfere with communication. Such speaking patterns are so divergent from what is typical and expected that they draw attention to the speaking act, thereby distracting the hearer's attention from the meaning of the message being sent. Such deviant speaking behavior can negatively affect the listener, the speaker, or both.

Speech is extremely important in contemporary society. Speaking ability can influence a person's success or failure in personal/social and professional arenas. Most people are about average in speaking ability, and they may envy those who are unusually articulate and pity those who have a difficult time with speech. What is it like to have a serious deficit in speaking ability? It is different for each individual, depending on the circumstances in which he or she operates and the severity of the deficit. The Case Study on Ricky (on page 306) illustrates the very personal nature of communication and speech disorders and their social/interpersonal impact.

People often carry strong emotional reactions to their speech that may significantly alter their behavior. Speech is so critical to functioning in society that speech disorders often have a significant impact on affected individuals. It is not difficult to imagine the impact that stuttering, for example, may have in classroom settings or in social encounters. Children may be ridiculed by peers, begin to feel inadequate, and suffer emotional stress. And that stress may continue into adulthood, limiting these individuals' social lives and influencing their vocational choices.

There are many different speech disorders and many theories about causes and treatment. Extensive volumes have focused solely on the topic. In this section, we will discuss fluency disorders, delayed speech, articulation disorders, and voice disorders.

CASE STUDY

RICKY

The following is a statement by Ricky Creech, a person with a serious communication disorder due to cerebral palsy. Ricky communicates by using a computer-controlled electronic augmentative communication device. He provides some insights into assumptions people make about individuals who cannot communicate. This is a portion of a presentation made at the National Institutes of Health.

"There is a great need for educating the public on how to treat physically limited people. People are still under the misconception that somehow the ability to speak, hear, see, feel, smell, and reason are tied together. That is, if a person loses one, he has lost the others.

The number-one question people ask my parents is "Can he hear?" When I reply that I can, they bend down where their lips are not two feet away from my eyes and say very loudly, "How—are—you? Do—you—like—that—talking—machine?" Now, I don't mind when that person is a pretty, young girl. But when it is an older or married woman, it is a little embarrassing. When the person is a man, I'm tempted to say something not very nice. . . .

I would make a great spy. When I am around, people just keep talking—because I can't speak, they think I can't hear or understand what is being said. I have listened to more private conversations than there are on the Watergate tapes. It is a good thing that I am not a blackmailer. If people knew that I hear and understand everything they say, some would die of embarrassment.

There is another conclusion which people make when first seeing me, which I don't kid about; I don't find it a bit humorous. That is, that I am mentally retarded.

The idea that if a person can't speak, something must be wrong with his mind is the prevalent belief in every class, among the educated as well as the not-so-educated. I have a very good friend who is a nuclear scientist, the most intelligent person I have ever known, but he admitted that when he first saw me, his first conclusion was that I was mentally retarded. This was in spite of my parents' assertions that I was not.

However, this man had a special quality—when he was wrong he could admit it with his mind and his heart—most people can't do both. There are people who know me who know with their minds that I am not mentally retarded, but they treat me as a child because in their hearts they have not really accepted that I have the mentality of an adult. I am an adult and I want to be treated as an adult. I have a tremendous amount of respect for anyone who does.

APPLICATION

1. Have you ever made the same error that the nuclear scientist made in the case study? Explain what you felt and how you acted.

2. Having read Ricky Creech's description, how would you react now?

3. As a professional, how would you explain Ricky's communication disorder to people so they would understand his abilities?

SOURCE: From "Consumers Speak Out on the Life of the Nonspeaker," by R. Creech and J. Viggiano, 1981, ASHA, 23, pp. 550–552. Reprinted by permission of the American Speech-Language-Hearing Association.

Fluency Disorders

In typical speech we are accustomed to a reasonably smooth flow of words and sentences. For the most part, it has a rhythm that is steady, regular, and rapid. Most of us also have times when we pause to think about what we are saying, either because we have made a mistake or because we want mentally to edit what we are about to say. However, these interruptions are infrequent and do not constitute a disturbance in the ongoing flow of our speaking. Our speech is generally fluent in speed and continuity.

Speech flow is a serious problem for people with a fluency disorder. Their speech is characterized by repeated interruptions, hesitations, or repetitions that interrupt the flow of communication. Some people have a fluency disorder known as cluttered speech, or **cluttering**, which is characterized by overly rapid speech that is disorganized, and occasionally filled with unnecessary words (Ramig & Dodge, 2005). Stuttering is the most recognized fluency disorder and has fascinated researchers for years.

STUTTERING. **Stuttering** occurs when the flow of speech is abnormally interrupted by repetitions, blocking, or prolongations of sounds, syllables, words, or phrases (Owens et al., 2007; Ramig & Shames, 2006). Although stuttering is a familiar concept to most people, it occurs rather infrequently, in between 1% and 5% of the general population, and has one of

➤ **Cluttering**
A speech disorder characterized by excessively rapid, disorganized speaking, often including words or phrases unrelated to the topic.

➤ **Stuttering**
A speech disorder that occurs when the flow of speech is abnormally interrupted by repetitions, blocking, or prolongations of sounds, syllables, words, or phrases.

the lowest prevalence rates among all speech disorders (e.g., Craig & Tran, 2005; Jones, Gebski, Onslow, & Packman, 2002). For example, articulation disorders (e.g., omitting, adding, or distorting certain sounds) occur in about 2% of 6- and 7-year-old children in the United States (American Psychiatric Association, 2000).

Laypeople's high awareness of stuttering comes partly from the nature of the behavior involved. Interruptions in speech flow are very evident to both speaker and listener, are perhaps more disruptive to communication than any other type of speech disorder, and often affect interpersonal relationships. Further, listeners often grow uncomfortable and may try to assist the stuttering speaker by providing missing or incomplete words (Davis, Howell, & Cooke, 2002; Gabel, Colcord, & Petrosino, 2002). The speaker's discomfort may be magnified by physical movements, gestures, or facial distortions that often accompany stuttering.

Parents often become concerned about stuttering as their children learn to talk. Anxiety is usually unnecessary; most children exhibit some normal nonfluencies that diminish and cease with maturation. However, these normal nonfluencies have historically played a role in some theories about the causes of stuttering.

Causation of Stuttering Current thinking suggests that stuttering may have a variety of causes (e.g., Max & Gracco, 2005; Sahin, Krespi, Yilmaz, & Coban, 2005; Yairi, 2004), and most behavioral scientists have abandoned the search for a single cause. Theories regarding causes follow three basic perspectives, regarding stuttering as a symptom of some emotional disturbance, as a result of biological makeup or some neurological problem, or as a learned behavior.

Some investigations of emotional problems have explored psychosocial factors emerging from the parent-child interaction, although this work is somewhat fragmentary. The emotional component has been included in many descriptions of contributors to stuttering, including speculation that stuttering may be caused by an individual's capacity being exceeded by demands. Such theories, however, often consider a person's cognitive, linguistic, and motor capacities as other contributors. Research on the relationship of stuttering to emotion continues only sporadically (Blomgren, Roy, Callister, & Merrill, 2005; Gregory, 2003a; Onslow, 2006). Many professionals have become less interested in emotional theories of the causation of stuttering. Investigation of this perspective is difficult because of problems with research methodology (e.g., Doehring, 2002).

Investigators continue to explore biological causation in a number of different areas. Limited evidence indicates that the brains or neurological structures of some who stutter may be organized or function differently than those of people without fluency disorders, although the nature of such differences remains unclear (Brown, Ingham, Ingham, Laird, & Fox, 2005;

FOCUS 5
Cite three factors that are thought to cause stuttering.

Neumann et al., 2005; Vartanov, Glozman, Kiselnikov, & Karpova, 2005). Some research also suggests that individuals who stutter use different sections of the brain to process information than do their counterparts with fluent speech. A few authors suggest that people who stutter may have differences in brain hemisphere function. For example, the hemispheres of the brain may compete with each other in information processing (e.g., Neumann et al., 2005; Subramanian & Yairi, 2006). Some researchers also suggest that nervous system damage, such as from an injury, can result in stuttering (Reilly, Douglas, & Oates, 2003). Other theories imply that a variety of problems may disrupt the person's precise timing ability, coordination, or capacity for synchrony, all of which are important elements in speech production (Alm, 2006; Max & Gracco, 2005; Sommer, Koch, Paulus, Weiller, & Buechel, 2002).

It has long been theorized that stuttering is learned behavior. According to this perspective, learned stuttering emerges from the normal nonfluency evident in early speech development. Language develops rapidly from 2 to 5 years of age, and stuttering often emerges in that general timeframe as well—between 3 and 5 years of age (e.g., Hulit, 2004; Owens et al., 2007; Venkatagiri, 2005). From a learning causation point of view, a typical child may become a stuttering child if considerable attention is focused on normal disfluencies at that stage of development. The disfluency of early stuttering may be further magnified by negative feelings about the self, as well as by anxiety (e.g., Blomgren et al., 2005; Stager et al., 2005). Interest in this theory persists, although, like others, it has its critics (e.g., Bloodstein, 2006; Onslow, 2006).

Theories about the causes of stuttering have included consideration of heredity (Gregory, 2003b; Subramanian & Yairi, 2006). Although this hypothesis remains speculative, some evidence suggests that stuttering may be gender-related, because males who stutter outnumber females about 4 to 1. Heredity has also been of interest because of the high incidence of stuttering and other speech disorders within certain families, as well as in twins (Ooki, 2005; Ramig & Shames, 2006). However, it is very hard to separate hereditary and environmental influences—a ubiquitous problem for research in human development (Drew & Hardman, 2007; Lytton & Gallagher, 2002).

Causation has been an especially elusive and perplexing matter for workers in speech pathology. Some recent literature has raised questions about definitions, assessment, and some of the theoretical logic related to stuttering. Researchers and clinicians continue their search for a cause, seeking more effective treatment and prevention (e.g., Craig, 2002; Venkatagiri, 2005).

Council for Exceptional Children

Standard 4: Instructional Strategies

Standard 7: Instructional Planning

Intervention Many approaches have been used to treat stuttering over the years, with mixed results. Interventions such as modeling, self-monitoring, counseling, and the involvement of support group assistance have been all studied and shown to be somewhat useful for children who stutter (e.g., Ramig & Dodge, 2005; Venkatagiri, 2005). Some research on medication treatment has shown improvements, although pharmacological intervention has not been widely employed (Stager et al., 2005; van Wattum, 2006). Hypnosis has been used to treat some cases of stuttering, but its success has been limited. Speech rhythm has been the focus of some therapy, as has developing the naturalness of speaking patterns. Relaxation therapy and biofeedback have also been used, since tenseness and anxiety are often observed in people who stutter (Craig & Tran, 2005; Max & Gracco, 2005; Ramig & Shames, 2006). In all the techniques noted, outcomes are mixed, and people who stutter are likely to try several approaches (Craig, 2002; Dayalu, Kalinowski, & Saltuklaroglu, 2002). The inability of any one treatment or cluster of treatments consistently to help people who stutter demonstrates the ongoing need for research in this area. There is also need for research on effective timing for intervention (e.g., Harris, Onslow, Packman, Harrison, & Menzies, 2002). Early intervention has long been popular in many exceptionality areas. However, it does carry a risk associated with labeling: the risk that a child may become what he or she is labeled (Jezer, 2006; Jones et al., 2005; Lattermann, Shenker, & Thordardottir, 2005).

For several years, treatment models have increasingly focused on direct behavioral therapy—that is, attempting to teach children who stutter to use fluent speech patterns (e.g., Block, Onslow, Packman, & Dacakis, 2006). In some cases, children are taught to monitor and manage their stuttering by speaking more slowly or rhythmically. Using this model, they are also taught to reward themselves for increasing periods of fluency. Some behavioral thera-

Preschool teachers should use all occasions possible to increase the vocabulary of a child with delayed speech. This child may be more comfortable using a puppet to interact with his teacher or other children.

pies include information regarding physical factors (such as regulating breathing) and direct instruction about correct speaking behaviors. The overall therapy combines several dimensions, such as an interview regarding the inconvenience of stuttering, behavior modification training, and follow-up. Because stuttering is a complex problem, effective interventions are likely to be complicated.

DELAYED SPEECH. **Delayed speech** is a deficit in communication ability in which the individual speaks like a much younger person. From a developmental point of view, this problem involves delayed speech and language development. Delayed speech may occur for many reasons and take various forms. Assessment and treatment differ accordingly (Flipsen, Hammer, & Yost, 2005; Paatsch, Blamey, & Sarant, 2006).

Delayed speech is often associated with other maturational delays. It may be associated with a hearing impairment, intellectual disabilities, emotional disturbance, or brain injury (e.g., Drew & Hardman, 2007; Kennedy, Watkin, & Worsfold, 2006). Young children can typically communicate, at least to some degree, before they learn verbal behaviors. They use gestures, gazing or eye contact, facial expressions, other physical movements, and nonspeech vocalizations, such as grunts or squeals. This early development illustrates the relationship among communication, language, and speech. Children with delayed speech often have few or no verbalizations that can be interpreted as conventional speech. Some communicate solely through physical gestures. Others may use a combination of gestures and vocal sounds that are not even close approximations of words. Still others may speak, but in a very limited manner, perhaps using single words (typically nouns without auxiliary words, such as *ball* instead of *my ball*), fewer syllables per word, or primitive sentences that are short or incomplete such as "Get ball" rather than "Would you get the ball?" (Flipsen, 2006; Flipsen et al., 2005). Such communication is normal for infants and very young children, but not for children beyond the age when most have at least a partially fluent speech (Bacon & Wilcox, 2006; Delgado et al., 2002).

Differences between stuttering and delayed speech are obvious, but the distinction between delayed speech and articulation disorders is less clear (Flipsen et al., 2005; Yavas, 2002). In fact, children with delayed speech usually make many articulation errors in their speaking patterns. However, their major problems lie in grammatical and vocabulary deficits, which are more matters of developmental delay. The current prevalence of delayed speech is not clear, and government estimates do not even regularly provide data on the provision of services for delayed speech (U.S. Department of Education, 2006). Such problems, along with definitional differences among studies, have led many to place little confidence in existing prevalence figures.

Causation of Delayed Speech Because delayed speech can take a variety of forms, the causes of these problems also vary greatly. Several types of environmental deprivation contribute to delayed speech. For example, partial or complete hearing loss may seriously limit an

➤ **Delayed speech**
A deficit in speaking proficiency whereby the individual performs like someone much younger.

FOCUS 6
Identify two ways in which learning theory and home environments are related to delayed speech.

individual's sensory experience and hence cause serious delays in speech development (e.g., Radziewicz & Antonellis, 2002; Owens, 2006; Szagun, 2002). For those with normal hearing, the broader environment may also contribute to delayed speech (e.g., Bernstein & Levey, 2002; Burgess, Hecht, & Lonigan, 2002). For example, in some children's homes there is minimal conversation, little chance for the child to speak, and thus little opportunity to learn speech. Other problems, such as cerebral palsy and emotional disturbance, may also contribute to delayed speech.

Negativism may be one cause of delayed speech. Negativism involves a conflict between parents' expectations and a child's ability to perform, and such a conflict often occurs as children develop speech. Considerable pressure is placed on children during the period when they normally develop their speaking skills: to go to bed when told, to control urination and defecation properly, and to learn appropriate eating skills, among other things. The demands are great, and they may exceed a child's performance ability. Children react in many ways when more is demanded than they are able to produce. They may refuse. They may simply not talk, seeming to withdraw from family interactions. In normal development, children occasionally refuse to follow the directions of adults. One very effective refusal is silence, to which the parents' reprisal options are few and may be ineffective. (As a parent, it is relatively simple to punish refusal to go to bed or to clean one's room, but it is a different matter when parents encounter the refusal to talk. It is not easy to force a child to talk through conventional punishment techniques.) Viewing negativism from another angle, children may be punished even to the point of abuse for talking in some situations. Parents may be irritated by a child's attempt to communicate. A child may speak too loudly or at inappropriate times, such as when adults are reading, watching television, resting, or talking with other adults (even more rules to learn at such a tender age). Delayed speech may occur in extreme cases of prolonged negativism related to talking (Gelfand & Drew, 2003; Owens, 2004).

Such unpleasant environments may raise concerns about the amount of love and caring in such a situation and the role that emotional health plays in learning to speak (e.g., Cohen, 2002; Molfese & Molfese, 2002). But delayed speech can also occur in families that exhibit great love and caring. In some environments, a child may have little need to learn speech. Most parents are concerned about satisfying their child's needs or desires. However, carrying this ambition to the extreme, a "superparent" may anticipate the child's wants (e.g., toys, water, or food) and provide them even before the child makes a verbal request. Such children need only gesture and their parents immediately respond, thereby rewarding gestures and not promoting the development of speech skills. Learning to speak is much more complex and demanding than making simple movements or facial grimaces. When gesturing is rewarded, speaking is less likely to be learned properly.

Intervention Treatment approaches for delayed speech are as varied as its causes. Whatever the cause, an effective treatment should teach the child appropriate speaking proficiency for his or her age level. In some cases, matters other than just defective learning, such as hearing impairments, must be considered in the treatment procedures (Owens, 2004; Radziewicz & Antonellis, 2002). Such cases may involve surgery and prosthetic appliances like hearing aids, as well as specially designed instructional techniques aimed at teaching speech.

Treatment is likely to focus on the basic principles of learned behavior if defective learning is the primary cause of delayed speech. In this situation, the stimulus and reinforcement patterns that are contributing to delayed speech must be changed so that appropriate speaking behaviors can be learned. Although the process sounds simple, learning language is very complex, and the identification and control of such contingencies are quite complicated (Annoussamy, 2006; Taatgen & Anderson, 2002). Some success has been achieved through direct instruction, as well as through other procedures aimed at increasing spontaneous speech. Such instruction emphasizes positive reinforcement of speaking to shape the child's behavior in the direction of more normal speech. Other interventions involve the collaborative efforts of speech clinicians, teachers, and parents (Tiegerman-Farber, 2002; Turner & Whitworth, 2006; Weiss, 2002) to focus on modifying the child's speech and the family environment that contributed to the problem. Because different elements cause the delay in each case, therapies must be individually tailored.

ARTICULATION DISORDERS. Articulation disorders represent the largest category of all speech problems, which are termed phonological disorders in DSM-IV and much speech and language research (American Psychiatric Association, 2000; Johnson & Beitchman, 2006; Schwartz, 2006). For most people with this type of difficulty, the label **functional articulation disorders** is used. This term refers to articulation problems that are not due to structural physiological defects, such as cleft palate and neurological problems, but, rather, are likely to have resulted from environmental or psychological influences.

Articulation disorders are characterized by abnormal production of speech sounds, resulting in the inaccurate or otherwise inappropriate execution of speaking. This category of problems often includes omissions, substitutions, additions, and distortions of certain sounds (Gibbon & Wood, 2002; Owens et al., 2007). Omissions most frequently involve dropping consonants from the ends of words (e.g., *los* for *lost*), although omissions may occur in any position in a word. Substitutions frequently include saying *w* for *r* (e.g., *wight* for *right*), *w* for *l* (e.g., *fowo* for *follow*), and *th* for *s* (e.g., *thtop* for *stop*, and *thoup* for *soup*). Articulation errors may also involve transitional lisps, where a *th* sound precedes or follows an *s* (e.g., *sthoup* for *soup* or *yeths* for *yes*) (Ferrand, 2007).

Articulation disorders are a rather prevalent type of speech problem. Research suggests that most problems encountered by speech clinicians involve articulation disorders (e.g., American Psychiatric Association, 2000; Owens et al., 2007). Although the vast majority of these difficulties are functional, some articulation problems may be attributed to physiological abnormalities.

Causation of Articulation Disorders Articulation disorders develop for many reasons. Some are caused by physical malformations, such as abnormal mouth, jaw, or teeth structures, and others result from nerve injury or brain damage (e.g., Ferrand, 2007; Ogar et al., 2006). Functional articulation disorders are often seen as caused by defective learning of the speaking act. However, such categories of causation overlap in practice, and even the line between functional and structural articulation disorders is indistinct. Furthermore, function and structure, though often related, are not perfectly correlated: Some people with physical malformations that "should" result in articulation problems do not have such problems, and vice versa.

Despite this qualifying note, we will examine the causes of articulation performance deficits in terms of two general categories: those due to physical oral malformations and those that are clearly functional because there is no physical deformity. These distinctions remain useful for instructional purposes, since it is the unusual individual who overcomes a physical abnormality and articulates satisfactorily.

In addition to physical abnormalities of the oral cavity, other types of physical defects, such as an abnormal or absent larynx, can affect articulation performance. Many different physical structures influence speech formulation, and all must be synchronized with learned muscle and tissue movements, auditory feedback, and a multitude of other factors. These coordinated functions are almost never perfect, but for most people they occur in a remarkably successful manner. Oral structure malformations alter the manner in which coordinated movements must take place, and sometimes they make normal or accurate production of sounds extremely difficult, if not impossible.

One faulty oral formation recognized by most people is the cleft palate, which is often referred to by speech pathologists as clefts of the lip or palate or both. The **cleft palate** is a gap in the soft palate and roof of the mouth, sometimes extending through the upper lip. The roof of the mouth serves an important function in accurate sound production. A cleft palate reduces the division between the nasal and mouth cavities, influencing the movement of air that is so important to articulation performance. Children with clefts often encounter substantial difficulties in articulation (Bressman, Klaiman, & Fischbach, 2006; Wermke, Hauser, Komposch, & Stellzig, 2002). Clefts are congenital defects that occur in about one of every 700 births and may take any of several forms (e.g., Marrinan & Shprintzen, 2006; Owens et al., 2007). Figure 11.4 on page 312 shows a normal palate in part (a) and unilateral and bilateral cleft palates in parts (b) and (c), respectively; it is easy to see how articulation would be impaired. These problems are caused by prenatal developmental difficulties and are often corrected by surgery.

Articulation performance is also significantly influenced by a person's dental structure. Because the tongue and lips work together with the teeth to form many sounds, dental abnormalities may

> **Functional articulation disorders**
Articulation problems that are not due to structural defects or neurological problems but are likely to have resulted from environmental or psychological influences.

> **Cleft palate**
A gap in the soft palate and roof of the mouth, sometimes extending through the upper lip.

FIGURE 11.4

Normal and Cleft Palate Configurations

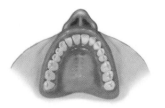
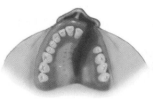
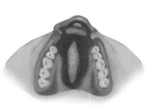

(a) Normal palate configuration   (b) Unilateral cleft palate   (c) Bilateral cleft palate   (d) Repaired cleft palate

➤ **Occlusion**

The closing and fitting together of dental structures.

➤ **Malocclusion**

An abnormal fit between the upper and lower dental structures.

result in serious articulation disorders. Some dental malformations are side effects of cleft palates, as shown in parts (b) and (c) of Figure 11.4, but other dental deformities not associated with clefts also cause articulation difficulties.

The natural meshing of the teeth in the upper and lower jaws is important to speech production. The general term used for the closure and fitting together of dental structures is **occlusion**, or dental occlusion. When the fit is abnormal, the condition is known as **malocclusion**. Occlusion involves several factors, including the biting height of the teeth when the jaws are closed, the alignment of teeth in the upper and lower jaws, the nature of curves in upper and lower jaws, and teeth positioning. A normal adult occlusion is illustrated in part (a) of Figure 11.5. The upper teeth normally extend slightly beyond those of the lower jaw, and the bite overlap of those on the bottom is about one third for the front teeth (incisors) when the jaw is closed.

Occlusion abnormalities take many forms, although we will discuss only two here. When the overbite of the top teeth is unusually large, the normal difference between the lower and upper dental structures is exaggerated. Such conditions may be due to the positioning of the upper and lower jaws, as illustrated in part (b) of Figure 11.5. In other cases nearly the opposite occurs, as illustrated in part (c) of Figure 11.5, forming another kind of jaw misalignment. Exaggerated overbites and underbites may result from atypical teeth positions or angles, as well as from atypical jaw alignment. All can cause articulation difficulties.

We turn now to functional articulation disorders. Many such disorders are thought to be due to faulty language learning. The sources of defective speech learning are frequently un-

FIGURE 11.5

Normal and Abnormal Dental Occlusions

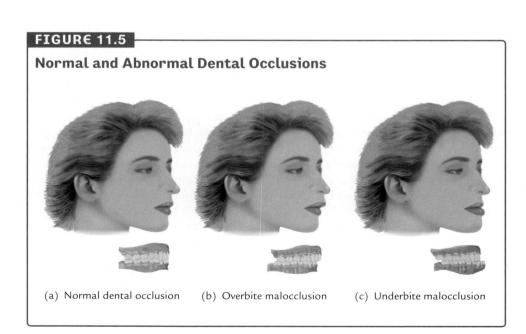

(a) Normal dental occlusion   (b) Overbite malocclusion   (c) Underbite malocclusion

known or difficult to identify precisely (Ehrhardt, Hixon, & Poling, 2006; Robinson & Robb, 2002; Silliman & Diehl, 2002). Like other articulation problems, those of a functional nature have numerous specific causes. For example, interactions between children and their adult caretakers (parents and others) make a major contribution to language acquisition (Bernstein & Levey, 2002; Gelfand & Drew, 2003; Hulit & Howard, 2006). In some cases, existing stimulus and reinforcement patterns may not support accurate articulation. For example, parents may be inconsistent in encouraging and prompting accurate articulation. Parents tend to be very busy. Routinely urging their children to speak properly may not be high on their priority list. However, such encouragement is important, particularly if misarticulation begins to emerge as a problem.

Also, adults may unthinkingly view some normal inaccuracies of speech in young children as cute or amusing. "Baby talk," for example, may be powerfully reinforced by parents asking the young child to say a particular word in the presence of grandparents or other guests and rewarding him or her with laughter and hugs and kisses. Such potent rewards can result in misarticulations that linger long beyond the time when normal maturation would diminish or eliminate them. Related defective learning may come from modeling. Parents (or other adults) may model and thus reinforce articulation disorders when they imitate the baby talk of young children or substantially change their manner of speaking in what has been called "parentese" (Owens, 2005). If parents and others realized the potential results of such behavior, they would probably change their verbal interchanges with young children. Modeling is a potent tool in shaping learned behavior. Although the negative influence of baby talk between parents and children has been questioned, modeling and imitation are used in interventions and are thought to influence natural verbal development (Uchikoshi, 2006; Wright, 2006).

Intervention Many types of treatment exist for articulation disorders. Clearly, the treatment for disorders due to physical abnormalities differs from that for functional disorders. In many cases, however, treatment may include a combination of procedures. The treatment of articulation disorders has also been somewhat controversial, partly because of the large number that are functional in nature. A predictable developmental progression occurs in a substantial number of functional articulation disorders. In such cases, articulation problems diminish and may even cease to exist as the child matures. For instance, the *r*, *s*, and *th* problems disappear for many children after the age of 5. Thus many school administrators are reluctant to treat functional articulation disorders in younger students. In other words, if a significant proportion of articulation disorders is likely to be corrected as the child continues to develop, why expend precious resources on early treatment? This logic has a certain appeal, particularly in times when there is a shortage of educational resources and their use is constantly questioned (see the nearby Debate Forum). However, this argument must be applied with considerable caution. In general, improvement of articulation performance continues until a child is about 9 or 10 years old. (see Reflect on This to hear from $7\frac{1}{2}$-year old Timothy.) If articulation problems persist beyond this age, they are unlikely to improve without intense intervention. Furthermore, the longer such problems are allowed to continue, the more difficult treatment will become and the less likely it is to be successful. Although some suggest that the impact of articulation difficulties is ultimately minimal, others believe that affected individuals may still have residual indications of the disorder many years later (e.g., Owens et al., 2007; Schwartz, 2006).

Deciding whether to treat articulation problems in young children is not easy, and interventions can be quite complex. One option is to combine articulation training with other instruction for all very young children. This approach may serve as an interim measure for those who have continuing problems, facilitate the development of articulation for others, and not overly tax school resources. It does, however, require some training for teachers of young children.

Considerable progress has been made over the years in various types of surgical repair for cleft palates. Current research addresses a number of related matters, such as complex patient assessment before and after intervention (Karnell, Bailey, & Johnson, 2005; Sell, 2005; Wermke et al., 2002). The surgical procedures may be intricate because of the dramatic nature of the structural defect. Some such interventions include Teflon implants in

FOCUS **7**
Identify two reasons why some professionals are reluctant to treat functional articulation disorders in young schoolchildren.

Council for
Exceptional
Children

Standard 4: Instructional Strategies

Standard 7: Instructional Planning

INCLUSION AND COLLABORATION THROUGH THE LIFESPAN

People with Communication Disorders

EARLY CHILDHOOD YEARS

Tips for the Family

- Model speech and language to your infant by talking to him or her in normal tones from a very early age, even though he or she may not yet be intentionally communicating directly with you.
- Respond to babbling and other noises the young child makes with conversation, reinforcing early verbal output.
- Do not overreact if your child is not developing speech at the same rate as someone else's infant; great variation is found between children.
- If you are concerned about your child's speech development, have his or her hearing tested to determine whether that source of stimulation is normal.
- Observe other areas of development to assure yourself that your child is progressing within the broad boundaries of normal variation.
- If you are seeking day care or a preschool program, search carefully for one that will provide a rich, systematic communication environment.
- Reach out and initiate communication with professionals who are involved with your child, such as preschool teachers, speech and language pathologists, and so on.
- Be proactive in collaborating and communicate across different professions to coordinate the child's services. Family members, especially parents or guardians, may play a central coordination role for the child's interactions and services with professionals.

Tips for the Preschool Teacher

- Encourage collaborative parent involvement in all dimensions of the program, including systematic speech and language stimulation at home.
- Consider all situations and events as opportunities to teach speech and language, perhaps initially focusing on concrete objects and later moving to the more abstract, depending on the individual child's functioning level.
- Ask "wh" questions, such as what, who, when, and where, giving the child many opportunities to practice speaking as well as thinking.
- Practice with the child the use of the prepositions *in*, *on*, *out*, and so forth.
- Use all occasions possible to increase the child's vocabulary.

Tips for Preschool Personnel

- Communicate with the young child and all of those that are interacting with him or her. Collaborate in either direct or indirect communication instruction, but do so in collaboration with the child's teacher and parent. Many times the informal communication in the hallway is more important than we think.

Tips for Neighbors and Friends

- Interact with young children with communication disorders as you would with any others, speaking to them normally and directly modeling appropriate communication.
- Intervene if you encounter other children ridiculing the speech and language of these youngsters, encourage sensitivity to individual differences among your own and other neighborhood children.

ELEMENTARY YEARS

Tips for the Family

- Stay proactively involved in your child's educational program through active participation with the school.
- Work in collaboration with the child's teacher on speaking practice, blending it naturally into family and individual activities.
- Communicate naturally with the child; avoid "talking down" and thereby modeling the use of "simpler language."

Tips for the General Education Classroom Teacher

- Continue collaborating with and promoting parents' involvement in their child's intervention program in whatever manner they can participate.
- Encourage the child with communication disorders to talk about events and things in his or her environment and to describe experiences in as much detail as possible.
- Use all situations possible to provide practice for the child's development of speech and language skills.
- Promote vocabulary enhancement for the child in different topic areas.

Tips for School Personnel

- Promote an environment where all who are available and in contact with the child are involved in communication instruction, if not directly then indirectly through interaction and modeling.
- Encourage student involvement in a wide array of activities that can also be used to promote speech and language development.

Tips for Neighbors and Friends

- Interact with children with communication disorders normally; do not focus on the speaking difficulties that may be evident.
- As a neighbor or friend, provide support for the child's parents, who may be struggling with difficult feelings about their child's communication skills.

Tips for the Family

- Children who still exhibit communication problems at this level are likely to perform on a lower cognitive level. In such cases communication may focus on functional matters such as grooming, feeding, and so on.
- For some children, communication may involve limited verbalization; consider other means of interacting.
- Interact with your child as much and as normally as possible.

Tips for the General Education Classroom Teacher

- Embed communication instruction in the context of functional areas (e.g., social interactions, requests for assistance, choice making).
- Consider adding augmented communication devices or procedures to the student's curriculum.

Tips for School Personnel

- Develop school activities that will encourage use of a broad variety of skill levels in speaking (i.e., not just the debate club).
- Collaborate and communicate with others in the school to find the best way you can contribute to the child's language or speech growth. Informal communication about daily activities may represent a very important growth and practice opportunity for the child.
- Promote school activities that permit participation through communication modes other than speaking (being careful to ensure that these efforts are consistent with therapy goals).

Tips for Neighbors and Friends

- To the degree that you are comfortable doing so, interact with children using alternative communication approaches (e.g., signs, gesturing, pantomiming).

Tips for the Family

- Interact with the adult who has a communication disorder on a level that is functionally appropriate for his or her developmental level. For some adults with communication disorders, the problem may be compounded by other disorders, such as intellectual disabilities. For others, the communication disorder is an inconvenience rather than another disability.

Tips for Therapists or Other Professionals

- Recognize the maturity level of the person with whom you are working. Do not assume you know the interests or inclinations of a younger client simply because the individual has a communication difficulty.
- Become aware of the lifestyle context of the adult before suggesting augmentative devices. Some techniques may not serve well a person who is employed or otherwise engaged in adult activities.

Tips for Neighbors and Friends

- Communicate in as normal a fashion as possible, given the severity and type of disorder. If the person uses alternative communication methods, consider learning about them to the degree that you feel comfortable.

I THINK I TALK OKAY, DON' YOU?

My name is Timothy. I am almost $7\frac{1}{2}$ years old. Mondays after school, I go to the university where I meet "wif a lady who help me talk betto. It was my teacha's idea 'cause she said I don' say "l" and "r" good an some othos too. I kinda like it [coming here] but I think I talk okay, don' you? I can say "l" good now all the time and "r" when I reeeally think about it.

I have lots of friends, fow, no—five. I don' talk to them about comin' hea, guess I'm jus not in the mood. Hey, you witing this down, is that good? You know the caw got hit by a semi this mowning and the doow hanle came off. I'm a little dizzy 'cause we wecked."

Timothy, age $7\frac{1}{2}$

the hard portion of the palate, as well as stretching and stitching together of the fleshy tissue. As Figure 11.4 suggests, surgery is often required for the upper lip and nose structures, and corrective dental work may be undertaken as well. It may also be necessary to train or retrain the individual in articulation and to assess his or her emotional status insofar as it is related to appearance or speech skills, depending on the child's age at the time of surgery (Ehrhardt et al., 2006). A child's continued development may introduce new problems later; for example, the physical growth of the jaw or mouth may create difficulties for someone who underwent surgery at a very young age. Although early correction has resulted in successful healing and speech for a very high percentage of treated cases, the permanence of such results is uncertain in light of later growth spurts.

Treatment of cleft palate may involve the use of prosthetic appliances as well. For example, a prosthesis that basically serves as the upper palate or at least covers the fissures may be em-

DEBATE FORUM

TO TREAT OR NOT TO TREAT?

Articulation problems represent about 80% of all speech disorders encountered by speech clinicians, making this type of difficulty the most prevalent of all communication disorders. It is also well known that young children normally make a number of articulation errors during the process of maturation as they are learning to talk. A substantial portion do not conquer all the rules of language and produce all the speech sounds correctly until they are 8 or 9 years old, yet they eventually develop normal speech and articulate properly. In lay terminology, they seem to "grow out of" early articulation problems. This maturation outcome and the prevalence of articulation problems raise serious questions about treatment in the early years.

POINT

Some school administrators are reluctant to treat young children who display articulation errors because the resources of school districts are in very short supply and budgets are extremely tight. If a substantial proportion of young children's articulation problems will correct themselves through maturation, then shouldn't the precious resources of school districts be directed to other, more pressing problems? Articulation problems should not be treated unless they persist beyond the age of 10 or 11.

COUNTERPOINT

Although articulation does improve with maturation, delaying intervention is a mistake. The longer such problems persist, the more difficult treatment will be. Even the claim of financial savings is an invalid one. If all articulation difficulties are allowed to continue, those children who do not outgrow such problems will be more difficult to treat later, requiring more intense and expensive intervention than they would have needed if treated early. Early intervention for articulation problems is vitally important.

ployed. Such an appliance may be attached to the teeth to hold it in position; it resembles the palate portion of artificial dentures.

Dental malformations other than those associated with clefts can also be corrected. Surgery can alter jaw structure and alignment. In some cases, orthodontic treatment may involve the repositioning of teeth through extractions and the use of braces. Prosthetic appliances, such as full or partial artificial dentures, may also be used. As in other types of problems, the articulation patient who has orthodontic treatment often requires speech therapy to learn proper speech performance.

Treatment of functional articulation disorders often focuses on relearning the speaking act; in some cases, muscle control and usage are the focus. Specific causes of defective learning are difficult to identify precisely, but the basic assumption in such cases is that an inappropriate stimulus and reinforcement situation (such as inappropriate early modeling or defective hearing) was present in the environment during speech development (Anderson, 2002; McAuliffe, Ward, & Murdoch, 2005; Schwartz, 2006). Accordingly treatment includes an attempt to correct that set of circumstances so that accurate articulation can be learned. Several behavior modification procedures have been employed successfully in treating functional articulation disorders. In all cases, treatment techniques are difficult to implement because interventions must teach proper articulation, must be tailored to the individual, and must promote generalization of the new learning to a variety of word configurations and diverse environments beyond the treatment setting (Anderson, 2002; Owens et al., 2007). Further research on articulation disorder intervention is badly needed, especially in view of its prevalence. Some moreover, call for improving the quality of measurement and research methods employed in this and other areas of communication disorders (Pring, 2004; Schlosser, 2005).

It should also be noted that differences in language and dialect can create some interesting issues regarding treatment. When a child's first language is other than English or involves an ethnic dialect, that youngster may demonstrate a distinctiveness of articulation that makes his or her speech different and perhaps hard to understand (Battle, 2002; Costa & Santesteban, 2006; Uchikoshi, 2006). Does this circumstance require an intervention similar to that applied for articulation disorders? Such a question involves cultural, social, and political implications far beyond those typically considered by professionals working with speech disorders.

VOICE DISORDERS. **Voice disorders** involve unusual or abnormal acoustical qualities in the sounds made when a person speaks. All voices differ significantly in pitch, loudness, and other features from the voices of others of the same gender, cultural group, and age. However, voice disorders involve acoustical qualities that are so different that they are noticeable and may divert a listener's attention from the content of a message.

Relatively little attention has been paid to voice disorders in the research literature, for several reasons. First, the determination of voice normalcy involves a great deal of subjective judgment. Moreover, what is normal varies considerably with the circumstances (e.g., football games, barroom conversation, or seminar discussion) and with geographical location (e.g., the West, a rural area, New England, or the Deep South). Another factor that complicates analysis of voice disorders is related to the acceptable ranges of normal voice. Most individuals' voices fall within acceptable ranges. Children with voice disorders are often not referred for help, and their problems are persistent when not treated (Boone, McFarlane, & Von Berg, 2005; Case, 2002; Gates, 2006).

Children with voice disorders often speak with an unusual nasality, hoarseness, or breathiness. Nasality involves either too little resonance from the nasal passages (**hyponasality** or **denasality**), which dulls the resonance of consonants and sounds as though the child has a continual cold or stuffy nose, or too much sound coming through the nose (**hypernasality**), which causes a twang in the speech. People with voice disorders of hoarseness have a constant husky sound to their speech, as though they had strained their voices by yelling. Breathiness is a voice disorder with very low volume, like a whisper; it sounds as though not enough air is flowing through the vocal cords. Other voice disorders include overly loud or soft speaking and pitch abnormalities (such as monotone speech).

➤ **Voice disorder**

A condition in which an individual habitually speaks with a voice that differs in pitch, loudness, or quality from the voices of others of the same sex and age in a particular cultural group.

➤ **Hyponasality**

A voice resonance disorder whereby too little air passes through the nasal cavity; also known as denasality.

➤ **Denasality**

A voice resonance problem that occurs when too little air passes through the nasal cavity; also known as hyponasality.

➤ **Hypernasality**

A voice resonance disorder that occurs when excessive air passes through the nasal cavity, often resulting in an unpleasant twanging sound.

Factors in voice disorders that interfere with communication are pitch, loudness, and quality. A voice disorder exists when these factors, singly or in combination, cause the listener to focus on the sounds being made rather than the message to be communicated.

Like so many speech problems, the nature of voice disorders varies greatly. Our description provides considerable latitude, but it also outlines the general parameters of voice disorders often dismissed in the literature: pitch, loudness, and quality. An individual with a voice disorder may exhibit problems with one or more of these factors, and they may significantly interfere with communication (that is, the listener will focus on the sound rather than the message) (Owens et al., 2007; Sapienza & Hicks, 2006).

Causation of Voice Disorders An appropriate voice pitch is efficient and is suited to the situation and the speech content, as well as to the speaker's laryngeal structure. Correct voice pitch permits inflection without voice breaks or excessive strain. Appropriate pitch varies as emotion and meaning change and should not distract attention from the message. The acoustical characteristics of voice quality include such factors as nasality, breathy speech, and hoarse-sounding speech. As for the other element of voice, loudness is subjective. A normal voice is not habitually characterized by undue loudness or unusual softness. The typical level of loudness depends greatly on circumstances.

Pitch disorders take several forms. The person's voice may have an abnormally high or low pitch, may be characterized by pitch breaks or a restricted pitch range, or may be monotonal or monopitched. Many individuals experience pitch breaks as they progress through adolescence. Although more commonly associated with young males, pitch breaks also occur in females. Such pitch breaks are a normal part of development, but if they persist much beyond adolescence, they may signal laryngeal difficulties. Abnormally high- or low-pitched voices may signal a variety of problems. They may be learned through imitation, as when a young boy attempts to sound like his older brother or father. They may also be learned from certain circumstances, as when a person in a position of authority believes a lower voice pitch evokes the image of power. And organic conditions, such as a hormone imbalance, may result in abnormally high- or low-pitched voices.

Voice disorders involving volume also have varied causes. Voices that are excessively loud or soft may be learned through imitation, perceptions and characteristics of the environment, and even aging (Boone et al., 2005; Rubin, Sataloff, & Korovin, 2002; Verdolini, Rosen, & Branski, 2006; Vilkman, 2000). An example is mimicking the soft speaking of a female movie star. Other cases of abnormal vocal intensity occur because an individual has not learned to monitor loudness. Organic problems may also be the culprit. For example, abnormally low vocal intensity may result from problems such as paralysis of vocal cords, laryngeal trauma (e.g., larynx surgery for cancer, damage through accident or disease), and pulmonary diseases such as asthma or emphysema (e.g., Benninger, 2002; Gray & Thibeault, 2002). Excessively loud speech may occur as a result of organic problems such as hearing impairments and brain damage.

Voice disorders related to the quality of speech include production deviances such as those of abnormal nasality. Hypernasality occurs essentially because the soft palate does not move upward and back to close off the airstream through the nose properly. Such conditions can be due to improper tissue movement in the speech mechanism, or they may result from physical flaws such as an imperfectly repaired cleft palate (Benninger, 2002). Excessive hypernasality may also be learned, as in the case of country music or certain rural dialects. Hyponasality or denasality is the type of voice quality experienced during a head cold or hay fever. In some cases, however, denasality is a result of learning or of abnormal physical structures, rather than these more common problems.

Intervention The approach to treatment for a voice disorder depends on its cause. In cases where abnormal tissue development and/or dental structures result in unusual voice production, surgical intervention may be necessary. Surgery may also be part of the intervention plan if removal of the larynx is required. Such an intervention will also involve relearning communication through alternative mechanisms, including prostheses, and learning communication techniques to replace laryngeal verbalizations (Benninger, 2002; Case, 2002). In some situations, treatment may include direct instruction to enhance the affected individual's learning or relearning of acceptable voice production. Such interventions entail counseling about the effects of unusual voice sounds on others and behavior modification procedures aimed at retraining the person's speaking. These efforts are more difficult if the behavior has been long-standing and is well ingrained.

Voice disorders are seldom the focus of referral and treatment in the United States. However, some researchers have argued that voice disorders should be treated more aggressively (Boone et al., 2005; Sapienza & Hicks, 2006). One important element in planning interventions for voice disorders is clear and open communication with the person seeking treatment (Gates, 2006). It is important to avoid setting unrealistic expectations about outcomes and to remember that those being treated are the ultimate arbiters of that treatment's success.

Standard 4: Instructional Strategies

Standard 7: Instructional Planning

Prevalence

We have already noted the difficulties involved in estimating the prevalence of other disorders: Many arise from differences in definitions and data collection procedures. The field of speech disorders is also vulnerable to these problems, so prevalence estimates vary considerably. It is typically claimed that speech disorders affect between 7% and 10% of the population. Nearly 19% of all children (ages 6 to 21) who were served in programs for those with disabilities were categorized as having speech or language impairments in 2004 (U.S. Department of Education, 2006). These figures do not deviate greatly from other estimates over the years, although some data have suggested substantial geographical differences (e.g., significantly higher percentages in some areas of California than in parts of the Midwest). These figures themselves present a problem when we consider the 12% ceiling for services to all students with disabilities, as specified in the Individuals with Disabilities Education Act (IDEA). Obviously, individuals with speech disorders of a mild nature cannot be eligible for federally funded services. However, the 24th Annual Report to Congress on the Implementation of IDEA cited speech or language impairments as the second most frequently occurring disability (next to learning disabilities) to receive special services during the 2000–2001 school year (U.S. Department of Education, 2006).

The frequency with which speech problems occur diminishes in the population as age increases. Speech disorders are identified in about 12% to 15% of children in kindergarten through grade 4. For children in grades 5 through 8, the figure declines to about 4% to 5%. The 5% rate remains somewhat constant after grade 8 unless treatment intervenes. Thus age and development diminish speech disorders considerably, though more so with certain types of problems (e.g., articulation difficulties) than with others.

FOCUS REVIEW

FOCUS 1 Identify four ways in which speech, language, and communication are interrelated.

- Both speech and language form part, but not all, of communication.
- Some components of communication involve language but not speech.
- Some speech does not involve language.
- The development of communication, that of language, and that of speech overlap to some degree.

FOCUS 2 Explain how language delay and language disorder differ.

- In language delay, the sequence of development is intact, but the rate is interrupted.
- In language disorder, the sequence of development is interrupted.

FOCUS 3 Identify three factors that are thought to cause language disorders.

- Defective or deficient sensory systems
- Neurological damage occurring through physical trauma or accident
- Deficient or disrupted learning opportunities during language development

FOCUS 4 Describe how treatment approaches for language disorders generally differ for children and for adults.

- Treatment for children generally addresses initial acquisition or learning of language.

- Treatment for adults involves relearning or reacquiring language function.

FOCUS 5 Cite three factors that are thought to cause stuttering.

- Learned behavior, emotional problems, and neurological problems can contribute to stuttering.
- Some research has suggested that brain organization differs in people who stutter.
- People who stutter may learn their speech patterns as an outgrowth of the normal nonfluency evident when speech development first occurs.

FOCUS 6 Identify two ways in which learning theory and home environments are related to delayed speech.

- The home environment may provide little opportunity to learn speech.
- The home environment may interfere with speech development, as when speaking is punished.

FOCUS 7 Identify two reasons why some professionals are reluctant to treat functional articulation disorders in young schoolchildren.

- Many articulation problems evident in young children are developmental in nature, so speech may improve "naturally" with age.
- Articulation problems are quite frequent among young children, and treatment resources are limited.

BUILDING YOUR PORTFOLIO

Council for Exceptional Children

If you are thinking about a career in special education, you should know that many states use national standards developed by the Council for Exceptional Children (CEC) to assess a teacher candidate's knowledge and skills for working with students with disabilities. See a complete listing of the ten CEC Content Standards on the inside front cover of this text.

CEC Content Standards Addressed in This Chapter

1 Foundations
2 Development and Characteristics of Learners
3 Individual Learning Differences
4 Instructional Strategies
5 Learning Environments and Social Interactions
6 Communication
7 Instructional Planning

Assess Your Knowledge of the CEC Standards Addressed in This Chapter

Some states require that teacher candidates develop a portfolio of products that demonstrate mastery of the CEC content standards. To assist in the development of products for this portfolio, you may wish to complete the following activities.

- Complete a written test of the chapter's content.

  If your instructor requires a written test of your content knowledge for this chapter, keep a copy for your portfolio. A practice test on the information covered in this chapter is available through the companion website (college.hmco.com/pic/hardman9e) and the Student Study Guide.

- Respond to the Application Questions for the Case Study "Ricky."

  Review the Case Study and respond in writing to the application questions. Keep a copy of the Case Study and of your written response for your portfolio.

- Participate in a Community Service Learning Activity.

  Community service is a valuable way to enhance your learning experience. Visit our companion website for suggested community service learning activities that correspond to the information presented in this chapter. Develop a reflective journal of the service learning experience for your portfolio.

WEB RESOURCES

Baby BumbleBee

http://www.babybumblebee.com/learningdifferences.htm

This commercial website provides a wide array of products for parents of children with language delays and challenges. These include language stimulation techniques that can be used in conjunction with interventions and therapies recommended by professionals.

The Nemours Foundation

http://kidshealth.org/teen/diseases_conditions/sight/speech_disorders.html

This website covers a number of issues related to teens' health. It seeks to communicate directly with teens who may have articulation disorders or other language challenges. Other topics that are addressed include food and fitness, drugs and alcohol, and sexual health.

AllRefer.com

http://health.allrefer.com/health/speech-disorders-info.html

This website covers a variety of health conditions and prominently features speech disorders, including articulation, disfluency, and voice disorders. The site is addressed to the general public and includes information on symptoms, prevention, diagnosis, and links.

Gus Communications

http://gusinc.com

This commercial website offers many different assistive technology products for a variety of conditions that result in language and communication disorders. Software is available for assisting people with aphasia, ALS (Lou Gehrig's disease), stroke, and other conditions.

FURTHER READINGS

Beckoff, M., & Allen, C. (Eds.). (2002). *The Cognitive Animal: Empirical and Theoretical Perspectives on Animal Cognition.* Cambridge, MA: M.I.T. Press.

Many scientists have asserted that cognition and language distinguish humans from other animals. This volume examines animal cognition and language in animals ranging from dolphins to chimpanzees.

Case, J. L. (2002). *Clinical Management of Voice Disorders.* Austin: PRO-Ed.

This volume examines the most commonly used approaches to assessing and treating voice disorders. Both medical procedures and instrumentation are discussed, and a wide array of voice function problems are covered.

Nelson, C. A., & Luciana, M. (2001). *Handbook of Developmental Cognitive Neuroscience.* Cambridge, MA: M.I.T. Press.

This volume includes original discussions on basic aspects of neural development, sensory and sensorimotor systems, language, cognition, and emotion. It examines how the human brain remains malleable and plastic throughout much of the lifespan, placing communication in the context of developmental science.

Wetherby, A. M., & Prizant, B. M. (Eds.). (2000). *Autism Spectrum Disorders: A Transactional Developmental Perspective.* Baltimore: Paul H. Brookes.

This is volume 9 in a series (Communication and Language Intervention) that provides comprehensive reviews of the research literature in communication and language. It examines issues related to augmentative and alternative communication and literacy for children with autism spectrum disorders.

COMPANION WEBSITE

Visit the companion website at college.hmco.com/pic/hardman9e for additional resources that support this text:

- HM Video Cases that present actual classroom scenarios that you may face every day as a teacher

- Practice ACE Exams that will help you prepare for quizzes, tests, and certfication exams
- Flashcards of key terms
- Weblinks

12

Severe and Multiple Disabilities

TO BEGIN WITH . . .

EVERYONE HAS THE RIGHT TO LIVE IN THE COMMUNITY

Children and adults with disabilities should have opportunities to develop relationships with neighbors, classmates, co-workers and community members. Adults, whether married or single, shall have the opportunity to make choices about where and with whom they shall live. The preferences of each individual should guide all aspects of the selection of housing, including the neighborhood, and whether the individual will live alone, with his/her family, extended family, spouse, partner or friends. The role of government, agencies and organizations is to determine the manner in which assistance is best provided and to provide requested supports to the individual in meeting his or her needs and preferences. Individuals with disabilities and families must be entitled to quality educational supports, decent and affordable housing, financial security, transportation, recreation and employment. (TASH, 2006a)

YVONNE BELONGS WITH US!

"Yvonne belongs with us!" we firmly told the psychiatrist when he insisted that we place our 2-year-old daughter in an institution. To us, Yvonne's sudden regression meant that she needed us more than ever—we could not abandon her, we could not reject her. At first we struggled on our own; there were no community supports. Then, together with other parents, we advocated for appropriate supports in the community for children who were labeled "severely mentally handicapped." We believed that Yvonne, and children like her, had a right to live at home, had a right to go to school, and had a right to participate in the life of the community. Our vision was shared and supported by some service providers, but other professionals opposed our view and worked against us. (Penner, 2006)

WHAT SHOULD I DO TO MAKE INCLUSION WORK FOR THE WHOLE CLASS?

For as long as she can remember, Mrs. Brown has been told that she and other general education teachers were not appropriately trained or qualified to teach students with a wide range of disabilities. She was told, "That's why we have special education classes and schools where students with special educational needs can get the specialized instruction they need." . . . Recently, people started talking about educating students with more significant disabilities in the general education classroom; they referred to it as "inclusive education." Mrs. Brown felt that she had never excluded children before because of their disabilities, but rather, was trying to help them by sending them to a place that would better meet their needs. Now, she was about to have a student with more significant disabilities in her class. She wondered how this would work and what she should do to make sure it worked for her whole class. (Giangreco & Doyle, 2000, pp. 51–52)

▼ SNAPSHOT

SARINA

Sarina never had the opportunity to go to preschool and didn't begin her formal education in the public schools until the age of 6. She is now 15 years old and goes to Eastmont Junior High—her neighborhood school. Sarina does not verbally speak, walk, hear, or see. Professionals have used several labels to describe her, including *severely disabled, severely multiply handicapped, deaf-blind,* and *profoundly mentally retarded.* Her teenage classmates at Eastmont call her Sarina.

Throughout the day, Sarina has a support team of administrators, teachers, paraprofessionals, and peers who work together to meet her instructional, physical, and medical needs. And she has many, many needs. Sarina requires some level of support in everything she does, ranging from eating and taking care of personal hygiene to communicating with others. In the last few years, she has learned to express herself through the use of assistive technology. Sarina has a personal communication board with picture symbols that keeps her in constant contact with teachers, friends, and family. Through the use of an electronic wheelchair and her ability to use various switches, Sarina is able to maneuver her way through just about any obstacle in her environment. She is also learning to feed herself independently.

Sarina lives at home with her family, including three older brothers. Her parents, siblings, and grandparents are very supportive, always looking for ways to help facilitate Sarina's participation in school, family, and community activities. What she loves to do most is go shopping with her mom at the local mall, eat with friends at a fast-food restaurant, relax on the lawn in the neighborhood park, and play miniature golf at Mulligan's Pitch and Putt.

arina, in the opening Snapshot, is a person with **severe and multiple disabilities**. In one way or another, she will require services and support in nearly every facet of her life. Some people with severe disabilities have significant intellectual, learning, and behavioral differences; others are physically disabled with vision and hearing loss. Most have significant, multiple disabilities. Sarina has multiple needs, one of which is communication. Yet, although she is unable to communicate verbally, she is able to express herself through the use of an assistive communication device, a language board. Thus, in many circumstances, a disability may be described as severe, but through today's technology and our understanding of how to adapt the environment, the impact on the person may be diminished.

Definitions

The needs of people with severe and multiple disabilities cannot be met by one profession. The nature of their disabilities extends equally into the fields of education, medicine, psychology, and social services. Because these individuals present such diverse characteristics and require the attention of several professionals, it is not surprising that numerous definitions have been used to describe them.

Standard 1: Foundations

Historical Descriptions of Severe Disabilities

Throughout history, terminology associated with severe disabilities has communicated a sense of hopelessness and despair. The condition was described as "extremely debilitating," "inflexibly incapacitating," or "uncompromisingly crippling." Abt Associates (1974) described individuals with severe handicaps as unable "to attend to even the most pronounced social stimuli, including failure to respond to invitations from peers or adults, or loss of contact with reality" (p. v). The definition went on to use terms such as *self-mutilation* (e.g., head banging, body scratching, and hair pulling), *ritualistic behaviors* (e.g., rocking and pacing), and *self-stimulation* (e.g., masturbation, stroking, and patting). The Abt definition focused almost exclusively on the individual's deficits and negative behavioral characteristics.

In 1976, Justen proposed a definition that moved away from negative terminology to descriptions of the individual's developmental characteristics. "The 'severely handicapped' refers to those individuals . . . who are functioning at a general development level of half or less than the level which would be expected on the basis of chronological age and who manifest learning and/or behavior problems of such magnitude and significance that they require extensive structure in learning situations" (p. 5).

Whereas Justen emphasized a discrepancy between normal and atypical development, Sailor and Haring (1977) proposed a definition that was oriented to the educational needs of each individual:

> A child should be assigned to a program for the severely/multiply handicapped according to whether the primary service needs of the child are basic or academic. . . . If the diagnosis and assessment process determines that a child with multiple handicaps needs academic instruction, the child should not be referred to the severely handicapped program. If the child's service need is basic skill development, the referral to the severely/multiply handicapped program is appropriate. (p. 68)

In 1991, Snell further elaborated on the importance of defining severe disabilities on the basis of educational need, suggesting that the emphasis be on supporting the individual in inclusive classroom settings. The Association for Severe Handicaps (Meyer, Peck, & Brown, 1991), agreeing in principle with Snell, proposed a definition that focused on inclusion in *all* natural settings: family, community, and school.

TASH and the People It Serves

TASH (formerly the Association for Severe Handicap) is an association of people with disabilities, their family members, other advocates, and professionals who promote full inclusion in family, school, and community life. A primary belief of this organization is that every individual has the right to direct her or his own life. TASH works on behalf of people with [intellectual disabilities], autism, cerebral palsy, physical disabilities, and other conditions that make full integration a challenge (TASH 2006b).

TASH defines the individuals it serves as follows:

> People with disabilities excluded from the mainstream of all ages, races, creeds, national origins, genders and sexual orientation who require ongoing support in one or more major life activities in order to participate in an integrated community and enjoy a quality of life similar to that available to all citizens. Support may be required for life activities such as mobility, communication, self-care, and learning as necessary for community living, employment, and self-sufficiency. (TASH, 2006c)

TASH focuses on the relationship of the individual with the environment (adaptive fit), the need to include people of all ages, and "ongoing support" in life activities. The adaptive fit between the person and the environment is a two-way street. First, it is important to determine the capability of the individual to cope with the requirements of family, school, and community environments. Second is the extent to which these various environments recognize and accommodate the need of the person with severe disabilities. The adaptive fit of the individual with the environment is a dynamic process requiring continuous adjustment that fosters a mutually supportive coexistence. The TASH definition suggests that an adaptive fit can be created only when there is ongoing support (formal and/or natural) for each person as he or she moves through various life activities, including social interactions, taking care of personal needs, and making choices about lifestyle, working, and moving from place to place.

The IDEA Definitions of Severe and Multiple Disabilities

The Individuals with Disabilities Education Act (IDEA) does not include the term *severe disabilities* as one of the categorical definitions of disability identified in federal regulations. Individuals with severe disabilities may be subsumed under any one of IDEA's categories, such as intellectual disabilities, autism, serious emotional disturbance, speech and language impairments, and so on. (These disability conditions are discussed in other chapters in this text.) Although *severe disabilities* is not a category within IDEA, *multiple disabilities* and *deaf-blindness* are categories in federal regulations.

MULTIPLE DISABILITIES. As defined in IDEA federal regulations, *multiple disabilities* means

> concomitant impairments (such as intellectual disabilities–blindness, intellectual disabilities–orthopedic impairment, etc.), the combination of which causes such severe educational needs that they cannot be accommodated in special education programs solely for one of the impairments. The term does not include deaf-blindness. 34 C.F.R. 300.8(c)(7) (August 14, 2006)

This definition includes multiple conditions that can occur in any of several combinations. One such combination is described by the term *dual diagnosis*. **Dual diagnosis** involves persons who have serious emotional disturbance or who present challenging behaviors in conjunction with severe intellectual disabilities. Estimates of the percentage of people with intellectual disabilities who also have serious challenging behaviors vary, ranging from 5% to 15% of those living in the community to a much higher percentage for people living in institutions (Beirne-Smith, Patton, & Kim, 2006). Why do people with intellectual disabilities and other developmental disabilities often have higher rates of challenging behaviors? These individuals are more likely to live in situations that are restrictive, are prejudicial, limit their independence, and result in victimization. For more insight into the life of a person with multiple disabilities, see the Reflect on This, "Mat's Story" on page 326.

DEAF-BLINDNESS. For some multiple disabilities, intellectual disabilities may not be a primary symptom. One such condition is deaf-blindness. The concomitant vision and hearing difficulties (sometimes referred to as **dual sensory impairments**) exhibited by people with **deaf-blindness** result in severe communication deficits as well as in developmental and

FOCUS **2**
Define the terms *multiple disabilities* and *deaf-blindness* as described in IDEA.

Council for Exceptional Children

Standard 1: Foundations

Standard 2: Development and Characteristics of Learners

➤ **Dual diagnosis**
Identification of both serious emotional problems and intellectual disabilities in the same individual.

➤ **Dual sensory impairments**
A condition characterized by both vision and hearing sensory impairments (deaf-blindness). The condition can result in severe communication problems as well as in developmental and educational difficulties that require extensive support across several professional disciplines.

➤ **Deaf-blindness**
A disorder involving simultaneous vision and hearing impairments.

Mat is a 23-year-old man with autism and intellectual disabilities. He lives in a home with one roommate and holds two jobs. One job involves cleaning at a local bar and restaurant for an hour each morning. The second job is delivering a weekly advertiser to 170 homes in his neighborhood. In addition to working in the community, Mat goes shopping, takes walks around a nearby lake, goes to the movies, attends concerts and special events, and eats at a fast-food restaurant where he uses a wallet-sized communication picture board to order his meal, independently.

Mat hasn't always been so integrated into his local community. In the past he engaged in a number of challenging behaviors, including removing pictures from the wall, taking down drapes and ripping them, dismantling his bed, ripping his clothing, breaking windows, smearing his bowel movements on objects, urinating on his clothing, hurting others, stripping naked, and similar behaviors. For almost one entire year Mat refused to wear clothing and spent most of his time wrapped in a blanket. He would often cover his head with the blanket and lie on the couch for hours. He frequently stripped in community settings, on those few occasions when staff were able to coax him to go out. After this had continued for months, the assistance of a behavioral analyst was sought. An analysis of the function that the behaviors served revealed that Mat's stripping and subsequent refusal to wear clothing were the result of his attempt to exert control over his environment, primarily to escape or avoid undesirable events. For this reason, the behavior analyst suggested not focusing directly on the issue of wearing clothing but, rather, addressing the development of a communication system for Mat.

Mat was reported to know over 200 signs, but he was rarely observed to use the signs spontaneously. When he did sign, others in his environment were unable to interpret his signing. Consequently, the behavior analyst and a consultant in augmentative and alternative communication suggested that a communication system using pictures or symbols be implemented to supplement his existing system.

The support program that was developed for Mat had two main components. The first was to enhance his communication and choice-making skills, and the second was to provide opportunities for him to participate in activities that were motivating and required him to wear clothing. To address communication and choice-making skills, several photographs were taken of people Mat knew and had worked with, activities he liked or was required to engage in (e.g. watching MTV, going to McDonald's, shaving, taking a shower), and a variety of objects (e.g. lotion, pop, cookies). Then, a minimum of four times each hour, Mat was presented with a choice. Mat would then pick one of the pictures, and staff would help him complete whatever activity he had chosen. Soon he had over 130 photographs in his communication system. The photographs were mounted on hooks in the hallway of the house where he lived, ensuring that he had easy access to them. Staff reported that over time, Mat began spontaneously using some of the pictures to request items. He would, for example, bring staff the photo of a Diet Pepsi to request a Diet Pepsi. Thus the communication served to enhance his ability to make his wants and needs known, as well as to help him understand choices presented to him.

While Mat's communication system was being developed, staff were also trying to address indirectly his refusal to wear clothes by capitalizing on the fact that he seemed to genuinely like to go out into the community. Staff would periodically encourage Mat to dress. On those occasions when he would dress, he was able to participate in a community activity that was reinforcing for him. The length of these outings was gradually increased.

SOURCE: Hewitt, A., & O'Nell, S. (2006). *A Little Help from My Friends.* Washington, DC: President's Committee on Intellectual Disabilities, Adapted from Piche, L., Krage, P., & Wiczek, C. (1991). Joining the community. *IMPACT, 4*(1), 3, 18. Retrieved October 10, 2006, from http://www.acf.hhs.gov/programs/pcpid/docs/help4.doc

educational difficulties that require extensive support across several professional disciplines. IDEA defines deaf-blindness as

> concomitant hearing and visual impairments, the combination of which causes such severe communication and other developmental and educational needs that they cannot be accommodated in special education programs solely for children with deafness or children with blindness. 34 C.F.R. 300.8(c)(2)(August 14, 2006)

The impact of both vision and hearing loss on the educational needs of the student is a matter of debate among professionals. One perspective on deaf-blindness is that individuals have such severe intellectual disabilities that both vision and hearing are also affected. Another view is that they have average intelligence and lost their hearing and sight after they acquired language. Intellectual functioning for persons with deaf-blindness may range from normal or gifted to severe intellectual disabilities. All people with deaf-blindness experience challenges in learning to communicate, access information, and comfortably move through their environment. These individuals may also have physical and behavioral disabilities. However, the specific needs of each person will vary enormously, depending on age, age at onset, and type of deaf-blindness (Deafblind International, 2006).

Students with deaf-blindness require extensive support to meet their educational needs, particularly in the area of communication.

Prevalence

People with severe and multiple disabilities constitute a very small percentage of the general population. Even if we consider the multitude of conditions, prevalence is no more than 0.1% to 1.0%. Approximately 4 out of every 1,000 persons have severe disabilities where the primary symptom is intellectual disabilities. The U.S. Department of Education (2006) reported that 131,682 students between the ages of 6 and 21 were served in the public schools under the label *multiple disabilities*. These students account for about 2% of the over 7 million students considered eligible for services under IDEA. The Department of Education also reported that 1,600 students between the ages of 6 and 21 were labeled as deaf-blind. These students account for 0.0002% of students with disabilities served under IDEA. Overall, about 14,000 individuals in the United States are identified as deaf-blind.

FOCUS **3**
Identify the estimated prevalence and causes of severe and multiple disabilities.

Council for Exceptional Children

Standard 2: Development and Characteristics of Learners

Causation

Multiple disabilities result from multiple causes. For the vast majority of people with severe and multiple disabilities, the differences are evident at birth. Severe disabilities may be the result of genetic or metabolic disorders, including chromosomal abnormalities, phenylketonuria, or Rh incompatibility. (See Chapter 10 for more indepth information on these disorders.) Most identifiable causes of severe intellectual disabilities and related developmental disabilities are genetic in origin (The ARC, 2006a). Other causes include prenatal conditions: poor maternal health during pregnancy, drug abuse, infectious diseases (e.g., HIV), radiation exposure, venereal disease, and advanced maternal age. Severe and multiple disabilities can also result from incidents or conditions that occur later in life, such as poisoning, accidents, malnutrition, physical and emotional neglect, and disease.

Characteristics

The multitude of characteristics exhibited by people with severe and multiple disabilities is mirrored by the numerous definitions associated with these conditions. A close analysis of these definitions reveals a consistent focus on people whose life needs cannot be met without substantial support from others, including family, friends, and society. With this support, however, people with severe and multiple disabilities have a much greater probability of escaping the stereotype that depicts them as totally dependent consumers of societal resources. People with severe disabilities can become contributing members of families and communities.

Giangreco (2006) suggests that "inclusion oriented people seek to establish an ethic that welcomes all children into their local schools and simultaneously pursues a range of individually meaningful learning outcomes through effective education practices" (p. 4). For Sarina in

FOCUS **4**
What are the characteristics of persons with severe and multiple disabilities?

Council for Exceptional Children

Standard 2: Development and Characteristics of Learners

the opening Snapshot, this would mean concentrating on educational outcomes that will decrease her dependence on others in her environment and create opportunities to enhance her participation at home, at school, and in the community. Instruction would be developed with these outcomes in mind, rather than on the basis of a set of general characteristics associated with the label *severely disabled*.

Intelligence and Academic Achievement

Most people with severe and multiple disabilities have intellectual disabilities as a primary condition. Thus their learning and memory capabilities are diminished. The greater the intellectual disabilities, the more difficulty the individual will have in learning, retaining, and applying information. People with severe and multiple disabilities will require specialized and intensive instruction in order to acquire and use new skills across a number of settings.

Given the diminished intellectual capability of many people with severe and multiple disabilities, academic learning is often a low instructional priority. The vast majority of students with severe disabilities are unable to learn from basic academic programs in reading, writing, and mathematics. Instruction in functional academic skills that facilitate access to the general curriculum is the most effective approach to academic learning. Basic academic subjects are taught in the context of daily living. For example, functional reading focuses on those words that facilitate a child's access to the environment (*restroom, danger, exit*, and the like). Functional math skill development involves developing strategies for telling time or the consumer's use of money. A more in-depth discussion on teaching functional skills to students with severe disabilities appears later in this chapter.

Adaptive Skills

The learning of **adaptive skills** is critical to success in natural settings. These skills involve both personal independence and social interaction. Personal independence skills range from the ability to take care of one's basic needs—eating, dressing, and hygiene—to living on one's own in the community (including getting and keeping a job, managing money, and finding ways to get around in the environment). Social interaction skills involve being able to communicate one's needs and preferences, as well as listening and appropriately responding to others. People with severe and multiple disabilities often do not have age-appropriate adaptive skills and need ongoing services and supports to facilitate learning and application in this area. We do know that when given the opportunity to learn adaptive skills through participation in inclusive settings with peers without disabilities, children with severe disabilities have a higher probability of maintaining and meaningfully applying this learning over time (Snell & Brown, 2006; Westling & Fox, 2004).

Speech and Language

People with severe and multiple disabilities generally have significant deficits and delays in speech and language skills, ranging from articulation and fluency disorders to an absence of any expressive oral language (Westling & Fox, 2004). Speech and language deficits and delays are positively correlated with the severity of intellectual disabilities (Moore-Brown & Montgomery, 2006). As is true for adaptive skill learning, people with severe and multiple disabilities will acquire and use appropriate speech and language if these skills are taught and applied in natural settings. Functional communication systems (such as signing, picture cards, communication boards, and gesturing) are also an integral part of instruction. Regardless of the communication system(s) used to teach speech and language skills, they must be applied across multiple settings. For example, if picture cards are used in the classroom, they must also be a part of the communication system used at home and in other environments.

Physical and Health

People with severe and multiple disabilities have significant physical and health care needs. For instance, these individuals have a higher incidence of congenital heart disease, **epilepsy**, respiratory problems, diabetes, and metabolic disorders. They also exhibit poor muscle tone and often have conditions such as **spasticity**, **athetosis**, and **hypotonia**. Such conditions require that professionals in the schools and other service agencies know how to administer medications, **catheterization**, **gastronomy tube feeding**, and **respiratory ventilation** (Rues, Graff, Ault, & Holvoet, 2006).

➤ **Adaptive skills**
Conceptual, social, and practical skills that facilitate an individual's ability to function in community, family, and school settings.

➤ **Epilepsy**
A condition that from time to time produces brief disturbances in the normal electrical functions of the brain, affecting a person's consciousness, bodily movements, or sensations for a short time and resulting in seizures. The intensity and length of these effects depend on the severity of the seizure.

➤ **Spasticity**
A condition that involves involuntary contractions of various muscle groups.

➤ **Athetosis**
A condition characterized by constant, contorted twisting motions in the wrists and fingers.

➤ **Hypotonia**
Poor muscle tone.

➤ **Catheterization**
The process of introducing a hollow tube (catheter) into body cavities to drain fluid, such as introducing a tube into an individual's bladder to drain urine.

➤ **Gastronomy tube feeding**
The process of feeding the individual through a rubber tube inserted into the stomach.

➤ **Respiratory ventilation**
Use of a mechanical aid (ventilator) to supply oxygen to an individual with respiratory problems.

Vision and Hearing

Although the prevalence of vision and hearing loss is not well documented among people with severe disabilities, sensory impairments do occur more frequently in people with severe disabilities than in the general population (Drew & Hardman, 2007). Some individuals, particularly those described as deaf-blind, have significant vision and hearing disorders that require services and supports beyond those for a person with blindness *or* deafness.

Educational Supports and Services

The axiom "the earlier, the better" is certainly applicable to educational services and supports for children with severe and multiple disabilities. Such services must begin at birth and continue throughout the lifespan.

Assessment

IDENTIFYING THE DISABILITY. Traditionally, there has been a heavy reliance on standardized measurements, particularly the IQ test, in identifying people with severe and multiple disabilities, particularly when the primary condition is intellectual disabilities (see Chapter 10). Some professionals (Brown & Snell, 2006; Bishop, 2004) have suggested that standardized tests, particularly the IQ test, do not provide information useful in either diagnosing the disability or providing instruction to individuals with severe disabilities. Others (McDonnell, Hardman, & McDonnell, 2003) believe that standardized tests may be appropriate as one tool in a battery of multidisciplinary assessment to determine eligibility for special education services, but that they provide no meaningful information for making curriculum decisions such as what and how to teach.

ASSESSING FOR INSTRUCTION. Assessments that focus on valued skills to promote independence and quality of life in natural settings are referred to as functional, ecological, or **authentic assessment** (Horner, Albin, Todd, & Sprague, 2006; McDonnell et al., 2003). These assessments focus on the match between the needs of the individual and the demands of the environment (adaptive fit). The purpose of the assessment is to determine what supports are necessary to achieve the intended outcomes of access and participation in natural settings. Skills are never taught in isolation from actual performance demands. Additionally, the individual does not "get ready" to participate in the community through a sequence of readiness stages as in the developmental model but, rather, learns and uses skills in the setting where the behavior is expected to occur.

SCHOOL ACCOUNTABILITY. During the past decade, there has been increasing emphasis on holding schools more accountable for student learning and progress. States are setting educational standards and then assessing how students progress toward the intended goals. A major challenge for education is to demonstrate accountability for all students, including those with the most significant disabilities.

> Regardless of one's perspective on the wisdom and implications of this [accountability] movement, it promises to have a significant effect on curricular guidance and foci for students with [severe] disabilities. . . . A major question facing eduators and parents is how can those concerned with the education of students with significant disabilities ensure a continued and focused emphasis on full membership and meaningful outcomes during this era? (Ford, Davern, and Schnorr, 2001, p. 215)

IDEA requires that schools must include students with disabilities in statewide or districtwide assessments of achievement or provide a statement of why that assessment is not appropriate for the child. The law also requires that individual modifications in the administration of statewide or districtwide assessments be provided as appropriate in order for the child to participate. Examples of student accommodations include large-print text, testing in a separate setting, and extended time. Ysseldyke, Olsen, and Thurlow (2006) estimate that about 85% of students with disabilities have mild or moderate disabilities and can take state

FOCUS **5**

Identify three types of educational assessments for students with severe and multiple disabilities.

Council for Exceptional Children

Standard 8: Assessment

➤ **Authentic assessment**

Assessment based on student progress in meaningful learning activities—and hence an alternative to the traditional use of standardized tests to measure student progress.

➤ **Alternate assessment**
Assessments mandated in IDEA for students who are unable to participate in required state- or districtwide assessments. It ensures that all students, regardless of the severity of their disabilities, are included in the state's accountability system.

or district assessments, either with or without accommodations. For many students with severe disabilities, these assessments are inappropriate, and such students are excluded from taking them. Schools are still accountable, however, for the progress of these students. IDEA mandated that states conduct **alternate assessments** to ensure that all students are included in the state's accountability system. Quenemoen and Thurlow (2006) identified five characteristics of good alternate assessments:

➤ There have been careful stakeholder and policymaker development and definition of desired student outcomes for the population, reflecting the best understanding of research and practice.

➤ Assessment methods have been carefully developed, tested, and refined.

➤ Professionally accepted standards are used to score evidence (e.g., adequate training, dual scoring third-party tie breakers, reliability tests and rechecks of scorer competence).

➤ An accepted standards-setting process has been used so that results can be included in reporting and accountability.

➤ The assessment process is continuously reviewed and improved.

Alternate assessment systems should include as key criteria the extent to which the system provides the supports and adaptations needed and trains the student to use them.

Alternate assessments may involve either normative or absolute performance standards (Ysseldyke & Olsen, 2006). If a normative assessment is used, then a student's performance is compared to that of peers (other students of comparable age or ability participating in the alternate assessment). If an absolute standard is used, then a student's performance is compared against a set criterion, such as being able to cross the street when the "walk" sign is flashing 100% of the time without assistance. (See the Reflect on This, "Alternate Assessment Strategies" above.)

Focus 6
Identify the features of effective services and supports for children with severe and multiple disabilities during the early childhood years.

The Early Childhood Years

Effective early intervention services that start when the child is born are critical to the prevention and amelioration of social, medical, and educational problems that can occur throughout

Effective programs for infants and toddlers with severe and multiple disabilities are both child- and family-centered. Therapists work closely with the infant and the family to promote early learning and development.

the life of the individual (Batshaw, 2003; Berk, 2005; Guralnick, 2001). During the early childhood years, services and supports are concentrated on two age groups: infants and toddlers, and preschool-age children.

Services and Supports for Infants and Toddlers

Effective programs for infants and toddlers with severe and multiple disabilities are both child- and family-centered. A child-centered approach is focused on identifying and meeting individual needs. Services begin with infant stimulation programs intended to elicit in newborns the sensory, cognitive, and physical responses that will connect them with their environment. As the child develops, health care, physical therapy, occupational therapy, and speech and language services may become integral components of a child-centered program.

Family-centered early intervention is characterized by a holistic approach that involves the child as a member of the family unit. The needs, structure, and preferences of the family drive the delivery of services and supports. The overall purpose of family-centered intervention is to enable family members first to cope with the birth of a child with a severe disability and eventually to grow together and support one another. Family-centered approaches build on and increase family strengths, address the needs of every family member, and support mutually enjoyable family relationships. Supports for families may include parent-training programs, counseling, and **respite care**.

Services and Supports for Preschool-Age Children

Preschool programs for young children with severe and multiple disabilities continue the emphasis on family involvement while extending the life space of the child to a school setting. McDonnell and colleagues (2003) suggest four goals for preschool programs serving children with severe disabilities:

1. Maximize the child's development in a variety of important developmental areas. These include social communication, motor skills, cognitive skills, preacademic skills, self-care, play, and personal management.

2. Develop the child's social interaction and classroom participation skills. Focus on developing peer relationships and teaching the child to follow adult directions, respond to classroom routines, and become self-directed (that is, to complete classroom activities without constant adult supervision).

3. Increase community participation through support to family members and other caregivers. Work to identify alternative caregivers so that the family has a broader base of support and more flexibility to pursue other interests. Help the family to identify activities within the neighborhood that their preschooler would enjoy in order to

Council for Exceptional Children

Standard 3: Individual Learning Differences

Standard 4: Instructional Strategies

Standard 7: Instructional Planning

► **Respite care**
Assistance provided by individuals outside of the immediate family, allowing parents and other children within the family time away from the child with a disability for a recreational event, a vacation, and so on. Some states provide funding to families to secure this kind of care.

provide the child with opportunities to interact with same-age peers. Activities may involve swimming or dancing lessons, joining a soccer team, attending a house of worship, and so on.

4. Prepare the child for inclusive school placements, and provide support for the transition to elementary school. The transition out of preschool will be facilitated if educators from the receiving elementary school work collaboratively with the family and preschool personnel.

To meet these goals, preschool programs for children with severe disabilities blend the principles and elements of developmentally appropriate practices (DAP), multicultural education, and special education. DAP was developed by the National Association for the Education of Young Children as an alternative to an academic curriculum for preschoolers. It emphasizes age-appropriate child exploration and play activities that are consistent with individual needs (see Chapter 3). Multicultural education emphasizes acceptance of people from different cultural and ethnic backgrounds within and across the preschool curriculum. Successful culturally inclusive programs blend principles and practices that guide special education, inclusive education, and multicultural education (Gollnick & Chinn, 2006). Special education focuses on assessing individual needs, providing intensive instruction, and teaching explicit skills within the context of an individualized education program (IEP). Families, educators, and other professionals committed to DAP, multicultural education, and special education work together to provide a quality experience for preschool-age children with severe disabilities.

The Elementary School Years

Historically, services and supports for students with severe and multiple disabilities have been oriented to protection and care. The objective was to protect the individual from society, and society from the individual. This philosophy resulted in programs that isolated the individual and provided physical care rather than preparation for life in a heterogeneous world. Today, educators working together with parents are concentrating their efforts on preparing students with severe and multiple disabilities to participate actively in the life of the family, school, and community. Given the emphasis on lifelong learning and living in natural settings, educators have identified several features that characterize quality programs for elementary-age students with severe and multiple disabilities:

➤ Self-determination is important—student preferences and needs are taken into account in developing educational objectives.

- The school values and supports parental involvement.
- Instruction focuses on frequently used functional skills related to everyday life activities.
- Assistive technology and augmentative communication are available to maintain or increase the functional capabilities of the student with severe and multiple disabilities.

Self-Determination

People with severe and multiple disabilities, like everyone else, must be in a position to make their own life choices as much as possible. School programs that promote self-determination enhance each student's opportunity to become more independent in the life of the family and in the larger community. Providing students with severe disabilities the opportunity to communicate their needs and preferences enhances autonomy, problem-solving skills, adaptability, and self-efficacy expectations (Bremer, Kachgal, & Schoeller, 2003; Morgan, Ellerd, Gerity, & Blair, 2000; Wehmeyer, Gragoudas, & Shogren, 2006).

Parental Involvement

Schools are more successful in meeting the needs of students when they establish positive relationships with the family. The important role that parents play during the early childhood years must continue and be supported during elementary school. Parents who actively participate in their child's educational program promote the development and implementation of instruction that is consistent with individual needs and preferences. Parental involvement can be a powerful predictor of postschool adjustment for students with severe and multiple disabilities. A strong home–school partnership requires that parents and educators acknowledge and respect each other's differences in values and culture, listen openly and attentively to each other's concerns, value varying opinions and ideas, discuss issues openly and in an atmosphere of trust, and share in the responsibility and consequences of making a decision.

Teaching Functional Skills

Effective educational programs focus on the functional skills that students with severe and multiple disabilities need to live successfully in the natural settings of family, school, and community. A functional skill is one that will have frequent and meaningful use across multiple environments. Instruction should involve the following elements:

- Many different people
- A variety of settings within the community
- Varied materials that will interest the learner and match performance demands

If the student with severe disabilities is to learn how to cross a street safely, shop in a grocery store, play a video game, or eat in a local restaurant, the necessary skills should be taught in the actual setting where the behavior is to be performed. It should not be assumed that a skill learned in a classroom will simply transfer to a setting outside of the school. Instruction in a more natural environment can ensure that the skill will be useful and will be maintained over time.

As suggested by Drew and Hardman (2007), a functional approach teaches academic skills in the context of environmental cues. The learning of new skills is always paired directly with environmental stimuli. Snell and Brown (2006) stressed that the teacher must use instructional materials that are real and meaningful to the student. Traditional materials, such as workbooks, basal readers, and flash cards, do not work for students with severe disabilities. Students must be taught using *real objects in real situations* in the home or community

An assistive device, such as this computerized touch screen language board, helps students who are nonverbal to communicate with parents, teachers, and friends.

Council for Exceptional Children

Standard 4: Instructional Strategies

Standard 7: Instructional Planning

In the vignette that follows Kimberly Voss describes how she taught her daughter Ashley, a child born with Down syndrome and severe disabilities, to learn reading through the use of assistive technology. Kimberley describes Ashley's odyssey through life as one of "getting Ashley out."

> Trapped inside a body that does not always do what she asks it to do, we have had to invent and create from scratch numerous methods that allow her to emerge. Her medical diagnosis and developmental label have not been an accurate measure of her human potential. Unwilling to accept "can't" as an option, we have focused on "what if." Ashley's determination, as well as mine, has been our key to unlocking door after door, every day revealing more of Ashley's abilities and character. While she lives with many challenging and complex disabilities, Ashley has emerged as an assertive, independent, loving and spirited young women with a zest for life and wonderfully keen sense of humor. She will face adversity throughout her life, but we will face it, as we have all the changes that came before, one day and one creative solution at a time. (Voss, 2005, pp. 9–10).

TEACHING ASHLEY TO READ USING ASSISTIVE TECHNOLOGY

When Ashley was quite young, I had the good fortune to attend a workshop Patricia Oelwein gave before her book *Teaching Reading to Children with Down Syndrome* (Woodbine House, 1995) was published. Her technique began by following a three-step progression (matching, selecting, and naming) and was very visual, initially teaching sight words rather than phonics or text decoding. Pat suggested starting off by playing simplified Lotto type games, matching text to text—for example, putting the word "Daddy" on "Daddy." After that was mastered, Pat suggested matching text to an image and then selecting the correct word from a set of different word choices. We would ask "Give me the card that says 'Daddy.'" This approach worked very well for Ashley.

For Ashley, teaching sight words held real potential. Because of her complex speech problems, Ashley could not verbally describe what letters she was seeing or what words she was reading, making it even more of a challenge to teach her to read. But Pat's approach of matching words and selecting words required no speech at all. Using these methods, Ashley was quickly able to learn to read a number of meaningful sight words, matching text to text, matching text to image, and then selecting a requested word from a set. Over time, she significantly increased her sight word vocabulary and eventually completed the final step of naming: expressively communicating her identification of many words using sign language. As she began to read and sign, lo and behold, along came speech.

Sight word cards really show the advantages of designing the materials by computer, including the opportunity to customize the word choices and to keep it constantly fresh and new. And the computer enables uniformity. If the words are to be matched, it is best if they are an exact copy of one another (so that they are truly visually the same) which they cannot be if handwritten. It is quick and easy to accomplish this using a computer.

SOURCE: Voss, K. S. (2005). *Teaching by Design.* Bethesda, MD: Woodbine House, pp. 9, 215.

setting. For example, when teaching the word *exit*, pair it with an actual exit sign in a movie theater. Or when teaching the word *stop*, pair it with a stop sign on a street corner.

Assistive Technology and Augmentative Communication

Assistive technology is any item, piece of equipment, or product system that can be used to increase, maintain, or improve the functional capabilities of students with disabilities (The Technology-Related Assistance for Individuals with Disabilities Act, PL 100-407, [20 U.S.C. Sec. 140(25)]). An assistive technology service "directly assists an individual with a disability in the selection, acquisition, or use of an assistive technology device" [20 U.S.C. Sec 140(26)]. Johnston (2003) identified several types of assistive technology:

➤ Aids for daily living (such as nonslip placement to hold a bowl, utensils with built-up handles to provide a better gripping surface, and two-handed mugs to allow for two-handed grasping)

➤ Communication aids (compuers with voice output, hearing aids)

➤ Aids for working, learning and playing (braces, artificial limbs, prosthetic hands)

➤ Mobility aids (wheelchairs, lifts, walkers)

➤ Positioning aids (cushions, pelvic strips or hip guides, head supports on a wheelchair)

Students with severe and multiple disabilities benefit from any one or more of these assistive devices or activities. For students with severe disabilities who are unable to use speech and need an additional communication mode, augmentative communication will nearly always be an integral component of their individualized education program. **Augmentative communication** involves adapting existing vocal or gestural abilities into meaningful communication; teaching manual signing (such as American Sign Language), static symbols, or icons (such as **Blissymbols**); and using manual or electronic communication devices (such as electric communication boards, picture cues, or synthetic speech) (Westling & Fox, 2004). For more insight into the use of assistive technology for a student with severe disabilities, see the Assistive Technology, "Meet Ashley" on page 334.

The Adolescent Years

Societal perceptions about the capabilities of people with severe and multiple disabilities have changed a great deal over the past several years. Until very recently, the potential of these individuals to learn, live, and work in community settings was significantly underestimated. People with severe and multiple disabilities can become active participants in the lives of their community and family. This realization has prompted professionals and parents to seek significant changes in the ways that schools prepare students for the transition to adult life.

In a review of the research on successful community living for people with severe disabilities, McDonnell and colleagues (2003) address four outcomes that are important in planning for the transition to adult life:

➤ Establish a network of friends and acquaintances.

➤ Develop the ability to use community resources on a regular basis.

➤ Secure a paid job that supports the use of community resources and interaction with peers.

➤ Establish independence and autonomy in making lifestyle choices.

Inclusive Education

Many professionals and parents argue that the provision of services and supports in an inclusive educational setting is a critical factor in delivering a quality program for students with severe and multiple disabilities (Giangreco, 2006; The ARC, 2006c). Effective educational programs include continual opportunities for interaction between students with severe disabilities and peers without disabilities. Frequent and age-appropriate interactions between students with disabilities and their peers without disabilities can enhance opportunities for successful participation in the community during the adult years. Social interaction can be enhanced by creating opportunities for these students to associate both during and after the school day. Successful inclusion efforts are characterized by the following features:

➤ Physical placement of students with severe and multiple disabilities in the general education schools and classes they would attend if they didn't have disabilities

➤ Systematic organization of opportunities for interaction between students with severe and multiple disabilities and students without disabilities

➤ Specific instruction in valued postschool outcomes that will increase the competence of students with severe and multiple disabilities in the natural settings of family, school, and community

For more insight into importance of friendships for students with severe disabilities, see the Case Study, "The Beginning of a New Circle of Friends" on page 338.

One of the most important characteristics of the postschool environments in which students ultimately must function is frequent interaction with people without disabilities. Consequently, it is logical to plan educational programs that duplicate this feature of the environment and that actively build skills required for successful inclusion.

➤ **Augmentative communication**
Communication systems that involve adapting existing vocal or gestural abilities into meaningful communication; teaching manual signing, static symbols, or icons; and using manual or electronic communication devices.

➤ **Blissymbols**
A system developed by C. K. Bliss that ties specific symbols to words. There are four types of Blissymbols: pictographic, ideographic, relational, and abstract.

FOCUS 8
Describe four outcomes that are important in planning for the transition from school to adult life for adolescents with severe and multiple disabilities.

Council for Exceptional Children
Standard 1: Foundations

FOCUS 9
Describe four features that characterize successful inclusive education for students with severe and multiple disabilities.

Council for Exceptional Children
Standard 5: Learning Environments and Social Interactions

INCLUSION AND COLLABORATION THROUGH THE LIFESPAN

People with Severe and Multiple Disabilities

EARLY CHILDHOOD YEARS

Tips for the Family

- During the infant and toddler years, seek out family-centered programs that focus on communication and the building of positive relationships among all individual members.
- Seek supports and services for your preschool-age child that promote communication and play activities with same-age peers without disabilities.
- Seek opportunities for friendships to develop between your child and children without disabilities in family and neighborhood settings.
- Use the individualized family service plan and the individualized education plan as a means for the multidisciplinary team to establish goals that develop your child's social interaction and classroom participation skills.

Tips for the Preschool Teacher

- Establish a classroom environment that promotes and supports diversity.
- Use a child-centered approach to instruction that acknowledges and values every child's strengths, preferences, and individual needs.
- Ignore whatever labels have been used to describe the child with severe and multiple disabilities. There is no relationship between the label and the instruction needed by the child to succeed in natural settings.
- Create opportunities for ongoing communication and play activities among children with severe disabilities and their same-age peers without disabilities. Nurture interactive peer relationships across a variety of instructional areas and settings.

Tips for Preschool Personnel

- Support the inclusion of young children with severe and multiple disabilities in all preschool classrooms and programs.
- Always refer to children by name, not label. If you must employ a label, use "child-first language." For example say, "children with severe disabilities," not "severely disabled children."
- Communicate genuine respect and support for all teachers, staff, and volunteers who look for ways to include children with severe disabilities in preschool classrooms and collaborative schoolwide activities.
- Welcome families into the preschool programs. Listen to what parents have to say about the importance of, or concerns about, including their child in school programs and activities.
- Create opportunities for parents to become involved in their child's program through collaborative projects with school personnel, including volunteering, school governance, and the like.

Tips for Neighbors and Friends

- First and foremost, see the child with severe disabilities as an individual who has needs, preferences, strengths, and weaknesses. Avoid the pitfalls of stereotyping and "self-fulfilling prophecies."
- Support opportunities for your children and those of friends and neighbors to interact and play with a child who has severe and multiple disabilities.
- Help children without disabilities build friendships with children who have severe and multiple disabilities, rather than merely playing care-giving roles.
- Provide a supportive and collaborative community environment for the family of a young child with severe and multiple disabilities. Encourage the family, including the child, to participate in neighborhood activities.

ELEMENTARY YEARS

Tips for the Family

- Actively collaborate with the multidisciplinary team in the development of your son's or daughter's individualized education program (IEP). Write down the priorities and educational goals that you see as important for your child in the natural settings of home, school, and community.
- Follow up at home on activities that the school suggests are important for helping your child generalize skills learned at school to other natural settings.
- Actively collaborate with school personnel whether it be in your child's classroom or in extracurricular activities. Demonstrate your appreciation and support for administrators, teachers, and staff who openly value and support the inclusion of your child in the school and classroom.
- Continually collaborate with administrators and teachers on the importance of children with severe disabilities being included with peers without disabilities during classroom and schoolwide activities (such as riding on the same school bus, going to recess and lunch at the same time, and participating in schoolwide assemblies).

Tips for the General Education Classroom Teacher

- See children with severe and multiple disabilities as individuals, not labels. Focus on their similarities with other children rather than on their differences.
- Openly value and support diversity and collaboration in your classroom. Set individualized goals and objectives for all children.
- Develop a classroom environment and instructional program that recognize multiple needs and abilities.
- Become part of a team that continually collaborates to meet the needs of all children in your classroom. View the special education teacher as a resource who can assist you in developing an effective instructional program for the child with severe and multiple disabilities.

Tips for School Personnel

- Communicate that diversity is a strength in your school. Openly value diversity by providing the resources necessary for teachers to work with students who have a range of needs and come from differing backgrounds.

- Integrate school resources as well as children. Develop schoolwide teacher-assistance or teacher-support teams that work collaboratively to meet the needs of every student.

- Collaborate with general and special education teachers in the development of peer-partner and support networks for students with severe and multiple disabilities.

- Include all students in the programs and activities of the school.

Tips for Neighbors and Friends

- Openly communicate to school personnel, friends, and neighbors your support of families who are seeking to have their child with severe and multiple disabilities be a part of an inclusive school setting.

- Communicate to your children and those of friends and neighbors the value of collaboration and inclusion. Demonstrate this value by creating opportunities for children with severe disabilities and their families to play an active role in the life of the community.

SECONDARY AND TRANSITION YEARS

Tips for the Family

- Seek opportunities for students from your son's or daughter's high school to visit your home. Help arrange get-togethers or parties involving students from the neighborhood and/or school.

- Communicate to the school what you see as priorities for your son or daughter as they transition from school into adult life. Suggest goals and objectives that promote and support social interaction and community-based activities with peers who are not disabled. Collaborate with the school to translate your goals into an individualized education plan that includes transition activities from school to adult life.

Tips for the General Education Classroom Teacher

- Become part of a schoolwide team that collaborates to meet the needs of all students in high school. Value the role of the special educator as teacher, collaborator, and consultant who can serve as a valuable resource in planning for the instructional needs of students with severe disabilities. Collaborate with special education teachers and other specialists to adapt subject matter in your classroom (e.g., science, math, or physical education) to the individual needs of students with severe and multiple disabilities.

- Communicate the importance of students with severe disabilities being included in school programs and activities. Although the goals and activities of this student may be different from those of other students, with support, she or he will benefit from working with you and other students in the class.

- Encourage the student with severe disabilities to become involved in extracurricular high school activities. If you are the faculty sponsor of a club or organization, explore whether this student is interested and how he or she could get involved.

Tips for School Personnel

- Advocate for parents of high-school-age students with severe and multiple disabilities to participate in the activities and governance of the school

- Collaborate with parents in the transition-planning process during the high school years by listening to parent input that focuses on a desire for their son or daughter to be included as a valued member of the high school community.

- Support high school special education or vocational teachers seeking to develop community-based instruction programs that focus on students learning and applying skills in actual community settings (e.g., grocery stores, malls, theaters, parks, work sites).

Tips for Neighbors, Friends, and Potential Employers

- Collaborate with the family and school personnel to create opportunities for students with severe and multiple disabilities to participate in community activities (such as going to the movies, "hanging out" with peers who are not disabled in the neighborhood mall, and going to high school sporting events) as often as possible.

- As a potential employer, collaborate with the high school to locate and establish community-based employment training sites for students with severe and multiple disabilities.

ADULT YEARS

Tips for the Family

- Develop an understanding of life after school during your son's or daughter's adult years. What are the formal (government-funded or parent organizations) and informal supports (family and friends) available in your community? What are the characteristics of adult service programs? Explore adult support systems in the local community in the areas of supported living, employment, and recreation/leisure.

Tips for Neighbors, Friends, and Potential Employers

- Become part of the community support network for the individual with severe and multiple disabilities. Be alert to ways in which this individual can become and remain actively involved in community employment, neighborhood recreational activities, and local church functions.

- As a potential employer in the community, seek information on employment of people with severe and multiple disabilities. Find out about programs (such as supported employment) that focus on establishing work for people with mental retardation while meeting your needs as an employer.

THE BEGINNING OF A NEW CIRCLE OF FRIENDS

Both Joanne and Jennifer are new students with disabilities in the fifth grade homeroom. It is mid-afternoon of their first day at the new school—and time for recess. The special education aide has a break now, so Tom and Maria, two students without disabilities, volunteer to help Jennifer outside to the playground. Halfway down the hall, Jennifer begins to wheel her chair—slowly, but by herself. Tom lights up. "Hey, I didn't know that you could do that. Why didn't you tell me before?"

Jennifer first smiles and then lets out a full laugh. The two other fifth graders join in. They continue slowly outside, where Tom leaves to play softball. Joanne, the other new student, has been invited to join an impromptu soccer game, serving, because of her height, as goalie. Maria, not wanting to leave Jennifer simply sitting by herself during recess, asks, "Do you want to play jump rope?"

Again, Jennifer smiles, and looks toward the group of girls next to the building who have already begun to play jump rope. Maria understands and helps Jennifer over a curb, as the two girls move on to the game. Once there, Maria asks, "Do you know how to twirl?"

Jennifer shakes her head, "no." So Maria places the end of the rope in her hand and holding says, "Okay, hold it like this, and go round this way." She guides her movements with her hand.

Soon Jennifer gets the hang of it, and Maria is able to let go. It's her turn to jump, so she leaves Jennifer's side, and begins her routine. She is able to jump longer than any of the other girls. As she spins around to complete a maneuver, she faces Jennifer as she jumps. Seeing her twirl, Maria sticks out her tongue, and both girls laugh. Unfortunately, the twirling stops, ending Maria's turn. It doesn't really matter, because a new game will start tomorrow, and Maria usually wins anyway.

In a moment Ms. Nelson calls to the students to return to class, and Maria and Jennifer come in together. As they enter the room, Ms. Nelson asks the classmates to take out their library books and use the remaining time to read silently. Marsha, who had been playing soccer with Joanne, asks her teacher if she could lend her one of her books to read. Ms. Nelson approves, and the girls go to the reading corner of the room to choose among Marsha's three books.

APPLICATION

1. Could this experience have occurred in a special school or if Jennifer had spent her entire day in a special education self-contained classroom?

2. What can be done to ensure that this relationship continues outside of school?

3. Why is being a "member" of the homeroom so important to establishing friendships for children with severe disabilities?

SOURCE: Adapted from *Introduction to Persons with Moderate and Severe Disabilities* (p. 194, 2nd ed.), by J. McDonnell, M. Hardman, & A. P. McDonnell, 2003, Boston: Allyn and Bacon, p. 297.

As students with severe and multiple disabilities are included in general education schools and classrooms, it is important to find ways to encourage social interactions between these students and students who are not disabled. Planned opportunities for interaction may include the use of in-class peer supports (tutors, circles of friends) as well as access to everyday school activities such as assemblies, recess, lunch, and field trips. For more tips on supporting people with severe and multiple disabilities in natural settings, see this chapter's Inclusion and Collaboration Through the Lifespan.

Severe Disabilities and Biomedical Dilemmas

Council for Exceptional Children

Standard 9: Professional and Ethical Practice

───

► **Bioethics**
The study of ethics in medicine.

Rapid advances in medical technology have resulted in the survival of an increasing number of infants with severe and multiple disabilities. Today, many such infants who would have died at birth only five to ten years ago often live well into their adult years. However, this decrease in infant mortality and increase in lifespan have raised a number of serious ethical issues regarding decisions about prevention, care, and selective nontreatment of infants with severe disabilities. In recent years, there has been an increasing awareness of and interest in **bioethics**, particularly as it is related to serious illness and severe disabilities. Bioethical issues include concerns about the purpose and use of genetic engineering, screening for genetic diseases, abortion, and the withholding of life-sustaining medical treatment. A number of questions have been raised by both professionals and parents. When do individual rights begin? Who should live, and who should die? What is personhood? Who defines quality of life? What are the rights of the person with severe disabilities in relationship to the obligations of a society? Who shall make the difficult decisions?

Genetic Engineering

The purpose of genetic engineering is to conquer disease. Through the identification of a faulty gene that causes a disease, such as cystic fibrosis, scientists are able to prevent future occurrence and treat those who have the condition. In 1990, the United States and the United Kingdom joined together with more than 3,000 research scientists in the **Human Genome Project**. The purpose of the project was to

> identify the 80,000 genes in human DNA.

> determine the sequences of the 3 billion chemical base pairs that make up human DNA.

> store this information in databases.

> develop tools for data analysis.

> address the ethical, legal, and social issues that may arise from the project. (U.S. Department of Energy, 2003)

In June 2000, scientists from the Human Genome Project and scientists from a private company, Celera Genomics of Rockville, Maryland, announced that they had successfully completed the first phase of the research. They had sequenced 99% of the human genome and had assembled more than 1 billion letters of genetic code. The next step, which may be the most challenging and controversial, is interpreting what all the codes mean.

The work of scientists to map the secrets of the genetic code has attracted the attention of professionals and parents concerned with the rights of people with severe and multiple disabilities. Although genetic engineering may be seen as holding considerable promise for reducing human suffering, it can also be viewed as a means of enhancing or perfecting human beings. Since the vast majority of people with severe and multiple disabilities have genetic disorders (such as fragile X syndrome and Down syndrome), they are greatly affected by this debate. The ARC of the United States (a national organization of and for people with intellectual disabilities and related developmental disabilities and their families) is concerned that people with severe disabilities have been subjected to a long history of discrimination. Thus it is important that the complex ethical issues surrounding the work of the Human Genome Project receive widespread public attention. The ARC (2006b) suggested numerous questions in the area of genetic engineering that have yet to be answered:

Should therapies for genetic conditions causing intellectual disabilities [severe disabilities] even be considered? Is there positive value in [human] diversity? How can we avoid stigmatizing those living with a genetic condition while [we are] trying to eliminate the condition in others? Are some conditions so destructive to the individual that if a therapy is possible it should be undertaken? Should parents include their newborn child in experimental gene therapy research?

┌ **FOCUS** 10
Describe four bioethical dilemmas that affect people with severe disabilities and their families.

> **Human genome project**
Project developed by the United States and the United Kingdom to identify the 80,000 genes in human DNA; determine the sequences of the 3 billion chemical base pairs that make up human DNA; store this information in databases; develop tools for data analysis; and address the ethical, legal, and social issues that may arise from the project.

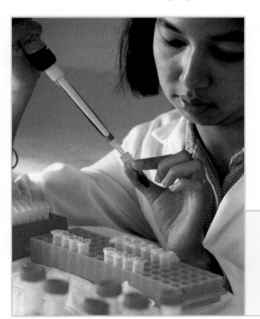

Although genetic engineering holds considerable promise for reducing human suffering, many ethical questions are yet to be answered.

Genetic Screening and Counseling

Genetic screening is a search for genes in the human body that are predisposed to disease, are already diseased, or may lead to disease in future generations of the same family. Genetic screening has become widespread throughout the world, but it is not without controversy and potential for abuse. The Human Genome Project has raised several ethical questions regarding genetic screening. As the availability of genetic information increases, how will society make sure that insurers, employers, courts, schools, adoption agencies, law enforcement, and the military use it in a fair and equitable manner and not to discriminate against certain groups of people? What psychological impact and stigmatization might be related to an individual's genetic differences? How does the information affect society's perceptions of that individual (The ARC, 2006b)?

The next step following genetic screening is counseling to ensure that family members understand the results and implications of the screening. The concerns surrounding genetic counseling focus on the neutrality of the counselor. The role of the genetic counselor is to provide information, not to become a "moral adviser" or psychotherapist for the family. Drew and Hardman (2007) noted that genetic counselors may find it difficult to maintain neutrality when they have personal beliefs and strong feelings about what should be done. However, counselors must remain neutral and not become directive in their attempts to help family members make the "right" decision in regard to future pregnancies or ongoing treatment of a condition.

Selective Abortion and Withholding Medical Treatment

No other issue polarizes society like the unborn child's right to life versus a woman's right to choose. Rapidly advancing medical technology makes the issue of abortion even more complex. A number of chromosomal and metabolic disorders that may result in severe and multiple disabilities can now be identified in utero. Thus parents and physicians are placed in the position of deciding whether to abort a fetus diagnosed with severe anomalies. On one side are those who argue that the quality of life for the child born with severe disabilities may be so diminished that, if given the choice, they would choose not to live under such circumstances. Additionally, the family may not be able to cope with a child who is severely disabled. On the other side are those who point out that no one has the right to decide for someone else whether life is "worth living." Major strides in education, medical care, technology, and social inclusion have enhanced quality of life for people with severe disabilities.

Controversy also surrounds the issue of denying medical treatment to a person with a disability (Drew & Hardman, 2007). The application of one standard for a person without disabilities and another for a person with a severe disability has resulted in some difficult issues in the medical field. For more insight into these controversial issues, see the Debate Forum, "Disabilities May Keep Brian Cortez from Heart Transplant."

Several national organizations (Association for Persons with Severe Handicaps [TASH], The ARC—A National Organization on Intellectual Disabilities, and the American Association on Intellectual Disabilities) have strongly opposed the withholding of medical treatment when the decision is based on the individual's having disabilities. These organizations hold that everyone is entitled to life and that society has an obligation to protect people from the ignorance and prejudices that may be associated with disability.

DISABILITIES MAY KEEP BRIAN CORTEZ FROM A HEART TRANSPLANT

Moving a step to his right, Brian Cortez dribbles the basketball and arcs a 15-foot shot that sails through the curbside hoop. He flashes a smile, and his fingers move quickly to sign his pleasure to his friends.

It is a happy moment in the troubled times of Cortez, 20. In a life filled with challenges, he is facing perhaps his most difficult.

Cortez is developmentally disabled, is almost deaf, and has lived in poverty since birth. Four years ago he was diagnosed with mild mental illness. Now his heart is sick and eventually will fail without a transplant.

Yet his limited mental abilities may disqualify him from the procedure. University of Washington physicians have said in an initial evaluation that they don't think Cortez, who lives in an adult home, can follow a strict medication regimen or articulate any problems after a transplant. A scarcity of donor hearts nationwide makes patients like Cortez less able to compete for a spot on the waiting list.

Advocates for Cortez—his teacher, his mother, adult-home caregivers, and case workers—disagree. They say University of Washington physicians and a social worker did not speak in depth with key people in the young man's support network. If they had, they would have learned that Cortez takes medications when asked, is aware of his physical condition, and can tell caregivers how he feels.

"They didn't have a true picture of his ability to deal with things," said Ted Karanson, deaf-education teacher at North Thurston High School, where Cortez was a student until his heart problems became worse this winter. "Brian deserves a chance at a transplant like anyone else."

Cortez's situation reflects the consequences of a national shortage of vital organs for transplantation. About 800 people a year die while waiting for heart transplants. More than 5,000 patients nationwide die while waiting for other organs.

The government-contracted agency that allocates organs nationally—the United Network for Organ Sharing—has an elaborate system to channel organs to patients who have the best chance of benefiting. And the law of supply and demand applies: Scarce organs go to those with the best chance of surviving an operation and caring for themselves afterward.

Laurence O'Connell, president of the Park Ridge Center, a Chicago bioethics institute, said the University of Washington is using a widely accepted standard, and the decision couldn't be more difficult:

"To offer the organ to this young man will almost certainly mean another patient will die," O'Connell said.

Brian Cortez's life began with a difficult birth, when his brain was briefly deprived of oxygen. Months later, he was diagnosed with severe hearing loss, impaired mental development,

poor fine-motor control, and a faulty heart valve. At age 16, he began occasionally hearing voices. He banged his head against his locker and mumbled threats at other students at North Thurston High School. He was diagnosed with a "thought disorder" and was prescribed medication that silences the voices most of the time. Through it all, Cortez has been undiscouraged and has struggled to learn, Karanson said. He has friends from school, reads the newspaper to keep up with the Seattle Sonics and Mariners, and has firm opinions about current affairs. He expresses himself through signing, speaking, and writing. Last year he worked two days a week for a landscape nursery as part of his school's job-training program.

With a successful transplant, "He could work a job, part time if not full time," said Lisa Flatt, a sign-language interpreter for the North Thurston School District. "He could do something repetitious—landscaping, assembly-line work, working in a mail room. . . . He would be really good at it." Cortez's medical record shows he was given test after test during his two-week stay at the University of Washington hospital. Communication was poor, his mother said, because he did not understand the hospital's sign-language interpreter. The tests and treatment frightened and angered him.

At one point he was restrained in bed because he was spitting at and biting nurses. He wet his bed and hoarded food. He was given heavy doses of anti-psychotic medications to calm him. In the end, doctors wrote in his record: "It was thought during his admission that, due to his developmental delay and inability to understand and comply with instructions, the patient was not a candidate for heart transplant. . . . Due to his mental and psychiatric condition, he is not a candidate for heart transplant and should be medically managed with medications as best as possible." David Smith, an Olympia physician who has seen Cortez in recent months, said he doesn't think doctors at the University of Washington or elsewhere exclude patients from scarce resources because they are disabled. Rather, they consider whether the patient's quality of life would improve with surgery and whether the patient can do his part to make it successful. Arthur Caplan, director of the University of Pennsylvania Center for Bioethics, said that the University of Washington's selection standard is appropriate. But he said it is essential that a patient's support system be considered when evaluating the chances of success.

Brian Cortez is clearly a qualified candidate for a heart transplant and should immediately be placed on the waiting list. His support network of family and caregivers have made a strong case that Brian is able to follow a strict medication regimen and communicate any problems he is having following the transplant. His disabilities should not in any way be a factor in the decision. Brian clearly qualifies on the basis of medical need. With reasonable accommodations and his strong family and caregivers support network, there is no reason to believe that Brian's chances for survival from the transplant would be less than anyone else's.

The primary issue here is a scarcity of organs that requires that difficult life-and-death decisions be made on the basis of who has the best chance of benefitting from the operation. To give to one person, means that another person must die. As suggested by Brian's behavior during his hospital stay, he has poor communication even with an interpreter; is easily upset by tests and medical treatment; and requires heavy doses of medication to calm him down. Clearly, his developmental disabilities make it difficult for him to understand the critical instructions necessary for him to meet the required medical regimen following the heart transplant. Brian's condition is better managed by medications and not a risky operation and difficult recovery that are beyond his abilities to cope with over the long run.

Update: Doctors at the University of Washington Medical Center eventually changed their position regarding Brian Cortez's qualifications for a heart transplant. Under threat of a lawsuit from Brian's mother and his special education teacher, doctors at the Medical Center completed a successful heart transplant on Brian in September 2001.

SOURCE: From "Disabilities May Keep Man from Transplant," by W. King, 2000, *Salt Lake Tribune,* May 2, pp. A1, A7.

FOCUS REVIEW

FOCUS 1 What are the three components of the TASH definition of severe disabilities?

- The relationship of the individual with the environment (adaptive fit)

- The inclusion of people of all ages

- The necessity of extensive ongoing support in life activities

FOCUS 2 Define the terms *multiple disabilities* and *deaf-blindness* as described in IDEA.

- The term *multiple disabilities* refers to concomitant impairments (such as intellectual disabilities–orthopedic impairments). The combination causes educational problems so severe that they cannot be accommodated in special education programs designed solely for one impairment. One such combination is "dual diagnosis," a condition characterized by serious emotional disturbance (challenging behaviors) in conjunction with severe intellectual disabilities.

- *Deaf-blindness* involves concomitant hearing and visual impairments. The combination causes communication and other developmental and educational problems so severe that they cannot be accommodated in special education programs designed solely for children who are deaf or blind.

FOCUS 3 Identify the estimated prevalence and causes of severe and multiple disabilities.

- Prevalence estimates generally range from 0.1% to 1% of the general population.

- Students with multiple disabilities recently accounted for about 2% of the 7 million students with disabilities served in the public schools. Approximately 0.0002% of students with disabilities were labeled deaf-blind.

- Many possible causes of severe and multiple disabilities exist. Most severe and multiple disabilities are evident at birth. Birth defects may be the result of genetic or metabolic problems. Most identifiable causes of severe intellectual disabilities and related developmental disabilities are genetic in origin. Factors associated with poisoning, accidents, malnutrition, physical and emotional neglect, and disease are also known causes.

FOCUS 4 What are the characteristics of persons with severe and multiple disabilities?

- Having intellectual disabilities is often a primary condition.

- Most children will not benefit from basic academics instruction in literacy and mathematics. Instruction in functional academics is the most effective approach to learning academic skills.

- People with severe and multiple disabilities often do not have age-appropriate adaptive skills and need ongoing services and supports to facilitate learning in this area.

- Significant speech and language deficits and delays are a primary characteristic.
- Physical and health needs are common, involving conditions such as congenital heart disease, epilepsy, respiratory problems, spasticity, athetosis, and hypotonia. Vision and hearing loss are also common.

FOCUS 5 Identify three types of educational assessments for students with severe and multiple disabilities.

- Traditionally, there has been a heavy reliance on standardized measurements, particularly the IQ test, in identifying people with severe and multiple disabilities.
- Assessments that focus on valued skills to promote independence and quality of life in natural settings are referred to as *functional, ecological,* or *authentic assessment.*
- Students with disabilities must participate in statewide and districtwide assessments of achievement, or the school must explain why that assessment is not appropriate for the child. For many students with severe disabilities, these assessments are inappropriate, and they are excluded from taking them. Alternate assessments are conducted instead.

FOCUS 6 Identify the features of effective services and supports for children with severe and multiple disabilities during the early childhood years.

- Services and supports must begin at birth.
- Programs for infants and toddlers are both child- and family-centered.
- The goals for preschool programs are to maximize development across several developmental areas, to develop social interaction and classroom participation skills, to increase community participation through support to family and caregivers, and to prepare the child for inclusive school placement.
- Effective and inclusive preschool programs have a holistic view of the child, see the classroom as a community of learners, base the program on a collaborative ethic, use authentic assessment, create a heterogeneous environment, make available a range of individualized supports and services, engage educators in reflective teaching, and emphasize multiple ways of teaching and learning.

FOCUS 7 Identify the features of effective services and supports for children with severe and multiple disabilities during the elementary school years.

- Self-determination is important—student preferences and needs are taken into account in developing educational objectives.
- The school values and supports parental involvement.
- Instruction focuses on frequently used functional skills related to everyday life activities.

- Assistive technology and augmentative communication are available to maintain or increase the functional capabilities of the student with severe and multiple disabilities.

FOCUS 8 Describe four outcomes that are important in planning for the transition from school to adult life for adolescents with severe and multiple disabilities.

- Establishing a network of friends and acquaintances
- Developing the ability to use community resources on a regular basis
- Securing a paid job that supports the use of community resources and interaction with peers
- Establishing independence and autonomy in making lifestyle choices

FOCUS 9 Describe four features that characterize successful inclusive education for students with severe and multiple disabilities.

- Physical placement of students with severe and multiple disabilities in the general education schools and classes they would attend if they didn't have disabilities
- Systematic organization of opportunities for interaction between students with severe and multiple disabilities and students without disabilities
- Specific instruction in valued postschool outcomes that will increase the competence of students with severe and multiple disabilities in the natural settings of family, school, and community

FOCUS 10 Describe four bioethical dilemmas that can affect people with severe disabilities and their families.

- Genetic engineering may be used to conquer disease or as a means to enhance or perfect human beings.
- Genetic screening may be effective in preventing disease but can also be used by insurance companies, employers, courts, schools, adoption agencies, law enforcement, and the military to discriminate against people with severe disabilities.
- Genetic counselors can provide important information to families, but they may also lose their objectivity and express their own personal beliefs about what the family should do.
- The availability of selective abortion and options for the withholding of medical treatment may enable parents to make the very personal decision about whether the quality of life for their unborn child may be so diminished that life would not be worth living. However, it can also be argued that no one has the right to decide for someone else whether a life is worth living.

BUILDING YOUR PORTFOLIO

If you are thinking about a career in special education, you should know that many states use national standards developed by the Council for Exceptional Children (CEC) to assess a teacher candidate's knowledge and skills for working with students with disabilities. See a complete listing of the ten CEC Content Standards on the inside front cover of this text.

CEC Content Standards Addressed in This Chapter

1 Foundations
2 Development and Characteristics of Learners
3 Individual Learning Differences
4 Instructional Strategies
5 Learning Environments and Social Interactions
7 Instructional Planning
8 Assessment
9 Professional and Ethical Practice

Assess Your Knowledge of the CEC Standards Addressed in This Chapter

Some states require that teacher candidates develop a portfolio of products that demonstrate mastery of the CEC content standards. To assist in the development of products for this portfolio, you may wish to complete the following activities.

- Complete a written test of the chapter's content.

  If your instructor requires a written test of your content knowledge for this chapter, keep a copy for your portfolio. A practice test on the information covered in this chapter is available through the companion website (college.hmco.com/pic/hardman9e) and the Student Study Guide.

- Read the Debate Forum in this chapter and then visit our companion website to complete the activity "Take a Stand." Keep a copy of this activity for your portfolio.

- Participate in a Community Service Learning Activity.

  Community service is a valuable way to enhance your learning experience. Visit our companion website for suggested community service learning activities that correspond to the information presented in this chapter. Develop a reflective journal of the service learning experience for your portfolio.

WEB RESOURCES

Association for Persons with Severe Handicaps (TASH)

http://www.TASH.org

TASH is an international advocacy association of people with disabilities, their family members, other advocates, and people who work in the disability field. This website contains TASH publications, products, legislative updates, and conference information.

Human Genome Project

http://www.ornl.gov/TechResources/Human_Genome/home.html

This site provides up-to-date information on what's new in human genome research, frequently asked questions about genetic engineering and research, and discussions on ethical, legal and social issues.

National Information Clearinghouse on Children Who Are Deaf-Blind

http://www.tr.wou.edu/dblink/

DB-LINK is a federally funded information and referral service that identifies, coordinates, and disseminates information related to children and youth who are deaf-blind (ages birth to 21 years). Four organizations have pooled their expertise into a consortium-based clearinghouse. This collaborative effort uses the expertise and resources of the American Association of the Deaf-Blind, Helen Keller National Center, the Perkins School for the Blind, and the Teaching Research Institute.

FURTHER READINGS

Downing, J. E., & Siegel, E. (2005). *Teaching communication skills to students with severe disabilities* (2nd ed.). Baltimore, MD: Paul H. Brookes.

Provides strategies for teaching communication skills to students with severe disabilities in inclusive school and community settings. Topics include assessing the student's communication ability, analyzing the environment, and alternative and augmentative communication techniques.

McDonnell, J., Hardman, M., & McDonnell, A. P. (2003). *Introduction to persons with moderate and severe disabilities* (2nd ed.). Boston: Allyn and Bacon.

Addresses the challenges that people with severe disabilities face in becoming full members of society. Using a lifespan approach, it provides information on promising practices for services and programs from birth through the adult years.

Snell, M. E. & Brown, F. (Eds.). (2006). *Instruction of students with severe disabilities* (6th ed.). Upper Saddle River, NJ: Merrill.

Provides teaching methods for work with students who have severe disabilities, including students with autism and functional skills needs. Covered are inclusive education, assessment, positive behavior support, health care, basic self-help skills, peer relationships, communication, and transition from school to adult life.

Visit the companion website at college.hmco.com/pic/hardman9e for additional resources that support this text:

- HM Video Cases that present actual classroom scenarios that you may face every day as a teacher

- Practice ACE Exams that will help you prepare for quizzes, tests, and certfication exams
- Flashcards of key terms
- Weblinks

13

Autism Spectrum Disorder

SOME ASSERT VACCINES CAUSE AUTISM

Some parents of children with autism have filed lawsuits against selected drug makers claiming that certain vaccines caused their children to develop the condition. While scientific evidence for this assertion is not clear, it is obviously a sensitive and emotional issue with many parents. (CBS News, 2003a)

I'LL MISS HIM

"Knowing Chris; he does not speak. He throws his food. When unrestrained, he often bangs his knee against his forehead. When he leaves, not only will I miss him; a small part of my personality will be gone too. . . . Next week, after two years here, Chris will be moved to another institution, one with better access to medical crisis intervention." (Whitaker, 2000, p. Z12)

GOING TO CAMP

If you're looking for a camp to accommodate a child with special needs, the search is getting easier. Accessing the Internet, one of several search sites will provide a multitude of choices, some of which are categorized by zip code to facilitate geographical identification. Programs like Camp Lee Mar in Pennsylvania work specifically with children having special needs. These camps provide youngsters with conditions like autism and Asperger syndrome autism a chance to have a camp experience with others who share their own and other disabilities. (ABCNEWS.com, 2006, pp. 1–5)

HORSES WORK "SMALL WONDERS"

Lisa Gatti's company uses horses as a therapeutic tool for a variety of children with disabilities, including autism. She believes that riding horses enhances self-esteem and helps teach discipline as well as enhancing muscle tone. Many parents support such claims, believing that there have been substantial benefits from their children's participation. (CBS News, 2003b)

FOCUS PREVIEW

1 Identify four areas of functional challenge often found in children with autism spectrum disorder.

2 What are the general prevalence estimates for autism and autism spectrum disorder?

3 Identify six characteristics of children with autism spectrum disorder.

4 Cite the two broad theoretical views regarding the causes of autism spectrum disorder.

5 Identify four major approaches to the treatment of autism spectrum disorder.

▼ SNAPSHOT

JOSH

Josh is in a general education class at his elementary school. His friend Marshall, who has learning disabilities, is a close friend to Josh. Marshall says, "Josh likes to dribble the basketball. Other people help Josh, but I help him a lot, too."

When Josh was born, his parents thought he was deaf, but tests showed he could hear. At age 30 months, Josh was diagnosed with autism. His parents couldn't afford a specialized clinic or treatment facility and felt at a loss for what to do. They visited a school with a separate unit for children with autism, mental retardation, and other disabilities. During the visit, Josh mingled with other children and mimicked their behavior—shouts, some violent movements. Josh's parents decided not to place Josh in that school.

Josh entered a general education class. The special education teacher at the school was concerned at first because Josh would bite his nails and scratch his legs. He wasn't interacting with the other students. Gradually, he started to talk and interact with the other students. His special education teacher says, "I think this wouldn't have happened if he were only interacting with other autistic children."

Josh's dad feels strongly about including students with disabilities in the general education classroom: "When wheelchairs come in (to school) in the morning and the Down syndrome (students) come in in the morning, and Josh comes in the morning, they are the students. They are not the special education students. It's a long process and it's just becoming comfortable."

BILLY

Billy is a blue-eyed, blond little boy of striking beauty; he is almost too perfect physically. His parents first became aware that Billy was different and had special problems when he was 5 years old but had not yet begun to talk. Some of his other behaviors also bothered Billy's parents a great deal. Billy didn't seem to play like other children. He would rock for long periods of time in his crib, and he had little interest in toys. At best, Billy would just spin the wheels of his trucks and stare as they turned. Most disturbing to Billy's parents was the fact that he showed little affection. Billy was not a warm baby. When his mother picked him up to cuddle, Billy would start to cry and arch his back until he was put back in his crib. Billy treated other children and adults as objects of no consequence in his life. He didn't care about people; he would rather be left alone.

Since Billy's behavior was recognized as different from normal, other changes have occurred. Billy developed language very slowly and in a strange way. His language is what specialists call "echolalic" in nature. When asked a question, Billy simply responds by echoing the question. Billy also has a great deal of trouble using pronouns and prepositions correctly when trying to talk. He will commonly reverse pronouns and refer to himself as "you" or refer to another person as "I." The correct use of prepositions also causes Billy a great deal of difficulty. Up or down, on or under, and a yes-or-no answer to a question are very confusing concepts for Billy. He simply answers yes or no at random. When viewed as a whole, Billy's language is not just delayed; it is also disturbed in some fundamental way. He simply does not learn. Over and over he makes the same language mistakes.

Aside from Billy's atypical language development, he now spends a great deal of time in repetitive, non-goal-oriented behavior called *self-stimulatory* or *stereotypic* behavior. He has progressed from simple rocking and spinning the wheels on his toys to flapping his hands and twirling in circles until he falls from dizziness. If made to stop this behavior, Billy will throw ferocious temper tantrums that include screaming, biting, and often head banging. This self-destructive behavior is very disconcerting because, in his tantrums, Billy not only breaks things but hurts himself as well.

Billy also has a tremendous need to protect himself against any sort of change, including changes in his daily routine or his physical environment. Billy's mother recently rearranged the furniture in the living room while he was napping. When Billy awoke and entered the rearranged room, he immediately started to cry and whine; then he had a tantrum until the furniture was returned to its original position. Changes in his daily schedule also produce near-panic reactions that end up in tantrums. It seems as though Billy has memorized his environment and daily schedule, and any change inflicts fear of the unknown. Adjustment and relearning are very difficult for him. Billy's behavior cripples his family as well as himself. The furniture arrangement episode is only one of many incidents in which Billy requires his parents' constant attention. If left alone for even short periods of time, Billy can hurt himself or break something. After claiming all the attention his parents and older brother can give, Billy returns little. He is not affectionate and will not even look his brother in the eye, nor does he seek his mother's affection. Billy suffers from a rare childhood developmental disorder known as infantile autism.

SOURCE: Adapted from *Understanding Child Behavior Disorders* (2nd ed., p. 288), by D. M. Gelfand, W. R. Jenson, and C. J. Drew, 1988, New York: Holt, Rinehart and Winston.

Council for
Exceptional
Children

Standard 1: Foundations

Focus 1
Identify four areas of functional challenge often found in children with autism spectrum disorder.

Federal law first recognized autism as a disability category in the Individuals with Disabilities Education Act of 1990 (IDEA). Although only recently acknowledged in federal law, autism began to appear in the research literature in the first half of the 20th century and is thought to have been described in the early 1800s (Spector & Volkmar, 2006; Volkmar, 2005). Even more recent is the perspective of autism spectrum disorder, which includes a broader range of functioning than narrower views of autism (Bregman, 2005; Gilberg, 2006; Ozonoff, Dawson, & McPartland, 2002). The term *autism* is taken from the Greek *autos,* meaning "self," to reflect the sense of isolation and detachment from the world around them that characterizes individuals with autism spectrum disorder.

Symptoms of autism spectrum disorder can emerge very early in a child's life (Maestro et al., 2005). Most cases become evident before the age of $2\frac{1}{2}$, and few are diagnosed after the age of 5. Autism spectrum disorder can be one of the most seriously disruptive of all childhood disabilities. It is characterized by combinations of varying degrees of deficiencies in language, interpersonal skills, emotional or affective behavior, and intellectual functioning (Bauminger, 2002; Bowler, 2006; Hobson, 2005). It is a disability that impairs the normal development of many areas of functioning.

Autism and autism spectrum disorder have received significant attention in the past several years from both researchers and the public media. Consider the words of Rick Whitaker in the chapter opening, which portray his son Chris both through the challenging behaviors he exhibits and also through the personal fingerprint he leaves on at least one individual who knows him. Although some of the more public portrayals of autism are perhaps not typical of the condition, they educate and capture the interest of a considerable segment of the lay public.

Definition

IDEA employs the following definition of autism:

> Autism means a developmental disability significantly affecting verbal and nonverbal communication and social interaction, generally evident before age 3, that adversely affects educational performance. Characteristics of autism include irregularities and impairments in communication, engagement in repetitive activities and stereotyped movements, resistance to environmental change or change in daily routines, and unusual responses to sensory experiences. (American Psychiatric Association, 2000; Bowler, 2006; McConkey, 2006)

The IDEA definition refers to the appearance of deviations from normal development before 3 years of age, because the symptoms of **autism** tend to emerge during the early years. The definition does not intend, however, to preclude a diagnosis of autism if a child develops symptoms after age 3. Although diagnosis occurs rarely before 3, characteristics can begin to emerge earlier (such as at 24 months) as well as later (Landa & Garrett-Mayer, 2006; Stone, 2006). Federal regulations also note that a diagnosis of autism should not be used in cases where children show characteristics of serious emotional disturbance, which is addressed elsewhere in the law. Such attention to autism is relatively recent. The 1991–1992 school year was the first during which data were collected on the number of children identified as having autism and served in the public schools (U.S. Department of Education, 2006).

Definitional statements provide a partial picture of autism, although most professionals are reluctant to make broad generalizations about people with autism. People with autism spectrum disorder are certainly not all alike, and it is more accurate to speak of characteristics than to characterize. Although autism has historically been assumed to imply a seriously reduced level of functioning, a broad range of capacity, from severe to mild impairments, occurs. Acknowledgment of this has led to use of the concept of **autism spectrum disorders**, which includes a range of functioning in the multiple skill areas of communication and language, intelligence, and social interaction (Anckarsater, 2006; Gillberg, 2006; Simpson, 2005). In some cases, debate has arisen about what represents functional variations within the same disability and what constitutes a separate disorder. One example of this is found with **Asperger syndrome**, or Asperger disorder, a condition that shares certain unusual social interactions and behaviors with autism but typically includes no general language delay (Gelfand & Drew, 2003; Raja, 2006). The Snapshot on Joseph illustrates some unusual behaviors, but the characteristics seem different from traditional descriptions of children with autism. Some researchers argue that Asperger disorder is distinct; others contend it is a higher-functioning version of autism spectrum disorders (Blakemore et al., 2006; Gillberg & Cederlund, 2005; Minshew & Meyer, 2006). Although this argument remains unresolved, the notion of a spectrum of disability severity has grown in acceptance and enables students and parents to begin to receive service

Council for Exceptional Children

Standard 2: Development and Characteristics of Learners

Standard 3: Individual Learning Differences

➤ **Autism**
A childhood disorder with onset prior to 36 months of age. It is characterized by extreme withdrawal, self-stimulation, intellectual deficits, and language disorders.

➤ **Autism spectrum disorders**
A term that reflects the range of functioning found, among those who exhibit symptoms of autism, in the multiple skill areas of communication and language, intelligence, and social interaction.

➤ **Asperger syndrome**
A condition that shares certain unusual social interactions and behaviors with autism but typically includes no general language delay.

This young girl loves the activity but has difficulty forming a personal attachment with the adult right behind her.

TABLE 13.1

Diagnostic Criteria for Autism and Asperger Disorder

AUTISM	ASPERGER DISORDER	CRITERIA
		Social Interaction
*	*	Qualitative impairment in social interaction manifested by:
X	X	• marked impairment in using multiple nonverbal behaviors such as eye-to-eye gaze, facial expressions, body postures, and gestures to regulate social interaction
X	X	• failure to develop peer relationships appropriate to developmental level
X	X	• lack of spontaneous seeking to share enjoyment, interests, or achievements with others
X	X	• lack of social or emotional reciprocity
**		Delay or abnormal functioning, with onset prior to age 3, in:
X		• social interaction
X		• language used in social communication
X		• symbolic or imaginative play
	X	The disturbance causes significant impairment in social, occupational, or other important functioning
		Stereotyped Behavior Patterns
**	**	Restricted repetitive and stereotyped behavior patterns, interests, and activities manifested by:
X	X	• preoccupation with one or more stereotyped, restricted interest patterns, abnormal in either intensity or focus
X	X	• inflexible adherence to specific, nonfunctional rituals
X	X	• stereotyped, repetitive motor mannerisms (e.g., hand flapping or twisting, whole-body movements)
X	X	• persistent preoccupation with parts of objects
		Language/Communication
**		Qualitative impairment in communication as manifested by:
X		• delay or total lack of spoken language development (not accompanied by alternative communication modes)
X		• marked impairment in initiating or sustaining conversations by those with adequate speech
X		• stereotyped and repetitive use of language or idiosyncratic language
X		• lack of varied, spontaneous play or social imitative play at appropriate developmental level
	X	No clinically significant general delay in language (i.e., single words used by age 2, phrases by age 3)
		Cognition
	X	No significant delay in cognitive development or age-appropriate self-help skills, adaptive behavior (other than social interaction), and curiosity about the environment
		Exclusions
X		Disturbance not better accounted for by Rett's or childhood disintegrative disorder
	X	Criteria are not met for another specific pervasive developmental disorder or schizophrenia

Note: A diagnosis of autism requires six (or more) identified behaviors from the social interaction, stereotyped behavior, and language/communication areas, with at least two from social interaction and one each from stereotyped behavior and language/communication.

*Requires at least two of these symptoms

**Requires at least one of these symptoms

SOURCE: American Psychiatric Association (2000), pp. 75, 84. Reprinted with permission from the *Diagnostic and Statistical Manual of Mental Disorders*, 4th ed., Text Revision, © 2000 APA.

SOURCE: Quoted in *Understanding Child Behavior Disorders* (p. 293), by D. M. Gelfand & C. J. Drew, 2003 (4th ed.), Belmont, CA: Wadsworth.

(Baron-Cohen & Klin, 2006; Beaumont & Newcombe, 2006; McConachie & Robinson, 2006). The diagnostic criteria outlined for autism and for Asperger disorder by the American Psychiatric Association are shown in Table 13.1. This side-by-side summary illustrates some of the similarities and differences between these conditions.

Table 13.1 also mentions in passing a disorder known as **Rett syndrome**. Rett syndrome is a neurological condition that primarily affects girls, emerges at a relatively young age (about 5 months to 4 years), and results in a slowed development and regression in several abilities (Kundert & Trimarchi, 2006; Lindberg, 2006). In many cases a child has developed some skills, such as purposeful use of hands and some mobility, only to exhibit a serious reversal of these capacities, such as stereotypy in hand movements and a reduction of steady mobility. Language and cognition likewise undergo a reversal of development (Baptista, Mercadante, Macedo, & Schwartzman, 2006; Hetzroni & Rubin, 2006). Researchers consider Rett syndrome as a part of the autism spectrum disorders but as a distinct neurological condition (Butler & Meany, 2005; Lindberg, 2006).

> **Rett syndrome**
A neurological condition primarily affecting girls who seem to develop normally until somewhere between 5 and 30 months of age. Thereafter, their development of skills slows and, in many cases, regresses significantly to a level of significant impairment.

Prevalence

Compared to other conditions, autism is relatively rare. The American Psychiatric Association recently estimated that the prevalence is about 5 cases per 10,000 (APA, 2000). Although this has been a commonly accepted prevalence range, some research suggests higher prevalence rates (up to 39 per 10,000), and the total prevalence for autism spectrum disorder is estimated at over 116 per 10,000 (Baird et al., 2006; Chakrabarti & Fombonne, 2005; Gillberg, 2006). Whether the variation in prevalence rates is due to definitional changes or to a genuine increase in incidence remains unclear (Conti-Ramsden, Simkin, & Botting, 2006; Reading, 2006; Scott, Baron-Cohen, Bolton, & Brayne, 2002). The wide range in prevalence may diminish over time, as greater consensus about what constitutes autism and autism spectrum disorder is achieved. Gender differences are evident in autism; males outnumber females substantially. Estimates of these prevalence differences vary from around 4 to 1 to as high as 8 to 1 (Baker, 2002; Renty & Roeyers, 2006; Scott et al., 2002). Some researchers attribute this gender difference to females with autism being less socially aberrant than males—and thus more difficult to identify (Soppitt, 2006).

Focus **2**
What are the general prevalence estimates for autism and autism spectrum disorder?

Characteristics

Unusual behaviors often appear very early in the lives of children with autism spectrum disorder. They may, for example, exhibit significant impairment in interpersonal interaction as babies. Parents often report that these babies may be particularly unresponsive to physical contact or affection (Bowler, 2006; Stone, 2006; Volkmar, 2005). It is not unusual for parents to note that their infants become rigid when picked up, that they are "not cuddly," and that they avoid eye contact, averting their gaze rather than looking directly at another person (Ozonoff, Williams, & Landa, 2005). Such behavior may continue in older children. Some children with autism spectrum disorder rely heavily on peripheral vision, rather than direct, face-to-face visual contact.

Children with autism spectrum disorders are often described in terms of social impairments, unresponsiveness, extreme difficulty relating to others and understanding or expressing emotion, and lowered ability to regulate affect (Begeer, Rieffe, Terwogt, & Stockmann, 2006; Bauminger, 2002; Konstantareas & Stewart, 2006). Often, these children seem to prefer interacting with inanimate objects, forming attachments to such objects rather than to people. They appear to be insensitive to the feelings of others and in many cases treat other people as objects, even physically pushing or pulling others around to suit their needs (Howlin, 2002; Shalom et al., 2006). Clearly, children with autism spectrum disorders interact with their environment in ways that are not typical, as though they have difficulty making sense of the world around them.

Focus **3**
Identify six characteristics of children with autism spectrum disorder.

Council for Exceptional Children

Standard 2: Development and Characteristics of Learners

Standard 3: Individual Learning Differences

Impaired or Delayed Language

> **Echolalia**
> A meaningless repetition or imitation of words that have been spoken.

Standard 2: Development and Characteristics of Learners

Standard 6: Communication

Children with autism spectrum disorders often exhibit impaired or delayed language development (Bishop & Norbury, 2002; Bowler, 2006; Dietz, Swinkels, van Daalen, van Engeland, & Buitelaar, 2006). Approximately half do not develop speech, and those who do often engage in strange language and speaking behavior, such as **echolalia** (speaking only to repeat what has been said to them) (Gleason, 2005; Tager-Flusberg, Paul, & Lord, 2005). In many cases, children with autism spectrum disorder who *do* speak reproduce parts of conversations that they have heard. But they do so in a very mechanical fashion, with no sign that they attach meaning to what was said. In other cases they appear to have a reduced ability to imitate language (Freitag, Kleser, & von Gontard, 2006; Walenski, Tager-Flusberg, & Ullman, 2006). All of these characteristics vary with the level of the individual's functioning.

Children with autism spectrum disorders who develop language often have a limited speaking repertoire, exhibit an uneven level of development between language skill areas, and fail to use pronouns in speech directed at other people (Tager-Flusberg, 2003; Spector & Volkmar, 2006; Tiegerman-Farber, 2002). These children seem to differ from their peers in failing to grasp grammatical complexity and making little use of semantics in sentence structure (e.g., Rhea, 2005; Tager-Flusberg, Rhea, & Lord, 2005; Perkins, Dobbinson, Boucher, Bol, & Bloom, 2006). Additionally, the tonal quality of their speech is often unusual or flat, and in some cases, their speech appears to serve the purpose of self-stimulation rather than communication. Further investigation of language development in children with autism spectrum disorders is needed, as are stronger and novel research methodologies (e.g., Harris, Chabris, & Clark, 2006; Rutter, 2005a; Tager-Flusberg, 2005).

Stereotypic Behavior

> **Stereotypic behavior**
> Repetitive behavior or stereotypy involving repetitive movements such as rocking, hand flicking, or object manipulation.

Although not always present, behavior of a self-stimulatory nature is often associated with autism spectrum disorder. These children may engage in physical forms of **stereotypic behavior** or stereotypy, sometimes termed self-stimulation, such as flicking their hands in front of their faces repeatedly (Chan, Fung, Tong, & Thompson, 2005; Smith, Lovaas, & Lovaas, 2002). They also tend to manipulate objects in a repetitive fashion that suggests self-stimulation to an observer. However, the purposes and origins of stereotypic behavior are not well understood (Symons, Sperry, Dropik, & Bodfish, 2005). For some, such activity may provide sensory input, whereas for others it may provide a sense of organization. Stereotypic behavior is one area, among others, where autobiographic material written by high-functioning indi-

---

▼ SNAPSHOT

JOSEPH

A BOY WITH ASPERGER SYNDROME

Joseph always seemed like a brilliant child. He began talking before his first birthday, much earlier than his older sister and brother. He expressed himself in an adult-like way and was always very polite. When his mother offered to buy him a treat at the movies, for example, Joseph said, "No thank you, M&Ms are not my preferred mode of snacking." He showed a very early interest in letters and by 18 months could recite the whole alphabet. He taught himself to read before his third birthday. Joseph wasn't much interested in typical toys, like balls and bicycles, preferring instead what his proud parents considered "grown-up" pursuits, such as geography and science. Starting at age 2, he spent many hours lying on the living room floor, looking at maps in the family's world atlas. By age 5, he could name anywhere in the world, given a description of its geographical location ("What is the northernmost city in Brazil?"). Just as his parents suspected, Joseph is brilliant. He also has Asperger syndrome.

SOURCE: *A Parent's Guide to Asperger Syndrome and High-Functioning Autism: How to Meet the Challenges and Help Your Child Thrive* (p. 3), by S. Ozonoff, G. Dawson, and J. McPartland, 2002, New York: Guilford Press.

viduals with autism spectrum disorders may significantly enhance our understanding (Barrett, 2006; Grandin, 2005; Stacey, 2003).

Stereotypic behavior such as spinning objects, rocking, or hand flapping may continue for hours. Some behaviors that seem to start as stereotypy or self-stimulation may worsen or take different forms and create the potential for injury to the child. Examples include face slapping, biting, and head banging (e.g., McCracken et al., 2002; Symons et al., 2005). Behavior that becomes self-injurious is more often found in low-functioning children and can cause great concern and stress for parents and others around them.

Resistance to Change in Routine

Intense resistance to change, or rigidity, is often mentioned in discussions of children with autism and autism spectrum disorder. Familiar routines—during meals or at bedtime, for example—are obsessively important to them, and any deviation from the set pattern may upset them immensely. Youngsters who are affected in this manner may insist on a particular furniture arrangement or on a particular food for a given meal (for example, a specific cereal for breakfast). They may even wash themselves in a particular pattern, in a manner reminiscent of obsessive-compulsive or repetitive behaviors (Dziobek, Fleck, & Rogers, 2006; Hess, 2006; Rossi, 2006). Often, items must be arranged in a symmetrical fashion to seem proper to the child with an autism spectrum disorder. There have also been reports relating the rigidity or perseveration of those with autism to obsessive behaviors, including self-mutilation (Greaves, Prince, & Evans, 2006; Rapin, 2002).

Such obsessive, ritualistic behaviors create numerous problems, as one might expect, particularly if an effort is made to integrate the child into daily life. For example, most people pay little attention to the exact route they take when driving to the grocery store or to the precise pattern of moving through the store once they arrive. For parents who try to take their child with autism spectrum disorder along, however, minor deviations may cause a serious crisis. Transitions from one activity to another may also present challenges for these children in both school and home activities. Research is beginning to address such matters and has revealed that structured verbal and visual cues facilitate communication and may smooth transitions from one activity to another (Bondy & Frost, 2002; Deruelle, Rondan, Gepner, & Fagot, 2006; Larson, 2006).

Intelligence

Most children with autism exhibit a lower intellectual functioning than other children; about 75% have measured IQs that would identify them as having intellectual disabilities at some level (Bowler, 2006; Drew & Hardman, 2007; Newsom & Hovanitz, 2006). The verbal and reasoning skills required in intelligence testing pose particular difficulty for these children. It has long been thought that they have a tendency to imitate what they hear, as evidenced by their echolalic speech. However, more recent thinking suggests that more systematic evidence is needed and that autism may be more appropriately viewed as one or more specific deficits in information processing or cognition (Blair, Frith, Smith, Abell, & Cipolotti, 2002; Edelson, 2006; Mandelbaum et al., 2006).

Intellectual ability varies among children with autism spectrum disorder, and high-functioning individuals may test at a normal or near-normal level. High-functioning individuals may have rather substantial vocabularies, but they do not always understand the appropriate use of terms that they can spell and define. In some cases, very high-functioning people with autism appear to use language quite well, although there may still

Council for Exceptional Children

Standard 2: Development and Characteristics of Learners

Council for Exceptional Children

Standard 2: Development and Characteristics of Learners

Standard 3: Individual Learning Differences

The teacher who works with a child with autism should be prepared to use different teaching strategies that compensate for the uneven skills development of the child.

be clues that something is different (Freitag et al., 2006; Sturm, Fernell, & Gillberg, 2004; Tager-Flusberg et al., 2005). Such is the case with the description of Mike FitzPatrick in the nearby Reflect on This.

Approximately 10% to 15% of those with autism spectrum disorders exhibit what are known as splinter skills—areas of ability in which levels of performance are unexpectedly high compared to those in other domains of functioning. For instance, a student with autism may perform unusually well at memory tasks or drawing but have serious deficiencies in language skills and abstract reasoning (Perkins et al., 2006; Rhea, 2005). For parents of such students, these splinter skills create enormous confusion. Although most parents realize very early that their child with autism has exceptionalities, they also hope that he or she is healthy. These hopes may be fueled by the child's demonstration of unusual skills. In some cases, the parents may believe that whatever is wrong is their fault, as portrayed in the Snapshot featuring Steven. A great deal about autism spectrum disorders remains unknown. For example, are the narrow islands of high (savant-like) performance portrayed in the movie *Rain Man* simply extremes of splinter skills? Can splinter skills be effectively exploited in a functional way to facilitate school or work activity? Some preliminary evidence suggests it is possible, and research in this fascinating area continues (e.g., Pring & Hermelin, 2002; Young, 2005).

▼SNAPSHOT

STEVEN

REFLECTIONS OF A PARENT

Steven was $2\frac{1}{2}$ years old when our daughter, Katherine, was born. This was the time when I seriously began to search for help. I knew something was wrong shortly after Steve's birth, but when I tried to describe the problem, no one seemed to understand what I was saying. In spite of chronic ear infections, Steve looked very healthy. He was slow in developing language, but that could easily be attributed to his ear trouble. Since he was our first baby, I thought that maybe we just weren't very good parents.

When he was $2\frac{1}{2}$, we enrolled Steven in a diagnostic nursery school. He did not seem to understand us when we spoke. I wondered whether he was retarded or had some other developmental problem. The nursery school gave us their opinion when he was 4. They said Steve seemed to have normal intelligence, but he perseverated, was behind socially, and did not seem to process verbs. The school said he had some signs of autism and some signs of a learning disability.

When Steve was $4\frac{1}{2}$, he did some amazing things. He began to talk, read, write, and play the piano. I was taking beginning adult piano lessons at the time, and Steve could play everything I did. In fact, he could play any song he heard and even added chords with his left hand. Relatives and friends began to tell us that he was a genius and that this accounted for his odd behavior. I really wanted to believe this genius theory.

I enrolled Steven in a public kindergarten at age 5. This teacher had another theory about Steve's strange behavior. She believed that we were not firm enough with him. She also sent the social worker to our home to see what we were doing with him.

I often wondered if we were just very poor parents. I certainly had enough people tell us so! Whenever I went to anyone for help, I was likely to begin crying. Then the doctor or whoever would start to watch my behavior closely. I could just see each of them forming a theory in his or her mind: The child is okay, but the mother is a mess. I wondered if I was a very cold mother. Maybe I was subtly rejecting my son. Then again, maybe it was his father. My mother always said he didn't spend enough time with Steve.

I didn't understand when the psychiatrist told me Steve had a pervasive developmental disorder. I began to get the picture when the other terms were used. I had heard of autism before. Something was terribly wrong, but it had a physical basis. It was not my fault at all. This was a relief but also a tremendous blow. It has really helped to have a name for the problem. We used to wonder whether Steve was lying awake nights, dreaming up new ways to get our attention. We lived from crisis to crisis. We would finally handle one problem, only to have a new one develop in its place. Steve still does unusual things, but it doesn't send us into a panic anymore.

—Sheri, Steve's mother

Learning Characteristics

The learning characteristics of children with autism spectrum disorder are frequently different from those of their normally developing peers and may present significant educational challenges. Some characteristics described earlier are prominent in this respect. For example, students who resist change may perseverate on a specific item to be learned and encounter cognitive-shifting difficulties in turning their attention to the next topic or problem in an instructional sequence (Bishop, Richler, & Lord, 2006; Deruelle et al., 2006; Larson, 2006). Because of problems understanding social cues and relating to people, students with autism spectrum disorder may experience difficulty interacting with teachers and other students in a school setting (Delano & Snell, 2006; Howlin, 2002; Pearson, Loveland, & Lachar, 2006).

Council for Exceptional Children

Standard 3: Individual Learning Differences

The abilities of children with autism spectrum disorder frequently develop unevenly, both within and among skill areas. These children may or may not generalize already-learned skills to other settings or topics (Lyons & Fitzgerald, 2005; Newsom & Hovanitz, 2006; Thioux, Stark, & Klaiman, 2006). They are often impulsive and inconsistent in their responses, which is a matter that teachers may have to address. Children with autism spectrum disorder frequently have difficulty with information processing and abstract ideas, and they may focus on one or more select stimuli while failing to understand the general concept (Bowler, 2006; Klin & Jones, 2006).

Some children with autism spectrum disorder possess certain qualities that can be viewed as educational strengths or at least can be focused on for instructional purposes. For example, although generalizations about these youngsters are difficult to make, individuals with autism spectrum disorder are sometimes noted as enjoying routine, which is consistent with their desire to maintain sameness. If a child shows this tendency, teachers can draw on it when practice or drill is warranted in learning a skill. In certain cases, splinter skills may be capitalized on for positive, productive purposes. Additionally, some individuals with autism spectrum disorder seem to have relatively strong, specific long-term memory skills, particularly for factual information such as names, numbers, and dates (Lyons & Fitzgerald, 2005; Pring & Hermelin, 2002). Once these students have learned a piece of information, they may not forget it. Their long-term memory skills may equal those of their normally developing peers.

Navigating college is especially tricky with autistic traits: Assignments overwhelm, dating becomes stalking, and the dining hall is just too scary.

Valerie Kaplan has an aptitude for math and scored a perfect 1600 on her SAT. When her high school classmates applauded the announcement at lunch, she was pleased. But less obvious signals—a raised eyebrow or impatient glance at a watch—elude her. In an advanced course at Carnegie Mellon called "Building Virtual Worlds," that problem caused classmates to sideline her in group projects. And during a critical meeting to win approval for her customized major, electronic art, she intently circled the freckles on her arm with a marker.

Miss Kaplan's behavioral quirks are agonizingly familiar to students with an autism spectrum disorder. Simply put, their brains are wired differently.

Children with classic autism exhibit language delays or deficits and have difficulty relating to others; they display rigid, often obsessive behaviors; deviation from routine disturbs them. Some are mentally retarded. Those with milder conditions on the spectrum—Asperger disorder is one of them—exhibit some or all of these characteristics to lesser degrees. But Asperger syndrome is also distinguished by average or above-average intelligence, an early acuity with language, and singular passions; Miss Kaplan, for example, has absorbed every detail of an animated 1990s television series called "ReBoot." People like Miss Kaplan have a disability, but to others they can seem merely gifted or difficult or odd. . . .

SOURCE: Excerpted and revised from Moore, A. S. (2006). A Dream Not Denied: Students on the Spectrum. *New York Times: Education Life* Section 4A/November 5, 28–29, 32.

Generalizations regarding children with autism spectrum disorder are difficult to make. Despite the many stereotypes about these individuals, they are highly variable. Learning characteristics—both limitations and strengths—must be individually assessed and considered in educational programming. Challenging behavior patterns found in children with autism often cause a variety of difficulties. Restricted behavioral repertoires, communication limitations, stereotypic self-stimulation, resistance to change, and unusual responses to their environment pose problems and may limit inclusion options for some individuals with autism (Dziobek et al., 2006; Hess, 2006; Greaves et al., 2006). Some evidence also suggests that the success of inclusion depends heavily on general education classmates, because inclusion is a social process as much as an academic one (Delano & Snell, 2006; Westling & Fox, 2004). Continued research is essential if these individuals are to achieve maximum inclusion in the community.

Causation

> **Psychodynamic perspective**
> An approach to psychological disorders that views unconscious conflicts and anxieties as the cause of such disorders.

Focus 4
Cite the two broad theoretical views regarding the causes of autism spectrum disorder.

Historically, two broad theories about the causes of autism spectrum disorder have been most prominent: psychodynamic and biological theories. The **psychodynamic perspective** has implicated family interactions as causal factors. Theorists who subscribe to this view have speculated that the child withdraws from rejection and erects defenses against psychological pain. In so doing, he or she retreats to an inner world and essentially does not interact with the outside environment that involves people. Psychodynamic theories have largely fallen out of favor, because research results have failed to support this position. However, some literature continues to explore this theoretical area by examining topics such as fears and the newborn's anxieties and by searching for the meaning of the child's symptoms. Similar theories have been extended to Asperger syndrome (Fonseca & Bussab, 2006; Rhode & Klauber, 2004).

Biological causation in a variety of forms, particularly genetics, dominates the current research on autism spectrum disorders (Cuccaro et al., 2003; Reichenberg et al., 2006; Ronald et al., 2006). For instance, damage to the chromosome structure in a condition known as

fragile X syndrome emerged in the late 1960s as a potential cause of autism spectrum disorder. Researchers found that this condition appeared in a certain percentage of males with autism spectrum disorder (e.g., Lewis et al., 2006; McCarthy, Cuskelly, van Kraayenoord, & Cohen, 2006; Volkmar, Wiesner, & Westphal, 2006). Work on this genetic linkage continues, although it appears that fragile X is simply associated with autism spectrum disorders, or co-occurring, rather than being a major cause (Lewis et al., 2006).

Research has established genetic causation in autism spectrum disorders, but it has not provided a clear and complete explanation of how causation occurs (e.g., Cuccaro et al., 2003; Minshew & Meyer, 2006). One problem in developing a body of genetic information arises from the relative infrequency with which autism spectrum disorder appears in the population at large. Although some research on twins has suggested a genetic link, additional evidence is clearly needed (Andres; 2002; Ronald et al., 2006).

Abnormal development received attention recently as a cause of autism spectrum disorders—along with other investigations of neurological problems, such as brain cell differences, absence of specialization in the brain hemispheres, arrested neurological development, and neurological chemical imbalances (Cohen, 2006; Pierce & Courchesne, 2002; Santos, Coelho, & Maciel, 2006). Major advances in technology have made possible research that once could be conducted only through autopsy, if at all. For example, some people with autism spectrum disorders appear to have an abnormality in a portion of the brain. One abnormal area, known as the **vermis** and located in the cerebellum (see Figure 13.1), may be related to the cognitive malfunctions found in autism spectrum disorder (Davis, Bockbrader, Murphy, Hetrick, & O'Donnell, 2006; Haist, Adamo, Westerfield, Courchesne, & Townsend, 2005). Further research is needed to confirm this.

Neurological damage to the central nervous system may be caused by a number of problems during prenatal development and early infancy. Maternal infections, alcohol abuse, and other problems during pregnancy have great potential to damage the developing fetus and have been associated with autism spectrum disorders and other disabilities involving the central nervous system (Akshoomoff, Pierce, & Courchesne, 2002; Berk, 2005; Martin & Fabes, 2006). In particular, viral infections such as rubella have been implicated, although a great deal of research is still needed to explore this area. Problems during the birth process are known causes of neurological injuries in babies, such as unusual hemorrhaging, difficult deliveries, and anoxia (Cook & Cook, 2007; Drew & Hardman, 2007). Children with autism spectrum disorders seem to have more frequent histories of delivery problems than children

➤ **Fragile X syndrome**

A condition involving damage to the chromosome structure, which appears as a breaking or splitting at the end of the X chromosome. This condition is found in some males with autism spectrum disorders.

Standard 1: Foundations

Standard 2: Development and Characteristics of Learners

➤ **Vermis**

A portion of the cerebellum that appears to be underdeveloped in children with autism spectrum disorders.

FIGURE 13.1

Cerebellum and Vermis

Vermis

Cerebellum

without disabilities. Despite the multitude of potential neurological causes, however, no single type of trauma has been consistently identified (Niehus & Lord, 2006).

Clearly, various causes of autism spectrum disorders remain unsolved puzzles in the face of ongoing research and widespread interest in the condition. Accumulated evidence has strongly implicated biological factors. Some biological malfunctions may be related to environmental influences, although evidence is only suggestive at this point (Bowers, 2002; Newsom & Hovanitz, 2006; Wing & Potter, 2002). Many current researchers have viewed autism spectrum disorders as a behavioral syndrome with multiple biological causes (Rutter, 2005b, 2006; Wilkerson, Volpe, Dean, & Titus, 2002). To date, researchers have not identified any single specific factor that causes autism spectrum disorders. Rather, autism spectrum disorder appears to be an assortment of symptoms instead of a specific disease, which is why it is sometimes called a syndrome. As with many areas of disability, an understanding of causation is important as we attempt to improve treatment. Research continues to unravel the sources of this perplexing disability, and improved research methodology is vital for further progress in the investigation of autism spectrum disorders (e.g., Rogers & Ozonoff, 2005; Rutter, 2005a).

Multidisciplinary Collaboration: Diagnosis and Intervention

FOCUS 5
Identify four major approaches to the treatment of autism spectrum disorder.

Council for Exceptional Children

Standard 4: Instructional Strategies

Standard 5: Learning Environments and Social Interactions

Throughout this book we have discussed collaboration between multiple disciplines as we have examined other disabilities. In each case, the discussion has involved various professionals, depending on the most prominent characteristics of the disability. This is also the case with autism spectrum disorders, and because of the wide variation of characteristics presented in this spectrum of disorders, the diversity of the collaboration team is quite broad (Chakrabarti, Haubus, Dugmore, Orgill, & Devine, 2005). This collaborative team most often includes professionals from medicine, psychology, and education, and it may also involve social workers or counselors, depending on the family circumstances (Chakrabarti & Frombonne, 2005; Margetts, LeCouteur, & Croom, 2006; Prelock & Vargas, 2004).

As we saw in the definition, the diagnosis of autism spectrum disorder most often emerges quite early, usually around 3 years of age. But parents often observe and worry about signals they see prior to that age, and a diagnosis may emerge later as well (Landa & Garrett-Mayer, 2006; Stone, 2006). Because of this relatively young age, parents often have a relationship with a physician (pediatrician), which puts the medical professional on the multidisciplinary team for collaboration very early. As the child's evaluation is begun, assessment is typically undertaken in multiple skill areas, including communication and language, intelligence, and social interaction (Anckarsater, 2006; Gillberg, 2006; Ozonoff et al., 2005). These evaluations quickly enlist additional disciplines, and the multidisciplinary team often includes school psychologists, behavior modification specialists, and specialists in psychiatry, language, and child development. Beyond the assessment process, this collaboration most often moves forward to include various elements of intervention, which are likely to include developmental specialists and education professionals. From the parents' perspective, the important outcome of this collaboration is to enable their child to begin to receive service (Baron-Cohen & Klin, 2006; Beaumont & Newcombe, 2006; McConachie & Robinson, 2006). The child with an autism spectrum disorder will often be the focus of communication and collaborative interventions from a very early age, and the nature of interventions and supports will evolve as he or she grows older, reaches adolescence, and transitions into adulthood (Henault, 2006; Howlin, 2004; Wolfe & Mash, 2006). The context and the nature of the collaboration evolve over time as circumstances change, but the need for multidisciplinary collaboration on assessments and intervention continues (e.g., Dowson, 2006).

Attempts to identify causes of autism spectrum disorders have gone hand in hand with efforts to discover effective treatments. Different approaches have been used as interventions. Some have been based on theories of causation, others have focused on specific observable behaviors, and empirical evidence supporting effectiveness is important in all cases (e.g., Delano & Snell, 2006; Ellis, Ala'i-Rosales, Glenn, Rosales-Ruiz, & Greenspoon, 2006; Kay, Harchik, & Luiselli, 2006). Significant progress has been made in successful interventions for people with autism spectrum disorders, although investigators continually emphasize the importance of further systematic research on the effectiveness of various treatment strategies.

Educational Interventions

The characteristics of autism spectrum disorders and the severity of specific problem areas vary significantly from individual to individual. Consequently, a wide variety of instructional options are required for the effective education of these children, and the multidisciplinary collaboration that evolves differs widely among the individuals served (Dowson, 2006; Henault, 2006; Wolfe & Mash, 2006). These alternatives range from specialized individual programs to integrated placement with support services. The unusual maladaptive behaviors mentioned earlier have led to the emergence of stereotypes about youngsters with autism spectrum disorders and to undue segregation. However, the current literature has emphasized integration for educational purposes to the greatest degree possible, with educational placement and instructional programming dependent on the student's age and functioning level (Arick, Krug, Fullerton, Loos, & Falco, 2005; Galinat, Barcalow, & Krivda, 2005; Spector & Volkmar, 2006). In most cases, the ultimate goal is to prepare individuals with autism spectrum disorders to live in their home community and in the least restrictive setting that is appropriate and possible. The research literature also supports early interventions as an important element in promoting growth for these children (Beeghly, 2006; Green, Brennan, & Fein, 2002; Pine, Luby, Abbacchi, & Constantino, 2006). Under IDEA, students with autism are entitled to a free appropriate education in the least restrictive environment possible.

Children with autism spectrum disorders should have an individualized education program (IEP), including statements of short- and long-term goals (Arick et al., 2005; Sherer & Schreibman, 2005). For most students with autism spectrum disorders, it is vital that the IEP have a central component of functional communication and social skills and that it focus on individual strengths and skills required for maximum independence. Functional skills and knowledge will vary among individuals. For some children, functional instruction will mean heavy use of language training; augmentative communication; and social, self-help, and self-protection skills (Goldstein, 2002; Koegel & Koegel, 2006; Legoff & Sherman, 2006). For others, functional instruction will focus on what may be traditional academic subjects, as well as on some subjects not always included in general education curricula, such as sexual awareness, sexual behavior, and sex education; other topics may be those of special concern to the children's parents (Dale, Jahoda, & Knott, 2006; Harrington, Patrick, & Edwards, 2006; U.S. Department of Education, 2006). Educational interventions for children with autism spectrum disorders and other disabilities are also beginning to include greater use of technology enhancements in the teaching process (Massaro & Bosseler, 2006; Parsons & Mitchell, 2002; Roblyer, 2006). Additional research on the effectiveness of such applications, and of using the Internet as a research and treatment tool, present intriguing possibilities as technology applications continue to mature (e.g., Brownlow & O'Dell, 2006; Gringras, Santosh, & Baird, 2006; Jayachandra, 2005).

Creative, innovative, and positive teachers are particularly important in providing effective education for students with autism spectrum disorders (e.g., Child, 2004; Moyes, 2003). As noted earlier, these children present some unique challenges for instruction. Some seemingly insignificant actions by teachers can create great difficulties for students who have autism spectrum disorders—difficulties that can easily be avoided if teachers are informed and receive training (Grey, Honan, McClean, & Daly, 2005; Wymbs et al., 2005). For example, many high-functioning individuals with autism spectrum disorders who have some language skills may interpret speech literally, so it is important to avoid using slang, idioms, and sarcasm. An individual with autism spectrum disorder might take such phrases literally and learn something very different from what was intended.

Parental participation in preparing children with autism spectrum disorders for school and other aspects of life can be of great assistance (Kay & Vyse, 2005; Schreibman & Koegel, 2005;

The IEP of a child with autism should focus on developing functional communication skills and social skills.

Council for Exceptional Children

Standard 4: Instructional Strategies

Standard 7: Instructional Planning

U.S. Department of Education, 2006). Such preparation can include objectives such as instilling a positive attitude in the child, helping him or her with scheduling, and teaching him or her how to find the way around in school. Also helpful is identifying a "safe" place and a "safe" person to seek out should the child become confused or encounter a particularly upsetting event. The accompanying Case Study illustrates parental involvement as we revisit Billy, the boy we met in the chapter-opening Snapshot.

Council for Exceptional Children

Standard 2: Development and Characteristics of Learners

Standard 5: Learning Environments and Social Interactions

Psychological and Medical Interventions

As we have noted, the multidisciplinary collaboration for individuals with autism spectrum disorders will include psychological and medical professionals, often from the very early stages of the child's life (Chakrabarti & Frombonne, 2005; Margetts et al., 2006; Prelock & Vargas, 2004). These supports will most often continue throughout the lifespan in a variety of forms, depending on the needs of the individual and the specific contextual circumstances (Dowson, 2006; Henault, 2006; Spector & Volkmar, 2006).

Interventions based on the psychodynamic theory of causation historically focused on repairing emotional damage and resolving inner conflict. This approach is aimed at remedying the presumably faulty relationship between the child and his or her parents, which, it is assumed, often involved parental rejection or absence and resulted in withdrawal by the child (e.g., Case, 2005; Holmes, 2005; Minazio, 2002). This treatment model has been criticized because there is little solid empirical evidence to support its effectiveness. The internal psychological nature of problems, as seen by this approach, makes evaluating it very difficult.

Various medical treatments have also been used for children with autism spectrum disorders. Some early medical therapies (for example, electroconvulsive shock and psychosurgery) have been discredited for use with these children, because these treatments appeared to have questionable re-

CASE STUDY

BILLY

What happens to a boy like Billy, whom we discussed in the chapter-opening snapshot? His parents are exhausted from years of caring for their son, who seems oblivious to their efforts. Placing him in the state hospital would be an easy answer, but Billy's parents sense that this would be disastrous for his development and later adjustment. If admitted to the state hospital, he could spend the rest of his life there.

This family was lucky. When Billy was ready to start school, the school district and the local mental health center arranged to place him in a special classroom within a regular public school. The classroom was well staffed, so he had individual instruction and treatment from a teacher who was trained to manage children with behavior disorders. Billy's disruptive self-stimulation and tantrums were decreased through the use of time-out procedures (seclusion for short periods of time). Intense language training was implemented, and slowly he has learned more appropriate language. His echolalia has begun to disappear. When his appropriate behavior becomes stabilized in the classroom, he will begin an academic program and learn reading and writing.

There have also been changes for Billy's family. The mental health center offered a series of child management classes that taught the family, including Billy's brother, how to handle his disruptive behavior. The classes also gave Billy's family a chance to see that other families had similar problems with their children who had disturbances. When the course was officially finished, the parents decided to continue meeting and planning for their children. The group members supported one another in times of need and worked actively to keep their children out of large institutions.

Although Billy is now making progress both behaviorally and academically, he will probably always have autism and be in need of special help. But great things are beginning to happen. The other day, just before the bus came to get Billy, he hugged his mother and kissed her good-bye for the first time.

APPLICATION

1. What impact do you think Billy's parents had on his ultimate prognosis as a child with autism?

2. How might the outcome have been different if they had placed him in the state hospital?

3. Is it realistic for his mother to expect him to "grow out of" his autistic behaviors?

SOURCE: Adapted from *Understanding Child Behavior Disorders* (2nd ed., p. 312) by D. M. Gelfand, W. R. Jenson, and C. J. Drew, 1988, New York: Holt, Rinehart and Winston.

sults and harmful side effects. Likewise, certain medications used in the past (such as D-lysergic acid, more commonly known as LSD) were of doubtful therapeutic value and were very controversial. Other medications used for people with autism spectrum disorders have often included antipsychotic drugs, anticonvulsants, and serotonin and dopamine (Kay & Vyse, 2005; Strauss, Unis, Cowan, Dawson, & Dager, 2002). Specific symptoms tend to be addressed with specific medication; obsessive-compulsive behaviors, for example, have been treated with clomipramine (e.g., King, Fay, & Wheildon, 2002; Lam, Aman, & Arnold, 2006; Rapp & Vollmer, 2005). Other antipsychotic drugs seem to help reduce some of the unusual speech patterns and self-injurious behaviors, particularly with older patients. Decreases in self-injury and social withdrawal have also been evident in some research on responses to other drugs (e.g., King & Bostic, 2006; Rattcliff-Schaub, Carey, & Reeves, 2005; Salgado-Pineda, Delaveau, Blin, & Nieoullon, 2005). However, other research on drug therapy has shown mixed results or no improvement in the condition (Handen & Hofkosh, 2005; Kemner et al., 2002; McDougle, Posey, & Stigler, 2006).

Generally, medication has shown some promise in the treatment of autism spectrum disorders. There appears to be potential for improvement, but such treatment should be used thoughtfully in conjunction with a multicomponent, comprehensive treatment plan (Johnson, 2002; Prelock & Vargas, 2004; Tsai, 2005). The tips found in this chapter's Inclusion and Collaboration Through the Lifespan illustrate how varied and complicated the overall environment is in terms of the various influences on an individual with autism spectrum disorders. Most authorities agree that autism spectrum disorders represent such a heterogeneous set of symptoms that no single treatment will effectively treat all children with the condition (e.g., Farmer, Donders, & Warschausky, 2006; Sherer & Schreibman, 2005; Wymbs et al., 2005).

Behavioral Interventions

Behavior modification represents an intervention strategy that has itself become multidisciplinary over the last 30 years. This model of intervention has been used in a wide array of circumstances within education, psychology, medicine, and family therapy. Interventions using behavioral treatment for children with autism spectrum disorders are undertaken without concern for the underlying cause(s) of the disability. This approach focuses on enhancing appropriate behaviors and reducing inappropriate or maladaptive behaviors (Blacher & McIntyre, 2006; Kimball, 2002; Rogers & Ozonoff, 2006). Behavior management for individuals with an autism spectrum disorder requires a statement of precise operational definition, careful observation, and the recording of data on behaviors viewed as appropriate and as inappropriate. Accurate and reliable data collection is a cornerstone of behavioral intervention, a process greatly enhanced by new technology (see the Assistive Technology, "Collecting Data: The Videx TimeWand" on page 364).

Behavioral interventions may focus on conduct such as self-stimulation, tantrum episodes, or self-inflicted injury. Behavioral therapy has substantially reduced or eliminated these problem behaviors in many cases (Britton, Carr, Landaburu, & Romick, 2002; Cummings & Carr, 2005; Westling & Fox, 2004). Behavioral treatment has also been effective in remediating deficiencies in fundamental social skills and language development, as well as in facilitating community integration for children with autism spectrum disorders (Bauminger, 2002; LeBlanc, Carr, Crossett, Bennett, & Detweiler, 2005; Lovaas, 2003). Furthermore, parental involvement in behavioral treatment has shown promising results. Research has demonstrated that certain students with autism spectrum disorders can be effectively taught to employ self-directed behavior management, which further enhances efficiency (Blacher & McIntyre, 2006; Ozonoff et al., 2002; Rogers & Ozonoff, 2006). However, finding reinforcements to use in behavioral treatments is sometimes difficult, as suggested in this chapter's Debate Forum on page 364.

It is important to emphasize that behavioral therapy does not claim to cure autism spectrum disorders. The procedures involved are very specific in focusing on limited behavioral areas that need attention. This approach seems effective for many children with autism spectrum disorders, prompting decreases in problem behaviors and potential improvement of survival skills (e.g., Cohen, Amerine-Dickens, & Smith, 2006; LeBlanc et al., 2005; Lovaas, 2003). Such gains constitute a significant step toward normalization for both the children and their families.

In the early 1990s, autism literature gave some attention to a treatment being used in Australia that specifically focused on communication problems for people with autism spectrum disorders. Known as facilitative communication, this procedure emphasizes the use of typing

Council for Exceptional Children

Standard 2: Development and Characteristics of Learners

Standard 5: Learning Environments and Social Interactions

INCLUSION AND COLLABORATION THROUGH THE LIFESPAN

People with Autism Spectrum Disorders

EARLY CHILDHOOD YEARS

Tips for the Family

- Seek out and read information regarding autism spectrum disorders, and become knowledgeable about the disabilities in all areas possible.

- Be an active partner in the treatment of your child. Collaborate proactively in the multidisciplinary team's planning for your child, facilitating communication and coordinating interventions.

- Learn about the simple applications of behavior modification in a home environment, perhaps by enrolling in a parent training class.

- When working with the child with an autism spectrum disorder, concentrate on one behavior at a time as the target for change; emphasize increasing appropriate behavior rather than focusing solely on inappropriate behavior.

- Involve all family members in learning about your child's disability.

- Protect your own health by obtaining respite care when you need a rest or a break. You may need to devise a family schedule that allows adequate time for ongoing sleep and respite. Plan ahead for respite; otherwise, when you need it most, you will be too exhausted to find it.

- Help prepare your child for school by instilling a positive attitude about it, helping him or her with the idea of a school schedule and indicating how to find a "safe" place and a "safe" person at school.

Tips for the Preschool Teacher

- Depending on the child's level of functioning, you may have to use physical cues or clear visual modeling to persuade him or her to do something; children with autism may not respond to social cues.

- Pair physical cues with verbal cues to begin teaching verbal compliance.

- Limit instruction to one thing at a time; focus on what is concrete rather than abstract.

- Avoid verbal overload by using short, directive sentences.

Tips for Preschool Personnel

- Encourage the development of programs where older children model good behavior and interact intensely with children with autism.

- Initiate and maintain communication with the child's parents or guardians to enhance the information flow and to promote consistent collaboration across environments in rules and reward structures.

- Promote ongoing collaborative relationships between the preschool and medical personnel who can provide advice and assistance for children with autism.

- Promote the initiation of parent-school relationships to assist parents and preschool personnel in working together.

- Promote the appropriate collaborative involvement of non-teaching staff through workshops that provide information and promote awareness. Consistent interaction and coordination of expectations are extremely important.

Tips for Neighbors and Friends

- Be supportive of the parents and siblings of a child with autism spectrum disorders. They may be under a great deal of stress and need moral support.

- Be positive with the parents. They may receive information that places blame on them, which should not be magnified by their friends.

- Offer parents a respite to the degree that you're comfortable; for example, you might give them a short but important time away to go to the store.

ELEMENTARY YEARS

Tips for the Family

- Be active in community efforts for children with autism spectrum disorders; join local or national parent groups to provide support to others and gain support from them.

- Consistently follow through with the basic principles of your child's treatment program at home. This may mean taking more workshops or training on various topics in order to effectively collaborate as part of the intervention team.

- Siblings of children with autism spectrum disorders may find it difficult to understand the level of attention afforded to the sibling with autism. Siblings and parents need support and information.

- Continue family involvement; be sensitive to the feelings of siblings who may be feeling left out or embarrassed by the child with an autism spectrum disorder.

- It may be necessary to take safety precautions in the home (e.g., installing locks on all doors).

Tips for the General Education Classroom Teacher

- Help with collaborative organizational strategies, assisting the student with autism spectrum disorders in matters that are difficult for him or her (e.g., remembering how to use an eraser).

- Avoid abstract ideas as much as possible unless they are necessary in instruction. Be as concrete as possible.

- Communicate with specific directions or questions, not vague or open-ended statements.

- If the child becomes upset, he or she may need to change activities or go to a place in the room that is "safe" for a period of time.

- Use rules and schedules that are written with accompanying pictures so that students will clearly understand what is expected of them. Communicate and collaborate with parents and other school personnel regarding a consistent set of rules and schedules.

- Begin preparing the child with an autism spectrum disorder for a more variable environment by programming and teaching adaptation to changes in routine. Involve the child in planning for the changes, mapping out what they might be.

Tips for School Personnel

- Promote an all-school environment where children model appropriate behavior and receive reinforcement for it. Proactively collaborate with all members of the team, including parents.

- Develop peer assistance programs, where older students can help tutor and model appropriate behavior for children with autism spectrum disorders.
- Encourage the development of a strong, ongoing collaborative school-parent relationship and of support groups working together to meet the child's needs. Consistent expectations are important.
- Do not depend on the child with an autism spectrum disorder to take messages home to parents for any reason except trying out this skill for him or her to learn. Communication is a major problem, and a note may be lost. Find other means of parent communication and collaboration.

Tips for Neighbors and Friends

- Insofar as possible, ignore trivial disruptions or misbehaviors; focus on positive behaviors.
- Don't take misbehaviors personally; the child is not trying to make your life difficult or to manipulate you.
- Avoid using nicknames such as "buddy" or "pal."
- Avoid sarcasm and idiomatic expressions, such as "beating around the bush." These children may not understand and may interpret what you say literally.

SECONDARY AND TRANSITION YEARS

Tips for the Family

- Be alert to developmental and behavioral changes as the child grows older, watching for any changing effects of a medication.
- Continue as a proactive collaboration partner in your child's educational and treatment program, planning for the transition to adulthood.
- Begin acquainting yourself with the adult services that will be available when your child leaves school. If he or she functions at a high level, consider or plan for adult living out of the family home.

Tips for the General Education Classroom Teacher

- Gradually increase the level of abstraction in teaching, remaining aware of the individual limitations the child with an autism spectrum disorder has.
- Continue preparing the student for an increasingly variable environment through specific instruction and example.
- Focus increasingly on matters of vital importance to the student as he or she matures (e.g., social awareness and interpersonal issues between the sexes).
- Teach the student with an eye toward postschool community participation, including matters such as navigating the community physically, activities, and employment. Teach the student about interacting with police in the community, since they require responses different from those appropriate for other strangers.*

Tips for School Personnel

- To the degree possible for children with autism spectrum disorders, promote involvement in social activities and clubs that enhance interpersonal interaction.
- Encourage the development of functional academic programs for students with autism spectrum disorders that are combined with transition planning and programs.

- Promote a continuing collaborative relationship with parents, other school staff, and agency personnel who might be involved in the student's overall treatment program (e.g., health care providers, social service agencies, etc.
- Work with other agencies (e.g., law enforcement) that may encounter the child in the community. Provide workshops, if possible, to inform officers regarding behavioral characteristics of people with autism.

Tips for Neighbors and Friends

- Encourage a positive understanding of people with autism spectrum disorders among other neighbors and friends who may be in contact with the child; help them to provide environmentally appropriate interaction.
- Promote the positive understanding of people with autism spectrum disorders by community agencies that may encounter these individuals at this stage of life (e.g., law enforcement officials, fire department personnel).
- Support the parents as they consider the issues of adulthood for their child. Topics such as guardianship and community living may be difficult for parents to discuss.

ADULT YEARS

Tips for the Family

- Continue to be alert for behavioral or developmental changes that may occur as the individual matures. Continued biological maturation may require medication adjustments as well as adjustments in behavioral intervention programming.
- Continue to seek out adult services that are available to individuals with disabilities.
- Seek legal advice regarding plans for the future when you are no longer able to care for the family member with an autism spectrum disorder. Plan for financial arrangements and other needs that are appropriate, such as naming an advocate. Backup plans should be made; do not always count on the youngster's siblings. Consider guardianship by other persons or agencies.

Tips for Therapists or Other Professionals

- Remain cognizant of the maturity level of the individual with whom you are working. Despite the presence of an autism spectrum disorder, some individuals have mature interests and inclinations. Do not treat the person as a child.
- Proactively promote collaboration between appropriate adult service agencies to provide the most comprehensive services.

Tips for Neighbors and Friends

- Encourage a positive understanding of people with autism spectrum disorders by other neighbors, friends, and community agencies (e.g., law enforcement, fire department).
- Support the family members as they consider the issues of adulthood for the individual. Topics such as guardianship and community living may be difficult for parents and siblings to discuss.

*The authors appreciate Cathy Pratt's review of and contribution to this material (1994).

SOURCE: A portion of this material is adapted from *High-Functioning Individuals with Autism: Advice and Information for Parents and Others Who Care*, by S. J. Moreno and A. M. Donellan, 1991, Crown Point, IN: Maap Services.

Most of us are familiar with the bar-code scanners used at checkout stands in many stores. The clerk passes the code symbol over a scanner, the price is instantly entered into the cash register, and a record of the sale is made for inventory control. This same technology is now being applied to coding and recording data on behavioral observations.

Known as the Videx TimeWand, this device simplifies reliable data collection for behavioral interventions with a variety of conditions, such as autism. Appropriate and inappropriate behaviors are defined very specifically, and then each is given a code, which is translated into a bar-code symbol much like those we see at the market. These bar codes are then placed on an observation sheet to be used by the observer. The observer also carries a small, portable bar-code reader with a wand that is passed over the relevant code symbol when that particular behavior is observed. Data on behavioral occurrences are recorded *and* clock-time stamped to indicate when the behavior occurred. These data are stored electronically (the unit will hold up to 16,000 characters of information) and transferred to a portable computer at the end of an observation session, for analysis and graphing.

Use of the TimeWand reduces the strain on therapists, who previously had to write down behavioral codes physically while attempting to continue observation. Use of this technology thereby improves the accuracy of data collection and also expedites data processing and translation into treatment action. Information regarding this automated data collection method is available from Walter Nelson and Gordon Defalco at the Fircrest School in Seattle, Washington, or from Richard Saunders at the Parson Research Center, University of Kansas.

as a means of communicating. A therapist-facilitator provides physical support by touching and putting light pressure on the student's arm or shoulder and provides interpersonal support via positive attitudes and interactions. Facilitative communication as a treatment for autism spectrum disorders has been sufficiently controversial to prompt a number of special programs on national television news shows, featuring both proponents and critics. Although

DEBATE FORUM

SELF-STIMULATION AS A REINFORCER?

Reinforcers as behavioral treatments are sometimes difficult to find for some children who have autism. Teachers must often take what the client gives them to work with and remain flexible in designing an intervention program.

Many individuals with autism do not respond to the same types of rewards that others do, and social rewards may not provide reinforcement or have any effect at all on these youngsters, at least in the initial stages of a treatment program. Research has also shown that even though tangible reinforcers may produce desired results, they often seem to lose their power for individuals with autism. Given these circumstances, some researchers have suggested that self-stimulation, which appears to be a powerful and durable reinforcer, should be used to assist in teaching appropriate behavior. Self-stimulation is very different for each child and may involve manipulation of items such as coins, keys, and twigs.

POINT

Because reinforcers are often difficult to identify for children with autism, it is important to use whatever is available and practical in teaching these youngsters. Self-stimulation has been recognized as providing strong reinforcement for those who engage in it. Although typically viewed as an inappropriate behavior, self-stimulation may be very useful in teaching the beginning phases of more adaptive behavior and other skill acquisition. For some children with autism, it may be the most efficient reinforcer available, so why not use it, at least initially?

COUNTERPOINT

Using inappropriate behavior as a reinforcer carries with it certain serious problems and in fact may be unethical. The use of self-stimulation as a reinforcer may cause an increase in this behavior, making it an even more pronounced part of the child's inappropriate demeanor. Should this occur, it may make self-stimulation more difficult to eliminate later.

advocates of this treatment are emphatic in their support, other researchers are unable to obtain results that support its effectiveness, which of course raises serious questions about its soundness (Emerson, Grayson, & Griffiths, 2001). Because of the facilitator's participation through touching the arm of the person, some question whether the person with autism or the facilitator is communicating.

Instruction in a general education elementary school classroom may be an important part of normalization for this young boy with autism.

Although some interest persists, little empirical evidence supports the effectiveness of facilitated communication with individuals who have autism spectrum disorders (Mostert, 2001).

Impact on the Family

The arrival or diagnosis of a child with an autism spectrum disorder presents a significant challenge to parents and other family members (Gray, 2002; Volkmar, Wiesner, & Westphal, 2006). Parents usually have to turn to multiple sources for assistance and information, and relations between professionals and parents are not simple or easy (McConachie & Robinson, 2006; Sallows & Graupner, 2005). Groups such as the Autism Society of America can offer a great deal of help and support from a perspective not available elsewhere. Parents may find that they have to become aggressive and vocal in their search for services from various agencies (Goin-Kochel, Mackintosh, & Myers, 2006; McConachie & Robinson, 2006). They must also be conscious of their own health and vitality, because their ability to cope will be significantly affected if they neglect their personal well-being. They are likely to need respite time and care from a number of sources—from the family as a whole and from outside agencies. Perhaps most difficult is realizing that there are no clear-cut answers to many of the questions they have. Intervention to help different families and family members must be tailored to the specific circumstances and individuals involved.

Council for Exceptional Children

Standard 5: Learning Environments and Social Interactions

The impact of a child with an autism spectrum disorder on his or her family members is enormous (Bowler, 2006; Weiss, 2002; Yazbak, 2002). Living with such a child is exhausting and presents many challenges, including strained relationships, vastly and permanently increased financial burdens, social isolation, grief, and considerable physical and emotional fatigue (Boyd, 2002; Lockshin, Gillis, & Romanczyk, 2005). The youngster with autism may sleep only a few hours each night and may spend many waking hours engaged in self-abusive or disruptive behavior. It is easy to see how parents may feel as though they are in a marathon, 24 hours a day, 7 days per week, with no respite. Not only is the family routine interrupted, but the constant demands are physically and emotionally draining, resulting in a number of problems for family members (such as high stress levels and depression) and in some affective disorders among mothers (Boyd, 2002; Lockshin et al., 2005; Weiss, 2002). And, as we have noted, the situation may be especially confusing for family members if the child with an autism spectrum disorder also has savant-like skills in some areas.

Siblings of children with autism spectrum disorders may experience a number of problems, particularly during the early years. They may have difficulty understanding their parents' distress regarding their brother or sister and the level of attention afforded this child, and they may manifest stress or some depression (Mascha & Boucher, 2006; Ozonoff et al., 2002; Ross & Cuskelly, 2006). Siblings may also have difficulty accepting the emotional detachment of the youngster, who may seem not to care for them

Temple Grandin, an assistant professor of animal science at Colorado State University, is a high-functioning person with autism. In addition to writing several hundred papers on autism, she has revolutionized the treatment of animals and barn design for animals that are being raised for consumption.

at all. Like the siblings of children with other disabilities, brothers and sisters of a child with autism spectrum disorders may be embarrassed and reluctant to bring friends home. However, if they can become informed and move beyond the social embarrassment, siblings can be a significant resource in assisting parents. Some research suggests fairly positive adjustment among siblings of children with autism spectrum disorders (Kaminsky & Dewey, 2002; Marks, Matson, & Barraza, 2005).

FOCUS REVIEW

FOCUS 1 Identify four areas of functional challenge often found in children with autism spectrum disorder.

- Language
- Interpersonal skills
- Emotional or affective behaviors
- Intellectual functioning

FOCUS 2 What are the general prevalence estimates for autism and autism spectrum disorder?

- Autism prevalence ranges from approximately 5 cases per 10,000 to 39 cases per 10,000.
- Autism spectrum disorder has a prevalence estimate of over 116 per 10,000.

FOCUS 3 Identify six characteristics of children with autism spectrum disorder.

- As infants, they are often unresponsive to physical contact or affection from their parents, and later they have extreme difficulty relating to other people.
- Most have impaired or delayed language skills, and about half do not develop speech at all.
- Those who have speech often engage in echolalia and other inappropriate behavior.

- They frequently engage in self-stimulatory behavior.
- Changes in their routine are met with intense resistance.
- Most have a reduced level of intellectual functioning.

FOCUS 4 Cite the two broad theoretical views regarding the causes of autism spectrum disorder.

- The psychoanalytic view places a great deal of emphasis on the interaction between the family and the child.
- The biological view attributes autism to neurological damage and/or to genetics.

FOCUS 5 Identify four major approaches to the treatment of autism spectrum disorder.

- Psychoanalytic-based therapy focuses on repairing the emotional damage presumed to have resulted from faulty family relationships.
- Medically based treatment often involves the use of medication.
- Behavioral interventions focus on enhancing specific appropriate behaviors or on reducing inappropriate behaviors.
- Educational interventions employ the full range of educational placements.

BUILDING YOUR PORTFOLIO

Council for Exceptional Children

If you are thinking about a career in special education, you should know that many states use national standards developed by the Council for Exceptional Children (CEC) to assess a teacher candidate's knowledge and skills for working with students with disabilities. See a complete listing of the ten CEC Content Standards on the inside front cover of this text.

CEC Content Standards Addressed in This Chapter

1 Foundations
2 Development and Characteristics of Learners
3 Individual Learning Differences
4 Instructional Strategies
5 Learning Environments and Social Interactions
6 Communication
7 Instructional Planning

Assess Your Knowledge of the CEC Standards Addressed in This Chapter

Some states require that teacher candidates develop a portfolio of products that demonstrate mastery of the CEC content standards. To assist in the development of products for this portfolio, you may wish to complete the following activities.

- Complete a written test of the chapter's content.

  If your instructor requires a written test of your content knowledge for this chapter, keep a copy for your portfolio. A practice test on the information covered in this chapter is available through the companion website (college.hmco.com/pic/hardman9e) and the Student Study Guide.

- Respond to the Application Questions for the Case Study "Billy."

  Review the Case Study and respond in writing to the application questions. Keep a copy of the Case Study and of your written response for your portfolio.

- Participate in a community service learning activity.

Community service is a valuable way to enhance your learning experience. Visit our companion website for suggested community service learning activities that correspond to the information presented in this chapter. Develop a reflective journal of the service learning experience for your portfolio.

WEB RESOURCES

Future Horizons, Inc.

http://www.futurehorizons-autism.com

This website features products, publications, and resources to people interacting with children and adolescents who have autism. In many cases, the resources will be of interest to family members who find themselves in ongoing and close relationships with such youngsters. The resources provided include conference information, magazines, and medical resources.

Autism Society of America

http://www.autism-society.org

This website provides opportunities for people who want to expand their network of resources related to autism. It provides a vehicle for joining ASA, as well as information about legislation and legal cases related to autism. ASA uses this website to encourage participation by people who have a relationship with someone who has autism or have a professional interest in autism.

The Autism Web

http://www.autismweb.com

This website is aimed at parents of children with autism and related pervasive developmental disorders. Clearly intended to enhance networking and provide support, this site includes community-based resources, information on conferences, and message boards to promote communication.

Autism Resources

http://www.autism-resources.com

This website provides information and links related to autism and Asperger syndrome. A simple and straightforward resource site offering a broad array of information.

FURTHER READINGS

Jackson, L. (2002). *Freaks, Geeks and Asperger Syndrome: A User Guide to Adolescence.* Philadelphia: Jessica Kingsley Publishers.

Luke Jackson has a number of challenges in his life, including having Asperger syndrome, one brother with ADHD, and another with autism. This is a delightful story that provides personal views of the world through the lens of a 13-year-old with high-functioning autism. If you think the teen years are a challenge, try seeing them through Luke's eyes.

Karasik, P., & Karasik, J. (2003). *The Ride Together: A Brother and Sister's Memoir of Autism in the Family.* New York: Atria Books.

This volume presents siblings' perspective on growing up with a brother who has autism. Paul and Judy (a cartoonist and book editor, respectively) provide a rarely found insight into their lives with brother David. This book also illustrates the changes in treatment approaches from the 1950s to the early 21st century.

Prince-Hughes, D. (Ed.). (2002). *Aquamarine Blue 5: Personal Stories of College Students with Autism.* Athens, GA: Swallow Press.

This volume includes the personal experiences of 12 people who encountered the challenges of autism or autism spectrum disorders for years without an explanation of what their diagnosis was. The title comes from one of these contributors who perceives numbers in color; her favorite is "5," which she sees as aquamarine. A nice resource for seeing the personal side of autism.

Stone, W. L. (2006). *Does My Child Have Autism? A Parent's Guide to Early Detection and Intervention in Autism Spectrum Disorders.* New York: Jossey-Bass.

This volume provides information for parents regarding what to look for if they are concerned that their child may have autism. It describes behavioral signals that may appear at very early ages, along with checklists for parents. The author also makes early intervention suggestions: what to do and how to obtain help from a variety of professionals.

COMPANION WEBSITE

Visit the companion website at college.hmco.com/pic/hardman9e for additional resources that support this text:

- HM Video Cases that present actual classroom scenarios that you may face every day as a teacher

- Practice ACE Exams that will help you prepare for quizzes, tests, and certification exams

- Flashcards of key terms

- Weblinks

14

Traumatic and Acquired Brain Injury

TO BEGIN WITH . . .

BRAIN INJURIES AND MASS CASUALTY EVENTS

■ An estimated 1.4 million Americans sustain a traumatic brain injury (TBI) each year, most often due to falls, motor vehicle–traffic crashes and being struck by persons or against objects.

■ The severity of a TBI can range from "mild," i.e., a brief change in mental status or consciousness, to "severe," i.e., an extended period of unconsciousness or amnesia after the injury.

■ In disaster events, such as the World Trade Center attack or the Oklahoma City bombing, TBIs can be caused by flying debris, falls, being trampled, or blast waves from an explosion.

■ In the chaos following mass casualty events, diagnosis of a TBI may be missed.

(Centers for Disease Control and Prevention, 2006)

NO BRUISES OR FRACTURES, NO BANDAGES AROUND MY HEAD. . .

I didn't even recognize my own face in the mirror. Nothing felt right. Daze. Paralyzed by fear, my first instinct was to run but I had nowhere to hide. Pain exploded like fireworks behind my eyeballs and there was a sizzling in my skull like a chain saw. I tried to speak but I had a knot in my throat and my tongue felt thick and woolly. I was terrified I was going to choke. Voices echoed, ricocheting across the room. I wished they sounded familiar.

I felt like an infant. Of course, I didn't fully comprehend how this brain injury had changed me; I only sensed that my life would never be the same. I remember crying, feeling alone and being defenseless, but only for a day. I recall an anonymous nurse who held my hand in comfort while I begged so frantically for my memories. This part of me was dead, yet I was fighting to resuscitate it.

I remember feeling totally anonymous. I didn't fully comprehend what had happened to me. I remember crying, feeling isolated. I was no longer the child my mother gave birth to. I did not feel like HER. I was HER reflection but I felt too ambiguous to be a real flesh and blood person. However, on the outside, I still looked like their daughter. I still looked like a normal average teenager. There were no bruises or fractures, no bandages around my head and no magic wand to reveal my imperfections.

When they dressed me up in HER clothes and showed me HER photograph, I thought she looked just like me too. That's when I began to feel threatened. Her shadow was beginning to haunt me and my family was trying to reincarnate her through me. I felt belittled by this overwhelming, overbearing ghost and everything that held a candle to her. It was as if I'd stepped through a mirror and here I was: the evil twin.

I'd been cheated. Cheated of my childhood. It was HER. It was all HER fault. SHE was the one. I blamed HER for my lack of memories. I HATED HER. (Calderwood, 2003, pp. 9–10)

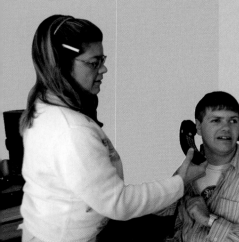

FOCUS PREVIEW

1 Identify three key elements of traumatic brain injury.

2 Cite four general characteristics of individuals with traumatic or acquired brain injuries.

3 Identify the most common causes of brain injury in children, youth, and adults.

4 Identify four common types of head injuries.

5 Describe five important elements of medical treatment for individuals with traumatic or acquired brain injuries.

6 Describe the focus of educational interventions for individuals with traumatic or acquired brain injuries.

▼ SNAPSHOT

SHANNON

Shannon works at Winegars, a food store [that] she describes as "sort of like heaven." That's not on account of the pay. She's not exactly on the fast track to making the Forbes list. Matter of fact, five months ago, right after she married her husband Jared, Shannon and Jared decided it would be great if they were wealthier, so Shannon left Winegars to look for higher pay.

What she got was a lot of doors shut in her face. People would take a sideways glance at the scar on her forehead and listen to her slightly slower speech and suddenly remember a pressing appointment. In all, she filled out 14 job applications. "We'll get back to you," she was told 14 times. No one did.

Winegars is one of those rare places of business that is infirmity-blind. Don't accuse them of hiring the handicapped, because they don't see handicaps. All they see is people.

As Shannon says, "Other places I've worked, the bosses treat me like I'm lower class; here, they treat me like I'm as high up as they are."

Shannon says this with the perspective of one who has been born twice. The first time was 28 years ago when she arrived on Earth. The second time was 12 years ago when she regained consciousness after a drunken driver ran a stop sign and smashed into the car she was riding in.

"It was no fender-bender," says Shannon. "I had to learn everything again, how to eat, how to walk, how to talk, everything."

Some brain damage was unavoidable, as were the scars. She knows she's not the same drop-dead gorgeous, intelligent blonde she was before the accident. Now she's a different kind of drop-dead gorgeous, intelligent blonde.

"It was so hard to get back to liking life at all after the accident," she admits. After a long, painful recovery, she finally got back to the business of taking care of herself. She worked at all sorts of jobs, as a hotel maid, at a movie theater, in child care, . . .

None were particularly easy, until along came Winegars, where manager Rod Lunceford routinely hires people used to getting doors slammed in their faces.

More often than not, it works out. In Shannon's case, for instance, the store's high expectations for her led to her own high expectations, and Winegars wound up with a public relations marvel.

Shannon's goal when she comes to work is to make sure that no one, no matter what they were wearing when they came in, leaves the store without a smile. She has proved so successful that management made a special badge she wears on her red apron.

"My badge says 'I'm a Customer Service Expert,'" says Shannon. "But really I'm a bagger."

Last October, when she and Jared tied the knot, half the people at their wedding reception were people whose groceries Shannon had bagged.

It was right after the wedding that she set out for other employment—a short-lived fling that only gave her more appreciation for a workplace where "if I have my hair a little out of place, I feel like no one's going to judge me."

"It's like a community here," she says, "there's a healing effect; I'm comfortable here. To shop here or work here, you don't have to be a special kind."

SOURCE: Adapted from "Winegars Is H(e)aven for Worker," *Deseret Morning News,* p. B01, April 30, 2006.

Children, youth, or adults who have experienced traumatic brain injuries are affected in many ways (Silver, McAllister, & Yudofsky, 2005). Memory loss, concentration problems, slowed information processing, seizures, vision problems, severe headaches—any and all of these problems may be present in individuals who have suffered severe head traumas. Think what it might be like to lose your sense of taste, to be able to think of things to say but not be able to actually speak them, and to know what it is like to throw a ball but not be able to release the ball from your hand. The challenges associated with traumatic brain injury (TBI) can be formidable (National Institutes of Neurological Disorders and Stroke, 2005).

Definition

Traumatic brain injury (TBI) occurs when there is a blow to the head or when the head slams against a stationary object. Such injuries happen, for example, in car accidents when the head hits the windshield and in bicycle accidents when the head hits the ground. The injury may occur in one of two ways:

> A closed-head injury occurs when the moving head is rapidly stopped, as when hitting a windshield, or when it is hit by a blunt object causing the brain to smash into the hard bony surface inside the skull. Closed-head injury may also occur without direct external trauma to the head if the brain undergoes a rapid forward or backward movement, such as when a person experiences whiplash. (Family Caregiver Alliance Clearing Houses, 2003, p. 1)

The trauma resulting from the rapid acceleration or deceleration of the brain may cause the tearing of important nerve fibers in the brain, the bruising of brain itself as it undergoes the impact with the skull, brain stem injuries, and brain swelling. Two types of brain damage, primary and secondary, are described by medical professionals. *Primary damage* is a direct outcome of the initial impact to the brain. *Secondary damage* develops over time as the brain responds to the initial trauma. For instance, an adolescent who is hit accidentally with a baseball bat may develop a hematoma—an area of internal bleeding within the brain. This may be the primary damage. However, with the passage of time, the brain's response to the initial injury may be pervasive swelling, which may cause additional insult to the brain.

In the school context, the Individuals with Disabilities Act (IDEA) defines traumatic brain injury as

> an acquired injury to the brain caused by an external force, resulting in total or partial functional disability or psychosocial impairment, or both, that adversely affects a student's educational performance. The term applies to open and closed head injuries resulting in impairments in one or more areas, such as cognition, language, memory, attention, reasoning, abstract thinking, judgment, problem-solving, sensory, perceptual, and motor abilities; psychosocial behavior, physical functions, information processing, and speech. The term does not apply to brain injuries that are congenital or degenerative or brain injuries induced by birth trauma. (*Federal Register, 57,* 189, pp. 44, 802)

Another term, **acquired brain injury (ABI)**, means

> an injury to the brain, which is not hereditary, congenital, degenerative, or induced by birth trauma. An acquired brain injury is an injury to the brain that has occurred after birth. (Brain Injury Association of America, 2006)

ABI may be caused by a lack of oxygen to the brain, airway obstruction, near-drowing, lightning or electrical shock, strangulation, loss of blood, tumors, infections, exposure to toxins, illegal drug use, and other types of poisoning.

These traumatic and acquired brain injuries result in disabilities that may adversely affect individuals' information processing, social behaviors, memory capacities, reasoning and thinking, speech and language skills, and sensory and motor abilities (Arlinghaus,

> ➤ **Traumatic brain injury (TBI)**
>
> Direct injury to the brain, such as tearing of nerve fibers, bruising of the brain tissue against the skull, brain stem trauma, and swelling.

FOCUS **1**
Identify three key elements of traumatic brain injury.

Council for Exceptional Children

Standard 1: Foundations

> ➤ **Acquired brain injury (ABI)**
>
> Injury that may result from TBI or from strokes and other vascular accidents, infectious diseases, anoxic injuries (hanging, near drowning), anesthetic accidents, severe blood loss, metabolic disorders, and ingestion of toxic products.

PEAT™ (the Planning and Execution Assistant and Trainer) provides unique assistance for people with cognitive impairments due to brain injury, attention-deficit disorder, autism, developmental disorders, and other causes. This handheld cognitive aid was designed by a NASA robotics researcher working to increase independence for autonomous spacecraft and Mars rovers. Like people, NASA robots need flexibility to replan and achieve goals in changing situations. PEAT applies this same technology to help users with executive function disorders, which disrupt attention, time management, and planning and execution of essential tasks. Individuals with these impairments are easily distracted and have difficulty completing daily activities without help.

PEAT provides cues (reminders) for daily activities, scheduled appointments and scripted behavior sequences. The Cue Card display reminds users when to stop or start activities (see figures below). Reminders include text prompts, personalized sound and voice recordings, digital photographs, and links to attached name and note information. PEAT's patented scheduling technology provides automatic planning, execution monitoring, and error correction to handle schedule conflicts and avoid missed deadlines. PEAT cues the user and automatically adjusts their schedule when delays or other changes occur. This flexible guidance enables users to stay on task and complete activities without help from a caregiver. PEAT can be customized for each user and configured for a wide range of user needs and capabilities. PEAT is made by Attention Control Systems (www.brainaid.com) in Mountain View, California.

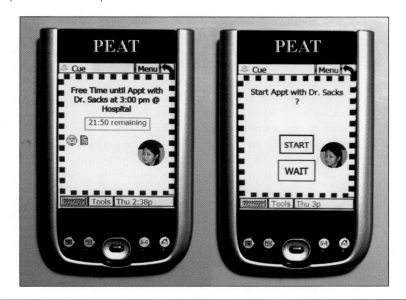

Shoaib, & Price, 2005; Best, Heller, & Bigge, 2005; Kapor & Ciuffreda, 2005; McCullagh & Feinstein, 2005; Richter, 2005; Silver & Yudofsky, & Anderson, 2005). See the nearby Assistive Technology to learn about a device designed to help those who have difficulty with these skills.

Prevalence

The statistics associated with traumatic brain injury are sobering. "At least 1.4 million people sustain TBIs. Of them, about 50,000 die, 235,000 are hospitalized, and 1.1 million are treated and released" (Langlois, Rutland-Brown, & Thomas, 2006, p. 1). About 475,000 TBIs take place with children (0 to 14 years of age). About 80,000 to 90,000 who have sustained TBIs are permanently disabled from their accidents or injuries. About 180 per 100,000 children under age 15 experience TBIs. Of that number, about 5% to 8% experience severe TBIs.

Most of the head injuries five million children experience annually could be prevented with the proper use of preventative aids such as helmets, seat belts, and child restraints.

It is now estimated that 5.3 million children and adults in the United States are living with the consequences of sustaining a traumatic brain injury. This number equals nearly 2% of the general population (Brain Injury Association, 2003; Kraus & Chu, 2005).

Of all the head injuries that occur, 40% involve children. About 2% to 5% of the children and youth who experience TBIs develop severe neurologic complications, others develop lasting behavior problems, and over one-third experience life-long disabilities (Pierangelo & Giuliani, 2001). Most of these injuries could be prevented with proper use of seat belts, air bags, child restraints, helmets, and guns (Elovic & Zafonte, 2005).

The incidence of TBI peaks during three specific age periods. Children below 5 years of age, individuals between 15 and 24 years of age, and individuals over 70 years of age are more likely to experience head injuries. The peaking of injuries between the ages of 15 and 24 is attributable to several factors, including increased participation in contact sports, greater access to and use of automobiles, more frequent use of racing and mountain bikes, and injuries sustained from firearms. The number of head injuries in males exceeds that in females. As a rule, males are two to three times more likely to sustain serious head injuries, particularly during the adolescent years (Max, 2005).

Obviously, medical care at the scene of the accident is crucial. Emergency treatment in the field and in the hospital can make a big difference in survival rates of injured individuals. As indicated earlier, many die as a result of severe head injuries (Langlois, Rutland-Brown, & Thomas, 2006).

Characteristics

Focus 2
Cite four general characteristics of individuals with traumatic or acquired brain injuries.

Council for Exceptional Children

Standard 2: Development and Characteristics of Learners

Individuals with traumatic or acquired brain injuries present a variety of challenges to families and professionals. The injuries may affect every aspect of an individual's life (see Figure 14.1 for effects on children). The resulting disabilities also have a profound effect on the individual's family (Cavallo & Kay, 2005; Max, 2005; Wright & Borgelt, 2003). Often the injuries radically change the individual's capacities for learning and making sense of different kinds of incoming information (verbal, written, nonverbal, visual, and so on) (Max, 2005). See the "Reflect on This" on page 374 for one person's response to a devastating accident.

Generally, individuals will need services and supports in four areas: cognition, speech and language, social and behavioral skills, as well as physical functioning (High, Sander, Struchen, & Hart, 2005; Keyser-Marcus et al., 2002). Cognitive problems have an impact on thinking and perception. For example, people who have sustained a brain injury may be unable to remember or retrieve newly learned or processed information. They may be unable to attend or concentrate for appropriate periods of time. Another serious problem is the inability to adjust or respond flexibly to changes in home, school, community, or work environments (Hux & Manasse, 2003).

FIGURE 14.1

Characteristics of Children with Traumatic Brain Injury

Medical/Neurological Symptoms

- Sensory deficits affecting vision, hearing, taste, smell or touch
- Decreased motor coordination
- Difficulty breathing
- Dizziness
- Headache
- Impaired balance
- Loss of intellectual capabilities
- Partial to full paralysis
- Poor eye–hand coordination
- Reduced body strength
- Seizure activity (possibly frequent)
- Sleep disorders
- Speech problems (e.g., stuttering, slurring)

Cognitive Symptoms

- Decreased attention
- Decreased organizational skills
- Decreased problem-solving ability
- Difficulties keeping up at school
- Difficulty with abstract reasoning
- Integration problems (e.g., sensory, thought)
- Poor organizational skills
- Memory deficits
- Perceptual problems
- Poor concentration
- Poor judgment
- Rigidity of thought

- Slowed information processing
- Poor short- and long-term memory
- Word-finding difficulty

Behavioral/Emotional Symptoms

- Aggressive behavior
- Denial of deficits
- Depression
- Difficulty accepting and responding to change
- Loss of reduction of inhibitions
- Distractibility
- Feelings of worthlessness
- Flat affect (expressionless, lacking emotion)
- Low frustration level
- Unnecessary or disproportionate guilt
- Helplessness
- Impulsivity
- Inappropriate crying or laughing
- Irritability

Social Skills Development

- Difficulties maintaining relationships with family members and others
- Inability to restrict socially inappropriate behaviors (e.g., disrobing in public)
- Inappropriate responses to the environment (e.g., overreactions to light or sound)
- Insensitivity to others' feelings
- Limited initiation of social interactions
- Social isolation

SOURCE: Adapted from *What Every Teacher Should Know About Students with Special Needs: Promoting Success in the Classroom* pp. 98–100, by R. Pierangelo and G. A. Guiliani (2001), Champaign, IL: Research Press. Copyright © 2001 by R. Pierangelo and G. A. Guilliani. Reprinted by permission.

A person with TBI may also struggle with speech, producing unintelligible sounds or indistinguishable words (Hux, 2003). Speech may be slurred and labored. The individual may know what he or she wants to say but be unable to express it. Professionals use the term **aphasia** to describe this condition. **Expressive aphasia** is an inability to express one's own thoughts and desires. Language problems may also be evident. For example, a school-age student may be unable to retrieve a desired word or expression, particularly in a "high-demand" instructional setting or during an anxiety-producing social situation. Given their difficulties with word retrieval, individuals with TBIs may reduce their overall speech output or use repetitive expressions or word substitutions. Many children with brain injuries express great frustration at knowing an answer to a question but being unable to retrieve it when called on by teachers. (See Chapter 11 for additional information on expressive aphasia.)

➤ **Aphasia**

An acquired language disorder that is caused by brain damage and is characterized by complete or partial impairment of language comprehension, formulation, and use.

➤ **Expressive aphasia**

An inability to express one's own thoughts and desires verbally.

I wish I could explain in words so that you can fully comprehend it. I want you to know how much this is hurting me. The car accident hurt me physically. This, you know. You are aware that I couldn't walk, talk, speak, swallow or even go to the bathroom at one point in time. You're aware that my dad's life was taken away from me. All this you know. I'm not trying to tell you this again just so you feel bad. That's not what I'm going to say at all actually. I want to let you know (just so that your aware) of the things that you may NOT know. The things that I'm suffering with TODAY.

Yes, it's been almost three years since everything. Three years! YOU may (or not, I don't know) think that I should be over it by now. But with the physical and emotional problems that I am likely to have for LIFE, I ask you to take a couple of minutes and just listen, hear me out and let me talk.

My dad left my life. He's dead. He left my life when I was only 16 years old. This you know. But what you may not know: I asked him to pick me up that day. I was the only reason that he was there, at that point in time. I am the one that will forever feel guilty and responsible for YOUR mistake.

I don't understand anything anymore. My brain, now ruined forever, it isn't the same.

I can't retain information. Probably the reason I'm failing. I try to convince myself that I'm just being lazy (or that I'm dumb) it helps me shield myself from the harsh reality that I'm really just incapable of doing it.

This whole letter of anger may seem like a lot to you. But to me I feel like I've missed SOOO much. That I can't even begin to properly explain to you the physical, emotional, cognitive, and mental problems that may just ruin me completely.

You go about your life. You think about it when you need to. When there's a court case, or something that involves you. Maybe I'm just being spiteful. Maybe you think about it all the time. But you COULD go a day without thinking about it—if you wanted if you really tried. Me? I can't! I have to notice how I can't do things.

There's an old saying. You can't go home again. Maybe that's the case. Maybe this guilt will keep me away from my family. The same family who slept in the hospital night after night with me who stayed until everything was ok who STILL comes to my surgical appointments with me. I love them. But maybe I should just accept responsibility and face the facts that I hurt them.

Then there's me—my friends think that I've turned into a bitter girl. They miss the Happy Beena (as they say) that I apparently once was and that they knew and miss. YOU tell me what to say to them.

I'm going to end this letter now, because otherwise I'll just write forever.

Beena

SOURCE: Excerpts from *Beena, A Place to Share*. Retrieved December 27, 2006, from http://tbihome.org/stories/beena2.htm

Standard 3: Individual Learning Differences

Social and behavioral problems may present the most challenging aspects of TBI and ABI. For many individuals, the injury produces significant changes in their personalities, their temperaments, their dispositions toward certain activities, and their behaviors (O'Shanick & O'Shanick, 2005; Robinson & Jorge, 2005; Silver, Yudofsky, & Anderson, 2005; Semrud-Clikeman, 2001; Warden & Labbate, 2005). These social and behavioral problems may worsen over time, depending on the nature of the injury, the preinjury status of the brain, the preinjury adjustment of the individual and family, the person's age at the time of the injury, and the treatment provided immediately after the injury (Eden & Stevens, 2006; Gennarelli & Graham, 2005). Behavior effects include increased irritability and emotionality, compromised motivation and judgment, an inability to restrict socially inappropriate behaviors, insensitivity to others, and low thresholds for frustration and inconvenience (Max, 2005; National Institutes of Neurological Disorders and Stroke, 2005; Ylvisaker et al., 2001).

Neuromotor and physical disabilities are also characteristic of individuals with brain injuries (Kapoor & Ciuffreda, 2005; Richter, 2005). Neuromotor problems may be exhibited through poor eye–hand coordination. For example, an adolescent may be able to pick up a ball but be unable to throw it to someone else. In addition, there may be impaired balance, an inability to walk unassisted, significantly reduced stamina, or paralysis. Impaired vision and hearing may also be present. The array and extent of the challenges faced by individuals with brain injuries and their families can be overwhelming and disheartening. However, with appropriate support and coordinated, interdisciplinary treatment, the individual and family can move forward with their lives and develop effective coping skills (Cavallo & Kay, 2005; National Institutes of Neurological Disorders and Stroke, 2005).

Causation

What most frequently causes brain injury varies with the age and developmental status of the individual. The highest incidence of injury in all age groups is motor vehicle crashes. Other transport-related crashes account for the next-highest incidence of injury. These include injuries derived from accidents involving bicycles, motorcyles, watercraft, and farm equipment (Eden & Stevens, 2006; Kraus & Chu, 2005). See the accompanying Reflect on This for a chilling account of what happens in a head-on auto accident.

For small children, the most common cause is a fall from a short distance. Such children may fall from a tree, playground equipment, their parents' arms, or furniture. Another major cause of injury in young children is physical abuse (Horton & Cruise, 2001). These injuries generally come from the shaking or striking of infants, which may cause sheering of brain matter or severe bleeding. Common causes of head injuries in older children include falls from playground swings or climbers, bicycles, or trees; blows to the head from baseball bats, balls, or other sports equipment; gunshot wounds; and pedestrian accidents. The Debate Forum on page 376 addresses the issue of gun control to reduce the number of brain injury fatalities from firearms.

The first signs of brain injury often manifest themselves in coma. The severity and nature of complications and the eventual outcomes of the trauma are a function of the location and degree of the injury to the brain (see Table 14.1 on page 377). Jennett and Teasdale (1974) developed a scale to assess the potential impact of head injuries in children and to predict their eventual functioning (see Table 14.2 on page 377). Scores of 3 to 5 generally indicate poor outcomes in children and youth over time.

The number of children and others who experience serious head trauma would be significantly reduced if seat belts and other child restraint devices were consistently used. Further reductions in such injuries would be achieved by significantly decreasing accidents due to driving under the influence of alcohol and other mind-altering substances (Elovic & Zafonte, 2005).

FOCUS **3**

Identify the most common causes of brain injury in children, youth, and adults.

Council for Exceptional Children

Standard 1: Foundations

REFLECT ON THIS

ALL THIS—WITHIN SEVEN TENTHS OF A SECOND

This is what happens in a head-on collision: In the first tenth of a second, the front bumper and grill collapse. In the second tenth, the hood crumples into the windshield and the rear of the car lifts off the ground with the wheels still spinning. The front fender starts to wrap itself around whatever object the car hit, and even though the front end of the car has stopped moving, the driver is still moving 55 miles per hour. Instinct causes the driver to stiffen the legs against the crash; that causes the knee joints to snap when the feet come in contact with the floorboard of the car. During the third tenth of a second, the driver is propelled toward the steering column. By the fourth tenth of a second, the front end of the car has 2 feet of damage, but the rear of the car is still moving at 35 miles per hour. The driver has not slowed down at all; he or she is still moving at 55 miles per hour. In the fifth tenth of a second, the steering column impales the driver's chest and blood rushes into the lungs. By the sixth tenth of a second, the driver's feet are ripped out of laced shoes, the brake pedal breaks off, the car frame buckles in the middle, and the driver's head bangs into the windshield. The rear wheels finally fall back to the ground. More structural damage occurs in the seventh tenth of a second as hinges break loose, doors open, and seats break free and strike the driver from behind. None of this matters, however, because the driver is already dead (Hux, 2003, pp. 3–4).

FIREARMS: SHOULDN'T WE PROTECT OUR CHILDREN AND YOUTH?

Hundreds of brain injuries could be avoided if parents limited children's access to firearms.

SCOPE OF THE PROBLEM

In 1992, firearms surpassed motor vehicles as the number one cause of brain injury fatalities in the United States.

It is estimated that every two hours in the United States, someone's child is killed with a loaded gun. Firearm violence is a uniquely American problem, with a rate 90 times greater than that of any similar country.

It is estimated that half of all American households have firearms.

Every day, 14 American children under the age of 20 are killed and many more are wounded by guns.

It costs more than $14,000 to treat each child wounded by gunfire—enough to pay for a full year at a private college.

FIREARM USAGE

Although firearms are often kept in the home for protection, they are rarely used for this

Lisa Kreutz, one of the Columbine High School seniors wounded in the school shooting, receives her diploma at commencement ceremonies with her mother and father. Two students of the class of 1999 were killed in the shootings, and three were injured.

purpose. Of 198 cases of home invasion crimes, only three victims (1.5%) used a gun for self-defense.

The risk of suicide is five times greater if there is a gun in the home, and the risk of domestic homicide is three times greater.

Most children who kill themselves or other children unintentionally while playing with a gun found it in their home or the home of a family member or friend.

News reports state that nearly 90% of accidental shootings involving children are linked to easy-to-find, loaded handguns in the home.

Over half of all handgun owners keep their guns loaded at least some of the time, and over half do not keep their guns locked up.

An estimated 30% of all unintentional shootings could be prevented by the presence of safety features such as trigger locks and loading indicators, but American-made guns are not subject to federal safety standards like other consumer products such as automobiles, aspirin bottles, and children's toys.

POINT

Gun control of any kind is repugnant to many individuals, particularly those who have strong feelings about the "right to bear arms." These individuals argue that controlling firearms is a violation of their civil rights. Any restriction of access to firearms or control of their use is seen by these individuals as undue government intervention and control.

COUNTERPOINT

As a society, we can no longer ignore the deaths and injuries to children and youth that are caused by firearms. We ought to treat firearms as we treat cars. Cars must have certain safety devices, or they are not available for purchase or use. Likewise, only those licensed to drive may legally get behind the wheel of a car. These governmental measures are directed at enhancing the safety of citizens. The same measures should apply to firearms. The essential goal is prevention, not control.

SOURCE: From *Firearm Safety,* developed by the Brain Injury Association of America, 2000b, Alexandria, Virginia.

Programs directed at reducing the number of individuals who drive while under the influence of alcohol or other substances should be vigorously supported. Likewise, children (and everyone else) should wear helmets when bicycling and should obey safety rules that reduce the probability of serious accidents.

TABLE 14.1

Descriptors of TBI Severity

DESCRIPTOR	SYMPTOMS
Minor	No loss of consciousness; head injury not seen by a physician; a minor bump.
Mild	Mild or transient loss of consciousness, if any; child may be lethargic and not be able to recall the injury; child may vomit (if more than three times, should be seen by emergency room staff).
Moderate	Loss of consciousness is typically less than 5 minutes; on recovery, the child may be able to move spontaneously and purposefully; opens eyes in response to pain. Older children or youth may be combative, telling others to "leave me alone."
Severe	Loss of consciousness ranges from 5 to 30 minutes. Surgery may be needed if skull is fractured significantly; neurologic consequences are common.
Serious	Loss of consciousness more that 30 minutes, notable neurologic consequences are typical.

SOURCE: Adapted from *Head Injuries* (p. 225), by J. L. Hill, 1999, Upper Saddle River, NJ: Merrill.

TABLE 14.2

Glasgow Coma Scale

ACTIVITY	SCORE	DESCRIPTION
Best Motor Response		
Obeys commands	6	Follows simple verbal directions
Localized pain	5	Moves arms and legs to escape painful stimuli
Withdrawal from pain	4	Normal reflex responses
Abnormal flexion	3	"Decorticate"—abnormal adduction of shoulder
Extensor posturing	2	"Decerebrate"—internal rotation of shoulder and pronation of forearm
No response	1	Limp, without evidence of spinal transection
Best Verbal Response		
Oriented	5	Aware of self, environment, time, and situation
Confused	4	Attention is adequate and patient is responsive, but responses suggest disorientation and confusion
Inappropriate	3	Understandable articulation, but speech is used in a nonconversational (exclamatory or swearing manner); conversation is not sustained
Incomprehensible	2	Verbal response (moaning) but without recognizable words
No response	1	
Eye Opening		
Spontaneous	4	Eyes are open; scored without reference to awareness
To speech	3	Eyes are open to speech or shout without implying a response to a direct command
To pain	2	Eyes are open with painful stimulus to limbs or chest.
None	1	No eye opening, not attributable to swelling

SOURCE: Adapted from *The Lancet*, 2, B. Jennett and G. Teasdale, "Assessment of Coma and Impaired Consciousness," pp. 81–84. Copyright © 1974, with permission from Elsevier.

A Multidisciplinary Approach

➤ **Computerized tomography (CT)**

An x-ray imaging technique by which computers create cross-sectional images of specific body areas or organs.

➤ **Magnetic resonance imaging (MRI)**

A magnetic imaging technique by which computers create cross-sectional images of specific body areas or organs.

➤ **Voxel-based morphometry**

A computational method for measuring differences in local concentrations of brain tissue, through comparisons of multiple brain images of normal and injured brains, all of which are conveyed visually through computer imaging.

➤ **Concussion**

The most common type of traumatic brain injury, which involves a transient loss of mental functioning. It can be caused by acceleration or deceleration forces or by a direct blow. Concussions are not generally associated with penetrating injuries. A jarring injury of the brain resulting in a disturbance of cerebral functioning.

➤ **Contusion**

Extensive damage to the brain resulting in intense stupor. This condition is often derived from brutal shaking, violent blows, or other serious impacts to the head.

➤ **Skull fracture**

A break, crack, or split of the skull resulting from a violent blow or other serious impact to the head.

➤ **Epidural hematoma**

The collecting of blood between the skull and the covering of the brain, which puts pressure on vital brain structures.

➤ **Subdural hematoma**

The collecting of blood between the covering of the brain and the brain itself, resulting in pressure on vital brain structures.

Medical and Psychological Services

Like other persons with disabilities, individuals with traumatic brain injuries profit significantly from systems of care—collaborative/multidisciplinary approaches and interventions that address unique family and individual needs (Cope & Reynolds, 2005). Because of the nature and number of the deficits that might result from a head injury, many specialists must be involved in a coordinated and carefully orchestrated fashion (Ylvisaker et al., 2001). Early comprehensive care is vital to the long-term, functional recovery of individuals with brain injuries.

Additionally, new medical technologies have revolutionized diagnostic and treatment procedures for traumatic and acquired brain injuries (Bigler, 2005). In previous decades, the vast majority of these individuals died within a short time of their accidents. With the development of **computerized tomography (CT)** scans, intracranial pressure monitors, **magnetic resonance imaging (MRI), voxel-based morphometry (VBM),** and the capacity to control bleeding and brain swelling, many individuals with traumatic brain injuries survive. Also, CT scans and voxel-based morphometry of individuals without brain injuries now enable physicians and other health care providers to compare the brain of an injured person with the uninjured brains of other individuals of the same age and gender. Voxel-based morphometry is a computational method for measuring differences in local concentrations of brain tissue, through comparisons of multiple brain images from individuals with and without injuries.

Head injuries may be described in terms of the nature of the injury. Injuries include concussions, contusions, skull fractures, and epidural and subdural hemorrhages (Gennarelli & Graham, 2005).

➤ *Concussions.* The most common effects of closed-head injuries, **concussions** occur most frequently in children and adolescents through contact sports such as football, hockey, and martial arts. Children who display weakness on one side of the body or a dilated pupil may have a concussion and should be examined immediately by a physician.

➤ *Contusions.* This kind of injury is characterized by extensive damage to the brain, including laceration of the brain, bleeding, swelling, and bruising. The resulting effect of a **contusion** is intense stupor or coma. Individuals with contusions should be hospitalized immediately.

➤ *Skull fractures.* The consequences of **skull fractures** depend on the location, nature, and seriousness of the fracture. Unfortunately, some fractures are not easily detectable through radiologic examination. Injuries to the lower back part of the head are particularly troublesome and difficult to detect. These basilar skull fractures may set the stage for serious infections of the central nervous system. Immediate medical care is essential for skull fractures to determine the extent of the damage and to develop appropriate interventions.

➤ *Epidural and subdural hemorrhages.* Hemorrhaging or bleeding is the central feature of epidural and subdural hematomas. Hematomas are collections of blood, usually clotted. An **epidural hematoma** is caused by damage to an artery (a thick-walled blood vessel carrying blood from the heart) between the brain and the skull (see Figure 14.2). If this injury is not treated promptly and appropriately, the affected individual will die. A **subdural hematoma** is caused by damage to tiny veins that draw blood from the outer layer of the brain (cerebral cortex) to the heart. The aggregation of blood between the brain and its outer covering (dura) produces pressure that adversely affects the brain and its functioning (see Figure 14.3). If the subdural bleeding is left untreated, death can result.

Medical treatment of traumatic and acquired brain injury proceeds generally in three stages: acute care, rehabilitation, and community intergration (Cavallo & Kay, 2005). During the acute stage, medical personnel focus on maintaining the child's life, treating the swelling and bleeding, minimizing complications, reducing the level of coma, and completing the initial neurologic examination. This stage of treatment is often characterized by strained interactions between physicians and parents. Many physicians are unable to respond satisfactorily to the overwhelming psychological needs of parents and family members

FIGURE 14.2

An Epidural Hematoma

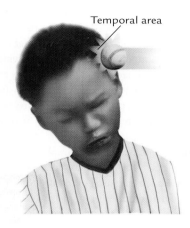

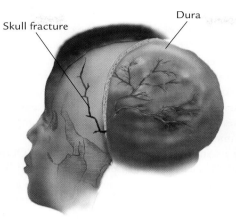

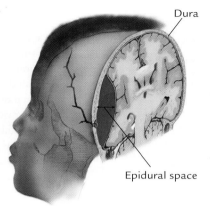

(a) A forceful injury occurs in the temporal area of the brain.

(b) The injury may result in a fractured skull, causing bleeding in the middle meningeal artery. Blood collects between the skull and the dura, a rough membrane covering the brain.

(c) As the blood collects, pressure builds on vital structures within the brain.

SOURCE: Adapted from "Common Neurological Disorders in Children," by Robert H. A. Haslam (p. 330) in R. H. A. Haslam & P. J. Valletutti (eds), *Medical Problems in the Classroom*. Copyright 1996, Austin, TX: Pro-Ed, Inc. Reprinted by permission.

FIGURE 14.3

A Subdural Hematoma

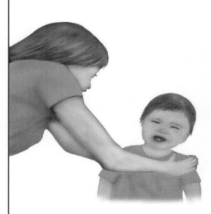

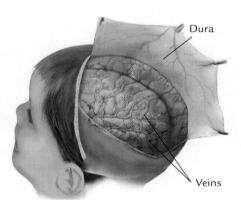

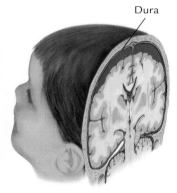

(a) Violently shaking or hitting a child may cause damage to the cerebral cortex.

(b) Trauma to the brain results in the rupturing of small veins.

(c) Blood gathers between the dura and the brain, resulting in pressure on vital brain structures.

SOURCE: Adapted from "Common Neurological Disorders in Children," by Robert H. A. Haslam (p. 332) in R. H. A. Haslam & P. J. Valletutti (eds.), *Medical Problems in the Classroom*. Copyright 1996, Austin, TX: Pro-Ed, Inc. Reprinted by permission.

FOCUS **4**
Identify four common types of head injuries.

Council for Exceptional Children

Standard 1: Foundations

FOCUS **5**
Describe five important elements of medical treatment for individuals with traumatic or acquired brain injuries.

because of the complex medical demands presented by the injured child (Cavallo & Kay, 2005; Max 2005). Other trained personnel (including social workers, psychologists, and clergy) play vital roles in supporting parents and other family members. Again, we see the importance of systems of care, where talented professionals work together to achieve optimal outcomes for all concerned.

If the child remains in a coma, medical personnel may use special stimulation techniques to reduce the depth of the coma. If the child becomes agitated by stimuli in the hospital unit, such as visitors' conversations, noises produced by housecleaning staff, intrusive light, or touching, steps may be taken to control or reduce these stimuli. As the injured individual comes out of the coma, orienting him or her to the environment becomes a priority. This may include explaining where the patient is located, introducing care providers, indicating where loved ones are, sharing what has happened since the injury, and responding to the individual's other questions. Many persons who have been injured do not remember the accident or the medical interventions administered.

The next stage of treatment is rehabilitation. During this phase the individual seeks to re-learn and adequately perform preinjury skills and behaviors. This treatment may take time and considerable effort—often months. Children and youth are prepared gradually for return to their homes and to appropriate school environments. Their families prepare as well, receiving ongoing support and counseling. Arrangements are also made for any speech/language, physical, and occupational therapies and for any specialized teaching necessary.

Many individuals return to their homes, schools, or employment settings as vastly different people. These differences often take the shape of unpredictable or extreme expressions of emotion. Furthermore, these individuals may have trouble recognizing and accepting their postinjury challenges and deficits (Bowe, 2000).

The last stage of intervention is community reintegration, which focuses on providing counseling and therapy to help individuals cope with their injuries and their residual ef-

The medical and psychological services available to Russian skater Elena Berezhnaya enabled her to successfully return to skating after receiving a traumatic head injury in practice. After months of care and rehabilitation, she and her partner were bronze medal winners in the XVIII Winter Olympics.

CASE STUDY

F.T.

F.T. is a 15-year-old . . . boy with a history of a TBI 5 years ago. He was referred for a neuropsychological assessment by his school district because educators were unsure of how to manage F.T.'s academic and behavior problems. F.T. had recently entered their school district as a ninth grader, and he was failing all of his classes except for a D- in science and a B+ in physical education. He had particular problems with written expression, with following oral and written directions, and with identifying the main idea in materials presented to him. Teachers were also concerned about his short attention span, staring spells, and poor work completion. F.T. had received special education services under a diagnosis of learning disabilities in his previous school district. This consisted of 1 hour per day of resource room assistance to help him organize his assignments and complete his homework. Since he entered the new school, F.T.'s attendance has been adequate, and teachers perceived him as a friendly, outgoing young man. However, they were considering a secondary educational diagnosis of behavior disorder because of the disruption caused by his impulsive and off-task behaviors.

F.T. sustained a severe TBI in an amusement park accident at the age of 10 years. He experienced full cardiopulmonary arrest at the scene of the accident and remained in a coma for 3 days. His initial Glasgow Coma Scale score was 6. A computerized tomography (CT scan) of the brain showed a large left tempoparietal contusion, but he had no other significant injuries. Upon transfer to acute rehabilitation 15 days postinjury, F.T. displayed a dense right-side hemiparesis and could not talk, but he could follow simple one-step commands. During rehabilitation, he showed a rapid recovery of physical mobility, self-care skills, and basic language functioning. His attention span was extremely short, his short-term memory was poor, and he was impulsive and noncompliant in therapies.

Behaviorally, F.T. was perceived somewhat differently by his teachers and parents. The teachers and his father reported clinically significant problems with attention/concentration, work production, and noncompliance. In addition to these problems, F.T.'s mother also indicated significant concerns about social withdrawal; aggressive behaviors (arguing, fighting, mood swings, temper tantrums); and delinquent behaviors (associating with bad companions, stealing, swearing, and truancy). On a behavioral self-report measure, F.T. [exhibited] mild . . . problems with daydreaming and arguing, suggesting a lack of insight and self-awareness.

F.T. certainly had multiple risk factors that could lead to poor long-term outcomes. He experienced a severe head injury with persistent cognitive and behavioral sequelae that interfered with his ability to keep up with same-age peers, as indicated by neuropsychological testing and by the decline in his IQ scores over time. Prior to his TBI, he had experienced academic problems that were probably associated with his history of physical and sexual abuse. His home environment was chaotic, and litigation over the TBI fueled family conflict and divisions. His single mother had multiple stressors, including the injury of two of her children and severe financial problems, and she did not exhibit strong behavioral management or limit-setting skills. F.T.'s recovery from TBI was affected by frequent family moves and inconsistent (and sometimes inadequate) educational services as a consequence of educators' inexperience and limited educational resources.

APPLICATION

1. What steps should be taken by medical and educational personnel in responding to F.T. and his particular needs?

2. What ongoing information should be delivered by the mother that would be helpful to F.T.'s teachers?

3. What ongoing information should be delivered by his teachers that would be helpful to F.T.'s mother?

4. How should other agencies and care providers in the community be involved with F.T. and his family?

SOURCE: From "Epilogue: An Ecological Systems Approach to Childhood Traumatic Injury," by J. E. Farmer. In *Childhood Traumatic Brain Injury: Diagnosis, Assessment, and Intervention,* edited by E. E. Bigler, E. Clark, & J. E. Farmer, 1997, pp. 177–190. Austin, TX: Pro-Ed, Inc.

---

fects; helping the families maintain the gains that have been achieved; terminating specific head injury services; and referring individuals to community agencies, educational programs, and vocational rehabilitation for additional services as needed (Cavallo & Kay, 2005; Wehman, 2001).

Educational Supports and Services

Educational supports focus on environmental changes that facilitate daily living and address critical transition issues that arise in preparing the child's or youth's return to appropriate school settings (Cavallo & Kay, 2005). Communication and collaboration are absolutely

Council for Exceptional Children

Standard 7: Instructional Planning

essential to the transition from the hospital or other care facility to the school environment. Three groups are involved in ensuring that the care and support are optimal: parents and teachers, professionals within the school, and school professionals working with clinical/medical personnel outside the school. It is essential that educators and health providers work together to blend clinical, educational, and family interventions effectively (Cavallo & Kay, 2005; Keyser-Marcus et al., 2002).

Unfortunately, many children with TBIs leave hospitals or rehabilitation settings without adequate preparation for the new environments in which they find themselves. They are not ready to return to school. And many teachers who receive these students are not adequately prepared to respond to their cognitive, academic, and behavioral needs.

Before the child or youth leaves the hospital or rehabilitation facility, several issues and questions need to be addressed by medical, psychological, and educational personnel (see Figure 14.4). Pertinent questions include the following:

➤ How severe was the injury? What is the prognosis for continued recovery?

➤ What are the major health-related needs of the child? Is an individual health plan needed to establish a protocol for treatment at school?

➤ Are seizures or other neurologic problems likely? What changes in behavior indicate that a physician should be contacted?

➤ Are activity restrictions needed to ensure safety and well-being?

➤ What medications are prescribed? Do they have side effects? Do they need to be administered at school?

➤ What is the impact of the brain injury on the child's ability to learn new information in verbal and visual-spatial modalities? Are problems with new learning due primarily to deficits in attention, comprehension, memory, response, speed of processing, or reasoning?

➤ In what areas (e.g., language arts, mathematics, science) is the child most likely to experience success?

➤ What content area may prove difficult or overwhelming for the learner? What modifications, if any, would facilitate the child's performance in those areas (reading partners, cooperative learning activities, peer tutoring, . . . calculators)? (Farmer, Clippard, Luehr-Wiemann, Wright, & Owings, 1997, pp. 40–41, 43, 49)

Addressing these questions provides valuable information for school personnel and others who must plan for and implement the youngster's reentry into school. Generally, a liaison or case manager works with other medical and health personnel to make certain that the child or youth is safe and sufficiently healthy to leave the health care facility. The transition liaison also ensures that parents and teachers are adequately prepared to receive and care for the child (Deidrick & Farmer, 2005).

Students with traumatic or acquired brain injuries may return to one of several school placements, depending on their needs. Appropriate teaching activities include establishing high expectations, reducing stimuli and conditions that elicit challenging behaviors, using appropriate reductive techniques for stopping or significantly reducing aggressive or noncompliant behaviors, eliminating rewards for negative or problematic behaviors, providing precise feedback, giving students strategies for organizing information, and providing many opportunities for practice (see Table 14.3 on page 386).

Educational services must be tailored to a student's specific needs. Effort should be directed at improving students' general behaviors, such as problem solving, planning, and developing insight. Teaching may also focus on appropriate social behaviors (such as performing in stressful situations, improving initiative taking, and working with others), expressive and receptive language skills (word retrieval, event description, understanding instructions, and reading nonverbal cues), and writing skills (sentence development, legibility, and so on) (see Figure 14.5 on page 387). Also, some individuals with TBI benefit greatly from assistive technology devices that aid in communication, information procession, learning, and recreation (Best, Reed, & Biggee, 2005). These technologies help individuals with TBIs and other disabilities communicate with others, display what they know, access information, and participate in various learning and recreational activities.

Focus 6
Describe the focus of educational interventions for individuals with traumatic or acquired brain injuries.

Council for Exceptional Children

Standard 5: Learning Environments and Social Interactions

FIGURE 14.4

Suggested School Reintegration Checklist

Student: _____   School/Grade: _____

Date of Injury: _____   Parent Name: _____   Phone #: _____

1. IMMEDIATELY FOLLOWING INJURY

A school representative will be assigned to the case by an administrator. The school representative will:

Contact parent(s) to:
- inquire about their child's condition
- obtain release for hospital contact (get release to and from school)

Contact the child's case manager at the hospital to:
- inform them of the school's concern

Meet with the child's classroom teacher(s) to:
- inform them of the child's condition
- obtain/review current educational records

2. AFTER STUDENT'S CONDITION HAS STABILIZED

The school representative will:

Arrange a meeting with the hospital care manager to:
- obtain information regarding the child's condition
- determine if/when to send schoolwork

3. PRIOR TO DISCHARGE

The school representative will:

Visit with student and rehabilitation staff

Obtain copies of hospital evaluations (psychological, educational, physical therapy/occupational therapy, speech)

Conduct in-service in school to:
- provide specific information about the school's condition
- provide more general information about TBI
- discuss potential modifications (ramp, wheelchair, lighting)

4. IMMEDIATELY AFTER HOSPITAL DISCHARGE

A school representative will:

Contact parent(s) to:
- determine if the child will be getting post-acute rehabilitation care
- set a tentative date for return to school if no further rehabilitation is being provided

Follow up with a hospital case manager to:
- get update on discharge condition/special needs (i.e., tracheotomy, ambulation)

Establish a TBI team and designate a case manager (if different from representative) to:
- develop a tentative plan for school reentry (consider need for environmental modifications, special education, 504, and related services)

5. ARRIVAL AT SCHOOL

The team will:
- assign further personnel to conduct initial evaluation and give feedback to teachers and parents
- further modify classroom environment to meet student's needs

6. AFTER FIRST WEEKS AT SCHOOL

The team will:
- reassess the student's needs and modify educational plan accordingly
- maintain contact with parents and teachers

SOURCE: From *Children and Adolescents with Traumatic Brain Injury: Reintegration Challenges in Educational Settings* (p. 202), by E. Clark, 1997, Austin, TX: Pro-Ed, Inc. Reprinted with permission.

The initial individualized education programs (IEPs) for students with brain injuries should be written for short periods of time, perhaps six to eight weeks. Moreover, these IEPs should be reviewed often to make adjustments based on the progress and growth of students. Often, students improve dramatically in the first year following their injuries. Children and youth with TBI generally experience the most gains in the first year following the injury and make little progress thereafter. Flexibility and responsiveness on the part of teachers and other support staff are essential to the well-being of students with traumatic and acquired brain injuries.

INCLUSION AND COLLABORATION THROUGH THE LIFE SPAN

PEOPLE WITH TRAUMATIC OR ACQUIRED BRAIN INJURY

EARLY CHILDHOOD YEARS

Tips for the Family

- Become fully informed about your child's condition.
- Become familiar with special services available in your school and with systems of care.
- Develop positive relationships with care providers.
- Seek out appropriate assistance through advocacy and support groups.
- Pursue family or individual counseling for persistent relationship-centered problems.
- Develop sensible routines and schedules for the child.
- Communicate with siblings, friends, and relatives; help them become informed about the injury and their role in the treatment process.

Tips for the Preschool Teacher

- Communicate and collaborate with parents, special education personnel, and health care providers to develop appropriate expectations, management, and instruction.
- Interact frequently with parents, special education personnel, and health care providers.
- Watch for abrupt changes in the child's behavior. If they occur, notify parents and other professionals immediately.
- Involve socially sophisticated and sensitive peers and other older children in working with the preschooler with TBI.
- Become familiar with events that "set the child off."
- Use management procedures that promote appropriate independence and foster learning.

Tips for Preschool Personnel

- Participate in team meetings with the preschool teacher.
- Develop an understanding of the child and the condition.
- Communicate frequently with the preschool teacher and his or her parents about concerns and promising developments.
- Employ the same management strategies used by the parents and the preschool teacher.
- Be patient with the rate of progress behaviorally, socially, and academically.
- Help other children understand the child.

Tips for Neighbors and Friends

- Offer to become educated about the condition and its impact on the child.
- Become familiar with recommended management procedures for directing the child.
- Inform your own children about the dynamics of the condition; help them understand how to react and respond to variations in behavior.
- Involve the child in appropriate family activities.

ELEMENTARY YEARS

Tips for the Family

- Remember that the transition back to school and family environments requires very explicit planning and preparation.
- Communicate and collaborate regularly with all care providers.
- Prepare siblings, peers, and neighbors for the child's return to the home and community.
- Learn about and use management procedures that promote the child's well-being and growth.
- Carefully plan with school personnel the child's reentry into school.
- Establish functional routines and schedules of activity.

Tips for the General Education Classroom Teacher

- Become fully familiar with the child's condition.
- Communicate with medical and other personnel about expectations, management strategies, and approaches for dealing with persistant problems.
- Use appropriate routines and schedules to foster learning and good behavior.
- Help other children understand how they can contribute to the child's growth and healing within the classroom setting.
- Let peers and older youngsters work with the student on academic and social tasks.
- Do not be reluctant to communicate and collaborate with other professionals and parents when problems arise.
- Remember that teamwork and coordination among caring professionals and parents is essential to the child's success.

Tips for School Personnel

- Become informed; seek to understand the unique characteristics of TBI.
- Behave as though the child were your own.
- Seek to understand and use instructional and management approaches that are well suited to the child's emerging strengths and challenges.
- Use the expertise that is available in the school and school system; collaborate with other specialists.

Tips for Neighbors and Friends

- Adopt an inclusive attitude about family and neighborhood events; invite the child or youth to join in family-centered activities, picnics, and holiday events.
- Learn how to respond effectively and confidently to the common problems that the child or youth may present.
- Communicate concerns and problems immediately in a compassionate fashion.

SECONDARY AND TRANSITION YEARS

Tips for the Family

- Prepare and plan for the secondary, transitional, and adult years.
- Work closely with school and adult services personnel in developing a transition plan.
- Develop a thoughtful and comprehensive transition plan that includes education, employment, housing, and use of leisure time.
- Become aware of all the services and resources that are available through state and national funding.
- Begin to develop plans for the individual's care and support over the lifespan.

Tips for the General Education Classroom Teacher

- Be sure that appropriate steps have been taken to prepare the youth to return to school and related activities.
- Realize that there will be significant changes in the youth's functioning—academically, socially, and behaviorally.
- Work closely with members of the multidisciplinary team in developing appropriate schooling and employment experiences.
- Report any changes in behavior immediately to parents and other specialists within the school.

Tips for School Personnel

- Determine what environmental changes need to be made.
- Employ teaching procedures that best fit the youth's current cognitive status and academic functioning.
- Consider having the youth gradually phased into a complete school day.
- Be prepared for anger, depression, and rebellion.
- Focus on the youth's current and emerging strengths.
- Help the youth develop appropriate compensatory skills.

Tips for Neighbors, Friends, and Potential Employers

- Remember that the injury may, and probably will, significantly alter the youth's personality and functioning in many areas.
- Involve the youth in appropriate family, neighborhood, and community activities, particularly youth activities and parties.
- Use successful management procedures employed in the home and school settings.
- Become informed about the youth's capacities and interests.
- Work with vocational and special education personnel in providing employment explorations and part-time employment.

ADULT YEARS

Tips for the Family

- Begin developing appropriate independence skills throughout the school years.
- Determine early what steps can be taken to prepare the youth for meaningful part-time or full-time employment.
- Become thoroughly familiar with postsecondary education opportunities and adult services for individuals with disabilities.
- Explore various living and housing options early in the youth's secondary school years.
- Provide opportunities for the young adult to experience different kinds of living arrangements.

Tips for Neighbors, Friends, and Employers

- Keep up a spirit of neighborliness.
- Create opportunities for the adult to be involved in age-relevant activities, including movies, sports events, going out to dinner, and so on.
- Work closely with educational and adult support services personnel in creating employment opportunities, monitoring performance on the job, and making appropriate adjustments.

TABLE 14.3

Representative Strategies for Developing Cognitive-Communicative Skills

	IMPAIRMENT	CLASSROOM BEHAVIORS	SKILLS AND TEACHING STRATEGIES
General Behaviors	Decreased judgment	Is impulsive	Establish a system of verbal or nonverbal signs to cue the student to alter behavior (e.g., call the student's name, touch the student, use a written sign or hand signal)
Social Behaviors	Rudeness, silliness, immaturity	Makes nasty or inappropriate comments to fellow students and teachers; laughs aloud during serious discussions or quiet seat work	Help the student develop better judgment by presenting "what if" situations and choices. Discuss the student's responses together; give the student opportunities to verbally express judgment and decision making regarding appropriate behavior, as well as opportunities to role-play such behaviors
Expressive Language	Word retrieval errors	Answers using many vague terms ("this," "that," "those things," "whatchamacallits"); has difficulty providing answers in fill-in-the-blank tests	To improve word recall, teach the student to use association skills and to give definitions of words he or she cannot recall; teach memory strategies
Receptive Language	Inability to read nonverbal cues	Is unaware that the teacher or other classmates do not want to be bothered while they are working	To raise social awareness, use preestablished nonverbal cues to alert the student that the behavior is inappropriate; explain what was wrong with the behavior and what would have been appropriate.
Written Language	Simplistic sentence structure and syntactic disorganization	Uses sentences and chooses topics that are simplistic compared with expectations for age and grade; writes themes that are short and dry	Provide the student with worksheets that focus on vocabulary, grammar, and proofreading skills

SOURCE: Adapted from "Creating an Effective Classroom Environment," by J. L. Blosser and R. De-Pomei in *Educational Dimensions of Acquired Brain Injury,* ed., R. C. Savage and G. F. Wolcott, 1994, pp. 413–451. Austin, TX: Pro-Ed, Inc. Reprinted by permission.

For students who want to move on to postsecondary education, interdisciplinary team members may contribute significantly to the transition process. Critical factors include the physical accessibility of the campus, living arrangements, support for academic achievement, social and personal support systems, and career/vocational training and placement.

Some individuals with TBI are greatly assisted by software programs that allow them to operate computers with speech sounds and commands to produce letters, graphic materials, presentations, and spreadsheets.

For students who might find it difficult to continue their schooling after high school, transition planning for employment is essential. Prior to leaving high school, these students with TBI should have skills associated with filling out job applications, interviewing for jobs, and participating in supervised work experiences. State vocational agencies also play key roles in assisting young people with TBI following high school. They provide services related to aptitude assessment, training opportunities after high school, and trial job placements.

Collaboration and cooperation are the key factors in achieving success with individuals who have traumatic and acquired brain injuries. A great deal can be accomplished when families, students, and care providers come together, engage in appropriate planning, and work collaboratively (Cope & Reynolds, 2005).

FIGURE 14.5

Classroom Strategies for Children and Youth with TBI

- **Study Guide or Content Outline.** Students may need an outline to follow so they can anticipate content.

- **Pictures or Visual Cues.** Signals are a good way to alert students that they need to do something differently.

- **Systematic Verbal Rehearsal.** Students may have to "practice" a verbal cue and what is expected of them.

- **Homework Assignment Book.** All assignments will need to be written down because of poor short-term memory.

- **Teach Memory Strategies.** Students may need to learn memory tricks such as mnemonics, pictures, or limericks.

- **Scribe or Note-Taker.** Classmates may want to take turns taking good notes and having them photocopied at the end of class to give to the student. TBI victims often can listen but cannot take notes and listen at the same time.

- **Recognition vs. Recall.** Do not assume, when students recognize information, that they recall how it fits into the big picture. Check for understanding.

- **Modify Work Amounts.** Because focusing may be a serious problem, shorten assignments to the minimum necessary. Increase assignments gradually if the students are successful.

- **Alternative Forms of Expression.** General statements and satire may go right over their heads. Be very specific and to the point.

- **Provide Feedback on Responses.** Always state that an answer is correct or needs more input. The students may not pick up on a smile or nod that would be affirming.

- **Classroom Aides.** It is often necessary to hire a classroom aide to help a student stay on task, organize, and plan homework.

- **Assist with Confusion.** Watch for the confused look. These students are not likely to raise their hands and ask questions.

- **Avoid Over-Reactions.** These students may ask the same question over and over because of poor short-term memory. Be patient. Repeat as needed.

- **Accept Inconsistencies in Performance.** These students may do very well on, say, Tuesday. This raises the bar for expectations. Remember that they may not be able to do this well the rest of the week.

- **Routine and Schedule.** Be prepared for problems if there is a late start, a substitute teacher, early dismissal, or shortened classes. Changes do not come easy to students with TBI.

- **Behavior Management Strategy.** Have a plan in mind for misbehavior. The regular plan may not work well. Preferably, talk with students ahead of time and let them know how you plan to discipline them.

- **Simple, Concrete Language.** Use short sentences that are to the point. Try to keep directions down to as few steps as possible.

- **Alert to Transitions.** State that the bell is going to ring in 5 minutes and that they should begin putting things away in an orderly fashion. It may help to state which class is next.

- **Communication Book.** While students are given time to do homework at the end of class, it would be good to communicate with parents how things are going in class, to note positives, and to discuss areas that need work.

SOURCE: Adapted from *TBI Classroom Strategies,* by Barbara Pytel. Retrieved from http://educationalissues.suite101.com/article.cfm/tbi_classroom_strategies

FOCUS REVIEW

FOCUS 1 Identify three key elements of traumatic brain injury.

- The brain is damaged by external forces that cause tearing, bruising, or swelling.

- Both primary and secondary injuries dramatically influence the individual's functioning in several areas, including psychosocial behavior, speech and language, cognitive performance, vision and hearing, and motor abilities.

- The brain injury often results in permanent disabilities.

FOCUS 2 Cite four general characteristics of individuals with traumatic or acquired brain injuries.

- Individuals with traumatic or acquired brain injuries often exhibit cognitive deficits, including problems with memory, concentration, attention, and problem solving.

- Speech and language problems are frequently evident, including word retrieval problems, slurred or unintelligible speech, and aphasia.

- These individuals may also present social and behavioral problems, including increased irritability, inability to

- suppress or manage socially inappropriate behaviors, low thresholds for frustration, and insensitivity to others.
- Neuromotor and physical problems may also be present, including impairments in eye–hand coordination, vision and hearing deficits, and paralysis.

FOCUS 3 Identify the most common causes of brain injury in children, youth, and adults.

- The most common causes of brain injury in young children are falls, neglect, and physical abuse.
- For children in the elementary grades, the most common causes are falls, pedestrian or bicycle accidents involving a motor vehicle, and sports.
- For high school students and adults, the most common causes are motor vehicle accidents and sports-related injuries.

FOCUS 4 Identify four common types of head injuries.

- Common head injuries include concussions, contusions, skull fractures, and epidural and subdural hemorrhages.

FOCUS 5 Describe five important elements of medical treatment for individuals with traumatic or acquired brain injuries.

- The first stage, acute care, is directed at preserving the individual's life, addressing swelling and bleeding, and minimizing complications.
- Once the individual regains consciousness or can benefit from more active therapies, the relearning of preinjury skills begins.

- The second stage, rehabilitation, focuses on preparing the individual to return to home, school, or work settings and on readying the individual to work with other health care and training providers.
- The last stage, community intergration, is also characterized by the provision of psychological services directed at helping individuals and their families cope with the injuries and their effects in home, school, community, and work settings.
- Throughout all the stages of treatment, interdisciplinary collaboration and cooperation are essential to the individual's success.

FOCUS 6 Describe the focus of educational interventions for individuals with traumatic or acquired brain injuries.

- Educational interventions are directed at improving the general behaviors of the individual, including problem solving, planning, and developing insight; at building appropriate social behaviors such as working with others, suppressing inappropriate behaviors, and using appropriate etiquette; at developing expressive and receptive language skills, such as retrieving words, describing events, and understanding instructions; and at developing writing skills.
- Other academic skills relevant to the students' needs and developmental level of functioning are also taught.
- Transition planning for postsecondary education and training is also essential to the well-being of the individual with traumatic or acquired brain injury.

BUILDING YOUR PORTFOLIO

If you are thinking about a career in special education, you should know that many states use national standards developed by the Council for Exceptional Children (CEC) to assess a teacher candidate's knowledge and skills for working with students with disabilities. See a complete listing of the ten CEC Content Standards on the inside front cover of this text.

CEC Content Standards Addressed in This Chapter

1 Foundations
2 Development and Characteristics of Learners
3 Individual Learning Differences
5 Learning Environments and Social Interactions
7 Instructional Planning
8 Assessment

Assess Your Knowledge of the CEC Standards Addressed in This Chapter

Some states require that teacher candidates develop a portfolio of products that demonstrate mastery of the CEC content standards. To

assist in the development of products for this portfolio, you may wish to complete the following activities.

- Complete a written test of the chapter's content.

  If your instructor requires a written test of your content knowledge for this chapter, keep a copy for your portfolio. A practice test on the information covered in this chapter is available through the companion website (college.hmco.com/pic/hardman9e) and the Student Study Guide.

- Respond to the Application Questions for the Case Study "F. T."

  Review the Case Study and respond in writing to the application questions. Keep a copy of the Case Study and of your written response for your portfolio.

- Participate in a community service learning activity.

  Community service is a valuable way to enhance your learning experience. Visit our companion website for suggested community service learning activities that correspond to the information presented in this chapter. Develop a reflective journal of the service learning experience for your portfolio.

WEB RESOURCES

National Information Center for Children and Youth with Disabilities (NICHCY)

http://www.nichcy.org

This is a national center committed to providing caregivers, parents, professionals, and educators with valuable information on disabilities and related issues.

Brain Injury Association of America

http://www.biausa.org

This website is a comprehensive source of information for individuals and families who are interested in learning more about brain injuries. The association consists of a national network of more than 40 state organizations that work together for the benefit of individuals who have brain injuries.

ABLEDATA

http://www.abledata.com

This website is a premier source for information about assistive technologies for children, youth, and adults. It is sponsored by the National Institute on Disability and Rehabilitation Research, U.S. Department of Education. The website describes a vast array of software and assistive devices that are useful to individuals with disabilities.

Family Caregiver Alliance

http://www.caregiver.org

The Family Caregiver Alliance focuses on helping families provide long-term care, at home, to individuals with disabilities and other challenging conditions. This website provides helpful information about caring for loved ones with Alzheimer's disease, stroke, traumatic brain injuries, and other debilitating cognitive disorders.

National Institute of Disability Management and Research

http://www.nidmar.ca

The National Institute of Disability Management and Research, a Canadian organization, focuses on workplace reintegration. The institute seeks to help workers return to meaningful employment through training and education.

Tbihome.org

http://www.tbihome.org/index.html

This peer-support website is for individuals with brain injury and their families and friends. The site offers stories, poems, galleries, and links to other helpful sites for individuals with TBIs.

FURTHER READINGS

Rocchio, C. (2004). *Ketchup on the Baseboard: Rebuilding Life after Brain Injury*. Wake Forest, NC: Lash and Associates Publishing/Training.

A wonderfully personal book written by a mother whose son sustained a severe head injury. She chronicles his growth and progress over twenty years, carefully sharing his road to recovery and the ongoing changes required of her and other family members to support and sustain his progress over time.

Ashley, M. J. (2004). *Traumatic Brain Injury: Rehabilitative Treatment and Case Management* (2nd ed.). Boca Raton, FL: CRC Press.

This second edition is a comprehensive source book for educators, psychologists, case managers, and others interested in issues and treatment of individuals with TBI. The book is carefully designed with outlines at the beginning of each chapter—a convenient means for assessing interest in the chapter and finding personally relevant information.

Silver, J., Yudofsky, S. C., & Hales, R. E. (2004). *Neuropsychiatry of Traumatic Brain Injury*. Arlington VA: American Psychiatric Publishing.

This edited book contains twenty-four chapters that describe various aspects of traumatic brain injury. Chapters include topics dealing with prevention, children and adolescents, assessment, personality changes, and various forms of treatment.

Westwood, P. S. (2003). *Commonsense Methods for Children with Special Educational Needs: Strategies for the Regular Classroom*. New York: RoutledgeFalmer.

This book is packed with strategies, not only for children and youth with traumatic brain injuries, but for persons with other disabling conditions. As its title implies, this book is designed for those who work in general education classrooms and settings.

Bruce, S., Gurdin, L. S., & Savage, R. (2006). *Strategies for Managing Challenging Behaviors of Students with Brain Injuries*. Wake Forest, NC: Lash and Associates Publishing/Training.

This is a manual for therapists and teachers who work with children with brain injuries. It provides a wealth of knowledge and resources for understanding and responding effectively to demanding and difficult behaviors.

COMPANION WEBSITE

Visit the companion website at college.hmco.com/pic/hardman9e for additional resources that support this text:

- HM Video Cases that present actual classroom scenarios that you may face every day as a teacher

- Practice ACE Exams that will help you prepare for quizzes, tests, and certfication exams

- Flashcards of key terms

- Weblinks

15

Hearing Loss

TO BEGIN WITH . . .

QUICK FACTS

Nearly 11 million people in the United States (6% of the population) have a significant irreversible hearing loss. Of those with a hearing loss, about 1 million are deaf. American Sign Language is the third most used language in the United States after English and Spanish. The first and oldest American school for the deaf was founded in 1817 in Hartford, Connecticut. Today, there are nearly 72,000 students between the ages of 6 and 21 with hearing impairments served under the Individuals with Disabilities Education Act in America's schools. Gallaudet University in Washington, DC, the world's only university in which all programs and services are specifically designed to accommodate students who are deaf or hard of hearing, has 1,850 enrolled students. Gallaudet was founded in 1864 by an act of Congress, and its charter was signed by President Abraham Lincoln. (Deaf World Web, 2006; U.S. Department of Education, 2006)

ARE MUSIC FANS LOSING THEIR HEARING?

In 1989, Pete Townshend admitted that he had sustained "very severe hearing damage." Since then, Neil Young, Beatles producer George Martin, Sting, Ted Nugent and Jeff Beck have all discussed their hearing problems. Fleetwood Mac drummer Mick Fleetwood first noticed that he was having trouble hearing conversations in crowded rooms about twelve years ago. "The world's worst is when you find yourself going like Mother Hubbard and cupping your hand behind your ear," says Fleetwood. "I was a major glutton for volume: 'Gotta feel it, gotta hear it.' Sooner or later you're going to pay . . . ." More than 28 million Americans currently have some degree of hearing loss, according to the National Institute on Deafness, and as baby boomers age, the number is expected to climb to as high as 78 million by 2030. For the iPod generation, the trouble could be worse. Twenty-two million American adults own an iPod or other digital-music player, and studies show that sustained listening, even at moderate volume, can cause serious harm. (Ringen, 2006)

STRIKE THREE . . . Y'ER OUT!!

Oblivious to jeering or cheering fans and focused on the slight movement of the ball to the left or right, Peter Rozynski finds solace behind the home plate where he calls balls and strikes as he sees them. Rozynski, an umpire [who is deaf], officiates high school softball games in New Jersey. He graduated from the New Jersey School for the Deaf in West Trenton, New Jersey, in 1970. He played junior varsity and varsity baseball at the New Jersey School for the Deaf when he was a student. Rozynski has been an umpire since 1988. Rozynski said of being an umpire, "The proper handling of any softball game demands me to hustle at all times. In addition, three factors are essential to my success: judgment, mechanics and techniques, and knowledge of the rules." There have been a few controversial calls and Rozynski has had to tell coaches to put the call behind them and move on. (Feldman, 2006)

1. Describe how sound is transmitted through the human ear.

2. Distinguish between the terms *deaf* and *hard of hearing*.

3. Why is it important to consider age of onset and anatomical site when defining a hearing loss?

4. What are the estimated prevalence and the causes of hearing loss?

5. Describe the basic intelligence, speech and language skills, educational achievement, and social development associated with people who are deaf or hard of hearing.

6. Identify four approaches to teaching communication skills to persons with a hearing loss.

7. Describe the uses of closed-caption television, computers, and the Internet for people with a hearing loss.

8. Why is the early detection of hearing loss so important?

9. Distinguish between an otologist and an audiologist.

10. Identify factors that may affect the social inclusion of people who are deaf into the hearing world.

▼ SNAPSHOT

TAMIKA

Tamika Catchings is the all-star forward for the W.N.B.A.'s Indiana Fever [and top overall vote-getter for the 2006 W.N.B.A all-star game]. . . . She proudly admits to being an organization freak—in high school she would plan her outfits a month in advance. [Tamika] speaks with a slight speech impediment, as if she hadn't quite come out from under a shot of Novocain. She was born with fairly severe hearing loss in both ears, so she cannot hear certain tones, pitches or sounds, like "ch" and "th," even in her own voice, an impairment that for years she tried, quite successfully, to hide from anyone outside her family. In third grade, fed up with the abuse from classmates, she tossed her hearing aids into a field and refused to wear new ones.

[Tamika's] hearing problem forced her to learn to read lips, which has left her with the habit of looking intently at anyone who is speaking to her (except while driving). For a professional athlete who was a four-time all-American in both high school and college, she can be surprisingly deferential. When Van Chancellor, the coach of the United States national women's basketball team, chewed out Catchings in practice by informing her that great players have to back on defense, Catchings wrote him a letter thanking him for thinking of her as a great player.

Almost every program in the country recruited her, and Catchings wrote thank-you notes to each of the 200 schools that contacted her. ("For me not to say anything would have been selfish," she says.) But she had wanted to go to [the University of] Tennessee since eighth grade, when she caught a glimpse of the Lady Vols coach, Pat Summitt, on TV. Summitt is perhaps the one on-court presence in basketball who is more intense than [Tamika]—she has been known to dent her rings by pounding her hands on the hardwood during a particularly trying game. She also demands that her players buy daily planners and schedule their days in minute increments.

[Tamika] had a rough start in Knoxville. "When I would say anything to her in practice, it would break her heart," Summitt recalls. Soon, however, Catchings bloomed under Summitt's exacting system. She already possessed a remarkably well-rounded game . . . but Summitt required Catchings to learn to play at more than one speed. "We had to slow her down," Summitt says.

Summitt also discovered that her star freshman wasn't comprehending much of what she was being told, especially in loud arenas when she was standing behind the coach. (As they returned to the court after a time-out, [Tamika] would ask a teammate to repeat what Summitt had said.) Summitt asked Catchings to start using a hearing aid. The difference on-court was minimal—"Everything was just magnified," [Tamika] says—but those around her noticed an immediate change in her confidence and ability to communicate. "It made a huge difference," Harvey Catchings says. For the first time in ten years, she could hear herself speak clearly.

SOURCE: "Elevated: Tamika Catchings Will Not Let Her Niceness, or Her Deafness, Prevent Her from Becoming the Best Player in the W.N.B.A.," by M. Adams, *New York Times Magazine,* May 25, 2003, pp. 26–29. Copyright © 2003, Mark Adams.

Although Tamika from the opening Snapshot is unable to hear many sounds, her life is one of independence, success, and fulfillment. For Tamika, just as for many people who are deaf or hard of hearing, the obstacles presented by the loss of hearing are not insurmountable.

In a world often controlled by sound and spoken language, the ability to hear and speak can be an important link in the development of human communication. Children who can hear learn to talk by listening to those around them. Everyday communication systems depend on sound. What, then, would it be like to live in a world that is silent? People talk, but you hear nothing. The television and movie screens are lit up with moving pictures, but you can't hear and understand what is going on. Your friends talk about their favorite music and hum tunes that have no meaning to you. A fire engine's siren wails as it moves through traffic, but you are oblivious to its warning. To people with hearing, the thought of such a world can be very frightening. To those without hearing, it is quite simply their world—a place that one day can be lonely, frustrating, and downright discriminatory, and in the next bring joy, fulfillment, and a life of endless possibilities no different from that experienced by "hearing people." Even so, the National Academy on an Aging Society (2006) indicated that compared to those with "normal" hearing, people with a hearing loss are less likely to participate in social activities; are less satisfied with their life; express greater dissatisfaction with their friendships, family life, health, and financial situation; are less healthy; and are underemployed.

People with a hearing loss are able to learn about the world around them in any number of ways, such as lipreading, gestures, pictures, and writing. Some people are able to use their residual hearing with the assistance of a hearing aid. For others, a hearing aid doesn't help because it only makes distorted sounds louder. To express themselves, some people prefer to use their voices; others prefer to use a visual sign language. Most people with a hearing loss use a combination of speech and signing. People with a hearing loss, such as Tamika from our opening snapshot, may seek and find success in the hearing world. Others seek to be part of a Deaf community or Deaf culture to share a common language (American Sign Language) and customs. In a Deaf culture, those within the community share a common heritage and traditions. People often marry others from within the community. They also have a shared literature and participate in the Deaf community's political, business, arts, and sports programs. People in the Deaf community do not see the loss of hearing as a disability. From their perspective, being deaf is not an impairment and should not be looked upon as a pathology or disease that requires treatment.

The Hearing Process

➤ **Audition**

The act or sense of hearing.

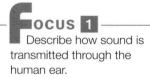

FOCUS **1**
Describe how sound is transmitted through the human ear.

Audition is the act or sense of hearing. The auditory process involves the transmission of sound through the vibration of an object to a receiver. The process originates with a vibrator—such as a string, reed, membrane, or column of air—that causes displacement of air particles. To become sound, a vibration must have a medium to carry it. Air is the most common carrier, but vibrations can also be carried by metal, water, and other substances. The displacement of air particles by the vibrator produces a pattern of circular waves that move away from the source.

This movement, which is referred to as a sound wave, can be illustrated by imagining the ripples resulting from a pebble dropped in a pool of water. Sound waves are patterns of pressure that alternately push together and pull apart in a spherical expansion. Sound waves are carried through a medium (e.g., air) to a receiver. The human ear is one of the most sensitive receivers there is; it is capable of being activated by incredibly small amounts of pressure and able to distinguish more than half a million different sounds. The ear is the mechanism through which sound is collected, processed, and transmitted to a specific area in the brain that decodes the sensations into meaningful language. The anatomy of the hearing mechanism is discussed in terms of the outer, middle, and inner ears. These structures are illustrated in Figure 15.1.

FIGURE 15.1

Structure of the Ear

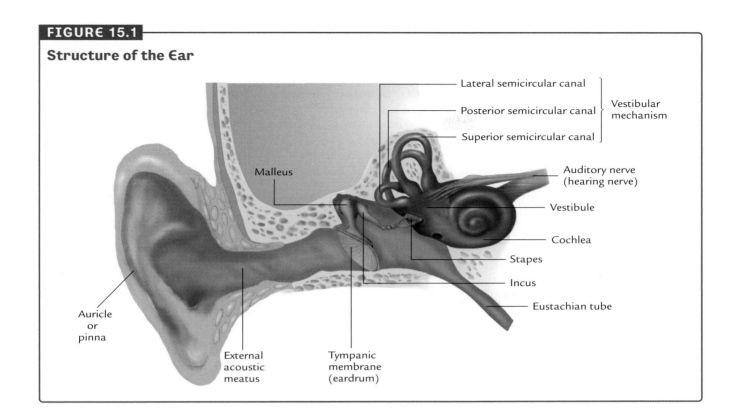

Lateral semicircular canal

Posterior semicircular canal — Vestibular mechanism

Superior semicircular canal

Malleus

Auditory nerve (hearing nerve)

Vestibule

Cochlea

Stapes

Incus

Eustachian tube

Auricle or pinna

External acoustic meatus

Tympanic membrane (eardrum)

The Outer Ear

The outer ear consists of a cartilage structure on the side of the head called the auricle, or pinna, and an outer ear canal referred to as the meatus. The only outwardly visible part of the ear, the auricle, is attached to the skull by three ligaments. Its purpose is to collect sound waves and funnel them into the meatus. The meatus secretes a wax called cerumen, which protects the inner structures of the ear by trapping foreign materials and lubricating the canal and eardrum. The eardrum, or tympanic membrane, is located at the inner end of the canal between the outer ear and middle ear. The concave membrane is positioned in such a manner that it can vibrate freely when struck by sound waves.

The Middle Ear

The inner surface of the eardrum is located in the air-filled cavity of the middle ear. This surface consists of three small bones that form the **ossicular chain**: the malleus, incus, and stapes, which are often referred to as the hammer, anvil, and stirrup because of similarities in shape to these common objects. The three bones transmit the vibrations from the external ear through the cavity of the middle ear to the inner ear.

The **eustachian tube**, extending from the throat to the middle-ear cavity, equalizes the air pressure on the eardrum with that of the outside by controlling the flow of air into the middle-ear cavity. Although air conduction is the primary avenue through which sound reaches the inner ear, conduction can also occur through the bones of the skull. Bone conduction is comparable to air conduction in that the patterns of displacement produced in the inner ear are similar.

The Inner Ear

The inner ear consists of a multitude of intricate passageways. The cochlea lies horizontally in front of the vestibule (a central cavity where sound enters directly from the middle ear), where it can be activated by movement in the ossicular chain. The cochlea is filled with fluid similar

Council for Exceptional Children

Standard 1: Foundations

Standard 2: Development and Characteristics of Learners

Standard 9: Professional and Ethical Practice

➤ **Ossicular chain**

The three small bones (malleus, incus, and stapes, or hammer, anvil, and stirrup) that transmit vibrations through the middle-ear cavity to the inner ear.

➤ **Eustachian tube**

A structure that extends from the throat to the middle-ear cavity and controls air flow into the cavity.

> **Vestibular mechanism**

A structure in the inner ear containing three semicircular canals filled with fluid. It is sensitive to movement and assists the body in maintaining equilibrium.

FOCUS **2**

Distinguish between the terms *deaf* and *hard of hearing*.

Council for Exceptional Children

Standard 1: Foundations

> **Hertz (Hz)**

A unit used to measure the frequency of sound in terms of the number of cycles that vibrating molecules complete per second.

> **Deafness**

A term used to describe individuals who have a hearing loss greater than 90 dB, have vision as their primary input, and cannot understand speech through the ear. As defined by IDEA, deafness means a hearing impairment that (1) is so severe that the child is impaired in processing linguistic information through hearing and (2) adversely affects educational performance.

> **Hard of hearing**

A term used to describe individuals whose hearing is deficient but somewhat functional.

in composition to cerebral spinal fluid. The cochlea contains highly specialized cells that translate vibrations into nerve impulses that are sent directly to the brain.

The other major structure within the inner ear is the **vestibular mechanism**, which contains the semicircular canals that control balance. The semicircular canals have enlarged portions at one end and are filled with fluid that responds to head movement. The vestibular mechanism integrates sensory input passing to the brain and assists the body in maintaining equilibrium. Motion and gravity are detected through this mechanism, allowing the individual to differentiate between sensory input associated with body movement and input coming from the external environment. Whenever the basic functions of the vestibular mechanism or any of the structures in the external, middle, and inner ear are interrupted, hearing loss may occur.

Definitions and Classification

Two terms, *deaf* and *partial hearing* (*or hard of hearing*), are commonly used to indicate the severity of a person's hearing loss. *Deaf* is often overused and misunderstood and is commonly applied to describe a wide variety of hearing loss. However, as discussed in this section, the term should be used in a more precise fashion.

Definitions

Deafness and hearing loss may be defined according to the degree of hearing impairment, which is determined by assessing a person's sensitivity to loudness (sound intensity) and pitch (sound frequency). The unit used to measure sound intensity is the decibel (dB); the range of human hearing is approximately 0 to 130 dB. Sounds louder than 130 dB (such as those made by jet aircraft at 140 dB) are extremely painful to the ear. Conversational speech registers at 40 to 60 dB, loud thunder at about 120 dB, and a rock concert at about 110 dB.

The frequency of sound is determined by measuring the number of cycles that vibrating molecules complete per second. The unit used to measure cycles per second is the **hertz (Hz).** The higher the frequency, the greater the measure in hertz. The human ear can hear sounds ranging from 20 to approximately 15,000 Hz. Speech sounds range in pitch from 300 to 4,000 Hz, whereas the pitches made by a piano keyboard range from 27.5 to 4,186 Hz. Although the human ear can hear sounds at the 15,000-Hz level, the vast majority of sounds in our environment range from 300 to 4,000 Hz.

DEAF AND HARD OF HEARING. Deafness describes people whose hearing loss is in the extreme: 90 dB or greater. Even with the use of hearing aids or other forms of amplification, for people who are deaf the primary means for developing language and communication is through the visual channel. **Deafness**, as defined by the Individuals with Disabilities Education Act (IDEA), means "a hearing impairment which is so severe that the child is impaired in processing linguistic information through hearing, with or without amplification, which adversely affects educational performance" (IDEA, 34 C.F.R. 300.7).

A person who is deaf is most often described as someone who cannot hear sound. Consequently, the individual is unable to understand human speech. Many people who are deaf have enough residual hearing to recognize sound at certain frequencies, but they still may be unable to determine the meaning of the sound pressure waves.

For persons defined as **hard of hearing**, audition is deficient but remains somewhat functional. Individuals who are hard of hearing have enough residual hearing that, with the use of a hearing aid, they are able to process human speech auditorily.

The distinction between deaf and hard of hearing, based on the functional use of residual hearing, is not as clear as many traditional definitions imply. New breakthroughs in the development of hearing aids, as well as improved diagnostic procedures, have enabled many children labeled deaf to use their hearing functionally under limited circumstances.

In addition to the individual's sensitivity to loudness and pitch, two other factors are involved in defining deafness and hard of hearing: the age of onset and the anatomical site of the loss.

AGE OF ONSET. Hearing loss may be present at birth (congenital) or acquired at any time during life. **Prelingual loss** occurs prior to the age of 2, or before out speech development. **Postlingual loss** occurs at any age following speech acquisition. In nine out of ten children, deafness occurs at birth or prior to the child's learning to speak. The distinction between a congenital and an acquired hearing loss is important. The age of onset will be a critical variable in determining the type and extent of interventions necessary to minimize the effect of the individual's disability. This is particularly true in relation to speech and language development. A person who is born with hearing loss has significantly more challenges, particularly in the areas of communication and social adaptation (Centers for Disease Control, 2006; Magnuson, 2000).

ANATOMICAL SITE OF THE HEARING LOSS. In terms of anatomical location, the two primary types of hearing loss are peripheral problems and central auditory problems. There are three types of peripheral hearing loss: conductive, sensorineural, and mixed. A **conductive hearing loss** results from poor conduction of sound along the passages leading to the sense organ (inner ear). The loss may result from a blockage in the external canal, as well as from an obstruction interfering with the movement of the eardrum or ossicle. The overall effect is a reduction or loss of loudness. A conductive loss can be offset by amplification (hearing aids) and medical intervention. Surgery has proved to be effective in reducing a conductive loss or even in restoring hearing.

A **sensorineural hearing loss** results from an abnormal sense organ and a damaged auditory nerve. A sensorineural loss may distort sound, affecting the clarity of human speech, and cannot presently be treated adequately through medical intervention. A sensorineural loss is generally more severe than a conductive loss and is permanent. Losses of greater than 70 dB are usually sensorineural and involve severe damage to the inner ear. One common way to determine whether a loss is conductive or sensorineural is to administer an air and bone conduction test. An individual with a conductive loss would be unable to hear a vibrating tuning fork held close to the ear, because of blocked air passages to the inner ear, but may be able to hear the same fork applied to the skull just as well as someone with normal hearing would. An individual with a sensorineural loss would not be able to hear the vibrating fork, regardless of its placement. This test is not always accurate, however, and must therefore be used with caution in distinguishing between conductive and sensorineural losses. **Mixed hearing loss**, a combination of conductive and sensorineural problems, can also be assessed through the use of an air and bone conduction test. In the case of a mixed loss, abnormalities are evident in both tests.

Although most hearing losses are peripheral, as are conductive and sensorineural problems, some occur where there is no measurable peripheral loss. This type of loss, which is referred to as a central auditory disorder, occurs when there is a dysfunction in the cerebral cortex. The cerebral cortex, the outer layer of gray matter of the brain, governs thought, reasoning, memory, sensation, and voluntary movement. Consequently, a central auditory problem is not a loss in the ability to hear sound but a disorder of symbolic processes, including auditory perception, discrimination, comprehension of sound, and language development (expressive and receptive).

Classification

Hearing loss may be classified according to the severity of the condition. The symptom severity classification system shown in Table 15.1 presents information relative to a child's ability to understand speech patterns at the various severity levels.

Classification systems based solely on a person's degree of hearing loss should be used with a great deal of caution when determining appropriate services and supports. These systems do not reflect the person's capabilities, background, or experience; they merely suggest parameters for measuring a physical defect in auditory function. As a young child, for example, Tamika from the opening snapshot was diagnosed as having a hearing loss in both ears, yet throughout her life she successfully adjusted to both school and community experiences. She went on to college and now has a successful career as a professional basketball player in the W.N.B.A. Clearly, many factors beyond the severity of the hearing loss must be assessed when determining an individual's potential. In addition to severity of loss, factors such as general intelligence,

➤ **Prelingual loss**
Pertaining to hearing impairments occurring before the age of 2 or before the time of speech development.

➤ **Postlingual loss**
Pertaining to hearing impairments occurring at any age following speech development.

➤ **Conductive hearing loss**
A hearing loss resulting from poor conduction of sound along the passages leading to the sense organ.

➤ **Sensorineural hearing loss**
A hearing loss resulting from an abnormal sense organ (inner ear) and a damaged auditory nerve.

➤ **Mixed hearing loss**
A hearing loss resulting from a combination of conductive and sensorineural problems.

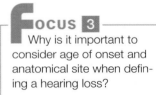

FOCUS **3**
Why is it important to consider age of onset and anatomical site when defining a hearing loss?

TABLE 15.1

Classification of Hearing Loss

HEARING LOSS IN DECIBELS (dB)	CLASSIFICATION	EFFECT ON ABILITY TO UNDERSTAND SPEECH
0–15	Normal hearing	None
16–25	Slight hearing loss	Minimal difficulty with soft speech
26–40	Mild hearing loss	Difficulty with soft speech
41–55	Moderate hearing loss	Frequent difficulty with normal speech
56–70	Moderate to severe hearing loss	Occassional difficulty with loud speech
71–90	Severe hearing loss	Frequent difficulty with loud speech
> 91	Profound hearing loss	Near total or total loss of hearing

emotional stability, scope and quality of early education and training, the family environment, and the occurrence of other disabilities must also be considered.

Prevalence

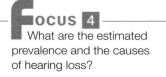

Focus 4
What are the estimated prevalence and the causes of hearing loss?

Council for Exceptional Children

Standard 2: Development and Characteristics of Learners

Hearing loss gets worse over time and increases dramatically with age. Estimates of hearing loss in the United States go as high as 28 million people. Of these 28 million, approximately 11 million people have significant irreversible hearing loss, and 1 million are deaf. Only 5% of people with hearing loss are under the age of 17, and nearly 43% are over the age of 65. Contrast this to the fact that only 12% of the general population is over the age of 65 years (Centers for Disease Control, 2006; National Academy on an Aging Society, 2006). Men are more likely than women to have a hearing loss; Caucasians are proportionately overrepresented among people with a hearing loss; and the prevalence of hearing loss decreases as family income and education increase (National Academy on an Aging Society, 2006).

The U.S. Department of Education (2006) indicated that 71,964 students defined as having a hearing impairment and between the ages of 6 and 21 are receiving special education services in the United States. These students account for approximately 1.5% of school-age students identified as having a disability. It is important to note that these figures represent only those students who receive special services; a number of students with hearing loss who could benefit from additional services do not receive them. Of the students with a hearing loss receiving special education, 38% were being served in general education classrooms for at least 80% of the school day. This is nearly double the number of students in these classrooms a decade ago. Another 43% spent at least a part of their day in a general education classroom, 7% in separate public or private day schools for students with a hearing loss, and 9% in public or private residential living facilities (U.S. Department of Education, 2006).

Causation

Council for Exceptional Children

Standard 8: Assessment

A number of congenital (existing at birth) or acquired factors may result in a hearing loss. Approximately one in a thousand children is born deaf because of factors associated with heredity, maternal rubella or German measles, or drugs taken during pregnancy. Substance abuse, disease, and constantly being subjected to loud noises are all causes of hearing loss. Loss of hearing is also a normal part of the aging process, beginning as early as the teen years when we lose some of the high-frequency hearing we had in childhood.

Congenital Factors

HEREDITY. Although more than 200 types of deafness have been related to hereditary factors, the cause of 33% of prelingual hearing loss remains unknown (Center for Assessment and Demograhic Studies, 2006). One of the most common diseases affecting the sense of hearing is **otosclerosis**. The cause of this disease is unknown, but it is generally believed to be hereditary and is manifested most often in early adulthood. About 10% of adults have otosclerosis, and it can be passed from one generation to the next but not manifest itself for several generations.

The disease is characterized by destruction of the capsular bone in the middle ear and the growth of web-like bone that attaches to the stapes. As a result, the stapes is restricted and unable to function properly. Hearing loss results in about 15% of all cases of otosclerosis and at a rate for females that is twice the rate for males. Victims of otosclerosis suffer from high-pitched throbbing or ringing sounds known as **tinnitus**, a condition associated with disease of the inner ear. There is no specific treatment or any medication that will improve the hearing in people with otosclerosis. Surgery (stapedectomy) may be recommended when the stapes (stirrup) bone is involved.

PRENATAL DISEASE. Several conditions, although not inherited, can result in sensorineural loss. The major cause of congenital deafness is infection, of which rubella, cytomegalovirus (CMV), and toxoplasmosis are the most common. The rubella epidemic of 1963–1965 dramatically increased the incidence of deafness in the United States. During the 1960s, approximately 10% of all congenital deafness was associated with women contracting rubella during pregnancy. For about 40% of the individuals who are deaf, the cause is rubella. About 50% of all children with rubella incur a severe hearing loss. Most hearing losses caused by rubella are sensorineural, although a small percentage may be mixed. In addition to hearing loss, children who have had rubella sometimes acquire heart disease (50%), cataracts or glaucoma (40%), and mental retardation (40%). Since the advent of the rubella vaccine, the elimination of this disease has become a nationwide campaign, and the incidence of rubella has dramatically decreased.

Congenital cytomegalovirus (CMV) is a viral infection that spreads by close contact with another person who is shedding the virus in body secretions. It is also spread by blood transfusions and from a mother to her newborn infant. CMV is the most frequently occurring virus among newborns; about 40,000 newborns contract the disease each year. CMV disease is characterized by jaundice, microcephaly, hemolytic anemia, mental retardation, hepatosplenomegaly (enlargement of the liver and spleen), and hearing loss. Although no vaccine is currently available to treat CMV, some preventive measures can be taken, such as ensuring safe blood transfusions and good hygiene and avoiding contact with persons who have the virus (Pediatric Bulletin, 2006). CMV is detectable in utero through amniocentesis.

Congenital toxoplasmosis infection is characterized by jaundice and anemia, but frequently the disease also results in central nervous system disorders (such as seizures, hydrocephalus, and microcephaly). Approximately 15% of infants born with this disease are deaf.

Other factors associated with congenital sensorineural hearing loss include maternal Rh-factor incompatibility and the use of ototoxic drugs. Maternal Rh-factor incompatibility does not generally affect a firstborn child, but as antibodies are produced during subsequent pregnancies, multiple problems can result, including deafness. Fortunately, deafness as a result of Rh-factor problems is no longer common. With the advent of an anti-Rh gamma globulin (RhoGAM) in 1968, the incidence of Rh-factor incompatibility has significantly decreased. If it is injected into the mother within the first 72 hours after the birth of the first child, she does not produce antibodies that harm future unborn infants.

Ototoxic drugs are so labeled because of their harmful effects on the sense of hearing. If taken during pregnancy, these drugs can result in a serious hearing loss in the infant. Congenital sensorineural loss can also be caused by congenital syphilis, maternal chicken pox, anoxia, and birth trauma.

A condition known as **atresia** is a major cause of congenital conductive loss. Congenital aural atresia results when the external auditory canal is either malformed or completely absent at birth. A congenital malformation may lead to a blockage of the ear canal through an accumulation of cerumen, which is a wax that hardens and blocks incoming sound waves from being transmitted to the middle ear.

➤ **Otosclerosis**

A disease of the ear characterized by destruction of the capsular bone in the middle ear and the growth of a web-like bone that attaches to the stapes. The stapes is restricted and unable to function properly.

➤ **Tinnitus**

High-pitched throbbing or ringing sounds in the ear, associated with disease of the inner ear.

➤ **Congenital cytomegalovirus (CMV)**

A viral infection that spreads by close contact with another person who is shedding the virus in body secretions.

➤ **Congenital toxoplasmosis infection**

A disease characterized by jaundice and anemia and often resulting in central nervous system disorders.

➤ **Atresia**

The absence of a normal opening or cavity.

Loud noise is a leading cause of hearing problems. Adolescents are subjected to damaging noise levels when headphones on CD, MP3, or DVD players are turned up too high.

Acquired Factors

POSTNATAL DISEASE. One of the most common causes of hearing loss in the postnatal period is infection. Postnatal infections—such as measles, mumps, influenza, typhoid fever, and scarlet fever—are all associated with hearing loss. Meningitis is an inflammation of the membranes that cover the brain and spinal cord and is a cause of severe hearing loss in school-age children. Sight loss, paralysis, and brain damage are further complications of this disease. The incidence of meningitis has declined, however, thanks to the development of antibiotics and chemotherapy.

➤ **Otitis media**
An inflammation of the middle ear.

Another common problem that may result from postnatal infection is known as **otitis media**, an inflammation of the middle ear. This condition, which results from severe colds that spread from the eustachian tube to the middle ear, is the most common cause of conductive hearing loss in younger children. Otitis media ranks second to the common cold as the most common health problem in preschool children. Three out of every four children have had at least one episode by the time they reach 3 years of age. The disease is difficult to diagnose, especially in infancy, at which time symptoms are often absent. Otitis media has been found to be highly correlated with hearing problems (National Institute on Deafness and Other Communication Disorders, 2006c).

ENVIRONMENTAL FACTORS. Environmental factors—including extreme changes in air pressure caused by explosions, physical abuse of the cranial area, impact from foreign objects during an accident, and loud music—also contribute to acquired hearing loss. Loud noise is rapidly becoming one of the major causes of hearing problems; about 30 million people are subjected to dangerous levels of noise in everyday life (National Institute on Deafness and Other Communication Disorders, 2006c). All of us are subjected to hazardous noise, such as noise from jet engines and loud music, more often than ever before. With the increasing use of headphones, such as those on portable compact disc or DVD players, many people (particularly adolescents) are subjected to damaging noise levels. Occupational noise (such as that from jackhammers, tractors, and sirens) is now the leading cause of sensorineural hearing loss. Other factors associated with acquired hearing loss include degenerative processes in the ear that may come with aging, cerebral hemorrhages, allergies, and intercranial tumors.

Focus 5
Describe the basic intelligence, speech and language skills, educational achievement, and social development associated with people who are deaf or hard of hearing.

Characteristics

The effects of hearing loss on the learning or social adjustment of individuals are extremely varied, ranging from far-reaching, as in the case of prelingual sensorineural deafness, to quite minimal, as in the case of a mild postlingual conductive loss. Fortunately, prevention, early detection, and intervention have recently been emphasized, resulting in a much improved prognosis for individuals who are deaf or hard of hearing.

Intelligence

Research on the intellectual characteristics of children with hearing loss has suggested that the distribution of IQ scores for these individuals is similar to that of hearing children (Marschark, Lang, & Albertini, 2002; Moores, 2001; Schirmer, 2000). Findings suggested that intellectual development for people with hearing loss is more a function of language development than of cognitive ability. Any difficulties in performance appear to be closely associated with speaking, reading, and writing the English language but are not related to level of intelligence. For example, children using sign language have to divide their attention between the signs and the instructional materials. Although the child may seem slower in learning, it may be that the child simply needs more time to process the information.

Speech and English Language Skills

Speech and English language skills are the areas of development most severely affected for those with a hearing loss, particularly for children who are born deaf. These children develop speech at a slower pace than their peers with normal hearing, and thus they are at greater risk for emotional difficulties and isolation from peers and family (Kaland & Salvatore, 2006). The effects of a hearing loss on English language development vary considerably. For children with mild and moderate hearing losses, the effect may be minimal. Even for individuals born with moderate losses, effective communication skills are possible because the voiced sounds of conversational speech remain audible. Although individuals with moderate losses cannot hear unvoiced sounds and distant speech, English language delays can be prevented if the hearing loss is diagnosed and treated early (Schirmer, 2000). The majority of people with hearing loss are able to use speech as the primary mode of English language acquisition.

For the person who is congenitally deaf, most loud speech is inaudible, even with the use of the most sophisticated hearing aids. These people are unable to receive information through speech unless they have learned to lip-read. Sounds produced by the person who is deaf may be extremely difficult to understand. Children who are deaf exhibit significant problems in articulation, voice quality, and tone discrimination. Even as early as 8 months of age, babies who are deaf appear to babble less than babies who can hear. One way to assist these babies in developing language is to provide early and extensive training in English language production and comprehension. Another approach is to teach them sign language long before they learn to speak. (See the Reflect on This, "A New Language for Baby" on page 400.)

Educational Achievement

The educational achievement of students with a hearing loss may be significantly delayed, compared to that of students who can hear. Students who are deaf or have a partial hearing loss have considerable difficulty succeeding in an educational system that depends primarily on the spoken word and written language to transmit knowledge. Low achievement is characteristic of students who are deaf (Marschark et al., 2002; Schirmer, 2000); they average 3 to 4 years below their age-appropriate grade levels. Reading is the academic area most negatively affected for students with a hearing loss. Any hearing loss, whether mild or profound, appears to have detrimental effects on reading performance (Gallaudet Research Institute, 2006). Students who are deaf obtain their highest achievement scores in reading during the first three years of school, but by third grade, reading performance is surpassed by both arithmetic and spelling performance. By the time students who are deaf reach adolescence (age 13), their reading performance is equivalent to that of about a third-grade child with normal hearing (Gallaudet Research Institute, 2006).

To counteract the difficulty with conventional reading materials, specialized instructional programs have been developed for students with a hearing loss (Marschark & Spencer, 2003; McNally Rose, Quigley, 2004). One such program is the Reading Milestones series (Quigley & King, 1985), which uses content that focuses on the interests and experiences of children with a hearing loss while incorporating linguistic controls: the careful pacing of new vocabulary, the clear identification of syntactic structures, and the movement from simple to complex in introducing new concepts (such as idioms, inferences). For more than two decades, Reading Milestones has been the most widely used reading program for students who are deaf.

Standard 2: Development and Characteristics of Learners

Standard 3: Individual Learning Differences

REFLECT ON THIS

A NEW LANGUAGE FOR BABY

Languishing in front of the tube, watching a gripping episode of *Teletubbies,* a baby of 10 months waves down Mom and signals for a bottle of the good stuff. No crying, no fuss. He just moves his hands in a pantomime of milking a cow—the international sign for *milk.* Mom smiles, signs back her agreement, and fetches Junior's bottle. No, this is not science fiction, but a portrayal of what's now possible at a U.S. university research facility where babies as young as 9 months old are taught sign language, long before they can speak. In a pilot program at Ohio State University, infants and their teachers learned to use a number of specific signs from American Sign Language to communicate with each other. Researcher Kimberlee Whaley says parents, when they think about it, won't be surprised to hear that children can communicate physically, before they can do so verbally. "Think of an infant raising his or her hands up in the air," says Ms. Whaley. "What does the baby want? To be picked up, and we all recognize that."

What we didn't recognize is that kids also have the cognitive ability, and the motor skills, to sign for simple words, such as *eat, more, stop,* and *share.*

It's almost spooky to think that babies who aren't even walking yet are capable of basic understanding and communication. That's not the half of it, says Dr. Whaley. She says it's not unusual for babies to teach the signs to adults who have forgotten them. It happened to Dr. Whaley when one baby girl indignantly reminded the researcher of the sign for *juice.* "I felt about two inches tall," said Dr. Whaley, an associate professor of human development and family science.

The sign language, she says, has allowed for much more effective communication between teachers and infants. "It is so much easier for our teachers to work with 12-month-olds who can sign that they want their bottle, rather than just cry and have us try to figure out what they want. This is a great way for infants to express their needs before they can verbalize them."

It's interesting, too, that some babies will grunt to be noticed and then use sign language to get more specific about what they want to say, she says.

The researchers are embarking on a larger, two-year study and hope to answer questions raised by the early study: How early can babies learn sign language? And is there a gender difference? Girls appear to learn or use sign language more easily. Dr. Whaley thinks children of 6 or 7 months, who are able to sit up on their own, will learn basic signs.

But what about at night? What happens to a hungry or wet baby when Mom and Dad are asleep? "They revert to crying," Dr. Whaley says.

SOURCE: "A New Language for Baby," by S. McKeen, *The Ottawa Citizen,* February 26, 1999. Retrieved October 4, 2006, from http://littlesigners.com/article3.html

When 20-year-old Terence Parkin arrived at the Sydney 2000 Olympic Games, his goal was to make his mark for South Africa and show the world what people who are deaf can accomplish. Terence, who was born with a severe hearing disability and uses sign language to communicate with his coach, achieved his goal by swimming to a silver medal in the 200-meter breaststroke. "I think it will confirm that deaf people can do things," he said afterwards. . . . "Other people will hopefully think now that we're just like other people. The only thing deaf people can't do is hear."

Social Development

A hearing loss modifies a person's capacity to receive and process auditory stimuli. People who are deaf or have a partial hearing loss receive a reduced amount of auditory information. That information is also distorted, compared to the auditory input received by those with normal hearing. Thus the perceptions of auditory information by people with a hearing loss, particularly those who are deaf, will differ from the those who can hear. Ultimately, this difference in perception has a direct effect on each individual's social adjustment to the hearing world.

ADJUSTMENT TO THE HEARING WORLD. Reviews of the literature on social and psychological development in children who are deaf have suggested that there are differences in development from that of children who can hear (Kaland & Salvatore, 2003; Scheetz, 2004). Different or delayed language acquisition may lead to more limited opportunities for social interaction. Children who are deaf may have more adjustment challenges when attempting to communicate with children who can hear. However, they appear to be more secure when conversing with peers who have a hearing loss.

THE DEAF CULTURE. For some people who are deaf, social isolation from the hearing world is not considered an adjustment problem. On the contrary, it is a natural state of being where people are bonded together by a common language, customs, and heritage. People in the

Council for Exceptional Children

Standard 5: Learning Environments and Social Interactions

DEBATE FORUM

LIVING IN A DEAF CULTURE

Deaf culture: a cultural group comprising persons who share similar and positive attitudes toward deafness. The "core Deaf culture" consists of those persons who have a hearing loss and who share a common language, values, and experiences and a common way of interacting with each other. The broader Deaf community is made up of individuals (both deaf and hearing) who have positive, accepting attitudes toward deafness which can be seen in their linguistic, social, and political behaviors. People in a Deaf culture seek each other out for social interaction and emotional support.

The inability to hear and understand speech may lead an individual to seek community ties and social relationships primarily with other individuals who are deaf. These individuals may choose to isolate themselves from hearing peers and to live, learn, work, and play in a social subculture known as "a Deaf culture or Deaf community."

POINT

The Deaf culture is a necessary and important component of life for many people who are deaf. The person who is deaf has a great deal of difficulty adjusting to life in a hearing world. Through the Deaf culture, he or she can find other individuals with similar problems, common interests, a common language (American Sign Language), and a common heritage and culture. Membership in the Deaf culture is an achieved status that must be earned by the individual who is deaf. The individual must demonstrate a strong identification with the Deaf world, understand and share experiences that come with being deaf, and be willing to participate actively in the Deaf community's educational, cultural, and political activities. The Deaf culture gives such persons a positive identity that can't be found among their hearing peers.

COUNTERPOINT

Participation in the Deaf culture only serves to isolate people who are deaf from those who hear. A separate subculture unnecessarily accentuates the differences between people who can and who cannot hear. The life of the person who is deaf need not be different from that of anyone else. Children who are deaf can be integrated into general education schools and classrooms. People who are deaf can live side by side with their hearing peers in local communities, sharing common bonds and interests. There is no reason why they can't participate together in the arts, enjoy sports, and share leisure and recreational interests. Membership in the Deaf culture will only further reinforce the idea that people who have disabilities should both grow up and live in a culture away from those who do not. The majority of people who are deaf do not seek membership in the Deaf culture. These people are concerned that the existence of such a community makes it all the more difficult for them to assimilate into society at large.

➤ **Deaf culture**

A culture where people who are deaf become bonded together by a common language (sign language), customs, and heritage and seek each other out for social interaction and emotional support.

Council for Exceptional Children

Standard 1: Foundations

Deaf culture seek each other out for social interaction and emotional support. The language of the culture is sign language, where communication is through hand signs, body language, and facial expressions. Sign language is not one universal language. American Sign Language (ASL) is different from Russian Sign Language (RSL), which is different from French Sign Language (FSL), and so on. ASL is not a form of English or of any other language. It has its own grammatical structure, which must be mastered in the same way as the grammar of any other language. (American Sign Language is discussed in greater detail later in this chapter.)

In addition to a common language, the Deaf culture also has it own unique set of interactive customs. For example, people value physical contact with one another even more than people in a hearing community. It is common to see visual and animated expressions of affection, such as hugs and handshakes in both greetings and departures. Regardless of the topic, discussions are frank, and there is no hesitation in getting to the point. Gatherings within the Deaf culture may last longer because people like to linger. This may be particularly true at a dinner, where it is perfectly okay to sign (talk) with your mouth full. It will obviously take longer to eat since it is difficult to sign and hold a knife and fork at the same time.

Within the Deaf community, the social identity of being a deaf person is highly valued, and there is a fierce internal loyalty. Everyone is expected to support activities within the Deaf culture, whether in sports, arts and literature, or political networks. The internal cohesion among the community's members includes a strong expectation that people will marry within the group. In fact, nine out of ten people in the Deaf culture marry others within the same community. This loyalty is so strong that deaf parents may hope for a deaf child in order to pass on the heritage and tradition of the Deaf culture to their offspring. Although hearing people may be welcomed within the Deaf community, they are seldom accepted as full members. (See the Debate Forum, "Living in a Deaf Culture" on page 401.)

Interdisciplinary Educational Services and Supports

In the United States, educational programs for children who are deaf or hard of hearing emerged in the early 19th century. The residential school for the deaf was the primary model for delivery of educational services; it was a live-in facility where students were segregated from the family environment. In the latter half of the 19th century, day schools were established in which students lived with their families while receiving an education in a special school exclusively for deaf students. As the century drew to a close, some public schools established special classes for children with a hearing loss within general education schools.

Council for Exceptional Children

Standard 5: Learning Environments and Social Interactions

Standard 7: Instructional Planning

The residential school continued to be a model for educational services well into the 20th century. However, with the introduction of electrical amplification, advances in medical treatment, and improved educational technology, more options became available within the public schools. Today, educational programs for students who are deaf or hard of hearing range from the residential school to inclusive education in a general education classroom with support services. For a more in-depth look at the importance of educational supports for students with hearing loss placed in general education settings, see the Case Study, "A Community of Learners."

Research strongly indicates that children with a hearing loss must receive early intervention as soon as possible if they are to learn the language skills necessary for reading and other academic subjects (Calderon & Naidu, 2000; Marschark et al., 2002). There is little disagreement that the education of the child with a hearing loss must begin at the time of the diagnosis. Educational goals for students with a hearing loss are comparable to those for students who can hear. The student with a hearing loss brings many of the same strengths and weaknesses to the classroom as the hearing student. Adjustment to learning experiences is often comparable for both groups, as well. Students with a hearing loss, however, face the formidable problems associated with being unable to communicate effectively with teachers and students who can hear. For more information on interacting with people who have a hearing loss, see this chapter's Inclusion and Collaboration Through the Lifespan.

CASE STUDY

A COMMUNITY OF LEARNERS

The Weld County School District 6 has housed the preschool through 12th-grade program for students who are deaf or hard of hearing at University Schools for more than 60 years. During this time, the school district has formed a strong working relationship with the professors from the Deaf Education program at the University of Northern Colorado. These mutually beneficial relationships have produced several innovative practices. For example, University Schools, in collaboration with the district, is one of a few programs in the United States that serves students who are deaf or hard of hearing using a co-enrollment model. This arrangement enables students who are deaf or hard of hearing to attend general education classrooms all day with their hearing peers. Two teachers— a general education teacher and a teacher of students who are deaf or hard of hearing—plan, teach, and share equal responsibility for the entire class throughout the day.

The 2002 to 2003 classroom contained 34 third- and fourth-grade students. Nine students had an individualized education program (IEP). Seven of the students who had IEPs were deaf or hard of hearing. Two hearing students also had IEPs. Eight students consistently performed well above grade level, three students were working below grade level, and the majority of students were on grade level in most academic areas. The two teachers both signed for themselves. There was no interpreter assigned to the classroom, although if interpreters had free time, they would often come into the classroom to help. Teachers conducted instruction using total communication—simultaneous sign and speech. The general education teacher had developed his signing skills by taking classes and by teaching in the co-taught classroom for the past six years.

When the co-taught program began, the school established the philosophy that it would strive to be a community of learners. The teachers knew that to establish such a community, everyone would need the skills to communicate with each other. To help students and teachers develop their signing skills, instruction in sign language was provided for all elementary-level students as a special, (like art, music, physical education, and Spanish). In addition, it has become well known throughout the school that sign and speech are used to communicate in this third- and fourth-grade classroom. Consequently, hearing students who had an interest in signing or who had been in the first- and second-grade co-taught classroom often asked to be placed in this class. The school believes that these actions, as well as interpreting at all school functions and expecting hearing students to sign for themselves, have been important ingredients in the development of a community of learners.

WELD'S TRANSFORMED LITERACY PROGRAM

The first major change implemented was to stop teaching reading, writing, and spelling as separate content areas. The teachers integrated these content areas into a single literacy block. Thus their literacy philosophy became "Read Like Writers and Write Like Readers." Literacy was taught every day from 7:55 until 11:00 a.m. Although this seemed like a large block of time for students to stay on task, they were often reluctant to stop for lunch.

Sustained Silent Reading. Each morning students were expected to read silently for 30 minutes. They could read from a variety of materials (fiction and nonfiction books, magazines, poetry, comics, or newspapers.) Also during this block of time, teachers had the opportunity to observe students reading or to have reading conferences with individual students or small groups of students.

Student Activities. The teachers used the remainder of the literacy block in a variety of ways. Activities included teacher-directed, whole-group reading, writing, and spelling lessons and time for students to work on individual or small-group projects. The end of the literacy block time was allocated for students to receive peer feedback on unfinished projects, present finished products to the class, reflect on what was learned through journal writing, and discuss what was learned in small- or whole-group settings.

Direct Instruction—with Accommodations. The initial teacher-directed lessons gave an overview of how reading comprehension strategies help readers understand what is being read. Each lesson included accommodations so that students who were deaf or hard of hearing had direct access to the information through graphic representations, closed captioning, or other aids. The teachers discovered that this practice was beneficial to all students.

APPLICATION

1. What does "a community of learners" mean in the schools at University Schools?
2. Why didn't the school assign interpreters to the classroom?
3. How did the school help students and teachers develop their signing skills?
4. What does the philosophy "Read Like Writers and Write Like Readers" mean to you?

SOURCE: Adapted from Wurst, D., Jones, D., & Luckner, J. (2005, May/June). "Promoting Literacy Development with Students who are Hard-of-Hearing, and Hearing." *Teaching Exceptional Children,* 37(5), pp. 56–57.

INCLUSION AND COLLABORATION THROUGH THE LIFESPAN

People with a Hearing Loss

EARLY CHILDHOOD YEARS

Tips for the Family

- Promote family learning about diversity in all people in the context of understanding the child with a hearing loss.

- Keep informed about organizations that can provide support to the young child with a hearing loss and also to the family.

- Get in touch with your local health, social services, and education agencies about infant, toddler, and preschool programs for children with a hearing loss. Become familiar with the individualized family service plan (IFSP) and how it can serve as a planning tool to support the inclusion of your child in early intervention programs and collaboration among professionals.

- Focus on the development of communication for your child. Collaborate with professionals to determine what mode of communication (oral, manual, and/or total communication) will be most effective in developing early language skills.

- Identify objects and people both visually and verbally as often as possible to provide the child with multiple sources of input.

Tips for the Preschool Teacher

- Language deficits are a fundamental problem for young children with a hearing loss. Focus on developing expressive and receptive communication in the classroom as early as possible. Collaborate with parents and other professionals to help children with a hearing loss understand words that are abstract, have multiple meanings, or are part of idiomatic expressions (e.g., "to run down the street" versus "to run for president").

- Help hearing classmates interact with the child with a hearing loss. Help hearing children be both verbal and visual with the student who is deaf or hard of hearing. If the child with a hearing loss doesn't respond to sound, have the hearing children learn to stand in the line of sight. Teach them to gain the attention of the child with a hearing loss without physical prompting.

- Work closely with parents so that early communication and skill development for the young child with a hearing loss are consistent across school and home environments.

- Become very familiar with acoustical devices (e.g., hearing aids) that may be used by the young child with a hearing loss. Make sure that these devices are worn properly and that they work in the classroom environment.

Tips for Preschool Personnel

- Support the inclusion of young children with a hearing loss in your classrooms and programs.

- Support teachers, staff, and volunteers as they attempt to create successful experiences for the young child with a hearing loss in the preschool setting.

- Collaborate with families to keep them informed and active members of the school community.

Tips for Neighbors and Friends

- Collaborate with the family of a young child with a hearing loss to seek opportunities for interactions with hearing children in neighborhood play settings.

- Focus on the capabilities of the young child with a hearing loss, rather than on the disabilities. Understand how the child communicates: orally? manually? or both? If the child uses sign language, take the time to learn fundamental signs that will enhance your communication with him or her.

ELEMENTARY YEARS

Tips for the Family

- Learn about your rights as parents of a child with a hearing loss. Actively collaborate with professionals in the development of your child's individualized education program (IEP). Through active participation, establish goals on the IEP that will focus on your child's developing social interaction and communication skills in natural settings.

- Participate in as many school functions for parents as possible (e.g., PTA, parent advisory groups, volunteering) to connect your family to the school.

- Seek information on in-school and extracurricular activities available that will enhance opportunities for your child to interact with hearing peers.

- Keep the school informed about the medical needs of your child. If he or she needs or uses acoustical devices to enhance hearing capability, help school personnel understand how these devices work.

Tips for the General Education Classroom Teacher

- Outline schoolwork (e.g., the schedule for the day) on paper or the blackboard so the student with a hearing loss can see it.

- As much as possible, require classroom work to be answered in complete sentences to provide the necessary practice.

- Remember that students with hearing loss don't always know how words fit together to make understandable sentences. Help students develop skills by always writing in complete sentences.

- Have the student with a hearing loss sit where he or she can see the rest of the class as easily as possible. Choose a buddy to sit nearby to help the student with a hearing loss stay aware of what is happening within the classroom.

- When lecturing, have the student with a hearing loss sit as close to you as possible.

- Don't be surprised to see gaps in learning. Demonstrations of disappointment or shock will make the student feel at fault.

- Be sure to help the student with a hearing loss know what is going on at all times (e.g., pass on announcements made over the intercom).

- Always give short, concise instructions and then make sure the student with a hearing loss understood them by having him or her repeat the information before performing the task.

- Type scripts (or outlines of scripts) for movies and videotapes used in class. Let the student read the script for the movie.

- When working with an interpreter, remember to:

- Introduce the interpreter to the class at the beginning of the year, and explain his or her role.

- Always speak directly to the student, not to the interpreter.

- Pause when necessary to allow the interpreter to catch up, since he or she may often be a few words behind.

- Face the class when speaking. (When using a blackboard, write on the board first, then face the class to speak.)

- Include students who are deaf in class activities, and encourage these students to participate in answering questions.

Tips for School Personnel

- Integrate school resources as well as children. Wherever possible, help general education classroom teachers access the human and material resources necessary to meet the needs of students with a hearing loss. For example:

  - The audiologist. Keep in close contact with this professional, and seek advice on the student's hearing and the acoustic devices being used.

  - The special education teacher trained in hearing loss. This professional is necessary both as a teacher of students with a hearing loss and as a consultant to general educators. Activities can range from working on the development of effective communication skills to dealing with behavioral difficulties. The general education teacher may even decide to work with the special education teacher on learning sign language, if appropriate.

  - Speech and language specialists. Many students with a hearing loss will need help with speech acquisition and application in the school setting.

- Help general and special education teachers to develop peer partner and support networks for students with a hearing loss. Peer partners may help by serving as tutors or just by reviewing for tests and class assignments.

- Collaborate with other professionals to help the student with a hearing loss strive for independence. Assistance from peers is sometimes helpful, but it should never reach the point where other students are doing work for the student with a hearing loss.

Tips for Neighbors and Friends

- Help families with a child who is deaf or hard of hearing to be an integral part of neighborhood and friendship networks. Seek ways to include the family and the child in neighborhood activities (e.g., outings, barbecues, outdoor yard and street cleanups, crime watches).

SECONDARY AND TRANSITION YEARS

Tips for the Family

- Become familiar with adult services systems (e.g., rehabilitation, Social Security, health care) while your son or daughter is still in high school. Understand the type of vocational or employment training needed prior to graduation.

- Create opportunities outside of school for your son or daughter to participate in activities with same-age hearing peers.

Tips for the General Education Classroom Teacher

- Collaborate with specialists in hearing loss and other school personnel to help students adapt to subject matter in your classroom (e.g., science, math, physical education).

- Become aware of the needs of students with a hearing loss in your classroom and with the resources available for them. Facilitate student learning by establishing peer support systems (e.g., note takers) to help students with a hearing loss be successful.

- Use diagrams, graphs, and visual representations whenever possible when presenting new concepts.

- Help the student with a hearing loss become involved in extracurricular high school activities. If you are the faculty sponsor of a club or organization, explore whether the student is interested and how he or she could get involved.

Tips for School Personnel

- Encourage parents of high-school-age students with a hearing loss to participate in school activities (such as committees and PTA).

- Parents will be more active when school personnel have general and positive contact with the family.

Tips for Neighbors, Friends, and Potential Employers

- Collaborate with family and school personnel to create opportunities for students with a hearing loss to participate in community activities as much as possible with individuals who are deaf or hard of hearing, as well as with those who are not.

- As a potential employer for people with a hearing loss, work with the high school and vocational rehabilitation counselors to locate and establish employment training sites.

ADULT YEARS

Tips for the Family

- Become aware of the supports and services available for your son or daughter in the local community in which they will live as adults. What formal supports are available in the community through government-funded programs or advocacy organizations for people with a hearing loss? through informal supports (family and friends)?

- Explore adult services in the local community in the areas of postsecondary education, employment, and recreation.

Tips for Neighbors, Friends, and Potential Employers

- Seek ways to become part of a community support network for individuals with a hearing loss. Be alert to ways in which these individuals can become and remain actively involved in community employment, neighborhood recreational activities, and local church functions.

- As potential employers in the community, seek out information on employment of people with a hearing loss. Find out about programs that focus on establishing employment opportunities for people with a hearing loss, while meeting your needs as an employer.

Teaching Communication Skills

Four approaches are commonly used in teaching communication skills to students with a hearing loss: auditory, oral, manual, and total communication. There is a long history of controversy regarding which approach is the most appropriate. However, no single method or combination of methods can meet the individual needs of all children with a hearing loss. Our purpose is not to enter into the controversy regarding these approaches but to present a brief description of each approach.

THE AUDITORY APPROACH. The auditory approach emphasizes the use of amplified sound and residual hearing to develop oral communication skills. The auditory channel is considered the primary avenue for language development, regardless of the severity or type of hearing loss. The basic principles of the auditory approach are as follows:

➤ Detecting hearing impairment as early as possible through screening programs, ideally in the newborn nursery and throughout childhood.

➤ Pursuing prompt and vigorous medical and audiologic management, including selection, modification, and maintenance of appropriate hearing aids, cochlear implants, or other sensory aids.

➤ Guiding, counseling, and supporting parents and caregivers as the primary models for spoken language through listening and to help them understand the impact of deafness and impaired hearing on the entire family.

➤ Helping children integrate listening into their development of communication and social skills.

➤ Supporting children's auditory–verbal development through one-to-one teaching.

➤ Helping children monitor their own voices and the voices of others in order to enhance the intelligibility of their spoken language.

➤ Using developmental patterns of listening, language, speech, and cognition to stimulate natural communication.

➤ Continually assessing and evaluating children's development in the above areas and, through diagnostic intervention, modifying the program when needed.

➤ Providing support services to facilitate children's educational and social inclusion in regular [general] education classes. (Auditory–Verbal International, 2006)

The auditory approach uses a variety of electroacoustic devices to enhance residual hearing, such as binaural hearing aids, acoustically tuned earmolds, and FM units. FM units employ a behind-the-ear hearing aid connected to a high-powered frequency-modulated radio-frequency (FM-RF) system. These units use a one-way wireless system on radio-frequency bands. The receiver unit (about the size of a deck of cards) is worn by the student, and a wireless microphone-transmitter-antenna unit is worn by the teacher. One advantage of using an FM-RF system is that the teacher can be connected to several students at a time.

THE ORAL APPROACH. The oral approach to teaching communication skills also relies on the use of amplified sound and residual hearing to develop oral language. This approach emphasizes the need for persons with a hearing loss to function in the hearing world. Individuals are encouraged to speak and be spoken to. In addition to electroacoustic amplification, the teacher may employ speechreading, reading and writing, and motokinesthetic speech training (feeling an individual's face and reproducing breath and voice patterns). **Speechreading** is the process of understanding another person's speech by watching lip movement and facial and body gestures. This skill is difficult to master, especially for the person who has been deaf since an early age and thus never acquired speech. Problems with speechreading include the fact that many sounds are not distinguishable on the lips and that the reader must attend carefully to every word spoken, a difficult task for preschool and primary-age children. Additionally, the speechreader must be able to see the speaker's mouth at all times.

Auditory–Verbal International (2006), a major international organization whose principal objective is to promote listening and speaking as a way of life for children who are deaf or

➤ **Speechreading**

The process of understanding another person's speech by watching lip movement and facial and body gestures.

hard of hearing, indicated that there is compelling evidence for the auditory and oral approaches to teaching communication skills:

➤ The majority of children with hearing loss have useful residual hearing.

➤ When properly aided, children with hearing loss can detect most, if not all, of the speech spectrum.

➤ Once residual hearing is accessed through amplification technology, a child will have the opportunity to develop language in a natural way through the auditory modality.

➤ In order for the child to benefit during the "critical periods" of neurological and linguistic development, appropriate amplification and medical technology and stimulation of hearing must occur as early as possible.

➤ If hearing is not accessed during the critical language-learning years, a child's ability to use acoustic input meaningfully will deteriorate as a consequence of physiological (retrograde deterioration of auditory pathways) and psychosocial (attention, practice, learning) factors.

➤ Current information about normal language development provides the framework and justification for the structure of auditory–verbal practice. That is, infants, toddlers, and children learn language most efficiently through consistent and continual meaningful interactions in a supportive environment with significant caretakers.

➤ As verbal language develops through the auditory input of information, reading skills can also develop.

➤ Parents in auditory–verbal programs do not have to learn sign language or cued speech. More than 90% of parents of children with hearing loss have normal hearing.

➤ Studies show that over 90% of parents with normal hearing do not learn sign language beyond a basic preschool level of competence.

If a severe or profound hearing loss automatically made an individual neurologically and functionally "different" from people with normal hearing, then the auditory–verbal philosophy would not be tenable. However, outcome studies show that individuals who have, since early childhood, been taught through the active use of amplified residual hearing are indeed independent, speaking, and contributing members of mainstream society.

THE MANUAL APPROACH. The manual approach to teaching communication skills stresses the use of signs in teaching children who are deaf to communicate. The use of signs is based on the premise that many such children are unable to develop oral language and consequently must have some other means of communication. Manual communication systems are divided into two main categories: sign languages and sign systems.

Sign languages are a systematic and complex combination of hand movements that communicate whole words and complete thoughts rather than the individual letters of the alphabet. One of the most common sign languages is the **American Sign Language (ASL)**, with a vocabulary of more than 6,000 signs. Examples of ASL signs are shown in Figure 15.2. ASL is currently the most widely used sign language among many adults who are deaf, because it is easy to master and has historically been the preferred mode of communication. It is a language, but it is not English. Its signs represent concepts rather than single words. The use of ASL in a school setting has been strongly recommended by some advocates for people who are deaf, because it is considered their natural language (National Institute on Deafness and Other Communication Disorders, 2006a).

Sign systems differ from sign languages in that they attempt to create visual equivalents of oral language through manual gestures. With finger spelling, a form of manual communication that incorporates all 26 letters of the English alphabet, each letter is signed independently on one hand to form words. Figure 15.3 on page 409 illustrates the manual alphabet. In recent years, finger spelling has become a supplement to ASL. It is common to see a person who is deaf using finger spelling when there is no ASL sign for a word. The four sign systems used in the United States are Seeing Essential English, Signing Exact English, Linguistics of Visual English, and Signed English.

There is a continuing debate regarding the use of ASL and signing English systems in providing academic instruction to students who are deaf. Should ASL or English be the primary

➤ **Sign language**
A systematic and complex combination of hand movements that communicate whole words and complete thoughts rather than the individual letters of the alphabet. One of the most common sign languages is the American Sign Language (ASL).

➤ **American Sign Language (ASL)**
A type of sign language commonly used by people with hearing impairments. ASL signs represent concepts rather than single words.

➤ **Sign systems**
Differing from sign languages, sign systems create visual equivalents of oral language through manual gestures. For example, finger spelling incorporates all 26 letters of the English alphabet, each letter being signed independently on one hand to form words.

FIGURE 15.2

Examples of "Faint" Expressed in American Sign Language

Faint: My mother fainted from the ammonia fumes.

Alabama, Hawaii

Arkansas, Florida, Maine,
Kentucky, Louisiana, Virginia,
North Carolina, South Carolina

California, Illinois, Utah

Colorado, Texas (1 of 2)

Massachusetts

Michigan, Ohio

SOURCE: Reprinted by permission of the publisher, from E. Shroyer and S. Shroyer, *Signs Across America,* (1984): 79–80. Washington, DC: Gallaudet University Press. Copyright © 1984 by Gallaudet University.

➤ **Bicultural–bilingual approach**

Instructional approach advocating ASL as the primary language, and English as the second language, for students who are deaf. ASL would thus serve as the foundation for learning English.

language for instruction? Those advocating a **bicultural–bilingual approach** believe that ASL should be the primary language and English the second language. As the primary language, ASL would then serve as the foundation for the learning of English. The rationale for ASL as the primary language emerges from the values held dear by the Deaf community: Children who are deaf must learn academic content in the language of their culture, their natural language. The primary language for children who are deaf is visual, not verbal. Children who are deaf should be considered bilingual students, not students with disabilities. As is true in bilingual education programs for students with differing language backgrounds, there is also the debate about whether ASL should be taught first and then English, or whether both should be taught simultaneously. One side emphasizes the importance of the child's first acquiring the natural language (ASL). The other stresses the need to expose the child to both ASL and English simultaneously and as early as possible. There is little research to support either position.

TOTAL COMMUNICATION. Total communication has roots traceable to the 16th century. Over the past four centuries, many professionals advocated for an instructional system that employed every method possible to teach communication skills: oral, auditory, manual, and written. This approach was known as the combined system or simultaneous method. The methodology of the early combined system was imprecise; essentially, any recognized approach to teaching communication was used as long as it included a manual component. The concept of total communication differs from the older combined system in that it is not used only when the oral method fails or when critical learning periods have long since passed. In fact, total communication is not a system at all, but a philosophy.

➤ **Total communication**

A communication philosophy and approach used by people with hearing impairments. It employs various combinations of elements from manual, oral, and any other techniques available to facilitate understanding.

The philosophy of **total communication** holds that the simultaneous presentation of signs and speech will enhance each person's opportunity to understand and use both systems more ef-

FIGURE 15.3

The American Manual Alphabet

The manual alphabet as the receiver sees it:

The manual alphabet as the sender sees it:

This teacher embraces the philosophy of total communication. Students use residual hearing, amplification, and speech reading in combination with sign language.

FIGURE 15.4

Milestones in Technology for the Deaf

1892

The first electrical hearing aid, which weighs several pounds, is invented.

1964

The teletypewriter, or TTY, which enables deaf people to call each other and type conversations, is invented by Robert Weitbrecht, who is deaf.

1972

The first television show featuring captioning—Julia Child's *The French Chef*—is broadcast on PBS.

1985

The FDA approves cochlear implants.

1990s and Beyond

All new televisions 13 inches or larger sold in the U.S. are required by the FCC to have decoding chips, which allow deaf people to view programs with captions.

New vibrating pagers are developed that provide deaf people with easy, on-the-go communication.

Computer technology— including laptops, e-mail and the Internet— gives deaf people a level playing field with the hearing world in job opportunities and social communication.

Advances include real-time captioning (spoken words typed simultaneously on a screen); video-relay interpreting (deaf and hearing people speak via a remote video interpreter); and signing avatars (onscreen figures who sign words spoken into a microphone).

SOURCE: "They're Breaking the Sound Barrier," by L.A. Walker, *Parade Magazine*, May 13, 2001, p. 4

FOCUS **7**

Describe the uses of closed-caption television, computers, and the Internet for people with a hearing loss.

➤ **Cued speech**

Cued speech facilitates the development of oral communication by combining eight different hand signals in four different locations near the person's chin. The hand signals provide information about sounds not identifiable by speechreading.

➤ **Closed-caption television**

Process by which people with hearing impairments are provided with translated dialogue, in the form of subtitles, from television programs. Also called the "line-21" system since the caption is inserted into blank line 21 of the picture.

Council for Exceptional Children

Standard 4: Instructional Strategies

---

fectively. Total communication programs use residual hearing, amplification, speechreading, speech training, reading, and writing in combination with manual systems. A method that may be used as an aid to total communication but is not a necessary component of the approach is cued speech. **Cued speech** facilitates the development of oral communication by combining eight different hand signals in four different locations near the person's chin. These hand signals provide additional information about sounds not identifiable by speechreading. The result is that an individual has access to all sounds in the English language through either the lips or the hands.

Assistive Technology

Educational and leisure opportunities for people with a hearing loss have been greatly expanded through technological advances such as closed-caption television, computers, and the Internet. In this section, we examine 21st-century technology for persons with a hearing loss.

CLOSED CAPTIONING. **Closed-caption television** translates dialogue from a television program into printed words (captions or subtitles). These captions are then converted into electronic codes that can be inserted into the television picture on sets specially adapted with decoding devices. The process is called the line-21 system because the caption is inserted into blank line 21 of the picture.

Captioning is not a new idea. In fact, it was first used on motion picture film in 1958. Most libraries in the United States distribute captioned films for individuals with a hearing loss. Available only since 1980, closed captioning on television has experienced steady growth over the past 20 years. In its first year of operation, national closed-caption programming was available about 30 hours per week. By 1987, more than 200 hours per week of national programming were captioned in a wide range of topics, from news and information to entertainment and commercials. By 1993, all major broadcast networks were captioning 100% of their prime-time broadcasts, national news, and children's programming. With the passage of the

Television Decoder Circuitry Act of 1993, the numbers of viewers watching closed-caption television expanded even more dramatically. This act required that all television sets sold in the United States that measure 13 inches or larger be equipped with a decoder that allows captions to be placed anywhere on the television screen. (This prevents captions from interfering with on-screen titles or other information displayed on the TV broadcast.) In 1997, the U.S. Congress passed the Telecommunications Act, which required virtually all new television programming to be captioned by January 2006. Although Congress provided for some exemptions (for example, non-English programming, commercials and public service announcements, and late night programs), the clear intent of the law was to perpetuate expanded access to television for millions of people who are deaf.

There is the mistaken belief that the Americans with Disabilities Act (ADA) mandates captioning for television and movies. In fact, the ADA requires captioning only on government-funded television public service announcements. Federal law does not extend beyond television because the Federal Communications Commission has jurisdiction only over the airwaves. Thus there is no law covering the captioning of movies in theaters or on videotapes or DVDs (Robson, 2006).

COMPUTERS AND THE INTERNET. Personal computers add an exciting dimension to information access for persons with a hearing loss. The computer places the person in an interactive setting with the subject matter. It is a powerful motivator. Most people find computers fun and interesting to work with on a variety of tasks. Furthermore, computer-assisted instruction can be individualized so that students can gain independence by working at their own pace and level.

Computer programs are now available for instructional support in a variety of academic subject areas, from reading and writing to learning basic sign language. Software is available that will display a person's speech in visual form on the screen to assist in the development of articulation skills. Another innovative computer system is called C-print, developed by the National Technical Institute for the Deaf. Using a laptop computer equipped with a computer shorthand system and commercially available software packages, C-print provides real-time translations of the spoken word. A trained operator is required to listen to speech and then type special codes representing words into the computer. These codes are transcribed into words that are shown almost simultaneously on a screen sitting atop an overhead projector. A printout of the transcription can be obtained as well. C-print provides a major service to students with a hearing loss as they attend college classes or oral lectures; they typically find note taking an extremely difficult activity, even when an oral interpreter is available (National Technical Institute for the Deaf, 2006).

The interactive videodisc is another important innovation in computer-assisted instruction. The videodisc, a record-like platter, is placed in a videodisc player that is connected to a microcomputer and television monitor. The laser-driven disc is interactive, allowing the individual to move through instruction at his or her own pace. Instant repetitions of subject matter are available to the learner at the touch of a button.

Perhaps the most important advance in technology for people with a hearing loss is access to information through the Internet. Through e-mail, interactive chatrooms, and the infinite number of websites, the World Wide Web offers people with a hearing loss access to all kinds of visual information through the quickest and most convenient means possible. Deaf Resources (http://www.deafresources.com/) and the American Sign Language Browser (http://commtechlab. msu.edu/sites/aslweb/) are just two examples of sites designed specifically for people who are deaf. For more in-depth information on the way assistive technology is opening up employment opportunities, entertainment, and communication for people who are deaf, see the Assistive Technology "They're Breaking the Sound Barrier." Additional information on web resources is available at the end of this chapter.

TELECOMMUNICATION DEVICES. A major advance in communication technology for people with a hearing loss is the telecommunication device (TDD). In 1990, the Americans with Disabilities Act renamed these devices **text telephones (TTs)**. TTs send, receive, and print messages through thousands of stations across the United States. People with a hearing loss can now dial an 800 number to set up conference calls, make appointments, or order merchandise or fast food. Anyone who wants to speak with a person using a TT can do so through the use of a standard telephone.

➤ **Text telephones (TTs)**
Telephones that send, receive, and print messages through thousands of stations across the United States.

ASSISTIVE TECHNOLOGY

THEY'RE BREAKING THE SOUND BARRIER

Marvin Herbold of Gaithersburg, Maryland, wanted a job in the computer game industry after college, so he e-mailed a résumé to Bethesda Softworks. The company asked him to write a simple computer program depicting a 3-D cube. Herbold went further. His 3-D program showed an entire chessboard and pieces. Impressed, Bethesda sent back an e-mail asking him to come for an interview. Herbold e-mailed to let the interviewer know he was deaf.

"Not a problem," was the reply.

After the interview, he was hired on the spot. "They were far more interested in what I could do," says Herbold, now 26, "than [in] any disabilities I may have had."

As recently as a decade ago, things were far more difficult for deaf people looking for employment. Few dared apply for white-collar jobs, unless they were in the "deaf job ghetto"—a handful of lowly government positions—or teaching deaf children.

Today, not only is technology opening up employment opportunities, it also has changed the ways deaf people socialize, receive entertainment, communicate with the hearing world and plan their futures.

I've seen it firsthand, in my own family. My mother and father are deaf, as were my aunt and uncle, and I signed even before I spoke. Not long ago, I went to a senior citizens' luncheon for deaf people in Indianapolis. As hands flew, I noticed something quite surprising about the conversations I was seeing among my parents' friends. These older people were wired! "Did you get my e-mail?" "When I was surfing the Web, I found a great new site. . . ." This was not the deaf world I knew growing up.

I was aware of these changes as I talked with some of the men and women who are using technology in their day-to-day lives. As a reporter, I have never used so many different methods for conducting interviews. Naturally, I communicated using American Sign Language. But I also used e-mail, faxes, and telephones with text. At times, I spoke by phone with a deaf person at the other end who used a sign-language interpreter to receive my words but was speaking for himself. During one conversation, the other person used an amplifying device hooked into a cochlear implant (a device that places electrodes directly into the cochlea, where sound waves are absorbed and interpreted by the auditory nerve).

[People who are deaf] now are able to be more plugged in to politics and other events than ever before. When I was home recently, I noticed my mother and father constantly zipping over to the computer to check the news. Not only did they receive regular updates on the happenings in the deaf world around the country, but there also were local deaf news bulletins being placed constantly. I asked my dad how technology had affected him. "My English has improved," he said. "With e-mails and faxes, I write and keep in touch with deaf people much more." And then he smiled. "My life is better than before."

SOURCE: From "They're Breaking the Sound Barrier," by L. A. Walker, *Parade Magazine,* May 13, 2001, pp. 4–5.

The teletypewriter and printer system (TTY) is another effective use of technology for people who are deaf. It allows them to communicate by phone via a typewriter that converts typed letters into electric signals through a modem. These signals are sent through the phone lines and then translated into typed messages and printed on a typewriter connected to a phone on the other end. Computer software is now available that can turn a personal computer into a TTY.

Health Care and Social Services

In this new century, advances in health care and social services are opening up vast new opportunities for people with a hearing loss. Health care plays a major role in the prevention, early detection, and remediation of a hearing loss. Community services and supports are helping to reduce the social isolation of people who are deaf or have a partial hearing loss. Societal perspectives on people with a hearing loss are changing dramatically, as evidenced in the life of Tamika Catchings in the opening Snapshot and of Marvin Herbold from the Assistive Technology feature above.

FOCUS 8

Why is the early detection of hearing loss so important?

Health Care

Several specialists are involved in health care assessment and intervention, including the geneticist, the pediatrician, the family practitioner, the otologist, the neurosurgeon, and the audiologist.

THE GENETICIST. Prevention of a hearing loss is a primary concern of the genetics specialist. A significant number of hearing losses are inherited or occur during prenatal, perinatal, and postnatal development. Consequently, the genetics specialist plays an important role in preventing disabilities through family counseling and prenatal screening.

THE PEDIATRICIAN AND FAMILY PRACTITIONER. Early detection of a hearing loss can prevent or at least minimize the impact of the disability on the overall development of an individual. Generally, it is the responsibility of the pediatrician or family practitioner to be aware of a problem and to refer the family to an appropriate hearing specialist. This requires that the physician be familiar with family history and conduct a thorough physical examination of the child. The physician must be alert to any symptoms (such as delayed language development) that indicate potential sensory loss.

THE OTOLOGIST. The **otologist** is a medical specialist who is most concerned with the hearing organ and its diseases. Otology is a component of the larger specialty of diseases of the ear, nose, and throat. The otologist, like the pediatrician, screens for potential hearing problems, but the process is much more specialized and exhaustive. The otologist also conducts an extensive physical examination of the ear to identify syndromes that are associated with conductive or sensorineural loss. This information, in conjunction with family history, provides data on the basis of which to recommend appropriate medical treatment.

Treatment may involve medical therapy or surgical intervention. Common therapeutic procedures include monitoring aural hygiene (e.g., keeping the external ear free from wax), blowing out the ear (e.g., a process to remove mucus blocking the eustachian tube), and administering antibiotics to treat infections. Surgical techniques may involve the cosmetic and functional restructuring of congenital malformations such as a deformed external ear or closed external canal (atresia). Fenestration is the surgical creation of a new opening in the labyrinth of the ear to restore hearing. A stapedectomy is a surgical process conducted under a microscope whereby a fixed stapes is replaced with a prosthetic device capable of vibrating, thus permitting the transmission of sound waves. A myringoplasty is the surgical reconstruction of a perforated tympanic membrane (eardrum).

Another widely used surgical procedure involves a **cochlear implant**. This electronic device is surgically placed under the skin behind the ear. It consists of four parts: (1) a microphone for picking up sound, (2) a speech processor to select and arrange sounds picked up by the microphone, (3) a transmitter and receiver/stimulator to receive signals from the speech processor and convert them into electric impulses, and (4) electrodes to collect the impulses from the stimulator and send them to the brain. The implant does not restore or amplify hearing. Instead, it provides people who are deaf or profoundly hard of hearing with a useful "sense" of sound in the world around them. The implant overcomes "nerve deafness" (sounds blocked from reaching the auditory nerve) by getting around damage to the tiny hair cells in the inner ear and directly stimulating the auditory nerve. An implant electronically finds useful or meaningful sounds, such as speech, and then sends these sounds to the auditory nerve.

Cochlear implants are becoming more widely used with both adults and children. More than 25,000 people worldwide (50% children and 50% adults) have had the surgery (National Institute on Deafness and Other Communication Disorders, 2006b). Some adults who were deafened in their later years reported useful hearing following the implant, and others still needed speechreading to understand the spoken word. Most children receive the implants between the ages of 2 and 6 years. Debate continues about which age is optimal for the surgery, but it appears that the earlier, the better. The Cochlear Implants Association (2006) suggests that children from 18 months to 17 years of age are appropriate candidates for an implant if they have profound hearing loss in both ears, little or no useful benefit from hearing aids, no medical contraindications, and high motivation and appropriate expectations (both child and family). The association also recommends that following surgery, the child be placed in an educational program that emphasizes development of auditory skills. Similar criteria are suggested for adults, with the additional caveat that the person must have a strong desire to be part of the hearing world.

The existing research suggests that cochlear implants assist in the learning of speech, language, and social skills, particularly for young children. However, there are still issues to be addressed, such as understanding the risk of possible damage to an ear that has some residual hearing, as well

Council for Exceptional Children

Standard 1: Foundations

Standard 8: Assessment

Standard 2: Development and Characteristics of Learners

➤ **Otologist**
One who is involved in the study of the ear and its diseases.

FOCUS 9
Distinguish between an otologist and an audiologist.

➤ **Cochlear implant**
A surgical procedure that implants an electronic device under the skin behind the ear. The implant overcomes "nerve deafness" by getting around damage to the cells in the inner ear and directly stimulating the auditory nerve.

as the risk of infection from the implant (McKinley & Warren, 2000). Some people who are deaf view cochlear implants as a direct attack on the values and heritage of the Deaf culture.

The media often describe deafness in a negative light, portraying deaf and hard of hearing children and adults as handicapped and second-class citizens in need of being "fixed" with cochlear implants. There is little or no portrayal of successful, well adjusted deaf and hard of hearing children and adults without implants. A major reason implantation and oral language training have been pursued so aggressively by the media, the medical profession, and parents is not simply because of the hoped-for benefits that come with being able to hear in a predominantly hearing society but more because of the perceived burdens associated with being deaf. Because cochlear implant technology continues to evolve, to receive mainstream acceptance, and to be acknowledged as part of today's reality, it is urgent to be aware of and responsive to the historical treatment of deaf persons. This perspective makes it possible to provide more realistic guidelines for parents of deaf and hard of hearing children and for pre-lingually and post-lingually deafened adults. (National Association of the Deaf, 2006)

Others people who are deaf, such as Mary Beth Green, view cochlear implants as a medical miracle. See the Reflect on This, "Cochlear Implant Fills Her Heart with Music."

THE AUDIOLOGIST. The degree of hearing loss, measured in decibel and hertz units, is determined by an audiologist, by means of a process known as audiometric evaluation. The

REFLECT ON THIS
COCHLEAR IMPLANT FILLS HER HEART WITH MUSIC

Mary Beth Green still remembers a life-altering experience she had while watching a PBS program six years ago. "There was this Irish tenor on TV," Green recalled, "and he touched my heart." What made this revelation unusual is that she never heard a single note [resounding] from Ronan Tynan. Green had spent the previous 40 years in a world of silence, but watching the tenor's passion as he sang inspired her to do something about her profound deafness. "I had to hear this man," she said.

Friends told her she [might] be a good candidate for a cochlear implant, a device that stimulates the inner ear to send sound signals to the brain. Green . . . considered the surgery but worried because a relative had died from a brain tumor. She didn't want doctors messing around with her head. Green lost her hearing as a teenager in a matter of hours, and her sudden deafness stumped her doctors. Through the next four decades of her life, she could still speak, but [she] was unable to hear anything until the Irish tenor led her to take a chance to bring sound back into her life.

The surgery involves attaching a thin electrical device to the cochlea, which resembles a snail's shell inside the ear, said Lisa Dahlstrom, a University Hospital audiologist. Green is one of about 60,000 people worldwide who have benefited from cochlear implants, according to the National Institute on Deafness and Other Communication Disorders. "It bypasses the inner ear and directly stimulates the nerves," which in turn signals the brain, Dahlstrom said. Not every kind of hearing problem is fixable through this or other types of surgical implants.

Cochlear implants are typically reserved for those with severe to profound deafness, in situations where traditional hearing aids don't work. Taking into account surgical expenses, the cost of the device and other factors. the total bill can run

as high as $70,000, Dahlstrom estimated. Other options can include a middle ear implant—which can cost up to $10,000 [for] surgery and equipment expenses—that bypasses the damaged middle ear area.

Another option is the bone-anchored hearing aid. This involves planting a metal fixture in the skull that can have a sound processor attached. The signal is sent through the bones of the head using vibrations. In Green's case, doctors saw the cochlear implant as the best bet. Her doctors warned her that voices would sound alien at first. Green quipped that this was all right, since she had never heard any aliens.

California surgeons began installing the cochlear implant in December 1999 and turned the device on in January 2000. "Oh my God, I can hear my voice," she repeated to herself. Then she noticed a strange voice—Green couldn't tell if it was male or female—calling her name. She turned around to see her father speaking her name, crying at the sight of his daughter being able to hear again.

Dahlstrom said it can take up to a year to train your brain how to hear again using such cochlear implants. Green now puts her hearing to good use with the Utah Public Services Commission, where she helps match hearing-impaired or visually impaired Utahns with modified communication devices. That new hearing also gets put to the test outside of work. Thanks to her cochlear implant, Green saw—and heard—the film "Lord of the Rings" seven times with a grandchild. Green also has several decades of music to catch up on. From country to musical sound tracks, she now dabbles in a wide variety of music. But that Irish tenor still holds a special place in her heart since the day of her surgery. "That night, I heard my Irish tenor sing Amazing Grace," she said. "You can't get any better than that."

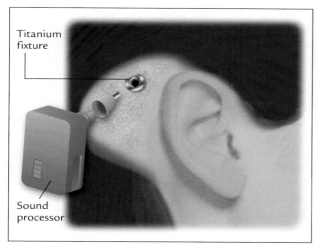

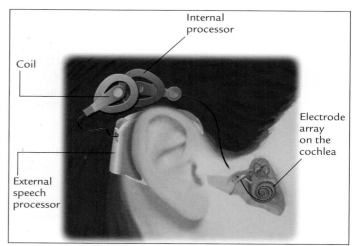

BAHA (BONE ANCHORED HEARING AID)

Best for: Those with chronic ear infections, congenital hearing loss and/or single-sided deafness.

How it works: A titanium fixture is installed in a bone near the ear. A sound processor, which picks up sound, is attached to the fixture. A signal is sent via bone vibrations.

Estimated total cost: $10,000*

COCHLEAR IMPLANT

Best for: Those with severe to profound sensorineural hearing loss.

How it works: A sound processor, worn on the ear, picks up sounds and sends signals to an internal implant. From there, the signal goes to an electrode array attached to the cochlea, which stimulates hearing nerves.

Estimated total cost: $70,000*

*Estimated costs includes device, surgery expenses and other factors.

SOURCE: "Cochlear Implant Fills Her Heart with Music," by G. Lavine, *Salt Lake Tribune*, August 30, 2005, pp. D1, D2.

listener receives tones that are relatively free of external noise (pure-tone audiometry) or spoken words, in which speech perception is measured (speech audiometry). An **audiometer** detects the person's response to sound stimuli, and a record (**audiogram**) is obtained from the audiometer that graphs the individual's threshold for hearing at various sound frequencies.

Whereas an otologist offers a biological perspective on hearing loss, an **audiologist** emphasizes the functional impact of losing one's hearing. The audiologist first screens the individual for a hearing loss and then determines both the nature and the severity of the condition. Social, educational, and vocational implications of the hearing loss are then discussed and explored. Although audiologists are not specifically trained in the field of medicine, these professionals interact constantly with otologists to provide a comprehensive assessment of hearing.

Working together, audiologists and otologists provide assistance in the selection and use of hearing aids. At one time or another, most people with a hearing loss will probably wear hearing aids. Hearing aids amplify sound, but they do not correct hearing. Hearing aids have been used for centuries. Early acoustic aids included cupping one's hand behind the ear as well as the ear trumpet. Modern electroacoustic aids do not depend on the loudness of the human voice to amplify sound but utilize batteries to increase volume. Electroacoustic aids come in three main types: body-worn aids, behind-the-ear aids, and in-the-ear aids. Which hearing aid is best for a particular person depends on the degree of hearing loss, the age of the individual, and his or her physical condition.

Body-worn hearing aids are typically worn on the chest, using a harness to secure the unit. The hearing aid is connected by a wire to a transducer, which is worn at ear level and delivers a signal to the ear via an earmold. Body-worn aids are becoming less common because of the disadvantages of their being chest-mounted, the location of the microphone, and inadequate high-frequency response. The behind-the-ear aid (also referred to as an ear-level aid) is a common electroacoustic device for children with a hearing loss. All components of the behind-the-ear aid are fitted in one case behind the outer ear. The case then connects to an earmold that delivers the signal directly to the ear. In addition to their portability, behind-the-ear aids have the advantage of producing the greatest amount of electroacoustic flexibility (amount of

> **Audiometer**

An electronic device used to detect a person's response to sound stimuli.

> **Audiogram**

A record obtained from an audiometer that graphs the faintest level of sound a person is able to hear in each ear at least half the time over several frequencies, including the range of normal speech.

> **Audiologist**

A specialist in the assessment of a person's hearing ability.

amplification across all frequencies). The primary disadvantage is problems with acoustic feedback. As discussed earlier in this chapter, the behind-the-ear aid may be used with an FM-RF system. These aids may be fitted monaurally (on one ear) or binaurally (on both ears).

The in-the-ear aid fits within the ear canal. All major components (microphone, amplifier, transducer, and battery) are housed in a single case that has been custom made for the individual user. The advantage of the in-the-ear aid is the close positioning of the microphone to the natural reception of auditory signals in the ear canal. In-the-ear aids are recommended for persons with mild hearing losses who do not need frequent changes in earmolds. Accordingly, these aids are not usually recommended for young children.

Although the quality of commercially available hearing aids has improved dramatically in recent years, they have distinct limitations. Commercial hearing aids make sounds louder, but do not necessarily make them more clear and distinct. The criteria for determining the effectiveness of a hearing aid must be based on how well it fits, as well as each individual's communication ability, and educational achievement.

The stimulation of residual hearing through a hearing aid enables most people with a hearing loss to function as hard of hearing. However, the use of a hearing aid must be implemented as early as possible, before sensory deprivation takes its toll on the child. It is the audiologist's responsibility to weigh all the factors involved (such as convenience, size, and weight) in the selection and use of an aid for the individual. The individual should then be directed to a reputable hearing-aid dealer.

Social Services

FOCUS 10

Identify factors that may affect the social inclusion of people who are deaf into the hearing world.

Council for Exceptional Children

Standard 1: Foundations

Standard 5: Learning Environments and Social Interactions

The social consequences of being deaf or hard of hearing are highly correlated with the severity of the loss. For the individual who is deaf, social inclusion may be extremely difficult because societal views of deafness have reinforced social isolation. The belief that such a person is incompetent has been predominant from the time of the early Hebrews and Romans, who deprived these people of their civil rights, to 20th-century America, where, in some areas, it is still difficult for adults who are deaf to obtain driver's licenses or adequate insurance coverage or to be gainfully employed. Individuals with the greatest difficulty are those born with congenital deafness. The inability to hear and understand speech has often isolated these people from those who can hear. For example, people who are deaf tend to marry other people who are deaf.

A segment of individuals who are deaf are actively involved in organizations and communities specifically intended to meet their needs. The National Association of the Deaf (NAD) was organized in 1880. The philosophy of the NAD is that every person who is deaf has the same rights as those in the hearing world—the right to life, liberty, and the pursuit of happiness. NAD emphasizes that the exercise of these rights must be to the satisfaction of those who are deaf, not merely to the satisfaction of their teachers and parents who do not have the condition. NAD serves individuals who are deaf in many capacities. Among its many contributions, NAD publishes books on deafness, sponsors cultural activities, and lobbies throughout the United States for legislation promoting the rights of persons who are deaf.

Another prominent organization is the Alexander Graham Bell Association for the Deaf and Hard of Hearing, which advocates the inclusion of persons with a hearing loss in the social mainstream. The major thrust of this approach is the improvement of proficiency in speech communications. As a clearinghouse for information for people who are deaf and their advocates, the association publishes widely in the areas of parent counseling, teaching methodology, speechreading, and auditory training. In addition, it sponsors national and regional conferences that focus on a variety of issues pertinent to the social adjustment of people who are deaf.

Today, most students with a hearing loss are educated side-by-side with hearing peers. Here a teacher signs to a young man with a hearing loss while his hearing classmate watches intently.

FOCUS 1 Describe how sound is transmitted through the human ear.

- A vibrator—such as a string, reed, or column of air—causes displacement of air particles.
- Vibrations are carried by air, metal, water, or other substances.
- Sound waves are displaced air particles that produce a pattern of auricular waves that move away from the source to a receiver.
- The human ear collects, processes, and transmits sounds to the brain, where they are decoded into meaningful language.

FOCUS 2 Distinguish between the terms *deaf* and *hard of hearing*.

- A person who is deaf typically has profound or total loss of auditory sensitivity and very little, if any, auditory perception.
- For the person who is deaf, the primary means of information input is through vision; speech received through the ears is not understood.
- A person who is hard of hearing (partially hearing) generally has residual hearing through the use of a hearing aid, which is sufficient to process language through the ear successfully.

FOCUS 3 Why is it important to consider age of onset and anatomical site when defining a hearing loss?

- Age of onset is critical in determining the type and extent of intervention necessary to minimize the effect of the hearing loss.
- Three types of peripheral hearing loss are associated with anatomical site: conductive, sensorineural, and mixed.
- Central auditory hearing loss occurs when there is a dysfunction in the cerebral cortex (the outer layer of gray matter in the brain).

FOCUS 4 What are the estimated prevalence and the causes of hearing loss?

- It has been extremely difficult to determine the prevalence of hearing loss. Estimates of hearing loss in the United States are as high as 28 million people; approximately 11 million people have significant irreversible hearing loss, and 1 million are deaf.
- Nearly 72,000 students between the ages of 6 and 21 have a hearing impairment and are receiving special education services in U.S. schools. These students account for approximately 1.5% of school-age students identified as having a disability.
- Although more than 200 types of deafness have been related to hereditary factors, the cause of 50% of all hearing loss remains unknown.

- A common hereditary disorder is otosclerosis (bone destruction in the middle ear).
- Nonhereditary hearing problems evident at birth may be associated with maternal health problems: infections (e.g., rubella), anemia, jaundice, central nervous system disorders, the use of drugs, sexually transmitted disease, chicken pox, anoxia, and birth trauma.
- Acquired hearing losses are associated with postnatal infections, such as measles, mumps, influenza, typhoid fever, and scarlet fever.
- Environmental factors associated with hearing loss include extreme changes in air pressure caused by explosions, head trauma, foreign objects in the ear, and loud noise. Loud noise is rapidly becoming one of the major causes of hearing problems.

FOCUS 5 Describe the basic intelligence, speech and language skills, educational achievement, and social development associated with people who are deaf or hard of hearing.

- Intellectual development for people with hearing loss is more a function of language development than of cognitive ability. Any difficulties in performance appear to be closely associated with speaking, reading, and writing the English language but are not related to level of intelligence.
- Speech and English language skills are the areas of development most severely affected for those with a hearing loss. The effects of a hearing loss on English language development vary considerably.
- Most people with a hearing loss are able to use speech as the primary mode for language acquisition. People who are congenitally deaf are unable to receive information through the speech process unless they have learned to speechread.
- Reading is the academic area most negatively affected for students with a hearing loss.
- Social and psychological development in children with a hearing loss is different from that in children who can hear. Different or delayed language acquisition may lead to more limited opportunities for social interaction. Children who are deaf may have more adjustment challenges when attempting to communicate with children who can hear, but they appear to be more secure when conversing with children who are also deaf. Some people who are deaf do not consider social isolation from the hearing world an adjustment problem. Rather, it is a natural state of being where people are bonded together by a common language, customs, and heritage.

FOCUS 6 Identify four approaches to teaching communication skills to persons with a hearing loss.

- The auditory approach to communication emphasizes the use of amplified sound and residual hearing to develop oral communication skills.

- The oral approach to communication emphasizes the use of amplified sound and residual hearing but may also employ speechreading, reading and writing, and motokinesthetic speech training.

- The manual approach stresses the use of signs in teaching children who are deaf to communicate.

- Total communication employs the use of residual hearing, amplification, speechreading, speech training, reading, and writing in combination with manual systems to teach communication skills to children with a hearing loss.

FOCUS **7** Describe the uses of closed-caption television, computers, and the Internet for people with a hearing loss.

- Closed-caption television translates dialogue from a television program into captions (subtitles) that are broadcast on the television screen. Closed-caption television offers the person with a hearing loss greater access to information and entertainment.

- Computers place people with a hearing loss in interactive settings with access to vast amounts of information. Computer programs are now available for instructional support in a variety of academic subject areas, from reading and writing to learning basic sign language. Certain software can display a person's speech in visual form on the screen to assist in the development of articulation skills.

- E-mail, interactive chatrooms, and the infinite number of websites offer people with a hearing loss access to many kinds of visual information.

- TT systems provide efficient ways for people who are deaf to communicate over long distances. TTY devices allow people who are deaf to use a personal computer or typewriter, modem, and printer to communicate over the phone.

FOCUS **8** Why is the early detection of hearing loss so important?

- Early detection of hearing loss can prevent or minimize the impact of the disability on the overall development of an individual.

FOCUS **9** Distinguish between an otologist and an audiologist.

- An otologist is a medical specialist who is concerned with the hearing organ and its diseases.

- An audiologist is concerned with the measurement of hearing loss and its sociological and educational impact on an individual.

- Both the audiologist and the otologist assist in the process of selecting and using a hearing aid.

FOCUS **10** Identify factors that may affect the social inclusion of people who are deaf into the hearing world.

- The inability to hear and understand speech has isolated some people who are deaf from the hearing world.

- Societal views of deafness may reinforce isolation.

BUILDING YOUR PORTFOLIO

Council for Exceptional Children

If you are thinking about a career in special education, you should know that many states use national standards developed by the Council for Exceptional Children (CEC) to assess a teacher candidate's knowledge and skills for working with students with disabilities. See a complete listing of the ten CEC Content Standards on the inside front cover of this text.

CEC Content Standards Addressed in This Chapter

1 Foundations
2 Development and Characteristics of Learners
3 Individual Learning Differences
4 Instructional Strategies
5 Learning Environments and Social Interactions
7 Instructional Planning
8 Assessment

Assess Your Knowledge of the CEC Standards Addressed in This Chapter

Some states require that teacher candidates develop a portfolio of products that demonstrate mastery of the CEC content standards. To assist in the development of products for this portfolio, you may wish to complete the following activities.

- Complete a written test of the chapter's content.

  If your instructor requires a written test of your content knowledge for this chapter, keep a copy for your portfolio. A practice test on the information covered in this chapter is available through the Human Exceptionality companion website (college.hmco.com/pic/hardman9e) and the Student Study Guide.

- Respond to the Application Questions for the Case Study "A Community of Learners."

  Review the Case Study and respond in writing to the application questions. Keep a copy of the Case Study and of your written response for your portfolio.

- Participate in a Community Service Learning Activity.

  Community service is a valuable way to enhance your learning experience. Visit our companion website for suggested community service learning activities that correspond to the information presented in this chapter. Develop a reflective journal of the service learning experience for your portfolio.

WEB RESOURCES

Alexander Graham Bell Association for the Deaf and Hard of Hearing

http://www.agbell.org

The Alexander Graham Bell website offers information on a wide range of programs and services for parents of children with hearing loss, educators, adults with hearing loss, and health professionals. The website has links on updated news and information, advocacy for people with a hearing loss, and publications and products.

American Speech-Hearing-Language Association (ASHA)

http://www.asha.org

ASHA is the professional, scientific, and credentialing association for more than 100,000 speech-language pathologists; audiologists; and speech, language, and hearing scientists in the United States and internationally. The ASHA website provides information and resources on speech-language pathology and audiology for family members, educators, clinicians, researchers, and the general public.

National Association of the Deaf (NAD)

http://www.nad.org

The NAD website provides information on programs and publications focused on advocacy, the deaf community and deaf culture, policy and research on deafness, and public awareness

FURTHER READINGS

Grayson, G. (2003). *Talking with Your Hands, Listening with Your Eyes: A Complete Photographic Guide to American Sign Language.* New York: Square One Publishers.

This book is designed to make it easier to understand, duplicate, and remember the vocabulary of American Sign Language. It covers more than 900 signs that represent nearly 1,800 words and phrases, with signs grouped by topic, such as common and polite phrases; mealtime and food; school and education; careers, jobs, and the workplace; and the body and health. Photos of professional signers demonstrating the sign formation accompany a discussion of each sign.

Matlin, M. (2002). *Deaf Child Crossing.* New York: Simon and Schuster.

Academy award–winning actor and producer Marlee Matlin writes about a topic she knows very well: the difficulties of growing up deaf. The book chronicles the relationship between Megan, a child who is deaf, and Cindy, her hearing friend. Together, they forge an unlikely friendship that is tested when the two attend summer camp together and meet another child who is deaf.

Mapp, I. (Ed.) (2005). *Essential Readings on Stress and Coping among Parents of Deaf and Hearing-Impaired Children.* Lincoln: Gordion Knot Books, University of Nebraska Press.

This book is intended to help parents of children who are deaf or hard of hearing to understand better the major sources of stress they confront, as well as the strategies and resources they can use to cope with the grief, depression, anxiety, and panic that often threaten their personal and family lives. The studies presented in this book dispel stereotypes about these parents by revealing differences in how they react to and cope with stressors—as individuals and as members of diverse social, ethnic, religious, and national groups. Leading experts in psychology, social work, sociology, and psychiatry address vital questions about parenting deaf and hearing-impaired children.

COMPANION WEBSITE

Visit the companion website at college.hmco.com/pic/hardman9e for additional resources that support this text:

- HM Video Cases that present actual classroom scenarios that you may face every day as a teacher

- Practice ACE Exams that will help you prepare for quizzes, tests, and certfication exams

- Flashcards of key terms

- Weblinks

16

Vision Loss

LIKE A SEEING EYE DOG THAT READS AND TALKS

Print-to-speech reading machines for the blind are now very small, inexpensive, palm-sized devices that can read books (those that still exist in paper form), other printed documents, and other real-world text such as signs and displays. These reading systems are equally adept at reading the trillions of electronic documents that are instantly available from the ubiquitous wireless worldwide network. After decades of ineffective attempts, useful navigation devices have been introduced that can assist blind people in avoiding physical obstacles in their path, and finding their way around, using global positioning system (GPS) technology. A blind person can interact with her personal reading–navigation systems through two-way voice communication, kind of like a Seeing Eye dog that reads and talks. (Kurzweil, 2006)

THAT ALL MAY READ

Braille readers can now read their books on the Internet thanks to a historic technological breakthrough by The Library of Congress called Web-Braille. Readers now have access to more than 2,700 electronic braille books recently placed on the Internet for the use of eligible braille readers by the library's National Library Service for the Blind and Physically Handicapped (NLS). Each year many hundreds of new titles will be added. Braille, a system of raised dots that is read with the fingers, has historically been embossed on paper. The system was invented by Louis Braille of France in the early 1800s. As a result of new computer technology, braille readers may now access Web-Braille digital braille book files with a computer and a refreshable braille display (electronic device that raises or lowers an array of pins to create a line of braille characters) or a braille embosser. These 2,700 braille book titles are available on the Internet for download or online use by eligible individuals, libraries, and schools with a computer and a braille output device. About 40 new titles per month are released in braille and immediately available online to users. (Library of Congress, 2006)

MILLIONS HAVE IMPAIRED EYESIGHT

From a practical point of view, if you can't count the fingers held up by someone ten feet away in broad daylight, you're blind. At least one million in [the United States] are legally blind, and 75,000 new cases develop every year. However, millions more, while not legally blind, have seriously impaired eyesight that, for example, prevents them from reading a newspaper even with glasses. (Rosenfeld, 2001, p. 12)

1 Why is it important to understand the visual process, as well as to know the physical components of the eye?

2 Distinguish between the terms *blind* and *partially sighted*.

3 What are the distinctive features of refractive eye problems, muscle disorders of the eye, and receptive eye problems?

4 What are the estimated prevalence and the causes of vision loss?

5 Describe how a vision loss can affect intelligence, speech and language skills, educational achievement, social development, physical orientation and mobility, and perceptual-motor development.

6 What is a functional approach to assessment for students with a vision loss?

7 Describe two content areas that should be included in educational programs for students with vision loss.

8 How can communication media facilitate learning for people with vision loss?

9 What educational placements are available to students with vision loss?

10 What steps can be taken to prevent and medically treat vision loss?

11 Why is the availability of appropriate social services important for people with vision loss?

▼SNAPSHOT

JOHN

Born prematurely and weighing only 1 pound 13 ounces, John is a child with vision loss. Now 9 years old, John lives with his parents and brother Michael, none of whom have any visual problems. John loves technology and has a CB radio, several TVs, a computer, and a tape recorder. He doesn't care for outdoor activities and isn't into sports. He uses braille to read and has a cane to help him find his way through the world.

John: "I really like to be blind, it's a whole lot of fun. The reason I like to be blind is because I can learn my way around real fast and I have a real fast thinking memory. I can hear things that some people can't hear and smell. Actually, my sense of hearing is the best. . . . I have a CB radio that [I] talk to different people on and sometimes I can talk to people in different places around the world."

John's parents: "John can do anything he wants to do if he puts his mind to it. He's smart enough, he loves all kinds of radio communications. He talks about being on the radio, on

TV, and there's no reason why he can't do that as long as he studies hard in school."

Michael: "I didn't want a blind brother."

John: "Sometimes my brother gets along good and sometimes he comes here in my room and under my desk there's a little power switch that controls all my TVs, scanner, CB, and tape recorder. He'll flip that then he'll laugh about it, run and go somewhere and I'll have to turn it back on, lock my door, and go tell Mom. So that's how he handles it and she puts him in time out."

John's third-grade teacher: "John is very well adjusted. He has a wonderful, delightful personality. He's intelligent. We were a little worried about his braille until this year. Probably because of his prematurity, [he has] a little trouble with the tactual. Of course, braille is all tactual. . . . But he's pulling out of that and that was his last problem with education. He's very bright. He could do many things. He loves computers."

John: "I'd like to be a few different things, and I'll tell you a few of them. I'd like to be a newscaster, an astronaut, or something down at NASA and a dispatcher. So that's three of the things out of a whole million or thousand things I'd like to be."

Through the visual process, we observe the world around us, develop an appreciation for the physical environment and a greater understanding of it. Vision is one of our most important avenues for the acquisition and assimilation of knowledge, but we often take it for granted. From the moment we wake up in the morning, our dependence on sight is obvious. We rely on our eyes to guide us around our surroundings, inform us through the written word, and give us pleasure and relaxation.

What if this precious sight were lost or impaired? How would our perceptions of the world change? Losing sight is one of our greatest fears, partly because of the misconception that people with vision loss are helpless and unable to lead satisfying or productive lives. It is not uncommon for people with sight to have little understanding of those with vision loss. People who are sighted may believe that most adults who are blind are likely to live a deprived socioeconomic and cultural existence. Children who have sight may believe that their peers who are blind are incapable of learning many basic skills, such as telling time and using a computer, or of enjoying leisure and recreational activities such as swimming and watching television. Throughout history, some religions have even promoted the belief that blindness is a punishment for sins.

As the opening Snapshot about John strongly suggests, these negative perceptions of people with vision loss are often inaccurate. John is an active child who has not allowed his vision loss to deprive him of the activities he values. To understand more clearly the nature of vision loss within the context of normal sight, we begin our discussion with an overview of the visual process. Because vision is basically defined as the act of seeing with the eye, we first review the physical components of the visual system.

FOCUS 1
Why is it important to understand the visual process, as well as to know the physical components of the eye?

The Visual Process

The physical components of the visual system include the eye, the **visual cortex** in the brain, and the **optic nerve**, which connects the eye to the visual cortex. The basic anatomy of the human eye is illustrated in Figure 16.1. The **cornea** is the external covering of the eye, and in the presence of light, it bends or refracts visual stimuli. These light rays pass through the **pupil**, which is an opening in the iris. The pupil dilates or constricts to control the amount of light entering the eye. The **iris**, the colored portion of the eye, consists of membranous tissue and muscles whose function is to adjust the size of the pupil. The **lens**, like the cornea, bends light rays so that they strike the retina directly. As in a camera lens, the lens of the eye reverses the images. The **retina** consists of light-sensitive cells that transmit the image to the brain via the optic nerve. Images from the retina remain upside down until they are neurally flipped over in the visual cortex occipital lobe of the brain.

The visual process is much more complex than suggested by a description of the physical components involved. The process is an important link to the physical world, helping us to gain information beyond the range of other senses, while also helping us to integrate the information acquired primarily through hearing, touch, smell, and taste. For example, our sense of touch can tell us that what we are feeling is furry, soft, and warm, but only our eyes must tell that it is a brown rabbit with a white tail and pink eyes. Our nose may perceive something with yeast and spices cooking, but our eyes must confirm that it is a large pepperoni pizza with bubbling mozzarella and green peppers. Our hearing can tell us that a friend sounds angry and upset, but only our vision can register the scowl, clenched jaw, and stiff posture. The way we perceive visual stimuli shapes our interactions with and reactions to the environment, while providing a foundation for the development of a more complex learning structure.

➤ **Visual cortex**

The visual center of the brain, located in the occipital lobe.

➤ **Optic nerve**

The nerve that connects the eye to the visual center of the brain.

➤ **Cornea**

The external covering of the eye.

➤ **Pupil**

The expandable opening in the iris of the eye.

➤ **Iris**

The colored portion of the eye.

➤ **Lens**

The clear structure of the eye that bends light rays so that they strike the retina directly.

➤ **Retina**

Light-sensitive cells in the interior of the eye that transmit images to the brain via the optic nerve.

The Parts of the Human Eye

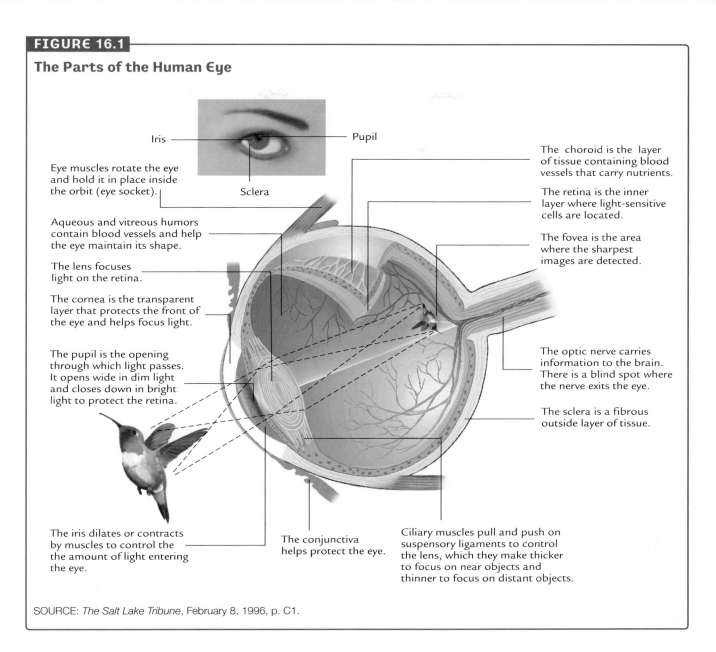

Iris — Pupil

Eye muscles rotate the eye and hold it in place inside the orbit (eye socket).

Sclera

Aqueous and vitreous humors contain blood vessels and help the eye maintain its shape.

The lens focuses light on the retina.

The cornea is the transparent layer that protects the front of the eye and helps focus light.

The pupil is the opening through which light passes. It opens wide in dim light and closes down in bright light to protect the retina.

The choroid is the layer of tissue containing blood vessels that carry nutrients.

The retina is the inner layer where light-sensitive cells are located.

The fovea is the area where the sharpest images are detected.

The optic nerve carries information to the brain. There is a blind spot where the nerve exits the eye.

The sclera is a fibrous outside layer of tissue.

The iris dilates or contracts by muscles to control the the amount of light entering the eye.

The conjunctiva helps protect the eye.

Ciliary muscles pull and push on suspensory ligaments to control the lens, which they make thicker to focus on near objects and thinner to focus on distant objects.

SOURCE: *The Salt Lake Tribune*, February 8, 1996, p. C1.

Definitions and Classification

The term *vision loss* encompasses people with a wide range of conditions, including those who have never experienced sight, those who had normal vision prior to becoming partially or totally blind, those who experienced a gradual or sudden loss of acuity across their field of vision, and those with a restricted field of vision.

Definitions

A variety of terms are used to define vision loss, and this has created some confusion among professionals in various fields of study. The rationale for the development of multiple definitions is directly related to their intended use. For example, eligibility for income tax exemptions or special assistance from the American Printing House for the Blind requires that individuals with vision loss qualify under one of two general subcategories: blind or partially sighted (low vision).

FOCUS **2**
Distinguish between the terms *blind* and *partially sighted*.

BLINDNESS. The term *blindness* has many meanings. In fact, there are over 150 citations for **blind** in an unabridged dictionary. **Legal blindness**, as defined by the Social Security Administration (2006), means either that vision cannot be corrected to better than 20/200 in the better eye or that the visual field is 20 degrees or less, even with a corrective lens. Many people who meet the legal definition of blindness still have some sight and may be able to read large print and get around without support (that is, without a guide dog or a cane).

As we have noted, the definition of legal blindness includes both acuity and field of vision. **Visual acuity** is most often determined by reading letters or numbers on a chart using the **Snellen Test** or by the use of an index that refers to the distance from which an object can be recognized. The person with normal eyesight is defined as having 20/20 vision. However, if an individual is able to read at 20 feet what a person with normal vision can read at 200 feet, then his or her visual acuity would be described as 20/200. Most people consider those who are legally blind to have some light perception; only about 20% are totally without sight. A person is also considered blind if his or her field of vision is limited at its widest angle to 20 degrees or less (see Figure 16.2). A restricted field is also referred to as **tunnel vision** (or pinhole vision or tubular vision). A restricted field of vision severely limits a person's ability to participate in athletics, read, or drive a car.

Blindness can also be characterized as an educational disability. Educational definitions of blindness focus primarily on students' ability to use vision as an avenue for learning. Children who are unable to use their sight and rely on other senses, such as hearing and touch, are described as functionally blind. Functional blindness, in its simplest form, may be defined in terms of whether vision is used as a primary channel of learning. Regardless of the definition used, the purpose of labeling a child as functionally blind is to ensure that he or she receives an appropriate instructional program. This program must assist the student who is blind in utilizing other senses as a means to succeed in a classroom setting and, in the future, as an independent and productive adult.

PARTIAL SIGHT (LOW VISION). People with partial sight or low vision have a visual acuity greater than 20/200 but not greater than 20/70 in the best eye after correction. The field of education also distinguishes between being blind and being partially sighted when determining what level and extent of additional support services a student requires. The term **partially sighted** describes students who are able to use vision as a primary source of learning.

A vision specialist often works with students with vision loss to make the best possible use of remaining sight. This includes the elimination of unnecessary glare in the work area, removal of obstacles that could impede mobility, use of large-print books, and use of special lighting to enhance visual opportunities. Although children with low vision often use printed materials and special lighting in learning activities, some use **braille** because they can see only

---

FIGURE 16.2

The Field of Vision

(a) 180°
Normal field of vision is about 180°.

(b) 20°
A person with a field of vision of 20° or less is considered blind.

shadows and limited movement. These children require the use of tactile or other sensory channels to gain maximum benefit from learning opportunities (Bishop, 2004).

There are two very distinct perspectives on individuals who are partially sighted and their use of residual vision. The first suggests that such individuals should make maximal use of their functional residual vision through the use of magnification, illumination, and specialized teaching aids (e.g., large-print books and posters), as well as any exercises that will increase the efficiency of remaining vision. This position is contrary to the more traditional philosophy of sight conservation, or sight saving, which advocates restricted use of the eye. It was once believed that students with vision loss could keep what sight they had much longer if it was used sparingly. However, extended reliance on residual vision in conjunction with visual stimulation training now appears actually to improve a person's ability to use sight as an avenue for learning.

Classification

Vision loss may be classified according to the anatomical site of the problem. Anatomical disorders include impairment of the refractive structures of the eye, muscle anomalies in the visual system, and problems of the receptive structures of the eye.

REFRACTIVE EYE PROBLEMS. **Refractive problems** are the most common type of vision loss and occur when the refractive structures of the eye (cornea or lens) fail to focus light rays properly on the retina. The four types of refractive problems are hyperopia, or farsightedness; myopia, or nearsightedness; astigmatism, or blurred vision; and cataracts.

Hyperopia occurs when the eyeball is excessively short from front to back (has a flat corneal structure), forcing light rays to focus behind the retina. The person with hyperopia can clearly visualize objects at a distance but cannot see them at close range. This individual may require convex lenses so that a clear focus will occur on the retina.

Myopia occurs when the eyeball is excessively long (has increased curvature of the corneal surface), forcing light rays to focus in front of the retina. The person with myopia can view objects at close range clearly but cannot see them from a distance (such as 100 feet). Eyeglasses may be necessary to assist in focusing on distant objects. Figure 16.3 illustrates the myopic and hyperopic eyeballs and compares them to the normal human eye.

Astigmatism occurs when the curvature or surface of the cornea is uneven, preventing light rays from converging at one point. The rays of light are refracted in different directions, producing unclear, distorted visual images. Astigmatism may occur independently of or in conjunction with myopia or hyperopia.

Cataracts occur when the lens becomes opaque, resulting in severely distorted vision or total blindness. Surgical treatment for cataracts (such as lens implants) has advanced rapidly in recent years, returning to the individual most of the vision that was lost.

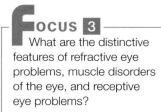

FOCUS 3
What are the distinctive features of refractive eye problems, muscle disorders of the eye, and receptive eye problems?

Council for Exceptional Children

Standard 1: Foundations

➤ **Refractive problems**
Visual disorders that occur when the refractive structures of the eye fail to properly focus light rays on the retina.

➤ **Hyperopia**
Farsightedness; a refractive problem wherein the eyeball is excessively short, focusing light rays behind the retina.

➤ **Myopia**
Nearsightedness; a refractive problem wherein the eyeball is excessively long, focusing light in front of the retina.

➤ **Astigmatism**
A refractive problem that occurs when the surface of the cornea is uneven or structurally defective, preventing light rays from converging at one point.

➤ **Cataract**
A clouding of the eye lens, which becomes opaque, resulting in visual problems.

FIGURE 16.3

Normal, Myopic, and Hyperopic Eyeballs

The image is focused on the retina upside down, but the brain immediately reverses it.

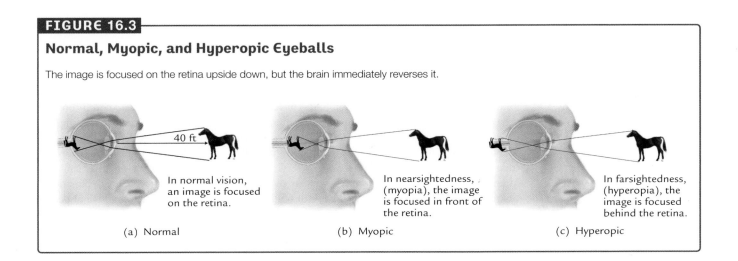

40 ft

In normal vision, an image is focused on the retina.

In nearsightedness, (myopia), the image is focused in front of the retina.

In farsightedness, (hyperopia), the image is focused behind the retina.

(a) Normal   (b) Myopic   (c) Hyperopic

MUSCLE DISORDERS. Muscular defects of the visual system occur when one or more of the major muscles within the eye are weakened in function, resulting in a loss of control and an inability to maintain tension. People with muscle disorders cannot maintain their focus on a given object for even short periods of time. The three types of muscle disorders are nystagmus (uncontrolled rapid eye movement), strabismus (crossed eyes), and amblyopia (an eye that appears normal but does not function properly). **Nystagmus** is a continuous, involuntary, rapid movement of the eyeballs in either a circular or a side-to-side pattern. **Strabismus** occurs when the muscles of the eyes are unable to pull equally, thus preventing the eyes from focusing together on the same object. Internal strabismus (**esotropia**) occurs when the eyes are pulled inward toward the nose; external strabismus (**exotropia**) occurs when the eyes are pulled out toward the ears. The eyes may also shift on a vertical plane (up or down), but this condition is rare. Strabismus can be corrected through surgical intervention. Persons with strabismus often experience a phenomenon known as double vision, because the deviating eye causes two very different pictures to reach to the brain. To correct the double vision and reduce visual confusion, the brain attempts to suppress the image in one eye. As a result, the unused eye loses its ability to see. This condition, known as **amblyopia**, can also be corrected by surgery or by forcing the affected eye into focus by covering the unaffected eye with a patch.

RECEPTIVE EYE PROBLEMS. Disorders associated with the receptive structures of the eye occur when there is a degeneration of or damage to the retina and the optic nerve. These disorders include optic atrophy, retinitis pigmentosa, retinal detachment, retinopathy of prematurity, and glaucoma. **Optic atrophy** is a degenerative disease that results from the deterioration of nerve fibers connecting the retina to the brain. **Retinitis pigmentosa**, the most common hereditary condition associated with loss of vision, appears initially as night blindness and gradually causes degeneration of the retina. Eventually, it results in total blindness.

Retinal detachment occurs when the retina separates from the choroid and the sclera. This detachment may result from disorders such as glaucoma, retinal degeneration, or extreme myopia. It can also be caused by trauma to the eye, such as a boxer's receiving a hard right hook to the face.

Retinopathy of prematurity (ROP), formerly known as *retrolental fibroplasia*, is one of the most devastating eye disorders in young children. It occurs when too much oxygen is administered to premature infants, resulting in the formation of scar tissue behind the lens of the eye, which prevents light rays from reaching the retina. ROP gained attention in the early 1940s, with the advent of better incubators for premature infants. These incubators substantially improved the concentration of oxygen available to the infant but resulted in a drastic increase in the number of children with vision loss. The disorder has also been associated with neurological, speech, and behavior problems in children and adolescents. Now that a relationship has been established between increased oxygen levels and blindness, premature infants can be protected by careful control of the amount of oxygen received in the early months of life.

➤ **Nystagmus**

Uncontrolled rapid eye movements.

➤ **Strabismus**

Crossed eyes (internal strabismus) or eyes that look outward (external strabismus).

➤ **Esotropia**

A form of strabismus in which the eyes are pulled inward toward the nose.

➤ **Exotropia**

A form of strabismus in which the eyes are pulled outward toward the ears.

➤ **Amblyopia**

Loss of vision due to an imbalance of eye muscles.

➤ **Optic atrophy**

A degenerative disease caused by deteriorating nerve fibers connecting the retina to the brain.

➤ **Retinitis pigmentosa**

A hereditary condition resulting from a break in the choroid.

➤ **Retinal detachment**

A condition that occurs when the retina is separated from the choroid and sclera.

➤ **Retinopathy of prematurity**

A disorder caused when too much oxygen is administered to a premature infant, resulting in the formation of scar tissue behind the lens of the eye, which prevents light rays from reaching the retina. Formerly called retrolental fibroplasia.

Focus 4
What are the estimated prevalence and the causes of vision loss?

Prevalence

The prevalence of vision loss is often difficult to determine. For example, although about 20% of children and adults in the United States have some vision loss, most of these conditions can be corrected to a level where they do not interfere with everyday tasks (such as reading and driving a car). Approximately 1 in 3,000 American children is considered legallly blind (Batshaw, 2003), while 3% of the total population (9 million people) have a significant vision loss that will require some type of specialized services and supports. About 5% of American children (approximately 1.2 million) have a serious eye disorder (KidSource, 2006). This figure increases to 20% for people over the age of 65. If cataracts are included, nearly 50% of people over the age of 65 have a significant vision loss The U.S. Department of Education (2006) reports that 26,113 school-age children with vision loss between the ages of 6 and 21 received specialized services in U.S. public schools.

Causation

Genetic Disorders

A number of genetic conditions can result in vision loss, including

➤ **albinism** (resulting in **photophobia** because of lack of pigmentation in eyes, skin, and hair)

➤ retinitis pigmentosa (degeneration of the retina)

➤ **retinoblastoma** (malignant tumor in the retina)

➤ optic atrophy (loss of function of optic nerve fibers)

➤ cataracts (opaque lens resulting in severely distorted vision)

➤ severe myopia associated with retinal detachment

➤ lesions of the cornea

➤ abnormalities of the iris (coloboma or aniridia)

➤ **microphthalmia** (abnormally small eyeball)

➤ **hydrocephalus** (excess cerebrospinal fluid in the brain) leading to optic atrophy

➤ **anophthalmia** (absence of the eyeball),

➤ **glaucoma** or **buphthalmos** (abnormal distention and enlargement of the eyeball).

Glaucoma results from increased pressure within the eye that damages the optic nerve if left untreated. It is responsible for about 4% of all blindness in children (Batshaw, 2003). The incidence of glaucoma is highest in persons over the age of 40 who have a family history of the disease. Glaucoma is treatable, either through surgery to drain fluids from the eye or through the use of medicated eye drops to reduce pressure.

Acquired Disorders

Acquired disorders can occur prior to, during, or after birth. Several factors present prior to birth, such as radiation or the introduction of drugs into the fetal system, may result in vision loss. A major cause of blindness in the fetus is infection, which may be due to diseases such as rubella and syphilis. Other diseases that can result in blindness include influenza, mumps, and measles.

One of the leading causes of acquired blindness in children worldwide is vitamin A deficiency (**xeropthalmia**). Xeropthalmia is ranked among the World Health Organization's top 10 leading causes of death through disease in developing countries (United Nations World Food Programme, 2006).

Another cause of acquired blindness is retinopathy of prematurity. As noted earlier, ROP results from administering of oxygen over prolonged periods of time to low-birthweight infants. Almost 80% of preschool-age blind children lost their sight as a result of ROP during the peak years of the disease (1940s through 1960s).

Vision loss after birth may be due to several factors. Trauma, infections, inflammations, and tumors are all related to loss of sight. **Cortical visual impairment (CVI)** is a leading cause of acquired blindness. CVI, which involves damage to the occipital lobes and/or the visual pathways to the brain, can result from severe trauma, asphyxia, seizures, infections of the central nervous system, drugs, poisons, or other neurological conditions. Most children with CVI have residual vision.

The most common cause of preventable blindness is **trachoma**. This infectious disease affects more than 150 million people worldwide. Trachoma is associated with compromised living standards and hygiene (such as lack of water and unsanitary conditions) within a community. Although the incidence of trachoma has been reduced worldwide, it remains a serious health risk to millions of people in underserved rural areas (International Trachoma Initiative, 2006).

The most common vision problems in adults, particularly those over the age of 60, are caused by **macular degeneration**. This condition is the result of a breakdown of the tissues in

---

➤ **Albinism**

Lack of pigmentation in eyes, skin, and hair.

➤ **Photophobia**

An intolerance to light.

➤ **Retinoblastoma**

A malignant tumor in the retina.

➤ **Microphthalmia**

An abnormally small eyeball.

➤ **Hydrocephalus**

Condition resulting in excess cerebrospinal fluid in the brain.

➤ **Anophthalmia**

Absence of the eyeball.

➤ **Glaucoma**

A disorder of the eye characterized by high pressure inside the eyeball.

➤ **Buphthalmos**

An abnormal distention and enlargement of the eyeball.

➤ **Xeropthalmia**

A condition that is caused by vitamin A deficiency and can lead to blindness. Vitamin A deficiency leads to a lack of production of mucus-producing cells (known as dry eye).

➤ **Cortical visual impairment (CVI)**

A leading cause of acquired blindness, which involves damage to the occipital lobes and/or the visual pathways to the brain. CVI can result from severe trauma, asphyxia, seizures, infections of the central nervous system, drugs, poisons, or various neurological conditions.

➤ **Trachoma**

A slowly progressing infectious bacterial disease associated with poor living standards and inadequate hygiene. Trachoma results in blindness over a period of many years due to repeated infections causing irritation and scars on the eyelid.

➤ **Macular degeneration**

An age-related condition in which the macula (tissues within the retina) break down, resulting in distorted and blurred central vision.

the macula (a small area in the middle of the retina). Macular degeneration affects more than 165,000 people each year, and 16,000 of them go blind as a result of the disease. Nearly two million Americans have impaired vision due to macular degeneration. With macular degeneration, central vision becomes distorted and blurry. The individual also has considerble difficulty differentiating among colors (Rosenfeld, 2001). New advances in the treatment of macular degeneration include laser surgery and drug theapy.

Characteristics

A vision loss present at birth will have a more significant effect on individual development than one that occurs later in life. Useful visual imagery may disappear if sight is lost prior to the age of 5. If sight is lost after the age of 5, it is possible for the person to retain some visual memories. These memories may be maintained for years to come, assisting the person to better understand newly learned concepts. Total blindness that occurs prior to age 5 has the greatest negative influence on overall functioning. However, many people who are blind from birth or early childhood are able to function at about the same level as sighted persons of equal ability.

Intelligence

Children with vision loss sometimes base their perceptions of the world on input from senses other than vision. This is particularly true of the child who is congenitally blind, whose learning experiences are significantly restricted by the lack of vision. Consequently, everyday learning opportunities that people with sight take for granted, such as reading the morning newspaper or watching television news coverage, may be substantially altered.

Reviews of the literature on intellectual development suggest that children with vision loss differ from children with sight in some areas of intelligence, ranging from understanding spatial concepts to a general knowledge of the world (Batshaw, 2003; McLinden & McCall, 2006). However, comparing the performances of individuals with and without sight may not be appropriate if those with sight have an advantage. The only valid way to compare the intellectual capabilities of these children must be based on tasks in which vision loss does not interfere with performance.

Speech and Language Skills

For children with sight, speech and language development occurs primarily through the integration of visual experiences and the symbols of the spoken word. Depending on the degree of loss, children with vision loss are at a distinct disadvantage in developing speech and language skills since they are unable to visually associate words with objects. Because of this, such children must rely on hearing or touch for input, and their speech may develop at a slower rate. Once these children have learned speech, however, it is typically fluent.

Preschool-age and school-age children with vision loss may develop a phenomenon known as **verbalisms**, or the excessive use of speech (wordiness), in which individuals may use words that have little meaning to them (e.g., "Crusaders are people of a religious sex" or "Lead us not into Penn Station"). Sacks and Silberman (2000) suggest that children with visual impairments may have a restricted oral vocabulary, compared to that of sighted peers, because they lack the visual input necessary for them to piece together all of the information available in a given experience.

Academic Achievement

The academic achievement of students with vision loss may be significantly delayed, compared to that of students with sight. Numerous factors may influence academic achievement for students with vision loss. In the area of written language, these students have more difficulty organizing their thoughts to write a composition because they lack the same opportunities as children with sight to read newspapers and magazines. Decoding in the area of reading may be delayed because students with visual impairments often use braille or large-print books as

➤ **Verbalisms**

Excessive use of speech (wordiness) in which individuals use words that have little meaning to them.

the media to decode. Decoding is a much slower process when the reader is using these two media. Reading comprehension is also affected because it depends so much on the experiences of the reader. Once again, the experience of students with visual impairments may be much more limited than that of students with sight, and therefore these children don't bring as much information to the reading task (Sacks & Silberman, 2000).

Young children with a vision loss often have limited opportunities to interact socially with peers who are not disabled. Thus they are less likely to initiate social contact.

Other possible reasons for delays in academic achievement range from excessive school absences due to the need for eye surgery or treatment to years of failure in programs that did not meet each student's specialized needs. On the average, children with vision loss lag two years behind sighted children in grade level. Thus any direct comparisons between students with vision loss and those with sight would indicate significantly delayed academic growth. However, this might have resulted from children with vision loss entering school at a later age, from frequent absence due to medical problems, or from lack of appropriate school resources and facilities. For more in-depth information about academic learning and children with a vision loss, see the Reflect on This, "Creating and Using Tactile Experience Books for Young Children with Visual Impairments" on page 430.

Social Development

The ability of children with vision loss to adapt to the social environment depends on a number of factors, both hereditary and experiential. It is true that each of us experiences the world in his or her own way, but common bonds provide a foundation on which to build perceptions of the world around us. One such bond is vision. Without vision, perceptions about ourselves and those around us can be drastically different.

For the person with vision loss, these differences in perception may produce some social-emotional challenges. Children with vision loss are less likely to initiate a social interaction and have fewer opportunities to socialize with other children (Leigh & Barclay, 2000). They are often unable to imitate the physical mannerisms of others and therefore do not develop one very important component of social communication: body language. Because the subtleties of nonverbal communication can significantly alter the intended meaning of spoken words, a person's inability to learn and use visual cues (such as facial expressions and hand gestures) has profound consequences for interpersonal interactions. The person with vision loss can neither see the visual cues that accompany the messages received from others nor sense the messages that he or she may be conveying through body language.

Differences between people with a vision loss and those who are sighted may also result from exclusion of the person with a vision loss from social activities that are integrally related to the use of sight (such as sports and movies). People with vision loss are often excluded from such activities without a second thought, simply because they cannot see. This reinforces the mistaken notion that they do not want to participate and would not enjoy these activities. Social skills can be learned and effectively used by a person with vision loss. Excluding them from social experiences more often stems from negative public attitudes than from the individuals' lack of social adjustment skills.

Orientation and Mobility

A unique limitation facing people with vision loss is the basic problem of getting from place to place. Such individuals may be unable to orient themselves to other people or objects in the environment simply because they cannot see them and therefore do not understand their own relative position in space. Consequently, they may be unable to move in the right direction and may fear getting injured, so they may try to restrict their movements in order to protect themselves. Parents and professionals may contribute to such fears by overprotecting the per-

CREATING AND USING TACTILE EXPERIENCE BOOKS FOR YOUNG CHILDREN WITH VISUAL IMPAIRMENTS

What do very young children learn about reading? According to many studies on developmental learning, young children develop an appreciation that the "reading" activities in which they engage are related to the words they speak and hear, and are further connected to the written symbols of our language. They observe others reading and writing within functional contexts and meaningful activities. At the same time, they develop important basic concepts about reading materials.

But what about children whose vision is limited, or children who are blind? How do they participate in early reading activities? This article explores ways in which educators, parents, and caregivers can ensure that *all* young children have a chance to learn to read.

LITERACY NEEDS OF CHILDREN WITH VISUAL IMPAIRMENTS

Obtaining access to the written symbols of language and observing adults and peers modeling reading and writing are not easily achieved for children with significant visual impairments. Visual impairment can directly interfere with the observation of symbols and events that are key to the development of early literacy skills. . . .

TACTILE ILLUSTRATIONS

For young children who are blind or who have severe visual impairments, the visual aspects of books written for emergent readers present a significant problem. The obvious solution to this accessibility issue is the use of raised-line drawings in conjunction with Braille text. Interpretation of raised-line drawings, however, is a far more difficult task than is recognition and identification of pictures. Raised line drawings attempt to present the three-dimensional world in two dimensions. Although we can visually see the relationship, a circle is really very unlike the way a ball feels; the outline of a birthday cake bears no resemblance to its tactile reality. Similarly, the outline of the "Cat in the Hat" holding a fish cannot be easily related to the outline of the Cat sitting in a chair. The details and constancy that make even abstract illustrations so identifiable visually cannot be reproduced in a tactile form. . . .

Books published for young children with vision feature text that is simple and often repetitive. This repetition helps the emerging reader to memorize the text, so that attention can be placed on the correspondence between the text and spoken words. This same practice can be used in tactile experience books published for young children with visual impairments. Although it is tempting to write long descriptive passages, young children benefit when there are few words on the page. They also benefit when phrases are repeated, such as "In my bathroom, there is a ____," or "When we fixed the doorknob, we used ____."

MARY'S TACTILE EXPERIENCE BOOK

Mary, who is totally deaf and blind, is in kindergarten in her local school district. A team of educators, including the second author, Joan, who is an orientation and mobility (O&M) specialist, provide support services to Mary. O&M specialists generally work on development of skills associated with travel, including use of the cane, body image, spatial concepts, sensory perception, and environmental-recognition skills. Joan decided that an "experience book" would be an ideal vehicle for reinforcing concepts of travel with Mary and approached the speech-language pathologist serving this student about working together on the project.

The two adults met with Mary and her interpreter in the school's courtyard garden and explored the area, which included flowers, trees, a gazebo, and even rabbits. Since Mary was not familiar with any garden, questions such as "What do you think might be in a garden?" were not helpful. Therefore, the adults asked Mary to move around the garden and look for items to the left or right, on the ground, or up high. As they explored, they discovered various natural items that were appropriate for an experience book; Mary picked these up and placed them in a large bag.

Joan then prepared the simple lines of the story in braille and print. During their next meeting, Mary assisted Joan in the assembly of the book. The process went slowly as Mary explored each garden item, used sign language to identify it, and helped position it on the page. Mary affixed the items with tape; later, Joan prepared more permanent mountings. Joan arranged short braille sentences at the bottom of each page. The last page was left for Mary and Joan to work on together. Mary not only chose the words for this page but also assisted in writing the sentences on the Braillewriter.

SOURCE: Lewis, S., & Tolla, J. (2003). "Creating and Using Tactile Experience Books for Young Children with Visual Impairments." *Teaching Exceptional Children, 35*(3), 22–25.

son who has vision loss from the everyday risks of life. Shielding the individual in this way will hinder acquisition of independent mobility skills and create an atmosphere that promotes lifelong overdependence on caregivers.

Vision loss can affect fine motor coordination and interfere with the ability to manipulate objects. Poor eye–hand coordination interferes with learning how to use tools related to job skills and daily living skills (such as using eating utensils, a toothbrush, or a screwdriver). Prevention or remediation of fine motor problems may require training in the use of visual aid magnifiers and improvement of basic fine motor skills. This training must begin early and focus directly on experiences that will enhance opportunities for independent living.

Perceptual-Motor Development

Perceptual-motor development is essential in the development of locomotion skills, but it is also important in the development of cognition, language, socialization, and personality. Most children with vision loss appear to have perceptual discrimination abilities (such as discriminating texture, weight, and sound) comparable to those of children with sight (Bishop, 2004). Children with vision loss do not perform as well on more complex tasks of perception, including form identification, spatial relations, and perceptual-motor integration (Bouchard & Tetreault, 2000).

Author and mountain climber Erik Wiehenmayer didn't let blindness interfere with his life's passion: to scale some of the world's highest mountains.

A popular misconception regarding the perceptual abilities of persons with vision loss is that because of their diminished sight, they develop greater capacity in other sensory areas. For example, people who are blind are supposedly able to hear or smell some things that people with normal vision cannot perceive. This notion has never been empirically validated.

Educational Supports and Services

Assessment

When assessing the cognitive ability, academic achievement, language skills, motor performance, and social-emotional functioning of a student with a vision loss, an IEP team must also focus on how the student utilizes any remaining vision (visual efficiency) in conjunction with other senses. The Visual Efficiency Scale (see Barraga and Erin, 2002) assesses the overall visual functioning of the individual to determine how he or she uses sight to acquire information. As suggested by Bishop (2004), if the individual has remaining vision, it is important that professionals and parents promote its use. It is a myth that remaining useful vision will be conserved by not using it.

A functional approach to assessment focuses on a person's visual capacity, attention, and processing. Visual capacity includes both acuity and field of vision, and it also encompasses the response of the individual to visual information. The assessment of visual attention involves observing the individual's sensitivity to visual stimuli (alertness), ability to use vision to select information from a variety of sources, attention to a visual stimulus, and ability to process visual information. Visual-processing assessment determines which, if any, of the components of normal visual functioning are impaired.

Mobility Training and Daily Living Skills

The educational needs of students with vision loss are comparable to those of their sighted counterparts. In addition, many instructional methods currently used with students who are sighted are appropriate for students with vision loss. However, educators must be aware that certain content areas that are generally unnecessary for sighted students are essential to the success, in a classroom, of students with vision loss. These areas include mobility and orientation training as well as acquisition of daily living skills.

FOCUS 6
What is a functional approach to assessment for students with a vision loss?

Council for Exceptional Children

Standard 3: Individual Learning Differences

Standard 4: Instructional Strategies

Standard 7: Instructional Planning

FOCUS 7
Describe two content areas that should be included in educational programs for students with vision loss.

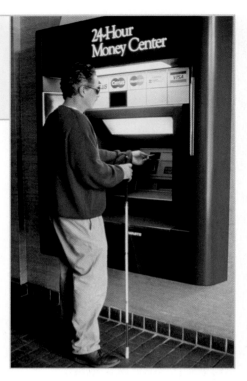

This talking ATM macine allows people with a vision loss to access their bank acount conveniently and complete a transaction.

The ability to move safely, efficiently, and independently through the environment enhances the individual's opportunities to learn more about the world and thus to be less dependent on others for survival. Lack of mobility restricts individuals with vision loss in nearly every aspect of educational life. Such students may be unable to orient themselves to physical structures in the classroom (desks, chairs, and aisles), hallways, rest rooms, library, and cafeteria. Whereas a person with sight can automatically establish a relative position in space, the individual with vision loss must be taught some means of compensating for a lack of visual input. This may be accomplished in a number of ways. It is important that students with vision loss not only learn the physical structure of their school but also develop specific techniques to orient themselves to unfamiliar surroundings.

These orientation techniques involve using the other senses. For example, the senses of touch and hearing can help identify cues that designate where the bathroom is in the school. Although it is not true that people who are blind have superior hearing abilities, they may learn to use their hearing more effectively by focusing on subtle auditory cues that often go unnoticed. The efficient use of hearing, in conjunction with the other senses (including any remaining vision), is the key to independent travel for people with vision loss.

Independent travel with a sighted companion, but without the use of a cane, guide dog, or electronic device, is the most common form of travel for young school-age children. The major challenges for children with low vision in moving independently and safely through their environment include

> knowing where landmarks are throughout the school setting

> being familiar with the layout of classsrooms and common areas, such as the library, gym, and cafeteria

> knowing where exits, restrooms, the main office, and other relevant [school and classroom] areas are [located]

> understanding the school's emergency procedures, such as fire, tornado, or earthquake drills (Cox & Dykes, 2001).

Other challenges for students with low vision include adapting to changes in lighting, negotiating stairs and curbs, and walking in bad weather.

With the increasing emphasis on instructing young children in orientation at an earlier age, use of the long cane (Kiddy Cane) for young children has become more common. As these children grow older, they may be instructed in the use of a Mowat Sensor. The **Mowat Sensor**, approximately the size of a flashlight, is a hand-held ultrasound travel aid that uses high-frequency sound to detect objects. Vibration frequency increases as objects become closer; the sensor vibrates at different rates to warn of obstacles in front of the individual. The device ignores everything but the closest object within the beam.

Guide dogs or electronic mobility devices may be appropriate for the adolescent or adult, since the need to travel independently increases significantly with age. A variety of electronic mobility devices are currently being used for everything from enhancing hearing efficiency to detecting obstacles.

The **Laser cane** converts infrared light into sound as light beams strike objects in the path of the person who is blind. It uses a range-finding technique with a semiconductor laser and a Position Sensitive Device (PSD). Proximity to an obstacle is warned by vibration at different levels of frequency.

> **Mowat Sensor**

A hand-held travel aid, approximately the size of a flashlight, used by people who are blind. It serves as an alternative to a cane for finding obstacles in the person's pathway.

> **Laser cane**

A mobility device for people who are blind. It converts infrared light into sound as light beams strike objects.

The **Sonicguide**, or Sonic Pathfinder, worn on the head, emits ultrasound and converts reflections from objects into audible noise in such a way that the individual can learn about the structure of objects. For example, loudness indicates size: The louder the noise, the larger the object. To use the Sonicguide effectively, the person with low vision should have mobility skills. It is designed for outdoor use in conjunction with a cane, a guide dog, or residual vision.

The acquisition of daily living skills is another content area important to success in the classroom and to overall independence. Most people take for granted many routine events of the day, such as eating, dressing, bathing, and toileting. A person with sight learns very early in life the tasks associated with perceptual-motor development, including grasping, lifting, balancing, pouring, and manipulating objects. These daily living tasks become more complex during the school years as a child learns personal hygiene, grooming, and social etiquette. Eventually, people with sight acquire many complex daily living skills that later contribute to their independence as adults. Money management, grocery shopping, doing laundry, cooking, cleaning, household repairs, sewing, mowing the lawn, and gardening are all daily tasks associated with adult life and are learned from experiences that are not usually a part of an individual's formal educational program.

For children with vision loss, however, routine daily living skills are not easily learned through everyday experiences. These children must be encouraged and supported as they develop life skills and must not be overprotected from everyday challenges and risks by family and friends.

Guide dogs and electronic mobility devices (such as this global positioning device) assist people who are blind in moving safely, efficiently, and independently through their environment.

➤ **Sonicguide**
An electronic mobility device for people who are blind, which is worn on the head, emits ultrasound, and converts reflections of objects into audible noise.

Instructional Content

Mobility training and daily living skills are components of an educational program that must also include an academic curriculum. (The Case Study, "Mary, Mike, and Josh" on page 434 illustrates classsroom strategies to improve academic learning for three students who have low vision and other disabilities.) Particular emphasis must be placed on developing receptive and expressive language skills. Students with vision loss must learn to listen in order to understand the auditory world more clearly. Finely tuned receptive skills contribute to the development of expressive language, which allows these students to describe their perceptions of the world orally. Koenig and Holbrook (2005) suggest the use of a language experience approach (LEA) as a means to develop language skills and prepare students for reading. The LEA involves several steps, as described in Figure 16.4.

Oral expression can be expanded to include handwriting as a means of communication. The acquisition of social and instructional language skills opens the door to many areas, including reading and mathematics. Reading can greatly expand the knowledge base for children with vision loss. For people who are partially sighted, various optical aids are available: video systems that magnify print, hand-held magnifiers, magnifiers attached to eyeglasses, and other telescopic aids. Another means to facilitate reading for partially sighted students is the use of large-print books, which are generally available in several print sizes through the American Printing House for the Blind and the Library of Congress. Other factors that must be considered in teaching reading to students who are partially sighted include adequate illumination and the reduction of glare. Advance organizers prepare students by previewing the instructional approach and materials to be used in a lesson. These organizers essentially identify the topics or tasks to be learned, give the student an organizational framework, indicate the concepts to be introduced, list new vocabulary, and state the intended outcomes for the student.

Abstract mathematical concepts may be difficult for students who are blind. These students will probably require additional practice in learning to master symbols, number facts, and higher-level calculations. As concepts become more complex, additional aids may be necessary to facilitate learning. Specially designed talking microcomputers, calculators, rulers, compasses, and the Crammer abacus have been developed to assist students in this area.

CASE STUDY

MARY, MIKE, AND JOSH

MARY

Mary, an 11-year-old with Down syndrome, is mainstreamed into a fourth-grade class 80% of her school day. She has mild myopia (nearsightedness) and often loses her place when reading unless she uses her finger as a guide. She has recently joined a dance class for children with special needs and enjoys it very much. Mary's parents bought her leotards, tights, and ballet shoes for the class. These articles now become a good topic for this activity.

The teacher (or her teacher's aide) shows three prices in a 1 × 3 grid—$25.00 for the leotard, $5.00 for tights, and $17.00 for ballet shoes. The grid is presented 7 feet in front of Mary. The teacher verbally tells her the prices on the three items and asks her to write down the price of one of the items in the 1 × 3 grid placed on her desk that corresponds to the one 7 feet away. Following Mary's correct response, the teacher then asks another question: "Among the three things, which one is the most expensive? Write the price in the matching box."

MIKE

Mike, a tenth grader, was born deaf and has recently been diagnosed with Usher syndrome. He has poor night vision and is slowly beginning to lose his visual fields. His visual acuity continues to be 20/20. In coping with his emerging field loss, Mike has been advised to move his head to scan the entire line or page when reading. Mike has special interests in planets and likes to read about the topic. A colorful planet poster hangs in his room.

Having Mike identify different planets would be a good topic for this activity. The teacher shows pictures of planets, describing each one, and has Mike identify which planet the teacher is referring to by spelling the name of the planet—that is, circling the letters in the letter chart in front of him. Because

Mike has difficulty with spelling, the teacher may need to provide assistance when necessary.

JOSH

Josh is an 8-year-old with cerebral palsy (mild diplegia) as a result of premature birth. He has excellent verbal skills but has difficulties with fine motor skills and any spatial-related tasks (such as drawing a tall tree on the left side of the house or writing the letter p, which is a stick with a "right" balloon. Josh is placed in a general education second grade classroom and possesses basic concepts comparable to that of a second grader without disabilities.

In this activity, Josh is asked to verbally illustrate as he draws a house or writes a letter within the grid or dots. If he has problems, the teacher demonstrates, for example, "drawing a line on the second row between the second and fourth dots, the chimney is sticking out between the third and fourth dots." If Josh is confused with rows and lines of dots, the teacher may number the dots so that he can follow the numbers instead of the lines and rows of dots. However, numbered dots should be faded out gradually so that Josh will use spatial concepts rather than numbers. For example, after Josh is comfortable with the numbered dots, then number the first and last dot of each row and line, next fade it out by numbering only the first dot, and eventually no numbers will appear along with dots.

APPLICATION

1. What strategies does the teacher use to accommodate Mary's vision loss when she is reading?

2. Mike, a student who both has a vision loss and was born deaf, is losing his visual fields. What strategies are used to assist Mike in coping with his emerging field loss?

3. Josh is a child with vision loss and cerebral palsy who has difficlties with fine motor skills and spatial-related tasks. Describe the activity that Josh uses to improve his skills in these two areas.

SOURCE: Li, A. (2004). Classroom Strategies for Improving and Enhancing Visual Skills in Students with Disabilities. *Teaching Exceptional Children, 36*(6), 38–46.

Focus 8
How can communication media facilitate learning for people with vision loss?

Communication Media

For students who are partially sighted, their limited vision remains a means of obtaining information. The use of optical aids in conjunction with auditory and tactile stimuli provides these individuals with an integrated sensory approach to learning. However, this approach is not possible for students who are blind. Because they do not have access to visual stimuli, they may have to compensate through the use of tactile and auditory media. Through these media, children who are blind develop an understanding of themselves and of the world around them. One facet of this development process is the acquisition of language, and one facet of language acquisition is learning to read.

For the student who is blind, the tactile sense represents entry into the symbolic world of reading. The most widely used tactile medium for teaching reading is the braille system.

General Steps in the Language Experience Approach

1. Arrange for and carry out a special event or activity for the child (or a group of children), such as a visit to the town's Post Office or a nearby farm. A naturally occurring experience like a classmate's birthday or a school assembly may also be used, but it is also important to continue to expand the child's experiences through unique and special activities (such as attending a circus or riding in a rowboat). Use a multisensory approach and active learning to immerse the child fully in the experience.

2. After the activity, have the child tell a story about what happened. If he or she has trouble getting started, use some brief prompts ("What happened first?"). As the child tells the story, write it down word for word with a braillewriter. Generally, the stories are relatively short at this stage in the student's literacy development. Three important points need to be emphasized:

   - Use a braillewriter (rather than a computer) to write the story so that the child knows that what he or she is saying is being recorded through writing. Have the child follow along with his or her finger just behind the embossing head, if appropriate.

   - Write the story in braille as the child is speaking. It is not instructionally effective to write it in print and later transcribe it into braille. Writing immediately in braille makes the child aware of the natural relationship between spoken and written words.

   - Write down the child's words exactly as he or she says them. Do not fix grammatical errors or attempt to control the vocabulary in any way. One of the goals of using this approach is to build the child's trust. If the child thinks that his or her story needs to be "fixed," then this feeling of trust is interrupted, and the child may be less willing to share his or her experiences and stories in the future.

3. Reread the story immediately with the child, using the shared reading strategy just discussed. The child will remember much of the story and will be able to read along, saying many of the words. Do not stop or pause during this step to have the child sound out or analyze words. The immediate rereading should be a holistic experience recounting the child's story.

4. Continue rereading the story through shared reading on subsequent days. Soon, the child will independently know more of the words and may even begin to recognize some of the words out of context.

5. Arrange contextually appropriate reading-strategy lessons based on the story, especially as the child approaches kindergarten. For example, if the story has several *p* words in it, talk about the initial /p/ sound. The child can scan to find the *p* words in the story and make a list, perhaps in a shared writing experience, of other *p* words. A comprehension activity may involve writing a new ending of the story by changing one feature (for example, "How would your story have ended if . . .?"). Related art activities or binding the story into a book may also be fun and motivating for the child.

SOURCE: Koenig, A. J., & Holbrook, M. C. (2005). Literacy Skills. In A. J. Koenig, & M. C. Holbrook (Eds.), *Foundations of Education: Volume II, Instructional Strategies for Teaching Children and Youths with Visual Impairments* (2nd Ed.). pp. 276–277. New York: AFB Press.

This system, which originated with the work of Louis Braille in 1829, is a code that utilizes a six-dot cell to form 63 different alphabetical, numerical, and grammatical characters. To become a proficient braille reader, a person must learn 263 different configurations, including alphabet letters, punctuation marks, short-form words, and contractions. Braille is not a tactile reproduction of the standard English alphabet but a separate code for reading and writing.

Braille is composed of from one to six raised dots depicted in a cell or space that contains room for two vertical rows of three dots each. On the left the dots are numbered 1, 2, and 3 from top to bottom; on the right the dots are numbered 4, 5, and 6 (see Figure 16.4). This makes it easy to describe braille characters. For example, a is dot 1, p is dots 1, 2, 3, and 4, and h is dots 1, 2, and 5. . . .

In braille any letter becomes a capital by putting dot 6 in front of it. For example, if *a* is dot 1, [then] A is dot 6 followed by dot 1, and if p is dots 1, 2, 3, and 4, [then] P is dot 6 followed by dots 1, 2, 3, and 4. This sure is easier than print, which requires different configurations for more than half of the capital letters. If h is dots 1, 2, and 5, what is H?

Council for
Exceptional
Children

Standard 4: Instructional Strategies

Standard 7: Instructional Planning

Standard 8: Assessment

Research has shown that the fastest braille readers use two hands. Using two hands also seems to make it easier for beginning braille readers to stay on the line. Do you think this might have something to do with two points constituting a line as my geometry teacher used to tell us? (Pester, 2006)

Braille is used by about one of every ten students who are blind and is considered by many to be an efficient means for teaching reading and writing. The American Printing House for the Blind produces about 28 million pages in English braille each year (Pester, 2006). Critics of the system argue that most readers who use braille are much slower than those who read from print and that braille materials are bulky and tedious. It can be argued, however, that without braille, people who are blind would be much less independent. Some people who are unable to read braille (such as people with diabetes who have decreased tactile sensitivity) are more dependent on sight readers and recordings. Simple tasks—such as labeling cans, boxes, or cartons in a bathroom or kitchen—become nearly impossible to complete.

Braille writing is accomplished through the use of a slate and stylus. Using this procedure, a student writes a mirror image of the reading code, moving from right to left. The writing process may be facilitated by using a braille writer, a hand-operated machine with six keys that correspond to each dot in the braille cell.

Innovations for braille readers that reduce some of the problems associated with the medium include the Mountbatten Brailler and the Braille 'n Speak. The Mountbatten Brailler is electronic and hence easier to operate than a manual unit. The Mountbatten Brailler weighs about 15 pounds and can be hooked up to a computer keyboard attachment to input information.

The Braille 'n Speak is a pocket-size battery-powered braille note taker with keyboard for data entry with voice output. The device can translate braille into synthesized speech or print. Files may be printed in formatted text to a printer designed to enable users to input information through a braille keyboard. The Braille 'n Speak has accessories for entering or reading text for a host computer, for reading computer disks, and for sending or receiving a fax.

In regard to educational programs for students who are blind, the U.S. Congress responded to concerns that services for these students were not addressing their unique educational and learning needs, particularly their needs for instruction in reading, writing, and composition. In IDEA, Congress mandated that schools make provision for instruction in braille and the use of braille unless the IEP team determines that such instruction and use are not appropriate to the needs of the student (U.S. Department of Education, 2000).

One tactile device that does not use the braille system is the Optacon Scanner. This machine exposes printed material to a camera and then reproduces it on a fingerpad, using a series of vibrating pins that are tactile reproductions of the printed material. Developed by J. C. Bliss, Optacons have been available commercially since 1971, and thousands are currently in use worldwide. Although the Optacon greatly expands access to the printed word, it has drawbacks as well. It requires tactile sensitivity, so reading remains a slow, laborious process. Additionally, considerable training is required for the individual to become a skilled user. These drawbacks, along with the development of reading machines, have resulted in the declining use and production of the Optacon Scanner.

Many of the newer communication systems do not make use of the tactile sense because it is not functional for all people who are blind (many, including some elderly people, do not have tactile sensitivity). Such individuals must rely solely on the auditory sense to acquire information. Specialized auditory media for people who are blind are becoming increasingly available. One example is the reading machine, hailed as a major breakthrough in technology

The Braille 'n Speak translates braille into synthesized speech and is so portable that it can be carried anywhere.

ASSISTIVE TECHNOLOGY

THE MAGIC MACHINES OF RAY KURZWEIL

In the late 1960s, Ray Kurzweil walked on stage, played a composition on an old upright piano, and then whispered to *I've Got a Secret* host Steve Allen, "I built my own computer." "Well that's impressive," Steve Allen replied, "but what does it have to do with the piece you just played?" Ray then whispered the rest of his secret: "The computer composed the piece I just played." . . . Ray programmed his computer to analyze the patterns in musical compositions by famous composers and then to compose original new melodies in a similar style. For the project, Ray won First Prize in the International Science Fair. From there, he went on to become one of the world's leading inventors, developing Kurzweil Computer Products and Optical Character Recognition (OCR)—teaching a computer to identify printed or typed characters regardless of type style and print quality.

For a while, this new technology was a solution in search of a problem. Then a chance plane flight sitting next to a man who was blind convinced Ray that the most exciting application of this new technology would be to create a machine that could read printed and typed documents out loud, thereby overcoming the reading disability of people who were visually impaired. This goal introduced new hurdles because there were no readily available scanners or speech synthesizers in the 1970s. Accordingly, Ray and his colleagues developed the first full text-to-speech synthesizer and combined these technologies into the first print-to-speech reading machine for people who are blind.

Ray, along with the National Federation of the Blind, announced the Kurzweil Reading Machine at a press conference on January 13, 1976, that was covered by all of the networks and leading print publications. Walter Cronkite used it to deliver his signature sign-off "And that's the way it was, January 13, 1976." Stevie Wonder happened to catch Ray demonstrating the Kurzweil Reading Machine on the *Today Show* and dropped by Kurzweil Computer Products to pick up their first production unit. This led to a long-term friendship between the inventor and the musical star, which led to Ray Kurzweil's subsequent innovations in computer-based music.

Today, the L&H Kurzweil Reading Systems are used by people with visual impairments around the world.

SOURCE: Adapted from Kurzweil Technologies (2006). *A Brief Biography of Ray Kurzweil*. Burlington, MA: Lernout & Hauspie. Retrieved November 5, 2006, from http://www.kurzweiltech.com/raybio.html

---

for persons with a vision loss. Reading machines convert printed matter into synthetic speech at a rate of 1 to 2.5 pages per minute. They can also convert print to braille. The costs associated with reading machines have decreased substantially in the past few years, and most can be purchased with computer accessories for about $1,000. Several advocacy organizations for those with blindness and many banks throughout America currently provide low-interest loans for people with vision loss so that they can purchase the device. The first reading machines were invented by Ray Kurzweil in the 1970s, culminating in the L&H Kurzweill 1000 Reading System in 1998. For more in-depth information on Kurzweil reading machines, see the Assistive Technology "The Magic Machines of Ray Kurzweil."

Other auditory aids that assist people who are blind include microcomputers with voice output, talking calculators, talking-book machines, compact disc players, and audiotape recorders. For example, the Note Teller is a small, compact machine that can identify denominations of U.S. currency using a voice synthesizer that communicates in either English or Spanish.

Communication media that facilitate participation of people with vision loss in the community include specialized library and newspaper services that offer books in large print, on cassette, and in braille. The *New York Times*, for example, publishes a weekly special edition with type three times the size of its regular type. The sale of large-print books has increased during the past ten years, and many have also become available through the Internet or on computer disk (electronic books).

Responding to a human voice, devices known as **personal digital assistants (PDAs)** can look up a telephone number and dial it. Using a synthesized voice, some PDAs can read a newspaper delivered over telephone lines, balance a checkbook, turn home appliances on and off, and maintain a daily appointment book.

Closed-circuit television (CCTV) systems are another means to enlarge the print from books and other written documents. Initially explored in the 1950s, CCTV systems became

> ► **Personal digital assistants (PDAs)**
>
> Hand-held computer device that can be programmed to perform multiple functions, such as dialing a telephone, reading a newspaper, or maintaining a daily calendar or address book.

> ► **Closed-circuit television (CCTV)**
>
> A TV system that includes a small television camera with a zoom lens, TV monitor, and sliding platform table, which allows an individual with vision loss to view printed material enlarged up to 60 times its original size.

more practical in the 1970s, and they are now in wider use than ever before. The components of the CCTV systems include a small television camera with variable zoom lens and focusing capacity, a TV monitor, and a sliding platform table for the printed materials. An individual sits in front of the television monitor to view printed material that can be enhanced up to 60 times its original size through the use of the TV camera and zoom lens. Some CCTVs are also available with split-screen capability to allow near and distant objects to be viewed together. These machines can also accept input directly from a computer as well as printed material.

Educating Students with Vision Loss in the Least Restrictive Environment

Focus **9**

What educational placements are available to students with vision loss?

Council for Exceptional Children

Standard 5: Learning Environments and Social Interactions

Historically, education for students with vision loss—specifically, blindness—was provided through specialized residential facilities. These segregated centers have traditionally been referred to as asylums, institutions, or schools. One of the first such facilities in the United States was the New England Asylum for the Blind, later renamed the Perkins School. This facility opened its doors in 1832 and was one of several eastern U.S. schools that used treatment models borrowed from well-established European institutions. For the most part, the early U.S. institutions operated as closed schools, where a person who was blind would live and learn in an environment that was essentially separate from the outside world. The philosophy was to get the person who was blind "ready for the outside world," even though this approach provided little actual exposure to it.

More recently, some residential schools have advocated an open system of intervention. These programs are based on the philosophy that children who are blind should have every opportunity to gain the same experiences that would be available if they were growing up in their own communities. Both open and closed residential facilities exist today as alternative intervention modes, but they are no longer the primary social or educational systems available to people who are blind. Just like John in the chapter-opening snapshot, the vast majority of people who are blind or partially sighted now live at home, attend local public schools, and interact within the community. For more information about including people with vision loss in family, school, and community, see this chapter's Inclusion and Collaboration Through the Lifespan.

Educational programs for students with vision loss are based on the principle of flexible placement. Thus a wide variety of services are available to these students, ranging from general education class placement, with little or no assistance from specialists, to separate residential schools. Between these two placements, the public schools generally offer several alternative classroom structures, including the use of consulting teachers, resource rooms, part-time special classes, or full-time special classes. Placement of a student in one of these programs depends on the extent to which the loss of vision affects his or her overall educational achievement. Many students with vision loss are able to function successfully within inclusive educational programs if the learning environment is adapted to meet their needs.

Some organizations advocating for students who are blind strongly support the concept of flexible placements within a continuum ranging from general education classroom to residential school (American Foundation for the Blind, 2006). The American Foundation for the Blind recommends a full continuum of alternative placements, emphasizing that students who are visually impaired are most likely to succeed in educational systems where appropriate instruction and services are provided in a full array of program options by qualified staff to address each student's unique educational needs. (See the Debate Forum, "General Education Schools versus Special Schools: Where Should Students Who Are Blind Be Educated?")

Whether the student is to be included in the general education classroom or taught in a special class, a vision specialist must be available, either to support the general education classroom teacher or to provide direct instruction to the student. A vision specialist has received concentrated training in the education of students with vision loss. This specialist and the rest of the educational support team have knowledge of appropriate educational assessment techniques, specialized curriculum materials and teaching approaches, and the

GENERAL EDUCATION SCHOOLS VERSUS SPECIAL SCHOOLS

WHERE SHOULD STUDENTS WHO ARE BLIND BE EDUCATED?

In 1900, the first class for students who were blind opened in the Chicago public schools. Prior to this, such children were educated in state residential schools, where they lived away from their families. Until 1950, the ratio of students attending schools for the blind to those in general education public schools was about 10 to 1. In that year, however, the incidence of children with retrolental fibroplasia (now known as retinopathy of prematurity) increased, resulting in significant numbers of children who were blind attending public schools. By 1960, more children with blindness were being educated with their nondisabled peers in general education public schools than in schools for the blind. Nonetheless, the issue of what is the most appropriate educational environment for children who are blind continues to be debated internationally.

POINT

Children who are blind should be educated in public schools and classrooms alongside their seeing peers. Inclusion enables children who are blind to remain at home with their families and live in a local neighborhood, which is just as important for these children as it is for their sighted friends. It also gives children who are blind greater opportunities for appropriate modeling of acceptable behaviors.

Schools for children who are blind have endeavored over the years to offer the best education possible, one intended to be equivalent to that offered to children who can see. However, these schools cannot duplicate the experiences of living at home and being part of the local community. Although it can be argued that the special school is geared entirely to the needs of the child who is blind, there is much more to education than a segregated educational environment can provide. During the growing years, the child must be directly involved in the seeing world in order to have the opportunity to adjust and become a part of society.

COUNTERPOINT

The special school for children who are blind provides a complete education that is oriented entirely to the unique needs of these individuals. The teachers in these schools have years of experience in working exclusively with children who are blind and are well aware of what educational experiences are needed to help them reach their fullest potential. Additionally, special schools are equipped with a multitude of educational resources developed for children who are blind. General education schools and classrooms cannot offer the intensive, individualized programs in areas such as music, physical education, and arts and crafts that are available through schools for the blind. The strength of the special school is that it is entirely geared to the specialized needs of the child who is blind. Thus, it can more effectively teach him or her the skills necessary to adapt to life experiences.

use of various communication media. Specialized instruction for students who have vision loss may include a major modification in curricula, including teaching concepts that children who are sighted learn incidentally (such as walking down the street, getting from one room to the next in the school building, getting meals in the cafeteria, and using public transportation).

Health Care and Social Services

Health care services for vision loss include initial screenings based on visual acuity; preventive measures that include genetic screening, appropriate prenatal care, and early developmental assessments; and treatment ranging from optical aids to surgery. Some people with vision loss may have social adjustment difficulties, including lack of self-esteem and general feelings of inferiority. To minimize these problems, social services should be made available as early as possible in the person's life.

Council for
Exceptional
Children

Standard 1: Foundations

Standard 8: Assessment

INCLUSION AND COLLABORATION THROUGH THE LIFESPAN

PEOPLE WITH VISION LOSS

EARLY CHILDHOOD YEARS

Tips for the Family

- Assist your child with vision loss in learning how to get around in the home environment. Then give your child the freedom to move freely about.

- Help your child become oriented to the environment by removing all unnecessary obstacles around the home (e.g., shoes left on the floor, partially opened doors, a vacuum cleaner left out). Keep your child informed of any changes in room arrangements.

- Instruction in special mobility techniques should begin as early as possible with the young child who has vision loss.

- Keep informed about organizations and civic groups that can provide support to the child and the family.

- Be collaborative with professionals. Get in touch and work closely with your local health, social services, and education agencies about infant, toddler, and preschool programs for children with vision loss. Become familiar with the individualized family service plan (IFSP) and how it can serve as a collaborative planning tool with professionals to provide early intervention programs.

Tips for the Preschool Teacher

- Mobility is a fundamental part of early intervention programs for children with vision loss. Help these children learn to explore the environment in the classroom, school, and local neighborhood.

- Help the child to develop a sense of touch and to use hearing to acquire information. The young child may also need assistance in learning to smile and make eye contact.

- Collaborate with the family to develop orientation and mobility strategies that can be learned and applied in both home and school settings.

- Help children in the classroom who have sight interact with the young child with vision loss by teaching them to speak directly in a normal tone of voice so as not to raise the noise level.

- Become very familiar with both tactile (e.g., braille) and auditory aids (e.g., personal readers) that may be used by the young child to acquire information.

Tips for Preschool Personnel

- Support the inclusion of young children with vision loss in your classrooms and programs.

- Collaborate with teachers, staff, and volunteers as they attempt to create successful experiences for the young child with vision loss in the preschool setting.

- Collaborate with families to keep them informed and active members of the school community.

Tips for Neighbors and Friends

- Never assume that because young children have a vision loss, they cannot or should not participate in family and neighborhood activities that are associated with sight (e.g., board games, sports, hide-and-seek).

- Collaborate with the young child's family to seek opportunities for interaction with sighted children in neighborhood play settings.

ELEMENTARY YEARS

Tips for the Family

- Learn about the programs and services available during the school years for your child with vision loss. Actively collaborate with professionals in the development of your child's individualized education program (IEP).

- Participate in as many school functions for parents as is reasonable (e.g., PTA, parent advisory groups, volunteering) to connect your family to the school.

- Seek information on in-school and extracurricular activities that will enhance opportunities for your child to interact with sighted peers.

- Keep the school informed about the medical needs of your child.

- If your child needs or uses specialized mobility devices to enhance access to the environment, help school personnel understand how these devices work.

Tips for the General Education Classroom Teacher

- Remove obstacles in the classroom that may interfere with the mobility of students with vision loss, from small things like litter on the floor to desks that are blocking aisles.

- The child with vision loss should also sit as close as possible to visual objects associated with instruction (e.g., blackboard, video monitor, classroom bulletin board).

- Be consistent in where you place classroom materials so that the child with vision loss can locate them independently.

- When providing instruction, always try to stand away from the windows. It is very difficult for a person with vision loss to look directly into a light source.

- Collaborate with a vision specialist to determine any specialized mobility or lighting needs for the student with vision loss (e.g., special desk lamp, cassette recorder, large-print books, personal reader).

- Help the student gain confidence in you by letting him or her know where you are in the classroom. It is especially helpful to let the student know when you are planning to leave the classroom.

Tips for School Personnel

- Integrate school resources as well as children. Wherever possible, help general education classroom teachers access the human and material resources necessary to collaboratively meet the needs of students with vision loss. For example:

  - A vision specialist. A professional trained in the education of students with vision loss can serve as an effective consultant to you and the children in several areas (e.g., mobility training, use of special equipment, communication media, instructional strategies).

- An ophthalmologist. Students with a vision loss often have associated medical problems. It is helpful for the teacher to understand any related medical needs that can affect the child's educational experience.

- Peer buddy and support systems. Peer support can be an effective tool for learning in a classroom setting. Peer buddy systems can be established in the school to help the child with initial mobility needs and/or to provide any tutoring that would help him or her succeed in the general education classroom.

- Support keeping the school as barrier-free as possible; this includes providing adequate lighting in classrooms and hallways.

- It is critical that children with vision loss have access to appropriate reading materials (e.g., braille books, large-print books, cassette recordings of books) in the school library and media center.

Tips for Neighbors and Friends

- Help the family of a child who is visually impaired become an integral part of the neighborhood and friendship networks. Seek ways to include the family and child wherever possible in neighborhood activities.

SECONDARY AND TRANSITION YEARS

Tips for the Family

- Become familiar with the adult services system (e.g., rehabilitation services, Social Security, health care) while your son or daughter is still in high school. Understand the type of vocational or employment training that he or she will need prior to graduation.

- Find out the school's view on what it should do to assist students with vision loss in making the transition from school to adult life.

- Create opportunities for your son or daughter to participate in out-of-school activities with same-age sighted peers.

Tips for the General Education Classroom Teacher

- Help students with vision loss to adapt to subject matter in your classroom while you adapt the classroom to meet their needs (e.g., in terms of seating, oral instruction, mobility, large-print or braille textbooks).

- Access to auditory devices (e.g., cassette recorders for lectures) can facilitate students' learning.

- Support the student with vision loss in becoming involved in extracurricular activities. If you are the faculty sponsor of a club or organization, explore whether the student is interested and how he or she could get involved.

Tips for School Personnel

- Encourage parents of students with vision loss to participate actively in school activities (e.g., parent/teacher groups and advisory committees).

- Maintain positive and ongoing contact with the family.

Tips for Neighbors, Friends, and Potential Employers

- Seek ways of becoming part of a community support network for individuals with a vision loss. Be alert to ways in which individuals can become and remain actively involved in community employment, neighborhood recreational activities, and local church functions.

- As potential employers in the local community, seek information on employment of people with a vision loss.

ADULT YEARS

Tips for the Family

- Become aware of the support and services available for your son and daughter in the local community. Identify the government-supported programs available to assist people with vision loss in the areas of postsecondary education opportunities, employment, and recreation/leisure. Identify informal supports, such as family and friends.

Tips for Neighbors, Friends, and Potential Employers

- Work with the person who has vision loss and the family to become part of a community support network for individuals with vision loss. Help the individual with vision loss to become and remain involved in community employment, neighborhood recreational activities, and local church functions.

- As an employer in the community, seek out information on the employment of people with vision loss. Find out about the programs that focus on establishing employment opportunities for people with vision loss, while meeting your needs as an employer.

FOCUS 10

What steps can be taken to prevent and medically treat vision loss?

Health Care

Initial screenings for vision loss are usually based on the individual's visual acuity. Visual acuity may be measured through the use of the Snellen Test, developed in 1862 by Dutch ophthalmologist Herman Snellen. This visual screening test is used primarily to measure central distance vision. The subject stands 20 feet from a letter chart, or E-chart (the standard eye-test chart), and reads each symbol, beginning with the top row. The different sizes of each row or symbol represent what a person with normal vision would see at the various distances indicated on the chart. As indicated earlier in this chapter, a person's visual acuity is then determined via an index that refers to the distance at which an object can be recognized. The person with normal eyesight is defined as having 20/20 vision.

Because the Snellen Test measures only visual acuity, it must be used primarily as an initial screening device that is supplemented by more in-depth assessments, such as a thorough ophthalmological examination. Parents, physicians, school nurses, and educators must also carefully observe the child's behavior, and a complete history of possible symptoms of a vision loss should be documented. These observable symptoms fall into three categories: appearance, behavior, and complaints. Table 16.1 describes some warning signs of vision loss. The existence of symptoms does not necessarily mean a person has a significant vision loss, but it does indicate that an appropriate specialist should be consulted for further examination.

PREVENTION. Prevention of vision loss is one of the major goals of the field of medicine. Since some causes of blindness are hereditary, it is important for the family to be aware of genetic services. One purpose of genetic screening is to identify those who are planning to have a family and who may possess certain detrimental genotypes (such as albinism or retinoblastoma) that can be passed on to their descendants. Screening may also be conducted after conception to determine whether the unborn fetus possesses any genetic abnormalities. Following screening, a genetic counselor informs the parents of the test results so that the family can make an informed decision about conceiving a child or carrying a fetus to term.

Adequate prenatal care is another means of preventing problems. Parents must be made aware of the potential hazards associated with poor nutritional habits, the use of drugs, and exposure to radiation (such as x-rays) during pregnancy. One example of preventive care during this period is the use of antibiotics to treat various infections (influenza, measles, and syphilis, for example), thus reducing the risk of infection to the unborn fetus.

Developmental screening is also a widely recognized means of prevention. (It was through early developmental screening that a medical specialist confirmed that John, from the chapter-opening snapshot, had a serious vision loss and would require the assistance of a trained vision specialist.) Early screening of developmental problems enables the family physician to analyze

---

TABLE 16.1

Warning Signs of Visual Problems

PHYSICAL SYMPTOMS	OBSERVABLE BEHAVIOR	COMPLAINTS
Eyes are crossed.	Blinks constantly	Frequent dizziness
Eyes are not functioning in unison.	Trips or stumbles frequently	Frequent headaches
Eyelids are swollen and crusted, with red rims.	Covers one eye when reading	Pain in the eyes
Eyes are overly sensitive to light.	Holds reading material either very close or very far away	Itching or burning of the eyes or eyelids
Sties occur frequently.	Distorts the face or frowns when concentrating on something in the distance	Double vision
Eyes are frequently bloodshot.	Walks cautiously	
Pupils are of different sizes.	Fails to see objects that are to one side or the other	
Eyes are constantly in motion.		

several treatment alternatives and, when necessary, refer the child to an appropriate specialist for a more thorough evaluation of developmental delays.

This screening—which includes examination of hearing, speech, motor, and psychological development—includes attention to vision as well. Early screening involves a medical examination at birth, assessing the physical condition of the newborn, and also obtaining a complete family medical history. The eyes should be carefully examined for any abnormalities, such as infection or trauma.

Early develomental screening for eye infection, trauma, and other abnormalities is widely recognized as an effective means of preventing future vision loss.

At 6 weeks of age, visual screening forms part of another general developmental assessment. This examination should include input from the parents about how their child is responding (e.g., smiling and looking at objects or faces). The physician should check eye movement and search for infection, crusting on the eyes, or **epiphora** (an overflow of tears resulting from obstruction of the lacrimal ducts).

The next examination should occur at about 6 months of age. A defensive blink should be present at this age, and eye movement should be full and coordinated. If any imbalance in eye movements is noted, a more thorough examination should be conducted. Family history is extremely important, since in many cases there is a familial pattern of vision problems.

Between the ages of 1 and 5 years, visual evaluation should be conducted at regular intervals. An important period occurs just prior to the child's entering school. Visual problems must not go undetected as children attempt to cope with the new and complex demands of the educational environment.

TREATMENT. In addition to medicine's emphasis on prevention of vision loss, significant strides have been made in the treatment of these problems. The nature of health care services depends on the type and severity of the loss. For people who are partially sighted, use of an optical aid can vastly improve access to the visual world. Most of these aids take the form of corrective glasses or contact lenses, which are designed to magnify the image on the retina. Some aids magnify the retinal image within the eye, and others clarify the retinal image. Appropriate use of optical aids, in conjunction with regular medical examinations, not only helps correct existing visual problems but may also prevent further deterioration of existing vision.

Surgery, muscle exercises, and drug therapy have also played important roles in treating persons with vision loss. Treatment may range from complex laser surgical procedures and corneal transplants to the process known as atropinization. **Atropinization** is the treatment for cataracts that involves washing out the eye with the alkaloid drug atropine, which permanently dilates the pupil.

Social Services

Social services can begin with infant stimulation programs and counseling for the family. As the child grows older, group counseling can help the family cope with their feelings about blindness and provide guidance in the area of human sexuality (limited vision may distort perception of the physical body). Counseling eventually extends into matters focusing on marriage, family, and adult relationships. For the adult with vision loss, special guidance may be necessary in preparation for employment and independent living.

Mobility of the person with vision loss can be enhanced in large cities by the use, at crosswalks, of auditory pedestrian signals known as audible traffic signals (ATS). The *walk* and *don't walk* signals are indicated by auditory cues, such as actual verbal messages (e.g., "Please do not cross yet"), different bird chirps for each signal, or a sonalert buzzer. ATS is somewhat controversial among people who are blind and professionals in the field. Those who do not support the use of ATS have two basic concerns. First, the devices promote negative public

➤ **Epiphora**
An overflow of tears from obstruction of the lacrimal ducts of the eye.

➤ **Atropinization**
Treatment for cataracts that involves washing the eye with atropine, permanently dilating the pupil.

FOCUS **11**
Why is the availability of appropriate social services important for people with vision loss?

Council for
Exceptional
Children

Standard 1: Foundations

Standard 5: Learning Environments and Social Interactions

Standard 8: Assessment

attitudes, indicating a presumption that such assistance is necessary for a person who is blind to be mobile. Second, the devices may actually contribute to unsafe conditions because they mask traffic noise for the person who is blind.

Restaurant menus, elevator floor buttons, and signs in buildings (such as rest rooms) can be produced in braille. Telephone credit cards, personal checks, ATM cards, special mailing tubes, and panels for household appliances are also available in braille. Access to community services is greatly enhanced by devices that use synthesized speech for purchasing subway and rail tickets and for obtaining money from automatic teller machines.

FOCUS REVIEW

FOCUS 1 Why is it important to understand the visual process, as well as to know the physical components of the eye?

- The visual process is an important link to the physical world, helping people to gain information beyond that provided by the other senses and also to integrate the information acquired primarily through sound, touch, smell, and taste.

- Our interactions with the environment are shaped by the way we perceive visual stimuli.

FOCUS 2 Distinguish between the terms *blind* and *partially sighted*.

- Legal blindness is determined by visual acuity of 20/200 or worse in the best eye after correction or by a field of vision of 20% or less.

- Educational definitions of blindness focus primarily on the student's inability to use vision as an avenue for learning.

- A person who is partially sighted has a visual acuity greater than 20/200 but not greater than 20/70 in the best eye after correction.

- A person who is partially sighted can still use vision as a primary means of learning.

FOCUS 3 What are the distinctive features of refractive eye problems, muscle disorders of the eye, and receptive eye problems?

- Refractive eye problems occur when the refractive structures of the eye (cornea or lens) fail to focus light rays properly on the retina. Refractive problems include hyperopia (farsightedness), myopia (nearsightedness), astigmatism (blurred vision), and cataracts.

- Muscle disorders occur when the major muscles within the eye are inadequately developed or atrophic, resulting in a loss of control and an inability to maintain tension. Muscle disorders include nystagmus (uncontrolled rapid eye movement), strabismus (crossed eyes), and amblyopia (loss of vision due to muscle imbalance).

- Receptive eye problems occur when the receptive structures of the eye (retina and optic nerve) degenerate or become damaged. Receptive eye problems in-

clude optic atrophy, retinitis pigmentosa, retinal detachment, retinopathy of prematurity, and glaucoma.

FOCUS 4 What are the estimated prevalence and the causes of vision loss?

- Approximately 20% of all children and adults have some vision loss; 3% (9 million people) have a significant vision loss that will require some type of specialized services and supports.

- Fifty percent of people over the age of 65 experience a significant loss of vision (includes cataracts).

- Over 26,000 students have visual impairments and received specialized services in U.S. public schools.

- A number of genetic conditions can result in vision loss, including albinism, retinitis pigmentosa, retinoblastoma, optic atrophy, cataracts, severe myopia associated with retinal detachment, lesions of the cornea, abnormalities of the iris, microphthalmia, hydrocephalus, anophthalmia, and glaucoma.

- Acquired disorders that can lead to vision loss prior to birth include radiation, the introduction of drugs into the fetal system, and infections. Vision loss after birth may be due to several factors, including trauma, infections, inflammations, and tumors.

- The leading cause of acquired blindness in children worldwide is vitamin A deficiency (xerophthalmia). Cortical visual impairment (CVI) is also a leading cause of acquired blindness.

FOCUS 5 Describe how a vision loss can affect intelligence, speech and language skills, educational achievement, social development, physical orientation and mobility, and perceptual-motor development.

- Performance on tests of intelligence may be negatively affected in areas ranging from spatial concepts to general knowledge of the world.

- Children with vision loss are at a distinct disadvantage in developing speech and language skills because they are unable to visually associate words with objects. They cannot learn speech by visual imitation but must rely on hearing or touch for input. Preschool-age and school-age children with vision loss may develop a phenomenon known as verbalisms, or the excessive use of speech (wordiness), in which individuals may use words that have little meaning to them.

- In the area of written language, students with vision loss have more difficulty organizing thoughts to write a composition. Decoding for reading may be delayed because such students often use braille or large-print books as the media to decode. Decoding is a much slower process with these two media. Reading comprehension is also affected because it depends so much on the experiences of the reader.

- Other factors that may influence the academic achievement include (1) late entry into school; (2) failure in inappropriate school programs; (3) loss of time in school due to illness, treatment, or surgery; (4) lack of opportunity; and (5) slow rate of acquiring information.

- People with vision loss are unable to imitate the physical mannerisms of sighted peers and thus do not develop body language, an important form of social communication. A person with sight may misinterpret what is said by a person with a vision loss because the latter's visual cues may not be consistent with the spoken word.

- People with vision loss are often excluded from social activities that are integrally related to the use of vision, thus reinforcing the mistaken idea that they do not want to participate.

- Lack of sight may prevent a person from understanding his or her own relative position in space. A vision loss may affect fine motor coordination and interfere with a person's ability to manipulate objects.

- The perceptual discrimination abilities of people with vision loss in the areas of texture, weight, and sound are comparable to those of sighted peers.

- People who are blind do not perform as well as people with sight on complex tasks of perception, including form identification, spatial relations, and perceptual-motor integration.

FOCUS 6 What is a functional approach to assessment for students with a vision loss?

- Assessment focuses specifically on how the student utilizes any remaining vision (visual efficiency) in conjunction with other senses to acquire information.

- A functional approach to assessment goes beyond determining visual acuity and focuses on capacity, attention, and processing.

FOCUS 7 Describe two content areas that should be included in educational programs for students with vision loss.

- Mobility and orientation training. The ability to move safely, efficiently, and independently through the environment enhances the individual's opportunities to learn more about the world and thus be less dependent on others. Lack of mobility restricts individuals with vision loss in nearly every aspect of educational life.

- The acquisition of daily living skills. For children with a vision loss, routine daily living skills are not easily learned through everyday experiences. These children must be encouraged and supported as they develop life skills, not overprotected from everyday challenges and risks by family and friends.

FOCUS 8 How can communication media facilitate learning for people with vision loss?

- Through communication media, such as optical aids, in conjunction with auditory and tactile stimuli, individuals with vision loss can better develop an understanding of themselves and the world around them.

- Tactile media, including the raised-dot braille system and the Optacon Scanner, can greatly enhance the individual's access to information.

- Specialized media—including personal readers, microcomputers with voice output, closed-circuit TV systems, personal digital assistants, talking calculators, talking-book machines, CD players, and audiotape recorders—provide opportunities for people with vision loss that were not thought possible even a few years ago.

FOCUS 9 What educational placements are available to students with vision loss?

- Residential facilities provide children who are blind with opportunities for the same kinds of experiences that would be available if they were growing up in their own communities.

- The vast majority of people with vision loss live at home, attend public schools, and interact within their own communities.

- Services available within the public schools range from general education class placement, with little or no assistance, to special day schools.

FOCUS 10 What steps can be taken to prevent and medically treat vision loss?

- Much vision loss can be prevented through genetic screening and counseling, appropriate prenatal care, and early developmental assessment.

- The development of optical aids, including corrective glasses and contact lenses, has greatly improved access to the sighted world for people with vision loss.

- Medical treatment may range from complex laser surgical procedures and corneal transplants to drug therapy (such as atropinization).

FOCUS 11 Why is the availability of appropriate social services important for people with vision loss?

- Social services address issues of self-esteem and feelings of inferiority that may stem from having a vision loss.

If you are thinking about a career in special education, you should know that many states use national standards developed by the Council for Exceptional Children (CEC) to assess a teacher candidate's knowledge and skills for working with students with disabilities. See a complete listing of the ten CEC Content Standards on the inside front cover of this text.

CEC Content Standards Addressed in This Chapter

1 Foundations

2 Development and Characteristics of Learners

3 Individual Learning Differences

4 Instructional Strategies

5 Learning Environments and Social Interactions

7 Instructional Planning

8 Assessment

Assess Your Knowledge of the CEC Standards Addressed in This Chapter

Some states require that teacher candidates develop a portfolio of products that demonstrate mastery of the CEC content standards. To assist in the development of products for this portfolio, you may wish to complete the following activities.

- Complete a written test of the chapter's content.

  If your instructor requires a written test of your content knowledge for this chapter, keep a copy for your portfolio. A practice test on the information covered in this chapter is available through the Human Exceptionality companion website (college.hmco.com/pic/hardman9e) and the Student Study Guide.

- Respond to the Application Questions for the Case Study "Mary, Mike, and Josh."

  Review the Case Study and respond in writing to the application questions. Keep a copy of the Case Study and of your written response for your portfolio.

- Participate in a Community Service Learning Activity

  Community Service is a valuable way to enhance your learning experience. Visit our companion website for suggested community service learning activities that correspond to the information presented in this chapter. Develop a reflective journal of the service learning experience for your portfolio.

WEB RESOURCES

American Foundation for the Blind

http://www.afb.org

The American Foundation for the Blind, to which Helen Keller devoted her life, focuses on eliminating barriers that prevent Americans who are blind or visually impaired from reaching their potential. This website provides resources on independent living, literacy, employment, and technology for people with visual impairments.

American Printing House for the Blind

http://www.aph.org/

The American Printing House for the Blind (APH) is the world's largest company devoted solely to creating products and services for people who are visually impaired. This website contains accessible publications and products, employment resources, and government links.

National Federation of the Blind

http://www.nfb.org/

The National Federation of the Blind (NFB) is the largest U.S. membership organization of people who are blind. The purpose of the National Federation of the Blind is to assist people with visual impairments in achieving greater self-confidence and self-respect, and to act as a vehicle for collective self-expression. This website includes information on accessible products and services, assistive technology, training and employment opportunities, and the use of braille.

FURTHER READINGS

Future Reflections

Future Reflections *is a magazine for parents and teachers of children who have a visual impairment. It is published quarterly by the National Organization of Parents of Blind Children, a Division of the National Federation of the Blind (NFB). The magazine covers the issues related to children with visual impairments as they grow from birth through college. Each issue provides resources and information for parents and teachers, as well as a positive philosophy about blindness. Future Reflections also offers a national network of contacts with other parents who have had similar experiences and who can provide information, support, and encouragement.*

Tenberken, S. (2005). *My Path Leads to Tibet: The Inspiring Story of How One Young Blind Woman Brought Hope to the Blind Children of Tibet.*

Defying everyone's advice and armed only with her rudimentary knowledge of Chinese and Tibetan, Sabriye Tenberken set out to do something about the appalling condition of Tibetan children who are blind and had been abandoned by society and left to die. Traveling on horseback throughout the country, she sought out the children, devised a braille alphabet in Tibetan, equipped the children with canes for the first time, and set up a school for the blind. She had such success that hundreds of young blind Tibetans, instilled with pride and equipped with an education, have now become self-supporting.

Weihenmayer, E. (2001) *Touch the Top of the World: A Blind Man's Journey to Climb Farther Than the Eye Can See.* New York: Plume.

This is a moving and adventure-packed autobiography of the author's adventures through life that eventually carry him to the summits of some of the world's highest mountains, as well as onto the frequently hazardous slopes of daily life as a person who is blind.

COMPANION WEBSITE

Visit the companion website at college.hmco.com/pic/hardman9e for additional resources that support this text:

- HM Video Cases that present actual classroom scenarios that you may face every day as a teacher

- Practice ACE Exams that will help you prepare for quizzes, tests, and certfication exams
- Flashcards of key terms
- Weblinks

Physical Disabilities and Health Disorders

LIVING INDEPENDENTLY

For many disabled Americans, . . . living independently can be an aspiration as well as a challenge. Started by disability rights activists, the Independent Living movement aims to achieve goals that make it possible for disabled Americans to live on their own—and on their own terms.

Based on the idea that people with disabilities should be in control of the support services that permit them to live independently, the movement advocates for accessible and affordable basic services such as housing, healthcare and transportation.

Finding safe, affordable and accessible housing can be a significant challenge for many disabled Americans. The Americans with Disabilities Act (A.D.A.) mandates that businesses, workplaces, government offices and public services provide accommodations for the disabled. But for many disabled Americans, access to one's own living quarters can be lacking.

Recent demands for housing "visitability" emphasize how inclusive design can be beneficial to all Americans—not only the disabled. As the National Organization for the Disabled states, "Housing that is accessible, attractive, affordable, and which welcomes disabled and aging Americans is an integral part of healthy, sustainable communities." Although visitability does not guarantee total access, it allows people with disabilities to enter the first floor of a home—as well as its rooms and bathrooms—without having to be lifted up.

Another major obstacle [to] independent living is inadequate or inaccessible transportation, making it difficult for many disabled Americans to get to work, school or perform other tasks that are essential to daily life.

SOURCE: Adapted from *PBS: Independent lens: Independent living*. Retrieved on August 17, 2006, from http://www.pbs.org/independentlens/onaroll/independentliving.html

EVERY DAY IN AMERICA

- 40,000 people miss school or work because of asthma.
- 30,000 people have an asthma attack.
- 5,000 people visit the emergency room because of asthma.
- 1,000 people are admitted to the hospital because of asthma.
- 14 people die from asthma.

SOURCE: *Asthma Facts and Figures, Fast Facts, Every Day in America*, Retrieved on August 19, 2006, from http://www.aafa.org/display.cfm?id=8&sub=42#over

1. Identify the disabilities that may accompany cerebral palsy.

2. What is spina bifida myelomeningocele?

3. Identify specific treatments for individuals with spinal cord injuries.

4. Describe the physical limitations associated with muscular dystrophy.

5. What are some of the key elements of treating adolescents with HIV and AIDS?

6. What are the basic interventions in treating individuals with asthma?

7. Describe the immediate treatment for a person who is experiencing a tonic/clonic seizure.

8. Identify three problems that individuals with diabetes may experience later in life.

9. Identify present and future interventions for the treatment of children and youth with cystic fibrosis.

10. Describe the impact on body tissues of the sickling of red blood cells.

11. Identify five factors that may contribute to child abuse and neglect.

12. Cite factors that may contribute to the increased prevalence of adolescent pregnancy.

13. Identify the potential effects of maternal substance abuse on the developing child.

▼ SNAPSHOT

ON A ROLL

Greg Smith, host and founder of the nationally syndicated *On A Roll* talk radio show, is one of the most dynamic voices in the disability movement today. Born in Bay Springs, Mississippi, in 1964, Smith was diagnosed with muscular dystrophy at the age of 3. At the time Smith's parents, Jim and Adelia, were teachers at Nichols High School in Biloxi, where Jim also served as the school's head football coach. The Smith family moved to upstate New York in 1968, and then to Chicago, where Jim worked in sales and marketing and Greg attended public schools.

By the time Smith reached the age of 13, his curving spine was starting to damage his internal organs. He underwent surgery to break and then straighten his spine, which was then fused with three metal rods. After this surgery, Smith could no longer walk, and he began using a power wheelchair.

In high school, Smith played percussion in the marching band and "marched" on the football field, using a foot control on his wheelchair. He also discovered his love for radio during this time, working as a play-by-play announcer for football, basketball, and baseball games on the student radio station. Smith later attended Arizona State University, where he earned a B.A. in broadcasting and was the sports director on the campus radio station. After graduating from college, Smith worked as the research and sales promotion director for KTAR/K-Lite Radio in Phoenix and as the host of *Cardinal Talk*, a call-in radio program that aired after NFL Cardinals games.

Smith started *On A Roll* as a local AM radio program in Phoenix in 1992, expanding it over the next 11 years to include more than 70 national stations. In 1999, he spoke at the Congressional Black Caucus on disability issues for African Americans and started a web-based discussion group to discuss unique cultural issues that face this "double minority" community. A year later Smith was the lead torchbearer during the 10th-anniversary celebration of the Americans with Disabilities Act.

A 2002 inductee into the esteemed National Speakers Association, Smith has dedicated his career to increasing disability awareness through the media and public speaking. His work has resulted in significant national media exposure, including profiles on CBS's *The Early Show* and National Public Radio's *All Things Considered*, as well as articles in the *Wall Street Journal*, the *New York Times*, the *Chicago Tribune*, and *Essence Magazine*. Smith is currently the host of a new syndicated radio show called *The Strength Coach*.

SOURCE: Adapted from *Greg Smith*, retrieved September 11, 2006, from http://www.pbs.org/independentlens/onaroll/greg.html

➤ **Orthopedic impairment**

An orthopedic impairment that adversely affects educational performance. The term includes impairments such as amputation, absence of a limb, cerebral palsy, poliomyelitis, and bone tuberculosis.

➤ **Physical disabilities**

Disabilities that can affect a person's ability to move about, to use arms and legs, and/or to breathe independently.

➤ **Other health impaired**

A category of disability under the Individuals with Disabilities Education Act that includes students with limited strength as a consequence of health problems.

➤ **Health disorders**

Disabling conditions characterized by limited stamina, vitality, or alertness due to chronic or acute health problems.

➤ **Medically fragile**

A disability category that includes people who are at risk for medical emergencies and often depend on technological support, such as a ventilator or nutritional supplements, to sustain health or even life.

➤ **Technologically dependent**

A disability category that includes people who require some technological assistance to breathe, to pass urine, or to meet other essential health needs while participating in home, school, or community activities.

FOCUS **1**
Identify the disabilities that may accompany cerebral palsy.

➤ **Cerebral palsy (CP)**

A neurological disorder characterized by motor problems, general physical weakness, lack of coordination, and perceptual difficulties.

P hysical disabilities can affect a person's ability to move about, to use arms and legs effectively, to swallow food, and/or to breathe independently. They may also affect other primary functions, such as vision, cognition, speech, language, hearing, and bowel control. The Individuals with Disabilities Education Act (IDEA) uses the term **orthopedic impairment** to describe students with **physical disabilities** and the term **other health impaired** to describe students with health disorders.

As described in IDEA, **health disorders** cause individuals to have "limited strength, vitality, or alertness, due to chronic or acute health problems such as a heart condition, tuberculosis, rheumatic fever, nephritis, asthma, sickle cell anemia, hemophilia, epilepsy, lead poisoning, leukemia, or diabetes which adversely affect . . . educational performance" (23 Code of Federal Regulations, Section 300.5 [7]). For example, children and youth with sickle cell anemia often experience periods of persistent pain in their arms, legs, abdomen, or back that frequently interferes with their school performance and also prevents them from participating in activities important to their social and emotional well-being.

In recent years, new subgroups have emerged within the health disorders area. They are often referred to as **medically fragile** and/or **technologically dependent** (Rivera & Oliden, 2006). These individuals are at risk for medical emergencies and often require specialized support in the form of ventilators or nutritional supplements. Often children or youth who are medically fragile have progressive diseases such as cancer or AIDS. Other children have episodic conditions that lessen their attentiveness, stamina, or energy. Sickle cell anemia and seizure disorders (epilepsy) are good examples of a conditions that are episodic in nature.

Physical disabilities and health disorders also affect how individuals with various conditions or diseases view themselves and how they are seen by others—parents, brothers and sisters, peers, teachers, neighbors, and employers. The impact of these disabilities is also felt on a number of social, educational, and psychological fronts. For example, children and youth who must spend significant periods of time away from their homes, neighborhoods, or schools for medical care or support may have limited opportunities to develop friendships with neighborhood and school peers, to attend special social events, and to develop essential social skills. The degree to which individuals with physical disabilities and health disorders participate in their neighborhoods and communities is directly related to the quality and timeliness of treatment received from various professionals; to the nurturing and encouragement provided by parents, siblings, and teachers; and to the support and acceptance offered by neighbors and other community members (Katsiyannis & Yell, 2000).

Individuals with physical disabilities and health disorders often require highly specialized interventions to realize their maximum potential. Moreover, the range of medical services, educational placements, and therapies is extremely diverse and highly specific to the person and his or her needs. Most students with physical disabilities and health disorders are served in general education classrooms and settings. However, some students may be served in other settings, including special day classes, their homes, hospital-based programs, and residential settings (Best, 2005c).

Physical Disabilities

Our discussion of physical disabilities will be limited to a representative sample of physically disabling conditions: cerebral palsy, spina bifida, spinal cord injuries, and muscular dystrophy. We will present pertinent information about definitions, prevalence, causation, and interventions.

Cerebral Palsy

DEFINITION AND CONCEPTS. **Cerebral palsy (CP)** represents a group of chronic conditions that affect muscle coordination and body movement. It is a neuromuscular disorder caused by damage to one or more specific areas of the brain, usually occurring during fetal development; before, during, or shortly following birth; or during infancy (Best & Bigge, 2005; Wescott & Goulet, 2005). *Cerebral* refers to the brain, *palsy* to muscle weakness and poor control. Secondary conditions can develop with CP, which may improve, worsen, or remain the same. Although CP is not "curable," carefully targeted interventions and therapies may improve an individual's functioning (United Cerebral Palsy, 2006).

Movement characteristics of individuals with CP fall into three categories: spastic—stiff and difficult movement; athetoid—involuntary and uncontrolled movement; and ataxic—disturbed depth perception and very poor sense of balance. Individuals with spastic CP may experience ongoing challenges with pain (Roscigno, 2002).

Cerebral palsy classified by location includes a description of what extremities/limbs are involved. The categories include **diplegia, hemiplegia,** and **quadriplegia** (see Table 17.1).

CP is a complicated and perplexing condition. Individuals with CP are likely to have mild to severe problems in nonmotor areas of functioning, such as hearing impairments, speech and language disorders, intellectual deficits, visual impairments, and general perceptual problems. Because of the multifaceted nature of this condition, many individuals with CP are considered persons with multiple disabilities. Thus CP cannot be characterized by any set of homogeneous symptoms; it is a condition in which a variety of problems may be present in differing degrees of severity (Fong, 2005, Wescott & Goulet, 2005).

PREVALENCE AND CAUSATION. In the United States, 500,000 children and adults present one or more of the features of CP (United Cerebral Palsy, 2006). The prevalence of CP in industrialized countries is about 1.5 to 2.45 per 1,000 live births (Odding, Roebroeck, & Stam, 2006; Piek, 2006). These figures fluctuate as a function of several variables. For example, some infants born with severe forms of CP do not survive, and the birth prevalence rate does not include these children who die. Other children may be diagnosed with CP several months or years after birth.

The causes of CP are varied (see Table 17.2). Any condition that can adversely affect the brain can cause CP. Chronic diseases, insufficient oxygen to the brain, premature birth, maternal infection, birth trauma, blood incompatibility, fetal infection, and postbirth infection may all be sources of this neurological-motor disorder. Most causes of CP are tied to intrauterine problems identified earlier (United Cerebral Palsy, 2006).

INTERVENTIONS. Rather than treating CP, professionals and parents work at managing the condition and its various manifestations. It is essential that the management and interventions begin as soon as CP is diagnosed. The interventions center on the child's movement, social and emotional development, learning, speech, and hearing (United Cerebral Palsy, 2006).

Effective interventions for the various forms of CP are based on accurate and continuous assessments. The motor deficits and other challenges associated with CP evolve over time. Continuous assessment enables care providers to adjust treatment programs and select placement options in accordance with the emerging needs of the child or youth.

Standard 1: Foundations

Standard 2: Development and Characteristics of Learners

TABLE 17.1

Topographical Descriptions of Paralytic Conditions

DESCRIPTION	AFFECTED AREA
Monoplegia	One limb
Paraplegia	Lower body and both legs
Hemiplegia	One side of the body
Triplegia	Three appendages or limbs, usually both legs and one arm
Quadriplegia	All four extremities and usually the trunk
Diplegia	Legs more affected than arms
Double hemiplegia	Both halves of the body, with one side more affected than the other

TABLE 17.2

Factors Influencing the Occurrence of Cerebral Palsy

PERIOD OF TIME	FACTORS
Preconception (parental background)	• Biological aging (parent or parents over age 35) • Biological immaturity (very young parent or parents) • Environmental toxins • Genetic background and genetic disorders • Malnutrition • Radiation damage
First trimester of pregnancy (0 to 3 months)	*Early weeks:* • Nutrition: malnutrition, vitamin deficiencies, amino acid intolerance • Toxins: alcohol, drugs, poisons, toxins from smoking *Late weeks:* • Maternal disease: thyrotoxicosis (abrupt oversecretion of thyroid hormone, resulting in elevated heart rate and potential coma), genetic disorders • Nutrition: malnutrition, amino acid intolerance
Second trimester of pregnancy (3+ to 6 months)	*Early weeks:* • Infection: CM (cytomegalo) virus, rubella, HIV, syphilis, chicken pox, uterine infection *Late weeks:* • Placental abnormalities, vascular blockages, fetal malnutrition, chronic hypoxia, growth factor deficiencies
Third trimester of pregnancy (6+ to 9 months)	*Early weeks:* • Prematurity and low birthweight • Blood factors: Rh incompatibility, jaundice • Cytokines: neurological tissue destruction • Inflammation and infection of the uterine lining *Late weeks:* • Prematurity and low birthweight • Hypoxia: insufficient blood flow to the placenta, perinatal hypoxia • Infection: listeria, meningitis, streptococcus group B (bacterial infection), septicemia (bacteria growing in the bloodstream), inflammation and infection of the uterine lining
Perinatal period and infancy (first 2 postnatal years)	• Endocrine: hypoglycemia, hypothyroidism • Hypoxia: perinatal hypoxia, respiratory distress syndrome • Infection: meningitis, encephalitis • Multiple births: death of a twin or triplet • Stroke: hemorrhagic or embolic stroke • Trauma: abuse, accidents

SOURCE: Adapted from "Cerebral Palsy: Contributing Risk Factors and Causes," Research Fact Sheets; September 1995; by United Cerebral Palsy Research and Education Foundation, Copyright 1995. Reprinted by permission.

Treatment of CP is a multifaceted process that involves many medical and human service specialties aggregated in interdisciplinary and transdisciplinary teams (Fong, 2005; United Cerebral Palsy, 2006). These teams, composed of medical experts, physical and occupational therapists, teachers, social workers, volunteers, and family members, join together to help children, youth, and adults with CP realize their full potential.

REFLECT ON THIS

WHAT IS AUGMENTATIVE AND ALTERNATIVE COMMUNICATION (AAC)?

AAC is any device, system or method that improves the ability of a child with a communication impairment to communicate effectively. Although the term is often used to refer to formal communication devices and systems such as sign language, communication boards, or voice output communication aids (VOCAs), it can include less sophisticated means of communication such as facial expressions, non-speech vocalizations, and idiosyncratic gestures. AAC is used when a child either does not develop communication in the normal fashion or experiences a significant delay in its development. AAC is not merely a substitute for how the child is currently communicating. It is used to augment that communication, replacing only elements that are unintelligible, socially unacceptable, or harmful to the child or others. Ideally, an AAC system includes more than one mode of communication, with the child using whichever is the most efficient given the persons, setting, and activity at hand. Very often one of the modes of communication in an AAC program is natural speech.

Broadly speaking, communication occurs with at least one other person, unfolds in the context of the environment, and serves the following functions:

- To indirectly control the environment—for example, to obtain or reject something.
- To regulate social interactions—for example, to express an emotion or interact with a friend.
- To receive and convey information and ideas.

The purpose of AAC is to increase a child's ability to achieve these functions in the environments and activities in which the child participates or is expected to participate.

In the past, some children with moderate to severe disabilities were considered too cognitively impaired to learn how to communicate effectively. These individuals were not even considered candidates for AAC. However, studies have since shown that children with multiple and diverse disabilities do benefit from AAC (Romski, Sevcik, Robinson, & Bakeman, 1994; Silverman, 1980). Currently, it is widely believed that any child, from those with severe and multiple disabilities to those with temporary impairments, can benefit from an AAC program that is appropriate and individualized. AAC, therefore, can include anything from a sophisticated electronic voice-output communication aid (VOCA) to teaching a child to extend a hand during snack to indicate the desire for another cookie.

SOURCE: Adapted from *Augmentative and Alternative Communication (AAC): How to Get Started.* Retrieved on September 11, 2006, from http://aac.unl.edu/yaack/b0.html

The thrust of management efforts depends on the nature of the problems and strengths presented by the individual child or youth. Generally, interventions are directed at preventing additional physical deformities; decreasing adverse symptoms; developing useful posture and movements; providing appropriate orthopedic surgery when needed to lengthen heel cords, hamstrings, or tendons; dealing with feeding and swallowing problems; developing appropriate motor skills; securing suitable augmentative communication and other assistive devices; prescribing appropriate medications (muscle relaxants); and developing mobility and independence (Beukelman & Mirenda, 2005; Piek, 2006). Because of the multifaceted nature of CP, other specialists may also be involved, including ophthalmologists, audiologists, massage therapists, speech and language clinicians, and vocational and rehabilitation specialists. The Reflect on This on page 453 describes some devices used to enhance communication with children who have a communication impairment. And the Assistive Technology describes an innovative garment designed to help with posture and mobility.

Medications play an increasingly important role in treating CP. Commonly prescribed medications include diazepam for controlling muscle tone, Botox for spasticity management, baclofen for central nervous system management/inhibition, and dantrolene for inhibiting contractions of muscle cells. Baclofen may be delivered directly to an individual's spinal fluid via a tube in the lower back with an infusion pump. This approach to medication carefully controls dosage rates and lessens the need for constant injections (Best & Bigge, 2005).

ASSISTIVE TECHNOLOGY

A SPECIALIZED SUIT FOR COLBY

Colby Christensen can ride a tricycle now, just like most other 4-year-old girls. She's even eating grapes with "righty," her once tightly clenched right fist, thanks to a new therapy for children with cerebral palsy.

Mom and daughter spent this past February in Mielno, a coastal city in Poland, where Colby worked six hours a day, six days a week, in a patented "Adeli" suit specially designed to help her small body learn correct posture (Israelsen, 2005).

The Adeli Suit consists of a vest, shorts, knee pads, and specially adapted shoes with hooks and elastic cords that help tell the body how it is supposed to move in space. Therapists use the Adeli Suit to hold the body in proper physical alignment. During specialized exercises, the therapists adjust the elastic connectors that topographically mirror flexor and extensor muscles, trunk rotators, and the lower limbs. Additional attach-

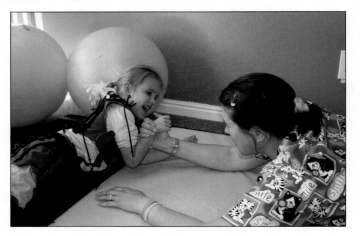

Colby benefited significantly from specialized therapies delivered in concert with the fitting and wearing of the Adeli Suit.

ments correcting the position of the feet, head, and other areas of the body have also been designed. While wearing the Adeli Suit, a patient goes through various exercises, including "how to walk." The suit works as an elastic frame surrounding the body and does not limit the amplitude of movement but adds an additional weight load on it within designed limits.

Research studies confirm that patients exhibit improved brain-to-muscle communication through increased blood flow to the brain and central artery, increased bioelectrical functions of the muscles (EMG readings), increased activity in the brain cortex (EEG readings), increased bone calcification, decreased ataxia (lack of coordination), and a decrease in the intensity of dysarthia (a speech fluency disorder). With Adeli Suit therapy new elements of stability occur, coordination increases, and speech articulation improves.

SOURCE: Adapted from *Suit* by Euromed, retrieved on August 11, 2006, from phttp://www.euromed.pl/en/index.php?ppg=adeli_suit:suit and from *Therapy Helping Children with CP* by Sara Israelsen, May 12, 2005, *Deseret News.*

Physical and occupational therapists play very significant roles in the lives of children and youth with CP (Martin, 2006; Westcott & Goulet, 2005). These individuals provide essentially three types of crucial services: assessments to detect deformities and deficits in movement quality; program planning such as assisting with the writing of IEPs, the selection of adaptive equipment and assistive devices, and the development of home programs for parents and other family members; and delivery of therapy services. School-centered services may include indirect treatment provided in the form of consultation, in-service training, and informal monitoring of student performance; direct service through regular treatment sessions in out-of-class settings; and in-class or multisite service delivery to students in general education classrooms, in their homes, or at other community sites (Pellegrino, 2001 & 2002) (see Figure 17.1).

Recent developments in augmentative communication and computer-centered technologies have had a tremendous impact on children, youth, and adults with CP and other conditions that impair speech and language production (Beukelman & Mirenda, 2006). Many augmentative communication devices are electronic or computer-based. These devices provide children, youth, and adults with symbols or icons that, when pressed or activated with an optical pointer in certain sequences, produce audio output such as "I'd like a *Quarter Pounder* with fries and a large *Coke*, please." "I need to go to the bathroom." "Do you know what we are having for lunch?" Selecting augmentative communication devices for a child or youth is a team effort. Teachers, parents, speech and language specialists, physical and occupational therapists, and rehabilitation engineers play important roles in assisting with the selection process (Heller & Bigge, 2005). Major benefits of augmentative and alternative communication in general education classrooms include increased interaction of students with disabilities with classroom peers, increased acceptance of students with disabilities, and greater connections with teachers—and thus improved relationships, greater learning, and better understanding of children with disabilities (Kent-Walsh, & Light, 2003).

As persons with CP move into adulthood, they may require various kinds of support, including continuing therapy, personal assistance services, independent living services, vocational training, and counseling (Chesson, Chisholm, & Zaw, 2004). Professionals are just beginning to understand the long-term needs and crucial dimensions of care for aging adults with CP. The Case Study "Living with Cerebral Palsy" is a first-person account of what one youngster wants to say about CP.

FIGURE 17.1

Suggestions for Teachers and Other Care Providers

- This may seem obvious, but sometimes the "look" of CP can give the mistaken impression that a child who has CP cannot learn as much as others.

- Focus on the individual child and learn firsthand what needs and capabilities he or she has.

- Tap into the strategies that teachers of students with learning disabilities use for their students.

- Become knowledgeable about different learning styles.

- Then you can use the approach best suited for a particular child, based on that child's learning abilities as well as physical abilities.

- Be inventive. Ask yourself (and others), "How can I adapt this lesson for this child to maximize *active, hands-on* learning?"

- Learn to love assistive technology.

- Find experts within and outside your school to help you. Assistive technology can mean the difference between dependence and independence for your student.

- Always remember that parents are experts, too.

- Talk candidly with your student's parents.

- They can tell you a great deal about their daughter's or son's special needs and abilities.

- Effective teamwork for the child with CP needs to bring together professionals with diverse backgrounds and expertise.

- The team must combine the knowledge of its members to plan, implement, and coordinate the child's services.

SOURCE: Adapted from *Tips for Teachers*. Retrieved on September 11, 2006, from http://www.nichcy.org/pubs/factshe/fs2txt.htm#teachers

CASE STUDY

LIVING WITH CEREBRAL PALSY

I do not know many scientific facts about CP (cerebral palsy), but I do know how it has affected my life. This is what I want to share with you. I hope it will help you to better understand people with CP.

When I was young, having cerebral palsy was never an issue in our home. I was treated no differently than my brothers or sisters. However, things changed when I started school. The first few years of school were great, to the best of my recollection. I was probably in the third or fourth grade when I became aware that children, in their innocence, can be cruel. I wore a brace on my leg and was faced with much teasing and ridicule. This caused me to become shy and introverted. I did not easily make friends and still don't!

My grandfather liked to take walks on sunny afternoons, so one day I went with him and was having a very pleasant time until we saw someone walking toward us. My grandpa made me change sides so that it would be harder to see that his granddaughter had cerebral palsy. That was a very hurtful thing to learn. I realized that he was ashamed of me.

People should be judged by their hearts and not by their looks. I have learned to judge myself harshly and I strive for perfection in all I attempt to do. Needless to say, I constantly fail miserably! It is easier not to try than to fail.

I need to learn to like me even with all my many imperfections. I need to learn that it is okay that not everyone I meet will like me.

APPLICATION

1. Given what you have learned about children and youth with disabilities and their families, how would you as a teacher help your students without disabilities treat children with disabilities well? How do we help children look beyond outward appearances?

2. How would you help your grandparents respond well to a new grandchild with a challenging disability?

3. How would you help a child with a disability deal with the teasing that is often inflicted by other children? How do we help children with disabilities become resilient and appropriately optimistic?

SOURCE: Adapted from "Living with cerebral palsy," Author, 2000. Retrieved from http://www.geocities.com/Athens/Ithaca/2418/cp.html

---

➤ **Spina bifida**

A developmental defect of the spinal column.

Focus 2

What is spina bifida myelomeningocele?

➤ **Spina bifida occulta**

A very mild form of spina bifida in which an oblique slit is present in one or several of the vertebral structures.

➤ **Spina bifida cystica**

A malformation of the spinal column in which a tumor-like sac is produced on the infant's back.

➤ **Spina bifida myelomeningocele**

A type of spina bifida cystica in which the characteristic tumor-like sac contains both spinal fluid and nerve tissue.

Spina Bifida

DEFINITIONS AND CONCEPTS. The most frequently occurring permanently disabling birth defect is **spina bifida** (SB) (Spina Bifida Association of America, 2006b). Various forms of SB are also referred to as neural tube defects (NTDs). SB is characterized by an abnormal opening in the spinal column. It originates in the first days of pregnancy, often before a mother even knows that she is expecting a child. Through the process of cell division and differentiation, a neural tube forms in the developing fetus. At about 26 or 27 days, for reasons not wholly understood, this neural tube fails to close completely. This failure results in various forms of spina bifida, frequently involving some paralysis of various portions of the body, depending on the location of the opening (Liptak, 2002). It may or may not influence intellectual functioning. Spina bifida is usually classified as either spina bifida occulta or spina bifida cystica.

Spina bifida occulta is a very mild condition in which a small slit is present in one or more of the vertebral structures. Most people with spina bifida occulta are unaware of its presence unless they have had a spinal x-ray for diagnosis of some other condition. Spina bifida occulta has little, if any, impact on a developing infant.

Spina bifida cystica is a malformation of the spinal column in which a tumor-like sac herniates through an opening or cleft on the infant's back (see Figure 17.2). Spina bifida cystica exists in many forms, two of the most prominent of which are spina bifida meningocele and **spina bifida myelomeningocele**. In spina bifida meningocele, the sac contains spinal fluid but no nerve tissue. In the myelomeningocele type, the sac contains nerve tissue.

Spina bifida myelomeningocele is the most serious form of neural tube defect. It generally results in weakness or paralysis in the legs and lower body, an inability to control the bladder or bowel voluntarily, and the presence of other orthopedic problems (such as club feet or

FIGURE 17.2

Side Views of the Spine

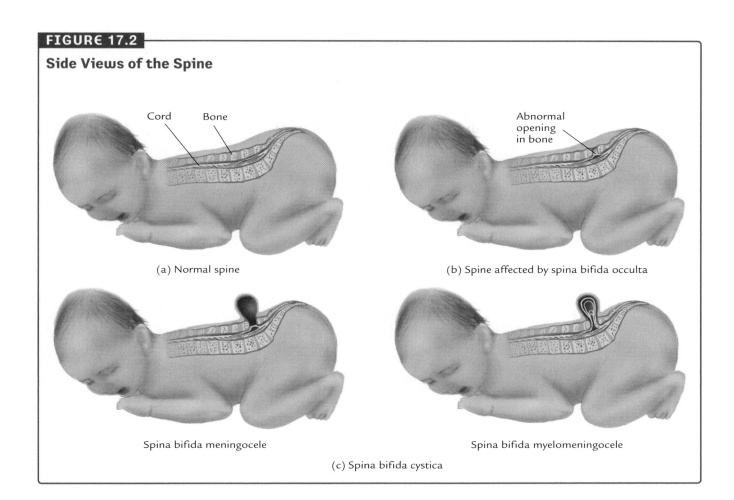

Cord   Bone

(a) Normal spine

Abnormal opening in bone

(b) Spine affected by spina bifida occulta

Spina bifida meningocele

Spina bifida myelomeningocele

(c) Spina bifida cystica

dislocated hip). There are two types of myelomeningocele. In one the tumor-like sac is open, revealing the neural tissue, and in the other the sac is closed or covered with a combination of skin and membrane.

Children with spina bifida occulta exhibit the normal range of intelligence. Most children with myelomeningocele also have normal IQs. For children whose learning capacity is normal or above average, no special education is needed or required.

PREVALENCE AND CAUSATION. Prevalence figures for spina bifida, both meningocele and myelomeningocele, vary. Spina bifida affects about 7 out of every 10,000 newborns in the United States (Spina Bifida Association of America, 2006a).

The exact cause of spina bifida is unknown, although there is a slight tendency for the condition to run in families. In fact, myelomeningocele appears to be transmitted genetically, probably as a function of certain prenatal factors interacting with genetic predispositions. It is also possible that certain harmful agents taken by the mother prior to or at the time of conception, or during the first few days of pregnancy, may be responsible for the defect. Several environmental factors play a role. These include nutrition, medication, and temperature (Best, 2005c).

Teratogens that may induce malformations in the spine include radiation, maternal hyperthermia (high fever), and excess glucose. Other causative factors include congenital rubella and chromosome abnormalities.

Folic acid deficiencies have been implicated strongly in the causation of spina bifida. Pregnant mothers should take particular care to augment their diets with 0.4 mg of folic acid each day. Folic acid is a common water-soluble B vitamin. Intake of this vitamin reduces the probability of neural tube defects in developing infants (Spina Bifida Association of America, 2006a).

Council for Exceptional Children

Standard 1: Foundations

➤ **Teratogens**

Substances or conditions that cause malformations.

INTERVENTIONS. Several tests are now available to identify babies with spina bifida myelomeningocele before they are born. One such test involves analysis of the mother's blood for the presence of a specific fetal protein (alfa-fetoprotein, AFT). This protein leaks from the developing child's spine into the amniotic fluid of the uterus and subsequently enters the mother's bloodstream. If blood tests prove positive for AFT, ultrasonic scanning of the fetus may be performed to confirm the diagnosis.

Confirmation of the myelomeningocele creates intense feelings in parents. If the diagnosis is early in the child's intrauterine development, parents are faced with the decision of continuing or discontinuing the pregnancy or subjecting the emerging fetus to intrauterine surgery. If parents decide to continue the pregnancy, they have time to process their intense feelings and to prepare for the child's surgery, birth, and care. If the decision is to discontinue the pregnancy, they must deal with the feelings produced by this action as well. If the condition is discovered at the time of the child's birth, it also produces powerful and penetrating feelings, the first of which is generally shock. All members of the health team (physicians, nurses, and social workers), as well as other persons (clergy, siblings, parents, and close friends), help parents cope with the feelings they experience and the decisions that must be made.

Immediate action is often called for when the child with myelomeningocele is born, depending on the nature of the lesion, its position on the spine, and the presence of other, related conditions. Decisions regarding medical interventions are extremely difficult to make, for they often entail problems and issues that are not easily or quickly resolved. For example, in 80% of children with myelomeningocele, a portion of the spinal cord is exposed, placing them at great risk for developing bacterial meningitis, which has a mortality rate of over 50%.

The decision to undertake surgery is often made quickly if the tissue sac is located very low on the infant's back. The purpose of the surgery is to close the spinal opening and lessen the potential for infection. Another condition that often accompanies myelomeningocele is hydrocephalus, which is characterized by excessive accumulation of cerebral fluid within the brain. More than 25% of children with myelomeningocele exhibit this condition at birth. Moreover, 70% to 90% of all children with myelomeningocele develop it after they are born (NICHY, 2006). Surgery may also be performed for this condition in the first days of life. The operation includes inserting a small, soft plastic tube between the ventricles of the brain and connecting this tube with an absorption site in the abdomen. The excessive spinal fluid is diverted from the ventricles of the brain to a thin layer of tissue, the peritoneum, that lines the abdominal cavity (see Figure 17.3).

FIGURE 17.3

Ventriculoperitoneal Shunt

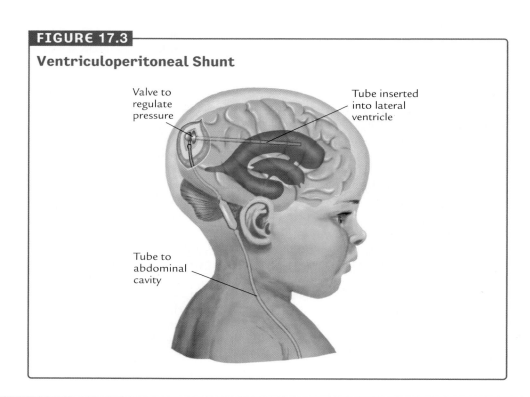

Valve to regulate pressure

Tube inserted into lateral ventricle

Tube to abdominal cavity

Children with spina bifida myelomeningocele may have little if any voluntary bowel or bladder control. This condition is directly attributable to the paralysis caused by malformation of the spinal cord and removal of the herniated sac containing nerve tissues. However, children as young as 4 years old can be taught effective procedures to manage bladder problems. As they mature, they can develop effective regimens and procedures for bowel management.

Physical therapists play a critical role in helping children as they learn to cope with the paralysis caused by myelomeningocele. Paralysis obviously limits the children's exploratory activities so critical to later learning and perceptual-motor performance. For this reason, many such children are fitted with modified skateboards or other wheeled devices, which enable them to explore their surroundings. Utilizing the strength in their arms and hands, they become quite adept at exploring their home environments. Gradually, they move to leg braces, crutches, a wheelchair, or a combination of the three. Some children are ambulatory and do not require the use of a wheelchair.

Education programs for students with serious forms of spina bifida vary according to the needs of each student. The vast majority of students with myelomeningocele are served in general education settings. School personnel can contribute to the well-being of these students in several ways: making sure that physical layouts permit students to move effectively with their crutches or wheelchairs through classrooms and other settings; supporting students' efforts in using various bladder and bowel management procedures and ensuring appropriate privacy in using them; requiring these students to be as responsible as anyone else in the class for customary assignments; involving them fully in field trips, physical education, and other school-related activities; and communicating regularly with parents. Additionally, if the student has a shunt, teachers should be alert to signs of its malfunctioning, including irritability, neck pain, headache, vomiting, reduced alertness, and decline in school performance. These symptoms may appear very quickly and may be mistaken for flu. Any of these aforementioned symptoms should be taken very seriously by teachers. As with all physical disabilities, collaboration and cooperation among all caregivers are vitally important to the well-being of each child or youth.

Standard 5: Learning Environments and Social Interactions

Spinal Cord Injury

DEFINITIONS AND CONCEPTS. Spinal cord injuries happen without any advance notice. They are generally a result of some normal or recreational activity: driving a car, hiking, skiing, sleding, or diving. About 11,000 spinal cord injuries take place each year in the United States (Liverman, Altevogt, Joy, & Johnson, 2005).

When the spinal cord is traumatized or severed, **spinal cord injury (SCI)** occurs. Trauma can result through extreme extension or flexing from a fall, an automobile accident, or a sports injury. The cord can also be severed through the same types of accidents, although such occurrences are extremely rare. Usually the cord is bruised or otherwise injured, after which swelling and (within hours) bleeding often occur. Gradually, a self-destructive process ensues, in which the affected area slowly deteriorates and the damage becomes irreversible (Spinal Cord Injury Resource Center, 2006).

➤ **Spinal cord injury (SCI)**
An injury in which the spinal cord is traumatized or transected.

Standard 1: Foundations

The overall impact of injury on an individual depends on the site and nature of the insult. If the injury occurs in the neck or upper back, the resulting paralysis and effects are usually quite extensive. If the injury occurs in the lower back, paralysis is confined to the lower extremities. Like individuals with spina bifida, those who sustain injuries in an SCI may experience loss of voluntary bowel and bladder function.

Spinal cord injuries rarely occur without individuals sustaining other serious damage to their bodies. Accompanying injuries may include head trauma, fractures of some portion of the trunk, and significant chest injuries.

The physical characteristics of spinal cord injuries are similar to those of spina bifida myelomeningocele except that there is no tendency for the development of hydrocephalus. The terms used to describe the impact of spinal cord injuries are *paraplegia, quadriplegia,* and *hemiplegia* (see Table 17.1 on page 451). Note, however, that these terms are global descriptions of functioning and are not precise enough to convey accurately an individual's actual level of motor functioning.

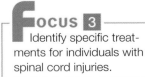

FOCUS **3**
Identify specific treatments for individuals with spinal cord injuries.

PREVALENCE AND CAUSATION. About 225,000 to 296,000 individuals live with SCI in the United States (Liverman, Altevogt, Joy, & Johnson, 2005). Causes include motor vehicle accidents (38.5%); violence, primarily gunshot wounds (24.5%); and falls (21.8%).

Twenty-five percent of the injuries are alcohol-related. Only 7.2% of the injuries are caused by sporting activities. The average age for SCI injuries is now 38 years (Spinal Cord Injury Information Network, 2006). About 5% of SCIs occur in children, primarily from automobile-related accidents and falls (Liverman, Altevogt, Joy, & Johnson, 2005).

INTERVENTIONS. The immediate care rendered to a person with SCI is crucial. The impact of the injury can be magnified if proper procedures are not employed soon after the accident or onset of the condition. Only properly trained personnel should move and transport a person with a suspected SCI (Huffman, Fontaine, & Price, 2003).

The first phase of treatment provided by a hospital is the management of shock. Quickly thereafter, the individual is immobilized to prevent movement and possible further damage. As a rule, surgical procedures are not undertaken immediately. The major goal of medical treatment at this point is to stabilize the spine, manage swelling, and prevent further complications. Pharmacological interventions are critical during this phase of treatment. Recent studies support the use of high and frequent doses of methylprednisolone. This medication often reduces damage to nerves cells, decreases swelling near the injury site, and improves the functional outcome for the affected individual, thus reducing secondary damage. Catheterization may be employed to control urine flow, and steps may be taken to reduce swelling and bleeding at the injury site. Traction may be used to stabilize certain portions of the spinal column and cord (National Institute of Neurological Disorders and Stroke, 2006b).

Medical treatment of spinal cord injuries is lengthy and often tedious. Once physicians have successfully stabilized the spine and treated other medical conditions, the rehabilitation process promptly begins. The individual is taught to use new muscle combinations and to take advantage of any and all residual muscle strength. He or she is also taught to use orthopedic equipment, such as handsplints, braces, reachers, headsticks (for typing), and plateguards. See the Reflect on This, "Superman's Wife" to learn more about the woman who did so much to inform and inspire people with SCIs and their families.

Traumatic SCI is accompanied by various pain syndromes—and sometimes by phantom pain. Relieving pain is a significant challenge over the lifespan of individuals with SCIs (Yarkony, Gittler, & Weiss, 2002).

Psychiatric and other support personnel are also engaged in rehabilitation activities. Psychological adjustment to SCI and its impact on the individual's functioning can take a great deal of time and effort. The goal of all treatment is to help the injured person become as independent as possible.

As the individual masters necessary self-care skills, other educational and career objectives can be pursued with the assistance of the rehabilitation team. The members of this collaborative team change constantly in accordance with the needs of the individual.

Education for individuals with spinal cord injuries is similar to that for uninjured children or adults. Teachers must be aware, however, that some individuals with spinal cord injuries will be unable to feel pressure and pain in the lower extremities, so pressure sores and skin

Council for
Exceptional
Children

Standard 5: Learning Environments and Social Interactions

Children with physical disorders profit greatly from real-life activities with same-age peers.

Dana Reeve was thrust into a public role after her husband became a quadriplegic as a result of a horseback riding accident in Culpeper, Virginia, on May 27, 1995. She then became a motivational speaker and activist for the quality of everyday life of the paralyzed and, after her husband's death, a proponent of the controversial human embryonic stem cell research. Reeve, in an editorial she wrote in October 2005, confessed that "I still have my soft spot for the quality-of-life grant programs and for the resource center, because it's really the people part. Chris used to be the visionary who went to Washington to lobby for funding, and I was the one who figured out, "Is there a wheelchair ramp so that our family can get into this movie theater?" I thought if that's hard for me, it's got to be much harder for the majority of people out there. She emphasized care over cure in her philosophy.

In 1996 the Reeves founded the Christopher Reeve Foundation, which funds research on paralysis and works to improve the lives of the disabled. The American Paralysis Association merged with the Christopher Reeve Foundation in 1999. Then, in 2005, the name was changed from *Christopher Reeve Paralysis Foundation* to the pre-merger name of *Christopher Reeve Foundation*. The organization names are interchangeable. To date, it has awarded more than $55 million in research grants and more than $8 million in quality-of-life grants.

On August 9, 2005, at the age of 44, Reeve announced that she had been diagnosed with lung cancer despite being

Dana Reeve, following the death of her husband, Christopher Reeve, became an articulate activist for individuals with various paralytic conditions.

a nonsmoker. She was exposed to second-hand smoke throughout her career as an entertainer in music clubs and as a waitress. Her exposure to other known lung carcinogens such as radon and asbestos dust is not known. The announcement of her diagnosis came two days after Peter Jennings of *ABC News* died from the same illness. Four months to the day after the death of her husband, her mother Helen, who was 71 years old, died of ovarian cancer. Reeve chose to disclose her illness after the *National Enquirer* announced that it planned to make the information public.

In 2005 Reeve received the "Mother of the Year Award" from the American Cancer Society for her dedication and determination in raising her son after the loss of her husband. In her final public appearances, she stated that the tumor had responded to therapy and was shrinking. She appeared at Madison Square Garden on January 12, 2006, to sing in honor of New York Rangers hockey player Mark Messier, whose number was retired that evening.

Dana Reeve died on March 6, 2006, at Memorial Sloan-Kettering Cancer Center in New York City, after losing her battle with lung cancer 11 days short of her 45th birthday. She is survived by her son; her father; two sisters, Deborah Morosini and Adrienne Morosini Heilman; and her late husband's two grown children, Matthew Exton and Alexandra Exton Reeve.

SOURCE: Adapted from *Dana Reeve*. Retrieved September 11, 2006, from http://en.wikipedia.org/wiki/Dana_Reeve

breakdown may occur in response to prolonged sitting. Opportunities for repositioning and movement will help prevent these problems. Parents and teachers should be aware of signs of depression that may accompany reentry into school.

Muscular Dystrophy

DEFINITIONS AND CONCEPTS. The term **muscular dystrophy** refers to a group of genetic diseases marked by progressive weakness, degeneration, and death of the skeletal, or voluntary, muscles that control movement (Best, 2005c). The muscles of the heart and some other involuntary muscles are also affected in some forms of muscular dystrophy, and a few forms involve other organs as well. Muscular dystrophy is a progressive disorder that may affect the muscles of the hips, legs, shoulders, and arms, progressively causing these individuals to lose their ability to walk and to use their arms and hands effectively

> ➤ **Muscular dystrophy**
>
> A group of inherited, chronic disorders that are characterized by gradual wasting and weakening of the voluntary skeletal muscles.

Focus 4

Describe the physical limitations associated with muscular dystrophy.

Council for Exceptional Children

Standard 1: Foundations

and functionally. The loss of ability is attributable to fatty tissue that gradually replaces muscle tissue.

Heart muscle may also be affected, resulting in symptoms of heart failure. There are actually nine different types of muscular dystrophy. The seriousness of the various dystrophies is influenced by heredity, age of onset, the physical location and nature of onset, and the rate at which the condition progresses.

Duchenne-type muscular dystrophy (DMD) is the most common form of childhood muscular dystrophy. DMD generally manifests itself between the ages of 2 and 6. Early in the second decade of life, individuals with DMD use wheelchairs to move from place to place. By the end of the second decade of life, or early in the third, young adults with DMD die from respiratory insufficiency or cardiac failure (Muscular Dystrophy Association, 2006).

DMD is first evidenced in the pelvic girdle, although it sometimes begins in the shoulder girdle muscles. With the passage of time, individuals begin to experience a loss of respiratory function and are unable to cough up secretions that may result in pneumonia. Also, severe spinal curvature develops over time with wheelchair use, although this curvature may be prevented with spinal fusion.

PREVALENCE AND CAUSATION. Abnormalities in muscle protein genes cause muscular dystrophies. Each human cell contains tens of thousands of genes. Each gene is a string of the chemical DNA and is the code or recipe for a given protein. If the recipe for a muscle-related protein is lacking or is missing a key ingredient, the results can be tragic. The missing or diminished ingredient is dystrophin, an essential and critical component of healthy muscle fibers. Without dystrophin, muscle cells explode and die (National Center for Biotechnology Information, 2006).

About 200,000 people are affected by muscular dystrophies and related disorders. About 1 in every 3,000 to 3,500 males is affected by DMD. Mothers who are carriers transmit this condition to 50% of their male offspring. One-third of the cases of DMD arise by mutation in families with no history of the disease.

Molecular genetics have contributed greatly to our understanding of neuromuscular diseases and their causes. In some cases, the specific genetic locus of the dystrophy can be identi-

REFLECT ON THIS

GENE THERAPY

Genes, those conceptual units composed of deoxyribonucleic acid—DNA, carry the information needed to make proteins, the building blocks of our bodies. The body buries genes deep in the heart of every cell, the nucleus, and organizes them in the chromosomes that hold the DNA. But when your DNA is damaged, it no longer makes all the needed proteins and disease results.

To reverse disease caused by genetic damage, researchers isolate normal DNA and package it into a vector, a molecular delivery truck usually made from a disabled virus. Doctors then infect a target cell—usually from a tissue affected by the illness, such as liver or lung cells—with the vector. The vector unloads its DNA cargo, which then begins producing the missing protein and restores the cell to normal.

Recently, French researchers reported dramatic results in treating a disease called severe combined immune deficiency (SCID), the disorder suffered by David, The Boy in the Bubble. A broken gene eliminates the production of an enzyme essential for the development of a normal immune system. Scientists isolated the normal copy of the gene and packaged it into a vector. In the laboratory, they then used the vector to transport the gene into the patient's own bone marrow cells. Bone marrow cells create the immune system. The treated bone marrow cells are then given back to the patient in a germ-free isolation room, where they reconstitute a normal, functioning immune system, freeing the patient from the need to remain in isolation.

SOURCE: Fundamentals of Gene Therapy, U.S. Food and Drug Administration, Retrieved March 12, 2007, from http://www.fda.gov/fdac/features/2000/gene.html

fied. Such is the case with DMD, which is tied to a sex-linked recessive gene. Additionally, the biochemical defects associated with various dystrophies can now be recognized.

INTERVENTIONS. There is no known cure for muscular dystrophy. The focus of treatment is maintaining or improving the individual's functioning and preserving his or her ambulatory independence for as long as possible. The first phases of maintenance and prevention are handled by physical therapists, who work to prevent or correct contractures (a permanent shortening and thickening of muscle fibers).

Drugs identified as *catabolic steroids* may have significant benefits for children and youth with DMD. The most often prescribed of these drugs is *prednisone*. It lessens the loss of muscle function or increases muscle strength in individuals with DMD. These drugs may lengthen the period of time in which individuals with DMD may be able to walk and to use their arms—several months to one or two years. However, prednisone also has many potentially damaging *side effects*, which can be severe over a prolonged period. These include loss of bone and muscle tissue, significant weight gain, thinning of the skin, elevated blood pressure and blood sugar, and serious psychological trouble, including depression, sleeping problems, and severely elevated mood (mania) (Muscular Dystrophy Association, 2006).

As DMD becomes more serious, treatment generally includes prescribing supportive devices, such as walkers, braces, nightsplints, surgical corsets, and hospital beds. Eventually, the person with muscular dystrophy will need to use a wheelchair.

The terminal nature of DMD and other health conditions poses challenging problems to affected individuals, their families, and caregivers. Major symptoms that may be experienced include pain, nausea, vomiting, seizures, convulsions, decreased appetite, mouth sores, fatigue, cough, difficulty swallowing foods, and skin problems.

Fortunately, significant progress has been made in helping individuals with terminal illnesses deal with death. Programs developed for families who have a terminally ill child, youth, or adult serve several purposes. They give children with terminal illnesses opportunities to ask questions about death; to express their concerns through writing, play, or other means; and to work through their feelings (Forsythe & Maddison, 2005; Huffman, Fontaine, & Price, 2003).

Programs for parents are designed to help them understand their children's conceptions about death, to suggest ways in which the parents might respond to certain questions or concerns, and to outline the steps they might take in successfully preparing for and responding to the child's death and related events. One such program is Compassionate Friends. This organization, which is composed of parents who have lost children to death, provides sensitive support and resources to other parents who have lost a child to injury or disease.

This chapter's Inclusion and Collaboration Through the Lifespan offers valuable suggestions for interacting with young children, school-age children, youth, and adults with physical disabilities and health disorders.

Health Disorders

Health disorders affect children, youth, and adults in a variety of ways. For example, a child with juvenile diabetes who has engaged in a vigorous game of volleyball with classmates may need to drink a little fruit juice or soda pop just before or after the activity to regulate blood sugar levels. An adult with diabetes may need to follow a special diet and regularly receive appropriate doses of insulin. By way of review, IDEA describes persons with health disorders as individuals with "limited strength, vitality, or alertness, due to chronic or acute health problems such as a heart condition, tuberculosis, rheumatic fever, nephritis, asthma, sickle cell anemia, hemophilia, epilepsy, lead poisoning, leukemia, or diabetes which adversely affect . . . educational performance" (23 Code of Federal Regulations, Section 300.5 [7]). The following health disorders will be reviewed in this section: acquired immune deficiency syndrome (AIDS), asthma, seizure disorders (epilepsy), diabetes, cystic fibrosis (CF), and sickle cell anemia (SCA).

> ➤ **Health disorders**
Disabling conditions characterized by limited stamina, vitality, or alertness due to chronic or acute health problems.

Council for Exceptional Children

Standard 1: Foundations

INCLUSION AND COLLABORATION THROUGH THE LIFESPAN

People with Physical Disabilities and Health Disorders

EARLY CHILDHOOD YEARS

Tips for the Family

- Work closely with medical personnel to lessen the overall impact of the disorder over time. This may include using prophylactic medications, monitoring the impact of certain medications, asking for reading materials, following dietary routines, communicating honest concerns, and asking questions about instructions not well understood.

- Give the child who has physical disabilities or health disorders opportunities to freely explore his or her environment to the maximum degree possible. This may require some adaptations or specialized equipment (e.g., custom-made wheelchairs, prosthetic devices).

- Involve the child with other children as time and energy permit. Only children can teach one another certain things. This may include inviting one or several children to your home for informal play, celebration of social events, and other age-appropriate activities.

- Join advocacy and support groups that provide the information and assistance you need.

Tips for the Preschool Teacher

- Be sure that the physical environment in the classroom lends itself to the needs of children who have physical disabilities or health disorders (e.g., aisles in the classroom must be wide enough for free movement in a wheelchair). Like any other children, these children benefit from moving around and fully exploring every inch of every environment. Also, it readies them in a gradual way to become appropriately independent.

- Become aware of specific needs of the child by consulting with parents. For example, the child may need to refrain from highly physical activities.

Tips for Preschool Personnel

- Be sure that other key personnel in the school who interact directly with the child are informed of his or her needs. Collaborate in offering the best services possible.

- Orient all the children in your classroom to the needs of the child with physical disabilities or health disorders. This could be done by you, the parents or siblings, or other educational personnel in the school. Remember, your behavior toward the child says more than words will ever convey.

- Be sure that arrangements have been made for emergency situations. For example, some peers may know exactly what to do if a fellow class member begins to have a seizure or an asthmatic attack. Additionally, classmates should know how they may be helpful in directing and assisting the child during a fire drill or other emergency procedures.

Tips for Neighbors and Friends

- Involve the child with physical disabilities or health disorders and his or her family in holiday gatherings. Be sensitive to dietary regimens, opportunities for repositioning, and alternative means of communicating.

- Become aware of things that you may need to do. For example, you may need to learn what to do if a child with insulin-dependent diabetes shows signs of glucose buildup.

ELEMENTARY YEARS

Tips for the Family

- Maintain a healthy and ongoing relationship with the care providers who are part of your child's life. Acknowledge their efforts and reinforce behaviors and actions that are particularly helpful to you and your child.

- Continue to be involved with advocacy and support groups.

- Stay informed by subscribing to newsletters that are produced and disseminated by advocacy organizations and governmental organizations.

- Develop and maintain good relationships with the people who teach and serve your child within the school setting. Collaboration is essential to your child's success.

Tips for the General Education Classroom Teacher

- Be informed and willing to learn about the unique needs of the child with physical disabilities or health disorders in your classroom. For example, before the year begins, schedule a conference with the child's parents to talk about medications, prosthetic devices, levels of desired physical activities, and so on.

- Inform the other children in the class. Help them become aware of their crucial roles in contributing to the well-being of the child with physical disabilities or health disorders.

- Use socially competent and mature peers to assist you (e.g., providing tutoring, physical assistance, social support in recess activities).

- Be sure that plans have been made and practiced for dealing with emergency situations (e.g., some children may need to be carried out of a building or room).

- If the child's condition is progressive and life-threatening, begin to discuss the ramifications of death and loss. Many excellent books about this topic are available for children.

Tips for School Personnel

- Be sure that all key personnel in the school setting who interact with the child on a regular basis are informed about treatment regimens, dietary requirements, and signs of potentially problematic conditions such as fevers and irritability.

- Meet periodically as professionals to deal with emergent problems, brainstorm for solutions, and identify suitable actions. Again, collaboration is vital to meeting the needs of these children and youth.
- Children can be involved periodically in brainstorming activities that focus on involving the child with physical disabilities or health disorders to the maximum degree possible.
- Institute cross-age tutoring and support. When possible, have the child with a physical disability or health disorder become a tutor.

Tips for Neighbors and Friends

- Involve the child with physical disabilities or health disorders in your family activities.
- Provide parents with some respite care. They will appreciate the time to themselves.
- Be informed! Be aware of the needs of the child by regularly talking to his or her parents. They will sincerely appreciate your concern.

SECONDARY AND TRANSITION YEARS

Tips for the Family

- Remember that for some individuals with physical disabilities or health disorders, the secondary or young adult years may be the most trying, particularly if the conditions are progressive in nature.
- Begin planning early in the secondary school years for the youth's transition from the public school to the adult world. Incorporate goals related to independent living in the IEP.
- Be sure that you are well informed about the adult services offered in your community and state.

Tips for the General Education Classroom Teacher

- Continue to be aware of the potential needs for accommodation and adjustment.
- Treat the individual as an adult.
- Realize that the youth's studies or work experiences may be interrupted from time to time for specialized or regular medical treatments or other important health care services.

Tips for School Personnel

- Acknowledge individuals by name, become familiar with their interests and hobbies, joke with them occasionally, and involve them in meaningful activities such as fundraisers, community service projects, and decorating for various school events.

- Provide opportunities for all students to receive recognition and be involved in school-related activities.
- Realize that peer assistance and tutoring may be particularly helpful to certain students. Social involvement outside the school setting (e.g., going to movies, attending concerts) should be encouraged.
- Use members of the multidisciplinary team to help with unique problems that surface from time to time. For example, you may want to talk with special educators about management ideas that may improve a given child's behavior in your classroom.

Tips for Neighbors, Friends, and Potential Employers

- Continue to be involved in the individual's life in meaningful ways.
- Be aware of assistance that you might provide in the event of a youth's gradual deterioration or death.
- Involve the individual in age-appropriate activities (e.g., cookouts, video nights, or community events).
- Encourage your own teens to volunteer as peer tutors or job coaches.
- If you are an employer, provide opportunities for job sampling, on-the-job training, or actual employment.

ADULT YEARS

Tips for the Family

- Make provisions for independent living away from home. Work with adult service personnel and advocacy organizations in lining up appropriate housing and related support services.
- Provide support for appropriate employment opportunities.
- Work closely with local and state adult services personnel. Know what your rights are and how you can qualify your son or daughter for educational or other support services.

Tips for Neighbors, Friends, and Employers

- Provide appropriate accommodations for leisure and work activities.
- Adopt an adult for regular recreational and social activities.
- Provide regular opportunities for recognition and informative feedback. When persons with disabilities are hired, be sure that they regularly receive specific information about their work performance. Feedback may include candid comments about their punctuality, rate of work completion, and social interaction with others. Withholding information, not making reasonable adjustments, and not expecting these individuals to be responsible for their behaviors are great disservices to them.

Human Immunodeficiency Virus (HIV) and Acquired Immune Deficiency Syndrome (AIDS)

DEFINITIONS AND CONCEPTS. Acquired immunodeficiency syndrome or acquired immune deficiency syndrome (AIDS) is a set of symptoms and infections resulting from the specific injury to the immune system caused by infection with the human immunodeficiency virus (HIV). AIDS in children and youth is defined by the following characteristics: (1) the presence of the **human immunodeficiency virus (HIV)**, a virus that attacks certain white blood cells within the body, and/or the presence of antibodies to HIV in the blood or tissues, as well as (2) recurrent bacterial diseases (Ladewig, London, & Davidson, 2006a).

The first reports regarding some of the features of AIDS, received by the Centers for Disease Control in the spring of 1981, dealt exclusively with young men who had a rare form of pneumonia. Simultaneously, the Centers for Disease Control received reports of an increased incidence of a rare skin tumor, Kaposi's sarcoma. Individuals who had developed these conditions were homosexual men in their thirties and forties. Many died or were severely debilitated within 12 months of diagnosis.

Prior to the spring of 1981, primary-care physicians in New York, San Francisco, and other large cities had seen many cases of swollen lymph nodes in homosexual men. Many of these individuals exhibited this condition for months or even years after their initial diagnosis without suffering serious side effects. However, those who developed **opportunistic infections** often experienced severe side effects or even death. Eventually, these opportunistic infections were linked to a breakdown in the functioning of the **immune system**. People affected with these infections exhibited pronounced depletions of a particular subset of white blood cells, T lymphocytes. White blood cells fight infections; without sufficient numbers and kinds of them, the body is defenseless. Individuals with this condition became subject to a wide range of opportunistic infections and tumors affecting the gastrointestinal system, central nervous system, and skin.

Individuals with AIDS move through a series of disease stages. The first stage is the exposure stage, or the period during which the transmission of the HIV occurs. Young people may be infected with HIV but not yet exhibit the life-threatening conditions associated with AIDS. The second stage is characterized by the production of antibodies in infected individuals. These antibodies appear about 2 to 12 weeks after the initial transmission of the virus. About 30% of individuals experience flu-like symptoms for a few days to several weeks. During the third stage, the immune system declines, and the virus begins to destroy cells of the immune system. However, many individuals with HIV are asymptomatic during this stage. This asymptomatic phase may continue for 3 to 10 years. About half of all individuals with HIV develop AIDS within 10 years.

For children, the onset of AIDS ranges from 1 to 3 years. At stage four, individuals begin to manifest symptoms of a damaged immune system, including weight loss, fatigue, skin rashes, and night sweats. In more severe cases, opportunistic diseases appear in individuals with AIDS. At stage five, recurrent and chronic diseases begin to take their toll on individuals. Gradually, the immune system fails and death occurs.

Researchers have identified several patterns of disease development in HIV-infected children. The mean age of onset in exposed children is about 4.1 years. About 33% of exposed children remain AIDS-free until up to 13 years of age. Often the most serious symptoms do not appear until these children enter school or begin their adolescent years.

PREVALENCE AND CAUSATION. Since the first cases of AIDS, infection with human immunodeficiency virus (HIV) has grown exponentially, resulting in an estimated 65 million infections and 25 million deaths. In the United States, between 1,039,000 and 1,185,000 individuals are living with HIV/AIDS, with 24% to 27% undiagnosed or totally unaware of their HIV status (Centers for Disease Control and Prevention, 2006b). Additionally, about 7,000 infants arrive each year at risk for developing HIV infection (Best, 2005b). Almost 9,500 children under age 13 in the United States have been diagnosed with AIDS (Centers for Disease Control and Prevention, 2006; Center for Disease Control & Prevention, 2006). About 420,000 individuals die of AIDS each year in the United States; about 5,000 of these are children or youth less than 15 years of age. The mean age for death

---

➤ **Human immunodeficiency virus (HIV)**

A virus that reduces immune system function and has been linked to AIDS.

➤ **Opportunistic infection**

An infection caused by germs that are not usually capable of causing infection in healthy people but can do so given certain changes in the immune system (opportunity).

➤ **Immune system**

The normally functioning system within a person's body that protects it from disease.

in children with AIDS is 9.4 years (Franks, Miller, Wolff, & Landry, 2004). Increasingly, heterosexual adolescents are at greater risk than infants in contracting the HIV virus—this is because of unprotected sexual activity (Advocates for Youth, 2006). In fact, in youth ages 13 to 19, 57% of the HIV infections occur in young women, and 43% surface in young men. These and other statistics accentuate the need for targeted, gender-sensitive, and culturally responsive prevention programs that lead to enhanced self-esteem, better decision-making skills, and positive behavior change.

Education is a key ingredient in preventing HIV/AIDS.

The cause of AIDS is the human immunodeficiency virus (HIV). This virus is passed from one person to another through contact that includes the exchange of bodily fluids, usually semen or vaginal secretions; blood exchange through injection drug use (IDU); and transfusions, perinatal contact, and breast milk (Best, 2005b; Centers for Disease Control & Prevention, 2006; Gold, 2004; Gostin, 2004). Mothers who are infected with HIV can dramatically reduce the chances of transmission of the virus to their yet-to-be-born children by taking zidovudine during the gestational period (Ladewig, London, & Davidson, 2006a).

Sixty percent of affected adolescents develop AIDS through sexual activity or intravenous drug use. Adolescent males acquire the HIV infection primarily through homosexual activity. Adolescent females generally acquire the infection through heterosexual activity and intravenous drug use.

Many children with AIDS do not grow normally, do not make appropriate weight gains, are slow to achieve important motor milestones (crawling, walking, and so on), and evidence neurological damage. As the HIV turns into AIDS, these children are attacked by life-threatening opportunistic infections. Also, many of the children, as indicated earlier, develop more serious neurological problems associated with mental retardation, cerebral palsy, and seizure disorders.

INTERVENTIONS. To date, there is no known cure for AIDS. The best cure for AIDS in children and youth is prevention. Treatment is generally provided by an interdisciplinary team composed of medical, educational, and health care professionals.

Much progress has been made in testing new antiretroviral therapies to combat AIDS and in developing agents to treat opportunistic infections. Nevertheless, there is still much work to be done to find satisfactory drugs and related therapies for HIV infections and AIDS. Despite this progress, 10% to 15% of infected children develop AIDS in the first months of life and die shortly thereafter, and another 15% to 20% develop AIDS following infancy. Some 65% to 75% of children who test positive for HIV thrive.

Early diagnosis of infants with HIV is crucial. Early antiviral therapy and prophylactic treatment of opportunistic diseases can contribute significantly to the infected child's well-being and prognosis over time. The frequency and nature of treatment depend on the age of onset and the age at which the child develops the first opportunistic infection.

Providing appropriate interventions for infants with AIDS can be challenging. These infants, like infants without AIDS, are totally dependent on others for their care. Many mothers who pass the AIDS virus on to their children are not adequately prepared to care effectively for their infants. Typically, these mothers come from impoverished environments with little access to health care and other appropriate support services. Additionally, these mothers are often intravenous drug users and thus are not reliable caregivers.

Treating adolescents with HIV and AIDS can be very challenging. For example, compliance with medical regimens for all age groups is difficult. However, for those who are

HIV-positive and have no obvious symptoms, keeping regular medical appointments and taking antiviral medications are not only highly problematic but also constant reminders of an impending fatal disease. Youth with HIV and AIDS need to learn how to make medical regimens a regular part of their lives to maintain good health and longevity. They also require assistance in dealing with the psychological reactions of anxiety and depression that often accompany the discovery of HIV infection. Finally, they and others benefit significantly from instruction directed at helping them to understand AIDS, to make wise decisions about their sexual behavior, to use assertiveness skills, and to communicate effectively with others.

Neither students with AIDS nor their parents are compelled by law to disclose their HIV medical status to school personnel. Nevertheless, the parents or students may share this information with a limited number of school-based personnel, including the school nurse, the principal, and the primary teacher. This information should be treated with the utmost confidentiality. Students with HIV who are on strict medical regimens will need time to take their medications. Missing a dosage could seriously jeopardize a student's health. Fatigue is a common occurrence in these students. Ample opportunities should be available for rejuvenation and respite from demanding physical activities.

Essential teacher-related behaviors in working with children and youth with AIDS include working collaboratively with care providers, providing sensitive and nonjudgmental services, heeding the guidelines to prevent blood-borne infections (see Figure 17.4), helping young people adhere to their medication regimens, modeling appropriate respectful behaviors, and maintaining privacy and confidentiality (Best, 2005b; Huffman, Fontaine, & Price, 2003). Also, teachers and parents play key roles providing instruction related to preventing AIDS and its tranmission.

Asthma

DEFINITIONS AND CONCEPTS. Think about what it must feel like to have difficulty breathing—being unable to inhale the air that you need. Twenty million Americans are affected by asthma. For many, the disease is a serious, life-threatening condition that impacts the quality of their lives. About 5,000 people die each year of asthma. Emergency physicians across the country experience more than 2 million visits as a result of asthma-related medical crises. More than 14 million school days are missed as a result of asthma. Asthma is the most

---

FIGURE 17.4

Universal Precautions and Their Benefits in School Settings

Universal Precautions

- Thorough hand washing, before and after contacting individuals, objects, or secretions
- Use of personal protective equipment (barrier protection, such as gloves and masks)
- Application of safe methods of disposing waste, cleaning up spills, and handling laundry
- Procedures for dealing with accidental exposure to potentially infectious materials

Benefits of Adhering to Universal Precautions

- Protecting infected individuals from further infection
- Protecting the privacy of infected individuals
- Protecting the health of service providers
- Protecting the health of other students

SOURCE: Adapted from *Preventing Infectious Disease Transmission and Implementing Universal Precautions* in S. J. Best, K. W. Heller, & J. L. Bigge, (Eds.), *Teaching Individuals with Physical or Multiple Disabilities* 2005, p. 79.

common chronic childhood disease, affecting one in 20 children in the United States (Asthma and Allergy Foundation of American, 2006).

Asthma, simply speaking, is evidenced by swelling and inflammation of the air passages that transport air from the mouth and nose to the lungs. This swelling within the affected passages causes them to narrow, thus limiting the air entering and exiting the individual's respiratory system. Symptoms can be activated by allergens, drugs, foods, inhalants, or other irritants that are drawn into the lungs, resulting in swollen, constricted, or blocked airways. Symptoms include diminished breathing capacity, coughing, wheezing, tightness in the chest, and excessive sputum. In severe cases, asthma can be life-threatening (Asthma and Allergy Foundation of America, 2006; Berger, 2004; Wolf, 2004).

PREVALENCE AND CAUSATION. Nearly one in ten children in the United States is affected by asthma. Prevalence rates vary from 7% to 10% of school-age children (Children and Asthma in America, 2006; Asthma and Allergy Foundation of America, 2006). In a little more than the past twenty years, the rate of asthma in children 4 to 14 years of age has grown a staggering 75%. (Environmental Protection Agency, 2005).

Asthma results from an abnormal immune response in the bronchial airways. These airways of children and youth are highly susceptible to certain triggers. In response to these triggers, the large airways (bronchi) contract into spasm. Swelling soon follows, leading to a further narrowing of the airways and excessive mucus production, which causes coughing and other breathing difficulties.

Triggers include allergens involving waste from common household insects (house dust mites, cockroaches, etc.), grass pollens, mold spores, and animal dander. Other triggers include medications, air pollution (ozone, nitrogen dioxide, sulfur dioxide, etc.), cleaning agents, tobacco smoke, and various chemicals and industrial compounds (Clark, 2003). Some early childhood infections, particularly respiratory infections, set the stage for the potential development of asthma. Emotional stress has also been implicated as a potential trigger (Asthma and Allergy Foundation of America, 2006; Shouldice, 2004). And there is a very strong genetic predisposition for the development of asthma and other allergy-related conditions (Silverman, Shapiro, Lomas, & Weiss, 2005; Wolf, 2004).

INTERVENTIONS. Several interventions are useful to persons with asthma. It is important for all age groups with asthma to eliminate or moderate exposure to potential triggers. Other interventions include increasing the anti-inflammatory mediation in advance of anticipated exposure to certain triggers, using appropriate bronchodilators for much the same purpose, and limiting the time of exposure to the potential or known triggers.

As we noted earlier, medications play a key role in treating and managing asthma. Bronchodilators, appropriately administered, reduce the swelling and inflammation in the affected airways and generally provide a short-term reprieve from common symptoms. Other physician-prescribed, anti-inflammatory medications regularly administered contribute significantly to the management of the disease and its symptoms. Generally, the side effects of the asthma-prescribed medications are minimal. However, frequent use of bronchodilators may indicate a need for further medical consultation. Also, some forms of asthma are induced by cold or exercise. In these cases, parents and other care providers will want to determine the benefit-to-risk ratios in having their children engage in activities that may activate asthma and its symptoms (Shouldice, 2004).

As is true of so many health conditions, teachers and others who have regular and frequent access to children and youth with asthma need to understand the disease and its consequences. Many families will have created an "asthma action plan" with two primary purposes: effectively managing the disease on a daily basis and creating a rescue plan in the event of a severe asthmatic attack. The plan outlines warning signs, identifies rescue medicines, provides steps to take in the event of an attack, and describes conditions that would warrant calling a doctor.

Frequently the symptoms associated with asthma are more evident during the day when children or youth participate in various school-related activities (recess, physical education, or other physically demanding activities). When there is some likelihood of severe asthmatic attacks, medications should be available in the school, teachers should know how to administer

Standard 1: Foundations

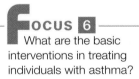
FOCUS **6**
What are the basic interventions in treating individuals with asthma?

Standard 5: Learning Environments and Social Interactions

them, and the medications should be stored in a secure cabinet, generally located in the school nurse's office. Communication and collaboration among and between teachers, parents, and other school personnel are vital to the successful treatment of asthma in children and youth (Shouldice, 2004; Wheeler, Boss, & Williams, 2004).

Several school-based, child-centered asthma education programs are beginning to take hold. These programs provide students with meaningful tools and knowledge to effectively manage their asthma symptoms and to lessen the likelihood of school absences or other asthma-related emergencies (Tinkelman & Schwartz, 2004). One of the most important tools is a peak-flow meter that enables children and youth to monitor their exhalation output frequently. If the output takes a dramatic drop, medication can be adjusted to give relief, or additional medical advice can be obtained (Clark, 2003).

Asthma by its very nature is a highly unpredictable disease, whose symptoms and crises may surface with little or no warning. As with so many health disorders, physicians, educators, and parents must collaborate in addressing the distinctively unique manifestations of asthma in each child, youth, and adult.

Seizure Disorders (Epilepsy)

DEFINITIONS AND CONCEPTS. "Epilepsy is a neurological condition that makes people susceptible to seizures. A **seizure** is a change in sensation, awareness, or behavior brought about by a brief electrical disturbance in the brain. Seizures vary from a momentary disruption of the senses, to short periods of unconsciousness or staring spells, to convulsions. Some people have just one type of seizure. Others have more than one type. Although they look different, all seizures are caused by the same thing: a sudden change in how the cells of the brain send electrical signals to each other" (Epilepsy Foundation, 2006, p. 1).

Several classification schemes have been employed to describe the various types of seizure disorders. We will briefly discuss two types of seizures: tonic/clonic and absence.

Generalized **tonic/clonic seizures**, formerly called *grand mal seizures*, affect the entire brain. The **tonic phase** of these seizures is characterized by a stiffening of the body, the **clonic phase** by repeated muscle contractions and relaxations. Tonic/clonic seizures are often preceded by a warning signal known as an **aura**, in which the individual senses a unique sound, odor, or physical sensation just prior to the onset of the seizure. In some instances, the seizure is also signaled by a cry or similar sound. The tonic phase of the seizure begins with a loss of consciousness, after which the individual falls to the ground. Initially, the trunk and head become rigid during the tonic phase. The clonic phase follows and consists of involuntary muscle contractions (violent shaking) of the extremities. Irregular breathing, blueness in the lips and face, increased salivation, loss of bladder and bowel control, and perspiration may occur (Donaghy, 2005; National Institute of Neurological Disorders and Stroke, 2006a).

The nature, scope, frequency, and duration of tonic/clonic seizures vary greatly from person to person. Such seizures may last as long as 20 minutes or less than 1 minute. One of the most dangerous aspects of tonic/clonic seizures is potential injury from falling and striking objects in the environment (see Figure 17.5).

A period of sleepiness and confusion usually follows a tonic/clonic seizure. The individual may exhibit drowsiness, nausea, headache, or a combination of these symptoms. Such symptoms should be treated with appropriate rest, medication, or other therapeutic remedies. The characteristics and aftereffects of seizures vary in many ways and should be treated with this in mind.

Absence seizures, formerly identified as *petit mal seizures*, are characterized by brief periods (moments or seconds) of inattention that may be accompanied by rapid eye blinking and head twitching. During these seizures, the brain ceases to function as it normally would. The individual's consciousness is altered in an almost imperceptible manner. Young people with this type of seizure disorder may experience these seizures as often as 100 times a day. Such inattentive behavior may be viewed as daydreaming by a teacher or work supervisor, but the episode is really due to a momentary burst of abnormal brain activity the individual cannot control. The lapses in attention caused by this form of epilepsy can greatly hamper the individual's ability to respond properly to or profit from a teacher's presentation or a supervisor's instruction (Donaghy, 2005). Treatment and control of absence seizures are generally achieved through prescribed medication.

➤ **Seizure**

A cluster of behaviors (altered consciousness, characteristic motor patterns, etc.) that occurs in response to abnormal neurochemical activity in the brain.

➤ **Tonic/clonic seizures**

Seizures in which the entire brain is affected. These seizures are characterized by stiffening of the body, followed by a phase of rapid muscle contractions (extreme shaking).

➤ **Tonic phase**

The phase of a seizure in which the entire body becomes rigid and stiff.

➤ **Clonic phase**

The phase of a seizure in which the muscles of the body contract and relax in rapid succession.

➤ **Aura**

A sensation that is experienced just before a seizure and that the person is able to remember.

➤ **Absence seizures**

Seizures characterized by brief lapses of consciousness, usually lasting no more than ten seconds. Eye blinking and twitching of the mouth may accompany these seizures.

Council for Exceptional Children

Standard 1: Foundations

FIGURE 17.5

First Aid for Seizures

1. Cushion the head.　　2. Loosen tight necktie or collar.　　3. Turn on side.　　4. Put nothing in the mouth.

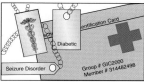

5. Look for identification.　　6. Don't hold the person down.　　7. Seizure ends.　　8. Offer help

SOURCE: Adapted from *Information and Education: First Aid for Seizures* (p.1), by the Epilepsy Foundation of America, 2006b. Retrieved from http://www.efa.org/education/firstaid/chart/html

PREVALENCE AND CAUSATION. Prevalence figures for seizure disorders vary, in part because of the social stigma associated with them. About two million people in the United States have some form of seizure disorders or epilepsy (Davis, King, & Shultz, 2005). Half of all the cases of seizure disorders in children appear before 10 years of age (Huffman, Fontaine, & Price, 2003). Unfortunately, large numbers of adults and children have seizure disorders that remain undiscovered and untreated.

The causes of seizure disorders are many, including perinatal factors, tumors of the brain, complications of head trauma, infections of the central nervous system, vascular diseases, alcoholism, infection, maternal injury or infection, and genetic factors. Also, some seizures are caused by ingestion of street drugs, toxic chemicals, and poisons. Nevertheless, no explicit cause can be found in seven out of ten individuals with seizure disorders (Davis, King, & Shultz, 2005; National Institute of Neurological Disorders and Stroke, 2006a). See Table 17.3 for more information about the causes of seizures for specific age groups.

Researchers are endeavoring to determine what specific biophysical features give rise to seizures. If they can discover the underlying parameters, they may be able to prevent seizures from occurring. This could be done through molecular genetic techniques (Milton & Jung, 2003).

INTERVENTIONS. The treatment of seizure disorders begins with a careful medical investigation in which the physician develops a thorough health history of the individual and completes an in-depth physical examination. Moreover, it is essential that the physician receive thorough descriptions of the seizure(s) (Mittan, 2005a). These preliminary steps may be followed by other diagnostic procedures, including blood tests, video capturing of seizure episodes, CT scans or MRIs, and spinal fluid taps to determine whether the individual has meningitis. EEGs (electroencephalograms) may also be performed to confirm the physician's clinical impressions (Manford, 2003). The electroencephalogram is a test to detect abnormalities in the electrical activity of the brain. However, it should be noted that many seizure disorders are not detectable through electroencephalographic measures. As indicated earlier, an accurate diagnosis is essential to providing effective treatments (National Institute of Neurological Disorders and Stroke, 2006a).

Many types of seizures can be treated successfully with precise drug management. Significant headway has been made with the discovery of effective drugs, particularly for children

FOCUS 7
Describe the immediate treatment for a person who is experiencing a tonic/clonic seizure.

TABLE 17.3

Common Causes of Seizures by Age

AGE RANGE	MAJOR CAUSES
Infant	Birth injury, hypoxia [lack of adequate oxygen]/ischemia [inadequate supply of blood to the brain], congenital malformations, and congenital infection
Childhood	Febrile [temperature-related] seizures, central nervous system infection, head trauma, birth injury, and idiopathic origins
Young adult	Head trauma, drugs, withdrawal from alcohol or sedatives, and idiopathic origin
Elderly	Strokes, brain tumor, cardiac arrest with hypoxia, and metabolic origin

SOURCE: Reprinted with permission from *Fundamentals of Neurologic Disease*, Text Revision (p. 156). Copyright © 2005, Demos Medical Publishing, Inc.

with tonic/clonic and absence seizures. Anticonvulsant drugs must be chosen very carefully, however. The potential risks and benefits of each medication must be balanced and weighed. Once a drug has been prescribed, families should be educated in its use, in the importance of noting any side effects, and in the need for consistent administration. Maintaining regular medication regimens can be very challenging for children or youth and their parents. In some instances, medication may be discontinued after several years of seizure-free behavior. This is particularly true for those young children who do not have some form of underlying brain pathology (Manford, 2003).

Other treatments for seizure disorders include surgery, stress management, and diet modifications. The goal of surgery is to remove the precise part of the brain that is damaged and is causing the seizures. Surgery is considered for those individuals with uncontrollable seizures—essentially those who have not responded to anticonvulsant medications. Using a variety of sophisticated scanning procedures, physicians attempt to isolate the damaged area of the brain that corresponds with the seizure activity. The outcomes of surgery for children and youth with well-defined foci of seizure activity are excellent. Fifty-five to 90% of individuals who undergo surgery experience positive outcomes (Epilepsy Foundation, 2006; National Institute of Neurological Disorders and Stroke, 2006a). Obviously, the surgery must be done with great care. Once removed, brain tissue is gone forever, and the function that the tissue performed is eliminated or only marginally restored. Unfortunately, only 1% of seizures disorders are treatable through surgery (Manford, 2003).

Stress management is designed to increase the child's or youth's general functioning. Because seizures are often associated with illnesses, inadequate rest, and other stressors, parents and other care providers work at helping children, youth, and adults understand the importance of attending consistently to their medication routines, developing emotional resilience, and maintaining healthful patterns of behavior.

Diet modifications are designed to alter the way the body uses energy from food. Typically, our bodies convert the carbohydrates we consume into glucose (sugar). Several types of seizures can be controlled by instituting a ketogenic diet. This diet focuses on consuming fats rather than carbohydrates. Instead of producing glucose, individuals on this diet produce ketones, a special kind of molecule. This change in food consumption causes alterations in the metabolism of the brain, which normally uses sugars to "fire" its functions. For reasons that are not completely understood, the brain is less receptive to certain kinds of seizures under this diet. However, the diet is extraordinarily difficult to maintain on a long-term basis and is now rarely used or recommended.

Individuals with seizure disorders need calm and supportive responses from teachers, parents, peers, and others. The treatment efforts of various professionals and family members must be carefully orchestrated. Educators should be aware of the basic fundamentals of seizure disorders and their management. They should also be aware of their critical role in observing seizures that may occur at school. The astute observations of a teacher may be invaluable to a health care team that is developing appropriate medical interventions for the child or youth with seizure disorders. Additionally, teachers should have "the skills needed to deal with a seizure before, during, and following its occurrence" (Vallettuti, 2004, p. 20). It is vitally important that teachers and parents be able to accurately and sensitively describe to other children and youth what has happened when a student experiences a seizure in their classrooms. This will reduce the chances for misunderstaning and the development of stigmas associated with seizure disorders (Mittan, 2005b).

Diabetes

DEFINITIONS AND CONCEPTS. The term **diabetes mellitus** refers to a developmental or hereditary disorder characterized by inadequate secretion or use of **insulin**, a substance that is produced by the pancreas and used to process carbohydrates. There are two types of diabetes mellitus: insulin-dependent diabetes mellitus (IDDM), commonly known as Type I or juvenile onset diabetes, and non-insulin-dependent diabetes mellitus (NIDDM), referred to as Type II or adult onset diabetes (American Diabetes Association, 2006a).

Glucose (a sugar, one of the end products of digesting carbohydrates) is used by the body for energy. Some glucose is used quickly, whereas some is stored in the liver and muscles for later use. However, muscle and liver cells cannot absorb and store the energy released by glucose without insulin, a hormone produced by the pancreas that converts glucose into energy that body cells use to perform their various functions. Without insulin, glucose accumulates in the blood, causing a condition known as hyperglycemia. Left untreated, this condition can cause serious, immediate problems for people with IDDM, leading to loss of consciousness or to a diabetic coma (American Diabetes Association, 2006a).

Typical symptoms associated with glucose buildup in the blood are extreme hunger, thirst, and frequent urination. Although progress has been made in regulating insulin levels, the prevention and treatment of the complications that accompany diabetes, which include blindness, cardiovascular disease, and kidney disease, still pose tremendous challenges for health care specialists.

Consider this revealing description provided by a talented professional: "A nine-year-old I interviewed, who was diagnosed with type 1 diabetes at age six, knew this well. She had pricked her finger for a blood test nine thousand times and received more than two thousand insulin shots in the past three years. She typically has four blood checks a day, eats on a relentlessly regular schedule, and may wake up out-of-kilter at night when her blood sugar level drops. The 'adjustments' necessitated by diabetes—which as far as she know will be lifelong—are wrenching" (Clark, 2003, p. 6). This brief vignette helps us sense the challenges experienced by many children and youth with diabetes.

IDDM, or juvenile onset diabetes, is particularly troublesome. Compared to the adult form, this disease tends to be more severe and progresses more quickly, thus increasing the likelihood of the onset of conditions associated with Type II diabetes.

> **Diabetes mellitus**

A disease characterized by inadequate use of insulin, resulting in disordered metabolism of carbohydrates, fats, and proteins.

> **Insulin**

A substance secreted by the pancreas that functions to process carbohydrates, enabling glucose to enter the body's cells.

FOCUS 8

Identify three problems that individuals with diabetes may experience later in life.

Consistent insulin monitoring is a key component of diabetes treatment.

Generally, the symptoms of Type I disabetes are easily recognized. The child develops an unusual thirst for water and other liquids. His or her appetite also increases substantially, but listlessness and fatigue occur despite increased food and liquid intake.

NIDDM is the most common form of diabetes and is often associated with obesity in individuals over age 40. Individuals with this form of diabetes are at less risk for diabetic comas, and most individuals can manage the disorder through exercise and dietary restrictions. If these actions fail, insulin therapy may be necessary.

PREVALENCE AND CAUSATION. It is estimated that 7% of the U.S. population has diabetes. The prevalence rate for children with insulin-dependent diabetes (those who must administer insulin) is approximately one per 400 to 500 children (Daneman & Frank, 2004). About 6.2 million people have diabetes and are unaware of it (American Diabetes Association, 2006a). Nearly 177,000 children and youth under 20 years of age have diabetes. Type II diabetes, a disease that once was seen primarily in adults over age 45, is becoming more common in children, largely as a result of the staggering growth of childhood obesity (National Diabetes Education Program, 2006).

The causes of diabetes remain obscure, although considerable research has been conducted on the biochemical mechanisms responsible for it. Diabetes develops gradually in individuals. Individuals with Type I diabetes have a genetic predisposition to the disease (Daneman & Frank, 2004). A youngster's environment and heredity interact in determining the severity and the long-term nature of the condition. However, even in identical twins, when one twin develops Type I diabetes, the other twin is affected only 25% to 50% of the time. There must be an environmental trigger that activates the onset of the disease. Some researchers believe that trigger to be a particular virus, *Coxsackie B.* Progressively, the body's immune system is affected, and the destruction of beta cells occurs. These are the cells in the pancreas that produce and regulate insulin production. Without insulin, the child develops the classic symptoms of Type I diabetes: excessive thirst, urination, and hunger, along with weight loss, fatigue, blurred vision, and high blood sugar levels.

INTERVENTIONS. Medical treatment centers on the regular administration of insulin, which is essential for children and youth with juvenile diabetes. Several exciting advances have been made in recent years in the monitoring of blood sugar levels and the delivery of insulin to people with diabetes. Recent success with pancreas transplants has virtually eliminated the disease for some individuals. Also, significant progress is being made in the development of the bioartificial pancreas and gene therapy.

Solid headway has been made in transplanting insulin-producing islet cells to individuals with Type I diabetes. However, this approach is complicated by shortages in available, whole pancreases and by the rejection of these new cells in recipients. Other sources of pancreatic tissue are present in fetal tissue. This controversial approach makes use of tissues derived from aborted fetuses. Animal islet cells are also being investigated, particularly islet cells derived from pigs, whose insulin differs by only one molecule from that of humans. However, transplantation of these cells poses similar rejection problems for recipients (American Diabetes Association, 2006b).

Hybrid technologies are also being pursued. Perhaps the most promising is the production of artificial beta cells that could be used in an artificial pancreas. This approach entails inserting, into naturally occurring cells, new genes that would produce insulin and be sensitive to the rise and fall of blood glucose.

Maintaining normal levels of glucose is now achieved in many instances with an insulin infusion pump, which is worn by persons with diabetes and powered by small batteries. The infusion pump operates continuously and delivers the dose of insulin determined by the physician and the patient. This form of treatment is effective only when used in combination with carefully followed diet and exercise programs. These pumps, if carefully monitored and operated, contribute greatly to "controlling" diabetes, thus reducing or slowing the onset and risks for eye disease, nerve damage, and kidney disease.

Juvenile diabetes is a lifelong condition that can have a pronounced effect on the child or youth in a number of areas. Complications for children with long-standing diabetes include blindness, heart attacks, and kidney problems. Many of these problems can be delayed or prevented by maintaining adequate blood sugar levels with appropriate food intake, exercise, and insulin injections.

Teachers and other care providers need to work carefully with parents and medical personnel in monitoring treatment and medication regimens, supporting efforts to monitor blood sugar, and being alert to changes in student behavior or performance that may warrant immediate action or consultation with medical or other therapeutic personnel. Also, teachers play key roles in helping children and youth embrace and engage in activities and events that enhance their physical well-being, lessening the likelihood of problems with childhood obesity and related conditions. Communication between teachers and parents is essential in caring for and educating children and youth with diabetes (Daneman & Frank, 2004; Huffman, Fontaine, & Price, 2003).

Cystic Fibrosis

DEFINITIONS AND CONCEPTS. **Cystic fibrosis (CF)** is "an autosomal recessive disease characterized by a cluster of symptoms including high levels of electrolytes in the sweat, pancreatic insufficiency, digestive problems, cirrhosis of the liver, infertility (in males), and an accumulation of thick mucus in the lungs accompanied by frequent infections and tissue scarring. There may also be damage to the right side of the heart because it is subjected to increased pressure as it attempts to pump blood through the damaged lungs. CF was originally called "cystic fibrosis of the pancreas" (Wailoo & Pemberton, 2006, p. 226).

PREVALENCE AND CAUSATION. Cystic fibrosis affects 30,000 children and adults in the United States. CF is virtually absent in Japan and China. Males and females appear to be affected in about equal numbers. CF manifests itself in slightly more than 3 infants in every 10,000 live births (Cytic Fibrosis Foundation, 2006a).

CF is a genetically transmitted disease. A child must inherit a defective copy of the CF gene from each parent to develop the disease. The gene for the CF transfer regulator (CFTR) is very large, and some 2,000 mutations have already been identified with the disease. CFTR, a protein, produces improper transportation of sodium and salt (chloride) within cells that line organs such as the lungs and pancreas. CFTR prevents chloride from exiting these cells. This blockage affects a broad range of organs and systems in the body, including reproductive organs in men and women, the lungs, sweat glands, and the digestive system (Cystic Fibrosis Foundation, 2006b).

INTERVENTIONS. The prognosis for an individual with CF depends on a number of factors. The two most critical are early diagnosis of the condition and the quality of care provided after diagnosis. If the diagnosis occurs late, irreversible damage may be present. With early diagnosis and appropriate medical care, most individuals with CF can achieve weight and growth gains similar to those of their normal peers. Early diagnosis and improved treatment strategies have lengthened the average lifespan of children with CF; more than half now live into their thirties.

The best and most comprehensive treatment is provided through CF centers located throughout the United States. These centers provide experienced medical and support staff (respiratory care personnel, social workers, dieticians, genetic counselors, and psychologists). Moreover, they maintain diagnostic laboratories especially equipped to perform pulmonary function testing and sweat testing. Sweat of children with CF has abnormal concentrations of sodium or chloride; in fact, sweat tests provide the definitive data for a diagnosis of CF in infants and young children (Cystic Fibrosis Foundation, 2006a).

Interventions for CF are varied and complex, and treatment continues throughout the person's lifetime. Consistent and appropriate application of the medical, social, educational, and psychological components of treatment enable these individuals to live longer and with less discomfort and fewer complications than in years past.

Treatment of CF is designed to achieve a number of goals. The first is diagnosis of the condition before any severe symptoms are exhibited. Other goals include control of chest infection, maintenance of adequate nutrition, education of the child and family regarding the condition, and provision of a suitable education for the child.

➤ **Cystic fibrosis (CF)**
An autosomal recessive disease characterized by a cluster of symptoms including high levels of electrolytes in the sweat, pancreatic insufficiency, digestive problems, cirrhosis of the liver, infertility (in males), and an accumulation of thick mucus in the lungs accompanied by frequent infections and tissue scarring.

Council for
Exceptional
Children

Standard 1: Foundations

FOCUS **9**
Identify present and future interventions for the treatment of children and youth with cystic fibrosis.

DEBATE FORUM

SHOULD WE FULLY USE OUR NEWLY ACQUIRED KNOWLEDGE?

It begins innocuously enough. A 6-month-old baby, previously thriving and cheerful, begins reacting differently to normal sounds such as clapping hands or closing doors. Her parents notice that her limbs twitch and her muscles are not developing properly. She has trouble swallowing and shows signs of mental retardation. What they can't see is her compromised brain tissue, which began degenerating when she was still in her mother's womb. Soon their once-healthy child is in the grips of an overwhelming illness. As the deterioration intensifies, fatty deposits overwhelm the nerve cells in her brain, and she experiences seizures and paralysis. Bright cherry red spots appear on the retinas of her eyes, and she is rendered blind. Their daughter lapses into a vegetative state, and by the age of 3 or 4 she is dead, often of complications from pneumonia.

If ever there were a clear case for using our knowledge of human genetics to end suffering, Tay-Sachs, a killer of children, is it. There is no cure for the disease. A single-gene disorder, Tay-Sachs is named for British ophthalmologist Warren Tay, who first described the cherry-red spot on Tay-Sachs victims' eyes in 1881, and for Bernard Sachs, a neurologist in New York who outlined the other progressive degenerations of the disease and noted the frequency of its occurrence among Ashkenazi Jews (Jews of Central and Eastern European descent). The rate of Tay-Sachs disease among Ashkenazi Jews is approximately one in every 3,000 births—nearly 100 times higher than the rate in other ethnic groups. Tay-Sachs is inherited in an autosomal recessive fashion, which means that both parents must be carriers of the defective gene to have an afflicted child. If both parents are carriers, they have a one in four chance—for each pregnancy—of having a child with Tay-Sachs.

Not long ago, information about a particular ethnic group's unique genetic characteristics was hardly so precise. It was known that certain diseases and disorders appear more frequently in particular populations. For instance, people of Mediterranean descent suffer from the group of blood disorders known as thalassemia; those of African descent experience higher rates of sickle cell anemia; and whites of Northern European descent are more likely to have children with cystic fibrosis. But only recently have we gained the power to pinpoint the genes that cause these specific conditions, among ethnic groups and in individuals.

As a result, our attention has moved beyond efforts to prevent germ-borne disease at the macro level—such as last century's crusades to eradicate diseases like smallpox and polio—to avoiding the genetic expression of disease at the micro level—the level of individual reproduction. In the future, an increasing number of people will prevent a range of genetic diseases by sidestepping the unions that create them, whether at the altar through "premarital genetic diagnosis" of genetic abnormalities, or in the petri dish through preimplantation genetic diagnosis (PGD) of embryos created using in vitro fertilization.

Only about 2% of all diseases, including Tay-Sachs, are caused by mutations in a single gene; the rest are the result of multiple genes acting together and in conjunction with assorted environmental factors. But our knowledge of both single-gene diseases and multi-gene diseases is increasing rapidly. Genetic tests for more than 800 conditions are now available, and more reach the market every year. For the most part, geneticists, physicians, and scientists are encouraging us to use this new knowledge about ourselves and our potential offspring to guide decisions about marriage and procreation. Why take a chance, they say, when we can prevent the birth of more "doomed babies"? The force of such an argument—and the terrible suffering endured by diseased children and their families—cannot be denied.

But such genetic guarantees necessarily come at a price, not least of which is the tacit judgment that individuals with certain genetic conditions are not fit to live or are better off never born. As genetic testing becomes more advanced and more widespread, the line between acting on a just concern for the well-being of the next generation and engaging in an inhuman project of weeding out the imperfect will become more difficult to draw. Different communities will draw different lines for different reasons—whether to protect the health and safety of children, to safeguard the life of the unborn, to expand the reproductive freedom of women, to heed the taboo against "playing God," or to perfect God's imperfect creation with human reason and human hands. And some of these reasons are clearly more justifiable than others. But no community—religious or secular, sacred or profane—will use such genetic powers without inviting the possibility of a new eugenics.

Management of respiratory disease caused by CF is critical. If respiratory insufficiency can be prevented or minimized, the individual's life will be greatly enhanced and prolonged. Antibiotic drugs, postural drainage (chest physical therapy), and medicated vapors play important roles in the medical management of CF.

Diet management is also essential for the child with CF. Generally, the child with this condition requires more caloric intake than his or her normal peers. The diet should be high in protein and should be adjusted if the child fails to grow and/or make appropriate weight gains. Individuals with CF benefit significantly from the use of replacement enzymes that assist with food absorption. The intake of vitamins is also very important to individuals with digestive system problems.

The major social and psychological problems of children with CF are directly related to chronic coughing, small stature, offensive stools, gas, delayed onset of puberty and secondary sex characteristics, and unsatisfying social relationships. These children and youth may spend significant amounts of time away from school settings. Thus teachers, counselors, and other support personnel play essential roles in helping these students feel at home in school, assisting them in making up past-due work, forming friendships, taking medications, obtaining appropriate privacy for restroom needs, helping other children and youth understand the condition, and receiving other appropriate school-based care. Collaboration between school personnel, parents, and health care providers is essential to the well-being of children and youth with CF (Best, 2005a). Moreover, support groups play important roles in helping students with CF to understand themselves and their disease and to develop personal resilience and ongoing friendships.

Emerging and exciting interventions for CF are being explored, including gene therapy, lung transplants, bone marrow transplant, mucus-thinning drugs, and the use of high doses of ibuprofen with young children. (Cystic Fibrosis Foundation, 2006b). However, CF continues to be a very challenging disease for children, youth, and their families. See the Debate Forum to consider the use of human genetics to combat genetically transmitted diseases.

Sickle Cell Anemia

DEFINITIONS AND CONCEPTS. **Sickle cell anemia** (SCA) is an inherited disorder that profoundly affects the structure and functioning of red blood cells. The hemoglobin molecule in the red blood cells of individuals with SCA is abnormal in that it is vulnerable to structural collapse when the blood oxygen level is significantly diminished. As the blood oxygen level declines, these blood cells become distorted and form bizarre shapes. This process, which is known as sickling, distorts the normal donut-like shapes of cells into shapes that resemble microscopic sickle blades. Obstructions in the vessels of affected individuals can lead to stroke and to damage of other organs in the body (Kelly, 2004; Sickle Cell Information Center, 2006).

People affected by sickle cell anemia experience unrelenting **anemia**. In some cases it is tolerated well; in others the condition is quite debilitating. Another aspect of SCA involves frequent infections and periodic vascular blockages, which occur as sickled cells block microvascular

FOCUS **10**
Describe the impact on body tissues of the sickling of red blood cells.

➤ **Sickle cell anemia (SCA)**
An inherited disease that has a profound effect on the structure and functioning of red blood cells and may lead to stroke and/or organ damage.

➤ **Anemia**
A condition in which the blood is deficient in red blood cells.

channels. These blockages can cause severe and chronic pain in the extremities, abdomen, or back. In addition, the disease may affect any organ system of the body. SCA also has a significant negative effect on the physical growth and development of infants and children (Sickle Cell Information Center, 2006).

PREVALENCE AND CAUSATION. Approximately one in 500 African American infants has SCA. Moreover, about 7% to 10% of African Americans carry the sickle cell gene. One in every 1,000 to 1,400 Hispanics is born with SCA. Sickle cell disease is most prevalent in areas of the world in which malaria is widespread. Individuals from the Mediterranean basin—from Greece, Italy, and Sardinia—may carry the mutant gene for SCA, as may individuals from India and the Arabian Peninsula (Huffman, Fontaine, & Price, 2003).

Sickle cell anemia is caused by various combinations of genes (Kelly, 2004). A child who receives a mutant S-hemoglobin gene from each parent exhibits SCA to one degree or another. The disease usually announces itself at 6 months of age and persists throughout the individual's lifetime.

INTERVENTIONS. A number of treatments may be employed to deal with the problems caused by sickle cell anemia, but the first step is early diagnosis. Babies, especially infants who are at risk for this disease, should be screened at birth. Early diagnosis lays the groundwork for the prophylactic use of antibiotics to prevent infections in the first five years of life. This treatment, coupled with appropriate immunizations and nutrition, prevents further complications of the disease. Moreover, these treatments significantly reduce the death rate associated with SCA.

Children, youth, and adults usually learn to adapt to their anemia and lead relatively normal lives. When their lives are interrupted by crises, a variety of treatment approaches can be used. For children, comprehensive and timely care is crucial. For example, children with SCA who develop fevers should be treated aggressively. In fact, parents of these children may be taught how to examine the spleen and recognize early signs of potentially serious problems. Hydration is also an important component of treatment. When necessary, pain management may be addressed with narcotic and nonnarcotic drugs.

Several factors predispose individuals to SCA crises: dehydration from fever, reduced liquid intake, and hypoxia (a result of breathing air that is poor in oxygen content). Stress, fatigue, and exposure to cold temperatures should be avoided by those who have a history of SCA crises.

Treatment of crises is generally directed at keeping the individual warm, increasing liquid intake, ensuring good blood oxygenation, and administering medication for infection. Assistance can be provided during crisis periods by partial-exchange blood transfusions with fresh, normal red cells. Transfusions may also be necessary for individuals with SCA who are preparing for surgery or are pregnant.

Teachers and other care providers may assist by dispensing medications in keeping with school regulations and policies, honoring recommendations for activity restrictions, making referrals to appropriate medical personnel if pain and fever become evident, encouraging affected students to dress warmly during cold weather, and moving with dispatch in the event of an SCA crises. As with all physical disabilities and health disorders, collaboration and communication among caregivers are key elements of serving children and youth so affected (Huffman, Fontaine, & Price, 2003).

Social and Health-Related Problems

This section reviews child abuse and neglect, adolescent pregnancy, and maternal drug and alcohol abuse. Although these conditions are not typically thought of as physical disabilities and health disorders, they influence significant numbers of families and place children and youth at risk for problems in their schools and communities.

Child Abuse and Neglect

DEFINITIONS AND CONCEPTS. For many of us, it is hard to imagine how anyone could hurt or neglect an infant or child, particularly one's own. Unfortunately, about 2.8 million children are physically abused each year, and many of them are injured or neglected by individuals they know—family members or close relatives (U.S. Department of Health and Human Services, 2006)

The Child Abuse and Prevention Treatment Act (CAPTA) (U.S. Code: 42 USC 5101 et seq; 42 USC §5106g), recently amended, defines child abuse and neglect as follows:

> ➤ Any recent act or failure to act on the part of a parent or caretaker which results in death, serious physical or emotional harm, sexual abuse or exploitation; or
> ➤ An act or failure to act which presents an imminent risk of serious harm.

Child abuse takes place in all ethnic and socioeconomic groups.

Within the standards set by CAPTA, each state is responsible for developing and defining child abuse and neglect for its citizenry. Generally, four types of child abuse and neglect are addressed in these definitions: physical abuse, sexual abuse, neglect, and emotional abuse (Child Welfare Information Gateway, 2006a; Ladewig, London, & Davidson, 2006a).

Physical abuse of children results in mild to serious physical harm or injury to the affected child and sometimes even causes death. The abuse occurs in the form of kickings, beatings, chokings, stabbings, burnings, or other violent acts. Abusive parents or caregivers often exhibit inconsistent childrearing practices, and their child management approaches are often hostile and aggressive. These abusive behaviors may be exacerbated by stress-eliciting problems arising from unemployment, adolescent parenthood, limited incomes, and related factors.

Sexual abuse is the exploitation of a child or youth for sexual gratification by a parent, caretaker, or other individuals. It may involve molestation, incest, rape, sodomy, prostitution, fondling, and other sexually related acts or behaviors. It may also include exploitation through the production of pornographic materials. Girls are at greater risk for sexual abuse than boys. And children and youth with disabilities are 1.75 times more likely than children without disabilities to be sexually abused (U.S. Department of Health and Human Services, 2003).

Behavioral indicators of sexual abuse include anxiety, depression, age-inappropriate knowledge about sex, running away from home, suicide attempts, substance abuse, and fantasies with sexual connotations. However, many children who have been sexually abused show no signs. Manifestations of their maltreatment may not surface until the adult years and are often reflected in problems with interpersonal relationships (Lehman, 2005).

Neglect is the failure of care providers to supply the essential needs of children or youth. Neglect may be physical (failure to provide appropriate supervision, shelter, or food), emotional (negligence in responding to a child's emotional needs, or failure to provide emotional nurturing), medical (failure to provide appropriate health care), and educational (failure to provide appropriate instruction and schooling opportunities).

Child neglect results when parents or other caregivers abandon their children or fail to care for them in healthy ways. In short, children who are not adequately cared for are considered neglected. These children are often malnourished, infrequently bathed or changed, left without suitable supervision, and rarely held or appropriately stimulated.

Neglect is evidenced in many ways. Some of these children are grossly underweight for their age. They often fail to thrive and yet display few medical problems. Some may exhibit persistent and severe diaper rashes because of inconsistent care.

> ➤ **Sexual abuse**
>
> It is the exploitation of a child or youth for sexual gratification by a parent, caretaker, or other individuals, involving any of the following: molestation, incest, rape, sodomy, prostitution, fondling, exploitation through the production of pornographic materials, and other sexually related acts or behaviors.

Emotional abuse is consistent pattern of behavior that interferes with a child's or youth's emotional development and feelings of worth. Moreover, it is often the result of behaviors related to rejecting, terrorizing, isolating, and exploiting. Outcomes of this kind of abuse are many and varied. Children who have been severely ignored are often lethargic and apathetic. Often they are developmentally delayed in physical development, language acquisition, and cognitive development. Emotional abuse is nearly always evident when other forms of abuse occur, but this form of abuse is also very difficult to prove or substantiate in legal proceedings.

Child abuse and **child neglect** can be regarded as maladaptive means of coping by parents. Abusive parents and caregivers are confronted with personal and family challenges that influence their responses to children. Some parents are able to cope with these challenges with adaptive behaviors that help their children; other parents, unfortunately, respond with maladaptive, harmful, sometimes violent behaviors (Howe, 2005).

PREVALENCE AND CAUSATION. Establishing accurate and precise prevalence estimates for child abuse is very difficult. In addition to the problem of underreporting, much of the difficulty is attributable to the lack of consistent criteria for child abuse and to the varying reporting procedures used in different states. Recent data from the National Child Abuse and Neglect Data System reveal that approximately 872,000 children are victims of child abuse or neglect each year. The maltreatment rate is about 11.9 per 1,000 children (Child Welfare and Information Gateway, 2006b).

Several factors may cause a parent or caregiver to be abusive. These include crises caused by unemployment, poverty, unwanted pregnancy, serious health problems, substance abuse, high levels of mobility, isolation from natural and community support networks, marital problems, death of a significant other, inadequate intellectual and moral development, and economic difficulties. Other parents or caregivers who neglect their children simply do not understand their children's behaviors and their own important role in caring for them. Moreover, many parents who neglect their children have very serious problems themselves, including substance abuse and psychiatric conditions (Scannepico & Cannell-Carrick, 2005).

Other potential factors include the withdrawal of spousal support, having a child at a very young age, having a particularly challenging infant (such as one with severe disabilities), and caring for a child not biologically related to the parent(s). Several personality traits often characterize abusive parents: poor impulse control, deficits in role taking and empathy, and low self-esteem.

Research suggests that parents who were abused as children are at risk of engaging in child abuse themselves. However, most children who were abused do not grow up to be abusive parents.

Child abuse and neglect occur among all ethnic groups and at all socioeconomic levels. Thus all educators of children and youth must be aware of its existence and willing to address it. State laws designate educators and other professionals who work with children (e.g., health care providers, police officers, social workers, clergy) as mandated reporters. This means that they have a legal responsibility to report suspected abuse or neglect to their administrators and/or appropriate law enforcement or child protection agencies. Laws vary from state to state; educators must become familiar with the definition of abuse used in their jurisdiction, as well as with their responsibilities in reporting.

Clearly, reporting child abuse or neglect is a serious matter, but the responsibility need not be intimidating. Although the reporter should have ample reason to suspect that abuse or neglect has occurred, he or she is not responsible for proving that it has. Moreover, laws often protect individuals who report abuse and neglect by ensuring some level of confidentiality. The reporter's primary consideration must be the welfare of the child or youth.

INTERVENTIONS. Treatment of child abuse and neglect is a multifaceted process. The entire family must be involved. The first goal is to treat the abused or neglected child for any serious injuries and simultaneously to prevent further harm or neglect. Hospitalization may be necessary to deal with immediate physical injuries or other complications, and during this time, the child protection and treatment team, in conjunction with the family, develops a comprehensive treatment plan. Once the child's immediate medical needs have been met, a variety of treatment options may be employed: individual play therapy, therapeutic playschool, regular preschool, foster care, residential care, hospitalization, and/or group treatment.

➤ **Child abuse**
Nonaccidental sexual, physical, and/or psychological trauma and/or injury inflicted on a child.

➤ **Child neglect**
A lack of interaction with a child on the part of other family members, which deprives that youngster of vital opportunities for development.

FOCUS **11**
Identify five factors that may contribute to child abuse and neglect.

Prevention and treatment programs for parents and families of abused and neglected children are directed at helping parents and other family members function more appropriately in responding to their children's needs as well as their own. These programs focus on behaviors and skills such as personal impulse control, alternative methods of disciplining, behavioral rehearsal, and anger management. Neglectful parents may receive one-on-one assistance with practical child care tasks such as feeding and diapering an infant, managing a challenging 2-year-old, and effectively dealing with various kinds of crying. Ways may be found to help parents provide adequate and nutritious food, suitable clothing, regular medical and dental care, and appropriate housing (Scannapieco & Connell-Carrick, 2005).

Some programs are directed at reducing economic and emotional stress by supplying affordable day care, delivering appropriate dental and medical care, helping parents become employable and remain employed, or providing opportunities for additional education and training. Also, collaboration among service providers is beginning to emerge. Such collaboration makes it possible for families to receive services that are tailored to their specific strengths and needs.

Interventions for children and youth who are abused are directed at the effects of the maltreatment. In some instances, the child or youth may receive treatment for depression, anxiety, stress, or even rage. Other children may need assistance with anger control or assertiveness training. Any number of problems or symptoms may surface as a result of abuse, including sleep disorders, regression in toileting and language development for young children, insomnia, eating disorders, and ulcers. Early and ongoing treatment for these problems and symptoms is essential for children and youth who have experienced abuse and neglect.

Once individual and family needs have be assessed and determined, an array of family-centered interventions may be set in action. These include the use and support of personal networks (family, friends), neighborhood and community services (self-help groups, church auxilliaries, parent groups), professsional programs (medical centers, day care, housing, employment), and highly specialized professional services (early intervention, residential placement, family preservation, drug abuse treatment). At the heart of these interventions are the following features: the development of trust with families and caregivers, significant support in addressing long-standing barriers and challenges (employment, drug abuse, child management), collaboration among service providers, development of new skills and dispositions, and developing long-term, natural connections with individuals, service providers, and support groups (Scannapieco & Connell-Carrick, 2005).

Young mothers experience a range of challenging problems in caring for their infants and continuing their education.

Adolescent Pregnancy

DEFINITIONS AND CONCEPTS. Adolescent pregnancy is the outcome of conception in girls 19 years old or younger. The impact of adolescent pregnancy is highly variable, depending on the age, class, and race of the individual. Between 80% and 90% of the pregnancies that occur during the adolescent years are unwanted. Of these, the vast majority of adolescent mothers remain unmarried—only 20% of couples continue any kind of relationship or connection; many leave school; most experience financial problems; and some become reliant on welfare. More than half of the unintended/unwanted pregancies conclude with induced or spontaneous abortions (Carson & Carson, 2004).

Teens undergo a number of developmental changes during adolescence: construction of an identity, development of personal relationships and responsibilities, gradual preparation for vocational or professional work through education, independence from their parents, and various adjustments to a complex society. Many—if not all—of these developmental changes are significantly affected by pregnancy (Ladewig, London, & Davidson, 2006b).

The risks and consequences associated with adolescent pregnancy are substantial, particularly if the young mother is 15 years of age or younger. Children born to these mothers experience higher rates of infant mortality, birth defects, mental retardation, central nervous system problems, and intelligence deficits. Generally, children born to adolescent mothers experience higher rates of medical and developmental problems, greater probability of being abused and neglected, increased likelihood of experiencing poverty over a lifetime, and increased odds for developing behavioral and emotional problems (Farber, 2003).

PREVALENCE AND CAUSATION. The birthrate for adolescent females 15 to 19 years of age is about 49 births per 1,000 teenagers. The United States has the highest rate of teen pregnancy among developed nations. The prevalence of adolescent pregnancy is staggering. About 1 million girls become pregnant each year in the United States. About 80% of these pregnancies are unplanned and unexpected. More than 50% of the young women who become pregnant keep their children (London, Ladewig, Ball, & Bindler, 2003). The communities highest in adolescent pregnancy and related birthrates are those that are socially disorganized, most economically challenged, and materially run down.

Adolescent girls become pregnant for a number of varied and complex reasons. In an early landmark study of teenage sexuality, pregnancy, and childbearing, Chilman (1980) wrote the following: "The causes of out-of-marriage childbearing are deceptively simple. Obviously, illegitimacy is a result of premarital coitus [sexual intercourse], premarital conception, lack of pregnancy interruption, and the birth of a child before marriage" (p. 199).

Other contributing factors include earlier sexual activity among young people, increased options for preventing pregnancy, childhood abuse and family dysfunction (lack of responsive and supportive parents), more resigned attitudes toward sexual activity and resultant pregnancy and childbirth, lack of knowledge about conception and sexuality, lack of access to or misuse of contraceptives, desire to escape family control, alcohol and drug consumption, and a lack of school or career plans (American Academy of Pediatrics, 2006; Deardorff et al., 2005; Farber, 2003; Klein, 2005). Additional societal factors also play a role in the increased number of adolescents who become pregnant: greater permissiveness and freedom, social pressure from peers, and continual exposure to sexuality through the media.

INTERVENTIONS. The goals of treatment for pregnant adolescents are varied. The first goal is to help the prospective mother cope with the discovery that she is pregnant. What emerges from this discovery is a crisis—for her, for the father, and for the families of both individuals, although responses vary among various ethnic and socioeconomic groups. Some adolescents may respond with denial, disbelief, bitterness, disillusionment, or a variety of other feelings. Parents often react to the announcement with anger, then shame and guilt.

Treatment during this period focuses on reducing interpersonal and intrapersonal strain and tension. A wise counselor involves the family in crisis intervention, which is achieved through careful mediation and problem solving. For many adolescents, this period involves some very intense decision making: Should I keep the baby? Should I have the baby and then put it up for adoption? Should I have an abortion? Should I get married? If the adolescent chooses to have the baby, nutritional support for the developing infant, quality prenatal and

FOCUS 12
Cite factors that may contribute to the increased prevalence of adolescent pregnancy.

perinatal care, training for eventual child care, education, and instruction in employment skills become the focus of the intervention efforts. Additionally, young expectant mothers are provided with assistance for managing smoking, alcohol consumption, and other drug use or abuse as appropriate (Ladewig, London, & Davidson, 2006b).

Treatment models for adolescent mothers vary. Some are school-based. Others are multi-disciplinary, focusing on medical care, economic self-sufficency through continued education and employment preparation, psychological support, and life skills support (Miller, Sage, & Winward, 2005). These programs or services are often delivered through medical centers or in ambulatory clinic settings, home-based programs, or early childhood centers. The young mother and the young infant receive care simultaneously. All of the programs focus on strengthening parenting skills, building parent-child relationships, encouraging or supporting the completion of essential education and employment training, and enhancing the mothers' personal functioning. These programs provide for prenatal and well-baby care, vocational training, and family-planning education. Also, every effort is made to help adolescent mothers stay in school, continue or conclude their secondary education, and focus on a positive future (Ladewig, London, & Davidson, 2006b; Miller, Sage, & Winward, 2005).

Unfortunately, many services rendered to pregnant adolescents fade after delivery of the child. One of the major hazards for these mothers is becoming pregnant again. Steps should be taken to help young mothers explore options and approaches that significantly reduce the likelihood of repeated pregnancies and other, related challenges. Problems do not cease with delivery; the development of functional life skills for independent living is a long-term educational and rehabilitation process.

Maternal Drug and Alcohol Abuse

DEFINITIONS AND CONCEPTS. Expectant mothers who use illegal drugs, alcohol, or tobacco place their children and themselves at risk for a variety of serious medical, psychological, and health-related problems (Bono, Dinehart, Claussen, Scott, Mundy, & Katz, 2005; Braun, Beaty, DiGuiseppi, & Steiner, 2005; Jaakkola & Gissler, 2004; Ladewig, London, & Davidson, 2006a; Newcomb & Locke, 2005). Consider this: 11 to 17.5 million children are being reared by a substance-abusing parent or guardian (Fraser & Macabee, 2004).

Substance-exposed infants are affected in several ways (see Figure 17.6). These infants are often of low birthweight and exhibit tremors, problems sleeping and eating, impaired cognitive development, learning problems, delayed expressive language, impeded motor development, and behavior problems (Bono et al., 2005; Noonan, Reichman, Corman, & Dave, 2005). There is also a strong relationship between maternal drug use and child maltreatment and neglect (Street, Harrington, Chiang, Cairns, & Ellis, 2004; Velez, et al., 2006).

Drug abuse in parents produces other problems that affect young children. Caring for infants and young children requires a great deal of selflessness and patience. If the children's parents are primarily concerned about obtaining and using drugs, they are not able to provide the nurturing, stimulation, and care that are essential for normal development and attachment (Barnard & McKeganey, 2004).

PREVALENCE AND CAUSATION. The actual prevalence of infants directly affected by substance abuse is difficult to determine. Many expectant mothers are reluctant to reveal their substance abuse for fear that they will be prosecuted for child maltreatment. Some 5% to 15% of all newborns are exposed prenatally to illegal drugs and/or alcohol (Nickel, 2000). Furthermore, about 3 million infants are prenatally affected by maternal alcohol consumption. Fetal alcohol syndrome (FAS) affects about 0.5 to 2 infants per 1,000 births in the United States. If we include FAS, alcohol-related neurodevelopmental disorder (ARND), and alcohol-related birth defects (ARBD), the rate jumps to 10 infants per 1,000 births (National Institute on Alcohol Abuse and Alcoholism, 2003). FAS is the leading known cause of mental retardation.

Maternal drug abuse and alcohol abuse affect infants in several ways. For example, cocaine is readily available, easily ingested, and highly addictive. In fact, it is the drug of choice for many substance abusers. Because of the low molecular weight of cocaine, it readily crosses the placenta to the developing fetus or child. Cocaine easily passes through the blood-brain barrier, thereby altering the chemistry and functioning of the emerging infant's brain. Cocaine may also be passed to the child from the mother through her breast milk. The regular presence

FOCUS **13**
Identify the potential effects of maternal substance abuse on the developing child.

FIGURE 17.6

The Effects of Maternal Cocaine Use on Mothers and Fetuses/Babies

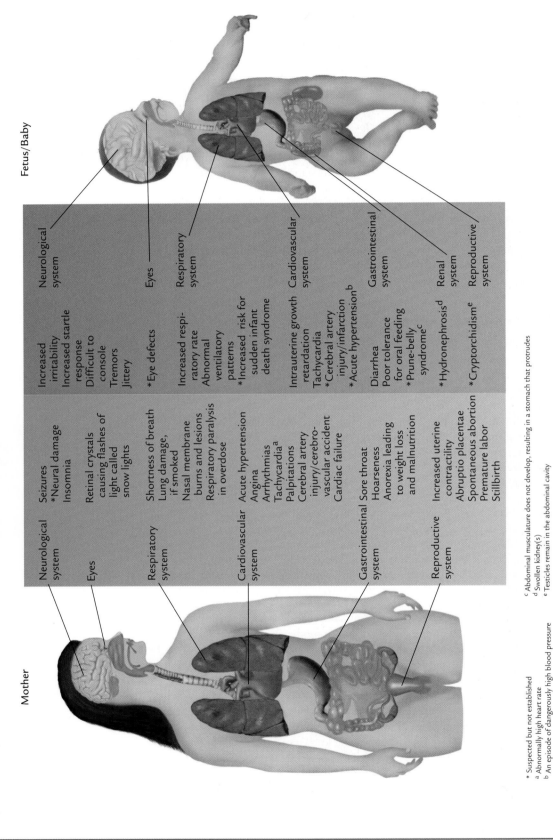

Mother

Neurological system	Seizures *Neural damage Insomnia
Eyes	Retinal crystals causing flashes of light called snow lights
Respiratory system	Shortness of breath Lung damage, if smoked Nasal membrane burns and lesions Respiratory paralysis in overdose
Cardiovascular system	Acute hypertension Angina Arrhythmias Tachycardia[a] Palpitations Cerebral artery injury/cerebro-vascular accident Cardiac failure
Gastrointestinal system	Sore throat Hoarseness Anorexia leading to weight loss and malnutrition
Reproductive system	Increased uterine contractility Abruptio placentae Spontaneous abortion Premature labor Stillbirth

Fetus/Baby

Neurological system	Increased irritability Increased startle response Difficult to console Tremors Jittery
Eyes	*Eye defects
Respiratory system	Increased respiratory rate Abnormal ventilatory patterns
Cardiovascular system	*Increased risk for sudden infant death syndrome Intrauterine growth retardation Tachycardia *Cerebral artery injury/infarction *Acute hypertension[b]
Gastrointestinal system	Diarrhea Poor tolerance for oral feeding *Prune-belly syndrome[c]
Renal system	*Hydronephrosis[d]
Reproductive system	*Cryptorchidism[e]

* Suspected but not established
[a] Abnormally high heart rate
[b] An episode of dangerously high blood pressure
[c] Abdominal musculature does not develop, resulting in a stomach that protrudes
[d] Swollen kidney(s)
[e] Testicles remain in the abdominal cavity

SOURCE: From "The Dangers of Prenatal Cocaine Use," by J. Smith, 1988, *American Journal of Maternal Child Nursing, 13*(3), p. 175. Copyright 1988 by *American Journal of Maternal Child Nursing.*

of cocaine in the developing fetus or child affects its development and functioning in a variety of detrimental ways (see Figure 17.6). Each drug (marijuana, heroin, LSD, ecstasy, amphetamines, etc.) creates its own havoc within the mother and the developing infant (American College of Obstetricians and Gynecologists, 2003; National Institutes of Health, 2003).

INTERVENTIONS. Implementing interventions for mothers and their babies who have been exposed to drugs is a challenging and complex process, particularly when the mother is addicted (Conners, Bokony, Whiteside-Mansell, Bradley, & Liu, 2004; Donohue, 2004; Newcomb & Locke, 2005). Mothers with histories of serious drug abuse may need as much treatment as their affected infants. Often, in fact, mothers need more assistance. Think for a moment about being a pediatrician or family physician faced with deciding whether to release an infant who is at risk and needs sophisticated care to a mother burdened with drug abuse. What action would you take?

Many infants born to drug-addicted or drug-using mothers may need to go through a withdrawal regimen themselves, carefully orchestrated by a team of medical professionals. Other challenges for these infants include respiratory distress, jaundice, and behavioral abnormalities. Long-term challenges may include motor-development problems, feeding difficulties, and delays in the development of expressive language. (Ladewig, London, & Davidson, 2006b).

Some infants are initially placed with grandparents or other caregivers until their mothers are capable of caring for them. Others are placed with relatives, foster parents, or respite care providers. Some are eventually adopted (Schilling, Mares, & El-Bassel, 2004).

Educationally oriented treatments for preschoolers affected by substance abuse focus on designing well-structured learning environments, creating small classes (eight children per teacher), and providing developmentally appropriate learning environments that are child-sized, visually interesting, and suitably stimulating. These environments also provide learning activities that are experiential rather than paper-and-pencil tasks. Programs for school-age children are beginning to emerge as practitioners and researchers learn more about the effects of substance abuse on the development and performance of young children. Many of these children benefit from early, comprehensive/wraparound services delivered by special education, medical and psychological specialists, and family service providers (O'Connor, Morganstern, Gibson, & Nakashian, 2005; Smith, Krisman, Strozier, & Marley, 2004).

Comprehensive models of treatment for drug-abusing women and their children are emerging (Altshuler, 2005). As we have noted, these models include intake screening and comprehensive health assessment; medical interventions for mothers, their children, and other family members; early intervention services for drug-exposed infants and toddlers; home-based support; counseling for HIV and AIDS; linkages to other service providers for outreach, residential, and outpatient services; substance abuse and psychological counseling; parenting education; health education; life skills education; training and remediation services; child care services; transportation support; housing assistance; and continuing care after intensive therapies and interventions have been applied (National Institute on Drug Abuse, 2003; O'Connor et al., 2005; Statham, 2004).

FOCUS REVIEW

FOCUS 1 Identify the disabilities that may accompany cerebral palsy.

- Often, individuals with cerebral palsy have several disabilities, including hearing impairments, speech and language disorders, intellectual deficits, visual impairments, and general perceptual problems.

FOCUS 2 What is spina bifida myelomeningocele?

- Spina bifida myelomeningocele is a type of spina bifida cystica that announces itself in the form of a tumor-like sac, on the back of the infant, that contains both spinal fluid and nerve tissue.

- Spina bifida myelomeningocele is the most serious variety of spina bifida in that it generally includes paralysis or partial paralysis of certain body areas, causing lack of bowel and bladder control.

FOCUS 3 Identify specific treatments for individuals with spinal cord injuries.

- The first step is immediate pharmacological interventions with high and frequent doses of methylprednisolone. These doses reduce the severity of the injury and improve the functional outcome over time.

- Stabilization of the spine is critical to the overall outcome of the injury.

- Once the spine has been stabilized, the rehabilitation process begins. Physical therapy helps the affected individual make full use of any residual muscle strength.

- The individual is taught to use orthopedic devices, such as handsplints, braces, reachers, headsticks, and other augmentative devices.

- Psychological adjustment is aided by psychiatric and psychological personnel.

- Rehabilitation specialists assist in retraining or reeducating the individual; they may also help the individual secure employment.

- Some individuals will need part-time or full-time attendant care for assistance with daily activities (e.g., bathing, dressing, and shopping).

FOCUS 4 Describe the physical limitations associated with muscular dystrophy.

- Individuals with muscular dystrophy progressively lose their ability to walk and to use their arms and hands effectively, because fatty tissue begins to replace muscle tissue.

FOCUS 5 What are some of the key elements of treating adolescents with HIV and AIDS?

- Regular administration of antiviral medications as proscribed by medical personnel

- Consistent attention to periodic medical appointments and checkups

- Support for maintaining essential medical regimens

- Delivery of needed psychological support for addressing anxiety, depression, or other emotional conditions

- Ongoing instuction about AIDS and related high-risk behaviors

- Development of good decision making, assertiveness, and communication skills

FOCUS 6 What are the basic interventions in treating individuals with asthma?

- Eliminate or moderate exposure to potential triggers.

- Increase the anti-inflammatory mediation in advance of anticipated exposure to certain triggers, using appropriate bronchodilators or other appropriate prescribed medications/treatments.

FOCUS 7 Describe the immediate treatment for a person who is experiencing a tonic/clonic seizure.

- Cushion the head.

- Loosen any tight necktie or collar.

- Turn the person on his or her side.

- Put nothing in the mouth of the individual.

- Look for identification.

- Don't hold the person down.

- As the seizure ends, offer help.

FOCUS 8 Identify three problems that individuals with diabetes may experience later in life.

- Structural abnormalities that occur over time may result in blindness, cardiovascular disease, and kidney disease.

FOCUS 9 Identify present and future interventions for the treatment of children and youth with cystic fibrosis.

- Drug therapy for prevention and treatment of chest infections

- Diet management, use of replacement enzymes for food absorption, and vitamin intake

- Family education regarding the condition

- Chest physiotherapy and postural drainage

- Inhalation therapy

- Psychological and psychiatric counseling

- Use of mucus-thinning drugs, gene therapy, and lung or lung/heart transplants

FOCUS 10 Describe the impact on body tissues of the sickling of red blood cells.

- Because sickled cells are more rigid than normal cells, they frequently block microvascular channels. The blockage of channels reduces or terminates circulation in these areas, and tissues in need of blood nutrients and oxygen die.

FOCUS 11 Identify five factors that may contribute to child abuse and neglect.

- Unemployment, poverty, and substance abuse
- Isolation from natural and community support networks
- Marital/relationship problems
- Having a particularly challenging, needy, or demanding infant
- Poor impulse control

FOCUS 12 Cite factors that may contribute to the increased prevalence of adolescent pregnancy.

- General factors include a lack of knowledge about conception and sexuality, a desire to escape family control, an attempt to be more adult, a desire to have someone to love, a need for attention and love, and an inability to make sound decisions.
- Societal factors include greater sexual permissiveness and freedom, social pressure from peers, and continual exposure to sexuality through the media.

FOCUS 13 Identify the potential effects of maternal substance abuse on the developing child.

- The effects include low birthweight, sleeping and eating disorders, heightened sensitivity, and challenging temperaments.
- Children exposed to cocaine are at greater risk for neurological problems, eye defects, respiratory problems, cardiovascular complications, and other health problems.

BUILDING YOUR PORTFOLIO

Council for Exceptional Children

If you are thinking about a career in special education, you should know that many states use national standards developed by the Council for Exceptional Children (CEC) to assess a teacher candidate's knowledge and skills for working with students with disabilities. See a complete listing of the ten CEC Content Standards on the inside front cover of this text.

CEC Content Standards Addressed in This Chapter

1 Foundations
2 Development and Characteristics of Learners
3 Individual Learning Differences
5 Learning Environments and Social Interactions

Assess Your Knowledge of the CEC Standards Addressed in This Chapter

Some states require that teacher candidates develop a portfolio of products that demonstrate mastery of the CEC content standards. To assist in the development of products for this portfolio, you may wish to complete the following activities.

- Complete a written test of the chapter's content.

  If your instructor requires a written test of your content knowledge for this chapter, keep a copy for your portfolio. A practice test on the information covered in this chapter is available through the companion website (college.hmco.com/pic/hardman9e) and the Student Study Guide.

- Respond to the Application Questions for the Case Study "Living with Cerebral Palsy."

  Review the Case Study and respond in writing to the application questions. Keep a copy of the Case Study and of your written response for your portfolio.

- Participate in a community service learning activity.

  Community service is a valuable way to enhance your learning experience. Visit our companion website for suggested community service learning activities that correspond to the information presented in this chapter. Develop a reflective journal of the service learning experience for your portfolio.

WEB RESOURCES

American Diabetes Association

http://www.diabetes.org/home.jsp
This website provides current and pertinent information for individuals with diabetes and their families. It addresses prevention, treatment, and research about diabetes and related conditions.

Asthma and Allergy Foundation of America

http://www.aafa.org
This is a fully functional/interactive site for individuals interested in asthma and allergies. At the site you can pose questions to allergists, explore the latest research regarding asthma, and access other valuable information.

Child Welfare Information Gateway

http://www.childwelfare.gov

This government-sponsored website provides up-to-date information about protecting children and nurturing families. It offers much high-quality information about caring for children and strengthening families.

Christopher Reeve Foundation

http://www.christopherreeve.org

This foundation raises funds for spinal cord injury research and administers the Christopher and Dana Reeve Paralysis Resource Center. It also provides current information for individuals and families affected by SCIs.

Cystic Fibrosis Foundation

http://www.cff.org/home/

If you are interested in virtually any aspect of cystic fibrosis, this should be your entry point. It provides current information on treatments, medications, research, and legislative issues of importance to individuals with cystic fibrosis.

Epilepsy Foundation

http://www.epilepsyfoundation.org

This website is a solid source of information about services and programs for individuals with epilepsy or seizure disorders. If you are interested in the latest research, legislation, or medical treatment for individuals with epilepsy, you should examine this website in some depth.

National Campaign to Prevent Teen Pregnancy

http://www.teenpregnancy.org

This website provides concerned parents and teens with information about preventing teen pregnancy, research related to adolescent pregnancy, and national media events.

National Information Center for Children and Youth with Disabilities (NICHCY)

http://www.nichcy.org

This is a national center committed to providing caregivers, parents, professionals, and educators with valuable information on disabilities and related issues.

National Rehabilitation Information Center (NARIC)

http://www.naric.com/public/

More than 75,000 resources are found at this site, including web resources, agencies, research, and other valuable information sources.

The National Spinal Cord Injury Association

http://www.spinalcord.org/

This site is an excellent source for current information and resources about spinal cord injury and its treatment. It also provides a current listing of resources available in each state.

New Mobility Magazine

http://newmobility.com/

This magazine and related online information are great resources for individuals with an interest in disability issues and related research.

Muscular Dystrophy Association

http://www.mdausa.org/

This is a very helpful and informative site for individuals interested in muscular dystrophy. It is rich with information about research, local support groups, legislation, and current treatments.

Sickle Cell Disease Association of America, Inc.

http://www.sicklecelldisease.org

This website is devoted to helping individuals with sickle cell anemia and their families by providing information about current research, treatments, and services available in each state.

FURTHER READINGS

Best, S. J., Heller, K. W, & Bigge, J. L. (2005). *Teaching Individuals with Physical and Multiple Disabilities* (5th ed.). Upper Saddle River, NJ: Merrill.

This is a carefully crafted reference book for teachers, parents, and others who are interested in caring for children with physical disabilities and health disorders.

Haslam, R. H. A., & Valletutti, P. J. (2004). *Medical Problems in the Classroom: The Teacher's Role in Diagnosis and Management* (4th ed.). Austin, TX: Pro-ed.

Written by medical and health care experts, this is a great resource for teachers who work with children and youth with physical disabilities and health disorders in general and special education settings.

Farber, N. (2003). *Adolescent Pregnancy.* New York: Springer.

This very readable, succinct review of the dimensions and factors associated with adolescent pregnancy also presents valuable information about prevention programs and related research.

Reeve, C. (2003). *Nothing Is Impossible: Reflections on a New Life.* Waterville, ME: Thorndike Press.

The title of this book says it all. Christopher Reeve talks about humor, the mind-body connection, parenting, religion, advocacy, recovery, faith, and hope. Wonderful photos, taken by his son Matthew, are included.

Huffman, D. M., Fontaine, K. L., & Price, B. K. (2003). *Health problems in the classroom PreK–6: An A–Z Reference Guide for Educators.* Thousand Oaks, CA: Corwin Press.

Designed for teachers of children (preschool through sixth grade), this is an information-rich guide for school personnel who must regularly deal with health problems in their classrooms.

Huffman, D. M., Fontaine, K. L., & Price, B. K. (2003). *Health Problems in the Classroom 6–12: An A–Z Reference Guide for Educators.* Thousand Oaks, CA: Corwin Press.

This is an excellent source of practical information for education professions (grades 6 through 12) who must regularly attend to and respond to health conditions of children and youth in classrooms.

Visit the companion website at college.hmco.com/pic/hardman9e for additional resources that support this text:

- HM Video Cases that present actual classroom scenarios that you may face every day as a teacher

- Practice ACE Exams that will help you prepare for quizzes, tests, and certfication exams

- Flashcards of key terms

- Weblinks

Gifted, Creative, and Talented

MARIA ELENA, SEVENTH GRADE

If I could just be in a gifted class that lasts all day. I get so bored in my regular class. The teacher repeats things over and over again. I lose interest many times. I love my gifted class. That's where I belong (Aguirre, 2003, p. 25)

WHAT A GREAT POTENTIAL LOSS!

It is generally recognized that gifted children as a whole do not receive the education and support they need. Underserved populations—those whose abilities seem "invisible," inconsistent, or not important enough to require special intervention—are the most vulnerable of all. Because of the unique challenges they face (e.g., language barriers, learning disabilities, low socioeconomic conditions), they are at the greatest risk of losing their talents due to lack of identification and support. (Smutny, 2003, p. 5)

ARE WE SQUANDERING A PRECIOUS RESOURCE?

- The United States is squandering one of its most precious resources—the gifts and talents of many of its students.

- These youngsters are not challenged to do their best work. They perform poorly in comparison with top students in other countries.

- America relies on its top-performing students to provide leadership in science, math, writing, politics, dance, art, business, history, health, and other human pursuits.

- Most gifted and talented students spend their school days without attention to their special learning needs; teachers make few if any provisions for gifted students.

- In elementary school, gifted students already have mastered 35 to 50 percent of the curriculum to be offered before they begin the school year. (Davis & Rimm, 2004, p. 9)

SOME QUESTIONS

Question: What group of students makes the lowest achievement gains in schools?
Answer: The brightest students.
Question: What group of students has been harmed most by the No Child Left Behind Act?
Answer: Our brightest students.
Question: How well is the United States preparing able students to compete in the world economy?
Answer: Very poorly.
Question: What group of special-needs students receives the least funding?
Answer: Our brightest students. (DeLacy, 2004, p. 40)

FOCUS PREVIEW

1 Briefly describe several historical developments directly related to the measurement of various types of giftedness.

2 Identify four major components of definitions that have been developed to describe giftedness.

3 Identify four problems inherent in accurately describing the characteristics of individuals who are gifted.

4 Identify three factors that appear to contribute significantly to the emergence of various forms of giftedness.

5 Indicate the range of assessment devices used to identify the various types of giftedness.

6 Identify eight strategies that are utilized to foster the development of children and adolescents who are gifted.

7 What are some of the social-emotional needs of students who are gifted?

8 Identify four challenges that females face in dealing with their giftedness.

9 Identify eight important elements of programs for gifted children who come from diverse backgrounds and who may live in poverty.

T.D. Egan, MD.

▾ SNAPSHOT

TALMAGE

Talmage's life is clear testimony to the power of home and family in fostering success. Talmage grew up in a home environment where each child's unique aptitudes and talents were cultivated and developed. The tenth of eleven children, Talmage was profoundly influenced by his older siblings, who represented a very diverse array of natural skills and capacities, ranging from excellence in music and art to high-level academic achievement and athletic prowess. A scholarly physician father and a gregarious, "life-of-the-party" mother inculcated into the children a sense of balance between work and play. Above all else, creativity was fostered and valued in their home. Talmage's parents focused on providing opportunities for the children to identify and explore their individual talents rather than pressuring them to conform to a uniform standard or path.

Talmage showed a proclivity toward academic pursuits from an early age. Using old-fashioned phonic puzzles, Talmage's mother taught him to read well before kindergarten, and Talmage took pride in being able to read stories to neighborhood kids who were older than he was. Just for fun, his mother would teach him difficult words and then encourage him to use them around adults in the neighborhood. Talmage still remembers the look of astonishment he would get from adults who were amazed at the little boy's vocabulary.

Talmage's siblings and parents helped provide opportunities to expand and develop his emerging intellectual talents and interests.

For example, after expressing an interest in chemistry one night at the dinner table, Talmage was surprised to find a new chemistry set outside his bedroom door a few mornings later (accompanied with a brochure about a career in chemical engineering). An older sibling once spent hours helping Talmage to build a set of mazes for a science project in junior high. Talmage got so much attention from his parents and siblings after earning straight-As on his first report card in junior high that he never settled for a B thereafter. Academic achievement was a way to establish a unique identity within his family, and his family reveled in his success.

With the support of his family, Talmage was able to develop other talents as well. Largely because of a very athletically gifted older brother's willingness to practice with him, Talmage was able to make the junior high and high school volleyball and basketball teams. The legacy of numerous brothers who had played on the school sports teams helped increase Talmage's visibility to the coaches and improve his chances for success. Another brother, one endowed with perfect pitch who had received formal and comprehensive musical training, made it possible for Talmage to become proficient as a bass guitar player through hours of one-on-one "jam sessions." Talmage played in the family band for many years and also made a living playing in a country combo during college and graduate school. Also, in large part because of a sense of family legacy with numerous brothers and sisters having served in student government, Talmage pursued elected office at school and served as both class president and student body president.

After serving as a volunteer for his church in Japan for two years as a young adult, Talmage entered college with an eye toward medical school. Talmage graduated from college and medical school with high honors and received postgraduate training in surgery and anesthesiology. He is now a tenured professor of medicine. He is highly engaged in the academic medical community, having served as president of a major professional society and as an associate editor for a major medical journal. He has published hundreds of papers on his original research, and he lectures around the world at major national and international medical meetings.

EDUARDO

Eduardo and his family are recent immigrants to the United States. At age 10, he has become quite adept at speaking English. His primary language is Spanish. He is the oldest of seven children.

Eduardo's father is a supervisor on a large farm in southern California. With a lot of effort, he developed sufficient English skills to be of great value to farm owners who now employ him full-time. They have hired him to work directly with migrant workers who regularly assist with the harvest of various kinds of produce and fruit. He is also skilled mechanically and, in the off-season, repairs equipment and farm machinery.

Eduardo's schooling was quite irregular until the past two years. Prior to having a stable residence, he traveled with his family up and down the West Coast of the United States, like many migrant families.

Eduardo's schoolmates really enjoy him. He has lots of friends and is invited frequently to birthday parties and social events. He seems to have a real knack for making friends, and adults like him.

Eduardo's parents view him as especially alert and bright. He seems to be interested in many topics and is rarely bored. At the moment, he is intrigued with tractors. His mother indicates that he always "questioned her to death." Moreover, he seems to be capable of easily entertaining himself. Recently, he spent an entire afternoon looking through a farm magazine and drawing farm equipment that caught his attention.

Since the beginning of this school year, Eduardo has made phenomenal gains in reading, math, and English. In fact, he has become an avid reader of both Spanish and English books that are available at his school. Although it has been difficult to assess his innate ability, he appears to be a child of some promise, intellectually and socially. However, his parents are worried about providing him with the resources he will need to utilize his curiosity and ability fully. They are also concerned about his late start with consistent schooling.

➤ **Gifted, creative, and talented**

Terms applied to people who have extraordinary abilities, and are capable of superior performance, in one or more areas.

Council for
Exceptional
Children

Standard 1: Foundations

The terms *gifted, creative,* and *talented* are associated with individuals who have extraordinary abilities in one or more areas of performance. The gifted, creative, and talented are a divserse set of children, youth, and adults (Landrum, 2006). In many cases we admire such individuals, and occasionally we are a little envious of their talents and abilities. Their ease in mastering diverse and difficult concepts is impressive. Because of their unusual abilities and skills, educators and policy makers frequently assume that these individuals will reach their full potential without any specialized programs or assistance.

For many years, behavioral scientists described children and youth with exceptionally high intelligence as being **gifted**. Only recently have researchers and practitioners included the adjectives **creative** and **talented** in their descriptions, to suggest domains of performance other than those measured by traditional intelligence tests. Not all individuals who get high scores on intelligence tests are creative. Capacities associated with creativity include *elaboration* (the ability to embellish or enrich an idea), *transformation* (the ability to construct new meanings or change an idea into something new and novel), and *visualization* (the capacity to manipulate ideas or images mentally). Individuals who are talented may display extraordinary skills in mathematics, sports, music, or other performance areas (Sternberg, 2006; Treffinger, 2004). Talmage is one of those individuals who is gifted, creative, *and* talented (see the chapter-opening Snapshot). Not only did he excel in intellectual (traditional academic) endeavors, but he also exhibited tremendous prowess in producing humor, speaking, and mimicking famous people. Certainly, the behaviors and traits associated with these terms interact with one another to produce the various constellations of giftedness. Some individuals soar to exceptional heights in the talent domain, others achieve in intellectual areas, and still others excel in creative endeavors. A few exhibit remarkable achievement across several domains.

Definitions that describe the unusually able in terms of intelligence quotients and creativity measures are recent phenomena (Passow, 2004; Treffinger, 2004). Not until the beginning of the 20th century was there a suitable method for quantifying or measuring the human attribute of intelligence. The breakthrough occurred in Europe when Alfred Binet, a French psychologist, constructed the first developmental assessment scale for children in the early 1900s. This scale was created by observing children at various ages to identify specific tasks that ordinary children were able to perform at each age. These tasks were then sequenced according to age-appropriate levels. Children who could perform tasks at a level well above what was typical for their chronological age were identified as being developmentally advanced.

Binet and Simon (1905, 1908) developed the notion of **mental age**. The mental age of a child was derived by matching the tasks (memory, vocabulary, mathematical, comprehension, etc.) that the child was able to perform according to the age scale (which gave the typical performance of children at various stages). Although this scale was initially developed and used to identify children with mental retardation in the Parisian schools, it eventually became an important means for identifying those who had higher than average mental ages, as well.

Lewis M. Terman, an American educator and psychologist, expanded the concepts and procedures developed by Binet. He was convinced that Binet and Simon had hit on an approach that would be useful for measuring intellectual abilities in all children. This belief prompted him to revise the Binet instrument, adding greater breadth to the scale. In 1916, Terman published the **Stanford-Binet Intelligence Scale** in conjunction with Stanford University. During this period, Terman introduced the term **intelligence quotient**, or **IQ**. The IQ score was obtained by dividing a child's mental age by his or her chronological age and multiplying that figure by 100 (MA/CA × 100 = IQ). For example, a child with a mental age of 12 and a chronological age of 8 would have an IQ of 150 (12/8 × 100 = 150).

FOCUS 1

Briefly describe several historical developments directly related to the measurement of various types of giftedness.

➤ **Mental age**

A concept used in psychological assessment and arrived at by matching the tasks the child is able to perform to a scale of typical performance of children at various stages.

➤ **Stanford-Binet Intelligence Scale**

A standardized individual intelligence test, originally known as the Binet-Simon Scales, which was revised and standardized by Lewis Terman at Stanford University.

➤ **Intelligence quotient (IQ)**

A score obtained from an intelligence test that provides a measure of mental ability in relation to age.

▼ SNAPSHOT

EVAN

Evan Feinberg was the state and national winner of the National Association for Gifted Children (NAGC) Nicolas Green Award in 2000 when he was in fourth grade. Here is a portion of the essay that he wrote for this competition at age 9:

Ever since I can remember, I have had a passion for science and astronomy, and mathematics. In my past, I focused on the solar system. Presently, I am fascinated by the field of cosmology, physics, and particle physics. Cosmology is the study of the universe's past, present, future, celestial objects, and the theoretical multiverse which is a web of different universes linked by black holes; particle physics is the opposite of cosmology, it is the study of the small such as elementary particles to superstrings. The cosmologist, Stephen Hawking, and especially the physicist, Albert Einstein inspired me to study these subjects and generate and spawn theories of my own concerning the universe and the multiverse. Stephen Hawking's discoveries of properties of black holes plus his creativeness of merging quantum mechanics (the study of the small and particles) and the theories of relativity (the theories of large scale) really made

me more and more interested in this field. Albert Einstein's biography, his theories of relativity (which are the special and general), and his contributions to the photoelectric effect has also had a great impact on my perspective of life and the universe around us. On a daily basis, I am lucky to have my teacher, Mr. Carbone, because he really inspired me in this subject. For example, he let me take the 4th grade telescope home to stargaze and look for celestial objects and constellations. In addition, he gave me a special research project to study a particular constellation, Bootes. His enthusiasm and love of learning has encouraged me to 'reach for the stars.' (Landrum, 2006, pp. 2–3).

This study and research triggered new life goals for me such as being a physicist or a cosmologist, proposing new theories, and aspiring to be like my role models, Stephen Hawking and Albert Einstein. My dream one day is to unlock the ultimate theory of the universe, called the theory of everything, and the ultimate question: the mind of G-D. Just as the very fabric of space-time expands and stretches since the big bang, so does my quest for grasping the ultimate theory: the theory of everything (Landrum, 2006, pp. 2–3).

Lewis Terman developed the term intelligence quotient, or IQ.

Gradually, more researchers became interested in studying the nature and assessment of intelligence. They tended to view intelligence as an underlying ability or capacity that expressed itself in a variety of ways. The unitary IQ scores that were derived from the Stanford-Binet tests were representative of and contributed to this notion.

Over time, however, other researchers came to believe that intellect was represented by a variety of distinct capacities and abilities (Cattell, 1971; Guilford, 1959). This line of thinking suggested that each distinct intellectual capacity could be identified and assessed. Several mental abilities were investigated, including memory capacity, divergent thinking, vocabulary usage, and reasoning ability (see Figure 18.1). Gradually, use of the multiple-ability approach outpaced the use of the unitary-intelligence notion. Its proponents were convinced that the universe of intellectual functions was extensive and that the intelligence assessment instruments utilized at that time measured a very small portion of an individual's true intellectual capacities.

One of the key contributors to the multidimensional theory of intelligence was J. P. Guilford (1950, 1959). He saw intelligence as a diverse range of intellectual and creative abilities. Guilford's work led many researchers to view intelligence more broadly, focusing their scientific efforts on the emerging field of creativity and its various subcomponents, such as divergent thinking, problem

---

FIGURE 18.1

Guilford's Structure of the Intellect Model

Each little cube represents a unique combination of one kind of operation, one kind of content, and one kind of product—and hence a distinctly different intellectual ability or function.

Operations

Cognition
Memory
Divergent production
Convergent production
Evaluation

Products

Units
Classes
Relations
Systems
Transformations
Implications

Contents

Visual
Symbolic
Semantic
Behavioral

SOURCE: From *Way Beyond the IQ: Guide to Improving Intelligence and Creativity* (p. 151), by J. P. Guilford, 1977, Buffalo, NY: Creative Education Foundation. Copyright 1977 by Creative Education Foundation. Reprinted by permission.

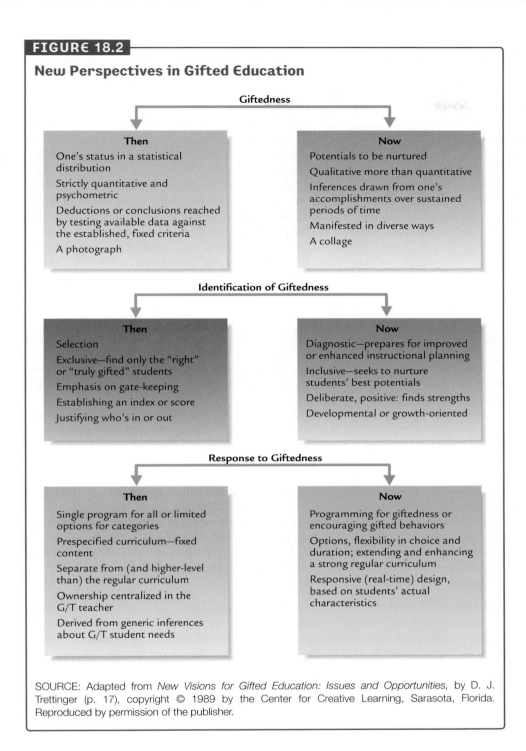

FIGURE 18.2

New Perspectives in Gifted Education

Giftedness

Then
- One's status in a statistical distribution
- Strictly quantitative and psychometric
- Deductions or conclusions reached by testing available data against the established, fixed criteria
- A photograph

Now
- Potentials to be nurtured
- Qualitative more than quantitative
- Inferences drawn from one's accomplishments over sustained periods of time
- Manifested in diverse ways
- A collage

Identification of Giftedness

Then
- Selection
- Exclusive—find only the "right" or "truly gifted" students
- Emphasis on gate-keeping
- Establishing an index or score
- Justifying who's in or out

Now
- Diagnostic—prepares for improved or enhanced instructional planning
- Inclusive—seeks to nurture students' best potentials
- Deliberate, positive: finds strengths
- Developmental or growth-oriented

Response to Giftedness

Then
- Single program for all or limited options for categories
- Prespecified curriculum—fixed content
- Separate from (and higher-level than) the regular curriculum
- Ownership centralized in the G/T teacher
- Derived from generic inferences about G/T student needs

Now
- Programming for giftedness or encouraging gifted behaviors
- Options, flexibility in choice and duration; extending and enhancing a strong regular curriculum
- Responsive (real-time) design, based on students' actual characteristics

SOURCE: Adapted from *New Visions for Gifted Education: Issues and Opportunities,* by D. J. Trettinger (p. 17), copyright © 1989 by the Center for Creative Learning, Sarasota, Florida. Reproduced by permission of the publisher.

solving, and decision making. Gradually, tests or measures of creativity were developed, using the constructs drawn from models created by Guilford and others (Treffinger, 2004).

In summary, conceptions of giftedness during the early 1920s were closely tied to the score that an individual obtained on an intelligence test. Thus a single score—one's IQ—was the index by which one was identified as being gifted. Commencing with the work of Guilford (1950, 1959) and Torrance (1961, 1965, 1968), notions regarding giftedness were greatly expanded. *Giftedness* began to be used to refer not only to those with high IQs but also to those who demonstrated high aptitude on creativity measures (Treffinger, 2004). More recently, the term *talented* has been added to the descriptors associated with giftedness. As a result, individuals who demonstrate remarkable skills in the visual or performing arts or who excel in other areas of performance may be designated as gifted. Figure 18.2 on page 495 reveals how our perspectives on giftedness have changed over time with the acceptance of new, multifaceted definitions of giftedness.

Currently, there is no federal mandate in the United States requiring educational services for students identified as gifted, as is the case with other exceptionalities. Some federal funding is provided through the Jacob K. Javits Gifted and Talented Students Act as a part of the No Child Left Behind legislation (National Association for Gifted Children, 2006). This act supports a national research center, demonstration programs, and activities for leadership and teaching personnel throughout the United States. The actual funding of services for individuals who are gifted is a state-by-state, local challenge, so there is tremendous variability in the quality and types of programs offered to students (Davis & Rimm, 2004).

In coming years, we will probably see *talent development* replace gifted education as the guiding concept (Baum, 2004; Cooper, 2004; Parke, 2003). This description suggests a kind of programming that is directed at all students, not just those identified as gifted (Davis & Rimm, 2004). A "benefit [of this kind of programming] is that the talent development orientation eliminates the awkwardness of the words *gifted* and, by exclusion, *not gifted*" (Davis & Rimm, 2004, p. 28).

Definitions and Concepts

Capturing the essence of any human condition in a definition can be very perplexing. This is certainly the case in defining the human attributes, abilities, and potentialities that constitute giftedness (Passow, 2004).

Definitions of giftedness serve several important purposes. For example, definitions may have a profound influence on the number and kinds of students ultimately selected in a school system, on the types of instruments and selection procedures used, on the scores students must obtain in order to qualify for specialized instruction, on the amount of funding required to provide services, and on the types of training that individuals need to teach students who are gifted and talented. Thus definitions are important from both practical and theoretical perspectives (Davis & Rimm, 2004).

Definitions of giftedness have been influenced by a variety of innovative and knowledgeable individuals (Cattell, 1971; Gardner, 1983; Guilford, 1959; Piirto, 1999; Ramos-Ford & Gardner, 1997; Renzulli & Reis, 2003; Sternberg, 1997; Torrance, 1966). As you will soon discover, there is no universally accepted definition of giftedness (Davis & Rimm, 2004).

Ross (1993) defined giftedness in the following manner:

Children and youth with outstanding talent perform or show the potential for performing at remarkably high levels of accomplishment when compared with others of their age, experience, or environment. These children and youth exhibit high performance capability in intellectual, creative, and/or artistic areas, possess an unusual leadership capacity, or excel in specific academic fields. They require services or activities not ordinarily provided by the schools. Outstanding talents are present in children and youth from all cultural groups, across all economic strata, and in all areas of human endeavor (p. 3).

The Elementary and Secondary Education Act (The No Child Left Behind Act, Public Law 107-110) defines giftedness as follows:

(22) Gifted and Talented.—The term "gifted and talented," when used with respect to students, children, or youth, means students, children, or youth who give evidence of high achievement capability in areas such as intellectual, creative, artistic, or leadership capacity, or in specific academic fields, and who need services or activities not ordinarily provided by the school in order to fully develop those capabilities (No Child Left Behind Act of 2001, Pubic Law No. 107-110, 115 Stat 1959, 2002.)

These definitions guide school personnel and others in pursuing several important objectives. These include identifying a variety of students across disciplines with diverse talents, using many different kinds of assessment measures to identify gifted students, identifying "achievement capabilities" (not necessarily demonstrated performance) in students, actively

FOCUS 2
Identify four major components of definitions that have been developed to describe giftedness.

FIGURE 18.3

Catalysts for the Development of Gifts and Talents

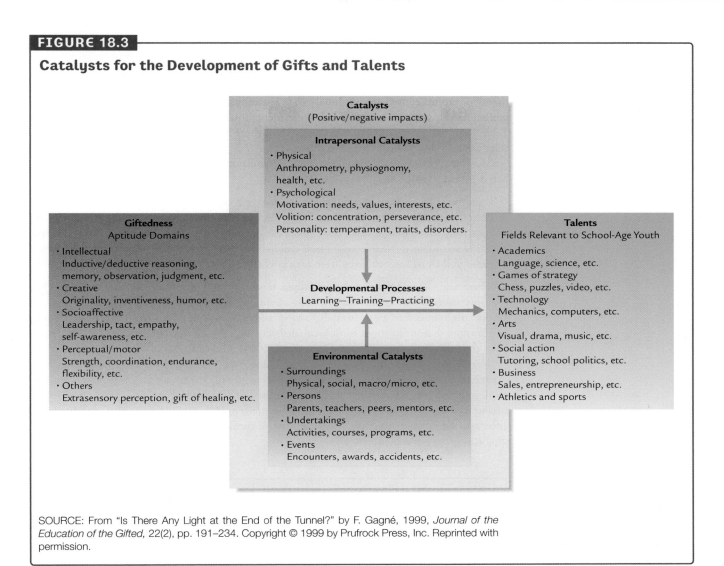

Catalysts
(Positive/negative impacts)

Intrapersonal Catalysts
- Physical
  Anthropometry, physiognomy,
  health, etc.
- Psychological
  Motivation: needs, values, interests, etc.
  Volition: concentration, perseverance, etc.
  Personality: temperament, traits, disorders.

Giftedness
Aptitude Domains
- Intellectual
  Inductive/deductive reasoning,
  memory, observation, judgment, etc.
- Creative
  Originality, inventiveness, humor, etc.
- Socioaffective
  Leadership, tact, empathy,
  self-awareness, etc.
- Perceptual/motor
  Strength, coordination, endurance,
  flexibility, etc.
- Others
  Extrasensory perception, gift of healing, etc.

Developmental Processes
Learning—Training—Practicing

Environmental Catalysts
- Surroundings
  Physical, social, macro/micro, etc.
- Persons
  Parents, teachers, peers, mentors, etc.
- Undertakings
  Activities, courses, programs, etc.
- Events
  Encounters, awards, accidents, etc.

Talents
Fields Relevant to School-Age Youth
- Academics
  Language, science, etc.
- Games of strategy
  Chess, puzzles, video, etc.
- Technology
  Mechanics, computers, etc.
- Arts
  Visual, drama, music, etc.
- Social action
  Tutoring, school politics, etc.
- Business
  Sales, entrepreneurship, etc.
- Athletics and sports

SOURCE: From "Is There Any Light at the End of the Tunnel?" by F. Gagné, 1999, *Journal of the Education of the Gifted*, 22(2), pp. 191–234. Copyright © 1999 by Prufrock Press, Inc. Reprinted with permission.

searching for giftedness in all student populations (cultural, economic, etc.), and considering students' drives and passions for achievement in various areas.

Furthermore, new conceptions of giftedness and intelligence have emerged from the theoretical and research literature (Ramos-Ford & Gardner, 1997; Sternberg, 1997; Passow, 2004). One of these approaches to intelligence is Sternberg's triarchic theory of human intelligence (Sternberg, 1997), according to which intellectual performance is divided into three parts: analytic, synthetic, and practical. Analytic intelligence is exhibited by people who perform well on aptitude and intelligence tests. Individuals with synthetic giftedness are unconventional thinkers who are creative, intuitive, and insightful. People with practical intelligence are extraordinarily adept in dealing with problems of everyday life and those that arise in their work environments.

Another conceptualization of giftedness or talent development has been proposed by Gagné (1999a). It centers on catalysts that have both positive and negative impacts (see Figure 18.3). These catalysts (intrapersonal and environmental) shape and influence developmental processes that give rise to talents. It is clear from this conceptualization of giftedness that the emergence of talents depends on environmental, motivational, and interpersonal factors (Piirto, 1999).

Gagné has also recommended the reexamination of IQ thresholds by which giftedness would be defined; the development of subcategories of talents, such as musical improvisation, mechanical prowess, and social precocity; and acknowledgment of talents in nontraditional areas of performance, including cooking, building, and farming (Piirto, 1999). These recommendations would democratize the field of gifted education, giving many more children and youth opportunities for talent development (Gagné, 1999b).

Another view of giftedness has been developed by Ramos-Ford and Gardner (1997). They have defined intelligence or giftedness as "an ability or set of abilities that permit an individual to solve problems or fashion products that are of consequence in a particular cultural setting" (Ramos-Ford & Gardner, 1991, p. 56). This perspective on giftedness is referred to as the theory of multiple intelligences. Intelligence is assumed to manifest itself in linguistic, logical-mathematical, spatial, musical, bodily-kinesthetic, interpersonal, and intrapersonal behaviors. Table 18.1 provides a brief definition of each of these behaviors, as well as the child and adult roles associated with each type of intelligence.

More recently, Piirto has constructed a pyramid of talent development (see Figure 18.4). She defines the gifted as

> those individuals who by way of learning characteristics such as superior memory, observational powers, curiosity, creativity, and the ability to learn school-related subject matters rapidly and accurately with a minimum of drill and repetition, have a right to an education that is differentiated according to their needs. These children become apparent early and should be served through their educational lives, from preschool through college. (Piirto, 1999, p. 28)

These and other definitions of giftedness have moved us from unitary measures of IQ to multiple measures of creativity, problem-solving ability, talent, and intelligence. However, despite the movement away from IQ scores and other changes in definitions of giftedness, critics argue that many if not most local, district, and state definitions are elitist in nature and favor the "affluent" and "privileged" (Borland, 2003; Ford, 2003).

The definitions of giftedness are diverse (Moon, 2006). Each of the definitions we have examined reveals the difficulty associated with defining the nature of giftedness. In a multicultural, pluralistic society, such as that of the United States, different abilities and capacities are encouraged and valued by different parents, teachers, and communities. Also, definitions of giftedness are often a function of educational, societal, and political priorities at a particular time and place (Gallagher, 2004).

TABLE 18.1

The Seven Intelligences

INTELLIGENCE	BRIEF DESCRIPTION	RELATED CHILD AND ADULT ROLES
Linguistic	The capacity to express oneself in spoken or written language with great facility	Superb storyteller, creative writer, or inventive speaker: Novelist, lyricist, lawyer
Logical-mathematical	The ability to reason inductively and deductively and to complete complex computations	Thorough counter, calculator, notation maker, or symbol user: Mathematician, physicist, computer scientist
Spatial	The capacity to create, manipulate, and represent spatial configurations	Creative builder, sculptor, artist, or skilled assembler of models: Architect, talented chess player, mechanic, navigator
Bodily-kinesthetic	The ability to perform various complex tasks or activities with one's body or part of the body	Skilled playground game player, emerging athlete or dancer: Surgeon, dancer, professional athlete
Musical	The capacity to discriminate musical pitches, to hear musical themes, and to sense rhythm, timbre, and texture	Good singer, creator of original songs or musical pieces: Musician, composer, director
Interpersonal	The ability to understand others' actions, emotions, and intents and to act effectively in response to verbal and nonverbal behaviors of others	Child organizer or orchestrator, child leader, or a very social child: Teacher, therapist, political social leader
Intrapersonal	The capacity to understand well and respond to one's own thoughts, desires, feelings, and emotions	A sensitive child, a resilient child, or an optimistic child: Social worker, therapist, counselor, hospice worker

FIGURE 18.4

The Piirto Pyramid of Talent Development

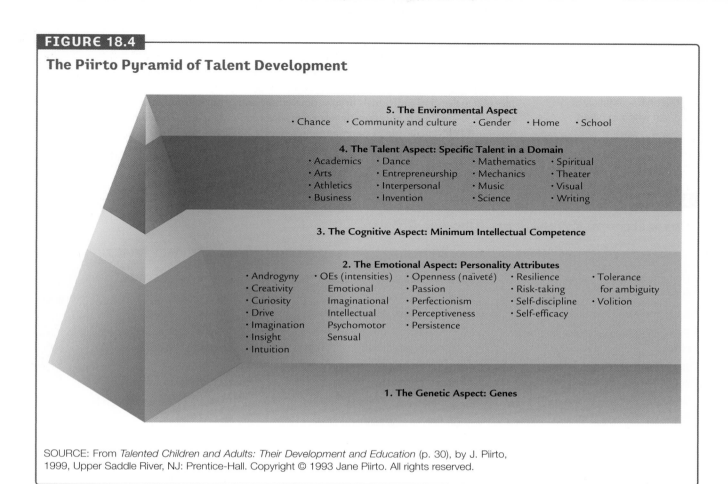

Prevalence

Determining the number of children who are gifted is a challenge. The complexity of the task is directly related to problems inherent in determining who is gifted and what constitutes giftedness (Gallagher, 2004). The numerous definitions of giftedness range from quite restrictive (in terms of the number of children to whom they apply) to very inclusive and broad descriptions. Consequently, the prevalence estimates are highly variable.

Prevalence figures compiled before the 1950s were primarily limited to the intellectually gifted: those identified for the most part by intelligence tests. At that time, 2% to 3% of the general population was considered gifted. During the 1950s, when professionals in the field advocated an expanded view of giftedness (Conant, 1959; DeHann & Havighurst, 1957), the prevalence figures suggested for program planning were substantially affected. Terms such as *academically talented* were used to refer to the upper 15% to 20% of the general school population.

Thus prevalence estimates have fluctuated, depending on the views of politicians, policy makers, researchers, and professionals during past decades. Currently, 3% to 25% of the students in the school population may be identified as gifted, depending on the regulations from state to state and the types of programs offered (Davis & Rimm, 2004).

Characteristics

Accurately identifying the characteristics of gifted people is a daunting task. Many characteristics attributed to those who are gifted have been generated by different types of studies (see

Table 18.2) (MacKinnon, 1962; Terman, 1925). Gradually, what emerged from these studies were oversimplified, inaccurate views of giftedness.

Unfortunately, much of the initial research related to the characteristics of giftedness was conducted with restricted population samples. Generally, the studies did not include adequate samples of females or of individuals from various ethnic and cultural groups; nor did early researchers carefully control for factors directly related to socioeconomic status. Therefore, the characteristics generated from these studies were not representative of gifted individuals as a whole but, rather, reflected the characteristics of gifted individuals from advantaged environments.

TABLE 18.2

Characteristics of Students Who Are Gifted

POSITIVE CHARACTERISTICS		NEGATIVE CHARACTERISTICS
Unusual alertness in infancy and later	Wide interests, interested in new topics	Uneven mental development
Early and rapid learning	High curiosity, explores how and why	Interpersonal difficulties, often due to intellectual differences
Rapid language development as a child	Multiple capabilities (multipotentiality)	Underachievement, especially in uninteresting areas
Superior language ability—verbally fluent, large vocabulary, complex grammar	High care ambitions (desire to be helpful to others)	Nonconformity, sometimes in disturbing directions
Enjoyment of learning	Overexcitability	Perfectionism, which can be extreme
Academic superiority, large knowledge base, sought out as a resource	Emotional intensity and sensitivity	Excessive self-criticism
Superior analytic ability	High alertness and attention	Self-doubt, poor self-image
Keen observation	High intellectual and physical activity level	Variable frustration and anger
Efficient, high-capacity memory	High motivation, concentrates, perseveres, persists, task-oriented	Depression
Superior reasoning, problem solving	Active—shares information, directs, leads, offers help, eager to be involved	
Thinking that is abstract, complex, logical, insightful	Strong empathy, moral thinking, sense of justice, honesty, intellectual honesty	
Insightful, sees "big picture," recognizes patterns, connects topics	Aware of social issues	
Manipulates symbol systems	High concentration, long attention span	
Uses high-level thinking skills, efficient strategies	Strong internal control	
Extrapolates knowledge to new situations, goes beyond what is taught	Independent, self-directed, works alone	
Expanded awareness, greater self-awareness	Inquisitive, asks questions	
Greater metacognition (understanding own thinking)	Excellent sense of humor	
Advanced interests	Imaginative, creative, solves problems	
Needs for logic and accuracy	Preference for novelty	
	Reflectiveness	
	Good self-concept	

SOURCE: Adapted from Rimm & Davis 2004, p. 33.

Children with gifts and talents come from every ethnic, cultural, and socioeconomic background. While some individuals achieve in intellectual endeavors, others excel through the arts.

Given the present multifaceted definitions of giftedness and emerging views of intelligence (Davis & Rimm, 2004), we must conclude that gifted individuals are members of a heterogeneous population. Consequently, research findings of the past must be interpreted with great caution as practitioners assess a particular youth's behavior, attributes, and talents.

Gifted students, who are intellectually able, demonstrate one resounding trait—"they are developmentally advanced in language and thought" (Davis & Rimm, 2004, p. 35). Many learn to speak and read very early. Their mental ages, as revealed in intelligence tests, far exceed their chronological ages. Moreover, their innate curiosity and capacity for asking questions can drive some parents and even teachers to the brink of exhaustion and desperation. These students can be unusually tenacious in pursuing ideas, concerns, and questions. They may also have interests that would be characteristic of older children and/or adults.

Council for Exceptional Children

Standard 2: Development and Characteristics of Learners

TABLE 18.3

Characteristics of Students Who Are Creative

POSITIVE TRAITS	APPROXIMATE SYNONYMS
Original	Imaginative, resourceful, flexible, unconventional, thinks metaphorically, challenges assumptions, irritated and bored by the obvious, avoids perceptual set, asks "what if?"
Aware of creativeness	Creativity-conscious, values originality, values own creativity
Independent	Self-confident, individualistic, nonconforming, sets own rules, unconcerned with impressing others, resists societal demands
Risk-taking	Not afraid to be different or to try something new, willing to cope with hostility, willing to cope with failure
Motivated	Energetic, adventurous, sensation-seeking, enthusiastic, excitable, spontaneous, impulsive, intrinsically motivated, perseveres, works beyond assigned tasks
Curious	Questions norms and assumptions, experiments, inquisitive, wide interests, is a problem-finder, asks "why?"
Sense of humor	Playful, plays with ideas, child-like freshness in thinking
Attracted to complexity	Attracted to novelty, asymmetry, the mysterious, theoretical and abstract problems; is a complex person; tolerant of ambiguity, disorder, incongruity
Artistic	Artistic and aesthetic interests, attracted to beauty and order
Open-minded	Receptive to new ideas, other viewpoints, new experiences, and growth; liberal, altruistic
Needs alone time	Reflective, introspective, internally preoccupied, sensitive, may be withdrawn, likes to work alone
Intuitive	Perceptive, sees relationships, finds order in chaos, uses all senses in observing
Intelligent	Verbally fluent, articulate, logical, good decision maker, detects gaps in knowledge, visualizes

SOURCE: Adapted from Davis & Rimm, 2004, p. 42.

Generally, gifted students are well adjusted and socially adept. There are, of course, exceptions. One of the more interesting attributes of gifted children and youth is their penchant for "emotional excitability" and "high sensitivity" (Rimm & Davis, 2004, p. 37). In this regard, their reactions can be more intense; that is, they may feel more joy and also experience greater sadness than age-mates. Table 18.2 lists characteristics often evident in gifted students.

Students who are described as creative share a number of salient personality attributes (Zimmerman, 2004). They often exhibit high energy and high motivation to succeed or perform. They have a real zest for pursuing tasks and seeking solutions to problems they encounter. They also have a proclivity for risk taking. They love to try new activities, to experiment with new behaviors, and to consider new ways of processing problems or creating things (artistic, mechanical, etc.). Table 18.3 on page 501 lists characteristics often evident in students described as creative.

No student who is identified as gifted will exhibit all of the characteristics described in this section. However, parents, teachers, coaches, and mentors have an opportunity, as well as an obligation, to encourage these traits, behaviors, and proclivities. Again, our collective focus as mentors and encouragers ought to be talent development (Baum, 2004; Rim & Davis, 2004).

Origins of Giftedness

Scientists have long been interested in identifying the origins of intelligence. Conclusions have varied greatly. For years, many scientists adhered to a hereditary explanation of intelligence: that people inherit their intellectual capacity at conception. Thus intelligence was viewed as an innate capacity that remained relatively fixed during an individual's lifetime. The prevailing belief then was that little could be done to enhance intellectual ability.

During the 1920s and 1930s, scientists such as John Watson began to explore the new notion of behavioral psychology, or behaviorism. Like other behaviorists who followed him, Watson believed that the environment plays an important role in the development of intelligence as well as personality traits. Initially, Watson largely discounted the role of heredity and its importance in intellectual development. Later, however, he moderated his views, moving somewhat toward a theoretical perspective in which both heredity and environment contributed to an individual's intellectual ability.

During the 1930s, many investigators sought to determine the relative influence of heredity and environment on intellectual development. Some proponents of genetics asserted that as much as 70% to 80% of an individual's capacity is determined by heredity and the remainder by environmental influences. Environmentalists believed otherwise. The controversy over the relative contributions of heredity and environment to intelligence (known as the **nature versus nurture** controversy) is likely to continue for some time, in part because of the complexity and breadth of the issues involved (Plomin & Price, 2003). However, important progress has been made in teasing apart the genetic and environmental contributors to high intelligence. "For example, developmental genetic research indicates that the heritability of intelligence increases with age, and that genetic factors contribute to age-to-age change, especially during the transition to middle childhood" (Plomin & Price, 2003, p. 121). To put it another way, as gifted children age and move to adulthood, they "actively select, modify, and even create environments conducive to the development of genetic proclivities" (Plomin & Price, 2003, p. 118).

For example, studies of identical twins raised in different environments suggest that 44% to 72% of their intelligence (general cognitive ability) is inherited. With regard to environmental factors, we are just beginning to understand the dynamic relationships between nature and nurture. Again, "bright children select and are selected by peers and educational programs that foster their abilities. They read and think more. This is the profound meaning of finding genetic influences on measures of the environment. Genes contribute to the experience itself" (Plomin & Price, 2003, p. 120). Plomin and Price (2003) captured it best when they said, "it may well be more appropriate to think about [general cognitive ability] as an appetite rather than an aptitude" (p. 121). This appetite enables gifted children and youth to profit more fully from environmental influences over their lifetimes.

Thus far, we have focused on the origins of intelligence rather than on giftedness per se. Many of the theories about the emergence or essence of giftedness have been derived from the

Standard 3: Individual Learning Differences

Focus **4**

Identify three factors that appear to contribute significantly to the emergence of various forms of giftedness.

Standard 1: Foundations

➤ **Nature versus nurture**

Controversy concerning how much of a person's ability is related to sociocultural influences (nurture) and how much is due to genetic factors (nature).

study of general intelligence. Few authors have focused directly on the origins of giftedness. Moreover, the ongoing changes in the definitions of giftedness have further complicated the precise investigation of its origins.

Tannenbaum (2003) proposed the "Star Model" (see Figure 18.5) for explaining the causes and antecedents of giftedness. It is composed of five elements, each of which contributes to gifted behavior. These elements are superior general intellect, distinctive special aptitudes, nonintellective factors, environmental supports, and chance. Associated with each are the descriptors *dynamic* and *static*. The static dimension includes factors that remain relatively constant or unchanged, such as the child's or youth's race and economic status. The dynamic dimension includes factors that are fluid and responsive to contextual or environmental changes or interventions.

The abilities associated with superior intelligence are generally factors assessed through intelligence tests (verbal, spatial, and memory capacity). Special abilities are those found, for example, in child prodigies who show extraordinary musical, mathematical, or other emerging talents.

FIGURE 18.5

The Star Model: Psychosocial Factors Accounting for Gifted Achievements

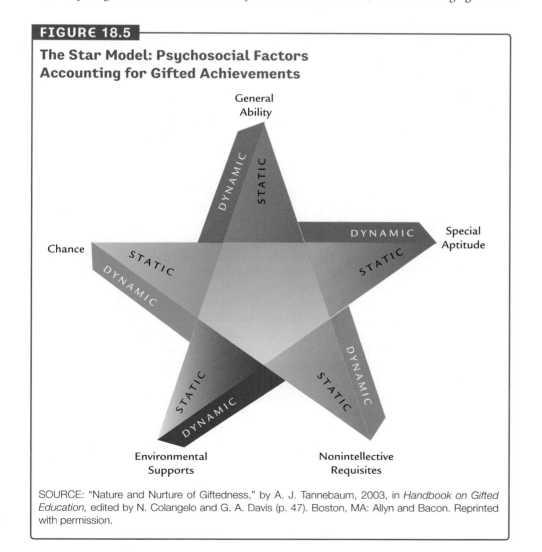

SOURCE: "Nature and Nurture of Giftedness," by A. J. Tannebaum, 2003, in *Handbook on Gifted Education,* edited by N. Colangelo and G. A. Davis (p. 47). Boston, MA: Allyn and Bacon. Reprinted with permission.

I can clearly remember the Sunday I was playing Toccata and Fugue in F Minor. I was twelve years old and organist at the First Presbyterian Church in Medina, New York. I made a chord mistake and spent the afternoon crying on my bed because I was such a failure in my own mind and heart. Every single week, I prepared the organ music for the Sunday services. All this was done between the ages of twelve and eighteen. Can you imagine? I thought I was failure because I would make an occasional playing error. Now I wonder how I could even assume that much responsibility at such a young and vulnerable age (Callard-Szulgit, 2003a, p. 39).

I am a recovering perfectionist. I never realized I was until twenty-five years ago, when I began teaching a self-contained fourth-grade class of gifted children in a suburban school district in Rochester, New York. Within two days, I was stunned to see personality traits of my students identical to those of myself. I saw so much of myself in my students—not wanting to make a mistake, not realizing when enough was really enough . . . , never feeling I was smart enough (in third grade I tested post-high school in all the achievement test scores), giving too much credit to what others thought rather than [to] what I was thinking or creating, worrying about things that in reality were not that important (age and hindsight are wonderful teachers) (Callard-Szulgit, 2003b, p. vii).

Nonintellective factors are a wide-ranging set of attributes, including, believe it or not, psychopathology and perfectionism. Many gifted artists and writers show clear signs of pathological deviance or emotional distress (Callard-Szulgit, 2003a). Other, more positive factors associated with this element include motivation, self-concept, and resilience. The influence of environmental support is obvious. "Giftedness requires [a] social context that enables it to mature. . . . Human potential needs nurturance, urgings, encouragement, and even pressures from a world that cares" (Tannenbaum, 2003, p. 54). Last is the element of chance. Often, external factors that coincide with one's preparation and talent development contribute to one's eventual imminence or greatness. All of these factors come together in a unique fashion to produce various kinds of giftedness.

Assessment

FOCUS 5
Indicate the range of assessment devices used to identify the various types of giftedness.

Council for Exceptional Children

Standard 8: Assessment

The focus of assessment procedures for identifying potential giftedness is beginning to change (Renzulli, 2004). Elitist definitions and exclusive approaches are being replaced with more defensible, inclusive methods of assessment (Briggs, Reis, Eckert, & Baum, 2006; Davis & Rimm, 2004; Richert, 2003). Tests for identifying persons with potential for gifted performance are being more carefully selected; that is, tests are being used with the children for whom they were designed. Children who were once excluded from programs for the gifted because of formal or standard cut-off scores that favored particular groups of students are now being included (Richert, 2003). Multiple sources of information are now collected and reviewed in determining who is potentially gifted (Chuska, 2005; Davis & Rimm, 2004; Renzulli, 2004; Richert, 2003). Ideally, the identification process is now directed at identifying needs and potentials rather than merely labeling individuals as gifted. Again, the new thrust is talent development as well as talent identification (Briggs, Reis, Eckert, & Baum, 2006; VanTassel-Baska & Stambaugh, 2006).

Several approaches have also been developed to identify children who are disadvantaged and also gifted. Some theorists and practitioners have argued for the adoption of a contextual paradigm or approach. Rather than using information derived solely from typical intelligence tests or other talent assessments, this approach relies on divergent views of giftedness as valued and determined by community members, parents, grandparents, and competent informants. Similar approaches focus on nontraditional measures of giftedness. These approaches use multiple criteria, broader ranges of scores for inclusion in special programs, peer nomination, assessments by persons other than educational personnel, and information provided by adaptive behavior assessments. Furthermore, these approaches seek to understand students' motivations, interests, capacity for communication, reasoning abilities, imagination, and humor

(Briggs, Reis, Eckert, & Baum, 2006; Davis & Rimm, 2004; Richert, 2003). For example, if 60% of students in a given school population come from a certain cultural minority group and only 2% are identified as gifted via traditional measures, the screening committee may want to reexamine and adjust its identification procedures.

Elementary and secondary students who are gifted are identified in a variety of ways. The first step is generally screening. During this phase, teachers, psychologists, and other school personnel attempt to select all students who are potentially gifted. A number of procedures are employed in the screening process. Historically, information obtained from group intelligence tests and teacher nominations has been used to select the initial pool of students. However, many other measures and data collection techniques have been instituted since the approach to assessment of giftedness changed from one-dimensional to multidimensional (Davis & Rimm, 2004; Richert, 2003). These techniques may include developmental inventories, classroom observations, parent and peer nominations, achievement tests, creativity tests, motivation assessments, teacher nominations, and evaluations of student projects (Renzulli, 2004).

Teacher Nomination

Teacher nomination has been an integral part of many screening approaches. It is fraught with problems, however. Teachers often favor children who are cooperative, well-mannered, and task-oriented. Bright underachievers and those who are bright, confrontive, and/or disruptive may be overlooked. Also, many teachers are unfamiliar with the general traits, behaviors, and dispositions that underlie giftedness.

Fortunately, some of these problems have been addressed. Several scales, approaches, and guidelines are now available to aid teachers and others who are responsible for making nominations (Davis & Rimm, 2004; Renzulli & Reis, 2003). Teachers who have a thorough understanding of the various kinds of giftedness are in a much better position to provide good information in the nomination, screening, and selection process.

Intelligence and Achievement Tests

Intelligence testing continues to be a major source of information for screening and identifying general ability or intellectual giftedness in children and adolescents. These tests must be carefully selected. For example, some intelligence tests have low ceilings; that is, they do not allow the participating children or youth to demonstrate their full potential. The same is true of some group-administered intelligence tests. They are not designed to identify students who may have exceptionally high intellectual abilities.

One advantage of intelligence testing is that it often identifies underachievers. Intelligence test scores frequently reveal students who have wonderful intellectual capacity that has gone unrecognized because of their poor school performance.

A serious limitation associated with intelligence tests emerges when they are administered to individuals for whom the tests were not designed. Very few intelligence tests adequately assess the abilities of children and adolescents who are substantially different from the core culture for whom the tests were created. However, some progress is being made in helping educators identify gifted children who are members of minority groups, underachievers, or at risk (Ford 2003; Richert, 2003; Renzulli, 2004).

Similar problems are inherent in achievement tests, which, like intelligence tests, are not generally designed to measure the true achievement of children who are academically gifted. Such individuals are often prevented from demonstrating their unusual prowess because of the restricted range of the test items. These **ceiling effects** prevent youth who are gifted from demonstrating their achievement at higher levels. However, achievement tests do play a very useful role in identifying students with specific academic talents (Davis & Rimm, 2004).

➤ **Ceiling effects**
A restricted range of test questions or problems that does not permit academically gifted students to demonstrate their true capacity or achievement.

Creativity Tests

Tests for creativity serve several purposes. Often they help the teacher or practitioner discover capacity that may not be evident in normal classroom interactions and performances. Also, these tests are useful in confirming attributes related to creativity. However, we must realize that creativity tests are difficult to construct. The degree to which they actually measure creativity is often called into question. Because of the nature of creativity and the many forms in which it can be expressed, developing tests to assess its presence and magnitude is a formidable task (Davis & Rimm, 2004; Renzulli, 2004; Treffinger, 2004). In spite of these challenges, a number of creativity tests have been formulated (Rimm, 1982; Rimm & Davis, 1983; Torrance, 1966; Williams, 1980). A typical question on a test of divergent thinking might read, "What would happen if your eyes could be adjusted to see things as small as germs?"

Once the screening steps have been completed, the actual identification and selection of students begin. During this phase, each of the previously screened students is carefully evaluated again, using more individualized procedures and assessment tools. Ideally, these techniques should be closely related to the definition of giftedness used by the district and to the program envisioned or offered to students (Eckert, 2006; Gubbins, 2006; Rogers, 2006).

Davis and Rimm (2004) have developed a series of recommendations and statements that summarize this section on assessment and identification (see Figure 18.6). If these recommendations are carefully followed, more appropriate and equitable decisions will be made in identifying and serving children and youth who are gifted or potentially gifted.

Services and Supports

Early Childhood

Parents can promote the early learning and development of their children in a number of ways (Jackson, 2003; Jin & Feldhusen, 2000). During the first 18 months of life, 90% of all social interactions with children take place during such activities as feeding, bathing, changing diapers, and dressing. Parents who are interested in advancing intellectual and social development use these occasions for stimulating and talking to their children; providing varied sensory experiences such as bare-skin cuddling, tickling, and smiling; and conveying a sense of trust. Early, concentrated, language-centered involvement with young children gives rise to solid cognitive, social, and linguistic skills.

As children progress through the infancy, toddler, and preschool periods, the experiences provided become more varied and uniquely suited to the child's emerging interests. Language and cognitive development are encouraged by means of stories that are read and told. Children are also urged to make up their own stories. Brief periods are reserved for discussions or spontaneous conversations that arise from events that have momentarily captured their attention. Requests for help in saying or printing a word are promptly fulfilled. Thus many children who are gifted learn to read before they enter kindergarten or first grade (Davis & Rimm, 2004; Jackson, 2003).

During the school years, parents continue to encourage their children's development by providing opportunities that correspond to their strengths and interests. The simple identification games played during the preschool period become more complex. Discussions frequently take place with peers and other interesting adults in addition to parents. The nature of the discussions and the types of questions asked become more sophisticated. Parents help their children move to higher levels of learning by asking questions that involve analysis (comparing and contrasting ideas), synthesis (integrating and combining ideas into new and novel forms), and evaluation (judging and disputing books, newspaper articles, and the like). Parents can also help by (1) furnishing books and reading materials on a broad range of topics; (2) providing appropriate equipment (such as microscopes, telescopes, or chemistry sets) as various interests surface; (3) encouraging regular trips to public libraries and other resource centers; (4) providing opportunities for participation in cultural events, lectures, and exhibits; (5) encouraging participation in extracurricular and community activities outside the home; and (6) fostering relationships with potential mentors and other resource people in the community.

Appropriate and early stimulation is vital to the development of all children.

Standard 5: Learning Environments and Social Interactions

PRESCHOOL PROGRAMS. A variety of preschool programs have been developed for young children who are gifted. Some children are involved in traditional programs, which focus on activities and curricula devoted primarily to the development of academic skills. Many of the traditional programs emphasize affective and social development as well. The entry criteria for these programs are varied, but the primary considerations are usually the child's IQ and social maturity.

Creativity programs are designed to help children develop their natural endowments in a number of artistic and creative domains (Treffinger, 2004). Another purpose of such programs is to help children discover their own areas of promise. Children in these programs are also prepared for eventual involvement in traditional academic areas of schooling.

Childhood and Adolescence

Giftedness in elementary and secondary students may be nurtured in a variety of ways. A number of service delivery systems and approaches are used in responding to the needs of students who are gifted (VanTassel-Baska & Stambaugh, 2006). The nurturing process has often been referred to as **differentiated education**—that is, an education uniquely and predominantly suited to the natural abilities and interests of individuals who are gifted (Chuska, 2005; Gagné, 2003; Karnes & Bean, 2001). It is differentiated in terms of "content, process, and content demands" (Vantassel-Baska, 2003, p. 3). Generally, programs for the gifted are targeted at delivering content more rapidly, using a variety of engaging instructional strategies, delivering more challenging content, examining content in greater depth, pursuing highly specialized content, and/or dealing with more complex and higher levels of subject matter (Brody, 2004).

➤ **Differentiated education**

Instruction and learning activities that are uniquely and predominantly suited to the characteristics, capacities, and interests of gifted students.

INSTRUCTIONAL APPROACHES. Instructional approaches are selected on the basis of a variety of factors. First, the school system must determine what types of giftedness it is capable of serving and supporting. It must also establish identification criteria and related measures that enable it to select qualified students fairly. For example, if the system is primarily interested in enhancing creativity, measures and indices of creativity should be utilized. If the focus

Standard 7: Instructional Planning

IS CALVIN GIFTED?

W hat follows is a series of cartoon strips from *Calvin and Hobbes.* They depict in part the relationship Calvin has with his dad.

APPLICATION

1. Is Calvin gifted, creative, and talented? Provide a rationale for your answer.

2. If Calvin's dad asked you how to handle Calvin's "giftedness," what recommendations would you make? Give a rationale for your answers.

3. If Calvin's dad were enrolled in your parenting class and asked for your counsel as the group leader, what would you recommend?

of the program is accelerating math achievement and understanding, instruments that measure mathematical aptitude and achievement should be employed. Second, the school system must select the organizational structures through which children who are gifted are to receive their differentiated education (Karnes & Bean, 2001; Schiever & Maker, 2003). Third, school personnel must select the instructional approaches to be utilized within each program setting. Fourth, school personnel must select continuous evaluation procedures and techniques that help them assess the overall effectiveness of the program (Chuska, 2005). Data generated from such evaluations can serve as catalysts for making appropriate and meaningful changes (Callahan, 2004; Davis & Rimm, 2004).

SERVICE DELIVERY SYSTEMS. Once the types of giftedness to be emphasized have been selected and appropriate identification procedures have been established, planning must be directed at selecting suitable service delivery systems. Organizational structures for students who are gifted are similar to those found in other areas of special education. Clark (1997) described several options that have been used to develop services for students who are gifted (see Figure 18.7). Each of the learning environments in the model has advantages and disadvantages. For example, students who are enrolled in general education classrooms and are given opportunities to spend time in seminars, resource rooms, special classes, and other novel learning environments profit from these experiences because they are allowed to work at their own levels of ability. Furthermore, such pull-out activities provide a means for students to interact with one another and to pursue interests to which the usual school curriculum offers little access. However, the disadvantages of such a program are numerous. The major part of the instructional week is spent doing things that may not be appropriate for students who are gifted, given their unique abilities and interests. Also, when they return to general education classes, they are frequently required to make up missed assignments.

Another example of Clark's alternatives for elementary, middle, and high schools is assignment to a special class, supplemented with opportunities for course work integrated with regular classes. This approach has many advantages. Students have the best of both worlds,

---

FIGURE 18.7

Clark's Continuum Model for Ability Grouping

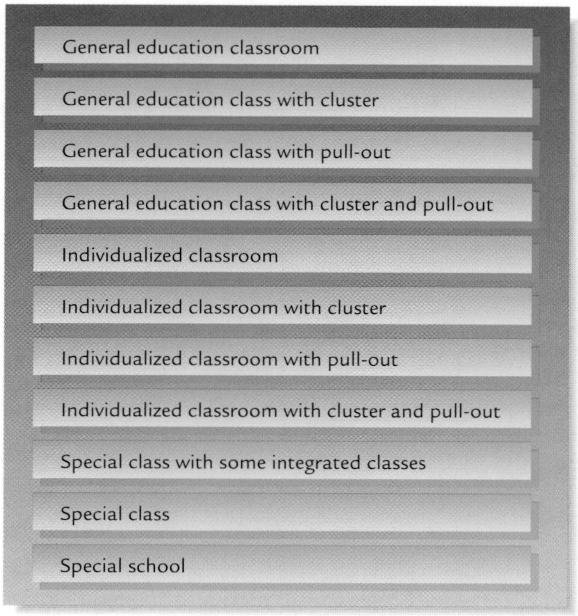

General education classroom

General education class with cluster

General education class with pull-out

General education class with cluster and pull-out

Individualized classroom

Individualized classroom with cluster

Individualized classroom with pull-out

Individualized classroom with cluster and pull-out

Special class with some integrated classes

Special class

Special school

SOURCE: From *Growing Up Gifted*, 5th ed., by Barbara Clark, Copyright © 1979. Adapted by permission of Prentice-Hall, Inc., Upper Saddle River, NJ.

INCLUSION AND COLLABORATION THROUGH THE LIFESPAN

People Who Are Gifted, Creative, and Talented

EARLY CHILDHOOD YEARS

Tips for the Family

- Realize that giftedness is evidenced in many ways (e.g., concentration, memory, pleasure in learning, sense of humor, social knowledge, task orientation, ability to follow and lead, capacity and desire to compete, information capacity).
- Provide, for children who are gifted, toys that may be used for a variety of activities.
- Take trips to museums, exhibits, fairs, and other places of interest.
- Provide an environment that is appropriately challenging.
- Supply proper visual, auditory, verbal, and kinesthetic stimulation.
- Talk to the child in ways that foster give-and-take conversation.
- Begin to expose the child to picture books and ask him or her to find certain objects or animals or to respond to age-appropriate questions.
- Avoid unnecessary restrictions.
- Provide play materials that are developmentally appropriate and may be a little challenging.

Tips for the Preschool Teacher

- Look for ways in which various talents and skills may be expressed (e.g., cognitive, artistic, leadership, socialization, motor ability, memory, special knowledge, imagination).
- Provide opportunities for the child who is gifted to express these talents.
- Collaborate with other professionals who are knowledgeable about identifying and serving gifted children.
- Capitalize on the child's curiosity. Develop learning activities related to his or her passions.
- Allow the child to experiment with all the elements of language—even written language—as he or she is ready.

Tips for Preschool Personnel

- Remember that conversation is critical to the child's development. Do not be reluctant to spend a great deal of time asking the child questions as he or she engages in various activities.
- Become a specialist in looking for gifts and talents across a variety of domains (e.g., artistic, social, cognitive).
- Allow for rapid mastery of concepts, and then allow the child to move on to other, more challenging activities rather than holding him or her back.

Tips for Neighbors and Friends

- Recognize that people have a variety of gifts and talents that can be encouraged.
- Provide preschool opportunities for all children who are potentially gifted to have the necessary environmental ingredients to use their talents or gifts fully—that is, support and encourage talent development.
- Enjoy and sometimes endure the neighborhood child who has chosen your home as his or her lab for various experiments in cooking, painting, and building.

ELEMENTARY YEARS

Tips for the Family

- Maintain the search for individual gifts and talents; some qualities may not be evident until the child is older.
- Collaborate with other professionals in your building in providing appropriate experiences and options for gifted learners.
- Provide out-of-school experiences that foster talent or skill development (e.g., artistic, physical, academic, social).
- Enroll the child who is gifted in summer programs offered by universities or colleges.
- Monitor the child's school environment to be sure that adequate steps are being taken to respond to your child's unique skills, interests, and abilities.
- Join an advocacy group for parents in your community or state.
- Subscribe to child publications that are related to your child's current interests.
- Encourage your child's friendships and associations with other children who have like interests and aptitudes.

Tips for the General Education Classroom Teacher

- Provide opportunities for enrichment as well as acceleration.
- Allow students who are gifted to pursue individual projects that require sophisticated forms of thinking, production, or problem solving.
- Become involved in professional organizations that provide assistance to teachers of students who are gifted.
- Take a course that specifically addresses the instructional strategies that might be used with children who are gifted.
- Encourage children to become active participants in various events that emphasize particular skills or knowledge areas (e.g., science fairs, music competitions).

Tips for School Personnel

- Develop clubs and programs that enable children who are gifted to pursue their talents.
- Create award programs that encourage talent development across a variety of domains.
- Involve and collaborate with community members (e.g., artists, engineers, writers) in offering enrichment and acceleration activities.

- Foster the use of inclusive procedures for identifying students who are potentially gifted from groups that are culturally diverse, are disadvantaged, or have disabilities.

Tips for Neighbors and Friends

- Contribute to organizations that foster talent development.
- Volunteer to serve as judges for competitive events.
- Be willing to share your talents with young, emergent scholars, musicians, athletes, and artists.
- Become a mentor for someone in your community.

SECONDARY AND TRANSITION YEARS

Tips for the Family

- Continue to provide sources of support for talent development outside of the home.
- Regularly counsel with your child about courses he or she may take—collaborate with counselors and other school personnel.
- Provide access to tools (e.g., computers, video cameras) and resources (e.g., specialists, coaches, mentors) that contribute to your child's development.
- Expect variations in performance from time to time—give your child appropriate breathing room.
- Provide opportunities for relaxation and rest from demanding schedules.
- Continue to encourage involvement with peers who have similar interests and aptitudes.

Tips for the General Education Classroom Teacher

- Provide a range of activities for students with varying abilities.
- Provide opportunities for students who are gifted to deal with real problems or develop actual products.
- Give opportunities for genuine enrichment activities, not just more work—collaborate with professional peers within your discipline and others in making these activities available.
- Remember that giftedness manifests itself in many ways. Determine how various types of giftedness may be expressed in your content domain.
- Help to eliminate the conflicting and confusing signals about career choices and fields of study that are often given to young women who are gifted.

Tips for School Personnel

- Provide, to the degree possible, a variety of curriculum options, activities, clubs, and the like.
- Acknowledge and celebrate excellence in a variety of performance areas (e.g., leadership, visual and performing arts, academics).

- Continue to use inclusive procedures in identifying individuals who are potentially gifted and talented.
- Encourage participation in competitive activities in which students are able to use their gifts and talents (e.g., science fairs, debate tournaments, music competitions).

Tips for Neighbors, Friends, and Potential Employers

- Provide opportunities for students to "shadow" talented professionals in your employment.
- Volunteer as a professional to work directly with students who are gifted in pursuing a real problem or producing an actual product.
- Become a mentor for a student who is interested in what you do professionally.
- Support the funding of programs for students who are gifted and talented and who come from disadvantaged environments.
- Provide summer internships for students who have a particular interest in your profession.
- Serve as an adviser for a high school club or other organization that gives students additional opportunities to pursue talent areas.

ADULT YEARS

Tips for the Family

- Continue to nurture appropriate interdependence and independence.
- Assist with the provision of specialized assistance.
- Celebrate the individuals' accomplishments and provide support for challenges.
- Let go.

Tips for Educational Personnel

- Exhibit behaviors associated with effective mentoring.
- Provide meaningful ways to deal with pressure.
- Allow the individuals to be themselves.
- Provide adequate time for discussion and interaction.
- Be aware of other demands in the individuals' lives.

Tips for Potential Employers

- Establish appropriately high expectations.
- Be sensitive to changing interests and needs.
- Encourage and support employees who wish to mentor young gifted students on a volunteer basis.

academically and socially. Directed independent studies, seminars, mentorships, and cooperative studies are possible through this arrangement. Students who are gifted are able to interact in an intensive fashion with other able students, as well as with regular students in their integrated classes. This program also has disadvantages, however. A special class requires a well-prepared, competent teacher, and many school systems simply do not have sufficient funds to hire specialists in gifted education. Without skilled teachers, special class instruction or other specialized learning activities may just be more of the general education curriculum.

Implementing service delivery and designing curricula for gifted students are significant but rewarding challenges (Burns, Purcell, & Hertberg, 2006). They demand the availability of sufficient financial and human resources, flexibility in determining student placement and progress, a focus on high-quality achievement and growth, and a climate of excellence characterized by high standards and significant student engagement (Cooper, 2006). Optimally, delivery systems should facilitate the achievement of specific curricular goals, should mesh with state standards, should correspond with the types of giftedness being nurtured, and should prepare students for other experiences yet to come in elementary, secondary and postsecondary settings (Adams, 2006; Tomlinson, Doubet, & Capper, 2006; VanTassel-Baska, 2004).

Conditions and strategies associated with successful classrooms and programs for gifted students include teachers who have advanced preparation and knowledge specifically related to gifted education, who relish change, and who enjoy working collaboratively with other professionals. Furthermore, these teachers believe in differentiated instruction and actively implement it, have access to a variety of strategies for delivering this kind of instruction, and have a disposition for leadership and some autonomy in fulfilling their teaching responsibilities (Chuska, 2005; Leppien & Westberg, 2006).

ACCELERATION. Traditionally, programs for students who are gifted emphasize the practices of **acceleration** and enrichment (Brody, 2004; Schiever & Maker, 2003). Acceleration enables gifted students to progress rapidly and learn at a rate commensurate with their abilities. Early entrance to kindergarten or college, part-time grade acceleration, and grade skipping are all examples of acceleration. In the past, grade skipping was a common administrative approach to meeting the needs of high-ability learners. But this practice has declined because some individuals believe that grade skipping may increase the likelihood of a student's becoming socially maladjusted. Others believe that accelerated students experience significant gaps in learning because of grade skipping. Acceleration is generally limited to two years in the typical elementary school program. In any case, acceleration unfortunately does not provide gifted students with a differentiated curriculum suited to their specific needs (Schiever & Maker, 2003).

Another practice related to grade skipping is telescoped or condensed schooling, which enables students to progress through the content of several grades in a significantly reduced time. An allied practice is allowing students to progress rapidly through a particular course or content offering. Acceleration of this nature provides students with the sequential, basic learning at a pace commensurate with their abilities. School programs that are ungraded are particularly suitable for telescoping. Regardless of their chronological ages, students may progress through a learning or curriculum sequence that is not constricted by artificial grade boundaries.

Other forms of condensed programming found at the high-school level include earning credit through examination, enrolling in extra courses for early graduation, reducing or eliminating certain course work, enrolling in intensive summer programs, and taking approved university courses while completing high school requirements. Many of these options enable students to enter college early or begin bachelor's programs with other advanced students. Many students who are gifted are ready for college-level course work at age 14, 15, or 16—and some at even younger ages. See this chapter's Debate Forum to consider what approach you would recommend for the education of one gifted youngster.

> **Acceleration**
A process whereby students are allowed to achieve at a rate that is consistent with their capacity and achievement.

Focus 6
Identify eight strategies that are utilized to foster the development of children and adolescents who are gifted.

Some gifted children and youth are ready for university-level instruction well in advance of their same-age peers.

Many children who are gifted are prevented from accelerating their growth and learning for fear that they will be hurt emotionally and socially.

Parents' comments such as these are common: She's so young. Won't she miss a great deal if she doesn't go through the fourth and fifth grades? What about her friends? Who will her friends be if she goes to college at such a young age? Will she have the social skills to interact with kids who are much older? If she skips these two grades, won't there be gaps in her learning and social development?

On the other hand, the nature of the questions or comments by parents about acceleration may also be positive: She is young in years only! She will adjust extremely well. Maybe she is emotionally mature enough to handle this type of acceleration. The increased opportunities provided through university training will give her greater chances to develop her talents and capacities. Perhaps the older students with whom she will interact are better suited to her intellectual and social needs.

Consider Jane, a child who is gifted. In third grade, she thrived in school, and just about everything associated with her schooling at that time was positive. Her teacher was responsive and allowed her and others to explore well beyond the usual "read-the-text-then-respond-to-the-ditto-sheet" routine. Much self-pacing was possible, and materials galore were presented for both independent studies and queries.

In the fourth and fifth grades, however, things began to change radically. Jane's teachers were simply unable to provide enough interesting and challenging work for her. It was during the latter part of the fourth grade that she began to view herself as different. Not only did she know, but her classmates knew, that learning came exceptionally easily to her. At this same time, Jane was beginning to change dramatically in her cognitive ca-

pacity. Unfortunately, her teachers persisted in unnecessary drills and other mundane assignments, and Jane gradually became bored and lapsed into a type of passive learning. Rather than attacking assignments with vigor, she performed them carelessly, often making many stupid errors. Gradually, what emerged was a child who was very unhappy in school. School had been the most interesting place for her to be before she entered fourth grade. Then it became a source of pain and boredom.

Jane's parents decided that they needed to know more about her capacities and talents. Although it was expensive and quite time-consuming, they visited a nearby university center for psychological services. Jane was tested, and the results were very revealing. For the first time, Jane's parents had some objective information about her capacities. She was in fact an unusually bright and talented young lady. Jane's parents then began to consider the educational alternatives available to her.

The counselor who provided the interpretation of the results at the university center strongly recommended that Jane be advanced to the seventh grade in a school that provided services to students who were talented and gifted. This meant that Jane would skip one year of elementary school and have an opportunity to move very rapidly through her junior and senior high school studies. Furthermore, she might be able to enter the university well in advance of her peers.

Jane's parents knew that her performance had diminished significantly in the last year. Moreover, her attitude and disposition about school seem to be worsening. What would you do as her parents? What factors would you consider important in making the decision? Or is the decision Jane's and hers alone?

POINT

Jane should be allowed to accelerate her educational pace. Moving to the seventh grade will benefit her greatly, intellectually and socially. Most girls develop more rapidly physically and socially than boys do. Skipping one grade will not hinder her social development at all. In fact, she will benefit from the interactions that she will have with other able students, some of whom will also have skipped a grade or two. Additionally, the research regarding the impact of accelerating students is positive, particularly if the students are carefully selected. Jane has been carefully evaluated and deserves to have the opportunity to be excited about learning and achieving again.

COUNTERPOINT

There are some inherent risks in having Jane skip her sixth grade experience and move on to the seventh grade. Jane is neither socially nor emotionally prepared to deal with the junior high environment. She may be very able intellectually, and her achievement may be superior, but this is not the time to move her into junior high. Socially, she is still quite awkward for her age. This awkwardness would be intensified in the junior high setting. Acceleration for Jane should be considered later on, when she has matured more socially.

She should be able to receive the acceleration that she needs in her present elementary school. Certainly, other able students in her school would benefit from joining together for various activities and learning experiences. The acceleration should take place in her own school, with other students who are gifted and of her own age. Maybe all Jane needs is some time to attend a class or two elsewhere. Using this approach, she could benefit from involvement with her same-age peers and still receive the stimulation that she so desperately needs. Allowing her to skip a grade now would hurt her emotionally and socially in the long run.

Again, research on acceleration and its impact reveals that carefully selected students profit greatly from such experiences (Assouline, 2003; Brody, 2004; Kulik, 2003; Shiever & Maker, 2003). Studies suggest that these accelerated students are well adjusted emotionally and socially, have positive self-concepts, and are on average not as troublesome as same-age peers (Gallagher, 2003). This is also true of gifted students who enter college earlier than peers. They perform well academically and benefit from the experiences associated with their university studies. Unfortunately, reform movements that stress equity have often reduced the number of specialized classes and experiences available for gifted students (Brody, 2004; Gallagher, 2003; Gottfredson, 2003).

> **Enrichment**
Educational experiences for gifted students that enhance their thinking skills and extend their knowledge in various areas.

ENRICHMENT. **Enrichment** experiences extend or broaden a person's knowledge (Parke, 2003; Schiever & Maker, 2003). Music appreciation, foreign languages, and mythology are enrichment courses that are added to a student's curriculum and are usually not any more difficult than other classes in which the student is involved. Other examples of enrichment involve experiences in which the student develops sophisticated thinking skills (synthesis, analysis, interpretation, and evaluation) or has opportunities to master advanced concepts in a particular subject area. Some forms of enrichment are actually types of acceleration. A student whose enrichment involves fully pursuing mathematical concepts that are well beyond his or her present grade level is experiencing a form of acceleration. Obviously, the two approaches are interrelated (Schiever & Maker, 2003).

Enrichment is the most common administrative approach to serving students who are gifted. It is also the most abused approach in that it is often applied in name only and in a sporadic fashion, without well-delineated objectives or rationales. There are also other problems with the enrichment approach. It is often implemented superficially, as a token response to the demands of parents of children who are gifted. Enrichment activities are viewed by some professionals as periods devoted to educational trivia or to instruction heavy in student assignments but light in content. Quality enrichment programs are characterized by carefully selected activities, modules, or units; challenging but not overwhelming assignments; and evaluations that are rigorous yet fair. Additionally, good enrichment programs focus on thoughtful and careful plans for student learning and on learning activities that stress higher-order thinking and application skills (Schiever & Maker, 2003).

Enrichment may include such activities as exploring exciting topics not normally pursued in the general curriculum, group-centered activities that focus on cognitive or affective skills and/or processes, and small-group investigations of actual, real-life problems (Renzulli & Reis, 2003). The keys to these endeavors are high student interest, excellent teaching, and superb mentoring (Feldhusen, 1998a & 1998b).

There is a paucity of systematic experimental research on enrichment programs (Schiever & Maker, 2003). Despite the limitations of current and past research, evidence supports the effectiveness of enrichment, particularly when it is delivered to specific ability groups and when the content and rigor of the curriculum coincide with the abilities of the targeted students (Schiever & Maker, 2003).

Enrichment activities do not appear to detract from the success that students experience on regularly administered achievement tests. Sociometric data on students who are pulled out of general education classrooms for enrichment activities are also positive. Students do not appear to suffer socially from involvement in enrichment programs that take place outside their general education classrooms. Acceleration and enrichment are complementary parts of curricular and service delivery systems for gifted children and youth (Schriever & Maker, 2003).

SPECIAL PROGRAMS AND SCHOOLS. Programs designed to nurture the talents of individuals in nonacademic areas, such as the visual and performing arts, have grown rapidly in recent years (Clasen & Clasen, 2003; Feldhusen, 2003; Kolloff, 2003; Olszewski-Kubilius, 2003; Winner & Martino, 2003). Students involved in these programs frequently spend half their school day working in academic subjects and the other half in arts studies. Often the arts instruction is provided by an independent institution, but some school systems maintain their own separate schools. Most programs provide training in the visual and performing arts, but a few emphasize instruction in creative writing, motion picture and television production, and photography. There are also residential schools for gifted students that specialize in developing stellar academic achievement and growth (Coleman, 2005). These schools become hothouses for rapid development and achievement in those academically able students whom they serve.

So-called governor's schools (distinctive summer programs generally held at university sites), talent identification programs, and specialized residential or high schools in various states also provide valuable opportunities for students who are talented and academically gifted (Davis & Rimm, 2004). Competitively selected students are provided with curricular experiences that are closely tailored to their individual aptitudes and interests. Faculties for these schools are meticulously selected for competence in various areas and for their ability to stimulate and motivate students. However, these schools and special programs are few and serve only a small number of the students who would profit from them.

CAREER EDUCATION. Career education, career guidance, and counseling are essential components of a comprehensive program for students who are gifted (Colangelo, 2003). Ultimately, career education activities and counseling are designed to help students make educational, occupational, and personal decisions. Because of their multipotentiality (their capacity for doing so many things well), it is frequently difficult for gifted students to make educational and career choices.

Differentiated learning experiences give elementary and middle school students opportunities to investigate and explore (Chuska, 2005). Many of these investigations and explorations are career-related and designed to help students understand what it might be like to be a zoologist, neurosurgeon, or film maker. Students also become familiar with the training and effort necessary for work in these fields. For gifted students in the elementary grades, these explorations often take place on Saturdays or weekends. They help such students understand themselves, their talents, and the preparations needed for entry into specific fields of advanced study.

In group meetings, gifted students and talented professionals may discuss the factors that influenced a scientist or group of researchers to pursue a given problem or conduct experiments that led to important discoveries or products. As students mature both cognitively and physically, the scope of their career education activities becomes more sophisticated and varied.

MENTORING. Some students are provided opportunities to work directly with research scientists, artists, musicians, or other professionals. Students may spend as many as three or four hours a day, two days a week, in laboratory facilities, mentored by the scientists and professionals with whom they work (Clasen & Clasen, 2003). Other students rely on intensive workshops or summer programs in which they are exposed to specialized careers through internships and individually tailored instruction (Olszewski-Kubilius, 2003).

The benefits of mentoring for gifted students are numerous. Students have sophisticated learning experiences that are highly motivating and stimulating. They gain invaluable opportunities to explore careers and to confirm their commitment to certain areas of study or reexamine their interests. Mentoring experiences may affirm potential in underachieving students or students with disabilities—potential that was not being tapped through conventional means. Mentoring may also promote the development of self-reliance, specific interpersonal skills, and life-long, productive friendships. As Clasen and Clasen (2003) indicated, "mentorships may mean the difference between a dream withered and a dream realized" (p. 265).

CAREER CHOICES AND CHALLENGES. Career interests, values, and dispositions appear to crystallize early in gifted students. In fact, their interests are neither broader nor more restricted than those of their classmates. Many gifted students know quite early what paths they will follow in postsecondary schooling. These paths often lead to careers in engineering, health professions, and physical sciences.

Counseling programs are particularly helpful to adolescents who are gifted. Often they know more about their academic content than they know about themselves (Colangelo, 2003). As gifted students come to understand themselves, their capacities, and their interests more fully, they will make better choices in selecting courses of study and professional careers (Moon, 2004).

Family counseling may also be helpful to parents and other family members. Problems caused by excessive or inappropriate parental expectations may need to be addressed in a family context. Counselors and therapists may help parents develop realistic expectations consistent with their child's abilities, aspirations, and true interests (Colangelo, 2003). As with other exceptionalities, counseling services are best provided through interdisciplinary/collaborative efforts.

PROBLEMS AND CHALLENGES OF GIFTEDNESS. Students who are gifted must cope with a number of problems. One problem is the expectations they have of themselves and those that have been explicitly and implicitly imposed by parents, teachers, and others. Students who are gifted frequently feel an inordinate amount of pressure to achieve high grades or to select particular professions. They often feel obligated or duty-bound to achieve excellence in every area, a syndrome called perfectionism (Colangelo & Davis, 2003; Callard-Szulgit, 2003a). Sadly, such pressure can foster a kind of conformity and prevent students from selecting avenues of endeavor that truly fit them and reflect their personal interests.

VanTassel-Baska (1989) identified several social-emotional needs that differentiate students who are gifted from their same-age peers:

➤ Understanding how they are different from and how they are similar to their peers

➤ Appreciating and valuing their own uniqueness as well as that of others

➤ Understanding and developing relationship skills

➤ Developing and valuing their high-level sensitivity

➤ Gaining a realistic understanding of their own abilities and talents

➤ Identifying ways of nurturing and developing their own abilities and talents

➤ Adequately distinguishing between the pursuit of excellence and the pursuit of perfection

➤ Developing behaviors associated with negotiation and compromise

Students who are gifted need ongoing and continual access to adult role models who have interests and abilities that parallel theirs; the importance of these role models cannot be overstated (Clasen & Clasen, 2003). Role models are particularly important for gifted students who grow up and receive their schooling in rural and remote areas. Such students often complete their public schooling without the benefit of having a mentor or professional person with whom they can talk or discuss various educational and career-related issues. Some students who live in rural or remote communities now have access to mentoring at a distance through telementoring or the Internet. Examples of this form of mentoring include the National Mentoring Partnership,

REFLECT ON THIS · A SAD LOSS

He started reading as a toddler, played piano at age 3 and delivered a high school commencement speech in cap and gown when he was just 10—his eyes barely visible over the podium.

Brandenn Bremmer was a child prodigy: He composed and recorded music, won piano competitions, breezed through college courses with an off-the-charts IQ, and mastered everything from archery to photography, hurtling through life precociously. Then, last Tuesday, Brandenn was found dead in his Nebraska home from an apparent self-inflicted gunshot wound to his head. He was just 14. He left no note.

"Sometimes we wonder if maybe the physical, earthly world didn't offer him enough challenges and he felt it was time to move on and do something great," his mother, Patricia, said from the family home in Venango, Nebraska, a few miles from the Colorado border. Brandenn exhibited no signs of depression, she said. He had just shown his family the art for the cover of his new CD that was about to be released.

He was, according to his family and teachers, an extraordinary blend of fun-loving child and serious adult. He loved Harry Potter and Mozart. He watched cartoons and enjoyed video games but gave classical piano concerts for hundreds of people—without a hint of stage fright. "He wasn't just talented, he was just a really nice young man," said David Wohl, an assistant professor at Colorado State University, where Brandenn studied music after high school. "He had an easy smile. He really was unpretentious."

Patricia Bremmer—who writes mysteries and has long raised dogs with her husband, Martin—said they both knew their son was special from the moment he was born. The brown-haired, blue-eyed boy was reading when he was 18 months old and was entering classical piano competitions by age 4. "He was born an adult," his mother said. "We just watched his body grow bigger." He scored 178 on one IQ test, a test his mother said he was too bored to finish.

Adapted from *Child Prodigy's Apparent Suicide: 'He Knew He Had to Leave,' Mother Says,* by Sharon Cohen, Associated Press, New York, March 19, 2005.

sponsored by the U.S. Department of Education; the SET (Study of Exceptional Talent) Mentor Program Center for Talented Youth, sponsored by John Hopkins University; and the Hewlett Packard Email Mentor Program (Clasen & Clasen, 2003).

Historically Neglected Groups

Females

Gifted females face several problems, particularly during the middle school years. During this time period, their confidence may wane. It may be eclipsed by uncertainty and diminished expectations for success. These girls begin to discount their intelligence and related abilities in an effort to enhance their chances for social acceptance and minimize their risk of social isolation.

The number of girls identified as gifted appears to decline with age. Olshen (1987) referred to this decline as the disappearance of giftedness in girls. This phenomenon is surprising when we consider that girls tend to walk and talk earlier than their male counterparts; that girls, as a group, read earlier; that girls score higher than boys on IQ tests during the preschool years; and that the grade-point averages of girls during the elementary years are higher than those of boys (Kerr & Nicpon, 2003).

Just exactly what happens to girls? Is the decline in the number of girls identified as gifted related to their socialization? Does some innate physiological or biological mechanism account for this decline? Why do some gifted females fail to realize their potential? To what extent do value conflicts about women's roles contribute to mixed achievement in gifted women? The answers to these and other important questions are gradually emerging (Kerr & Nicpon, 2003; Reis, 2003).

One of the explanations given for this decline is the gender role socialization that girls receive. Behaviors associated with competitiveness, risk taking, and independence are not generally encouraged in girls. Behaviors that are generally fostered in girls include dependence, cooperation, and nurturing. The elimination of independent behaviors in girls is viewed by Silverman (1986) as the most damaging aspect of their socialization. More recent research suggests that girls who develop social self-esteem, "the belief that one has the ability to act effectively and to make decisions independently," are more likely to realize their potential (Davis & Rimm, 2004). Without independence, the development of high levels of creativity, achievement, and leadership are severely limited. Overcoming the impact of sociocultural influences requires carefully applied interventions, counseling, and heightened levels of awareness (Davis & Rimm, 2004; Kerr & Nicpon, 2003; Maltby & Devlin, 2000). The Reflect on This "Encouraging giftedness in girls" lists ways in which families and teachers of gifted girls can help them realize their full potential.

Females who are gifted and talented experience additional problems (Davis & Rimm, 2004), including fear of appearing "unfeminine" or unattractive when competing with males, competition between marital and career aspirations, stress induced by traditional cultural and societal expectations, and self-imposed and/or culturally imposed restrictions related to educational and occupational choices. Although many of these problems are far from being resolved at this point, some progress is being made. Women in greater numbers are choosing to enter professions traditionally pursued by men (Davis & Rimm, 2004; Kerr & Nicpon, 2003).

Fortunately, multiple role assignments are emerging in many families, wherein the tasks traditionally performed by mothers are shared by all members of the family or are completed by someone outside the family. Cultural expectations are changing, and as a result, options for women who are gifted are rapidly expanding (Davis & Rimm, 2004; Kerr & Nicpon, 2003).

Persons with Disabilities

For some time, intellectual giftedness has been largely associated with high IQs and high scores on aptitude tests. These tests, by their very nature and structure, measure a

FOCUS 8
Identify four challenges that females face in dealing with their giftedness.

Council for Exceptional Children

Standard 1: Foundations

The world benefits significantly from gifted women like Madeline Albright who served in vitally important government, business, education, and service arenas.

SUGGESTIONS FOR THE FAMILY

Hold high expectations for daughters.

Do not purchase gender-role-stereotyped toys.

Avoid overprotectiveness.

Encourage high levels of activity.

Allow girls to get dirty.

Instill beliefs in their capabilities.

Support their interests.

Identify them as gifted during their preschool years.

Find for them playmates who are gifted to identify with and emulate.

Foster interests in mathematics outside of school.

Consider early entrance and other opportunities to accelerate.

Encourage enrollment in mathematics courses.

Introduce them to professional women in many occupations.

Encourage their mothers to acknowledge their own giftedness.

Encourage their mothers to work at least part-time outside the home.

Encourage fathers to spend time alone with daughters in so-called masculine activities.

Share household duties equally between the parents.

Assign chores to siblings on a nonsexist basis.

Discourage the use of sexist language or teasing in the home.

Monitor television programs for sexist stereotypes, and discuss these with children of both genders.

Encourage siblings to treat each other equitably, rather than according to the traditional gender role stereotypes they may see outside the home.

SUGGESTIONS FOR TEACHERS AND COUNSELORS

Believe in girls' logicomathematical abilities, and provide many opportunities for them to practice mathematical reasoning within other subject areas.

Accelerate girls through the science and mathematics curriculum whenever possible.

Have special clubs in mathematics for girls who are high-achieving.

Design coeducational career development classes in which both girls and boys learn about career potentialities for women.

Expose boys and girls to role models of women in various careers.

Discuss nontraditional careers for women, including salaries for men and women and schooling requirements.

Help girls set long-term goals.

Discuss underachievement among females who are gifted and ask how they can combat it in themselves and others.

Have girls read biographies of famous women.

Arrange opportunities for girls to "shadow" a female professional for a few days to see what her work entails.

Discourage sexist remarks and attitudes in the classroom.

Boycott sexist classroom materials, and write to the publishers for their immediate correction.

Discuss sexist messages in the media.

Advocate special classes and after-school enrichment opportunities for students who are gifted.

Form support groups for girls with similar interests.

SOURCE: From "What Happens to the Gifted Girl?" by L. K. Silverman. In *Critical Issues in Gifted Education, Vol. 1*: *Defensible Programs for the Gifted,* edited by C. J. Maker, 1986, pp. 43–89. Austin, TX: Pro-Ed. (Copyright owned by author.) Adapted by permission.

limited range of mental abilities. Because of such limitations, they have not been particularly helpful in identifying persons with disabilities who are intellectually or otherwise gifted. However, persons with disabilities such as cerebral palsy, learning disabilities, emotional and behavior disorders, and other disabling conditions can be gifted (Baum, 2004; Montgomery, 2003; Newman & Sternberg, 2004; Davis & Rimm, 2004). Helen Keller, Vincent van Gogh, and Ludwig van Beethoven are prime examples of individuals with disabilities who were also gifted. Some theorists and practitioners suggest that as many as 2% of individuals with disabilities are gifted. Fortunately, we have begun to look for various kinds of giftedness in children and youth with disabilities.

In this context, individuals who are gifted and disabled are persons with exceptional ability or potential and who achieve high performance despite such disabilities as hearing, speech, orthopedic, or emotional impairments, learning disabilities, or health problems, either singly or in combination (Davis & Rimm, 2004). Although many challenges are still associated with identifying individuals with disabilities who are gifted, much progress has been made.

Unfortunately, the giftedness of children with disabilities is often invisible to parents and teachers. Factors critical to the recognition of giftedness include (1) environments that elicit signs of talent and capacity and (2) availability of information about the individual's performance gathered from many sources. With regard to these eliciting environments, it is important that the child be given opportunities to perform tasks on which his or her disabling condition is no impediment. Also, if and when tests of mental ability are used, they must be appropriately adapted, in both administration and scoring (Davis & Rimm, 2004). Furthermore, the identification screening should occur at regular intervals. Some children with disabilities change dramatically with appropriate instruction and related assistive technologies. The developmental delays present in children with disabilities and the disabilities themselves pose the greatest challenges to identification efforts (Baum, 2004; Davis & Rimm, 2004).

Itzhak Perlman is one of the most gifted violinists of our time. Performing here with the University of Southern Mississippi Symphony Orchestra, he has been a friend and mentor to countless numbers of young musicians. He was struck with polio at the age of four and has been a tireless advocate for the rights of persons with disabilities throughout his life.

Differential education for children with disabilities who are gifted is still in its infancy. A great deal of progress has been made, particularly in the adaptive uses of computers and related technologies, but much remains to be done. Additionally, a great deal is still unknown about the service delivery systems and materials that are best suited for these individuals. One of the best things that parents and teachers can do for children and youth with disabilities who are gifted is to foster self-confidence and independence. Unfortunately, the need for one-to-one instruction frequently gives rise to dependence and undermines self-confidence (Davis & Rimm, 2004).

Children and Youth from Diverse Cultural, Linguistic, Ethnic, and Economic Backgrounds

Very rarely are culturally diverse and economically disadvantaged youth identified as gifted (Baldwin, 2004; Davis & Rimm, 2004). These youth are dramatically underrepresented in programs for the gifted and talented (Briggs, Reis, Eckert, & Baum, 2006; Esquivel & Houtz, 2000; Smutny, 2003). Ford (2003) has suggested that this underrepresentation is a function of several factors: excessive reliance on testing and test scores that may not accurately capture potential and talent in these youth, IQ-based definitions of giftedness, identification based on achievement test scores, and polices and practices that are exclusive rather than inclusive. As suggested at the beginning of this chapter, we are now focusing more on inclusive practices in identifying giftedness and are paying more attention to talent development.

Identification procedures often fail to identify children as being gifted when they come from minority groups or disadvantaged environments (Baldwin, 2004). Consider this insight provided by Aquirre (2003): "It is paradoxical that many educators continue to believe that English language proficiency is essential prior to placement in gifted programs. Giftedness is not a trait inherent to native English speakers. Gifted programs must mirror the population of any given community" (p. 17). Many practitioners are now using multiple criteria to reveal potential giftedness in children who are poor or from diverse cultural and linguistic backgrounds (Davis & Rimm, 2004). Past research conducted by VanTassel-Baska and Chepko-Sade (1986) has suggested that as many as 15% of the gifted population may be children from diverse cultural, linguistic, and economic backgrounds.

Effective instructional programs for children and adolescents who are disadvantaged and gifted have several key components. First and foremost, the teachers in these programs are well trained in adapting and differentiating instruction for these students. They understand learning styles, how to build and capitalize on students' interests, and how to maximize students' affective, cognitive, and ethical capacities. In addition to providing the typical curricular options for enrichment, acceleration, and talent development, the best programs for these children and youth embrace and celebrate ethnic diversity, provide extracurricular cultural enrichment, attend to differences in learning styles, provide counseling, foster parent support groups and community connections, and give these children and youth access to significant role models (Davis & Rimm, 2004).

FOCUS 9
Identify eight important elements of programs for gifted children who come from diverse backgrounds and who may live in poverty.

There is general agreement that programs for these children and youth should begin early and should be tailored to the needs and interests of each identified child. They should focus on individual potentialities rather than deficits and should help parents and others understand their roles in fostering giftedness and talent development (Baum, 2004). Often, the emphasis in the early years is on reading instruction, language development, and foundation skills. Other key components include experiential education that provides children with many opportunities for hands-on learning, activities that foster self-expression, plentiful use of mentors and role models who represent the child's cultural or ethnic group, involvement of the community, and counseling throughout the school years that gives serious consideration to the cultural values of the family and the child who is gifted. Finally, the programs are enhanced by collaborative approaches in which mentors, parents, teachers, and other community members work collaboratively to meet the needs of these very special children.

▼SNAPSHOT

SADIKIFU

Sadi's mother, Thelma, who was one week shy of her 41st birthday when her only child was born, considers her son a gift from Allah. He was unexpected and unplanned. Thelma and Sadi's father, who never married, became Muslims in the 1970s, and they gave their son an Islamic name—Sadikifu—which means "truthful and honest."

Because Thelma never had been around children, and Sadi was her only child, she talked to him like a peer. That is one reason, she believes, why he is so bright and articulate. In the third grade he was classified as gifted by the school district when he scored in the 95th percentile on a national achievement test. In the fourth grade he won an oratorical contest, sponsored by a local bank, for a speech on homelessness. Thelma still proudly displays the trophy—next to a picture of Elijah Muhammad—in her small, immaculate two-bedroom apartment (p. 32).

Sadi, unfortunately, went the wrong way. In the ninth grade, he enrolled in Crenshaw's gifted program, but after only two months of high school he was thrown out for instigating a fight between his tagging crew and a rival set. Although his mother was livid, Sadi's expulsion probably saved his life because the next afternoon his best friend was shot to death by a rival tagging crew called "Nothin' But Trouble." Sadi always spent every day after school with his friend, whose street name was Chaos. Sadi knew that if he had not been stuck all afternoon enrolling in his new high school, he would have been walking down Vermont Avenue with Chaos. He probably would have been killed, too (pp. 33–34).

On Sadi's first day of school he discovered he was the only black student in his gifted classes. When students passed out worksheets, they skipped him. When he asked for the assignments, the students invariably said, "I thought you were here for detention."

Although he was now attending a suburban high school far from South-Central, at night and on weekends he was immersed in the gang life. He had graduated from his tagging crew to the Front Hood 60s and was known by his street name—Little Cloudy. And even though he had been arrested several times, three of his homies had recently been killed in drive-bys, and about ten were in jail, he kept gangbanging.

One weekday afternoon, when school was canceled because of an earthquake, he and two other 60s were walking down Western Avenue, on their way to buy some Thunderbird at a liquor store near 69th Street. They spotted a teenager across the street whom they did not recognize. Sadi and his two homies threw up the hand sign for the Front Hood 60s. The gangbanger across the street threw up the sign for the Eight-Tray Gangsters, a bitter rival of the 60s. One of Sadi's homies pulled out a semiautomatic .380-caliber pistol and fired at the Eight-Tray. Then everyone sprinted for cover. Two LAPD officers in a patrol car heard the shots, pulled up, and grabbed Sadi and another 60. The shooter and the Eight-Tray, who had not been hit, escaped.

Sadi and his homie were handcuffed, arrested, and taken to the 77th Street Division station. They were questioned by detectives, who then dabbed their hands with a sticky aluminum tab that tests for gunshot residue. When the test came back negative and a witness told detectives that neither of them was the shooter, they were released. But the incident precipitated an epiphany for Sadi.

Seeing the flash of the gun, just inches away, marked a turning point for him. It inalterably changed the course of his life. In an instant, he realized how transitory life was, how transitory *his* life was. How all his decisions were wrong. How he was destined to die in a drive-by or languish in prison. He realized that maybe his mother had been right about school. Maybe his intelligence was, as his mother told him, a gift from Allah (pp. 34–35).

SOURCE: From *And Still We Rise* (pp. 32–35), by M. Corwin, 2000, New York: Morrow.

FOCUS REVIEW

FOCUS 1 Briefly describe several historical developments directly related to the measurement of various types of giftedness.

- Alfred Binet developed the first developmental scale for children during the early 1900s. Gradually, there emerged the notion of mental age, a representation of what the child was capable of doing compared with age-specific developmental tasks.
- Lewis M. Terman translated the Binet scale and made modifications suitable for children in the United States.
- Gradually, the intelligence quotient, or IQ, became the gauge for determining giftedness.
- Intelligence was long viewed as a unitary structure or underlying ability. But this view gradually changed, and researchers began to believe that intelligence was represented in a variety of distinct capacities and abilities.
- J. P. Guilford and other social scientists began to develop a multidimensional theory of intelligence, which prompted researchers to devise models and assessment devices for examining creativity.
- Programs to foster creativity in young people were gradually developed.
- More recently, V. Ramos-Ford and H. Gardner developed the theory of multiple intelligences, which manifest themselves in linguistic, logical-mathematical, spatial, musical, bodily-kinesthetic, interpersonal, and intrapersonal behaviors.

FOCUS 2 Identify four major components of definitions that have been developed to describe giftedness.

- Children and youth with outstanding talent perform, or show the potential for performing, at remarkably high levels of accomplishment when compared with others of their age, experience, or environment.
- Gifted children and youth exhibit high performance capability in intellectual, creative, and/or artistic areas, possess an unusual leadership capacity, or excel in specific academic fields.
- Gifted children and youth require services or activities not ordinarily provided by schools.
- Outstanding talents are present in children and youth from all cultural groups, across all economic strata, and in all areas of human endeavor.

FOCUS 3 Identify four problems inherent in accurately describing the characteristics of individuals who are gifted.

- Individuals who are gifted vary significantly on a variety of characteristics; they are not a homogeneous group.
- Because research on the characteristics of people who are gifted has been conducted with different population groups, the characteristics that have surfaced tend to represent the population studied rather than the gifted population as a whole.

- Many early studies of individuals who are gifted led to a stereotypical view of giftedness.
- Historically, studies on the characteristics of individuals who are gifted have not included adequate samples of females, minority or ethnic groups, or the poor.

FOCUS 4 Identify three factors that appear to contribute significantly to the emergence of various forms of giftedness.

- Genetic endowment certainly contributes to giftedness.
- Environmental stimulation provided by parents, teachers, coaches, tutors, and others contributes significantly to the emergence of giftedness.
- The interaction of innate abilities with environmental influences and encouragement fosters the development and expression of giftedness.

FOCUS 5 Indicate the range of assessment devices used to identify the various types of giftedness.

- Developmental checklists and scales
- Parent and teacher inventories
- Intelligence and achievement tests
- Creativity tests
- Other diverse observational information provided by parents, grandparents, and other knowledgeable informants

FOCUS 6 Identify eight strategies that are utilized to foster the development of children and adolescents who are gifted.

- Environmental stimulation provided by parents from infancy through adolescence.
- Differentiated education and specialized service delivery systems that provide enrichment activities and/or possibilities for acceleration. Examples include early entrance to kindergarten or school; grade skipping; early admission to college; honors programs at the high school and college levels; specialized schools in the performing and visual arts, math, and science; mentor programs with university professors and other talented individuals; and specialized counseling services.

FOCUS 7 What are some of the social-emotional needs of students who are gifted?

- Understanding, appreciating, and valuing their own uniqueness as well as that of others
- Understanding the importance and the development of relationship skills
- Expanding and valuing their high-level sensitivity
- Gaining a realistic understanding of their own abilities and talents
- Identifying ways of nurturing and developing their own abilities and talents

- Adequately distinguishing between the pursuit of excellence and the pursuit of perfection
- Developing behaviors associated with negotiation and compromise

FOCUS 8 Identify four challenges that females face in dealing with their giftedness.

- Fear of appearing "unfeminine" or unattractive when competing with males
- Competition between marital and career aspirations
- Stress induced by traditional cultural and societal expectations
- Self-imposed and/or culturally imposed restrictions related to educational and occupational choices

FOCUS 9 Identify eight important elements of programs for gifted children who come from diverse backgrounds and who may live in poverty.

- The programs are staffed with skilled and competent teachers and other support personnel.

- The staff members work as a collaborative team.
- Teachers and others responsible for shaping the learning experience understand learning styles, students' interests, and how to build students' affective, cognitive, and ethical capacities.
- The programs maintain and encourage ethnic diversity, provide extracurricular cultural enrichment, offer counseling, foster parent support groups, and give children and youth access to significant models.
- The programs focus on students' strengths, not on their deficits.
- The programs help parents understand their key role in developing their children's talents and giftedness.
- The programs provide many opportunities for hands-on learning, activities that foster self-expression, and generous use of mentors and role models from the child's cultural or ethnic group.
- The programs are characterized by a team approach involving parents, teachers, mentors, and other family members.

BUILDING YOUR PORTFOLIO

Council for Exceptional Children

If you are thinking about a career in special education, you should know that many states use national standards developed by the Council for Exceptional Children (CEC) to assess a teacher candidate's knowledge and skills for working with students with disabilities. See a complete listing of the ten CEC Content Standards on the inside front cover of this text.

CEC Content Standards Addressed in This Chapter

1 Foundations
2 Development and Characteristics of Learners
3 Individual Learning Differences
5 Learning Environments and Social Interactions
7 Instructional Planning
8 Assessment

Assess Your Knowledge of the CEC Standards Addressed in This Chapter

Some states require that teacher candidates develop a portfolio of products that demonstrate mastery of the CEC content standards. To assist in the development of products for this portfolio, you may wish to complete the following activities.

- Complete a written test of the chapter's content.

  If your instructor requires a written test of your content knowledge for this chapter, keep a copy for your portfolio. A practice test on the information covered in this chapter is available through the companion website (college.hmco.com/pic/hardman9e) and the Student Study Guide.

- Respond to the Application Questions for the Case Study "Is Calvin Gifted?"

  Review the Case Study and respond in writing to the application questions. Keep a copy of the Case Study and of your written response for your portfolio.

- Participate in a Community Service Learning Activity.

  Community service is a valuable way to enhance your learning experience. Visit our companion website for suggested community service learning activities that correspond to the information presented in this chapter. Develop a reflective journal of the service learning experience for your portfolio.

WEB RESOURCES

National Association for Gifted Children

http://www.nagc.org

This nonprofit organization is composed of parents, teachers, educators, and other professionals. It promotes programs, polices, and legislation that benefit gifted children and youth. This website provides valuable information for individuals who are interested in promoting educational and other support services for children and youth who are gifted, talented, or creative.

National Research Center on the Gifted and Talented

http://www.gifted.uconn.edu/nrcgt.html

This center is funded by the Jacob K. Javits Gifted and Talented Students Education Act. It represents a national array of researchers, practitioners, policy makers, and other individuals who are interested in promoting the development of gifted young people from preschool through postsecondary levels. Its website contains many resources for parents, teachers, and professionals interested in gifted education.

Center for Talented Youth at Johns Hopkins University

http://www.jhu.edu/gifted/

This website describes the programs and opportunities offered through the center, which identifies academically talented students in grades 2 through 8 and provides distinctive educational programs through their first and second years of high school. This identification takes place through a talent search in which students are sought out because of their high national test scores in mathematics. The center also sponsors summer programs and conferences tailored to the special interests of gifted students.

Duke University Talent Identification Program

http://www.tip.duke.edu/

This website provides information for educational leaders who are interested in identifying and providing innovative programs for gifted children and youth. The site also offers valuable information about developing model programs for academically able children and youth.

Center for Gifted Education Policy

http://www.apa.org/ed/cgep.html

This website promotes public awareness of gifted children and youth. It also provides current information about research and innovative programs for gifted children and youth. The website focuses on programs and initiatives for all kinds of giftedness, including academics, sports, and the performing arts.

FURTHER READINGS

Colangelo, N., & Davis, G. A. (2003). *Handbook on Gifted Education.* Boston: Allyn and Bacon.

This graduate-level text explores the many and varied aspects of the education of gifted people. The contributing authors are all respected and eminently qualified scholars.

Parke, N. P. (2003). *Discovering Programs for Talent Development.* Thousand Oaks, CA: Corwin Press.

This book is designed for general educators who work regularly, in their classrooms, with children who are gifted. Outlined are 65 programs that advance talent development in gifted learners.

Purcell, J. H., & Eckert, R. D. (2006). *Designing Services and Programs for High-Ability Learners: A Guidebook for Gifted Education.* Thousand Oaks, CA: Corwin Press and National Association for Gifted Children.

This handbook, edited and authored by authorities in the field of gifted education, is an excellent resource for educators. It provides information about all aspects of services and programming for gifted children and youth.

Coleman, L. J. (2005). *Nurturing Talent in High School.* New York: Teachers College, Columbia University.

This is an intriguing study of a residential high school for gifted students. It comprehensively reveals in precise detail the lives of students who attend the Greenhouse Institute, describes the connections that the school established and nourishes with parents and families, and even shares the pranks and other antics of its able students.

COMPANION WEBSITE

Visit the companion website at college.hmco.com/pic/hardman9e for additional resources that support this text:

- HM Video Cases that present actual classroom scenarios that you may face every day as a teacher

- Practice ACE Exams that will help you prepare for quizzes, tests, and certfication exams

- Flashcards of key terms

- Weblinks

Appendix: What Every Teacher Should Know About IDEA 2004

Myrna Mandlawitz

MRM Associates, Legislative and Consulting Services

Abbreviations Key

AYP: adequate yearly progress

FAPE: free appropriate public education

HOUSSE: High Objective Uniform State Standard of Education

IAES: interim alternative educational setting

IDEA: Individuals with Disabilities Education Act

IEP: individualized education program

IFSP: individualized family service plan

LEA: local educational agency (local school district)

LRE: least restrictive environment

NCLB: No Child Left Behind Act of 2001

NIMAC: National Instructional Materials Access Center

NIMAS: National Instructional Materials Accessibility Standard

SEA: State educational agency

"Secretary": United States Secretary of Education

Table of Contents

PART A: General Provisions

Section 602: Definitions

Several new definitions have been added to the IDEA, reflecting the continuing evolution of the law and the desire to align the IDEA with the No Child Left Behind Act of 2001 (NCLB).

IDEA '97 (P.L. 105-17)	IDEA '04 (P.L. 108-446)
Sec. 602(1). "Assistive Technology Device." Any item, equipment, or product used to increase, maintain, or improve functional capabilities.	**Sec. 602(1)(B). "Assistive Technology Device."** Adds that term does not include surgically implanted medical device or replacement of such a device.

"Assistive Technology Device." This exception arose in part from a concern, heightened by several due process hearings, that school districts might be held responsible for provision of cochlear implants for children with hearing impairments.

IDEA '97 (P.L. 105-17)	IDEA '04 (P.L. 108-446)
Sec. 602. "Core Academic Subjects." No comparable language in IDEA '97.	**Sec. 602(4). "Core Academic Subjects."** Adds NCLB definition (Sec. 9101) "Core Academic Subjects" are English, reading and language arts, mathematics, science, foreign languages, civics and government, economics, arts, history, and geography.

Sec. 602. "Highly Qualified." No comparable language in IDEA '97.	**Sec. 602(10). "Highly Qualified."**
	1. Requirements for All Special Education Teachers:
	  a. All special education teachers come under NCLB definition (Sec. 9101); *PLUS, special education teachers must*
	  b. Have State special education certification OR have passed State licensing exam AND have license to teach special education;
	  c. Have not had certification or licensure waived on emergency, temporary, or provisional basis; AND
	  d. Have at least a bachelor's degree.
	
	2. Special Education Teachers Teaching Students under Alternate Achievement Standards:
	Used for teachers teaching core academic subjects *only* to children assessed against alternate standards, as established under NCLB regulations.
	  a. Must EITHER meet NCLB Highly Qualified requirements (Sec. 9101) for any teacher new or not new to the profession, OR
	  b. Meet NCLB requirements for elementary teachers or middle or high school teachers with subject knowledge appropriate to the level of instruction being provided.
	
	3. Special Education Teachers Teaching Multiple Subjects:
	Applicable to those teaching two or more core academic subjects *only* to children with disabilities.
	  a. Must EITHER meet NCLB highly qualified requirements for any teacher new or not new to the profession; OR
	  b. If not a new teacher, must demonstrate competence in all subjects taught, as under NCLB, which may include "high objective uniform State standard of evaluation" (HOUSSE) covering multiple subjects; OR
	  c. If a new teacher who is highly qualified in math, language arts, or science, must demonstrate competence in other core subjects taught, as under NCLB, which may include a HOUSSE, *not later than 2 years after being hired.*

4. This definition does not create a right of action by a single student or a class of students for failure of the teacher to be highly qualified.

5. Teachers deemed highly qualified under this provision are considered highly qualified for purposes of NCLB.

"Highly Qualified." The addition of this definition to the IDEA is very significant. The NCLB definition of "highly qualified" refers to "any public elementary or secondary school teacher" and requires those teachers to meet this standard by the close of school year 2005–2006. Considerable debate has occurred since the passage of NCLB on whether special education teachers, who are not specifically mentioned in NCLB, were also required to meet the "highly qualified" provisions of that law. The debate was particularly intense because NCLB requires that new teachers teaching multiple core subjects, as defined in NCLB and now in the IDEA, have an academic major or advanced degree, or pass a competency exam in each subject area taught. Teachers not new to the profession under NCLB may demonstrate competency based on a "high objective uniform State standard of evaluation" (HOUSSE), which may involve multiple measures of teacher competency as established by the individual State.

Because middle or high school special education teachers working in a resource capacity provide assistance to students in the full range of academic subject areas, the standard for new teachers would have proven particularly difficult for most special education teachers to meet. Therefore, the IDEA allows special educators teaching multiple core subjects to (a) meet either the NCLB requirements for teachers new or not new to the profession; (b) meet the HOUSSE option; or, (c) for teachers already deemed highly qualified in math, language arts, or science, establish competence not later than two years after being hired in any other core areas taught.

According to the conference report accompanying the IDEA amendments (H. Rep. No. 108-77, Nov. 17, 2004, p. 171), special education teachers providing only consultative services to general education teachers should be considered "highly qualified" if they meet the requirements for "all special education teachers," as outlined above (Sec. 602(10)(a)). Consultative services do not include direct instruction in core academic subjects, but may include adjustments to the learning environment, modification of instructional methods, and curriculum adaptations.

Sec. 602. "Homeless Children." No comparable language in IDEA '97.

Sec. 602(11). "Homeless Children." Adds definition from McKinney-Vento Homeless Assistance Act (Sec. 725): Children who don't have a regular, adequate nighttime residence, including children (a) sharing others' housing due to loss of housing, economic hardship, or similar reason; living in motels, hotels, trailer parks, or campgrounds due to lack of alternative adequate accommodations; living in emergency or transitional shelters; abandoned in hospitals; or awaiting foster care placement; (b) whose primary nighttime residence is a public or private place not designed for or ordinarily used for regular sleeping accommodation; (c) living in cars, public spaces, abandoned buildings, substandard housing, bus or train stations, or similar settings; and, (d) who are migratory youth living in circumstances described in (a)–(c).

Sec. 602. "Limited English Proficient." No comparable language in IDEA '97.

Sec. 602(18). "Limited English Proficient." Adds definition from NCLB (Sec. 9101): An individual, aged 3–21, enrolled or preparing to enroll in an elementary or secondary school,

1. (a) who wasn't born in the U.S. or whose native language isn't English; (b) who is a Native American or Alaska Native, or native resident of the outlying areas and comes from an environment where a language other than English has significantly impacted level of English language proficiency; or (c) ho is migratory, with a native language other than English, from an environment where a language other than English is dominant; and

2. whose difficulties in speaking, reading, writing, or understanding English may be sufficient to deny the child (a) ability to meet proficient level of achievement on State

	assessments; (b) ability to successfully achieve in class where instruction is in English; or (c) opportunity to participate fully in society.
Sec. 602. "Ward of the State." No comparable language in IDEA '97.	*Sec. 602(36). "Ward of the State."* Adds new definition: A child who, as determined by State of residence, is a foster child, ward of the State, or in custody of a public child welfare agency. Does not include foster children whose foster parents meet IDEA "parent" definition.

"Homeless Children," "Limited English Proficient," and "Ward of the State." These additions clarify that every child who is a "child with a disability" under the law must be provided special education and related services and receive the protections of the IDEA, regardless of socioeconomic, language, or other differences. While the spirit and intent of the law has always been that all children with disabilities needing special education and related services are located and served, the law has never specified these categories of children.

Sec. 602(19). "Parent." Includes legal guardians and surrogate parents.	*Sec. 602(23). "Parent."* Adds "natural, adoptive, or foster parent"; guardian (but not the State if child is a ward of the State); or a person acting in place of a natural or adoptive parent with whom the child lives or who is legally responsible for the child.
Sec. 602(22). "Related Services." Transportation, and developmental, corrective, and supportive services. A number of specific services are mentioned, but the list is not intended to be exclusive.	*Sec. 602(26). "Related Services."* Adds "school nurse services" and "interpreting services."
Sec. 602(30). "Transition Services." Services designed to promote movement from school to postschool activities based on students' needs and taking into account preferences and interests.	*Sec. 602(34). "Transition Services."* Adds that services must be focused on improving academic and functional achievement, and that the student's strengths must also be taken into account.
Sec. 602. "Universal Design." No comparable language in IDEA '97.	*Sec. 602(35). "Universal Design."* Adds definition from the Assistive Technology Act of 1998 (Sec. 3): "A concept or philosophy for designing and delivering products and services that are usable by people with the widest possible range of functional capabilities, which include products and services that are directly usable (without requiring assistive technologies) and products and services that are made usable with assistive technologies."

"Universal Design." With few exceptions, children with disabilities are expected to meet the same high academic standards as children without disabilities using the general education curriculum. The dearth of instructional materials and assessment tools that are accessible, valid, and appropriate for use with children with a broad range of disabilities has made this goal more difficult. The concept of universal design is incorporated throughout the amendments to the law. The law allows States to use federal funds to support technology with universal design principles, requires that States and school districts develop and administer assessments, to the extent feasible, using these principles; and, directs research toward incorporating universal design into the development of standards, assessments, curricula, and instructional methods.

Sections 607–609: Requirements for Prescribing Regulations; State Administration; Paperwork Reduction

IDEA '97 (P.L. 105-17)

IDEA '04 (P.L. 108-446)

Sec. 607. Requirements for Prescribing Regulations. Public shall have at least 90 days to comment on proposed regulations. Regulations may not be implemented in any way that lessens protections of the law.	***Sec. 607. Requirements for Prescribing Regulations.*** Public comment period is changed to not less than 75 days. Regulations are limited only to those necessary to ensure compliance with requirements of the law.
Sec. 608. State Administration. No comparable language in IDEA '97.	***608. State Administration.*** States must notify LEAs and the Secretary in writing of any State rules, regulations, or policies not required by federal law or regulation. States must minimize the number of such rules, regulations, or policies, and those that are issued must be designed to enable students to meet academic achievement standards.
Sec. 609. Paperwork Reduction. No comparable language in IDEA '97.	***Sec. 609. Paperwork Reduction.*** Authorizes a 15-State pilot program authorizing waivers of Part B statutory or regulatory requirements to reduce "excessive paperwork and non-instructional time burdens" that do not improve students' educational or functional results. Requirements pertaining to civil rights or procedural safeguards may not be waived, and waivers may not affect the right to a free appropriate public education (FAPE). The Secretary will include information in an annual report to Congress on the effectiveness of waivers, including recommendations for broader implementation of waivers.

PART B: Assistance for Education of All Children with Disabilities

Section 611: Allotment and Use of Funds; Authorization of Appropriations

IDEA '97 (P.L. 105-17)

IDEA '04 (P.L. 108-446)

Sec. 611. Technical Assistance. No comparable language in IDEA '97.	***Sec. 611(c). Technical Assistance.*** Secretary may reserve not more than $\frac{1}{2}$ of 1% of Part B funds for technical assistance to States under the monitoring and enforcement section (Sec. 616).
Sec. 611(f). State-Level Activities. IDEA '97 provides a list of required activities paid out of State activity funds from which States may choose.	***Sec. 611(e)(2)(B). Required Activities; (C). Authorized Activities.*** States, as in IDEA '97, are required to use reserved funds for monitoring, enforcement, and complaint investigation, and to implement mediation. The law now includes a list of discretionary uses for State activity funds. These activities include: reducing paperwork; assisting LEAs to provide positive behavioral supports and interventions, and appropriate mental health services; improving classroom use of technology; developing transition programs, alternative programs for expelled students, and appropriate accommodations and alternate assessments; and, providing technical assistance to schools identified for improvement under NCLB.

Sec. 611. *Local Educational Agency Risk Pool.* No comparable language in IDEA '97.

Sec. 611(e)(3). *Local Educational Agency Risk Pool.* States may opt to reserve annually 10% of funds reserved for State-level activities to establish a high-cost fund and to support innovative ways of cost sharing.

1. The State must develop a plan that
   a. includes a definition of a "high-need child with a disability," addresses the financial impact on LEAs' budgets, and ensures that the cost of a high-need child exceeds three times the State's average per pupil expenditure;
   b. establishes eligibility criteria for LEA participation, accounting for number and percentage of high-need children served; and,
   c. develops mechanism and schedule for annual distribution of funds.

2. Costs associated with high-need children are only those incurred in the provision of direct special education and related services. Funds may not be used for legal fees or costs otherwise paid by Medicaid.

3. This provision does not limit or condition the right to FAPE or to authorize an SEA or LEA to limit the amount spent on a child's education.

4. For States having existing pools, those funds may be used if the current program meets eligibility criteria developed under this provision.

Sec. 611. *Flexibility in Using Funds for Part C.* No comparable language in IDEA '97.

Sec. 611(e)(7). *Flexibility in Using Funds for Part C.* States eligible to receive preschool grants (Sec. 619) may develop and implement a policy, with the Part C lead agency, to provide Part C services to children who were previously served in that program and are now eligible for preschool services, until the children are eligible for kindergarten.

Flexibility in Using Funds for Part C. The details of this program are found in Part C, Sec. 635(c). The Part C program, which serves infants and toddlers with disabilities ages birth through 2, and the Section 619 Preschool program, which serves children ages 3 through 5, operate under significantly different rules and regulations. The State designates a lead agency, not necessarily the State education agency, that is responsible for implementation of Part C. Services to the child and the family are delivered in the "natural environment," most often the home or childcare setting, by a variety of providers under an Individualized Family Service Plan (IFSP), and the lead agency may require that parents pay for certain services based on a sliding fee scale.

The Preschool program operates under the same rules and regulations as the Part B program serving students ages 5–21. Children receive a free appropriate public education (FAPE), based on an Individualized Education Program (IEP), provided in the least restrictive environment, which may be a public preschool program if available or a private program paid for by the school district.

Under this new provision, parents must receive an explanation of the differences between Part C and the Preschool program, including possible costs to the family. Parents would then have the option to keep their child in Part C or move him or her to the Preschool program.

Sec. 611(j). *Authorization of Appropriations.* For the purposes of carrying out Part B, serving children with disabilities ages 3–21, except for Sec. 619 (Preschool Grants), Congress authorizes such sums as may be necessary.

Sec. 611(i). *Authorization of Appropriations.* The law includes specific appropriations levels for federal Fiscal Years 2005–2011 and provides "such sums as may be necessary" for Fiscal Year 2012 and beyond.

Authorization of Appropriations. Since its original enactment in 1975, federal aid to States for students with disabilities has been based on the number of students receiving services adjusted by a uniform percentage of the national average per pupil expenditure. The law states that the adjustment should be 40% of the per pupil expenditure; however, the current percentage paid to States by the federal government is slightly less than half that amount. Debate has also focused on whether or not the appropriations for IDEA should be mandatory, i.e., an entitlement program, or discretionary, in which congressional appropriations committees decide annually what, if any, increase in funding to provide. The new provision provides appropriations targets to reach the 40% "full funding" amount by 2011, but leaves discretion for reaching these targets to the annual congressional appropriations process.

Section 612: State Eligibility

IDEA '97 (P.L. 105-17)	IDEA '04 (P.L. 108-446)
Sec. 612. State Flexibility. No comparable language in IDEA '97.	**Sec. 612(a)(1)(C). State Flexibility.** States having a policy allowing Part C services for preschool-aged children (see Sec. 611(e)(7)) are not required to provide a free appropriate public education (FAPE) to children choosing to continue in Part C.
Sec. 612(a)(3). Child Find. States are required to identify, locate, and evaluate all children with disabilities, including private school students, regardless of the severity of their disabilities, who are in need of special education and related services. The law does not require that children be classified by disability, as long as they meet the definition of "child with a disability" (Sec. 602(3)).	**Sec. 612(a)(3). Child Find.** Adds that "homeless children" and "wards of the State" who may be children with disabilities in need of special education and related services must also be identified, located, and evaluated.
Sec. 612(a)(10). Children in Private Schools. Children enrolled by their parents in private schools are eligible for special education and related services. The amount spent for those services shall be equal to a proportionate amount of federal funds available under Part B. Services may be provided on premises of private and parochial schools. The LEA is not required to reimburse costs for parentally placed students, unless a court or hearing officer determines that the LEA did not provide FAPE to the student.	**Sec. 612(a)(10). Children in Private Schools.** Additions include: 1. State and local funds may supplement, but not supplant, the proportionate amount of federal funds that must be spent. 2. LEA must report to the State the number of children evaluated, determined eligible, and served under this provision. 3. Child find process must ensure equitable participation of parentally placed private school children and an accurate count of those children. 4. Costs of child find and evaluations may not be counted in determining whether the LEA has met its obligation under this provision. 5. The LEA must consult with representatives of the private school and the parents regarding the following: Child find and equitable participation; determination of proportionate amount of federal funds; how, when, and by whom services will be provided; and, provision of a written explanation of why the LEA chooses not to provide services to a child. 6. Private school may submit State complaint alleging that LEA did not engage in meaningful consultation or consider private school's views.
Sec. 612(a)(13). Comprehensive System of Personnel Development. State is required to develop a system to ensure an adequate supply of qualified special and regular education teachers and related services personnel to meet the State's needs.	**Comprehensive System of Personnel Development:** *was eliminated.* The State Personnel Development Grants (Part D, Subpart 1) incorporates much of what was previously included in this section.

Sec. 612(a)(15). Personnel Standards.	***Sec. 612(a)(14). Personnel Qualifications.*** Throughout the law, the word *standards* has been replaced by the word *qualifications* in regard to personnel issues. The "highest requirement" language has been eliminated. Other changes include:

Sec. 612(a)(15). Personnel Standards.

1. States must establish and maintain standards to ensure that personnel are appropriately and adequately prepared and trained. Standards must be consistent with any State-approved or recognized certification or licensure or other comparable requirements.

2. To the extent those standards are not based on the highest State requirements applicable to a specific profession or discipline, the State is taking steps to retrain or hire personnel that meet the highest requirements.

3. State standards shall allow appropriately trained and supervised paraprofessionals and assistants to assist in provision of services.

4. States may require LEAs to make ongoing good faith efforts to recruit and hire appropriately and adequately trained personnel, including where there are shortages, individuals who will meet the highest standard within three years.

Sec. 612(a)(14). Personnel Qualifications. Throughout the law, the word *standards* has been replaced by the word *qualifications* in regard to personnel issues. The "highest requirement" language has been eliminated. Other changes include:

1. Qualifications established for related services personnel must ensure that those individuals meet any State-approved or State-recognized certification, licensure, registration, or other comparable requirements. Licensure or certification may not have been waived on an emergency, temporary, or provisional basis.

2. Special education teachers must be highly qualified by the NCLB deadline (not later than the end of the 2005–06 school year).

3. Language regarding three-year waiver to meet highest standard has been eliminated. Instead, the State must adopt a policy that requires LEAs to take "measurable steps to recruit, hire, train, and retain highly qualified personnel."

4. This provision does not create a right of action for the failure of a staff person to be highly qualified. However, parents may file a State complaint about staff qualifications.

Personnel Qualifications. In the conference report, the Conference Committee states its intention that SEAs establish "rigorous qualifications" (p. 192) for related services personnel. The Committee felt that SEAs needed greater flexibility and should consult with other State agencies, LEAs, and the professional organizations representing the service providers in establishing these standards.

Sec. 612(a)(16). Performance Goals and Indicators. States must establish performance goals consistent with standards for students without disabilities. States must have performance indicators to assess progress toward meeting performance goals that, at a minimum, address performance on assessments and dropout and graduation rates.

Sec. 612(a)(15). Performance Goals and Indictors. Additions include:

1. Performance goals must be the same as the State's definition of adequate yearly progress, including the State's objectives for progress by children with disabilities, as required under NCLB.

2. States report annually on progress toward meeting goals, which may include elements of the reports required under NCLB.

Performance Goals and Indicators. Performance goals for students with disabilities must conform to the State's definition of "adequate yearly progress" (AYP) under NCLB. AYP is a measure established by each State to demonstrate students' progress in meeting proficiency on assessments keyed to the State's academic achievement standards. Students with disabilities constitute a specific subgroup under NCLB, and data on those students' progress must be disaggregated and publicly reported.

Sec. 612(a)(17). Participation in Assessments. Children with disabilities will be included in general State- and district-wide assessments, with appropriate accommodations.

1. State or LEA, as appropriate, develops guidelines for participation and develops and conducts alternate assessments.

2. State must report, with the same frequency as for children without disabilities, on the number of children with disabilities taking regular and alternate assessments and on the performance on those assessments.

Sec. 612(a)(16) Participation in Assessments. Adds the following:

1. *All* children with disabilities participate in *all* assessments, with accommodations and alternate assessments as indicated on the IEP.

2. State, or, for district-wide assessments, the LEA guidelines must provide for alternate assessments aligned with the State's academic content and achievement standards. If the State has adopted alternate achievement standards, students working under those standards are assessed on those standards.

3. State must report on the number of students provided accommodations on regular assessments, the number taking alternate assessments based on alternate standards, and a comparison of performance of students with disabilities with all students, including students with disabilities, on those assessments.

4. State or LEA must, to the extent feasible, use universal design principles in developing and administering any assessments.

Participation in Assessments. Under NCLB, States may develop alternate achievement standards for students with significant cognitive disabilities, as defined by each State, as indicated on their IEPs. Students whose instruction is based on alternate achievement standards will take alternate assessments keyed to those standards. There is no limit on the number of students who may take alternate assessments based on alternate standards; however, a cap of up to 1% of those scores may be used in the AYP calculation.

Sec. 612(a)(21). State Advisory Panel. State establishes advisory panel for purpose of providing policy guidance on special education and related services. Panel advises on unmet needs, evaluations, data reporting, and coordinating services and provides comments on proposed rules and regulations.

Sec. 612(a)(21). State Advisory Panel. The following new members have been added: an official responsible for carrying out the McKinney-Vento Homeless Assistance Act and a representative of the State child welfare agency responsible for foster care.

Sec. 612(a)(22). Suspension and Expulsion Rates. State examines data for significant discrepancies in rates of long-term suspensions and expulsions among LEAs in the State and compared to rates for students without disabilities.

Sec. 612(a)(22). Suspension and Expulsion Rates. Data must now be disaggregated by race and ethnicity.

Sec. 612. Access to Instructional Materials. No comparable language in IDEA '97.

Sec. 612(a)(23). Access to Instructional Materials.

1. States must adopt the National Instructional Materials Accessibility Standard (NIMAS) to provide instructional materials to blind persons or those with disabilities in relation to print.

2. States do not have to coordinate with the National Instructional Materials Access Center (NIMAC), but must assure that they will provide materials to blind or print-disabled individuals in a timely manner.

3. If State coordinates with NIMAC, no later than two years after enactment of IDEA '04 the State must contract with publishers to provide electronic files of print instructional materials to NIMAC using the NIMAS or must buy materials in specialized formats.

Sec. 612. Overidentification and Disproportionality. No comparable language in IDEA '97.

Sec. 612(a)(24). Overidentification and Disproportionality. State adopts policies and procedures designed to prevent inappropriate identification or disproportionate representation by race and ethnicity of children as children with disabilities.

Sec. 612. Prohibition on Mandatory Medication. No comparable language in IDEA '97.

Sec. 612(a)(25). Prohibition on Mandatory Medication.

1. State shall prohibit State and local education agency personnel from requiring a child to obtain a prescription for medications covered by the Controlled Substances Act as a condition of school attendance or receiving an evaluation or services.

| | 2. This provision shall not create a prohibition against teachers or other school personnel consulting or sharing classroom observations with parents regarding academic and functional performance, behavior, or the need for an evaluation for special education and related services. |

Section 613: Local Educational Agency Eligibility

IDEA '97 (P.L. 105-17)	IDEA '04 (P.L. 108-446)
Sec. 613(a)(2)(C). Treatment of Federal Funds in Certain Fiscal Years. In any year in which the federal appropriation for Part B exceeds $4.1 billion, the LEA may treat as local funds up to 20% of federal funds it receives that exceed the amount received in the previous fiscal year.	**Sec. 613(a)(2)(C). Adjustment to Local Fiscal Effort in Certain Fiscal Years.** The provision is changed as follows: 1. In any year in which the LEA's federal allocation exceeds the previous year's amount, the LEA may reduce its level of expenditures by not more than 50% of the amount of excess. 2. If the LEA chooses to reduce its level of expenditure, it must use an amount equal to the reduction for activities authorized under NCLB. 3. Funds spent by the LEA on "early intervening" (Sec. 613(f)) shall count toward the maximum amount the LEA may reduce.
Sec. 613(a)(4). Permissive Use of Funds. LEA may use funds for services and aids that also benefit nondisabled students and for a coordinated service system.	**Sec. 613(a)(4). Permissive Use of Funds.** Deletes Coordinated Services System, and adds the following permitted uses of funds: 1. Develop and implement coordinated, early intervention educational services system (Sec. 613(f)); 2. Establish and implement cost- or risk-sharing funds, consortia, or cooperatives for high-cost special education and related services (Sec. 611(e)(3)); 3. Purchase technology for record-keeping, data collection, and other case management activities.
Sec. 613. Purchase of Instructional Materials. No comparable language in IDEA '97.	**Sec. 613(a)(6). Purchase of Instructional Materials.** No later than two years after enactment of IDEA '04, LEAs opting to coordinate with NIMAC shall acquire materials in the same manner and under the same conditions as the State (Sec. 612(a)(23)).
Sec. 613. Records Regarding Migratory Children with Disabilities. No comparable language in IDEA '97.	**Sec. 613(a)(9). Records Regarding Migratory Children with Disabilities.** LEA works with the Secretary under NCLB (Sec. 1308) to provide among States an electronic exchange of health and educational information on migratory children.
Sec. 613(f). Coordinated Services System. LEAs may use up to 5% of federal funds annually to implement a system to improve results for all children, including children with disabilities. Activities allowed under this provision include developing strategies that promote accountability for results, service coordination and case management, developing interagency financing strategies, and interagency personnel development for personnel working on coordinated services.	**Coordinated Services System.** *Was eliminated.*

Sec. 613. *Early Intervening Services.* No comparable language in IDEA '97.	**Sec. 613(f). *Early Intervening Services.***

Sec. 613(f). *Early Intervening Services.*

1. An LEA may use up to 15% of its federal allotment annually, in combination with other funds, to develop and implement coordinated early intervention services for students, grades K–12 (focusing on K–3), who have not been identified as needing special education and related services, but who need extra academic and behavioral support to succeed in the general education environment.

2. Activities may include professional development to deliver scientifically based academic and behavioral interventions, and provision of educational and behavioral evaluations, services, and supports.

3. This provision neither limits nor creates a right to FAPE.

4. LEA will report annually to the State on the number of students served for two years under this provision, and the number who subsequently receive special education and related services.

5. These funds may be used for services aligned with NCLB, if funds are used to supplement and not supplant NCLB funds.

Early Intervening Services. This provision specifically targets at-risk general education students and has generated some controversy, since IDEA funds will be used for students who are not identified as needing special education and related services. A number of school districts already use systems whereby struggling students receive classroom interventions of varying levels of intensity over a period of time. If students are not successful after a series of these interventions, they may be referred for evaluation for special education and related services.

LEAs are required to report on students served in this program for two years to determine if this program reduces the number of referrals for special education and related services. The two-year period applies to the two years after the child has received these services. (Conf. Report, p. 199.)

Sec. 613(g). *School-Based Improvement Plan.* LEAs may use federal funds to permit schools to implement school-based improvement plans to improve educational and transitional results for children with and without disabilities.	**School-Based Improvement Plan.** *Was eliminated.*

Sec. 613. *State Agency Flexibility.* No comparable language in IDEA '97.	**Sec. 613(j). *State Agency Flexibility.***

Sec. 613(j). *State Agency Flexibility.*

1. In any year in which the State's Part B allotment exceeds the amount received the previous year, and, if the State in school year 2003–04 or any subsequent school year pays or reimburses all LEAs for 100% of the nonfederal share of special education and related services, the SEA may reduce the level of expenditures from State sources by not more than 50% of the amount of excess.

2. If the Secretary determines that the State cannot meet the requirements of the law and needs assistance or intervention under Sec. 616, the Secretary shall prohibit the State from using this authority.

3. If the State uses this authority, the SEA shall use funds from State sources in an amount equal to the reduction to support activities authorized under NCLB or to support need-based or teacher higher education programs.

Section 614: Evaluations, Eligibility Determinations, Individualized Education Programs, and Educational Placements

IDEA '97 (P.L. 105-17)	IDEA '04 (P.L. 108-446)

IDEA '97 (P.L. 105-17)

Sec. 614(a). Initial Evaluation and Reevaluation.

1. Initial Evaluation:
   a. SEA or LEA shall conduct an initial evaluation to determine eligibility for services and educational needs.
   b. LEA must obtain parents' informed consent before conducting evaluation, and consent shall not be construed as consent for placement.
   c. If parents refuse consent, LEA may pursue evaluation through mediation and due process procedures.

2. Reevaluation:
   a. LEA shall conduct reevaluation if conditions warrant or if parents or child's teacher requests such, but at least once every 3 years.
   b. Parents' informed consent should be secured prior to reevaluation; however, informed consent is not necessary if the LEA can demonstrate that reasonable measures were taken to obtain consent and parents did not respond.

IDEA '04 (P.L. 108-446)

Sec. 614(a)(1)(B). Request for Initial Evaluation. Changes include:

1. Initial Evaluation:
   a. Either parents or the SEA, other state agency or LEA may request an initial evaluation.
   b. Eligibility determination must be made within 60 days of receiving parental consent for evaluation, or, if the State has an established time frame for evaluation, that time frame may be used.
   c. The time frame does not apply
      if (1) the child enrolls after the relevant time frame has begun and before the eligibility determination is made by the child's previous LEA, but only if the new LEA is making sufficient progress to ensure prompt completion of the evaluation, and the parent and the new LEA agree to a specific time for completion of the evaluation.
      (2) the parent repeatedly fails or refuses to produce the child for evaluation.

2. Parental Consent for Services:
   a. Agency responsible for providing FAPE shall seek to obtain parents' informed consent before providing special education and related services.
   b. If parents refuse to provide consent for services, LEA shall not provide services by utilizing the due process procedures
   c. LEA shall not be considered to be in violation of the requirement to provide FAPE if parents refuse to consent or refuse to respond to request for consent, nor shall LEA be required to convene an IEP meeting or develop an IEP.
   d. Consent for Wards of State:
      (1) If the child is a ward of the State and not residing with parents, agency shall make reasonable efforts to obtain parents' informed consent for initial evaluation.
      (2) Agency shall not be required to obtain parents' informed consent for initial evaluation if, despite reasonable efforts, agency cannot find the parent, parents' rights have been terminated, or the right to make educational decisions has been assigned by a court to another individual.

3. Screening of a student by a teacher or specialist to determine instructional strategies shall not be considered evaluation for eligibility for special education and related services.

4. Reevaluation:
   a. LEA shall ensure reevaluation if it determines that educational or related needs, including improved academic and functional performance, warrant.
   b. Reevaluation shall occur not more often than once a year, unless parent and LEA agree otherwise, but should occur at least once every three years, unless parent and LEA agree that reevaluation is not necessary.

Initial Evaluation and Reevaluation. The law clarifies that both parents and agency personnel may request an initial evaluation and establishes a time frame within which the evaluation must be completed. The law also prohibits school districts from providing services without parental consent. In the past, school districts could use the due process procedures to provide services even without parental consent, but the new provisions bar districts from using those procedures for this purpose.

IDEA '97 (P.L. 105-17)

Sec. 614(b). Evaluation Procedures.

1. LEA shall provide notice to parents describing any evaluation procedures to be conducted.

2. LEA shall use a variety of assessment tools, including information provided by parents; shall not use any single procedure to make determination of eligibility; and, shall use technically sound instruments to assess cognitive, behavioral, physical, and developmental factors.

3. Other requirements
   a. Evaluation materials must be selected and administered so as not to be racially or culturally discriminatory.
   b. Tests must be administered in the child's native language or other mode of communication, unless not feasible to do so.
   c. Child must be assessed in all areas of suspected disability.
   d. Assessments must provide information to determine educational needs.

4. A team of qualified professionals and the parents will determine if the child meets eligibility requirements.

5. Eligibility cannot be determined based on lack of reading or math instruction or based on limited English proficiency.

6. If an IEP team determines that no additional data are needed to determine continued eligibility, LEA must notify parents of that determination and of the parents' right to request an assessment, and shall not be required to conduct an assessment unless parents so request.

7. LEA shall evaluate the child before determining that the child is no longer a child with a disability.

IDEA '04 (P.L. 108-446)

Sec. 614(b). Evaluation Procedures. Changes and additions include:

1. Conduct of Evaluation:
   a. Assessments must be provided and administered in "the language and form most likely to yield accurate information on what the child knows and can do academically, developmentally, and functionally. . . ."
   b. Assessments of a child who transfers to another school district during the school year are coordinated between prior and subsequent schools for expeditious completion of evaluation.
   c. Child will not be determined a "child with a disability" if the determining factor is "lack of appropriate instruction in reading, including in the essential components of reading instruction" (as defined in NCLB, Sec. 1208(3)).

2. Specific Learning Disabilities:
   a. When determining if a child has a specific learning disability, the "LEA shall not be required to take into consideration whether [the] child has a severe discrepancy between achievement and intellectual ability in oral expression, listening comprehension, written expression, basic reading skill, reading comprehension, mathematical calculation, or mathematical reasoning."
   b. In making this determination, LEA may use "a process that determines if the child responds to scientific, research-based intervention" as a part of the regular special education evaluation procedures.

3. Evaluation before change in eligibility:
   a. Evaluation is not required before eligibility is terminated due to graduation with a regular diploma or to exceeding the age requirement for provision of FAPE under State law.
   b. For a child whose eligibility ends due to graduation with regular diploma or exceeding the age requirement, the LEA shall provide a summary of the child's academic achievement and functional performance, including recommendations on how to assist the child in meeting postsecondary goals.

Evaluation Procedures/Specific Learning Disabilities. The IQ-discrepancy model has always been quite controversial, particularly in recent years, since over 50% of all students with disabilities receiving services under the IDEA are identified as having specific learning disabilities. The model uses a severe discrepancy between the student's intellectual ability, as measured by an IQ test, and actual achievement and performance as the primary indicator of a learning disability.

The controversy has arisen for several reasons. First, despite the fact that the law has never required the use of an IQ-discrepancy model and, in fact, requires the use of a variety of assessment tools and strategies to make a determination of eligibility under any disability category, some school districts have adopted this model as the sole criterion for determining specific learning disabilities. Second, a broad range of researchers and advocates believe that using this model as the sole criterion has resulted in over- and misidentification of learning disabilities and does not account for other possible factors resulting in academic failure, such as poor instruction or lack of appropriate interventions.

These provisions clarify that school districts do not have to find a severe discrepancy between ability and achievement to determine a child eligible for special education and related services under the category of specific learning disabilities. In addition, the law allows school districts to try research-based interventions in the general education setting as part of the evaluation process. If these interventions result in academic improvement, school personnel should consider whether or not the child has a true learning disability or his or her academic difficulties are due to lack of proper instruction or other factors.

IDEA '97 (P.L. 105-17)

Sec. 614(d)(1)(A). Individualized Education Programs.
The Individualized Education Program (IEP) includes statements of:

1. Present levels of educational performance, including how the disability affects involvement and progress in the general curriculum, or for preschoolers, how disability affects participation in appropriate activities.
2. Annual goals and short-term objectives.
3. Special education and related services and supplementary aids and services needed to advance toward annual goals and to be involved and make progress in the general curriculum.
4. The extent to which the child will not participate in the regular classroom.
5. Modifications needed to participate in assessments, and if an assessment is not appropriate, how the child will be assessed.
6. Frequency and location of services and modifications.
7. Transition service needs, beginning at age 14, and, at age 16, transition services, including interagency responsibilities.
8. Information regarding transfer of rights at the age of majority.
9. How child's progress will be measured and how parents will be informed.

Sec. 614(d). IEP Team Attendance; IEP Team Transition; Meetings. No comparable language in IDEA '97.

IDEA '04 (P.L. 108-446)

Sec. 614(d)(1)(A). Individualized Education Programs.
Deleted

1. **Benchmarks** or short-term objectives: Retained only for children who take alternate assessments aligned to alternate achievement standards.
2. Transition requirement at age 14.

Added

IEP must include a statement, beginning not later than the first IEP in effect when the student is 16 and updated annually, of "appropriate measurable postsecondary goals based on age appropriate transition assessments related to training, education, employment, and where appropriate, independent skills." Will also include transition services, including courses, needed to assist in reaching goals, contained previously in the age-14-transition requirement.

Sec. 614(d)(1)(C), (D); 614(3)(D)–(F). IEP Team Attendance, IEP Team Transition; Meetings.

1. IEP team attendance:
   a. A team member is not required to attend a meeting if parents and LEA agree that the member's attendance is not necessary because the member's curriculum area or related service will not be discussed.
   b. Member may be excused from attendance when his or her curriculum area or related service is being discussed if parents and LEA consent, and member submits written input to parents and team before the meeting.
   c. Parents' agreement and consent under these sections must be in writing.

2. IEP team transition:
   For child previously served under Part C, at parents' request, Part C service coordinator or other Part C representatives shall be invited to the initial IEP meeting to assist in the smooth transition of services.

3. Meetings:
   a. Parents and LEA may agree not to convene an IEP meeting to make changes that are needed after the annual IEP meeting, but instead may develop a written document to amend or modify the current IEP.

b. LEA shall encourage consolidation of reevaluation and other IEP meetings.

c. Changes to the IEP may be made either by the entire team, or by amending rather than redrafting the entire IEP. Parents may request a revised copy with amendments incorporated.

d. For IEP and placement meetings and administrative matters under the Procedural Safeguards section (sec. 615), parents and LEA may agree to use alternative means of meeting participation, e.g., video-conferences or conference calls.

IEP Team Transition. Allowing parents to have a Part C representative at an initial IEP meeting may provide a smoother transition for children moving into the Preschool program. The Part C and Preschool programs differ in the types of services provided, as well as duration, frequency, and location of services. Program representatives should help parents understand these changes as an IEP is developed.

Sec. 614(d). Program for Children Who Transfer School Districts. No comparable language in IDEA '97.

Sec. 614(d)(2)(C). Program for Children Who Transfer School Districts.

1. Transfer within the same State:
   If a child with an IEP in effect transfers to another school district within the State during the school year, the new LEA shall provide FAPE, including services comparable to the previous IEP, in consultation with parents, until new LEA adopts the previous IEP or develops and implements a new IEP.

2. Transfer outside State:
   If a child with an IEP in effect transfers to a school in another state during the school year, the new LEA shall provide FAPE, including services comparable to the previous IEP, in consultation with parents, until new LEA conducts an evaluation, if deemed necessary, and develops a new IEP.

3. Transmittal of Records:
   Child's new school shall take reasonable steps to promptly obtain records, including the IEP and other documents relating to the provision of special education and related services. The previous school shall take reasonable steps to respond promptly to such request.

Sec. 614(d). Multiyear IEP Demonstration. No comparable language in IDEA '97.

Sec. 614(d)(5). Multiyear IEP Demonstration.

1. Authorizes 15-State pilot program for an optional multiyear (not to exceed three years) IEP. Secretary will report to Congress within two years on effectiveness of the pilot and provide any recommendations for broader implementation.

2. Program must be optional to parents, and parents must provide informed consent before multiyear IEP is developed.

3. The IEP must include:
   a. Measurable goals to enable the child to make progress in the general education curriculum and meet other needs that coincide with natural transition points (preschool to elementary; elementary to middle; middle to secondary; secondary to postsecondary, but in no case longer than three years); and,

| | b. Measurable annual goals for determining progress toward meeting academic goals. |
| | 4. Program must include process for review and revision of IEPs, including:
a. Review at natural transition points;
b. In years other than natural transition points, an annual review to determine current levels of progress and whether goals are being met, and a requirement to amend IEP, as appropriate, to allow continued progress toward goals;
c. Requirement, if team determines that child isn't making sufficient progress toward meeting goals, that LEA ensures a more thorough review of the IEP within 30 days; and,
d. At parents' request, requirement that the team conduct a review of the IEP rather than or subsequent to an annual review. |

Multiyear IEP. This pilot program attempts to address excessive paperwork burdens by streamlining the number of IEP meetings and revisions to the document. Districts and parents will most likely find that a multiyear IEP is more appropriate for children with mild to moderate disabilities, rather than those who receive multiple services that may require more frequent review of the IEP.

Section 615: Procedural Safeguards and Discipline Provisions

IDEA '97 (P.L. 105-17)

Sec. 615(b). Procedural Safeguards — Types of Procedures. The law requires the following:

1. Opportunity for parents to examine all records; to participate in meetings regarding identification, evaluation, and placement, and provision of FAPE; and, to have an independent evaluation;

2. Protection of child's rights when LEA, after reasonable efforts, cannot locate parents;

3. Written prior notice to parents when LEA proposes to initiate or change or refuses to initiate or change identification, evaluation, or placement, or provision of FAPE;

4. Assurance that written prior notice fully informs parents, in native language unless not feasible, of all safeguards;

5. Opportunity for parents to present complaints;

6. Opportunity for mediation;

7. Provision of notice regarding a complaint to the SEA or LEA by parents or their attorney that includes (a) child's name, address, and school, (b) description of and facts related to the problem, and (c) proposed resolution to the problem; and,

8. Development of model form by SEA to assist parents in filing complaints.

IDEA '04 (P.L. 108-446)

Sec. 615(b). Types of Procedures. Changes and additions include:

1. Regarding surrogates making educational decisions:
   a. In the case of a ward of the State, judge overseeing child's care may appoint a surrogate.
   b. LEA appoints a surrogate for unaccompanied homeless youth.
   c. State shall make reasonable efforts to ensure appointment of surrogate within 30 days after determination of need.

2. "Any party" may present a complaint that alleges a violation occurring not more than two years before the party knew or should have known about the alleged action that is the basis of the complaint. If there is already a State time limitation for presenting complaints, that time line may be used.

3. State must establish procedures that require either a party or that party's attorney to provide *due process complaint notice* (See Sec. 615(c)(2) below) to the other party and forward a copy of the notice to the SEA. Notice must include (a) child's name, address, and school the child attends; (b) for homeless child, available contact information and school the child attends; (c) description of and facts related to the problem; and (d) proposed resolution. May not have a due process hearing until the party or party's attorney files the due process complaint notice.

4. State must develop model due process complaint notice.

Types of Procedures. The law now establishes that both parents and local school districts may file complaints. The IDEA '97 regulations stated that "a parent or a public agency may initiate a hearing" (34 CFR Sec. 300.507); however, the statutory language was not as clear. Also, the law includes a statute of limitations for filing complaints. The previous law did not limit the amount of time that could elapse between the alleged violation and bringing a complaint. This sometimes resulted in complaints being raised that allegedly occurred a number of years earlier, making fact-finding more difficult and possibly resulting in orders for compensatory education long after the violation had been cured or the student had exited the school system. The statute of limitations may also serve to reduce the number of hearings and to encourage attempts to resolve complaints outside the hearing process through mediation or other alternative dispute resolution mechanisms.

IDEA '97 (P.L. 105-17)

Sec. 615(c), (d). Content of Prior Written Notice; Procedural Safeguards Notice.

1. Prior written notice must include (a) the action proposed or refused by the LEA; (b) why the LEA proposed or refused to take action; (c) other actions considered and why rejected; and (d) other relevant factors. It must also include a statement that includes (a) that the parents have protections under the law's procedural safeguards, (b) how a copy may be obtained, and (c) sources where parents may obtain assistance to understand these protections.

2. Procedural Safeguards Notice:
   a. Must be given to parents at least at initial referral for evaluation, at each notification of an IEP meeting and reevaluation, and when complaints are filed.
   b. Notice must include a full explanation of the procedural safeguards, written in family's native language, if feasible, and in easily understandable language.
   c. Notice covers regulations related to independent evaluation; prior written notice; parental consent; access to educational records; opportunity to present complaints; child's placement during due process proceedings; procedures for a child in an interim alternative educational setting; requirements for placement of the child by parents in a private school at public expense; mediation; due process hearings; appeals; civil actions; and, attorneys' fees.

IDEA '04 (P.L. 108-446)

Sec. 615(c), (d). Notification Requirements; Procedural Safeguards Notice.

1. No changes in Prior Written Notice requirements.

2. Due Process Complaint Notice (new notice requirement):
   a. Notice is deemed sufficient unless receiving party gives written notification to the hearing officer (within 15 days of receiving complaint) and the other party that the receiving party believes the notice hasn't met the requirements of Sec. 615(b).
   (1) Within five days of receipt of notification, hearing officer must make a determination as to whether the notice meets requirements.
   (2) A party may amend a complaint notice only if (a) the other party gives written consent to an amendment and has an opportunity to resolve the complaint through the "resolution session" (Sec. 615(f)); or, (b) the hearing officer grants permission no later than five days before due process hearing occurs.
   b. LEA's response to complaint:
   (1) If LEA hasn't sent prior written notice to parents on a subject in the complaint notice, LEA must, within ten days of receiving the complaint, send a response to parents that includes (a) why the LEA proposed or refused to take action raised in the complaint; (b) other options that were considered and why they were rejected; each evaluation procedure, assessment, record or records used by the agency as basis for action; and (c) other relevant factors.
   (2) LEA's response does not preclude it from asserting that parents' due process complaint notice was insufficient.
   c. Other party's response: Noncomplaining party must, within ten days of receiving complaint, send response that specifically addresses issues raised.
   d. Parents are not precluded from filing a separate due process complaint on issues separate from the complaint already filed.

3. Procedural Safeguards Notice:
   a. Notice shall be given to parents only once a year, except that it shall also be given at (1) initial referral or parental request for evaluation; (2) first filing of a complaint; and, (3) parents' request.
   b. LEA may put notice on web site.
   c. Notice requirements are same as IDEA '97, except that they must include regulations related to time line for filing and LEA's opportunity to resolve complaints, and time line for filing civil actions.

4. Parents may opt to receive notices by email, if that option is available.

Sec. 615(e). Mediation.

1. Mediation must be voluntary; may not be used to deny or delay parents' right to a hearing or other rights under the law; must be conducted by qualified impartial mediator from the State's list; and agreement must be in writing.

2. LEA or SEA may have procedures to require parents who do not choose mediation to meet with a disinterested party to urge its use and explain the benefits of mediation.

3. Mediation discussions are confidential and may not be used in subsequent hearings or civil proceedings.

Sec. 615(e). Mediation. Procedures are the same, with the following addition: If a resolution is reached through the mediation, the parties shall execute a "legally binding agreement" signed by parents and an authorized agency representative. Agreement is enforceable in State court or U.S. district court.

Sec. 615(f). Impartial Due Process Hearings.

1. Whenever a complaint is received, parents shall have the opportunity for a hearing.

2. SEA or LEA personnel involved in the child's education shall not conduct the hearing.

3. At least five business days before a hearing, each party must disclose all evaluations and recommendations that each intends to use at the hearing. Failure to disclose may result in a bar to introduction at the hearing without the other party's consent.

Sec. 615(f). Impartial Due Process Hearing.

1. Resolution Session:
   Before opportunity for a hearing and within 15 days of receiving notice of a complaint, LEA shall convene a meeting with parents and relevant members of the IEP team with specific knowledge of the facts of the complaint. During this meeting, parents discuss the issues in the complaint, and the LEA has an opportunity to resolve those issues.
   a. Parents and LEA may agree in writing to waive this meeting or to use the mediation process.
   b. Meeting must include LEA representative with decision-making authority, and it may not include LEA's attorney, unless parents bring an attorney.
   c. If LEA hasn't resolved the complaint to parents' satisfaction within 30 days of receipt of complaint, a hearing may occur and all applicable time lines for a hearing will begin to run.
   d. If resolution is reached, parties shall execute a legally binding agreement signed by the parents and authorized agency representative, which is enforceable in State court or U.S. district court. Either party may void the agreement within three business days of agreement's execution.

2. Limitations on Hearing:
   a. A hearing officer (1) shall not be an SEA or LEA employee involved in the child's education or care; (2) shall not have professional interest that would conflict with objectivity; (3) shall have knowledge and understanding of the law and regulations and legal interpretations; and (4) shall have the ability to conduct hearings under standard legal practice.
   b. Party requesting a hearing shall not be allowed to raise issues at hearing not previously raised in the due process complaint notice.
   c. Parent or LEA shall request hearing within two years of when the party "knew or should have known about the alleged action" on which the complaint is based.
   (1) If State has a time limitation for requesting hearing, that time line is used.
   (2) Time line does not apply to parents if they were prevented from requesting a hearing due to (a) specific misrepresentations by the LEA that it had resolved the issue in the complaint; or (b) LEA withheld information that it was required to divulge.

3. Hearing officer decisions:
   a. Such decisions must be made on substantive grounds based on a determination of whether child received FAPE.
   b. Where procedural violations are alleged, hearing officer may find that child did not receive FAPE only if procedural "inadequacies"(1) impeded child's right to FAPE; (2) "significantly impeded" parents' opportunity to participate in decision-making process regarding provision of FAPE; or, (3) caused deprivation of educational benefits.
   (3) Hearing officer is not precluded from ordering LEA to comply with procedural requirements.
   (4) This section shall not be construed to affect parents' right to file a complaint with the SEA.

Impartial Due Process Hearing. The resolution session is an attempt to reduce the number of due process hearings and to encourage less adversarial means of dispute resolution. Hearing officer requirements have been moved from the regulations to statute.

This section also clarifies that complaints based solely on procedural violations will be successful only if those violations are significant. This addition addresses a continuing concern that the IDEA has focused too much on process and not enough on improving educational outcomes for students with disabilities. Requiring that the basis of complaints be on substantive rather than procedural grounds reinforces the focus on results.

Sec. 615(i). Administrative Procedures.

1. Civil Action: Any party aggrieved by a hearing officer's decision or by a civil action, or who does not have a right to an administrative appeal shall have the right to bring a civil action.

2. Attorneys' Fees: The court, in its discretion, may award reasonable attorneys' fees to parents who are the prevailing party.

Sec. 615(i). Administrative Procedures. Changes and additions include:

1. Civil Action: A party bringing a civil action shall have 90 days from the date of the hearing officer's decision to bring an action, or, if the State has an explicit time line, shall follow the State law time line.

2. Attorneys' Fees:
   a. In addition to award of fees to parents, court may award fees to:
      (1) Prevailing SEA or LEA against parents' attorney (a) who files complaint or other cause of action that is frivolous, unreasonable, or without foundation; or, (b) who continues to litigate after litigation clearly became frivolous, unreasonable, or without foundation.
      (2) Prevailing SEA or LEA against parents' attorney *or against parent* if complaint or subsequent cause of action was presented for "any improper purpose," e.g., to harass, cause unnecessary delay, or needlessly increase cost of litigation.
   b. Attorneys' fees are not available for prehearing "resolution session."
   c. Fees may be reduced if parent *or parents' attorney* unreasonably protracted final resolution of controversy.

Administrative Procedures. This section includes another new time line. Also, it provides for attorneys' fees under certain circumstances to a school district that is a prevailing party. Award of attorneys' fees to the school district under the stated circumstances comports with provisions under other civil rights laws.

IDEA '97 (P.L. 105-17)	IDEA '04 (P.L. 108-446)

Sec. 615(k). Placement in Alternative Educational Setting.

1. School personnel may order a change in placement to an appropriate interim alternative educational setting (IAES), another setting, or suspension for not more than ten school days, and to an IAES for not more than 45 days for violations involving weapons or drugs.

2. LEA must conduct a functional behavioral assessment and develop a behavioral intervention plan or review an existing plan not later than 10 days after disciplinary action is taken.

3. Hearing officers may order change in placement to IAES for not more than 45 days if they decide that keeping the student in the current placement is substantially likely to result in injury to the child or others. That decision is based on determination of appropriateness of placement, whether the LEA made reasonable efforts to minimize harm in the placement, and whether the IAES meets legal requirements of this section.

4. IAES must be a setting where the child can continue to participate in the general curriculum and receive IEP services and services to address the behavior.

5. Manifestation Determination: The IEP team must determine whether there is a connection between the disability and the behavior. It may determine that behavior was not a manifestation of the disability only if the team considers all relevant information and determines that (a) placement and IEP were appropriate, (b) disability did not impair child's ability to understand impact and consequences of behavior, and (c) disability did not impair ability to control the behavior.
   a. If behavior is not a manifestation of the disability, the child may be disciplined under a general conduct code.
   b. If parents disagree with manifestation determination, they may request and will receive an expedited hearing.

6. For a child in IAES, that placement is where the child remains, for the allowable time of 45 days, during a hearing. School personnel may decide that it is too dangerous to return child to original placement at the end of the 45-day period and may request an expedited hearing to maintain the child in the IAES until a decision is reached.

7. Children not yet determined to be eligible for special education and related services that violate the conduct code may assert protections of IDEA if LEA had "knowledge" that child was "child with a disability" before the incident occurred.

8. Agency may report crime to appropriate authorities and must ensure that special education and disciplinary records are transmitted to authorities.

Sec. 615(k). Placement in Alternative Educational Setting.
Changes and additions include:

1. Authority of School Personnel:
   a. Personnel may consider unique circumstances on case-by-case basis when deciding whether to order change in placement for violation of student conduct code.
   b. May remove child who *violates student conduct code* from current placement to IAES, another setting, or suspension for not more than ten schooldays to the extent that such alternatives are applied to a child without disabilities.
   c. If they seek to order change in placement exceeding ten schooldays and behavior is *not* a manifestation of the disability, they may apply same disciplinary action applicable to children without disabilities "in the same manner and for the same duration," although it may be in an IAES.
   d. Continuation of Services: Whether or not behavior is a manifestation of disability, a child removed from current placement shall continue to receive educational services enabling progress toward IEP goals and participation in general education curriculum, and shall receive, as appropriate, a functional behavioral assessment and behavioral intervention services and modifications.
   e. Manifestation Determination:
      (1) Except for short-term removals, within ten schooldays of decision to change placement, LEA, parents, and relevant IEP team members (as determined by LEA and parents) shall review all relevant information (including IEP, teacher observations, and relevant information provided by parents) to determine if:
         (a) the conduct was "caused by, or had a direct and substantial relationship to" child's disability; or,
         (b) the conduct was a "direct result of LEA's failure to implement the IEP."
      (2) If either instance above applies, the conduct is a manifestation of the disability, and the IEP team shall:
         (a) conduct a functional behavioral assessment, if one was not done prior to the incident, and implement a behavioral intervention plan or review previous plan for modification, as needed; and,
         (b) except when violations involve weapons, drugs, or serious bodily injury, return child to previous placement, unless parents and LEA agree to a change in placement as part of modification of behavioral intervention plan.
   f. Special Circumstances: Child may be removed to IAES for not more than 45 days, *without regard to whether or not behavior is a manifestation of the disability,* for violations involving weapons, drugs, or infliction of serious bodily injury.

2. Appeal:
   a. Either parents or LEA may request an appeal. SEA or LEA must arrange for an expedited hearing, which must occur within 20 schooldays of date the hearing is requested and must result in a decision within ten schooldays after hearing.

b. During appeal, child remains in IAES pending decision or until expiration of time period allowed for students without disabilities, whichever occurs first, unless parents and LEA agree otherwise.

c. In reaching a decision, the hearing officer may order a change in placement to (1) placement from which child was removed or (2) an IAES for not more than 45 schooldays if he or she determines that there is substantial likelihood in current placement of injury to child or others.

3. Protections for Children Not Yet Eligible for IDEA Services: This section is basically the same as IDEA '97, with the following changes:

a. LEA is deemed to have knowledge that the child is a child with a disability if (1) parents expressed concern in writing to *supervisory or administrative* personnel or *a teacher of the child* that child needs services; or, (2) teacher or other LEA personnel expressed "specific concerns about a pattern of behavior . . . directly" to the special education director or other "supervisory" personnel.

b. LEA is not deemed to have knowledge if parent has not allowed an evaluation or has refused services, or child has been evaluated and was determined not to be eligible.

Placement in Alternative Educational Setting. Prior to IDEA '97, the law did not mention disciplinary actions. These provisions were, in large measure, a result of serious discussion regarding whether or not schools employ a dual system of discipline. Once it was apparent that discipline provisions would become part of the law, advocates focused on how imposing disciplinary measures would be balanced with addressing behaviors that might arise as a manifestation of the child's disability. The concern about a dual disciplinary system carried over into the discussions of the 2004 amendments, resulting in a broader use of general disciplinary measures and explicit language allowing students with disabilities to be removed for any violation of the student conduct code. For infractions resulting in 45-day removals for students with disabilities, including the addition of "serious bodily injury," removals may now extend beyond the 45-day period if longer removals are applicable to students without disabilities. The caveat remains that students with disabilities removed for longer than ten schooldays in a school year must receive educational services and behavioral interventions. In fact, a number of States have now passed laws that require continuation of services for all students removed for disciplinary action. These legislative actions bolster the view of some researchers that suspension and expulsion do little to improve behavior and may, in fact, leave students who act out due to academic failure even farther behind.

The manifestation determination has been considerably streamlined to ease and improve implementation. School administrators expressed frustration that the determination required considerable staff time and almost always resulted in finding some connection between the behavior and the disability. The provision now requires that the conduct was "caused by, or had a direct and substantial relationship to, the child's disability." Previously the law specifically addressed only what the school district must do when the behavior was not a manifestation of the disability. Now the law addresses what actions will be taken if the behavior is or is not a manifestation. Students may be removed to an interim alternative educational setting without a manifestation determination when the violation involves weapons, drugs, or serious bodily injury.

The House bill had eliminated the functional behavioral assessment, which was retained in the final legislation. The functional behavioral assessment involves a review of how the child functions across settings—school, home, community—and is used to develop a plan that addresses the underlying cause of the behavior.

Section 616: Monitoring, Technical Assistance, and Enforcement

IDEA '97 (P.L. 105-17)

Sec. 616. Monitoring, Technical Assistance, and Enforcement. No comparable language in IDEA '97.

IDEA '04 (P.L. 108-446)

Sec. 616. Monitoring, Technical Assistance, and Enforcement.

1. Federal and State Monitoring:
   a. Secretary shall (1) monitor implementation of law through oversight of general supervisory responsibility and the State performance plan (see below), and (2) require States to monitor LEAs.
   b. Primary focus of monitoring shall be on improving "educational results and functional outcomes for all children with disabilities."
   c. Monitoring priorities will be (1) provision of FAPE in least restrictive environment (LRE), (2) State's general supervisory authority, and (3) disproportionate representation of ethnic and racial minorities resulting in inappropriate identification.

2. State Performance Plans:
   States must have a performance plan to evaluate implementation efforts and describe how implementation will be improved. Secretary approves plans, and State reviews them at least once every six years.
   a. State establishes "measurable and rigorous targets" for indicators under priority areas, collects data on priorities, and reports annually to Secretary.
   b. States use targets to analyze and report annually to the public on LEAs' performance and to the Secretary on State's performance.
   c. Secretary annually reviews performance plan and determines if the State meets the law's requirements or needs assistance to implement the law.

3. Enforcement:
   a. "Needs Assistance": If, for two consecutive years, Secretary determines that State needs assistance in implementing the law, Secretary shall do one or more of the following: (1) advise State of technical assistance sources; (2) direct use of State-level funds to where assistance is needed; or, (3) identify State as high-risk grantee and impose conditions on grant.
   b. "Needs Intervention": If, for three or more consecutive years, Secretary determines that State needs intervention, he or she may take any of the actions described in (a) and shall do one or more of the following: (1) require corrective action or improvement plan if problem is correctable in one year; (2) require compliance agreement if it is not correctable in one year; (3) for each year of determination, withhold not less than 20% or more than 50% of State's funds until problems are corrected; (4) seek to recover funds; (5) withhold some or all of payments; or, (6) refer State for appropriate enforcement, including to the Department of Justice.
   c. "Needs Substantial Intervention": Secretary shall do one or more of the following: (1) recover funds; (2) withhold some or all of payments; (3) refer to U.S.

	Department of Education Inspector General; or, (4) refer for appropriate enforcement, including to the Department of Justice.
	d. Opportunity for Hearing: Before withholding funds, Secretary must provide notice and opportunity for hearing. Pending outcome of hearing, payments and/or authority to obligate funds may be suspended.
	e. Secretary reports to Congress within 30 days of action taken.
	4. State Enforcement: If State finds that LEA is not meeting requirements, State shall prohibit LEA from reducing maintenance of effort for any year.
	5. Data Capacity: Secretary shall review States' data collection and analysis capacity and provide technical assistance as needed to improve capacity.

Monitoring, Technical Assistance, and Enforcement. The previous law stated that, when a State had not substantially complied with the requirements of the law, the Secretary could withhold payments or refer the matter for appropriate action, including to the Department of Justice. The new law directs federal and State monitoring to focus more heavily on improving educational results than it had in the past, at which time the emphasis had been mainly on process; law also provides for a series of sanctions for several levels of noncompliance.

Sections 617 and 618: Administration; Program Information

IDEA '97 (P.L. 105-17)	IDEA '04 (P.L. 108-446)
Sec. 617. Administration. Secretary shall: 1. Provide technical assistance to States to implement the law. 2. Issue regulations only to the extent necessary to ensure compliance. 3. Assure confidentiality of personally identifiable information.	***Sec. 617. Administration.*** Provisions on regulations have been deleted from this section. Additions include: 1. Federal government cannot "mandate, direct, or control" specific instructional content, academic standards and assessments, curriculum, or program of instruction of any SEA, LEA, or individual school. 2. Secretary will provide model forms for IEP, IFSP, and procedural safeguards and prior written notices.
Sec. 618. Program Information. States submit data annually, by race, ethnicity, and disability on 1. Number of infants and toddlers (by race/ethnicity only) and children receiving FAPE or early intervention services. 2. Number of children participating in regular education, in separate classes, schools, or facilities, or in residential facilities. 3. Number of students, ages 14–21, who stopped receiving services and why, and ages birth to 2 (by race/ethnicity) who stopped early intervention services. 4. Number of students removed to interim alternative educational settings and subject to long-term suspensions and expulsions, and the acts causing removals. 5. Number of infants and toddlers (by race/ethnicity) at risk of substantial developmental delay and receiving early intervention services. 6. Significant discrepancies in rate of long-term suspensions and expulsions among LEAs in a State or compared to rates for nondisabled students.	***Sec. 618. Program Information.*** Data will be collected by both number and percentage of students and by race, ethnicity, limited English proficiency, gender, and disability categories. 1. New data collections include such data as: a. Incidence and duration of disciplinary actions, including suspensions of one day or more. b. Comparison of students with and without disabilities removed to alternative settings or expelled. c. Number of (1) due process complaints filed and hearings conducted; (b) hearings requested under discipline provisions and resulting changes in placement; and, (c) mediations held and settlements reached 2. Secretary may provide technical assistance to States on data collection and reporting. 3. LEAs with policies resulting in significant disproportionality must reserve maximum amount allowed (Sec. 613(f)) for early intervening services, particularly to serve students in groups significantly overidentified.

Section 619: Preschool Grants

IDEA '97 (P.L. 105-17)

Sec. 619. Preschool Grants.

1. Grants are provided to States under this section to serve children with disabilities, ages 3 through 5, and, at the State's discretion, 2-year-olds turning 3 during the school year. States receiving grants must provide FAPE to children served.

2. States shall use funds reserved for State-level activities for support services, direct services, a coordinated services system, and meeting State performance goals.

3. Part C does not apply to any children receiving FAPE under this section.

IDEA '04 (P.L. 108-446)

Sec. 619. Preschool Grants. State reserve funds may be used for two new activities:

1. Provision of Part C early intervention services to children eligible for preschool who previously received Part C services, until they enter or are eligible for kindergarten; or,

2. At a State's discretion, to continue service coordination or case management for families receiving services under Part C.

PART C: Infants and Toddlers with Disabilities

IDEA '97 (P.L. 105-17)

Secs. 631–644.

1. Grants are provided to assist states to establish and maintain a coordinated, multidisciplinary, interagency system of early intervention services for infants and toddlers with disabilities and their families.

2. The Statewide system (Sec. 635) must include the following components, among others:
   a. Definition of "developmental delay."
   b. Policy ensuring services are available to all eligible infants and toddlers and their families, including Indian children residing on reservations.
   c. Comprehensive multidisciplinary evaluation of each child and identification of the family's needs in assisting in child's development.
   d. Individualized family service plan, including service coordination, for each eligible child and family.
   e. Child-find system, including referral system.
   f. Public awareness program focusing on early identification.
   g. State interagency coordinating council.
   h. Systems of personnel development and personnel standards.
   i. Policy ensuring that services are provided, to the maximum extent appropriate, in the natural environment.

2. States must submit a grant application (Sec. 637) containing, among other items:
   a. Designation of lead agency responsible for administration.
   b. If State provides services to at-risk infants and toddlers, description of those services.
   c. Policies and procedures to ensure smooth transitions from Part C to preschool or other appropriate services.

IDEA '04 (P.L. 108-446)

Sec. 635. Requirements for Statewide System. Additions to the system include:

1. Services are based, *to the extent practicable, on scientifically based research* and available to infants/ toddlers with disabilities, including *homeless children.*

2. Child find includes "rigorous standards" of identification to reduce need for future services.

3. Public awareness targets parents of premature infants or those with other physical risk factors associated with learning or developmental problems.

4. Training is provided for personnel in the social and emotional development of young children.

Sec. 635. Flexibility to Serve 3-Year-Olds Until Elementary School.

SEA and Part C lead agency may develop a joint system allowing Part C children eligible for Preschool services to continue in Part C until they enter or are eligible for kindergarten.

1. System must ensure:
   a. Annual notice to parents of right to receive B or C services with an explanation of program differences, including possible costs to parents for Part C services.
   b. Services, including an educational component promoting school readiness and incorporating preliteracy, language, and numeracy skills.
   c. Child may receive FAPE under Part B, if parents so choose.
   d. IFSP services continue while eligibility determination is made.
   e. Informed written consent before child turns 3 is required for continuation of Part C services.
   f. In substantiated cases of trauma due to exposure to family violence, evaluation referral for Part C is made.

IDEA '97 (P.L. 105-17)	IDEA '04 (P.L. 108-446)
3. States must provide procedural safeguards to families, similar to Part B procedures.	2. State reports on number/percentage of children eligible for Preschool but continuing under Part C.
4. Secretary establishes the Federal Interagency Coordinating Council to minimize duplication of programs and activities across federal, State, and local agencies, ensure effective coordination of federal early intervention and preschool services across agencies, identify gaps in programs and services, and identify barriers to interagency cooperation.	3. State is not required to provide FAPE for preschool-aged children served under Part C.
	Sec. 637. State Application and Assurances. Application includes description of (a) policies requiring referral for children involved in substantiated cases of neglect/abuse or affected by substance abuse; and, (b) efforts to promote collaboration among Early Head Start, early education and child care programs, and Part C.
	Added:
	Sec. 640(b): Obligations Related to and Methods of Ensuring Services. Basically the same as Part B, Sec. 612(a)(12) establishing financial responsibility for services through interagency agreements.
	Sec. 641. State Interagency Coordinating Council (SICC). (*NOTE:* Federal Interagency Coordinating Council was eliminated.) New SICC members include representatives of the Medicaid program, education programs for homeless children, and agencies responsible for foster care and for children's mental health.
	Sec. 643(e). Reservation for State Incentive Grants. In any year when the federal appropriation for Part C exceeds $460 million, the Secretary shall reserve 15% of the increase for State grants for flexibility provisions (see Sec. 635 above).

PART D: National Activities to Improve Education of Children with Disabilities

Part D programs provide support for the Part B and Part C grant programs through research, professional development, and technical assistance. These programs have been reorganized in P.L. 108-446, although most of the same functions and activities remain. There are new focuses on coordinating grants with requirements under the No Child Left Behind Act and ensuring that academic achievement of students with disabilities improves as a result of these grants. Other major themes include ensuring that programs and services are based on scientifically based research, and also ensuring appropriate training for both general and special education personnel, including related services personnel and administrators, to meet the needs of students with disabilities. Several new sections in Part D are highlighted below.

Subpart 1: State Personnel Development Grants

IDEA '97 (P.L. 105-17)	IDEA '04 (P.L. 108-446)
Subpart 1. State Program Improvement Grants. Competitive grants awarded to States to reform and improve educational, early intervention, and transition systems to improve student results. Required that at least 75% of funds be used to ensure sufficient numbers of personnel.	***Subpart 1. State Personnel Development Grants.***
	1. In any year when appropriation for this section is less than $100 million, competitive grants will be awarded, with priority to States with greatest personnel shortages or that demonstrate greatest difficulty in meeting "Personnel Qualifications" requirements (see Sec. 612(a)(14)).
	2. In years in which the appropriation equals or exceeds $100 million, formula grants will be awarded to all States.
	3. Requires a State Personnel Development Plan, and not less than 90% of the grant must be used for professional development.

Subpart 2: Personnel Preparation, Technical Assistance, Model Demonstration Projects, and Dissemination of Information

IDEA '97 (P.L. 105-17)	IDEA '04 (P.L. 108-446)
Subpart 2. Sec. 664(c). Accountability for Students Held to Alternative Achievement Standards. No comparable language in IDEA '97.	**Subpart 2. Sec. 664(c). Accountability for Students Held to Alternative Achievement Standards.** National studies to examine criteria States use in determining eligibility for alternate assessments, validity and reliability of instruments and procedures, alignment with State content standards, and use and effectiveness in appropriately measuring progress and outcomes specific to individualized instructional need.
Subpart 2. Sec. 665. Interim Alternative Educational Settings, Behavioral Supports, and Systemic School Interventions. No comparable language in IDEA '97.	**Subpart 2. Sec. 665. Interim Alternative Educational Settings, Behavioral Supports, and Systemic School Interventions.** Grants awarded to support safe learning environments that foster academic achievement by improving quality of interim settings and providing increased behavioral supports and systemic interventions. Funds may support activities such as training for staff on identification and preferral and referral procedures, and on positive behavioral supports and interventions and classroom management; stronger links between school-based and community mental health services; and use of behavioral specialists and related services personnel to implement behavioral supports. Funds may also be used to improve interim alternative educational settings by improving staff training, providing referrals for counseling services, increasing the use of instructional technology, and promoting interagency coordination of service delivery.
Subpart 2. Sec. 682. Parent Training and Information Centers. Grants to parent organizations to support centers that provide training and information to parents, particularly to underserved parents and parents of children inappropriately identified, and to assist parents to understand their rights under the law.	**Subpart 2. Sec. 682. Parent Training and Information Centers.** Has become Subpart 3. Sec. 671. Parent Training and Information Centers.

Subpart 3: Supports to Improve Results for Children with Disabilities

IDEA '97 (P.L. 105-17)	IDEA '04 (P.L. 108-446)
	Subpart 3. Sec. 671. Parent Training and Information Centers. New required activities include:
	1. Providing training and information to parents to enable their children to meet "developmental and functional goals" and challenging academic achievement goals and be prepared for independent living.
	2. Providing training and information meeting needs of low-income parents and parents of limited English proficient children.
	3. Helping parents participate in school activities that benefit their children.
	4. Helping parents understand, prepare for, and participate in "resolution sessions" (Sec. 615(f)(1)(B)).

IDEA '97 (P.L. 105-17)	IDEA '04 (P.L. 108-446)
Subpart 3. Sec. 674(e). National Instructional Materials Access Center. No comparable language in IDEA '97.	***Subpart 3. Sec. 674(e). National Instructional Materials Access Center.*** Secretary establishes and supports NIMAC to receive and maintain a catalog of print instructional materials prepared in the National Instructional Materials Accessibility Standard, to provide access to these materials, and to adopt procedures to protect against copyright infringement.

TITLE II: National Center for Special Education Research

IDEA '97 (P.L. 105-17)	IDEA '04 (P.L. 108-446)

National Center for Special Education Research. No comparable language in IDEA '97.	1. Title II establishes the National Center for Special Education Research.
	
	2. The Center will carry out research activities that are consistent with its mission to:
	   a. Sponsor research to expand knowledge and understanding of the needs of infants, toddlers, and children with disabilities in order to improve developmental, educational, and transitional results.
	   b. Sponsor research to improve services under the law in order to improve:
	   (1) academic achievement, functional outcomes, and educational results.
	   (2) developmental outcomes for infants and toddlers with disabilities.
	   c. Evaluate implementation and effectiveness of the IDEA.
	
	3. Commissioner of Special Education Research will direct the Center and will propose a research plan to the Director of the Institute, developed in collaboration with the Assistant Secretary of Education for Special Education and Rehabilitative Services, that (a) is consistent with the priorities and mission of the Institute and the Center; (b) is consistent with purposes of the IDEA; (c) has appropriate balance across all age ranges and types of disabilities; and (d) provides for objective research and uses measurable indicators to assess progress and results.

National Center for Special Education Research. Title II amends the Education Sciences Reform Act of 2002 (20 U.S.C. 9501 et. seq.) and becomes Part E of that Act. The Education Sciences Reform Act established the Institute, which replaces the Office of Educational Research and Information (OERI) as the main research branch of the U.S. Department of Education. Special education research previously was not housed under OERI, but will now become a part of the larger Department of Education research function.

TITLE III, Sec. 302: Effective Dates

" Parts A, B, C, and Subpart 1 of Part D take effect on July 1, 2005.

" The requirements of Sec. 602(10) "Highly Qualified" provisions took effect on the date of enactment.

" Subparts 2, 3, and 4 of Part D took effect on the date of enactment.

" Title II, "National Center on Special Education Research," took effect on the date of enactment; Sec. 201(a)(2), which deals with development of the research plan, takes effect on October 1, 2005.

References

CHAPTER 1

Ability Magazine. (2006). FDR's splendid deception. Retrieved May 15, 2006, from http://www .abilitymagazine.com/FDR_story .html

Autism Society of Michigan. (2006). Person first language: Guidelines for discussing people with disabilities. Retrieved May 12, 2006, from http://www.autism-mi.org/ aboutautism/TeacherTools12-04 .html

Baron, R. A., Byrne, D., & Branscombe, N. R. (2006). *Social psychology: Understanding human interaction* (11th ed.). Boston: Allyn and Bacon.

Blatt, B., & Kaplan F. (1974). *Christmas in purgatory: A photographic essay on mental retardation*. Syracuse, NY: Human Policy Press.

Braddock, D., & Parish, S. L. (2002). An institutional history of disability. In D. Braddock (Ed.), *Disability at the dawn of the 21st century and the state of the states* (pp. 1–61). Washington, DC: American Association on Mental Retardation.

Carlson, N. R., Heath, D., Miller, H. L., Donahoe, J. W., Buskist, W., & Martin, N. (2007). *Psychology: The science of behavior* (6th ed.). Boston: Allyn and Bacon.

Cook, B. G. (2001). A comparison of teachers' attitudes toward their included students with mild and severe disabilities. *Journal of Special Education, 34*(4), 203–213.

Dajini, K. F. (2001, January). What's in a name? Terms used to refer to people with disabilities. *Disabilities Studies Quarterly, 21*(3), 196–209.

Drew, C. J., & Hardman, M. L. (2007). *Intellectual disabilities across the lifespan* (9th ed.). Columbus, OH: Merrill.

Fox-Grage, W., Folkemer, D., Straw, T, & Hansen, A. (2002). *The states' response to the Olmstead decision: A work in progress*. Washington, DC: National Conference of State Legislatures.

Goodwin, D. (2006). Person of the century runner-up: Franklin Delano Roosevelt. *Time Magazine*. Retrieved May 17, 2006, from http://www.time.com/time/ time100/poc/magazine/franklin_ delano_rooseve9a.html

Hardman, M. L. & Nagle, K. (2004). Policy issues. In A. McCray, H. Rieth, & P. Sindelar (Eds.), *Contemporary issues in special education: Access, diversity, and accountability* (pp. 277–292). Boston: Allyn and Bacon.

Hastings, R. P., & Remington, B. (1993). Connotations of labels for mental handicap and challenging behavior: A review and research evaluation. *Mental Handicap Research, 6,* 237–249.

Hastings, R. P., Songua-Barke, E. J. S., & Remington, B. (1993). An analysis of labels for people with learning disabilities. *British Journal of Clinical Psychology, 32,* 463–465.

James, W. (1890). *Principles of psychology*. New York: Henry Holt.

Johnson, M. (2006). The Super-crip stereotype: Press victimization of disabled people. Retrieved May 16, 2006, from http://www.journalism. indiana.edu/gallery/Ethics/sup_crip .html

National Council on Disability. (2000, January). *From privileges to rights: People labeled with psychiatric disabilities speak for themselves*. Washington, DC: Author.

National Organization on Disability (N.O.D.) (2006). Top ten reasons to hire people with disabilities. Retrieved May 3, 2006, from http:// www.nod.org/index.cfm?fuseaction =page.viewPage&pageID=1430 &nodeID=1&FeatureID=480& redirected=1&CFID=7245299& CFTOKEN=6043927

N.O.D./Harris, L., & Associates. (1995). *National Organization on Disability/Harris Survey of Americans with Disability*. New York: Author.

N.O.D./Harris, L., & Associates. (2000). *National Organization on Disability/Harris Survey of Americans with Disability*. New York: Author.

N.O.D./Harris, L., & Associates. (2002). *National Organization on Disability/Harris Survey of Americans with Disability*. New York: Author.

N.O.D./Harris, L., & Associates. (2004). *National Organization on Disability/Harris Survey of Americans with Disability*. New York: Author.

Parish, S. L. (2002). Forces shaping developmental disabilities services in the states: A comparative study. In D. Braddock (Ed.), *Disability at the dawn of the 21st century and the state of the states* (pp. 353–475). Washington, DC: American Association on Mental Retardation.

Persaud, N. (2000). *Labeling: Its effects on labeled students*. International Special Education Congress 2000: Including the Excluded. Manchester, England: University of Manchester School of Education in association with Manchester Metropolitan University.

Rosenhan, D. I. (1973). On being sane in insane places. *Science, 179,* 250–258.

Sidey/Washington, H. (2006). What becomes a legend most? FDR True to life. *Time Magazine*. Retrieved May 17, 2006, from http://www .time.com/time/archive/preview/ 0,10987,998990,00.html

United States Department of Justice. (2006). A resort community improves access to city programs and services for residents and vacationers. *On-line*. Available: http://www .usdoj.gov/crt/ada/fernstor.htm. Retrieved May 4, 2006.

United States Department of Justice, Equal Employment Opportunity Commission. (2006). Americans with Disabilities Act: Questions and Answers. *On-line*. Available: http://www.ada.gov/q&aeng02 .htm.Retrieved May 1, 2006.

Watson, J. B., & Rayner, R. (1920). Conditioned emotional reactions. *Journal of Experimental Psychology, 3,* 1–14.

Wolfensberger, W. (1975). *The origin and nature of our institutional models*. Syracuse, NY: Human Policy Press.

Woolfolk, A. (2004). *Educational psychology* (9th ed.). Boston: Allyn and Bacon.

CHAPTER 2

Brown v. Topeka, Kansas, Board of Education, 347 U.S. 483 (1954).

Brownell, M. T., Sindelar, P. T., Bishop, A. G., Langley, L. K., & Seo, S. (2002). Special education teacher supply and teacher quality: The problems, the solutions. *Focus on Exceptional Children, 35*(2), 1–16.

Byrnes, M. A. (2002). *Taking sides: Clashing views on controversial issues in special education*. Guilford, CT: McGraw-Hill Dushkin.

Cassidy, V. M., & Stanton, J. E. (1959). *An investigation of factors involved in the educational placement of mentally retarded children: A study of differences between children in special and regular classes in Ohio*. (U.S. Office of Education Cooperative Research Program, Project No. 043). Columbus: Ohio State University.

Children's Defense Fund. (2005). *The state of America's children*. Washington, DC: Author.

Darling-Hammond, L., & Young, P. (2002). Defining "highly qualified teachers": What does "scientifically based research" actually tell us? *Educational Researcher, 31*(9), 13–25.

Elbaum, B. E., Vaughn, S., Hughes, M., & Moody, S. W. (2000). How effective are one-to-one tutoring programs in reading for elementary students at risk for reading failure? *Journal of Educational Psychology, 92*(4), 605–619.

Friend, M. P. & Bursuck, W. D. (2006). *Including students with special needs: A practical guide for classroom teachers* (4th ed). Boston: Allyn and Bacon.

Hahne, K. (2000). One parent's struggle with inclusion. In S. E. Wade (Ed.), *Inclusive education: A casebook and readings for prospective and practicing teachers*. London: Lawrence Erlbaum.

Hardman, M., & McDonnell, J. M. (in press). Perspectives and purposes of disability classification systems in research and clinical practice: Implications for teacher education. In M. McLaughlin & L. Florian (Eds.), *Issues in the classification of children in education: Perspectives and purposes of disability classification systems*. London: Corwin Press.

Hardman, M., & Mulder, M. (2004). Critical issues in public education: Federal reform and the impact on students with disabilities. In L. M. Bullock, & R. A. Gable (Eds.). *Quality personnel preparation in emotional/behavior disorders* (pp. 12–36). Dallas, TX: Institute for Behavioral and Learning Differences.

Hartwig, E. P., & Ruesch, G. M. (2000). Disciplining students in special education. *The Journal of Special Education, 33*(4), 240–247.

Hehir, T. (2002). IDEA 2002 Reauthorization: An opportunity to improve educational results for students with disabilities. *A timely IDEA: Rethinking federal education programs for children with disabilities*. Washington, DC: Center on Educational Policy.

Hendrick Hudson District Board of Education v. Rowley, 458 U.S. 176 (1982).

Hocutt, A. M. (1996). Effectiveness of special education: Is placement the critical factor? In The Center for the Future of Children, *Special education for students with disabilities*, (pp. 77–102). Los Angeles, CA: The Center for the Future of Children.

Huefner, D. S. (2006). *Getting comfortable with special education law*. Norwood, MA: Christopher-Gordon Publishers.

Jarrow, J. (1999, spring). Understanding the law to give students with disabilities full potential. *Opportunity Outlook: The Journal of the Council for Opportunity in Education*, 1–5.

Johnson, G. O. (1961). *A comparative study of the personal and social adjustment of mentally handicapped children placed in special classes with mentally handicapped children who remain in regular classes.* Syracuse, NY: Syracuse University Research Institute, Office of Research in Special Education and Rehabilitation.

Johnson, G. O. (1962). Special education for the mentally handicapped—A paradox. *Exceptional Children, 29*, 62–69.

Johnson, J., Duffett, A., Farkas, S., & Wilson, L. (2002). *When it's your own child: A report on special education from the families who use it.* Baltimore: The Annie E. Casey Foundation.

Jordan, A. M., & deCharms, R. (1959). Personal-social traits of mentally handicapped children. In T. G. Thurstone (Ed.), *An evaluation of educating mentally handicapped children in special classes and regular classes.* Chapel Hill: School of Education, University of North Carolina.

Kauffman, J. M. (1999). Commentary: Today's special education and its messages for tomorrow. *Journal of Special Education, 32*(4), 244–254.

Mastropieri, M. A., & Scruggs, T. E. (2007). *The inclusive classroom: Strategies for effective instruction.* Upper Saddle River, NJ: Merrill.

McLaughlin, M. (2002). Issues for consideration in the reauthorization of Part B of the Individuals with Disabilities Education Act. *A timely IDEA: Rethinking federal education programs for children with disabilities.* Washington, DC: Center on Educational Policy.

McLaughlin, M. J., Fuchs, L., & Hardman, M. (1999). Individual rights to education and students with disabilities: Some lessons from U.S. policy. In H. Daniels & P. Garner (Eds.), *Inclusive education: World yearbook of education 1999* (pp. 24–35). London: Kogan Page.

McLaughlin, M. J., & Tilstone, C. (2000). Standards and curriculum. The core of educational reform. In M. Rouse & M. J. McLaughlin (Eds.), *Special education and school reform in the United States and Britain* (pp. 38–65). London: Routledge.

Mercer, C. D., & Mercer, A. R. (2001). *Teaching students with learning problems.* Upper Saddle River, NJ: Merrill.

Mills v. District of Columbia Board of Education, 348 F. Supp. 866 (D.D.C. 1972).

National Center for Education Statistics. (2002). *Indicators of school crime and safety.* Washington, DC: Author.

National Commission on Teaching and America's Future. (1996). *What matters most: Teaching and America's future.* New York: Author.

National Council on Disability. (2000). *Back to school on civil rights.* Washington, DC: Author.

National Information Center for Children and Youth with Disabilities. (2003). *Office of Special Education Programs IDEA 97 Training Package.* Washington, DC: Author. Retrieved February 25, 2003, from http://www.nichcy.org/Trainpkg/trainpkg.htm

Nolet, V., & McLaughlin, M. J. (2000). *Assessing the general curriculum: Including students with disabilities in standards-based reform.* Thousand Oaks, CA: Corwin.

O'Connor, R. (2000). Increasing the intensity of intervention in kindergarten and first grade. *Learning Disabilities Research and Practice, 15*, 43–54.

Pennsylvania Association for Retarded Citizens v. Commonwealth of Pennsylvania, 334 F. Supp. 1257 (E.D.Pa. 1971).

Peterson, M. (2000). *Key elements of whole schooling.* Detroit: Renaissance Community Press, Wayne State University.

Peterson, J. M., & Hittie, M. M. (2005). *Inclusive teaching: Creating effective schools for all learners: Mylabschool edition.* Boston: Allyn and Bacon.

President's Commission on Excellence in Special Education. (2002). *A new era: Revitalizing special education for children and their families.* Washington, DC: Education Publications Center, U.S. Department of Education.

Rosenberg, M., Sindelar, P., & Hardman, M. (2004). Preparing highly qualified teachers for students with emotional and behavioral disorders: The impact of NCLB and IDEA. *Behavioral Disorders, 29*(3), 266–278.

Schaller, J., Ynag, N. K., & Chang, S. C. (2004.) Contemporary issues in rehabilitation counseling: Interface with and implications for special education. In A. M. Sorrells, H. J. Rieth, & P. T. Sindelar (Eds.), *Critical issues in special education: Access, diversity, and accountability* (pp. 226–242). Boston: Allyn and Bacon.

Sebba, J., Thurlow, M. L., & Goertz, M. (2000). Educational accountability and students with disabilities in the United States and England and Wales. In M. J. McLaughlin & M. Rouse (Eds.), *Special education and school reform in the United States and Britain* (pp. 98–125). New York: Routledge.

Thurlow, M. L. (2000). Standards-based reform and students with disabilities: Reflections on a decade of change. *Focus on Exceptional Children, 33*(3), 1–15.

Thurstone, T. G. (1959). *An evaluation of educating mentally handicapped children in special classes and regular classes* (U.S. Office of Education, Cooperative Research Project No. OE-SAE 6452). Chapel Hill: University of North Carolina.

U.S. Department of Education. (2003). *Introduction to No Child Left Behind.* Retrieved March 1, 2003, from http://www.nclb.gov/next/overview/index.html

U.S. Department of Education. (2006). To assure the free appropriate public education of all children with disabilities. *Twenty-sixth annual report to Congress on the implementation of the Individuals with Disabilities Education Act.* Washington, DC: U.S. Government Printing Office.

Vaughn, S., Bos, C. S., & Schumm, J. S. (2005). *Teaching exceptional, diverse, and at-risk students: IDEA 2004 update edition.* Boston: Allyn and Bacon.

Wood, J. W. (2002). *Adapting instruction to accommodate students in inclusive settings* (4th ed.). Upper Saddle River, NJ: Prentice-Hall.

CHAPTER 3

Adams, G., & Carnine, D. (2003). Direct instruction. In H. L. Swanson, K. Harris, & S. Graham (Eds.), *Handbook of learning disabilities* (pp. 403–416). New York: Guilford.

Batshaw, M. (2003). *Children with disabilities* (4th ed.). Baltimore: Paul H. Brookes.

Berk, L. E. (2005). *Development through the lifespan.* Boston: Allyn and Bacon.

Bloom, B. S. (1964). *Stability and change in human characteristics.* New York: Wiley & Sons.

Bruder, M. B. (2001). Inclusion of infants and toddlers: Outcomes and ecology. In M. J. Guralnick (Ed.), *Early childhood inclusion: Focus on change* (pp. 203–228). Baltimore: Paul H. Brookes.

Byrnes, M. (2002). Does full inclusion deliver a good education? In M. Byrnes (Ed.), *Taking sides: Clashing views on controversial issues in special education* (p. 219). Guilford, CT: McGraw-Hill Dushkin.

Carnine, D. (2000). *Why education experts resist effective practices (and what it would take to make education more like medicine).* Washington, DC: Fordham Foundation.

Chesley, G. M., & Calaluce, P. D. (2002). The deception of inclusion. In M. Byrnes (Ed.), *Taking sides: Clashing views on controversial issues in special education* (pp. 215–218). Guilford, CT: McGraw-Hill Dushkin.

Darling-Hammond, L. (2006) *Powerful teacher education: Lessons from exemplary programs.* San Francisco: Jossey-Bass.

Devore, S., & Hanley-Maxwell, C. (2000). "I wanted to see if we could make it work": Perspectives on inclusive childcare. *Exceptional Children, 66*(2), 241–255.

Division for Early Childhood, Council for Exceptional Children (2006). *Position statement on inclusion.*

Retrieved July 17, 2006, from http://www.decsped.org/pdf/positionpapers/Position%20Inclusion .pdf

Dorn, S., & Fuch, D. (2004). Trends in placement issues. In A. M. Sorrells, H. J. Rieth, & P. T. Sindelar (Eds.), *Critical issues in special education: Access, diversity, and accountability* (pp. 57–72). Boston: Allyn and Bacon.

Drew, C. J., & Hardman, M. L. (2007). *Mental retardation* (9th ed.). Upper Saddle River, NJ: Prentice-Hall.

Dunn, L. M. (1968). Special education for the mildly retarded. Is much of it justifiable? *Exceptional Children, 35*, 229–237.

Edyburn, D. L., (2003). *What every teacher should know about assistive technology.* Boston: Allyn and Bacon.

Eggen, P., & Kauchak, D. (2004). *Educational psychology: Windows on classrooms* (6th ed.). Upper Saddle River, NJ: Merrill Prentice-Hall.

Falvey, M. A., Rosenberg, R. L., Monson, D., & Eschilian, L. (2006). Facilitating and supporting transition. In P. Wehman (Ed.), *Life beyond the classroom: Transition strategies for youth with disabilities.* (pp. 165–181). Baltimore: Paul H. Brookes.

Friend, M. P., & Bursuck, W. D. (2006). *Including students with special needs: A practical guide for classroom teachers* (4th ed.). Boston: Allyn and Bacon.

Friend, M. P., & Cook, L. (2003). *Interactions: Collaboration skills for school professionals.* Boston: Allyn and Bacon.

Gartin, B. C., Murdick, N. L., Imbeau, M., & Perner, D. E. (2002). *How to use differentiated instruction with students with developmental disabilities in the general education classroom.* Alexandria, VA: Council for Exceptional Children.

Gillies, R. M., & Ashman, A. F. (2000). The effects of cooperative learning on students with learning difficulties in the lower elementary school. *Journal of Special Education, 34*, 19–27.

Gollnick, D., & Chinn, P. C. (2006). *Multicultural education in a diverse society* (7th ed.). Upper Saddle River, NJ: Prentice-Hall.

Haager, D., & Klinger, J. K. (2005). *Differentiating instruction in inclusive classrooms: The special educator's guide.* Boston: Allyn and Bacon.

Hallahan, D. P. (2002). We need more intensive instruction. In M. Byrnes (Ed.), *Taking sides: Clashing views on controversial issues in special education* (pp. 204–206). Guilford, CT: McGraw-Hill Dushkin

Harden, T. (2003, April 13). The disabilities you can see may be easier to deal with than the ones you can't. *New York Times,* p. 4A25–4A26.

Hobbs, T. (1997). *Planning for inclusion: A comparison of individual and cooperative procedures.* Unpublished doctoral dissertation, Florida State University, Tallahassee.

Hollins, E. R., & Guzman, M. T. (2005). Research on preparing teachers for diverse populations. In M. Cochran-Smith & K. M. Zeichner (Eds.), *Studying teacher education: The report of the AERA panel on research and teacher education* (pp. 477–548). Mahwah, NJ: Lawrence Erlbaum Associates.

Horner, R. H., Albin, R. W., Sprague, J. R., & Todd, A. W. (2006). Positive behavior support. In M. E. Snell & F. Brown (Eds.), *Instruction of students with severe disabilities* (pp. 206–250). Baltimore: Paul H. Brookes.

Hosp, M. K., & Hosp, J. L. (2003). Curriculum-based measurement for reading, spelling, and math: How to do it and why. *Preventing School Failure, 48*(1), 10–17.

Howell, K. W., & Nolet, V. (2000). *Curriculum-based evaluation.* Stamford, CT: Wadsworth.

Huefner, D. S. (2006). *Getting comfortable with special education law.* Norwood, MA: Christopher Gordon.

Hunt, J. M. (1961). *Intelligence and experience.* New York: Ronald Press.

Johnson, J., & Duffett, A. (2002). *When it's your own child: A report on special education and the families who use it.* New York: The Public Agenda.

Kavale, K. A., & Forness, S. R. (2000). History, rhetoric, and reality. *Remedial and Special Education, 21*(5), 279–296.

Klein, M. D., Cook, R. E., & Richardson-Gibbs, A. M. (2001). *Strategies for including children with special needs in early childhood settings.* Albany, NY: Delmar.

Landers, M. F., & Weaver, M. F. (1997). *Inclusive education: A process, not a placement.* Swampscott, MA: Watersun.

Lane, H., Hoffmeister, R., & Bahan, B. (2002). Are residential schools the least restrictive environment for deaf children? In M. Byrnes (Ed.), *Taking sides: Clashing views on controversial issues in special education* (pp. 222–228). Guilford, CT: McGraw-Hill Dushkin.

Lewis, A., & Norwich, B. (2005). Overview and discussion: Overall conclusions. In A. Lewis & B. Norwich (Eds.), *Special teaching for special children? Pedagogies for inclusion* (pp. 206–221). Berkshire, England: Open University Press.

Lipsky, D. K., & Gartner, A. (2002). Taking inclusion into the future. In M. Byrnes (Ed.), *Taking sides: Clashing views on controversial issues in special education* (pp. 198–203). Guilford, CT: McGraw-Hill Dushkin.

Maheady, L., Harper, G. F., & Mallette, B. (2001). Peer-mediated instruction and interventions and students with disabilities. *Remedial and Special Education, 22*(1), 4–14.

Mastropieri, M. A., & Scruggs, T. E. (2007). *The inclusive classroom: Strategies for effective instruction.* Upper Saddle River, NJ: Merrill.

McDonnell, J., Hardman, M., & Mc-Donnell, A. P. (2003). *Introduction to persons with moderate and severe disabilities* (p. 299). Boston: Allyn and Bacon.

Meyer, L. H. (2001). The impact of inclusion on children's lives: Multiple outcomes, and friendship in particular. *International Journal of Disability, Development, and Education, 48*(1), 9–31.

National Association for the Education of Young Children. (2006). *NAEYC position statement.* Retrieved July 16, 2006, from http://www.naeyc.org/about/positions/pdf/PSDAP98.PDF

National Association of School Psychologists. (2003). *Position Statement on Inclusive Programs for Students with Disabilities.* Retrieved: March 20, 2003, from http://www.nasponline.org/information/pospaper_ipsd.html

National Organization on Disability (NOD.), & Harris, L., & Associates. (2004). *National Organization on Disability/Harris Survey of Americans With Disabilities.* New York: Author.

National Institute for Urban School Improvement. (2003). *Improving education: The promise of inclusive schooling.* Denver: Author.

Niccols, A., Atkinson, L., & Pepler, D. (2003). Mastery movitation in young children with Down syndrome: Relations with cognitive and adaptive competence. *Journal of Intellectual Disability Research, 47,* 121–133.

Odom, S. L., & Bailey, D. B. (2001). Inclusive preschool programs: Classroom ecology and child outcomes. In M. J. Guralnick (Ed.), *Early childhood inclusion: Focus on change* (pp. 253–276). Baltimore: Paul H. Brookes.

Peterson, J. M., & Hittie, M. M. (2005). *Inclusive teaching: Creating effective schools for all learners: Mylabschool edition.* Boston: Allyn and Bacon.

Pettig, K. L. (2000). On the road to differentiated practice. *Educational Leadership, 58*(1), 14–18

Piaget, J. (1970). Piaget's theory. In P. H. Mussen (Ed.), *Carmichael's manual of child psychology* (3rd ed., Vol. 1). New York: Wiley.

Phillips, D. A., & Cabrera, N. J. (2006). *Beyond the blueprint: Directions for research on Head Start families.* Retrieved July 19, 2006, from http://search.nap.edu/readingroom/books/blueprint/.

Pugach, M. C. (2005). Research on preparing general education teachers to work with students with disabilities. In M. Cochran-Smith & K. M. Zeichner (Eds.), *Studying teacher education: The report of the AERA panel on research and teacher education* (pp. 549–590). Mahwah, NJ: Lawrence Erlbaum Associates.

Resources for Young Children and Families. (2000). *The individualized family service plan.* Colorado Springs, CO: Author. Retrieved from http://www.rycf.org/ifsp.html

Rose, D. H., & Meyer, A. (2002). *Teaching every student in the digital age: Universal design for learning.* Alexandria, VA: Association for Supervision and Development.

Rosenkoetter, S. E., Whaley, K. T., Hains, A. H., & Pierce, L. (2001). The evolution of transition policy for young children with special needs and their families: Past, present, and future. *Topics in Early Childhood Education, 21,* 3–15.

Sailor, W., Gee, K., & Karasoff, P. (2000). Inclusion and school restructuring. In M. Snell & F. Brown (Eds.), *Instruction of students with severe disabilities* (5th ed., pp. 1–30). Columbus, OH: Charles Merrill.

Sainato, D. M., & Morrison, R. S. (2001). Transition to inclusive environments for young children with disabilities. In M. J. Guralnick (Ed.), *Early childhood inclusion: Focus on change* (pp. 293–306). Baltimore: Paul H. Brookes.

Shapiro-Barnard, S., Tashie, C., Martin, J., Malloy, J., Schuh, M., Piet, J., Lichenstein, S., & Nisbet, J. (2002). Petroglyphs: The writing on the wall. In M. Byrnes (Ed.), *Taking sides: Clashing views on controversial issues in special education* (pp. 210–214). Guilford, CT: McGraw-Hill Dushkin.

Siegler, R. S. (2003). Thinking and intelligence. In L. Davidson & M. H. Bornstein (Eds.), *Well-being: Positive development across the life course* (pp. 311–320). Mahwah, NJ: Erlbaum.

Spencer, S. (2005). Lynne Cook and June Downing: The practicalities of collaboration in special education service delivery (Interview). *Intervention in School and Clinic, 40,* 296–300.

Study of Personnel Needs in Special Education. (2006). *General education teachers' role in special education (fact sheet).* Retrieved July 20, 2006, from http://ferdig.coe.ufl.edu/spense/

University of Northern Iowa. (2006). Children that learn together, learn to live together. Cedar Falls, Iowa, University of Northern Iowa, Department of Special Education. Retrieved July 24, 2006, from http://www.uni.edu/coe/inclusion/standards/index.html

United Nations Educational, Scientific, and Cultural Organization. (2003). *The Salmanca Statement and Framework for Action on Special Needs Education.* Retrieved May 7, 2003, from http://www.unesco.org/education/educprog/sne/files_pdf/framew_e.pdf

U.S. Department of Health and Human Services (2006). *Head Start Program Fact Sheet.* Washington, DC: Administration on Families and Children. Retrieved July 6, 2006, from http://www.acf.hhs.gov/programs/hsb/research/2006.htm

Vaughn, S., Bos, C. S., & Schumm, J. S. (2005). *Teaching exceptional, diverse, and at-risk students: IDEA 2004 update edition.* Boston: Allyn and Bacon.

Wade, S. E., & Zone, J. (2000). Creating inclusive classrooms: An overview. In S. E. Wade (Ed.), *Inclusive education: A casebook and readings for prospective and practicing teachers* (pp. 1–27). Mahwah, NJ: Lawrence Erlbaum Associates.

White, B. L. (1975). The first three years of life. Englewood Cliffs, NJ: Prentice Hall. *Journal of the Division for Early Childhood Education, 9,* 11–26.

CHAPTER 4

Algozzine, B., Browder, D., Karvonen, M., Test, D. W., & Wood, W. M. (2001). Effects of interventions to promote self-determination for individuals with disabilities. *Review of Educational Research, 71,* 219–277.

Babbitt, B. C., & White, C. M. (2002). RU ready? Helping students assess their readiness for postsecondary education. *Teaching Exceptional Children, 35*(2), 62–66.

Bambara, L. M, Browder, D. M., & Koger, F. (2006). Home and community. In M. E. Snell & F. Brown (Eds.), *Instruction of students with severe disabilities* (6th Ed. pp. 526–568). Upper Saddle River, NJ: Merrill/Prentice-Hall.

Braddock, D., Hemp, R., Rizzolo, M. C., Parish, S., & Pomeranz, A. (2002). The state of the state in developmental disabilities. In D. Braddock (Ed.), *Disability at the dawn of the 21st century and the state of the states* (pp. 83–130). Washington, DC: American Association on Mental Retardation.

Bremer, C. D., Kachgal, M., & Schoeller, K. (2003, April). Self-determination: Supporting successful transition. *Research to Practice Brief of the National Center on Secondary Education and Transition, 2*(1), 1–5.

Browder, D., Ahlgrim-Delzell, L., Courtade-Little, G., & Snell, M. E. (2006). General curriculum access. In M. E Snell & F. Brown (Eds.), *Instruction of students with severe disabilities* (6th Ed., pp. 489–525). Upper Saddle River, NJ: Merrill/Prentice-Hall.

deFur, S. (2000). Designing individualized education (IEP) transition plans. *ERIC Digest (EDO-EC-00-7).* Reston, VA: Council for Exceptional Children/ERIC Clearinghouse on Disabilities and Gifted Education.

Drew, C. J., & Hardman, M. L. (2007). *Intellectual disabilities across the lifespan* (9th ed.). Upper Saddle River, NJ: Merrill.

Fennick, E. (2001, July/August). Co-teaching: An inclusive curriculum for transition. *Teaching Exceptional Children*, 60–66.

Friend, M. P., & Bursuck, W. D. (2006). *Including students with special needs: A practical guide for classroom teachers* (4th ed.). Boston: Allyn and Bacon.

Getzel, E. E., & Gugerty, J. J. (2001). Applications for youth with learning disabilities. In P. Wehman (Ed.), *Life beyond the classroom: Transition strategies for young people with disabilities*, 3rd ed., pp.371–398). Baltimore: Paul H. Brookes.

Hasazi, S. B., Furney, K. S., & Destefano, L. (1999). Implementing the IDEA transition initiatives. *Exceptional Children, 65*(4), 555–566.

Hodapp, R., Glidden, L. M., & Kaiser, A. (2005). Siblings of persons with disabilities: Toward a research agenda. *Mental Retardation, 43*(5), 334–338.

Inge, K., & Moon, M. S. (2006). Vocational preparation and transition. In M. E. Snell & F. Brown (Eds.), *Instruction of students with severe disabilities* (pp. 569–609). Upper Saddle River, NJ: Merrill.

Kregel, J. (2001). Promoting employment opportunities for individuals with mild cognitive limitations: A time for reform. In A. J. Tymchuk, K. C. Lakin, & R. Luckasson (Eds.), *The forgotten generation: The status and challenges of adults with mild cognitive limitations* (pp. 87–98). Baltimore: Paul H. Brookes.

McDonnell, J. M., Hardman, M. L., & McDonnell, A. P. (2003). *Introduction to persons with moderate and severe disabilities*. Boston: Allyn and Bacon.

McDonnell, J. M., Hardman, M. L., & McGuire, J. (2007). Teaching and learning in secondary education. In L. Florian (Ed.), *Handbook of special education*. London: Sage.

Morgan, R. L., Ellerd, D. A., Jensen, K., & Taylor, M. J. (2000). A survey of community placements: Where are youth and adults with disabilities working? *Career Development for Exceptional Individuals, 23*, 73–86.

Morgan, R. L., Ellerd, D. A., Gerity, B. P., & Blair, R. J. (2000). That's the job I want: How technology helps young people in transition. *Teaching Exceptional Children, 32*(4), 44–49.

Murawski, W. W., & Dieker, L. A. (2004). Tips and strategies for co-teaching at the secondary level. *Teaching Exceptional Children 36*(5), 52–58

N.O.D. & Harris, L., & Associates. (2004). *National Organization on Disability/Harris Survey of Americans with Disabilities*. New York: Author.

Prouty, R. W., Smith, G., & Lakin, K. C. (2001, June). *Residential services for persons with developmental disabilities: Status and trends through 2000*. Minneapolis: University of Minnesota, College of Education and Human Development, Institute in Community Integration, Research and Training Center on Community Living.

Ryan, D. J. (2000). *Job search handbook for people with disabilities*. Indianapolis, Indiana: Jist.

Steere, D. E., Rose, E., & Cavaiuolo, D. (2007). *Growing up: Transition to adult life for students with disabilities*. Boston: Allyn and Bacon.

The ARC. (2006). The Individual with Disabilities Education Act: Transition from School to Work and Community Life. Retrieved August 10, 2006, http://www.thearc.org/faqs/qa-idea-transition.html

Thomas, S.B. (2000). College students and disability law. *Journal of Special Education, 33*(4), 248–257.

Tymchuk, A. J., Lakin, K. C., & Luckasson, R. (2001). Life at the margins: Intellectual demographic, economic, and social circumstances of adults with mild cognitive limitations. In A. J. Tymchuk, K. C. Lakin, & R. Luckasson (Eds.), *The forgotten generation: The status and challenges of adults with mild cognitive limitations* (pp. 21–38). Baltimore: Paul H. Brookes.

University of Illinois at Chicago National Research and Training Center, (2003). *Self-determination framework for people with psychiatric disabilities*. Chicago: Author. Retrieved May 20, 2003, from http://www.psych.uic.edu/UICNRTC/sdframework.pdf

U.S. Department of Education, (2006). *To assure the free appropriate public education of all children with disabilities: Twenty-sixth annual report to Congress on the implementation of the Individuals with Disabilities Education Act*. Washington, DC: U.S. Government Printing Office.

Wagner, M., & Blackorby, J. (1996). Transition from high school to work or college: How special education students fare. *In The Center for the Future of Children, Special Education for Students with Disabilities, 6*(1),(103–120). Los Angeles: The Center for the Future of Children.

Wagner, M., Newman, L., Cameto, R., & Levine, P. (2005). *Changes over time in the early postschool outcomes of youth with disabilities. A report from the National Longitudinal Study (NLTS) and the National Longitudinal Transition Study-2 (NLTS2)*. Menlo Park, CA: SRI International.

Wehman, P. (2006a). Individualized transition planning. In P. Wehman (Ed.), *Life beyond the classroom: Transition strategies for young people with disabilities* (4th ed., pp. 71–96).Baltimore: Paul H. Brookes, pp. 78–95.

Wehman, P. (2006b). Transition: The bridge to adulthood. In P. Wehman (Ed.), *Life beyond the classroom: Transition strategies for young people with disabilities* (4th ed., pp. 3–42). Baltimore: Paul H. Brookes.

Wehmeyer, M. L., Gragoudas, S., & Shogren, K. A. (2006). Self-determination, student involvement, and leadership development. In P. Wehman (2006). *Life beyond the classroom: Transition strategies for young people with disabilities* (4th ed., pp. 41–69). Baltimore: Paul H. Brookes.

CHAPTER 5

Abernathy, T. J., Webster, G., & Vermeulen, M. (2002). Relationship between poverty and health among adolescents. *Adolescence*, 37(145), 55–68.

Anderson, K. V. (2004). Educating America's Latino youth: A critical review of dropout-prevention literature. *Dissertation Abstracts International: Section B: The Sciences and Engineering, 65*(6-B), 3141.

Arredondo, P., & Perez, P. (2006). Historical perspectives on the multicultural guidelines and contemporary applications. *Professional Psychology: Research and Practice, 37*, 1–5.

Baca, L., & Baca, E. (2004). Bilingualism and bilingual education. In L. M. Baca & H. T. Cervantes (Eds.), *The bilingual special education interface* (4th ed., pp. 24–99). Columbus, OH: Merrill/Macmillan.

Baca, L. M., & Cervantes, H. T. (2004). *The bilingual special education interface* (4th ed.). Columbus, OH: Merrill/Macmillan.

Baldwin, J. R., Faulkner, S. L., & Hecht, M. L. (2006). *Redefining culture: Perspectives across the disciplines*. Mahwah, NJ: Lawrence Erlbaum.

Banks, J. A., & Banks, C. A. (2006). *Multicultural education: Issues and perspectives* (6th ed.). New York: Wiley.

Barranti, C. C. R. (2005). Family health social work practice with Mexican migrant and seasonal farmworking families. In F. K. O. Yuen (Ed.), *Social work practice with children and families* (pp. 117–142). Binghamton, NY: Haworth Social Work Practice Press.

Barnum-Martin, L., Mehta, P. D., Fletcher, J. M., Carlson, C. D., Ortiz, A., Carlo, M., & Francis, D. J. (2006). Bilingual phonological awareness: Multilevel construct validation among Spanish-speaking kindergartners in transitional bilingual education classrooms. *Journal of Educational Psychology, 98*, 170–181.

Barrera, M. (2006). Roles of definitional and assessment models in the identification of new or second language learners of English for special education. *Journal of Learning Disabilities, 39*, 142–156.

Barrett, K. H. (2005). Case examples: Addressing racism, discrimination, and cultural bias in the interface of psychology and law. In K. H. Barrett & W. H. George (Eds.), *Race, culture, psychology, and law*. Thousand Oaks, CA: Sage.

Battle, D. E. (2002). Language and communication disorders in culturally and linguistically diverse children. In D. K. Bernstein & E. Tiegerman-Farber (Eds.), *Language and communication disorders in children* (5th ed., pp. 354–386). Boston: Allyn and Bacon.

Bratter, J. L., & Eschbach, K. (2005). Race/ethnic differences in nonspecific psychological distress: Evidence from the National Health Interview Survey. *Social Science Quarterly, 86*, 620–644.

Buckner, J. C., Bassuk, E. L., & Weinreb, L. F. (2002). Predictors of academic achievement among homeless and low-income housed children. *Journal of School Psychology, 39*, 45–69.

Causey, V. E., Thomas, C. D., & Armento, B. J. (2000). Culture diversity is basically a foreign term to me: The challenges of diversity for preservice teacher education. *Teaching and Teacher Education, 16*, 33–45.

Charles, C. Z., Dinwiddie, G., & Massey, D. S. (2004). The continuing consequences of segregation: Family stress and college academic performance. *Social Science Quarterly, 85*, 1353–1373.

Chiappe, P., Siegel, L. S, & Gottardo, A. (2002). Reading-related skills of kindergartners from diverse linguistic backgrounds. *Applied Psycholinguistics, 23*, 95–116

Choi, Y., & Harachi, T. W. (2002). The cross-cultural equivalence of the Suinn-Lew Asian Self-Identity Acculturation Scale among Vietnamese and Cambodian Americans. *Journal of Social Work Research and Evaluation, 3*, 5–17.

Cohen, G. L., & Steele, C. M. (2002). A barrier of mistrust: How negative stereotypes affect cross-race mentoring. In J. Aronson (Ed.), *Improving academic achievement: Impact of psychological factors on education* (pp. 303–327). San Diego, CA: Academic Press.

Cohen, L. G., & Spenciner, L. J. (2007). *Assessment of children and youth with special needs* (3rd ed.). Boston: Allyn & Bacon.

Cohen, M. N. (2002). An anthropologist looks at "race" and IQ testing. In J. M. Fish (Ed.), *Race and intelligence: Separating from myth* (pp. 201–223). Mahwah, NJ: Lawrence Erlbaum.

Collier, C. (2004). Including bilingual exceptional children in the general education classroom. In L. M. Baca & H. T. Cervantes (Eds.), *The bilingual special education interface* (4th ed., pp. 298–335). Columbus, OH: Merrill/Macmillan.

Cuffe, S. P., McKeown, R. E., Addy, C. L., & Garrison, C. Z. (2005). Family and psychosocial risk factors in a longitudinal epidemiological study of adolescents. *Journal of the American Academy of Child & Adolescent Psychiatry, 44,* 121–129.

Deaux, K., Reid, A., & Martin, D. (2006). Ideologies of diversity and inequality: Predicting collective action in groups varying in ethnicity and immigrant status. *Political Psychology, 27,* 123–146.

Dettmer, P., Thurston, L. P., & Dyck, N. J. (2005). *Consultation, collaboration, and teamwork for students with special needs* (5th ed.). Boston: Allyn & Bacon.

de Valenzuela, J. S., & Baca, L. (2004). Issues and theoretical considerations in the assessment of bilingual children. In L. M. Baca & H. T. Cervantes (Eds.), *The bilingual special education interface* (4th ed., pp. 162–183). Columbus, OH: Merrill/Macmillan.

De Von Figueroa-Moseley, C., Ramey, C. T., & Keltner, B. (2006). Variations in Latino parenting practices and their effects on child cognitive developmental outcomes. *Hispanic Journal of Behavioral Sciences, 28,* 102–114.

Diana v. State Board of Education (1970, 1973). C-70, 37 RFP (N.D. Cal., 1970, 1973).

Dika, S. L., & Singh, K. (2002). Applications of social capital in educational literature: A critical synthesis. *Review of Educational Research, 72,* 31–60.

Dong, Y. R. (2002). Integrating language and content: How three biology teachers work with non-English-speaking students. *International Journal of Bilingual Education and Bilingualism, 5,* 40–57.

Downing, S. M. & Haladyna, T. M. (2006). *Handbook of test development.* Mahwah, NJ: Lawrence Erlbaum.

Drew, C. J., & Hardman, M. L. (2007). *Intellectual disabilities across the lifespan* (9th ed.). Columbus, OH: Merrill.

Durant, N. A. (2004). Mental health professionals, minorities, and the poor. *American Journal of Psychiatry, 161,* 382–383.

Edelsky, C. (2006). *With literacy and justice for all: Rethinking the social in language and education* (3rd ed.). Mahwah, NJ: Lawrence Erlbaum.

Erevelles, N., Kanga, A., & Middleton, R. (2006). How does it feel to be a problem? Race, disability, and exclusion in educational policy. In E. A. Brantlinger (Ed.). *Who benefits from special education? Remediating (fixing) other people's children* (pp. 77–99). Mahwah, NJ: Lawrence Erlbaum.

Farmer, T. W., Price, L. N., O'Neal, K. K., Leung, M. C., Goforth, J. B., Cairns, B. D., & Reese, L. E. (2004). Exploring risk in early adolescent African American youth.

American Journal of Community Psychology, 33, 51–59.

Feldman, S. (2005). The war for children. *Professional Psychology: Research and Practice, 36,* 615–617.

Ferrell, C. B., Beidel, D. C., & Turner, S. M. (2004). Assessment and treatment of socially phobic children: A cross cultural comparison. *Journal of Clinical Child and Adolescent Psychology, 33,* 260–268.

Fiese, B. H., Eckert, T., & Spagnola, M. (2006). Family context in early childhood: A look at practices and beliefs that promote early learning. In B. Spodek & O. N. Saracho (Eds.), *Handbook of research on the education of young children* (2nd ed.) (pp. 393–409). Mahwah, NJ: Lawrence Erlbaum.

Ferri, B. A., & Connor, D. J. (2005). Tools of exclusion: Race, disability, and (re)segregated education. *Teachers College Record, 107, Special Issue: Brown Plus Fifty.* 453–474.

Friend, M., & Cook, L. (2007). *Interactions: Collaboration skills for school professionals* (5th ed.). Boston: Allyn & Bacon.

Gallo, L. C., & Matthews, K. A. (2003). Understanding the association between socioeconomic status and physical health: Do negative emotions play a role? *Psychological Bulletin, 129,* 10–51.

Gelfand, D. M., & Drew, C. J. (2003). *Understanding child behavior disorders* (4th ed.). Belmont, CA: Wadsworth.

Gollnick, D. M., & Chinn, P. C. (2006). *Multicultural education in a pluralistic society* (7th ed.). Columbus, OH: Merrill.

Green, T. D., McIntosh, A. S., & Cook-Morales, V. J. (2005). From old schools to tomorrow's schools: Psychoeducational assessment of African American students. *Remedial and special education, 26,* 82–92.

Gregory, R. J. (2007). *Psychological testing: History, principles, and applications* (5th ed.). Boston: Allyn & Bacon.

Guadarrama, I. (2000). The empowering role of service learning in preparation of teachers. In C. R. O'Grady (Ed.), *Integrating service learning and multicultural education in colleges and universities* (pp. 227–243). Mahwah, NJ: Lawrence Erlbaum.

Halfon, N., & McLearn, K. T. (2002). Families with children under 3: What we know and implications for results and policy. In N. Halfon and K. T. McLearn (Eds.), *Child rearing in America: Challenges facing parents with young children* (pp. 367–412). New York: Cambridge University Press.

Hambleton, R. K., Merenda, P. F., & Spielberger, C. D. (2006). *Adapting educational psychological tests for cross-cultural assessment.* Mahwah, NJ: Lawrence Erlbaum.

Harrington, M. M., & Brisk, M. E. (2006). *Bilingual education: From compensatory to quality schooling* (2nd ed.). Mahwah, NJ: Lawrence Erlbaum.

Hendrick, J., & Weissman, P. (2007). *The whole child: Developmental curriculum for the young child* (7th ed.). Upper Saddle River, NJ: Pearson/Merrill, Prentice-Hall.

Heredia, R. R., & Altarriba, J. (2002). *Bilingual sentence processing.* San Diego, CA: Elsevier Science.

Hoover, J., & Collier, C. (2004). Methods and materials for bilingual special education. In L. M. Baca & H. T. Cervantes (Eds.), *The bilingual special education interface* (4th ed., pp. 274–297). Columbus, OH: Merrill/Macmillan.

Jozefowicz, D. M. (2003). Why do they leave? Why do they stay? A quantitative and qualitative examination of high school dropout. *Dissertation Abstracts International: Section A: Humanities and Social Sciences, 63(10-A),* 3729.

Kroeger, S. D., & Bauer, A. M. (2004). *Exploring diversity: A video case approach.* Upper Saddle River, NJ: Pearson/Merrill Prentice-Hall.

Larry P. v. Riles. (1972). C-71-2270 US.C, 343 F. Supp. 1306 (N.D. Cal. 1972).

Larry P. v. Riles. (1979). 343 F. Supp. 1306, 502 F. 2d 963 (N.D. Cal. 1979).

Lau v. Nichols. (1974). 414, U.S., 563–572 (1974, January 21).

Li, S. C. (2003). Biocultural orchestration of developmental plasticity across levels: The interplay of biology and culture in shaping the mind and behavior across the life span. *Psychological Bulletin, 129,* 171–194.

Linn, R. L. (2002). Constructs and values in standards-based assessment. In H. I. Braun and D. N. Jackson, (Eds.), *The role of constructs in psychological and educational measurement* (pp. 231–254). Mahwah, NJ: Lawrence Erlbaum.

Linn, R. L., & Miller, M. D. (2005). *Measurement and assessment in teaching* (9th ed.). Upper Saddle River, NJ: Pearson/Merrill Prentice-Hall.

Locke, D. C. (1995). Counseling interventions with African American youth. In C. C. Lee (Ed.), *Counseling for diversity* (pp. 21–40). Boston: Allyn and Bacon.

Manly, J. J., & Jacobs, D. M. (2002). Future directions in neuropsychological assessment with African Americans. In F. R. Ferraro (Ed.), *Minority and cross-cultural aspects of neuropsychological assessment. Studies on neuropsychology, development, and cognition* (pp. 79–96). Bristol, PA: Swets & Zeitlinger.

Martinez, C. R., Jr., DeGarmo, D. S., & Eddy, J. M. (2004). Promoting academic success among Latino youths. *Hispanic Journal of Behavioral Sciences, 26,* 128–151.

McDonough, P., Sacker, A., & Wiggins, R. D. (2005). Time on my side? Life course trajectories of poverty and health. *Social Science and Medicine, 61,* 1795–1808.

McGee, G. W. (2004). Closing the achievement gap: Lessons from Illinois' golden spike high-poverty high-performing schools. *Journal of Education for Students placed at Risk, 9,* 97–125.

McKinnon, J. (2001). *The black population: 2000.* U.S. Census Bureau, U.S. Department of Commerce, C2KBR/01-5.

McKinnon, J. (2003). *The black population in the United States: March 2002.* U.S. Census Bureau, U.S. Department of Commerce, P20–541.

McMillan, J. H. (2007). *Classroom assessment: Principles and practice for effective standards-based instruction* (4th ed.). Boston: Allyn & Bacon.

Merrell, K. W. (2003). *Behavioral, social, and emotional assessment of children and adolescents* (2nd ed.). Mahwah, NJ: Lawrence Erlbaum.

Mirel, J. (2002). Civic education and changing definitions of American identity, 1900–1950. *Educational Review, 54,* 143–152.

Montgomery, D. (2006, May 19). Senate backs English in a symbolic stand. *Salt Lake Tribune,* A11.

Morrison, G. S. (2007). *Early childhood education today* (10th ed.). Upper Saddle River, NJ: Pearson/Merrill Prentice-Hall.

Nakagawa, K., Stafford, M. E., Fisher, T. A., & Matthews, L. (2002). The "city migrant" dilemma: Building community at high-mobility urban schools. *Urban Education, 37,* 96–125.

Neven, R. S. (2005). Under fives counseling—opportunities for growth, change and development for children and parents. *Journal of Child Psychotherapy, 31,* 189–208.

Ornstein, E., & Moses, H. (2005). One nation many voices. *School Social Work Journal, 30,* 87–89.

Oyserman, D., Coon, H. M., & Kemmelmeier, M. (2002). Rethinking individualism and collectivism: Evaluation of theoretical assumptions and metaanalyses. *Psychological Bulletin, 128,* 3–72.

Pena, E., Iglesias, A., & Lidz, C. S. (2001). Reducing test bias through dynamic assessment of children's word learning ability. *American Journal of Speech Language Pathology, 10*(2), 138–154.

Proctor, B. D. (1998). *Poverty. Population Profile of the United States: 1997.* (pp. 40–41). U.S. Bureau of the Census, Current Population Reports, Series P23–194. Washington, DC: U.S. Government Printing Office.

Puckett, M., & Black, J. K. (2005). *The young child: Development from prebirth through age 8* (4th ed.). Upper Saddle River, NJ: Pearson/Merrill Prentice-Hall.

Quezada, R., & Osajima, K. (2005). The challenges of diversity: Moving toward cultural proficiency. In Hughes, L. W. (Ed.). *Current issues in school leadership* (pp. 163–182). Mahwah, NJ: Lawrence Erlbaum.

Quinones-Mayo, Y., & Dempsey, P. (2005). Finding the bicultural balance: Immigrant Latino mothers raising 'American' adolescents. *Child Welfare Journal, 84,* 649–668.

Ram, R. (2005). Income inequality, poverty, and population health: Evidence from recent data for the United States. *Social Science and Medicine, 61,* 2568–2576.

Reynolds, C. R., Livingston, R., & Willson, V. (2006). *Measurement and assessment in education.* Boston: Allyn & Bacon.

Rueda, R., & Yaden, D. B., Jr. (2006). The literacy education of linguistically and culturally diverse young children: An overview of outcomes, assessment, and large-scale interventions. In B. Spodek and O. N. Saracho (Eds.). *Handbook of research on the education of young children* (2nd ed., pp. 167–186). Mahwah, NJ: Lawrence Erlbaum.

Scheffner-Hammer, C., Pennock-Roman, M., Rzasa, S., & Tomblin, J. B. (2002). An analysis of the Test of Language Development—Primary for item bias. *American Journal of Speech Language Pathology, 11,* 274–284.

Separate and unequal. (1993, December 13) *U.S. News & World Report,* pp. 46–60.

Skiba, R. J., Poloni-Staudinger, L., & Simmons, A. B. (2005). Unproven links: Can poverty explain ethnic disproportionality in special education? *Journal of Special Education, 39,* 130–144.

Snyder, C. R., Shorey, H. S., & Rand, K. L. (2006). Using hope theory to teach and mentor academically at-risk students. In W. Buskist & S. F. Davis (Eds.), *Handbook of the teaching of psychology* (pp. 170–174). Malden, MA: Blackwell.

Solarsh, B., Alant, E. (2006). The challenge of cross-cultural assessment—The test of ability to explain for Zulu speaking children. *Journal of Communication Disorders, 39,* 109–138.

Spangenberg, E. R., & Sprott, D. E. (2006) Self-monitoring and susceptibility to the influence of self-prophecy. *Journal of Consumer Research, 32,* 550–556.

Spinelli, C. (2006). *Classroom assessment for students in special and general education* (2nd ed.). Upper Saddle River, NJ: Pearson/Prentice-Hall.

Taylor, A. C. (2005). Improving the academic achievement of African American males: A case study of African American male perceptions of attempted instructional strategies. *Dissertation Abstracts International:*

Section A: Humanities and Social Sciences, 66(5-A), 1643.

Trawick-Smith, J. (2006). *Early childhood development: A multicultural perspective* (4th ed.). Upper Saddle River, NJ: Pearson/Prentice-Hall.

Trouilloud, D., Sarrazin, P., & Bressoux, P. (2006). Relation between teachers' early expectations and students' later perceived competence in physical education classes: Autonomy-supportive climate as a moderator. *Journal of Educational Psychology, 98,* 75–86.

Twenge, J. M., & Crocker, J. (2002). Race and self-esteem revisited: Reply to Hafdahl and Gray-Little (2002). *Psychological Bulletin, 128,* 417–420.

U.S. Bureau of the Census. (1998). *Population Profile of the United States: 1997.* U.S. Bureau of the Census, Current Population Reports, Series P23–194. U.S. Washington, DC: Government Printing Office.

U.S. Bureau of the Census. (2000). *Poverty in the United States: 2000.* Retrieved from http://www.census.gov/dmd

Vasquez, M. J. T., Lott, B., & Garcia-Vazquez, E. (2006). Personal reflections: Barriers and strategies in increasing diversity in psychology. *American Psychologist, 61,* 157–172.

Vaughn, S., Linan-Thompson, S., Mathes, P. G., Cirino, P. T., Carlson, C. D., Pollard-Durodola, S. D., Gardenas-Hagan, E., & Francis, D. J. (2006). Effectiveness of Spanish intervention for first-grade English language learners at risk for reading difficulties. *Journal of Learning Disabilities, 39,* 56–73.

Venn, J. J. (2004). Assessing children with special needs (4th ed.). Upper Saddle River, NJ: Pearson/Prentice-Hall.

Webb, F. J. (2004). Mental health professionals, minorities, and the poor. *Journal of Behavioral Health Services and Research, 31,* 343.

Wiese, A. M. (2006). Educational policy in the United States regarding bilinguals in early childhood education. In B. Spodek (Ed.). *Handbook of research on the education of young children* (2nd ed.). Mahwah, NJ: Lawrence Erlbaum Associates.

Willingham, W. W. (2002). Seeking fair alternatives in construct design. In H. I. Braun and D. N. Jackson (Eds) *The role of constructs in psychological and educational measurement* (pp. 231–254). Mahwah, NJ: Lawrence Erlbaum.

Wolfendale, S. (2005). Children, families and schools: Developing partnerships for inclusive education. *European Journal of Special Needs Education, 20,* 447–448.

Zapata, J. T. (1995). Counseling Hispanic children and youth. In C. C. Lee (Ed.), *Counseling for Diversity* (pp. 85–108). Boston: Allyn and Bacon.

Zigler, E. F., Finn-Stevenson, M., & Hall, N. W. (2002). *The first three years and beyond: Brain development and social policy.* New Haven, CT: Yale University Press.

CHAPTER 6

Adams, J. F. (2001). Impact of parent training on family functioning. *Child and Family Behavior Therapy, 23,* 29–42.

Affleck, G., & Tennen, H. (1993). Cognitive adaptation to adversity: Insights from parents of medically fragile infants. In A. P. Turnbull, J. M. Patterson, S. K. Behr, D. L. Murphy, J. G. Marguis, & M. J. Blue-Banning (Eds.), *Cognitive coping, families, and disability* (pp. 135–150). Baltimore, MD: Brookes.

Anton, G. (2002). Back toward normal: How our family recovered after Alison was born. *The Exceptional Parent, 32,* 28–32.

Banks, M. E. (2003). Disability in the family: A life span perspective. *Cultural Diversity and Ethnic Minority Psychology, 9(4),* 367–384.

Baranowski, M. D., & Schilmoeller, G. L. (1999). Grandparents in the lives of grandchildren with disabilities: Mothers' perceptions. *Education and Treatment of Children, 22,* 427–446.

Baskin, A., & Fawcett, H. (2006). *More than a Mom: Living a full and balanced life when your child has special needs.* Bethesda, MD: Woodbine House.

Baxter, C., Cummins, R. A., & Yiolitis, L. (2000). Parental stress attributed to family members with and without disability: A longitudinal study. *Journal of Intellectual & Developmental Disability, 25,* 105–118.

Blacher, J. (2002). The mystery of family research: Parents magically change from invisible to prominent. *Exceptional Parent, 32,* 46–48.

Blue-Banning, M., Summers, J. A., Frankland, H. C., Nelson, L. L., & Beegle, G. (2004). Dimensions of family and professional partnerships: Constructive guidelines for collaboration. *Council for Exceptional Children, 70(2),* 167–184.

Boscardin, M. L., Brown-Chidsey, R., & Gonzalez-Martinez, J. C. (2001). The essential link for students with disabilities from diverse backgrounds. *Journal of Special Education Leadership, 14(2),* 89–95.

Brown, G. (2004). Family-centered care, mothers' occupations of caregiving and home therapy programs. In S. A. Esdaile & J. A. Olson (Eds.), *Mothering occupations: Challenge, agency, and participation* (pp. 346–371). Philadelphia: F.A. Davis.

Bruder, M. B. (2000). Family-centered early intervention: Clarifying our values for the new millennium. *Topics In Early Childhood Special Education, 20,* 105–15, 22.

Bui, Y. N., & Turnbull, A. (2003). East meets West: Analysis of person-centered planning in the context of Asian American values. *Education and Training and Mental Retardation and Developmental Disabilities, 38(1),* 18–31.

Buschbacher, P., Fox, L., & Clarke, S. (2004). Recapturing desired family routines: A parent-professional behavioral collaboration. *Research and Practice for Persons with Severe Disabilities, 2(1),* 25–39.

Cantu, C. (2002). Early intervention services: A family-professional partnership. *Exceptional Parent, 32(12),* 47–50.

Carpenter, B. (2000). Sustaining the family: Meeting the needs of families of children with disabilities. *British Journal of Special Education, 27,* 135–144.

Chambers, C. R., Hughes, C., & Carter, E. W. (2004). Parent and sibling perspectives on the transition to adulthood. *Education and Training in Developmental Disabilities, 39(2),* 79–94.

Chan, J. B., & Sigafoos, J. (2000). A review of child and family characteristics related to the use of respite care in developmental disability services. *Child and Youth Care Forum, 29,* 27–37.

Connors, C., & Stalker, K. (2003). *The views and experiences of disabled children and their siblings: A positive outlook.* London: Jessica Kingsley.

Correa, I., Hudson, R. F., & Hayes, M. T. (2004). Preparing early childhood special educators to serve culturally and linguistically diverse children and families: Can a multicultural education course make a difference? *Teacher Education and Special Education, 27(4),* 323–341.

Correa, V. I., & Jones, H. (2000). Multicultural issues related to families of children with disabilities. In M. J. Fine, & R. L. Simpson (Eds.), *Collaboration with parents and families of children with exceptionalities* (2nd ed., pp. 133–154). Austin, TX: PRO-ED.

Darley, S., Porter, J., Werner, J., & Eberly, S. (2002). Families tell us what makes families strong. *The Exceptional Parent, 32,* 34–36.

Devlin, S. D., & Harber, M. M. (2004). Collaboration among parents and professionals with discrete trial training in the treatment of autism. *Education and Training in Developmental Disabilities, 39(4),* 291–300.

Dollahite, D. C. (2001, August). Beloved children, faithful fathers: Caring for children with special needs. *Marriage and Families,* 16–21.

Dunst, Carl J. (2002). Family-centered practices: Birth through high school. *The Journal of Special Education, 36,* 139–147.

Epstein, S. H., & Bessel, A. G. (2002). A parent's determination and a pre-K dream realized. *The Exceptional Parent, 32,* 56–60.

Ferguson, P. M. (2002). A place in the family: An historical interpretation of research on parental reactions to having a child with a disability. *Journal of Special Education, 36,* 124–130.

Fine, M. J., & Nissenbaum, M. S. (2000). The child with disabilities and the family: Implications for professionals. In M. J. Fine, & R. L. Simpson (Eds.), *Collaboration with parents and families of children with exceptionalities* (2nd ed., pp. 3–26). Austin, TX: PRO-ED.

Fine, M. J., & Simpson, R. L. (2000). *Collaboration with parents and families of children with exceptionalities* (2nd ed.). Austin, TX: PRO-ED.

Fischer, S. (2003). Fathers are caregivers too! [Online]. Available: http://www.fathersnetwork.org/572.html

Fish, M. C. (2000). Children with special needs in nontraditional families. In M. J. Fine, & R. L. Simpson (eds.), *Collaboration with parents and families of children with exceptionalities* (2nd ed., pp. 49–68). Austin, TX: PRO-ED.

Ford, A. (2003). *Laughing Allegra.* New York: Newmarket Press.

Fox, L., & Dunlap, G. (2002). Family-centered practices in positive behavior support. *Beyond Behavior,* 24–26.

Fox, L., Vaughn, B. J., Wyatte, M. L., & Dunlap, G. (2002). "We can't expect other people to understand": Family perspectives on problem behavior. *Exceptional Children, 68,* 437–450.

Frankland, H. C., Edmonson, H., & Turnbull, A. P. (2001). Positive behavioral support: Family, school, and community partnerships. *Beyond Behavior,* 7–9.

Frankland, H. C., Turnbull, A. P., Wehmeyer, M. L., & Blackmountain, L. (2004). An exploration of the self-determination construct and disability as it relates to the Diné (Navajo) culture. *Education and Training in Developmental Disabilities, 39*(3), 191–205.

Friend, M., & Cook, L. (2003). *Interactions: Collaboration skills for school professionals* (4th ed.). Boston: Allyn and Bacon.

Frost, J. (2002). Sarah syndrome: A mother's view of having a child with no diagnosis. *Exceptional Parent Magazine, 32,* 70–71.

Fuller, M. L., & Olsen, G. (1998). *Home-school relations: Working successfully with parents and families.* Boston: Allyn and Bacon.

Furlong, P. (2005). Parent project muscular dystrophy. *Exceptional Parent, 35*(2), 61–62.

Gallagher, P. A., Rhodes, C. H., & Darling, S. M. (2004). Parents as professionals in early intervention. *Topics in Early Childhood Special Education, 24*(1), 5–13.

Geisthardt, C., Brotherson, M., & Cook, C. (2002). Friendships of children with disabilities in the home environment. *Education and Training in Mental Retardation and Developmental Disabilities, 37,* 235–252.

Goeke, J. (2003). Parents speak out: Facial plastic surgery for children with Down syndrome. *Education and Training in Developmental Disabilities, 38*(3), 323–333.

Gorman, J. C. (2004). *Working with challenging parents of students with special needs.* Thousand Oaks, CA: Corwin Press.

Gray, D. E. (2002). Ten years on: A longitudinal study of families of children with autism. *Journal of Intellectual and Developmental Disability, 27,* 215–222.

Grissom, M. O., & Borkowski, J. G. (2002). Self-efficacy in adolescents who have siblings with or without disabilities. *American Journal on Mental Retardation, 107*(2), 79–90.

Harland, P., & Cuskelly, M. (2000). The responsibilities of adult siblings of adults with dual sensory impairments. *International Journal of Disability Development and Education, 47,* 293–307.

Harris, S. L., & Glasberg, B. A. (2003). Siblings of children with autism: A guide for families (2nd ed.). Bethesda, MD: Woodbine House.

Hastings, R. P., Daley, D., Burns, C., & Beck, A. (2006). Maternal distress and expressed emotion: Cross-sectional and longitudinal relationships with behavior problems of children with intellectual disabilities. *American Journal on Mental Retardation, 111*(1), 48–61.

Hastings, R. P., & Taunt, H. M. (2002). Positive perceptions in families of children with developmental disabilities. *American Journal on Mental Retardation, 107,* 116–27.

Hauser-Cram, P. (2006). Young children with developmental disabilities and their families: Needs, policies, and services. In K. M. Thies & J. F. Travers (Eds.), *Handbook of human development for health care professionals* (pp. 287–305). Boston: Jones and Bartlett.

Hauser-Cram, P., Warfield, M. E., Shonkoff, J. P., & Krauss, M. W. (2001). Children with disabilities: A longitudinal study of child development and parent well-being. *Monographs of the Society for Research in Child Development, 66,* 1–114.

Herbert, M. J., Klemm, D., & Schimanski, C. (1999). Giving the gift of support: From parent to parent. *Exceptional Parent, 29*(8), 58–62.

Jackson, C. W., & Turnbull, A. (2004). Impact of deafness on family life: A review of the literature. *TECSE, 24*(1), 15–29.

Johnson, C. (2000). What do families need? *Journal of Positive Behavior Interventions, 2,* 115–117.

Kolb, S. M., & Hanley-Maxwell, C. (2003). Critical social skills for adolescents with high incidence disabilities: Parental perspectives. *Council for Exceptional Children, 69,* 163–179.

Lake, J. F., & Billingsley, B. S. (2000). An analysis of factors that contribute to parent-school conflict in special education. *Remedial and Special Education, 21,* 240–251.

Lamb, M. E., & Meyer, D. J. (1991). Fathers of children with special needs. In M. Seligman (Ed.), *The family with a handicapped child* (2nd ed., pp. 151–180). Boston: Allyn and Bacon.

Larson, E. A. (2000). The orchestration of occupation: The dance of mothers. *American Journal of Occupational Therapy, 54,* 269–280.

Last, E. C. (2001). I have learned.... In S. D. Klein & K. Schive (Eds.), *You will dream new dreams* (pp. 56–60). New York: Kensington Books.

Lee, A. L., Strauss, L., Wittman, P., Jackson, B., & Carstens, A. (2001). The effects of chronic illness on roles and emotions of caregivers. *Occupational Therapy in Health Care, 14,* 47–60.

Levinson, E. M., McKee, L., & Dematteo, F. J. (2000). The exceptional child grows up: Transition from school to adult life. In M. J. Fine, & R. L. Simpson (Eds.), *Collaboration with parents and families of children with exceptionalities* (2nd ed., pp. 409–436). Austin, TX: PRO-ED.

Lobato, D. J., Faust, D., & Spirito, A. (1988). Examining the effects of chronic disease and disability on children's sibling relationships. *Journal of Pediatric Psychology, 13,* 389–407.

Luckner, J. L. & Velaski, A. (2004). Healthy families of children who are deaf. *American Annals of the Deaf, 149*(4), 324–335.

Martin, J. E., Van Dycke, J. L., Greene, B. A., Gardner, J. E., Christensen, W. R., Woods, L. L., & Lovett, D. L. (2006). Direct observation of teacher-directed IEP meetings: Establishing the need for student IEP meeting instruction. *Council for Exceptional Children, 72*(2), 187–200.

Masson E. J., Kruse, L. A., Farabaugh, A., Gershberg, R., & Kohler, M. S. (2000). Children with exceptionalities: Opportunities for collaboration between family and school. In M. J. Fine & R. L. Simpson (Eds.), *Collaboration with parents and families of children with exceptionalities* (2nd ed., pp. 69–88). Austin, TX: PRO-ED.

McHugh, M. (2003). *Special siblings: Growing up with someone with a disability.* Baltimore, MD: Paul H. Brooks.

McHatton, P. A., & Correa, V. (2005). Stigma and discrimination: Perspectives from Mexican and Puerto Rican mothers of children with special needs. *Topics in Early Childhood Education, 25*(3), 131–142.

McKay, M. M. (2000). What we can do to increase involvement of urban children and families in mental health services and prevention programs. *Report on Emotional and Behavioral Disorders in Youth, 1,* 11–12, 20.

Meyer, D. (Ed.). (2005). *The Sibling Slam Book: What it's really like to have a brother or sister with special needs.* Bethesda, MD: Woodbine House.

Meyer, D. J. (1995). *Uncommon fathers: Reflections on raising a child with a disability.* Bethesda, MD: Woodbine House.

Muscott, H. S. (2002). Exceptional partnerships: Listening to the voices of families. *Preventing School Failure, 46,* 66–69.

Park, J., Turnbull, A. P., & Turnbull, H. R. III (2002). Impacts of poverty on quality of life in families of children with disabilities. *Exceptional Children, 68,* 151–170.

Pipp-Siegel, S., Sedey, A. L., Yoshinaga-Itano, C. (2002). Predictors of parental stress in mothers of young children with hearing loss. *Journal of Deaf Studies and Deaf Education, 7,* 1–17.

Poston, D., Turnbull, A., Park, J., Mannan, H., Marquis, J., & Wang, M. (2003). Family quality of life: A qualitative inquiry. *American Association on Mental Health, 41*(5), 313–328.

Poston, D. J., & Turnbull, A. P. (2004). Role of spirituality and religion in family quality of life for families of children with disabilities. *Education and Training in Developmental Disabilities, 39*(2), 95–108.

Raver, S. A. (2005). Using family-based practices for young children with special needs in preschool programs. *Childhood Education, 82*(1), 9–13.

Rieger, A. (2004). Explorations of the functions of humor and other types of fun among families of children with disabilities. *Research and Practice for Persons with Severe Disabilities, 29*(3), 194–209.

Risdal, D., & Singer, G. H. S. (2004). Marital adjustment in parents of children with disabilities: A historical review and meta-analysis. *Research & Practice for Persons with Severe Disabilities, 29*(2), 95–103.

Rivers, K. O. (2000). Working with caregivers of infants and toddlers with special needs from culturally and linguistically diverse backgrounds. *Infant Toddler Intervention: The Transdisciplinary Journal, 10,* 61–72.

Rupiper, M., & Marvin, C. (2004). Preparing teachers for family centered services: A survey of preservice curriculum content. *Teacher Education and Special Education, 27*(4), 384–395.

Russell, L. M., & Grant, A. E. (2005). *Planning for the future: Providing a meaningful life for a child with a disability after your death.* Palatine, IL: Planning for the Future.

Sandler, A. G., Warren, S. H., & Raver, S. A. (1995, August). Grandparents as a source of support for parents of children with disabilities. A brief report. *Mental Retardation, 33,* 248–250.

Santarelli, G., Koegel, R. L., Casas, J. M., & Koegel, L. K. (2001). Culturally diverse families participating in behavior therapy parent education programs for children with developmental disabilities. *Journal of Positive Behavior Interventions, 3,* 120–123.

Scherman, A., Gardner, J. E., & Brown, P. (1995, April/May). Grandparents' adjustment to grandchildren with disabilities. *Educational Gerontology, 21,* 261–273.

Segal, R. (2004). Mother time: The art and skill of scheduling in families of children with attention deficit hyperactivity disorders. In S. A. Esdaile & J. A. Olson (Eds.), *Mothering occupations: Challenge, agency, and participation* (pp. 324–345). Philadelphia: F.A. Davis.

Seligman, M., & Darling, R. B. (1989). *Ordinary families, special children.* New York: Guilford.

Seltzer, M. M., Greenberg, J. S., Floyd, F. J., Pettee, Y., & Hong, J. (2001). Life course impacts of parenting a child with a disability. *American Journal on Mental Retardation, 106*(3), 265–286.

Shelden, M. L., & Rush, D. D. (2001). The ten myths about providing early intervention services in natural environments. *Infants and Young Children, 14,* 1–13.

Simmerman, S., Blacher, J., & Baker, B. L. (2001). Fathers' and mothers' perceptions of father involvement in families with young children with a disability. *Journal of Intellectual and Developmental Disability, 26,* 325–338.

Simpson, R. L., & Zurkowski, J. K. (2000). Parent and professional collaborative relationships in an era of change. In M. J. Fine & R. L. Simpson (Eds.), *Collaboration with parents and families of children with exceptionalities* (2nd ed., pp. 89–102). Austin, TX: PRO-ED.

Singer, G., Marquis, J. G., Powers, L. K., Blanchard, L., DiVenere, N., Santelli, B., & Ainbinder, J. (1999). A multi-site evaluation of parent to parent programs for parents of children with disabilities. *Journal of Early Intervention, 22*(3), 217–229.

Snow, K. (2001). *Disability is natural: Revolutionary common sense for raising successful children with disabilities.* Woodland Park, CO: BraveHeart Press.

Stone, J. H. (Ed.). (2005). *Culture and disability: Providing culturally competent services.* London: Sage.

Stoneman, Z., & Gavidia-Payne, S. (2006). Marital adjustment in families of young children with disabilities: Associations with daily hassles and problem-focused coping. *American Journal of Mental Retardation, 111*(1), 1–14.

Strohm, K. (2005). *Being the other one: Growing up with a brother or sister who has special needs.* Boston: Shambhala.

Taylor, J. M, & Baglin, C. A. (2000). Families of young children with disabilities: Perceptions in the early childhood special education literature. *Infant Toddler Intervention: The Transdisciplinary Journal, 10,* 239–257.

Turbiville, V. P., & Marquis, J. G. (2001). Father participation in early education programs. *Topics in Early Childhood Special Education, 21,* 223–231.

Turbiville, V. (1997). *Literature review: Fathers, their children, and disability.* Lawrence, KS: The Beach Center on Families and Disability, The University of Kansas.

Turnbull, A. P., & Turnbull, H. R. (2002), From the old to the new paradigm of disabilities and families: Research to enhance family quality and life outcomes. In J. L. Paul, C. D. Lavely, A. Cranston-Gingras, & E. L. Taylor (Eds.), *Rethinking professional issues in special education* (pp. 83–118). Westport, CT: Ablex.

Turner, M. H. (2000). The developmental nature of parent-child relationships: The impact of disabilities. In M. J. Fine & R. L. Simpson (Eds.), *Collaboration with parents and families of children with exceptionalities* (2nd ed., pp. 103–130). Austin, TX: PRO-ED.

Tynan, W. D., Wornian, K. (2002). Parent management training: Efficacy, effectiveness, and barriers to implementation. *Report on Emotional and Behavioral Disorders in Youth, 2,* 57–58, 71–72.

Ulrich, M. E. (2003). Levels of awareness: A closer look at communication between parents and professionals. *TEACHING Exceptional Children, 35*(6), 20–23.

Vacca, J., & Feinberg, E. (2000). Why can't families be more like us?: Henry Higgins confronts Eliza Doolittle in the world of early intervention. *Infants and Young Children, 13,* 40–48.

Wang, M., Turnbull, A. P., Summers, J. A., Little, T. D., Poston, D. J., Mannan, H., & Turnbull, R. (2004). Severity of disability and income as predictors of parents' satisfaction with their family quality of life during early childhood years. *Research & Practice for Persons with Severe Disabilties, 29*(2), 82–94.

Ward, M. J., Cronin, K. B., Renfro, P. D., Lowman, D. K., & Cooper, P. D. (2000). Oral motor feeding in the neonatal intensive care unit: Exploring perceptions of parents and occupational therapists. *Occu-pational Therapy in Health Care, 12,* 19–37.

Worthington, J., Hernandez, M., Friedman B., & Uzzell, D. (2001). *Systems of care: Promising practices in children's mental health, 2001 Series, Volume 11.* Washington, DC: Center for Effective Collaboration and Practice, American Institutes for Research.

Young, D. M., & Roopnarine, J. L. (1994). Fathers' childcare involvement with children with and without disabilities. *Topic in Early Childhood Special Education, 14* (Winter), 488–502.

Zhang, C., & Bennett, T. (2001). Multicultural views of disability: Implications for early intervention professionals. *Infant Toddler Intervention: The Transdisciplinary Journal, 11,* 143–154.

CHAPTER 7

Aiken, L. R., & Groth-Marnat, G. (2006). *Psychological testing and assessment* (12th ed.). Boston: Allyn & Bacon.

Airasian, P. W. (2005). *Classroom assessment: Concepts and applications* (5th ed.). New York: McGraw-Hill.

Allsopp, D. H., Minskoff, E. H., & Bolt, L. (2005). Individualized course-specific strategy instruction for college students with learning disabilities and ADHD: Lessons learned from a model demonstration project. *Learning Disabilities Research & Practice, 20,* 103–118.

American Psychiatric Association. (2000). Diagnostic and statistical manual of mental disorders (4th ed., text revision). Washington, DC: Author.

Ardoin, S. P. (2006). The response in response to intervention: Evaluating the utility of assessing maintenance of intervention effects. *Psychology in the schools, 43,* 713–725.

Atkinson, D. (2006). Editorial. *British Journal of Learning Disabilities, 34,* 1–2.

Barrett, L. F., Tugade, M. M., & Engle, R. W. (2004). Individual differences in working memory capacity and dual-process theories of the mind. *Psychological Bulletin, 130,* 553–573.

Baum, S. M., & Olenchak, F. R. (2002). The alphabet children: GT, ADHD, and more. *Exceptionality, 10*(2), 77–91.

Bauminger, N., Edelsztein, H. S., & Morash, J. (2005). Social information processing and emotional understanding in children with LD. *Journal of Learning Disabilities, 38,* 45–60.

Baxter, J. A., Woodward, J., & Olson, D. (2005). Writing in mathematics: An alternative form of communication for academically low-achieving students. *Learning Disabilities Research and Practice, 20,* 119–135.

Bayliss, D. M., Jarrold, C., & Baddeley, A. D. (2005). *Journal of Experimental Child Psychology, 92,* 76–99.

Bender, W. N. (2004). *Learning disabilities: Characteristics, identification, and teaching strategies* (5th ed.). Boston: Allyn and Bacon.

Bender, W. N. (2005). Differentiating instruction for students with learning disabilities. Thousand Oaks, CA: Sage.

Berry, R. A. W. (2006). Beyond strategies: Teacher beliefs and writing instruction in two primary inclusion classrooms. *Journal of Learning Disabilities, 39,* 11–24.

Bishop, A., & Jones, P. (2002). Promoting inclusive practice in primary initial teacher training: Influencing hearts as well as minds. *Support for Learning, 17*(2), 58–63.

Bitter, G. G., & Pierson, M. E. (2005). *Using technology in the classroom* (6th ed.). Boston: Allyn and Bacon.

Boets, B., Wouters, J., & van Wieringen, A. (2006). Auditory temporal information processing in pre-school children at family risk for dyslexia: Relations with phonological abilities and developing literacy skills. *Brain and Language, 97,* 64–79.

Booth, T., Booth, W., & McConnell, D. (2005). The prevalence and outcomes of care proceedings involving parents with learning difficulties in the family courts. *Journal of Applied Research in Intellectual Disabilities, 18,* 7–17.

Bradley, R., Danielson, L., & Doolittle, J. (2005). Response to intervention. *Journal of Learning Disabilities, 38,* 485–486.

Brook, U. & Boaz, M. (2005). Attention deficit and hyperactivity disorder (ADHD) and learning disabilities (LD): Adolescents perspective. *Patient Education and Counseling, 58,* 187–191.

Brosvic, G. M., Dihoff, R. E., & Epstein, M. L. (2006). Feedback facilitates the acquisition and retention of numerical fact series by elementary school students with mathematics learning disabilities. *Psychological Record, 56,* 35–54.

Brown, G., & Coldwell, B. (2006). Developing a controlled drinking programme for people with learning disabilities living in conditions of medium security. *Addiction Research and Theory, 14,* 87–95.

Brumback, R. A., & Coffey, C. E. (2006). Neuropsychiatric contributions. In R. T. Ammerman (Ed.). *Comprehensive handbook of personality and psychopathology,* Vol. 3. (pp. 29–37). Hoboken, NJ: John Wiley & Sons.

Bryan, T. (2005). Science-based advances in the social domain of learning disabilities. *Learning Disability Quarterly, 28,* 119–121.

Burns, M. K., & Senesac, B. V. (2005). Comparison of dual discrepancy criteria to assess response to intervention. *Journal of School Psychology, 43,* 393–406.

Butler, D. L., Beckingham, B., & Lauscher, H. J. N. (2005). Promoting strategic learning by eighth-grade students struggling in mathematics: A report of three case studies. *Learning Disabilities Research & Practice, 20,* 156–174.

Butin, D. W. (2005). Is anyone listening? Educational policy perspectives on the social foundations of education. *Educational Studies: Journal of the American Educational Studies Association, 38,* 286–297.

Carter, E. W., Lane, K. L., & Pierson, M. R. (2006). Self-determination skills and opportunities of transition-age youth with emotional disturbance and learning disabilities. *Exceptional Children, 72,* 333–346.

Cartledge, G. (2005). Learning disabilities and social skills: Reflections. *Learning Disability Quarterly, 28,* 179–181.

Chalk, J. C., Hagan-Burke, S., & Burke, M. D. (2005). The effects of self-regulated strategy development on the writing process for high school students with learning disabilities. *Learning Disability Quarterly, 28,* 75–87.

Chang, F., Early, D. M., & Winton, P. J. (2005). Early childhood teacher preparation in special education at 2- and 4-year institutions of higher education. *Journal of Early Intervention, 27,* 110–124.

Chapman, M., Gledhill, P., Jones, P., Burton, M., & Soni, S. (2006). The use of psychotropic medication with adults with learning disabilities: Survey findings and implications for services. *British Journal of Learning Disabilities, 34,* 28–35.

Chitsabesan, P., & Bailey, S. (2006). Mental health, educational and social needs of young offenders in custody and in the community. *Current Opinion in Psychiatry, 19,* 355–360.

Cleary, T. J., & Zimmerman, B. J. (2006). Teachers' perceived usefulness of strategy microanalytic assessment information. *Psychology in the Schools, 43,* 149–155.

Collishaw, S., Maughan, B., & Pickles, A. (2005). "Confounding factors for depression in adults with mild learning disability": Reply. *British Journal of Psychiatry, 187,* 89–90.

Compton, D. L., Fuchs, D., & Fuchs, L. S. (2006). Selecting at-risk readers in first grade for early intervention: A two-year longitudinal study of decision rules and procedures. *Journal of Educational Psychology, 98,* 394–409.

Cone-Wesson, B. (2005). Prenatal alcohol and cocaine exposure: Influences on cognition, speech, language, and hearing. *Journal of Communication Disorders, 38,* 279–302.

Cornett-DeVito, M. M., & Worley, D. W. (2005). A front row seat: A phenomenological investigation of learning disabilities. *Communication Education, 54,* 312–333.

Coyne, M. D., Kame'enui, E. J., & Simmons, D. C. (2001). Prevention and intervention in beginning reading: Two complex systems. *Learning Disabilities Research and Practice, 16*(2), 62–73.

Cummings, E. M., Davies, P., & Campbell, S. (2002). *Developmental psychopathology and family processes, theory, research, and clinical implications.* New York: Guilford.

Daley, D. (2006). Attention deficit hyperactivity disorder: A review of the essential facts. *Child: Care, Health and Development, 32,* 193–204.

Dean, V. J., Burns, M. K., & Grialou, T. (2006). Comparison of ecological validity of learning disabilities diagnostic models. *Psychology in the Schools, 43,* 157–168.

De Haan, E. (2006). Effective treatment of OCD? *Journal of the American Academy of Child & Adolescent Psychiatry, 45,* 383.

Deshler, D. D., Mellard, D. F., & Tollefson, J. M. (2005). Research topics in responsiveness to intervention: Introduction to the special series. *Journal of Learning Disabilities, 38,* 483–484.

DeSimone, J. R., & Parmar, R. S. (2006). Middle school mathematics teachers' beliefs about inclusion of students with learning disabilities. *Learning Disabilities Research & Practice, 21,* 98–110.

Dettmer, P. A., Thurston, L. P., & Dyck, N. J. (2005). *Consultation, collaboration, and teamwork for students with special needs* (5th ed.). Boston: Allyn and Bacon.

Dietz, S., & Montague, M. (2006). Attention deficit hyperactivity disorder comorbid with emotional and behavioral disorders and learning disabilities in adolescents. *Exceptionality, 14,* 19–33.

Donfrancesco, R., Mugnaini, D., & Dell'Uomo, A. (2005). Cognitive impulsivity in specific learning disabilities. *European Child & Adolescent Psychiatry, 14,* 270–275.

Drew, C. J., & Hardman, M. L. (2007). *Intellectual disabilities across the lifespan* (9th ed.). Columbus, OH: Merrill.

DuPaul, G. J., & Weyandt, L. L. (2006). School-based intervention for children with attention deficit hyperactivity disorder: Effects on academic, social, and behavioural functioning. *International Journal of Disability, Development and Education, 53,* 161–176.

Eckert, T. L., Dunn, E. K., Codding, R. S., Begeny, J. C., & Kleinmann, A. E. (2006). Assessment of mathematics and reading performance: An examination of the correspondence between direct assessment of student performance and teacher report. *Psychology in the Schools, 43,* 247–265.

Edelman, S., & Remond, L. (2005). Group cognitive behavior therapy program with troubled adolescents: A learning experience. *Child & Family Behavior Therapy, 27,* 47–59.

Eisenmajer, N., Ross, N., & Pratt, C. (2005). Specificity and characteristics of learning disabilities. *Journal of Child Psychology and Psychiatry, 46,* 1108–1115.

Englert, C. S., Wu, X., & Shao, Y. (2005). Cognitive tools for writing: Scaffolding the performance of students through technology. *Learning Disabilities Research and Practice, 20,* 184–198.

Estrada, L., Dupoux, E., & Wolman, C. (2006). The relationship between locus of control and personal-emotional adjustment and social adjustment to college life in students with and without learning disabilities. *College Student Journal, 40,* 43–54.

Filippatou, D. N., & Livaniou, E. A. (2005). Comorbidity and WISC-III profiles of Greek children with attention deficit hyperactivity disorder, learning disabilities, and language disorders. *Psychological Reports, 97,* 485–504.

Flanagan, D. P., Bernier, J., Keiser, S., & Ortiz, S. O. (2003). *Diagnosis of learning disability in adulthood.* Boston: Allyn and Bacon.

Flanagan, D., & Harrison, P. (2005). *Contemporary intellectual assessment: Theories, tests and issues* (2nd ed.). London: The Guilford Press.

Fletcher, J. M. (2005). Predicting math outcomes: Reading predictors and comorbidity. *Journal of Learning Disabilities, 38,* 308–312.

Fletcher, J. M., Denton, C., & Francis, D. J. (2005). Validity of alternative approaches for the identification of learning disabilities: Operationalizing unexpected underachievement. *Journal of Learning Disabilities, 38,* 545–552.

Fletcher, J. M., Francis, D. J., & Morris, R. D. (2005). Evidence-based assessment of learning disabilities in children and adolescents. *Journal of Clinical Child and Adolescent Psychology, 34,* 506–522.

Floyd, K. (2006). Physiology and human relationships. *Journal of Social and Personal Relationships, 23,* 187–188.

Francis, D. J., Fletcher, J. M., & Steubing, K. K. (2005). Psychometric approaches to the identification of LD: IQ and achievement scores are not sufficient. *Journal of Learning Disabilities, 38,* 98–108.

Fuchs, D., & Fuchs, L. S. (2006). Introduction to response to intervention: What, why, and how valid is it? *Reading Research Quarterly, 41,* 93–99.

Fuchs, L. S. (2005). Prevention research in mathematics: Improving outcomes, building identification models, and understanding disabil-

ity. *Journal of Learning Disabilities, 38,* 350–352.

Fussell, J. J., Macias, M. M., & Saylor, C. F. (2005). Social skills and behavior problems in children with disabilities with and without siblings. *Child Psychiatry and Human Development, 36,* 227–241.

Galaburda, A. M. (2005). Neurology of learning disabilities: What will the future bring? The answer comes from the successes of the recent past. *Learning Disability Quarterly, 28,* 107–109.

Gall, M. D., Gall, J. P., & Borg, W. R. (2007). *Educational research: An introduction* (8th ed.). Boston: Allyn & Bacon.

Gangadharan, S., Bretherton, K., & Johnson, B. (2001). Pattern of referral to a child learning disability service. *British Journal of Developmental Disabilities, 47*(93, Pt. 2), 99–104.

Garrett, A. J., Mazzocco, M. M. M., & Baker, L. (2006). Development of the metacognitive skills of prediction and evaluation in children with or without math disability. *Learning Disabilities Research & Practice, 21,* 77–88.

Geary, D. C., & Hoard, M. K. (2005). Learning disabilities in arithmetic and mathematics: Theoretical and empirical perspectives. In J. I. D. Cambell (Ed.). *Handbook of mathematical cognition* (pp. 253–267). New York: Psychology Press.

Gelfand, D. M., & Drew, C. J. (2003). *Understanding child behavior disorders* (4th ed.). Belmont, CA: Wadsworth.

Gerber, M. M. (2005). Response to tough teaching: The 2% solution. *Learning Disability Quarterly, 28,* 189–190.

Gerber, M., & Durgunoglu, A. Y. (2004). Reading risk and intervention for young English learners: Evidence from longitudinal intervention research. *Learning Disabilities Research & Practice, 19,* 199–201.

Gersten, R., & Jordan, N. C. (2005). Early screening and intervention in mathematics difficulties: The need for action. *Journal of Learning Disabilities, 38,* 291–292.

Gettinger, M., & Seibert, J. K. (2002). Contributions of study skills to academic competence. *School Psychology Review, 31,* 350–365.

Gonzalez, J. E. J. (2002). Reading disabilities in a language with transparent orthography. In E. Witruk & A. D. Friederici (Eds.), *Basic functions of language, reading and reading disability. Neuropsychology and cognition,* Vol. 20 (pp. 251–264). Dordrecht, Netherlands: Kluwer Academic Publishers.

Graham, S., Struck, M., Santoro, J., & Berninger, V. W. (2006). Dimensions of good and poor handwriting legibility in first and second graders: Motor programs, visual-spatial arrangement, and letter formation parameter settings. *Developmental Neuropsychology, 29,* 43–60.

Graner, P. S., Faggetta-Luby, M. N., & Frischmann, N. S. (2005). An overview of responsiveness to intervention: What practitioners ought to know. *Topics in Language Disorders, 25,* 93–105.

Gregg, N., Coleman, C., Stennett, R. B., & Davis, M. (2002). Discourse complexity of college writers with and without disabilities: A multidimensional analysis. *Journal of Learning Disabilities, 35,* 23–38, 56.

Gregory, R. J. (2007). *Psychological testing: History, principles, and applications* (5th ed.). Boston: Allyn & Bacon.

Gresham, F. M. (2006). Response to intervention. In G. G. Bear and K. M. Minke (Eds.). *Children's needs III: Development, prevention, and intervention* (pp. 525–540). Washington, DC: National Association of School Psychologists.

Grigorenko, E. L. (2006). Learning disabilities in juvenile offenders. *Child and Adolescent Psychiatric Clinics of North America, 15,* 353–371.

Gronlund, N. E. (2004). *How to write and use instructional objectives* (7th ed.). Columbus, OH: Merrill/Prentice-Hall.

Gronlund, N. E. (2006). *Assessment of student achievement* (8th ed.). Boston: Allyn and Bacon.

Grunow, H., Spaulding, T. J., Gomez, R. L., & Plante, E. (2006). The effects of variation on learning word order rules by adults with and without language-based learning disabilities, *Journal of Communication Disorders, 39,* 158–170.

Gutstein, S. E., & Sheely, R. K. (2002). *Relationship development intervention with young children: Social and emotional development activities for Asperger Syndrome, autism, PPD and NLD.* London, England: Jessica Kingsley Publishers.

Haager, D., & Klinger, J. K. (2005). *Differentiating instruction in inclusive classrooms: The special educator's guide.* Boston: Allyn and Bacon.

Hardman, M. L. (2005). Special teaching for special children? Pedagogies for inclusion. *European Journal of Special Needs Education, 20,* 347–348.

Hartman-Hall, H. M., & Haaga, D. A. F. (2002). College students' willingness to seek help for their learning disabilities. *Learning Disability Quarterly, 25,* 263–276.

Hayiou-Thomas, M. E., Oliver, B., & Plomin, R. (2005). Genetic influences on specific versus nonspecific language impairment in 4-year-old twins. *Journal of Learning Disabilities, 38,* 222–232.

Hechtman, L. (2005). Journeys from childhood to midlife: Risk, resilience, and recovery. *Transcultural Psychiatry, 42,* 684–686.

Hetzroni, O. E., & Shrieber, B. (2004). Word processing as an assistive technology tool for enhancing academic outcomes of students with writing disabilities in the general classroom. *Journal of Learning Disabilities, 37,* 143–154.

Holman, A. (2006). In conversation: Hilary Burton and Brendan Gogarty. *British Journal of Learning Disabilities, 34,* 3–5.

Hudson, B. (2006). Making and missing connections: Learning disability services and the transition from adolescence to adulthood. *Disability and Society, 21,* 47–60.

Huefner, D. S. (2006). *Getting comfortable with special education law.* Norwood, MA: Christopher Gordon-Publishers.

Hynd, G. W., & Reynolds, C. R. 2005). School neuropsychology: The evolution of a specialty in school psychology. In R. C. D'Amato, E. Fletcher-Janzen, and C. R. Reynolds (Eds.). *Handbook of school neuropsychology* (pp. 3–14). Hoboken, NJ: John Wiley & Sons.

Individuals with Disabilities Education Improvement Act of 2004 (IDEA, 2004). 20 USC 1400, H.R. 1350.

Jitendra, A. K., Sczesniak, E., & Deatline-Buckman, A. (2005). An exploratory validation of curriculum-based mathematical word problem-solving tasks as indicators of mathematics proficiency for third graders. *School Psychology Review, 34,* 358–371.

Jorgensen, S., Fichten, C. S., & Havel, A. (2005). Academic performance of college students with and without disabilities: An archival study. *Canadian Journal of Counselling, 39,* 101–117.

Kaiser, A. J. (2005). College students with learning disabilities: Using psychoeducational test results to predict accommodations and learning disability type. *Dissertation Abstracts International: Section B: The Sciences and Engineering, 65(7-B).*

Kamhi, A. G., & Catts, H. W. (2002). The language basis of reading: Implications for classification and treatment of children with reading disabilities. In K. G. Bulter & E. R. Silliman (Eds.), *Speaking, reading, and writing in children with language learning disabilities: New paradigms in research and practice* (pp. 45–72). Mahwah, NJ: Lawrence Erlbaum.

Kamhi, A. G., & Catts, H. W. (2005a). Language and reading: Convergences and divergences. In H. W. Catts & A. G. Kamhi (Eds.). *Language and reading disabilities* (2nd ed.). (pp. 1–25). Boston: Allyn & Bacon.

Kamhi, A. G., & Catts, H. W. (2005b). Reading development. In H. W. Catts & A. G. Kamhi (Eds.). *Language and reading disabilities* (2nd ed.). (pp. 1–25). Boston: Allyn & Bacon.

Kelly, B. D. (2006). Psychiatry in contemporary Irish cinema: A qualitative study. *Irish Journal of Psychological Medicine, 23,* 74–79.

Kennemar, K., & Goldstein, S. (2005). Incidence of ADHD in adults with severe mental health problems. *Applied Neuropsychology, 12,* 77–82.

Keogh, B. K. (2005). Revisiting classification and identification. *Learning Disability Quarterly, 28,* 100–102.

Kirk, S. A. (1963). Behavioral diagnosis and remediation of learning disabilities. Proceedings: Conference on exploration into the problems of the perceptually handicapped (Vol. 1). First Annual Meeting, Chicago.

Klassen, R. M., Neufeld, P., & Munro, F. (2005). When IQ is irrelevant to the definition of learning disabilities: Australian School Psychologists? Beliefs and practice. *School Psychology International, 26,* 297–316.

Klinger, J. K., & Vaughn, S. (2002). The changing roles and responsibilities of an LD specialist. *Learning Disability Quarterly, 25,* 19–31.

Klingner, J. K., & Edwards, P. A. (2006). Cultural considerations with response to intervention models. *Reading Research Quarterly, 41,* 108–117.

Kozlof, M. A. (2005). Fads in general education: Fad, fraud, and folly. In J. W. Jacobson, R. M. Foxx, and J. A. Mulick (Eds.). *Controversial therapies for developmental disabilities: Fad, fashion and science in professional practice* (pp. 159–173). Mahwah, NJ: Lawrence Erlbaum Associates.

Larsen, S. (1978). Learning disabilities and the professional educator. *Learning Disability Quarterly, 1*(1), 5–12.

Lerner, J., & Kline, F. (2006). *Learning disabilities and related disorders* (10th ed.). Boston: Houghton Mifflin.

Lighthouse, A. G. (2006). The relationship between SAT scores and grade point averages among postsecondary students with disabilities. *Dissertation Abstracts International Section A: Humanities and Social Sciences, 66(7-A).*

Linn, R. L., & Miller, M. D. (2005). *Measurement and assessment in teaching* (9th ed.). Columbus, OH: Pearson/Prentice-Hall.

Lipka, O., & Siegel, L. S. (2006). Learning disabilities. In D. A. Wolfe and E. J. Mash (Eds.). *Behavioral and emotional disorders in adolescents: Nature, assessment, and treatment* (pp. 410–443). New York: Guilford.

Litt, J., Taylor, H. G., & Klein, N. (2005). Learning disabilities in children with very low birthweight: Prevalence, neuropsychological correlates, and educational interventions. *Journal of Learning Disabilities, 38,* 130–141.

Loomis, J. W. (2006). Learning disabilities. In R. T. Ammerman (Ed.).

Comprehensive handbook of personality and psychopathology Vol. 3. (pp. 272–284). Hoboken, NJ: John Wiley & Sons.

Luftig, R. L., & Muthert, D. (2005). Patterns of employment and independent living of adult graduates with learning disabilities and mental retardation of an inclusionary high school vocational program. *Research in Developmental Disabilities, 26,* 317–325.

Luna, C. (2003). (Re)Writing the discourses of schooling and of "learning disabilities": The development of critical literacy in a student action group. *Reading and Writing Quarterly, 19,* 253–280.

Maag, J. W., & Reid, R. (2006). Depression among students with learning disabilities: Assessing the risk. *Journal of Learning Disabilities, 39,* 3–10.

Macy, M. G., Bricker, D. D., & Squires, J. K. (2005). Validity and reliability of a curriculum-based assessment approach to determine eligibility for part C services. *Journal of Early Intervention, 28,* 1–16.

Mammarella, I. C., & Cornoldi, C. (2005). Sequence and space: The critical role of a backward spatial span in the working memory deficit of visuospatial learning disabled children. *Cognitive Neuropsychology, 22,* 1055–1068.

Manning, M. A., Bear, G. G., & Minke, K. M. (2006). Self-concept and self-esteem. In G. G. Bear & K. M. Minke (Eds.). *Children's needs III: Development, prevention, and intervention* (pp. 341–356). Washington, DC: National Association of School Psychologists.

Manset-Williamson, G., & Nelson, J. M. (2005). Balanced, strategic reading instruction for upper-elementary and middle school students with reading disabilities: A comparative study of two approaches. *Learning Disability Quarterly, 28,* 59–74.

Martin, G. (2005). Support for people with learning disabilities: The role of primary care. *Primary Care & Community Psychiatry, 10,* 133–142.

Mather, N., & Gregg, N. (2006). Specific learning disabilities: Clarifying, not eliminating a construct. *Professional Psychology: Research and Practice, 37,* 99–106.

Mather, N., & Ofiesh, N. (2005). Resilience and the child with learning disabilities. In S. Goldstein & R. B. Brooks (Eds.). *Handbook of resilience in children* (pp. 239–255). New York: Kluwer Academic/Plenum Publishers.

Mayes, S. D., & Calhoun, S. L. (2005). Test of the definition of learning disability based on the difference between IQ and achievement. *Psychological Reports, 97,* 109–116.

Mayes, S. D., & Calhoun, S. L. (2006). Frequency of reading, math, and writing disabilities in children with clinical disorders. *Learning and Individual Differences, 16,* 145–157.

Mazzocco, M. M., & Thompson, R. E. (2005). Kindergarten predictors of math learning disability. *Learning Disabilities Research & Practice, 20,* 142–155.

McDougal, J. L., Chafouleas, S. M., & Waterman, B. (2006). *Functional behavioral assessment and intervention in schools: A practitioner's guide—grades 1–8.* Champaign, IL: Research Press.

McGlaughlin, S. M., Knoop, A. J., & Holliday, G. A. (2005). Differentiating students with mathematics difficulty in college: Mathematics disabilities vs. no diagnosis. *Learning Disability Quarterly, 28,* 223–232.

McMillan, J. H. (2007). *Classroom assessment: Principles and practice for effective standards-based instruction* (4th ed.). Boston: Allyn & Bacon.

McNamara, J. K., Willoughby, T., & Chalmers, H. (2005). Psychosocial status of adolescents with learning disabilities with and without co-morbid attention deficit hyperactivity disorder. *Learning Disabilities Research and Practice, 20,* 234–244.

McNergney, R. F., & McNergney, J. M. (2007). *Education: The practice and profession of teaching* (5th ed.) Boston: Allyn & Bacon.

Mellard, D. F., Deshler, D. D., & Barth, A. (2004). LD identification: It's not simply a matter of building a better mousetrap. *Learning Disability Quarterly, 27,* 229–242.

Milsom, A., & Hartley, M. T. (2005). Assisting students with learning disabilities transitioning to college: What school counselors should know. *Professional School Counseling, 8,* 436–441.

Moore, D. (2001). Friend or foe? A selective review of the literature concerning abuse of adults with learning disability by those employed to care for them. *Journal of Learning Disabilities, 5,* 245–258.

National Joint Committee on Learning Disabilities. (1998). Operationalizing the NJCLD definition of learning disabilities for ongoing assessment in schools. *Learning Disability Quarterly, 24,* 186–193.

National Research Center on Learning Disabilities (2002). Finding common ground: Consensus statements. NRCLD Information Digest 2 [Online]. www.nrcld.org.

O'Bannon, B. W., & Puckett, K. (2007). *Preparing to use technology: A practical guide to curriculum integration.* Boston: Allyn & Bacon.

O'Brien, G. (2006). Young adults with learning disabilities: A study of psychosocial functioning at transition to adult services. *Developmental Medicine & Child Neurology, 48,* 195–199.

Okada, S., Goto, H., & Ueno, K. (2005). Effect of social skills training including rehearsal of game activities: Comparison of children with LD, ADHD, and Asperger Syndrome. *Japanese Journal of Educational Psychology, 53,* 565–578.

Pavri, S. (2006). Introduction: School-based interventions to promote social and emotional competence in students with reading difficulties. *Reading & Writing Quarterly: Overcoming Learning Difficulties, 22,* 99–101.

Pelham, W. E., Hoza, B., Pillow, D. R., Gnagy, E. M., Kipp, H. L., Greiner, A. R., Waschbusch, D. A., Trane, S. T., Greenhouse, J., Wolfson, L., & Fitzpatrick, E. (2002). Effects of methyphenidate and expectancy on children with ADHD: Behavior, academic performance, and attributions in a summer treatment program and regular classroom settings. *Journal of Consulting and Clinical Psychology, 70,* 320–335.

Persampieri, M., Gortmaker, V., Daly, E. J., Sheridan, S. M., & McCurdy, M. (2006). Promoting parent use of empirically supported reading interventions: Two experimental investigations of child outcomes. *Behavioral Interventions, 21,* 31–57.

Peterson, J. M., & Hittie, M. M. (2005). *Inclusive teaching: Creating effective schools for all learners* (Mylabschool edition). Boston: Allyn and Bacon.

Petrill, S. A., Deater-Deckard, K., & Thompson, L. A. (2006). Reading skills in early readers: Genetic and shared environment. *Journal of Learning Disabilities, 39,* 48–55.

Picton, T. A., & Karki, C. (2002). Referral patterns of children to a psychiatric learning disability service. *British Journal of Developmental Disabilities, 48*(94, Pt. 1), 53–59.

Pierangelo, R., & Giuliani, G. A. (2006). *Learning disabilities: A practical approach to foundations, assessment, diagnosis, and teaching.* Boston: Allyn & Bacon.

Plomin, R., & Kovas, Y. (2005). Generalist genes and learning disabilities. *Psychological Bulletin, 131,* 592–617.

Porter, J. (2005). Awareness of number in children with severe and profound learning difficulties: Three exploratory case studies. *British Journal of Learning Disabilities, 33,* 97–101.

Prater, M. A. (2003). She will succeed! Strategies for success in inclusive classrooms. *Teaching Exceptional Children, 35,* 58–64.

Prater, M. A. (2007). *Teaching strategies for students with mild to moderate disabilities.* Boston: Allyn & Bacon.

Pretorius, E., Naude, H., & Becker, J. (2002). Can excess bilirubin levels cause learning difficulties? *Early Child Development and Care, 172,* 391–404.

Proctor, B. E., Hurst, A., Prevatt, F., Petscher, Y., & Adams, B. E. (2006). Study skills profiles of normal-achieving and academically struggling college students. *Journal of College Student Development, 47,* 37–51.

Rapport, M. D., & Moffitt, C. (2002). Attention deficit/hyperactivity disorder and methylphenidate. A review of height/weight, cardiovascular and somatic complaint side effects. *Clinical Psychology Review, 22,* 1107–1131.

Rath, K. A., & Royer, J. M. (2002). The nature and effectiveness of learning disability services for college students. *Educational Psychology Review, 14,* 353–381.

Reiff, H. B. (2004). Reframing the learning disabilities experience redux. *Learning Disabilities Research & Practice, 19,* 185–198.

Richards, T., Berninger, V., Nagy, W., Parsons, A., Field, K., & Richards, A. (2005). Brain activation during language task contrasts in children with and without dyslexia: Inferring mapping processes and assessing responses to spelling instruction. *Educational and Child Psychology, 22,* 62–80.

Ring, E., & Travers, J. (2005). Barriers to inclusion: A case study of a pupil with severe learning difficulties in Ireland. *European Journal of Special Needs Education, 20,* 41–56.

Rix, J. (2006). Inclusive education—Readings and reflections. *Journal of Learning Disabilities, 34,* 57–58.

Roblyer, M. D. (2006). *Integrating technology into teaching* (4th ed.). Upper Saddle River, NJ: Prentice-Hall.

Romi, S., & Leyser, Y. (2006). Exploring inclusion preservice training needs: A study of variables associated with attitudes and self-efficacy beliefs. *European Journal of Special Needs Education, 21,* 85–105.

Rock, M. L. (2005). Use of strategic self-monitoring to enhance academic engagement, productivity, and accuracy of students with and without exceptionalities. *Journal of Positive Behavior Interventions, 7,* 3–17.

Rodger, S., & Brown, G. T. (2005). Profile of paediatric occupational therapy practice in Australia. *Australian Occupational Therapy Journal, 52,* 311–325.

Roer-Strier, D. (2002). University students with learning disabilities advocating for change. *Disability and Rehabilitation: An International Multidisciplinary Journal, 24,* 914–924.

Romani, C., Olson, A., & Di Betta, A. M. (2005). Spelling disorders. In M. J. Hulme, & C. Hulme (Eds.). *The science of reading: A handbook* (pp. 431–447). Malden, MA: Blackwell.

Sabornie, E. J., Cullinan, D., & Osborne, S. S. (2005). Intellectual, academic, and behavioral functioning of students with high-incidence disabilities: A cross-categorical meta-analysis. *Exceptional Children, 72,* 47–63.

Salkind, N. J. (2006). *Exploring research* (6th ed.). Upper Saddle River, NJ: Prentice-Hall.

Sams, K., Collins, S., & Reynolds, S. (2006). Cognitive therapy abilities in people with learning disabilities. *Journal of Applied Research in Intellectual Disabilities, 19,* 25–33.

Sanson, J. (2005). Invited editorial. *Pediatric Rehabilitation, 8,* 1–3.

Savage, R. S., Frederickson, N., & Goodwin, R. (2005). Relationships among rapid digit naming, phonological processing, motor automaticity, and speech perception in poor, average, and good readers and spellers. *Journal of Learning Disabilities, 38,* 12–28.

Schmidt, R. J., Rozendal, M. S., & Greenman, G. G. (2002). Reading instruction in the inclusion classroom: Research-based practices. *Remedial and Special Education, 23*(3), 130–140.

Scott, M. S., Delgado, C. F., & Tu, S. (2005). Selecting and validating tasks from a kindergarten screening battery that best predict third grade educational placement. *Education and Training in Developmental Disabilities, 40,* 377–389.

Seidman, L. J., Biederman, J., Valera, E. M., Monuteaux, M. C., Doyle, A. E., & Faraone, S. V. (2006). Neuropsychological functioning in girls with attention-deficit/hyperactivity disorder with and without learning disabilities. *Neuropsychology, 20,* 166–177.

Semrud-Clikeman, M. (2005). Neuropsychological aspects for evaluating learning disabilties. *Journal of Learning Disabilities, 38,* 563–568.

Shaywitz, B. A., Shaywitz, S. E., Pugh, K. R., Mencl, W. E., Fulbright, R. K., Skudlarkski, P., Constable, R. T., Marchione, K. E., Fletcher, J. M., Lyon, G. R., & Gore, J. C. (2002). Disruption of posterior brain systems for reading in children with developmental dyslexia. *Biological Psychiatry, 52*(2), 101–110.

Shireman, T. I., Reichard, A., & Rigler, S. K. (2005). Psychotropic medication use among Kansas Medicaid youths with disabilities. *Journal of Child and Adolescent Psychopharmacology, 15,* 107–115.

Siegel, L. S., & Smythe, I. S. (2005). Reflections on research on reading disability with special attention to gender issues. *Journal of Learning Disabilities, 38,* 473–477.

Silliman, E. R., Bahr, R. H., & Peters, M. L. (2006). Spelling patterns in preadolescents with atypical language skills: Phonological, morphological, and orthographic factors. *Neuropsychology, 29,* 93–123.

Silliman, E. R., & Scott, C. M. (2006). Language impairment and reading disability: Connections and complexities. Introduction to the special issue. *Learning Disabilities Research and Practice, 21,* 1–7.

Singer, E (2005). The strategies adopted by Dutch children with dyslexia to maintain their self-esteem when teased at school. *Journal of Learning Disabilities, 38,* 411–423.

Smith, B. H., Barkley, R. A., & Shapiro, C. J. (2006). Attention-deficit/hyperactivity disorder. In E. J. Mash & R. A. Barkley (Eds.). *Treatment of childhood disorders* (3rd ed.) (pp. 65–136). New York: Guilford Press.

Smith, C. R. (2004). *Learning disabilities: The interaction of learner, task, and setting* (5th ed.). Boston: Allyn and Bacon.

Smith, L. A., & Williams, J. M. (2005). Developmental differences in understanding the causes, controllability, and chronicity of disabilities. *Child: Care, Health and Development, 31,* 479–488.

Sparks, R. L., Javorsky, J., & Philips, L. (2005). Comparison of the performance of college students classified as ADHD, LD, and LDADHD in foreign language courses. *Language Learning, 55,* 151–177.

Stanovich, K. E. (2005). The future of a mistake: Will discrepancy measurement continue to make the learning disabilities field a pseudoscience? *Learning Disability Quarterly, 28,* 103–106.

Stecker, P. M. (2006). Using curriculum-based measurement to monitor reading progress in inclusive elementary settings. *Reading & Writing Quarterly: Overcoming Learning Difficulties, 22,* 91–97.

Stone, C. A., & Carlisle, J. F. (2006). From the outgoing editors. *Learning Disabilities Research & Practice, 21,* v.

Stone, C. A., & May, A. L. (2002). The accuracy of academic self-evaluations in adolescents with learning disabilities. *Journal of Learning Disabilities, 35,* 370–383.

Stuebing, K. K., Fletcher, J. M., LeDoux, J. M., Lyon, G. R., Shaywitz, S. E., & Shaywitz, B. A. (2002). Validity of IQ-discrepancy classifications of reading disabilities: A meta-analysis. *American Educational Research Journal, 39,* 469–518.

Sullivan, M. M. (2005). Teaching mathematics to college students with mathematics-related learning disabilities: Report from the classroom. *Learning Disability Quarterly, 28,* 205–220.

Sutcliffe, P. (2006). Comorbid attentional factors and frequency discrimination performance in a child with reading difficulties. *International Journal of Disability, Development and Education, 53,* 195–208.

Suter, W. N. (2006). *Introduction to educational research.* Thousand Oaks, CA: Sage Publications.

Swanson, H. L., & Howard, C. B. (2005). Children with reading disabilities: Does dynamic assessment help in the classification? *Learning Disability Quarterly, 28,* 17–34.

Tarleton, B., & Ward, L. (2005). Changes and choices: Finding out what information young people with learning disabilities, their parents and supporters need at transition. *British Journal of Learning Disabilities, 33,* 70–76.

Taylor, E., & Rogers, J. W. (2005). Practitioner Review: Early adversity and developmental disability. *Journal of Child Psychology and Psychiatry, 46,* 451–467.

Tomblin, J. B. (2006). A normativist account of language-based learning disability. *Learning Disabilities Research & Practice, 21,* 8–18.

Tournaki, N. (2003). The differential effect of teaching addition through strategy instruction versus drill and practice to students with and without learning disabilities. *Journal of Learning Disabilities, 36,* 449–458.

Troia, G. A. (2005). Responsiveness to intervention: Roles for speech-language pathologists in the prevention and identification of learning disabilities. *Topics in Language Disorders, 25,* 106–119.

Troia, G. A., & Graham, S. (2002). The effectiveness of a highly explicit, teacher-directed strategy instruction routine: Changing the writing performance of students with learning disabilities. *Journal of Learning Disabilities, 35*(4), 290–305.

Trusdell, M. L., & Horowitz, I. W. (2002). *Understanding learning disabilities: A parent guide and workbook* (3rd ed.). Timonium, MD: York Press.

Tsal, Y., Shalev, L., & Mevorach, C. (2005). The diversity of attention deficits in ADHD: The prevalence of four cognitive factors in ADHD versus controls. *Journal of Learning Disabilities, 38,* 142–157.

Twyman, T., McCleery, J., Tindal, G. (2006). Using concepts to frame history content. *Journal of Experimental Education, 74,* 331–349.

Ullman, J. G. (2005). *Making technology work for learners with special needs: Practical skills for teachers.* Boston: Allyn & Bacon.

Ungerleider, D., & Maslow, P. (2001). Association of educational therapists: Position paper on the SAT. *Journal of Learning Disabilities, 34,* 311–314.

Unruh, D., & Bullis, M. (2005). Female and male juvenile offenders with disabilities: Differences in the barriers to their transition to the community. *Behavioral Disorders, 30,* 105–117.

U.S. Department of Education, Office of Special Education Programs. (2006a). Twenty-sixth annual report to Congress on the implementation of the Individuals with Disabilities Education Act. Washington, DC: Author.

U.S. Department of Education (2006b). IDEA 2004 Part B regulations. *Federal Register,* August 14, Section [300.541, p. 12457].

Vadasy, P. F., Sanders, E. A., & Peyton, J. A. (2005). Relative effectiveness of reading practice or word-level instruction in supplemental tutoring: How text matters. *Journal of Learning Disabilities, 38,* 364–380.

Vaid, J., Singh, M., Sakhuja, T., & Gupta, G. C. (2002). Stroke direction asymmetry in figure drawing: Influence of handedness and reading/writing habits. *Brain and Cognition, 48*(2–3), 597–602.

van Aarle, E. J. M., van den Bercken, J. H. L., & Krol, N. P. C. M. (2005). The identification of valid syndromes in disturbed reading and spelling behavior. *Journal of Psychoeducational Assessment, 23,* 53–68.

Van der Bijl, C., Alant, E., & Lloyd, L. (2006). A comparison of two strategies of sight word instruction in children with mental disability. *Research in Developmental Disabilities, 27,* 43–55.

van Lang, N. D. J., Bouma, A., & Sytema, S. (2006). A comparison of central coherence skills between adolescents with an intellectual disability with and without comorbid autism spectrum disorder. *Research in Developmental Disabilities, 27,* 217–226.

Vellutino, F. R., Scanlon, D. M., Small, S., & Fanuele, D. P. (2006). Response to intervention as a vehicle for distinguishing between children with and without reading disabilities: Evidence for the role of kindergarten and first-grade interventions. *Journal of Learning Disabilities, 39,* 157–169.

Voss, K. S. (2005). *Teaching by design: Using your computer to create materials for students with learning differences.* Bethesda, MD: Woodbine House.

Wadsworth, S. J., & DeFries, J. C. (2005). Genetic etiology of reading difficulties in boys and girls. *Twin Research and Human Genetics, 8,* 594–601.

Wakely, M. B., Hooper, S. R., & de Kruif, R. E. L. (2006). Subtypes of written expression in elementary school children: A linguistic-based model. *Developmental Neuropsychology, 29,* 125–159.

Walker, B., Alberto, P., Houchins, D. E., & Cihak, D. F. (2005). Using the expressive writing program to improve the writing skills of high school students with learning disabilities. *Learning Disabilities Research & Practice, 20,* 175–183.

Walker, S. O., & Plomin, R. (2005). The nature-nurture question: Teachers' perceptions of how genes and the environment influence educationally relevant behaviour. *Educational Psychology, 25,* 509–516.

Wallach, G. P. (2005). A conceptual framework in language learning disabilities: School-age language disorders. *Topics in Language Disorders, Special Issue: Language Disorders and Learning Disabilities: A Look Across 25 Years, 25,* 292–301.

Watkins, M. W., Kush, J. C., & Schaefer, B. A. (2002). Diagnostic utility of the Learning Disability Index. *Journal of Learning Disabilities, 35,* 98–103.

Wenar, C., & Kerig, P. (2006). *Developmental psychopathology* (5th ed.). New York: McGraw-Hill.

Whitaker, S. (2004). Hidden learning disability. *Journal of Learning Disabilities, 32,* 383–395.

Wilber, A., & Cushman, T. P. (2006). Selecting effective academic interventions: An example using brief experimental analysis for oral reading. *Psychology in the Schools, 43,* 79–84.

Wilkinson, C. Y., Ortiz, A. A., Robertson, P. M., & Kushner, M. I. (2006). English language learners with reading-related LD: Linking data from multiple sources to make eligibility determinations. *Journal of Learning Disabilities, 39,* 129–141.

Woltz, D. J. (2003). Implicit cognitive processes as aptitudes for learning. *Educational Psychologist, 38,* 95–104.

Xin, Y. P., Jitendra, A. K., & Deatline-Buckman, A. (2005). Effects of mathematical word problem-solving instruction on middle students with learning problems. *Journal of Special Education, 39,* 181–192.

Young, A. F., & Chesson, R. A. (2006). Obtaining views on health care from people with learning disabilities and severe mental health problems. *British Journal of Learning Disabilities, 34,* 11–19.

Young, A. R. (2005). Learning disorders in girls. In D. J. Bell, S. L. Foster, and E. J. Mash (Eds.), *Handbook of behavioral and emotional problems in girls* (pp. 263–283). New York: Kluwer Academic/Plenum Publishers.

Youngstrom, N. (1991). Most child clinicians support prescribing. *APA Monitor, 22*(3), 21.

Zuvekas, S. H., Vitiello, B., & Norquist, G. S. (2006). Recent trends in stimulant medication use among U.S. children. *American Journal of Psychiatry, 163,* 579–585.

CHAPTER 8

Adler, L. A., Barkley, R. A., Wilens, T. E., & Ginsberg, D. L. (2006). Differential diagnosis of attention-deficit/hyperactivity disorder and comorbid conditions. *Primary Psychiatry, 13,* 1–14.

Ambalavanan, G., & Molten, K. B. (2005). How should we evaluate and treat ADHD in children and adolescents? *Journal of Family Practice, 54,* 1058–1059.

American Academy of Pediatrics. (2000). Diagnosis and evaluation of the child with attention-deficit/hyperactivity disorder (AC0002). *Pediatrics, 105,* 1158–1170.

American Psychiatric Association. (2000). *Diagnostic and statistical manual of mental disorders* (4th ed.–text revision). Washington, DC: Author.

Archibald, S. J., Kerns, K. A., Mateer, C. A., & Ismay, L. (2006). Evidence of utilization behavior in children with ADHD. *Journal of the International Neuropsychological Society, 11*, 367–375.

ARMC News. (2006). ADHD: It's not just for kids anymore. *Athens Regional Medical Center News.* Retrieved http://www.armc.org

Bank, C. (2000, February 1). Coping with attention deficit disorder. MSNBC report by Philadelphia, PA Channel 10, NBC. Retrieved http://www.msnbc.com/local/WCAU/245787.asp

Barkley, R. A. (2006). Attention-deficit/hyperactivity disorder. In D. A. Wolfe & E. J. Mash (Eds.), *Behavioral and emotional disorders in adolescents: Nature, assessment, and treatment* (pp. 91–152). New York: Guilford.

Barkley, R. A., Fischer, M., Smallish, L., & Fletcher, K. (2002). The persistence of attention-deficit/hyperactivity disorder into young adulthood as a function of reporting source and definition of disorder. *Journal of Abnormal Psychology, 111*, 279–289.

Barkley, R. A., Fischer, M., Smallish, L., & Fletcher, K. (2006). Young adult outcome of hyperactive children: Adaptive functioning in major life activities. *Journal of the American Academy of Child & Adolescent Psychiatry, 45*, 192–202.

Barry, T. D., Dunlap, S. T., Cotton, S. J., Lochman, J. E., & Wells, K. C. (2005). The influence of maternal stress and distress on disruptive behavior problems in boys. *Journal of the American Academy of Child & Adolescent Psychiatry, 44*, 265–273.

Biederman, J. (2005). Mixed amphetamine salts extended release for the treatment of ADHD. *CNS Spectrums, 10* (12, Supplement 20), 5.

Bender, W. N. (2004). *Learning disabilities: Characteristics, identification, and teaching strategies* (5th ed.). Boston: Allyn and Bacon.

Bettencourt, B. A., Talley, A., Benjamine, A. J., & Valentine, J. (2006). Personality and aggressive behavior under provoking and neutral conditions: A meta-analytic review. *Psychological Bulletin, 132*, 751–777.

Button, T. M. M., Thapar, A., & McGuffin, P. (2005). Relationship between antisocial behaviour, attention-deficit hyperactivity disorder and maternal prenatal smoking. *British Journal of Psychiatry, 187*, 155–160.

Brand, N., Geenen, R., Oudenhoven, M., Lindeborn, B., van-der-Ree, A., Cohen-Kettenis, P., & Buitelaar, J. K. (2002). Brief report: Cognitive functioning in children with Tourette's syndrome with and without comorbid ADHD. *Journal of Pediatric Psychology, 27*, 203–208.

Brook, U. & Boaz, M. (2005). Attention deficit and hyperactivity disorder (ADHD) and learning disabilities (LD): Adolescents'

perspective. *Patient Education and Counseling, 58*, 187–191.

Brown, T. E. (2006). Executive functions and attention deficit hyperactivity disorder: Implications of two conflicting views. *International Journal of Disability, Development and Education, 53*, 35–46.

Burns, G. L., & Walsh, J. A. (2002). The influence of ADHD-hyperactivity/impulsivity symptoms on the development of oppositional defiant disorder symptoms in a 2-year longitudinal study. *Journal of Abnormal Child Psychology, 30*, 245–256.

Canivez, G. L., & Sprouls, K. (2005). Assessing the construct validity of the adjustment scales for children and adolescents. *Journal of Psychoeducational Assessment, 23*, 3–14.

CBS News. (2002, December 13). Diagnosis: ADHD not airhead girls. *The Early Show: Health News.*

CBS News. (2002, September 6). Out of control: Imperfect solutions. *48 Hours Investigates.*

Chang, F., Early, D. M., & Winton, P. (2005). Early childhood teacher preparation in special education at 2- and 4-year institutions of higher education. *Journal of Early Intervention, 27*, 110–124.

Chronis, A. M., Jones, H. A., & Raggi, V. L. (2006). Evidence-based psychosocial treatments for children and adolescents with attention-deficit/hyperactivity disorder. *Clinical Psychology Review, 26*, 486–502.

Codding, R. S., Lewandowski, L., & Eckert, T. (2005). Examining the efficacy of performance feedback and goal-setting interventions in children with ADHD: A comparison of two methods of goal setting. *Journal of Evidence-Based Practices for Schools, 6*, 42–58.

Coghill, D., Nigg, J., Rothenberger, A., Sonuga-Barke, E., & Tannock, R. (2005). Wither causal models in the neuroscience of ADHD? *Developmental Science, 8*, 105–114.

Connor, D. F. (2002). Preschool attention deficit hyperactivity disorder: A review of prevalence, diagnosis, neurobiology, and stimulant treatment. *Journal of Developmental and Behavioral Pediatrics, 23* (Supplement 1), S1–S9.

Cuffe, S. P., Moore, C. G., & McKeown, R. E. (2005). Prevalence and correlates of ADHD symptoms in the national health interview survey. *Journal of Attention Disorders, 9*, 392–401.

Cukrowicz, K. C., Taylor, J., Schatschneider, C., & Iacono, W. G. (2006). Personality differences in children and adolescents with attention-deficit/hyperactivity disorder, conduct disorder, and controls. *Journal of Child Psychology and Psychiatry, 47*, 151–159.

Daley, D. (2006). Attention deficit hyperactivity disorder: A review of the essential facts. *Child: Care, Health and Development, 32*, 193–204.

Danforth, J. S., Harvey, E., Ulaszek, W. R., & McKee, T. E. (2006). The outcome of group parent training for families of children with attention-deficit hyperactivity disorder and defiant/aggressive behavior. *Journal of Behavior Therapy and Experimental Psychiatry, 37*, 188–205.

Davids, E., & Gastpar, M. (2005). Attention deficit hyperactivity disorder and borderline personality disorder. *Progress in Neuro-Psychopharmacology & Biological Psychiatry, 29*, 865–877.

Dehon, C., & Scheeringa, M. S. (2006). Screening for preschool posttramatic stress disorder with the Child Behavior Checklist. *Journal of Pediatric Psychology, 31*, 431–435.

Derks, E. M., Hudziak, J. J., & Dolan, C. V. (2006). The relations between DISC-IV and multi-informant CBCL-AP syndrome scores. *Comprehensive Psychiatry, 47*, 116–122.

Derks, E. M., Hudziak, J. J., Dolan, C. V., Ferdinand, R. F., & Boomsma, D. I. (2006). The relations between DISC-IV DSM diagnoses of ADHD and multi-informant CBCL-AP syndrome scores. *Comprehensive Psychiatry, 47*, 116–122.

DeSimone, J. R., & Parmar, R. S. (2006). Middle school mathematics teachers' beliefs about inclusion of students with learning disabilities. *Learning Disabilities Research & Practice, 21*, 98–110.

Diamond, G., Panichelli-Mindel, S. M., Shera, D., Dennis, M., Tims, F., & Ungemack, J. (2006). Psychiatric syndromes in adolescents with marijuana abuse and dependency in outpatient treatment. *Journal of Child & Adolescent Substance Abuse, 15*, 37–54.

Dierker, L. C., Canino, G., & Merikangas, K. R. (2006). Association between parental and individual psychiatric/substance use disorders and smoking stages among Puerto Rican adolescents. *Drug and Alcohol Dependence, 84*, 144–153.

Dietz, S., & Montague, M. (2006). Attention deficit hyperactivity disorder comorbid with emotional and behavioral disorders and learning disabilities in adolescents. *Exceptionality, 14*, 19–33.

Diller, L. (2006). The rise of Ritalin: Triumph and tragedy in children's mental health. In S. Olfman (Ed.), *No child left different* (pp. 143–161). Westport, CT: Praeger/Greenwood.

Donovan, S. J. (2006). Childhood conduct disorder and the antisocial spectrum. In E. Hollander & D. J. Stein (Eds.), *Clinical manual of impulse-control disorders* (pp. 39–62). Washington, DC: American Psychiatric.

Dowson, J. H. (2006). Pharmacological treatments for attention-deficit/hyperactivity disorder (ADHD) in adults. *Current Psychiatry Reviews, 2*, 317–331.

Drabick, D. A. G., Gadow, K. D., & Sprafkin, J. (2006). Co-occurrence of conduct disorder and depression in a clinic-based sample of boys with ADHD. *Journal of Child Psychology and Psychiatry, 47*, 766–774.

Drew, C. J., & Hardman, M. L. (2007). *Intellectual disabilities across the lifespan* (9th ed.). Columbus, OH: Merrill.

DuPaul, G. J. (2006a). School-based intervention for children with attention deficit hyperactivity disorder: Effects on academic, social, and behavioural functioning. *International Journal of Disability, Development and Education, 53*, 161–176.

DuPaul, G. J. (2006b). Academic achievement in children with ADHD. *Journal of the American Academy of Child & Adolescent Psychiatry, 45*, 766.

Efron, D. (2005). ADHD: The need for system change. *Journal of Paediatrics and Child Health, 41*, 621–622.

Ehringer, M. A., Rhee, S. H., Young, S., Corley, R., & Hewitt, J. K. (2006). Genetic and environmental contributions to common psychopathologies of childhood and adolescence: A study of twins and their siblings. *Journal of Abnormal Child Psychology, 34*, 1–17.

Evans, S. W. (2005). Introduction to special issue on school-based treatment of children and adolescents with ADHD. *Journal of Attention Disorders, 9*, 245–247.

Evans, S. W., Timmins, B., Sibley, M., White, L. C., Serpell, Z. N., & Schultz, B. (2006). Developing coordinated, multimodal, school-based treatment for young adolescents with ADHD. *Education & Treatment of Children, 29*, 359–378.

Faraone, S. V., & Biederman, J. (2005). What is the prevalence of adult ADHD? Results of a population screen of 966 adults. *Journal of Attention Disorders, 9*, 384–391.

Fassbender, C., & Schweitzer, J. B. (2006). Is there evidence for neural compensation in attention deficit hyperactivity disorder? A review of the functional neuroimaging literature. *Clinical Psychology Review, 26*, 445–465.

Fredericksen, K. A., Cutting, L. E., Kates, W. R., Mostofsky, S. H., Singer, H. S., Cooper, K. L., Lanham, D. C., Denckla, M. B., & Kaufmann, W. E. (2002). Disproportionate increases of white matter in right frontal lobe in Tourette syndrome. *Neurology, 58*, 85–89.

Frick, P. J., Silverthorn, P., & Evans, C. S. (1994). Assessment of childhood anxiety using structured interviews: Patterns of agreement among informants and association with maternal anxiety. *Psychological Assessment, 6*, 372–379.

Galili-Weisstub, E., & Segman, R. H. (2003). Attention deficit and hyperactivity disorder: Review of genetic association studies. *Israel Journal of Psychiatry and Related Sciences, 40,* 57–66.

Gelfand, D. M., & Drew, C. J. (2003). *Understanding child behavior disorders* (4th ed.). Belmont, CA: Wadsworth.

Gorman, E. B., Klorman, R., Thatcher, J. E., & Borgstedt, A. D. (2006). Effects of methylphenidate on subtypes of attention-deficit/hyperactivity disorder. *Journal of the American Academy of Child & Adolescent Psychiatry, 45,* 808–816.

Gureasko-Moore, S., DuPaul, G. J., & White, G. P. (2006). The effects of self-management in general education classrooms on the organizational skills of adolescents with ADHD. *Behavior Modification, 30,* 159–183.

Hall, J. D., Ashley, D. M., Bramlett, R. K., Dielmann, K. B., & Murphy, J. J. (2005). ADHD assessment: A comparison of negative versus positive symptom formats. *Journal of Applied School Psychology, 21,* 163–173.

Halperin, J. M., & Schulz, K. P. (2006). Revisiting the role of the prefrontal cortex in the pathophysiology of attention-deficit/hyperactivity disorder. *Psychological Bulletin, 132,* 560–581.

Happe, F., Booth, R., & Charlton, R. (2006). Executive function deficits in autism spectrum disorders and attention-deficit/hyperactivity disorder. Examining profiles across domains and ages. *Brain and Cognition, 61,* 25–39.

Harris, K. R., Friedlander, B. D., Saddler, B., Frizzelle, R., & Graham, S. (2006). Self-monitoring of attention versus self-monitoring of academic performance: Effects among students with ADHD in the general education classroom. *Journal of Special Education, 39,* 145–156.

Hechtman, L., Abikoff, H. B., & Jensen, P. S. (2005). Multimodal therapy and stimulants in the treatment of children with attention-deficit/hyperactivity disorder. In E. D. Hibbs & P. S. Jensen (Eds.), *Psychosocial treatments for child and adolescent disorders: Empirically based strategies for clinical practice* (2nd ed., pp. 411–437). Washington, DC: American Psychological Association.

Heiman, T. (2005). An examination of peer relationships of children with and without attention deficit hyperactivity disorder. *School Psychology International, 26,* 330–339.

Hepperlen, T. M., Clay, D. L., Henly, G. A., & Barke, C. R. (2002). Measuring teacher attitudes and expectations toward students with ADHD: Development of the Test of Knowledge About ADHD (KADD). *Journal of Attention Disorders, 5*(3), 133–142.

Higgins, K., Boone, R., & Lovitt, T. C. (2002). Adapting challenging textbooks to improve content area learning. In M. R. Shinn, H. M.

Walker, & G. Stoner (Eds.), *Interventions for academic and behavior problems II: Preventive and remedial approaches* (pp. 755–790). Washington, DC: National Association of School Psychologists.

Hirshfeld-Becker, D. R., Biederman, J., Faraone, S. V., Violette, H., Wrightsman, J., & Rosenbaum, J. F. (2002). Temperamental correlates of disruptive behavior disorders in young children: Preliminary findings. *Biological Psychiatry, 51,* 563–574.

Hoerger, M. L., & Mace, F. C. (2006). A computerized test of self-control predicts classroom behavior. *Journal of Applied Behavior Analysis, 39,* 147–159.

Hoza, B., Mrug, S., Gerdes, A. C., Hinshaw, S. P., Bukowski, W. M., Gold, J. A., Kraemer, H. C., Pelham, W. E., Jr., Wigal, T., & Arnold, L. E. (2005). What aspects of peer relationships are impaired in children with attention-deficit/hyperactivity disorder. *Journal of Consulting and Clinical Psychology, 73,* 411–423.

Jackson, D. A. (2002). The negative halo effect of oppositional defiant behaviors on teacher ratings of ADHD: Impact of child gender. *Dissertation Abstracts International Section B: The Sciences and Engineering, 62*(9-B), 4221.

Jarratt, K. P., Riccio, C. A., & Siekierski, B. M. (2005). Assessment of attention deficit hyperactivity disorder (ADHD) using the BASC and BRIEF. *Applied Neuropsychology, 12,* 83–93.

Jensen, P. S., & Members of the MTA Cooperative Group. (2002). ADHD comorbidity findings from the MTA Study: New diagnostic subtypes and their optimal treatments. In J. E. Helzer & J. J. Hudziak (Eds.), *Defining psychopathology in the 21st century: DSM-V and beyond* (pp. 169–192). Washington, DC: American Psychiatric Publishing.

Jensen, P. S., & Members of the MTA Cooperative Group. (2005). Cost-effectiveness of ADHD treatments: Findings from the multimodal treatment study of children with ADHD. *American Journal of Psychiatry, 162,* 1628–1636.

Johnson, J. H., & Reader, S. K. (2002). Assessing stress in families of children with ADHD: Preliminary development of the Disruptive Behavior Stress Inventory (DBSI). *Journal of Clinical Psychology in Medical Settings, 9,* 51–62.

Kamphaus, R. W., & Frick, P. J. (1996). *Clinical assessment of child and adolescent personality and behavior.* Needham Heights, MA: Allyn and Bacon, p. 131.

Kapalka, G. M. (2005). Avoiding repetitions reduces ADHD children's management problems in the classroom. *Emotional & Behavioural Difficulties, 10,* 269–279.

Kazdin, A. E. (2005). *Parent management training, treatment for oppositional, aggressive, and antisocial behavior in children and adolescents.* New York: Oxford University Press.

Kessler, R. C., Adler, L., Barkley, R., Biederman, J., Conners, C. K., Demler, O., Faraone, S. V., Greenhill, L. L., Howes, M. J., Secnik, K., Spencer, T., Ustun, T. B., Walters, E. E., & Zaslavsky, A. M. (2006). The prevalence and correlates of adult ADHD in the United States: Results from the national comorbidity survey replication. *American Journal of Psychiatry, 163,* 716–723.

Klingberg, T., Forssberg, H., & Westerberg, H. (2002). Training of working memory in children with ADHD. *Journal of Clinical and Experimental Neuropsychology, 24,* 781–791.

Knopik, V. S., Sparrow, E. P., Madden, P. A. F., Bucholz, K. K., Hudziak, J. J., Reich, W., Slutske, W. S., Grant, J. D., McLaughlin, T. L., Todorov, A., Todd, R. D., & Heath, A. C. (2005). Contributions of parental alcoholism, prenatal substance exposure, and genetic transmission to child ADHD risk: A female twin study. *Psychological Medicine, 35,* 625–635.

Krain, A. L., & Castellanos, F. X. (2006). Brain development and ADHD. *Clinical Psychology Review, 26,* 433–444.

Kratochvil, C. J., Egger, H., Greenhill, L. L., & McGough, J. J. (2006). Pharmacological management of preschool ADHD. *Journal of the American Academy of Child & Adolescent Psychiatry, 45,* 115–118.

Kurlan, R. (2005). *Handbook of tourette's syndrome and related tic and behavioral disorders* (2nd ed.). New York: Marcel Dekker.

Kutcher, S. (2002). *Practical child and adolescent psychopharmacology.* New York: Cambridge University Press.

Lambert, N. (2005). The contribution of childhood ADHD, conduct problems, and stimulant treatment to adolescent and adult tobacco and psychoactive substance abuse. *Ethical Human Psychology and Psychiatry, 7,* 197–221.

Lee, C. Y., Chang, Y. Y., & Lung, F. W. (2006). The marriage-related risk factors during maternal pregnancy in children with attention-deficit hyperactivity disorder. *Child: Care, Health and Development, 32,* 205–211.

Livni, E. (2000). Misdiagnosing misbehavior?: First Lady calls for a closer look at psychotropics for kids. ABC News, March 20.

Lohman, M. C. (2002). Cultivating problem-solving skills through problem-based approaches to professional development. *Human Resource Development Quarterly, 13,* 243–261.

MacArthur, C. A., & Haynes, J. B. (1995). Student assistant for learn-

ing from text (SALT): A hypermedia reading aid. *Journal of Learning Disabilities, 28,* 150–159.

Marshal, M. P., & Molina, B. S. G. (2006). Antisocial behaviors moderate the deviant peer pathway to substance abuse with ADHD. *Journal of Clinical Child and Adolescent Psychology, 35,* 216–226.

Martell, R. F., & Evans, D. P. (2005). Source-monitoring training: Toward reducing rater expectancy effects in behavioral measurement. *Journal of Applied Psychology, 90,* 956–963.

Martin, N. C., Levy, F., Pieka, J., & Hay, D. A. (2006). A genetic study of attention deficit hyperactivity disorder, conduct disorder, oppositional defiant disorder and reading disability: Aetiological overlaps and implications. *International Journal of Disability, Development and Education, 53,* 21–34.

Masi, G., Perugi, G., Toni, C., Millepiedi, S., Mucci, M., Bertini, N., & Pfanner, C. (2006). Attention-deficit hyperactivity disorder—bipolar comorbidity in children and adolescents. *Bipolar Disorders, 8,* 373–381.

Mathews, C. A., Bimson, B., Lowe, T. L., Herrera, L. D., Budman, C. L., Erenberg, G., Naarden, A., Bruun, R. D., Freimer, N. B., & Reus, V. I. (2006). Association between maternal smoking and increased symptom severity in Tourette's Syndrome. *American Journal of Psychiatry, 163,* 1066–1073.

Mayes, S. D., & Calhoun, S. L. (2006). Frequency of reading, math, and writing disabilities in children with clinical disorders. *Learning and Individual Differences, 16,* 145–157.

McCabe, S. E., Teter, C. J., & Boyd, C. J. (2006). Medical use, illicit use and diversion of prescription stimulant medication. *Journal of Psychoactive Drugs, 38,* 43–56.

McGoey, K. E., Eckert, T. L., & DuPaul, G. J. (2002). Early intervention for preschool-age children with ADHD: A literature review. *Journal of Emotional and Behavioral Disorders, 10,* 14–28.

McGough, J. J., McBurnett, K., Bukstein, O., Willens, T. E., Greenhill, L., Lerner, M., & Stein, M. (2006). Once-daily OROS methylphenidate is safe and well tolerated in adolescents with attention-deficit/hyperactivity disorder. *Journal of Child and Adolescent Psychopharmacology, 16,* 351–356.

Mill, J., Caspi, A., Williams, B. S., Craig, I., Taylor, A., Polo-Tomas, M., Berridge, C. W., Poulton, R., & Moffit, T. E. (2006). Prediction of heterogeneity in intelligence and adult prognosis by genetic polymorphisms in the dopamine system among children with attention-deficit/hyperactivity disorder. *Archives of General Psychiatry, 63,* 462–469.

Miller, C. J., Miller, S. R., Trampush, J., Mckay, K. E., Newcorn, J. H., & Halperin, J. M. (2006). Family and cognitive factors: Modeling risk for aggression in children with ADHD. *Journal of the American Academy of Child & Adolescent Psychiatry, 45,* 355–363.

Miranda, A., Jarque, S., & Tarraga, R. (2006). Interventions in school settings for students with ADHD. *Exceptionality, 14,* 35–52.

Monastra, V. J. (2005). Everybody doesn't have a little bit of ADHD! *Parenting children with ADHD: 10 lessons that medicine cannot teach* (pp. 11–26). Washington, DC: American Psychological Association.

Montague, M., & Dietz, S. (2006). Attention deficit hyperactivity disorder. *Exceptionality, 14,* 1–2.

Moore, C. M., Biederman, J., Wozniak, J., Mick, E., Aleardi, M., Wardrop, M., Dougherty, M., Harpold, T., Hammerness, P., Randall, E., & Renshaw, P. F. (2006). Differences in brain chemistry in children and adolescents with attention deficit hyperactivity disorder with and without comorbid bipolar disorder: A proton magnetic resonance spectroscopy study. *American Journal of Psychiatry, 163,* 316–318.

Nadeau, K. G., & Quinn, P. O. (2002). An overview of coexisting conditions for women with AD/HD. In K. G. Nadeau & P. O. Quinn (Eds.), Understanding women with AD/HD (pp. 152–176). Silver Spring, MD: Advantage Books.

Nash, K., Rovet, J., Greenbaum, R., Fantus, E., Nulman, I., & Koren, G. (2006). Identifying the behavioural phenotype in fetal alcohol spectrum disorder: Sensitivity, specificity and screening potential. *Archives of Women's Mental Health, 9,* 181–186.

National Institutes of Health. (1998). Diagnosis and treatment of attention deficit hyperactivity disorder. *NIH Consensus Statement Online, 16*(2), 1–37.

Nigg, J. T., Hinshaw, S. P., & Huang-Pollock, C. (2006). Disorders of attention and impulse regulation. In D. Cicchetti & D. J. Cohen (Eds.), *Developmental psychopathology, Vol 3: Risk, disorder, and adaptation* (2nd ed., pp. 358–403). Hoboken, NJ: John Wiley & Sons.

Null, G., & Feldman, M. (2005). The benefits of going beyond conventional therapies for ADHD. *Journal of Orthomolecular Medicine, 20,* 75–88.

Oldehinkel, A. J., Veenstra, R., Ormel, J., de Winter, A. F., & Verhulst, F. C. (2006). Temperament, parenting, and depressive symptoms in a population sample of preadolescents. *Journal of Child Psychology and Psychiatry, 47,* 684–695.

Orford, E. (2006). Re-thinking ADHD—Integrated approaches to helping children at home and at school. An illness of our time. *Journal of Child Psychotherapy, 32,* 114–115.

Pappadopulos, E., Woolston, S., Chait, A., Perkins, M., Connor, D. F., & Jensen, P. S. (2006). Pharmacotherapy of aggression in children and adolescents: Efficacy and effect size. *Journal of the Canadian Academy of Child and Adolescent Psychiatry, 15,* 27–39.

Pappas, D. (2006). ADHD rating scale-IV: Checklists, norms, and clinical interpretation. *Journal of Psychoeducational Assessment, 24,* 172–178.

Pelletier, J., Collett, B., Gimpel, G., & Crowley, S. (2006). Assessment of disruptive behaviors in preschoolers: Psychometric properties of the Disruptive Behavior Disorders Rating Scale and School Situations Questionnaire. *Journal of Psychoeducational Assessment, 24,* 3–18.

Pelham, W. E., Hoza, B., Pillow, D. R., Gnagy, E. M., Kipp, H. L., Greiner, A. R., Waschbusch, D. A., Trane, S. T., Greenhouse, J., Wolfson, L., & Fitzpatrick, E. (2002). Effects of methylphenidate and expectancy on children with ADHD: Behavior, academic performance, and attributions in a summer treatment program and regular classroom settings. *Journal of Consulting and Clinical Psychology, 70,* 320–335.

Pelham, W. E., Jr., Manos, M. J., Ezzell, C. E., Tresco, K. E., Gnagy, E. M., Hoffman, M. T., Onyango, A. N., Fabiano, G. A., Lopez-Williams, A., Wymbs, B. T., Caserta, D., Chronis, A. M., Burrows-Maclean, L., & Morse, G. (2005). A dose-ranging study of a methylphenidate transdermal system in children with ADHD. *Journal of the American Academy of Child & Adolescent Psychiatry, 44,* 522–529.

Pliszka, S. R., Glahn, D. C., Semrud-Clikeman, M. Franklin, C., Perez, R., III., Xiong, J., & Liotti, M. (2006). Neuroimaging of inhibitory control areas in children with attention deficit hyperactivity disorder who were treatment naïve or in long-term treatment. *American Journal of Psychiatry, 163,* 1052–1060.

Power, T. J., Werba, B. E., Watkins, M. W., Angelucci, J. G., Eiraldi, R. B. (2006). Patterns of parent-reported homework problems among ADHD-referred and non-referred children. *School Psychology Quarterly, 21,* 13–33.

Prater, M. A. (2007). *Teaching strategies for students with mild to moderate disabilities.* Boston: Allyn & Bacon.

Radford, P. M., & Ervin, R. A. (2002). Employing descriptive functional assessment methods to assess low-rate, high-intensity behaviors: A case example. *Journal of Positive Behavior Interventions, 4*(3), 146–155.

Rafalovich, A. (2004). *Framing ADHD children: A critical examination of the history, discourse, and everyday experience of attention deficit/hyperactivity disorder.* Lanham, MD: Rowman & Littlefield.

Rafalovich, A. (2005). Exploring clinician uncertainty in the diagnosis and treatment of attention deficit hyperactivity disorder. *Sociology of Health & Illness, 27,* 305–323.

Rappley, M. D. (2005). Attention deficit-hyperactivity disorder. *New England Journal of Medicine, 352,* 165–173.

Ravenel, S. D. (2002). A new behavioral approach for ADD/ADHD and behavioral management without medication. *Ethical Human Sciences and Services, 4*(2), 93–106.

Reich, W., Huang, H., & Todd, R. D. (2006). ADHD medication use in a population-based sample of twins. *Journal of the American Academy of Child & Adolescent Psychiatry, 45,* 801–807.

Robertson, M. M. (2006). Attention deficit hyperactivity disorder, tics and tourette's syndrome: The relationship and treatment implications. A commentary. *European Child & Adolescent Psychiatry, 15,* 1–11.

Robison, L. M., Skaer, T. L., Sclar, D. A., & Galin, R. S. (2002). Is attention deficit hyperactivity disorder increasing among girls in the U.S.? Trends in diagnosis and the prescribing of stimulants. *CNS Drugs, 16*(2), 129–137.

Rowland, A. S., Lesesne, C. A., & Abramowitz, A. J. (2002). The epidemiology of attention-deficit/hyperactivity disorder (ADHD): A public health view. *Mental Retardation and Developmental Disabilities Research Reviews, 8*(3), 162–170.

Rush, C. R., Higgins, S. T., Vansickel, A. R., Stoops, W. W., Lile, J. A., & Glaser, P. E. A. (2005). Methylphenidate increases cigarette smoking. *Psychopharmacology, 181,* 781–789.

Santosh, P. J., Baird, G., Pityaratstian, N. (2006). Impact of comorbid autism spectrum disorders on stimulant response in children with attention deficit hyperactivity disorder: A retrospective and prospective effectiveness study. *Child: Care, Health and Development, 32,* 575–583.

Schmidt, A. T., & Georgieff, M. K. (2006). Early nutritional deficiencies in brain development: Implications for psychopathology. In D. Cicchetti & D. J. Cohen (Eds.), *Developmental psychopathology, Vol 2: Developmental neuroscience* (2nd ed., pp. 259–291). Hoboken, NJ: John Wiley & Sons.

Seidman, L. J. (2006). Neuropsychological functioning in people with ADHD across the lifespan. *Clinical Psychology Review, 26,* 466–485.

Seidman, L. J., Biederman, J., Valera, E. M., Monuteaux, M. C., Doyle, A. E., & Fafaone, S. V. (2006). Neuropsychological functioning in girls with attention-deficit/hyperactivity disorder with and without learning disabilities. *Neuropsychology, 20,* 166–177.

Smith, B. H., Barkley, R. A., & Shapiro, C. J. (2006). Attention-deficit/hyperactivity disorder. In E. J. Mash & R. A. Barkley (Eds.). *Treatment of childhood disorders* (3rd ed., pp. 65–136). New York: Guilford.

Spencer, T. J. (2005). Mixed amphetamine salts extended release for the treatment of ADHD in adolescents: Current evidence. *CNS Spectrums, 10* (10, Supplement 15), 5.

Sutcliffe, P. (2006). Comorbid attentional factors and frequency discrimination performance in a child with reading difficulties. *International Journal of Disability, Development and Education, 53,* 195–208.

Swanson, J. M., Arnold, L. E., Vitiello, B., Abikoff, H. B., Wells, K. C., Pelham, W. E., March, J., S., Hinshaw, S. P., Hoza, B., Epstein, J. N., Elliot, G. R., Greenhill, L. L., Hechtman, L., Jensen, P. S., Kraemer, H. C., Kotkin, R., Molina, B., Newcorn, J. H., Owens, E. B., Severe, J., Hoagwood, K., Simpson, S., Wigal, T., & Hanley, J. (2002). Response to commentary on the Multimodal Treatment Study of ADHD (MTA): Mining the meaning of the MTA. *Journal of Abnormal Child Psychology, 30,* 327–332.

Termine, C., Balottin, U., Rossi, G., Maisano, F., Salini, S., DiNardo, R., & Lanzi, G. (2006). Psychopathology in children and adolescents with tourette's syndrome: A controlled study. *Brain & Development, 28,* 69–75.

Thapar, A., van den Bree, M., Fowler, T., Langley, K., & Whittinger, N. (2006). Predictors of antisocial behaviour in children with attention deficit hyperactivity disorder. *European Child & Adolescent Psychiatry, 15,* 118–125.

Toner, M., O'Donoghue, T., & Houghton, S. (2006). Living in chaos and striving for control: How adults with attention deficit hyperactivity disorder deal with their disorder. *International Journal of Disability, Development and Education, 53,* 247–261.

Tripp, G., & Schaughency, E. A. (2006). Parent and teacher rating scales in the evaluation of attention-deficit hyperactivity disorder: Contributions to diagnosis and differential diagnosis in clinically referred children. *Journal of Developmental & Behavioral Pediatrics, 27,* 209–218.

U.S. Department of Education, Office of Special Education Programs. (2004). *Teaching children with attention deficit hyperactivity disorder: Instructional strategies and practices.* Washington, DC: Author.

U.S. Department of Education, Office of Special Education Programs. (2006). Twenty-sixth annual report to Congress on the implementation of the Individuals with Disabilities Education Act. Washington, DC: Author.

Vile Junod, R. E., DuPaul, G. J., Jitendra, A. K., Volpe, R. J., & Cleary, K. S. (2006). Classroom observations of students with and without ADHD: Differences across types of engagement. *Journal of School Psychology, 44,* 87–104.

Wells, K. C., Chi, T. C., & Hinshaw, S. P. (2006). Treatment-related changes in objectively measured parenting behaviors in the multimodal treatment study of children with attention-deficit/hyperactivity disorder. *Journal of Consulting and Clinical Psychology, 74,* 649–657.

White, B. P., Becker-Blease, K. A., Grace-Bishop, K. (2006). Stimulant medication use, misuse, and abuse in an undergraduate and graduate student sample. *Journal of American College Health, 54,* 261–268.

Wilens, T. E., & Biederman, J. (2006). Alcohol, drugs, and attention-deficit/hyperactivity disorder: A model for the study of addictions in youth. *Journal of Psychopharmacology, 20,* 580–588.

Wigg, K., Zai, G., Schachar, R., Tannock, R., Roberts, W., Malone, M., Kennedy, J. L., & Barr, C. L. (2002). Attention deficit hyperactivity disorder and the gene for dopamine beta-hydroxylase. *American Journal of Psychiatry, 159,* 1046–1048.

Winstanley, C. A., Eagle, D. M., & Robbins, T. W. (2006). Behavioral models of impulsivity in relation to ADHD: Translation between clinical and preclinical studies. *Clinical Psychology Review, 26,* 379–395.

Wolraich, M. L., Bickman, L., Lambert, E. W., Simmons, T., & Doffing, M. A. (2005). Intervening to improve communications between parents, teachers, and primary care providers of children with ADHD or at high risk for ADHD. *Journal of Attention Disorders, 9,* 354–368.

Zahn-Waxler, C., Crick, N. R., Shirtcliff, E. A., & Woods, K. E. (2006). The origins and development of psychopathology in females and males. In D. Cicchetti & D. J. Cohen (Eds.), *Developmental psychopathology, Vol. 1: Theory and method* (2nd ed., pp. 76–138). Hoboken, NJ: John Wiley & Sons.

CHAPTER 9

Achenbach, T. M. (1966). The classification of children's psychiatric symptoms: A factor analytic study. *Psychological Monographs: General and Applied, 615,* 1–37.

Achenbach, T. M. (1991a). *Manual for the child behavior checklist/4B18 and 1991 profile.* Burlington, VT: University of Vermont, Department of Psychiatry.

Achenbach, T. M. (1991b). *Manual for the teachers report form and 1991 profile.* Burlington, VT: University of Vermont, Department of Psychiatry.

Achenbach, T. M. (2000). Assessment of psychopathology. In A. J. Sameroff, M. Lewis, & S. M. Miller (Eds.), *Handbook of developmental psychopathology* (2nd ed.) (pp. 41–56). New York: Kluwer Academic/Plenum.

Adelman, H. S., & Taylor, L. (2006). *The implementation guide to student learning supports in the classroom and schoolwide.* Thousand Oaks, CA: Corwin Press.

Algozzine, B., & White, R. (2002). Preventing problem behaviors using schoolwide discipline. In Algozzine, B., & Kay, P. (Eds.), *Preventing problem behaviors* (pp. 85–103). Thousand Oaks, CA: Corwin Press.

Algozzine, B., Serna, L., & Patton, J. R. (2001). *Childhood behavior disorders: Applied research and educational practices* (2nd ed.). Austin: Pro-Ed.

Anderson, J. A., & Mohr, W. K. (2003). A developmental ecological perspective in systems of care for children with emotional disturbances and their families. *Education and Treatment of Children, 26*(1), 52–47.

Barber, B. K., Stolz, H. E., & Olsen, J. A. (2005). Parental control, psychological control, and behavioral control: Assessing relevance across time, culture, and method. *Monographs of the Society for Research in Child Development, 70*(4), 1–137.

Barton-Arwood, S. M., Wehby, J. H., & Falk, K. B. (2005). Reading instruction for elementary-age students with emotional and behavioral disorders: Academic and behavioral outcomes. *Council for Exceptional Children, 72*(1), 7–27.

Beard, K. Y., & Sugai, G. (2004). First step to success: An early intervention for elementary children at risk for antisocial behavior. *Behavioral Disorders, 29*(4), 396–409.

Benitez, D. T., Lattimore, J., & Wehmeyer, M. L. (2005). Promoting the involvement of students with emotional and behavioral disorders in career and vocational planning and decision-making: The self-determined career development model. *Behavioral Disorders, 30*(4), 431–447.

Benner, G. J., Nelson, J. R., & Epstein, M. H. (2002). Language skills of children with EBD: A literature review. *Journal of Emotional and Behavioral Disorders, 10,* 43–59.

Booth, P., & O'Hara, D. (2005). Using Theraplay to interrupt a three-generation pattern of inadequate parenting. In C. W. LeCroy & J. M. Daley (Eds.), *Case studies in child, adolescent, and family treatment* (pp. 91–2). Belmont, CA: Thomson Brooks/Cole.

Borg, M. B., & Dalla, M. R. (2005). Treatment of gangs/gang behavior in adolescence. In T. P. Gullotta & G. R. Adams (Eds.), *Handbook of adolescent behavioral problems* (pp. 519–542). New York: Springer Science & Business Media.

Bower, E. M. (1959). The emotionally handicapped child and the school. *Exceptional Children, 26,* 6–11.

Bradley, R., Henderson, K., & Monfore, D. A. (2004). A national perspective on children with emotional disorders. *Behavioral Disorders, 29*(3), 211–223.

Bullis, M. (2001). Job placement and support considerations in transition programs for adolescents with emotional disabilities. In L. M. Bullock, & R. A. Gable (Eds.), *Addressing the social, academic, and behavioral needs of students with challenging behavior in inclusive and alternative settings* (pp. 31–36). Las Vegas, Nevada: Council for Children with Behavioral Disorders.

Bullis, M., & Yovanoff, P. (2006). Idle hands: Community employment experiences of formerly incarcerated youth. *Journal of Emotional and Behavioral Disorders, 14*(2), 71–85.

Burrell, S., & Warboys, L. (2000, July). Special education and the juvenile justice system. *Juvenile Justice Bulletin,* 1–15.

Capaldi, D. M., & Eddy, J. M. (2005). Oppositional defiant disorder and conduct disorder. In T. P. Gullotta & G. R. Adams (Eds.), *Handbook of adolescent behavioral problems* (pp. 283–308). New York: Springer Science & Business Media.

Carter, E. W., & Wehby, J. H. (2003). Job performance of transition-age youth with emotional and behavioral disorders. *Council for Exceptional Children, 69*(4), 449–465.

Carter, E. W., Wehby, J. H., Hughes, C., Johnson, S. M., Plank, D. R., Barton-Arwood, S. M., & Lunsford, L. B. (2005). Preparing adolescents with high-incidence disabilities for high-stakes testing with strategy instruction. *Preventing School Failure, 49*(2), 55–62.

Carter, E. W., & Lunsford, L. B. (2005). Meaningful work: Improving employment outcomes for transition-age youth with emotional and behavioral disorders. *Preventing School Failure, 49*(2), 63–69.

Cassidy, E., James, A., & Wiggs, L. (2001). The prevalence of psychiatric disorder in children attending a school for pupils with emotional and behavioral difficulties. *British Journal of Special Education, 28,* 167–173.

Christle, C. A., Jolivette, K., & Nelson, C. M. (2005). Breaking the school to prison pipeline: Identifying school risk and protective factors for youth delinquency. *Exceptionality, 13*(2), 69–88.

Coleman, M. C., & Webber, J. (2002). *Emotional and behavioral disorders:*

Theory and practice. Boston: Allyn & Bacon.

Conroy, M. A., & Brown, W. H. (2004). Early identification, prevention, and early intervention with young children at risk for emotional or behavioral disorders: Issues, trends, and a call for action. *Behavioral Disorders, 29*(3), 224–236.

Conroy, M. A., Hendrickson, J. M., & Hester, P. P. (2004). Early identification and prevention of emotional and behavioral disorders. In R. B. Rutherford, M. M. Quinn, & S. R. Mathur (Eds.), *Handbook of research in emotional and behavioral disorders* (pp. 199–215). New York: Guilford.

Cross, M. (2004). *Children with emotional and behavioural difficulties and communication problems: There is always a reason.* London: Jessica Kingsley Publications.

Crosson-Tower, C. (2002). *When children are abused: An educator's guide to intervention.* Boston: Allyn & Bacon.

Cullinan, D. (2004). Classification and definition of emotional and behavioral disorders. In R. B. Rutherford, M. M. Quinn, & S. R. Mathur (Eds.), *Handbook of research in emotional and behavioral disorders* (pp. 32–53). New York: Guilford.

DuCharme, R. W., & McGrady, K. A. (2005). Pervasive developmental delay. In T. P. Gullotta & G. R. Adams (Eds.), *Handbook of adolescent behavioral problems* (pp. 309–329). New York: Springer Science & Business Media.

Duchnowski, A. J., & Friedman, R. M. (1990). Children's mental health: Challenges for the nineties. *Journal of Mental Health Administration, 17*(1), 3–12.

EasyChild Software. (2006). *EasyChild: Encouragement system.* Retrieved June 6, 2006, from www.easychild.com/index.htm

Eber, L., & Keenan, S. (2004). Collaboration with other agencies: Wraparound and systems of care for children and youths with emotional and behavioral disorders. In R. B. Rutherford, M. M. Quinn, & S. R. Mathur (Eds.), *Handbook of research in emotional and behavioral disorders* (pp. 502–516). New York: Guilford.

Eber, L., Sugai, G., Smith, C., & Scott, T. (2002). Wraparound and positive behavioral interventions and supports in the schools. *Journal of Emotional and Behavioral Disorders, 10,* 171–180.

Eddy, J. M., Reid, J. B., & Fetrow, R. A. (2000). An elementary school-based prevention program targeting modifiable antecedents of youth delinquency and violence: Linking the interests of families and teachers (LIFT). *Journal of Emotional and Behavioral Disorders, 8,* 165–176.

Epstein, M. H., & Sharma, J. M. (1997). *Behavior and Emotional*

Rating Scale. Austin, TX: PRO-ED.

Essa, E. (2003). *A practical guide to solving preschool behavior problems* (5th ed.). Australia: Thompson/Delmar Learning.

First, M. B., & Tasman, A. (Eds.). (2004). *DSM-IV-TR mental disorders: Diagnosis, etiology, and treatment.* Chichester, England: John Wiley & Sons.

Forness, S. R. (2004). Characteristics of emotional and behavioral disorders [Introduction]. In R. B. Rutherford, M. M. Quinn, & S. R. Mathur (Eds.), *Handbook of research in emotional and behavioral disorders* (pp. 235–241). New York: Guilford.

Forness, S. R., & Kavale, K. A. (2001). ADHD and a return to the medical model of special education. *Education and Treatment of Children, 24,* 224–247.

Forness, S. R., & Knitzer, J. (1992). A new proposed definition and terminology to replace "Serious Emotional Disturbance" in Individuals with Disabilities Education Act. *School Psychology Review, 21,* 12–20.

Gable, R. A. (2004). Hard times and an uncertain future: Issues that confront the field of emotional/behavioral disorders. *Education and Treatment of Children, 27*(4), 341–352.

Goh, D. S. (2004). *Assessment accommodations for diverse learners.* Boston: Allyn & Bacon.

Graczyk, P. A., Connolly, S. D., & Corapci, F. (2005). Anxiety disorders in children and adolescents: Theory, treatment, and prevention. In T. P. Gullotta & G. R. Adams (Eds.), *Handbook of adolescent behavioral problems* (pp. 131–157). New York: Springer Science & Business Media.

Greenberg, M. T., Domitrovich, C., & Bumbarger, B. (2001, March). The prevention of mental disorders in school-aged children: Current state of the field. *Prevention & Treatment, 4*(1)1a.

Guerra, N. G., Boxer, P., & Kim, T. E. (2005). A cognitive-ecological approach to serving students with emotional and behavioral disorders: Application to aggressive behavior. *Behavioral Disorders, 30*(3), 277–288.

Hansen, S. D., & Lignugaris-Kraft, B. (2005). Effects of a dependent group contingency on the verbal interactions of middle school students with emotional disturbances. *Behavioral Disorders, 30*(2), 170–184.

Heilbrun, A. B. (2004). *Disordered and deviant behavior: Learning gone awry.* Lanham, MD: University Press of America.

Henley, M. (2003). *Teaching self-control: A curriculum for responsible behavior.* Bloomington, IN: National Education Service.

Henry, D. B., Tolan, P. H., Gorman-Smith, D. (2001). Longitudinal family and peer group effects on violence and nonviolent delinquency. *Journal of Clinical Child Psychology, 30,* 172–186.

Hernandez, M., Gomez, A., Lipien, L., Greenbaum, P. E., Armstrong, K. H., Gonzalez, P. (2001). Use of the system-of-care practice review in the national evaluation: Evaluating the fidelity of practice to system-of-care principles. *Journal of Emotional and Behavioral Disorders, 9,* 43–52.

Hester, P. P., Baltodano, H. M., Hendrickson, J. M., Tonelson, S. W., Conroy, M. A., & Gable, R. A. (2004). Lessons learned from research on early intervention: What teachers can do to prevent children's behavior problems. *Preventing School Failure, 49*(1), 5–10.

Hieneman, M., Dunlap, G., & Kincaid, D. (2005). Positive support strategies for students with behavioral disorders in general education settings. *Psychology in the Schools, 42*(8), 779–794.

Horton, C. B., & Cruise, T. K. (2001). *Child abuse & neglect: The school's response.* New York: Guilford.

Howell, J. C. (2003). Youth gangs: Prevention and intervention. In P. Allen-Meares & M. W. Fraser (Eds.), *Intervention with children and adolescents: An interdisciplinary perspective* (pp. 493–404). Boston: Allyn & Bacon.

Howell, J. C., & Egley, A. (2005). Moving risk factors into developmental theories of gang membership. *Youth Violence and Juvenile Justice, 3*(4), 334–354.

Hughes, T. L., & Bray, M. A. (2004). Differentiation of emotional disturbance and social maladjustment: Introduction to the special issue. *Psychology in the Schools, 41*(8), 819–821.

Ialongo, N., Poduska, J., Werthamer, L., & Kellam, S. (2001). The distal impact of two first-grade preventive interventions on conduct problems and disorder in early adolescence. *Journal of Emotional and Behavioral Disorders, 9,* 146–160.

Joseph, G. E., & Strain, P. S. (2003). Comprehensive evidence-based social-emotional curricula for young children: An analysis of efficacious adoption potential. *Topics in Early Childhood Special Education, 23*(2), 65–76.

Kauffman, J. M. (2005). *Characteristics of emotional and behavioral disorders of children and youth.* Upper Saddle River, NJ: Prentice-Hall.

Kauffman, J. M., Bantz, J., & McCullough, J. (2002). Separate and better: A special public school class for students with emotional and behavioral disorders. *Exceptionality, 10,* 149–170.

Kavale, K. A., & Forness, S. R. (2000). History, rhetoric, and reality: Analysis of the inclusion debate. *Remedial and Special Education, 21,* 279–296.

Kea, C. D., Cartledge, G., & Bowman, L. J. (2002). Interventions for African American learners with behavioral problems. In F. E. Obiaker, & B. A. Ford (Eds.), *Creating successful learning environments for African American learners with exceptionalities* (pp. 79–94). Thousand Oaks, CA: Corwin Press.

Kendler, K. S., & Eaves, L. J. (Eds.). (2005). Psychiatric genetics. In *Review of Psychiatry.* Arlington, VA: American Psychiatric Publishing.

Kendziora, K. T. (2004). Early intervention for emotional and behavioral disorders. In R. B. Rutherford, M. M. Quinn, & S. R. Mathur (Eds.), *Handbook of research in emotional and behavioral disorders* (pp. 327–351). New York: Guilford.

Kendziora, K., Bruns, E., Osher, D., Pacchiano, D., & Mejia, B. (2001). Systems of care: Promising practices in children's mental health, 2001 series, volume I. Washington, DC: Center for Effective Collaboration and Practice, American Institutes for Research.

Kennedy, C. H., Long, T., Jolivette, K., Cox, J., Tang, J., & Thompson, T. (2001). Facilitating general education participation for students with behavior problems by linking positive behavior supports and person-centered planning. *Journal of Emotional and Behavioral Disorders, 9,* 161–171.

Knitzer, J. (1982). *Unclaimed children: The failure of public responsibility to children and adolescents in need of mental health services.* Washington, DC: Children's Defense Fund.

Knitzer, J., Steinberg, Z., & Fleisch, B. (1990). *At the schoolhouse door: An examination of programs and policies for children with behavioral and emotional problems.* New York: Bank Street College of Education.

Konopasek, D. E., & Forness, S. R. (2004). Psychopharmacology in the treatment of emotional and behavioral disorders. In R. B Rutherford, M. M. Quinn, & S. R. Mathur (Eds.), *Handbook of research in emotional and behavioral disorders* (pp. 352–368). New York: Guilford.

Koyanagi, C., & Feres-Merchant, D. (2000). For the long haul: Maintaining systems of care beyond the federal investment. *Systems of care: Promising practices in children's mental health,* 2000 series, volume III. Washington, DC: Center for Effective Collaboration and Practice, American Institutes for Research.

Lane, K. L. (2004). Academic instruction and tutoring interventions for students with emotional and behavioral disorders: 1990 to the present. In R. B. Rutherford, M. M. Quinn, & S. R. Mathur (Eds.), *Handbook of research in emotional and behavioral disorders* (pp. 462–486). New York: Guilford.

Lane, K. L., Menzies, H. M., Barton-Arwood, S. M., Doukas, G. L., & Munton, S. M. (2005). Designing, implementing, and evaluating social skills interventions for elementary students: Step-by-step procedures based on actual school-based investigations. *Preventing School Failure, 49*(2), 18–26.

Lane, K. L., Wehby, J., & Barton-Arwood, S. M. (2005). Students with and at risk for emotional and behavioral disorders: Meeting their social and academic needs. *Preventing School Failure, 49*(2), 6–9.

Lane, K. L., Wehby, J. H., Little, M. A., & Cooley, C. (2005). Students educated in self-contained classrooms and self-contained schools: Part II-How do they progress over time? *Behavioral Disorders, 30*(4), 363–374.

Levitt, J. L., Sansone, R. A., & Cohn, L. (Eds.). (2004). *Self-harm behavior and eating disorders: Dynamics, assessment, and treatment.* New York: Brunner-Routledge.

Lewis, T. J., Lewis-Palmer, T., Newcomer, L., & Stichter, J. (2004). Applied behavior analysis and the education and treatment of students with emotional and behavioral disorders. In R. B. Rutherford, M. M. Quinn, & S. R. Mathur (Eds.), *Handbook of research in emotional and behavioral disorders* (pp. 523–545). New York: Guilford.

Lewis, T. J., Hudson, S., Richter, M., & Johnson, N. (2004). Scientifically supported practices in emotional and behavioral disorders: A proposed approach and brief review of current practices. *Behavioral Disorders, 29*(3), 247–259.

Liaupsin, C. J., Jolivette, K., & Scott, T. M. (2004). Schoolwide systems of behavior support. In R. B. Rutherford, M. M. Quinn, & S. R. Mathur (Eds.), *Handbook of research in emotional and behavioral disorders* (pp. 487–501). New York: Guilford.

Lien-Thorne, S., & Kamps, D. (2005). Replication study of the first step to success early intervention program. *Behavioral Disorders, 31*(1), 18–32.

Lopez, J. (2005). Intervention with students with learning, emotional, and behavioral disorders: Why do we take so long to do it? *Education and Treatment of Children, 28*(4), 345–360.

Lyons, J. S. (1997). *Child and adolescent strengths assessment.* Chicago, IL: Northwest University, Department of Psychiatry and Behavioral Sciences.

Mattison, R. E., Hooper, S. R., & Carlson, G. A. (2006). Neuropsychological characteristics of special education students with serious emotional/behavioral disorders. *Behavioral Disorders, 31*(2), 176–188.

Mayer, M., Lochman, J., & Van Acker, R. (2005). Introduction to the special issue: Cognitive-behavioral interventions with students with EBD. *Behavioral Disorders, 30*(3), 197–212.

McEvoy, A., & Welker, R. (2000). Antisocial behavior, academic failure, and school climate: A critical review. *Journal of Emotional and Behavioral Disorders, 8,* 130–140.

Meadows, N. B., & Stevens, K. B. (2004). Teaching alternative behaviors to students with emotional and behavioral disorders. In R. B. Rutherford, M. M. Quinn, & S. R. Mathur (Eds.), *Handbook of research in emotional and behavioral disorders* (pp. 385–398). New York: Guilford.

Merrell, K. W., & Walker, H. M. (2004). Deconstructing a definition: Social maladjustment versus emotional disturbance and moving the EBD field forward. *Psychology in the Schools, 41*(8), 899–910.

Miller, M. J., Lane, K. L., & Wehby, J. (2005). Social skills instruction for students with high-incidence disabilities: A school-based intervention to address acquisition deficits. *Preventing School Failure, 49*(2), 27–39.

Morse, W. C., Cutler, R. L., & Fink, A. H. (1964). *Public school classes for emotionally handicapped: A research analysis.* Washington, DC: Council for Exceptional Children.

National Center for Education Statistics. (2006). *Table 50. Children 3 to 21 years old served in federally supported programs for the disabled, by type of disability: Selected years, 1976–77 through 2003–04.* Retrieved June 10, 2006, from http://nces.ed.gov/programs/digest/d05/tables/ dt05_050.asp

National Mental Health Information Center. (2006). *National systems of care a promising solution for children with serious emotional disturbances and their families.* Washington, DC: Author. Retrieved July 19, 2006, from http://www.mentalhealth.samhsa.gov/publications/allpubs/Ca-0030/default.asp

Nelson, J. R., Benner, G. J., Lane, K., & Smith, B. W. (2004). Academic achievement of K-12 students with emotional and behavioral disorders. *Council for Exceptional Children, 71*(1), 59–73.

Newcomer, P. L. (2003). *Understanding and teaching emotionally disturbed children and adolescents* (3rd ed.). Austin: Pro-Ed.

Nungesser, N. R., & Watkins, R. V. (2005). Preschool teachers' perceptions and reactions to challenging classroom behavior: Implications for speech-language pathologists. *Language, Speech, and Hearing Services in Schools, 36,* 139–151.

Obiakor, F. E., Enwefa, S. E., Utley, C., Obi, S. O., Gwalla-Ogisi, N., & Enwefa, R. (2004). Serving culturally and linguistically diverse students with emotional and behavioral disorders. In *Meeting the diverse needs of children and youth with E/BD: Evidence-based programs and practices.* Arlington, VA: Council for Children with Behavioral Disorders.

Osher, D., Cartledge, G., Oswald, D., Sutherland, K. S., Artiles, A. J., & Coutinho, M. (2004). Cultural and linguistic competency and disproportionate representation. In R. B. Rutherford, M. M. Quinn, & S. R. Mathur (Eds.), *Handbook of research in emotional and behavioral disorders* (pp. 54–77). New York: Guilford.

Panacek, L. J., & Dunlap, G. (2003). The social lives of children with emotional and behavioral disorders in self-contained classrooms: A descriptive analysis. *Council for Exceptional Children, 69*(3), 333–348.

Peacock Hill Working Group. (1990). *Problems and promises in special education and related services for children and youth with emotional and behavioral disorders.* Charlottesville, VA: Author.

Peterson, N. L. (1987). *Early intervention for handicapped and at-risk children: An introduction to early childhood special education.* Denver: Love.

Pierce, C. D., Reid, R., & Epstein, M. H. (2004). Teacher-mediated interventions for children with EBD and their academic outcomes. *Remedial and Special Education, 25*(3), 175–188.

Place, M., Wilson, J., Martin, E., & Hulsmeier, J. (1999). Attention deficit disorder as a factor in the origin of behavioural disturbance in schools. *British Journal of Special Education, 26,* 158–163.

Polsgrove, L. & Smith, S. (2004). Informed practice in teaching students self-control. In Rutherford, R., Quinn, & Mathur, S. (Eds.), *Research in Emotional and Behavioral Disorders.* New York: Guilford.

Quay, H. C. (1975). Classification in the treatment of delinquency and antisocial behavior. In N. Hobbs (Ed.), *Issues in the classification of children* (Vol. 1, pp. 377–392). San Francisco: Jossey-Bass.

Quay, H. C. (1979). Classification. In H. C. Quay & J. S. Werry (Eds.), *Psychopathological disorders of childhood* (2nd ed., pp. 1–41). New York: Wiley.

Quinn, M. M., & Poirier, J. M. (2004). Linking prevention research with policy: Examining the costs and outcomes of the failure to prevent emotional and behavioral disorders. In R. B. Rutherford, M. M. Quinn, & S. R. Mathur (Eds.), *Handbook of research in emotional and behavioral disorders* (pp. 78–97). New York: Guilford.

Reid, R., Trout, A. L., & Schartz, M. (2005). Self-regulation interventions for children with attention deficit/hyperactivity disorder. *Council for Exceptional Children, 71*(4), 361–377.

Reinke, W. M., Herman, K. C., & Tucker, C. M. (2006). Building and sustaining communities that prevent mental disorders: Lessons from the field of special education. *Psychology in the Schools, 43*(3), 313–329.

Roberts, C., & Bishop, B. (2005). Depression. In T. P. Gullotta & G. R. Adams (Eds.), *Handbook of adolescent behavioral problems* (pp. 205–230). New York: Springer Science & Business Media.

Rosenberg, M. S., Wilson, R., Maheady, L., & Sindelar, P. T. (2004). *Educating students with behavior disorders* (3rd ed.). Boston: Allyn & Bacon.

Rutter, M. (2006). *Genes and behavior: Nature-nurture interplay explained.* Malden, MA: Blackwell.

Ryan, J. B., Reid, R., & Epstein, M. H. (2004). Peer-mediated intervention studies on academic achievement for students with EBD: A review. *Remedial and Special Education, 25*(6), 330–341.

Safran, S. P., & Oswald, K. (2003). Positive behavior supports: Can schools reshape disciplinary practices? *Council for Exceptional Children, 69*(3), 361–373.

Sampers, J., Anderson, K. G., Hartung, C. M., & Scambler, D. J. (2001). Parent training programs for young children with behavior problems. *Infant Toddler Intervention: The Transdisciplinary Journal, 11,* 91–110.

Seifert, K. (2000). Juvenile violence: An overview of risk factors and programs. *Reaching Today's Youth, 4,* 60–71.

Shores, R. E., & Wehby, J. H. (1999). Analyzing the classroom social behavior of students with EBD. *Journal of Emotional and Behavioral Disorders, 7*(4), 194–199.

Shriner, J. G., & Wehby, J. H. (2004). Accountability and assessment for students with emotional and behavioral disorders. In R. B. Rutherford, M. M. Quinn, & S. R. Mathur (Eds.), *Handbook of research in emotional and behavioral disorders* (pp. 216–231). New York: Guilford.

Simpson, J. S., Jivanjee, P., Koroloff, N., Doerfler, A., & Garcia, M. (2001). Promising practices in early childhood mental health. *Systems of care: Promising practices in children's mental health,* 2001 series, volume III. Washington, DC: Center for Effective Collaboration and Practice, American Institutes for Research.

Sitlington, P. L., & Neubert, D. A. (2004). Preparing youths with emotional or behavioral disorders for transition to adult life: Can it be done within the standards-based reform movement? *Behavioral Disorders, 29*(3), 279–288.

Smolak, L. (2005). Eating disorders in girls. In D. J. Bell, S. L. Foster, & E. J. Mash (Eds.), *Handbook of behavioral and emotional problems in girls* (pp. 463–487). New York: Kluwer Academic/Plenum Publishers.

Stainback, W., & Stainback, S. (1992). *Curriculum considerations in inclusive classrooms: Facilitating learning for all students.* Baltimore: Brookes.

Stroul, B. A., & Friedman, R. M. (1986). *A system of care for severely emotionally disturbed children and youth.* Washington, DC: Georgetown University.

Thornberry, T. P., Krohn, M. D., Lizotte, A. J., Smith, C. A., & Tobin, K. (2003). *Gangs and delinquency in developmental perspective.* Cambridge, UK: Cambridge University Press.

U.S. Department of Education. (1999). To assure the free appropriate public education of all children with disabilities: Twenty-first annual report to Congress on the implementation of the Individuals with Disabilities Act. Washington, DC: Author.

U.S. Department of Education. (2005). Twenty-fifth annual (2003) report to Congress on the implementation of the Individuals with Disabilities Act (vol. 1). Washington, DC: Author.

U.S. Department of Education. (2006). *Federal Register,* August 14, 2006, Part II, 34 CFR Parts 300 and 301. Assistance to states for the education of children with disabilities and preschool grants for children; Final rule. Washington, DC: Author.

Von Isser, A., Quay, H. C., & Love, C. T. (1980). Interrelationships among three measures of deviant behavior. *Exceptional Children, 46*(4), 272–276.

Walker, H. M., & Severson, H. H. (1992). *Systematic screening for behavior disorders.* Longmont, CO: Sopris West.

Walker, H. M., Ramsey, E., & Gresham, F. M. (2004). *Antisocial behavior in school: Strategies and best practices* (2nd ed.). Pacific Grove, CA: Brooks/Cole.

Weaster, K. (2004). Reading and behavioral disorders: Searching for meaning under the streetlight. *Intervention in School and Clinic, 40*(1), 59–62.

Wicks-Nelson, R., & Israel, A. C. (2006). *Behavior disorders of childhood* (6th ed.). Upper Saddle River, NJ: Prentice Hall.

Witt, J. C., Daly, E. M., & Noell, G. (2000). *Functional assessments: A step-by-step guide to solving academic and behavior problems.* Longmont, CO: Sopris West.

Witt, J. C., VanDerHeyden, A. M., & Gilbertson, D. (2004). Instruction and classroom management. In R. B. Rutherford, M. M. Quinn, & S. R. Mathur (Eds.), *Handbook of research in emotional and behavioral disorders* (pp. 426–445). New York: Guilford.

Woodruff, D. W., Osher, D., Hoffman, C. C., Gruner, A., King, M. A.,

Snow, S. T., & McIntire, J. C. (1999). The role of education in a system of care: Effectively serving children with emotional or behavioral disorders. *Systems of Care: Promising Practices in Children's Mental Health, 1998 Series, Vol. III*. Washington, DC: Center for Effective Collaboration and Practice, American Institutes for Research.

Worthington, J., Hernandez, M., Friedman, B., & Uzzell, D. (2001). *Systems of care: Promising Practices in Children's Mental Health, 2001 Series, Volume II*. Washington, DC: Center for Effective Collaboration and Practice, American Institutes for Research.

Yeh, M., Forness, S. R., Ho, J., McCabe, K., & Hough, R. L. (2004). Parental etiological explanations and disproportionate racial/ethnic representation in special education services for youths with emotional disturbances. *Behavioral Disorders, 29*(4), 348–358.

Zahn-Waxler, C., Race. E., & Duggal, S. (2005). Mood disorders and symptoms in girls. In D. J. Bell, S. L. Foster, & E. J. Mash (Eds.), *Handbook of behavioral and emotional problems in girls* (pp. 25–77). New York: Kluwer Academic/Plenum Publishers.

CHAPTER 10

AAIDD (AAMR) Ad Hoc Committee on Terminology and Classification. (2002). *Mental retardation: Definition, classification, and systems of support* (10th ed.). Washington, DC: American Association on Intellectual and Developmental Disabilities (formally known as the American Association on Mental Retardation), p. 42.

Batshaw, M. (2003). *Children with disabilities* (4th ed.). Baltimore: Paul H. Brookes.

Beirne-Smith, M., Patton, J. R., & Kim., S. H. (2006). *Mental retardation: An introduction to intellectual disability* (7th edition). Upper Saddle River, NJ: Merrill.

Berk, L. E. (2005). *Development through the lifespan*. Boston: Allyn and Bacon.

Bonn, H., & Bonn, B. (2000a). In the best interests of the child. In S. E. Wade (Ed.), *Inclusive education: A casebook and readings for prospective and practicing teachers* (pp. 173–180). Mahwah, NJ: Lawrence Erlbaum Associates.

Bonn, H., & Bonn, B. (2000b). Part B of the case: "In the best interests of the child." In S. E. Wade (Ed.), *Preparing teachers for inclusive education* (pp. 209–211). Mahwah, NJ: Lawrence Erlbaum Associates.

Braddock, D., Hemp, R., Rizzolo, M. C., Parish, S., & Pomeranz, A. (2002). *The state of the states in developmental disabilities: 2002 study summary*. Boulder, CO: Coleman

Institute for Cognitive Disabilities and the Department of Psychiatry, University of Colorado.

Browder, D. M., Ahlgrim-Delzell, L. A., Courtade-Little, G., & Snell, M. E. (2006). General curriculum access. In M. E. Snell & F. Brown (Eds.), *Introduction to students with severe disabilities* (6th ed., pp. 489–525). Upper Saddle River, NJ: Merrill.

Centers for Disease Control. (2006). Maternal Smoking During Pregnancy Increases Children's Risk for Mental Retardation. Retrieved September 4, 2006, from http://www.cdc.gov/tobacco/research_data/health_consequences/matsmkg.htm

Children's Defense Fund. (2005). *The state of America's children*. Washington, DC: Author.

Corum, S. (2003, May 18). Life is short. *Washington Post*, D, 1.

National Down Syndrome Society. (2006). Down syndrome: Myths and Truths. Retrieved September 27, 2006, from http://www.ndss.org/content.cfm?fuseaction=NDSS.article&article=443

Drew, C. J., & Hardman, M. L. (2007). *Intellectual disabilities across the lifespan* (9th ed.). Columbus, OH: Merrill.

Guralnick, M. J. (2001). A framework for change in early childhood inclusion. In M. J. Guralnick (Ed.), *Early childhood inclusion: Focus on change* (pp. 3–35). Baltimore: Paul H. Brookes.

Horvat, M. (2000). Physical activity of children with and without mental retardation in inclusive recess settings. *Education and Training in Mental Retardation, 35*(2), 160–167.

Kaiser, A. P. (2000). Teaching functional communication skills. In M. E. Snell & F. Brown (Eds.), *Instruction of persons with severe disabilities* (5th ed., pp. 453–492). Columbus, OH: Merrill.

Katims, D. S. (2000). Literacy instruction for people with mental retardation: Historical highlights and contemporary analysis. *Education and Training in Mental Retardation and Developmental Disabilities, 35*(1), 3–15.

Kittler, P., Krinsky-McHale, S. J., & Devenny, D. A. (2004). Semantic and phonological loop effects on visual working memory in middle-age adults with mental retardation. *American Journal on Mental Retardation, 109*(6), 467–480.

Kowalski, J. T. (2006). *HIV AIDS and Mental Retardation*. Silver Springs, MD: The ARC- A National Organization on Mental Retardation. Retrieved September 18, 2006, from http://www.thearc.org/faqs/hiv.html

Kregel, J. (2001). Promoting employment opportunities for individuals with mild cognitive limitations: A time for reform. In A. J. Tymchuk, K. C. Lakin, & R. Luckasson (Eds.), *The forgotten generation: The status

and challenges of adults with mild cognitive limitations* (pp. 87–98). Baltimore: Paul H. Brookes.

Lakin, C. (2005). Introduction. In K. C. Lakin & A. Turnbull (Eds.), *National goals for people with intellectual and developmental disabilities* (pp. 1–13). Washington, DC: The ARC of the U.S. and the American Association on Intellectual and Developmental Disabilities (formerly AAMR).

Lee, S., Yoo, S., & Bak, S. (2003). Characteristics of friendships among children with and without mild disabilities. *Education and Training in Developmental Disabilities, 38*(2), 157–166.

McDonnell, J., Hardman, M., & McDonnell, A. P. (2003). *Introduction to persons with moderate and severe disabilities*. Boston: Allyn and Bacon.

Moore-Brown, B. J., & Montgomery, J. K. (2006). *Making a difference for America's children: Speech–language pathologists in public schools*. Eau Claire, WI: Thinking Publications.

Morgan, R. L., Ellerd, D. A., Gerity, B. P., & Blair, R. J. (2000). "That's the job I want": How technology helps young people in transition. *Teaching Exceptional Children, 32*(4), 44–49.

National Organization on Fetal Alcohol Syndrome. (2006). *What is fetal alcohol syndrome?* Retrieved September 21, 2006, from http://www.nofas.org/faqs.aspx?id=12

Nirje, B. (1970). The normalization principle and its human management implications. *Journal of Mental Subnormality, 16*, 62–70.

Otley, K. (2006). The keys are mine. In T. Fields & C. Lakin (Eds.), *Consumer controlled housing* (pp. 24). Minneapolis, MN: ARC-Minnesota and the Institute on Community Integration.

President's Committee for People with Intellectual Disabilities. (2006). Fact Sheet: *The Role of the PCPID*. Retrieved September 11, 2006, from http://www.acf.hhs.gov/programs/pcpid/pcpid_fact.html

Sailor W., Gee, K., & Karasoff, P. (2000). Inclusion and school restructuring. In M. Snell & F. Brown (Eds.), *Instruction of students with severe disabilities* (5th ed., pp. 1–30). Columbus, OH: Charles Merrill.

Shonkoff, J. P. & Phillips, D. A. (Eds.). (2000). *From neurons to neighborhoods: The science of early childhood development*. Washington, DC: Committee on Integrating the Science of Early Childhood Development, Board on Children, Youth, and Families, National Academies Press.

Stainback, S., Stainback, W., & Ayres, B. (1996). Schools as inclusive communities. In W. Stainback & S. Stainback (Eds.), *Controversial issues confronting special education:

Divergent perspectives* (pp. 31–43). Boston: Allyn and Bacon.

Sternberg, R. J. (2003). *Cognitive Psychology* (3rd edition). Florence, KY: Wadsworth.

The Arc. (2006). *Causes and prevention of mental retardation*. Retrieved September 14, 2006, from http://www.thearc.org/faqs/causesandprev.pdf/

U.S. Department of Education. (2006). To assure the free appropriate public education of all children with disabilities. *Twenty-sixth annual report to Congress on the implementation of the Individuals with Disabilities Education Act*. Washington, DC: U.S. Government Printing Office.

Warren, S. F. (2002, May/June). Mental retardation: Curse, characteristic, or coin of the realm? *AAMR News and Notes, 1*, 10–11.

Wehman, P. (2006). Transition: The bridge to adulthood. In P. Wehman (Ed.), *Life beyond the classroom: Transition strategies for young people with disabilities* (4th ed., pp. 3–42). Baltimore: Paul H. Brookes.

Westling, D. & Fox, L. (2004). *Teaching students with severe disabilities* (3rd ed.) Upper Saddle River, NJ: Merrill/Prentice Hall.

CHAPTER 11

Alexander, L. B., & Solomon, P. (2006). *The research process in the human services: Behind the scenes*. Belmont, CA: Thomson, Brooks/Cole.

Alison, R., Winslow, I., Marchant, P., & Brumfitt, S. (2006). Evaluation of communication, life participation and psychological well-being in chronic aphasia: The influence of group intervention. *Aphasiology, 20*, 427–448.

Alm, P. A. (2006). Stuttering and sensory gating: A study of acoustic startle prepulse inhibition. *Brain and Language, 97*, 317–321.

American Psychiatric Association. (2000). Diagnostic and statistical manual of mental disorders (4th ed.–text revision). Washington, DC: Author.

Anderson, N. B., & Shames, G. H. (2006). *Human communication disorders: An introduction* (7th ed.). Boston: Allyn and Bacon.

Anderson, N. B., Shames, G. H., & Chabon, S. (2006). Introduction: Human communication disorders: A philosophy and practice of service. In N. B. Anderson & G. H. Shames (Eds.), *Human communication disorders: An introduction* (7th ed., pp. 1–21). Boston: Allyn and Bacon.

Anderson, R. T. (2002). Onset clusters and the sonority sequencing principle in Spanish: A treatment efficacy study. In F. Windsor, L. M. Kelly, & N. Hewlett (Eds.), *Investigations in clinical phonetics and linguistics* (pp. 213–224). Mahwah, NJ: Lawrence Erlbaum.

Annoussamy, D. (2006). Psychological aspects of language acquisition. *Journal of the Indian Academy of Applied Psychology, 32,* 119–127.

Bacon, C. K., & Wilcox, M. J. (2006). Developmental language delay in infancy and early childhood. In N. B. Anderson & G. H. Shames (Eds.), *Human communication disorders: An introduction* (7th ed., pp. 325–351). Boston: Allyn and Bacon.

Bartens, A. (2000). *Ideophones and sound symbolism in Atlantic creoles.* Helsinki, Finland: Academia Scientiarum Fennica.

Basso, A. (2003). *Aphasia and its therapy.* New York: Oxford University Press.

Battle, D. E. (2002). Language and communication disorders in culturally and linguistically diverse children. In D. K. Bernstein & E. Tiegerman-Farber (Eds.), *Language and communication disorders in children* (5th ed., pp. 354–386). Boston: Allyn and Bacon.

Benninger, M. S. (2002). *Benign disorders of the voice.* Alexandria, VA: American Academy of Otolaryngology–Head & Neck Surgery Foundation.

Bernstein, D. K. (2002). The nature of language and its disorders. In D. K. Bernstein & E. Tiegerman-Farber (Eds.), *Language and communication disorders in children* (5th ed., pp. 2–26). Boston: Allyn and Bacon.

Bernstein, D. K., & Levey, S. (2002). Language development: A review. In D. K. Bernstein & E. Tiegerman-Farber (Eds.), *Language and communication disorders in children* (5th ed., pp. 27–94). Boston: Allyn and Bacon.

Beveridge, M. A., & Crerar, M. A. (2002). Remediation of asyntactic sentence comprehension using a multimedia microworld. *Brain and Language, 82,* 243–295.

Block, S., Onslow, M., Packman, A., & Dacakis, G. (2006). Connecting stuttering management and measurement: IV. Predictors of outcome for a behavioural treatment for stuttering. *International Journal of Language & Communication Disorders, 41,* 395–406.

Blomgren, M., Roy, N., Callister, T., & Merrill, R. M. (2005). Intensive stuttering modification therapy: A multidimensional assessment of treatment outcomes. *Journal of Speech, Language, and Hearing Research, 48,* 509–523.

Bloodstein, O. (2006). Some empirical observations about early stuttering: A possible link to language development. *Journal of Communication Disorders, 39,* 185–191.

Boone, D. R., McFarlane, S. C., & Von Berg, S. L. (2005). *The voice and voice therapy* (7th ed.). Boston: Allyn and Bacon.

Bowen, C. (2002). Speech and language development in infants and young children [Online]. www.members .tripod.com/Caroline_Bowen/devel1 .htm. Retrieved September 6, 2002.

Bressman, T., Klaiman, P., & Fischbach, S. (2006). Same noses, different nasalance scores: Data from normal subjects and cleft palate speakers for three systems for nasalance analysis. *Clinical Linguistics & Phonetics, 20,* 163–170.

Bromfield, J., & Dodd, J. (2004). Children with speech and language disability: Caseload characteristics. *International Journal of Language & Communication Disorders, 39,* 303–324.

Brown, S., Ingham, R. J., Ingham, J. C., Laird, A. R., & Fox, P. T. (2005). Stuttered and fluent speech production: An ALE meta-analysis of functional neuroimaging studies. *Human Brain Mapping, 25,* 105–117.

Burgess, S. R., Hecht, S. A., & Lonigan, C. J. (2002). Relations of the home literacy environment (HLE) to the development of reading-related abilities: A one-year longitudinal study. *Reading Research Quarterly, 37,* 408–426.

Case, J. L. (2002). *Clinical management of voice disorders* (4th ed.). Austin, TX: PRO-ED.

Cohen, N. J. (2002). Developmental language disorders. In P. Howlin and O. Udwin (Eds.), *Outcomes in neurodevelopmental and genetic disorders: Cambridge child and adolescent psychiatry* (pp. 26–55). New York: Cambridge University Press.

Costa, A., & Santesteban, M. (2006). The control of speech production by bilingual speakers: Introductory remarks. *Language and Cognition, 9,* 115–117.

Craig, A. R. (2002). Fluency outcomes following treatment for those who stutter. *Perceptual and Motor Skills, 94*(3, Pt. 1), 772–774.

Craig, A. R., & Tran, Y. (2005). The epidemiology of stuttering: The need for reliable estimates of prevalence and anxiety levels over the lifespan. *Advances in Speech Language Pathology, 7,* 41–46.

Culatta, B., & Wiig, E. H. (2006). Language disabilities in school-age children and youth. In N. B. Anderson & G. H. Shames (Eds.) *Human communication disorders: An introduction* (7th ed., pp. 352–385). Boston: Allyn and Bacon.

Davis, S., Howell, P., & Cooke, F. (2002). Sociodynamic relationships between children who stutter and their non-stuttering classmates. *Journal of Child Psychology and Psychiatry and Allied Disciplines, 43,* 939–947.

Dayalu, V. N., Kalinowski, J., & Saltuklaroglu, T. (2002). Active inhibition of stuttering results in pseudofluency: A reply to Craig. *Perceptual and Motor Skills, 94*(3, Pt. 1), 1050–1052.

Delgado, C. E. F., Mundy, P., Crowson, M., Markus, J., Yale, M., & Schwartz, H. (2002). Responding to joint attention and language development: A comparison of target locations. *Journal of Speech, Language, and Hearing Research, 45,* 715–719.

Doehring, D. G. (2002). *Research strategies in human communication disorders* (3rd ed.). Austin, TX: PRO-ED.

Drew, C. J., & Hardman, M. L. (2007). *Intellectual disabilities across the lifespan* (9th ed.). Columbus, OH: Merrill.

Ehrhardt, K., Hixon, M., & Poling, A. (2006). Craniofacial anomalies. In L. Phelps (Ed.), *Chronic health-related disorders in children: Collaborative medical and psychoeducational interventions* (pp. 57–66). Washington, DC: American Psychological Association.

Fager, S., Hux, K., Beukelman, D. R., & Karantounis, R. (2006). Augmentative and alternative communication use and acceptance by adults with traumatic brain injury. *AAC: Augmentative and Alternative Communication, 22,* 37–47.

Farmer, M., & Oliver, A. (2005). Assessment of pragmatic difficulties and socioemotional adjustment in practice. *International Journal of Language & Communication Disorders, 40,* 403–429.

Feldman, L. B., Barac-Cikoja, D., & Kostic, A. (2002). Semantic aspects of morphological processing: Transparency effects in Serbian. *Memory and Cognition, 30,* 629–636.

Ferrand, C. T. (2007). *Speech science: An integrated approach to theory and clinical practice* (2nd ed.). Boston: Allyn and Bacon.

Fink, R. B., Brecher, A., Sobel, P., & Schwartz, M. F. (2005). Computer-assisted treatment of word retrieval deficits in aphasia. *Aphasiology, 19,* 943–954.

Flipsen, P. Jr. (2006). Syllables per word in typical and delayed speech acquisition. *Clinical Linguistics & Phonetics, 20,* 293–301.

Flipsen, P., Jr., Hammer, J. B., & Yost, K. M. (2005). Measuring severity of involvement in speech delay: Segmental and whole-word measures. *American Journal of Speech-Language Pathology, 14,* 298–312.

Fridriksson, J., Nettles, C., Davis, M., Morrow, L., & Montgomery, A. (2006). Functional communication and executive function in aphasia. *Clinical Linguistics & Phonetics, 20,* 401–410.

Gabel, R. M., Colcord, R. D., & Petrosino, L. (2002). Self-reported anxiety of adults who do and do not stutter. *Perceptual and Motor Skills, 94*(3, Pt. 1), 775–784.

Gates, J. (2006). Working with children's voice disorders. *International Journal of Language & Communication Disorders, 41,* 112–113.

Gelfand, D. M., & Drew, C. J. (2003). *Understanding child behavior disorders* (4th ed.). Belmont, CA: Wadsworth.

Gibbon, F. E., & Wood, S. E. (2002). Articulatory drift in the speech of children with articulation and phonological disorders. *Perceptual and Motor Skills, 95,* 295–307.

Gleason, J. B. (2005). *The development of language* (6th ed.). Boston: Allyn and Bacon.

Gray, S. D., & Thibeault, S. L. (2002). Diversity in voice characteristics—Interaction between genes and environment, use of microarray analysis. *Journal of Communication Disorders, 35,* 347–354.

Gregory, H. H. (2003a). Implications of research for evaluation and treatment. In H. H. Gregory (Ed.), *Stuttering therapy: Rationale and procedures* (pp. 22–70). Boston: Allyn and Bacon.

Gregory, H. H. (2003b). Essential background information. In H. H. Gregory (Ed.), *Stuttering therapy: Rationale and procedures* (pp. 1–21). Boston: Allyn and Bacon.

Harris, V., Onslow, M., Packman, A., Harrison, E., & Menzies, R. (2002). An experimental investigation of the impact of the Lidcombe Program on early stuttering. *Journal of Fluency Disorders, 27*(3), 203–214.

Hickin, J., Best, W., Herbert, R., Howard, D., & Osborne, F. (2002). Phonological therapy for word-finding difficulties: A reevaluation. *Aphasiology, 16,* 981–999.

Holland, A. L. (2006). Aphasia and related acquired language disorders. In N. B. Anderson & G. H. Shames (Eds.), *Human communication disorders: An introduction* (7th ed., pp. 409–435). Boston: Allyn and Bacon.

Hopper, T., Holland, A., & Rewega, M. (2002). Conversational coaching: Treatment outcomes and future directions. *Aphasiology, 16,* 745–761.

Horiuchi, V. (1999, April 10). Assistive devices help to level playing field: Machines can be key to productive life and individual self-esteem. *Salt Lake Tribune,* D8.

Hulit, L. M. (2004). *Straight talk on stuttering: Information, encouragement, and counsel for stutterers, caregivers, and speech-language clinicians* (2nd ed.). Springfield, IL: Charles C. Thomas.

Hulit, L. M., & Howard, M. R. (2006). *Born to talk: An introduction to speech and language development* (4th ed.). Boston: Allyn and Bacon.

Jezer, M. (2006). Spit it out. *Journal of Fluency Disorders, 31,* 66–67.

Johnson, C. J., & Beitchman, J. H. (2006). Specific developmental disorders of speech and language. In C. Gillberg and R. Harrington (Eds.), *A clinician's handbook of child and adolescent psychiatry* (pp. 388–416). New York: Cambridge University Press.

Johnston, S. S., Reichle, J., & Evans, J. (2004). Supporting augmentative and alternative communication use by beginning communicators with severe disabilities. *American Journal of Speech-Language Pathology, 13,* 20–30.

Jones, M., Gebski, V., Onslow, M., & Packman, A. (2002). Statistical power in stuttering research: A tutorial. *Journal of Speech, Language, and Hearing Research, 45,* 243–255.

Jones, M., Onslow, M., Packman, A., Williams, S., Ormond, T., Schwarz, L., & Gebski, V. (2005). Randomised controlled trial of the Lidcombe programme of early stuttering intervention. *BMJ: British Medical Journal, 331,* 7518.

Karnell, M. P., Bailey, P., & Johnson, L. (2005). Facilitating communication among speech pathologists treating children with cleft palate. *Cleft Palate—Craniofacial Journal, 42,* 585–588.

Kennedy, C., Watkin, P., & Worsfold, S. (2006). Language ability after early detection of hearing impairment: Commentary reply. *New England Journal of Medicine, 355,* 734.

Kumin, L. (2002). Maximizing speech and language in children and adolescents with Down syndrome. In W. I. Cohen and L. Nadel (Eds.), *Down syndrome: Visions for the 21st century* (pp. 407–419). New York: Wiley-Liss.

Lattermann, C., Shenker, R. C., Thordardottir, E. (2005). Progression of language complexity during treatment with the Lidcombe program for early stuttering intervention. *American Journal of Speech-Language Pathology, 14,* 242–253.

Lederer, S. H. (2001). Efficacy of parent–child language group intervention for late-talking toddlers. *Infant Toddler Intervention, 11*(3–4), 223–235.

Lerner, J., & Kline, F. (2006). *Learning disabilities and related disorders* (10th ed.). Boston: Houghton Mifflin.

Locke, J. L. (2006). Parental selection of vocal behavior: Crying, cooking, babbling, and the evolution of language. *Human Nature, 17,* 155–168.

Long, S. H. (2005). Language and children with learning disabilities. In Reed, V. A. *An Introduction to Children with Language Disorders* (3rd ed.). Boston: Allyn and Bacon.

Lytton, H., & Gallagher, L. (2002). Parenting twins and the genetics of parenting. In M. H. Bornstein (Ed.), *Handbook of parenting: Vol. 1: Children and parenting* (2nd ed., pp. 227–253). Mahwah, NJ: Lawrence Erlbaum.

Markham, C., & Dean, T. (2006). Parents' and professionals' perceptions of quality of life in children with speech and language difficulty. *International Journal of Language & Communication Disorders, 41,* 189–212.

Marrinan, E., & Shprintzen, R. J. (2006). Cleft palate and craniofacial disorders. In N. B. Anderson &

G. H. Shames (Eds.) *Human communication disorders: An introduction* (7th ed., pp. 254–290). Boston: Allyn and Bacon.

Max, L., & Gracco, V. L. (2005). Coordination of oral and laryngeal movements in the perceptually fluent speech of adults who stutter. *Journal of Speech, Language, and Hearing Research, 48,* 524–542.

McAuliffe, M. J., Ward, E. C., & Murdoch, B. E. (2005). Articulatory function in hypokinetic dysarthria: An electropalatographic examination of two cases. *Journal of Medical Speech-Language Pathology, 13,* 149–168.

McCauley, R. J., & Fey, M. E. (2006). Introduction to treatment of language disorders in children. In R. J. McCauley & M. E. Fey (Eds.), *Treatment of language disorders in children* (pp. 1–17). Baltimore: Paul H. Brookes.

Mechling, L. C., & Cronin, B. (2006). Computer-based video instruction to teach the use of augmentative and alternative communication devices for ordering at fast-food restaurants. *Journal of Special Education, 39,* 234–245.

Melton, A. K., & Shadden, B. B. (2005). Linguistic accommodations to older adults in the community: The role of communication disorders and partner motivation. *Advances in Speech Language Pathology, 7,* 233–244.

Mildenberger, K., Noterdaeme, M., Sitter, S., & Amorosa, H. (2001). Behavioural problems in children with specific and pervasive developmental disorders, evaluated with the psychopathological documentation (AMDP). *Praxis der Kinderpsychologie und Kinderpsychiatrie, 50,* 649–663.

Molfese, V. J., & Molfese, D. L. (2002). Environmental and social influences on reading skills as indexed by brain and behavioral responses. *Annals of Dyslexia, 52,* 121–137.

Moore-Brown, B. J., & Montgomery, J. K. (2001). *Making a difference for America's children: Speech-language pathologists in public schools.* Eau Claire, WI: Thinking Publications.

Nelson, N. W. (2002). Language intervention in school settings. In D. K. Bernstein and E. Tiegerman-Farber (Eds.), *Language and communication disorders in children* (5th ed., pp. 315–353). Boston: Allyn and Bacon.

Neumann, K., Preibisch, C., Euler, H. A., Lanfermann, H., Gall, V., & Giraud, A. L. (2005). Cortical plasticity associated with stuttering therapy. *Journal of Fluency Disorders, 30,* 23–39.

Nicolosi, L., Harryman, E., & Kresheck, J. (2003). *Terminology of communication disorders, speech, language and hearing* (5th ed.). Philadelphia: Lippincott Williams & Wilkins.

Noens, I., van Berckelaer-Onnes, I., Verpoorten, R., & van Duijn, G., (2006). The ComFor: An instrument for the indication of augmentative communication in people with autism and intellectual disability. *Journal of Intellectual Disability Research, 50,* 621–632.

Ogar, J., Willock, S., Baldo, J., Wilkins, D., Ludy, C., & Dronkers, N. (2006). Clinical and anatomical correlates of apraxia of speech. *Brain and Language, 97,* 343–350.

Onslow, M. (2006). Connecting stuttering management and measurement: V. Deduction and induction in the development of stuttering treatment outcome measures and stuttering treatments. *International Journal of Language & Communication Disorders, 41,* 407–421.

Ooki, S. (2005). Genetic and environmental influences on stuttering and tics in Japanese twin children. *Twin Research, 8,* 69–75.

Ogar, J., Willock, S., Baldo, J., Wilkins, D., Ludy, C., & Dronkers, N. (2006). Clinical and anatomical correlates of apraxia of speech. *Brain and Language, 97,* 343–350.

Owens, R. E., Jr. (2004). *Language disorders: A functional approach to assessment and intervention* (4th ed.). Needham Heights, MA: Allyn and Bacon.

Owens, R. E., Jr. (2005). *Language development: An introduction* (6th ed.). Boston: Allyn and Bacon.

Owens, R. E., Jr. (2006). Development of communication, language, and speech. In N. B. Anderson & G. H. Shames (Eds.), *Human communication disorders: An introduction* (7th ed., pp. 22–58). Boston: Allyn and Bacon.

Owens, R. E., Metz, D. E., & Haas, A. (2007). *Introduction to communication disorders: A lifespan approach* (3rd ed.). Boston: Allyn and Bacon.

Paatsch, L. E., Blamey, P. J., & Sarant, J. Z. (2006). The effects of speech production and vocabulary training on different components of spoken language performance. *Journal of Deaf Studies and Deaf Education, 11,* 39–55.

Payne, K. T., & Taylor, O. L. (2006). Multicultural differences in human communication and disorders. In N. B. Anderson & G. H. Shames (Eds.), *Human communication disorders: An introduction* (7th ed., pp. 93–125). Boston: Allyn and Bacon.

Petrill, S. A., Deater-Deckard, K., & Thompson, L. A. (2006). Genetic and environmental effects of serial naming and phonological awareness on early reading outcomes. *Journal of Educational Psychology, 98,* 112–121.

Pring, T. (2004). *Research methods in communication disorders.* London: Whurr.

Radziewicz, C., & Antonellis, S. (2002). Considerations and implications for habilitation of hearing impaired

children. In D. K. Bernstein & E. Tiegerman-Farber (Eds.), *Language and communication disorders in children* (5th ed., pp. 565–598). Boston: Allyn and Bacon.

Ramig, P. R., & Dodge, D. (2005). *The child and adolescent stuttering treatment and activity resource guide.* Clifton Park, NY: Thomson-Delmar Learning.

Ramig, P. R., & Shames, G. H. (2006). Stuttering and other disorders of fluency. In N. B. Anderson & G. H. Shames (Eds.) *Human communication disorders: An introduction* (7th ed., pp. 183–221). Boston: Allyn and Bacon.

Reed, V. A. (2005). *An introduction to children with language disorders* (3rd ed.). Boston: Allyn and Bacon.

Reilly, S., Douglas, J., & Oates, J. (2003). *Evidence based practice in speech pathology.* London: Whurr.

Robinson, N. B., & Robb, M. P. (2002). Early communication assessment and intervention: A dynamic process. In D. K. Bernstein and E. Tiegerman-Farber (Eds.), *Language and communication disorders in children* (5th ed., pp. 155–196). Needham Heights, MA: Allyn and Bacon.

Rubin, J. S., Sataloff, R. T., & Korovin, G. S. (2002). *Diagnosis and treatment of voice disorders* (2nd ed.). San Diego, CA: Singular Publishing Group.

Sahin, H. A., Krespi, Y., Yilmaz, A., & Coban, O. (2005). Stuttering due to ischemic stroke. *Behavioural Neurology, 16,* 37–39.

Sapienza, C., & Hicks, D. M. (2006). Voice Disorders. In N. B. Anderson and G. H. Shames (Eds.) *Human communication disorders: An introduction* (7th ed., pp. 222–253). Boston: Allyn and Bacon.

Schauer, G. A. (2006). Pragmatic awareness in ESL and EFL contexts: Contrast and development. *Language Learning, 56,* 269–318.

Schlosser, R. W. (2005). Meta-analysis of single-subject research: How should it be done? *International Journal of Language & Communication Disorders, 40,* 375–377.

Schwartz, R. G. (2006). Articulatory and phonological disorders. In N. B. Anderson & G. H. Shames (Eds.), *Human communication disorders: An introduction* (7th ed., pp. 149–182). Boston: Allyn and Bacon.

Sell, D. (2005). Issues in perceptual speech analysis in cleft palate and related disorders: A review. *International Journal of Language & Communication Disorders, 40,* 103–121.

Silliman, E. R., & Diehl, S. F. (2002). Assessing children with language disorders. In D. K. Bernstein & E. Tiegerman-Farber (Eds.), *Language and communication disorders in children* (5th ed., pp. 181–255). Boston: Allyn and Bacon.

Sims, C. P. (2005). Tribal languages and the challenges of revitalization.

Anthropology & Education Quarterly, 36, 104–105.

Sommer, M., Koch, M. A., Paulus, W., Weiller, C., & Buechel, C. (2002). Disconnection of speech-relevant brain areas in persistent developmental stuttering. *Lancet, 360,* 380–383.

Spreen, O. (2002). *Assessment of aphasia.* New York: Oxford University Press.

Stager, S. V., Calis, K., Grothe, D., Block, M., Berensen, N. M., Smith, P. J., & Braun, A. (2005). Treatment with medications affecting dopaminergic and serotonergic mechanisms: Effects on fluency and anxiety in persons who stutter. *Journal of Fluency Disorders, 30,* 319–335.

Stark, J., Martin, N., & Fink, R. B. (2005). Current approaches to aphasia therapy: Principles and applications. *Aphasiology, 19,* 903–905.

Stromswold, K. (2006). Why aren't identical twins linguistically identical? Genetic, prenatal and postnatal factors. *Cognition, 101,* 333–384.

Subramanian, A., & Yairi, E. (2006). Identification of traits associated with stuttering. *Journal of Communication Disorders, 39,* 200–216.

Szagun, G. (2002). Learning the h(e)ard way: The acquisition of grammar in young German-speaking children with cochlear implants and with normal hearing. In F. Windsor, L. M. Kelly, & N. Hewlett (Eds.), *Investigations in clinical phonetics and linguistics* (pp. 131–144). Mahwah, NJ: Lawrence Erlbaum.

Taatgen, N. A., & Anderson, J. R. (2002). Why do children learn to say "broke"? A model of learning the past without feedback. *Cognition, 86,* 123–155.

Theodore, L. A., Bray, M. A., Kehle, T. J., & DioGuardi, R. J. (2006). Language-related disorders in childhood. In L. Phelps (Ed.), *Chronic health-related disorders in children: Collaborative medical and psychoeducational interventions* (pp. 139–155). Washington, DC: American Psychological Association.

Tiegerman-Farber, E. (2002). Interactive teaming: The changing role of the speech-language pathologist. In D. K. Bernstein & E. Tiegerman-Farber (Eds.), *Language and communication disorders in children* (5th ed., pp. 96–125). Boston: Allyn and Bacon.

Tomasello, M. (2003). *Constructing a language: A usage-based theory of language acquisition.* Cambridge, MA: Harvard University Press.

Turner, S., & Whitworth, A., (2006). Clinicians' perceptions of candidacy for conversation partner training in aphasia: How do we select candidates for therapy and do we get it right? *Aphasiology, 20,* 616–643.

Uchikoshi, Y. (2006). English vocabulary development in bilingual kindergartners: What are the best predictors? *Bilingualism: Language and Cognition, 9,* 33–49.

U.S. Department of Education. (2006). *Twenty-sixth annual report to Congress on the implementation of the Individuals with Disabilities Education Act.* Washington, DC: Author.

Van-Slyke, P. A. (2002). Classroom instruction for children with Landau-Kleffner syndrome. *Child Language Teaching and Therapy, 18,* 23–42.

Van Wattum, P. J. (2006). Stuttering improved with risperidone. *Journal of the American Academy of Child & Adolescent Psychiatry, 45,* 133.

Vartanov, A. V., Glozman, Z. M., Kiselnikov, A. A., & Karpova, N. L. (2005). Cerebral organization of verbal action in stutterers. *Human Physiology, 31,* 132–136.

Venkatagiri, H. S. (2005). Recent advances in the treatment of stuttering: A theoretical perspective. *Journal of Communication Disorders, 38,* 375–393.

Verdolini, K., Rosen, C. A., & Branski, R. C. (2006). *Classification manual for voice disorders-I.* American Speech-Language-Hearing Association. Mahwah, NJ: Lawrence Erlbaum Associates.

Verhoeven, L., & Vermeer, A. (2002). Communicative competence and personality dimensions in first and second language learners. *Applied Psycholinguistics, 23,* 361–374.

Vilkman, E. (2000). Voice problems at work: A challenge for occupational safety and health arrangement. *Folia Phoniatrica et Logopaedica, 52,* 120–125.

Waller, A. (2006). Communication access to conversational narrative. *Topics in Language Disorders, 26,* 221–239.

Weigel, D. J., Martin, S. S., Bennett, K. K. (2006). Contributions of the home literacy environment to preschool-aged children's emerging literacy and language skills. *Early Child Development and Care, 176,* 357–378.

Weiss, A. L. (2002). Planning language intervention for young children. In D. K. Bernstein & E. Tiegerman-Farber (Eds.), *Language and communication disorders in children* (5th ed., pp. 256–314). Boston: Allyn and Bacon.

Wermke, K., Hauser, C., Komposch, G., & Stellzig, A. (2002). Spectral analysis of prespeech sounds (spontaneous cries) in infants with unilateral cleft lip and palate (UCLP): A pilot study. *Cleft Palate Craniofacial Journal, 39,* 285–294.

Wilkins, M., & Ertmer, D. J. (2002). Introducing young children who are deaf or hard of hearing to spoken language: Child's voice, an oral school. *Language, Speech, and Hearing Services in Schools, 33*(3), 196–204.

Wolpaw, J. R., Birbaumer, N., McFarland, D. J., Pfurtscheller, G., & Vaughan, T. M. (2002). Brain-computer interfaces for communication and control. *Clinical Neurophysiology, 113,* 767–791.

Worrall, L., McCooey, R., Davidson, B., Larkins, B., & Hickson, L. (2002). The validity of functional assessments of communication and the Activity/Participation components of the ICIDH-2: Do they reflect what really happens in real-life? *Journal of Communication Disorders, 35*(2), 107–137.

Wright, A. N. (2006). The role of modeling and automatic reinforcement in the construction of the passive voice. *Analysis of Verbal Behavior, 22,* 153–169.

Yairi, E. (2004). *Early childhood stuttering.* Austin, TX: Pro-Ed.

Yavas, M. (2002). Voice onset time patterns in bilingual phonological development. In F. Windsor, L. M. Kelly, and N. Hewlett (Eds.), *Investigations in clinical phonetics and linguistics* (pp. 341–349). Mahwah, NJ: Lawrence Erlbaum.

CHAPTER 12

Abt Associates. (1974). *Assessments of selected resources for severely handicapped children and youth. Vol I: A state-of-the-art paper.* Cambridge, MA: Author (ERIC Document Reproduction Service No. ED 134 614).

Batshaw, M. (2003). *Children with disabilities* (4th ed.). Baltimore: Paul H. Brookes.

Berk, L. E. (2005). *Development through the lifespan.* Boston: Allyn and Bacon.

Beirne-Smith, M., Patton, J. R., & Kim, S. H (2006). *Intellectual disabilities: An introduction to intellectual disability* (7th ed.). Upper Saddle River, NJ: Merrill.

Bishop, V. (2004). *Teaching visually impaired children.* Springfield, IL: Charles C. Thomas.

Bremer, C. D., Kachgal, M., & Schoeller, K. (2003, April). Self-determination: Supporting successful transition. *Research to Practice Brief of the National Center on Secondary Education and Transition, 2*(1), 1–5.

Brown, F., & Snell, M. (2006). Measurement, analysis, and evaluation. In M. E. Snell & F. Brown (Eds.), *Introduction to students with severe disabilities* (6th ed., pp. 170–205). Upper Saddle River, NJ: Merrill.

Deafblind International. (2006). *What is deafblindness?* Retrieved September 23, 2006, from http://www .deafblindinternational.org/ standard/about.html

Drew, C. J., & Hardman, M. L. (2007). *Intellectual disabilities across the lifespan* (9th ed.). Columbus: OH: Merrill.

Ford, A., Davern, L., & Schnorr, R. (2001, July/August). Learners with significant disabilities: Curricular relevance in an era of standards-based reform. *Remedial and Special Education, 22*(4), 214–222.

Giangreco, M. F., & Doyle, M. B. (2000). Curricular and instructional considerations for teaching students with disabilities in general education classrooms. In S. E. Wade (Ed.), *Inclusive education: A casebook and readings for prospective and practicing teachers* (pp. 51–70). Mahwah, NJ: Lawrence Erlbaum Associates.

Giangreco, M. (2006). Foundational concepts and practices for educating students with severe disabilities. In M. E. Snell & F. Brown (Eds.), *Introduction to students with severe disabilities* (6th ed., pp. 1–27). Upper Saddle River, NJ: Merrill.

Gollnick, D., & Chinn, P. C. (2006). *Multicultural education in a diverse society* (7th ed.). Upper Saddle River, NJ: Prentice-Hall.

Guralnick, M. J. (2001). A framework for change in early childhood inclusion. In M. J. Guralnick (Ed.), *Early childhood inclusion: Focus on change* (pp. 3–35). Baltimore: Paul H. Brookes.

Hewitt, A., & O'Nell, S. (2006). *A little help from my friends.* Washington, DC: President's Committee on Intellectual Disabilities. Retrieved October 10, 2006, from http:// www.acf.hhs.gov/programs/pcpid/ docs/help4.doc

Horner, R. H., Albin, R. W., Todd, A. W., & Sprague, J. (2006). Positive behavior support for individuals with severe disabilities. In M. E. Snell & F. Brown (Eds.), *Introduction to students with severe disabilities* (6th ed., pp. 206–250). Upper Saddle River, NJ: Merrill.

Johnston, S. (2003). Assistive technology. In J. McDonnell, M. Hardman, & A. McDonnell, *Introduction to persons with severe disabilities* (pp. 138–159). Boston: Allyn and Bacon.

Justen, J. (1976). Who are the severely handicapped? A problem in definition. *AAESPH Review, 1*(5), 1–11.

King, W. (2000, May 2). Disabilities may keep man from transplant. *Salt Lake Tribune,* A1, A7.

Massanari, C. (2006). Alternate assessment: Questions and answers. IDEA practices. Retrieved October 12, 2006, from http://www1.usu.edu/ mprrc/infoserv/pubs/q&aaa.pdf

McDonnell, J., Hardman, M., & McDonnell, A. P. (2003). *Introduction to persons with moderate and severe disabilities* (2nd ed.). Boston: Allyn and Bacon.

Meyer, L. H., Peck, C. A., & Brown, L. (1991). Definitions and diagnosis. In L. H. Meyer, C. A. Peck, & L. Brown (Eds.), *Critical issues in the lives of people with disabilities* (p. 17). Baltimore: Paul H. Brookes.

Moore-Brown, B. J., & Montgomery, J. K. (2006). *Making a difference for America's children: Speech–language pathologists in public schools.* Eau Claire, WI: Thinking Publications.

Morgan, R. L., Ellerd, D. A., Gerity, B. P., & Blair, R. J. (2000). That's the job I want: How technology helps young people in transition. *Teaching Exceptional Children, 32*(4), 44–49.

Oelwein, P. (1995) *Teaching reading to children with Down syndrome.* Bethesda, MD: Woodbine House.

Penner, I. (2006). *The right to belong: The story of Yvonne.* Retrieved September 17, 2006, from http://www3.nb.sympatico.ca/ipenner/

Quenemoen, R., & Thurlow, M. (2006). *NCEO policy directions: Including alternate assessment results in accountability decisions.* Retrieved June 10, 2006, from http://education.umn.edu/nceo/OnlinePubs/Policy13.htm

Rues, J. P., Graff, J. C., Ault, M. M., & Holvoet, J. F. (2006). Special health care procedures. In M. E. Snell & F. Brown (Eds.), *Introduction to students with severe disabilities* (6th ed.) (pp. 251–290). Upper Saddle River, NJ: Merrill.

Sailor, W., & Haring, N. (1977). Some current directions in the education of the severely/multiply handicapped. *AAESPH Review, 2,* 67–86.

Snell, M. E. (1991). Schools are for all kids: The importance of integration for students with severe disabilities and their peers. In J. Lloyd, N. N. Singh, & A. C. Repp (Eds.), *The regular education initiative: Alternative perspectives on concepts, issues, and models* (pp. 133–148). Sycamore, IL: Sycamore.

Snell, M. E., & Brown, F. (2006) Designing and implementing instructional programs. In M. E. Snell & F. Brown (Eds.), *Introduction to students with severe disabilities* (6th ed., pp. 111–169). Upper Saddle River, NJ: Merrill.

TASH. (2006a). *TASH resolution on life in the community.* Retrieved October 2, 2006, from http://www .tash.org/IRR/resolutions/res02community.htm

TASH. (2006b). *Who we are.* Retrieved September 29, 2006, from http://www.tash.org/who_we_are.html

TASH. (2006c). *TASH resolution on the people for whom TASH advocates.* Retrieved October 8, 2006, from http://www.tash.org/IRR/resolutions/res02advocate.htm

The ARC. (2006a). *Causes and prevention of mental retardation.* Retrieved September 14, 2006, from http://www.thearc.org/faqs/causesandprev.pdf

The ARC. (2006b). *Genetic issues in mental retardation.* Retrieved October 14, 2006, from http://www.thearc.org/depts/gbr01.html

The ARC. (2006c). *Position statement on education.* Retrieved October 10, 2006, from http://www.thearc.org/posits/educationpos.doc

U.S. Department of Education. (2006). *To assure the free appropriate public education of all children with disabilities. Twenty-sixth annual report to Congress on the implementation of the Individuals with Disabilities Education Act.* Washington, DC: U.S. Government Printing Office.

U.S. Department of Energy. (2003). *Human Genome Project information.* Retrieved June 12, 2003, http://www.ornl.gov/hgmis/

Voss, K. S. (2005). *Teaching by design.* Bethesda, MD: Woodbine House.

Wehmeyer, M. L., Gragoudas, S., & Shogren, K. A. (2006). Self-determination, student involvement, and leadership development. In P. Wehman (Ed.), *Life beyond the classroom: Transition strategies for young people with disabilities* (4th ed., pp. 41–69). Baltimore: Paul H. Brookes.

Westling, D., & Fox, L. (2004). *Teaching students with severe disabilities* (3rd ed.). Upper Saddle River, NJ: Merrill/Prentice Hall.

Ysseldyke, J. E., & Olsen, K. (2006). *Putting alternate assessments into practice: What to measure and possible sources of data. NCEO Synthesis Report 28.* Minneapolis: The National Center on Educational Outcomes, University of Minnesota. Retrieved August 18, 2006, from http://education.umn.edu/NCEO/OnlinePubs/Synthesis28.htm

Ysseldyke, J. E., Olsen, K., & Thurlow, M. (2003). *Issues and considerations in alternate assessments. NCEO Synthesis Report 27.* Minneapolis: The National Center on Educational Outcomes, University of Minnesota. Retrieved June 3, 2006, from http://education.umn.edu/NCEO/OnlinePubs/Synthesis27.htm

CHAPTER 13

ABCNEWS.com. (2006). *Search for camps and special needs.* Retrieved http://infospace.abcnews.com

Akshoomoff, N., Pierce, K., & Courchesne, E. (2002). The neurobiological basis of autism from a developmental perspective. *Development and Psychopathology, 14,* 613–634.

American Psychiatric Association (APA). (2000). Diagnostic and statistical manual of mental disorders (DSM-IV-TR) (4th ed.—text rev.). Washington, DC: Author.

Anckarsater, H. (2006). Central nervous changes in social dysfunction: Autism, aggression, and psychopathology. *Brain Research Bulletin, 69,* 259–265.

Andres, C. (2002). Molecular genetics and animal models in autistic disorder. *Brain Research Bulletin, 57,* 109–119.

Arick, J. R., Krug, D. A., Fullerton, A., Loos, L., & Falco, R. (2005). School-based programs. In F. R. Volkmar, P. Rhea, A. Klin, & D. Cohen, (Eds.), *Handbook of autism*

and pervasive developmental disorders, Vol. 2: Assessment, interventions and policy (3rd ed., pp. 1003–1028). Hoboken, NJ: John Wiley & Sons.

Baird, G., Simonoff, E., Pickles, A., Chandler, S., Loucas, T., Meldrum, D., & Charman, T. (2006). Prevalence of disorders of the autism spectrum in a population cohort of children in South Thames: The special needs and autism project (SNAP). *Lancet, 368,* 210–215.

Baker, H. C. (2002). A comparison study of autism spectrum disorder referrals, 1997 and 1989. *Journal of Autism and Developmental Disorders, 32*(2), 121–125.

Baptista, P. M., Mercandante, M. T., Macedo, E. C., & Schwartzman, J. S. (2006). Cognitive performance in Rett syndrome girls: A pilot study using eyetracking technology. *Journal of Intellectual Disability Research, 50,* 662–666.

Baron-Cohen, S., & Klin, A. (2006). What's so special about asperger syndrome? *Brain and Cognition, 61,* 1–4.

Barrett, M. (2006). 'Like dynamite going off in my ears': Using autobiographical accounts of autism with teaching professionals. *Educational Psychology in Practice, 22,* 95–110.

Bauminger, N. (2002). The facilitation of social-emotional understanding and social interaction in high-functioning children with autism: Intervention outcomes. *Journal of Autism and Developmental Disorders, 32,* 283–298.

Beaumont, R., & Newcombe, P. (2006). Theory of mind and central coherence in adults with high-functioning autism or asperger syndrome. *Autism, 10,* 365–382.

Beeghly, M. (2006). Translational research on early language development: Current challenges and future directions. *Development and Psychopathology, 18,* 737–757.

Begeer, S., Rieffe, C., Terwogt, M. M., & Stockmann, L. (2006). Attention to facial emotion expressions in children with autism. *Autism, 10,* 37–51.

Berk, L. E. (2005). *Infants and children: Prenatal through middle childhood* (5th ed.). Boston: Allyn & Bacon.

Bishop, D. V. M., & Norbury, C. F. (2002). Exploring the borderlands of autistic disorder and specific language impairment: A study using standardised diagnostic instruments. *Journal of Child Psychology and Psychiatry and Allied Disciplines, 43,* 917–929.

Bishop, S. L., Richler, J., & Lord, C. (2006). Association between restricted and repetitive behaviors and nonverbal IQ in children with autism spectrum disorders. *Child Neuropsychology, 12,* 247–267.

Blacher, J., & McIntyre, L. L. (2006). Syndrome specificity and behavioural disorders in young adults with intellectual disability: Cultural

differences in family impact. *Journal of Intellectual Disability Research, 50,* 184–198.

Blair, R. J. R., Frith, U., Smith, N., Abell, F., & Cipolotti, L. (2002). Fractionation of visual memory: Agency detection and its impairment in autism. *Neuropsychologia, 40,* 108–118.

Blakemore S. J., Tavossoli, T., Calo, S., Thomas, R. M., Catmur, C., Frith, U., & Haggard, P. (2006). Tactile sensitivity in asperger syndrome. *Brain and Cognition, 61,* 5–13.

Bondy, A., & Frost, L. (2002). *A picture's worth: PECS and other visual communication strategies in autism.* Bethesda, MD: Woodbine House.

Bowler, D. (2006). *Autism spectrum disorders: Psychological theory and research.* New York: John Wiley & Sons.

Bowers, L. (2002). An audit of referrals of children with autistic spectrum disorder to the dietetic service. *Journal of Human Nutrition and Dietetics, 15,* 141–144.

Boyd, B. A. (2002). Examining the relationship between stress and lack of social support in mothers of children with autism. *Focus on Autism and Other Developmental Disabilities, 17,* 208–215.

Bregman, J. D. (2005). Definitions and characteristics of the spectrum. In D. Zager (Ed.), *Autism spectrum disorders: Identification, education, and treatment* (3rd ed.). Mahwah, NJ: Lawrence Erlbaum Associates.

Britton, L. N., Carr, J. E., Landaburu, H. J., & Romick, K. S. (2002). The efficacy of non-contingent reinforcement as treatment for automatically reinforced stereotypy. *Behavioral Interventions, 17*(2), 93–103.

Brownlow, C., & O'Dell, L. (2006). Constructing an autistic identity: AS voices online. *Mental Retardation, 44,* 315–321.

Butler, M., & Meaney, F. J. (2005). *Genetics of developmental disabilities.* Boca Raton, FL: Taylor and Francis.

Case, C. (2005). *Imagining animals: Art, psychotherapy and primitive states of mind.* New York: Routledge.

CBSNEWS.com. (2003a). *Scrapping late favors in homeland law.* Retrieved January 11, 2006, from www.cbsnews.com

CBSNEWS.com. (2003b). *Using horses for "small wonders."* Retrieved February 19, 2006, from www .cbsnews .com

Chan, S., Fung, M. Y., Tong, C. W., & Thompson, D. (2005). The clinical effectiveness of a multisensory therapy on clients with developmental disability. *Research in Developmental Disabilities, 26,* 131–142.

Chakrabarti, S., & Fombonne, E. (2005). Pervasive developmental disorders in preschool children: Confirmation of high prevalence. *American Journal of Psychiatry, 162,* 1133–1141.

Chakrabarti, S., Haubus, C., Dugmore, S., Orgill, G., & Devine, F. (2005). A model of early detection and diagnosis of autism spectrum disorder in young children. *Infants & Young Children, 18,* 200–211.

Child, D. (2004). *Psychology and the teacher.* London: Continuum.

Cohen, B. I. (2006). Ammonia (NH3), nitric oxide (NO) and nitrous oxide (N2O)—The connection with infantile autism. *Autism, 10,* 221–223.

Cohen, H., Amerine-Dickens, M., & Smith, T. (2006). Early intensive behavioral treatment: Replicaton of the UCLA model in a community setting. *Journal of Developmental & Behavioral Pediatrics, 27*(Suppl. 2), S145–155.

Conti-Ramsden, G., Simkin, Z., & Botting, N. (2006). The prevalence of autistic spectrum disorders in adolescents with a history of specific language impairment. *Journal of Child Psychology and Psychiatry, 47,* 621–628.

Cook, J. L., & Cook, G. (2007). *The world of children.* Boston: Allyn and Bacon.

Cuccaro, M. L., Shao, Y., Bass, M. P., Abramson, R. K., Ravan, S. A., Wright, H. H., Wolpert, C. M., Donnelly, S. L., & Pericak-Vance, M. A. (2003). Behavioral comparisons in autistic individuals from multiplex and singleton families. *Journal of Autism and Developmental Disorders, 33,* 87–91.

Cummings, A. R., & Carr, J. E. (2005). Functional analysis and treatment of joint dislocation associated with hypermobility syndrome: A single-case analysis. *Journal of Developmental and Physical Disabilities, 17,* 225–236.

Dale, E., Jahoda, A., & Knott, F. (2006). Mothers' attributions following their child's diagnosis of autistic spectrum disorder: Exploring links with maternal levels of stress, depression and expectations about their child's future. *Autism, 10,* 463–479.

Davis, R. A. O., Bockbrader, M. A., Murphy, R. R., Hetrick, W. P., & O'Donnell, B. F. (2006). Subjective perceptual distortions and visual dysfunction in children with autism. *Journal of Autism and Developmental Disorders, 36,* 199–210.

Delano, M., & Snell, M. E. (2006). The effects of social stories on the social engagement of children with autism. *Journal of Positive Behavior Interventions, 8,* 29–42.

Deruelle, C., Rondan, C., Gepner, B., & Fagot, J. (2006). Processing of compound visual stimuli by children with autism and asperger syndrome. *International Journal of Psychology, 41,* 97–106.

Dietz, C., Swinkels, S., van Daalen, E., van Engeland, H., & Buitelaar, J. K. (2006). Screening for autistic spectrum disorder in children aged 14–15 Months. II: Population screening with the early screening of autistic traits questionnaire (ESAT). Design and general findings. *Journal of Autism and Developmental Disorders, 36,* 713–722.

Dowson, J. H. (2006). Pharmacological treatments for attention-deficit/hyperactivity disorder (ADHD) in adults. *Current Psychiatry Reviews, 2,* 317–331.

Drew, C. J., & Hardman, M. L. (2007). *Intellectual disabilities across the lifespan* (9th ed.). Columbus, OH: Merrill.

Dziobek, I., Fleck, S., & Rogers, K. (2006). The "amygdala theory of autism" revisited: Linking structure to behavior. *Neuropsychologia, 44,* 1891–1899.

Edelson, M. G. (2006). Are the majority of children with autism mentally retarded? A systematic evaluation of the data. *Focus on Autism and Other Developmental Disabilities, 21,* 66–83.

Ellis, E. M., Ala'i-Rosales, S. S., Glenn, S. S., Rosales-Ruiz, J., & Greenspoon, J. (2006). The effects of graduated exposure, modeling, and contingent social attention on tolerance to skin care products with two children with autism. *Research on Developmental Disabilities, 27,* 585–598.

Emerson, A., Grayson, A., & Griffiths, A. (2001). Can't or won't? Evidence relating to authorship in facilitated communication. *International Journal of Language and Communication Disorders, 36*(Suppl.), 98–103.

Farmer, J. E., Donders, J., & Warschausky, S. (2006). *Treating neurodevelopmental disabilities: Clinical research and practice.* New York: Guilford.

Fonseca, V. R., & Bussab, V. S. R. (2006). Self, other and dialogical space in autistic disorders. *International Journal of Psychoanalysis, 87,* 439–455.

Freitag, C. M., Kleser, C., & von Gontard, A. (2006). Imitation and language abilities in adolescents with autism spectrum disorder without language delay. *European Child & Adolescent Psychiatry, 15,* 282–291.

Galinat, K., Barcalow, K., & Krivda, B. (2005). Caring for children with autism in the school setting. *Journal of School Nursing, 21,* 208–217.

Gelfand, D. M., & Drew, C. J. (2003). *Understanding child behavior disorders* (4th ed.). Belmont, CA: Wadsworth.

Gillberg, C. (2006). Autism spectrum disorders. In C. Gillberg, R. Harrington, & H. C. Steinhausen (Eds.). *A clinician's handbook of child and adolescent psychiatry* (pp. 447–488). New York: Cambridge University Press.

Gillberg, C., & Cederlund, M. (2005). Asperger syndrome: Familial and pre- and perinatal factors. *Journal of Autism and Developmental Disorders, 35,* 159–166.

Gleason, J. B. (2005). *The development of language* (6th ed.). Boston: Allyn and Bacon.

Goin-Kochel, R. P., Mackintosh, V. H., & Myers, B. J. (2006). How many doctors does it take to make an autism spectrum diagnosis? *Autism, 10,* 439–451.

Goldstein, H. (2002). Communication intervention for children with autism: A review of treatment efficacy. *Journal of Autism and Developmental Disorders, 32,* 373–396.

Grandin, T. (2005). A personal perspective of autism. In F. R. Volkmar, P. Rhea, A. Klin, & D. Cohen, (Eds.), *Handbook of autism and pervasive developmental disorders, Vol. 2: Assessment, interventions and policy* (3rd ed., pp. 1276–1286). Hoboken, NJ: John Wiley & Sons.

Gray, D. E. (2002). Ten years on: A longitudinal study of families of children with autism. *Journal of Intellectual and Developmental Disability, 27,* 215–222.

Greaves, N., Prince, E., & Evans, D. W. (2006). Repetitive and ritualistic behaviour in children with Prader Willi syndrome and children with autism. *Journal of Intellectual Disability Research, 50,* 92–100.

Green, G., Brennan, L. C., & Fein, D. (2002). Intensive behavioral treatment for a toddler at high risk for autism. *Behavior Modification, 26,* 69–102.

Grey, I. M., Honan, R., McClean, B., & Daly, M. (2005). Evaluating the effectiveness of teacher training in applied behaviour analysis. *Journal of Intellectual Disabilities, 9,* 209–227.

Gringras, P., Santosh, P., & Baird, G. (2006). Development of an internet-based real-time system for monitoring pharmacological interventions in children with neurodevelopmental and neuropsychiatric disorders. *Child: Care, Health and Development, 32,* 591–600.

Haist, F., Adamo, M., Westerfield, M., Courchesne, E., & Townsend, J. (2005). The functional neuroanatomy of spatial attention in autism spectrum disorder. *Developmental Neuropsychology, 27,* 425–458.

Handen, B. L., & Hofkosh, D. (2005). Secretin in children with autistic disorder: A double-blind, placebo-controlled trial. *Journal of Developmental and Physical Disabilities, 17,* 95–106.

Harrington, J. W., Patrick, P. A., & Edwards, K. S. (2006). Parental beliefs about autism: Implications for the treating physician. *Autism, 10,* 452–462.

Harris, G. J., Chabris, C. F., & Clark, J. (2006). Brain activation during semantic processing in autism spectrum disorders via functional magnetic resonance imaging. *Brain and Cognition, 61,* 54–68.

Henault, I. (2006). *Asperger's syndrome and sexuality: From adolescence through adulthood.* London: Jessica Kingsley.

Hess, L. (2006). I would like to play but I don't know how: A case study of pretend play in autism. *Child Language Teaching & Therapy, 22,* 97–116.

Hetzroni, O. E., & Rubin, C. (2006). Identifying patterns of communicative behaviors in girls with rett syndrome. *AAC: Augmentative and Alternative Communication, 22,* 48–61.

Hobson, P. (2005). Autism and emotion. In F. R. Volkmar, P. Rhea, A. Klin, & D. Cohen, (Eds.), *Handbook of autism and pervasive developmental disorders, Vol. 2: Assessment, interventions and policy* (3rd ed., pp. 406–422). Hoboken, NJ: John Wiley & Sons.

Holmes, J. (2005). Notes on mentalizing—old hat, or new wine? *British Journal of Psychotherapy, 22,* 179–197.

Howlin, P. (2002). Autistic disorders. In P. Howlin and O. Udwin (Eds.), *Outcomes in neurodevelopmental and genetic disorders: Cambridge child and adolescent psychiatry* (pp. 136–168). New York: Cambridge University Press.

Howlin, P. (2004). *Autism and asperger syndrome: Preparing for adulthood* (2nd ed.). London: Routledge.

Jayachandra, S. (2005). Need for internet based scoring system for autism treatment evaluation. *Journal of Autism and Developmental Disorders, 35,* 684.

Johnson, C. R. (2002). Mental retardation. In M. Hersen (Ed.), *Clinical behavior therapy: Adults and children* (pp. 420–433). New York: Wiley.

Kaminsky, L., & Dewey, D. (2002). Psychosocial adjustment in siblings of children with autism. *Journal of Child Psychology and Psychiatry and Allied Disciplines, 43,* 225–232.

Kay, S., Harchik, A. F., & Luiselli, J. K. (2006). Elimination of drooling by an adolescent student with autism attending public high school. *Journal of Positive Behavior Interventions, 8,* 24–28.

Kay, S., & Vyse, S. (2005). Helping parents separate the wheat from the chaff: Putting autism treatments to the test. In J. W. Jacobson, R. M. Foxx, & J. A. Mulick (Eds.), *Controversial therapies for developmental disabilities: Fad, fashion and science in professional practice* (pp. 265–277). Mahwah, NJ: Lawrence Erlbaum Associates.

Kemner, C., Willemsen-Swinkels, S. H. N., de-Jonge, M., Tuynman-Qua, H., & van-Engeland, H. (2002). Open-label study of olanzapine in children with pervasive developmental disorder. *Journal of Clinical Psychopharmacology, 22,* 455–460.

Kimball, J. W. (2002). Behavior analytic instruction for children with autism: Philosophy matters. *Focus on Autism and Other Developmental Disabilities, 17*(2), 66–75.

King, B. H., & Bostic, J. Q. (2006). An update on pharmacologic treatments for autism spectrum disorders. *Child and Adolescent Psychiatric Clinics of North America, 15,* 161–175.

King, R., Fay, G., & Wheildon, H. (2002). Re: Clomipramine vs. haloperidol in the treatment of autistic disorder: A double-blind, placebo, crossover study. *Journal of Clinical Psychopharmacology, 22,* 525–526.

Klin, A., & Jones, W. (2006). Attributing social and physical meaning to ambiguous visual displays in individuals with higher-functioning autism spectrum disorders. *Brain and Cognition, 61,* 40–53.

Koegel, R. L., & Koegel, L. K. (2006). *Pivotal response treatments for autism: Communication, social, & academic development.* Baltimore: Paul H. Brookes.

Konstantareas, M. M., & Stewart, K. (2006). Affect regulation and temperament in children with autism spectrum disorder. *Journal of Autism and Developmental Disorders, 36,* 143–154.

Kundert, D. K., & Trimarchi, C. L. (2006). Pervasive developmental disorders. In L. Phelps (Ed.), *Chronic health-related disorders in children: Collaborative medical and psychoeducational interventions* (pp. 213–235). Washington, DC: American Psychological Association.

Lam, K. S. L., Aman, M. G., & Arnold, L. E. (2006). Neurochemical correlates of autistic disorder: A review of the literature. *Research in Developmental Disabilities, 27,* 254–289.

Landa, R., & Garrett-Mayer, E. (2006). Development in infants with autism spectrum disorder: A prospective study. *Journal of Child Psychology and Psychiatry, 47,* 629–638.

Larson, E. (2006). Caregiving and autism: How does children's propensity for routinization influence participation in family activities? *OTJR: Occupation, Participation and Health, 26,* 69–79.

LeBlanc, L. A., Carr, J. E., Crossett, S. E., Bennett, C. M., & Detweiler, D. D. (2005). Intensive outpatient behavioral treatment of primary urinary incontinence of children with autism. *Focus on Autism and Other Developmental Disabilities, 20,* 98–105.

Legoff, D. B., & Sherman, M. (2006). Long-term outcome of social skills intervention based on interactive LEGO play. *Autism, 10,* 317–329.

Lewis, P., Abbeduto, L., Murphy, M., Richmond, E., Giles, N., Bruno, L., & Schroeder, S. (2006). Cognitive, language and social-cognitive skills of individuals with fragile X

syndrome with and without autism. *Journal of Intellectual Disability Research, 50,* 532–545.

Lindberg, B. (2006). *Understanding Rett syndrome: A practical guide for parents, teachers, and therapists* (2nd rev. ed.). Ashland, OH: Hogrefe & Huber.

Lockshin, S. B., Gillis, J. M., & Romanczyk, R. G. (2005). *Helping your child with autism spectrum disorder: A step-by-step workbook for families.* Oakland, CA: New Harbinger.

Lovaas, O. I. (2003). *Teaching individuals with developmental delays: Basic intervention techniques.* Austin, TX: PRO-ED.

Lyons, V., & Fitzgerald, M. (2005). Early memory and autism. *Journal of Autism and Developmental Disorders, 35,* 683.

Maestro, S., Muratori, F., Cesari, A., Cavallaro, M. C., Paziente, A., Pecini, C., Grassi, C., Manfredi, A., & Sommario, C. (2005). Course of autism signs in the first year of life. *Psychopathology, 38,* 26–31.

Mandelbaum, D. E., Stevens, M., Rosenberg, E., Wiznitzer, M., Steinschneider, M., Filipek, P., & Rapin, I. (2006). Sensorimotor performance in school-age children with autism, developmental language disorder or low IQ. *Developmental Medicine & Child Neurology, 48,* 33–39.

Margetts, J. K., LeCouteur, A., & Croom, S. (2006). Families in a state of flux: The experience of grandparents in autism spectrum disorder. *Child: Care, Health and Development, 32,* 565–574.

Marks, S., Matson, A., & Barraza, L. (2005). The impact of siblings with disabilities on their brothers and sisters pursuing a career in special education. *Research and Practice for Persons with Severe Disabilities, 30,* 205–218.

Martin, C. L., & Fabes, R. (2006). *Discovering child development.* Boston: Allyn and Bacon.

Mascha, K., & Boucher, J. (2006). Preliminary investigation of a qualitative method of examining siblings' experiences of living with a child with ASD. *British Journal of Developmental Disabilities, 52,* 19–28.

Massaro, D. W., & Bosseler, A. (2006). Read my lips: The importance of the face in a computer-animated tutor for vocabulary learning by children with autism. *Autism, 10,* 495–510.

McCarthy, A., Cuskelly, M., van Kraayenoord, C. E., & Cohen, J. (2006). Predictors of stress in mothers and fathers of children with fragile X syndrome. *Research in Developmental Disabilities, 27,* 688–704.

McConachie, H., & Robinson, G. (2006). What services do young children with autism spectrum dis-

order receive? *Child: Care, Health and Development, 32,* 553–557.

McConkey, R. (2006). Transition toolkit: A framework for managing change and successful transition planning for children and young people with autism spectrum disorder. *Journal of Intellectual Disabilities, 10,* 293–294.

McCracken, J. T., McGough, J., Shah, B., Cronin, P., Hong, D., Aman, M. G., Arnold, L. E., Lindsay, R., Nash, P., Hollway, J., McDougle, C. J., Posey, D., Swiezy, N., Kohn, A., Scahill, L., Martin, A., Koenig, K., Volkmar, F., Carroll, D., Lancor, A., Tierney, E., Ghuman, J., Gonzalez, N. M., Grados, M., Vitiello, B., Ritz, L., Davies, M., Robinson, J., & McMahon, D. (2002). Risperidone in children with autism and serious behavioral problems. *New England Journal of Medicine, 347*(5), 314–321.

McDougle, C. J., Posey, D. J., & Stigler, K. A. (2006). Pharmacological treatments. In S. O. Moldin & J. L. R. Rubenstein (Eds.), *Understanding autism: From basic neuroscience to treatment* (pp. 417–442). Boca Raton, FL: CRC Press.

Minazio, N. (2002). Autistic states: Are these a figure of defeat of the psyche? *Revue Française de Psychanalyse, 66,* 1771–1778.

Minshew, N. J., & Meyer, J. A. (2006). Autism and related conditions. In M. J. Farah & T. E. Feinberg (Eds.), *Patient-based approaches to cognitive neuroscience* (2nd ed., pp. 419–431). Cambridge, MA: The MIT Press.

Mostert, M. P. (2001). Facilitated communication since 1995: A review of published studies. *Journal of Autism and Developmental Disorders, 31,* 287–313.

Moyes, R. (2003). Incorporating social goals in the classroom—A guide for teachers and parents of children with high functioning autism and Asperger syndrome. *British Journal of Educational Psychology, 73,* 138–139.

Newsom, C., & Hovanitz, C. A. (2006). Autistic spectrum disorders. In E. J. Mash, & R. A. Barkley (Eds.), *Treatment of childhood disorders* (3rd ed., pp. 455–511). New York: Guilford Press.

Niehus, R., & Lord, C. (2006). Early medical history of children with autism spectrum disorders. *Journal of Developmental & Behavioral Pediatrics, 27* (Suppl. 2), S120–S127.

Owens, R. E., Jr. (2004). *Language disorders: A functional approach to assessment and intervention* (4th ed.). Needham Heights, MA: Allyn and Bacon.

Ozonoff, S., Dawson, G., & McPartland, J. (2002). *A parent's guide to Asperger syndrome and high-functioning autism: How to meet the challenges and help your child thrive.* New York: Guilford Press.

Ozonoff, S., Williams, B. J., & Landa, R. (2005). Parental report of the early development of children with regressive autism: The delays-plus-regression phenotype. *Autism, 9,* 461–486.

Parsons, S., & Mitchell, P. (2002). The potential of virtual reality in social skills training for people with autistic spectrum disorders. *Journal of Intellectual Disability Research, 46,* 430–443.

Pearson, D. A., Loveland, K. A., & Lachar, D. (2006). A comparison of behavioral and emotional functioning in children and adolescents with autistic disorder and PDD-NOS. *Child Neuropsychology, 12,* 321–333.

Perkins, M. R., Dobbinson, S., Boucher, J., Bol, S., & Bloom, P. (2006). Lexical knowledge and lexical use in autism. *Journal of Autism and Developmental Disorders, 36,* 795–805.

Pierce, K., & Courchesne, E. (2002). "A further support to the hypothesis of a link between serotonin, autism and the cerebellum": Reply. *Biological Psychiatry, 52,* 143.

Pine, E., Luby, J., Abbacchi, A., & Constantino, J. N. (2006). Quantitative assessment of autistic symptomatology in preschoolers. *Autism, 10,* 344–352.

Prelock, P. A., & Vargas, C. M. (2004). The role of partnerships in program development for adolescents with autism spectrum disorders. In C. M. Vargas & P. A. Prelock (Eds.), *Caring for children with neurodevelopmental disabilities and their families: An innovative approach to interdisciplinary practice* (pp. 275–301). Mahwah, NJ: Lawrence Erlbaum.

Pring, L., & Hermelin, B. (2002). Numbers and letters: Exploring an autistic savant's unpractised ability. *Neurocase, 8,* 330–337.

Raja, M. (2006). The diagnosis of asperger's syndrome. *Directions in Psychiatry, 26,* 89–104.

Rapin, I. (2002). The autistic-spectrum disorders. *New England Journal of Medicine, 347*(5), 302–303.

Rapp, J. T., & Vollmer, T. R. (2005). Stereotypy II: A review of neurobiological interpretations and suggestions for an integration with behavioral methods. *Research in Developmental Disabilities, 26,* 548–564.

Rattcliff-Schaub, K., Carey, T., & Reeves, G. D. (2005). Randomized controlled trial of transdermal secretin on behavior of children with autism. *Autism, 9,* 256–265.

Reading, R. (2006). Comment on "Prevalence of disorders of the autism spectrum in a population cohort of children in Sough Tames: The special needs and autism project (SNAP)." *Child: Care, Health and Development, 32,* 752–753.

Reichenberg, A., Gross, R., Weiser, M., Bresnahan, M., Silverman, J., Harlap, S., Rabinowitz, J., Shulman, C., Malaspina, D., Lubin, G.,

Knobler, H. Y., Davidson, M., & Susser, E. (2006). Advancing paternal age and autism. *Archives of General Psychiatry, 63,* 1026–1032.

Renty, J., & Roeyers, H. (2006). Satisfaction with formal support and education for children with autism spectrum disorder: The voices of the parents. *Child: Care, Health and Development, 32,* 371–385.

Rhea, P. (2005). Assessing communication in autism spectrum disorders. In F. R. Volkmar, P. Rhea, A. Klin, & D. Cohen, (Eds.), *Handbook of autism and pervasive developmental disorders, Vol. 2: Assessment, interventions and policy* (3rd ed., pp. 799–816). Hoboken, NJ: John Wiley & Sons.

Rhode, M., & Klauber, T. (2004). *The many faces of aspergers' syndrome.* London: Karnac Books.

Roblyer, M. D. (2006). *Integrating technology into teaching* (4th ed.). Upper Saddle River, NJ: Prentice-Hall.

Rogers, S. J., & Ozonoff, S. (2005). Annotation: What do we know about sensory dysfunction in autism? A critical review of the empirical evidence. *Journal of Child Psychology and Psychiatry, 46,* 1255–1268.

Rogers, S. J., & Ozonoff, S. (2006). Behavioral, educational, and developmental treatments for autism. In S. O. Moldin & J. L. R. Rubenstein (Eds.), *Understanding autism: From basic neuroscience to treatment* (pp. 443–473). Boca Raton, FL: CRC Press.

Ronald, A., Happe, F., Bolton, P., Butcher, L. M., Price, T. S., Wheelwright, S., Baron-Cohen, S., & Plomin, R. (2006). Genetic heterogeneity between the three components of autism spectrum: A twin study. *Journal of the American Academy of Child & Adolescent Psychiatry, 45,* 691–699.

Ross, P., & Cuskelly, M. (2006). Adjustment, sibling problems and coping strategies of brothers and sisters of children with autistic spectrum disorder. *Journal of Intellectual & Developmental Disability, 31,* 77–86.

Rossi, L. (2006). Obsessive-compulsive disorder and related conditions. *Psychiatric Annals, 36,* 514–517.

Rutter, M. (2005a). Autism research: Lessons from the past and prospects for the future. *Journal of Autism and Developmental Disorders, 35,* 241–257.

Rutter, M. (2005b). Aetiology of autism: Findings and questions. *Journal of Intellectual Disability Research, 49,* 231–238.

Rutter, M. (2006). Introduction: Autism: Its recognition, early diagnosis, and service implications. *Journal of Developmental & Behavioral Pediatrics, 27* (Suppl. 2), S54–S58.

Salgado-Pineda, P., Delaveau, P., Blin, O., & Nieoullon, A. (2005). Dopaminergic contribution to the regulation of emotional perception. *Clinical Neuropharmacology, 28,* 228–237.

Sallows, G. O., & Graupner, T. D. (2005). Intensive behavioral treatment for children with autism: Four-year outcome and predictors. *American Journal on Mental Retardation, 110,* 417–438.

Santos, M., Coelho, P. A., & Maciel, P. (2006). Chromatin remodeling and neuronal function: Exciting links. *Genes, Brain & Behavior, 5* (Suppl. 2), 80–91.

Schreibman, L., & Koegel, R. L. (2005). Training for parents of children with autism: Pivotal responses, generalization, and individualization of interventions. In E. D. Hibbs & P. S. Jensen (Eds.), *Psychosocial treatments for child and adolescent disorders: Empirically based strategies for clinical practice* (2nd ed., 605–631). Washington, DC: American Psychological Association.

Scott, F. J., Baron-Cohen, S., Bolton, P., & Brayne, C. (2002). Brief report: Prevalence of autism spectrum conditions in children aged 5–11 years in Cambridgeshire, UK. *Autism, 6,* 231–237.

Shalom, D. B., Mostofsky, S. H., Hazlett, R. L., Goldberg, M. C., Landa, R. J., Faran, Y., McLeod, D. R., & Hoehn-Saric, R. (2006). Normal physiological emotions but differences in expression of conscious feelings in children with high-functioning autism. *Journal of Autism and Developmental Disorders, 36,* 395–400.

Sherer, M. R., & Schreibman, L. (2005). Individual behavioral profiles and predictors of treatment effectiveness for children with autism. *Journal of Consulting and Clinical Psychology, 73,* 525–538.

Siceloff, J. (1999). A simple man: Autistic man wrongly accused of robbery. Retrieved December 13, 1999, from http://ABCNEWS.com

Simpson, R. L. (2005). *Autism spectrum disorders: Interventions and treatments for children and youth.* Thousand Oaks, CA: Corwin Press.

Smith, T., Lovaas, N. W., & Lovaas, O. I. (2002). Behaviors of children with high-functioning autism when paired with typically developing versus delayed peers: A preliminary study. *Behavioral Interventions, 17*(3), 129–143.

Soppitt, R. (2006). Clinical observations in children with autistic spectrum disorders. *Autism, 10,* 429.

Spector, S. G., & Volkmar, F. R. (2006). Autism spectrum disorders. In D. A. Wolfe & E. J. Mash (Eds.), *Behavioral and emotional disorders in adolescents: Nature, assessment, and treatment* (pp. 444–460). New York: Guilford.

Stacey, P. (2003). *The boy who loved windows.* Cambridge, MA: Da Capo Press.

Stone, W. L. (2006). *Does my child have autism?: A parent's guide to early detection and intervention in autism spectrum disorders.* New York: Jossey-Bass.

Strauss, W. L., Unis, A. S., Cowan, C., Dawson, G., & Dager, S. R. (2002). Fluorine magnetic resonance spectroscopy measurement of brain fluvoxa-mine and fluoxetine in pediatric patients treated for pervasive developmental disorders. *American Journal of Psychiatry, 159,* 755–760.

Sturm, H., Fernell, E., & Gillberg, C. (2004). Autism spectrum disorders in children with normal intellectual levels: Associated impairments and subgroups. *Developmental Medicine & Child Neurology, 46,* 444–447.

Symons, F. J., Sperry, L. A., Dropik, P. L., & Bodfish, J. W. (2005). The early development of stereotypy and self-injury: A review of research methods. *Journal of Intellectual Disability Research, 49,* 144–158.

Tager-Flusberg, H. (2003). Language impairment in children with complex neurodevelopmental disorders: The case of autism. In Y. Levy & J. Schaeffer (Eds.), *Language competence across populations: Toward a definition of specific language impairment* (pp. 297–321). Mahwah, NJ: Lawrence Erlbaum.

Tager-Flusberg, H. (2005). Designing studies to investigate the relationships between genes, environments, and developmental language disorders. *Applied Psycholinguistics, 26,* 29–39.

Tager-Flusberg, H., Reah, P., & Lord, C. (2005). Language and communication in autism. In F. R. Volkmar, P. Rhea, A. Klin, & D. Cohen, (Eds.), *Handbook of autism and pervasive developmental disorders, Vol. 2: Assessment, interventions and policy* (3rd ed., pp. 335–364). Hoboken, NJ: John Wiley & Sons.

Thioux, M., Stark, D. E., & Klaiman, C. (2006). The day of the week when you were born in 700 ms: Calendar computation in an autistic savant. *Journal of Experimental Psychology: Human Perception and Performance, 32,* 1155–1168.

Tiegerman-Farber, E. (2002). Autism spectrum disorders: Learning to communicate. In D. K. Bernstein & E. Tiegerman-Farber (Eds.), *Language and communication disorders in children* (5th ed., pp. 510–564). Boston: Allyn and Bacon.

Tsai, L. Y. (2005). Medical treatment in autism. In D. Zager (Ed.) *Autism spectrum disorders: Identification, education, and treatment* (3rd ed., pp. 395–492). Mahwah, NJ: Lawrence Erlbaum.

U.S. Department of Education. (2006). *Twenty-sixth annual report to Congress on the implementation of the Individuals with Disabilities Education Act.* Washington, DC: Author.

Volkmar, F. R. (2005). International perspectives. In F. R. Volkmar, R. Paul, A. Klin, & D. Cohen (Eds.), *Handbook of autism and pervasive developmental disorders, Vol. 2: Assessment, interventions, and policy* (3rd ed.). Hoboken, NJ: John Wiley & Sons.

Volkmar, F. R., Wiesner, L. A., & Westphal, A. (2006). Healthcare issues for children on the autism spectrum. *Current Opinion in Psychiatry, 19,* 361–366.

Walenski, M., Tager-Flusberg, H., & Ullman, M. T. (2006). Language in autism. In S. O. Moldin & J. L. Rubenstein (Eds.), *Understanding autism: From basic neuroscience to treatment* (pp. 175–203). Boca Raton, FL: CRC Press.

Weiss, M. J. (2002). Hardiness and social support as predictors of stress in mothers of typical children, children with autism, and children with mental retardation. *Autism, 6,* 115–130.

Westling, D. L., & Fox, L. (2004). *Teaching students with severe disabilities* (3rd ed.). Columbus, OH: Merrill/Prentice-Hall.

Whitaker, R. (2000). Knowing Chris. *Washington Post,* March 21, Z12.

Wilkerson, D. S., Volpe, A. G., Dean, R., & Titus, J. B. (2002). Perinatal complications as predictors of infantile autism. *International Journal of Neuroscience, 112,* 1085–1098.

Wing, L., & Potter, D. (2002). The epidemiology of autistic spectrum disorders: Is prevalence rising? *Mental Retardation and Developmental Disabilities Research Reviews, 8*(3), 151–161.

Wolfe, D. A., & Mash, E. J. (2006). Behavioral and emotional problems in adolescents: Overview and issues. In D. A. Wolfe & E. J. Mash (Eds.), *Behavioral and emotional disorders in adolescents: Nature, assessment, and treatment* (pp. 3–20). New York: Guilford.

Wymbs, B. T., Robb, J. A., Chronis, A. M., Massetti, G. M., Fabiano, G. A., Arnold, F. W., Brice, A. C., Gnagy, E. M., Pelham, W. E., Jr., Burrows-MacLean, L., & Hoffman, M. T. (2005). Long-term, multimodal treatment of a child with asperger's syndrome and comorbid disruptive behavior problems: A case illustration. *Cognitive and Behavioral Practice, 12,* 338–350.

Yazbak, K. (2002). Connections: The new autism: One family's perspective. *Clinical Child Psychology and Psychiatry, 7,* 505–517.

Young, R. (2005). Neurobiology of savant syndrome. In C. Stough (Ed.), *Neurobiology of exceptionality* (pp. 199–215). New York: Kluwer Academic/Plenum.

CHAPTER 14

Arlinghaus, K. A., Shoaib, A. M., & Price, T. R. P (2005). Neuropsychiatric Assessment. In J. M. Silver, T. W. McAllister, & S. C. Yudofsky (Eds.), *Textbook of traumatic brain* injury (pp. 59–78). Arlington, VA: American Psychiatric Publishing.

Best, S. J., Heller K. W., & Bigge, J. L. (2005). *Teaching individuals with physical or multiple disabilities* (5th ed.). Upper Saddle River, NJ: Pearson.

Best, S. J., Reed, P., & Bigge, J. L. (2005). Assistive Technology. In S. J. Best, K. W. Heller, & J. L. Bigge (Eds.), *Teaching individuals with physical or multiple disabilities* (5th ed.) (pp. 179–226). Upper Saddle River, NJ: Pearson Education.

Bigler, E. D. (2005). Structural Imaging. In J. M. Silver, T. W. McAllister, & S. C. Yudofsky (Eds.), *Textbook of traumatic brain injury* (pp. 79–105). Arlington, VA: American Psychiatric Publishing.

Bowe, F. (2000). *Physical, sensory, and health disabilities.* Upper Saddle River, NJ: Merrill.

Brain Injury Association of America. (2003). *TBI incidence.* Retrieved May 23, 2003, from http://www.biausa.org

Brain Injury Association of America. (2006). *Acquired brain injury.* Retrieved July 28, 2006, from http://www.biausa.org/Pages/types_of_brain_injury.html#acquired

Brainsource. (2006). *The amazing brain.* Retrieved July 28, 2006, from http://www.brainsource.com/amazing%20brain.htm

Calderwood, L. (2003). *Cracked: Recovering after traumatic brain injury.* Philadelphia: Jessica Kingsley Publishers.

Cavallo, M. M., & Kay, T. (2005). The family system. In J. M. Silver, T. W. McAllister, & S. C. Yudofsky (Eds.), *Textbook of traumatic brain injury* (pp. 533–558). Arlington, VA: American Psychiatric Publishing.

Centers for Disease Control and Prevention. (2006). *Brain injuries and mass casualty events: Information for clinicians: Traumatic brain injury facts.* Retrieved July 28, 2006, from http://www.bt.cdc.gov/masscasualties/braininjuriespro.asp

Cope, D. N., & Reynolds, W. E. (2005). Systems of care. In J. M. Silver, T. W. McAllister, & S. C. Yudofsky (Eds.), *Textbook of traumatic brain injury* (pp. 559–569). Arlington, VA: American Psychiatric Publishing.

Deidrick, K. K. M., & Farmer, J. E. (2005). School reentry following traumatic brain injury. *Preventing School Failure, 49*(4), 23–33.

Eden, J., & Stevens, R. (Eds.). (2006). *Evaluating the HRSA traumatic brain injury program.* Washington, DC: The National Academies Press.

Elovic, E., & Zafonte, R. (2005). Prevention. In J. M. Silver, T. W. McAllister, & S. C. Yudofsky (Eds.), *Textbook of traumatic brain injury* (pp. 727–747). Arlington, VA: American Psychiatric Publishing.

Family Caregiver Alliance Clearinghouse. (2003). *Definition.* Retrieved May 17, 2003, from http://www.caregiver.org/factsheets/diagnoses/head_injury.html

Farmer, J. E., Clippard, D. S., Luehr-Wiemann, Y., Wright, E., & Owings, S. (1997). Assessing children with traumatic brain injury during rehabilitation: Promoting school and community reentry. In E. D. Bigler, E. Clark, & J. E. Farmer (Eds.), *Childhood traumatic brain injury: Diagnosis, assessment, and intervention* (pp. 33–62). Austin, TX: Pro-Ed.

Gennarelli, T. A., & Graham, D. I. (2005). Neuropathology. In J. M. Silver, T. W. McAllister, & S. C. Yudofsky (Eds.), *Textbook of traumatic brain injury* (pp. 27–50). Arlington, VA: American Psychiatric Publishing.

High, W. M., Sander, A. M., Struchen, M. A., & Hart, K. A. (Eds). (2005). *Rehabilitation for traumatic brain injury.* New York: Oxford University Press.

Horton, C. B., & Cruise, T. K. (2001). *Child abuse and neglect: The school's response.* New York: Guilford Press.

Hux, K. (Ed.). (2003). *Assisting survivors of traumatic brain injury: The role of speech-language pathologists.* Austin, TX: Pro-Ed.

Hux, K., & Manasse, N. (2003). Assessment and treatment of cognitive-communication impairments. In K. Hux (Ed.), *Assisting survivors of traumatic brain injury: The role of speech-language pathologists* (pp. 93–133). Austin, TX: Pro-Ed.

Jennett, B., & Teasdale, G. (1974). Assessment of coma and impaired consciousness. *Lancet, 2,* 81–84.

Kapoor, N., & Ciuffreda, K. J. (2005). Vision problems. In J. M. Silver, T. W. McAllister, & S. C. Yudofsky (Eds.), *Textbook of traumatic brain injury* (pp. 405–415). Arlington, VA: American Psychiatric Publishing.

Keyser-Marcus, L., Briel, L., Sherron-Targett, P., Yasuda, S., Johnson, S., & Wehman, P. (2002). Enhancing the schooling of students with traumatic brain injury. *Teaching Exceptional Children, 34,* 62–67.

Kraus, J. F., & Chu, L. D. (2005). Epidemiology. In J. M. Silver, T. W. McAllister, & S. C. Yudofsky (Eds.), *Textbook of traumatic brain injury* (pp. 3–26). Arlington, VA: American Psychiatric Publishing.

Langlois, J. A., Rutland-Brown, W., & Thomas, K. E. (2006). *Traumatic brain injury in the United States: Emergency department visits, hospitalizations, and deaths.* Atlanta: Centers for Disease Control and Prevention, National Center for Injury Prevention and Control.

Max, J. E. (2005). Children and adolescents. In J. M. Silver, T. W. McAllister, & S. C. Yudofsky (Eds.), *Textbook of traumatic brain injury*

(pp. 477–494). Arlington, VA: American Psychiatric Publishing.

McCullagh, S., & Feinstein, A. (2005). Cognitive changes. In J. M. Silver, T. W. McAllister, & S. C. Yudofsky (Eds.), *Textbook of traumatic brain injury* (pp. 321–335). Arlington, VA: American Psychiatric Publishing.

National Institutes of Neurological Disorders and Strokes. (2005). What you need to know about traumatic brain injury. In S. J. Judd (Ed.), *Brain disorders sourcebook* (pp. 206–225). Detroit: Omnigraphics.

O'Shanick, G. J., & O'Shanick, A. M. (2005). Personality Disorders. In J. M. Silver, T. W. McAllister, & S. C. Yudofsky (Eds.), *Textbook of traumatic brain injury* (pp. 245–258). Arlington, VA: American Psychiatric Publishing.

Pierangelo, R., & Giuliani, G. A. (2001). *What every teacher should know about students with special needs: Promoting success in the classroom.* Champaign, IL: Research Press.

Richter, E. F. (2005). Balance problems and dizziness. In J. M. Silver, T. W. McAllister, & S. C. Yudofsky (Eds.), *Textbook of traumatic brain injury* (pp. 393–404). Arlington, VA: American Psychiatric Publishing.

Robinson, R. G., & Jorge, R. E. (2005). Mood disorders. In J. M. Silver, T. W. McAllister, & S. C. Yudofsky (Eds.), *Textbook of traumatic brain injury* (pp. 201–212). Arlington, VA: American Psychiatric Publishing.

Semrud-Clikeman, M. (2001). *Traumatic brain injury in children and adolescents: Assessment and intervention.* New York: Guilford Press.

Silver, J. M., McAllister, T. W., & Yudofsky, S. C. (Eds.). (2005). *Textbook of traumatic brain injury.* Arlington, VA: American Psychiatric Publishing.

Silver, J. M., Yudofsky, S. C., & Anderson, K. E. (2005). Aggressive disorders. In J. M. Silver, T. W. McAllister, & S. C. Yudofsky (Eds.), *Textbook of traumatic brain injury* (pp. 259–277). Arlington, VA: American Psychiatric Publishing.

Warden, D. L., & Labbate, L. A. (2005). Posttraumatic stress disorder and other anxiety disorders. In J. M. Silver, T. W. McAllister, & S. C. Yudofsky (Eds.), *Textbook of traumatic brain injury* (pp. 231–243). Arlington, VA: American Psychiatric Publishing.

Wehman, P. (2001). *Life beyond the classroom: Transition strategies for young people with disabilities* (3rd ed.). Baltimore: Paul H. Brooks.

Wright, C., & Borgelt, C. E. (2003). Family issues. In K. Hux (Ed.), *Assisting survivors of traumatic brain injury: The role of speech-language pathologists* (pp. 317–331). Austin, TX: Pro-Ed.

Ylvisaker, M., Todis, B., Glang, A., Urbanczyk, B., Franklin, C., DePompei, R., Feeney, T., Maxwell, N. M., Pearson, S., & Tyler, J. S. (2001). Educating students with TBI:

Themes and recommendations. *Journal of Head Trauma Rehabilitation, 16*(1), 76–93.

CHAPTER 15

Adams, M. (2003, May 25). Elevated: Tamika Catchings will not let her niceness, or her deafness, prevent her from becoming the best player in the W.N.B.A. *New York Times Magazine, 26–29.*

Auditory–Verbal International. (2006). *Principles of auditory-verbal practice.* Retrieved October 25, 2006, from http://deafness.miningco.com/health/deafness/gi/dynamic/offsite.htm?site=http://www.auditory%2Dverbal.org/

Calderon, R., & Naidu S. (2000). Further support for the benefits of early identification and intervention for children with hearing loss. *The Volta Review, 100*(5), 53–84.

Center for Assessment and Demographic Studies. (2006). *2001–2002 Annual survey of deaf and hard of hearing children and youth.* Washington, DC: Gallaudet University. Retrieved October 19, 2006, from http://gri.gallaudet.edu/Demographics/2002_National_Summary.pdf

Centers for Disease Control. (2006). *Hearing loss.* Retrieved October 19, 2006, from http://www.cdc.gov/ncbddd/dd/hi4.htm

Cochlear Implants Association. (2006). *What is a cochlear implant?* Retrieved August 17, 2006, from http://www.cici.org/factsheets.html

Deaf World Web. (2006). *Deaf America Web.* Retrieved August 1, 2006, from http://deafworldweb.org/int/us/

Feldman, S. (2006). *Strike y'er out. Atlantic Canada Opportunities Agenda.* Retrieved July 6, 2006, from http://www.cbbaseball.ca/nationals/ Strike%20Three.htm

Gallaudet Research Institute. (2006). *Literacy and deaf students.* Washington, DC: Author. Retrieved October 30, 2006, from http://gri.gallaudet.edu/Literacy/

Kaland, M., & Salvatore, K. (2006). *Psychology of hearing loss.* Retrieved July 19, 2006, from http://www.asha.org/about/publications/leader-online/archives/2002/q1/020319d.htm

Lavine, G. (2005, August 30). Cochlear implant fills her heart with music. *Salt Lake Tribune,* D1, D2.

Magnuson, M. (2000). Infants with congenital deafness: On the importance of early sign language acquisition. *American Annals of the Deaf, 145*(1), 6–14.

Marschark, M., Lang, H. G., Albertini, J. A. (2002). *Educating deaf students: From research to practice.* New York: Oxford University Press.

Marschark, M., & Spencer, P. E. (2003). *Oxford handbook of deaf studies, language, and education.* New York: Oxford University Press.

McKeen, S. (2006). A new language for baby. *The Ottowa Citizen*. Retrieved October 4, 2006, from http://littlesigners.com/article3.html

McNally, P. L., Rose, S., & Quigley, S. P. (2004). *Language learning practices with deaf children* (3rd ed.). Austin, TX: Pro Ed.

McKinley, A. M., & Warren, S. F. (2000). The effectiveness of cochlear implants for children with prelingual deafness. *Journal of Early Intervention, 23*, 252–263.

Melich, M. (1996, October 14). Now hear this. *Salt Lake Tribune*, c1, c8.

Moores, D. F. (2001). *Educating the deaf: Psychology, principles and practices* (5th ed.). Boston: Houghton-Mifflin.

National Academy on an Aging Society. (2006). *Hearing loss: A growing problem that affects quality of life, 2*, 1–6. Retrieved July 28, 2006, from http://www.agingsociety.org/agingsociety/pdf/hearing.pdf

National Association of the Deaf. (2006). *I have heard that deaf people are against technology. Is that true?* Silver Springs, MD: Author. Retrieved October 14, 2006, from http://www.nad.org/site/pp.asp?c=foINKQMBF&b=180439

National Institute on Deafness and Other Communication Disorders. (2006a). *American Sign Language. Health information: Hearing and balance.* Retrieved October 30, 2006, from http://www.nidcd.nih.gov/health/hearing/asl.asp

National Institute on Deafness and Other Communication Disorders. (2006b). *Cochlear implants. Health information: Hearing and balance.* Retrieved September 10, 2006, from http://www.nidcd.nih.gov/health/hearing/coch.asp

National Institute on Deafness and Other Communication Disorders. (2006c). *Otitis media. Health information: Hearing and balance.* Retrieved September 10, 2006, from http://www.nidcd.nih.gov/health/hearing/otitism.asp

National Technical Institute for the Deaf. (2006). *Welcome to C-Print.* Rochester, NY: Author. Retrieved November 6, 2006, from http://www.ntid.rit.edu/cprint/index.php

Pediatric Bulletin. (2006). *Congenital cytomegalovirus infection and disease.* Retrieved October 4, 2006, from http://home.coqui.net/myrna/cmv.htm

Quigley, S. P., & King, C. (Eds.). (1985). *Reading milestones.* Beaverton, OR: Dormac.

Ringen, J. (2006). *Music making fans deaf? How the ipod generation may be losing its hearing without even knowing it.* Retrieved November 4, 2006, from http://www.rollingstone.com/news/story/8841090/music_making_fans_deaf

Robson, G. (2006). Captioning and the law. *Journal of Court Reporting.*

Retrieved October 12, 2006, from http://www.captioncentral.com/

Scheetz, N. A. (2004). *Psychosocial aspects of deafness.* Boston: Pearson Education.

Schirmer, B. R. (2000). *Language and literacy development in children who are deaf* (2nd Ed.). Boston : Allyn and Bacon.

Smith, J. D. (1998). *Inclusion: Schools for all students.* Belmont, CA: Wadsworth.

U.S. Department of Education. (2006). To assure the free appropriate public education of all children with disabilities. *Twenty-sixth annual report to Congress on the implementation of the Individuals with Disabilities Education Act.* Washington, DC: U.S. Government Printing Office.

Walker, L. A. (2001, May 13). They're breaking the sound barrier. *Parade Magazine, 5.*

Wurst, D., Jones, D., & Luckner, J. (2005, May/June). Promoting literacy development with students who are hard-of-hearing, and hearing. *Teaching Exceptional Children, 37*(5) 56–62.

CHAPTER 16

American Foundation for the Blind. (2006). *Educating students with visual impairments for inclusion in society: A paper on the inclusion of students with visual impairments.* Louisville, KY: Author. Retrieved November 15, 2006, from http://www.afb.org/Section.asp?SectionID=44&TopicID=189&DocumentID=1344

Barraga, N. C., & Erin, J. N. (2002). *Visual handicaps and learning* (4th ed.). Austin, TX: Pro-Ed.

Batshaw, M. L. (2003). *Children with disabilities* (5th ed.). Baltimore: Paul H. Brookes.

Bishop, V. E. (2004). *Teaching visually impaired children* (3rd ed.). Springfield, IL: Charles C. Thomas.

Bouchard, D., & Tetreault, S. (2000). The motor development of sighted children and children with moderate low vision aged 8–13. *Journal of Visual Impairments and Blindness, 94*, 564–573.

Cox, P. R., & Dykes, M. K. (2001 July/August). Effective classroom adaptations for students with visual impairments. *Teaching Exceptional Children, 33*(6), 68–74.

International Trachoma Initiative. (2006). *About Trachoma.* Retrieved October 14, 2006, from http://www.trachoma.org/trachoma.php

KidSource. (2006). *Undetected Vision Disorders Are Blinding Children: Earlier Testing Needed to Preserve Good Eyesight.* Retrieved October 24, 2006, from http://www.kidsource.com/kidsource/content/news/vision.html

Koenig, A. J., & Holbrook, M. C. (2005). Literacy skills. In A. J.

Koenig, & M. C. Holbrook (Eds.), *Foundations of education* (2nd ed.): *Volume II Insructional strategies for teaching children and youths with visual impairments* (pp. 264–312). New York: AFB Press.

Kurzweil Technologies. (2006). *A Brief Biography of Ray Kurzweil.* Burlington, MA: Lernout & Hauspie. Retrieved November 5, 2006, from http://www.kurzweiltech.com/raybio.html

Kurzweil, R. (2006). The age of spiritual machines. New York: Penguin Putnam. Retrieved November 2, 2006, from http://www.kurzweilai.net/meme/frame.html?main=memelist.html?m=7%23622.

Leigh, S. A., & Barclay, L. A. (2000). High school braille readers: Achieving academic success. *RE:view, 32,* 123–131.

Lewis, S., & Tolla, J. (2003). Creating and using tactile experience books for young children with visual impairments. *Teaching Exceptional Children, 35*(3), p. 22–25.

Li, A. (2004). Classroom strategies for improving and enhancing visual skills in students with disabilities. *Teaching Exceptional Children, 36*(6), 38–46.

Library of Congress. (2006). *That All May Read.* National Library Service for the Blind and Physically Handicapped (NLS). Retrieved July 30, 2006, from http://www.loc.gov/nls/nls-wb.html

McLinden, M., & McCall, S. (2006). *Learning through touch: Supporting children with visual impairments and additional difficulties.* Milton Park Abingdon, UK: David Fulton Publishers.

Pester, P. (2006). *Braille bits.* Louisville, KY: American Printing House for the Blind. Retrieved November 12, 2006, from http://www.aph.org/edresearch/bits898.htm

Rosenfeld, I. (2001, July 8). When you can't see what's in front of you. *Parade Magazine,* 12–13.

Sacks, S. Z., & Silberman, R. K. (2000). Social skills. In A. J. Koenig & M. C. Holbrook (Eds.), *Foundations of education* (2nd ed.), *Volume II: Insructional strategies for teaching children and youths with visual impairments* (pp. 616–652). New York: AFB Press.

Social Security Administration. (2006). *Disability planner: Special rules for people who are blind.* Washington, DC: Author. Retrieved October 31, 2006, from http://www.ssa.gov/dibplan/dqualify8.htm

United Nations World Food Programme. (2006). *Hunger, humanity's oldest enemy.* Retrieved October 23, 2006, from http://www.wfp.org/aboutwfp/introduction/hunger_what.asp?section=1&sub_section=1

U.S. Department of Education. (2000, June). *Educating blind and visually impaired students; policy guidance.* Washington, DC: Office of Special

Education and Rehabilitative Services, 65 FR 36586.

U.S. Department of Education. (2006). To assure the free appropriate public education of all children with disabilities. *Twenty-sixth annual report to Congress on the implementation of the Individuals with Disabilities Education Act.* Washington, DC: U.S. Government Printing Office.

CHAPTER 17

Advocates for Youth. (2006). *Adolescents and HIV/AIDS.* Retrieved September 5, 2006, from http://www.advocatesforyouth.org/PUBLICATIONS/factsheet/fshivaid.pdf#search=%22Adolescents%20and%20HIV%22

Altshuler, S. J. (2005). Drug-endangered children need a collaborative community response. *Child Welfare, 84*(2), 171–190.

American Academy of Pediatrics. (2006). *Prevention of unintended adolescent pregnancy an important goal.* Retrieved September 2, 2006, from http://www.aap.org/advocacy/releases/july05pregnancy.htm

American College of Obstetricians and Gynecologists. (2003). *Illegal drugs and pregnancy.* Retrieved June 6, 2003, from http://www.medem.com/MedLB/article_detaillb.cfm?article_ID=AAANOX8997C&sub_cat=2005

American Diabetes Association. (2006a). *All about diabetes.* Retrieved August 23, 2006, from http://www.diabetes.org/about-diabetes.jsp

American Diabetes Association. (2006b). *Cure.* Retrieved August 23, 2006, from http://www.diabetes.org/for-parents-and-kids/what-is-diabetes/cure.jsp

Asthma and Allergy Foundation of America. (2006). *Asthma facts and figures.* Retrieved August 11, 2006, from http://www.aafa.org/display.cfm?id=8&sub=42#over

Barnard, M., & McKeganey, N. (2004). The impact of parental problem drug use on children: What is the problem and what can be done to help? *Addiction, 99*(5), 552–559.

Berger, W. E. (2004). *Asthma for dummies.* Hoboken, NJ: Wiley.

Best, S. J. (2005a). Definitions, supports, issues, and services in schools and communities. In S. J. Best, K. W. Heller, & J. L Bigge (Eds.), *Teaching individuals with physical or multiple disabilities* (pp. 3–29). Upper Saddle River, NJ: Pearson.

Best, S. J. (2005b). Health impairments and infectious diseases. In S. J. Best, K. W. Heller, & J. L Bigge (Eds.), *Teaching individuals with physical or multiple disabilities* (pp. 59–85). Upper Saddle River, NJ: Pearson.

Best, S. J. (2005c). Physical disabilities. In S. J. Best, K. W. Heller, & J. L

Bigge (Eds.), *Teaching individuals with physical or multiple disabilities* (pp. 31–58). Upper Saddle River, NJ: Pearson.

Best, S. J., & Bigge, J. L. (2005). Cerebral Palsy. In S. J. Best, K. W. Heller, & J. L Bigge (Eds.), *Teaching individuals with physical or multiple disabilities* (pp. 87–109). Upper Saddle River, NJ: Pearson.

Beukelman, D. R., & Mirenda, P. (2005). *Augmentative and alternative communication: Supporting children and adults with complex communication needs* (3rd ed.). Baltimore: Paul H. Brooks.

Bono, K. E., Dinehart, L. H. B., Claussen, A. H., Scott, K. G., Mundy, P. C., & Katz, L. F. (2005). Early intervention with children prenatally exposed to cocaine: Expansion with multiple cohorts. *Journal of Early Intervention, 27*(4), 268–284.

Braun, P. A., Beaty, B. L., DiGuiseppi, C., & Steiner, J. F. (2005). Recurrent early childhood injuries among disadvantaged children in primary care settings. *Injury Prevention, 11*(4), 251–255.

Carson, G. D., & Carson, S. L. (2004). Sexual development, function, and consequences. In R. H. Haslam & P. J. Valletutti (Eds.), *Medical problems in the classroom: The teacher's role in diagnosis and management* (4th ed., pp. 565–608). Austin, TX: PRO-ED,.

Centers for Disease Control and Prevention. (2006). What we have learned from HIV/AIDS surveillance? Retrieved August 17, 2006, from http://www.cdc.gov/hiv/topics/surveillance/basic.htm#aidscases

Chesson, R. A., Chisholm, D., & Zaw, W. (2004). Counseling children with chronic physical illness. *Patient Education and Counseling, 55,* 331–338.

Child Welfare Information Gateway. (2006a). *What is child abuse and neglect?* Retrieved August 24, 2006, from http://www.childwelfare.gov/pubs/factsheets/whatiscan.pdf

Child Welfare and Information Gateway. (2006b). *National and state statistics.* Retrieved August 24, 2006, from http://www.childwelfare.gov/can/prevalence/stats.cfm

Chilman, C. (1979, November). Teenage pregnancy: A research review. *Social Work, 24*(6), 492–498.

Chilman, C. S. (1980). *Adolescent pregnancy and childbearing: Findings from research.* Washington, DC: U.S. Department of Health and Human Services, National Institutes of Health.

Clark, C. D. (2003). *In sickness and in play: Children coping with chronic illness.* Piscataway, NJ: Rutgers University Press.

Conners, N. A., Bokony, P., Whiteside-Mansell, L., Bradley, R. H., & Liu,

J. (2004). Addressing the treatment needs of children affected by maternal addiction: Challenges and solutions. *Evaluation and Program Planning, 27*(2), 241–247.

Cystic Fibrosis Foundation. (2006a). What is cystic fibrosis? Retrieved August 24, 2006, from http://www.cff.org/about_cystic_fibrosis/index.cfm?dspPrintReady=Y

Cystic Fibrosis Foundation. (2006b). CF drug development pipeline. Retrieved August 24, 2006, from http://www.cff.org/research/CFDrugDevelopmentPipeline/

Daneman, D., & Frank, M. (2004). The student with diabetes mellitus. In R. H. A. Haslam & P. J. Valletutti (Eds.), *Medical problems in the classroom: The teacher's role in diagnosis and management* (4th ed., pp. 109–129). Austin, TX: PRO-ED.

Davis, L. E., King, M. K., & Schultz, J. L. (2005). *Fundamentals of neurologic disease.* New York: Demos Medical.

Deardorff, J., Christopher, F. S., & Millsap, R. E. (2005). Early puberty and adolescent pregnancy: The influence of alcohol use. *Pediatrics, 116*(6), 1451–1456.

Donaghy, M. (2005). *Neurology* (2nd ed.). New York: Oxford University Press.

Donohue, B. (2004). Coexisting child neglect and drug abuse in young mothers: Specific recommendations for treatment based on a review of the outcome literature. *Behavior Modification, 28*(2), 206–233.

Environmental Protection Agency. (2005). *Asthma research results highlights.* Washington, DC: United States Environmental Protection Agency, Office of Research and Development.

Epilepsy Foundation. (2006). *Surgical and social outcomes.* Retrieved August 22, 2006, from http://www.epilepsyfoundation.org/answerplace/Medical/treatment/surgery/outcomes.cfm

Farber, N. (2003). *Adolescent pregnancy: Policy and prevention services. (Springer Series on Social Work.)* New York: Springer.

Fong, H. D. (Ed.). (2005). *Focus on cerebral palsy research.* New York: Nova Science.

Forsyth, C., & Maddison, J. (2005). Terminal Care. In A. Peebles, G. Connett, J. Maddison, & J. Gavin (Eds.), *Cystic fibrosis care: A practical guide* (pp. 279–284). New York: Elsevier Limited.

Franks, B. A., Miller, M. D., Wolff, E. J., & Landry, K. (2004). HIV/AIDS and the teachers of young children. *Early Childhood Development and Care, 174*(3), 229–241.

Fraser, J. J., & Mcabee, G. N. (2004). Commission on Medical Liability. Dealing with the parent whose judgment is impaired by alcohol or drugs: Legal and ethical considerations. *Pediatrics, 114*(3), 869–873.

Gold, R. (2004). What every teacher should know about infectious diseases. In R. H. A. Haslam & P. J. Valletutti (Eds.), *Medical problems in the classroom: The teacher's role in diagnosis and management* (4th ed., pp. 61–79). Austin, TX: PRO-ED.

Gostin, L. (2004). The interconnected epidemics of drug dependency and AIDS. In A. Alexandrova (Ed.), *AIDS, drugs and society* (Rev. ed., pp. 52–67). New York: The International Debate Education Association.

Heller, K. W., & Bigge, J. L. (2005). Augmentative and alternative communication. In S. J. Best, K. W. Heller, & J. L. Bigge, *Teaching individuals with physical or multiple disabilities* (pp. 227–274). Upper Saddle River, NJ: Pearson.

Howe, D. (2005). *Child abuse and neglect: Attachment, development, and intervention.* New York: Palgrave Macmillan.

Huffman, D. M., Fontaine, K. L., & Price, B. K. (2003). *Health problems in the classroom 6–12: An a–z reference guide for educators.* Thousand Oaks, CA: Corwin Press.

Israelsen, S. (2005, May 12). Therapy helping children with CP. *The Deseret News.*

Jaakkola, J. J. K., & Gissler, M. (2004). Maternal smoking in pregnancy, fetal development, and childhood asthma. *American Journal of Public Health, 94*(1), 136–140.

Katsiyannis, A., & Yell, M. L. (2000). The Supreme Court and school health services: *Cedar Rapids v. Garret F. Exceptional Children, 66*(3), 317–326.

Kelly, T. E. (2004). The role of genetic mechanisms in childhood disabilities. In R. H. Haslam & P. J. Valletutti (Eds.), *Medical problems in the classroom: The teacher's role in diagnosis and management* (4th ed., pp. 147–186). Austin, TX: PRO-ED.

Kent-Walsh, J. E., & Light, J. C. (2003, June). General education teachers' experiences with inclusion of students who use augmentative and alternative communication. *Augmentative and Alternative Communication, 19*(2), 104–124.

Klein, J. D. (2005, July). Adolescent pregnancy: Current trends and issues. *Pediatrics, 116*(1), 281–286.

Ladewig, P. W., London, M. L., & Davidson, M. R. (2006a). *Contemporary maternal-newborn nursing care* (6th ed.). Upper Saddle River, NJ: Pearson.

Ladewig, P. W., London, M. L., & Davidson, M. R. (2006b). Adolescent Pregnancy. In P. W. Ladewig, M. L. London, & M. R. Davidson, *Contemporary maternal-newborn nursing care* (6th ed., pp. 257–271). Upper Saddle River, NJ: Pearson.

Lehman, C. (2005). *Strong at the heart: How it feels to heal from sexual abuse.* New York: Melanie Kroupa Books.

Liptak, G. S. (2002). Neural tube defects. In M. L. Batshaw (Ed.), *Children*

with disabilities (5th ed., 592–552). Baltimore: Paul H. Brookes.

Liverman, C. T., Altevogt, B. M., Joy, J. E., & Johnson, R. T. (Eds.). (2005). *Spinal cord injury: Progress, promise, and priorities.* Washington, DC: National Academies Press.

London, M. L., Ladewig, P. W., Ball, J. W., & Bindler, R. M. (2003). *Maternal-newborn and child nursing: Family-centered care.* Upper Saddle River, NJ: Pearson.

Manford, M. (2003). *Practical guide to epilepsy.* Burlington, MA: Butterworth Heinemann.

Martin, S. (2006). *Teaching motor skills to children with cerebral palsy and similar movement disorders.* Bethesda: Woodbine House.

Miller, B. C., Sage, R., & Winward, B. (2005). Adolescent pregnancy. In T. P. Gullotta & G. R. Adams (Eds.), *Handbook of adolescent behavioral problems: Evidence-based approaches to prevention and treatment* (pp. 567–587). New York: Springer.

Milton, J., & Jung, P. (Eds.). (2003). *Epilepsy as a dynamic disease.* New York: Springer-Verlag.

Mittan, R. J. (2005a). Beating bad seizures. *The Exceptional Parent, 35*(6), 32–39.

Mittan, R. J. (2005b). S.E.E. program parents' manual: How to raise a child with epilepsy, part two: Coping with stigma. *The Exceptional Parent, 35*(11), 58–66.

Muscular Dystrophy Association. (2006). Medications. Retrieved August 16, 2006, from http://www.mda.org/publications/fa-dmdbmd-treat.html#meds

National Center for Biotechnology Information. (2006). *Duchenne muscular dystrophy.* Retrieved August 16, 2006, from http://www.ncbi.nlm.nih.gov/books/bv.fcgi? call=bv.View.ShowSection&rid=gnd.section.161

National Diabetes Education Program. (2006). *Overview of diabetes in children and adolescents.* Retrieved September 12, 2006, from http://www.ndep.nih.gov/diabetes/youth/youth_FS.htm#Type2

National Institute on Alcohol Abuse and Alcoholism. (2003). *Estimating the prevalence of fetal alcohol syndrome: A summary* [Online]. Retrieved June 7, 2003, from http://www.niaaa.nih.gov/publications/arh25–3/159–167.htm

National Institute of Neurological Disorders and Strokes. (2006a). *Seizures and epilepsy: Hope through research.* Retrieved August 21, 2006, from http://www.ninds.nih.gov/disorders/epilepsy/detail_epilepsy.htm

National Institute of Neurological Disorders and Stroke. (2006b). *What are the immediate treatments for spinal cord injury?* Retrieved August 16, 2006, from http://www.ninds.nih.gov/disorders/sci/detail_sci.htm#55653233

National Institute on Drug Abuse. (2003). *Principles of drug addiction treatment: A research based guide.* Retrieved June 6, 2003, from http://www.nida.nih.gov/PODAT/PODAT10.html#Matrix

National Institutes of Health. (2003). *NIH news release: Significant deficits in mental skills observed in toddlers exposed to cocaine before birth.* Retrieved June 6, 2003, from http://www.nih.gov/news/pr/apr2002/nida19.htm

Newcomb, M. D., & Locke, T. F. (2005). Childhood adversity and poor mothering: Consequences of polydrug abuse use as a moderator. *Addictive Behaviors, 30*(5), 1061–1064.

NICHY. (2006). *Spina bifida.* Retrieved on August 10, 2006, from http://www.nichcy.org/pubs/factshe/fs12txt.html

Nickel, R. E. (2000). Human immunodeficiency virus infection. In R. E. Nickel & L. W. Desch, (Eds.), *The physician's guide to caring for children with disabilites and chronic conditions* (pp. 391–424). Baltimore: Paul H. Brookes.

Noonan, K., Reichman, N., Corman, H., & Dave, D. (2005, June). Prenatal drug use and the production of infant health. In *NBER Working Paper Series.* Cambridge, MA: National Bureau of Economic Research.

O'Connor, L. A., Morgenstern, J., Gibson, F., & Nakashian, M. (2005). "Nothing about me without me": Leading the way to collaborative relationships with families. *Child Welfare, 84*(2), 153–170.

Odding, E., Roebroeck, M. E., & Stam, H. J. (2006, February 28). The epidemiology of cerebral palsy: Incidence, impairments and risk factors. *Disability Rehabilitation, 28*(4), 183–191.

Pellegrino, L. (2001). Cerebral palsy. In M. L. Batshaw (Ed.), *When your child has a disability* (pp. 275–287). Baltimore: Paul H. Brookes.

Piek, J. P. (2006). *Infant motor development.* Champaign, IL: Human Kinetics.

Public Broadcasting Service. (2006). *Independent lens: Independent living: Greg Smith.* Retrieved August 17, 2006, from http://www.pbs.org/independentlens/onaroll/greg.html

Rivera, K., & Oliden, F. (2006*). Children who are technologically dependent and medically fragile: Medical issues and health concerns.* Retrieved August 9, 2006, from http://www.csun.edu/~hfedu009/innovations/html/medicalresource.html

Roscigno, C. I. (2002). Addressing spasticity-related pain in children with spastic cerebral palsy. *Journal of Neuroscience Nursing, 34*(3), 123–133.

Scannapieco, M., & Connell-Carrick, K. (2005). *Understanding child maltreatment: An ecological and developmental perspective.* New York: Oxford University Press.

Schilling, R., Mares, A., & El-Bassel, N. (2004). Women in detoxification: Loss of guardianship of their children. *Children and Youth Services Review, 26*(5), 463–480.

Shouldice, M. (2004). Chronic illness in children. In R. H. A. Haslam & P. J. Valletutti (Eds.), *Medical problems in the classroom: The teacher's role in diagnosis and management* (4th ed., pp. 131–146). Austin, TX: PRO-ED.

Sickle Cell Information Center. (2006). What is sickle cell anemia? Retrieved August 24, 2006, from http://www.scinfo.org/sicklept.htm

Silverman, E. K., Shapiro, S. D., Lomas, D. A., & Weiss, S. T. (Eds.). (2005). *Respiratory Genetics.* London: Hodder Education.

Smith, A., Krisman, K., Strozier, A. L., & Marley, M. A. (2004). Breaking through the bars: Exploring the experiences of addicted incarcerated parents whose children are cared for by relatives. *Families in Society, 85*(2), 187–195.

Spina Bifida Association of America. (2006a). *What can be done to reduce the risk?* Retrieved August 10, 2006, from http://www.sbaa.org/site/PageServer?pagename=nrc_faqreducerisk

Spina Bifida Association of America. (2006b). *How often does spina bifida occur?* Retrieved August 10, 2006, from http://www.sbaa.org/site/PageServer?pagename=nrc_faqoccurrence

Spina Bifida Association of America. (2006c). *About spina bifida.* Retrieved August 10, 2006, from http://www.sbaa.org/site/PageServer?pagename=about_sb

Spinal Cord Injury Information Network. (2006). *Facts and figures at a glance—June 2005.* Retrieved on August 11, 2006, from http://www.spinalcord.uab.edu/show.asp?durki=21446

Spinal Cord Injury Resource Center. (2006). *Spinal cord 101.* Retrieved on August 15, 2006, from http://www.spinalinjury.net/html/_spinal_cord_101.html

Statham J. (2004). Effective services to support children in special circumstances. *Child: Care, Health and Development, 30*(6), 589–598.

Street, K., Harrington, J., Chiang, W., Cairns, P., & Ellis, M. (2004). How great is the risk of abuse in infants born to drug-using mothers? *Child: Care, Health and Development, 30*(4), 325–330.

Tinkelman, D., & Schwartz, A. (2004). School-based asthma disease management. *Journal of Asthma, 41*(4), 455–462.

United Cerebral Palsy. (2006). *Cerebral palsy—Facts & figures.* Retrieved on August 10, 2006, from http://www.ucp.org/ucp_generaldoc.cfm/1/9/37/37-37/447

U.S. Department of Health and Human Services. (2006). *Child Mal-*

treatment 2004. Retrieved August 25, 2006, from http://www.acf.hhs.gov/programs/cb/pubs/cm04/index.htm

U.S. Department of Health and Human Services. (2003). *In Focus: The risk and prevention of maltreatment of children with disabilities.* Retrieved June 5, 2003, from http://www.calib.com/nccanch/prevention/publications/risk.cfm#scope

Valletutti, P. J. (2004). The crucial role of the teacher. In R. H. A. Haslam & P. J. Valletutti (Eds.), *Medical problems in the classroom: The teacher's role in diagnosis and management* (4th ed., pp. 1–28). Austin, TX: PRO-ED.

Velez, M. L., Montoya, I. D., Jansson, L. M., Walters, V., Svikis, D., Jones, H. E., Chilcoat, H., & Campbell, J. (2006). Exposure to violence among substance-dependent pregnant women and their children. *Journal of Substance Abuse Treatment, 30*(1), 31–38.

Wailoo, K., & Pemberton, S. (2006). *The troubled dream of genetic medicine.* Baltimore: John Hopkins University Press.

Westcott, S. L., & Goulet, C. (2005). Neuromuscular system: Structures, functions, diagnoses, and evaluation. In S. K. Effgen (Ed.), *Meeting the physical therapy needs of children* (pp. 185–244). Philadelphia: F. A. Davis.

Wheeler, L. S., Boss, L. P., & Williams, P. V. (2004). School-based approaches to identifying students with asthma. *Journal of School Health, 74*(9), 378–380.

Wolf, R. L. (2004). *Essential pediatric allergy, asthma, and immunology.* New York: McGraw-Hill.

Yarkony, G. M., Gittler, M. S., & Weiss, D. J. (2002). Pain syndromes following spinal cord injury. In T. N Monga & M. Grabois (Eds.), *Pain management in rehabilitation* (pp. 56–72). New York: Demos Medical.

CHAPTER 18

Adams, C. M. (2006). Articulating gifted education program goals. In J. H. Purcell & R. D. Eckert (Eds.), *Designing services and programs for high-ability learners: A guidebook for gifted education* (pp. 62–72). Thousand Oaks, CA: Corwin Press.

Aguirre, N. (2003). ESL students in gifted education. In J. A. Castellano (Ed.), *Special populations in gifted education: Working with diverse gifted learners* (pp. 17–27). New York: Pearson.

Assouline, S. G. (2003). Psychological and educational assessment of gifted children. In N. Colangelo & G. A. Davis (Eds.), *Handbook of gifted education* (pp. 124–145). Boston: Pearson.

Baldus, C. (2003). Gifted education in rural schools. In J. A. Castellano (Ed.), *Special populations in gifted education: Working with diverse gifted learners* (pp. 163–176). New York: Pearson.

Baldwin, A. Y. (Ed.). (2004). Introduction to culturally diverse and underserved populations of gifted students [Introduction]. In *Culturally diverse and underserved populations of gifted students* (pp. xxiii–xxxi). Thousand Oaks, CA: Corwin Press.

Baum, S. (Ed.). (2004). Introduction to twice-exceptional and special populations of gifted students [Introduction]. In *Twice-exceptional and special populations of gifted students* (pp. xxiii–xxxiii). Thousand Oaks, CA: Corwin Press.

Binet, A., & Simon, T. (1905). Méthodes nouvelles pour le diagnostique du nivea intellectual des anomaux. *L'Année Psychologique, 11,* 196–198.

Binet, A., & Simon, T. (1908). Le dévelopment de l'intelligence chez les enfants. *L'Année Psychologique, 14,* 1–94.

Borland, J. H. (2003). Evaluating gifted programs: A broader perspective. In N. Colangelo & G. A. Davis (Eds.), *Handbook of gifted education* (pp. 293–307). Boston: Pearson.

Briggs, C. J., Reis, S. M., Eckert, R. D., & Baum, S. (2006). Providing programs for special populations of gifted and talented students. In J. H. Purcell & R. D. Eckert (Eds.), *Designing services and programs for high-ability learners: A guidebook for gifted education* (pp. 32–48). Thousand Oaks, CA: Corwin Press.

Brody, L. E. (Ed.). (2004). Introduction to grouping and acceleration practices in gifted education [Introduction]. In *Grouping and acceleration practices in gifted education* (pp.xxiii–xxxii). Thousand Oaks, CA: Corwin Press.

Burns, D. E., Purcell, J. H., & Hertberg, H. L. (2006). Curriculum for gifted education students. In J. H. Purcell & R. D. Eckert (Eds.), *Designing services and programs for high-ability learners: A guidebook for gifted education* (pp. 87–111). Thousand Oaks, CA: Corwin Press.

Callahan, C. M. (Ed.). (2004). Introduction to program evaluation in gifted education [Introduction]. In *Program evaluation in gifted education* (pp. xxiii–xxxi). Thousand Oaks, CA: Corwin Press.

Callard-Szulgit, R. (2003a). *Parenting and teaching the gifted.* Lanham, MD: Scarecrow Press.

Callard-Szulgit, R. (2003b). *Perfectionism and gifted children.* Lanham, MD: Scarecrow Press.

Cattell, R. B. (1971). *Abilities: Their structure, growth, and action.* Boston: Houghton Mifflin.

Chuska, K. R. (2005). *Gifted learners K–12: A practical guide to effective* curriculum and teaching (2nd ed.). Bloomington, IN: National Educational Service.

Clark, B. (1997). *Growing up gifted* (5th ed.). Columbus, OH: Merrill.

Clasen, D. R., & Clasen, R. E. (2003). Mentoring the gifted and talented. In N. Colangelo & G. A. Davis (Eds.), *Handbook of gifted education* (3rd ed., pp. 254–267). Boston: Pearson.

Colangelo, N. (2003). Counseling gifted students. In N. Colangelo & G. A. Davis (Eds.), *Handbook of gifted education* (3rd ed., pp. 373–387). Boston: Pearson.

Colangelo, N., & Davis, G. A. (2003). *Handbook of gifted education* (3rd ed.). Boston: Allyn and Bacon.

Coleman, L. J. (2005). *Nurturing talent in high school: Life in the fast lane.* New York: Teachers College Press.

Conant, J. B. (1959). *The American high school today.* New York: McGraw-Hill.

Cooper, C. R. (2004). For the good of humankind: Matching the budding talent with a curriculum of conscience. In J. J. Gallagher (Ed.), *Public policy in gifted education* (pp. 147–158). Thousand Oaks, CA: Corwin Press.

Cooper, C. R. (2006). Creating a comprehensive and defensible budget for gifted programs and services. In J. H. Purcell & R. D. Eckert (Eds.), *Designing services and programs for high-ability learners: A guidebook for gifted education* 31 (pp. 125–136). Thousand Oaks, CA: Corwin Press.

Cusick, P. A. (2005). *A passion for learning: The education of seven eminent Americans.* New York: Teachers College Press.

Davis, G. A., & Rimm, S. B. (2004). *Education of the gifted and talented* (5th ed.). San Francisco: Allyn and Bacon.

DeHann, R., & Havighurst, R. J. (1957). *Educating gifted children.* Chicago, IL: University of Chicago Press.

DeLacy, M. (2004, June 23). The "No Child" law's biggest victims? An answer that may surprise. *Education Week, 23*(41), 40.

Eckert, R. D. (2006). Developing a mission statement on the educational needs of gifted and talented students. In J. H. Purcell & R. D. Eckert (Eds.), *Designing services and programs for high-ability learners: A guidebook for gifted education* (pp. 15–22). Thousand Oaks, CA: Corwin Press.

Esquivel, G. B., & Houtz, J. C. (Eds.). (2000). *Creativity and giftedness in culturally diverse students.* Cresskill, NJ: Hampton Press.

Feldhusen, J. F. (1998a). Programs and services at the elementary level. In J. VanTassel-Baska (Ed.), *Excellence in educating gifted and talented learners* (3rd ed., pp. 211–223). Denver: Love.

Feldhusen, J. F. (1998b). Programs and services at the elementary level. In

J. VanTassel-Baska (Ed.), *Excellence in educating gifted and talented learners* (3rd ed., pp. 235–240). Denver: Love.

Feldhusen, J. F. (2003). Talented youth at the secondary level. In N. Colangelo & G. A. Davis (Eds.), *Handbook of gifted education* (3rd ed., pp. 229–237). Boston: Pearson.

Ford, D. Y. (2003). Equity and excellence: Culturally diverse students in gifted education. In N. Colangelo & G. A. Davis (Eds.), *Handbook of gifted education* (3rd ed., pp. 506–520). Boston: Pearson.

Gagné, F. (1999a). Is there any light at the end of the tunnel? *Journal for the Education of the Gifted, 22*(2), 191–234.

Gagné, F. (1999b). My convictions about the nature of abilities, gifts, and talents. *Journal for the Education of the Gifted, 22*(2), 109–136.

Gagné, F. (2003). Transforming gifts into talents: The DMGT as a developmental theory. In N. Colangelo & G. A. Davis (Eds.), *Handbook of gifted education* (3rd ed., pp. 60–74). Boston: Pearson.

Gallagher, J. J. (2003). Issues and challenges in the education of gifted students. In N. Colangelo & G. A. Davis (Eds.), *Handbook of gifted education* (3rd ed., pp. 11–23). Boston: Pearson.

Gallagher, J. J. (Ed.). (2004). *Public policy in gifted education. In Essential Readings in Gifted Education.* Thousand Oaks, CA: Corwin Press.

Gardner, H. (1983). *Frames of mind: The theory of multiple intelligences.* New York: Basic Books.

Gottfredson, L. S. (2003). The science and politics of intelligence in gifted education. In N. Colangelo & G. A. Davis (Eds.), *Handbook of gifted education* (3rd ed., pp. 24–40). Boston: Pearson.

Gubbins, E. J. (2006). Constructing identification procedures. In J. H. Purcell & R. D. Eckert (Eds.), *Designing services and programs for high-ability learners: A guidebook for gifted education* (pp. 49–61). Thousand Oaks, CA: Corwin Press.

Guilford, J. P. (1950). Creativity. *American Psychologist, 5,* 444–454.

Guilford, J. P. (1959). Three faces of intellect. *American Psychologist, 14,* 469–479.

Jackson, N. E. (2003). Young gifted children. In N. Colangelo & G. A. Davis (Eds.), *Handbook of gifted education* (3rd ed., pp. 470–482). Boston: Pearson.

Jin, S., & Feldhusen, J. F. (2000). Parent identification of the talents of gifted students. *Gifted Education International, 14,* 230–236.

Karnes, F. A., & Bean, S. M. (Eds.). (2001). *Methods and materials for teaching the gifted.* Waco, TX: Prufrock Press.

Kerr, B. A., & Nicpon, M. F. (2003). Gender and giftedness. In

N. Colangelo & G. A. Davis (Eds.), *Handbook of gifted education* (3rd ed., pp. 493–505). Boston: Allyn and Bacon.

Kolloff, P. B. (2003). State-supported residential high school. In N. Colangelo & G. A. Davis (Eds.), *Handbook of gifted education* (3rd ed., pp. 238–246). Boston: Pearson.

Kulik, J. A. (2003). Grouping and tracking. In N. Colangelo & G. A. Davis (Eds.), *Handbook of gifted education* (3rd ed., pp. 268–281). Boston: Pearson.

Landrum, M. S. (2006). Identifying student cognitive and affective needs. In J. H. Purcell & R. D. Eckert (Eds.), *Designing services and programs for high-ability learners: A guidebook for gifted education* (pp. 1–14). Thousand Oaks, CA: Corwin Press.

Leppien, J. H., & Westberg, K. L. (2006). Roles, responsibilities, and professional qualifications of key personnel for gifted education services. In J. H. Purcell & R. D. Eckert (Eds.), *Designing services and programs for high-ability learners: A guidebook for gifted education* (pp. 161–182). Thousand Oaks, CA: Corwin Press.

MacKinnon, D. W. (1962). The nature and nurture of creative talent. *American Psychologist, 17*(7), 484–495.

Maltby, F., & Devlin, M. (2000). Breaking through the glass ceiling without bruising: The breakthrough programme for high ability girls. *Gifted Education International, 14,* 112–124.

Montgomery, D. (2003). *Gifted & talented children with special education needs.* London: David Fulton.

Moon, S. M. (Ed.). (2004). Social and emotional issues, underachievement, and counseling [Introduction]. In *Social/emotional issues, underachievement, and counseling of gifted and talented students* (pp. xxiii–xxxviii). Thousand Oaks, CA: Corwin Press.

Moon, S. M. (2006). Developing a definition of giftedness. In J. H. Purcell & R. D. Eckert (Eds.), *Designing services and programs for high-ability learners: A guidebook for gifted education* (pp. 23–31). Thousand Oaks, CA: Corwin Press.

National Association for Gifted Children. (2007). *Background information: The No Child Left Behind Act, "Does the No Child Left Behind Act 'do' anything for gifted students?"* Retrieved January 8, 2006, from http://www.nagc.org/CMS400Min/index.aspx?id=999

Newman, T. M., & Sternberg, R. J. (Eds.). (2004). Students with both gifts and learning disabilities: Identification, assessment, and outcomes. In *Neuropsychology and Cognition.* New York: Kluwer Academic/Plenum.

No Child Left Behind Act of 2001, Pub. L. no. 107-110, 115 Stat 1959 (2002).

Olshen, S. R. (1987). The disappearance of giftedness in girls: An intervention strategy. *Roeper-Review, 9*(4), 251–254.

Olszewski-Kubilius, P. (2003). Special summer and Saturday programs for gifted students. In N. Colangelo & G. A. Davis (Eds.), *Handbook of gifted education* (3rd ed., pp. 219–228). Boston: Pearson.

Parke, B. N. (2003). *Discovering programs for talent development.* Thousand Oaks, CA: Corwin Press.

Passow, A. H. (2004). The nature of giftedness and talent. In R. J. Sternberg (Ed.), *Definitions and conceptions of giftedness* (pp. 1–11). Thousand Oaks, CA: Corwin Press.

Piirto, J. (1999). *Talented children and adults: Their development and education.* Upper Saddle River, NJ: Prentice-Hall.

Plomin, R., & Price, T. S. (2003). The relationship between genetics and intelligence. In N. Colangelo & G. A. Davis (Eds.), *Handbook of gifted education* (3rd ed., pp. 113–123). Boston: Pearson.

Ramos-Ford, V., & Gardner, H. (1991). Giftedness from a multiple intelligences perspective. In N. Colangelo & G. A. Davis (Eds.), *Handbook of gifted education* (pp. 55–64). Boston: Allyn and Bacon.

Ramos-Ford, V., & Gardner, H. (1997). Giftedness from a multiple intelligences perspective. In N. Colangelo & G. A. Davis (Eds.), *Handbook of gifted education* (2nd ed., pp. 54–66). Boston: Allyn and Bacon.

Reis, S. M. (2003). Gifted girls, twenty-five years later: Hopes realized and new challenges found. *Roeper Review, 25*(4), 154–157.

Renzulli, J. S. (Ed.) (2004). Identification of students for gifted and talented programs. In *Essential Readings in Gifted Education.* Thousand Oaks, CA: Corwin Press.

Renzulli, J. S., & Reis, S. M. (2003). The schoolwide enrichment model: Developing creative and productive giftedness. In N. Colangelo & G. A. Davis (Eds.), *Handbook of gifted education* (3rd ed., pp. 184–203). Boston: Pearson.

Richert, E. S. (2003). Excellence with justice in identification and programming. In N. Colangelo & G. A. Davis (Eds.), *Handbook of gifted education* (3rd ed., pp. 146–161). Boston: Pearson.

Rimm, S. B. (1982). *PRIDE: Preschool and primary interest descriptor.* Watertown, WI: Educational Assessment Service.

Rimm, S. B., & Davis, G. A. (1983, September/October). Identifying creativity, Part II. *G/C/T, 19*–23.

Rogers, K. B. (2006). Connecting program design and district policies. In J. H. Purcell & R. D. Eckert (Eds.), *Designing services and* programs for high-ability learners: A guidebook for gifted education (pp. 207–223). Thousand Oaks, CA: Corwin Press.

Ross, P. O. (1993). National excellence: A case for developing America's talent. Washington, DC: Office of Educational Research and Improvement, U.S. Department of Education.

Schiever, S. W., & Maker, C. J. (2003). New directions in enrichment and acceleration. In N. Colangelo & G. A. Davis (Eds.), Handbook of gifted education (3rd ed., pp. 163–173). Boston: Pearson.

Silverman, L. K. (1986). What happens to the gifted girl? In C. J. Maker (Ed.), Critical issues in gifted education: Defensible programs for the gifted, Vol. 1 (pp. 43–89). Austin, TX: PRO-ED.

Smutny, J. F. (Ed.). (2003). Underserved gifted populations: Responding to their needs and abilities. Cresskill, NJ: Hampton Press.

Sternberg, R. J. (1997). A triarchic view of giftedness: Theory and practice. In N. Colangelo & G. A Davis (Eds.), Handbook of gifted education (2nd ed., pp. 43–53). Boston: Allyn and Bacon.

Sternberg, R. J. (2006, February 22). Creativity is a habit. Education Week, 25(24), 64.

Tannenbaum, A. J. (2003). Nature and nurture of giftedness. In N. Colangelo & G. A Davis (Eds.), Handbook of gifted education (3rd ed., pp. 45–59). Boston: Allyn and Bacon.

Terman, L. M. (1925). Genetic studies of genius: Vol. 1. Mental and physical traits of a thousand gifted children. Stanford, CA: Stanford University Press.

Tomlinson, C. A., Doubet, K. J., & Capper, M. R. (2006). Aligning gifted education services with general education. In J. H. Purcell & R. D. Eckert (Eds.), Designing services and programs for high-ability learners: A guidebook for gifted education (pp. 224–238). Thousand Oaks, CA: Corwin Press.

Torrance, E. P. (1961). Problems of highly creative children. Gifted Child Quarterly, 5, 31–34.

Torrance, E. P. (1965). Gifted children in the classroom. New York: Macmillan.

Torrance, E. P. (1966). Torrance tests of creative thinking. Bensenville, IL: Scholastic Testing Service.

Torrance, E. P. (1968). Finding hidden talent among disadvantaged children. Gifted and Talented Quarterly, 12, 131–137.

Treffinger, D. J. (2004). Creativity and giftedness. In Essential Readings in Gifted Education. Thousand Oaks, CA: Corwin Press.

VanTassel-Baska, J. (1989). Counseling the gifted. In J. Feldhusen, J. VanTassel-Baska, & K. Seeley (Eds.), Excellence in educating the gifted. Denver, CO: Love.

VanTassel-Baska, J. (2003). Content-based curriculum for high-ability learners: An introduction. In J. VanTassel-Baska & C. A. Little (Eds.), Content-based curriculum for high-ability learners. Waco, TX: Prufrock Press.

VanTassel-Baska, J. (Ed.). (2004). Introduction to curriculum for gifted and talented students: A 25-year retrospective and prospective [Introduction]. In Curriculum for gifted and talented students (pp. xxiii–xxxiii). Thousand Oaks, CA: Corwin Press.

VanTassel-Baska, J., & Chepko-Sade, D. (1986). An incidence study of disadvantaged gifted students in the Midwest. Evanston, IL: Center for Talent Development, Northwestern University.

VanTassel-Baska, J., & Stambaugh, T. (2006). Comprehensive curriculum for gifted learners (3rd ed.). Boston: Pearson.

Williams, F. E. (1980). Creativity assessment packet. East Aurora, NY: DOK.

Winner, E., Martino, G. (2003). Artistic giftedness. In N. Colangelo & G. A. Davis (Eds.), Handbook of gifted education (pp. 335–349). Boston: Pearson.

Zimmerman, E. (2004). Introduction to artistically and musically talented students [Introduction]. In Artistically and musically talented students (pp. xxiii–xxxiv). Thousand Oaks, CA: Corwin Press.

Author Index

Abbacchi, A., 359
Abbeduto, L., 357
ABCNEWS.com, 346
Abell, F., 353
Abernathy, T.J., 127
Abikoff, H.B., 217, 220
Abramowitz, A.J., 214
Abramson, R.K., 356, 357
Abt Associates, 324
Achenbach, T.M., 230
Adamo, M., 357
Adams, B.E., 193, 194
Adams, C.M., 512
Adams, G., 80
Adams, J.F., 152
Adams, M., 391
Addy, C.L., 116
Adelman, H.S., 246, 247
Adler, L.A., 205, 210
Advocates for Youth, 467
Affleck, G., 138
Aguirre, N., 490, 519
Ahlgrim-Delzell, L., 96, 272, 284
Aiken, L.R., 179
Ainbinder, J., 152
Airasian, P.W., 179
Akshoomoff, N., 357
Ala'i-Rosales, S.S., 358
Alant, E., 118, 121, 186
Albertini, J.A., 399, 402
Alberto, P., 160, 183, 191
Albin, R.W., 69, 329
Aleardi, M., 216
Alexander, C.P., 171
Alexander, L.B., 298
Algozzine, B., 96, 226
Algozzine, R., 235
Alison, R., 303
Allsopp, D.H., 198
Alm, P.A., 308
Altarriba, J., 118
Altevogt, B.M., 459, 460
Altshuler, S.J., 485
Aman, M.G., 353, 361
Ambalavanan, G., 210
American Academy of
    Pediatrics, 482
American Association on
    Intellectual and Devel-
    opmental Disabilities

(AAIDD), 265, 266, 267
American Association on
    Mental Retardation
    (AAMR), 277
American College of Obste-
    tricians and Gynecolo-
    gists, 485
American Diabetes Associa-
    tion, 473, 474
American Foundation for the
    Blind, 438
American Psychiatric Associa-
    tion, 165, 207, 208,
    209, 307, 311, 349,
    350, 351
Amerine-Dickens, M., 361
Amorosa, H., 300
Anckarsater, H., 349, 358
Anderson, J.A., 239, 246
Anderson, J.R., 310
Anderson, K., 371, 374
Anderson, K.G., 239
Anderson, K.V., 116
Anderson, N.B., 292, 298,
    300, 302
Anderson, R.T., 317
Andres, C., 357
Angelucci, J.G., 211, 212, 213
Annoussamy, D., 301, 310
Anton, G., 138
Antonellis, S., 310
ARC, The, 86, 273, 274,
    327, 335, 339, 340
Archibald, S.J., 216
Ardoin, S.P., 182
Arick, J.R., 359
Arlingaus, K.A., 370
ARMC News, 202
Armento, B.J., 122
Armstrong, K.H., 247
Arnold, F.W., 359, 361
Arnold, L.E., 215, 220, 353,
    361
Arredondo, P., 114
Artiles, A.J., 235, 244
Ashley, D.M., 213
Ashman, A.F., 64
Assouline, S.G., 514
Asthma and Allergy Founda-
    tion of America, 469

Atkinson, D., 196
Atkinson, L., 66
Auditory-Verbal Interna-
    tional, 406
Ault, M.M., 328
Autism Society of Michigan, 2

Babbitt, B.C., 90, 94, 95
Baca, E., 118
Baca, L., 118, 120, 125
Baca, L.M., 122, 124
Bacon, C.K., 298, 302, 309
Baddeley, A.D., 172, 175
Baglin, C.A., 154
Bahan, B., 59
Bahr, R.H., 173
Bailey, P., 313
Bailey, S., 192
Baird, G., 210, 351, 359
Bak, S., 271
Baker, B.L., 141
Baker, H.C., 351
Baker, L., 191
Baldo, J., 311
Baldwin, A.Y., 519
Baldwin, J.R., 114
Ball, J.W., 482
Balottin, U., 206
Baltodano, H.M, 240, 247,
    249
Bambara, L.M., 96
Banks, C.A., 110, 116, 124
Banks, J.A., 110, 116, 124
Banks, M.E., 139, 140
Bantz, J., 254, 258, 259
Baptista, P.M., 351
Barac-Cikoja, D., 295
Baranowski, M.D., 148
Barber, B.K., 239
Barcalow, K., 359
Barclay, L.A., 429
Barke, C.R., 213
Barkley, R., 210, 214
Barkley, R.A., 177, 202, 204,
    205, 209, 210, 215,
    217, 221
Barnard, M., 483
Barnum-Martin, L., 118
Baron, R.A., 6
Baron-Cohen, S., 351, 356,
    357, 358

Barr, C.L., 216
Barraga, N.C., 431
Barranti, C.C.R., 128
Barrera, M., 118
Barrett, K.H., 120
Barrett, L.F., 175, 176
Barrett, M., 353
Barry, T.D., 213
Bartens, A., 298
Barth, A., 179
Barton-Arwood, S.M., 237,
    249
Baskin, A., 136, 137, 138,
    141, 143, 150
Bass, M.P., 356, 357
Basso, A., 300, 301
Bassuk, E.L., 116, 128
Batshaw, M., 65, 279, 331,
    428
Batshaw, M.L., 426, 427
Battle, D.E., 121, 317
Bauer, A.M., 124
Baum, S., 496, 502, 504,
    505, 518, 519, 520
Baum, S.M., 176
Bauminger, N., 175, 181,
    348, 351, 361
Baxter, C., 138
Baxter, J.A., 172
Bayliss, D.M., 172, 175
Bean, S.M., 507, 509
Bear, G.G., 177
Beard, K.Y., 249, 254
Beaty, B.L., 483
Beaumont, R., 351, 358
Beck, A., 136
Becker, J., 175
Becker-Blease, K.A., 217
Beckingham, B., 173
Beeghly, M., 359
Beegle, G., 150
Begeer, S., 351
Begeny, J.C., 169, 170
Beidel, D.C., 116
Beirne-Smith, M., 270, 271,
    284, 325
Beitchman, J.H., 311
Bender, W.N., 169, 170,
    173, 175, 178, 189,
    190, 191, 194
Benitez, D.T., 256

AUTHOR INDEX 587

Subject Index

Page numbers in **bold** indicate definitions; page numbers followed by *f* or *t* indicate figures or tables, respectively

Adulthood (continued)
person-centered approach to transition planning, 91–94
planning and services, 90–91
secondary school's role, 94–101
Adult service agencies, **93**, 93–94
Adult services, 103–105
Advocacy groups
for the blind, 436
family advocates, 253–254
history of, 9
African Americans. *See also* Cultural diversity; Minorities, cultural and ethnic
dropout rates of, 116
in gifted programs, 116
overrepresentation in special education, 115–116, 117
parents, 122
population growth, 116–117
in poverty, 126
role in American history, 114
sickle cell anemia in, 478
African Americans
emotional and behavioral disorders, 235
AFT. *See* Alfa-fetoprotein (AFT)
Age-appropriate classrooms in neighborhood school, 59
Age-appropriate placement, 70–**71**
Age of onset
of hearing loss, 395
for mental retardation, 267
Aggression
ADHD and, 214
conduct disorder and, 231, 239
socialized, 231, **236**
undersocialized, 237
AIDS. *See* Acquired immunodeficiency syndrome (AIDS)
Air Carrier Access Act, 14
Albert, conditioning experiment with, 18
Albinism, **427**
Alcohol-related birth defects (ARBD), 483
Alcohol-related neurodevelopmental disorder (ARND), 483
Alcohol use/abuse
fetal alcohol effects (FAE) and, 277
fetal alcohol syndrome (FAS) and, **277**, 483
learning disabilities and, 192
maternal, 277, 483–485
Alexander Graham Bell Association for the Deaf and the Hard of Hearing, 416
website, 419

Alfa-fetoprotein (AFT), 457
AllRefer.com website, 319
Alternate assessments, **36**, 182, **330**
Alternative communication. *See* Augmentative communication
Amblyopia, **426**
American Academy of Pediatrics, 209*f*
American Association on Intellectual and Developmental disabilities (AAIDD), **265**
definition of mental retardation, 265–267
website, 290
American Association on Mental Deficiency, 9
American Association on Mental Retardation, 9n. *See* American Association on Intellectual and Developmental disabilities (AAIDD)
American Federation for the Blind, 9
American Foundation for Suicide Prevention website, 488
American Foundation for the Blind website, 446
American Indians, 123, 298
American Printing House for the Blind, 436
website, 446
American Psychiatric Association (APA), 9, 165
definition of ADHD, 207
DSM-IV-TR, 231–234
American Sign Language, 402, **407**–410, 408*f*, 409*f*
American Sign Language Browser, 411
American Speech-Hearing-language Association (ASHA) website, 419
Americans with Disabilities Act (1990), 10, **10**–12, 26*t*, 91
closed-captioning and, 411
comparison of IDEA with, 48*t*
definition of disability, 11
enforcing compliance with, 14–16
public endorsement of, 10
purpose of, 10
reasonable accommodations, 12–14, 14, 194, 195
students with disabilities and, 48
text telephones in, **411**–412
website, 21
Analytic intelligence, 496
Anemia, **477**
sickle cell, 450, **477**–478
Anencephaly, **278**
Anophthalmia, **427**
Anorexia nervosa, 232

Anoxia, **278**
Antibiotics
for cystic fibrosis, 477
for sickle cell anemia, 478
Anticonvulsants, **277**, 472
Antidepressants, 218*t*
Antipsychotic drugs, 361
Antiretroviral therapies to combat AIDS, 467
Anti-Rh gamma globulin (Rhogam), 277, 397
Antisocial behaviors, 239–240
ADHD and, 212, 214–215
Anxiety, sibling's feelings of, 145
Anxiety disorders, 231, 233–234
Anxiety-withdrawal, 231, 236
Aphasia, 163, **300, 373**
expressive, **373**
interventions to remediate, 303–304
APSE, The Network on Employment website, 107
ARC, A National Organization on Mental Retardation, 9n, **269**
website, 290
Arithmetic learning disabilities, 173–174, 186
Arithmetic skills. *See* Mathematics
Articulation problems, **272**, 307, 311–317
causation, 311–313
delayed speech *vs.,* 310
functional, **311**, 311–317
intervention, 313–317
Asian Americans, 122
Asperger syndrome, **349**, 350*t,* 352, 356
Assessment, 27, 34*t. See also specific disorders*
of ADHD, 210–213
alternate, **36**, 182, **330**
authentic, 72*t*, 182, **329**
of children's learning and development, 70
court cases on, 120
criterion-referenced, **179**, 180
cultural bias and error in, 120
curriculum-based (CBA), **79**–81, **179**
of emotional/behavioral disorders, 240–246
formal, 179–182
functional, **69**, 70*t*
functional behavioral (FBA), 241–243, 244*f,* 254
of giftedness, 504–507, 506*t*
informal, 179–182
insurance as factor in, 211

language differences and, 26t, 121–122
of learning disabilities, 167, 179–182
multidisciplinary, 29, 119–122
nondiscriminatory, 29, **119,** 119–121
norm-referenced, **179,** 180
preparation of professionals for, 122
for preschool special education services, 69
of severe and multiple disabilities, 329–330
strength-based, **243**
of student eligibility and educational need, 34t, 35
traditional, 79
vision loss and, 431
Assistive communication. *See* Augmentative communication
Assistive technology, **78**–79, 80, **268,** 333. *See also* Computer-assisted instruction
  Adeli Suit, 454
  autism spectrum disorder and, 364
  communication aids, 281, 284
  for hearing loss, 406, **410**–412, 410*f,* 416
  for language disorders, 304, 305
  severe and multiple disabilities and, 323, 333, 334–335
  transition services and, 287
  traumatic brain injury and, 371
  vision loss and, 431–433
  wheelchairs, 462
Association for Children with Learning Disabilities, 9
The Association for Persons with Severe Handicaps (TASH), 324–325
  definition of severe disabilities, 324–325
  website, 344
Asthma, 448, 468–470, 468*f*
Astigmatism, **425**
Ataxic cerebral palsy, 451
Athetoid cerebral palsy, 451
Athetosis, **328**
Atresia, **397**
Atropinization, **443**
Attachment
  mother-child, 142–143
  reactive attachment disorder, 234
Attention, selective, **175**
Attention-deficit and disruptive disorders, 232
Attention-deficit/hyperactivity disorder (ADHD), 177, 202–225, **204,** 232

in adolescence, 221, 223
in adulthood, 221, 223
assessment and diagnosis, 210–213
causes of, 216–223
characteristics, 213–214
definitions, 207–209
diagnostic criteria for, 207t, 208*f*
disabilities/conditions comorbid with, 205–207
in elementary school years, 217–221
emotional/behavioral disorders and, 237
gender and, 209–210
inclusion through lifespan of people with, 221–223
interventions for, 216–223
  classroom setting, 219–220
  medications, 197, 218
  multimodal treatments, 220
learning disabilities and, 177
as lifelong condition, 202, 204
prevalence estimates for, 209–210
subcategories of, 207
Attention problems, learning disabilities and, 175–176
Attitude of family toward exceptionality, 122
Audible traffic signals (ATS), 443
Audiogram, **415**
Audiologist, **415**
Audiometer, **415**
Audition, **392**. *See also* Hearing loss
Auditory aids for the blind, 436
Auditory approach to teaching communication skills, 406
Auditory association, **176**
Auditory blending, **176**
Auditory discrimination, **176**
Auditory memory, **176**
Auditory perception problems, 176
Augmentative communication, **304,** 305, 334–335, **335,** 453–454
Aura, **470**
Auricle, 393
Authentic assessment, 72t, 182, **329**
Autism, **28**. *See also* Autism spectrum disorder
  definition, **349**
Autism Resources website, 367
Autism Society of America, 365
  website, 367
Autism spectrum disorder, 231, 346–367
  causation, 356–358
  characteristics, 351–356
    diagnostic criteria, 350t
    impaired or delayed language, 352

intelligence, 353–354
learning characteristics, 355–356
resistance to change in routine, 343
self-stimulation, 353, 364
stereotypic behavior, **352**–353
definition, **349,** 349–351
impact on family, 365–366
inclusion and, 362–363
interventions, 358–359
  behavioral, 361–365
  educational, 359–360
  psychological and medical, 360–361
prevalence, 351
Autism Web website, 367
Automobile-related accidents, traumatic brain injury and, 375–378

Baby Bumblebee website, 321
Baby-sitter, finding, 142
Baby talk, 313
Background knowledge, use in reading, 171
Barrier-free community, 11, 14
Barrier-free facility, **14**
Basal ganglia, **216**
Basal readers, 186–187
BASC-TRS. *See* Behavior Assessment System for Children-Teacher Rating Scales (BASC-TRS)
Beach Center website, 158
BEH, 25
Behavioral approach, 238
Behavioral contracts, **189**
Behavioral factors
  in emotional and behavioral disorders, 241–243
  in mental retardation, **277**
  in traumatic brain injury, 372, 373t, 374
Behavioral inhibition, ADHD and difficulty in, 216–217
Behavioral intervention plan, 34, 242–243
Behavioral therapy/treatment, 249
  for autism, 361–365
  cognitive-behavioral therapy, **247**
  for learning disabilities, 189
  positive behavioral support (PBS), 151, 244–246, 253–254
  for stuttering, 308–309
  Videx TimeWand for data collection in, 364
Behavior and Emotional Rating Scale (BERS), 243, 245*f*
Behavior Assessment System for Children-Teacher Rating Scales (BASC-TRS), 211

sexual, 479, **479**
traumatic brain injury and, 375
Child Abuse and Prevention Treatment Act (CAPTA), 479
Child Behavior Checklist (CBCL), 211
example of profile, 212
representative items, 245*f*
Childbirth. *See* Birth
Child care
finding baby-sitters, 142
involvement of fathers, 141, 143–144
Child-find system, **68**
Child management, emotional/behavioral disorders and, 239–240
Child neglect, 126, 240, **479**, 479–482, **480**
Children. *See also* Adolescent(s); Early childhood; Elementary school; Infant(s) and toddlers; *specific disabilities*
bringing about change for, 63–65
legal precedents affecting, 26, 26*t*, 64–65
in poverty (*See* Poverty)
Children's Television Workshop, 155
Children with Disabilities website, 158
Child Welfare Information Gateway website, 488
Choice making, promoting, 97*f*
Christopher Reeve Foundation, 461
website, 488
Chromosomal abnormalities, **274–275,** 457
Circle of friends/circle of support, **93**
Civil rights, 9. *See also* Americans with Disabilities Act (1990)
Civil Rights Act (1964), **10**
Class as community, 72*t*
Cleft palate, **311,** 312, 312*f,* 319
surgery for, 312, 313–317
Clinical interview in ADHD assessment, 213
Clinically derived classification systems, 231–234
Clomipramine, 361
Clonic phase, **470**
Closed-caption television, **410**–411, 410*f*
Closed-circuit television (CCTV), **437**
Closed-head injury, 378, 379*f. See also* Traumatic brain injury
Cluttering, **306**
CMV. *See* Cytomegalovirus (CMV)
Cocaine, maternal use of, 483, 484*f*
Cochlea, 393–394
Cochlear implant, 410*f,* **413**–414, 415*f*

Cognition, **175**. *See also* Intelligence
learning disabilities and, 175–176
traumatic brain injury and, 372, 373*t*
Cognitive-behavioral therapies, ADHD and, 220
Cognitive-behavioral therapy, **247**
Cognitive coping, 138
Cognitive instruction, learning disabilities and, 183
Collaboration, **60**–64
in inclusive preschool program, 72*t*
key characteristics, 60–64
models of professional, 63*t*
between parents and professionals, 61, 150–151
special educator's role as collaborator, 73–74
training for professionals in, 154–155
Collaboration, needs of culturally and linguistically diverse students, 119–122
Collaborative ethic, 60
College
giftedness and early enrollment in, 513–514
learning disabilities in, 193
transition to, 86, 95*f,* 192–195
Coma, 375, 380
diabetic, 473
Glasgow Coma Scale, 377*t*
Communication
augmentative, **304,** 305, 334–335, **335,** 453–454
conceptual model of language, speech and, 294*f*
facilitative, 361–364
sensitivity in, cultural diversity and, 123
total, **408**–410
training for professionals in, 154–155
Communication disorders, 292–321
inclusion and, 314–315
language disorders and, 298–305
speech disorders and, 305–319
Communication media, vision loss and, 434–437
Communication skills
mental retardation and, 281–282
teaching, hearing loss and, 399, 406–410
Community-based interventions for emotional/behavioral disorders, 247
Community living
changes over time in postschool outcomes, 89

social activities and, 89
transition to, 87
Community reintegration, in traumatic brain injury, 380–381
Community settings
barrier-free access in, 11, 14
historical perspective on, 8–9
living and learning in, 14
medical model and, 17, 18
participation in, mental retardation and, 266–267, 285–286
Comorbidity, **169**
of ADHD and other disabilities, 205–207
Comorbidity research, 169
Compassionate Friends, 466
Compensatory skills, 191
Comprehensive Strategy Framework (CSF), 258
Computer-assisted instruction
for math skills, 186
for reading, 186, 188
for writing, 187
Computerized tomography (CT) scans, **378**
Computer(s). *See also* Assistive technology
communication media, vision loss and, 436
hearing loss and information access with, 411, 412
Concussions, **378**
Condensed schooling, 512–514
Conditioning, **18**
Conduct disorder, 228, 231, 236, 237
ADHD and, 206
diagnostic criteria for, 233*t*
and gang membership, 257
Conductive hearing loss, **395**
Conferences, parent-teacher, 241
Conformity, 6
Congenital cytomegalovirus (CMV), **397**
Congenital rubella, **277**
Congenital toxoplasmosis infection, **397**
Consent
informed, 34–35
in special education, 29, 48*t*
Consistency, general education's goal of achieving, 115
Consultant, as special educator's role, 74
Consultative services, 32*f,* **44**
Consulting teacher, 62
Context information, using, 171
Continuum model for ability grouping, 509*f*

cystic fibrosis, 461, **475–477**
diabetes, 472–475
HIV and acquired immune defi-
    ciency syndrome (AIDS),
    466–471
inclusion and, 465–466
seizure disorders (epilepsy), 470–473
sickle cell anemia, 450, **477–478**
Health insurance
    assessment of ADHD and, 211
    custody *versus* care issue, 252
    Medicare and Medicaid, **103**
    Work Incentives Improvement Act
        and, 91
Health services
    learning disabilities, 197
Hearing aids, 399, 406, 410*f*, 415–416,
    415*f*
Hearing loss, 390–419
    age of onset, 395
    anatomical site of, 395
    assistive technology, 410–411
        closed-caption television,
            410–411, 410*f*
        computers and Internet, 411, 412
        telecommunication devices, 406,
            416
    causation, 396–398
        acquired factors, 398
        congenital factors, 397
    characteristics, 398–402
    classification, 395–396, 396*t*
    communication skills, teaching
        manual approach, 407–408
        total communication, **408**–410
    conductive, **395**
    deaf-blindness, **325**, 325–327
    definitions, 394–396
    delayed speech and, 302
    inclusion and, 402–412
    medical services, 412–416
    mixed, **395**
    postlingual, **395**
    prelingual, **395**
    prevalence, 396
    sensorineural, **395**
    severe and multiple disabilities and,
        329
    social services, 416
Hearing process, 392–394
Hematoma, 378, 379*f*
Hemiplegia, **451, 459**
*Hendrick Hudson District Board of Edu-
    cation v. Rowley* (1982), 26*t*, 29
Heredity. *See* Genetic factors
    in ADHD, 216
    hearing loss in, 397

Hertz (Hz), **394**
Heterogeneity classification of learning
    disabilities, 165
Heterogeneous grouping in inclusive
    preschool program, 72*t*
Higher education. *See* College
Highly qualified teachers, 42
High school. *See also* Secondary school
    changes over time in postschool out-
        comes, 89
    completion, 88–90
    diploma, 99
Hispanics. *See* Latinos/Hispanics
HIV. *See* Human immunodeficiency
    virus (HIV)
Hoarseness, voice disorders of, 317
Hobsen v. Hansen (1969), 26*t*
Holistic view of child development, 72*t*
Home-based services. *See also* Family-
    centered services and programs
    early intervention, 66–67
    emotional/behavioral disorders and,
        249
Homebound programs, 31*f*, 32, 32*f*
Home environment. *See* Family(ies)
Horses, as therapeutic tool in autism,
    346
Hospital education programs, 31*f*, 32,
    32*f*
Housing
    physical disabilities and health disor-
        ders, 448
Housing services, 104
Human Genome Project, **339,** 340
    website, 344
Human immunodeficiency virus. *See
    also* Acquired immunodeficiency
    syndrome (AIDS)
Human immunodeficiency virus (HIV),
    277, 466, 466–468. *See also* Ac-
    quired immunodeficiency syn-
    drome (AIDS)
Hydration, for sickle cell anemia, 478
Hydrocephalus, **278, 427,** 458, 459
Hyperactivity, **177, 204**
    ADHD and, 213–214, 217
    learning disabilities and, 177
    medication for, 197–198
Hyperglycemia, 473
Hyperkinetic behavior, 163, **177**
Hypernasality, **317,** 319
Hyperopia, **425,** 425*f*
Hyponasality, **317,** 319
Hypotonia, **328**

IB 367, 476
IC. *See* Individualized care (IC)

IDDM. *See* Insulin-dependent diabetes
    mellitus (IDDM)
IDEA. *See* Individuals with Disabilities
    Education Act (1990)
IDEA 97. *See* Individuals with Disabili-
    ties Education Act amendments
    (1997)
IDEA 2004. *See* Individuals with Dis-
    abilities Education Act (2004)
IDEA Partnerships: Results for Kids Re-
    sources website, 52
Identical twins, 178
Idiot savants, 354
IEP. *See* Individualized education pro-
    gram (IEP)
IEP diploma, 99
IFSP. *See* Individualized family service
    plan (IFSP)
ILP. *See* Individualized language plans
    (ILPs)
Immaturity, 231, 236
Immigration status, 123. *See also* Cul-
    tural diversity
    migrant families and, 127–128
Immune system, **466**
Impairment, 163
Impulsivity, ADHD and, 213–214, 217
Inclusion, 54–60
    ADHD and, 220, 222–223
    autism and, 362–363
    bilingual-bicultural inclusion models,
        125*f*
    communication disorders and,
        314–315
    continuum of placements and, 31*f*,
        32
    Down syndrome and, 285
    emotional/behavioral disorders,
        250–251
    family-centered support and, 149
    formal supports in, **59**
    full, **57,** 58–59, **256,** 258–259
    giftedness and, 504–505, 510–511
    hearing loss and, 402–412
    history of, 8–9
    learning disabilities and, 184–185, 196
    mental retardation and, 282–283,
        287, 288
    natural supports in, 59
    partial, **57**
    physical disabilities and health disor-
        ders, 465–466
    severe and multiple disabilities and,
        322, 335–338
    traumatic and acquired brain injury
        and, 384–385
    vision loss and, 440–441

by medical descriptors, 268
by severity of condition, 268
cultural differences in view of, 122
cultural-familial retardation, **274**
definition, 265–267
distinctions between learning disabilities and, 175
educational services and supports, 278–287
  early childhood years, 279
  elementary school years, 279–280
  transition from school to adult life, 283, 284–287, 285*f*
evolving terminology, 265
fathers of children with, 144
fetal alcohol syndrome and, 483
inclusion and, 282–283, 285, 287, 288
prevalence of, 269–270, 270*f*
Mentoring of gifted students, 515, 516
Metabolic disorders, **275**
Metacognition, 191, 271
Methylphenidate (Ritalin), 197, 217–219
Methylprednisolone, 460
Microphthalmia, **427**
Middle ear, 393
Migrant families, children in, 127–128
Mild mental retardation, 268
Mills v. District of Columbia Board of Education (1972), 26*t*, 27
Minimal brain dysfunction, 163
Minorities, cultural and ethnic. *See* Cultural diversity
Mirror writing, **173**
Misdiagnosis, 116
Mixed hearing loss, **395**
Mobility, vision loss and, 429–430, 443
Mobility of migrant families, effect of, 127–128
Mobility training, 431–433
Moderate mental retardation, 268, 273*t*
Morphology, 295
Mothers. *See also* Maternal drug and alcohol abuse; Maternal infections; Parent(s)
  adolescent, 482–483, 482*f*
  mother-child relationships, 140, 142–143
  overprotectiveness of, 143
  spousal relationship, 140–142
  trauma and strain experienced by, 139–140
Motivation, mental retardation and, 272
Motor skills, mental retardation and, 280
Mountbatten Brailler, 435–436

Mowat Sensor, **432**
MRI. *See* Magnetic resonance imaging (MRI)
Multicultural education, 110–133, **113**. *See also* Cultural diversity; Language diversity
  beliefs and assumptions underlying, 124–125
  cultural pluralism addressed by, 114–115
  individualized education plan and, 124
  other diversity issues, 126–129
  severe and multiple disabilities and, 332
  special education and, 115–119
    individualized education plan, 124
    least restrictive environment, 124–126
    nondiscriminatory and multidisciplinary assessment, 28, 29, **119,** 119–121
    parental involvement, 122–124
    specialized instruction, 129
Multicultural issues, 110–133
Multidimensional theory of intelligence, 494
Multidisciplinary assessment, 29, 119–122
Multidisciplinary model of professional collaboration, 63*t*
Multidisciplinary perspectives on people with disabilities, 16–19
Multidisciplinary schoolwide assistance teams (SWATs), 63
Multilevel instruction, 77–78
Multimodal treatments, ADHD and, 220
Multiple disabilities, 325, 326. *See also* Severe and multiple disabilities
  cerebral palsy and, 451
Multiple intelligences, theory of, **77,** 498, 498*t*
Muscular defects of visual system, 426
Muscular dystrophy, 449, **461**–463
Muscular Dystrophy Association website, 488
Musical intelligence, 498*t*
Mutism, elective, 234
Myopia, **425,** 425*f,* 427
Myringoplasty, 413

NAD. *See* National Association for the Deaf (NAD)
NARC. *See* National Association for Retarded Children
Nasality, voice disorders of, 317

National Alliance for the Mentally Ill (NAMI) website, 261
National Association for Multicultural Education website, 132
National Association for Retarded Children, 9
National Association for the Deaf (NAD), 9, 416
  website, 419
National Association for the Education of Young Children (NAEYC), 69
National Association of School Psychologists website, 261
National Campaign to Prevent Teen Pregnancy website, 488
National Center for Learning Disabilities website, 200
National Center for Secondary Education and Transition website, 107
National Council on Disability (NCD), 10
  website, 21
National Down Syndrome Society website, 290
National Federation of the Blind website, 446
National Information Center for Children and Youth with Disabilities (NICHCY)
  website, 52, 158
National Information Center for Children and Youth with Disabilities (NICHCY) website, 389, 488
National Information Clearinghouse on Children Who Are Deaf-Blind website, 344
National Institute of Disability Management and Research website, 389
National Institutes of Health Consensus Statement, 211
National Joint Committee for Learning Disabilities, 163
National Longitudinal Transition Study (USDE), 90
National Mental Health and Special Education Coalition, 229
National Mentoring Partnership, 516
National Organization on Disability (N.O.D.), 10
  website, 21
National Organization on Fetal Alcohol Syndrome, 277
National Rehabilitation Information Center (NARIC) website, 488
National Research Center on Learning Disabilities, 192

suggested school reintegration checklist, 383

inclusion and, 384–385

medical and psychological services, 378–381

types of head injuries, 378–379

prevalence, 371–372

severity descriptors, 377*t*

Travel aids, visual loss and, 432–433

Treatment. *See* Interventions; *specific disabilities*

Trephining, 18

Triarchic theory of human intelligence, 496–497

Trisomy 21, **275**

Troubled Teen Advisor website, 225

Tuberous sclerosis, **277**

Tunnel vision, **424**

Tutoring

cross-age, **63**

peer, **63**

Twin studies, 178

Tympanic membrane, 393

Type I/II diabetes. *See* Diabetes mellitus

Undersocialized aggression, 237

United Cerebral Palsy Organization (UCP), 9

United States, population growth by ethnic background in, 116–117

Universal design for learning (UDL), **78,** 79*t*

Universal health care, **152**

Universal health care, debate over, 252

U.S. Department of Education, National Longitudinal Transition Study, 90

U.S. Department of Justice, 14

U.S. Supreme Court, 14

Vaccine(s)

autism and, 346

rubella, 396, 397

Vagus nerve stimulation (VNS), 473

Ventriculoperitoneal shunt, 458*f*

Verbalisms, **429**

Vermis, **357,** 357*f*

Vestibular mechanism, **394**

Videx Timewand, 364

Violence

firearm, 49, 376

gang membership and, 257

safe schools legislation and, 47–49

Vision

field of, 424, 425*f*

low, 424–425

tunnel, **424**

Vision loss, 420–447, **423**

age of onset and, 428

causation, 427–428

acquired disorders, 427–428

genetic disorders, 427–428

characteristics, 428–430

classification, 425–427

muscle disorders, 426

receptive eye problems, 426–427

refractive problems, **425**–426

deaf-blindness, **325,** 325–327

definitions, 424–425

educational supports and services, 431–438

assessment, 431

communication media, 434–437

instructional content, 433–434

in least restrictive environment, 437–438

mobility training and daily living skills, 431–433

inclusion and, 440–441

medical services, 437, 439–443

negative perceptions of people with, 422

prevalence, 426–427

severe and multiple disabilities and, 329

social services, 439, 443

warning signs of, 442*t*

Vision specialist, 437

Visual acuity, **424,** 439

Visual attention, 431

Visual capacity, 431

Visual cortex, **422**

Visual discrimination, **176**

Visual Efficient Scale, 431

Visualization, 492

Visual perception problems, 176

Visual process, 422

Visual-processing, assessment of, 431

Visual screening, 443

Vitamin A deficiency (xerophthalmia), 427

VNS. *See* Vagus nerve stimulation (VNS)

Vocational rehabilitation, **104**

Vocational Rehabilitation Act, 10, 91. *See also* Section 504

Voice disorders, **317**–319

Voice problems, **272**

Volume, voice disorders involving, 318

Voxel-based morphometry, **378**

Watson, John, 18–19, 501

Web-Braille, 420

Web resources, 21, 52, 83, 84, 107, 108, 132, 133, 158, 159, 188, 200, 201, 225, 261, 290, 291, 321, 344, 345, 367, 389, 419, 446, 447, 488, 489, 523

Weihenmayer, Erik, 431*f*

Wheelchairs, 462

Whole-language strategies, 187

Wild boy of Aveyon, 17

Williams syndrome, **275**

Wilson, Woodrow, 195

Word knowledge and word recognition, 171

Work Incentives Improvement Act, 91

Wraparound approach (WRAP), 246–247, 253–256, 253*f,* **256**

WRITE, P.L.E.A.S.E. learning strategy, 191

Writing

braille, 435

learning disabilities and, 172–173, 191

mirror, **173**

software for, 187

traumatic brain injury and, 386*t*

vision loss and, 429

Wundt, Wilhelm, 18

Xerophthalmia, **427**

Young adults. *See* Adolescent(s); Adulthood; Transition to adult life, planning for

Zero-exclusion principle, **27**

Zero-tolerance, 47–**49**

Photo Credits

CHAPTER 1
Page 2: John Henley/Corbis; p. 4: Margaret Suckley/Franklin D. Roosevelt Library; p. 5: Chuck Savage/Corbis; p. 7: top row, left: Topham/The Image Works; top row, center and right: Corbis; middle row, left and center: AP Images; middle row, right: Bettmann/Corbis; bottom row, left to right: Bettmann/Corbis; Stephanie Cardinale/Sygma/Corbis; AP Images; p. 11, top: Jose Carillo/PhotoEdit; bottom: James Shaffer/PhotoEdit; p. 14: Corbis; p. 15: Ariel Skelley/Corbis; p. 17: ©Stockbyte Platinum/Alamy Royalty Free.

CHAPTER 2
Page 22: AP Images/Rusty Kennedy; p. 26: Charles Gupton/Corbis; p. 30: Laura Dwight Photography; p. 35: Elizabeth Crews Photography; p. 41: AP Images; p. 49: Phil Mislinski/Liaison/Getty Images.

CHAPTER 3
Page 54: AP Images/Jessica Griffin; p. 57: Ellen Senisi/The Image Works; p. 61: Robin Nelson/PhotoEdit; p. 62: Ray Chernush/Image Bank/Getty Images; p. 64: Gabe Palmer/Corbis; p. 68: Jonathan Nourok/PhotoEdit; p. 71: AP Images; p. 75: Elizabeth Crews/The Image Works; p. 79: Courtesy of Recording for the Blind and Dyslexic, Princeton, NJ.

CHAPTER 4
Page 86: Tracy Ferrero/Alamy; p. 94: Purestock/SuperStock Royalty Free; p. 98: Bob Daemmrich/The Image Works; p. 105: Bob Daemmrich/PhotoEdit.

CHAPTER 5
Page 110: David Young-Wolff/Alamy; p. 113: David Young-Wolff/PhotoEdit; p. 116: Will Hart/PhotoEdit; p. 120: Bob Daemmrich/The Image Works; p. 123: Jose Luis Pelaez/Corbis; p. 124: Elizabeth Crews Photography.

CHAPTER 6
Page 134: Christopher Fitzgerald/The Image Works; p. 137: Spencer Grant/PhotoEdit; p. 141: Rick Gomez/Corbis; p. 142: Chris Ware/The Image Works; p. 144: Ron Chapple/Taxi/Getty Images; p. 145: Cathy Melloan Resources/PhotoEdit; p. 147, top: SuperStock Royalty Free; bottom: Photodisc/Getty Images Royalty Free; p. 149: A. Ramey/PhotoEdit; p. 154: AP Images/John Amis; p. 155: Courtesy of Emily Kingsley.

CHAPTER 7
Page 160: AP Images/Jessica Griffin; p. 161: SW Productions/Photodisc/Getty Images Royalty Free; p. 167: Purestock/Alamy Royalty Free; p. 168: Bettann/Corbis; p. 169: Science Photo Library/Photo Researchers, Inc. p. 170: Mug Shots/Corbis; p. 174: Brian Smith; p. 190: Photodisc Blue/Getty Images Royalty Free.

CHAPTER 8
Page 202: Bananastock/SuperStock Royalty Free; p. 204: David Young Wolff/PhotoEdit; p. 211: Michael Malyszko/Taxi/Getty Images; p. 214: Geostock/Taxi/Getty Images; p. 215: Chip Henderson/Stone-Allstock/Getty Images.

CHAPTER 9
Page 226: Lifestock/Image Bank/Getty Images; p. 231: Maggie Leonard/Rainbow; p. 232: Express Newspapers/Liaison/Getty Images; p. 236: Robert Harbison; p. 239: Tom & Dee Ann McCarthy/Corbis; p. 240: Peggy & Ronald Barnett/Corbis; p. 241: Randy Faris/Corbis; p. 244: Michael Newman/PhotoEdit; p. 249: David H. Wells/Corbis; p. 254: Tom Lindfors Photography; p. 257: A. Ramey/PhotoEdit; p. 258: Stone-Allstock/Getty Images.

CHAPTER 10
Page 262: Grace/zefa/Corbis; p. 267: Corbis Royalty Free; p. 269: Richard Hutchings/PhotoEdit; p. 272: Bob Daemmrich/PhotoEdit; p. 275: Lynn Johnson/Black Star; p. 278: David H. Wells/Corbis; p. 280: Dan McCoy/Rainbow; p. 286: Mika/zefa/Corbis.

CHAPTER 11
Page 292: Robin Sachs/PhotoEdit; p. 296: Tom Prettyman/PhotoEdit; p. 303: Martin Poole/Getty Images Rights-Ready; p. 305: Courtesy of Norma Velez; p. 307: Robert Brenner/PhotoEdit; p. 309: Michael Newman/PhotoEdit; p. 318: Mary Kate Denny/PhotoEdit.

CHAPTER 12
Page 322: Ellen Senisi/The Image Works; p. 327: Robin Sachs/PhotoEdit; p. 331: Eric Fowke/PhotoEdit; p. 332: David Young-Wolff/PhotoEdit; p. 333: Robin Nelson/PhotoEdit; p. 339: Taxi/Getty Images.

CHAPTER 13
Page 346: AP Images/The Plain Dealer, Chuck Crow; p. 349: Jonathan Nourok/PhotoEdit; p. 353: Bob Daemmrich/PhotoEdit; p. 359: Brian Smith; p. 365, top: Brian Smith; bottom: Michael Schwartz/Liaison/Getty Images.

CHAPTER 14
Page 368: AP Images/Toby Talbot; p. 371: Courtesy of Steve Farmer; p. 372: Nick Pardo/The Image Bank/Getty Images; p. 376: Rick Wilking/Hulton Archive/Getty Images; p. 380: AP Images; p. 386: Elizabeth Crews Photography.

CHAPTER 15
Page 390: Robin Sachs/PhotoEdit; p. 391: AP Images/ John Harrell; p. 398: SuperStock, Inc.; p. 400: AP Images; p. 409: Will Hart; p. 416: Bob Daemmrich/The Image Works.

CHAPTER 16
Page 420: Stockbyte/SuperStock Royalty Free; p. 429: Tony Freeman/PhotoEdit; p. 431: Didrik Johnck/Sygma/Corbis; p. 432: David Young-Wolff/PhotoEdit; p. 433: AP Images/Robert F. Bukaty; p. 436: Robin Sachs/PhotoEdit; p. 443: Corbis Royalty Free.

CHAPTER 17
Page 448: Tom Stoddart/Exclusive by Getty Images Exclusive; p. 449: Courtesy of Greg Smith; p. 453: Richard Hutchings/PhotoEdit; p. 454: Courtesy of The Christensen Family; p. 460: Elizabeth Crews Photography; p. 461: AP Images/Kathy Willens; p. 467: Mark Richards/PhotoEdit; p. 473: Tony Freeman/PhotoEdit; p. 479: Bill Aron/PhotoEdit; p. 481: Paul Costello/Stone/Getty Images.

CHAPTER 18
Page 490: Bonnie Kamin/PhotoEdit; p. 491: Courtesy Talmage D. Egan, M.D., p. 494: Archives of the History of American Psychology; p. 501, left: Bob Daemmrich/PhotoEdit; p. 501, right: David Young-Wolff/PhotoEdit; p. 503: Mark Peterson/Corbis; p. 507: Blend Images/SuperStock Royalty Free; p. 512: Rochester Democrat & Chronicle /Sygma/Corbis; p. 517: Karin Cooper/AFP/Getty Images; p. 519: AP Images/David Budny.